Proposed DSM-5 Diagnoses

NEURODEVELOPMENTAL DISORDERS

Intellectual Developmental Disorders
Intellectual Developmental Disorder

Communication Disorders
Language Impairment / Late Language Emergence / Specific Language Impairment / Social Communication Disorder / Speech Sound Disorder / Childhood Onset Fluency Disorder / Voice Disorder

Autism Spectrum Disorder
Autism Spectrum Disorder

Attention-Deficit / Hyperactivity Disorder
Attention-Deficit / Hyperactivity Disorder

Learning Disorders
Learning Disorder / Dyslexia / Dyscalculia

Motor Disorders
Developmental Coordination Disorder / Stereotypic Movement Disorder / Tourette's Disorder / Chronic Motor or Vocal Tic Disorder / Provisional Tic Disorder

SCHIZOPHRENIA SPECTRUM DISORDERS

Schizophrenia / Schizotypal Personality Disorder / Schizophreniform Disorder / Brief Psychotic Disorder / Delusional Disorder / Schizoaffective Disorder / Attenuated Psychosis Syndrome

BIPOLAR AND RELATED DISORDERS

Bipolar I Disorder / Bipolar II Disorder (Recurrent Major Depressive Episodes with Hypomania) / Cyclothymic Disorder

DEPRESSIVE DISORDERS

Disruptive Mood Dysregulation Disorder / Major Depressive Disorder / Chronic Depressive Disorder (Dysthymia) / Premenstrual Dysphoric Disorder / Mixed Anxiety Depression

ANXIETY DISORDERS

Panic Disorder / Agoraphobia / Specific Phobia / Social Anxiety Disorder (Social Phobia) / Generalized Anxiety Disorder

OBSESSIVE-COMPULSIVE AND RELATED DISORDERS

Obsessive-Compulsive Disorder / Body Dysmorphic Disorder / Hoarding Disorder / Hair-Pulling Disorder (Trichotillomania) / Skin Picking Disorder

TRAUMA- AND STRESSOR-RELATED DISORDERS

Reactive Attachment Disorder / Disinhibited Social Engagement Disorder / Posttraumatic Stress Disorder in Preschool Children / Acute Stress Disorder / Posttraumatic Stress Disorder / Adjustment Disorders

DISSOCIATIVE DISORDERS

Depersonalization / Derealization Disorder / Dissociative Amnesia / Dissociative Identity Disorder

SOMATIC SYMPTOM DISORDERS

Complex Somatic Symptom Disorder / Simple Somatic Symptom Disorder / Illness Anxiety Disorder / Functional Neurological Disorder (Conversion Disorder)

FEEDING AND EATING DISORDERS

Pica / Rumination Disorder / Avoidant/Restrictive Food Intake Disorder / Anorexia Nervosa / Bulimia Nervosa /Binge Eating Disorder

ELIMINATION DISORDERS

Enuresis / Encopresis

SLEEP-WAKE DISORDERS

Insomnia Disorder / Primary Hypersomnia / Narcolepsy without Cataplexy / Kleine Levin Syndrome / Narcolepsy / Hypocretin Deficiency / Obstructive Sleep Apnea Hypopnea Syndrome / Primary Central Sleep Apnea / Primary Alveolar Hypoventilation / Circadian Rhythm Sleep Disorder / Disorder of Arousal / Nightmare Disorder / Rapid Eye Movement Behavior Disorder / Restless Legs Syndrome

SEXUAL DYSFUNCTIONS

Erectile Disorder / Female Orgasmic Disorder / Delayed Ejaculation / Early Ejaculation / Sexual Interest-Arousal Disorder in Women / Hypoactive Sexual Desire in Men / Genito-Pelvic Pain / Penetration Disorder

GENDER DYSPHORIA

Gender Dysphoria in Children; in Adolescents or Adults

DISRUPTIVE, IMPULSE CONTROL, AND CONDUCT DISORDERS

Oppositional Defiant Disorder / Pyromania / Kleptomania / Intermittent Explosive Disorder / Conduct Disorder

SUBSTANCE USE AND ADDICTIVE DISORDERS

Alcohol Use Disorder / Amphetamine Use Disorder / Cannabis Use Disorder / Cocaine Use Disorder / Hallucinogen Use Disorder / Inhalant Use Disorder / Nicotine Use Disorder / Opioid Use Disorder / Phencyclidine Use Disorder / Sedative, Hypnotic, or Anxiolytic Use Disorders / Tobacco Use Disorder

NEUROCOGNITIVE DISORDERS

Delirium / Mild Neurocognitive Disorder / Major Neurocognitive Disorder

PERSONALITY DISORDERS

Antisocial Personality Disorder / Avoidant Personality Disorder / Borderline Personality Disorder / Narcissistic Personality Disorder / Obsessive-Compulsive Disorder / Personality Disorder / Schizotypal Personality Disorder

PARAPHILIAS

Exhibitionistic Disorder / Fetishistic Disorder / Frotteuristic Disorder / Pedohebephilic Disorder / Sexual Masochism Disorder / Sexual Sadism Disorder / Transvestic Disorder / Voyeuristic Disorder

OTHER DISORDERS

Non-Suicidal Self-Injury / Factitious Disorder

OTHER CONDITIONS THAT MAY BE A FOCUS OF CLINICAL ATTENTION

Mental Disorders Affecting Medical Condition / Psychological Symptoms Affecting Medical Condition / Personality Traits or Coping Style Affecting Medical Condition / Maladaptive Health Behaviors Affecting Medical Condition / Stress-Related Physiological Responses Affecting Medical Condition / Other or Unspecified Psychological Factors Affecting Medical Condition

Proposed DSM-5 Classification System
Psychiatric & Medical Diagnoses

Neurodevelopmental Disorders
Schizophrenia Spectrum and Other Psychotic Disorders
Bipolar and Related Disorders
Depressive Disorders
Anxiety Disorders
Obsessive-Compulsive and Related Disorders
Trauma- and Stressor-Related Disorders
Dissociative Disorders
Somatic Symptom Disorders
Feeding and Eating Disorders
Elimination Disorders
Sleep-Wake Disorders
Sexual Dysfunctions
Gender Dysphoria
Disruptive, Impulse Control, and Conduct Disorders
Substance Use and Addictive Disorders
Neurocognitive Disorders
Personality Disorders
Paraphilias
Other Disorders

www.wileyplus.com

WileyPLUS is a research-based online environment for effective teaching and learning.

WileyPLUS builds students' confidence because it takes the guesswork out of studying by providing students with a clear roadmap:

- **what to do**
- **how to do it**
- **if they did it right**

It offers interactive resources along with a complete digital textbook that help students learn more. With *WileyPLUS*, students take more initiative so you'll have greater impact on their achievement in the classroom and beyond.

For more information, visit www.wileyplus.com

Abnormal Psychology
Twelfth Edition

International Student Version

Abnormal Psychology
Twelfth Edition

International Student Version

Ann M. Kring
University of California, Berkeley

Sheri L. Johnson
University of California, Berkeley

With former contributions from
Gerald C. Davison
University of Southern California

John M. Neale
State University of New York at Stony Brook

And Contributions From
Nicky Edelstyn
Keele University

Dora Brown
University of Surrey

WILEY

John Wiley & Sons, Inc.

ISBN: 978-1-118-09241-5

Printed in Asia

10 9 8 7 6 5 4 3 2 1

To

Angela Hawk

Daniel Rose

About the Authors

ANN M. KRING is Professor of Psychology at the University of California at Berkeley, where she is a former Director of the Clinical Science Program and Psychology Clinic. She received her B.S. from Ball State University and her M.A. and Ph.D. from the State University of New York at Stony Brook. Her internship in clinical psychology was completed at Bellevue Hospital and Kirby Forensic Psychiatric Center, in New York. From 1991 to 1998, she taught at Vanderbilt University. She received a Distinguished Teaching Award from UC Berkeley in 2008. She is on the editorial board of *Schizophrenia Bulletin, Journal of Abnormal Psychology,* and *Psychological Science in the Public Interest*, an Associate Editor for *Applied and Preventive Psychology,* and a former Associate Editor for *Journal of Abnormal Psychology* and *Cognition and Emotion.* She is a former member of the Executive Board of the International Society for Research on Emotion.

She has won several awards, including a Young Investigator Award from the National Alliance for Research on Schizophrenia and Depression in 1997 and the Joseph Zubin Memorial Fund Award in recognition of her research in schizophrenia in 2006. In 2005, she was named a fellow of the Association for Psychological Science. Her research has been supported by grants from the Scottish Rite Schizophrenia Research program, the National Alliance for Research on Schizophrenia and Depression, and the National Institute of Mental Health. She is a co-editor (with Denise Sloan) of the book *Emotion Regulation and Psychopathology* (Guilford Press) and is the author on more than 70 articles and chapters. Her current research focus is on emotion and psychopathology, with a specific interest in the emotional features of schizophrenia, assessing negative symptoms in schizophrenia, and the linkage between cognition and emotion in schizophrenia.

SHERI L. JOHNSON is Professor of Psychology at the University of California at Berkeley, where she directs the Cal Mania (Calm) program, and is a visiting professor at the University of Lancaster, England. She received her B.A. from Salem College and her Ph.D. from the University of Pittsburgh. She completed an internship and postdoctoral fellowship at Brown University, and she was a clinical assistant professor at Brown from 1993 to 1995. From 1995 to 2008, she taught in the Department of Psychology at the University of Miami, where she was recognized three times with the Excellence in Graduate Teaching Award. In 1993, she received the Young Investigator Award from the National Alliance for Research in Schizophrenia and Depression. She is an Associate Editor for *Applied and Preventive Psychology,* and she serves on the editorial board for *Psychological Bulletin* and *International Journal of Cognitive Therapy.* She is a member of the Executive Board for the Society for Research in Psychopathology and a Fellow of the Academy of Behavioral Medicine Research and the Association for Psychological Science.

For the past 25 years, her work has focused on understanding the factors that predict the course of mania and depression. She uses social, psychological, and neurobiological paradigms to understand these processes. Her work has been funded by the National Alliance for Research on Schizophrenia and Depression and by the National Institute of Mental Health. She has published over 100 articles and chapters, and her findings have been published in leading journals such as the *Journal of Abnormal Psychology* and the *American Journal of Psychiatry.* She is co-editor of several books, including *Psychological Treatment of Bipolar Disorder* (Guilford Press).

A bit of authorship history...

Nearly 40 years ago, Gerald Davison and John Neale sat down to share their experiences teaching the undergraduate abnormal psychology course at the State University of New York at Stony Brook. Arising from that conversation was the outline of a textbook on which they decided to collaborate, one that was different from the texts available at the time. The first edition of this book, co-authored by Davison and Neale, was published in 1974. Ann Kring joined the team in 2001, and she invited Sheri Johnson to join in 2004, when Kring and Johnson took over full authorship responsibilities. The legacy of Davison and Neale remains in this and every edition, and we are forever indebted to these two pioneering authors who developed and wrote many editions of this textbook. Near the end of our work on the twelfth edition, we learned that John Neale had passed away after a long illness. He will be greatly missed by many.

Photo by Christine McDowell.

GERALD C. DAVISON is Professor of Psychology at the University of Southern California. Previously he was Professor and Chair of the Department of Psychology at USC and served also as Director of Clinical Training. He recently served as Dean of the USC Davis School of Gerontology. He earned his B.A. in social relations from Harvard and his Ph.D. in psychology from Stanford. He is a Fellow of the American Psychological Association, a Charter Fellow of the Association for Psychological Science, and a Distinguished Founding Fellow of the Academy of Cognitive Therapy. Among his other honors are the USC Associates Award for Excellence in Teaching, and the Outstanding Educator Award and the Lifetime Achievement Award of the Association for Behavioral and Cognitive Therapies. Among his more than 150 publications is his book Clinical Behavior Therapy, co-authored in 1976 with Marvin Goldfried and reissued in expanded form in 1994. It is one of two publications that have been recognized as Citation Classics by the Social Sciences Citation Index. He is also on the editorial board of several professional journals. His research has emphasized experimental and philosophical analyses of psychopathology, assessment, therapeutic change, and the relationships between cognition and a variety of behavioral and emotional problems via his articulated thoughts in simulated situations paradigm.

JOHN M. NEALE was Professor of Psychology at the State University of New York at Stony Brook, retiring in 2000. He received his B.A. from the University of Toronto and his M.A. and Ph.D. from Vanderbilt University. He won numerous awards, including the American Psychological Association's Early Career Award (1974), the Distinguished Scientist Award from the American Psychological Association's Society for a Science of Clinical Psychology (1991), and the Sustained Mentorship Award from the Society for Research in Psychopathology (2011). Besides his numerous articles in professional journals, he published books on the effects of televised violence on children, research methodology, schizophrenia, case studies in abnormal psychology, and psychological influences on health. Schizophrenia was a major focus of his research, and he also conducted research on the influence of stress on health.

Preface

It has been nearly 40 years since the first edition of this book was published. From the beginning, the focus of the book has always been on the balance and blending of research and clinical application; on the use of paradigms as an organizing principle; and on the effort to involve the reader in the problem solving engaged in by clinicians and scientists. These qualities have continued to be the cornerstones of subsequent editions, and we have been both surprised and delighted at the favorable reception the book has received and, perhaps more importantly, the impact it has had on the lives of so many students of psychopathology throughout the years.

With the twelfth edition, we continue to emphasize the recent and comprehensive research coverage that has been the hallmark of the book as well as to expand the pedagogical features. We have added additional clinical cases, figures, tables, and clarifying writing to make this material accessible to a broad audience. Now more than ever, we emphasize an integrated approach, showing how psychopathology is best understood by considering multiple perspectives and how these varying perspectives can provide us with the clearest accounting of the causes of these disorders as well as the best possible treatments.

The cover image is a satellite image of the Great Sandy Desert in Australia. The light-colored, fan-like parts of the image are of the scars left by a wildfire that tore through the desert in the year 2000. Wildfires are a necessary part of the life cycle of a healthy ecosystem, and they are a powerful means for reshaping the landscape. Beyond the beauty of this image, it illustrates a number of key principles about our book. Like landscapes, humans are shaped by neurobiology and environmental events, which is what the study of psychopathology is all about: different paradigms (genetic, neuroscience, cognitive–behavioral) coming together to shape the development and course of different psychological disorders. This is also how science works. New discoveries help to reshape the landscape of scientific inquiry. Our book is first and foremost grounded in the latest science of mental illness. However, just as landscapes continually change and shift, so does the field of psychopathology. As new discoveries and new treatments are developed, our understanding shifts toward a better conceptualization of mental illness.

Goals of the Book

With each new edition, we update, make changes, and streamline features to enhance both the scholarly and pedagogical characteristics of the book. We also devote considerable effort to couching complex concepts in prose that is sharp, clear, and vivid. In the past 40 years, the domains of psychopathology and intervention have become increasingly multifaceted and technical. Therefore, a good abnormal psychology textbook must engage the careful and focused attention of students so that they can acquire a deep and critical understanding of the issues and the material. Some of the most exciting breakthroughs in psychopathology research and treatment that we present in the book have come in areas that are complex, such as molecular genetics, neuroscience, and cognitive science. Rather than oversimplify these complex issues, we have instead added a number of pedagogical features to enhance understanding of this vital material.

We endeavor to present up-to-date theories and research in psychopathology and intervention as well as to convey some of the intellectual excitement that is associated with the search for answers to some of the most puzzling questions facing humankind. A reviewer of an earlier edition once said that our book reads like a detective story, for we do more than just state the problem and then its solution. Rather, we try to involve the student in the search for clues, the follow-up of hunches, and the evaluation of evidence—all of which are part and parcel of the science and art of the field. We try to encourage students to participate with us in a process of discovery as we sift through the evidence on the origins of psychopathology and the effectiveness of specific interventions.

In this edition, we continue to emphasize ways in which we can do away with the stigma that is unfortunately still associated with mental illness. Psychopathology is something that affects all of us in one way or another. As many as half of us may experience a psychological disorder at some time or another, and most of us know someone who has had a mental disorder. Despite the ubiquity of psychopathology, the stigma associated with it can keep some from seeking treatment, keep our legislatures from providing adequate funding for treatment and research, and keep some terms as accepted popular vernacular (e.g., *crazy, nuts*). Thus, another of our goals for the book is to combat this stigma and present a positive and hopeful view on the causes and treatments of mental illness.

Organization of the Twelfth Edition

In Chapters 1 through 4, we place the field in historical context, present the concept of paradigms in science, describe the major paradigms in psychopathology, preview the forthcoming fifth edition of the *Diagnostic and Statistical Manual of Mental Disorders* (DSM-5), critically discuss its validity and reliability, provide an overview of major approaches and techniques in clinical assessment, and then describe the major research methods of the field. These chapters are the foundation on which the later chapters can be interpreted and understood. As in the eleventh edition, specific disorders and their treatment are discussed in Chapters 5 through 15. However, we have reorganized these chapters for better flow in a typical abnormal psychology course. In Chapter 16, we discuss legal and ethical issues.

A recurrent theme in the book is the importance of perspectives, or, to use Kuhn's (1962/1970) phrase, paradigms. Throughout the book we discuss three major paradigms: genetic, neuroscience, and cognitive behavioral. We also emphasize the importance of factors that are important to all paradigms, including emotion, gender, culture, ethnicity, socioeconomic status, and interpersonal relationships. A related issue is the use of more than one paradigm in studying abnormal psychology. Rather than force an entire field into, for example, a cognitive behavioral paradigm, we argue from the available information that different problems in psychopathology are amenable to analyses within different frameworks. For instance, genetic factors are important in bipolar disorder and attention-deficit/hyperactivity disorder, but genes do their work via the environment. In disorders such as depression, cognitive behavioral factors are essential, but neurotransmitters also exert an influence. For still other disorders—for example, dissociative disorders—cognitive factors involving consciousness are important to consider. Furthermore, the importance of a diathesis–stress approach remains a cornerstone to the field. Emerging data indicate that nearly all mental disorders arise from subtle interactions between genetic or psychological predispositions and stressful life events.

We continue to include considerable material on culture and ethnicity in the study of psychopathology and intervention. In Chapter 2, we present a separate section that emphasizes the importance of culture and ethnicity in all paradigms. We point to the important role of culture and ethnicity in the other chapters as well. For example, in the Diagnosis and Assessment chapter (3), we discuss cultural bias in assessment and ways to guard against this selectivity in perception. We have expanded and updated information on ethnicity with respect to how stress impacts health in Chapter 2, we have provided new findings about families and culture in schizophrenia (Chapter 9), and we have updated coverage of culture and ethnicity in substance use disorders (Chapter 10).

We continue to emphasize and expand our discussion of genetics and psychopathology throughout the book. We repeatedly emphasize that psychopathology is best understood by considering how genes do their work via the environment. Thus, rather than asking whether genes or the environment is more important in a particular disorder, we emphasize that both of these factors are important. Exciting new discoveries have made it clear that nature and nurture work together, not in opposition to each another. Without the genes, a behavior might not be possible. But without the environment, genes could not express themselves and thus contribute to the behavior. Genes are remarkably flexible at responding to different types of environments. In turn, human beings are quite flexible at adapting to different environments.

New to This Edition

The twelfth edition has many new and exciting additions and changes. By the time current students graduate and join our field, DSM-5 will be in use. Our goal is to help prepare them for this. Thus, we have added significant new material about the forthcoming DSM-5 in every chapter. We have added two new chapters to reflect the changing organization of the DSM-5. We have also added many new tables and figures throughout the book to illustrate the similarities and differences between the forthcoming DSM-5 and older diagnostic symptoms.

In addition, we continue to update and innovate. We no longer apologetically cover theories that don't work or don't have empirical support. As the research on each disorder has burgeoned, we've moved to just highlighting the most exciting and accepted theories, research, and treatments. This edition, as always, contains hundreds of updated references. Throughout the book, we have further streamlined the writing to increase the clarity of presentation and to highlight the key issues in the field. We have included many more figures to carefully illustrate the genetics and brain networks involved in different disorders.

One of our major changes was to shift the chapter structure of the book to make the material more integrated and accessible. First, we have reorganized the order of chapters so that the disorder chapters are presented in an order that maximizes their similarities and research base. In past editions, we included a chapter late in the book on therapies, and yet we covered therapies throughout the book as well. In this edition, we've integrated the material on the different types of therapies in each and every chapter, and we introduce these concepts in Chapters 1 and 2. So that students will be equipped to understand the state of research on treatments as they consider each disorder, we've described how to evaluate treatment outcome studies early in the book, as we discuss other research methods in Chapter 4. To bring treatment to life, we've added new Clinical Cases throughout the chapters on specific disorders.

We have continued to add additional pedagogy based on feedback from students and professors. In addition to the new Clinical Case boxes, we have also added a number of new Focus on Discovery boxes in order to illustrate what the different disorders look like in the context of real people's lives. In addition, we have modified and added new Check Your Knowledge questions so that students can do a quick check to see if they are learning and integrating the material. There are many new photos to provide students with additional real-world examples and applications of psychopathology. The end-of-chapter summaries continue to be consistent across the chapters, using a bulleted format and summarizing the descriptions, causes, and treatments of the disorders covered.

New and Expanded Coverage

We are really excited about the new features of this edition. Some of the major new material in this twelfth edition includes:

Chapter 1: Introduction and Historical Overview

New research on stigma and mental illness

New material on the likely DSM-5 definition of mental disorder

Expanded section on the history of psychoanalysis and psychodynamic thought

New Focus on Discovery box on Freud and depression

New section on cognition

New material on the mental health professions

Chapter 2: Current Paradigms in Psychopathology

Paradigms reorganized to include genetic, neuroscience, and cognitive behavioral

New section on interpersonal factors that cut across paradigms, including discussion of interpersonal psychotherapy

New material on cutting-edge molecular genetics, including SNPs, CNVs, and genome-wide association studies, including new figures to illustrate these issues

Genetics section revised to amplify how genes interact with the environment

Updated coverage on cognitive science contributions to cognitive behavioral paradigm

New Clinical Case in the cognitive behavioral paradigm section

Expanded coverage of factors that cut across paradigms: emotion, sociocultural factors, and interpersonal factors

Three new Focus on Discovery boxes on: (1) gender and health, (2) socioeconomics and health, (3) couples and family therapies

New Check Your Knowledge questions

Chapter 3: Diagnosis and Assessment

Completely reorganized section on diagnosis to reflect the upcoming publication of DSM-5

New tables and figures comparing DSM-IV-TR to DSM-5

New Focus on Discovery box on the history of stress research

Expanded section on the assessment of stress, including current methods for comprehensively assessing stress with interviews and self-report checklists

New research on IQ assessment

Updated and expanded coverage of cultural factors in diagnosis and assessment

Chapter 4: Research Methods in Psychopathology

Updated section on molecular genetics research methods

New material on methods and issues involved in evaluating treatments, including the randomized controlled clinical trial, to give students a more solid understanding of treatment issues as they read through that material in each of the chapters on psychopathology

New material on the issue of nonrepresentative samples and its impact on research

New material on dissemination efforts designed to diminish the gap between research and practice

Chapter 5: Mood Disorders

New evidence for the lower rates of depression among immigrants to the United States

New evidence for light therapy as a successful treatment for nonseasonal forms of affective disorder

New evidence about the prevalence of bipolar disorder worldwide

Discussion of base rates of bipolar II disorder in the context of the growing awareness of the low reliability of structured interviews for the disorder

Substantially updated material on the neurobiology (brain imaging) findings for depression, including experimental manipulations using deep brain stimulation and new neurobiological models of emotion regulation

Removal of research that has not been well replicated

Three new Focus on Discovery boxes on (1) cardiovascular disease and depression, (2) non-suicidal self-injury, and (3) the overlap between anxiety and depression

Several new tables to provide an overview of the subtype specifiers for depression and bipolar disorder, key neurobiological models of mood disorders, and key terms in suicidality

Substantial updates to cognitive theories of depression, including new research on information processing and rumination

New figure to illustrate the basic components of hopelessness theory

New research on sleep deprivation and schedule disruption as a predictor of manic symptoms

More succinct coverage of the history of research and debate regarding the efficacy of cognitive therapy

New findings showing that computerized cognitive therapy can be helpful

New findings on suicide prevention

Entire section on suicide streamlined and updated to cover recent evidence of the role of the social environment

Chapter 6: Anxiety Disorders

Chapter reorganized to reflect removal of OCD and PTSD from the main anxiety disorders chapter in the DSM-5

Most of the risk factors are now general to the different anxiety disorders, making this a simpler chapter for students to comprehend

Recent findings on the neurobiology of fear conditioning and, in the treatment section, on how neurobiology helps us understand extinction

Etiology section reorganized with clarity and current research in mind

New material on the use of computerized interventions and virtual reality

Focus in treatment sections on the principles and efficacy across anxiety disorders, reflecting the growing research base on commonalities across anxiety disorders

Chapter 7: Obsessive-Compulsive-Related and Trauma-Related Disorders

Brand new chapter for this edition, covering obsessive-compulsive disorder, hoarding disorder, body dysmorphic disorder, post-traumatic stress disorder, and acute stress disorder

Chapter 8: Dissociative Disorders and Somatic Symptom Disorders

Reorganized to fit with likely DSM-5 combination of pain, somatoform, and hypochondriasis disorders—reflected in the clinical description, etiology, and treatment sections, which are now much simpler

New section on neurobiology of somatic symptoms and pain

New Clinical Case on factitious disorder

Chapter 9: Schizophrenia

New information on DSM-5

New Focus on Discovery box on attenuated psychosis syndrome

Outdated material on genetics trimmed and new research on GWAS studies, including a new figure, added

Developmental section reorganized to distinguish familial high-risk from clinical high-risk studies

New material on schizophrenia and the brain

New material on culture and expressed emotion

New section on environmental factors impacting the cause of schizophrenia, including cannabis use

Updated material on second-generation antipsychotic medications

Updated material on cognitive remediation treatments

New section on psychoeducation

Chapter 10: Substance Use Disorders

New material on likely DSM-5 changes, including abuse and dependence as indicators of severity of alcohol and drug use disorders

New statistics and two new figures on use of all drugs

New material on cravings for substances

New figures on use of drugs and emergency room visits for pain medications (nonmedical uses)

New material on medical marijuana

New treatment studies for smoking, heroin, alcohol, and cocaine

New information on drug replacement treatment

New information on treatment instead of prison for drug offenders

Chapter 11: Eating Disorders

Expanded section on binge eating disorder, consistent with its likely inclusion in DSM-5, including physical consequences and prognosis

New Clinical Case on binge eating disorder

Updated material on obesity

Updated section on family factors

Updated material on family treatment for anorexia

New material on treatment for binge eating disorder

Updated sections on symptoms, physical consequences, and prognosis for all eating disorders

Chapter 12: Sexual Disorders

Gender identity disorder no longer covered, as we believe this diagnosis stigmatizes more than it helps; this diagnosis placed in cultural and historical context

Similarly, transvestic fetishism longer covered, given the lack of evidence that this behavior causes harm

Likely DSM-5 changes in sexual dysfunction and paraphilias described

Lack of validity for Kaplan's phases of the sexual response cycle in women described

Graph added to show rates of HIV diagnoses by age, showing highest incidence among people in their early 20s

Material on rape covered in a new Focus on Discovery box

New material from the first randomized controlled trial for CBT among sex offenders, showing poor outcomes

Chapter 13: Disorders of Childhood

New figures and tables showing the likely changes in DSM-5 for these disorders

Updated material on conduct disorder types and traits

Major revision to section on intellectual developmental disorder, including use of new name likely to be adopted in DSM-5

Updated material on dyslexia and dyscalculia

Updated material on genetics in autism spectrum disorder

Updated material in the Focus on Discovery box covering controversies in the field

Updated material on treatment for ADHD, longitudinal studies of the course of ADHD, and environmental toxins and ADHD

Updated material on depression and anxiety in children

Two new Focus on Discovery boxes on (1) asthma and (2) history of autism

Chapter 14: Late-Life and Neurocognitive Disorders

Chapter substantially reorganized to focus mostly on neurocognitive disorders

Updated material on methods and issues involved in understanding late life

New material on mild cognitive impairment, Alzheimer's disease, frontotemporal dementia, and preclinical risk for Alzheimer's disease

New material to show how lifestyle factors such as exercise, cognitive engagement, and depression can influence the onset and course of Alzheimer's disease

New material to capture recent findings on the emotional and social deficits associated with frontotemporal dementia

Updated sections on treatments, with a discussion of the emergent focus on early identification

Chapter 15: Personality and Personality Disorders

Chapter substantially reorganized to reflect the fact that DSM-5 changes to personality and personality disorders are more fundamental than those for any other aspect of diagnosis

New section on the differences between DSM-IV-TR and DSM-5

New focus on the six personality disorder types likely to be included in the DSM-5, leading the entire chapter to feel much more research-oriented since these are the personality disorder types with the most research available

New material on mentalization-based treatment, which has shown effects across an 8-year follow-up period for the treatment of borderline personality disorder

Treatment section reorganized and simplified

New material demonstrating comorbidity, etiological overlap, and treatment parallels of obsessive-compulsive personality disorder type with obsessive-compulsive disorder and of schizotypal personality disorder type with schizotypy

Chapter 16: Legal and Ethical Issues

Material on the insanity defense trimmed and reorganized

New material on violence and mental illness

New material on competency to stand trial

Overall chapter trimmed and tightened up

Special Features for the Student Reader

Several features of this book are designed to make it easier for students to master and enjoy the material.

Clinical Case Boxes We have expanded and added a number of new Clinical Cases throughout the book to provide a clinical context for the theories and research that occupy most of our attention in the chapters and to help make vivid the real-life implications of the empirical work of psychopathologists and clinicians.

Focus on Discovery Boxes There are many in-depth discussions of selected topics encased in Focus on Discovery boxes throughout the book. This feature allows us to involve readers in specialized topics in a way that does not detract from the flow of the regular text. Sometimes a Focus on Discovery box expands on a point in the text; sometimes it deals with an entirely separate but relevant issue, often a controversial one. We have added a number of new boxes in this edition, replacing a number of the older ones. Additional boxes feature real-life examples of individuals living with different disorders.

Quick Summaries We include short summaries throughout the chapters to allow students to pause and assimilate the material. These should help students keep track of the multifaceted and complex issues that surround the study of psychopathology.

End-of-Chapter Summaries Summaries at the end of each chapter have been rewritten in bulleted form. In Chapters 5–15, we organize these by clinical descriptions, etiology, and treatment—the major sections of every chapter covering the disorders. We believe this format will make it easier for readers to review and remember the material. In fact, we even suggest that students read the summary before beginning the chapter itself in order to get a good sense of what lies ahead. Then re-reading it after completing the chapter itself will enhance students' understanding and provide an immediate sense of what has been learned in just one reading of the chapter.

Check Your Knowledge Questions Throughout each chapter, we provide between three and six boxes that ask questions about the material covered in the chapter. These questions are intended to help students assess their understanding and retention of the material as well as provide them with samples of the types of questions that often are found in course exams. The answers to the questions in these boxes are at the end of each chapter, just before the list of key terms. We believe that these will be useful aids for students as they make their way through the chapters.

Glossary When an important term is introduced, it is boldfaced and defined or discussed immediately. Most such terms appear again later in the book, in which case they will not be highlighted in this way. All these terms are listed again at the end of each chapter, and definitions appear at the end of the book in a glossary.

DSM-5 Table The endpapers of the book contain a summary of the proposed psychiatric nomenclature for of the fifth edition of the *Diagnostic and Statistical Manual of Mental Disorders*, known as DSM-5. This provides a handy guide to where particular disorders appear in

the "official" taxonomy or classification. We make considerable use of DSM-5, though in a selective and sometimes critical vein. Sometimes we find it more effective to discuss theory and research on a particular problem in a way that is different from DSM's conceptualization.

Supplements

Teaching and Learning Program: Learn More at www.wileyplus.com

WileyPlus is an online teaching and learning environment that builds confidence because it takes the guesswork out of studying, providing students with a clear roadmap of what to do, how to do it, and whether they have done it correctly. Powered by tested and proven technology, WileyPlus has enriched the education of millions of students in over 20 countries around the world.

What do Instructors Receive with WileyPlus for *Abnormal Psychology*?

WileyPlus provides reliable, customizable resources that reinforce course goals inside and outside the classroom. WileyPLUS also provides instructors with powerful assessment tools that enable instructors to track individual student progress, as well as overall mastery levels achieved by an entire class or class section.

Powerful Multimedia Resources for Classroom Presentations:

- **Case Study Videos** presents an encompassing view of 16 psychological disorders. Produced by documentary filmmaker Nathan Friedkin in collaboration with Ann Kring and Sheri Johnson, each case study video is about 7-10 minutes long and features patients and their families, in the context of their lives, describing symptoms from their own perspectives. In addition to the patient experience, each video also provides concise information about the available treatment options and commentary from a professional clinician.

- **Wiley Psychology Videos**, which is available to all instructors regardless of whether their students adopt WileyPlus, represent a collection of over 50 brief clips applying the concepts of clinical psychology to current events.

- *Media-enriched PowerPoint slides,* authored by Michael Nina of New York University, outline key concepts in the chapter and contain illustrations from the text as well as embedded web links to Wiley's video program.

- *Image Gallery,* which features line art from the textbook in a flexible digital format instructors can use for in-class presentations.

Pre-created teaching materials and assessments connected to a WileyPlus grade book help instructors optimize their time and deliver assignments customized to their learning objectives:

- *The Instructor's Resource Manual,* prepared by Kathleen Tillman of SUNY New Palz, includes chapter summaries, "lecture launcher" discussion stimulators, perspectives on the causes and treatment of each disorder, key points students should know, key terms, guides to instructional films and websites, and more.

- A **Test Bank**, written by Jean Ranieski of the University of Houston, contains over 2,000 multiple-choice questions.

- Both the *Case Study* and *Wiley Psychology Videos* are assignable to students in WileyPlus and each is paired with a suite of questions that measure student understanding of the video's content, as well as its connection to related concepts discussed in the textbook. The *Case Studies Videos* are further supported within WileyPlus by a series of pre- and post-activities, written by Tiffany Wilson of Des Moines Area Community College, that test comprehension and measure student empathy levels relating to each of the presented mental disorders.

- *A library of 16 complete research articles* from leading academic journals have been selected by Richard Williams of SUNY Potsdam and connected to each chapter in **Abnormal Psychology.** Each research article is accompanied by a series of assessment questions that test students understanding of the methodologies, outcomes and objectives of each research study. Instructors can assign articles and accompanying assessments in WileyPLUS, providing students with valuable experience analyzing current research.

- Chapter exams and quizzes, prepared by Courtney Worley of the University of Alabama and Kathy Sexton of Elmhurst College, give students a way to test themselves on course material before exams. Each question is also linked by a specific learning objective within the book to aid in concept mastery.

- Flashcards. This interactive module gives students the opportunity to easily test their knowledge of vocabulary

Other Resources

Book Companion Website (www.wiley.com/go/global/kring) containing additional online resources for instructors and students.

To Learn More

To review samples of the **Abnormal Psychology** rich program of teaching and learning material, please visit www.wiley.com/go/global/kring or contact your local Wiley representative to arrange a live demonstration of WileyPLUS.

What do Students Receive with WileyPlus?

WileyPlus builds student confidence and proficiency by providing a clear easy-to-follow study roadmap. Throughout each study session, students can assess their progress and gain immediate feedback. WileyPlus provides precise reporting of strengths and weaknesses, as well as individualized quizzes so that students can feel confident that they are spending their time on the right activities and come to class better prepared to engage with the instructor.

WileyPlus Student Resources

- A digital version of the complete textbook with integrated videos, study tools, and quizzes.

- **Case Study Videos** presents an encompassing view of 16 psychological disorders. Produced by documentary filmmaker, Nathan Friedkin in collaboration with Ann Kring and Sheri Johnson, each case study video is about 7-10 minutes long and features patients and their families, in the context of their lives, describing symptoms from their own perspectives. In addition to the patient experience, each video also provides concise information about the available treatment options and commentary from a professional clinician.

- **Wiley Psychology Videos** represent a collection of over 50 brief clips applying the concepts of clinical psychology to current events.

- *A library of 16 complete research articles* from leading academic journals have been selected by Richard Williams of SUNY Potsdam and connected to each chapter in *Abnormal Psychology 12th edition*. Each research article is accompanied by a series of assessment questions that test students understanding of the methodologies, outcomes and objectives of each research study. Instructors can assign articles and accompanying assessments in WileyPLUS, providing students with valuable experience analyzing current research.

Acknowledgments

We are grateful for the contributions of our colleagues and staff, for it was with their assistance that the twelfth edition was able to become the book that it is. In particular, we thank Doug Mennin at CUNY Hunter College and Bob Krueger at the University of Minnesota. We are also extremely appreciative of the work done by Andrew Kennedy, Natalyn Daniels, and Jessica Jayne Yu, who did a huge amount of work to create, manage, and edit our ever-expanding reference section. We also thank Janelle Caponigro and Luma Muhtadie from UC Berkeley who compiled the research articles from Wiley journals to be used in the library of research articles.

We have also benefited from the skills and dedication of the folks from Wiley. For this edition, we have many people to thank. Specifically, we thank Executive Editor, Chris Johnson; Marketing Manager, Margaret Barrett; Production Editor, William Murray; Photo Editors and Researchers, Sheena Goldstein and Teri Stratford; Senior Illustration Editor, Sandra Rigby; and the Outside Production Service, Suzanne Ingrao of Ingrao Associates. We also are grateful for the generous help and timely support from Maura Gilligan, Editorial Assistant.

From time to time, students and faculty colleagues have written us their comments on the book; these communications are always welcome. Readers can e-mail us at akring@berkeley.edu, sljohnson@berkeley.edu.

Finally and most importantly, our heartfelt thanks go to the most important people in our lives for their continued support and encouragement along the way. A great big thanks to Angela Hawk (AMK) and Daniel Rose (SLJ), to whom this book is dedicated with love and gratitude.

DECEMBER 2011

Ann M. Kring, *Berkeley, CA*

Sheri L. Johnson, *Berkeley, CA*

Brief Contents

Contents

4

Research Methods in Psychopathology   104

5

Mood Disorders   131

6

Anxiety Disorders   174

7

Obsessive-Compulsive-Related and Trauma-Related Disorders   203

8

Dissociative Disorders and Somatic Symptom Disorders   226

9

Schizophrenia   252

10

Substance Use Disorders   287

1 Introduction and Historical Overview

Clinical Case: A family perspective on living with schizophrenia

The lifetime emotional, social, and financial consequences experienced by individuals with schizophrenia have significant effects on their families. In a qualitative study of parents' experiences of caring for sons and daughters with schizophrenia, Knudson and Coyle (2002) found the greatest areas of concern expressed by parents related to difficulties in obtaining comprehensive, accurate information about schizophrenia, particularly in the early stages. Participants described the onset of schizophrenia in a son or daughter as a bewildering and often frightening experience. This was compounded by the fact that, as Joan said, their knowledge about the condition was often limited or misinformed by social myths.

Joan's experience, for example, was shared by many:

Joan: Nobody ever tells you anything, and I think in the early stages you need a lot of support and you need a lot of information and explanation and so on.

Interviewer: Specifically, what kind of information do you think you needed at that point?

Joan: Well, I needed information about the course of the illness, the medicines and the symptoms. Because this is like, you know, it hit me, and people don't know anything about schizophrenia and they think it's a dual personality, don't they?

The second area of major concern identified by Knudson and Coyle related to the perceived failure of the mental health system to include them in the treatment process. They describe one particular experience of Sonia and her feelings of exclusion.

Sonia: 'We ourselves, really, have been largely side-lined. Uh, things were said "Well, these are now confidential matters" and, um, we still find that very difficult because, uh, how can you be not informed about somebody that you're caring for? Um…and you need to know certain things – otherwise you can't care properly for that person'.

Clinical Case: Molly

Molly describes her school days as some of the unhappiest times of her life. She was frequently called 'stupid' by her teachers and given detentions after school because she'd repeatedly handed her homework late and failed to pay attention in class. Instead of listening to the teacher, she'd much prefer to watch a bird outside the window or an aeroplane flying in the sky. But ask Molly now, aged 27 years, about her attention deficit hyperactivity disorder (ADHD), and she'll tell that she'd "never trade (her) ADHD for the chance to be a non-ADHDer." Adding "I may never have experienced the thrill of taking on challenges that many people have no desire to do, like bungee jumping, parachuting, climbing steep cliffs and learning to fly. Crash landing my first plane because I forgot to check my fuel gauge was another ADHD 'oops,' but I survived...although my plane didn't!"

But when asked to reflect on the question of whether her life would be different if she didn't have ADHD, Molly responded that she would have finished college the *first* time, she would have held down the same job for more than 2 or 3 years. She would get to places on time, rather than always arriving at least 20 minutes later. Her bills would be paid on time, and her parents would feel a sense of her having accomplished something in life. On a personal level, Molly thought she'd probably be a nicer person and have more friends. She knew that she frequently came across as being rude or arrogant, and had trouble controlling her anger when she became frustrated. Her parents were also nagging to be more careful, as Felicia was frequently sporting new bruises as she was, according to them, clumsy and didn't take care of herself or the things around her.

WE ALL TRY TO understand other people. Determining why another person does or feels something is not easy to do. In fact, we do not always understand our own feelings and behavior. Figuring out why people behave in normal, expected ways is difficult enough; understanding seemingly abnormal behavior, such as the behavior of Molly, can be even more difficult.

In this book, we will consider the description, causes, and treatments of a number of different mental disorders. We will also demonstrate the numerous challenges professionals in this field face. As you approach the study of **psychopathology**, the field concerned with the nature, development, and treatment of mental disorders, keep in mind that the field is continually developing and adding new findings. As we proceed, you will see that the field's interest and importance is ever growing.

One challenge we face is to remain objective. Our subject matter, human behavior, is personal and powerfully affecting, making objectivity difficult. The pervasiveness and potentially disturbing effects of psychopathology intrude on our own lives. Who has not experienced irrational thoughts, or feelings? Most of us have known someone, a friend or a relative, whose behavior was upsetting and impossible to fathom, and we realize how frustrating and frightening it can be to try to understand and help a person suffering psychological difficulties. You can see that this personal impact of our subject matter requires us to make a conscious, determined effort to remain objective.

The other side of this coin is that our closeness to the subject matter adds to its intrinsic fascination; undergraduate courses in abnormal psychology are among the most popular in the entire college curriculum, not just in psychology departments. Our feeling of familiarity with the subject matter draws us to the study of psychopathology, but it also has a distinct disadvantage: we bring to the study our preconceived notions of what the subject matter is. Each of us has developed certain ways of thinking and talking about mental disorders, certain words and concepts that somehow seem to fit. As you read this book and try to understand the psychological disorders it discusses, we may be asking you to adopt different ways of thinking and talking from those to which you are accustomed.

Perhaps most challenging of all, we must not only recognize our own preconceived notions of mental disorders, but we must also confront and work to change the stigma we often associate with these conditions. **Stigma** refers to the destructive beliefs and attitudes held by a society that are ascribed to groups considered different in some manner, such as people with mental illness. More specifically, stigma has four characteristics (see Figure 1.1):

1. A label is applied to a group of people that distinguishes them from others (e.g., "crazy").

2. The label is linked to deviant or undesirable attributes by society (e.g., crazy people are dangerous).

3. People with the label are seen as essentially different from those without the label, contributing to an "us" versus "them" mentality (e.g., we are not like those crazy people).

4. People with the label are discriminated against unfairly (e.g., a clinic for crazy people can't be built in our neighborhood).

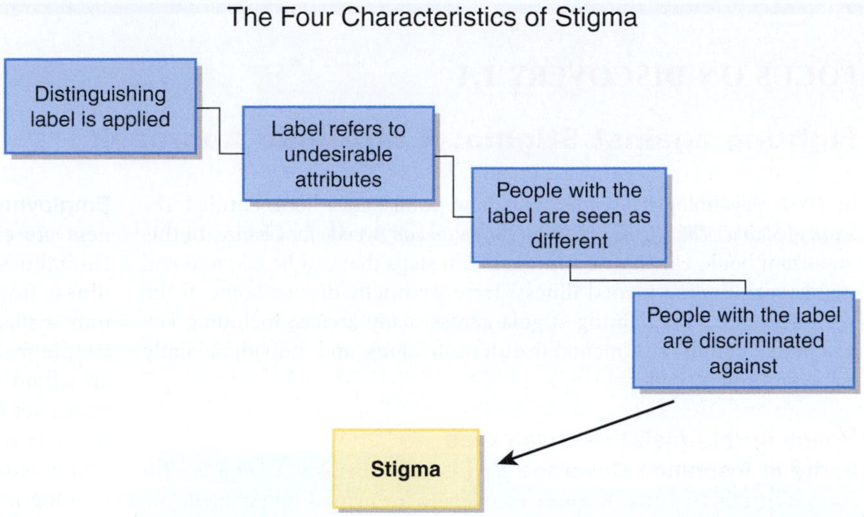

The first clinical case of this chapter illustrates how stigma can lead to discrimination. Some people assume that schizophrenics will be violent. This belief is based more in fiction than reality, however. A person with mental illness is not necessarily any more likely to be violent than a person without mental illness (Steadman et al., 1998; Swanson et al., 1990).

As we will see, the treatment of individuals with mental disorders throughout recorded history has not generally been good, and this has contributed to their stigmatization, to the extent that they have often been brutalized and shunned by society. Torturous treatments have been described to the public as miracle cures, and even today, terms such as *crazy, insane, retard,* and *schizo* are tossed about without thought of the people who actually suffer from mental illnesses and for whom these insults and the intensely distressing feelings and behaviors they refer to are a reality of daily life. The case of Molly illustrates how hurtful using such careless and mean-spirited names can be.

Mental illness remains one of the most stigmatized of conditions in the twenty-first century, despite advances in the public's knowledge about the origins of mental disorders (Hinshaw, 2007). In 1999, David Satcher, then Surgeon General of the United States, wrote that stigma is the "most formidable obstacle to future progress in the arena of mental illness and mental health" in his groundbreaking report on mental illness (U.S. Department of Health and Human Services, 1999). Sadly, this remains true more than 10 years later.

Throughout this book, we hope to fight this stigma by showing you the latest evidence about the nature, causes, and treatments for these disorders, dispelling myths and other misconceptions as we go. As part of this effort, we will try to put a human face on mental disorders, by including descriptions of actual people with these disorders in the chapters that follow. Additional ways to fight stigma are presented in Focus on Discovery 1.1.

But you will have to help in this fight, for the mere acquisition of knowledge does not ensure the end of stigma (Penn, Chamberlin, & Mueser, 2003). As we will see in Chapter 2, we have learned a great deal about neurobiological contributors to mental illness, such as neurotransmitters and genetics, in the last 20 years. Many mental health practitioners and advocates hoped that the more people learned about the neurobiological causes of mental disorders, the less stigmatized these disorders would be. However, results from a recent study shows that this may not be true (Pescosolido et al., 2010). People's knowledge has increased, but unfortunately stigma has not decreased. In the study, researchers surveyed people's attitudes and knowledge about mental disorders at two time points: in 1996 and 2006. Compared to 1996, people in 2006 were more likely to believe that mental disorders like schizophrenia, depression, and alcohol addiction had a neurobiological cause, but stigma toward these disorders did not decrease. In fact, in some cases it increased. For example, people in 2006 were less likely to want to have a person with schizophrenia as their neighbor compared to people in 1996. Clearly, there is work to be done to reduce stigma.

In this chapter, we first discuss what we mean by the term *mental disorder.* Then we look briefly at how our views of mental disorders have evolved through history to the more scientific perspectives of today. We conclude with a discussion of the current mental health professions.

The Four Characteristics of Stigma

Distinguishing label is applied

Label refers to undesirable attributes

People with the label are seen as different

People with the label are discriminated against

Stigma

Figure 1.1 The four characteristics of stigma.

FOCUS ON DISCOVERY 1.1

Fighting against Stigma: A Strategic Approach

In 2007, psychologist Stephen Hinshaw published a book entitled *The Mark of Shame: The Stigma of Mental Illness and an Agenda for Change*. In this important book, Hinshaw outlines several steps that can be taken to end stigma surrounding mental illness. Here we briefly discuss some of the key suggestions for fighting stigma across many arenas, including law and policy, community, mental health professions, and individual/family behaviors and attitudes.

Policy and Legislative Strategies

Parity in Insurance Coverage In 1996, the Federal Mental Health Parity Act required that insurance coverage for mental illness be at the same level as for other illnesses, which was an important first step. However, the law had a number of problems (e.g., addiction was not included; companies could set limits on coverage). In March 2008, the U.S. House of Representatives passed an even broader parity bill, the Paul Wellstone Mental Health Parity and Addiction Equity Act, which comes closer to offering true parity. With this law, insurance companies cannot charge higher co-payments or deductibles for mental illness than they do for other types of illnesses. House and Senate committees produced a bill that was signed into law on October 3, 2008, and rules regarding the implementation of the law were put into place in early 2010.

Discriminatory Laws Some states have rules banning people with mental illness from voting, marrying, serving on juries, or holding public office. In an analysis of bills submitted for consideration in state legislatures in 2002, there were about as many bills to take away liberties as there were to grant liberties to people with mental illness. Similarly, there were roughly equal numbers of new bills that would effectively increase discrimination against people with mental illness as there were bills that would diminish discrimination (Corrigan et al., 2005). Speaking to state legislators about the importance of nondiscriminatory laws is something we can all do to help fight stigma in this arena.

Employment Unemployment rates among people with mental illness are extremely high, despite provisions of the Americans with Disabilities Act (ADA) that make it illegal to keep someone with mental illness from obtaining or keeping a job. The cruel irony here is that only a small number of ADA claims deal with job discrimination for people with mental illness (likely because people with mental illness are afraid to come forward due to the stigma surrounding their illness), yet these claims are among the easiest, at least in terms of cost, to fix (e.g., contrast the cost of allowing time off for therapy to the cost of redesigning and building a wheelchair-accessible area). Further training in job-relevant skills, such as provision of extra educational benefits to those whose education might have been curtailed by mental illness, would help with employment opportunities. Similarly, training in social skills relevant to the workplace and other structured programs to enhance workplace success is an important goal.

Decriminalization People with mental illness, particularly substance use disorders, often end up in jail rather than a hospital. Large urban jails, such as the Los Angeles County jail, Riker's Island in New York, and Cook County jail in Chicago, now house more people with mental illness than any hospital, public or private, in the United States. Many substance-related problems are first detected within the criminal justice system, and people may need more intensive treatment to address underlying substance use problems. Minimal or no treatment is provided in jail, and this is thus not an optimal place for people with mental illness. Many states have adopted assisted outpatient treatment (AOT) laws that provide court-mandated outpatient treatment rather than jail time for people with mental illness.

Community Strategies

Housing Options Rates of homelessness in people with mental illness are too high, and more programs to provide community residences and group homes are needed. However, many neighborhoods are reluctant

Defining Mental Disorder

A difficult but fundamental task facing those in the field of psychopathology is to define **mental disorder.** The best current definition of mental disorder is one that contains several characteristics. The definition of *mental disorder* presented in the fourth edition of the American diagnostic manual, the *Diagnostic and Statistical Manual of Mental Disorders* (DSM-IV-TR), as well as the proposed definition for the fifth edition of the DSM (DSM-5), which is scheduled for release in May 2013, includes a number of characteristics essential to the concept of mental disorder (Stein et al., 2010), including the following:

- The disorder occurs within the individual.
- It causes personal distress or disability.
- It is not a culturally specific reaction to an event (e.g., death of a loved one).
- It is not primarily a result of social deviance or conflict with society.

In the following sections, we consider in more detail some of the key characteristics of the mental disorder definition including disability, distress, violation of social norms, and to embrace the idea of people with mental illness living too close. Lobbying legislatures and community leaders about the importance of adequate housing is a critically important step toward providing housing and reducing stigma.

Personal Contact Providing greater housing opportunities for people with mental illness will likely mean that people with mental illness will shop and eat in local establishments alongside people without mental illness. Research suggests that this type of contact—where status is relatively equal—can reduce stigma. Informal settings, such as local parks and churches, can also help bridge the personal contact gap between people with and without mental illness.

Education Educating people about mental illness (one of the goals of this book!) is an important step toward reducing stigma. Education alone won't completely eradicate stigma, however. By learning about mental illness, though, people may be less hesitant to interact with people who have different disorders. Many of you already know someone with a mental disorder. Sadly, though, stigma often prevents people from disclosing their history with mental illness. Education may help lessen the hesitancy of people to talk about their illnesses.

Mental Health and Health Profession Strategies

Mental Health Evaluations Many children see their pediatricians for well-baby or well-child exams. The goal of these is to prevent illness before it occurs. Hinshaw (2007) makes a strong case for the inclusion of similar preventive efforts for mental illness among children and adolescents by, for example, including rating scale assessments from parents and teachers in order to help identify problems before they become more serious.

Education and Training Mental health professionals should receive training in stigma issues. This type of training would undoubtedly help professionals recognize the pernicious signs of stigma, even within the very profession that is charged with helping people with mental illness. In addition, mental health professionals need to keep current in their knowledge of the descriptions, causes, and empirically supported treatments for mental illness. This would certainly lead to better interactions with patients and might also help in educating the public about the important work that is done by mental health professionals.

Individual and Family Strategies

Education for Individuals and Families It can be frightening and disorienting for families to learn that a loved one has been diagnosed with an illness, and this may be particularly true for mental illness. Receiving current information about the causes and treatments of mental illness is crucial because it would help to alleviate blame and stereotypes families might hold about mental illness. Educating people with mental illness is also extremely important. Sometimes termed *psychoeducation*, this type of information is built into many types of treatments, whether they are pharmacological or psychosocial. In order for people to understand why they should adhere to certain treatment regimens, it is important for them to know the nature of their illness and the treatment alternatives available.

Support and Advocacy Groups Participating in support or advocacy groups can be a helpful adjunct to treatment for people with mental illness and their families. Websites such as Mind Freedom International (http://www.mindfreedom.org) are designed to provide a forum for people with mental illness to find support. Some such groups also encourage people not to hide their mental illness, but rather to consider it a point of pride—"Mad Pride" events are scheduled all over the world. Many people with mental illness have created their own blogs to discuss their illness and help to demystify and therefore destigmatize it. For example, the nonprofit BringChange2Mind is a group that seeks to demystify mental illness in several ways, including a blog that is written by people with mental illness (http://bringchange2mind.wordpress.com/). The site Patients Like Me (http://www.patientslikeme.com/) is a social networking site for people with all sorts of different illnesses. These sites, developed and run by people with mental illness, contain useful links, blogs, and other helpful resources. In-person support groups are also helpful, and many communities have groups supported by the National Alliance on Mental Illness (www.nami.org). Finding peers in the context of support groups can be beneficial, especially for emotional support and empowerment.

dysfunction. We will see that no single characteristic can fully define the concept, although each has merit and each captures some part of what might be a full definition. Consequently, mental disorder is usually determined based on the presence of several characteristics at one time, as the DSM definition exemplifies. Figure 1.2 shows the different characteristics of the definition of mental disorder.

Personal Distress

One characteristic used to define mental disorder is personal distress—that is, a person's behavior may be classified as disordered if it causes him or her great distress. Molly felt distress about her difficulty with paying attention and the social consequences of this difficulty—that is, being called names by other schoolgirls. Personal distress also characterizes many of the forms of mental disorder considered in this book—people experiencing anxiety disorders and depression suffer greatly. But not all mental disorders cause distress. For example, an individual with the antisocial type of personality disorder may treat others coldheartedly and violate the law

Figure 1.2 Key characteristics in the definition of mental disorder.

Clinical Case: José

José didn't know what to think about his nightmares. Ever since he returned from the war, he couldn't get the bloody images out of his head. He woke up nearly every night with nightmares about the carnage he witnessed as a soldier stationed in Fallujah. Even during the day, he would have flashbacks to the moment his Humvee was nearly sliced in half by a rocket-propelled grenade. Watching his friend die sitting next to him was the worst part; even the occasional pain from shrapnel still embedded in his shoulder was not as bad as the recurring dreams and flashbacks. He seemed to be sweating all the time now, and whenever he heard a loud noise, he jumped out of his chair. Just the other day, his grandmother stepped on a balloon left over from his

"welcome home" party. To José, it sounded like a gunshot, and he immediately dropped to the ground.

His grandmother was worried about him. She thought he must have *ataque de nervios*, just like her father had back home in Puerto Rico. She said her father was afraid all the time and felt like he was going crazy. She kept going to Mass and praying for José, which he appreciated. The army doctor said he had posttraumatic stress disorder (PTSD). José was supposed to go to the Veterans Administration (VA) hospital for an evaluation, but he didn't really think there was anything wrong with him. Yet his buddy Jorge had been to a group session at the VA, and he said it made him feel better. Maybe he would check it out. He wanted these images to get out of his head.

without experiencing any guilt, remorse, anxiety, or other type of distress. And not all behavior that causes distress is disordered—for example, the distress of hunger due to religious fasting or the pain of childbirth.

Disability

Personal distress can be part of the definition of mental disorder.
(© VojtechVlk/Shutterstock.)

Disability—that is, impairment in some important area of life (e.g., work or personal relationships)—can also characterize mental disorder. For example, substance use disorders are defined in part by the social or occupational disability (e.g., serious arguments with one's spouse or poor work performance) created by substance abuse. Being rejected by peers, as Molly was, is also an example of this characteristic. Phobias can produce both distress and disability—for example, if a severe fear of flying prevents someone living in California from taking a job in New York. Like distress, however, disability alone cannot be used to define mental disorder, because some, but not all, disorders involve disability. For example, the disorder bulimia nervosa involves binge eating and compensatory purging (e.g., vomiting) in an attempt to control weight gain but does not necessarily involve disability. Many people with bulimia lead lives without impairment, while bingeing and purging in private. Other characteristics that might, in some circumstances, be considered disabilities—such as being blind and wanting to become a professional race car driver—do not fall within the domain of psychopathology. We do not have a rule that tells us which disabilities belong in our domain of study and which do not.

Violation of Social Norms

In the realm of behavior, social norms are widely held standards (beliefs and attitudes) that people use consciously or intuitively to make judgments about where behaviors are situated on such scales as good–bad, right–wrong, justified–unjustified, and acceptable–unacceptable. Behavior that violates social norms might be classified as disordered. For example, the repetitive rituals performed by people with obsessive-compulsive disorder (see Chapter 7) and the conversations with imaginary voices that some people with schizophrenia engage in (see Chapter 9) are behaviors that violate social norms. José's dropping to the floor at the sound of a popping balloon does not fit within most social norms. Yet this way of defining mental disorder is both too broad and too narrow. For example, it is too broad in that criminals violate social norms but are not usually studied within the domain of psychopathology; it is too narrow in that highly anxious people typically do not violate social norms.

Also, of course, social norms vary a great deal across cultures and ethnic groups, so behavior that clearly violates a social norm in one group may not do so at all in another. For example, in some cultures but not in others it violates a social norm to directly disagree with someone. In Puerto Rico, Josè's behavior would not likely have been interpreted in the same way as it would be in the United States. Throughout this book, we will address this important issue of cultural and ethnic diversity as it applies to the descriptions, causes, and treatments of mental disorders.

Dysfunction

In an influential and widely discussed paper, Wakefield (1992) proposed that mental disorders could be defined as **harmful dysfunction.** This definition has two parts: a value judgment ("harmful") and an objective, scientific component—the "dysfunction." A judgment that a behavior is harmful requires some standard, and this standard is likely to depend on social norms and values, the characteristic just described. Dysfunctions are said to occur when an internal mechanism is unable to perform its natural function—that is, the function that it evolved to perform. By grounding this part of the definition of mental disorder in evolutionary theory, Wakefield hoped to give the definition scientific objectivity.

Numerous critics have argued that the dysfunction component of Wakefield's definition is not so easily and objectively identifiable in relation to mental disorders (e.g., Houts, 2001; Lilienfeld & Marino, 1999). One difficulty is that the internal mechanisms involved in mental disorders are largely unknown; thus, we cannot say exactly what may not be functioning properly. Wakefield (1999) has tried to meet this objection by, in part, referring to plausible dysfunctions rather than proven ones. For example, hallucinations (hearing voices) could be construed as a failure of the mind to "turn off" unwanted sounds. Nevertheless, we have a situation in which we judge a behavior or set of behaviors to be harmful and then decide that the behavior represents a mental disorder because we believe it is caused by a dysfunction of some unknown internal mechanism. Clearly, like the other definitions of mental disorder, Wakefield's concept of harmful dysfunction has its limitations.

The DSM definition provides a broader concept of dysfunction, which is supported by our current body of evidence. Specifically, the DSM definition of dysfunction refers to the fact that behavioral, psychological, and biological dysfunctions are all interrelated. That is, the brain impacts behavior, and behavior impacts the brain; thus dysfunction in these is interrelated. This broadening does not entirely avoid the problems that Wakefield's definition suffers from, but it is an attempt that formally recognizes the limits of our current understanding.

Indeed, it is crucial to keep in mind that this book presents human problems that are currently considered mental disorders. Over time, because the field is continually evolving, the disorders discussed in books like this will undoubtedly change, and so will the definition of mental disorder. It is also quite possible that we will never be able to arrive at a definition that captures mental disorder in its entirety and for all time. Nevertheless, at the current time, the characteristics that are included in the definition constitute a useful partial definition, but keep in mind that they are not equally or invariably applicable to every diagnosis.

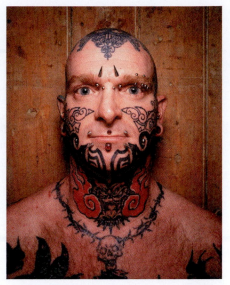

To some people, extreme tatoos are a social norm violation. However, social norm violations are not necessarily signs of a mental disorder. (Roger Spooner/GettyImages, Inc.)

Quick Summary

The focus of this book is on the description, causes, and treatments of a number of different mental disorders. It is important to note at the outset that the personal impact of our subject matter requires us to make a conscious, determined effort to remain objective. Stigma remains a central problem in the field of psychopathology. Stigma has four components that involve the labels for mental illness and their uses. Even the use of everyday terms such as *crazy* or *schizo* can contribute to the stigmatization of people with mental illness.

Defining mental disorder remains difficult. A number of different definitions have been offered, but none can entirely account for the full range of disorders. Whether or not a behavior causes personal distress can be a characteristic of mental disorder. But not all behaviors that we consider to be part of mental disorders cause distress. Behaviors that cause a disability or are unexpected can be considered part of a mental disorder. But again, some behaviors do not cause disability, nor are they unexpected. Behavior that violates social norms can also be considered part of a mental disorder. However, not all such behavior is considered part of a mental disorder, and some behaviors that are characteristic of mental disorders do not necessarily violate social norms. Harmful dysfunction involves both a value component and a scientific component. Like the other definitions, however, it cannot fully account for what we study in psychopathology. Taken together, each definition of mental disorder has something helpful to offer in the study of psychopathology.

Check Your Knowledge 1.1 (Answers are at the end of the chapter.)

1. Characteristics of stigma include all of the following *except*:
   a. a label reflecting desirable characteristics
   b. discrimination against those with the label
   c. focus on differences between those with and without the label
   d. labeling a group of people who are different
2. Which of the following definitions of mental disorder is currently thought best?
   a. personal distress
   b. harmful dysfunction
   c. norm violation
   d. none of the above

3. Why is the DSM definition of mental disorder perhaps the best current definition?
   a. It includes information about both violation of social norms and dysfunction.
   b. It includes many components, none of which alone can account for mental disorder.
   c. It is part of the current diagnostic system.
   d. It recognizes the limits of our current understanding.

History of Psychopathology

Many textbooks begin with a chapter on the history of the field. Why? It is important to consider how concepts and approaches have changed (or not) over time, because we can learn not to make the same mistakes made in the past and because we can see that our current concepts and approaches are likely to change in the future. As we consider the history of psychopathology, we will see that many new approaches to the treatment of mental illness throughout time appear to go well at first and are heralded with much excitement and fanfare. But these treatments eventually fall into disrepute. These are lessons that should not be forgotten as we consider more contemporary approaches to treatment and their attendant excitement and fanfare.

The search for causes of mental disorders has gone on for a considerable period of time. At different periods in history, explanations for mental disorders have been supernatural, biological, and psychological. As we quickly travel through these different periods, ask yourself what level of explanation was operating at different times.

Early Demonology

Before the age of scientific inquiry, all good and bad manifestations of power beyond human control—eclipses, earthquakes, storms, fire, diseases, the changing seasons—were regarded as supernatural. Behavior seemingly outside individual control was also ascribed to supernatural causes. Many early philosophers, theologians, and physicians who studied the troubled mind believed that disturbed behavior reflected the displeasure of the gods or possession by demons.

The doctrine that an evil being or spirit can dwell within a person and control his or her mind and body is called **demonology**. Examples of demonological thinking are found in the records of the early Chinese, Egyptians, Babylonians, and Greeks. Among the Hebrews, odd behavior was attributed to possession of the person by bad spirits, after God in his wrath had withdrawn protection. The New Testament includes the story of Christ curing a man with an unclean spirit by casting out the devils from within him and hurling them onto a herd of swine (Mark 5:8–13).

The belief that odd behavior was caused by possession led to treating it by **exorcism**, the ritualistic casting out of evil spirits. Exorcism typically took the form of elaborate rites of prayer, noisemaking, forcing the afflicted to drink terrible-tasting brews, and on occasion more extreme measures, such as flogging and starvation, to render the body uninhabitable to devils.

Christ driving the evil spirits out of a possessed man. (© SuperStock/SuperStock.)

Early Biological Explanations

In the fifth century B.C., Hippocrates (460?–377? B.C.), often called the father of modern medicine, separated medicine from religion, magic, and superstition. He rejected the prevailing Greek belief that the gods sent mental disturbances as punishment and insisted instead that such illnesses had natural causes and hence should be treated like other, more common maladies, such as colds and constipation. Hippocrates regarded the brain as the organ of consciousness, intellectual life, and emotion; thus, he thought that disordered thinking and behavior were indications of some kind of brain pathology. Hippocrates is often considered one of the earliest proponents of the notion that something wrong with the brain disturbs thought and action.

Hippocrates classified mental disorders into three categories: mania, melancholia, and phrenitis, or brain fever. Further, Hippocrates believed that normal brain functioning, and therefore mental health, depended on a delicate balance among four humors, or fluids of the body, namely, blood, black bile, yellow bile, and phlegm. An imbalance of these humors produced disorders. If a person was sluggish and dull, for example, the body supposedly contained a preponderance of phlegm. A preponderance of black bile was the explanation for melancholia; too much yellow bile explained irritability and anxiousness; and too much blood, changeable temperament.

Through his teachings, the phenomena associated with mental disorders became more clearly the province of physicians rather than priests. The treatments Hippocrates suggested were quite different from exorcism. For melancholia, for example, he prescribed tranquility, sobriety, care in choosing food and drink, and abstinence from sexual activity. Because Hippocrates believed in natural rather than supernatural causes, he depended on his own keen observations and made valuable contributions as a clinician. He also left behind remarkably detailed records clearly describing many of the symptoms now recognized in seizure disorders, alcohol dependence, stroke, and paranoia.

Hippocrates' ideas, of course, did not withstand later scientific scrutiny. However, his basic premise—that human behavior is markedly affected by bodily structures or substances and that odd behavior is produced by some kind of physical imbalance or even damage—did foreshadow aspects of contemporary thought. In the next seven centuries, Hippocrates' naturalistic approach to disease and disorder was generally accepted by other Greeks as well as by the Romans, who adopted the medicine of the Greeks after their empire became the major power in the ancient European world.

The Greek physician Hippocrates held a biological view of mental illness, considering mental disorders to be diseases of the brain. (© Bruce Miller/Alamy.)

The Dark Ages and Demonology

Historians have often pointed to the death of Galen (A.D. 130–200), the second-century Greek who is regarded as the last great physician of the classical era, as the beginning of the so-called Dark Ages in western European medicine and in the treatment and investigation of mental disorders. Over several centuries of decay, Greek and Roman civilization ceased to be. The Church gained in influence, and the papacy was declared independent of the state. Christian monasteries, through their missionary and educational work, replaced physicians as healers and as authorities on mental disorder.[1]

The monks in the monasteries cared for and nursed the sick, and a few of the monasteries were repositories for the classic Greek medical manuscripts, even though the monks may not have made use of the knowledge in these works. Monks cared for people with mental disorders by praying over them and touching them with relics; they also concocted fantastic potions for them to drink in the waning phase of the moon. Many people with mental illness roamed the countryside, destitute and progressively becoming worse. During this period, there was a return to a belief in supernatural causes of mental disorders.

The Persecution of Witches   Beginning in the thirteenth century, in response to widespread social unrest and recurrent famines and plagues, people in Europe turned to demonology to explain these disasters. Witchcraft, now viewed as instigated by Satan, was seen as a heresy and

Galen was a Greek physician who followed Hippocrates' ideas and is regarded as the last great physician of the classical era. (Corbis Images.)

---

[1]The teachings of Galen continued to be influential in the Islamic world. For example, the Persian physician al-Razi (865–925) established a facility for the treatment of people with mental illness in Baghdad and was an early practitioner of psychotherapy.

In the dunking test, if the woman did not drown, she was considered to be in league with the devil (and punished accordingly); this is the ultimate no-win situation. (Corbis-Bettmann.)

a denial of God. Then, as today, when faced with inexplicable and frightening occurrences, people tended to seize on whatever explanation seemed most plausible. The times conspired to heap enormous blame on those regarded as witches, who were persecuted with great zeal.

In 1484, Pope Innocent VIII exhorted the clergy of Europe to leave no stone unturned in the search for witches. He sent two Dominican monks to northern Germany as inquisitors. Two years later they issued a comprehensive and explicit manual, *Malleus Maleficarum* ("the witches' hammer"), to guide the witch hunts. This legal and theological document came to be regarded by Catholics and Protestants alike as a textbook on witchcraft. Those accused of witchcraft should be tortured if they did not confess, those convicted and penitent were to be imprisoned for life, and those convicted and unrepentant were to be handed over to the law for execution. The manual specified that a person's sudden loss of reason was a symptom of demonic possession and that burning was the usual method of driving out the supposed demon. Records of the period are not considered reliable, but it is thought that over the next several centuries hundreds of thousands of people, particularly women and children, were accused, tortured, and put to death.

Modern investigators initially believed that many of the people accused of being witches during the later Middle Ages were mentally ill (Zilboorg & Henry, 1941). The basis for this belief was the confessions of the accused that investigators interpreted as delusional beliefs or hallucinations.

More detailed research into this historical period, however, indicates that many of the accused were not mentally ill. Careful analyses of the witch hunts reveal that more healthy than ill people were tried. Confessions were typically obtained during brutal torture, having been suggested to the accused witches both by their accusers and by the prevailing beliefs of the times. Indeed, in England, where torture was not allowed, the confessions did not usually contain descriptions resembling delusions or hallucinations (Schoeneman, 1977).

Lunacy Trials Evaluations of other sources of information also indicate that mental illness was not primarily ascribed to witchcraft. From the thirteenth century on, as the cities of Europe grew larger, hospitals began to come under secular jurisdiction. Municipal authorities, gaining in power, tended to supplement or take over some of the activities of the Church, one of these being the care of people who were mentally ill. The foundation deed for the Holy Trinity Hospital in Salisbury, England, dating from the mid-fourteenth century, specified the purposes of the hospital, among them that the "mad are kept safe until they are restored of reason." English laws during this period allowed people with mental illness to be hospitalized. Notably, the people who were hospitalized were not described as being possessed (Allderidge, 1979).

Beginning in the thirteenth century, lunacy trials to determine a person's mental health were held in England. As explained by Neugebauer (1979), the trials were conducted under the Crown's right to protect the people with mental illness, and a judgment of insanity allowed the Crown to become guardian of the lunatic's estate. The defendant's orientation, memory, intellect, daily life, and habits were at issue in the trial. Usually, strange behavior was attributed to physical illness or injury or to some emotional shock. In all the cases that Neugebauer examined, only one referred to demonic possession. Interestingly, the term *lunacy* comes from a theory espoused by the Swiss physician Paracelsus (1493–1541), who attributed odd behavior to a misalignment of the moon and stars (the Latin word for "moon" is *luna*). This lunar explanation, even if unsubstantiated, was a welcome alternative to explanations involving demons or witches. Even today, many people believe that a full moon is linked to odd behavior; however, there is no scientific evidence to support this belief.

Development of Asylums

Until the fifteenth century, there were very few hospitals for people with mental illness in Europe. However, there were many hospitals for people with leprosy—for example, in the twelfth century, England and Scotland had 220 leprosy hospitals serving a total population of a million and a half. Leprosy gradually disappeared from Europe, probably because with the end of wars came a break with the Eastern sources of the infection. With hospitals now underused, attention seems to have turned to people with mental illness. Leprosariums were converted to **asylums**, refuges for the confinement and care of people with mental illness.

Bethlehem and Other Early Asylums The Priory of St. Mary of Bethlehem was founded in 1243. Records indicate that in 1403 it housed six men with mental illness. In 1547, Henry VIII handed it over to the city of London, thereafter to be a hospital devoted solely to the confinement of people with mental illness. The conditions in Bethlehem were deplorable. Over the years the word *bedlam*, the popular name for this hospital, came to mean a place or scene of wild uproar and confusion. Bethlehem eventually became one of London's great tourist attractions, by the eighteenth century rivaling both Westminster Abbey and the Tower of London. Even as late as the nineteenth century, viewing the patients was considered entertainment, and people bought tickets to see them. Similarly, in the Lunatics Tower, which was constructed in Vienna in 1784, patients were confined in the spaces between inner square rooms and the outer walls, where they could be viewed by passersby.

Obviously, confining people with mental illness in hospitals and placing their care in the domain of medicine did not necessarily lead to more humane and effective treatment. Medical treatments were often crude and painful. Benjamin Rush (1745–1813), for example, began practicing medicine in Philadelphia in 1769 and is considered the father of American psychiatry. Yet he believed that mental disorder was caused by an excess of blood in the brain, for which his favored treatment was to draw great quantities of blood from disordered individuals (Farina, 1976). Rush also believed that many people with mental illness could be cured by being frightened. Thus, one of his recommended procedures was for the physician to convince the patient that death was near!

In this eighteenth-century painting by Hogarth, two upper-class women find amusement in touring St. Mary's of Bethlehem (Bedlam). (Corbis-Bettmann.)

Pinel's Reforms Philippe Pinel (1745–1826) has often been considered a primary figure in the movement for humanitarian treatment of people with mental illness in asylums. In 1793, while the French Revolution raged, he was put in charge of a large asylum in Paris known as La Bicêtre. A historian described the conditions at this particular hospital:

> [The patients were] shackled to the walls of their cells, by iron collars which held them flat against the wall and permitted little movement. They could not lie down at night, as a rule. Oftentimes there was a hoop of iron around the waist of the patient and in addition chains on both the hands and the feet. These chains [were] sufficiently long so that the patient could feed himself out of a bowl, the food usually being a mushy gruel—bread soaked in a weak soup. Since little was known about dietetics, [no attention] was paid to the type of diet given the patients. They were presumed to be animals and not to care whether the food was good or bad. (Selling, 1940, p. 54)

Many texts assert that Pinel removed the chains of the people imprisoned in La Bicêtre, an event that was memorialized in well-known paintings. Pinel is said to have begun to treat the patients

The freeing of the patients at La Bicêtre (supposedly by Pinel, as pictured here) is often considered to mark the beginning of more humanitarian treatment of people with mental illness. (Archives Charmet/The Bridgeman Art Library International.)

as sick human beings rather than as beasts. Light and airy rooms replaced dungeons. Many who had been completely unmanageable became calm. Patients formerly considered dangerous now strolled through the hospital and grounds without creating disturbances or harming anyone. Some patients who had been incarcerated for years were apparently restored to health and eventually discharged from the hospital.

Historical research, however, indicates that it was not Pinel who released the patients from their chains. Rather, it was a former patient, Jean-Baptiste Pussin, who had become an orderly at the hospital. In fact, Pinel was not even present when the patients were released (Weiner, 1994). Several years later, though, Pinel did praise Pussin's efforts and began to follow the same practices.

Consistent with the egalitarianism of the new French Republic, Pinel came to believe that patients in his care were first and foremost human beings, and thus these people should be approached with compassion and understanding and treated with dignity. He surmised that if their reason had left them because of severe personal and social problems, it might be restored to them through comforting counsel and purposeful activity.

Pinel did much good for people with mental illness, but he was no paragon of enlightenment and egalitarianism. He reserved the more humanitarian treatment for the upper classes; patients of the lower classes were still subjected to terror and coercion as a means of control, with straitjackets replacing chains.

Moral Treatment   For a time, mental hospitals established in Europe and the United States were relatively small, privately supported, and operated along the lines of the humanitarian changes at La Bicêtre. In the United States, the Friends' Asylum, founded in 1817 in Pennsylvania, and the Hartford Retreat, established in 1824 in Connecticut, were established to provide humane treatment. In accordance with this approach, which became known as **moral treatment**, patients had close contact with attendants, who talked and read to them and encouraged them to engage in purposeful activity; residents led lives as close to normal as possible and in general took responsibility for themselves within the constraints of their disorders. Further, there were to be no more than 250 patients in a given hospital (Whitaker, 2002).

Moral treatment was largely abandoned in the latter part of the nineteenth century. Ironically, the efforts of Dorothea Dix (1802–1887), a crusader for improved conditions for people with mental illness who fought to have hospitals created for their care, helped effect this change. Dix, a Boston schoolteacher, taught a Sunday school class at the local prison and was shocked at the deplorable conditions in which the inmates lived. Her interest spread to the conditions at mental hospitals and to people with mental illness who had nowhere to go for treatment. She campaigned vigorously to improve the lives of people with mental illness and personally helped see that 32 state hospitals were built. These large public hospitals took in many of the patients whom the private hospitals could not accommodate. Unfortunately, the small staffs of these new hospitals were unable to provide the individual attention that was a hallmark of moral treatment (Bockhoven, 1963). Moreover, the hospitals came to be administered by physicians, most of whom were interested in the biological aspects of illness and in the physical, rather than the psychological well-being of patients with mental illness. The money that had once paid the salaries of personal attendants now paid for equipment and laboratories. (See Focus on Discovery 1.2 for an examination of whether the conditions in today's mental hospitals have improved.)

In the nineteenth century, Dorothea Dix played a major role in establishing more mental hospitals in the United States. (Corbis Images.)

FOCUS ON DISCOVERY 1.2

The Mental Hospital Today

In the late 1960s and early 1970s, concerns about the restrictive nature of confinement in a mental hospital led to the so-called deinstitutionalization (i.e., release from the hospital) of a large number of people with mental illness. Budget cuts beginning in the 1980s and continuing today have caused this trend to continue. But sometimes people with mental illness do need treatment in a hospital setting, and unfortunately, we still do not do a good job of this, even in the twenty-first century (as we will discuss in more detail in Chapter 16). Treatment in public mental hospitals today is often "just enough" to provide some protection, food, shelter, and in most cases medication. Indeed. people with mental illness in a public hospital may receive little treatment beyond medication; their existence is monotonous and sedentary for the most part.

Public mental hospitals in the United States are usually funded either by the federal government or by the state where they are located. Many Veterans Administration hospitals and general medical hospitals also contain units for people with mental illness. Since 1970, the number of public mental hospitals has decreased substantially. In 1969, there were 310 state or county hospitals; by 1998, there were just 229 (Geller, 2006).

With the decreasing numbers of state and county hospitals, you might guess that more private mental hospitals were built to provide services once available through public hospitals. This was indeed the case beginning in the 1970s. In 1969, there were 150 private hospitals, but in 1998, there were 348 (Geller, 2006). This trend toward increasing private hospitals, however, peaked in 1992. Since then, private hospitals have also declined in number. The physical facilities and professional care in private hospitals tend to be superior to those of public hospitals for one reason: the private hospitals have more money.

A somewhat specialized mental hospital, sometimes called a forensic hospital, is reserved for people who have been arrested and judged unable to stand trial and for those who have been acquitted of a crime by reason of insanity (see Chapter 16). Although these patients have not been sent to prison, security staff and other tight security measures regiment their lives. Treatment of some kind is supposed to take place during their stay.

One of the unfortunate consequences of fewer public and private mental hospitals today is overcrowding in the existing hospitals. A recent longitudinal study of 13 public mental hospitals in Finland showed that nearly half the hospitals were overcrowded (defined as having more than 10 percent occupancy than the hospital was designed for). The researchers also found that overcrowding was associated with an increased risk of violence against hospital staff by patients (Virtanen et al., 2011). Although we have developed more effective treatments for many mental disorders, as we will see throughout this book, the mental hospital of today is still in need of improvement.

Most rooms at state mental hospitals are bleak and unstimulating.
(© Amanda Brown/StarLedger/© Corbis.)

Quick Summary

Early concepts of mental illness included not only demonology (possession by demons) but also biological approaches, as evidenced by the ideas of Hippocrates. During the Dark Ages, some people with mental illness were cared for in monasteries, but many simply roamed the countryside. Some were persecuted as witches, but this was relatively rare (later analyses indicated that many of the people accused of being witches were not mentally ill). Treatments for people with mental illness have changed over time, though not always for the better. Exorcisms did not do much good. Treatments in asylums could also be cruel and unhelpful, but pioneering work by Pinel, Dix, and others made asylums more humane places for treatment. Unfortunately, their good ideas did not last, as the mental hospitals became overcrowded and understaffed.

Check Your Knowledge 1.2

True or false?
1. Benjamin Rush is credited with beginning moral treatment in the United States.
2. The most recent historical research has found that nearly all of the people persecuted as witches were mentally ill.
3. Hippocrates was one of the first to propose that mental illness had a biological cause.
4. The term *lunatic* is derived from the ideas of Paracelsus.

The Evolution of Contemporary Thought

As horrific as the conditions in Bethlehem hospital were, the physicians at the time were nonetheless interested in what caused the maladies of their patients. Table 1.1 lists the hypothesized causes of the illnesses exhibited by patients in 1810 that were recorded by William Black, a physician working at Bethlehem at the time (Appignannesi, 2008). It is interesting to observe that about half of the presumed causes were biological (e.g., fever, hereditary, venereal) and half were psychological (e.g., grief, love, jealousy). Only around 10 percent of the causes were spiritual.

Contemporary developments in biological and psychological approaches to the causes and treatments of mental disorders were heavily influenced by theorists and scientists working in the late nineteenth and early twentieth centuries. We will discuss, compare, and evaluate these approaches more fully in Chapter 2. In this section, we review the historical antecedents of these more contemporary approaches.

Recall that in the West, the death of Galen and the decline of Greco-Roman civilization temporarily ended inquiries into the nature of both physical and mental illness. Not until the late Middle Ages did any new facts begin to emerge, thanks to an emerging empirical approach to medical science, which emphasized gathering knowledge by direct observation.

Biological Approaches

Discovering Biological Origins in General Paresis and Syphilis The anatomy and workings of the nervous system were partially understood by the mid-1800s, but not enough was known to let investigators conclude whether the structural brain abnormalities presumed to cause various mental disorders were present or not. Perhaps the most striking medical success was the elucidation of the nature and origin of syphilis, a venereal disease that had been recognized for several centuries.

The story of this discovery provides a good illustration of how an empirical approach, the basis for contemporary science, works. Since the late 1700s it had been known that a number of people with mental illness manifested a syndrome characterized by a steady deterioration of both mental and physical abilities, including symptoms such as delusions of grandeur (i.e., the belief that you hold special and great power or can accomplish more than any other person on the planet) and progressive paralysis; the presumed disease associated with this syndrome was given the name **general paresis**. Soon after these symptoms were recognized, investigators realized that these people never recovered. By the mid-1800s, it had been established that some patients with general paresis also had syphilis, but a connection between the two conditions had not yet been made.

In the 1860s and 1870s, Louis Pasteur established the germ theory of disease, which posited that disease is caused by infection of the body by minute organisms. This theory laid the groundwork for demonstrating the relation between syphilis and general paresis. Finally, in 1905, the specific microorganism that causes syphilis was discovered. For the first time, a causal link had been established between infection, destruction of certain areas of the brain, and a form of psychopathology (general paresis). If one type of psychopathology had a biological cause, so could others. Biological approaches gained credibility, and searches for more biological causes were off and running.

Table 1.1 Causes of Maladies Observed among Patients in Bethlehem iny 1810

Cause	Number of Patients
Childbed*	79
Contusions/fractures of skull	12
Drink/intoxication	58
Family/hereditary	115
Fevers	110
Fright	31
Grief	206
Jealousy	9
Love	90
Obstruction	10
Pride	8
Religion/Methodism	90
Smallpox	7
Study	15
Venereal	14
Ulcers/scabs dried up	5

Source: Adapted from Appignannesi (2008), Hunter & Macalpine (1963).

*Childbed refers to childbirth—perhaps akin to what we now call postpartum depression.

Genetics Francis Galton (1822–1911), often considered the originator of genetic research with twins, because of his study of twins in the late 1800s in England, attributed many behavioral characteristics to heredity. He is credited with coining the terms *nature* and *nurture* to talk about differences in genetics (nature) and environment (nurture). In the early twentieth century, investigators became intrigued by the idea that mental illness may run in families, and beginning at that time, a number of studies documented the heritability of mental illnesses such as schizophrenia, bipolar disorder, and depression. These studies would set the stage for later theories about the causes of mental illness.

Unfortunately, Galton is also credited with creating the eugenics movement in 1883 (Brooks, 2004). Advocates of this movement sought to eliminate undesirable characteristics from the population by restricting the ability of certain people to have children (e.g., by enforced sterilization). Many of the early efforts in the United States to determine whether mental illness could be inherited were associated with the eugenics movement, and this stalled research progress. Indeed, in a sad page from U.S. history, state laws in the late 1800s and early 1900s prohibited people with mental illness from marrying and forced them to be sterilized in order to prevent them from "passing on" their illness. Such laws were upheld by the U.S. Supreme Court in 1927 (Chase, 1980), and it wasn't until the middle of the twentieth century that these abhorrent practices were halted. Nevertheless, much damage had been done: by 1945, more than 45,000 people with mental illness in the United States had been forcibly sterilized (Whitaker, 2002).

Biological Treatments The general warehousing of patients in mental hospitals earlier in the twentieth century, coupled with the shortage of professional staff, created a climate that allowed, perhaps even subtly encouraged, experimentation with radical interventions. In the early 1930s, the practice of inducing a coma with large dosages of insulin was introduced by Sakel (1938), who claimed that up to three-quarters of the people with schizophrenia whom he treated showed significant improvement. Later findings by others were less encouraging, and insulin-coma therapy—which presented serious risks to health, including irreversible coma and death—was gradually abandoned.

In the early twentieth century, **electroconvulsive therapy (ECT)** was originated by two Italian physicians, Ugo Cerletti and Lucino Bini. Cerletti was interested in epilepsy and was seeking a way to induce seizures experimentally. Shortly thereafter he found that by applying electric shocks to the sides of the human head, he could produce full epileptic seizures. Then, in Rome in 1938, he used the technique on a patient with schizophrenia.

In the decades that followed, ECT was administered to people with schizophrenia and severe depression, usually in hospital settings. As we will discuss in Chapter 5, it is still used today for people with severe depression. Fortunately, important refinements in the ECT procedures have made it less problematic, and it remains an effective treatment.

In 1935, Egas Moniz, a Portuguese psychiatrist, introduced the *prefrontal lobotomy*, a surgical procedure that destroys the tracts connecting the frontal lobes to other areas of the brain. His initial reports claimed high rates of success (Moniz, 1936), and for 20 years thereafter thousands of people with mental illness underwent variations of this psychosurgery. The procedure was used especially for those whose behavior was violent. Many people did indeed quiet down and could even be discharged from hospitals, largely because their brains were damaged. During the 1950s, this intervention fell into disrepute for several reasons. After surgery, many people became dull and listless and suffered serious losses in their cognitive capacities—for example, becoming unable to carry on a coherent conversation with another person—which is not surprising given the destruction of parts of their brains that support thought and language.

Francis Galton is considered the originator of genetics research. (© Bettmann/Corbis.)

Psychological Approaches

The search for biological causes dominated the field of psychopathology until well into the twentieth century, no doubt partly because of the exciting discoveries made about the brain and genetics. But beginning in the late eighteenth century, various psychological points of view emerged that attributed mental disorders to psychological malfunctions. These theories were fashionable first in France and Austria, and later in the United States, leading to the development of psychotherapeutic interventions based on the tenets of the individual theories.

Scene from *One Flew over the Cuckoo's Nest*. The character portrayed by Jack Nicholson was lobotomized in the film. (Photofest.)

Mesmer's procedure for manipulating magnetism was generally considered a form of hypnosis. (Jean-Loup Charnet/Photo Researchers, Inc.)

In this famous painting, the French neurologist Jean Charcot lectures on hysteria (note the woman suffering hysterical symptoms). Charcot was an important figure in reviving interest in psychological approaches. (©Bettmann/©Corbis.)

Mesmer and Charcot During the eighteenth century in western Europe, many people were observed to be subject to *hysteria*, which referred to physical incapacities, such as blindness or paralysis, for which no physical cause could be found. Franz Anton Mesmer (1734–1815), an Austrian physician practicing in Vienna and Paris in the late eighteenth century, believed that hysteria was caused by a particular distribution of a universal magnetic fluid in the body. Moreover, he felt that one person could influence the fluid of another to bring about a change in the other's behavior.

Mesmer conducted meetings cloaked in mystery and mysticism, at which afflicted patients sat around a covered wooden tub, with iron rods protruding through the cover from bottles underneath that contained various chemicals. Mesmer would enter the room, take various rods from the tub, and touch afflicted parts of his patients' bodies. The rods were believed to transmit animal magnetism and adjust the distribution of the universal magnetic fluid, thereby removing the hysterical disorder. Later, Mesmer perfected his routines by simply looking at patients rather than using rods. Whatever we may think of this questionable explanation and strange procedure, Mesmer apparently helped many people overcome their hysterical problems.

Although Mesmer regarded hysteria as having strictly biological causes, we discuss his work here because he is generally considered one of the earlier practitioners of modern-day hypnosis (the word *mesmerism* is a synonym for *hypnotism*; the phenomenon itself was known to the ancients of many cultures, where it was part of the sorcery and magic of conjurers and faith healers).

Mesmer came to be regarded as a quack by his contemporaries, which is ironic, since he had earlier contributed to the discrediting of an exorcist, Father Johann Gassner, who was performing similar rituals (Harrington, 2008). Nevertheless, hypnosis gradually became respectable. The great Parisian neurologist Jean Martin Charcot (1825–1893) also studied hysterical states. Although Charcot believed that hysteria was a problem with the nervous system and had a biological cause, he was also persuaded by psychological explanations. One day, some of his enterprising students hypnotized a healthy woman and, by suggestion, induced her to display certain hysterical symptoms. Charcot was deceived into believing that she was an actual patient with hysteria. When the students showed him how readily they could remove the symptoms by waking the woman, Charcot became interested in psychological interpretations of these very puzzling phenomena. Given Charcot's prominence in Parisian society, his support of hypnosis as a worthy treatment for hysteria helped to legitimize this form of treatment among medical professionals of the time (Harrington, 2008; Hustvedt, 2011).

Breuer and the Cathartic Method In the nineteenth century, a Viennese physician, Josef Breuer (1842–1925), treated a young woman, whose identity was disguised under the pseudonym Anna O., with a number of hysterical symptoms, including partial paralysis, impairment of sight and hearing, and, often, difficulty speaking. She also sometimes went into a dreamlike state, or "absence," during which she mumbled to herself, seemingly preoccupied with troubling thoughts. Breuer hypnotized her, and while hypnotized, she began talking more freely and, ultimately, with considerable emotion about upsetting events from her past. Frequently, on awakening from a hypnotic session she felt much better. Breuer found that the relief of a particular symptom seemed to last longer if, under hypnosis, she was able to recall the event associated with the first appearance of that symptom and if she was able to express the emotion she had felt at the time. Reliving an earlier emotional trauma and releasing emotional tension by expressing previously forgotten thoughts about the event was called catharsis, and Breuer's method became known as the **cathartic method**. In 1895, Breuer and a younger colleague, Sigmund Freud (1856–1939), jointly published *Studies in Hysteria*, partly based on the case of Anna O.

The case of Anna O. became one of the best-known clinical cases in the psychoanalytic literature. Ironically, later investigation revealed that Breuer and Freud reported the case incorrectly. Historical study by Henri Ellenberger (1972) indicates that the young woman was helped only temporarily by Breuer's talking cure. This is supported by Carl Jung, a renowned colleague of Freud's, who is quoted as saying that during a conference in 1925, Freud told him that Anna O. had never been cured. Hospital records discovered by Ellenberger confirmed that Anna O. continued to rely on morphine to ease the "hysterical" problems that Breuer is reputed to have cured by catharsis.

Freud and Psychoanalysis   The apparently powerful role played by factors of which patients seemed unaware led Freud to postulate that much of human behavior is determined by forces that are inaccessible to awareness. The central assumption of Freud's theorizing, often referred to as **psychoanalytic theory**, is that psychopathology results from unconscious conflicts in the individual. In the next sections, we take a look at Freud's theory. See Focus on Discovery 1.3 for a look at Freud's theory of personality development and Focus on Discovery 1.4 for Freud's ideas about depression.

Josef Breuer, an Austrian physician and physiologist, collaborated with Freud in the early development of psychoanalysis. (Corbis-Bettmann.)

Structure of the Mind   Freud divided the mind, or the **psyche**, into three principal parts: id, ego, and superego. According to Freud, the **id** is present at birth and is the repository of all of the energy needed to run the psyche, including the basic urges for food, water, elimination, warmth, affection, and sex. Trained as a neurologist, Freud saw the source of the id's energy as biological, and he called this energy **libido**. The individual cannot consciously perceive this energy—it is **unconscious**, below the level of awareness.

The id seeks immediate gratification of its urges, operating on what Freud called the **pleasure principle.** When the id is not satisfied, tension is produced, and the id impels a person to eliminate this tension as quickly as possible. For example, a baby feels hunger and is impelled to move about, sucking, in an attempt to reduce the tension arising from the unsatisfied drive. A person may also attempt to obtain gratification by generating images—in essence, fantasies—of what is desired. For instance, the hungry baby imagines sucking at the mother's breast and thereby obtains some substitute, short-term satisfaction. Of course, fantasizing cannot really satisfy such urges. This is where the ego comes in.

According to Freud, the **ego** begins to develop from the id during the second 6 months of life. Unlike the contents of the id, those of the ego are primarily conscious. The id may resort to fantasy when seeking satisfaction, but the task of the ego is to deal with reality. The ego thus operates on what Freud termed the **reality principle** as it mediates between the demands of reality and the id's demands for immediate gratification.

The **superego**—the third part of the psyche in Freud's theory—can be roughly conceived of as a person's conscience. Freud believed that the superego develops throughout childhood, arising from the ego much as the ego arises from the id. As children discover that many of their impulses—for example, biting and bed-wetting—are not acceptable to their parents, they begin to incorporate parental values as their own in order to receive the pleasure of parental approval and avoid the pain of disapproval.

Defense Mechanisms   According to Freud, and as elaborated by his daughter Anna (A. Freud, 1946/1966), herself an influential psychoanalyst, discomforts experienced by the ego as it attempts to resolve conflicts and satisfy the demands of the id and superego can be reduced in several ways. A **defense mechanism** is a strategy used by the ego to protect itself from anxiety. Examples of defense mechanisms are presented in Table 1.2.

Sigmund Freud developed psychoanalytic theory, a theory of the structure and functions of the mind (including explanations of the causes of mental disorders), and psychoanalysis, a new method of therapy based on it. (Corbis-Images.)

Psychoanalytic Therapy   Psychotherapy based on Freud's theory is called **psychoanalysis** or psychoanalytic therapy. It is still practiced today, although not as commonly

Table 1.2 Selected Defense Mechanisms

Defense Mechanism	Definition	Example
Repression	Keeping unacceptable impulses or wishes from conscious awareness	A professor starting a lecture she dreaded giving says, "In conclusion".
Denial	Not accepting a painful reality into conscious awareness	A victim of childhood abuse does not acknowledge it as an adult.
Projection	Attributing to someone else one's own unacceptable thoughts or feelings	A man who hates members of a racial group believes that it is they who dislike him.
Displacement	Redirecting emotional responses from their real target to someone else	A child gets mad at her brother but instead acts angrily toward her friend.
Reaction formation	Converting an unacceptable feeling into its opposite	A person with sexual feelings toward children leads a campaign against child sexual abuse.
Regression	Retreating to the behavioral patterns of an earlier stage of development	An adolescent dealing with unacceptable feelings of social inadequacy attempts to mask those feelings by seeking oral gratification.
Rationalization	Offering acceptable reasons for an unacceptable action or attitude	A parent berates a child out of impatience, then indicates that she did so to "build character."
Sublimation	Converting unacceptable aggressive or sexual impulses into socially valued behaviors	Someone who has aggressive feelings toward his father becomes a surgeon.

as it once was. In psychoanalytic and newer psychodynamic treatments, the goal of the therapist is to understand the person's early-childhood experiences, the nature of key relationships, and the patterns in current relationships. The therapist is listening for core emotional and relationship themes that surface again and again (see Table 1.3 for a summary of psychoanalysis techniques).

Freud developed a number of techniques in his efforts to help people resolve repressed conflicts. With **free association,** a patient reclines on a couch, facing away from the analyst, and is encouraged to give free rein to his or her thoughts, verbalizing whatever comes to mind, without censoring anything.

Another key component of psychoanalytic therapy is the analysis of **transference**. Transference refers to the patient's responses to his or her analyst that seem to reflect attitudes and ways of behaving toward important people in the patient's past, rather than reflecting actual aspects of the analyst–patient relationship. For example, a patient might feel that the analyst is generally bored by what he or she is saying and as a result might struggle to be entertaining; this pattern of response might reflect the patient's childhood relationship with a parent rather than what's actually going on between the patient and the analyst. Through careful observation and analysis of these transferred attitudes, Freud believed the analyst could gain insight into the childhood origins of the patient's repressed conflicts. In the example above, the analyst might find that the patient was made to feel boring and unimportant as a child and could only gain parental attention through humor.

In the technique of **interpretation**, the analyst points out to the patient the meanings of certain of the patient's behaviors. Defense mechanisms are a principal focus of interpretation. For instance, a man who appears to have trouble with intimacy may look out the window and change the subject whenever anything touches on closeness during the course of a session.

Table 1.3 Major Techniques of Psychoanalysis

Technique	Description
Free association	The patient tries to say whatever comes to mind without censoring anything.
Interpretation	The analyst points out to the patient the meaning of certain of the patient's behaviors.
Analysis of transference	The patient responds to the analyst in ways that the patient has previously responded to other important figures in his or her life, and the analyst helps the patient understand and interpret these responses.

FOCUS ON DISCOVERY 1.3

Stages of Psychosexual Development

Freud conceived of the personality as developing through a series of four distinct psychosexual stages. He used the term *psychosexual* because, at each stage, a different part of the body is the most sensitive to sexual excitation and, therefore, the most capable of satisfying the id.

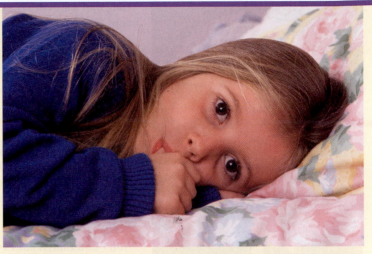

According to Freud, too much or too little gratification during one of the psychosexual stages may lead to regression to this stage during stress. (Jennie Woodcock; Reflections Photolibrary/Corbis Images.)

In Freud's theory, the first stage of psychosexual development is the oral stage, during which pleasure is obtained from feeding. (© SvetlanaFedoseyeva/Shutterstock.)

The **oral stage** is the first stage. From birth to about 18 months, the demands of an infant's id are satisfied primarily by feeding and the sucking and biting associated with it. The body parts through which the infant receives gratification at this stage are the lips, mouth, gums, and tongue. During the **anal stage**, from about 18 months to 3 years of age, a child receives pleasure mainly via the anus, by passing and retaining feces. The **phallic stage** extends from age 3 to age 5 or 6; during this stage, maximum gratification of the id is obtained through genital stimulation. Between the ages of 6 and 12, the child is in a **latency period**; during these years the id impulses do not play a major role in motivating behavior. The final and adult stage is the **genital stage**, during which heterosexual interests predominate.

During each stage, the developing person must resolve the conflicts between what the id wants and what the environment will provide. How this is accomplished is believed, in Freud's view, to determine basic personality traits that last throughout the person's life. A person who experiences either excessive or deficient amounts of gratification at a particular stage develops a **fixation** and is likely to regress to that stage when stressed.

The analyst will attempt at some point to interpret the patient's behavior, pointing out its defensive nature in the hope of helping the patient acknowledge that he is in fact avoiding the topic.

Neo-Freudian Psychodynamic Perspectives Several of Freud's contemporaries met with him periodically to discuss psychoanalytic theory and therapy. As often happens when a brilliant leader attracts brilliant followers and colleagues, disagreements arose about many general issues, such as the relative importance of id versus ego, of biological versus sociocultural forces on psychological development, of unconscious versus conscious processes, and of childhood versus adult experiences; whether sexual urges drive behaviors that are not obviously sexual; and the role of reflexlike id impulses versus that of purposive behavior governed primarily by conscious ego deliberations. We discuss two influential historical figures here: Carl Jung and Alfred Adler.

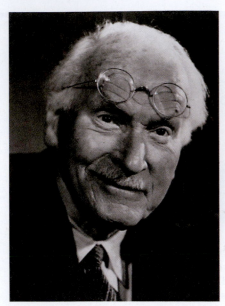

Carl Jung was the founder of analytical psychology. (Topham/The Image Works.)

Alfred Adler was the founder of individual psychology. (Corbis-Bettmann.)

Jung and Analytical Psychology Carl Gustav Jung (1875–1961), a Swiss psychiatrist originally considered Freud's heir apparent, broke with Freud in 1914 on many issues, after a 7-year period of intense correspondence about their disagreements. Jung proposed ideas radically different from Freud's, ultimately establishing **analytical psychology.**

Jung hypothesized that in addition to the personal unconscious postulated by Freud, there is a **collective unconscious,** the part of the unconscious that is common to all human beings and that consists primarily of what Jung called *archetypes,* or basic categories that all human beings use in conceptualizing about the world. In addition, Jung asserted that each of us has masculine and feminine traits that are blended and that people's spiritual and religious urges are as basic as their id urges. Jung also catalogued various personality characteristics; perhaps most important among them are extraversion (an orientation toward the external world) versus introversion (an orientation toward the inner, subjective world). This personality dimension continues to be regarded as very important, and we will encounter it again in our discussion of personality disorders in Chapter 15.

Adler and Individual Psychology Alfred Adler (1870–1937), also an early adherent of Freud's theories, came to be even less dependent on Freud's views than was Jung, and Freud remained quite bitter toward Adler after their relationship ended. Adler's theory, which came to be known as **individual psychology,** regarded people as inextricably tied to their society because he believed that fulfillment was found in doing things for the social good. Like Jung, he stressed the importance of working toward goals (Adler, 1930).

A central element in Adler's work was his focus on helping individual patients change their illogical and mistaken ideas and expectations; he believed that feeling and behaving better depend on thinking more rationally, an approach that anticipated contemporary developments in cognitive behavior therapy (discussed in Chapter 2).

Continuing Influences of Freud and His Followers Freud's original ideas and methods have been heavily criticized over the years. For example, Freud conducted no formal research on the causes and treatments of mental illness. This remains one of the main criticisms today: because they are based on anecdotal evidence gathered during therapy sessions, some psychodynamic theories are not grounded in objectivity and therefore are not scientific. However, other contemporary psychodynamic theories, such as object relations theory (discussed in Chapter 2), have built a limited base of supportive research. Offshoots of object relations theory, such as attachment theory and the idea of the relational self (discussed in Chapter 2), have accumulated a good bit of empirical support, both in children and adults.

Though perhaps not as influential as it once was, the work of Freud and his followers continues to have an impact on the field of psychopathology (Westen, 1998). This influence is most evident in the following three commonly held assumptions:

1. *Childhood experiences help shape adult personality.* Contemporary clinicians and researchers still view childhood experiences and other environmental events as crucial. They seldom focus on the psychosexual stages about which Freud wrote, but some emphasize problematic parent–child relationships in general and how they can influence later adult relationships in negative ways.

FOCUS ON DISCOVERY 1.4

Freud's Ideas on Depression

In his celebrated paper "Mourning and Melancholia," Freud (1917/1950) drew from clinical observations to develop a model of depression. He theorized that the potential for depression is created early in childhood, during the oral period. If the child's needs are insufficiently or excessively gratified, the person becomes fixated in the oral stage. This arrest in development may cause the person to become excessively dependent on other people for the maintenance of self-esteem.

Why do people with this childhood history come to suffer from depression? Freud hypothesized that after the loss of a loved one—whether by death, separation, or withdrawal of affection—the mourner identifies with the lost one, perhaps in a fruitless attempt to undo the loss. Freud asserted that the mourner unconsciously resents being deserted and feels anger toward the loved one for the loss. In addition, the mourner feels guilt for real or imagined sins against the lost person. According to the theory, the mourner's anger toward the lost one becomes directed inward, developing into ongoing self-blame and depression. In this view, depression can be described as anger turned against oneself. Overly dependent persons are believed to be particularly susceptible to this process, and, as noted above, people fixated in the oral stage are overly dependent on others.

Although this theory was interesting at the time, not much research has been carried out to test it, and the little information available does not strongly support it. Contrary to the idea that depression is a result of anger turned inward, people with depression express much more anger than do people without depression (Biglan et al., 1988). Despite

this, some of Freud's ideas continue to influence more recent models of depression, as we discuss in Chapter 5. For example, Freud maintained that depression could be triggered by the loss of a loved one. A large body of evidence indicates that episodes of major depressive disorder are precipitated by stressful life events, which often involve losses. Researchers have consistently shown that people who are high in dependency are prone to depressive symptoms after a rejection (Nietzel & Harris, 1990), a finding that is also congruent with Freud's theory. Although some of Freud's ideas still influence theories of depression, researchers have gone far beyond the clinical observations that were the foundation of his ideas.

2. *There are unconscious influences on behavior.* As we will discuss in Chapter 2, the unconscious is a focus of contemporary research in cognitive neuroscience and psychopathology. This research shows that people can be unaware of the causes of their behavior. However, most current researchers and clinicians do not think of the unconscious as a repository of id instincts.

3. *The causes and purposes of human behavior are not always obvious.* Freud and his followers sensitized generations of clinicians and researchers to the nonobviousness of the causes and purposes of human behavior. Contemporary psychodynamic theorists continue to caution us against taking everything at face value. A person expressing disdain for another, for example, may actually like the other person very much yet be fearful of admitting positive feelings. This tendency to look under the surface, to find hidden meanings in behavior, is perhaps the best-known legacy of Freud.

Quick Summary

The nineteenth and twentieth centuries saw a return to biological explanations for mental illness. Developments outside the field of psychopathology, such as the germ theory of disease and the discovery of the cause of syphilis, illustrated how the brain and behavior are linked. Early investigations into the genetics of mental illness led to a tragic emphasis on eugenics and the enforced sterilization of many thousands of people with mental illness. Such biological approaches to treatment as induced insulin coma and lobotomy eventually gave way to drug treatments. Psychological approaches to psychopathology began with Mesmer's manipulation of "magnetism" to treat hysteria (late eighteenth century), proceeded through Breuer's

conceptualization of the cathartic method in his treatment of Anna O. (late nineteenth century), and culminated in Freud's psychoanalytic theories and treatment techniques (early twentieth century). Jung and Adler took Freud's basic ideas in a variety of different directions. The theories of Freud and other psychodynamic theorists do not lend themselves to systematic study, which has limited their acceptance by some in the field. Although Freud's early work is often criticized, his theorizing has been influential in the study of psychopathology in that it has made clear the importance of early experiences, the notion that we can do things without conscious awareness, and the insight that the causes of behavior are not always obvious.

Check Your Knowledge 1.3

Fill in the blanks.

1. _____ was a French neurologist who was influenced by the work of _____.

2. _____ developed the cathartic method, which _____ later built on in the development of psychoanalysis.

3. The _____ is driven by the pleasure principle, but the _____ is driven by the reality principle.

4. In psychoanalysis, _____ refers to interpreting the relationship between therapist and client as indicative of the client's relationship to others.

5. _____ developed the concept of the collective unconscious; _____ developed the technique of free association; _____ is associated with individual psychology.

John B. Watson, an American psychologist, was the major figure in establishing behaviorism. (Underwood &Underwood/ Corbis Images.)

Ivan Pavlov, a Russian physiologist and Nobel laureate, made important contributions to the research and theory of classical conditioning. (Culver Pictures, Inc.)

The Rise of Behaviorism   After some years, many in the field began to lose faith in Freud's approach. This dissatisfaction was brought to a head by John B. Watson (1878–1958), who in 1913 revolutionized psychology with his views.

Watson looked to the experimental procedures of the psychologists who were investigating learning in animals, and because of his efforts, the dominant focus of psychology switched from thinking to learning. **Behaviorism** focuses on observable behavior rather than on consciousness or mental functioning. We will look at three types of learning that influenced the behaviorist approach in the early and middle parts of the twentieth century and that continue to be influential today: classical conditioning, operant conditioning, and modeling.

STIMULI

Classical Conditioning   Around the turn of the twentieth century, the Russian physiologist and Nobel laureate Ivan Pavlov (1849–1936) discovered **classical conditioning,** quite by accident. As part of his study of the digestive system, Pavlov gave a dog meat powder to make it salivate. Before long, Pavlov's laboratory assistants became aware that the dog began salivating when it saw the person who fed it. As the experiment continued, the dog began to salivate even earlier, when it heard the footsteps of its feeder. Pavlov was intrigued by these findings and decided to study the dog's reactions systematically. In the first of many experiments, a bell was rung behind the dog and then the meat powder was placed in its mouth. After this procedure had been repeated a number of times, the dog began salivating as soon as it heard the bell and before it received the meat powder.

In this experiment, because the meat powder automatically elicits salivation with no prior learning, the powder is termed an **unconditioned stimulus (UCS)** and the response of salivation an **unconditioned response (UCR).** When the offering of meat powder is preceded several times by a neutral stimulus, the ringing of a bell, the sound of the bell alone (the **conditioned stimulus,** or **CS)** is able to elicit the salivary response (the **conditioned response,** or **CR)** (see Figure 1.3). As the number of paired presentations of the bell and the meat powder increases, the number of salivations elicited by the bell alone increases. What happens to an established CR if the CS is no longer followed by the UCS—for example, if repeated soundings of the bell are not followed by meat powder? The answer is that fewer and fewer CRs (salivations) are elicited, and the CR gradually disappears. This is termed **extinction.**

Classical conditioning can even instill pathological fear. A famous but ethically questionable experiment conducted by John Watson and Rosalie Rayner (1920) involved introducing a white rat to an 11-month-old boy, Little Albert. The boy showed no fear of the animal and appeared to want to play with it. But whenever the boy reached for the rat, the experimenter made a loud noise (the UCS) by striking a steel bar behind Albert's head. This caused Little Albert great fright (the UCR). After five such experiences, Albert became very frightened (the CR) by the sight of the white rat, even when the steel bar

Figure 1.3 The process of classical conditioning. (*a*) Before learning, the meat powder (UCS) elicits salivation (UCR), but the bell (CS) does not. (*b*) A training or learning trial consists of presentations of the CS, followed closely by the UCS. (*c*) Classical conditioning has been accomplished when the previously neutral bell elicits salivation (CR).

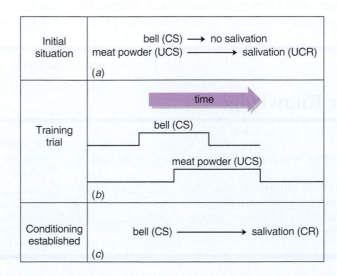

was not struck. The fear initially associated with the loud noise had come to be elicited by the previously neutral stimulus, the white rat (now the CS). This study suggests a possible relationship between classical conditioning and the development of certain disorders, in this instance a phobia. It is important to note that this type of study could never be done today because it breaches ethical standards.

CONSEQUENCES

Operant Conditioning In the 1890s, Edward Thorndike (1874–1949) began work that led to the discovery of another type of learning. Rather than investigate the association between stimuli, as Pavlov did, Thorndike studied the effects of consequences on behavior. Thorndike formulated what was to become an extremely important principle, the **law of effect:** behavior that is followed by consequences satisfying to the organism will be repeated, and behavior that is followed by noxious or unpleasant consequences will be discouraged.

B. F. Skinner (1904–1990) introduced the concept of **operant conditioning,** so called because it applies to behavior that operates on the environment. Renaming Thorndike's "law of effect" the "principle of reinforcement," Skinner distinguished two types of reinforcement. **Positive reinforcement** refers to the strengthening of a tendency to respond by virtue of the presentation of a pleasant event, called a positive reinforcer. For example, a water-deprived pigeon will tend to repeat behaviors (operants) that are followed by the availability of water. **Negative reinforcement** also strengthens a response, but it does so via the removal of an aversive event, such as the cessation of electric shock.

Operant conditioning principles may contribute to the persistence of aggressive behavior, a key feature of conduct disorder (see Chapter 13). Aggression is often rewarded, as when one child hits another to secure the possession of a toy (getting the toy is the reinforcer). Parents may also unwittingly reinforce aggression by giving in when their child becomes angry or threatens violence to achieve some goal, such as staying up late to watch TV.

Modeling Learning often goes on even in the absence of reinforcers. We all learn by watching and imitating others, a process called **modeling.** In the 1960s, experimental work demonstrated that witnessing someone perform certain activities can increase or decrease diverse kinds of behavior, such as sharing, aggression, and fear. For example, Bandura and Menlove (1968) used a modeling treatment to reduce fear of dogs in children. After witnessing a fearless model engage in various activities with a dog, initially fearful children showed an increase in their willingness to approach and touch a dog. Children of parents with phobias or substance abuse problems may acquire similar behavior patterns, in part through observation.

Behavior Therapy **Behavior therapy** emerged in the 1950s. In its initial form, this therapy applied procedures based on classical and operant conditioning to alter clinical problems. Sometimes the term *behavior modification* is used as well, and therapists who use operant conditioning as a treatment often prefer that term. Behavior therapy was an attempt to change behavior, thoughts, and feelings by applying in a clinical context the methods used and the discoveries made by experimental psychologists.

One important behavior therapy technique that is still used to treat phobias and anxiety today is called **systematic desensitization.** Developed by Joseph Wolpe in 1958, it includes two components:

B. F. Skinner originated the study of operant conditioning and the extension of this approach to education, psychotherapy, and society as a whole. (Kathy Bendo for John Wiley & Sons.)

Skinner boxes are often used in studies of operant conditioning to demonstrate how behavior can be shaped by reinforcing it. (BILL ROTH/ASSOCIATED PRESS.)

Aggressive responses in children are often rewarded, which makes them more likely to occur in the future. In this photo, the more aggressive child gets to keep the toy. (Ken Cavanagh/Photo Researchers.)

Appraisals are an important part of cognitive therapy. As illustrated, appraisals can change the meaning of a situation. (© 2000 Bil Keane, Inc. King Features Syndicate.)

(1) deep muscle relaxation and (2) gradual exposure to a list of feared situations, starting with those that arouse minimal anxiety and progressing to those that are the most frightening. Wolpe hypothesized that a state or response opposite to anxiety is substituted for anxiety as the person is exposed gradually to stronger and stronger doses of what he or she fears. We will cover this technique in more detail in Chapter 2, as it remains an important part of current forms of cognitive behavior therapy.

Modeling was also included in behavior therapy starting in the 1960s. For example, people reduced their fear of snakes by viewing both live and filmed encounters in which other people gradually approached and successfully handled snakes (Bandura, Blanchard, & Ritter, 1969). Fears of surgery and dental work have also been treated in a similar manner (Melamed & Siegel, 1975).

Operant techniques such as systematically rewarding desirable behavior and extinguishing undesirable behavior have been particularly successful in the treatment of many childhood problems (Kazdin & Weisz, 1998). Once contingencies shape a behavior, a key goal is to maintain the effects of treatment. If a therapist or a teacher has been providing reinforcement, one might not expect this person to keep providing reinforcement forever. This issue has been addressed in several ways. Because laboratory findings indicate that intermittent reinforcement—rewarding a response only a portion of the times it appears—makes new behavior more enduring, many operant programs move away from continuous schedules of reinforcement once desired behavior is occurring regularly. For example, if a teacher has succeeded in helping a disruptive child spend more time sitting by praising the child generously for each math problem finished while seated, the teacher will gradually reward the child for every other success, and ultimately only infrequently.

The Importance of Cognition   Although behaviorism remains influential in many ways today, clinicians and researchers have begun to recognize the limitations of focusing only on behavior. Human beings don't just behave, they think and feel, too! Early behavior theories did not leave much room for cognition and emotion. Beginning in the 1960's, the study of cognition began to become very prominent. Researchers and clinicians realized that the ways in which people think about, or *appraise,* situations can influence behavior in dramatic ways. For example, walking into a room of strangers can elicit thoughts such as "Great! I am so excited to meet all sorts of new and interesting people" or "I do not know any of these people and I am going to look and sound like a complete moron!" A person who has the first thought is likely to join a group of people enthusiastically and join in the conversation. The person who has the second thought, however, is likely to turn right around and leave the room.

Cognitive Therapy   Cognitive therapy, as mentioned earlier, is based on the idea that people not only behave, they also think and feel. All cognitive approaches have one thing in common. They emphasize that how people construe themselves and the world is a major determinant of psychological disorders. In cognitive therapy, the therapist typically begins by helping clients become more aware of their maladaptive thoughts. By changing cognition, therapists hope that people can change their feelings, behaviors, and symptoms.

The roots of cognitive therapy included Aaron Beck's cognitive therapy (discussed in Chapter 2) and Albert Ellis's **rational-emotive behavior therapy (REBT).** Ellis's (1913–2007) principal thesis was that sustained emotional reactions are caused by internal sentences that people repeat to themselves; these self-statements reflect sometimes unspoken assumptions— irrational beliefs—about what is necessary to lead a meaningful life. In Ellis's REBT (Ellis, 1993, 1995), the aim is to eliminate self-defeating beliefs. A person with depression, for example, may say several times a day, "What a worthless jerk I am." Ellis proposed that people interpret what is happening around them, that sometimes these interpretations can cause emotional turmoil, and that a therapist's attention should be focused on these beliefs rather than on historical causes or, indeed, on overt behavior.

Albert Ellis, a cognitive behavior therapist and founder of rational-emotive behavior therapy, focused on the role of irrational beliefs as causes of psychopathology. (© Bettmann/© Corbis.)

Ellis used to list a number of irrational beliefs that people can harbor. He later (1991; Kendall et al., 1995) shifted from a cataloguing of specific beliefs to the more general concept of "demandingness," that is, the musts or shoulds that people impose on themselves and on others. Thus, instead of wanting something to be a certain way, feeling disappointed, and then perhaps engaging in some behavior that might bring about the desired outcome, the person demands that it be so. Ellis hypothesized that it is this unrealistic, unproductive demand that creates the kind of emotional distress and behavioral dysfunction that bring people to therapists.

Quick Summary

Behaviorism began its ascendancy in the 1920s and continues to be an important part of various psychotherapies. John Watson built on the work of Ivan Pavlov in showing how some behaviors can be conditioned. B. F. Skinner, building on the work of Edward Thorndike, emphasized the contingencies associated with behavior, showing how positive and negative reinforcement could shape behavior. Research on modeling helped to explain how people can learn even when no obvious reinforcers are present. Early behavior therapy techniques that are still used today include systematic desensitization, intermittent reinforcement, and modeling. The study of cognition became popular beginning in the 1960s. Cognitive therapy was developed, and one of its pioneers, Albert Ellis, developed an influential treatment that is still used today. Rational-emotive behavior therapy emphasizes that the thoughts and "demands" that people impose on themselves (I should do this; I must do that) are counterproductive and lead to different types of emotional distress.

Check Your Knowledge 1.4

True or false?
1. Positive reinforcement refers to increasing a desired behavior, while negative reinforcement refers to eliminating an undesirable behavior.
2. Systematic desensitization involves meditation and relaxation.

3. A cat comes running at the sound of a treat jar rattling, and his human friend then gives him a treat. The conditioned stimulus in this example is the sound of the jar rattling.
4. REBT focuses on changing emotions first so that thoughts can then change.

The Mental Health Professions

As views of mental disorders have evolved, so, too, have the professions associated with the field. Professionals authorized to provide psychological services include clinical psychologists, psychiatrists, psychiatric nurses, counseling psychologists, social workers, and marriage and family therapists. The need for such professions has never been greater. For example, a recent study found that the cost of mental disorders in the United States is nearly $200 billion a year in lost earnings (Kessler et al., 2008). People with serious mental illness are often not able to work due to their illness, and as a result their yearly earnings are substantially less than those of people without mental illness (by as much as $16,000 a year!). In addition, people with mental disorders are more likely to be without health insurance than people without mental disorders (Garfield et al., 2011), a situation that will hopefully change in the United States with the new health care legislation (the Patient Protection and Affordable Care Act) passed in 2010. In this section, we discuss the different types of mental health professionals who treat people with mental disorders, the different types of training they receive, and a few related issues.

Clinical psychologists (such as the authors of this textbook) must have a Ph.D. or Psy.D. degree, which entails 4 to 8 years of graduate study. Training for the Ph.D. in clinical psychology is similar to that in other psychological specialties, such as developmental or cognitive

Clinical psychologists are trained to deliver psychotherapy. (© PhotoStock-Israel/Alamy.)

neuroscience. It requires a heavy emphasis on research, statistics, neuroscience, and the empirically based study of human behavior. As in other fields of psychology, the Ph.D. is basically a research degree, and candidates are required to write a dissertation on a specialized topic. But candidates in clinical psychology learn skills in two additional areas, which distinguish them from other Ph.D. candidates in psychology. First, they learn techniques of assessment and diagnosis of psychopathology; that is, they learn the skills necessary to determine whether a person's symptoms or problems indicate a particular disorder. Second, they learn how to practice **psychotherapy**, a primarily verbal means of helping people change their thoughts, feelings, and behavior to reduce distress and to achieve greater life satisfaction. Students take courses in which they master specific techniques and treat patients under close professional supervision; then, during an intensive internship, they assume increasing responsibility for the care of patients.

Another degree option for clinical psychologists is the Psy.D. (doctor of psychology), for which the curriculum is similar to that required of Ph.D. students, but with less emphasis on research and more on clinical training. The thinking behind this approach is that clinical psychology has advanced to a level of knowledge and certainty that justifies intensive training in specific techniques of assessment and therapeutic intervention rather than combining practice with research. On the other hand, conducting assessment or therapy without a sufficient empirical basis is professionally dubious. As of 2002, there were nearly 90,000 clinical psychologists in the United States (Duffy et al., 2004). By 2003, estimates suggested that there were more clinical psychologists than needed to adequately deliver services and that this was negatively impacting clinical psychologists' salaries (Robiner, 2006). Nevertheless, psychologists are three times as likely to be providers of psychotherapy compared to social workers according to a recent survey of nearly 2,000 people receiving mental health services (Olfson & Marcus, 2010).

Psychiatrists hold an M.D. degree and have had postgraduate training, called a residency, in which they have received supervision in the practice of diagnosis and pharmacotherapy (administering medications). By virtue of the medical degree, and in contrast to psychologists, psychiatrists can function as physicians—giving physical examinations, diagnosing medical problems, and the like. Most often, however, the only aspect of medical practice in which psychiatrists engage is prescribing **psychoactive medications**, chemical compounds that can influence how people feel and think. Psychiatrists may receive some training in psychotherapy as well, though this is not a strong focus of training. In contrast to clinical psychologists, there is a shortage of psychiatrists, largely due to budget cuts in residency training programs. In 2000, there were over 40,000 psychiatrists in the United States (Robiner, 2006).

Over the past 20 years, there has been a lively and sometimes acrimonious debate about whether to allow clinical psychologists with suitable training to prescribe psychoactive medications. Such a move is opposed not only by psychiatrists, whose turf would be invaded, but also by many psychologists, who view it as an ill-advised dilution of the basic behavioral science focus of psychology. Also at issue is the question of whether a non-M.D. can learn enough about neurobiology and neurochemistry to monitor the effects of drugs and protect patients from adverse side effects and drug interactions. Currently two states (New Mexico and Louisiana) allow psychologists to prescribe medication following the receipt of additional training; several other states are considering similar legislation.

A **psychiatric nurse** typically receives training at the bachelor's or master's level. Nurses can also receive more specialized training as a nurse practitioner that will allow them to prescribe psychoactive medications. There are currently over 18,000 psychiatric nurses in the United States, but the trend appears to be more toward emphasizing training as a nurse practitioner in order to secure prescription privileges (Robiner, 2006).

Other graduate programs are more focused on clinical practice than are the traditional Ph.D. programs. One of these is **counseling psychology**. Counseling psychologists originally dealt mostly with vocational issues; their focus today may be quite similar to that in clinical psychology, though still with less of an emphasis on mental disorders and more of an emphasis on prevention, education, and general life problems. Counseling psychologists work in a variety of settings, including schools, mental health agencies, industry, and community health centers. In 2002, there were 85,000 counseling psychologists working in mental health (Robiner, 2006).

Social workers have an M.S.W. (master of social work) degree. Training programs are shorter than Ph.D. programs, typically requiring 2 years of graduate study. The focus of training is on psychotherapy. Those in social work graduate programs do not receive training in psychological assessment. In 2002, there were close to 100,000 social workers in the United States who provided direct mental health services and were also members of the National Association of Social Workers (Duffy et al., 2004).

Marriage and family therapists treat families or couples, focusing on the ways in which these relationships impact a variety of mental health issues. Specialized programs in marriage and family therapy can be at the master's or doctoral level. Some M.S.W. programs offer specialized training and certification in marriage and family therapy. In 2002, there were just over 47,000 marriage and family therapists in the United States, the majority having training at the master's level.

Summary

- The study of psychopathology is a search for the reasons why people behave, think, and feel in unexpected, sometimes odd, and possibly self-defeating ways. Unfortunately, people who have a mental illness are often stigmatized. Reducing the stigma associated with mental illness remains a great challenge for the field.

- In evaluating whether a behavior is part of a mental disorder, psychologists consider several different characteristics, including personal distress, disability, violation of social norms, and dysfunction. Each characteristic tells us something about what can be considered mental disorder, but no one by itself provides a fully satisfactory definition. The DSM definition includes all of these characteristics.

- Since the beginning of scientific inquiry into mental disorders, supernatural, biological, and psychological points of view have vied for attention. More supernatural viewpoints included early demonology, which posited that people with mental illness are possessed by demons or evil spirits, leading to treatments such as exorcism. Early biological viewpoints originated in the writings of Hippocrates. After the fall of Greco-Roman civilization, the biological perspective became less prominent in western Europe, and demonological thinking gained ascendancy, as evidenced by the persecution of so-called witches. Beginning in the fifteenth century, people with mental illness were often confined in asylums, such as Bethlehem; treatment in asylums was generally poor or nonexistent until various humanitarian reforms were instituted. In the twentieth century, genetics and mental illness became an important area of inquiry, though the findings from genetic studies were used to the detriment of people with mental illness during the eugenics movement.

- Psychological viewpoints emerged in the nineteenth century from the work of Charcot and the writings of Breuer and Freud. Freud's theory emphasized stages of psychosexual development and the importance of unconscious processes, such as repression and defense mechanisms that are traceable to early-childhood conflicts. Therapeutic interventions based on psychoanalytic theory make use of techniques such as free association and the analysis of transference in attempting to overcome repression so that patients can confront and understand their conflicts and find healthier ways of dealing with them. Later theorists such as Jung and Adler made various modifications to Freud's basic ideas and emphasized different factors in their perspectives on therapy.

- Behaviorism suggested that behavior develops through classical conditioning, operant conditioning, or modeling. B. F. Skinner introduced the ideas of positive and negative reinforcement and showed that operant conditioning can influence behavior. Behavior therapists try to apply these ideas to change undesired behavior, thoughts, and feelings.

- The study of cognition became widespread in the 1960's. Appraisals and thinking are part of cognitive therapy. Ellis was an influential theorist in cognitive therapy.

- There are a number of different mental health professions, including clinical psychologist, psychiatrist, counseling psychologist, psychiatric nurse, social worker, and marriage and family therapist. Each involves different training programs of different lengths and with different emphases on research, psychological assessment, psychotherapy, and psychopharmacology.

Answers to Check Your Knowledge Questions

1.1 1. a; 2. d; 3. b
1.2 1. F; 2. F; 3. T; 4. T

1.3 1. Charcot, Mesmer; 2. Breuer, Freud; 3. id, ego; 4. transference; 5. Jung, Freud, Adler
1.4 1. F; 2. T; 3. T; 4 F

Key Terms

anal stage	cathartic method	conditioned stimulus (CS)	electroconvulsive therapy (ECT)
analytical psychology	classical conditioning	counseling psychologist	exorcism
asylums	clinical psychologist	defense mechanism	extinction
behavior therapy	collective unconscious	demonology	fixation
behaviorism	conditioned response (CR)	ego	free association

general paresis
genital stage
harmful dysfunction
id
individual psychology
interpretation
latency period
law of effect
libido
marriage and family therapist

mental disorder
modeling
moral treatment
negative reinforcement
operant conditioning
oral stage
phallic stage
pleasure principle
positive reinforcement
psyche

psychiatric nurse
psychiatrist
psychoactive medications
psychoanalysis
psychoanalytic theory
psychopathology
psychotherapy
rational-emotive behavior
    therapy (REBT)
reality principle

social worker
stigma
superego
systematic desensitization
transference
unconditioned response (UCR)
unconditioned stimulus (UCS)
unconscious

2 Current Paradigms in Psychopathology

AS WE NOTED IN Chapter 1, we face an enormous challenge to remain objective when trying to understand and study psychopathology scientifically. Science is a human enterprise that is bound by scientists' human limitations; it is also bound by the current state of scientific knowledge. We cannot ask questions or investigate phenomena that go beyond what human beings can understand, and it is very difficult even to go beyond what we currently understand. Our view is that every effort should be made to study psychopathology according to scientific principles. But science is not a completely objective and certain enterprise. Rather, as suggested by philosopher of science Thomas Kuhn (1970), subjective factors as well as our human limitations enter into the conduct of scientific inquiry.

Central to scientific activity, in Kuhn's view, is the notion of a **paradigm**, a conceptual framework or approach within which a scientist works—that is, a set of basic assumptions, a general perspective, that defines how to conceptualize and study a subject, how to gather and interpret relevant data, even how to think about a particular subject.[1] A paradigm has profound implications for how scientists operate at any given time. Paradigms specify what problems scientists will investigate and how they will go about the investigation.

In this chapter we consider current paradigms of psychopathology and treatment. We present three paradigms that guide the study and treatment of psychopathology: genetic, neuroscience, and cognitive behavioral. We also consider the important role of emotion and sociocultural factors in psychopathology. These factors cut across all the paradigms and are significant in terms of the description, causes, and treatments of all the disorders we will discuss in this book.

Current thinking about psychopathology is multifaceted. The work of clinicians and researchers is informed by an awareness of the strengths and limitations of all the paradigms. For this reason, current views of psychopathology and its treatment typically integrate several paradigms. At the end of this chapter we describe another paradigm—diathesis–stress—that provides the basis for an integrative approach.

---

[1]O'Donohue (1993) has criticized Kuhn's use of the concept of paradigm, noting that he was inconsistent in its definition. The complexities of this argument are beyond the scope of this book. Suffice to say that we find it useful to organize our thinking about mental disorders around the paradigm concept. We use the term to refer to the general perspectives that constrain the way scientists collect and interpret information in their efforts to understand the world.

For researchers and clinicians, the choice of a paradigm has important consequences for the way in which they define, investigate, and treat psychopathology. Our discussion of paradigms will lay the groundwork for the topics covered in the rest of the book. We note at the outset that no one paradigm offers the "complete" conceptualization of psychopathology. Rather, for most disorders, each paradigm offers some important information with respect to etiology and treatment, but only part of the picture.

The Genetic Paradigm

Genes do not, on their own, make us smart, dumb, sassy, polite, depressed, joyful, musical, tone-deaf, athletic, clumsy, literary or incurious. Those characteristics come from a complex interplay within a dynamic system. Every day in every way you are helping to shape which genes become active. Your life is interacting with your genes. (Shenk, 2010, p. 27)

In 2003, we celebrated the fiftieth anniversary of the discovery of human DNA's double-helix structure. That has been augmented with the virtual explosion of information regarding human genetics in just the past 10 years. The **genetic paradigm** has guided a number of discoveries regarding human behavior since the early part of the twentieth century. However, the changes that have occurred recently have transformed the way we think about genes and behavior. We no longer have to wonder, "Is nature or nurture responsible for human behavior?" We now know (1) almost all behavior is heritable to some degree (i.e., involves genes) and (2) despite this, genes do not operate in isolation from the environment. Instead, throughout the life span, the environment shapes how our genes are expressed, and our genes also shape our environments (Plomin et al., 2003; Rutter & Silberg, 2002; E. Turkheimer, 2000).

The more contemporary way to think about genes and the environment is cast as "nature via nurture" (Ridley, 2003). In other words, researchers are learning how environmental influences, such as stress, relationships, and culture (the nurture part), shape which of our genes are turned on or off and how our genes (the nature part) influence our bodies and brain. We know that without genes, a behavior might not be possible. But without the environment, genes could not express themselves and thus contribute to the behavior.

When the ovum, the female reproductive cell, is joined by the male's sperm, a zygote, or fertilized egg, is produced. It has 46 chromosomes, the number characteristic of a human being. Each chromosome is made up of many **genes**, the carriers of the genetic information (DNA) passed from parents to child.

In 2001, two different groups of researchers announced that the human genome consisted of around 30,000 genes. This number was later revised downward to between 20,000 and 25,000 (Human Genome Project, 2008). At first, this news was surprising, since researchers had been thinking the human genome consisted of closer to 100,000 genes. After all, the mere fruit fly has around 14,000 genes—researchers had thought that surely human beings were several times more complex than that! As it turns out, however, one of the exciting things about this discovery was the revelation from dozens of other genetic labs that the number of genes was not all that important. Instead, it is the sequencing, or ordering, of these genes as well as their expression that make us unique. What genes *do* matters more than the number of genes we have. What genes do is make proteins that in turn make the body and brain work. Some of these proteins switch, or turn, on and off other genes, a process called **gene expression**. Learning about the flexibility of genes and how they switch on or off has closed the door on beliefs about the inevitability of the effects of genes, good or bad. As we will illustrate throughout this book, the data do not support the supposition that if you have the genes for **x**, you will necessarily get **x**. What matters is how your genes interact with the environment. With respect to most mental illnesses, there is not one gene that contributes vulnerability. Instead, psychopathology is **polygenic**, meaning several genes, perhaps operating at different times during the course of development, turning themselves on and off as they interact with a person's environment is the essence of genetic vulnerability.

Thus, we do not inherit mental illness from our genes; we develop mental illness through the interaction of our genes with our environments (Shenk, 2010). This is a subtle but very important point. It is easy to fall into the trap of thinking a person inherits schizophrenia from his or her genes. What genetics research today is telling us, however, is that a person *develops* schizophrenia from the interaction between genes and the environment [as well as the body (e.g. hormones), brain, and other genes].

An important term that will be used throughout the book is **heritability**. Unfortunately, it is a term that is easily misunderstood and often misused. Heritability refers to the extent to which variability in a particular behavior (or disorder) in a population can be accounted for by genetic factors. There are two important points about heritability to keep in mind.

1. Heritability estimates range from 0.0 to 1.0: the higher the number, the greater the heritability.
2. Heritability is relevant *only* for a large population of people, not a particular individual. Thus, it is incorrect to talk about any one person's heritability for a particular behavior or disorder. Knowing that the heritability of attention-deficit/hyperactivity disorder (ADHD) is around 0.70 does not mean that 70 percent of Jane's ADHD is because of her genes and 30 percent is due to other factors. It means that in a population (e.g., a large sample in a study), the variation in ADHD is understood as being attributed to 70 percent genes and 30 percent environment. There is no heritability in ADHD (or any disorder) for a particular individual.

Other factors that are just as important as genes in genetic research are environmental factors. **Shared environment** factors include those things that members of a family have in common, such as family income level, child-rearing practices, and parents' marital status and quality. **Nonshared environment** (sometimes referred to as *unique environment*) factors are those things believed to be distinct among members of a family, such as relationships with friends or specific events unique to a person (e.g., being in a car accident or on the swim team), and these are believed to be important in understanding why two siblings from the same family can be so different. Consider an example. Jason is a 34-year-old man who is dependent on alcohol and struggling to keep his job. His sister Joan is a 32-year-old executive in a computer company in San Jose and has no alcohol or drug problems. Jason did not have many friends as a child; Joan was one of the most popular girls in high school. Jason and Joan shared several influences, including their family atmosphere growing up. They also had unique, nonshared experiences, such as differences in peer relationships. Behavior genetics research suggests that the nonshared, or unique, environmental experiences have much more to do with the development of mental illness than the shared experiences.

We now turn to review two broad approaches in the genetic paradigm, including behavior genetics and molecular genetics. We then discuss the exciting evidence on the ways in which genes and environments interact. This sets the stage for our discussion of an integrative paradigm later in the chapter.

Behavior Genetics

Behavior genetics is the study of the degree to which genes and environmental factors influence behavior. To be clear, behavior genetics is not the study of *how* genes or the environment determine behavior. Many behavior genetics studies estimate the heritability of a mental illness, without providing any information about how the genes might work. The total genetic makeup of an individual, consisting of inherited genes, is referred to as the **genotype** (physical sequence of DNA); the genotype cannot be observed outwardly. In contrast, the totality of observable behavioral characteristics, such as level of anxiety, is referred to as the **phenotype**.

Shared environment refers to things families have in common, like marital quality. (© Aletia/Shutterstock.)

Nonshared environment refers to factors that are distinct among family members, such as having different groups of friends. (Pixland/SuperStock, Inc.)

Behavior genetics studies the degree to which characteristics, such as physical resemblance or psychopathology, are shared by family members because of shared genes. (Tony Freeman/ PhotoEdit.)

We defined gene expression earlier: the genotype should not be viewed as a static entity. Genes switch off and on at specific times, for example, to control various aspects of development. Indeed, genetic programs are quite flexible—they respond in remarkable ways to things that happen to us.

The phenotype changes over time and is the product of an interaction between the genotype and the environment. For example, a person may be born with the capacity for high intellectual achievement, but whether he or she develops this genetically given potential depends on environmental factors such as upbringing and education. Hence, intelligence is an index of the phenotype.

A study by Turkheimer and colleagues (2003) shows how genes and environment may interact to influence IQ. A number of studies have demonstrated high heritability for IQ (e.g., Plomin, 1999). What Turkheimer and colleagues found, though, was that heritability depends on environment. The study included 319 twin pairs of 7-year-olds (114 identical, 205 fraternal). Many of the children were living in families either below the poverty line or with a low family income. Among the families of lower socioeconomic status (SES), 60 percent of the variability in children's IQ was attributable to the environment. Among the higher-SES families, the opposite was found. That is, variability in IQ was more attributable to genes than to environment. Thus, being in an impoverished environment may have deleterious effects on IQ, whereas being in a more affluent environment may not help out all that much. It is important to point out that these interesting findings deal with IQ scores, a measure of what psychologists consider to be intelligence, not achievement (we discuss this more in Chapters 3 and 13). Such interactions between genes and environments are the "new look" to behavior genetics research (Moffitt, 2005), and we discuss additional studies illustrating how genes and environments work together below. In Chapter 4, we will discuss the major research designs used in behavior genetics research—including family, twin, and adoption studies—to estimate the heritability of different disorders.

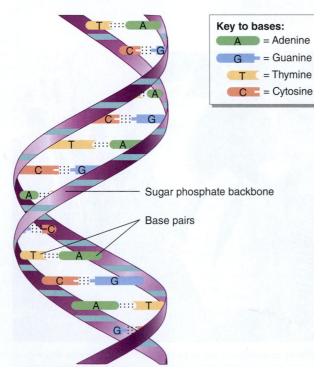

Key to bases:

- A = Adenine
- G = Guanine
- T = Thymine
- C = Cytosine

Sugar phosphate backbone

Base pairs

Figure 2.1 This figure shows a strand of DNA with four chemical bases: A(adenine), T(thymine), G(guanine), and C(cytosine).

Molecular Genetics

Molecular genetics studies seek to identify particular genes and their functions. Recall that a human being has 46 chromosomes (23 chromosome pairs) and that each chromosome is made up of hundreds or thousands of genes that contain DNA (see Figure 2.1). Different forms of the same gene are called **alleles**. The alleles of a gene are found at the same location, or locus, of a chromosome pair. A genetic **polymorphism** refers to a difference in DNA sequence on a gene that has occurred in a population.

The DNA in genes is transcribed to RNA. In some cases, the RNA is then translated into amino acids, which then form proteins, and proteins make cells (see Figure 2.2). Gene expression involves particular types of DNA called *promoters*. These promoters are recognized by particular proteins called *transcription factors*. Promoters and transcription factors are the focus of much research in molecular genetics and psychopathology. All of this is a remarkably complex system, and variations along the way, such as different combinations or sequences of events, lead to different outcomes.

In the past 10 years, molecular genetics research has focused on identifying differences between people in the *sequence* of their genes and in the *structure* of their genes. One area of interest in the study of gene sequence involves identifying what are called **single nucleotide polymorphisms** or **SNPs** (pronounced *snips*). A SNP refers to differences between people in a single nucleotide (A, T, G, or C; see Figure 2.3) in the DNA sequence of a particular gene. Figure 2.1 illustrates what a SNP looks like in a strand of DNA. The SNP is circled, pointing to the single nucleotide difference between the two strands. These are the most common types of polymorphisms in the

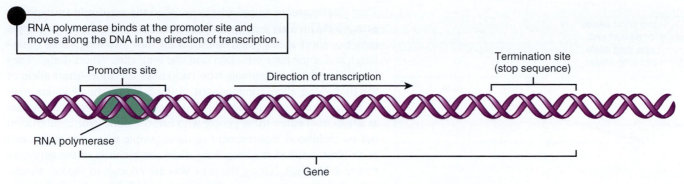

Figure 2.2 This figure shows gene **transcription**, the process by which DNA is transcribed to RNA. In some cases, the RNA is then translated into amino acids, which then form proteins, and proteins make cells.

human genome, with nearly 10 million different SNPs identified thus far. SNPs have been studied in schizophrenia, autism, and the mood disorders to name but a few disorders.

Another area of interest is the study of differences between people in gene structure, including the identification of what are called **copy number variations (CNVs)**. A CNV can be present in a single gene or multiple genes. The name refers to an abnormal copy of one or more sections of DNA within the gene(s). These abnormal copies can be *additions*, where extra copies are abnormally present, or *deletions*, where copies are missing. As much as 5 percent of the human genome contains CNVs, which can be inherited from parents or can be what are called spontaneous (*de novo*) mutations—appearing for the first time in an individual. We will discuss studies that have identified CNVs in different disorders, particularly schizophrenia (Chapter 9), autism, and ADHD (Chapter 13).

Researchers studying animals can actually manipulate specific genes and then observe the effects on behavior. Specific genes can be taken out of mice DNA—these are called knockout studies because a particular gene is knocked out of the animal's system. For example, the gene that is responsible for a specific receptor for the neurotransmitter serotonin, called 5-HT$_{1A}$, has been knocked out in mice before their birth. As adults, they show what could be described as an anxious phenotype. Interestingly, one study that employed a novel technique to knock out this gene only temporarily found that its restoration early in development prevented the development of anxious behavior in the adult mice (Gross et al., 2002). This is a major area of molecular genetic work. Linking the findings from these animal studies to humans remains a challenge for the field, however.

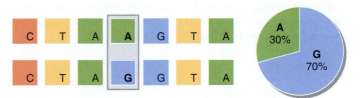

Figure 2.3 Illustration of what a single nucleotide polymorphism, or SNP, looks like in a comparison of two people. The two strands are the same except for a single nucleotide. To the right, an illustration showing that the position of G in the sequence is far more common in a large population of people compared to the position of A in the sequence.

Gene–Environment Interactions

As we noted earlier, we know now that genes and environments work together. Life experience shapes how our genes are expressed, and our genes guide us in behaviors that lead to the selection of different experiences. A **gene–environment interaction** means that a given person's sensitivity to an environmental event is influenced by genes.

Take a simple (and made-up) example. If a person has gene XYZ, he or she might respond to a snakebite by developing a fear of snakes. A person without the XYZ gene would not develop a fear of snakes after being bitten. This simple relationship involves both genes (the XYZ gene) and an environmental event (snakebite).

A different (and true) example of a gene–environment interaction involves depression. In one longitudinal study, a large sample of children in New Zealand was followed across time from the age of 5 until their mid–20s (Caspi et al., 2003). Across this time, the researchers assessed a number of variables, including early childhood maltreatment (abuse) and depression as an adult.

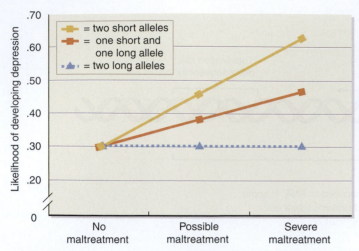

Figure 2.4 A gene–environment interaction is illustrated here. Having both the short allele of the 5-HTT gene and childhood maltreatment were associated with the greatest probability of developing depression as an adult. Adapted from Caspi et al. (2003).

Baby rats who are raised by a mother who does a lot of licking are more likely to do this when they grow up to be mothers, even if they were raised by an adoptive mother. (Courtesy Darlene Francis.)

They also measured a particular gene called the **serotonin transporter gene** (5-HTT). This gene has a polymorphism such that some people have two short alleles (short–short), some have two long alleles (long–long), and some have one short and one long allele (short–long). They found that those individuals who had either the short–short allele or the short–long allele combinations of the 5-HTT gene *and* were mal-treated as children were more likely to have major depressive disorder as adults than either those people who had the same gene combination but no childhood maltreatment or those people who were maltreated as children but had the long–long allele combination of the gene (see Figure 2.4). Thus, having the gene was not enough to predict an epi-sode of depression, nor was the presence of childhood maltreatment. Rather, it was the specific combination of the gene configuration and environmental events that predicted depression. They found the same gene–environment interaction for having at least one short allele of the gene and reports of stressful life events. That is, those people who reported more severe stressful life events and had at least one short allele of the 5-HTT gene were at greater risk of developing depression. Importantly, findings from this study have been replicated by several different groups of researchers (see Chapter 4 for the importance of replication), particularly when studies have incorporated careful inter-view measures of stress, as we discuss in Chapter 3 (Caspi et al., 2010).

Other exciting developments in this area have emerged in animal research. In these studies, different environments are manipulated and then changes in behavior and gene expression are measured. The study of how the environment can alter gene expression or function is called **epigenetics**. The term *epigenetic* means "above or outside the gene" and refers to the chemical "marks" that are attached to and protect the DNA in each gene. These epigenetic marks are what control gene expression, and the environment can directly influence the work of these marks (Karg et al., 2011; Zhang & Meaney, 2010).

In a series of fascinating studies with rats, Darlene Francis has shown that parenting behaviors can be passed on to offspring in a nongenetic way. Good parenting among rats consists of a lot of licking and grooming (LG) and what is called arched-back nursing (ABN). Mothers differ in the extent to which they do these LG-ABN behaviors, but mothers who do it more tend to have pups that grow up to be less reactive to stress. Francis and colleagues (1999) found that pups born to mothers who were low in this LG-ABN behavior but raised by mothers high in LG-ABN (called a cross-fostering adoptee method, discussed in more detail in Chapter 4) grew up to be low in stress reactivity and as mothers themselves exhibited the high LG-ABN style. And when they had their own pups, these "grandpups" were also low in stress reactivity and became high LG-ABN mothers. Thus, this parenting style was trans-mitted across two generations after an adoption. Does this suggest that genes are not important? The adoptive parent's behavior was what was transmitted across genera-tions, not the biological parent's behavior, which would suggest that this is an environmental effect.

However, a later study showed that this transmission of good mothering was due in part to the fact that it triggered an increase in the expression of a certain gene among the adopted offspring (Weaver et al., 2004). Using cross-fostering again, pups with a low LG-ABN biological mother who were raised by a high LG-ABN mother had increases in expression of a certain gene (glucocorticoid receptor) in the same way that pups with a biological high LG-ABN mother did (but pups with a biological low LG-ABN mother did not). The environment (mothering) was responsible for turning on (or turning up) the expression of a particular gene. Once it was on, the mothering style seemed to continue across generations.

We will continue to see these types of studies in animals and humans. Understanding how environments influence the expression of genes will be important for understanding the causes of psychopathology.

Reciprocal Gene–Environment Interactions

Another important way in which genes are important in psychopathology is in how they may promote certain types of environments. This is called a **reciprocal gene–environment interaction** (Plomin et al., 2003; Rutter & Silberg, 2002). The basic idea is that genes may predispose us to seek out certain environments that then increase our risk for developing a particular disorder. For example, a genetic risk for alcohol use disorder may predispose persons to life events that put them in high-risk situations for alcohol use such as being in trouble with the law. One study found that genetic vulnerability to depression may promote certain life events, such as breaking up with a boyfriend or difficulties with parents, that can trigger depression among adolescent girls (Silberg et al., 1999). More broadly, one type of stressful life events, called dependent life events, appears to be influenced by genes more than by random bad luck. That is, people seem to select environments that increase the likelihood of certain kinds of stressful life events at least in part based on their genes (Kendler & Baker, 2007). Researchers now try to distinguish between these dependent life events and those that are outside of an individual's control, a topic we return to in Chapter 3 when we discuss life event assessment.

Evaluating the Genetic Paradigm

Our discussion of each paradigm will conclude with an evaluation section. Genetics is an important part of the study of psychopathology, and there are many ways in which genes might be involved in psychopathology. The models that will help us understand how genes are implicated in psychopathology are the ones that take the contemporary view that genes do their work *via* the environment. Perhaps the biggest challenge facing scientists working within the genetic paradigm is to specify exactly how genes and environments reciprocally influence one another. This is more easily done in tightly controlled laboratory studies with animals. Making the leap to understanding how genes interact with complex human environments throughout the course of development is of course a greater challenge. Nevertheless, this is an exciting time for genetics research, and important discoveries about genes, environments, and psychopathology are being made at a rapid rate. In addition, some of the most exciting breakthroughs in genetics have involved a combination of methods from genetics and neuroscience. For example, findings from neuroscience have illuminated the ways in which genes and environments exert their influence via the brain (Caspi & Moffitt, 2006). Although we present the genetic and neuroscience paradigms separately, they go hand in hand when it comes to understanding the possible causes of psychopathology.

Quick Summary

The genetic paradigm focuses on questions such as whether certain disorders are heritable and, if so, what is actually inherited. Heritability is a population statistic, not a metric of the likelihood a particular person will inherit a disorder. Environmental effects can be classified as shared and nonshared (sometime called unique). Molecular genetics studies seek to identify differences in the sequence and structure of genes as well as gene polymorphisms, such as SNPs, that may be involved in psychopathology. Research has emphasized the importance of gene–environment interactions. Genes do their work via the environment in most cases. Recent examples of genetic influence being manifested only under certain environmental conditions (e.g., poverty and IQ; early maltreatment and depression) make clear that we must look not just for the genes associated with mental illness but also for the conditions under which these genes may be expressed.

Check Your Knowledge 2.1 (Answers are at the end of the chapter.)

1. The process by which genes are turned on or off is referred to as:
   a. heritability
   b. gene expression
   c. polygenic
   d. gene switching
2. Sam and Sally are twins raised by their biological parents. Sam excelled in music and was in the high school band; Sally was the star basketball player on the team. They both received top-notch grades, and they both had part-time jobs at the bagel store. An example of a shared environment variable would be _____; an example of a nonshared environment variable would be _____.
   a. school activities; their parents' relationship
   b. band for Sam; basketball for Sally
   c. their parents' relationship; work
   d. their parents' relationship; school activities
3. _____ refers to different forms of the same gene; _____ refers to different genes contributing to a disorder.
   a. Allele; polygenic
   b. Polygenic; allele

   c. Allele; polymorphism
   d. Polymorphism; allele
4. SNPs tell us about the _____ of genes, and CNVs tell us about the_____ of genes.
   a. DNA; RNA
   b. sequence; structure
   c. structure; sequence
   d. DNA; polymorphism
5. In the Caspi and colleagues (2003) gene–environment interaction study of depression, those who were at highest risk for developing depression were:
   a. those who were maltreated as children and had a biological parent with depression
   b. those who were maltreated as children and had at least one long allele of the 5-HTT gene
   c. those who were maltreated as children and had at least one short allele of the 5-HTT gene
   d. those who were not maltreated as children but had at least one short allele of the 5-HTT gene

The Neuroscience Paradigm

The **neuroscience paradigm** holds that mental disorders are linked to aberrant processes in the brain. Considerable literature deals with the brain and psychopathology. For example, some depressions are associated with neurotransmitter problems within the brain; anxiety disorders may be related to a defect within the autonomic nervous system that causes a person to be too easily aroused; dementia can be traced to impairments in structures of the brain. In this section, we look at three components of this paradigm in which the data are particularly interesting: neurons and neurotransmitters, brain structure and function, and the neuroendocrine system. We then consider some of the key treatments that follow from the paradigm.

Neurons and Neurotransmitters

The cells in the nervous system are called neurons, and the nervous system is comprised of billions of neurons. Although neurons differ in some respects, each **neuron** has four major parts: (1) the cell body; (2) several dendrites, the short and thick extensions; (3) one or more axons of varying lengths, but usually only one long and thin axon that extends a considerable distance from the cell body; and (4) terminal buttons on the many end branches of the axon (Figure 2.5). When a neuron is appropriately stimulated at its cell body or through its dendrites, a **nerve impulse** travels down the axon to the terminal endings. Between the terminal endings of the sending axon and the cell membrane of the receiving neuron there is a small gap, called the **synapse** (Figure 2.6).

For neurons to send a signal to the next neuron so that communication can occur, the nerve impulse must have a way of bridging the synaptic space. The terminal buttons of each axon contain synaptic vesicles, small structures that are filled with **neurotransmitters.** Neurotransmitters are chemicals that allow neurons to send a signal across the synapse to another neuron. As the neurotransmitter flows into the synapse, some of the molecules reach the receiving, or postsynaptic, neuron. The cell membrane of the postsynaptic neuron contains receptors. Receptors are configured so that only specific neurotransmitters can fit into them. When a neurotransmitter fits into a receptor site, a message can be sent to the postsynaptic cell.

What actually happens to the postsynaptic neuron depends on integrating thousands of similar messages. Sometimes these messages are excitatory, leading to the creation of a nerve impulse in the postsynaptic cell; at other times the messages are inhibitory, making the postsynaptic cell less likely to create a nerve impulse.

Once a presynaptic neuron (the sending neuron) has released its neurotransmitter, the last step is for the synapse to return to its normal state. Not all of the released neurotransmitter has found its way to postsynaptic receptors. Some of what remains in the synapse is broken down by enzymes, and some is taken back into the presynaptic cell through a process called **reuptake**.

Several key neurotransmitters have been implicated in psychopathology, including **dopamine**, **serotonin**, **norepinephrine**, and **gamma-aminobutyric acid (GABA)**. Serotonin and dopamine may be involved in depression, mania, and schizophrenia. Norepinephrine is a neurotransmitter that communicates with the sympathetic nervous system, where it is involved in producing states of high arousal and thus may be involved in the anxiety disorders and other stress-related conditions (see Focus on Discovery 2.1 for more on the sympathetic nervous system). GABA inhibits nerve impulses throughout most areas of the brain and may be involved in the anxiety disorders.

Early theories linking neurotransmitters to psychopathology sometimes proposed that a given disorder was caused by either too much or too little of a particular transmitter (e.g., mania is associated with too much norepinephrine, anxiety disorders with too little GABA). Later research has uncovered the details behind these overly simple ideas. Neurotransmitters are synthesized in the neuron through a series of metabolic steps, beginning with an amino acid. Each reaction along the way to producing an actual neurotransmitter is catalyzed by an enzyme. Too much or too little of a particular neurotransmitter could result from an error in these metabolic steps. Similar disturbances in the amounts of specific transmitters could result from alterations in the usual processes by which transmitters are deactivated after being released into the synapse. For example, a failure to pump leftover neurotransmitter back into the presynaptic cell (reuptake) would leave excess transmitter in the synapse. Then, if a new nerve impulse causes more neurotransmitter to be released into the synapse, the postsynaptic neuron would, in a sense, get a double dose of neurotransmitter, making it more likely for a new nerve impulse to be created.

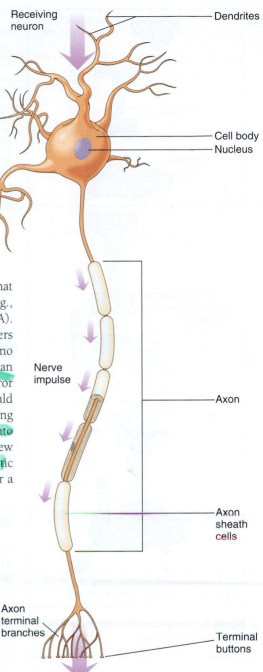

Figure 2.5 The neuron, the basic unit of the nervous system.

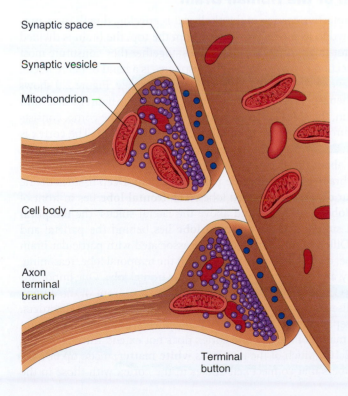

Figure 2.6 A synapse, showing the terminal buttons of two axon branches in close contact with a very small portion of the cell body of another neuron.

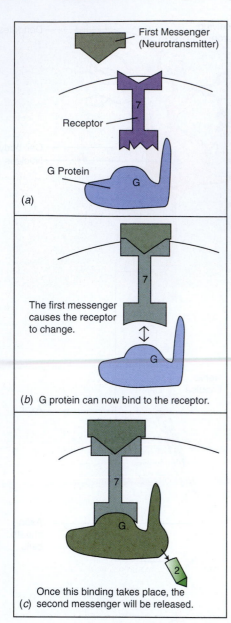

First Messenger (Neurotransmitter)

Receptor

G Protein

(a)

The first messenger causes the receptor to change.

(b)   G protein can now bind to the receptor.

Once this binding takes place, the
(c)   second messenger will be released.

Figure 2.7 The process by which a second messenger is released.

Other research has focused on the possibility that the neurotransmitter receptors are at fault in some disorders. If the receptors on the postsynaptic neuron were too numerous or too easily excited, the result would be akin to having too much transmitter released. There would simply be more sites available with which the neurotransmitter could interact, increasing the chances that the postsynaptic neuron would be stimulated. The delusions and hallucinations of schizophrenia, for example, may result from an overabundance of dopamine receptors.

Many mechanisms control the sensitivity of postsynaptic neurons. For example, if a receptor has been activated extensively over time, the cell may retune the sensitivity of the receptor so that it becomes more difficult to create a nerve impulse. When a cell has been firing more frequently, this receptor releases **second messengers** (see Figure 2.7). Once second messengers are released, they play a role in adjusting the sensitivity of postsynaptic receptors to dopamine, norepinephrine, or serotonin (Duman, Heninger, & Nestler, 1997; Shelton, Mainer, & Sulser, 1996). One can think of second messengers as helping a neuron adjust receptor sensitivity when it has been overly active. Current research on depression suggests that antidepressant medications may be effective in part due to their ability to impact second messengers

One method that investigators use to study how neurotransmitters are working in the brain is to have people take a drug that stimulates a particular neurotransmitter's receptors. This kind of drug is referred to as an **agonist**. A serotonin agonist, for example, is a drug that stimulates serotonin receptors to produce the same effects as serotonin does naturally. By contrast, an **antagonist** is a drug that works on a neurotransmitter's receptors to dampen the activity of that neurotransmitter. For example, many drugs used to treat schizophrenia are dopamine antagonists that work by blocking dopamine receptors (see p. 266 in Chapter 9).

Although neurons and neurotransmitters have been studied the most in psychopathology, we introduce another important type of brain cell here called a **glial cell** (see Figure 2.8; Fields, 2011). There are several different types of glial cells, all with long and strange sounding names, such as astrocytes, oligodendrocytes, and microglial cells. Research has discovered that these glial cells not only interact with neurons but also help to control how neurons work. These cells have been implicated in disorders we discuss in the book, including types of dementia (Chapter 14) and schizophrenia (Chapter 9).

Structure and Function of the Human Brain

The brain is located within the protective coating of the skull and is enveloped with three protective layers of membranes referred to as meninges. Viewed from the top, the brain is divided by a midline fissure into two mirror-image cerebral hemispheres; together they constitute most of the cerebrum. The major connection between the two hemispheres is a band of nerve fibers, called the **corpus callosum**, that allows the two hemispheres to communicate. Figure 2.9 shows the surface of one of the cerebral hemispheres. The cortex is comprised of the neurons that form the thin outer covering of the brain, the so-called **gray matter** of the brain. The cortex consists of six layers of tightly packed neurons, estimated to number close to 16 billion. The cortex is vastly convoluted; the ridges are called gyri, and the depressions between them sulci, or fissures. If unfolded, the cortex would be about the size of a formal dinner napkin. The sulci are used to define different regions of the brain, much like guide points on a map. Deep fissures divide the cerebral hemispheres into four distinct areas called lobes. The **frontal lobe** lies in front of the central sulcus; the **parietal lobe** is behind it and above the lateral sulcus; the **temporal lobe** is located below the lateral sulcus; and the **occipital lobe** lies behind the parietal and temporal lobes (see Figure 2.9). Different functions tend to be associated with particular brain areas: vision with the occipital lobe; discrimination of sounds with the temporal lobe; reasoning, problem solving, working memory, and emotion regulation with the frontal lobe. One important area of the cortex is called the **prefrontal cortex**. This region, in the very front of the cortex, helps to regulate the amygdala (discussed below) and is important in many different disorders.

If the brain is sliced in half, separating the two cerebral hemispheres, additional important structures can be seen. The gray matter of the cerebral cortex does not extend throughout the interior of the brain (see Figure 2.10). Much of the interior is **white matter**, made up of large tracts of myelinated (sheathed) fibers that connect cell bodies in the cortex with those in the spinal cord and in other centers lower in the brain. In certain areas, called *nuclei*, sets of nerves converge and messages are integrated from different centers.

One important set of areas, collectively referred to as the *basal ganglia*, is located deep within each hemisphere. The basal ganglia help regulate starting and stopping both motor and cognitive activity. Also deep within the brain are cavities called **ventricles**. These ventricles are filled with cerebrospinal fluid. Cerebrospinal fluid circulates through the brain through these ventricles, which are connected with the spinal cord.

The **thalamus** is a relay station for all sensory pathways except the olfactory. The nuclei making up the thalamus receive nearly all impulses arriving from the different sensory areas of the body before passing them on to the cortex, where they are interpreted as conscious sensations. The **brain stem**, comprised of the *pons* and the *medulla oblongata*, functions primarily as a neural relay station. The pons contains tracts that connect the cerebellum with the spinal cord and with motor areas of the cerebrum. The medulla oblongata serves as the main line of traffic for tracts ascending from the spinal cord and descending from the higher centers of the brain. The **cerebellum** receives sensory nerves from the vestibular apparatus of the ear and from muscles, tendons, and joints. The information received and integrated relates to balance, posture, equilibrium, and the smooth coordination of the body when in motion.

A set of deeper, mostly subcortical, structures are often implicated in different forms of psychopathology. There is a long history of referring to different groupings of these structures as the *limbic system,* a term that most contemporary neuroscientists consider outdated. These structures, shown in Figure 2.11, support the visceral and physical expressions of emotion—quickened heartbeat and respiration, trembling, sweating, and alterations in facial expressions—and the expression of appetitive and other primary drives, namely, hunger, thirst, mating, defense, attack, and flight. Important structures are the **anterior cingulate**, which is an area just above the corpus callosum; the **septal area**, which is anterior to the thalamus; the **hippocampus**,

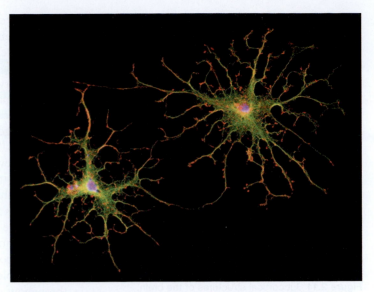

Figure 2.8 Glial cells are other important cells in our brain. (DR JAN SCHMORANZER/SCIENCE PHOTO LIBRARY/Photo Researchers, Inc.)

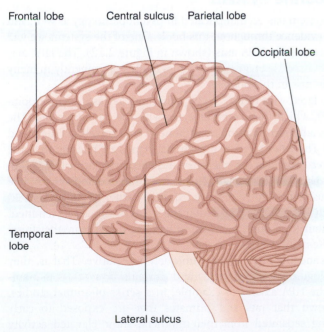

Figure 2.9 Surface of the left cerebral hemisphere, showing the four lobes and the central and lateral sulci.

Frontal lobe
Central sulcus
Parietal lobe
Occipital lobe
Temporal lobe
Lateral sulcus

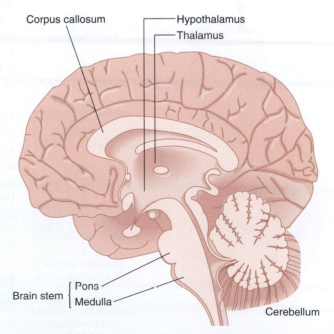

Figure 2.10 Slice of brain showing some of the internal structures.

Corpus callosum
Hypothalamus
Thalamus
Brain stem { Pons / Medulla
Cerebellum

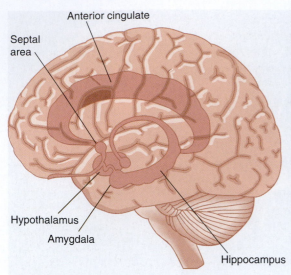

Figure 2.11 Subcortical structures of the brain.

which stretches from the septal area into the temporal lobe; the **hypothalamus**, which regulates metabolism, temperature, perspiration, blood pressure, sleeping, and appetite; and the **amygdala**, which is embedded in the tip of the temporal lobe. The amygdala is also an important area for attention to emotionally salient stimuli and memory of emotionally relevant events. This is one of the key brain structures for psychopathology researchers, given the ubiquity of emotional problems in the psychological disorders. For example, people with depression show more activity in the amygdala when watching pictures of emotional faces than do people without depression (Sheline et al., 2001).

The development of the human brain is a complex process that begins early in the first trimester of pregnancy and continues into early adulthood. It has been estimated that about a third of our genes are expressed in the brain, and many of these genes are responsible for laying out the structure of the brain. The development of the cells and migration of these cells to the appropriate layers of cortex comprise an intricate dance. Unfortunately, missteps can happen, and current thinking about a number of disorders, such as schizophrenia, places the beginnings of the problem in these early developmental stages. Brain development continues throughout childhood, adolescence, and even into adulthood. What is happening during this time is cell development and a honing of the connections between cells and brain areas. The gray matter of the brain continues to develop, filling with cells, until early adolescence. Then, somewhat surprisingly, a number of synaptic connections begin to be eliminated—a process called **pruning**. Throughout early adulthood, the connections in the brain may become fewer, but they also become faster. The areas that develop the quickest are areas linked to sensory processes, like the cerebellum and occipital lobe. The area that develops last is the frontal lobe.

We will discuss a number of these brain areas throughout the book. For example, people with schizophrenia have been found to have enlarged ventricles of the brain (Chapter 9); the size of the hippocampus is reduced among some people with posttraumatic stress disorder, depression, and schizophrenia, perhaps due to overactivity of their stress response systems (Chapters 5, 7, and 9); brain size among some children with autism expands at a much greater rate than it should in typical development (Chapter 13).

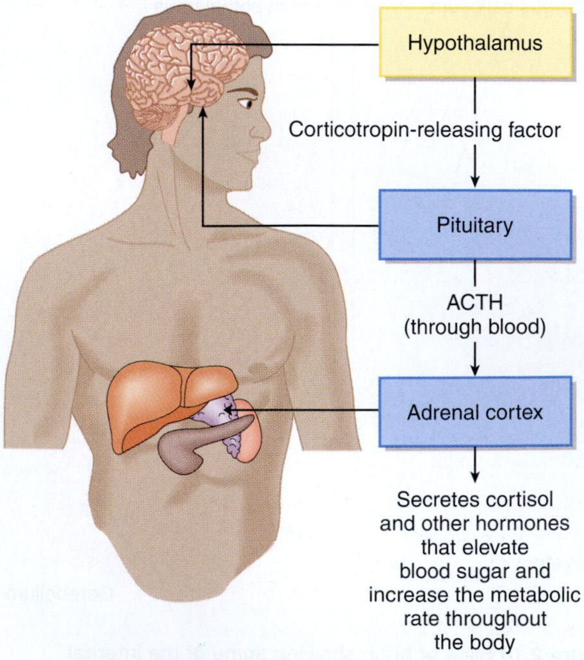

The Neuroendocrine System

The neuroendocrine system has been implicated in psychopathology as well, and we will consider this evidence throughout this book. One of the systems we will return to again and again is the **HPA axis** (shown in Figure 2.12). The HPA axis is central to the body's response to stress, and stress figures prominently in many of the disorders we discuss in this book.

When people are faced with threat, the hypothalamus releases corticotropin-releasing factor (CRF), which then communicates with the *pituitary gland*. The pituitary then releases adrenocorticotropic hormone, which travels via the blood to the adrenal glands. The outer layers of the adrenal glands are referred to as the *adrenal cortex*; this area promotes the release of the hormone cortisol. Cortisol is often referred to as the stress hormone. This is not a fast-moving system, like the autonomic nervous system, to be reviewed shortly. Rather, it takes about 20 to 40 minutes for cortisol release to peak. After the stress or threat has remitted, it can take up to an hour for cortisol to return to baseline (i.e., before the stress) levels (Dickerson & Kemeny, 2004).

Studies of stress and the HPA axis are uniquely integrative. That is, they begin with a psychological concept (stress) and examine how stress is manifested in the body (the HPA axis). For example, in a series of animal studies, researchers have shown that rats and primates that are exposed to early trauma, such as being separated from their mothers, show elevated activity in the HPA axis when they are exposed to stressors later in life (Gutman & Nemeroff, 2003). Like our discussion of gene–environment interactions above,

Hypothalamus

Corticotropin-releasing factor

Pituitary

ACTH (through blood)

Adrenal cortex

Secretes cortisol and other hormones that elevate blood sugar and increase the metabolic rate throughout the body

Figure 2.12 The HPA axis.

FOCUS ON DISCOVERY 2.1

The Autonomic Nervous System

The autonomic nervous system (ANS) innervates the endocrine glands, the heart, and the smooth muscles that are found in the walls of the blood vessels, stomach, intestines, kidneys, and other organs. This nervous system is itself divided into two parts, the **sympathetic nervous system** and the **parasympathetic nervous system** (Figure 2.13). A simple way to think about these two components of the ANS is that the sympathetic nervous system prepares the body for "fight or flight" and the parasympathetic nervous system helps "calm down" the body. Things are not actually that simple, though. The sympathetic portion of the ANS, when energized, accelerates the heartbeat, dilates the pupils, inhibits intestinal activity, increases electrodermal activity (i.e., sweat on the skin), and initiates other smooth muscle and glandular responses

that prepare the organism for sudden activity and stress. Division of activities is not quite so clear-cut, however, for it is the parasympathetic system that increases blood flow to the genitals during sexual excitement.

The autonomic nervous system figures prominently in many of the anxiety disorders, such as panic disorder and posttraumatic stress disorder. For example, people with panic disorder tend to misinterpret normal changes in their nervous system, such as shortness of breath after running up a flight of stairs. Instead of attributing this to being out of shape, people with panic disorder may think they are about to have another panic attack. In essence, they come to fear the sensations of their own autonomic nervous system.

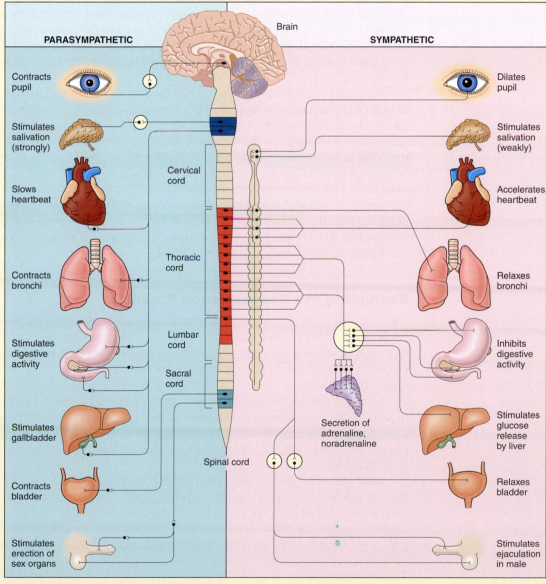

Figure 2.13 The autonomic nervous system.

it is hard to consider biology and environment separately—biology may create increased reactivity to the environment, and early experiences may influence biology. As we will see, chronic stress and its effects on the HPA axis are linked to disorders as diverse as schizophrenia, depression, and posttraumatic stress disorder.

Another important system, the **autonomic nervous system (ANS)**, is discussed in Focus on Discovery 2.1. Much of our behavior is dependent on a nervous system that operates very quickly, generally without our awareness, and that has traditionally been viewed as beyond voluntary control; hence, the term *autonomic*.

Neuroscience Approaches to Treatment

The use of psychoactive drugs has been increasing dramatically. For example, between 1988 and 2000 antidepressant use among adults nearly tripled (National Center for Health Statistics, 2004). Spending on antipsychotic drugs increased from $1.3 billion in 1997 to $5.6 billion in 2006 (Barber, 2008). Antidepressants, such as Prozac, increase neural transmission in neurons that use serotonin as a neurotransmitter by inhibiting the reuptake of serotonin. Benzodiazepines, such as Xanax, can be effective in reducing the tension associated with some anxiety disorders, perhaps by stimulating GABA neurons to inhibit other neural systems that create the physical symptoms of anxiety. Antipsychotic drugs, such as Olanzapine, used in the treatment of schizophrenia, reduce the activity of neurons that use dopamine as a neurotransmitter by blocking their receptors and also impact serotonin. Stimulants, such as Adderall, are often used to treat children with attention-deficit/hyperactivity disorder; they operate on several neurotransmitters that help children pay attention.

Although you might assume that we have learned which neurotransmitters are involved in a disorder and then used that to determine pharmacological treatments, this is often not the case. Rather, the reverse has often happened: a drug is found that influences symptoms, and then researchers are inspired to study the neurotransmitters influenced by that drug. But as we will see, the evidence linking neurotransmitters as causal factors in psychopathology is not all that strong.

It should be noted that a person could hold a neuroscience view about the nature of a disorder and yet recommend psychological intervention. Contemporary scientists and clinicians also appreciate that nonbiological interventions can influence brain functioning. For example, psychotherapy that teaches a person how to stop performing compulsive rituals, which is an effective and widely used behavioral treatment for obsessive-compulsive disorder, has measurable effects on brain activity (Baxter et al., 2000).

Evaluating the Neuroscience Paradigm

Over the past three decades, neuroscientists have made great progress in elucidating brain–behavior relationships. Neuroscience research on both the causes and treatment of psychopathology is proceeding at a rapid rate, as we will see when we discuss specific disorders in later chapters. Although we view these developments in a positive light, we also want to caution against reductionism.

Reductionism refers to the view that whatever is being studied can and should be reduced to its most basic elements or constituents. In the case of mental disorders, reductionism happens when scientists try to reduce complex mental and emotional responses to biology. In its extreme form, reductionism asserts that psychology and psychopathology are ultimately nothing more than biology.

Basic elements, such as individual nerve cells, are organized into more complex structures or systems, such as neural networks or circuits. The properties of these neural circuits cannot be deduced from the properties of the individual nerve cells. The whole is greater than the sum of its parts. A good example is provided by computers. Students writing papers for their courses use word-processing programs like Word or Google Docs. These software programs consist of many levels of code that communicate with the computer. The word-processing program necessarily involves low-level communication with the computer, involving a series of 0's and 1's and even electronics. Yet we don't conceptualize the program in terms of binary digits or electrical impulses. If the spell-checker stopped working, our first place to begin repairs would not be with the computer chips. Instead, we would want the programmer to fix the bug in the program. To be sure, the program could not run without the computer, but the program is more than just the impulses sent by the chips. In the same way, although a complex behavior like a hallucination necessarily involves the brain and nerve impulses, it is not likely that we can fully capture this by knowing about specific nerve impulses.

Certain phenomena emerge only at certain levels of analysis and will be missed by investigators who focus only at the molecular level. In the field of psychopathology, problems such as delusional beliefs, dysfunctional attitudes, and catastrophizing cognitions may well be impossible to explain neurobiologically, even with a detailed understanding of the behavior of individual neurons (Turkheimer, 1998).

Quick Summary

The neuroscience paradigm is concerned with the ways in which the brain contributes to psychopathology. Neurotransmitters such as serotonin, norepinephrine, dopamine, and GABA have been implicated in a number of disorders. A number of different brain areas are also a focus of research. The autonomic nervous system, which includes the sympathetic and parasympathetic nervous systems, is also implicated in the manifestations of some disorders.

The HPA axis is responsible for the body's response to stress and thus is relevant for several stress-related disorders. Biological treatments, primarily medications, are effective for different disorders, but they are not necessarily treating the cause of the problems. Although the brain plays an important role in our understanding of the causes of psychopathology, we must be careful to avoid reductionism.

Check Your Knowledge 2.2

Fill in the blanks.

1. The so-called limbic system of the brain includes the following brain areas: _____, _____, _____, _____, and _____.
2. The _____ matter of the brain consists of the tracts of myelinated fibers that connect cells; the _____ matter of the brain refers to the brain's cells or neurons.

3. Neurotransmitters that are studied in psychopathology include _____, which can produce states of high arousal, and _____, which inhibits nerve impulses.
4. The HPA axis consists of the _____, _____, and _____.

The Cognitive Behavioral Paradigm

The **cognitive behavioral paradigm** traces its roots to learning principles and to cognitive science. As we willl see, the basic principles from classical and operant conditioning as well as cognitive science have shaped the development of many cognitive behavioral therapies.

Influences from Behavior Therapy

One of the key influences from behaviorism is the notion that problem behavior is likely to continue if it is reinforced. Generally, problem behavior is thought to be reinforced by four possible consequences: getting attention, escaping from tasks, generating sensory feedback (such as results from the hand flapping often seen in children with autism spectrum disorder),

Time-out is a behavioral therapy technique based on operant conditioning; the consequence for misbehavior is removal to an environment with no positive reinforcers. (© Harvey Fitzhugh/Shutterstock.)

and gaining access to desirable things or situations (Carr et al., 1994). Once the source of reinforcement has been identified, treatment is then tailored to alter the consequences of the problem behavior. For example, if it was established that getting attention reinforced the problem behavior, the treatment might be to ignore the behavior. Alternatively, the problem behavior could be followed by **time-out**—the person is sent for a period of time to a location where positive reinforcers are not available. Today, time-out is a commonly used parenting technique for children who exhibit a problematic behavior of some sort.

Another technique used to increase the frequency of desirable behavior is making positive reinforcers contingent on behavior. For example, a socially withdrawn child could be reinforced for playing with others. Similarly, positive reinforcement has been used to help children with autistic disorder develop language, to remediate learning disabilities, and to help children with mental retardation develop necessary living skills.

Operant techniques such as systematically rewarding desirable behavior and extinguishing undesirable behavior have been particularly successful in the treatment of many childhood problems (Kazdin & Weisz, 1998). Once contingencies shape a behavior, a key goal is to maintain the effects of treatment. If a therapist or a teacher has been providing reinforcement, one might not expect this person to keep providing reinforcement forever. This issue has been addressed in several ways. Because laboratory findings indicate that intermittent reinforcement—rewarding a response only a portion of the times it appears—makes new behavior more enduring, many operant programs move away from continuous schedules of reinforcement once desired behavior is occurring regularly. For example, if a teacher has succeeded in helping a disruptive child spend more time sitting by praising the child generously for each math problem finished while seated, the teacher will gradually reward the child for every other success, and ultimately only infrequently.

Another successful example of operant conditioning is **behavioral activation (BA) therapy** of depression (Jacobson, Martell, & Dimidjian, 2011), which involves helping a person engage in tasks that provide an opportunity for positive reinforcement.

We introduced the technique called systematic desensitization in Chapter 1. Recall that this involves two components: (1) deep muscle relaxation and (2) gradual exposure to a list of feared situations, starting with those that arouse minimal anxiety and progressing to those that are the most frightening. The still-influential contribution from this behavioral approach is the **exposure** component of this treatment. The basic idea is that the anxiety will extinguish if the person can face the object or situation for long enough with no actual harm occurring. Sometimes this exposure can be conducted **in vivo**—that is, in real-life situations. For example, if someone has a fear of flying, you might have him or her take an actual flight. At times, exposure cannot be conducted in real life, so *imaginal exposure* will be used to address fears, such as rape, trauma, or contamination. In other situations, both types of exposure are used.

Exposure treatment is one of the most well-supported approaches for anxiety disorders. (Michael Newman/PhotoEdit.)

To illustrate exposure and systematic desensitization, consider a person who suffers from a fear of snakes. The person is taught to relax deeply. Next, the person develops a list of situations with snakes that vary in how frightening or anxiety producing they are. Examples of hierarchy items for someone who has a specific phobia of snakes might include the following:

- You hear the word *snake*.
- You look at an illustration of a snake in a children's book.
- You look at a photo of a snake.
- You look at a nature program on DVD about snakes.

- You look at a snake in a glass case at the zoo.
- You look at a live snake from several feet away.
- You look at a live snake up close.

Step-by-step, while relaxed, the person imagines the graded series of situations with snakes. The relaxation tends to inhibit any anxiety that might otherwise be elicited by the imagined scenes of snakes. The fearful person becomes able to tolerate increasingly more difficult imagined situations as he or she climbs the hierarchy over a number of therapy sessions.

Exposure continues to be a centrally important component of many forms of cognitive behavior therapy today. In the years since exposure treatments such as systematic desensitization were first developed, much has been learned about them. For instance, exposure to the real thing (in vivo exposure), when practical, is more effective than imagining situations. Also, even though relaxation training helps people experience less arousal when they first face the feared stimulus, there is no evidence that such training is required for good outcomes; as a result, it has been possible to develop briefer psychological treatments that do not include relaxation training.

As influential as these behavior therapy techniques were (and still are), behaviorism and behavior therapy were often criticized for minimizing the importance of two important factors: thinking and feeling. In other words, the way we think and feel about things undoubtedly influences our behavior. Yet behaviorists did not often take this into account when conceptualizing or treating psychological problems. These limitations of behavioral points of views, plus the explosion of research in the 1960s and 1970s in cognitive science, led some behavioral researchers and clinicians to include cognitive variables in their conceptualizations of psychopathology and therapy.

Cognitive Science

Cognition is a term that groups together the mental processes of perceiving, recognizing, conceiving, judging, and reasoning. Cognitive science focuses on how people (and animals) structure their experiences, how they make sense of them, and how they relate their current experiences to past ones that have been stored in memory.

At any given moment, we are bombarded by far more stimuli than we can possibly respond to. How do we filter this overwhelming input, put it into words or images, form hypotheses, and arrive at a perception of what is out there?

Cognitive scientists regard people as active interpreters of a situation, with people's past knowledge imposing a perceptual funnel on the experience. A person fits new information into an organized network of already-accumulated knowledge, often referred to as a **schema**, or cognitive set (Neisser, 1976). New information may fit the schema; if not, the person reorganizes the schema to fit the information or construes the information in such a way as to fit the schema. The following situation illustrates how a schema may alter the way in which information is processed and remembered.

> The man stood before the mirror and combed his hair. He checked his face carefully for any places he might have missed shaving and then put on the conservative tie he had decided to wear. At breakfast, he studied the newspaper carefully and, over coffee, discussed the possibility of buying a new washing machine with his wife. Then he made several phone calls. As he was leaving the house he thought about the fact that his children would probably want to go to that private camp again this summer. When the car didn't start, he got out, slammed the door and walked down to the bus stop in a very angry mood. Now he would be late. (Bransford & Johnson, 1973, p. 415)

Now read the excerpt again, but add the word *unemployed* before the word *man*. Now read it a third time, substituting *investment banker* for *man*. Notice how differently you understand the passage. Ask yourself what parts of the newspaper these men read. If you were asked on a questionnaire to recall this information and you no longer had access to the excerpt, you might answer "the want ads" for the unemployed man and "the financial pages" for the investment banker. Since the passage does not specify which part of the paper was read, these answers are wrong, but in each instance the error would have been a meaningful, predictable one.

Black	Pink
Red	White
Blue	Red
Green	Black
Yellow	Purple
Blue	Green
Red	Blue
White	Yellow

Figure 2.14 In the Stroop task, participants must name the color of the ink instead of reading the words.

Other important contributions from cognitive science include the study of attention. As we will see, people with disorders as diverse as anxiety disorders, mood disorders, and schizophrenia have problems with attention. For example, individuals with anxiety disorders tend to focus their attention on threatening or anxiety-producing events or situations in the environment. People with schizophrenia have a hard time concentrating their attention for a period of time.

One of the ways in which researchers have studied attention is with the Stroop task. In this task, the participant sees a set of color names printed in inks of *different* colors and must name the ink color of each word as rapidly as possible (see Figure 2.14). To do this, participants have to resist the natural impulse to say the printed word. For example, a participant might see the word *blue* written in green ink. The participant is instructed to name the ink color (green) as fast as possible without making mistakes (saying the word *blue*). It is difficult to say *green* and "inhibit" the more natural tendency to say *blue*. Interference, measured as a lengthening of response time, occurs because the words are more "attention grabbing" than the ink color.

The Stroop task has been modified to focus on emotion rather than colors. In this emotion Stroop task, participants are still instructed to name the color of the ink rather than saying the word. However, the list of words now contains emotion words instead of color words. So, for example, words such as *threat, danger, happy*, or *anxious* are written in different ink colors. In such an emotion Stroop task, individuals with anxiety disorders find that some of the emotion words are so attention grabbing that the impulse to say the word is especially strong. As in the original Stroop task, the more attention grabbing the word is, the more interference and the slower the response. Research has shown that people with anxiety disorders show more interference for threatening words (i.e., they say these words more slowly) than for nonthreatening words; this is used as evidence of an attention bias toward threatening information (see Chapter 6).

Of course, the concepts of schema and attention are related to each other. If a person has a particular set or schema about the world (e.g., the world is dangerous), that person may be more likely to pay attention to threatening or dangerous things in the environment. Furthermore, this person may be more likely to interpret ambiguous things in the environment as threatening. For example, seeing a stranger standing on a front porch may be interpreted as a sign of danger to someone with such a "danger" schema. For someone without such a schema, this person may be viewed simply as the person who lives in that house.

Cognitive explanations are now central in the search for the causes of psychopathology and for new methods of intervention. A widely held view of depression, for example, places the blame on a particular cognitive set, namely, the individual's overriding sense of hopelessness. Many people who are depressed believe that they have no important effect on their surroundings regardless of what they do. Their destiny seems to them to be out of their hands, and they expect their future to be negative. If depression does develop from a sense of hopelessness, this fact could have implications for how clinicians treat the disorder. Cognitive theorizing will be included in discussions of most of the disorders presented in subsequent chapters.

The Role of the Unconscious

As far back as Freud (see Chapter 1), much of human behavior was presumed to be unconscious, or outside the awareness of the individual. Later followers of Freud continued to emphasize the role of the unconscious in human behavior and psychopathology, but the way in which the unconscious has been discussed and even empirically studied has changed throughout the years (see also Focus on Discovery 8.3).

The unconscious has been a hot topic of study among cognitive psychologists for over 30 years, and cognitive neuroscientists have more recently explored how the brain supports behavior that is outside conscious awareness. For example, the concept of *implicit memory* refers to the idea that a person can, without being aware of it, be influenced by prior learning. A person may be shown a list of words so quickly that he or she cannot identify the words. Later, the person will be able to recall those words even though the words were not consciously perceived during the rapid initial presentation. Thus, a memory is formed implicitly (i.e., without conscious awareness). Implicit memory paradigms have been adopted by psychopathology researchers, who have found, for example, that people with social anxiety and depression have trouble with these tasks (Amir, Foa, & Coles, 1998; Watkins, 2002).

Contemporary studies of the unconscious, such as studies of implicit memory, are a long way from Freud's original theorizing about the unconscious. For cognitive neuroscientists, the unconscious reflects the incredible efficiency and automaticity of the brain. That is, there are simply too many things going on around us all the time for us to be aware of everything. Thus, our brains have developed the capacity to register information for later use even if we are not aware of it.

Cognitive Behavior Therapy

Cognitive behavior therapy (CBT) incorporates theory and research on cognitive processes. Cognitive behavior therapists pay attention to private events—thoughts, perceptions, judgments, self-statements, and even tacit (unconscious) assumptions—and have studied and manipulated these processes in their attempts to understand and modify overt and covert disturbed behavior. **Cognitive restructuring** is a general term for changing a pattern of thought. People with depression may not realize how often they think self-critically, and those with anxiety disorders may not realize that they tend to be overly sensitive to possible threats in the world. Therapists hope that people can change their feelings, behaviors, and symptoms by changing their cognition. The therapist begins by tracking the daily thoughts a person experiences but then moves to understanding more about core cognitive biases and schemata that might shape those daily negative thoughts.

Beck's Cognitive Therapy   Psychiatrist Aaron Beck, one of the leading cognitive behavior therapists, developed a cognitive therapy for depression based on the idea that depressed mood is caused by distortions in the way people perceive life experiences (Beck, 1976; Salkovskis, 1996). For example, a person with depression may focus exclusively on negative happenings and ignore positive ones. Imagine that a woman's romantic partner both praises and criticizes her. If the woman attends to the praise and remembers it the next day, she is likely to feel happy. But if she focuses on the criticism and continues to dwell on it the next day, she is likely to feel unhappy. Beck proposed that the attention, interpretation, and recall of negative and positive information are biased in depression. These effects on attention and memory are called

Aaron Beck developed a cognitive theory of depression and a cognitive behavioral therapy for people with depression. (Courtesy Dr. Aaron T. Beck.)

Clinical Case: An Example of Beck's Cognitive Therapy

The examples here illustrate ways of beginning to help a person change negative cognitions.

Therapist: You said that you feel like a failure since Bill left you. How would you define "failure"?

Patient: Well, the marriage didn't work out.

Therapist: So, you believe that the marriage didn't work out because you, as a person, are a failure?

Patient: If I had been successful, then he would still be with me.

Therapist: So, would we conclude that we can say, "People whose marriages don't work out are failures"?

Patient: No, I guess I wouldn't go that far.

Therapist: Why not? Should we have one definition of failure for you and another for everyone else?

People who define *failure* as less than "extraordinarily successful" can see that their definitions are polarized in all-or-nothing terms—that is, "complete success" vs. "complete failure." A variation on this technique is to ask the patient how others would define "success" or "failure."

Therapist: You can see that your definition of failure is quite different from the way other people might see it. Few people would say that a person who is divorced is a failure. Let's focus on the positive end right now. How would most people define "success" in a person?

Patient: Well, they might say that someone has success when they accomplish some of their goals.

Therapist: OK. So, would we say that if someone accomplishes some goals they have success?

Patient: Right.

Therapist: Would we also say that people can have different degrees of success? Some people accomplish more goals than others?

Patient: That sounds right.

Therapist: So, if we applied this to you, would we say that you have accomplished some of your goals in life?

Patient: Yes, I did graduate from college and I have been working for the past six years. I've been busy raising Ted—he had some medical problems a couple of years ago, but I got the right doctors for him.

Therapist: So, would we call these some successful behaviors on your part?

Patient: Right, I've had some successes.

Therapist: Is there a contradiction, then, in your thinking—calling yourself a "failure" but saying that you have had several successes?

Patient: Yes, that doesn't make sense, does it? (quoted in Leahy, 2003, pp. 38–39).

information-processing biases. Beck's therapy, which has now been adapted for other disorders in addition to depression, addresses these biases by trying to persuade patients to change their opinions of themselves and the way in which they interpret life events. When a depressed person expresses feelings that nothing ever goes right, for example, the therapist offers counter-examples, pointing out how the client has overlooked favorable happenings. The general goal of Beck's therapy is to provide people with experiences, both inside and outside the therapy room, that will alter their negative schemas, enabling them to have hope rather than despair.

There have also been many recent innovations in CBT. These treatments include dialecti-cal behavior therapy (see Chapter 15), mindfulness-based cognitive therapy (see Chapter 5), and acceptance and commitment therapy. The newer treatments differ from traditional CBT by incorporating a focus on spirituality, values, emotion, and acceptance. Another theme involves strategies to minimize emotional avoidance. For example, in acceptance and commitment therapy (Hayes, 2005), a person might be taught that much of the destructive power of emo-tions lies in the way we respond to them cognitively and behaviorally. An overarching goal of these therapies is to help a person learn to be more aware of emotions but to avoid immediate, impulsive reactions to that emotion. In the case of mindfulness-based cognitive therapy, this is facilitated through the use of meditation (Segal, Williams, & Teasdale, 2003). Overall, a rich array of cognitive behavioral approaches has been developed.

Evaluating the Cognitive Behavioral Paradigm

Cognitive behavioral explanations of psychopathology tend to focus more on current determi-nants of a disorder and less on historical, childhood antecedents. Some cognitive explanations of psychopathology do not appear to explain much. That a person with depression has a nega-tive schema tells us that the person thinks gloomy thoughts. But such a pattern of thinking is actually part of the diagnosis of depression. What is distinctive in the cognitive behavioral paradigm is that the thoughts are given causal status; that is, the thoughts are regarded as causing the other features of the disorder, such as sadness. Left unanswered is the question of where the negative schema came from in the first place. Much of the current research is focused on understanding what types of mechanisms sustain the biased thoughts shown in different psychopathologies.

Quick Summary

The cognitive behavioral paradigm reflects influences from behavior therapy and cognitive science. Treatment techniques designed to alter the consequences or reinforcers of a behavior, such as in time-out and exposure, are still used today. Cognitive science focuses on concepts such as schemas (a network of accumulated knowl-edge or set), attention, memory, and the unconscious, and these concepts are part of cognitive behavioral theories and treatments of psychopathology. For example, research on implicit memory promoted acceptance of the ideas of unconscious influences on behavior. Cognitive behavior therapy uses behavior therapy tech-niques and cognitive restructuring. Aaron Beck is an influential cognitive behavior therapist.

Check Your Knowledge 2.3

True or false?
1. In the Stroop task, interference is measured by how long it takes to name the color of the ink in a list of words.
2. Beck's theory suggests people have distortions in the way they perceive life's experiences.
3. Current research on the unconscious is conducted in much the same way as it was when Freud talked about the unconscious.

Factors That Cut across the Paradigms

Three important sets of factors that we will consider throughout this book are emotion, socio-cultural, and interpersonal factors. Some type of disturbance in emotion can be found in nearly all mental disorders. In addition, we will see that gender, culture, ethnicity, and social relationships bear importantly on the descriptions, causes, and treatments of the different disorders. In the next sections, we introduce these concepts and give some examples of why they are so important in psychopathology, regardless of what paradigm has been adopted.

Emotion and Psychopathology

Emotions influence how we respond to problems and challenges in our environment; they help us organize our thoughts and actions, both explicitly and implicitly, and they guide our behavior. Perhaps because our emotions exert such widespread influence, we spend a good deal of time trying to regulate how we feel and how we present our emotions to others. Given their centrality, it is not surprising that disturbances in emotion figure prominently in many different forms of psychopathology. By one analysis, as many as 85 percent of psychological disorders include disturbances in emotional processing of some kind (Thoits, 1985).

What is emotion? The answer to that question could fill an entire textbook on its own. Emotions are believed to be fairly short-lived states, lasting for a few seconds, minutes, or at most hours. Sometimes the word *affect* is used to describe short-lasting emotional feelings. Moods, on the other hand, are emotional experiences that endure for a longer period of time.

Most contemporary emotion theorists and researchers suggest that emotions are comprised of a number of components—including (but not limited to) expressive, experiential, and physiological components—that are typically coordinated within the individual. The expressive, or behavioral, component of emotion typically refers to facial expressions of emotion. Many people with schizophrenia display very few facial expressions. The experience, or subjective feeling, component of emotion refers to how someone reports he or she feels at any given moment or in response to some event. For example, learning that you received an A on your midterm might elicit feelings of happiness, pride, and relief. Learning you received a C might elicit feelings of anger, concern, or embarrassment. The physiological component of emotion involves changes in the body, such as those due to the autonomic nervous system activity that accompanies emotion. For example, if a car almost runs you down as you are crossing the street, you may show a frightened look on your face, feel fear, and experience an increase in your heart rate, breathing rate, and skin conductance.

When we consider emotional disturbances in psychopathology, it will be important to consider which of the emotion components are affected. In some disorders, all emotion components may be disrupted, whereas in others, just one might be problematic. For example, people with schizophrenia do not readily express their emotions outwardly, but they report feeling emotions very strongly. People with panic disorder experience excessive fear and anxiety when no actual danger is present. People with depression may experience prolonged sadness and other negative feelings. A person with antisocial personality disorder does not feel empathy. We will try to be clear in the book as to what component of emotion is being considered.

Another important consideration in the study of emotion and psychopathology is the concept of *ideal affect*, which simply refers to the kinds of emotional states that a person ideally wants to feel. At first glance, you might presume that happiness is the ideal affect for everyone. After all, who doesn't want to feel happy? However, recent research shows that ideal affects vary depending on cultural factors (Tsai, 2007). Thus, people from Western cultures, such as the United States, do indeed value happiness as their ideal state. However, people from East Asian cultures, like China, value less arousing positive emotions, such as calmness, more than happiness (Tsai, Knutson, & Fung, 2006). Tsai

Emotion consists of many components, including expression (shown here), experience, and physiology.
(© Tyler Stalman/iStockphoto.)

and colleagues have also shown a linkage between people's ideal affect and drug usage; if the ideal affect is a state of low arousal, like calmness, a person is less likely, for example, to use cocaine (Tsai, Knutson, & Rothman, 2007). Cross-nationally, more people in the United States seek treatment for cocaine and amphetamines, drugs that are stimulating and associated with feelings of excitement and happiness; more people in China seek treatment for heroin, a drug that has calming effects (Tsai, 2007; for more on the effects of these drugs, see Chapter 10).

The study of emotion figures prominently in the work of neuroscientists who are examining the ways in which the brain contributes to the different emotion components. Geneticists have also begun to examine how tendencies to experience a lot of positive or negative emotion may run in families. Emotions such as anger figured prominently in Freud's views; more contemporary psychodynamic treatments also focus on changing emotion. Even cognitive behavioral therapies consider how emotion influences thinking and behavior. Emotion thus cuts across the paradigms and can be studied from multiple perspectives, depending on the paradigm that is adopted.

Sociocultural Factors and Psychopathology

A good deal of research has focused on the ways in which sociocultural factors, such as gender, race, culture, ethnicity, and socioeconomic status, can contribute to different psychological disorders. Researchers who study such sociocultural factors and psychopathology all share the premise that environmental factors can trigger, exacerbate, or maintain the symptoms that make up the different disorders. But the range of variables considered and the ways of studying those variables cover a lot of ground.

Several studies consider the role of gender in different disorders. These studies have shown that some disorders affect men and women differently. For example, depression is nearly twice as common among women as among men. On the other hand, antisocial personality disorder and alcohol use disorder are more common among men than women. Childhood disorders, such as attention-deficit/hyperactivity disorder, affect boys more than girls, but some researchers question whether this reflects a true difference between boys and girls or a bias in the diagnostic criteria. Current research is looking beyond whether men and women differ in the prevalence rates of certain disorders to asking questions about risk factors that may differently impact men and women in the development of certain disorders. For example, father-to-son genetic transmission appears to be an important risk factor in the development of alcohol use disorder for men, whereas sociocultural standards of thinness may be a risk factor in the development of eating disorders for women.

Other studies show that poverty is a major influence on psychological disorders. For example, poverty is related to antisocial personality disorder, anxiety disorders, and depression. We discuss the role of these factors in overall health in Focus on Discovery 2.2.

Cultural and ethnic factors in psychopathology have also been examined. Some questions, such as whether or not the disorders we diagnose and treat in the United States are observed in other parts of the world, have been fairly well studied. This research has demonstrated that a number of disorders are observed in diverse parts of the world. Indeed, no country or culture is without psychopathology of some sort. For example, Murphy (1976) examined whether schizophrenia symptoms could be observed in cultures as diverse as the Eskimo and Yoruba. She found that both cultures have a concept of being "crazy" that is quite similar to the Western definition of schizophrenia. The Eskimo's *nuthkavihak* includes talking to oneself, refusing to talk, delusional beliefs, and bizarre behavior. The Yoruba's *were* encompasses similar symptoms. Notably, both cultures also have shamans but draw a clear distinction between their behavior and that of mentally ill people. In Chapter 6, we discuss a number of anxiety conditions across the world that look very similar to the symptoms of panic disorder.

Although some disorders appear to occur in different cultures, other disorders appear to be specific to particular cultures. In Chapter 11, we consider the evidence that eating disorders are specific to Western culture. The Japanese term *hikikomori* refers to a condition where a person completely withdraws from his social world (although women are affected, it is observed predominantly among men). People with hikikomori may completely shut themselves into their room or house—in some cases, for many years—refusing to interact with other people and leaving only occasionally to buy food. As we discuss in the next chapter, the current diagnostic system includes cultural factors in the discussion of every category of disorder, and this may be an important step toward increasing research in this area.

Even though there are some cross-cultural similarities in the presence of mental illnesses across cultures, there are also a number of profound cultural influences on the symptoms expressed in different disorders, the availability of treatment, and the willingness to seek treatment. We consider these issues throughout this book.

We must also consider the role of ethnicity in psychopathology. Some disorders, such as schizophrenia, are diagnosed more often among African Americans than Caucasians. Does this mean schizophrenia occurs more often in this group, or does it mean that some type of ethnic bias might be operating in diagnostic assessments? The use of drugs and their effects vary by ethnicity. Whites are more likely to use or abuse many drugs, such as nicotine, hallucinogens, methamphetamine, prescription painkillers, and, depending on the age group, alcohol. Yet African American smokers are more likely to die from lung cancer. Eating disturbances and body dissatisfaction are greater among white women than black women, particularly in college, but differences in actual eating disorders, particularly bulimia, do not appear to be as great. The reasons for these differences are not yet well understood and are the focus of current research. Table 2.1 shows data on ethnic and racial differences in the lifetime prevalence of DSM-IV-TR disorders.

Sociocultural factors have become more prominent in recent years in genetics and neuroscience. For example, *social neuroscience* seeks to understand what happens in the brain during complex social situations. Gene—environment interaction studies are uncovering the ways in which the social environment in combination with certain genes can increase the risk for disorders, as illustrated by the Caspi and colleagues (2003) study of childhood maltreatment, adult depression, and the 5-HTT gene discussed earlier. A multinational project called the 1,000 Genomes Project seeks to sequence the genomes of a representative sample of people around the world. An initial study found that people from each country had about the same number of rare variants in the genomes (Gravel et al., 2011). However, the rare variants were not the same in the different countries, suggesting that culture may also be influencing gene expression. Cognitive behavioral traditions have tended to focus more on the individual rather than how the individual interacts with the social world. However, this, too, is changing. New efforts are under way, for example, to develop cognitive behavior therapy for people from different cultures and ethnicities.

Culture and ethnicity play an important role in the descriptions, causes, and treatments of mental disorders. (Betsie Van der Meer/Stone/Getty Images.)

Table 2.1 Lifetime Prevalence Rates of DSM-IV-TR Disorders among Different Ethnic Groups

Disorder	White	Hispanic	Black
ADHD	4.6	4.6	3.4
Alcohol abuse or dependence	13.4	15.0*	9.5
Bipolar disorder	3.2	4.3	4.9*
Depression	17.9*	13.5	10.8
Drug abuse or dependence	7.9	9.1	6.3
Generalized anxiety disorder	8.6*	4.8	5.1
Panic disorder	4.9	5.4	3.1
PTSD	6.8	5.9	7.1

Table values are percentages. * indicates group with significantly highest prevalence rate.

Source: Adapted from Breslau et al. (2006). Sample came from the National Comorbidity Survey-Replication study, which included a representative sample of people age 18 or older in the United States.

FOCUS ON DISCOVERY 2.2

Sociocultural Factors and Health

Not only are sociocultural factors like gender, race, ethnicity, and socioeconomic status important for understanding psychopathology, these factors are also important for understanding overall health. The many demonstrations of the pervasive role of these types of factors in health form the basis for the fields of **behavioral medicine** and **health psychology.** Since the 1970s, these fields have dealt with the role of psychological factors in all facets of health and illness. Beyond examining the role of stress in the exacerbation or maintenance of illness, researchers in these fields study psychological treatments (e.g., stress management) and the health care system itself (e.g., how better to deliver services to underserved populations) (Appel et al., 1997; Stone, 1982). Here we consider how sociocultural factors have been studied in health psychology.

Gender and Health

At every age from birth to 85 and older, more men die than women. Men are more than twice as likely to die in automobile accidents and of homicide, cirrhosis, heart disease, lung cancer and other lung diseases, and suicide. Women, however, have higher rates of morbidity (i.e., poor health). That is, general poor health is more frequent among women, and women have a higher incidence of several specific diseases. For example, women have higher rates of diabetes, anemia, gastrointestinal problems, depression, and anxiety; and they report more visits to physicians, use more prescription drugs, and account for two-thirds of all surgical procedures performed in the United States.

What are some of the possible reasons for the differences in mortality and morbidity rates in men and women? It might be that women have some biological mechanism that protects them from certain life-threatening diseases. For example, epidemiological and observational studies suggested that estrogen might offer protection from **cardiovascular disease**. Based on this evidence, many women began hormone replacement therapy (HRT) following menopause (when estrogen naturally declines) in an attempt to reduce the risk of cardiovascular disease. However, randomized clinical trials of HRT for postmenopausal women (Hulley et al., 1998: Writing Group for the Women's Health Initiative Investigators, 2002) failed to find any such protective effects. In fact, the large prospective study called the Women's Health Initiative (WHI) had to end earlier than planned because women receiving estrogen plus progesterone therapy (so-called combined therapy) actually had an *increased* risk of breast cancer. A follow-up study (Heiss et al., 2008) concluded that women were not at greater risk for developing cardiovascular disease, but neither the combined therapy nor estrogen alone decreased the risk of cardiovascular disease (WHI, 2004).

Other research has examined psychological risk factors for cardiovascular disease, such as anger and hostility. The evidence suggests that anger is not necessarily more commonly experienced and expressed by men, contrary to stereotypes about gender and emotion (Kring, 2000; Lavoie et al., 2001). However, increased hostility and both the suppression and expression of anger are associated with risk factors for cardiovascular disease among women (Matthews et al., 1998; Rutledge et al., 2001). In addition, anxiety and depression are more common among women than men (see Chapters 5, 6, and 7) and are also linked to cardiovascular disease (e.g., Suls & Bunde, 2005).

Research shows that women live longer than men but women have more health problems than men. (Thomas Langreder VISUM/The Image Works.)

Although the mortality rate is higher for men than women, the gender difference is shrinking. Why? In the early twentieth century, most deaths were due to infectious diseases, but now most deaths result from diseases that are affected by lifestyle. One possibility, then, is that lifestyle differences between men and women account for the sex difference in mortality and that these lifestyle differences are decreasing. Although men still smoke more than women and consume more alcohol, women are catching up in their use of alcohol and cigarettes. Not surprisingly, then, these behavior changes in women are paralleled by increases in lung cancer and by the failure of the mortality rate for cardiovascular disease to decrease among women (lung cancer has been the leading cause of cancer death among women since 1987).

Other explanations focus on the identification and treatment of disease in women. For example, even though cardiovascular disease is the number-one killer of women and more women than men have died from heart disease since 1984 (more than one in four women who died in 2006 died of cardiovascular disease), there is still a widespread belief that men should be more concerned with heart disease than women. Furthermore, a common diagnostic procedure for heart disease risk, the so-called stress test, which involves measuring heart rate while on a treadmill, is not a good predictor of heart problems among women (Mora et al., 2003), particularly women who do not have chest pains (L.J. Shaw et al., 2006). In addition, a low dose of aspirin does not appear to prevent myocardial infarction in women as it does in men (though it does appear to prevent stroke in women, which is not true for men) (Ridker et al., 2005). Other research shows that women are less likely to be referred to a cardiovascular rehabilitation program following a heart attack, perhaps contributing to their persistent rates of mortality from cardiovascular disease (Abbey & Stewart, 2000).

Why do women have poorer health in general than men? There are several possible explanations. First, because women live longer than men, they may be more likely to experience certain diseases that are associated with aging. Second, women may be more attentive to their health than are men and thus may be more likely to visit physicians and be diagnosed. Third, women are exposed to more stress than men and they rate stress as having a greater impact on them, particularly stress related to major life events (Davis, Matthews, & Twamley, 1999). Fourth, physicians tend to treat women's health concerns and complaints less seriously than men's concerns (Weisman & Teitelbaum, 1985). Finally, evidence indicates that women's morbidity differs depending on socioeconomic and demographic variables, such as income, education, and ethnicity. For example, having more education and having a higher income are associated with fewer risk factors for cardiovascular disease, including obesity, smoking, hypertension, and reduced amounts of exercise. In the United States, women tend to have lower income than men. Also, 16.5 million women in the United States do not have health insurance.

Socioeconomic Status, Ethnicity, and Health

Low socioeconomic status (SES) is associated with higher rates of health problems and mortality from all causes. A recent study attributed 133,000 deaths in the year 2000 to poverty (Galea et al., 2011). That may not seem like a large number, but each year fewer people die from accidents (119,000) and only slightly more die from lung cancer (156,000). A number of explanations have been proposed for the correlation between SES and poor health and mortality, but many of these are still in need of empirical support. Recent research attempts to trace the connections between health and SES, encompassing economic, societal, relationship, individual, and biological factors. For example,

Poverty is stressful and is associated with poor health.
(Jeff Greenberg/PhotoEdit)

one risk factor for poor health has to do with environmental factors that reinforce poor health behaviors. Poorer neighborhoods often have high numbers of liquor stores, grocery stores offering fewer healthy food choices, and fewer opportunities for exercise at health clubs or parks. Given these environmental constraints, it is perhaps not surprising to learn that lower-SES people are more likely than higher-SES people to engage in behaviors that increase the risk of disease, such as smoking, eating fewer fruits and vegetables, and drinking more alcohol (Lantz et al., 1998).

Other risk factors include limited access to health services and greater exposure to stressors. Certainly discrimination and prejudice are sources of chronic stress, and these abhorrent social conditions continue to affect people of color as well as people of lower SES and, in turn, impact health (Mayes, Cochran, & Barnes, 2007). Since people of color are found in high numbers among lower-SES groups, ethnicity has also been a feature of research into the relationship of SES to health. Consider, for example, that the mortality rate for African Americans is nearly twice as high as it is for whites in the United States (Williams, 1999). Why might this be? The reasons are complex and not completely understood. Some research suggests that certain risk factors for disease are more common in people of color. For example, risk factors for cardiovascular disease (such as smoking, obesity, hypertension, and reduced exercise) are higher among women from ethnic minorities than among white women. This finding holds even when members of the two groups are comparable in SES (Winkleby et al., 1998). The increased prevalence of some of these risk factors shows up in studies of children as young as 6 to 9 years of age. For example, African American and Mexican American girls in this age range have higher body mass indexes and higher fat intake than do non-Hispanic white girls (Winkleby et al., 1999). Other studies have found that increased stress associated with discrimination is linked to cardiovascular reactivity among African American women (Guyll, Matthews, & Bromberger, 2001).

Consideration of SES at multiple levels, including the individual, family, and neighborhood, is also important (Mayes et al., 2007). For example, lower family SES and neighborhood SES were found to be associated with greater cardiovascular reactivity for African American children and adolescents, but only lower family SES was associated with greater cardiovascular reactivity among white children and adolescents (Gump et al., 1999). In sum, both SES and ethnicity are important factors in health.

Interpersonal Factors and Psychopathology

Beyond the role of culture, ethnicity, and poverty, thousands of articles have been published on how the quality of relationships influences different disorders. Family and marital relationships, social support, and even the amount of casual social contact all play a role in influencing the course of disorders. In Focus on Discovery 2.3 we discuss couples and family approaches to psychotherapy. Within relationships, researchers have looked for ways to measure not only the relative closeness and support offered but also the degree of hostility.

One tradition involves examining problem-solving interactions of family members to try to capture key dimensions in relationships. In a typical family interaction task, researchers might ask family members to discuss a topic that has been a source of concern, like whether the family is spending enough time together. An interviewer talks with each family member independently to capture the basics of his or her position. Then, in a family meeting, the interviewer briefly summarizes each person's perspective and asks the family to discuss the topic for 10 to 15 minutes and try to come to some resolution. Researchers then might code various dimensions from watching videotapes, like how family members share power, express positive sentiments, or deal with negative emotions.

Other researchers are interested in understanding the role of trauma, serious life events, and stress in psychopathology. We will describe some of the ways people measure life events in the next chapter. But the influence of stress within the context of social relationships plays a role in just about all the disorders we will consider.

FOCUS ON DISCOVERY 2.3

Couples and Family Therapies

Given that interpersonal factors are important in nearly all disorders we discuss in this book, it is not surprising that therapies have been developed to focus on these relationships. In addition to interpersonal therapy, discussed in the text, we consider here two additional types of therapies: couples therapy and family therapy.

Couples Therapy

Conflict is inevitable in any long-term partner relationship, whether the two people are married or not, or of the opposite sex or not. About 50 percent of marriages in the United States end in divorce, and most of these divorces happen within the first seven years of marriage (Snyder, Castellani, & Whisman, 2006). People in a distressed marriage are two to three times as likely to experience a psychological disorder (Whisman & Uebelacker, 2006). In some couples, distress may be a consequence of the psychological disorder, but it is also clear that distress can trigger many psychological disorders. Couples therapy is often used in the treatment of psychological disorders, particularly when they occur in the context of major relationship distress.

In couples therapy, the therapist works with both partners together to reduce relationship distress. Most couples treatments focus on

When a problem involves a couple, treatment is most effective if the couple is seen together. (© Anton Gvozdikov/Shutterstock.)

improving communication, problem solving, satisfaction, trust, and positive feelings. To enhance communication, each partner is trained to listen empathically to the other and to state clearly to the partner what he or she understands is being said and what feelings underlie those remarks.

Family Therapy

Family therapy is based on the idea that the problems of the family influence each member and that the problems of each member influence the family. As such, family therapy is used to address specific symptoms of a given family member, particularly for the treatment of childhood problems.

Over time, family therapy approaches have evolved to include a broader array of strategies (Sexton, Alexander, & Mease, 2004), often carefully integrated into the school and community (Liddle, 1999). Some family therapists focus on roles within the family, asking questions about whether parents assume an appropriate level of responsibility. Sometimes family therapists attend to whether a given person in the family has been "scapegoated," or unfairly blamed for a broader issue in the family. Many family therapists teach strategies to help families communicate and problem-solve more effectively.

Clinical Case: Clare

Clare, a 17-year-old female who lived with her parents and her 15-year-old brother, was referred for family-focused treatment (FFT) of bipolar disorder as an adjunct to medication treatment. She had received a diagnosis of bipolar I disorder in early adolescence and was treated with lithium carbonate and quetiapine but had never fully responded to medications.

During an individual assessment session, Clare explained that she thought about suicide almost daily and had made two prior attempts, both by overdosing on her parents' medications. Clare had kept both attempts secret from her parents. Ethically, clinicians need to take steps to keep a client safe, and in this case, one measure would be to let Clare's parents know about her suicidality. The clinician explained this to Clare.

The first goal in FFT is to provide psychoeducation about bipolar disorder. As the symptoms of bipolar disorder were being reviewed, the clinician asked Clare to discuss her suicide attempts with her parents. When Clare did so, her parents were surprised. Her father, who had experienced his own father's suicide, was particularly concerned.

After psychoeducation, a goal in FFT is to choose one problem for the family to address and to help them learn new problem-solving skills in the process. In this family, the focus of problem solving was how to keep Clare safe from her suicidal impulses. To begin problem solving, the therapist worked with the family to define the problem and its context. The therapist asked the family to discuss situations that seemed to place Clare at most risk for suicide. The family was able to pinpoint that both previous attempts had followed interpersonal losses.

The next phase of problem solving is to generate potential solutions. To help with this process, the clinician framed questions in the problem-solving process for the family, including whether Clare could share her suicidal thoughts with her parents, how to establish whether she was safe, what responses would be helpful from them, and what other protective actions should be taken. Using this structure, the family was able to agree on the plan that Clare would phone or page her parents when she was feeling self-destructive. Clare and her parents generated a plan in which her parents would help Clare engage in positive and calming activities

until her suicidal thoughts were less intrusive. Clare and her parents reported feeling closer and more optimistic.

The therapist then began to conduct the next phase of therapy, which focused directly on symptom management. This phase consisted of training Clare to monitor her moods, to identify triggers for mood changes, and to help her cope with those triggers.

As is typical in FFT, the clinician introduced the communication enhancement module during session eight. A goal of this module is to role-play new communication skills. Family members practice skills such as "active listening" by paraphrasing and labeling the others' statements and by asking clarifying questions. At first, Clare and her brother protested against the role-play exercises.

Clare experienced another loss during this period, in that her one and only close long-term friend announced that she was going to be moving out of state. Clare took an overdose of Tylenol as a suicide attempt. Afterward, she became afraid, induced vomiting, and later told her parents about the attempt.

The next session focused on the suicide attempt. Her parents, particularly her father, were hurt and angry. Clare reacted angrily and defensively. The therapist asked the family to practice active listening skills regarding Clare's suicidality. Clare explained that she had acted without even thinking about the family agreement because she had been so distressed about the idea of losing her friend. Clare's parents were able to validate her feelings using active listening skills. The therapist reminded the parents that suicidal actions are common in bipolar disorder and noted that Clare's ability to be honest about her suicide attempt was an indicator of better family connectedness. The therapist also recommended that Clare see her psychiatrist, who increased her dosage of lithium.

By the end of treatment after nine months, Clare had not made any more suicide attempts, had become more willing to take her medications, and felt closer to her parents. Like many people with bipolar disorder, though, she remained mildly depressed. Clare and her family continued to see the therapist once every three months for ongoing support. [Adapted from Miklowitz and Taylor (2005) with permission of the author.]

Family therapy is often tailored to the specific disorder. In family approaches for conduct disorder, the therapist may focus on improving parental monitoring and discipline. For adolescents with other externalizing problems, the goal of family therapy may be to improve communication, to change roles, or to address a range of family problems. With disorders like schizophrenia and bipolar disorder, family therapy often includes psychoeducation as a supplement for the medication treatment provided to the individual. Psychoeducation focuses on improving understanding of the disorder, reducing expressed family criticism and hostility, and helping families learn skills for managing symptoms, as in the clinical case of Clare (Miklowitz et al., 2003). For people with substance disorders, family therapy has been used to help clients recognize the need for treatment. In anorexia nervosa, family members are used strategically to help the adolescent gain weight. In sum, the goals and strategies of family therapy will be adjusted to meet the needs of different clients.

Recall from Chapter 1 that one of the central features of psychoanalysis is transference, which refers to a patient's responses to the analyst that seem to reflect attitudes and ways of behaving towards important people in the patient's past, rather than reflecting actual aspects of the analyst–patient relationship. Contemporary psychodynamic theorists have built on the concept of transference to emphasize the importance of a person's interpersonal relationships for psychological well-being. One example is **object relations theory,** which stresses the importance of long-standing patterns in close relationships, particularly within the family, that are shaped by the ways in which people think and feel. The "object" refers to another person in most versions of this theory. This theory goes beyond transference to emphasize the way in which a person comes to understand, whether consciously, how the self is situated in relation to other people. For example, a woman may come to understand herself as a worthless person based on her cold and critical relationship with her mother.

Another influential theory, **attachment theory,** grew out of object relations theory. John Bowlby (1907–1990) first proposed this theory in 1969, and Mary Ainsworth (1913–1999) and colleagues (1978) developed a method to measure attachment styles in infants. The essence of the theory is that the type or style of an infant's attachment to his or her caregivers can set the stage for psychological health or problems later in life. For example, infants who are securely attached to their caregivers are more likely to grow up to be psychologically healthy adults, whereas infants who are anxiously attached to their caregivers are more likely to experience psychological difficulties. Attachment theory has been extended to adults (Main, Kaplan, & Cassidy, 1985; Pietromonaco & Barrett, 1997) and couples (e.g., Fraley & Shaver, 2000), and therapies based on attachment theory have been developed for children and adults, though these have not yet been empirically scrutinized.

Children who are securely attached to parents are more likely to be psychologically healthy adults. (© grublee/Shutterstock)

Social psychologists have integrated both of these theories into the concept of the *relational self,* which refers to the self in relation to others (Andersen & Chen, 2002; Chen, Boucher, & Parker Tapias, 2006). The concept of the relational self has garnered a tremendous amount of empirical support. For example, people will describe themselves differently depending on what other close relationships they have been asked to think about (Chen et al., 2006). Other studies show that describing a stranger in terms that are similar to a description of a close significant other will trigger positive feelings and facial expressions, presumably linked to the view of the self in relation to the close other person (Andersen et al., 1996). Thus, if you are given a description of a stranger you must interact with that resembles a description of a close friend from high school, you will be more likely to smile, perhaps as a result of thinking about yourself and your interactions with your high school friend. The idea of the relational self has not yet been fully extended to the study of psychopathology, but given its theoretical basis and empirical support, it is ripe for translation to the study of interpersonal difficulties across many different psychological disorders.

Interpersonal Therapy   Interpersonal therapy (IPT) emphasizes the importance of current relationships in a person's life and how problems in these relationships can contribute to psychological symptoms. The therapist first encourages the patient to identify feelings about his or her relationships and to express these feelings, and then helps the patient generate solutions to interpersonal problems. IPT has been shown to be an effective treatment for depression (a topic we turn to in more detail in Chapter 5). IPT has also been used to treat eating disorders, anxiety disorders, and personality disorders.

In IPT, four interpersonal issues are assessed to examine whether one or more might be impacting symptoms:

- *Unresolved grief*—for example, experiencing delayed or incomplete grieving following a loss

- *Role transitions*—for example, transitioning from child to parent or from worker to retired person

- *Role disputes*—for example, resolving different relationship expectations between romantic partners

- *Interpersonal or social deficits*—for example, not being able to begin a conversation with an unfamiliar person or finding it difficult to negotiate with a boss at work

In sum, the therapist helps the patient understand that psychopathology occurs in a social or relationship context and that getting a better handle on relationship patterns is necessary to reduce symptoms of psychopathology.

Unresolved grief is one of the issues discussed in interpersonal therapy. (© Lisa F. Young/Shutterstock.)

Quick Summary

Disturbances in emotion figure prominently in psychopathology, but the ways in which emotions can be disrupted vary quite a bit. Emotions guide our behavior and help us to respond to problems or challenges in our environment. It is important to distinguish between components of emotion, including expression, experience, and physiology. In addition, mood can be distinguished from emotion. The concept of ideal affect points to important cultural differences in emotion that may be important in psychopathology. Psychological disorders have different types of emotion disturbances, and thus it is important to consider which of the emotion components are affected. In some disorders, all emotion components may be disrupted, whereas in others, just one might be problematic. Emotion is an important focus in the paradigms.

Sociocultural factors, such as culture, ethnicity, gender, and socioeconomic status, are important factors in the study of psychopathology. Some disorders appear to be universal across cultures, like

schizophrenia or anxiety, yet their manifestations may differ somewhat and the ways in which society regards them may also differ. Other disorders, like eating disorders or hikikomori, may be specific to particular cultures. Some disorders are more frequently diagnosed in some ethnic groups compared to others. It is not clear whether this reflects a true difference in the presence of disorder or perhaps a bias on the part of diagnosticians.

Current research is also examining whether risk factors associated with various disorders differ for men and women. Sociocultural factors have recently become the focus of people working in the other paradigms, and this trend will continue. Interpersonal relationships can be important buffers against stress and have benefits for physical and mental health. Object relations theory, which stresses the importance of relationships, and its offshoot, attachment theory, which emphasizes the role of attachment styles in infancy through adulthood, are also important in psychopathology research.

Check Your Knowledge 2.4

True or false?

1. Emotion consists of at least three components: expression, experience, and physiology.
2. Sociocultural factors such as gender, culture, ethnicity, and social relationships are less important to consider in the neuroscience paradigm.
3. Examining problem-solving interactions of family members is useful for understanding key dimensions in relationships.
4. The relational self is a concept from social psychology that incorporates ideas from object relations and attachment theories.
5. Interpersonal therapy may focus on four types of interpersonal problems including unresolved grief, role transitions, role disputes, and social deficits.

Diathesis–Stress: An Integrative Paradigm

Psychopathology is much too diverse to be explained or treated adequately by any one of the current paradigms. Most of the disorders we will discuss in this book likely develop through an interaction of neurobiological and environmental factors, a view that we turn to next.

The **diathesis–stress** paradigm is an integrative paradigm that links genetic, neurobiological, psychological, and environmental factors. It is not limited to one particular school of thought, such as cognitive behavioral, genetic, or neurobiological. The diathesis–stress concept was introduced in the 1970s as a way to account for the multiple causes of schizophrenia (Zubin & Spring, 1977). Its appeal continues today for many disorders, however, because, like the gene–environment interaction models reviewed above, it is a model that focuses on the interaction between a predisposition toward disease—the **diathesis**—and environmental, or life, disturbances—the stress. Diathesis refers most precisely to a constitutional predisposition toward illness, but the term may be extended to any characteristic or set of characteristics of a person that increases his or her chance of developing a disorder.

In the realm of neurobiology, for example, a number of disorders considered in later chapters appear to have a genetically transmitted diathesis. Although the precise nature of these genetic diatheses is currently unknown (e.g., we don't know exactly what is inherited that makes one person more vulnerable than another to develop bipolar disorder), it is clear that a genetic predisposition is an important component of many disorders. Other neurobiological diatheses include oxygen deprivation at birth, poor nutrition, and a maternal viral infection or smoking during pregnancy. Each of these conditions may lead to changes in the brain that predispose the individual toward psychopathology.

In the psychological realm, a diathesis for depression may be a particular cognitive schema or the chronic feeling of hopelessness sometimes found in people with depression. Other psychological diatheses include the ability to be easily hypnotized, which may be a diathesis for dissociative identity disorder (formerly called multiple personality disorder), and an intense fear of becoming fat, which is a vulnerability factor for some eating disorders.

Possessing the diathesis for a disorder increases a person's risk of developing it but does not by any means guarantee that a disorder will develop. The stress part of diathesis–stress is meant to account for how a diathesis may be translated into an actual disorder. In this context stress generally refers to some noxious or unpleasant environmental stimulus that triggers psychopathology. Psychological stressors include major traumatic events (e.g., becoming unemployed, divorce, death of a spouse) as well as more mundane happenings that many of us experience (e.g., car breakdown). By including these environmental events, the diathesis–stress model goes beyond the major paradigms we have already discussed.

The key point of the diathesis–stress model is that both diathesis and stress are necessary in the development of disorders. Some people, for example, have inherited a predisposition

Stressors that may activate a diathesis range from minor, such as having car trouble, to major, such as the aftermath of a hurricane. (Left: © fbmadeira/Shutterstock; Right: AFP/Getty Images.)

that places them at high risk for mania (see Chapter 5); a certain amount of stress increases the possibility of developing mania. Other people, those at low genetic risk, are not likely to develop mania regardless of how difficult their lives are.

Another major feature of the diathesis–stress paradigm is that psychopathology is unlikely to result from the impact of any single factor. Like our discussion of the reciprocal relationships between genes and the environment above, a genetically transmitted diathesis may be necessary for some disorders, but it is embedded in a network of other factors that also contribute to the disorder. These factors could include genetically transmitted diatheses for other personality characteristics; childhood experiences that shape personality, the development of behavioral competencies, and coping strategies; stressors encountered in adulthood; cultural influences; and numerous other factors.

Finally, we should note that within this framework, the data gathered by researchers holding different paradigms are not incompatible with one another. For example, stress may be needed to activate a predisposition toward a problem in neurotransmitter systems. Some of the differences between the paradigms also appear to be more linguistic than substantive. A cognitive behavioral theorist may propose that maladaptive cognitions cause depression, whereas a neurobiological theorist may speak of the activity of a certain neural pathway. The two positions are not contradictory but merely reflect different levels of description, just as we could describe a table as pieces of wood in a particular configuration or as a collection of atoms.

In Focus on Discovery 2.4 we present a case example to illustrate how adopting one paradigm to the exclusion of others can bias your view of what the critical targets for treatment might be.

FOCUS ON DISCOVERY 2.4

Multiple Perspectives on a Clinical Problem

To provide a concrete example of how it is possible to conceptualize a clinical case using multiple paradigms, we present a case and discuss how information provided is open to a number of interpretations, depending on the paradigm adopted.

Clinical Case: Sam

Sam's childhood had not been a particularly happy one. His mother died suddenly when he was only six, and for the next 10 years, he lived either with his father or with a maternal aunt. His father drank heavily, seldom managing to get through any day without some alcohol. His father's income was so irregular that he could seldom pay bills on time and they always lived in poor neighborhoods. At times Sam's father was totally incapable of caring for himself, let alone his son. Sam would then spend weeks, sometimes months, with his aunt in a nearby town. Despite these early life circumstances, Sam completed secondary school and entered university. During these university years, he felt an acute self-consciousness with people who he felt had authority over him—his lecturers, and even some of his classmates, with whom he compared himself unfavorably.

Two years after graduating, Sam married his girlfriend. Sam could never quite believe that his wife, as intelligent as she was beautiful, really cared for him. As the years wore on, his doubts about himself and about her feelings toward him continued to grow. He felt she was far brighter than he and he worried that she would make more money than he would. After their marriage, Sam began a job at a publishing company, serving as an assistant editor. This job proved to be even more stressful than university. The deadlines and demands of the senior editors were difficult. He constantly questioned whether he had what it took to be an editor. Like his father, he often drank to deal with this stress.

Now 32 years old, with a fairly secure job that pays reasonably well and a young son, he and his wife are arguing more often. She continually complains about his drinking (he is drinking a bottle of wine a night). He denies there is a problem, although he has noticed a slight tremor and seems to catch every cold going round the office. His brooding over his home and work life has led him to drink even more heavily throughout the day and the only thing that gets him started each morning seems to be a drink. Sam realized that his drinking is out of control and that he needs help after one Saturday morning when he went into town. As usual, he had been drinking secretly at home before he went out. Taking his son with him, he called into the first couple of shops, but then forgot about his son and went onto the next shop. Eventually, he returned home, alone. If it hadn't been for another mother, who recognized the boy from nursery school, Sam doesn't know what would have happened to his son. He realized that if he didn't seek help immediately, his marriage wouldn't last and he would lose the two people he loved most in his life.

A psychodynamic point of view casts Sam in yet another light. Believing that events in early childhood are of great importance in later patterns of adjustment, you may hypothesize that Sam is still grieving for his mother and has blamed his father for her early death. Such strong anger at the father has been repressed, and this plus the death of his mother is negatively impacting his adult relationships with others. For treatment, you may choose interpersonal therapy to work on Sam's relationships and to deal openly and consciously with his buried anger toward his father.

Now suppose that you are committed to a cognitive behavioral perspective, which encourages you to analyze human behavior in terms of reinforcement patterns as well as cognitive variables. You may focus on Sam's self-consciousness at college, which seems related to the fact that compared with his fellow students, he grew up with few advantages. Economic insecurity and hardship may have made him unduly sensitive to criticism and rejection. Alcohol has been his escape from such tensions. But heavy drinking, coupled with persistent doubt about his own worth as a human being, has worsened an already deteriorating marital relationship, further undermining his confidence. As a cognitive behavior therapist, you may employ systematic desensitization, in which you teach Sam to relax deeply as he imagines a hierarchy of situations in which he is being evaluated by others. Or you may decide on cognitive behavior therapy to convince Sam that he need not obtain universal approval for every undertaking.

If you adopt a diathesis–stress perspective, you might follow more than one of these strategies. You would acknowledge the likely genetic contribution to Sam's alcohol dependence, but you would also identify key triggers (e.g., job stress) that might lead to greater bouts of drinking. You would likely employ many of the therapeutic techniques noted above.

Summary

- A paradigm is a conceptual framework or general perspective. Because the paradigm within which scientists and clinicians work helps to shape what they investigate and find, understanding paradigms helps us to appreciate subjective influences that may affect their work.

- The genetic paradigm holds that psychopathology is caused, or at least influenced, by heritable factors. Recent genetic findings show how genes and the environment interact, and it is this type of interaction that will figure prominently in psychopathology. Moleculer genetics research is identifying differences in gene sequence and structure that may be associated with vulnerability to psychopathology.

- The neuroscience paradigm emphasizes the role of the brain, neurotransmitters, and other systems, such as the HPA axis. Biological treatments, including medications, attempt to rectify the specific problems in the brain.

- The cognitive behavioral paradigm emphasizes schemas, attention, and cognitive distortions about life experiences and their influence on behavior as major factors in psychopathology. Cognitive neuroscience research follows from the early work of Freud, highlighting the importance of childhood expriences, the unconscious, and the fact that the causes of behavior are not always obvious. Cognitive behavior therapists such as Beck focus on altering patients' negative schemas and thoughts about events in their lives.

- Emotion plays a prominent role in many disorders. It is important to distinguish among components of emotion that may be disrupted, including expression, experience, and physiology. Emotion disturbances are the focus of study across the paradigms.

- Sociocultural factors, including culture, ethnicity, gender, and poverty, are also important in conceptions of psychopathology. The prevalence and meaning of disorders may vary by culture and ethnicity, men and women may have different risk factors for different disorders, and social relationships can be an important buffer against stress.

- Interpersonal factors, including social support and relationships, are also factors that cut across paradigms. Social relationships can be an important buffer against stress, and relationships, including current conceptualizations of attachment and the relational self, are important. Sociocultural and interpersonal factors are included in the work of geneticists, neuroscientists, and cognitive behaviorists.

- Because each paradigm seems to have something to offer to our understanding of mental disorders, an integrative paradigm is perhaps the most comprehensive. The diathesis–stress paradigm, which integrates several points of view, assumes that some people are predisposed to react adversely to environmental stressors. The diathesis may be genetic, neurobiological, or psychological and may be caused by early-childhood experiences, genetically influenced personality traits, or sociocultural influences, among other things.

Answers to Check Your Knowledge Questions

2.1   1. b; 2. d; 3. a; 4. b; 5.c

2.2   1. hypothalamus, anterior cingulate, septal area, hippocampus, amygdala; 2. white, gray; 3. norepinephrine, GABA; 4. hypothalamus, pituitary gland, adrenal cortex

2.3   1. T; 2. T; 3. F

2.4   1. T; 2. F; 3. T; 4. T; 5. T

Key Terms

agonist
allele
amygdala
antagonist
anterior cingulate
attachment theory
autonomic nervous system (ANS)
behavioral activation (BA) therapy
brain stem
behavior genetics
behavior medicine
cardiovascular disease
cerebellum
cognition
cognitive behavior therapy (CBT)
cognitive behavioral paradigm
cognitive restructuring
copy number variation (CNV)

corpus callosum
cortisol
diathesis
diathesis–stress
dopamine
emotion
epigenetics
exposure
frontal lobe
gamma-aminobutyric acid (GABA)
gene
gene expression
gene–environment interaction
genetic paradigm
genotype
glial cells
gray matter
health psychology
heritability
hippocampus

HPA axis
hypothalamus
in vivo
interpersonal therapy (IPT)
molecular genetics
nerve impulse
neuron
neuroscience paradigm
neurotransmitters
nonshared (unique) environment
norepinephrine
object relations theory
occipital lobe
paradigm
parasympathetic nervous system
parietal lobe
phenotype
polygenic
polymorphism

prefrontal cortex
pruning
reciprocal gene–environment interaction
reuptake
schema
second messengers
septal area
serotonin
serotonin transporter gene
shared environment
single nucleotide polymorphism (SNP)
sympathetic nervous system
synapse
temporal lobe
thalamus
time-out
transcription
ventricles
white matter

3 Diagnosis and Assessment

Clinical Case: Aaron

Hearing the sirens in the distance, Aaron realized that someone must have called the police. He didn't mean to get upset with the people sitting next to him at the bar, but he just knew that they were talking about him and plotting to have his special status with the CIA revoked. He could not let this happen again. The last time people conspired against him, he wound up in the hospital. He did not want to go to the hospital again and endure all of the evaluations. Different doctors would ask him all sorts of questions about his work with the CIA, which he simply was not at liberty to discuss. They asked other odd questions, such as whether he heard voices or believed others were putting thoughts into his head. He was never sure how they knew that he had those experiences, but he suspected that there were electronic bugging devices in his room at his parents' house, perhaps in the electrical outlets.

Just yesterday, Aaron began to suspect that someone was watching and listening to him through the electrical outlets. He decided that the safest thing to do was to stop speaking to his parents. Besides, they were constantly hounding him to take his medication. But when he took this medication, his vision got blurry and he had trouble sitting still. He reasoned that his parents must somehow be part of the group of people trying to remove him from the CIA. If he took this medication, he would lose his special powers that allowed him to spot terrorists in any setting, and the CIA would stop leaving messages for him in phone booths or in the commercials on Channel 2. Just the other day, he found a tattered paperback book in a phone booth, which he interpreted to mean that a new assignment was imminent. The voices in his head were giving him new clues about terrorist activity. They were currently telling him that he should be wary of people wearing the color purple, as this was a sign of a terrorist. If his parents were trying to sabotage his career with the CIA, he needed to keep out of the house at all costs. That was what had led him to the bar in the first place. If only the people next to him wouldn't have laughed and looked toward the door. He knew this meant that they were about to expose him as a CIA operative. If he hadn't yelled at them to stop, his cover would have been blown.

DIAGNOSIS AND ASSESSMENT are the critically important "first steps" in the study and treatment of psychopathology. In the case of Aaron, a clinician may begin treatment by determining whether Aaron meets the diagnostic criteria for a mood disorder, schizophrenia, or perhaps a substance-related disorder. Diagnosis can be the first major step in good clinical care. Having a correct **diagnosis** will allow the clinician to describe base rates, causes, and treatment for Aaron and his family, all of which are important aspects of good clinical care. More broadly, imagine that your doctor told you, "There is no diagnosis for what you have." Rather than this alarming scenario, hearing a diagnosis can provide relief in several different ways. Often, a diagnosis can help a person begin to understand why certain symptoms are occurring, which can be a huge relief. Many disorders are extremely common, such as depression, anxiety, and substance abuse—knowing that his or her diagnosis is common can also help a person feel less unusual.

Diagnosis enables clinicians and scientists to communicate accurately with one another about cases or research. Without agreed-on definitions and categories, our field would face a situation like the Tower of Babel (Hyman, 2002), in which different scientists and clinicians would be unable to understand each other.

Diagnosis is important for research on causes and treatments. Sometimes researchers discover unique causes and treatments associated with a certain set of symptoms. For example, autism was only recognized in the *Diagnostic and Statistical Manual* in 1980. Since that time, research on the causes and treatments of autism has grown exponentially.

To help make the correct diagnosis, clinicians and researchers use a variety of assessment procedures, beginning with a clinical interview. Broadly speaking, all clinical assessment procedures are more or less formal ways of finding out what is wrong with a person, what may have caused problems, and what can be done to improve the person's condition. Assessment procedures can help in making a diagnosis, and they can also provide information beyond a diagnosis. Indeed, a diagnosis is only a starting point. In the case of Aaron, for example, many other questions remain to be answered. Why does Aaron behave as he does? Why does he believe he is working for the CIA? What can be done to resolve his conflicts with his parents? Has he performed up to his intellectual potential in school and in his career? What obstacles might interfere with treatment? These are also the types of questions that mental health professionals address in their assessments.

In this chapter, we will describe the official diagnostic system used by many mental health professionals, as well as the strengths and weaknesses of this system. We will then turn to a discussion of the most widely used assessment techniques, including interviews, psychological assessment, and neurobiological assessment. We then conclude the chapter with an examination of a sometimes neglected aspect of assessment, the role of cultural bias. Before considering diagnosis and assessment in detail, however, we begin with a discussion of two concepts that play a key role in diagnosis and assessment: reliability and validity.

Cornerstones of Diagnosis and Assessment

The concepts of reliability and validity are the cornerstones of any diagnostic or assessment procedure. Without them, the usefulness of our methods is seriously limited. That said, these two concepts are quite complex. There are several kinds of each, and an entire subfield of psychology—psychometrics—exists primarily for their study. Here, we provide a general overview.

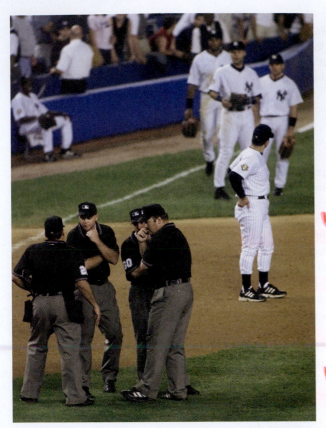

Reliability is an essential property of all assessment procedures. One means of establishing reliability is to determine whether different judges agree, as happens when two umpires witness the same event in a baseball game. (Reuters/NewMedia Inc./Corbis Images.)

Reliability

Reliability refers to consistency of measurement. An example of a reliable measure would be a wooden ruler, which produces the same value every time it is used to measure an object. In contrast, an unreliable measure would be a flexible, elastic-like ruler whose length changes every time it is used. Several types of reliability exist, and here we will discuss the types that are most central to assessment and diagnosis.

Interrater reliability refers to the degree to which two independent observers agree on what they have observed. To take an example from baseball, two umpires may or may not agree as to whether the ball is fair or foul.

Test–retest reliability measures the extent to which people being observed twice or taking the same test twice, perhaps several weeks or months apart, receive similar scores. This kind of reliability makes sense only when we can assume that the people will not change appreciably between test sessions on the underlying variable being measured; a prime example of a situation in which this type of reliability is typically high is in evaluating intelligence tests. On the other hand, we cannot expect people to be in the same mood at a baseline and a follow-up assessment 4 weeks later.

Sometimes psychologists use two forms of a test rather than giving the same test twice, perhaps when there is concern that test takers will remember their answers from the first round of taking the test and aim merely to be consistent. This approach enables the tester to determine **alternate-form reliability**, the extent to which scores on the two forms of the test are consistent.

Finally, **internal consistency reliability** assesses whether the items on a test are related to one another. For example, one would expect the items on an anxiety questionnaire to be interrelated, or to correlate with one another, if they truly tap anxiety. A person who reports a dry mouth in a threatening situation would be expected to report increases in muscle tension as well, since both are common characteristics of anxiety.

Validity

Validity is a complex concept, generally related to whether a measure measures what it is supposed to measure. For example, if a questionnaire is supposed to measure a person's hostility, does it do so? Before we describe types of validity, it is important to note that validity is related to reliability—unreliable measures will not have good validity. Because an unreliable measure does not yield consistent results (recall our example of a ruler whose length is constantly changing), it will not relate very strongly to other measures. For example, an unreliable measure of coping is not likely to relate well to how a person adjusts to stressful life experiences. Reliability, however, does not guarantee validity. Height can be measured very reliably, but height would not be a valid measure of anxiety.

Content validity refers to whether a measure adequately samples the domain of interest. For example, later in this chapter we will describe an interview that is often used to make an Axis I diagnosis. It has excellent content validity because it contains questions about all the symptoms that are involved in most Axis I diagnoses. For certain uses, though, the interview might have poor content validity. The interview doesn't cover questions about kleptomania (a disorder characterized by a compulsive need to steal). If one were trying to assess kleptomania, this interview would have poor content validity.

Criterion validity is evaluated by determining whether a measure is associated in an expected way with some other measure (the criterion). If both variables are measured at the same point in time, the resulting validity is referred to as **concurrent validity**. For example, below we will describe a measure of the overly negative thoughts that are believed to play an important role in depression. Criterion validity for this measure of negative thoughts could be established by showing that people with depression score higher on the test than do people without depression. Alternatively, criterion validity can be assessed by evaluating the ability of the measure to predict some other variable that is measured at some point in the future, often referred to as **predictive validity**. For example, IQ tests were originally developed to predict future school performance. Similarly, a measure of negative thinking could be used to predict the development of depression in the future. In summary, concurrent and predictive validity are both types of criterion validity.

Construct validity is a more complex concept. It is relevant when we want to interpret a test as a measure of some characteristic or construct that is not observed simply or overtly (Cronbach, 1955; Hyman, 2002). A construct is an inferred attribute, such as anxiousness or distorted cognition. Consider an anxiety-proneness questionnaire as an example. If the questionnaire has construct validity, people who obtain different scores on our test really will differ in anxiety proneness. Just because the items seem to be about the tendency to become anxious ("I find that I become anxious in many situations"), it is not certain that the test is a valid measure of the construct of anxiety proneness.

Construct validity is evaluated by looking at a wide variety of data from multiple sources (compare this to criterion validity, where a test is typically evaluated against just one other piece of data). For example, people diagnosed as having an anxiety disorder and people without such a diagnosis could be compared on their scores on our self-report measure of anxiety proneness. The self-report measure would achieve some construct validity if the people with anxiety disorders scored higher than the people without anxiety disorders. Greater construct validity would be achieved by showing that the self-report measure was related to other measures thought to reflect anxiety, such as observations of fidgeting and trembling, and physiological indicators, such as increased heart rate and rapid breathing. When the self-report measure is associated with these multiple measures (diagnosis, observational indicators, physiological measures), its construct validity is increased.

More broadly, construct validity is related to theory. For example, we might hypothesize that being prone to anxiety is in part caused by a family history of anxiety. We could then obtain further evidence for the construct validity of our questionnaire by showing that it relates to a family history of anxiety. At the same time, we would also have gathered support for our theory of anxiety proneness. Thus, construct validation is an important part of the process of theory testing.

Construct validity is also centrally important to diagnostic categories. Below, we consider in more detail the issue of construct validity and the DSM-5.

Classification and Diagnosis

Clinical Case: Rachel

Rachel is a middle-aged woman who was brought to the local accident and emergency department by the police. They had found her running through a crowded street, laughing loudly and knocking into people. Her clothes were dirty and torn. When questioned, her speech was loud, rapid and difficult to understand. At the hospital, she wrestled free of the police and began running down the hallway. She knocked over two staff members during her flight, while bellowing at the top of her lungs: "I am God...my best work is yet to come!" She was brought back to the examination room, and the staff began to form hypotheses. Clearly, she was hyperactive, euphoric and her thought processes were speeded up. She also displayed grandiose delusions. Unfortunately, the staff were unable to gain much information from an interview due to her rapid and pressured speech. Instead, Rachel sat restlessly, occasionally laughing and shouting; and treatment could not proceed without understanding the reason for her unusual behavior. When efforts to calm Rachel failed, police helped the hospital staff to contact family members, who were relieved to hear that Rachel was safe. She had disappeared from home the day before. Family members described a long history of bipolar disorder (formerly known as manic depression), and they reported having been concerned for the past couple of weeks because Rachel had stopped taking medications for her bipolar disorder and for her high blood pressure. Valproate was prescribed based on the idea that Rachel was experiencing a new manic episode of her long-standing bipolar disorder. Her antihypertensive medication was resumed.

The Diagnostic System of the American Psychiatric Association: Toward DSM-5

In this section, we focus on the official diagnostic system used by mental health professionals, the *Diagnostic and Statistical Manual of Mental Disorders* (DSM). The DSM is now in its fourth edition, commonly referred to as DSM-IV-TR. A draft of the DSM-5 is now available (www.dsm5.org). This draft edition is being reviewed and tested, and the final release of DSM-5 is expected in 2013. Because the DSM-5 will be in use by the time most of you are working in clinical and research settings, we will focus on the likely DSM-5 in this book. We recognize, though, that this is an interesting time in the field—the DSM-IV-TR remains in use, even as the DSM-5 is anticipated soon. Throughout the chapters of this book, then, we will note major differences between the DSM-IV-TR and the proposed DSM-5. In this chapter, we will review the history of the DSM and the major features of the latest versions of the DSM, and then we will review some strengths and criticisms of the DSM as well as of diagnosis in general.

In 1952, the American Psychiatric Association published its *Diagnostic and Statistical Manual* (DSM). The publication of the DSM was informed by earlier systems of classification (for a review, see Focus on Discovery 3.1), and it has been revised five times since 1952. DSM-IV was published in 1994, and in June 2000, a "text revision," DSM-IV-TR, followed. Almost no changes were made to the diagnostic categories and criteria in the 2000 revision. Rather, DSM-IV-TR provided a summary of new research findings on prevalence rates, course, and etiology (causes).

Each version of the DSM has included improvements. Beginning with the third edition of DSM and continuing today, an effort was made to create more reliable and valid diagnostic categories. Two major innovations were introduced in DSM-III that have been retained by each edition since.

1. Specific diagnostic criteria—the symptoms for a given diagnosis—are spelled out precisely, and clinical symptoms are defined in a glossary. Table 3.1 compares the descriptions of a manic episode given in DSM-II with the diagnostic criteria given in the likely DSM-IV-TR. Notice how DSM-IV-TR is much more detailed and concrete.

2. The characteristics of each diagnosis are described much more extensively than they were in DSM-II. For each disorder there is a description of essential features, then of associated

---

FOCUS ON DISCOVERY 3.1

A History of Classification and Diagnosis

By the end of the nineteenth century, diagnostic procedures improved as physicians began to understand the advantages of tailoring treatments to different illnesses. Impressed by the successes that followed the development of classification systems in other scientific disciplines, physicians sought to develop their own classification scheme. Unfortunately, progress in classifying mental disorders was not gained easily.

Early Efforts at Classification of Mental Illness

Emil Kraepelin (1856–1926) authored an influential early classification system in his textbook of psychiatry first published in 1883 where he attempted to establish the biological nature of mental illnesses.

Kraepelin noted that certain symptoms clustered together as a *syndrome*. He labeled a set of syndromes and hypothesized that each had its own biological cause, course, and outcome. Even though effective treatments had not been identified, at least the course of the disease could be predicted. Kraepelin proposed two major groups of severe mental illnesses: dementia praecox and manic-depressive psychosis, early terms for schizophrenia and bipolar disorder, respectively. He suggested a chemical imbalance as the cause of dementia praecox and an irregularity in metabolism as the explanation of manic-depressive psychosis. Though his theories about causes are not this straightforward, Kraepelin's classification scheme nonetheless influenced the current diagnostic categories.

features, such as laboratory findings (e.g., enlarged ventricles in schizophrenia) and results from physical exams (e.g., electrolyte imbalances in people who have eating disorders). Next, a summary of the research literature provides information about age of onset, course, prevalence and sex ratio, familial pattern, and differential diagnosis (i.e., how to distinguish similar diagnoses from each other).

The DSM-IV and DSM-IV-TR introduced more focus on cultural issues as well as separate dimensions, or axes, to rate people. As shown in Figure 3.2, DSM-IV-TR includes five axes. This **multiaxial classification system,** by requiring judgments on each of the five axes, forces the diagnostician to consider a broad range of information. The DSM-IV-TR Axis I includes all

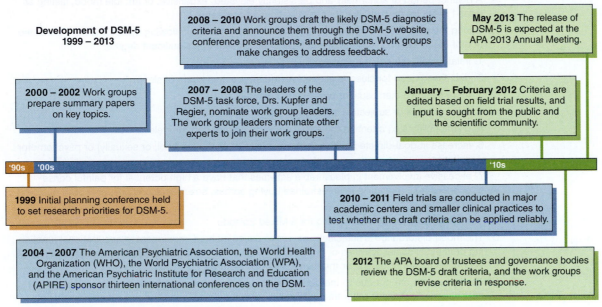

Development of DSM-5
1999 – 2013

2008 – 2010 Work groups draft the likely DSM-5 diagnostic criteria and announce them through the DSM-5 website, conference presentations, and publications. Work groups make changes to address feedback.

May 2013 The release of DSM-5 is expected at the APA 2013 Annual Meeting.

2000 – 2002 Work groups prepare summary papers on key topics.

2007 – 2008 The leaders of the DSM-5 task force, Drs. Kupfer and Regier, nominate work group leaders. The work group leaders nominate other experts to join their work groups.

January – February 2012 Criteria are edited based on field trial results, and input is sought from the public and the scientific community.

'90s '00s   '10s

1999 Initial planning conference held to set research priorities for DSM-5.

2010 – 2011 Field trials are conducted in major academic centers and smaller clinical practices to test whether the draft criteria can be applied reliably.

2004 – 2007 The American Psychiatric Association, the World Health Organization (WHO), the World Psychiatric Association (WPA), and the American Psychiatric Institute for Research and Education (APIRE) sponsor thirteen international conferences on the DSM.

2012 The APA board of trustees and governance bodies review the DSM-5 draft criteria, and the work groups revise criteria in response.

Figure 3.1 Timeline for the development of DSM-5.

Development of the WHO and DSM Systems

There are currently two widely established systems for classifying mental disorders - Chapter V of the International Classification of Diseases (ICD-10) produced by the World Health Organization (WHO) and the Diagnostic and Statistical Manual of Mental Disorders (DSM) produced by the American Psychiatric Association (APA). Other classification schemes may be in use more locally, such as the Chinese Classification of Mental Disorders, or by others of an alternative theoretical persuasion, for example, the Psychodynamic Diagnostic Manual.

In 1939 the WHO added mental disorders to the International List of Causes of Death (ICD). In 1948 the list was expanded to become the International Statistical Classification of Diseases, Injuries, and Causes of Death, a comprehensive listing of all diseases, including a classification of abnormal behaviour. Unfortunately, the mental disorders section was not widely accepted. Even though American psychiatrists had played a prominent role in the WHO effort, the APA published its own DSM in 1952. The WHO published a new classification system in 1969, which was more widely accepted. A second version of the DSM, DSM-II (1968), was similar to the WHO system, but true consensus was still lacking. Even though both specified some symptoms of diagnoses, the two systems defined different symptoms for a given disorder! Thus diagnostic practices still varied widely. In 1980 the APA published an extensively revised diagnostic manual, DSM-III, with further revisions (DSM-III-R) following in 1987 and (DSM-IV) in 1994.

The DSM-IV was updated with text revisions (DSM-IV TR) in 2000 to incorporate features such as culture, age, gender-related issues, prevalence, course, and familial pattern of mental disorders. Work on the fifth edition (DSM-V) was begun in 1999 with an expected release date early in 2013. Key additions will include sections on developmental issues, disability and impairment, neuroscience, nomenclature and cross-cultural issues.

Table 3.1 Description of Mania in DSM-II versus DSM-IV-TR

DSM-II (1968, p. 36)

Manic-depressive illness, manic type. This disorder consists exclusively of manic episodes. These episodes are characterized by excessive elation, irritability, talkativeness, flight of ideas, and accelerated speech and motor activity. Brief periods of depression sometimes occur, but they are never true depressive episodes.

DSM-IV-TR (2000, p. 362)

Diagnostic Criteria for a Manic Episode

A. A distinct period of abnormally and persistently elevated, expansive, or irritable mood, lasting at least 1 week (or any duration if hospitalization is necessary).

B. During the period of mood disturbance, three (or more) of the following symptoms have persisted (four if the mood is only irritable) and have been present to a significant degree:

   1. inflated self-esteem or grandiosity

   2. decreased need for sleep (e.g., feels rested after only 3 hours of sleep)

   3. more talkative than usual or pressure to keep talking

   4. flight of ideas or subjective experience that thoughts are racing

   5. distractibility (i.e., attention too easily drawn to unimportant or irrelevant external stimuli)

   6. increase in goal-directed activity (either socially, at work or school, or sexually) or psychomotor agitation

   7. excessive involvement in pleasurable activities that have a high potential for painful consequences (e.g., engaging in unrestrained buying sprees, sexual indiscretions, or foolish business investments)

C. The symptoms do not meet criteria for a Mixed Episode.

D. The mood disturbance is sufficiently severe to cause marked impairment in occupational functioning or in usual social activities or relationships with others, or to necessitate hospitalization to prevent harm to self or others, or there are psychotic features.

E. The symptoms are not due to the direct physiological effects of a substance (e.g., a drug of abuse, a medication, or other treatment) or a general medical condition (e.g., hyperthyroidism).

Note: DSM-IV-TR material reprinted with permission from the DSM-II, copyright 1968, and the DSM-IV-TR copyright 2000, American Psychiatric Association.

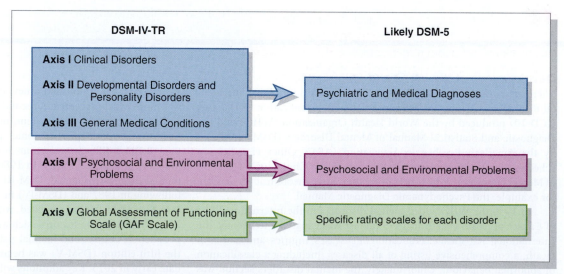

Figure 3.2 Multiaxial classification system in DSM-IV-TR and proposed DSM-5.

diagnostic categories except the personality disorders and mental retardation, which make up Axis II. Thus Axes I and II cover the classification of mental disorders. Axis III covers general medical conditions. For many diagnoses, the DSM includes a provision for indicating that the disorder is due to a medical condition or substance abuse. On Axis IV, the clinician codes psychosocial problems that may contribute to the disorder, including occupational problems, housing problems, economic problems, or interpersonal difficulties. Finally, on Axis V, the clinician indicates the person's current level of adaptive functioning, using ratings from 0 to 100 on the Global Assessment of Functioning (GAF) scale to consider social relationships, occupational functioning, and use of leisure time. As we discuss next, these axes are likely to change in DSM-5.

The DSM-5 will likely include many changes from DSM-IV-TR. Indeed, even conventions for labeling the edition have shifted—the Roman numerals used to denote the edition (e.g., DSM-IV) are replaced with Arabic numbers (i.e., DSM-5) to facilitate electronic printing. We will cover many of the changes as we discuss specific disorders in the chapters throughout this book. Here, then, we cover some of the major debates and changes that have implications across diagnoses.

Changes to the Multiaxial System As shown in Figure 3.2, the multiaxial system developed for DSM-IV-TR is changed substantially in DSM-5. The five axes of DSM-IV-TR are reduced to one axis for clinical syndromes and one for psychosocial and environmental problems. The codes for the Psychosocial and Environmental Problems Axis are changed to be more similar to those used by the international community in the World Health Organization's (WHO) International Classification of Diseases (ICD). The DSM-IV-TR axis V is removed in DSM-5; instead, clinicians will be asked to rate severity along a continuum using scales developed specifically for each disorder.

Organizing Diagnoses by Causes DSM-IV-TR defines diagnoses entirely on the basis of symptoms. Some have argued that advances in our understanding of etiology (causes) could help us rethink this approach. For example, schizophrenia and schizotypal personality disorder share a great deal of genetic overlap. Could these ties be reflected in the diagnostic system? Others have proposed organizing diagnoses based on parallels in neurotransmitter activity, temperament, emotion dysregulation, or social triggers. After considerable review, it became clear that our knowledge base is not yet strong enough to organize diagnoses around etiology (Hyman, 2010). With the exception of IQ tests for intellectual developmental disorder (formerly know as mental retardation) or polysomnography for sleep disorders, we have no laboratory tests, neurobiological markers, or genetic indicators to use in making diagnoses. The DSM-5 will continue to use symptoms as the basis for diagnosis.

On the other hand, some changes have been made to reflect growing knowledge of etiology. The DSM-IV-TR diagnoses are clustered into chapters based on similarity of symptoms. In the DSM-5, the chapters are reorganized to reflect patterns of comorbidity and shared etiology (see Figure 3.3). For example, in DSM-IV-TR, obsessive-compulsive disorder is included as an anxiety disorder. The etiology of this disorder, though, seems to involve distinct genetic and neural influences compared to other anxiety disorders, as we discuss in Chapter 7. To reflect this, the DSM-5 includes a new chapter for obsessive-compulsive and other related disorders. This new chapter includes three disorders that often co-occur and share some risk factors: obsessive-compulsive disorder, hoarding disorder, and body dysmorphic disorder.

DSM-IV-TR is the current diagnostic system of the American Psychiatric Association. DSM-5 is expected in 2013. (Teri Stratford/Six-Cats Research Inc.)

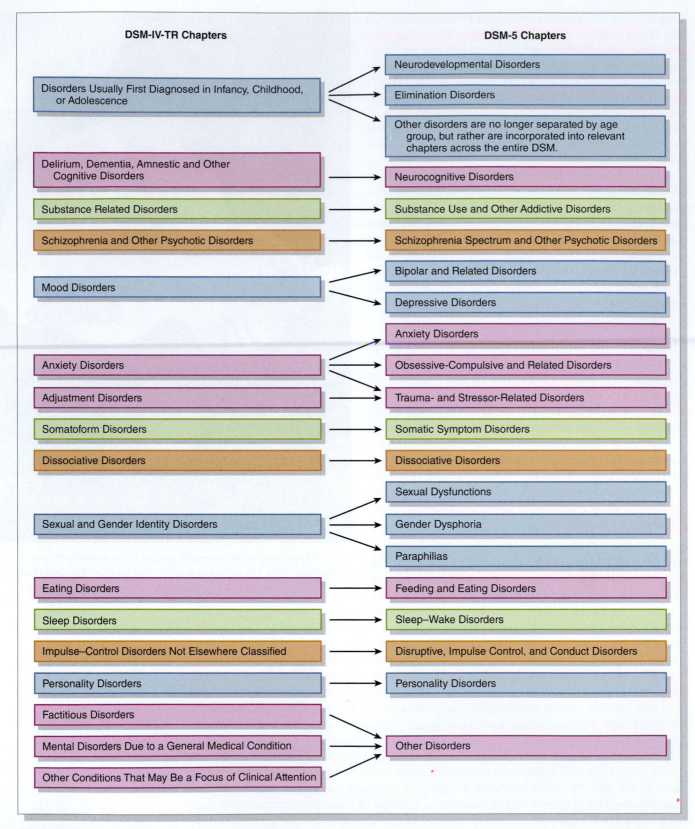

DSM-IV-TR Chapters

- Disorders Usually First Diagnosed in Infancy, Childhood, or Adolescence
- Delirium, Dementia, Amnestic and Other Cognitive Disorders
- Substance Related Disorders
- Schizophrenia and Other Psychotic Disorders
- Mood Disorders
- Anxiety Disorders
- Adjustment Disorders
- Somatoform Disorders
- Dissociative Disorders
- Sexual and Gender Identity Disorders
- Eating Disorders
- Sleep Disorders
- Impulse–Control Disorders Not Elsewhere Classified
- Personality Disorders
- Factitious Disorders
- Mental Disorders Due to a General Medical Condition
- Other Conditions That May Be a Focus of Clinical Attention

DSM-5 Chapters

- Neurodevelopmental Disorders
- Elimination Disorders
- Other disorders are no longer separated by age group, but rather are incorporated into relevant chapters across the entire DSM.
- Neurocognitive Disorders
- Substance Use and Other Addictive Disorders
- Schizophrenia Spectrum and Other Psychotic Disorders
- Bipolar and Related Disorders
- Depressive Disorders
- Anxiety Disorders
- Obsessive-Compulsive and Related Disorders
- Trauma- and Stressor-Related Disorders
- Somatic Symptom Disorders
- Dissociative Disorders
- Sexual Dysfunctions
- Gender Dysphoria
- Paraphilias
- Feeding and Eating Disorders
- Sleep–Wake Disorders
- Disruptive, Impulse Control, and Conduct Disorders
- Personality Disorders
- Other Disorders

Figure 3.3 Chapters in DSM-IV-TR and proposed DSM-5.

Including a Continuous Severity Rating to Supplement Categorical Classification   In the DSM-IV-TR clinical diagnoses are based on **categorical classification**. Does the patient have schizophrenia or not? This type of classification does not consider continuity between normal and abnormal behavior. For example, in Table 3.1 we see that the diagnosis of mania requires the presence of three symptoms from a list of seven, or four if the person's mood is irritable. But why require three symptoms rather than two or five? A categorical system forces clinicians to define one threshold as "diagnosable." There is often little research support for the threshold defined. Categorical diagnoses foster a false impression of discontinuity (Widiger, 2005).

It may be more helpful to know the severity of symptoms as well as whether they are present. In contrast to categorical classification, **dimensional** systems describe the *degree* of an entity that is present (e.g., a 1-to-10 scale of anxiety, where 1 represents minimal and 10, extreme). (See Figure 3.4 for an illustration of the difference between dimensional and categorical approaches.)

One reason categorical systems are popular is that they define a threshold for treatment. Consider high blood pressure (hypertension). Blood pressure measurements form a continuum, which clearly fits a dimensional approach; yet by defining a threshold for high blood pressure, doctors can feel more certain about when to offer treatment. Similarly, a threshold for clinical depression may help demarcate a point where treatment is recommended. Although the cutoffs are likely to be somewhat arbitrary, they can provide helpful guidance.

Despite some debate, DSM-5 preserves a categorical approach to diagnosis. The categories, though, are supplemented by a severity rating for each disorder. See Figure 3.5 for an example of one of the severity rating scales proposed for DSM-5. The severity rating provides a more precise estimate of how serious an illness is (Kraemer, 2007).

The severity ratings do not address all of the concerns raised about categorical diagnosis—severity ratings will not be considered unless a person is first diagnosed with a categorical diagnosis. Up to half of the people seeking treatment have mild symptoms that fall just below the threshold for a diagnosis (Helmuth, 2003). Many of these people with subthreshold symptoms of a diagnosis still receive extensive treatment (Johnson, 1992). As with DSM-IV-TR, the DSM-5 will likely include the category "not otherwise specified" to be used when a person meets many but not all of the criteria for a diagnosis. Just as with DSM-IV-TR, it is probable that far too many people will fit the "not otherwise specified" category.

Changes in Personality Disorder Diagnoses   DSM-IV-TR includes 10 different personality disorder categories. The proposed DSM-5 will include criteria for deciding if a personality disorder is present and then will specify five types. Rating scales will be provided to assess how well a person's symptoms fit with the different types. We discuss this in more detail in Chapter 15.

New Diagnoses   Several new diagnoses are proposed in the DSM-5. For example, disruptive mood dysregulation disorder is included to address the growing number of children and adolescents who are seen by clinicians due to severe mood changes and irritability as well as some of the symptoms of mania. Many of these youth do not meet the full criteria for mania (the defining feature of bipolar disorder) but were often falsely labeled with bipolar disorder because no other category seemed to fit their symptoms. It is hoped that by including this diagnosis, the overdiagnosis of bipolar disorder in children and adolescents will be lessened. Other new diagnoses include mixed anxiety depressive disorder, language impairment disorder, premenstrual dysphoric disorder, simple somatic symptom disorder, and illness anxiety disorder.

Combining Diagnoses   Some of the DSM-IV-TR diagnoses have been combined because there is not enough evidence for differential etiology, course, or treatment response to justify labeling the conditions separately. For example, the DSM-IV-TR diagnoses of substance abuse and dependence are replaced with the DSM-5 diagnosis of substance use disorder. The DSM-IV-TR

Categorical Classification

Dimensional Classification

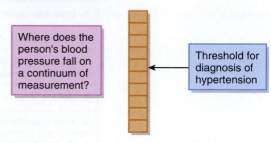

Figure 3.4 Categorical versus dimensional systems of diagnosis.

Name: _John Q. Sample_   **Date:** _____

Over the *last 2 weeks*, how often have you been bothered by any of the following problems? (use "√" to indicate your answer)

	Not at all	Several days	More than half the days	Nearly every day
1. Little interest or pleasure in doing things	0	1	2 ✓	3
2. Feeling down, depressed, or hopeless	0	1 ✓	2	3
3. Trouble falling or staying asleep, or sleeping too much	0	1	2 ✓	3
4. Feeling tired or having little energy	0	1	2	3 ✓
5. Poor appetite or overeating	0	1 ✓	2	3
6. Feeling bad about yourself—or that you are a failure or have let yourself or your family down	0	1	2 ✓	3
7. Trouble concentrating on things, such as reading the newspaper or watching television	0	1	2 ✓	3
8. Moving or speaking so slowly that other people could have noticed. Or the opposite—being so fidgety or restless that you have been moving around a lot more than usual	0	1	2 ✓	3
9. Thoughts that you would be better off dead, or of hurting yourself in some way	0 ✓	1	2	3

Add columns: __2__ + __10__ + __3__

TOTAL: = __15__

10. If you checked off *any* problems, how *difficult* have these problems made it for you to do your work, take care of things at home, or get along with other people?	Not difficult at all _____
	Somewhat difficult ✓
	Very difficult _____
	Extremely difficult _____

Figure 3.5 Example of a possible severity rating scale for major depression in the DSM-5. Developed by Drs. Robert Spitzer, Janet B.W. Williams, Kurt Kroenke, and colleagues, with an educational grant from Pfizer Inc. Drawn from Pfizer.com.

diagnoses of hypoactive sexual desire disorder and female sexual arousal disorder are replaced with the DSM-5 diagnosis of sexual interest/arousal disorder in women.

Clearer Criteria   For many disorders, criteria have been rewritten to provide clearer guidance about thresholds for diagnosis. For example, duration and intensity rules have been added for some diagnoses. For some diagnoses, criteria have been changed to reflect new information. Across diagnoses, many criteria have been reworded for clarity.

Ethnic and Cultural Considerations in Diagnosis   Mental illness is universal. There is not a single culture in which people are free of mental illness. But there are many different cultural influences on the risk factors for mental illness (e.g., social cohesion, poverty, access to drugs of abuse, and stress), the types of symptoms experienced, the willingness to seek help, and the treatments available. Sometimes these differences across cultures are profound. For example, although mental health care is widely available in the United States, it is estimated that there is only one psychiatrist for every 2 million people living in sub-Saharan Africa (World Health Organization, 2001, p. 17).

Cultural differences do not always play out in the way one might expect. For example, even with the access to medical care in the United States, a major study found that outcomes for schizophrenia were more favorable in Nigeria, India, and Colombia than in more industrialized countries, including the United States (Sartorius, 1986). People who immigrate from Mexico to the United States are initially about half as likely to meet criteria for mental illness as native born citizens in the United States, but over time, they and their children begin to show an increase in certain disorders, such as substance abuse, such that their risk for disorder begins to approximate that of people born in the United States (Alegria, 2008). As shown in Table 3.2, rates of mental illnesses tend to be higher in the United States than in many other countries. If we hope to understand how culture influences risk, symptom expression, and outcomes, we need a diagnostic system that can be applied reliably and validly in different countries and cultures.

Table 3.2 Twelve-Month Prevalence Rates of the Most Common DSM-IV-TR Diagnoses by Country

Country	Anxiety Disorders	Mood Disorders	Substance Disorders	Any Psychological Disorder
Americas				
Colombia	10.0	6.8	2.8	17.8
Mexico	6.8	4.8	2.5	12.2
United States	18.2	9.6	3.8	26.4
Europe				
Belgium	6.9	6.2	1.2	12.0
France	12.0	8.5	0.7	18.4
Germany	6.2	3.6	1.1	9.1
Italy	5.8	3.8	0.1	8.2
Netherlands	8.8	6.9	3.0	14.9
Spain	5.9	4.9	0.3	9.2
Middle East and Africa				
Lebanon	11.2	6.6	1.3	16.9
Nigeria	3.3	0.8	0.8	4.7
Asia				
Japan	5.3	3.1	1.7	8.8
Beijing	3.2	2.5	2.6	9.1

Source: The WHO World Mental Health Survey Consortium (2004).
Anxiety disorders include agoraphobia, generalized anxiety disorder, obsessive-compulsive disorder, panic disorder, posttraumatic stress disorder, social phobia, and specific phobia. Mood disorders include bipolar I and II disorders, dysthymia, and major depressive disorder. Substance disorders include alcohol or drug abuse or dependence. Diagnoses were assessed with the Composite International Diagnostic Interview. Values are percentages.

Note: In the European countries, bipolar disorders and non-alcohol-related substance use disorders were not assessed. Obsessive-compulsive disorder was not assessed in Asian countries.

Previous editions of the DSM were criticized for their lack of attention to cultural and ethnic variations in psychopathology. DSM-IV-TR enhanced cultural sensitivity in three ways: (1) by providing a general framework for evaluating the role of culture and ethnicity, (2) by

The core symptoms of depression appear to be similar cross-culturally. (© redstone/Shutterstock.)

describing cultural factors and ethnicity for each disorder, and (3) by listing culture-bound syndromes in an appendix.

In the general framework, clinicians are cautioned not to diagnose symptoms unless they are atypical and problematic within a person's culture. People vary in the degree to which they identify with their cultural or ethnic group. Some value assimilation into the majority culture, whereas others wish to maintain close ties to their cultural background. In general, clinicians are advised to be constantly mindful of how culture and ethnicity influence diagnosis and treatment.

Attention is paid to how culture can shape the symptoms and expression of a given disorder. For example, the symptoms of both schizophrenia (e.g., delusions and hallucinations) and depression (e.g., depressed mood and loss of interest or pleasure in activities) are similar cross-culturally (Draguns, 1989). But as we will discuss in Chapter 6, it is more likely in Japan than in the United States for anxiety to be focused around fears of offending others (Kirmayer, 2001). In evaluating symptoms, clinicians also need to be aware that cultures may shape the language used to describe distress. In many cultures, for example, it is common to describe grief or anxiety in physical terms—"I am sick in my heart" or "My heart is heavy"—rather than in psychological terms.

The DSM includes 25 culture-bound syndromes in the appendix. Culture-bound syndromes are diagnoses that are likely to be seen within specific regions. It is important to note that these culture-bound syndromes are not just found in cultures outside the United States. For example, some argued for listing bulimia nervosa as a Western culture-bound syndrome, a topic we return to in more detail in Chapter 11. The following are some examples of syndromes listed in the DSM appendix.

- *Amok.* A dissociative episode in which there is a period of brooding followed by a violent and sometimes homicidal outburst. The episode tends to be triggered by an insult and is found primarily among men. Persecutory delusions are often present as well. The term is Malaysian and is defined by the dictionary as a murderous frenzy. You may have heard the phrase "run amok."

- *Ghost sickness.* An extreme preoccupation with death and those who have died, found among certain Native American tribes.

- *Drat.* A term used in India to refer to severe anxiety about the discharge of semen.

- *Koru.* Reported in South and East Asia, an episode of intense anxiety about the possibility that the penis or nipples will recede into the body, possibly leading to death.

- *Shenjing shuairuo* (neurasthenia). A common diagnosis in China, a syndrome characterized by fatigue, dizziness, headaches, pain, poor concentration, sleep problems, and memory loss.

- *Taijin kyofusho.* The fear that one could offend others through inappropriate eye contact, blushing, a perceived body deformation, or one's own foul body odor. This disorder is most common in Japan, but cases have been reported in the United States. Japanese cultural norms appear to prescribe more careful attention to social appropriateness and hierarchy, perhaps intensifying the risk of these symptoms (Fabrega, 2002).

- *Hikikomori* (withdrawal). This refers to a syndrome observed in Japan, Taiwan, and South Korea in which an individual, most often an adolescent boy or young adult man, shuts himself into a room (e.g., bedroom) for a period of 6 months or more and does not socialize with anyone outside the room.

Some have argued that we should try to identify broad syndromes that can be identified across cultures and, in this light, have argued against the inclusion of culture-bound syndromes (Lopez-Ibor, 2003). In support of this position, they point toward a number of culture-bound syndromes that are not so different from the main DSM diagnoses. For example, Kleinman (1986) interviewed 100 Chinese people who had been diagnosed with *shenjing shuairuo* and

Clinical Case: Lola: An Example of Diagnosis

Lola is a 17-year-old high school junior. She moved to the United States from Mexico with her parents and brother when she was 14 years old. A few months after they arrived, Lola's father returned to Mexico to attend the funeral of his brother. He was denied reentry to the United States due to a problem with his visa, and he has been unable to reunite with the family for nearly 3 years. Lola's mother has found it difficult to make ends meet on her salary as a bookkeeper, and the family was forced to move to a rougher neighborhood a year ago. Lola's English was fairly good when she came to the United States, and she has picked up many of the nuances of the language since arriving in the country. For the past 2 years, she has been dating a boy in her school. They have been fairly constant companions, and she describes him as the one person she would turn to if she was feeling upset. If her mother had any previous concern about Lola, it was that she seemed to rely on her boyfriend too much—she asked for his advice with small and large decisions, and she seemed wary of social interactions when he wasn't present. Lola's mother stated, "It is as though she is afraid to think for herself." Lola's mother noted that she had always been a bit shy and had tended to count on her brother a lot for decisions and social support when she was younger.

With little warning, her boyfriend announced that he wanted to break up with her. Lola was extremely distressed by this change and reported that almost immediately she was unable to sleep or eat. She lost weight rapidly and found herself unable to concentrate on her schoolwork. Friends complained that she no longer wanted to talk during lunch or by phone. After 2 weeks of steadily feeling worse, Lola left a suicide note and disappeared. Police found her the next day in an abandoned home, holding a bottle of medicines. She reported that she had been sitting there all night, considering ending her life. Lola's mother reported that she had never seen her this distressed but noted that a few other family members had struggled with periods of sadness. Still, these family members in Mexico had not made suicide attempts nor had they received any formal treatment. Instead, the family learned to give these family members support and time to heal on their own. After the police found Lola, she was hospitalized for intensive treatment.

DSM-IV-TR Diagnosis

Axis I   Major depressive disorder

Axis II   Dependent personality disorder

Axis III   None

Axis IV   Problems with primary support group (father not with family); problems related to social environment (acculturation stress; relationship with boyfriend)

Axis V   GAF: 25

Likely-DSM-5 Diagnosis

Major depressive disorder

Personality disorder trait specified
    Level of functioning: 1
    Traits of submissiveness and
    separation insecurity

found that 87 percent of them met criteria for major depressive disorder. Many of those responded to antidepressant medications. Suzuki and colleagues (2003) have pointed out that the symptoms of *taijin kyofusho* overlap with those of social phobia (excessive fear of social interaction and evaluation) and body dysmorphic disorders (the mistaken belief that one is deformed or ugly), which are more commonly diagnosed in the United States. Other syndromes may reflect the common concerns of anxiety and distress, with the content shaped by life circumstances and values (Lopez-Ibor, 2003). Hence, some researchers believe it is important to look for commonalities across cultures. In contrast, others believe that culture-bound syndromes are central, because local and personal meanings are a key issue in understanding mental illness (Gaw, 2001).

In the planning process for DSM-5, one study group was dedicated to considering gender and culture issues. They recommended ways to keep culture salient for clinicians. As one example, the DSM-IV-TR includes an appendix on culture and diagnosis. More than half of clinicians surveyed reported that they didn't realize the appendix existed (Kirmayer et al., 2008). In the proposed DSM-5, this material is included in the introductory material on diagnostic assessment (Alarcón et al., 2009).

A therapist must be mindful of the role of cultural differences in the ways in which patients describe their problems. (© Chris Schmidt/iStockphoto.)

Returning to Clinical Case: Rachel: A Second Example of a Multiaxial Diagnosis

Previously, we described the case of Rachel, who was brought to the accident and emergency department by the police. A multiaxial diagnosis for Rachel might look as follows.

Axis I	Bipolar I disorder, Manic
Axis II	None
Axis III	High blood pressure
Axis IV	Problems with housing (homeless)
Axis V	GAF: 20

Quick Summary

Because diagnosis provides the first step in thinking about the causes of symptoms, it is the first step in planning treatment. Because psychopathology is diagnosed on the basis of symptoms, clinical interviews are used to make diagnoses.

With all assessments, the reliability (the consistency of measurement) and validity (whether an assessment measures what it is designed to measure) should be evaluated. Reliability can be estimated by examining how well raters agree, how consistent test scores are over time, how alternate forms of a test compare, or how well items correlate with each other. There are many different forms of validity, including content, criterion, and construct validity.

Diagnostic systems for mental illness have changed a great deal in the past 100 years. DSM-III introduced explicit rules for diagnosis. The system in use currently, the DSM-IV-TR, introduced several features to improve cultural sensitivity, such as providing a framework for clinicians to evaluate the role of culture, detailing the ways in which culture might influence symptoms of disorder, and including an appendix to describe culture-bound symptoms. DSM-5 has been drafted and is in the process of being reviewed and tested. Key changes include severity ratings that are specific to each disorder, a new approach to diagnosing personality disorder, and a reduction in the number of axes to be rated. Drawing on research evidence, the DSM-5 chapters are reorganized to reflect current knowledge of etiology. Some disorders are added, some are removed, and others are combined. The release of the final DSM-5 is expected in 2013.

Check Your Knowledge 3.1 (Answers are at the end of the chapter.)

Answer the questions.
1. Major changes in the likely DSM-5 include (circle all that apply):
   a. more axes
   b. inclusion of severity ratings
   c. a greater number of personality disorder diagnoses
   d. many fewer diagnoses
2. Which type of reliability or validity is tested with the following procedures?
   _____ A group of high school students is given the same IQ test 2 years in a row.
   _____ A group of high school students is given an IQ test, and their scores are correlated with a different IQ test they took the year before.

_____ A measure of the tendency to blame oneself is developed, and researchers then test whether it predicts depression, whether it is related to childhood abuse, and whether it is related to less assertiveness in the workplace.

_____ Patients are interviewed by two different doctors. Researchers examine whether the doctors agree about the diagnosis.
   a. interrater reliability
   b. test–retest reliability
   c. criterion validity
   d. construct validity

Specific Criticisms of the DSM

Some specific questions and concerns have been raised about the DSM. We review some of these concerns in the following sections.

Too Many Diagnoses? DSM-IV-TR contains almost 300 different diagnoses. Some have critiqued the burgeoning number of diagnostic categories (see Table 3.3). As one example, the DSM-IV and likely DSM-5 include a category for acute stress disorder in order to capture symptoms in the first month after a severe trauma. Should these relatively common reactions to trauma be pathologized by diagnosing them as a mental disorder (Harvey & Bryant, 2002)? By expanding its coverage, the authors of the DSM seem to have made too many problems into psychiatric disorders, without good justification for doing so.

Others argue that the system includes too many minute distinctions based on small differences in symptoms. One side effect of the huge number of diagnostic categories is a phenomenon called **comorbidity**, which refers to the presence of a second diagnosis. Comorbidity is the norm rather than the exception. Among people who meet criteria for at least one DSM-IV-TR psychiatric diagnosis, 45 percent will meet criteria for at least one more psychiatric diagnosis (Kessler, 2005). Some argue that this overlap is a sign that we are dividing syndromes too finely (Hyman, 2010).

A more subtle issue about the large number of diagnoses is that many risk factors seem to trigger more than one disorder. For example, some genes increase the risk for externalizing disorders as a whole (Kendler et al., 2003). Early trauma, dysregulation of stress hormones, tendencies to attend to and remember negative information about the self, and neuroticism all seem to increase risk for a broad range of anxiety disorders as well as mood disorders (Harvey et al., 2004). Anxiety and mood disorder also seem to share overlap in genes (Kendler, 2003), diminished function of a brain region called the prefrontal cortex (Hyman, 2010), and low serotonin function (Carver, Johnson, & Joormann, 2008). Similarly, selective serotonin reuptake inhibitors (SSRIs), such as Prozac, often seem to relieve symptoms of anxiety as well as depression (Van Ameringen, 2001). Different diagnoses do not seem to be distinct in their etiology or treatment.

Does this mean that we should lump some of the disorders into one category? Beliefs about lumping versus splitting differ. Some think we should keep the finer distinctions, whereas others believe we should lump (Watson, 2005). Among people who think there are too many diagnostic categories, several researchers have considered ways to collapse into broader categories. To begin, some disorders seem to co-occur more frequently than do others. For example, a person with antisocial personality disorder is highly likely to meet diagnostic criteria for a substance use disorder. In the DSM, these are diagnosed as separate disorders. Some have argued that childhood conduct disorder, adult antisocial personality disorder, alcohol use disorder, and substance use disorder co-occur so often that they should be considered different manifestations of one underlying disease process or vulnerability (Krueger, 2005). These different types of problems could be jointly considered "externalizing disorders."

The authors of DSM-5 took modest steps toward addressing these concerns. In a few cases, two disorders were combined into one disorder. For example, as noted previously, the DSM-IV-TR diagnoses of substance abuse and dependence are replaced with the proposed DSM-5 diagnosis of substance use disorder. The new diagnosis of mixed anxiety depressive disorder is included in the likely DSM-5 because of the large number of people who present with both anxiety and depressive symptoms. The changes in DSM-5 are small, though. It includes more than 300 diagnoses, and comorbidity will remain the norm.

Reliability of the DSM in Everyday Practice Suppose you were concerned about your mental health, and you went to see two psychologists. Consider the distress you would feel if the two psychologists disagreed—one told you that you had schizophrenia, and the other told you that you had bipolar disorder. Diagnostic systems must have high interrater reliability to be useful. Before DSM-III, reliability for DSM diagnoses was poor, mainly because the criteria for making a diagnosis were not clear (see Figure 3.6 for an illustration of interrater reliability).

Table 3.3 Number of Diagnostic Categories per Edition of DSM

Edition of DSM	Number of Categories
DSM I	106
DSM-II	182
DSM-III	265
DSM-III-R	292
DSM-IV-TR	297
Proposed DSM-5	>300

Source: Pincus et al. (1992).

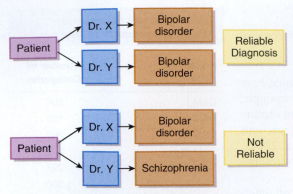

Figure 3.6 Interrater reliability. In this example, the diagnosis of the first patient is reliable—both clinicians diagnose bipolar disorder—whereas the diagnosis of the second is not reliable.

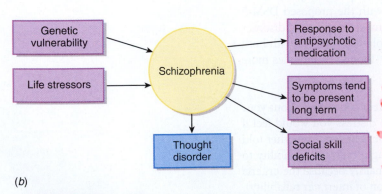

(a)

(b)

Figure 3.7 Construct validity. An example of the types of information a diagnosis might help predict.

The increased explicitness of the DSM criteria has improved reliability (see Table 3.1). Nonetheless, because clinicians might not rely on the criteria precisely, the reliability of the DSM in everyday usage may be lower than that seen in research studies. Even when following criteria, there is some room for disagreement in DSM-5. Consider again the criteria for mania in Table 3.1. What does it mean to say that mood is "abnormally" elevated . . . ? Or when is "involvement in pleasurable activities that have a high potential for painful consequences" excessive? Such judgments set the stage for the insertion of cultural biases as well as the clinician's own personal ideas of what the average person should be doing. Because different clinicians may adopt different definitions for symptoms like "elevated mood," achieving high reliability can be a challenge.

How Valid Are Diagnostic Categories? The DSM diagnoses are based on a pattern of symptoms. A diagnosis of schizophrenia, then, does not have the same status as a diagnosis of, say, diabetes, for which we have laboratory tests.

One way of thinking about diagnosis is to ask whether the system helps organize different observations (see Figure 3.7). Diagnoses have construct validity if they help make accurate predictions. What types of predictions should a good diagnostic category facilitate? One would hope that a diagnosis would inform us about related clinical characteristics and about functional impairments. The DSM specifies that impairment or distress must be present to meet criteria for a diagnosis, so perhaps it is not surprising that diagnoses are related to functional impairments such as marital distress and missed days at work (see Table 3.4). Beyond capturing the most common difficulties for a person with a diagnosis, one would hope that a diagnosis would inform us about what to expect next—the likely course of the disorder and response to different treatments. Perhaps most importantly, one would hope that the diagnosis relates to possible causes of the disorder, for example, a genetic predisposition or a biochemical imbalance. A diagnosis with strong construct validity should help predict a broad range of characteristics.

The central question, then, is whether diagnoses made with the DSM criteria reveal anything useful about patients. We have organized this book around the major DSM diagnostic categories because we believe that they do indeed possess some construct validity. Certain categories have less validity than others, however, and we will discuss some gaps in the validity of specific diagnostic categories in later chapters.

General Criticisms of Diagnosing Mental Illness

Although we described many advantages of diagnosis in the beginning of this chapter, it is also clear that diagnoses can have negative effects on a person. Consider how your life might be changed by receiving the diagnosis of schizophrenia. You might become worried that someone will recognize your disorder. Or you might fear the onset of another episode. You might worry about your ability to deal with new challenges. The fact that you are a "former mental patient" could have a stigmatizing effect. Friends and loved ones might treat you differently, and employment might be hard to find.

There is little doubt that hearing a diagnosis can be difficult. Research shows that many view people with mental illness negatively, and patients and their families often encounter stigma against

Table 3.4 Rates of Marital Distress and Missed Work Days among People with Mental Illness in the Past Year

Disorder	Odds of Marital Distress for a Given Diagnosis Compared to No Mental Illness	Odds of Missed Work Days for a Given Diagnosis Compared to No Mental Illness
Panic disorder	1.28	3.32
Specific phobia	1.34	2.82
Social phobia	1.93	2.74
Generalized anxiety disorder	2.54	1.15
Posttraumatic stress disorder	2.30	2.05
Major depressive disorder	1.68	2.14
Bipolar I or II disorder	3.60	Not assessed
Alcohol use disorder	2.78	2.54

Note: Age, gender, education, and race/ethnicity are controlled for in marital distress analyses, and age and gender are controlled for in work-loss analyses. Diagnoses were based on the Composite International Diagnostic Interview. Marital distress was measured using a 14-item version of the Dyadic Adjustment Scale. Missed work days were measured during the month before the interview.

Source: Information on marital distress drawn from M. A. Whisman (2007). Information on work-loss days drawn from The ESEMeD/MHEDEA 2000 investigators (2004).

mental illness (Wahl, 1999), which, as we discussed in Chapter 1, remains a huge problem. Many have raised concerns that a diagnosis might contribute to stigma. To study this, researchers have given people brief written descriptions of a target individual. Beyond including a bit of information about the person's life and personality, the descriptions include either a mental health diagnosis (such as schizophrenia or bipolar disorder), a description of their symptoms (such as periods of high moods, decreased sleep, and restlessness), both (a diagnosis and symptoms), or neither. In this way, researchers can examine whether people tend to be more negative about labels or behavior. Research clearly shows that people tend to view the behaviors negatively. Sometimes labels may actually relieve stigma by providing an explanation for the symptomatic behavior (Lilienfeld et al., 2010). Of course, making a diagnosis is still a serious process that warrants sensitivity and privacy. But it may not be fair to presume that diagnostic labels are the major source of stigma.

Another concern is that when a diagnostic category is applied, we may lose sight of the uniqueness of that person. Because of this concern, the American Psychological Association recommends that people avoid using words like *schizophrenic* or *depressive* to describe people. Consider that we do not call people with medical illnesses by their disease (e.g., you aren't likely to hear someone with cancer described as the *canceric*). Rather, psychologists are encouraged to use phrases such as *a person with schizophrenia.*

Even with more careful language, some maintain that diagnosis leads us to focus on illnesses and, in doing so, to ignore important differences among people. Unfortunately, this criticism ignores a fundamental truth: it is human nature to categorize whenever we think about anything. Some would argue, then, that if we use categories anyway, it is best to systematically develop the categories. If one accepts this perspective, then the question is how well the current system does in grouping similar illnesses.

Quick Summary

Despite the major improvements in the DSM, a number of problems remain. Some argue that there are too many diagnoses. Reliability is substantially higher than it was for DSM-II, but there is still some disagreement across clinicians regarding some diagnoses, and the reliability achieved in practice may not be as high as the reliability achieved in research studies. Finally, the field as a whole faces a huge challenge; researchers are focused on validating this diagnostic system by trying to identify the causal patterns, symptom patterns, and treatment that can be predicted by a given diagnosis. In sum, although the DSM is continually improving, it is far from perfect. Regardless of which diagnostic system is used, there are certain problems inherent in diagnosing people with mental illness. It is important to be aware of the tendency to ignore a person's strengths when focusing on diagnoses. The American Psychological Association recommends using phrases such as *person with schizophrenia* rather than *schizophrenic* as one way to acknowledge that a person is much more than his or her diagnosis. Although many worry that stigma can be increased by applying labels, diagnoses can sometimes relieve stigma by providing a way of understanding symptoms.

Check Your Knowledge 3.2

Answer the questions.
1. List three reason why some think DSM should lump diagnoses.

2. What are three broad types of characteristics that a valid diagnosis should help predict?

Psychological Assessment

To make a diagnosis, mental health professionals can use a variety of assessment measures and tools. Beyond helping to make a diagnosis, psychological assessment techniques are used in other important ways. For example, assessment methods are often used to identify appropriate therapeutic interventions. And repeated assessments are very useful in monitoring the effects of treatment over time. In addition, assessments are fundamental to conducting research on the causes of disorder.

We will see that beyond the basic interview, many of the assessment techniques stem from the paradigms presented in Chapter 2. Here we discuss clinical interviews; measures for assessing stress; personality tests, including objective and projective tests; intelligence tests; and behavioral and cognitive assessment techniques. Although we present these methods individually, a complete psychological assessment of a person will often entail combining several assessment techniques. The data from the various techniques complement each other and provide a more complete picture of the person. In short, there is no one best assessment measure. Rather, using multiple techniques and multiple sources of information will provide the best assessment.

Clinical Interviews

Most of us have probably been interviewed at one time or another, although the conversation may have been so informal that we did not regard it as an interview. For mental health professionals, both formal and structured as well as informal and less structured clinical interviews are used in psychopathological assessment.

Characteristics of Clinical Interviews One way in which a **clinical interview** is different from a casual conversation is the attention the interviewer pays to how the respondent answers questions—or does not answer them. For example, if a person is recounting marital conflicts, the clinician will generally be attentive to any emotion accompanying the comments. If the person does not seem upset about a difficult situation, the answers probably will be understood differently from how they would be interpreted if the person was crying or agitated while relating the story.

Although it is illegal to discriminate based on mental illness, many employers do so. Stigma must be considered when giving a person a diagnosis of a mental disorder. (Ryan McVay/PhotoDisc, Inc./Getty Images.)

Great skill is necessary to carry out good clinical interviews. Clinicians, regardless of the paradigm adopted, recognize the importance of establishing rapport with the client. The interviewer must obtain the trust of the person; it is naive to assume that a client will easily reveal information to another, even to an authority figure with the title "Doctor." Even a client who sincerely, perhaps desperately, wants to recount intensely personal problems to a professional may not be able to do so without help.

Most clinicians empathize with their clients in an effort to draw them out and to encourage them to elaborate on their concerns. An accurate summary statement of what the client has been saying can help sustain the momentum of talk about painful and possibly embarrassing events and feelings, and an accepting attitude toward personal disclosures dispels the fear that revealing "secrets of the heart" (London, 1964) to another human being will have disastrous consequences.

Interviews vary in the degree to which they are structured. In practice, most clinicians probably operate from only the vaguest outlines. Exactly how information is collected is left largely up to the particular interviewer and depends, too, on the responsiveness and responses of the interviewee. Through years of training and clinical experience, each clinician develops ways of asking questions that he or she is comfortable with and that seem to draw out the information that will be of maximum benefit to the client. Thus, to the extent that an interview is unstructured, the interviewer must rely on intuition and general experience. As a consequence, reliability for unstructured clinical interviews is probably lower than for structured interviews; that is, two interviewers may reach different conclusions about the same patient.

Structured Interviews   At times, mental health professionals need to collect standardized information, particularly for making diagnostic judgments based on the DSM. To meet that need, investigators use a **structured interview,** in which the questions are set out in a prescribed fashion for the interviewer. One example of a commonly used structured interview is the Structured Clinical Interview (SCID) for Axis I of DSM-IV (Spitzer, Gibbon, & Williams, 1996). (Plans are under way to revise this and other structured interviews to cover DSM-5 criteria.)

The SCID is a branching interview; that is, the client's response to one question determines the next question that is asked. It also contains detailed instructions to the interviewer concerning when and how to probe in detail and when to go on to questions about another diagnosis. Most symptoms are rated on a three-point scale of severity, with instructions in the interview schedule for directly translating the symptom ratings into diagnoses. The initial questions pertaining to obsessive-compulsive disorder (discussed in Chapter 7) are presented in Figure 3.8. The interviewer begins by asking about obsessions. If the responses elicit a rating of 1 (absent), the interviewer turns to questions about compulsions. If the patient's responses again elicit a rating of 1, the interviewer is instructed to go to the questions for posttraumatic stress disorder. On the other hand, if positive responses (2 or 3) are elicited about obsessive-compulsive disorder, the interviewer continues with further questions about that problem.

Results of several studies demonstrate that the SCID achieves good interrater reliability for most diagnostic categories. As shown in Table 3.5, interrater reliability is a bit low for some of the anxiety disorders. Other structured interviews with good reliability have been developed for diagnosing personality disorders and for more specific disorders, such as the anxiety disorders, and for diagnosing disorders of childhood (DiNardo, 1993; Shaffer, 2000). With adequate training, interrater reliability for structured interviews is generally good (Blanchard & Brown, 1998).

In practice, most clinicians review the DSM symptoms in an informal manner without using a structured interview. Note, however, that clinicians using unstructured diagnostic interviews tend to miss comorbid diagnoses that often accompany a primary diagnosis (Zimmerman, 1999). When clinicians use an informal interview rather than a structured interview, the reliability of diagnoses also tends to be much lower (Garb, 2005).

Table 3.5 Interrater Reliability of Selected DSM-IV-TR Diagnoses

Diagnosis	Kappa
Axis I disorders	
Major depressive disorder	.80
Dysthymic disorder	.76
Bipolar disorder	.84
Schizophrenia	.79
Alcohol dependence/abuse	1.00
Other substance dependence/abuse	1.00
Panic disorder	.65
Social phobia	.63
Obsessive-compulsive disorder	.57
Generalized anxiety disorder	.63
Posttraumatic stress disorder	.88
Any eating disorder	.77
Personality disorders	
Avoidant	.97
Obsessive-compulsive	.83
Schizotypal	.91
Narcissistic	.98
Borderline	.91
Antisocial	.95

Note: The numbers here are a statistic called kappa, which measures the proportion of agreement over and above what would be expected by chance. Generally, kappas over 0.70 are considered good.

Sources: Estimates for bipolar disorder are based on a study using DSM-III-R criteria (Williams et al., 1992), which are largely comparable to DSM-IV-TR. Estimates for schizophrenia are drawn from Flaum et al. (1998). Other Axis I estimates are drawn from Zanarini et al. (2000), and Axis II estimates are based on Maffei et al. (1997).

Structured interviews are widely used to make reliable diagnoses. (© BSIP/Phototake.)

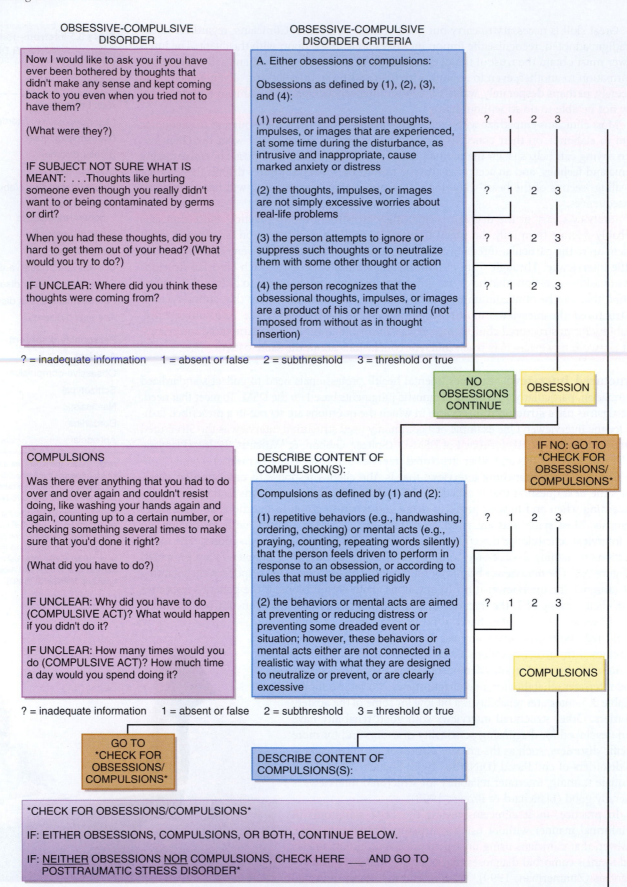

OBSESSIVE-COMPULSIVE DISORDER

Now I would like to ask you if you have ever been bothered by thoughts that didn't make any sense and kept coming back to you even when you tried not to have them?

(What were they?)

IF SUBJECT NOT SURE WHAT IS MEANT: . . .Thoughts like hurting someone even though you really didn't want to or being contaminated by germs or dirt?

When you had these thoughts, did you try hard to get them out of your head? (What would you try to do?)

IF UNCLEAR: Where did you think these thoughts were coming from?

OBSESSIVE-COMPULSIVE DISORDER CRITERIA

A. Either obsessions or compulsions:

Obsessions as defined by (1), (2), (3), and (4):

(1) recurrent and persistent thoughts, impulses, or images that are experienced, at some time during the disturbance, as intrusive and inappropriate, cause marked anxiety or distress — ? 1 2 3

(2) the thoughts, impulses, or images are not simply excessive worries about real-life problems — ? 1 2 3

(3) the person attempts to ignore or suppress such thoughts or to neutralize them with some other thought or action — ? 1 2 3

(4) the person recognizes that the obsessional thoughts, impulses, or images are a product of his or her own mind (not imposed from without as in thought insertion) — ? 1 2 3

? = inadequate information   1 = absent or false   2 = subthreshold   3 = threshold or true

NO OBSESSIONS CONTINUE

OBSESSION

IF NO: GO TO *CHECK FOR OBSESSIONS/ COMPULSIONS*

COMPULSIONS

Was there ever anything that you had to do over and over again and couldn't resist doing, like washing your hands again and again, counting up to a certain number, or checking something several times to make sure that you'd done it right?

(What did you have to do?)

IF UNCLEAR: Why did you have to do (COMPULSIVE ACT)? What would happen if you didn't do it?

IF UNCLEAR: How many times would you do (COMPULSIVE ACT)? How much time a day would you spend doing it?

DESCRIBE CONTENT OF COMPULSION(S):

Compulsions as defined by (1) and (2):

(1) repetitive behaviors (e.g., handwashing, ordering, checking) or mental acts (e.g., praying, counting, repeating words silently) that the person feels driven to perform in response to an obsession, or according to rules that must be applied rigidly — ? 1 2 3

(2) the behaviors or mental acts are aimed at preventing or reducing distress or preventing some dreaded event or situation; however, these behaviors or mental acts either are not connected in a realistic way with what they are designed to neutralize or prevent, or are clearly excessive — ? 1 2 3

COMPULSIONS

? = inadequate information   1 = absent or false   2 = subthreshold   3 = threshold or true

GO TO *CHECK FOR OBSESSIONS/ COMPULSIONS*

DESCRIBE CONTENT OF COMPULSIONS(S):

CHECK FOR OBSESSIONS/COMPULSIONS

IF: EITHER OBSESSIONS, COMPULSIONS, OR BOTH, CONTINUE BELOW.

IF: NEITHER OBSESSIONS NOR COMPULSIONS, CHECK HERE ___ AND GO TO POSTTRAUMATIC STRESS DISORDER*

Figure 3.8 Sample item from the SCID. Reprinted by permission of New York State Psychiatric Institute Biometrics Research Division. Copyright © 2004 Biometrics Research/New York State Psychiatric Institute.

Assessment of Stress

Given its centrality to nearly all the disorders we consider in this book, measuring stress is clearly important in the total assessment picture. To understand the role of stress, we must first be able to define and measure it. Neither task is simple, as stress has been defined in many ways. See Focus on Discovery 3.2 for influential antecedents to our current conceptualizations of stress. Broadly, **stress** can be conceptualized as the subjective experience of distress in response to perceived environmental problems. Life stressors can be defined as the environmental problems that trigger the subjective sense of stress. Various scales and methods have been developed to measure life stress. Here we examine the most comprehensive measure of life stress: the Life Events and Difficulties Schedule (LEDS) as well as self-report checklist measures of stress.

Stress can include major life events or daily hassles. (© Artens/Shutterstock.)

The Bedford College Life Events and Difficulties Schedule This assessment is widely used to study life stressors (Brown & Harris, 1978). The LEDS includes an interview that covers over 200 different kinds of stressors. Because the interview is only semistructured, the interviewer can tailor questions to cover stressors that might only occur to a small number of people. The interviewer and the interviewee work collaboratively to produce a calendar of each of the major events within a given time period (see Figure 3.10 for an example). After the interview, raters evaluate the severity and several other dimensions of each stressor. The LEDS was designed to address a number of problems in life stress assessment, including the need to evaluate the importance of any given life event in the context of a person's life circumstances. For example, pregnancy might have quite a different meaning for an unmarried 14-year-old girl compared to a 38-year-old woman who has been trying to conceive for a long time. A second goal of the LEDS is to exclude life events that might just be consequences of symptoms. For example,

---

FOCUS ON DISCOVERY 3.2

A Brief History of Stress

The pioneering work by the physician Hans Selye set the stage for our current conceptualizations of stress. He introduced the term *general adaptation syndrome* (GAS) to describe the biological response to sustained and high levels of stress (see Figure 3.9). In Selye's model there are three phases of the response:

Figure 3.9 Selye's general adaptation syndrome.

1. During the first phase, the alarm reaction, the autonomic nervous system is activated by the stress.
2. During the second phase, resistance, the organism tries to adapt to the stress through available coping mechanisms.
3. If the stressor persists or the organism is unable to adapt effectively, the third phase, exhaustion, follows, and the organism dies or suffers irreversible damage (Selye, 1950).

In Selye's syndrome, the emphasis was on the body's response, not the environmental events that trigger that response. Psychological researchers later broadened Selye's concept to account for the diverse stress responses that people exhibited, including emotional upset, deterioration of performance, or physiological changes such as increases in the levels of certain hormones. The problem with these response-focused definitions of stress is that the criteria are not clear-cut. Physiological changes in the body can occur in response to a number of things that we would not consider stressful (e.g., anticipating a pleasurable event).

Other researchers defined stress as a stimulus, often referred to as a stressor, rather than a response, and identified stress with a long list of environmental conditions, such as electric shock, boredom, catastrophic life events, daily hassles, and sleep deprivation. Stimuli that are considered stressors can be major (the death of a loved one), minor (daily hassles, such as being stuck in traffic), acute (failing an exam), or chronic (a persistently unpleasant work environment). For the most part, they are experiences that people regard as unpleasant, but they can also be pleasant events.

Like response-based definitions of stress, stimulus-based definitions present problems. It is important to acknowledge that people vary widely in how they respond to life's challenges. A given event does not elicit the same amount of stress in everyone. For example, a family that has lost its home in a flood but has money enough to rebuild and strong social support from a network of friends nearby will experience less stress from this event than will a family that has neither adequate money to rebuild nor a network of friends to provide social support.

Current conceptualizations of stress emphasize that how we perceive, or *appraise*, the environment determines whether a stressor is present. Stress is perhaps most completely conceptualized as the subjective experience of distress in response to perceived environmental problems. A final exam that is merely challenging to some students may be highly stressful to others who do not feel prepared to take it (whether their concerns are realistic or not).

The LEDS focuses on major stressors, such as deaths, job losses, and romantic breakups. (Bob Falcetti Reportage/Getty Images News and Sport Services.)

if a person misses work because he or she is too depressed to get out of bed, any consequent job problems should really be seen as symptoms of the disorder rather than a triggering life event. Finally, the LEDS includes a set of strategies to carefully date when a life stressor occurred. Using this more careful assessment method, researchers have found that life stressors are robust predictors of episodes of anxiety, depression, schizophrenia, and even the common cold (Brown & Harris, 1989b; Cohen et al., 1998).

Self-Report Stress Checklists Because intensive interview measures like the LEDS are so comprehensive, they take a good deal of time to administer. Often clinicians and researchers want a quicker way to assess stress and thus may turn to self-report checklists, such as the List of Threatening Experiences (LTE; Brugha & Cragg, 1990) or the Psychiatric Epidemiological Research Interview Life Events Scale (PERL; Dohrenwend et al., 1978). These checklists typically list different life events (e.g., death of a spouse, serious physical illness, major financial crisis), and participants are asked to indicate whether or not these events happened to them in a specified period of time. One difficulty associated with these types of measures is that there is a great deal of variability in how people view these events (Dohrenwend, 2006).

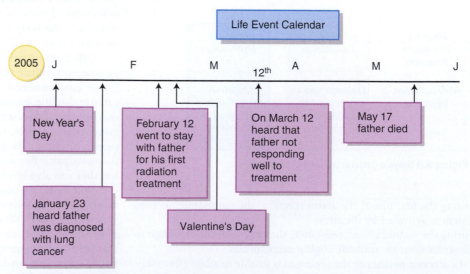

Figure 3.10 Example of a life events timeline. The LEDS interview is designed to capture the major stressors a person has encountered in the past year.

For example, the death of a spouse could be the most horrible event ever for someone in a loving relationship. However, for someone in an abusive relationship, it might be the source of relief rather than stress. Other problems with such self-report checklists include difficulties with recall (Dohrenwend, 2006). For example, people may forget about some events. There is also evidence that people who are feeling depressed or anxious when they complete the measure may be biased in their responses. Perhaps because of these various issues influencing recall, test–retest reliability for life stress checklists can be low (McQuaid et al., 1992).

Personality Tests

Psychological tests further structure the process of assessment. The two most common types of psychological tests are personality tests and intelligence tests. Here we will examine the two types of personality tests: self-report personality inventories and projective personality tests.

Self-Report Personality Inventories   In a **personality inventory,** the person is asked to complete a self-report questionnaire indicating whether statements assessing habitual tendencies apply to him or her. When these tests are developed, they are typically administered to many people to analyze how certain kinds of people tend to respond. Statistical norms for the test can thereby be established. This process is called **standardization.** The responses of a particular person can then be compared with the statistical norms.

Perhaps the best known of these tests is the **Minnesota Multiphasic Personality Inventory (MMPI),** developed in the early 1940s by Hathaway and McKinley (1943) and revised in 1989 (Butcher et al., 1989). The MMPI is called multiphasic because it was designed to detect a number of psychological problems. Over the years, the MMPI has been widely used to screen large groups of people for whom clinical interviews are not feasible.

In developing the test, the investigators used several steps. First, many clinicians provided statements that they considered indicative of various mental problems. Second, patients diagnosed with particular disorders and people with no diagnoses were asked to rate whether hundreds of statements described them. Items were selected for the final version of the test if patients in one clinical group responded to them more often in a certain way than did those in other groups.

With additional refinements, sets of these items were established as scales for determining whether a respondent should be diagnosed in a particular way. If a person answered many of the items in a scale in the same way as had a certain diagnostic group, his or her behavior was expected to resemble that of the particular diagnostic group. The 10 scales are described in Table 3.6.

The revised MMPI-2 (Butcher et al., 1989) was designed to improve validity and acceptability. The original sample assessed 65 years ago was composed mainly of white people from Minnesota and lacked representation of ethnic minorities. The new version was standardized using a sample that was much larger and more representative of 1980 U.S. census figures. Several items containing allusions to sexual adjustment, bowel and bladder functions, and excessive religiosity were removed because they were judged in some testing contexts to be needlessly intrusive and objectionable. Sexist wording was eliminated, along with outmoded idioms. New scales deal with substance abuse, emotions, and marital problems.

Aside from these differences, the MMPI-2 is otherwise quite similar to the original, having the same format, yielding the same scale scores and profiles (Ben-Porath & Butcher, 1989; Graham, 1988), and in general providing continuity with the vast literature already existing on the original MMPI (Graham, 1990). An extensive research literature shows that the MMPI-2 is reliable and has adequate criterion validity when it is related to diagnoses made by clinicians and to ratings made by spouses (Ganellan, 1996; Vacha-Hasse et al., 2001).

Like many other personality inventories, the MMPI-2 is typically administered and scored by computer. Many available computer programs even provide narratives about the respondent. Of course, the validity of the computer analysis is only as good as the program, which in turn is only as good as the competency and experience of the psychologist who wrote it. Figure 3.11 shows a hypothetical profile. Such profiles can be used in conjunction with a therapist's evaluation to help diagnose a client, assess personality functioning and coping style, and identify likely obstacles to treatment.

Table 3.6 Typical Clinical Interpretations of Items Similar to Those on the MMPI-2

Scale		Sample Item	Interpretation
?	(Cannot say)	This is merely the number of items left unanswered or marked both true and false.	A high score indicates evasiveness, reading difficulties, or other problems that could invalidate results of the test. A very high score could also suggest severe depression or obsessional tendencies.
L	(Lie)	I approve of every person I meet. (True)	Person is trying to look good, to present self as someone with an ideal personality.
F	(Infrequency)	Everything tastes sweet. (True)	Person is trying to look abnormal, perhaps to ensure getting special attention from the clinician.
K	(Correction)	Things couldn't be going any better for me. (True)	Person is guarded, defensive in taking the test, wishes to avoid appearing incompetent or poorly adjusted.
1.	Hs (Hypochondriasis)	I am seldom aware of tingling feelings in my body. (False)	Person is overly sensitive to and concerned about bodily sensations as signs of possible physical illness.
2.	D (Depression)	Life usually feels worthwhile to me. (False)	Person is discouraged, pessimistic, sad, self-deprecating, feeling inadequate.
3.	Hy (Hysteria)	My muscles often twitch for no apparent reason. (True)	Person has somatic complaints unlikely to be due to physical problems; also tends to be demanding and histrionic.
4.	Pd (Psychopathy)	I don't care about what people think of me. (True)	Person expresses little concern for social mores, is irresponsible, has only superficial relationships.
5.	Mf (Masculinity–Femininity)	I like taking care of plants and flowers. (True, female)	Person shows nontraditional gender characteristics (e.g., men with high scores tend to be artistic and sensitive.
6.	Pa (Paranoia)	If they were not afraid of being caught, most people would lie and cheat. (True)	Person tends to misinterpret the motives of others, is suspicious and jealous, vengeful and brooding.
7.	Pt (Psychasthenia)	I am not as competent as most other people I know. (True)	Person is overanxious, full of self-doubts, moralistic, and generally obsessive-compulsive.
8.	Sc (Schizophrenia)	I sometimes smell things others don't sense. (True)	Person has bizarre sensory experiences and beliefs, is socially reclusive.
9.	Ma (Hypomania)	Sometimes I have a strong impulse to do something that others will find appalling. (True)	Person has overly ambitious aspirations and can be hyperactive, impatient, and irritable.
10.	Si (Social Introversion)	Rather than spend time alone, I prefer to be around other people. (False)	Person is very modest and shy, preferring solitary activities.

Note: The first four scales assess the validity of the test; the numbered scales are the clinical or content scales.
Sources: Hathaway & McKinley (1943); revised by Butcher et al. (1989).

You may wonder whether it would be easy to fake answers that suggest no psychopathology. For example, a superficial knowledge of contemporary psychopathology research could alert someone that to be regarded as psychologically healthy, he or she must not admit to worrying a great deal about receiving messages from television.

As shown in Table 3.6, the MMPI-2 includes several "validity scales" designed to detect deliberately faked responses. In one of these, the lie scale, a series of statements sets a trap for the person who is trying to look too good. An item on the lie scale might be, "I read the newspaper editorials every day." The assumption is that few people would be able to endorse such a statement honestly. Persons who endorse a large number of the statements in the lie scale might be attempting to present themselves in a good light. High scores on the F scale also discriminate between people trying to fake psychopathology and real patients (Bagby et al., 2002). If a person obtains high scores on the lie or F scale, his or her profile might be viewed with skepticism. People who are aware of these validity scales, however, can effectively fake a normal profile (Baer & Sekirnjak, 1997; Walters & Clopton, 2000). In most testing circumstances, however, people do not want to falsify their responses because they want to be helped. Focus on Discovery 3.3 discusses other issues surrounding the validity of self-report questionnaires.

Projective Personality Tests   A **projective test** is a psychological assessment tool in which a set of standard stimuli—inkblots or drawings—ambiguous enough to allow variation in responses is presented to the person. The assumption is that because the stimulus materials are unstructured and ambiguous, the person's responses will be determined primarily by

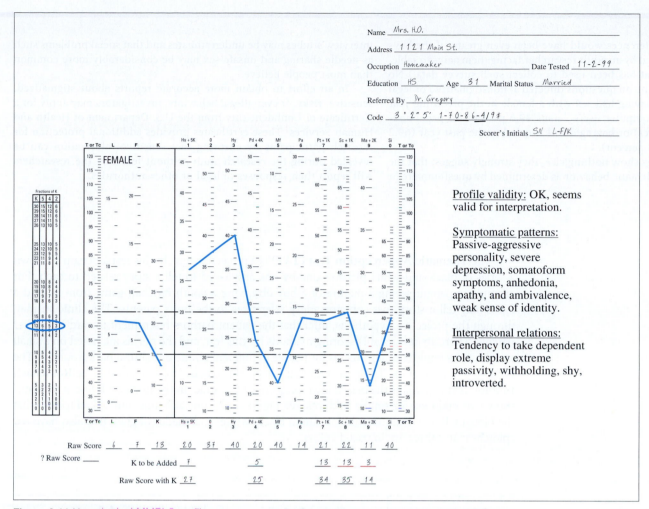

Name __Mrs. H.O.__

Address __1121 Main St.__

Occupation __Homemaker__ Date Tested __11-2-99__

Education __HS__ Age __31__ Marital Status __Married__

Referred By __Dr. Gregory__

Code __3'2"5' 1-7 0-8 6-4/9#__

Scorer's Initials __SN L-F/K__

Profile validity: OK, seems valid for interpretation.

Symptomatic patterns: Passive-aggressive personality, severe depression, somatoform symptoms, anhedonia, apathy, and ambivalence, weak sense of identity.

Interpersonal relations: Tendency to take dependent role, display extreme passivity, withholding, shy, introverted.

Raw Score __6__ __7__ __13__ __20__ __37__ __40__ __20__ __40__ __14__ __21__ __22__ __11__ __40__

? Raw Score ____

K to be Added __7__ __5__ __13__ __13__ __3__

Raw Score with K __27__ __25__ __34__ __35__ __14__

Figure 3.11 Hypothetical MMPI-2 profile.

unconscious processes and will reveal his or her true attitudes, motivations, and modes of behavior. This notion is referred to as the **projective hypothesis.** If a patient reports seeing eyes in an ambiguous inkblot, for example, the projective hypothesis might be that the patient tends toward paranoia. The use of projective tests assumes that the respondent would be either unable or unwilling to express his or her true feelings if asked directly. As you might have guessed, projective techniques are derived from the work of Freud and his followers (see Chapter 1).

FOCUS ON DISCOVERY 3.3

Underreporting of Stigmatized Behaviors

A survey of self-reported drug use, sexual behavior, and violence highlights the importance of the setting in establishing the validity of what people will tell about their actions and attitudes (Turner et al., 1998). Findings from self-report questionnaires were compared with results from a novel self-report method—boys and young men (ages 15 to 19) listened by themselves through headphones to questions probing risky, often stigmatized behavioral practices and then indicated whether they had engaged in those behaviors by pressing keys on a computer keyboard labeled Yes and No.

Compared to a matched control group who responded to the same items on a paper-and-pencil questionnaire, many more of the computer respondents admitted to having engaged in a range of high-risk behaviors. For example, they were almost 14 times more likely to report having had sex with an intravenous drug user (2.8 percent versus 0.2 percent), more than twice as likely to report having been paid for sex (3.8 percent versus 1.6 percent), and almost twice as likely to report having used cocaine (6.0 percent versus 3.3 percent). (One can safely assume that the differences would have been even greater if the boys had been interviewed by an adult researcher facing them across a table, another method that has been used to collect such survey data.) No differences showed up on questions directed at nonstigmatized or legal behaviors such as having had sex with a female in the preceding year (47.8 percent for computer users versus 49.6 percent for paper-and-pencil questionnaires) or having drunk alcohol in the past year (69.2 percent versus 65.9 percent).

If these findings show nothing else, they strongly suggest that the frequencies of problematic behavior as determined by questionnaire or interview studies may be underestimates and that social problems such as needle sharing and unsafe sex may be considerably more common than most people believe.

In an effort to obtain more accurate reports about stigmatized, sensitive, risky, or even illegal behaviors, investigators may apply for a Certificate of Confidentiality from the U.S. Department of Health and Human Services. These certificates provides additional protection for research participants by ensuring that sensitive information can be revealed during the research study without fear that the researchers will report their responses to legal or other authorities.

The **Thematic Apperception Test (TAT)** is a projective test. In this test a person is shown a series of black-and-white pictures one-by-one and asked to tell a story related to each. For example, a patient seeing a picture of a boy observing a youth baseball game from behind a fence may tell a story that contains angry references to the boy's parents. The clinician may, through the projective hypothesis, infer that the patient harbors resentment toward his or her parents. There are few reliable scoring methods for this test, and the norms are based on a small and limited sample (i.e., few norms for people of different ethnic or cultural backgrounds). The construct validity of the TAT is also limited (Lilienfeld, Wood, & Garb, 2000). The **Rorschach Inkblot Test** is perhaps the best-known projective technique. In the Rorschach test, a person is shown 10 inkblots (for similar inkblots, see Figure 3.12), one at a time, and asked to tell what the blots look like. Half the inkblots are in black, white, and shades of gray; two also have red splotches; and three are in pastel colors.

Figure 3.12 In the Rorschach test, the client is shown a series of inkblots and is asked what the blots look like.

Exner (1978) designed the most commonly used system for scoring the Rorschach test. The Exner scoring system concentrates on the perceptual and cognitive patterns in a person's responses. The person's responses are viewed as a sample of how he or she perceptually and cognitively organizes real-life situations (Exner, 1986). For example, Erdberg and Exner (1984) concluded from the research literature that respondents who express a great deal of human movement in their Rorschach responses (e.g., "The man is running to catch a plane") tend to use inner resources when coping with their needs, whereas those whose Rorschach responses involve color ("The red spot is a kidney") are more likely to seek interaction with the environment. Rorschach suggested this approach to scoring in his original manual, *Psychodiagnostics: A Diagnostic Test Based on Perception* (1921), but he died only 8 months after publishing his 10 inkblots, and his immediate followers devised other methods of interpreting the test.

The Exner scoring system has norms, although the sample on which they are based was rather small and did not represent different ethnicities and cultures well. Regarding its reliability and validity, this work has enthusiastic supporters as well as equally harsh critics (e.g., Hunsley & Bailey, 1999; Lilienfeld et al., 2000; Meyer & Archer, 2001). Perhaps trying to make a blanket statement about the validity of the Rorschach (or the MMPI-2) is not the right approach. The test appears to have more validity in assessing some issues more than others. For example, limited evidence suggests that the Rorschach may have validity in identifying schizophrenia, borderline personality disorder, and dependent personality traits, but it remains unclear whether it does so better than other assessment techniques (Lilienfeld et al., 2000). In other words, it is unclear whether the Rorschach provides information that could not be obtained more simply—for example, through an interview.

Intelligence Tests

Alfred Binet, a French psychologist, originally constructed tests to help the Parisian school board predict which children were in need of special schooling. Intelligence testing has since developed into one of the largest psychological industries. An **intelligence test**, often referred to as an IQ test, is a way of assessing a person's current mental ability. IQ tests are based on the assumption that a detailed sample of a person's current intellectual functioning can predict how well he or she will perform in school, and most are individually administered. The most commonly administered tests include the Wechsler Adult Intelligence Scale, 4th edition (WAIS-IV, 2008); the Wechsler Intelligence Scale for Children, 4th edition (WISC-IV, 2003); the Wechsler Preschool and Primary Scale of Intelligence, 3rd edition (WPPSI-III, 2002); and the Stanford–Binet, 5th edition (SB5, 2003); IQ tests are regularly updated, and, like personality inventories, they are standardized.

Beyond predicting school performance, intelligence tests are also used in other ways:

- In conjunction with achievement tests, to diagnose learning disorders and to identify areas of strengths and weaknesses for academic planning
- To help determine whether a person has intellectual developmental disorder (formerly known as mental retardation; see Chapter 13)
- To identify intellectually gifted children so that appropriate instruction can be provided them in school
- As part of neuropsychological evaluations; for example, periodically testing a person believed to be suffering from dementia so that deterioration of mental ability can be followed over time

IQ tests tap several functions believed to constitute intelligence, including language skills, abstract thinking, nonverbal reasoning, visual-spatial skills, attention and concentration, and speed of processing. Scores on most IQ tests are standardized so that 100 is the mean (i.e., the average score) and 15 or 16 is the standard deviation (a measure of how scores are dispersed above and below the average). Approximately 65 percent of the population receives scores between 85 and 115. Approximately 2.5 percent of the population falls below 70 or above 130 (i.e., 2 standard deviations below or above the mean score of 100). In Chapter 14 we discuss people whose IQ falls at the low end of the distribution.

During a ride in the country with his two children, Hermann Rorschach (1884–1922), a Swiss psychiatrist, noticed that what they saw in the clouds reflected their personalities. From this observation came the famous inkblot test. (Courtesy National Library of Medicine.)

The French psychologist Alfred Binet developed the first IQ test to predict how well children would do in school. (Archives of the History of American Psychology, The Center for the History of Psychology-The University of Akron.)

IQ tests are highly reliable (e.g., Canivez & Watkins, 1998) and have good criterion validity. For example, they distinguish between people who are intellectually gifted and those with intellectual developmental disorder and between people with different occupations or educational attainment (Reynolds et al., 1997). They also predict educational attainment and occupational success (Hanson, Hunsley, & Parker, 1988), at least among Caucasians (see below for a discussion of cultural bias in assessment). Although IQ and educational attainment are positively correlated (see Chapter 4 for a discussion of correlational methods), what remains less clear is whether more education causes an increase in IQ or whether IQ causes one to attain more education (Deary & Johnson, 2010). Furthermore, although correlations between IQ scores and school performance are statistically significant, IQ tests explain only a small part of school performance; much more is unexplained by IQ test scores than is explained.

Of interest to the subject matter of this book, IQ is also correlated with mental health. In one study of over one million Scandinavian men, lower IQ scores at age 20 were associated with a greater risk of hospitalization for schizophrenia, mood disorders, or substance dependence some 20 years later, even after controlling for other possible contributing factors, such as the participants' families' socioeconomic status (Gale et al., 2010). A recent meta-analysis of 16 prospective, longitudinal studies (see Chapter 4 for a description of these methods) found that lower IQ scores in early adulthood were associated with greater morality risk (i.e., death) later in life, even after controlling for other variables such as socioeconomic status and educational attainment (Calvin et al., 2010).

Regarding construct validity, it is important to keep in mind that IQ tests measure only what psychologists consider intelligence. Factors other than what we think of as intelligence, however, also play an important role in how people will do in school, such as family and circumstances, motivation to do well, expectations, performance anxiety, and difficulty of the curriculum. Another factor relevant to IQ test performance is called stereotype threat. It suggests that the social stigma of poor intellectual performance borne by some groups (e.g., African Americans do poorly on IQ tests; women perform more poorly than men on mathematics tests) actually interferes with their performance on these tests. In one study demonstrating this phenomenon, groups of men and women were given a difficult mathematics test. In one condition the participants were told that men scored higher than women on the test they were going to take (stereotype threat condition), while in the other condition they were told there were no gender differences in performance on the test. Only when the test was described as yielding gender differences did the women perform more poorly than the men (Spencer, Steele, & Quinn, 1999).

Unfortunately, awareness of these stereotypes develops early. For example, a study revealed that children develop awareness of stereotypes regarding ethnicity and ability between the ages of 6 and 10, with 93 percent of children being aware of such stereotypes by age 10 (McKown & Weinstein, 2003). This awareness seems to influence stereotype threat (and performance). In the McKown and Weinstein (2003) study, children were asked to complete a puzzle task. Half of the children received instructions that the task reflected their ability (stereotype threat condition), and half the children received instructions that the test did not reflect their ability. African American children who were aware of the stereotype about ethnicity and ability showed evidence of stereotype threat. Specifically, among African American children, those who received the ability instructions performed more poorly on the puzzle task than the children who did not, suggesting that the instructions activated the stereotype and thus influenced their performance.

Behavioral and Cognitive Assessment

Thus far, we have discussed assessment methods that measure personality traits and intellectual ability. Other types of assessment focus on behavioral and cognitive characteristics, including the following:

IQ tests have many subtests, including this test to assess spatial ability. (Bob Daemmrich/The Image Works.)

- Aspects of the environment that might contribute to symptoms (e.g., an office location next to a noisy hallway might contribute to concentration problems)

- Characteristics of the person (e.g., a client's fatigue may be caused in part by a cognitive tendency toward self-deprecation manifested in such statements as "I never do anything right, so what's the point in trying?")

- The frequency and form of problematic behaviors (e.g., procrastination taking the form of missing important deadlines)

- Consequences of problem behaviors (e.g., when a client avoids a feared situation, his or her partner offers sympathy and excuses, thereby unwittingly keeping the client from facing up to his or her fears)

The hope is that understanding these aspects of cognition and behavior will guide the clinician toward more effective intervention targets.

The information necessary for a behavioral or cognitive assessment is gathered by several methods, including direct observation of behavior in real life as well as in laboratory or office settings, interviews and self-report measures, and various other methods of cognitive assessment (Bellack & Hersen, 1998). We turn to these now.

Direct Observation of Behavior   It is not surprising that cognitive behavior therapists have paid considerable attention to careful observation of behavior in a variety of settings, but it should not be assumed that they simply go out and observe. Like other scientists, they try to fit events into a framework consistent with their points of view. In formal behavioral observation, the observer divides the sequence of behavior into various parts that make sense within a learning framework, including such things as the antecedents and consequences of particular behaviors. Behavioral observation is also often linked to intervention (O'Brien & Haynes, 1995). The cognitive behavioral clinician's way of conceptualizing a situation typically implies a way to try to change it.

It is difficult to observe most behavior as it actually takes place, and little control can be exercised over where and when it may occur. For this reason, many therapists contrive artificial situations in their consulting rooms or in a laboratory so they can observe how a client or a family acts under certain conditions. For example, Barkley (1981) had a mother and her child spend time together in a laboratory living room, complete with sofas and a television set. The mother was given a list of tasks for the child to complete, such as picking up toys or doing arithmetic problems. Observers behind a one-way mirror watched the proceedings and reliably coded the child's reactions to the mother's efforts to control as well as the mother's reactions to the child's compliant or noncompliant responses. These **behavioral assessment** procedures yielded data that could be used to measure the effects of treatment.

Self-Observation   Cognitive behavior therapists and researchers have also asked people to observe and track their own behavior and responses, an approach called **self-monitoring.** Self-monitoring is used to collect a wide variety of data of interest to both clinicians and researchers, including moods, stressful experiences, coping behaviors, and thoughts (Hurlburt, 1979; Stone et al., 1998).

Another method of self-observation is called **ecological momentary assessment,** or **EMA.** EMA involves the collection of data in real time as opposed to the more usual methods of having people reflect back over some time period and report on recently experienced thoughts, moods, or stressors. The methods for implementing EMA range from having people complete diaries at specified times during the day (perhaps signaled by a wristwatch that beeps at those times) to supplying them with smartphones that not only signal when reports

Behavioral assessment often involves direct observation of behavior, as in this case, where the observer is behind a one-way mirror. (© Spencer Grant/Alamy Limited.)

Self-monitoring generally leads to increases in desirable behaviors and decreases in undesirable ones. (ANDREW GOMBERT/ EPA/Landov LLC.)

are to be made but also allow them to enter their responses directly into the device (Stone & Shiffman, 1994).

Given the problems in retrospective recall, some theories in the field of psychopathology can best be tested using EMA. For example, current theories of both anxiety disorders and depression propose that emotional reactions to a life event are triggered in part by the thoughts that the event elicits. It is unlikely, however, that these thoughts can be recalled accurately in retrospect.

EMA may also be useful in clinical settings, revealing information that traditional assessment procedures might miss. For example, Hurlburt (1997) describes a case of a man with severe attacks of anxiety. In clinical interviews, the patient reported that his life was going very well, that he loved his wife and children, and that his work was both financially and personally rewarding. No cause of the anxiety attacks could be discerned. The man was asked to record his thoughts as he went about his daily routine. Surprisingly, about a third of his thoughts were concerned with annoyance with his children (e.g., "He left the fence gate open again and the dog got out").

Once the high frequency of annoyance thoughts was pointed out to him, he . . . accepted that he was in fact often annoyed with his children. However, he believed that anger at his children was sinful and felt unfit as a father for having such thoughts and feelings. . . . [He] entered into brief therapy that focused on the normality of being annoyed by one's children and on the important distinction between being annoyed and acting out aggressively. Almost immediately, his anxiety attacks disappeared. (Hurlburt, 1997, p. 944)

Although some research indicates that self-monitoring or EMA can provide accurate measurement of such behavior, considerable research indicates that behavior may be altered by the very fact that it is being self-monitored—that is, the self-consciousness required for self-monitoring affects the behavior (Haynes & Horn, 1982). The phenomenon wherein behavior changes because it is being observed is called **reactivity**. In general, desirable behavior, such as engaging in social conversation, often increases in frequency when it is self-monitored (Nelson, Lipinski, & Black, 1976), whereas behavior the person wishes to reduce, such as cigarette smoking, diminishes (McFall & Hammen, 1971). Therapeutic interventions can take advantage of the reactivity that is a natural by-product of self-monitoring. Smoking, anxiety, depression, and health problems have all undergone beneficial changes in self-monitoring studies (Febbraro & Clum, 1998). Beyond reactivity, self-monitoring with portable electronic devices like smart phones has also been included effectively in cognitive behavior therapy for different anxiety disorders (Przeworski & Newman, 2006).

Cognitive-Style Questionnaires Cognitive questionnaires tend to be used to help plan targets for treatment as well as to determine whether clinical interventions are helping to change overly negative thought patterns. In format, some of these questionnaires are similar to the personality tests we have already described.

One self-report questionnaire that was developed based on Beck's theory (see Chapters 2 and 8) is the Dysfunctional Attitude Scale (DAS). The DAS contains items such as "People will probably think less of me if I make a mistake" (Weissman & Beck, 1978). Supporting construct validity, researchers have shown that they can differentiate between depressed and nondepressed people on the basis of their scores on this scale and that scores decrease (i.e., improve) after interventions that relieve depression. Furthermore, the DAS relates to other aspects of cognition in ways consistent with Beck's theory (Glass & Arnkoff, 1997).

Cognitive assessment focuses on the person's perception of a situation, realizing that the same event can be perceived differently. For example, moving could be regarded as a very negative event or a very positive one, resulting in very different levels of stress. (Fuse/Getty Images, Inc.)

Table 3.7 Psychological Assessment Methods

Interviews	Clinical interviews	The clinician learns about the patient's problems through conversation. The paradigm of the interviewer shapes the content of the interview.
	Structured interviews	Questions to be asked are spelled out in detail in a booklet. The Structured Clinical Interview for Axis I Disorders is a structured interview that is commonly used to make a diagnosis.
Stress measures		Self-report scales or interviews that assess stressful events and responses to these events.
Psychological tests	Personality tests	Self-report questionnaires, used to assess either a broad range of characteristics, as in the MMPI-2, or a single characteristic, such as dysfunctional attitudes.
	Projective tests	Ambiguous stimuli, such as inkblots (Rorschach test), are presented and responses are thought to be determined by unconscious processes.
	Intelligence tests	Assessments of current mental functioning. Used to predict school performance and identify cognitive strengths and weaknesses.
Direct observation		Used by clinicians to identify problem behaviors as well as antecedents and consequences.
Self-observation		People monitor and keep records of their own behavior, as in ecological momentary assessment.

Quick Summary

The psychological assessments we have described are summarized in Table 3.7. A comprehensive psychological assessment draws on many different methods and tests. Interviews can be structured, with the questions predetermined and followed in a certain order, or unstructured to follow more closely what the client tells the interviewer. Structured interviews are more reliable. Rapport is important to establish regardless of the type of interview.

Stress is best assessed via a semistructured interview that captures the importance of any given life event in the context of a person's life circumstances, as in the LEDS. Self-report checklists are also used to assess stress, but they have poorer reliability and validity than the LEDS.

The MMPI-2 is a standardized and objective personality inventory. The test has good reliability and validity and is widely used. Projective personality tests, like the Rorschach or TAT, are not as widely used today, likely due to their poor validity. Reliability can be achieved using scoring systems such as Exner's. Intelligence tests have been used for a number of years and are quite reliable. Like any test, there are limits to what an IQ test can tell a clinician or researcher.

Direct observation of behavior can be very useful in assessment, though it can take more time than a self-report inventory. Other behavioral and cognitive assessment methods include ecological momentary assessment (EMA).

Check Your Knowledge 3.3

True or false?
1. If conducted properly, a psychological assessment typically includes just one measure most appropriate to the client.
2. Unstructured interviews may have poor reliability, but they can still be quite valuable in a psychological assessment.
3. The MMPI-2 contains scales to detect whether someone is faking answers.
4. The projective hypothesis is based on the idea that a person does not really know what is bothering him or her; thus, a subtler means of assessment is needed.
5. Intelligence tests are highly reliable.
6. EMA is a method to assess unwanted impulses.

Neurobiological Assessment

Recall from Chapters 1 and 2 that throughout history people interested in psychopathology have assumed, quite reasonably, that some symptoms are likely to be due to or at least reflected in malfunctions of the brain or other parts of the nervous system. We turn now to contemporary work in neurobiological assessment. We'll look at four areas in particular: brain imaging, neurotransmitter assessment, neuropsychological assessment, and psychophysiological assessment (see Table 3.8 for a summary of these methods).

Table 3.8 Neurobiological Assessment Methods	
Brain imaging	CT and MRI scans reveal the structure of the brain. PET reveals brain function and, to a lesser extent, brain structure. fMRI is used to assess both brain structure and brain function.
Neurotransmitter assessment	Includes postmortem analysis of neurotransmitters and receptors, assays of metabolites of neurotransmitters, and PET scans of receptors.
Neuropsychological assessment	Behavioral tests such as the Halstead–Reitan and Luria–Nebraska assess abilities such as motor speed, memory, and spatial ability. Deficits on particular tests help point to an area of brain dysfunction.
Psychophysiological assessment	Includes measures of electrical activity in the autonomic nervous system, such as skin conductance, or in the central nervous system, such as EEG.

Brain Imaging: "Seeing" the Brain

Because many behavioral problems can be brought on by brain dysfunction, neurological tests—such as checking the reflexes, examining the retina for any indication of blood vessel damage, and evaluating motor coordination and perception—have been used for many years to identify brain dysfunction. Today, devices have become available that allow clinicians and researchers a much more direct look at both the structure and functioning of the brain.

Computerized axial tomography, the **CT** or **CAT scan**, helps to assess structural brain abnormalities (and is able to image other parts of the body for medical purposes). A moving beam of X-rays passes into a horizontal cross section of the person's brain, scanning it through 360 degrees; the moving X-ray detector on the other side measures the amount of radioactivity that penetrates, thus detecting subtle differences in tissue density. A computer uses the information to construct a two-dimensional, detailed image of the cross section, giving it optimal contrasts. Then the machine scans another cross section of the brain. The resulting images can show the enlargement of ventricles (which can be a sign of brain tissue degeneration) and the locations of tumors and blood clots.

Other devices for seeing the living brain include **magnetic resonance imaging,** also known as **MRI,** which is superior to the CT scan because it produces pictures of higher quality and does not rely on even the small amount of radiation required by a CT scan. In MRI the person is placed inside a large, circular magnet, which causes the hydrogen atoms in the body to move. When the magnetic force is turned off, the atoms return to their original positions and thereby produce an electromagnetic signal. These signals are then read by the computer and translated into pictures of brain tissue. This technique provides an enormous advance. For example, it has allowed physicians to locate delicate brain tumors that would have been considered inoperable without such sophisticated methods of viewing brain structures.

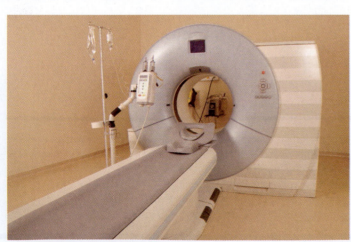

An fMRI scanner is a long tubelike structure. (© Levent Konuk/ Shutterstock.)

An even greater advance has been a technique called **functional MRI (fMRI)**, which allows researchers to measure both brain structure and brain function. This technique takes MRI pictures so quickly that metabolic changes can be measured, providing a picture of the brain at work rather than of its structure alone. fMRI measures blood flow in the brain, and this is called the **BOLD** signal, which stands for blood oxygenation level dependent. As neurons fire, blood flow increases to that area. Therefore, blood flow in a particular region of the brain is a reasonable proxy for neural activity in that brain region.

Positron emission tomography, the **PET scan**, a more expensive and invasive procedure, also allows measurement of both brain structure and brain function, although the measurement of brain structure is not as precise as with MRI or fMRI. A substance used by the brain is labeled with a short-lived radioactive isotope and injected into the bloodstream. The radioactive molecules of the substance emit a particle called a positron, which quickly collides with an electron. A pair of high-energy light particles shoot out from the skull in opposite directions and are detected by the scanner. The computer analyzes millions of such recordings and converts them into a picture of the functioning brain. The images are in color; fuzzy spots of lighter and warmer colors are areas in which metabolic rates for the substance are higher. Because this is more invasive than fMRI, it is now used less often as a measure of brain function.

Visual images of the working brain can indicate sites of seizures, brain tumors, strokes, and trauma from head injuries, as well as the distribution of psychoactive drugs in the brain. fMRI and to a lesser extent PET are being used to study possible abnormal brain processes that are linked to various disorders, such as the failure of the prefrontal cortex of patients with schizophrenia to become activated while they attempt to perform a cognitive task. Current neuroimaging studies in psychopathology are attempting to identify not only areas of the brain that may be dysfunctional (e.g., the prefrontal cortex) but also deficits in the ways in which different areas of the brain communicate with one another. This type of inquiry is often referred to as functional connectivity analysis since it aims to identify how different areas of the brain are connected with one another.

Neurotransmitter Assessment

It might seem that assessing the amount of a particular neurotransmitter or the quantity of its receptors in the brain would be straightforward. But as we began to discuss in Chapter 2, it is not. Most of the research on neurotransmitters and psychopathology has relied on indirect assessments.

In postmortem studies, the brains of deceased patients are removed and the amount of specific neurotransmitters in particular brain areas can then be directly measured. Different brain areas can be infused with substances that bind to receptors, and the amount of binding can then be quantified; more binding indicates more receptors.

In studies of participants who are alive, one common method of neurotransmitter assessment involves analyzing the metabolites of neurotransmitters that have been broken down by enzymes. A **metabolite**, typically an acid, is produced when a neurotransmitter is deactivated. These by-products of the breakdown of

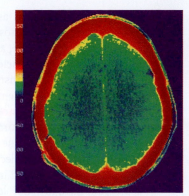
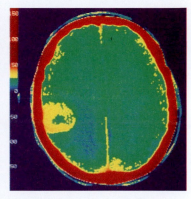

These two CT scans show a horizontal "slice" through the brain. The one on the left is normal; the one on the right has a tumor on the left side. (Dan McCoy/Rainbow.)

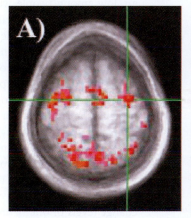
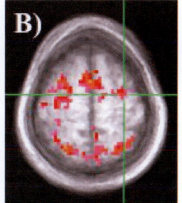

Functional magnetic resonance images (fMRI). With this method, researchers can measure how brain activity changes while a person is doing different tasks, such as viewing an emotional film, completing a memory test, looking at a visual puzzle, or hearing and learning a list of words. (Reprinted from J. E. McDowell et al., Neural correlates of refixation saccades and antisaccades in normal and schizophrenia subjects. *Biological Psychiatry, 51,* 216-223 2002 with permission from Elsevier.)

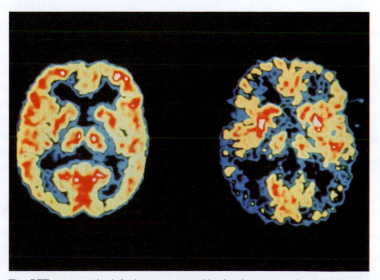

The PET scan on the left shows a normal brain; the one on the right shows the brain of a patient with Alzheimer's disease. (Dr. Robert Friedland/Photo Researchers, Inc.)

neurotransmitters, such as norepinephrine, dopamine, and serotonin, are found in urine, blood serum, and cerebrospinal fluid (CSF; the fluid in the spinal column and in the brain's ventricles). For example, a major metabolite of dopamine is homovanillic acid; of serotonin, 5-hydroxyindoleacetic acid. A high level of a particular metabolite presumably indicates a high level of a neurotransmitter, and a low level indicates a low level of the transmitter.

But there is a problem with measuring metabolites from blood or urine; such measures are not direct reflections of levels of neurotransmitters in the brain; metabolites measured in this way could reflect neurotransmitters anywhere in the body. A more specific measure can be taken of metabolites in the CSF fluid drawn from a person's spinal cord. Even with CSF fluid, however, metabolites reflect activity throughout the brain and spinal cord, rather than regions that are directly involved in psychopathology. We will see in Chapter 5 that some people with depression have low CSF levels of the main metabolite of serotonin—a fact that has played an important role in the serotonin theory of depression.

Another problem with metabolite studies is that they are correlational. In Chapter 4, we discuss the limits of correlational research, including the fact that causation cannot be determined from a correlational study. That is, when researchers find that neurotransmitter levels are low among people with a particular disorder, such as depression, this could be because neurotransmitter levels cause depression, because depression causes neurotransmitter changes, or because a third variable causes shifts in both neurotransmitters and depression. For example, dopamine, norepinephrine, and serotonin levels change in response to stress. To test whether neurotransmitter levels could cause symptoms, experimental evidence is needed.

To provide more experimental data on whether these neurotransmitter systems actually help cause psychopathology, one strategy is to administer drugs that increase or decrease levels of neurotransmitters. For example, a drug that raises the level of serotonin should alleviate depression; one reducing it should trigger depressive symptoms. This strategy also has its problems, though. One might wonder about whether it is ethical to do these studies if the goal of an experiment is to produce symptoms. On this front, it is reassuring that most studies find very temporary effects of these medications; neurotransmitter systems quickly return to normal levels, allowing for recovery from these brief mood episodes. Another issue is that drugs that change levels of one neurotransmitter often tend to influence other neurotransmitter systems. We will see examples of these types of studies throughout this book.

Clinicians and researchers in many disciplines are currently using brain imaging and neurotransmitter assessment techniques both to discover previously undetectable brain problems and to conduct inquiries into the neurobiological contributions to thought, emotion, and behavior. It is a very lively and exciting area of research and application. Indeed, one might reasonably assume that researchers and clinicians, with the help of such procedures and technological devices as fMRI, could observe the brain and its functions more or less directly and thus assess all brain abnormalities. Results to date, however, are not strong enough for these methods to be used in diagnosing psychopathology. Moreover, many brain abnormalities involve alterations in structure so subtle or slight in extent that they have thus far eluded direct examination. Furthermore, the problems in some disorders are so widespread that finding the contributing brain dysfunction is a daunting task. Take, for example, schizophrenia, which affects thinking, feeling, and behavior. Where in the brain might there be dysfunction? Looking for areas that influence thinking, feeling, and behavior requires looking at just about the entire brain.

Measures of neurotransmitter metabolites in blood or urine levels do not provide a very accurate index of neurotransmitter levels in the brain. (© MilanMarkovic/Shutterstock.)

Neuropsychological Assessment

It is important at this point to note a distinction between neurologists and neuropsychologists, even though both specialists are concerned with the study of the central nervous system. A **neurologist** is a physician who specializes in diseases or problems that affect the nervous system, such as stroke, muscular dystrophy, cerebral palsy, or Alzheimer's disease. A **neuropsychologist** is a psychologist who studies how dysfunctions of the brain affect the way we think, feel, and behave. Both kinds of specialists contribute much to each other as they work in different ways, often collaboratively, to learn how the nervous system functions and how to ameliorate problems caused by disease or injury to the brain.

Neuropsychological tests are often used in conjunction with the brain imaging techniques just described, both to detect brain dysfunction and to help pinpoint specific areas of behavior that are impacted by problems in the brain. Neuropsychological tests are based on the idea that different psychological functions (e.g., motor speed, memory, language) rely on different areas of the brain. Thus, for example, neuropsychological testing might help identify the extent of brain damage suffered during a stroke, and it can provide clues about where in the brain the damage may exist that can then be confirmed with more expensive brain imaging techniques. There are numerous neuropsychological tests used in psychopathology assessment. Here, we highlight two widely used batteries of tests.

One neuropsychological test is Reitan's modification of a battery, or group, of tests previously developed by Halstead, called the Halstead–Reitan neuropsychological test battery. The following are three of the Halstead–Reitan tests.

1. **Tactile Performance Test—Time.** While blindfolded, the patient tries to fit variously shaped blocks into spaces of a form board, first using the preferred hand, then the other, and finally both.

2. **Tactile Performance Test—Memory.** After completing the timed test, the participant is asked to draw the form board from memory, showing the blocks in their proper location. Both this and the timed test are sensitive to damage in the right parietal lobe.

3. **Speech Sounds Perception Test.** Participants listen to a series of nonsense words, each comprising two consonants with a long-*e* sound in the middle. They then select the "word" they heard from a set of alternatives. This test measures left-hemisphere function, especially temporal and parietal areas.

Extensive research has demonstrated that the battery is valid for detecting behavior changes linked to brain dysfunction resulting from a variety of conditions, such as tumors, stroke, and head injury (Horton, 2008).

The Luria–Nebraska battery (Golden, Hammeke, & Purisch, 1978), based on the work of the Russian psychologist Aleksandr Luria (1902–1977), is also widely used (Moses & Purisch, 1997). The battery includes 269 items divided into 11 sections designed to determine basic and complex motor skills, rhythm and pitch abilities, tactile and kinesthetic skills, verbal and spatial skills, receptive speech ability, expressive speech ability, writing, reading, arithmetic skills, memory, and intellectual processes. The pattern of scores on these sections, as well as on the 32 items found to be the most discriminating and indicative of overall impairment, helps reveal potential damage to the frontal, temporal, sensorimotor, or parietal-occipital area of the right or left hemisphere.

The Luria–Nebraska battery can be administered in $2\frac{1}{2}$ hours and can be scored in a highly reliable manner (e.g., Kashden & Franzen, 1996). Criterion validity has been established by findings that test scores can correctly distinguish 86 percent of neurological patients and controls (Moses et al., 1992). A particular advantage of the Luria–Nebraska tests is that one can control for educational level so that a less educated person will not receive a lower score solely because of limited educational experience (Brickman et al., 1984). Finally, a version for children ages 8 to 12 (Golden, 1981a, 1981b) has been found useful in helping to pinpoint brain damage and in evaluating the educational strengths and weaknesses of children (Sweet et al., 1986).

Neuropsychological tests assess various performance deficits in the hope of detecting a specific area of brain malfunction. Shown here is the Tactile Performance Test. (Richard Nowitz/Photo Researchers, Inc.)

Psychophysiological Assessment

The discipline of **psychophysiology** is concerned with the bodily changes that are associated with psychological events. Experimenters have used measures such as heart rate, tension in the muscles, blood flow in various parts of the body, and electrical activity in the brain (so-called brain waves) to study physiological changes when people are afraid, depressed, asleep, imagining, solving problems, and so on. Like the brain-imaging methods we have already discussed, the assessments we describe here are not sensitive enough to be used for diagnosis. They can, however, provide important information about a person's reactivity and can also be used to compare individuals. For example, in using exposure to treat a patient with an anxiety disorder, it would be useful to know the extent to which the patient shows physiological reactivity when exposed to the stimuli that create anxiety. Patients who show more physiological reactivity may be experiencing more fear, which predicts more benefit from the therapy (Foa et al., 1995).

The activities of the autonomic nervous system (also discussed in Chapter 2) are often assessed by electrical and chemical measurements to understand aspects of emotion. One important measure is heart rate. Each heartbeat generates electrical changes, which can be recorded by electrodes placed on the chest that convey signals to an electrocardiograph or a polygraph. The signal is graphically depicted in an **electrocardiogram (EKG)**, which may be seen as waves on a computer screen or on a roll of graph paper.

A second measure of autonomic nervous system activity is **electrodermal responding**, or skin conductance. Anxiety, fear, anger, and other emotions increase activity in the sympathetic nervous system, which then boosts sweat-gland activity. Increased sweat-gland activity increases the electrical conductance of the skin. Conductance is typically measured by determining the current that flows through the skin as a small voltage is passed between two electrodes on the hand. When the sweat glands are activated, this current shows a pronounced increase. Since the sweat glands are activated by the sympathetic nervous system, increased sweat-gland activity indicates sympathetic autonomic excitation and is often taken as a measure of emotional arousal. These measures are widely used in research in psychopathology.

Brain activity can be measured by an **electroencephalogram (EEG)**. Electrodes placed on the scalp record electrical activity in the underlying brain area. Abnormal patterns of electrical activity can indicate seizure activity in the brain or help in locating brain lesions or tumors. EEG indices are also used to measure attention and alertness.

As with the brain-imaging techniques reviewed earlier, a more complete picture of a human being is obtained when physiological functioning is assessed while the person is engaging in some form of behavior or cognitive activity. If experimenters are interested in psychophysiological responding in patients with obsessive-compulsive disorder, for example, they would likely study the patients while presenting stimuli, such as dirt, that would elicit the problematic behaviors.

A Cautionary Note about Neurobiological Assessment

A cautionary note regarding neurobiological assessment methods is in order here. Inasmuch as psychophysiology and brain imaging employ highly sophisticated electronic machinery, and many psychologists aspire to be as scientific as possible, researchers and clinicians sometimes believe uncritically in these apparently objective assessment devices without appreciating their real limitations and complications. Many of the measurements do not differentiate clearly among emotional states. Skin conductance, for example, increases not only with anxiety but also with other emotions—among them, happiness. In addition, being in a scanner is often a threatening experience. Thus, the investigator interested in measuring brain changes associated with emotion using fMRI must also take the scanning environment into account. It is also important to keep in mind that brain-imaging techniques do not allow us to manipulate brain activity and then measure a change in behavior (Feldman Barrett, 2003). In a typical study, we

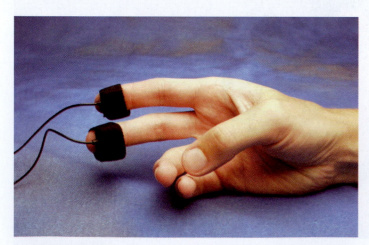

In psychophysiological assessment, physical changes in the body are measured. Skin conductance can be measured with sensors on two fingers. (Courtesy of BIOPAC Systems, Inc. (biopac.com).)

show people a list of emotionally evocative words and then measure blood flow in the brain. Does a person who fails to show the same level of activation in emotion regions during this task have a brain-based emotion deficit? Not necessarily. The person might not have paid attention, might not have understood the words, or might be focused on the loud clanging noises that the fMRI machine is making. It is important to be extremely careful in considering alternative explanations for the effects found in these studies.

Neither is there a one-to-one relationship between a score on a given neuropsychological test or a finding on an fMRI scan on the one hand and psychological dysfunction on the other. The reasons for these sometimes loose relationships have to do with such factors as how the person has, over time, reacted to and coped with the losses brought about by the brain dysfunction. And the success of coping, in turn, has to do with the social environment in which the person has lived, for example, how understanding parents and associates have been or how well the school system has provided for the special educational needs of the person. Furthermore, the brain changes in response to these psychological and socioenvironmental factors over time. Therefore, in addition to the imperfect nature of the neurobiological assessment instruments themselves and our incomplete understanding of how the brain actually functions, clinicians and researchers must consider these environmental factors that operate over time to contribute to the clinical picture. In other words, a complete assessment must include multiple methods (clinical interviews, psychological and neurobiological methods).

A final caution is reflected in the simple yet often unappreciated fact that in attempting to understand the neurocognitive consequences of any brain dysfunction, one must understand the preexisting abilities that the patient had prior to diagnosis with a mental disorder. This straightforward truth brings to mind the story of the man who, recovering from an accident that has broken all the fingers in both hands, earnestly asks the surgeon whether he will be able to play the piano when his wounds heal. "Yes, I'm sure you will," says the doctor reassuringly. "That's wonderful," exclaims the man, "I've always wanted to be able to play the piano."

Quick Summary

Advances in technology have allowed clinicians and researchers to "see" the living brain. Different imaging techniques, such as CT, MRI, and fMRI, have the potential to show areas of the brain that might not be working optimally. Direct assessment of neurotransmitters is not done often. Rather, examinations of the metabolites of neurotransmitters provide a rough way to estimate how neurotransmitters are functioning. Another approach is to administer drugs that increase or decrease the levels of a neurotransmitter. Postmortem exams also allow for measurements of neurotransmitters, particularly receptors.

Neuropsychological tests are tests that have been developed to show how changes in behavior may reflect damage or disturbance in particular areas of the brain. Psychophysiological assessment methods can show how behaviors and cognitions are linked to changes in nervous system activity, such as heart rate, skin conductance, or brain activity. These methods have as many or more limitations as other assessment measures, and the key concepts of reliability and validity are just as relevant with neurobiological assessment as with other forms of assessment.

Check Your Knowledge 3.4

True or false?
1. MRI is a technique that shows both the structure and function of the brain.
2. Neurotransmitter assessment is most often done using indirect methods.
3. A neuropsychologist is a psychologist who studies how dysfunctions of the brain affect the way we think, feel, and behave.
4. Brain activity can be measured with the psychophysiological method called EKG.

Cultural and Ethnic Diversity and Assessment

Studies of the influences of culture and ethnicity on psychopathology and its assessment have proliferated in recent years. As you read about some of this research, it is critical to keep in mind that there are typically more differences within cultural, ethnic, and racial groups than there are between them. Remembering this important point can help avoid the dangers of stereotyping members of a culture.

We should also note that the reliability and validity of various forms of psychological assessment have been questioned on the grounds that their content and scoring procedures reflect the culture of white European Americans and so may not accurately assess people from other cultures. In this section we discuss problems of cultural bias and what can be done about them.

Cultural Bias in Assessment

The issue of cultural bias in assessment refers to the notion that a measure developed for one culture or ethnic group may not be equally reliable and valid with a different cultural or ethnic group. Some tests that were developed in the United States, however, have been translated into different languages and used in different cultures successfully. For example, a Spanish-language version of the WAIS has been available for over 40 years (Wechsler, 1968) and can be useful in assessing the intellectual functioning of people from Hispanic or Latino cultures (Gomez, Piedmont, & Fleming, 1992). Additionally, the MMPI-2 has been translated into more than two dozen languages (Tsai et al., 2001).

Simply translating words into a different language, however, does not ensure that the meaning of those words will be the same across different cultures. Several steps in the translation process, including working with multiple translators, back-translating, and testing with multiple native speakers, can help to ensure that the test is similar in different languages. This approach has been successful in achieving equivalence across different cultures and ethnic groups for some instruments, such as the MMPI-2 (Arbisi, Ben-Porath, & McNulty, 2002). Even with the MMPI-2, however, there are cultural differences that are not likely attributable to differences in psychopathology. For example, among Asian Americans who are not heavily assimilated into American culture, scores on most MMPI-2 scales are higher than those of Caucasians (Tsai & Pike, 2000). This is unlikely to reflect truly higher emotional disturbance among Asians. For children, the latest version of the WISC has not only been translated into Spanish (WISC-IV Spanish); it also has a complete set of norms for Spanish-speaking children in the United States, and the items have been designed explicitly to minimize cultural bias.

Despite these efforts, the field has a way to go in reducing cultural and ethnic bias in clinical assessment. These cultural assumptions or biases may cause clinicians to over- or underestimate psychological problems in members of other cultures (Lopez, 1989, 1996). African American children are overrepresented in special education classes, which may be a result of subtle biases in the tests used to determine such placement (Artiles & Trent, 1994). At least since the 1970s, studies have found that African Americans are more likely to receive a diagnosis of schizophrenia than are Caucasian Americans, but it is still unclear whether this reflects an actual difference or a form of ethnic bias on the part of clinicians (Arnold et al., 2004; Trierweiler et al., 2000). Yet take the example of an Asian American man who is very emotionally withdrawn. Should the clinician

Assessment must take the person's cultural background into account. Believing in possession by spirits is common in some cultures and thus should not always be taken to mean that the believer is psychotic. (Tony Savino/The Image Works.)

consider that lower emotional expressiveness in men is viewed more positively in Asian cultures than in European American culture? A clinician who quickly attributes the behavior to a cultural difference may overlook an emotional problem that he or she would be likely to diagnose if the patient were a white male.

How do such biases come about? Cultural factors may affect assessment in various ways. Language differences, differing religious and spiritual beliefs, the alienation or timidity of members of ethnic groups when being assessed by clinicians of the European American culture—all these factors can play a role. For example, clinicians who encounter clients claiming to be surrounded by spirits might view this belief as a sign of schizophrenia. Yet in Puerto Rican cultures, such a belief is common; therefore, believing that one is surrounded by spirits should probably not be taken as a sign of schizophrenia in a Puerto Rican person (Rogler & Hollingshead, 1985).

Cultural and ethnic differences in psychopathology must be examined more closely. Unfortunately, the cultural and ethnic biases that can creep into clinical assessment do not necessarily yield to efforts to compensate for them. There is no simple answer. The DSM-5's emphasis on cultural factors in the discussion of every category of disorder may well sensitize clinicians to the issue, a necessary first step. When practitioners were surveyed, they overwhelmingly reported taking culture into account in their clinical work (Lopez, 1994), so it appears that the problem, if not the solution, is clearly in focus.

Strategies for Avoiding Cultural Bias in Assessment

Clinicians can—and do—use various methods to minimize the negative effects of cultural biases when assessing patients. Perhaps the place to begin is with graduate training programs. Lopez (2002) has noted three important issues that should be taught to graduate students in clinical psychology programs. First, students must learn about basic issues in assessment, such as reliability and validity. Second, students must become informed about the specific ways in which culture or ethnicity may impact assessment rather than relying on more global stereotypes about a particular cultural or ethnic group. Third, students must consider that culture or ethnicity may not impact assessment in every individual case.

Assessment procedures can also be modified to ensure that the person truly understands the requirements of the task. For example, suppose that a Native American child performed poorly on a test measuring psychomotor speed. The examiner's hunch is that the child did not understand the importance of working quickly and was overly concerned with accuracy instead. The test could be administered again after a more thorough explanation of the importance of working quickly without worrying about mistakes. If the child's performance improves, the examiner has gained an important understanding of the child's test-taking strategy and avoids diagnosing psychomotor speed deficits.

Finally, when the examiner and client have different ethnic backgrounds, the examiner may need to make an extra effort to establish a rapport that will result in the person's best performance. For example, when testing a shy Hispanic preschooler, one of the authors was unable to obtain a verbal response to test questions. However, the boy was overheard talking in an animated and articulate manner to his mother in the waiting room, leading to a judgment that the test results did not represent a valid assessment of the child's language skills. When testing was repeated in the child's home with his mother present, advanced verbal abilities were observed.

As Lopez (1994) points out, however, "the distance between cultural responsiveness and cultural stereotyping can be short" (p. 123). To minimize such problems, clinicians are encouraged to be particularly tentative about drawing conclusions regarding patients from different cultural and ethnic backgrounds. Rather, they are advised to make hypotheses about the influence of culture on a particular client, entertain alternative hypotheses, and then test those hypotheses.

Cultural differences can lead to different results on an aptitude or IQ test. For example, Native American children may lack interest in the individualistic, competitive nature of IQ tests because of the cooperative, group-oriented values instilled by their culture. (© Gabe Palmer/Alamy Limited.)

Training in cultural awareness is truly important, as a clinician's biases can influence diagnosis. As an example, schizophrenia is often overdiagnosed among African Americans, leading to high dosages of antipsychotic medications and too many hospitalizations (Alarcón et al., 2009). One way to combat these biases is to use structured diagnostic interviews, like the SCID described above. When clinicians use structured interviews, they are less likely to overdiagnose minority patients (Garb, 2005).

Summary

- In gathering diagnosis and assessment information, clinicians and researchers must be concerned with both reliability and validity. Reliability refers to whether measurements are consistent and replicable; validity, to whether assessments are tapping into what they are meant to measure. Assessment procedures vary greatly in their reliability and validity. Certain diagnostic categories are more reliable than others.

Diagnosis

- Diagnosis is the process of assessing whether a person meets criteria for a mental disorder. Having an agreed-on diagnostic system allows clinicians to communicate effectively with each other and facilitates the search for causes and treatments. Clinically, diagnosis provides the foundation for treatment planning.
- *The Diagnostic and Statistical Manual of Mental Disorders* (DSM), published by the American Psychiatric Association, is an official diagnostic system widely used by mental health professionals. The last edition of the manual, referred to as DSM-IV–TR, was published in 2000, and the publication of DSM-5 is expected in 2013.
- Reliability of diagnosis has been improved dramatically by including specific criteria for each diagnosis. Criticisms of the DSM include the proliferation of diagnoses that are often related to the same risk factors and tend to co-occur; the fact that reliability in practice may be lower than that achieved in research studies; and the ongoing need to validate diagnoses against etiology, course, and treatment. Most researchers and clinicians, though, recognize that the DSM is an enormous advance compared to historical systems.
- Some critics of the DSM argue against diagnosis in general. They point out that diagnostic classifications may ignore important information. Although many worry that diagnostic labels will increase stigma, there is some data that a diagnosis can reduce stigma by providing an explanation for worrisome behavior.

Assessment

- Clinicians rely on several modes of psychological and neurobiological assessment in trying to find out how best to describe an individual, search for the reasons the person is troubled, arrive at an accurate diagnosis, and design effective treatments. The best assessment involves multiple types of methods.
- Psychological assessments include clinical interviews, assessments of stress, psychological tests, and behavioral and cognitive assessments.
- Clinical interviews are structured or relatively unstructured conversations in which the clinician probes the patient for information about his or her problems. Assessing stress is key to the field of psychopathology. A number of useful methods for assessing stress have been developed, including the LEDS.
- Psychological tests are standardized procedures designed to assess personality or measure performance. Personality assessments range from empirically derived self-report questionnaires, such as the Minnesota Multiphasic Personality Inventory, to projective tests in which the patient interprets ambiguous stimuli, such as the Rorschach test. Intelligence tests, such as the Wechsler Adult Intelligence Scale, evaluate a person's intellectual ability and predict how well he or she will perform academically.
- Behavioral and cognitive assessment is concerned with how people act, feel, and think in particular situations. Approaches include direct observation of behavior, interviews, and self-report measures that are situational in their focus.
- Neurobiological assessments include brain-imaging techniques, such as fMRI, that enable clinicians and researchers to see various structures and access functions of the living brain; neurochemical assays that allow clinicians to make inferences about levels of neurotransmitters; neuropsychological tests, such as the Luria-Nebraska battery, that seek to identify brain defects based on variations in responses to psychological tests; and psychophysiological measurements, such as heart rate and electrodermal responding, that are associated with certain psychological events or characteristics.
- Cultural and ethnic factors play a role in clinical assessment. Assessment techniques developed on the basis of research with Caucasian populations may be inaccurate when used with clients of differing ethnic or cultural backgrounds, for example. Clinicians can have biases when evaluating ethnic minority patients, which can lead to minimizing or exaggerating a patient's psychopathology. Clinicians use various methods to guard against the negative effects of cultural biases in assessment.

Answers to Check Your Knowledge Questions

3.1 1. b; 2. b, c, d, a
3.2 1. high comorbidity, many different diagnoses are related to the same causes, symptoms of many different diagnoses respond to the same treatments; 2. any three of the following: etiology, course, social functioning, treatment

3.3 1. F; 2. T; 3. T; 4. T; 5. T; 6. F
3.4 1. F; 2. T; 3. T; 4. F

Key Terms

alternate-form reliability
behavioral assessment
BOLD
categorical classification
clinical interview
comorbidity
concurrent validity
construct validity
content validity
criterion validity
CT or CAT scan
Diagnostic and Statistical Manual of Mental Disorders
diagnosis

dimensional diagnostic system
ecological momentary assessment (EMA)
electrocardiogram (EKG)
electrodermal responding
electroencephalogram (EEG)
functional magnetic resonance imaging (fMRI)
intelligence test
internal consistency reliability
interrater reliability
magnetic resonance imaging (MRI)
metabolite

Minnesota Multiphasic Personality Inventory (MMPI)
multiaxial classification system
neurologist
neuropsychological tests
neuropsychologist
personality inventory
PET scan
predictive validity
projective hypothesis
projective test
psychological tests
psychophysiology

reactivity
reliability
Rorschach Inkblot Test
self-monitoring
standardization
stress
structured interview
test–retest reliability
Thematic Apperception Test (TAT)
validity

4 Research Methods in Psychopathology

1. Be able to define science and the scientific method.

2. Be able to describe the advantages and disadvantages of case studies, correlational designs, and experimental designs.

3. Be able to identify common types of correlational and experimental designs.

4. Be able to explain the standards and issues in conducting psychotherapy outcome research.

5. Be able to describe the basic steps in conducting a meta-analysis.

OUR ABILITY TO CONCEPTUALIZE and treat mental illness has improved vastly over the past 50 years. Nonetheless, there are still important unanswered questions about the causes and treatments of psychological disorders. Because there are unanswered questions, it is important to pursue new discoveries using scientific research methods. This chapter discusses the methods used in psychopathology research.

Science and Scientific Methods

The term *science* comes from the Latin *scire*, "to know." At its core, science is a way of knowing. More formally, science is the systematic pursuit of knowledge through observation. Science involves forming a theory and then systematically gathering data to test the theory.

A **theory** is a set of propositions meant to explain a class of observations. Usually, the goal of scientific theories is to understand cause–effect relationships. A theory permits the generation of more specific **hypotheses**—expectations about what should occur if a theory is true. For example, if the classical conditioning theory of phobias is valid, people with phobias should be more likely than those in the general population to have had traumatic experiences with the situations they fear, such as flying. By collecting such data, you could test this hypothesis.

People sometimes assume that a scientist formulates a theory by simply considering data that were previously collected and then deciding, in a rather straightforward fashion, that one way of thinking about the data is the most useful. Although some theory building follows this course, not all does. Theory building often involves creativity—a theory sometimes seems to leap into the scientist's head in a wonderful moment of insight. New ideas suddenly occur, and connections that were overlooked before are grasped. Formerly obscure observations might make a new kind of sense within the framework of the new theory.

What makes a good theory? A scientific approach requires that ideas be stated clearly and precisely. This is needed for scientific claims to be exposed to systematic tests that could negate the scientist's expectations. That is, regardless of how plausible a theory seems, it must be subject to disproof. Science proceeds by disproving theories, never by "proving theories." Because of this, it is not enough to assert that traumatic experiences during childhood cause psychological maladjustment in adulthood. This is no more than a possibility. According to a scientific point of view, a hypothesis must be amenable to systematic testing that could show it to be false. That is, the focus of testing is on disproving rather than proving a theory.

A set of principles must be considered in testing a theory. Each scientific observation must be replicable. Each facet of a study must be carefully defined so that findings can be replicated. Much of this depends on using assessments with strong reliability and validity, as discussed in Chapter 3. Beyond choosing measures carefully, though, researchers in psychopathology choose among a set of different types of research designs. In this chapter, we discuss the pros and cons of some common types of research designs.

It is worth noting at the outset that many aspects of research involve ethical issues. For example, researchers must consider whether participants are fully informed, whether any coercion is involved in a study, and what the long-term implications of findings are. Ethical issues in the conduct of research are covered in Chapter 16.

As we review the theories and evidence about the causes of and treatments for abnormal behavior, we will often encounter complexities and shortcomings in the research literature. Even if we knew all the variables controlling behavior—and no one would claim that we do—our ability to predict would be limited by many unexpected and uncontrollable factors that are likely to affect a person over a period of time. People do not behave in a social vacuum. Research participants and therapy clients live moment-to-moment in exquisitely complex interaction with others who themselves are affected on a moment-to-moment basis by hundreds of factors that are impossible to anticipate. We are not scientific nihilists; rather, we want to counsel humility, even awe, in an enterprise that tries to understand how things go awry with the human condition. Consequently, simple cause–effect statements are exceedingly difficult to construct with confidence.

Check Your Knowledge 4.1 (Answers are at the end of the chapter.)

True or false?
1. A good theory can be proven.
2. Researchers always build a theory by examining data, making rational assumptions, and then carefully testing the next small step—intuition is rarely involved.

3. Hypotheses are broader and more abstract than a theory is.

Approaches to Research on Psychopathology

In this section we describe the most common research methods in the study of abnormal behavior: the case study, correlational methods, and experimental methods. These methods will be seen in the studies described throughout this book, and we will describe some of the typical ways these different research methods are used in psychopathology research. Table 4.1 provide a summary of the strengths and weaknesses of each.

The Case Study

The **case study**, perhaps the most familiar method of observing human behavior, involves recording detailed information about one person at a time. The clinical cases described in the last chapter are examples of case studies. A comprehensive case study would cover developmental milestones, family history, medical history, educational background, jobs held, marital history, social adjustment, personality, environment and experiences in therapy across the life course.

Table 4.1 Research Methods in Psychopathology

Method	Description	Evaluation
Case study	Collection of detailed biographical information	Excellent source of hypotheses Can provide information about novel cases or procedures Can disconfirm a relationship that was believed to be universal Cannot provide causal evidence because cannot rule out alternative hypotheses May be biased by observer's theoretical viewpoint
Correlation	Study of the relationship between two or more variables; measured as they exist in nature	Widely used because we cannot manipulate many risk variables (such as personality, trauma, or genes) or diagnoses in psychopathology research with humans Often used by epidemiologists to study the incidence, prevalence, and risk factors of disorders in a representative sample Often used in behavioral genetics research to study the heritability of different mental disorders Cannot determine causality because of the directionality and third-variable problems
Experiment	Includes a manipulated independent variable, a dependent variable, preferably at least one control group, and random assignment	Most powerful method for determining causal relationships Often used in studies of treatment Also used in analogue studies of the risk factors for mental illness Single-case experimental designs also common but can have limited external validity

Case studies lack the control and objectivity of other research methods. That is, the validity of the information gathered in a case study is sometimes questionable. The objectivity of case studies is limited because the clinician's paradigm will shape the kinds of information reported in a case study. To take one example, case studies by psychodynamic clinicians typically contain more information about the client's early childhood and parental conflicts than do reports by behavioral clinicians.

Despite their relative lack of control, case studies still play an important role in the study of abnormal behavior. Specifically, the case study can be used:

1. To provide a rich description of a clinical phenomenon
2. To disprove an allegedly universal hypothesis
3. To generate hypotheses that can be tested through controlled research

We discuss each of these uses next.

The Case Study as a Rich Description Because it focuses on a single person, the case study can include much more detail than other research methods typically do. This is particularly helpful when a report covers a rare clinical phenomenon. Another typical use is to provide a detailed description of how a new intervention works. See Focus on Discovery 4.1 for an example of the level of detail that can be gathered with a case study.

The Case Study Can Disprove but Not Prove a Hypothesis Case histories can provide examples that contradict an assumed universal relationship. Consider, for example, the proposition that depressive episodes are always preceded by life stress. Finding even a single case of non-stress-related depression would negate the theory.

Even though case studies can disprove a hypothesis, they do not provide good evidence in support of a particular theory because they do not provide a way to rule out alternative hypotheses. To illustrate this problem, consider the sleep/wake intervention described in Focus on Discovery 4.1. Although it would be tempting to conclude that the therapy is effective, such a conclusion cannot be drawn legitimately because other factors could have produced the change. A stressful situation in the client's life may have resolved, or the client may have adopted better coping skills during the time period of the intervention. Thus, several plausible rival hypotheses could account for the clinical improvement. The data yielded by the case study do not allow us to determine the true cause of the change.

Using the Case Study to Generate Hypotheses Although the case study may not provide valid support for hypotheses, it does help generate hypotheses about causes and treatments for disorders. As they hear the life histories of many different clients, clinicians may notice patterns and then formulate important hypotheses that they could not have formed otherwise. For example, in his clinical work, Kanner (1943) noticed that some disturbed children showed a similar constellation of symptoms, including failure to develop language and extreme isolation from other people. He therefore proposed a new diagnosis—infantile autism—that was subsequently confirmed by larger-scale research and adopted into the DSM (see p. 432).

The Correlational Method

A great deal of psychopathology research relies on the **correlational method**. Correlational studies address questions of the form "Do variable *X* and variable *Y* vary together (co-relate)?" In correlational research, variables are measured as they exist in nature. This is distinct from experimental research (discussed on pp. 115), in which the researcher manipulates variables.

To illustrate the difference, consider that the role of stress in hypertension (high blood pressure) can be assessed with either a correlational or an experimental design. In a correlational study, we might measure stress levels by interviewing people about their recent stressful experiences. Stress would then be correlated with blood pressure measurements collected from these same people. In an experimental study, in contrast, the experimenter might create stress in the laboratory; for example, some participants might be asked to give a speech to an audience about the aspect of their personal appearance that they find least appealing (see Figure 4.1). The key difference between these methods is whether or not a variable is manipulated. Psychopathologists will rely on correlational methods when there are ethical reasons not to manipulate a variable; for example, no researcher would try to manipulate genes, trauma, severe stressors, or neurobiological deficits in humans.

Although the information yielded by a case study does not fare well as a source of evidence, it is an important source of hypotheses. (Greg Smith/Cortis Images.)

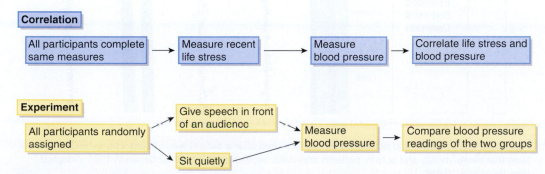

Figure 4.1 Correlational versus experimental studies.

FOCUS ON DISCOVERY 4.1

An Example of the Advantages and Disadvantages of Case Studies

Bipolar disorder, defined by episodes of mania, is one of the most severe of psychological illnesses. Manic episodes are defined by extreme happiness or anger, along with increased confidence, energy, talkativeness, goal-directed behavior, and decreased need for sleep. Of particular concern, when people are manic they may not be aware of potential dangers, and so they are likely to engage in reckless behaviors, such as driving too fast, spending too much money, or being more sexual. Beyond the manic episodes, depressive episodes are also common for people with this disorder. The manic and the depressive symptoms both take a toll on jobs, relationships, and self-esteem.

Although bipolar disorder is believed to be inherited, sleep loss can trigger episodic symptoms of bipolar disorder (Colombo, Benedetti, Barbini, et al., 1999). Wehr and his colleagues (1998) noted that electric lights might disrupt our natural sleep schedules and that this might be of particular concern for people with this disorder. Given this, they theorized that a more natural light–dark cycle that mirrored the natural rhythm of the sun might help protect sleep and thereby reduce symptoms in bipolar disorder. To test the influence of natural light–dark cycles on the course of bipolar disorder, Wehr's group tried a unique treatment idea: they asked a person with bipolar disorder to extend his hours of bedrest.

At the time the case study began, the patient was a 51-year-old married man who had worked as a chief engineer in a technology firm. He had always had a great deal of energy and drive. He reported that his mother had a history of depression. The patient developed depression in 1990 and was treated with two antidepressants. As is relatively common for people diagnosed with bipolar disorder (Ghaemi & Goodwin, 2003), the antidepressants triggered mild manic symptoms. In his case, though, the symptoms of depression and mania continued for more than 2 years, despite the addition of mood-stabilizing medications such as lithium and divalproex. Antidepressants were discontinued, but then he became depressed. When a new antidepressant

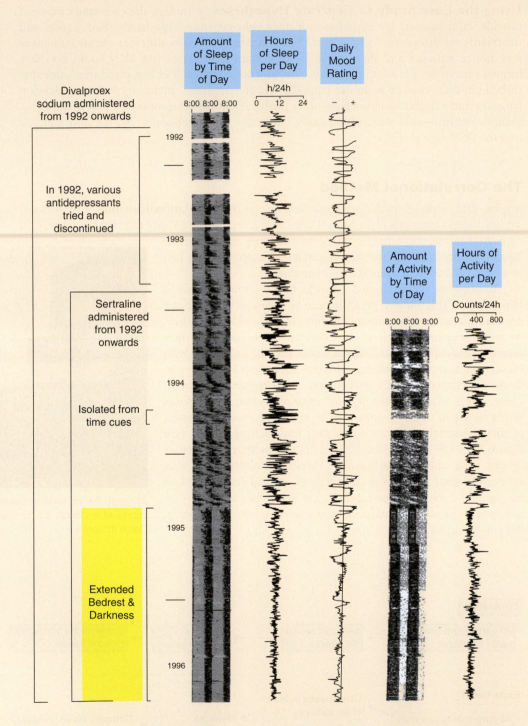

Figure 4.2 Sleep, mood, and activity patterns before and after a patient was treated with extended bedrest. Note that sleep, mood, and activity patterns improved once extended bedrest began in 1995. Adapted from Wehr et al. (1998).

was started, he developed manic symptoms again. Over a period of several years, he frequently shifted between depression and mania. During his manic periods, he was overly active, slept only 3–4 hours, and woke up before dawn. When he was depressed, he would spend long hours of the day inactive, then sleep for 10 or 12 hours, waking up late in the morning or even during the afternoon.

After several years of monitoring the client's symptoms and trying different medications, Wehr and his colleagues began the novel sleep/wake intervention in May 1995. For the first 3 months, he slept in a bedroom on a research ward where lights could be carefully controlled. The room was sealed to protect against accidental light exposure. During the dark period, he was asked not to take part in any activities and even to avoid using the radio, TV, or telephone. During the first part of the intervention, he was asked to spend 14 hours resting in the dark each night. Over the next 18 months, the dark period was gradually reduced to 10 hours. Medications were kept stable throughout the sleep/wake intervention phase.

As shown in Figure 4.2, the number of hours per night that the client slept varied a good deal up until 1995, when the intervention began. At that point, the number of hours of sleep per night became much more routine. Also at that time, the amount of daily activity began to vary much less; the patient no longer displayed days of extreme inactivity or days of extreme hyperactivity. Most importantly, almost all of his mood ratings after the sleep/wake intervention began were in a neutral range,

neither depressed nor manic. Hence the increased bedrest appeared to be an effective way to bolster the effects of medication.

Although the findings were encouraging, this case study leaves many questions unanswered. These include whether the critical ingredient in the intervention is time spent sleeping, time spent resting, or just a focus on calmer routines. It is also possible that something other than sleep/wake cycles changed for this patient during the period of the intervention, such that the symptom reductions were unrelated to sleep/wake. Perhaps most importantly, case studies can never reveal whether a treatment will work well for other patients.

Fortunately, several researchers have extended these findings. In other case studies (Wirz-Justice, Quinto, Cajochen, et al., 1999) and uncontrolled studies (Barbini, Benedetti, Colombo, et al., 2005), researchers have achieved good results with encouraging people with bipolar disorder to extend their time spent in bed. Other researchers have tried to help people with bipolar disorder to create more stable patterns of daily activities, along with improving sleep routines (Frank, 2005; Shen, Sylvia, Alloy, et al., 2008; Totterdell & Kellett, 2008). Hence this early case report helped to generate interest in whether treatments focused on sleep could enhance the effects of medication in bipolar disorder. In short, case studies provide a way to demonstrate new and interesting treatments. Case studies, though, cannot address whether treatment is the sole cause of the change, nor can they address whether findings can be applied to other people.

Numerous examples of **correlation** can be drawn from mental health research. For example, depression tends to correlate with anxiety; people who feel depressed tend to report feeling anxious. It is worth highlighting that comparisons of people with and without a diagnosis can be correlational as well. See Table 4.2 for a description of how such data might be coded. For example, two diagnostic groups may be compared to see how much stress was experienced before the onset of their disorders. In other words, questions are asked about relationships between a given diagnosis and some other variable; for example, "Is schizophrenia related to social class?" or "Are anxiety disorders related to neurotransmitter function?"

In the next sections, we discuss how to measure the relationship (correlation) between two variables, how to test whether the relationship is statistically and clinically significant, and some issues involved in determining whether variables are causally related. Then we discuss two specific types of research that tend to use correlational designs: epidemiology as well as behavior and molecular genetics.

Measuring Correlation The first step in determining a correlation is to obtain pairs of observations of the two variables in question. One example would be the height and weight of each participant. Another example would be the intelligence of mothers and daughters. Once such pairs of measurements are obtained, the strength of the relationship between the paired observations can be computed to determine the **correlation coefficient**, denoted by the symbol r. This statistic may take any value between −1.00 and +1.00, and it measures both the magnitude and the direction of a relationship. The higher the absolute value of r, the stronger the relationship between the two variables. That is, an r of either +1.00 or −1.00 indicates the strongest possible, or perfect, relationship, whereas an r of .00 indicates that the variables are unrelated. If the sign of r is positive, the two variables are said to be positively related; in other words, as the values for variable X increase, those for variable Y also tend to increase. Table 4.3 shows data for a correlation of +.88 between height and weight, indicating a very strong positive relationship; as height increases, so does weight. Conversely, when the sign of r is negative,

Table 4.2 Data for a Correlational Study with Diagnosis

Participant	Diagnosis	Stress Score
1	1	65
2	1	72
3	0	40
4	1	86
5	0	72
6	0	21
7	1	65
8	0	40
9	1	37
10	0	28

Note: Diagnosis—having an anxiety disorder or not, with having an anxiety disorder designated as 1 and not as 0—is correlated with an assessment of recent life stress on a 0–100 scale. Higher scores indicate greater recent stress. To make the point clearly, we present a smaller sample of cases than would be used in an actual research study. Notice that diagnosis is associated with recent life stress. Patients with an anxiety disorder tend to have higher stress scores than people without an anxiety disorder. In this example, the correlation between stress and anxiety scores = +.60.

Table 4.3 Data for Determining a Correlation

	Height	Weight in Pounds
John	5'10"	170
Asher	5'10"	140
Eve	5'4"	112
Gail	5'3"	105
Jerry	5'10"	177
Gayla	5'2"	100
Steve	5'8"	145
Margy	5'5"	128
Gert	5'6"	143
Sean	5'10"	140
Kathleen	5'4"	116

Note: For this data set, the *r* of height and weight = +.88.

variables are said to be negatively related; as scores on one variable increase, those for the other tend to decrease. For example, the number of hours spent watching television is negatively correlated with grade point average.

One way to think about the strength of a correlation is to plot the two variables. In Figure 4.3, each point represents the scores for a given person on variable *X* and variable *Y*. In a perfect correlation, all the points fall on a straight line; if we know the value of only one of the variables for a person, we can know the value of the other variable. Similarly, when the correlation is relatively large, there is only a small degree of scatter about the line of perfect correlation. The values tend to scatter increasingly far from the line as the correlations become lower. When the correlation reaches .00, knowledge of a person's score on one variable tells us nothing about his or her score on the other.

Statistical and Clinical Significance Thus far we have established that the magnitude of a correlation coefficient tells us the strength of a relationship between two variables. But scientists use **statistical significance** for a more rigorous test of the importance of a relationship. (Significance is considered with many different statistics. Here we focus on correlation coefficients, but significance is also relevant when we describe experiments below.) A statistically significant correlation is unlikely to have occurred by chance. A nonsignificant correlation may have occurred by chance, so it does not provide evidence for an important relationship. What do scientists mean by chance? Imagine that a researcher conducted the same study again and again. You would not expect to see exactly the same results every time. For example, there might be differences in who signed up for the study that would influence the pattern of findings. This random variation, or chance, must be considered in evaluating the findings of any study. When a correlation is not statistically significant, it is highly likely that no significant relationship will be observed if the study is repeated.

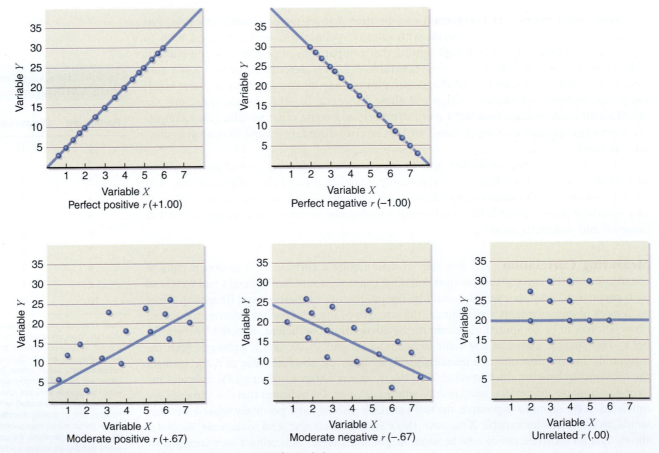

Figure 4.3 Scatter diagrams showing various degrees of correlation.

A statistical finding is usually considered significant if the probability that it is a chance finding is 5 or less in 100. This level of significance is called the alpha level, commonly written as $p < .05$ (the p stands for probability). In general, as the absolute size of the correlation coefficient increases, the result is more likely to be statistically significant. For example, a correlation of .80 is more likely than a correlation of .40 to be significant.

Statistical significance is influenced not only by the size of the relationship between variables but also by the number of participants in a study. The more people studied, the smaller the correlation needs to be to reach statistical significance. For example, a correlation of $r = .30$ is statistically significant when the number of observations is large—say, 300—but is not significant if only 20 observations were made. Thus, if the alcohol consumption of 30 men was studied and the correlation between depression and drinking was found to be .32, the correlation would not be statistically significant. The same correlation, however, would be significant if 300 men were studied.

Beyond statistical significance, it is important to consider **clinical significance.** Clinical significance is defined by whether a relationship between variables is large enough to matter. In a survey as large as the U.S. Census, almost every correlation you could conceive of would be statistically significant. Because of this issue, researchers also attend to whether a correlation is large enough to be of clinical significance. For example, one might want to see that a risk factor has a moderately strong relationship with the severity of symptoms. Clinical significance is also considered with statistics other than correlations. For a treatment effect to be considered clinically significant, a researcher might want to see that symptoms in the active treatment condition were decreased by 50 percent or that patients appeared comparable to those without disorder at the end of treatment. In other words, researchers should evaluate not only whether an effect is statistically significant but also whether the effect is large enough to be meaningful in predicting or treating a clinical disorder (Jacobson, Roberts, Berns, et al., 1999).

Problems of Causality   Even though it is commonly used, the correlational method has a critical drawback: it does not allow determination of cause–effect relationships. A large correlation between two variables tells us only that they are related to each other, but we do not know if either variable is the cause of the other. For example, a correlation has been found between the diagnosis of schizophrenia and social class; lower-class people are diagnosed with schizophrenia more often than middle- and upper-class people are. One possible explanation is that the stress of living in poverty could cause an increase in the prevalence of schizophrenia. But a second hypothesis has been supported. It may be that the disorganized behavior patterns of persons with schizophrenia cause them to perform poorly in their occupational endeavors and thus to become impoverished.

The **directionality problem** is present in most correlational research designs—hence the often-cited dictum "correlation does not imply causation." One way of overcoming the directionality problem is based on the idea that causes must precede effects. In a **longitudinal design,** the researcher tests whether causes are present before a disorder has developed. This is in contrast to a **cross-sectional design,** in which the causes and effects are measured at the same point in time. A classic longitudinal design to study the development of schizophrenia, for example, would involve selecting a large sample of babies, measuring risk variables repeatedly throughout development, and following the sample for 45 years to determine who develops schizophrenia. But such a method would be prohibitively expensive, for only about 1 person in 100 eventually develops schizophrenia. The yield of data from such a longitudinal study would be small indeed.

The **high-risk method** overcomes this problem; with this approach, only people with above-average risk of developing schizophrenia would be studied. For example, several research programs involve studying people who have a parent diagnosed with schizophrenia (having a parent with schizophrenia increases a person's risk for developing schizophrenia). The high-risk method is also used to study several other disorders, and we will examine these findings in subsequent chapters.

Even if a high-risk study identifies a variable that precedes schizophrenia, a researcher still faces the **third-variable problem:** a third factor may have produced the correlation. Such factors are often labeled as *confounds.* Consider the following example, which points out an obvious third variable:

In some epidemiological research, interviewers go door-to-door to conduct interviews. (© Pixsooz/Shutterstock.)

One regularly finds a high positive correlation between the number of churches in a city and the number of crimes committed in that city. That is, the more churches a city has, the more crimes are committed in it. Does this mean that religion fosters crime, or does it mean that crime fosters religion? It means neither. The relationship is due to a particular third variable—population. The higher the population of a particular community, the greater . . . the number of churches and . . . the frequency of criminal activity. (Neale & Liebert, 1986, p. 109)

Psychopathology research offers numerous examples of third variables. Biochemical differences between people with and without schizophrenia are often reported. These differences could reflect the influence of medications used for schizophrenia or even dietary differences between groups; the differences might not reveal anything about the nature of schizophrenia. Are there ways to resolve the third-variable problem? Although some strategies can help reduce it, the solutions are only partially satisfactory. Take the example of diet as a potential confound in biochemical differences in schizophrenia. Researchers can try to control for diet in statistical analyses, but they may not measure the most important aspects of diet. It is not feasible to measure every possible confound. Because of the third-variable problem, causal inferences cannot be made from correlational data.

One Example of Correlational Research: Epidemiological Research

Epidemiology is the study of the distribution of disorders in a population. That is, data are gathered about the rates of a disorder and its correlates in a large sample. Epidemiological research focuses on three features of a disorder:

1. **Prevalence.** The proportion of people with the disorder either currently or during their lifetime
2. **Incidence.** The proportion of people who develop *new* cases of the disorder in some period, usually a year
3. **Risk factors.** Variables that are related to the likelihood of developing the disorder

Epidemiological studies of risk factors are usually correlational studies because they examine how variables relate to each other without manipulating any of the variables.

Epidemiological studies are designed to be *representative* of the population being studied—researchers test a group of people who match the population on key characteristics, like gender, economic status, and ethnicity. Unfortunately, much of mental health research does not follow these principles but rather draws on samples that are not representative. For example, many studies use undergraduate samples. Undergraduates, though, are likely to be wealthier and more educated than the general population. If we only studied undergraduates with anxiety disorders, we could end up concluding that people with anxiety disorders are above average in intelligence. Other studies use samples drawn from treatment centers. But people who seek treatment may be those with the more severe forms of disorders. For example, estimates of suicide rates for a given disorder are much higher when measured in hospitalized samples as compared to rates in representative community samples. These types of bias can skew our perceptions of factors related to mental disorders. Epidemiological studies, then, are needed to carefully identify risk variables and outcomes for disorders.

The National Comorbidity Survey–Replication is an example of one large-scale national survey that used structured interviews to collect information on the prevalence of several diagnoses (Kessler, Berglund, Demler, et al., 2005). Table 4.4 shows some data from this study. The table presents lifetime prevalence rates—the proportion of people who experienced a disorder during their lifetime. From the table, we can see that major depression, alcoholism, and anxiety disorders are very common—so common, in fact, that as many as half (46.4 percent) of the people in the United States describe meeting criteria for a mental disorder at some point during their lives. Knowing that mental disorders will strike one out of every two people should help reduce stigma. People who experience the disorders may take comfort in knowing that so many other people struggle with similar issues.

Table 4.4 Lifetime Prevalence Rates of Selected Diagnoses

Disorder	Male	Female	Total
Major depressive disorder	13.2	20.2	16.6
Bipolar I or II disorder	na	na	3.9
Dysthymia	1.8	3.1	2.5
Panic disorder	3.1	6.2	4.7
Social anxiety disorder	11.1	13.0	12.1
Specific phobia	8.9	15.8	12.5
Generalized anxiety disorder	na	na	5.7
Alcohol abuse	19.6	7.5	13.2
Drug abuse	11.6	4.8	7.9

Source: From data collected in the National Comorbidity Survey—Replication (Kessler et al., 2005).

Epidemiological research has shown that mood disorders, anxiety disorders, and substance abuse are extremely common. (© nemke/Shutterstock.)

Knowledge about risk factors may provide clues to the causes of disorders. For example, depression is about twice as common in women as in men. Thus, gender is a risk factor for depression. In Chapter 5, we will review theories about this gender difference. The results of epidemiological research may inform us about risk factors (like gender and social class) that can be more thoroughly investigated using other research methods.

Another Example of Correlational Research: Behavior and Molecular Genetics

Research on behavior genetics has relied on three basic methods to uncover whether a genetic predisposition for psychopathology is inherited—comparison of members of a family, comparison of pairs of twins, and investigation of adoptees. In each case, researchers are interested in whether relatives demonstrate similarity (correlations) in their patterns of disorder. Research on molecular genetics is designed to evaluate whether specific genes contribute to the presence of a disorder.

The **family method** can be used to study a genetic predisposition among members of a family because the average number of genes shared by two blood relatives is known. Children receive a random sample of half their genes from one parent and half from the other, so on average siblings as well as parents and their children share 50 percent of their genes. People who share 50 percent of their genes with a given person are called first-degree relatives of that person. Relatives who are not as closely related share fewer genes. For example, nephews and nieces share 25 percent of the genetic makeup of an uncle and are called second-degree relatives. If a predisposition for a mental disorder can be inherited, a study of the family should reveal a relationship between the proportion of shared genes and the *concordance* of the disorder in relatives (that is, whether the relatives are matched on presence or absence of a disorder).

The starting point in such investigations is the collection of a sample of persons with the diagnosis in question. These people are referred to as **index cases** or **probands.** Then relatives are studied to determine the frequency with which the same diagnosis might be applied to them. If a genetic predisposition to the disorder being studied is present, first-degree relatives of the index cases should have the disorder at a rate higher than that found in the general population. This is the case with schizophrenia: about 10 percent of the first-degree relatives of index cases with schizophrenia can be diagnosed as having this disorder, compared with about 1 percent of the general population.

Although the methodology of family studies is clear, the data they yield are not always easy to interpret. For example, children of parents with agoraphobia—people suffering from a fear of being in places from which it would be hard to escape if they were to become highly anxious—are themselves more likely than average to have agoraphobia. Does this mean that a predisposition for this anxiety disorder is genetically transmitted? Not necessarily. The greater number of family members with agoraphobia could reflect the child-rearing practices and modeling of the phobic parents. In other words, family studies show that agoraphobia runs in families but not necessarily that a genetic predisposition is involved.

In the **twin method** both **monozygotic (MZ) twins** and **dizygotic (DZ) twins** are compared. MZ, or identical, twins develop from a single fertilized egg and are genetically the same. DZ, or fraternal, pairs develop from separate eggs and are on average 50 percent alike genetically, no more alike than are any two siblings. MZ twins are always of the same sex, but DZ twins can be either the same sex or opposite in sex. Twin studies begin with diagnosed cases and then search for the presence of the disorder in the other twin. When the twins are similar diagnostically, they are said to be concordant. To the extent that a predisposition for a mental disorder can be inherited, **concordance** for the disorder should be greater in genetically identical MZ pairs than in DZ pairs. When the MZ concordance rate is higher than the DZ rate, the characteristic being studied is said to be heritable. We will see in later chapters that the concordance for many forms of psychopathology is higher in MZ twins than in DZ twins.

The **adoptees method** studies children who were adopted and reared completely apart from their biological parents. Though infrequent, findings from this method are more clear-cut because the child is not raised by the parent with a disorder. If a high frequency of agoraphobia was found in children reared apart from their parents who also had agoraphobia, we would have convincing support for the heritability of the disorder. In another adoptee method called **cross-fostering**, children are adopted and reared completely apart from their biological parents. In this case, however, the adoptive parent has a particular disorder, not the biological parent. The adoptee method is also used to examine gene–environment interactions. For example, one study found that adoptees who had a biological parent with antisocial personality disorder (APD) and were raised in an unhealthy adoptive family (e.g., parental conflict, abuse, alcohol/drugs in the adoptive family) were more likely to develop APD than two other groups of adoptees: (1) adoptees who had a biological parent with APD but were raised in a healthy family and (2) adoptees who had no biological parent with APD but were raised in an unhealthy adoptive family (Cadoret, Yates, Troughton, et al., 1995). Thus, genes (APD in a biological parent) and environment (unhealthy adoptive family) worked together to increase the risk for developing antisocial personality disorder.

Molecular genetics methods are designed to identify specific genes or combinations of genes that may be associated with the presence of a particular disorder in a large population of people. One method used in molecular genetics is called an **association study**. In these studies, researchers examine the relationship between a specific allele (i.e., different forms of the same gene; see Chapter 2) and a trait or behavior in the population. Because the researchers are measuring a specific allele rather than the general chromosome location, association studies can be precise. Association studies have become much more common as technologies for measuring alleles have become more affordable. In Chapter 14, we will describe a particular allele called APOE-4 that is related to later-onset Alzheimer's disease. Not all people with Alzheimer's have this allele, and not all people who have APOE-4 develop Alzheimer's. Still, there is a strong association between this allele and Alzheimer's disease (Williams, 2003).

A special type of association research called **genome-wide association studies** (**GWAS**, pronounced *gee-waas*) examines the entire genome of a large group to identify variation between people. For example, a GWAS study in schizophrenia might include hundreds (or ideally thousands) of people with schizophrenia and hundreds of people without schizophrenia (a control group). Using extremely powerful computers, researchers look at all 22,000+ genes for all of these people to isolate differences in the sequence of genes between groups. The entire genome of individuals can be obtained from a simple swab on the inside of the cheek. The saliva is then analyzed to reveal the sequence of the thousands of genes for each person. GWAS researchers are most often looking for genetic variations called mutations in the genome, such as the single nucleotide polymorphisms, or SNPs, discussed in Chapter 2. If certain SNPs are found more often in the group of people with schizophrenia, they are said to be associated with schizophrenia. We will see that SNPs have been studied in several disorders, including schizophrenia (Chapter 9), depression (Chapter 5), and autism (Chapter 13).

Quick Summary

Science is the systematic pursuit of knowledge through observation. The first step of science is to define a theory and related hypotheses. A good theory is precise and could be disproven.

The case study is an excellent way of examining the behavior of a single person in rich detail and of generating hypotheses that can be evaluated by controlled research. Sometimes the evidence disconfirms a theory; other times it illustrates a rare disorder or technique. But findings from a case study may or may not be valid—they may be biased by the observer's theories, and the patterns observed in one case may not apply to others. Furthermore, the case study cannot provide satisfactory evidence concerning cause–effect relationships because alternative hypotheses are not examined.

Correlational studies allow a researcher to gather data about variables and to see if these variables covary. No variables are manipulated; rather, the researcher assesses whether a naturally occurring relationship is large enough to appear statistically significant and clinically meaningful. Psychopathologists are forced to make heavy use of the correlational method because there

are many key variables, including diagnosis, genes, trauma, and neurobiological deficits, that they do not have the freedom to manipulate in humans. But correlational findings are clouded by third-variable and directionality problems. High-risk designs, in which people with elevated risk of developing a psychological disorder are recruited and followed over time, overcome the directionality problem.

Studies of epidemiology and behavior genetics often use correlational designs. Researchers use epidemiological studies to assess how common disorders are (incidence and prevalence) and what risk factors are associated with them. Behavior genetics research uses the family method, to see how the presence of a disorder varies by the proportion of genes shared by family members; the twin method, to see whether monozygotic twins with more shared genes are at greater risk for developing a disorder than are dizygotic twins; and the adoptees method, to help separate genetic and environmental effects. Molecular genetics research includes genome-wide association studies to identify SNPs.

Check Your Knowledge 4.2

Answer the questions.

1. Which of the following are good uses of case studies (circle all that apply)?
   a. to illustrate a rare disorder or treatment
   b. to show that a theory does not fit for everyone
   c. to prove a model
   d. to show cause and effect
2. Correlational studies involve:
   a. manipulating the independent variable
   b. manipulating the dependent variable
   c. manipulating the independent and dependent variable
   d. none of the above
3. What is the most central problem that is unique to correlational studies, regardless of how carefully a researcher designs a study?
   a. Findings are qualitative rather than statistical.
   b. It is impossible to know which variable changes first.

c. Third variables may explain a relationship observed.
   d. Findings may not generalize.
4. Incidence refers to:
   a. the number of people who will develop a disorder during their lifetime
   b. the number of people who report a disorder at the time of an interview
   c. the number of people who develop a disorder during a given time period
   d. none of the above
5. In behavior genetics studies, researchers can rule out the influence of parenting variables most carefully if they conduct studies using the:
   a. correlational method
   b. family method
   c. twin method
   d. adoptees method

The Experiment

The **experiment** is the most powerful tool for determining causal relationships. It involves the **random assignment** of participants to conditions, the manipulation of an **independent variable,** and the measurement of a **dependent variable.** We will begin with a brief overview of the basic features of an experiment. We will provide more detail on specific issues in designing experiments when we describe treatment outcome studies, the most common form of experiment in psychopathology research.

As an introduction to the basics of experimental research, consider a study of how emotional expression relates to health (Pennebaker, Kiecolt-Glaser, & Glaser, 1988). In this experiment, 50 undergraduates came to a laboratory for 4 consecutive days. On each of the 4 days, half the students wrote a short essay about a past traumatic event. They were instructed as follows:

> During each of the four writing days. I want you to write about the most traumatic and upsetting experiences of your entire life. You can write on different topics each day or on the same topic for all four days. The important thing is that you write about your deepest thoughts and feelings. Ideally, whatever you write about should deal with an event or experience that you have not talked with others about in detail.

The remaining students also came to the laboratory each day but wrote essays describing topics like their daily activities, a recent social event, the shoes they were wearing, and their plans for the rest of the day.

Information about how often the participants used the university health center was available for the 15-week period before the study began and for the 6 weeks after it had begun. Figure 4.4 shows these data. Members of the two groups had visited the health center about equally before the experiment. After writing the essays, however, the number of visits declined for students who wrote about their traumatic experiences and increased for the remaining students. (This increase may have been due to seasonal variation in rates of visits to the health center. The second measure of number of visits was taken in February, just before midterm exams.) From these data the investigators concluded that expressing emotions has a beneficial effect on health. The idea that daily writing (journaling) might help people cope with difficult experiences and emotions has become popular, and this article has been cited more than 750 times.

Basic Features of Experimental Design The emotional expression study just discussed illustrates many of the basic features of an experiment:

1. The investigator manipulates an independent variable. In this study, the independent variable was the writing topic.

2. Participants are assigned to the two conditions (traumatic experiences versus mundane happenings) by random assignment.

3. The researcher measures a dependent variable that is expected to vary with conditions of the independent variable. The dependent variable in this study was the number of visits to the health center.

4. Differences between conditions on the dependent variable are called the **experimental effect**. In this example, the experimental effect is the difference in the mean number of visits for those who wrote about traumatic experiences compared to those who wrote about mundane happenings.

Internal Validity **Internal validity** refers to the extent to which the experimental effect can be attributed to the independent variable. For a study to have internal validity, the researchers must include at least one **control group**. The control group does not receive the experimental treatment and is needed to claim that the effects of an experiment are due to the independent variable. In the Pennebaker study, the control group wrote about mundane happenings. The data from a control group provide a standard against which the effects of an independent variable can be assessed. We will describe control groups in more detail as we discuss treatment outcome studies.

The inclusion of a control group does not ensure internal validity, however. Random assignment is also important. To randomly assign participants in a two-group experiment, for example, the researchers could toss a coin for each participant. If the coin turned up heads, the participant would be assigned to one group; if tails, to the other group. Random assignment helps ensure that groups are similar on variables other than the independent variable.

Consider a treatment study in which participants can enroll in their choice of two experimental conditions—psychotherapy or medication. In this study, the researcher cannot claim that group differences are the result of treatment because a competing hypothesis cannot be disproven: patients in the two conditions might have differed in baseline characteristics such as their willingness to discuss difficult emotional issues or their beliefs about medications. This

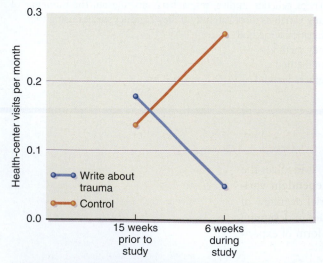

Figure 4.4 Health-center visits for the periods before and during the experiment. Visits for students who wrote about traumas decreased, while visits for those who wrote about mundane events actually rose. After Pennebaker (1988).

study design is poor because the researchers did not use random assignment. Without true random assignment, potential confounds make results hard to interpret.

External Validity   **External validity** is defined as the extent to which results can be generalized beyond the study. If investigators find that a particular treatment helps a particular group of patients, they will want to conclude that this treatment will be effective for other similar patients, at other times, and in other places. For example, Pennebaker and his colleagues would hope that their findings would generalize to other instances of emotional expression (e.g., confiding to a close friend), to other situations, and to people other than undergraduates.

Determining the external validity of the results of an experiment is extremely difficult. For example, participants in studies often behave in certain ways because they are being observed, and thus results that are produced in the laboratory may not automatically be produced in the natural environment. External validity may also be threatened by including only a select group of persons in a study, such as college students (Coyne, 1994) or Caucasian middle-class Americans (Hall, 2001). Indeed, in a review of articles published in six journals of the American Psychological Association between 2003 and 2007, 68 percent of participants in studies were from the United States and 96 percent were from Western industrialized countries (Arnett, 2008). Researchers must be alert to the extent to which they can claim findings are likely to generalize to people and settings other than those studied in the experiment. Often they must perform similar studies in new settings or with a different sample to test whether findings generalize.

Quick Summary

The experimental method entails the manipulation of an independent variable and the measurement of the effect on a dependent variable. Generally, participants are randomly assigned to one of at least two groups: an experimental group, which experiences the active condition of the independent variable, and a control group, which does not. The researcher tests to see if the independent variable had an effect (the experimental effect) by looking for differences between the experimental and control groups on the dependent variable.

Internal validity refers to whether an effect can be confidently attributed to the independent variable. External validity refers to whether experimental effects can be generalized to situations and people outside of this specific study. Experimental designs can provide internal validity, but external validity is sometimes of concern. Correlational studies can provide solid external validity but poorer internal validity.

One Example of Experimental Research: Treatment Outcome Research   **Treatment outcome research** is designed to address a simple question: does treatment work? The clear answer is yes. Here we will focus on the issues in testing psychotherapy, but many of these same issues must be considered in evaluating medication treatments.

Hundreds of studies have examined whether people who receive psychotherapy fare better than those who do not. In meta-analyses of more than 300 studies, researchers have found that there is a moderately positive effect of treatment. About 75 percent of people who enter treatment achieve at least some improvement (Lambert & Ogles, 2004). As shown in Figure 4.5, these effects appear to be more powerful than the passage of time or support from friends and family. On the other hand, it is also clear from this figure that therapy does not always work. That is, about 25 percent of people do not improve in therapy.

What are the standards for treatment outcome research to be seen as valid? Several different working groups have come up with slightly different answers to this question. At a minimum, most researchers agree that a treatment study should include the following criteria:

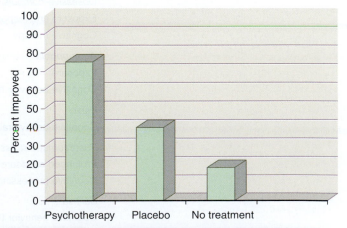

Figure 4.5 Summary of the percent of people who achieve improvement across outcome for psychotherapy, placebo, and no treatment across studies. Drawn from Lambert, M.J. (2004). Psychotherapeutically speaking-updates from the Division of Psychotherapy (29). Available by web at http://www.divisionofpsychotherapy.org/updates.php

- A clear definition of the sample being studied, such as a description of diagnoses
- A clear description of the treatment being offered, as in a treatment manual (described below)
- Inclusion of a control or comparison treatment condition
- Random assignment of clients to treatment or comparison conditions
- Reliable and valid outcome measures (see Chapter 3 for definitions of reliability and validity)
- A large enough sample for statistical tests

Studies in which clients are randomly assigned to receive active treatment or a comparison (either no treatment, a placebo, or another treatment) are called **randomized controlled trials (RCTs)**. In this type of experiment, the independent variable is the treatment and the dependent variable is the clients' outcome.

The American Psychological Association (APA) publishes a report on the therapies that have received empirical support using these standards (Task Force on Promotion and Dissemination of Psychological Procedures, 1995). Some of the therapies it has found to have empirical support are shown in Table 4.5. The goal is to help clinicians, consumers, managed care agencies, and insurance companies draw more easily on this rapidly growing literature

Table 4.5 Examples of Empirically Supported Treatments for Adult Disorders

Generalized anxiety disorder	*Depression*
Cognitive therapy	Cognitive therapy
Applied relaxation	Behavior therapy
	Interpersonal psychotherapy
Social phobia	Problem-solving therapy
Exposure	Self-management/self-control therapy
Cognitive behavioral group therapy	
Systematic desensitization	*Schizophrenia*
	Family psychoeducation
Simple phobia	Cognitive behavioral therapy
Exposure	Social learning/token economy programs
Guided mastery	Cognitive remediation
Systematic desensitization	Social skills training
	Behavioral family therapy
Obsessive-compulsive disorder	Supported employment programs
Exposure and response prevention	Assertive community treatment
Cognitive therapy	
	Alcohol abuse and dependence
Agoraphobia	Community reinforcement approach
Exposure	
Cognitive behavior therapy	*Relationship distress*
	Behavioral couples therapy
Panic	Emotion-focused therapy
Cognitive behavioral therapy	Insight-oriented couples therapy
Posttraumatic stress disorder	
Prolonged exposure	*Sexual dysfunctions*
Cognitive processing therapy	Partner-assisted sexual skills training
Bulimia	*Borderline personality disorder*
Cognitive behavior therapy	Dialectical behavior therapy
Interpersonal psychotherapy	
Anorexia nervosa	
Family-based treatment	

Drawn from Task Force on Promotion and Dissemination of Psychological Treatments (1995).

about **empirically supported treatments**. We will describe empirically supported treatments throughout this book when we discuss specific psychological disorders.

Some aspects of the APA report on empirically supported treatments have been hotly debated. For example, failure for a treatment to appear on the APA list of empirically supported treatments (Table 4.5) could simply reflect a lack of careful studies. As you can see, most of the treatments listed are cognitive behavioral. Research on other treatments has not met the APA's strict research standards.

We now turn to some of the major decisions researchers face as they design treatment outcome studies. These issues include defining the treatment procedures, choosing the best possible control group, and recruiting an appropriate sample of patients. Once a treatment has been shown to work well in a tightly controlled treatment outcome study, effectiveness research is designed to test how well treatments fare in the real world. As evidence accrues that a treatment works, dissemination is needed to ensure that the treatment is adopted by therapists in the community. Throughout the process of testing a treatment, there is growing acknowledgment of the need to consider whether some treatments may be harmful (see Focus on Discovery 4.2).

Defining the Treatment Condition: The Use of Treatment Manuals Treatment manuals are detailed books on how to conduct a particular psychological treatment; they provide specific procedures for the therapist to follow at each stage of treatment. With manuals, someone reading a psychotherapy study can have an idea of what happened in therapy sessions. The use of manuals is widely recommended for psychotherapy research (e.g., Nathan & Gorman, 2002) and for graduate training in clinical psychology (Crits-Christoph, Chambless, Frank, et al., 1995).

Treatment manuals are designed to help therapists be more similar in what they do. This leads to some debate. Some have expressed concern that manuals might constrain therapists such that they might not be as sensitive to a client's unique concerns (Haaga & Stiles, 2000). Evidence suggests that the clear guidelines provided by manuals seem to help novice therapists more than experienced therapists (Multon, Kivlighan, & Gold, 1996). The challenge, then, might be to provide manuals that give therapists a clear

Troubled people may talk about their problems with friends or seek professional therapy. Treatment is typically sought by those for whom the advice and support of family or friends have not provided relief. (Top: © Blaj Gabriel/Shutterstock; Bottom: © Gladskikh Tatiana/Shutterstock.)

FOCUS ON DISCOVERY 4.2

Can Therapy Be Harmful?

Despite the substantial evidence that therapies, on average, tend to be helpful, this does not mean that they help everyone. Indeed, a small number of people may be in worse shape after therapy. Estimating how often therapy is harmful is not easy. Up to 10 percent of people are more symptomatic after therapy than they were before therapy began (Lilienfeld, 2007). Does this mean that therapy harmed them? Maybe not. Without a control group, it is hard to know whether symptoms would have worsened even without therapy. Unfortunately, few researchers report the percentage of people who worsened in the different branches of RCTs.

Nonetheless, it is important to be aware that several treatments have been found to be harmful to some people. The list in Table 4.6 was compiled by identifying treatments that related to worsened outcomes in randomized controlled trials or in multiple case reports (Lilienfeld, 2007). We should note that harmful effects of treatment are not exclusive to therapy; the U.S. Food and Drug Administration has issued warnings that antidepressants and antiseizure medications can increase the risk of suicidality and that antipsychotic medications can increase the risk of death among the elderly.

Table 4.6 Examples of Treatments Found to Be Harmful in Multiple Studies or Case Reports

Treatment	Negative Effects
Critical incident stress debriefing	Heightened risk for posttraumatic symptoms
Scared Straight	Exacerbation of conduct problems
Facilitated communication	False accusations of child abuse against family members
Attachment therapies (e.g., rebirthing)	Death and serious injury to children
Recovered-memory techniques	Production of false memories of trauma
Dissociative identity disorder-oriented therapy	Induction of "alter" personalities
Grief counseling for people with normal bereavement reactions	Increases in depressive symptoms
Expressive-experiential therapies	Exacerbation of painful emotions
DARE programs	Increased intake of alcohol and cigarettes

Drawn from Lilienfeld (2007).

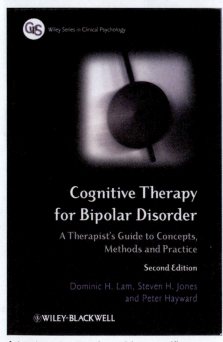

A treatment manual provides specific procedures for a therapist to use in working with a client. They are standard in treatment outcome studies. (Cognitive Therapy for Bipolar Disorder: A Therapist's Guide to Concepts, Methods and Practice, 2e by Dominic H. Lam, Steven H. Jones and Peter Hayward. © 2010 John Wiley & Sons.)

road map and enough flexibility. One way to do this is to develop manuals that give therapists lots of freedom—for example, promoting the goal of exposure treatment for anxiety disorders but also giving a menu of options of how to conduct exposure (Kendall & Beidas, 2007).

Defining Control Groups To illustrate the importance of a control group, consider a study of a particular therapy for anxiety. Let us assume that persons with anxiety disorders receive therapy and that, from the start to the end of a 16-week program, their anxiety symptoms diminish. With no control group against which to compare the improvement, we cannot argue that changes are due to the treatment. The improvement in anxiety could have been due to factors other than the treatment, such as the passage of time or support from friends. Without a control group, any changes during treatment are difficult to interpret.

Many different types of control groups can be used in treatment outcome research. A no-treatment control group allows researchers to test whether the mere passage of time helps as much as treatment does. A stricter test compares the treatment group to a **placebo** control group. In psychotherapy research, the placebo might be a therapy that consists of support and encouragement (the "attention" component) but not the active ingredient of therapy under study (e.g., exposure to a feared stimulus in a behavioral treatment of a phobia). In medication studies, a placebo might be a sugar pill that is described to the patient as a proven treatment. A placebo condition allows researchers to control for expectations of relief. The strictest type of design includes an active-treatment control group, in which researchers compare the new treatment against a well-tested treatment. This type of design allows researchers to make comparative statements about two treatments.

Some have argued that placebos and no-treatment controls are unethical, in that active treatment is being withheld from patients who might suffer as a consequence (Wolitzky, 1995). An active-treatment control group may not raise ethical concerns, but it can be hard to show a difference between different types of active treatments. Choosing the best control group, then, is a difficult decision!

If a researcher decides to use a placebo condition, there are a number of considerations. When including a placebo condition in a medication trial, researchers use a **double-blind procedure**. That is, the psychiatrist and the patient are not told whether the patient receives active medication or a placebo, so as to reduce bias in evaluating outcomes. A double-blind procedure can be hard to implement. Treatment providers and patients may guess who is getting the active treatment because medications are much more likely to produce side effects than are placebos (Salamone, 2000). Researchers often measure whether participants guessed that they were in the placebo condition, as well as how much they expected their treatment to help them.

The **placebo effect** refers to a physical or psychological improvement that is due to a patient's expectations of help rather than to any active ingredient in a treatment. The placebo effect is often significant and even long-lasting. For example, a meta-analysis of 75 research studies revealed that 29.7 percent of patients with depression improved after they received a placebo (Walsh, Seidman, Sysko, et al., 2002). Among depressed patients who respond to antidepressant medication, many may actually be showing a placebo response (Kirsch, 2000). Because the placebo effect can be so powerful, many researchers continue to believe this is an important type of control condition to consider using.

The effects of pilgrimages to shrines, such as Fatima, may be placebo effects. (Hans Georg Roth/Corbis Images.)

Defining a Sample Randomized controlled trials (RCTs) typically focus on treating people who have a certain DSM diagnosis, such as major depressive disorder or panic disorder. Most studies, though, also exclude many potential participants, a process that can limit the external validity of findings. For example, researchers might exclude people who have more than one disorder or who are acutely suicidal (for ethical reasons). Some participants might be unwilling to enroll in a study in which they might be assigned to an ineffective treatment (the control condition). As it turns out, some studies exclude almost as many people as they enroll (Westen, Novotny, & Thompson-Brenner, 2004).

One of the major gaps in treatment outcome studies has been the exclusion of people from diverse cultural and ethnic backgrounds. Most studies enroll predominantly white, non-Latino clients, so samples are often not diverse enough to examine how treatment effects vary for differing groups of people. This problem may reflect a more general tendency for members of minority groups and those from non-Western cultures to be less likely to seek treatment. For example, people from minority groups are about half as likely to receive mental health treatment as are white, non-Hispanic adults in the United States [U.S. Department of Health and Human Services (USDHHS), 2008]. As shown in Table 4.7, there are also dramatic differences in rates of treatment seeking by country among people with psychological disorders (Wang, Simon, Avorn, et al., 2007). Cultural and ethnic differences in willingness to seek treatment, particularly treatment in a research study, can limit the relevance of findings to minority populations.

Overall, there are far too few studies on whether treatments are valid for any specific minority group (Chambless & Ollendick, 2001). Nonetheless, several studies have tested whether empirically supported treatments work well for culturally diverse populations. For example, a group version of interpersonal psychotherapy for depression was found to be efficacious for people living in Ugandan villages (Bolton, Bass, Neugebauer, et al., 2003). Several studies support the efficacy of cognitive behavioral therapy (CBT) for anxiety disorders among African American clients (Miranda et al., 2006). Two studies have found comparable efficacy for CBT of childhood anxiety disorders across ethnicities, and findings of several studies indicate that the effects of treatments for childhood disruptive disorders, including CBT and family therapy, do not differ by ethnicity (Miranda et al., 2005). In sum, at least some results from treatment outcome studies appear to generalize to minority populations. See Focus on Discovery 4.3 for other ways to consider culture and ethnicity in treatment.

Assessing How Well Treatments Work in the Real World Controlled RCTs, typically conducted in academic research settings, are designed to determine the **efficacy** of a treatment, that is, whether a treatment works under the purest of conditions. Because of the kinds of concerns just raised, academic research might not inform us about how these treatments work with broader samples in the hands of nonacademic therapists. That is, the external validity of controlled RCTs is sometimes criticized. We need to determine not just the

Table 4.7 Percent of People Who Sought Treatment in the Past 12 Months for Emotions, Nerves, Mental Health, or Drug/Alcohol Concerns by Country (N = 84,850)

Country	Percent of People Seeking Treatment
Nigeria	1.6
China	3.4
Italy	4.3
Lebanon	4.4
Mexico	5.1
Colombia	5.5
Japan	5.6
Spain	6.8
Ukraine	7.2
Germany	8.1
Israel	8.8
Belgium	10.9
Netherlands	10.9
France	11.3
New Zealand	13.8
South Africa	15.4
United States	17.9

Drawn from a World Health Organization study reported by Wang, Aguilar-Gaxiola, et al. (2007).

FOCUS ON DISCOVERY 4.3

The Importance of Culture and Ethnicity in Psychological Treatment

It is important to consider some of the issues that may limit how well therapies work for people from different backgrounds as well as ways to improve treatments for people from diverse backgrounds. We do want to raise one caveat about the risks of stereotyping. People from minority groups can differ as much from each other as their racial or ethnic group differs from another racial or ethnic group. It is important to consider the degree to which the person is *assimilated* into the majority culture and holds the same values as the majority culture (Sue & Sue, 2008). Nonetheless, a consideration of group characteristics is important and is part of a specialty called ethnic-minority mental health.

Many minority clients report that they would prefer to see someone from a similar background (Lopez, Lopez, & Fong, 1991). Many clients believe that therapists of similar background, perhaps even of the same gender, will understand their life circumstances better and more quickly. Despite this assumption, it has *not* been demonstrated that better outcomes are achieved when client and therapist are similar in race or ethnicity (Beutler, Machado, & Neufeldt, 1994) or that clients are more likely to continue treatment when there is such a match (Maramba & Nagayama-Hall, 2002). **Cultural competence** may matter more than ethnic matching. A therapist who is not a member of the same racial or ethnic group as the client might still understand the client and create a good therapeutic relationship if he or she is familiar with the client's culture (USDHHS, 2002).

In developing cultural competence, therapists need to consider that many members of minority groups have encountered prejudice and racism, and many have been subjected to hate crimes (USDHHS, 2002). Many families come to the United States from other countries to escape political turmoil and persecution, and these traumas may intensify the risks of posttraumatic stress disorder and emotional distress (Sue & Sue, 2008). Cultural background may shape values and beliefs about emotion, as well as how to interact with authorities like treatment providers. These values and beliefs will influence the therapeutic interview. For example, Asian Americans may initially describe stress in physical terms, such as headaches and fatigue, even though they are aware of emotional symptoms and will endorse those when asked directly (Chang et al., 2008). Latino culture may prohibit men from expressing weakness and fear (USDHHS, 2002). Native American children may avoid making eye contact with authorities as a way of expressing respect (Everett, Proctor, & Cartmell, 1989). Hence cultural background may shape not only experiences relevant to the development of symptoms but also how people will communicate in treatment.

Even though there is a small amount of evidence that established treatments are helpful for minority populations, many theorists argue that

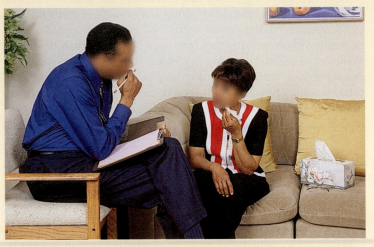

Although many minority clients report that they would like to see a minority therapist, cultural sensitivity appears to be more important to outcome than a match of ethnicity between the client and therapist. (Lew Merrim/ Photo Researchers, Inc.)

treatments should be adapted to be more culturally sensitive. As an example of modifying the content of cognitive behavioral treatment (CBT) for depression to be more specific to the concerns of African American women, one team has provided a manual that includes a set of innovative suggestions. Their approach provides more emphasis on the social isolation, family concerns, and trauma that are common in this population, as well as strategies to challenge myths of the superhuman African American woman. African American women stated that they would rather receive the tailored intervention, and it produced a significantly larger reduction in depressive symptoms than a traditional CBT intervention (Kohn, Oden, Munoz, et al., 2002).

Another approach to developing culturally sensitive interventions is to draw on strengths that might be promoted by a given culture. For example, Latino culture emphasizes family values and spirituality. One team modified CBT for depression to incorporate more emphasis on family values. Puerto Rican adolescents who received culturally sensitive CBT demonstrated significantly more decrease in depressive symptoms than did those who received interpersonal psychotherapy or a control condition (Rossello, Bernal, & Rivera-Medina, 2008).

In sum, therapists can and should learn to work with people from many different backgrounds. This quest, though, would be helped by more researchers working to adapt treatments for people from diverse backgrounds.

efficacy of a treatment but also its **effectiveness**, that is, how well the treatment works in the real world. Studies of effectiveness might include clients with a broader range of problems and provide less intensive supervision of therapists. Often effectiveness studies rely on briefer assessments as well. As you might expect, when clients have more serious diagnostic complications and providers have less support, psychotherapies and even medications tend to look less powerful than they do in careful efficacy studies (Rush, Trivedi, Wisniewski, et al., 2006).

Effectiveness studies do provide support for CBT of anxiety (Wade, Treat, & Stuart, 1998) and depression (Persons, Bostrom, & Bertagnolli, 1999), and for several psychotherapies as supplements to medication for bipolar disorder (Miklowitz, Otto, Frank, et al., 2007).

The Need for Dissemination of Treatment Outcome Findings At this point, hundreds of studies have shown that certain psychological treatments work well. Many treatments have fared well not just in efficacy studies but in effectiveness studies as well. Despite this, many therapists in the community report that they do not use empirically supported treatments. There is a large gap between science and practice in this field, and several approaches are being used to narrow this gap.

Dissemination is the process of facilitating adoption of efficacious treatments in the community, most typically by offering clinicians guidelines about the best available treatments along with training on how to conduct those treatments. Major policy efforts in England and in the U.S. Veterans Administration have focused on dissemination (McHugh & Barlow, 2010).

Even with better dissemination efforts, though, some clinicians find that the currently available empirically supported treatments are not applicable for some unique symptom presentations or for some clients from diverse backgrounds. What should a therapist do when a given client has a profile that does not fit with the available treatment studies? In 2006, an APA task force provided guidelines for evidence-based practice. Evidence-based practice is a way of combining knowledge gained from treatment outcome research with clinical expertise, so that therapists can be sensitive to unique characteristics influencing the therapy process. In doing so, it is hoped that therapists consider the scientific evidence carefully, particularly knowing that inappropriate treatments could cause harm (Stuart & Lilienfeld, 2007).

Check Your Knowledge 4.3

Circle all that apply for the following questions.

1. In an experimental design, the researcher manipulates:
   a. the independent variable
   b. the dependent variable
2. Dr. Jones is interested in whether a new treatment for autism will be helpful. She recruits 30 participants, and she randomly assigns 15 to receive drug X and 15 to receive a placebo. After 3 weeks of treatment, she measures social engagement. In this study, the independent variable is:
   a. medication condition
   b. drug X
   c. social engagement
   d. autism

3. The dependent variable in question 2 is:
   a. treatment
   b. drug X
   c. social engagement
   d. autism
4. Which of the following are the elements of an RCT by definition?
   a. randomization
   b. a comparison condition
   c. medications
   d. double-blind procedures
5. The goal of effectiveness studies is to determine whether a treatment works
   a. under the best possible conditions
   b. under real-world conditions

Analogue Experiments The experimental method is the clearest way to determine cause–effect relationships. Even though experiments are typically used to test treatments, there are many situations in which the experimental method cannot be used to understand the causes of abnormal behavior. Why?

Suppose that a researcher has hypothesized that emotionally charged, overly dependent maternal relationships cause generalized anxiety disorder. An experimental test of this hypothesis would require randomly assigning infants to either of two groups of mothers. The mothers in one group would undergo an extensive training program to ensure that they would be able to create a highly emotional atmosphere and foster overdependence in children. The mothers in the second

Studies of college students with mild symptoms may not provide a good analogue for major mental illness. (B. Daemmrich/The Image Works.)

Harlow's famous analogue research examined the effects of early separation from the mother on infant monkeys. Even a cloth surrogate mother is better than isolation for preventing subsequent emotional distress and depression. (Martin Rogers/Woodfin Camp/Photoshot.)

group would be trained not to create such a relationship with their children. The researcher would then wait until the participants in each group reached adulthood and determine how many of them had developed generalized anxiety disorder. Clearly, this is unethical.

In an effort to take advantage of the power of the experimental method, researchers sometimes use an **analogue experiment**. Investigators attempt to create or observe a related phenomenon—that is, an analogue—in the laboratory to allow more intensive study. Because a true experiment is conducted, results with good internal validity can be obtained. The problem of external validity arises, however, because the researchers are no longer studying the actual phenomenon of interest.

In one type of analogue study, temporary symptoms are produced through experimental manipulations. For example, lactate infusion can elicit a panic attack, hypnotic suggestion can produce blindness similar to that seen in conversion disorder, and threats to self-esteem can produce anxiety or sadness. If mild symptoms can be experimentally induced by such manipulations, this may provide clues into the causes of more severe symptoms.

In another type of analogue study, participants are selected because they are considered similar to people with certain diagnoses. Thousands of studies, for example, have been conducted with college students who received high scores on questionnaire measures of anxiety or depression.

A third type of analogue study involves using animals as a way to understand human behavior. For example, researchers found that dogs that were exposed to electrical shocks they could not control developed many of the symptoms of depression, including seeming despair, passivity, and decreased appetite (Seligman, Maier, & Geer, 1968). Similarly, researchers interested in studying anxiety disorders in humans sometimes study how animals become conditioned to fear previously unthreatening stimuli (Grillon, 2002). Such animal models have helped us understand more about the neurotransmitter systems involved in depression and anxiety disorders in humans.

The key to interpreting such studies lies in the validity of the analogue. Is a stressor encountered in the laboratory fundamentally similar to the death of a parent or other serious stressors? Are distressed college students similar to people with clinically diagnosable depression? Are lethargy and decreased eating in dogs akin to depressive symptoms in humans? Some would argue against such approaches overall, even when researchers are careful to discuss the limits of generalizability. For example, Coyne (1994) has argued that clinical depression is caused by different processes than those that cause common distress. He would argue that analogue studies with undergraduates have poor external validity.

We believe that analogue studies can be very helpful but that findings from these types of studies must be considered conjointly with studies that do not rely on analogues. Science often depends on comparing the results of experimental analogue studies to those of longitudinal correlational studies. For example, analogue studies have shown that people with depression respond more negatively to laboratory stressors (an analogue of life stress), and correlational studies have shown that severe life events predict the onset of clinical depression. Because the findings from correlational and analogue studies complement each other, this provides strong support for life event models of depression. Analogue studies can provide the precision of an experiment (high internal validity), whereas correlational studies provide the ability to study very important influences that cannot be manipulated, like the influence of death and trauma (high external validity).

Single-Case Experiments We have been discussing experimental research with groups of participants, but experiments do not always have to be conducted on groups. In **single-case experimental design**, the experimenter studies how one person responds to manipulations of the independent variable. Unlike the traditional case studies described above, single-case experimental designs can have high internal validity.

Chorpita, Vitali, and Barlow (1997) provide an example of how single-case studies can provide well-controlled data. They describe their treatment of a 13-year-old girl with a phobia (intense fear) of choking, such that she was no longer able to eat solid foods. At times, her fear was so intense that she would experience a fast heart rate, chest pain, dizziness, and other symptoms. She reported that the most frightening foods were hard foods, such as raw vegetables.

A behavioral treatment was designed based on exposure, a common strategy for treating anxiety. During the first 2 weeks, baseline ratings were taken of the amount of different foods eaten, along with her level of discomfort in eating those foods. Discomfort ratings were made on a "subjective units of distress scale" (SUDS) ranging from 0 to 9. Figure 4.6 shows her SUDS ratings and eating behavior over time for each food group. During the third week, she was asked to begin eating foods she described as mildly threatening—crackers and cookies—in three 4-minute blocks each day. The authors hoped that exposure to feared foods would reduce her anxiety. Despite this intervention, though, the patient's SUDS ratings and food consumption did not improve. When the therapist talked with the client and her parents, he discovered that the patient was eating only the absolute minimum of foods, such that she was not getting enough exposure to the feared stimulus. To increase her exposure to foods, reinforcement was added to the program—her parents were instructed to give her ice cream at the end of any day in which the patient had consumed at least three servings of the target food. Within a week, she reported being able to consume crackers and cereals without distress. Gradually, she was asked to begin eating more frightening foods. One week, she was asked to begin consuming soft vegetables, pasta, and cheese, followed the next week by meat, and the next week by raw vegetables, salad, and hard fruit. As shown by the graphs, with the introduction of exposure to each new food group, the client experienced a reduction in SUDS ratings within the next week; effects do not look like they were due to just simply time or maturation, as anxiety was reduced only after the client began exposure for the new food group. The repeated decrements in anxiety are hard to explain using any variable other than treatment. Gains were maintained through a 19-month follow-up.

In one form of single-case design, referred to as a **reversal design** or **ABAB design**, the participant's behavior must be carefully measured in a specific sequence:

1. An initial time period, the baseline (A)
2. A period when a treatment is introduced (B)
3. A reinstatement of the conditions of the baseline period (A)
4. A reintroduction of the treatment (B)

If behavior in the experimental period is different from that in the baseline period, reverses when the treatment is removed, and re-reverses when the treatment is again introduced, there is little doubt that the manipulation, rather than chance or uncontrolled factors, has produced the change. Hence, even though there is no control group, there are time periods that serve as control comparisons for the treatment (Hersen & Barlow, 1976).

The reversal technique cannot always be employed, however, because the initial state of a participant may not be recoverable. Remember that most treatments aim to produce enduring change, so just removing an intervention may not return a person to the pretreatment state. This reversal technique, then, is most applicable when researchers believe that the effects of their manipulation are temporary.

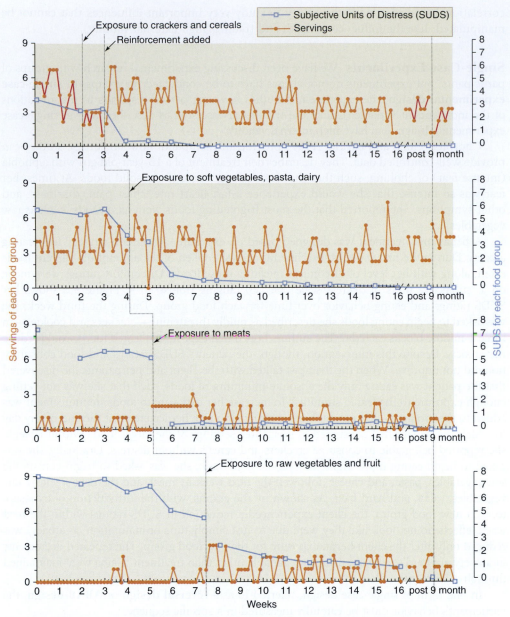

Figure 4.6 Effects of exposure treatment and reinforcement for food phobia in a single-case design. Note the rapid shifts in SUDS ratings as exposure for each new food group is introduced. Reprinted from Chorpita et al., Behavioral treatment of choking phobia in adolescent: An experimental analysis, *Journal of Behavior Therapy and Experimental Psychiatry, 28,* 307–315, copyright 1997, with permission from Elsevier.

Perhaps the biggest drawback of single-case designs is the potential lack of external validity. The fact that a treatment works for a single person does not necessarily imply that it will be effective for others. Findings may relate to a unique aspect of that one person. Some researchers use single-case experimental research to decide whether research with larger groups is warranted. Other researchers conduct a series of single-case experiments to see if findings generalize. In doing so, it is important to include participants who differ. With replication across varied participants, single-case designs can provide a strong approach for testing hypotheses. Indeed, single-case experimental research can be used as evidence that a treatment is efficacious. The APA task force (1995) will consider a treatment to have gained empirical support if it has shown success compared to a well-designed control condition in at least nine single-case experiments.

Quick Summary

Treatment outcome studies are the most common form of experiment in the psychopathology field. These studies focus on whether a given treatment works well. A number of groups have attempted to provide clear standards for psychotherapy research and to summarize the current state of knowledge about the validity of psychotherapy. It is generally agreed that treatment outcome researchers should use treatment manuals, clearly define the sample, randomly assign participants to the active treatment or control comparison, and include reliable and valid measures of outcome.

There is some debate about the best type of control condition, in that no-treatment and placebo-condition control groups involve withholding active treatments for those who may be suffering. Placebo conditions, though, are informative, in that many people demonstrate symptom reduction after taking a placebo.

The external validity of randomized controlled trials (RCTs) is often criticized because so many people are excluded or do not take part in studies. There is a particular need for more research on the efficacy of treatments for minority populations. Effectiveness studies focus on whether treatment findings generalize to the real world.

Analogue studies use an experimental design to study an analogue to a psychological disorder. Common approaches in analogue studies include testing milder or temporary forms of symptoms or risk factors (usually in undergraduate samples) and testing animal models of psychopathology.

Single-case experimental designs observe the effects of manipulating an independent variable in a single person. These designs can have high internal validity, particularly if reversal (ABAB) designs are employed. External validity can be limited for single-case experimental designs.

Integrating the Findings of Multiple Studies

Understanding the pros and cons of different research designs should suggest a natural conclusion—there is no perfect research study. Rather, a body of research studies is often needed to test a theory. When an important research finding emerges, a key goal is to replicate the finding by conducting the study again and seeing if the same pattern of results emerges. Over time, dozens of studies may emerge on important topics. Sometimes the results of different studies will be similar, but more often, differences will emerge across studies. Researchers must synthesize the information across studies to arrive at a general understanding of findings.

How does a researcher go about drawing conclusions from a series of investigations? A simple way of drawing general conclusions is to read individual studies, mull them over, and decide what they mean overall. The disadvantage with this approach is that the researcher's biases and subjective impressions can play a significant role in determining what conclusion is drawn. It is fairly common for two scientists to read the same set of studies and reach very different conclusions.

Meta-analysis was developed as a partial solution to this problem (Smith, Glass, & Miller, 1980). The first step in a meta-analysis is a thorough literature search, so that all relevant studies are identified. Because these studies have typically used different statistical tests, meta-analysis then puts all the results into a common scale, using a statistic called an *effect size*. For example, in treatment studies, the effect size offers a way of standardizing the differences in improvement between a therapy group and a control group so that the results of many different studies can be averaged. Figure 4.7 summarizes the steps in a meta-analysis.

In their often-cited report, Smith and colleagues (1980) meta-analyzed 475 psychotherapy outcome studies involving more than 25,000 patients and 1,700 effect sizes; they came to conclusions that have attracted considerable attention and some controversy. Most importantly, they concluded that psychotherapies produce more improvement than does no treatment. Specifically, treated patients were found to be better off than almost 80 percent of untreated patients. Subsequent meta-analyses have confirmed that therapy appears effective (Lambert & Ogles, 2004).

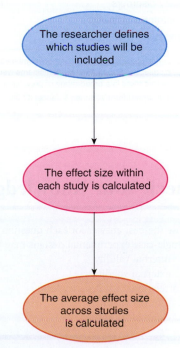

Figure 4.7 Steps in conducting a meta-analysis.

Meta-analysis has been criticized by a number of researchers. The central problem is that researchers sometimes include studies that are of poor quality in a meta-analysis. Smith and colleagues gave equal weight to all studies, so that a poorly controlled outcome study (such as one that did not evaluate what the therapists actually did in each session) received as much weight as a well-controlled one (such as a study in which therapists used a manual that specified what they did with each research participant). When Smith and colleagues attempted to address this problem by comparing effect sizes of good versus poor studies and found no differences, they were further criticized for the criteria they employed in separating the good from the not so good (Rachman & Wilson, 1980)! O'Leary and Wilson (1987) concluded that the ultimate problem is that someone has to make a judgment of good versus poor quality in research and that others can find fault with that judgment. A good meta-analysis, though, will be clear about the criteria for including or excluding studies.

Table 4.8 provides another example of a meta-analysis. In this meta-analysis, researchers integrated the findings of 21 epidemiological studies conducted in Europe on the 12-month prevalence of mental disorders (Wittchen & Jacobi, 2005). Across these studies, more than 155,000 participants were interviewed. Prevalence estimates from the different studies were fairly varied. Tallying the findings across studies should give a stronger estimate of how common the disorders are.

Table 4.8 An Example of a Meta-Analysis: One-Year Prevalence Rates for Mental Illness across 21 European Studies

DSM-IV Diagnosis	Number of Studies	Combined *N*	12-Month Prevalence (%) across the Combined Sample	Range of Prevalence Estimates within Different Studies
Alcohol dependence	12	60,891	3.3	0.1–6.6
Illicit substance dependence	6	28,429	1.1	0.1–2.2
Psychotic disorders	6	27,291	0.9	0.2–2.6
Major depressive disorder	17	152,044	6.4	3.1–10.1
Bipolar I disorder	6	21,848	0.8	0.2–1.1
Anxiety disorders	12	53,597	1.6	0.7–3.1
Somatoform disorders	7	18,894	6.4	1.1–11
Eating disorders	5	19,761	4.8	0.2–0.7

Note: In this meta-analysis, researchers combined the findings of 27 major epidemiological studies on the 12-month prevalence of psychiatric disorders in European countries. Across these studies, more than 155,000 participants were interviewed. Researchers were able not only to determine the percentage of participants who met criteria for diagnoses but also to illustrate that there is a broad range of prevalence estimates across different studies.

Source: Adapted from Wittchen & Jacobi (2005).

Check Your Knowledge 4.4

Choose the best answer for each question.

1. Single-case experimental designs may lack:
   a. internal validity
   b. external validity
2. Correlational studies may lack:
   a. internal validity
   b. external validity

3. The step in meta-analysis that has received extensive criticism is:
   a. determining which studies should be included
   b. calculating the effect size of each study
   c. calculating the average effect size across studies
   d. none of the above

Summary

Science and Scientific Methods

- Science involves forming a theory and developing hypotheses based on that theory, and then systematically gathering data to test the hypotheses. It is important for researchers to replicate findings from a given study, which requires being precise about the methods used.

Approaches to Research on Psychopathology

- Common methods for studying abnormal behavior include case studies, correlational studies, and experimental studies. Each method has strengths and weaknesses.

Case Studies

- Case studies provide detailed descriptions of rare phenomena or novel procedures. Case studies also can disconfirm that a relationship is universal and can generate hypotheses that can be tested through controlled research. Case studies, however, may not always be valid, and they are of limited value in providing evidence to support a theory.

Correlational Research

- Correlational methods are the most common way to study the causes of abnormal behavior, because we cannot manipulate most of the major risk factors in psychopathology, nor can we manipulate diagnosis.
- Conclusions drawn from cross-sectional correlational studies cannot be interpreted in cause–effect terms because of the directionality problem. Longitudinal studies help address which variable came first but can still suffer from the third-variable problem.
- One form of correlational study, epidemiological research, involves gathering information about the prevalence and incidence of disorders in populations and about risk factors that relate to higher probability of developing a disorder. Epidemiological studies avoid the sampling biases seen in studies of people drawn from undergraduate psychology classes or from treatment clinics.
- Studies of behavior genetics often rely on correlational techniques as well. The most common behavior genetics methods include the family method, the twin method, and the adoptees method. Molecular genetics research includes association studies and genome-wide association studies (GWAS) to identify specific genes that are related to a disorder.

Experimental Research

- In the experimental method, the researcher randomly assigns people to an experimental group or a control group. Effects of the independent variable on a dependent variable are then tested. Treatment outcome studies and analogue studies are common types of experimental research in psychopathology. Single-case experimental designs can provide well-controlled data.
- Generally, experimental methods help enhance internal validity, but correlational methods sometimes offer greater external validity.
- Research on the efficacy of various forms of psychological treatments has been conducted for many decades. Overall, this research suggests that about 75 percent of people gain some improvement from therapy. Therapy also seems to be more helpful than a placebo or the passage of time.
- Efforts have been made to define standards for research on psychotherapy trials and to summarize current knowledge on which psychological treatments work. These standards typically include the need to use a treatment manual, to randomly assign participants to treatment or a control condition, to define the sample carefully, and to use reliable and valid outcome measures. It is hoped that efforts to summarize these findings will help disseminate the best available therapeutic practices to clinicians, clients, and insurance companies.
- Researchers have also begun to identify treatments that may cause harm.
- Many people are excluded or will not take part in clinical trials, and cultural diversity is lacking in most trials. There are a small number of studies demonstrating that psychotherapy can be helpful with minority populations.
- A broader concern is that a gap exists between what happens in the research world and the real world. Efficacy research focuses on how well therapies work in carefully controlled experiments, whereas effectiveness research focuses on how well therapies work in the real world with a broader array of clients and therapists.

Integrating the Findings of Multiple Studies

- Meta-analysis is an important tool for reaching conclusions from a group of research studies. It entails putting the statistical comparisons from single studies into a common format—the effect size—so the results of many studies can be averaged.

Answers to Check Your Knowledge Questions

4.1 1. F; 2. F; 3. F
4.2 1. a and b; 2. d; 3. c; 4. c; 5. d

4.3 1. a; 2. a; 3.c; 4. a and b; 5. b
4.4 1. b; 2. a; 3. a

Key Terms

ABAB design
adoptees method
analogue experiment
association study
case study
clinical significance
concordance
control group
correlation
correlation coefficient
correlational method
cross-fostering
cross-sectional design

cultural competence
dependent variable
directionality problem
dissemination
dizygotic (DZ) twins
double-blind procedure
effectiveness
efficacy
empirically supported treatments
epidemiology
experiment
experimental effect
external validity

family method
genome-wide association studies
   (GWAS)
high-risk method
hypothesis
incidence
independent variable
index cases
internal validity
longitudinal design
meta-analysis
monozygotic (MZ) twins
placebo

placebo effect
prevalence
probands
random assignment
randomized controlled trials (RCTs)
reversal designs
risk factor
single-case experimental design
statistical significance
theory
third-variable problem
treatment outcome research
twin method

5 Mood Disorders

Clinical Case: Lily

Lily, a 38-year-old mother of four children, had been deeply depressed for about 2 months when she first went to see her doctor. Twelve months earlier, her husband had been promoted at work which should have been great, but the accompanying (small) increase in pay was offset by an even larger decrease in their housing benefit. The shortfall amounted to £30 per week which meant, that after paying the bills, Lily had little money left to buy food. She ended up visiting a crisis centre on a weekly basis and taking home a free box of food. On the one hand Lily felt incredibly grateful for the donation, but she also felt humiliated and a failure for not being able to provide for her family and having to receive charity. Each night, she struggled to fall asleep. She had little appetite and as a result had lost 5.5 kilos. Lily felt exhausted all the time, housework became impossible for her to do, and she lost her interest in sex. She and her husband argued frequently, which upset their children and left Lily feeling isolated. Finally, realizing that something serious had happened to his wife, Lily's husband cajoled her into making an appointment with their GP. (You will read about the outcome of Lily's treatment later in this chapter.)

MOOD DISORDERS INVOLVE DISABLING disturbances in emotion—from the extreme sadness and disengagement of depression to the extreme elation and irritability of mania. In this chapter, we begin by discussing the clinical description and the epidemiology of the different mood disorders. Next, we consider various perspectives on the etiology of these disorders, and then we consider approaches to treating them. We conclude with an examination of suicide, an action far too often associated with mood disorders.

Clinical Descriptions and Epidemiology of Mood Disorders

The proposed DSM-5 recognizes two broad types of **mood disorders**: those that involve only depressive symptoms and those that involve manic symptoms (bipolar disorders). Table 5.1 presents a summary of the symptoms of each of these disorders. We begin by describing the signs of depression, the formal criteria for diagnosis of the depressive disorders (including major depressive disorder and dysthymia), and the epidemiology and consequences of depressive disorders.

After describing depressive disorders, we turn to bipolar disorders. There, we describe the signs of mania, followed by the formal criteria for diagnosing bipolar I disorder, bipolar II disorder, and cyclothymic disorder, and then the epidemiology and consequences of bipolar disorders. After covering the basic diagnostic categories, we describe the proposed DSM-5 subtypes that are used to further define depressive disorders and bipolar disorders.

As shown in Figure 5.1, the likely DSM-5 includes many changes. The DSM-5 proposes three new depressive disorders: mixed anxiety/depressive disorder, premenstrual dysphoric disorder, and disruptive mood dysregulation disorder. Later in the chapter, we discuss mixed anxiety/depressive disorder in Focus on Discovery 5.5 as part of a broader discussion of the overlap between anxiety and depressive disorders. We briefly discuss the rationale for disruptive mood dysregulation, a diagnosis specific to children and adolescents, in Focus on Discovery 14.3. Because so little is known, we include the diagnostic criteria but do not discuss these new diagnoses further.

Depressive Disorders

The cardinal symptoms of depression include profound sadness and/or an inability to experience pleasure. Most of us experience sadness during our lives, and most of us say that we are "depressed" at one time or another. But most of these experiences do not have the intensity and duration to be diagnosable. The author William Styron (1990) wrote about his depression, "Like anyone else I have always had times when I felt deeply depressed, but this was something altogether new in my experience—a despairing, unchanging paralysis of the spirit beyond anything I had ever known or imagined could exist."

Table 5.1 Diagnoses of Mood Disorders

DSM-5 Diagnoses	Likely Key Changes	Major Features
Major depressive disorder	• Bereavement-related symptoms are no longer excluded	• Five or more depressive symptoms, including sad mood or loss of pleasure, for 2 weeks
Dysthymia	• Chronic major depressive disorder is included in dysthymia	• Low mood and at least two other symptoms of depression at least half of the time for 2 years
Mixed anxiety/depressive disorder	• New category proposed for DSM-5	• Symptoms of depression and anxiety are present, but diagnostic criteria for another anxiety or depressive disorder are not met
Premenstrual dysphoric disorder	• New category proposed for DSM-5	• Depressive or physical symptoms in the week before menses
Disruptive mood dysregulation disorder	• New category proposed for DSM-5	• Severe recurrent temper outbursts and persistent negative mood for at least 1 year beginning before age 10
Bipolar I disorder	• Abnormally increased activity and energy included as a required symptom of mania	• At least one lifetime manic episode
Bipolar II disorder	• Abnormally increased activity and energy included as a required symptom of hypomania	• At least one lifetime hypomanic episode and one major depressive episode
Cyclothymia	• No changes	• Recurrent mood changes from high to low for at least 2 years, without manic or depressive episodes

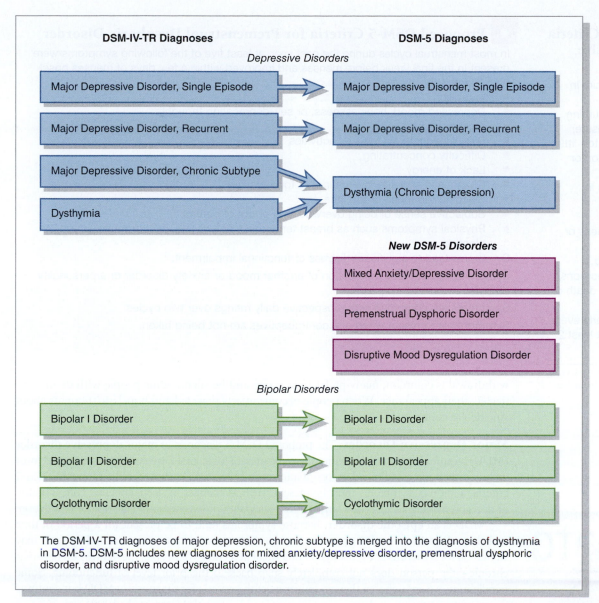

DSM-IV-TR Diagnoses

DSM-5 Diagnoses

Depressive Disorders

DSM-IV-TR		DSM-5
Major Depressive Disorder, Single Episode	→	Major Depressive Disorder, Single Episode
Major Depressive Disorder, Recurrent	→	Major Depressive Disorder, Recurrent
Major Depressive Disorder, Chronic Subtype	→	Dysthymia (Chronic Depression)
Dysthymia	→	

New DSM-5 Disorders

Mixed Anxiety/Depressive Disorder

Premenstrual Dysphoric Disorder

Disruptive Mood Dysregulation Disorder

Bipolar Disorders

DSM-IV-TR		DSM-5
Bipolar I Disorder	→	Bipolar I Disorder
Bipolar II Disorder	→	Bipolar II Disorder
Cyclothymic Disorder	→	Cyclothymic Disorder

The DSM-IV-TR diagnoses of major depression, chronic subtype is merged into the diagnosis of dysthymia in DSM-5. DSM-5 includes new diagnoses for mixed anxiety/depressive disorder, premenstrual dysphoric disorder, and disruptive mood dysregulation disorder.

Figure 5.1 Diagnoses of mood disorders.

When people develop a depressive disorder, their heads may reverberate with self-recriminations. Like Lily, described in the Clinical Case, they may become focused on their flaws and deficits. Paying attention can be so exhausting that they have difficulty absorbing what they read and hear. They often view things in a very negative light, and they tend to lose hope.

Physical symptoms of depression are also common, including fatigue and low energy as well as physical aches and pains. These symptoms can be profound enough to convince afflicted persons that they must be suffering from some serious medical condition, even though the symptoms have no apparent physical cause (Simon, Von Korff, Piccinelli, et al., 1999). Although people with depression typically feel exhausted, they may find it hard to fall asleep and may wake up frequently. Other people sleep throughout the day. They may find that food tastes bland or that their appetite is gone, or they may experience an increase in appetite. Sexual interest disappears. Some may find their limbs feel heavy. Thoughts and movements may slow for some (**psychomotor retardation**), but others cannot sit still—they pace, fidget, and wring their hands (**psychomotor agitation**). Beyond these cognitive and physical symptoms, initiative may disappear. Social

Some people with depression have trouble falling asleep and staying asleep. Others find themselves sleeping for more than 10 hours but still feeling exhausted. (Shannon Fagan/Stone/Getty Images.)

withdrawal is common; many prefer to sit alone and be silent. Some people with depression neglect their appearance. When people become utterly dejected and hopeless, thoughts about suicide are common.

Major Depressive Disorder The proposed DSM-5 diagnosis of **major depressive disorder (MDD)** requires five depressive symptoms to be present for at least 2 weeks. These symptoms must include either depressed mood or loss of interest and pleasure. As shown in the proposed DSM-5 criteria, additional symptoms must be present, such as changes in sleep, appetite, concentration or decision making, feelings of worthlessness, suicidality, or psychomotor agitation or retardation.

MDD is an **episodic disorder**, because symptoms tend to be present for a period of time and then clear. Even though episodes tend to dissipate over time, an untreated episode may stretch on for 5 months or even longer. For a small percentage of people, the depression becomes chronic—the person does not completely snap back to the prior level of functioning. Some people improve enough that they no longer meet the criteria for diagnosis of MDD but continue to experience subclinical depression for years (Judd, Akiskal, Maser, et al., 1998).

Major depressive episodes tend to recur—once a given episode clears, a person is likely to experience another episode. About two-thirds of people with an episode of major depression will experience at least one more episode during their lifetime (Solomon, Keller, Leon, et al., 2000). The average number of episodes is about four (Judd, 1997). With every new episode that a person experiences, his or her risk for experiencing another episode goes up by 16 percent (Solomon et al., 2000).

There is controversy about whether a person with five symptoms lasting 2 weeks (i.e., someone who meets the criteria for diagnosis with MDD) is distinctly different from someone who has only three symptoms for 10 days (i.e., someone who meets the criteria for so-called *subclinical depression*). A study of twins found that subclinical depression predicted the occurrence of future episodes of MDD and even the diagnosis of MDD in a co-twin. That is, when one twin had subclinical depression, both twins were likely to have future episodes of major depression (Kendler & Gardner, 1998). Even a few symptoms of depression can result in impairment, but it does appear that impairment levels are higher when more depressive symptoms are present (Judd, Akiskal, Zeller, et al., 2000).

Chronic Depressive Disorder (Dysthymia) People with **dysthymia** are chronically depressed—more than half of the time for at least 2 years, they feel blue or derive little pleasure from usual activities and pastimes. In addition, they have at least two of the other symptoms of depression.

Kirsten Dunst has described her problems with major depressive disorder (MDD). One out of every five women will experience an episode of depression during her lifetime. (Allstar Picture Library/Alamy.)

<table>
<tr>
<td>

Proposed DSM-5 Criteria for Disruptive Mood Dysregulation Disorder

- Severe recurrent temper outbursts in response to common stressors, including verbal or behavioral expressions of temper that are out of proportion in intensity or duration to the provocation.
- Temper outbursts are inconsistent with developmental level.
- The temper outbursts tend to occur at least three times per week.
- Persistent negative mood between temper outbursts most days, and the negative mood is observable to others.
- These symptoms have been present for at least 12 months and do not clear for more than 3 months at a time.
- Temper outbursts or negative mood are present in at least two settings (at home, at school, or with peers) and are severe in at least one setting.
- Age 6 or higher (or equivalent developmental level).
- Onset before age 10.
- In the past year, there has not been a distinct period lasting more than 1 day during which elevated mood and at least three other manic symptoms were present.
- The behaviors do not occur exclusively during the course of another psychotic or mood disorder and are not better accounted for by another mental disorder.
- This diagnosis can coexist with oppositional defiant disorder, attention-deficit/hyperactivity disorder, conduct disorder, and substance use disorders.

</td>
<td>

Proposed DSM-5 Criteria for Chronic Depressive Disorder (Dysthymia)

Depressed mood for most of the day more than half of the time for 2 years (or 1 year for children and adolescents).
At least two of the following during that time:
- Poor appetite or overeating
- Sleeping too much or too little
- Poor self-esteem
- Low energy
- Trouble concentrating or making decisions
- Feelings of hopelessness
The symptoms do not clear for more than 2 months at a time.

Note: DSM-IV-TR but not DSM-5 criteria specify that no major depressive episode was present during the first 2 years of symptoms.

</td>
</tr>
</table>

The DSM-IV-TR distinguishes chronic MDD from dysthymia, but DSM-5 criteria do not make this distinction. Rather, the DSM-5 combines these two chronic forms of depression. This places emphasis on the chronicity of symptoms, which has been shown to be a stronger predictor of poor outcome than the number of symptoms; among people who have experienced depressive symptoms for at least 2 years, those who do and do not have a history of major depressive disorder appear similar in their symptoms and treatment response (McCullough, Klein, Keller, et al., 2000). The DSM-5 criteria are also consistent with findings from one longitudinal study which found that 95 percent of people with dysthymia developed MDD over a 10-year period (Klein, Shankman, & Rose, 2006). Findings like these suggest that it does not make sense to try to differentiate these two forms of chronic depression.

Epidemiology and Consequences of Depressive Disorders MDD is one of the most prevalent psychiatric disorders. One large-scale epidemiological study in the United States estimated that 16.2 percent of people meet the criteria for diagnosis of MDD at some point in their lives (Kessler, Berglund, Demler, et al., 2005). Dysthymia is rarer than MDD: about 2.5 percent of people meet criteria for dysthymia as defined by DSM-IV-TR during their lives (Kessler et al., 2005).

MDD is twice as common among women as among men (see Focus on Discovery 5.1 for a discussion of possible reasons for this gender difference). Socioeconomic status also matters—that is, MDD is three times as common among people who are impoverished compared to those who are not (Kessler et al., 2005).

The prevalence of depression varies considerably across cultures. In a major cross-cultural study using the same diagnostic criteria and structured interview in each country, prevalence of MDD varied from a low of 1.5 percent in Taiwan to a high of 19 percent in Beirut, Lebanon (Weissman et al., 1996). Similar findings have emerged in a study of depression rates among 26,000 people receiving care through primary care doctors in 14 countries (Simon, Goldberg, Von Korff, et al., 2002).

Another study yielded the intriguing result that people who have moved to the United States from Mexico have lower rates of MDD and other psychiatric disorders than do people of Mexican descent who were born in the United States (Vega, Kolody, Aguilar-Gaxiola, et al., 1998). Since then, the same team has found that in general, minorities who move to the United States have lower rates of depression than those who were born in the United States (Gonzalez, Vega, Williams, et al., 2010). Why? The resiliency of people who are able to immigrate could be protective.

FOCUS ON DISCOVERY 5.1

Gender Differences in Depression

Major depression occurs about twice as often in women as in men. Similar gender ratios in the prevalence of depression have been documented in many countries around the world, including the United States, France, Lebanon, and New Zealand (Weissman & Olfson, 1995). Intriguingly, the ratio does not hold in some cultural groups. For example, this gender difference does not hold between Jewish adults, because depression is more common among Jewish men than among other men (Levav, Kohn, Golding, et al., 1997). But for most ethnic and cultural groups, a clear gender difference in MDD begins to emerge during early adolescence and is documented consistently by late adolescence. Some of you might wonder if these findings just reflect a tendency for men to be less likely to describe symptoms. So far, evidence does not support that idea (Kessler, 2003). Although a fair amount of research has focused on hormonal factors that could explain the vulnerability of women, findings have been mixed for this idea, too (Brems, 1995). Evidence suggests that the gender ratio in depression is more pronounced in cultures with more traditional gender roles (Seedat, Scott, Angermeyer, et al., 2009). Several social and psychological factors may help explain this gender difference (Nolen-Hoeksema, 2001):

- Twice as many girls as boys are exposed to childhood sexual abuse.
- During adulthood, women are more likely than men to be exposed to chronic stressors such as poverty and caretaker responsibilities.
- Acceptance of traditional social roles among girls may intensify self-critical attitudes about appearance. Adolescent girls worry more than adolescent boys about their body image, a factor that appears tied to depression (Hankin & Abramson, 2001).

- Traditional social roles may interfere with pursuit of some potentially rewarding activities that are not considered "feminine."
- Exposure to childhood and chronic stressors, as well as the effects of female hormones, could change the reactivity of the HPA axis, a biological system guiding reactions to stress.
- A focus on gaining approval and closeness within interpersonal relationships, which is more commonly endorsed by women, may intensify reactions to interpersonal stressors (Hankin, Mermelstein, & Roesch, 2007).
- Social roles promote emotion-focused coping among women, which may then extend the duration of sad moods after major stressors. More specifically, women tend to spend more time ruminating about sad moods or wondering about the reasons why unhappy events have occurred. Men tend to spend more time using distracting or action-focused coping, such as playing a sport or engaging in other activities that shake off the sad mood. As we discuss when we review cognitive factors in depression, a fair amount of research suggests that rumination will intensify and prolong sad moods.

In all likelihood, gender differences in depression are related to multiple factors. In considering these issues, bear in mind that men are more likely to demonstrate other types of disorders, such as alcohol and substance abuse as well as antisocial personality disorder (Seedat et al., 2009). Hence, understanding gender differences in psychopathology is likely to require attending to many different risk factors and syndromes.

The gender difference in depression does not emerge until adolescence. At that time, young women encounter many stressors and more pressure concerning social roles and body image, and they tend to ruminate about the resulting negative feelings. (© paul hill/iStockphoto.)

Symptoms of depression also show some cross-cultural variation, probably resulting from differences in cultural standards regarding acceptable expressions of emotional distress. For example, people in South Korea are less likely to describe a sad mood or suicidal thoughts than are people in the United States (Chang, Hahm, Lee, et al., 2008). Complaints of nerves and headaches are common in Latino culture, and reports of weakness, fatigue, and poor concentration are common in some Asian cultures. On the other hand, these symptom differences do not appear to be major enough to explain the differing rates of depression across countries (Simon et al., 2002).

It is tempting to assume that differences in prevalence rates by country indicate a strong role for culture. It turns out that differences between countries in rates of depression may be fairly complex. As described in Focus on Discovery 5.2, one factor may be distance from the equator. Rates of winter depression, or seasonal affective disorder, are higher farther from the equator, where days are shorter. There is also a robust correlation of per capita fish consumption with depression; countries with more fish consumption, such as Japan and Iceland, have much lower rates of MDD and bipolar disorder (Hibbeln, Nieminen, Blasbalg, et al., 2006). Undoubtedly, cultural and economic factors, such as wealth disparity and family cohesion, play an important role in rates of depression as well.

In most countries, the prevalence of MDD increased steadily during the mid to late twentieth century (Klerman, 1988); at the same time, the age of onset decreased. Figure 5.2 shows that the age of onset has become lower for each recent generation of people in the United States: Among people in their 60s, less than 5 percent reported that they had experienced an episode

FOCUS ON DISCOVERY 5.2

Seasonal Subtype of MDD (SAD): The Winter Blues

Criteria for SAD specify that a person experiences depression during 2 consecutive winters with symptom resolution during the summer. Phenomenology typically include low mood, lethargy, hypersomnia, social withdrawal, decreased libido, increased appetite (most often carbohydrate craving) and weight gain. SAD appear to be more common in temperate than in periequatorial climates, where depressive symptoms, if anything, are more prevalent in summer than in autumn/winter (Ito, et al., 1992) and are related to excessive heat and humidity (Morrissey et al., 1996).

An evolutionary perspective on SAD suggests the "condition" may have originated in a set of behavior changes linked to hibernation. Certainly people with SAD report that in the autumn/winter months they "just want to hibernate", and the symptoms (listed above) overlap with lower-order mammalian hibernation. So, whilst for mammals living in the wild, a slower metabolism in the winter could have been a lifesaver during periods of

This woman is having light therapy. (David White/ Alamy.)

scarce food, but for modern day humans, these behaviors have now lost their advantageous effects on survival.

The mechanism underlying SAD is believed to be associated with changes in melatonin levels in the brain. Melatonin is sensitive to light and dark cycles and is only released during dark periods, and research suggests that people with SAD show greater changes in melatonin in the winter than people without SAD (Wehr, et al., 2001).

The therapeutic effects of light therapy have been shown to be equal to, or larger than, those found in most antidepressant pharmacotherapy trials (Westrin & Lam, 2007) and there is also evidence it helps relieve depression even among those without a seasonal pattern to their depressions (Lieverse, et al., 2011).

Fortunately, several treatment options are available for SAD. Like other subtypes of depression, SAD responds to antidepressant medications and cognitive behavioral therapy (Rohan, et al., 2007).

---

of MDD by age 20, whereas among people ages 18–29, almost 10 percent reported that they had experienced an episode of MDD by age 20. The median age of onset is now the late teens to early 20s. One possible explanation for the increasing depression rates lies in the social changes that have occurred over the past 100 years. Support structures—such as tightly knit extended families and marital stability, which were more widespread in the past—are often absent for people today. Yet there are no clear data about why depression seems to strike earlier and earlier. Beyond the prevalence rates, the symptoms of depression vary somewhat across the life span. Depression in children often results in somatic complaints, such as headaches or stomachaches. In older adults, depression is often characterized by distractibility and complaints of memory loss.

Both MDD and dysthymia are often associated, or comorbid, with other psychological problems. About 60 percent of people who meet the criteria for diagnosis of MDD during their lifetime also will meet the criteria for diagnosis of an anxiety disorder at some point (Kessler, Berglund, Demler, et al., 2003a). See Focus on Discovery 5.5 later in the chapter for more discussion of the overlap of anxiety disorders and depressive disorders. Other common comorbid conditions include substance-related disorders, sexual dysfunctions, and personality disorders.

Depression has many serious consequences. As we will discuss later, suicide is a real risk. MDD is also one of the world's leading causes of disability (Murray & Lopez, 1996); it is estimated that MDD is associated with $31 billion per year in lost productivity in the United States (Stewart, Ricci, Chee, et al., 2003). MDD is also related to a higher risk of other health problems, including death from medical diseases (Mykletun, Bjerkeset, Overland, et al., 2009). There is particularly strong evidence that depression is related to the onset and more severe course of cardiovascular disease (Surtees, Wainwright, Luben, et al., 2008). See Focus on Discovery 5.3 for more discussion of the links between depression and cardiovascular disease.

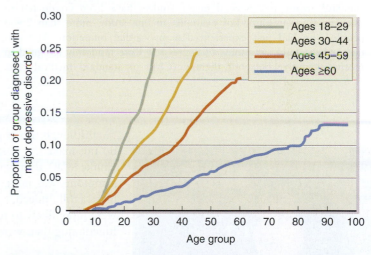

Figure 5.2 With each generation, the median age of onset for major depressive disorder gets younger. Adapted from Kessler, Berglund, Demler, et al. (2003b). *JAMA, 289,* 3095–3105.

FOCUS ON DISCOVERY 5.3

Depression and Cardiovascular Disease

Depression is all too common after cardiovascular events. For example, after a stroke, about 30 percent of people will experience depression (Teper & O'Brien, 2008). Not only does cardiovascular health predict depression but vice versa—depression can also predict cardiovascular health. Indeed, in one meta-analysis, authors compiled the findings of 22 prospective studies that controlled for baseline medical and cardiovascular factors. Across those studies, depression was found to be related to a 90 percent increase in the onset of cardiovascular disease and a 60 percent increase in the severity of cardiovascular disease over time (Nicholson, Kuper, & Hemingway, 2006). These effects of depression on cardiovascular disease can be observed even in younger populations (Lee, Lin, & Tsai, 2008). A separate meta-analysis shows that depression is also related to increased risk of death from cardiovascular disease, even after controlling for baseline cardiovascular health (Barth, Schumacher, & Herrmann-Lingen, 2004).

There are likely many reasons for the overlap of depression and cardiovascular outcomes. Both conditions can involve stress reactivity, as well as related changes in neurotransmitters, cortisol regulation, immune function, and the balance of parasympathetic to sympathetic nervous system activity (Grippo, 2009; Wolkowitz, Epel, Reus, et al., 2010). Untangling the role of these interrelated processes will require careful longitudinal research.

Beyond understanding the basic mechanisms, a high priority has been placed on studying whether these depressions are relieved by standard treatments. Several major studies have been conducted to examine this question. For example, in one study, more than 2,400 people who had just experienced a myocardial infarction (MI) and had at least mild symptoms of depression were randomly assigned to receive cognitive behavior therapy (CBT) or standard medical care.

If people receiving CBT continued to show high levels of depression after five sessions, sertraline was prescribed as well. Active intervention led to significant reductions in depression compared to placebo treatment (Berkman, Blumenthal, Burg, et al., 2003). These findings suggest that treatments work in this population.

Researchers have also examined how well antidepressants work in this population. Tricyclic antidepressants are not recommended, because they have been found to be associated with twice the risk of subsequent MI as compared to placebos in this population (Cohen, Gibson, & Alderman, 2000). Better findings have emerged for selective serotonin reuptake inhibitors (SSRIs), such as fluoxetine (Prozac), among people who are depressed after an MI. For example, in one study, 369 people were randomly assigned to receive sertraline (an SSRI) or a placebo for 24 weeks. Sertraline was effective—and particularly effective for the people with severe and recurrent depression (Glassman, O'Connor, Califf, et al., 2002).

Most studies have not been large enough to examine whether treatment can reduce the risk of death from cardiovascular disease (Glassman & Bigger, 2011). In one careful analysis of people prescribed antidepressants after an MI, the degree of actual improvement in depression predicted greater likelihood of survival (Carney, Blumenthal, Freedland, et al., 2004). This would suggest that it may be important to offer aggressive treatment in order to ensure full relief from depression.

A major goal, then, is to help medical teams to routinely screen for depression and provide treatment. Many physicians are likely to dismiss symptoms of depression in a patient who has just had a heart attack, assuming that people might be understandably distressed by their recent change in health. However, depression relief may be an important facet of medical recovery.

Although the diagnostic criteria for dysthymia require fewer symptoms than for MDD, do not make the mistake of thinking that dysthymia is a less severe disorder than MDD. Unlike MDD, dysthymia is chronic. One study found that the average duration of dysthymic symptoms was more than 5 years (Klein et al., 2006). The chronicity of these symptoms takes a toll. Indeed, a study following patients for 5 years found that people with dysthymia were more likely to require hospitalization, to attempt suicide, and to be impaired in their functioning than were people with MDD (Klein, Schwartz, Rose, et al., 2000).

Bipolar Disorders

The proposed DSM-5 recognizes three forms of bipolar disorders: bipolar I disorder, bipolar II disorder, and cyclothymic disorder. Manic symptoms are the defining feature of each of these disorders. The bipolar disorders are differentiated by how severe and long-lasting the manic symptoms are.

These disorders are labeled "bipolar" because most people who experience mania will also experience depression during their lifetime (mania and depression are considered opposite poles). An episode of depression is not required for a diagnosis of bipolar I, but it is required for a diagnosis of bipolar II disorder.

Mania is a state of intense elation or irritability accompanied by other symptoms shown in the diagnostic criteria. During manic episodes, people will act and think in ways that are highly unusual compared to their typical selves. They may become louder and make an

Margaret Trudeau, the former first lady of Canada, has become an advocate for better mental health services since her own diagnosis with bipolar disorder. (Neil Burstyn/Newscom.)

incessant stream of remarks, sometimes full of puns, jokes, rhymes, and interjections about nearby stimuli that have attracted their attention (like Wayne in the Clinical Case on the next page). They may be difficult to interrupt and may shift rapidly from topic to topic, reflecting an underlying **flight of ideas**. During mania, people may become sociable to the point of intrusiveness. They can also become excessively self-confident. Unfortunately, they can be oblivious to the potentially disastrous consequences of their behavior, which can include imprudent sexual activities, overspending, and reckless driving. They may stop sleeping but stay incredibly energetic. Attempts by others to curb such excesses can quickly bring anger and even rage. Mania usually comes on suddenly over a period of a day or two.

The proposed DSM-5 also includes criteria for **hypomania** (see diagnostic criteria for mania and hypomania). *Hypo-* comes from the Greek for "under"; hypomania is "under"—less extreme than—mania. Although mania involves significant impairment, hypomania does not. Rather, hypomania involves a change in functioning that does not cause serious problems. The person with hypomania may feel more social, flirtatious, energized, and productive.

Bipolar I Disorder   In the proposed DSM-5, the criteria for diagnosis of **bipolar I disorder** (formerly known as manic-depressive disorder) include a single episode of mania during the course of a person's life. Note, then, that a person who is diagnosed with bipolar I disorder may or may not be experiencing current symptoms of mania. In fact, even someone who experienced only 1 week of manic symptoms years ago is still diagnosed with bipolar I disorder. Even more than episodes of MDD, bipolar episodes tend to recur. More than half of people with bipolar I disorder experience four or more episodes (Goodwin & Jamison, 1990).

Bipolar II Disorder   The proposed DSM-5 also includes a milder form of bipolar disorder, called **bipolar II disorder**. To be diagnosed with bipolar II disorder, a person must have experienced at least one major depressive episode and at least one episode of hypomania.

Cyclothymic Disorder   Also called *cyclothymia,* **cyclothymic disorder** is a second chronic mood disorder (the other is dysthymia). As with the diagnosis of dysthymia, the proposed DSM-5 criteria require that symptoms be present for at least 2 years among adults (see diagnostic criteria). In cyclothymic disorder, the person has frequent but mild symptoms of depression, alternating with mild symptoms of mania. Although the symptoms do not reach the severity

In his book *Electroboy*, Andy Berhman describes receiving incorrect diagnoses of his bipolar disorder for years, a problem that is all too common. (NY Daily News via Getty Images.)

Proposed DSM-5 Criteria for Manic and Hypomanic Episodes

Distinctly elevated or irritable mood for most of the day nearly every day.

Abnormally increased activity and energy.

At least three of the following are *noticeably changed from baseline* (four if mood is irritable):

- Increase in goal-directed activity or psychomotor agitation
- Unusual talkativeness; rapid speech
- Flight of ideas or subjective impression that thoughts are racing
- Decreased need for sleep
- Increased self-esteem; belief that one has special talents, powers, or abilities
- Distractibility; attention easily diverted
- Excessive involvement in activities that are likely to have undesirable consequences, such as reckless spending, sexual behavior, or driving

For a manic episode:

- Symptoms last for 1 week or require hospitalization
- Symptoms cause significant distress or functional impairmen

For a hypomanic episode:

- Symptoms last at least 4 days
- Clear changes in functioning that are observable to others, but impairment is not marked
- No psychotic symptoms are present

Note: Italics reflect changes introduced in DSM-5.

Proposed DSM-5 Criteria for Cyclothymic Disorder

For at least 2 years (or 1 year in children or adolescents):

- Numerous periods with hypomanic symptoms that do not meet criteria for a manic episode
- Numerous periods with depressive symptoms that do not meet criteria for a major depressive episode.

The symptoms do not clear for more than 2 months at a time.

Symptoms cause significant distress or functional impairment.

Clinical Case: Wayne

Wayne, a 32-year-old insurance appraiser, had been married for 8 years. He and his wife and their two children lived comfortably and happily in a middle-class neighborhood. He had not experienced any clear symptoms until age 32. One morning, Wayne told his wife that he was bursting with energy and ideas, that his job was unfulfilling, and that he was just wasting his talent. That night he slept little, spending most of the time at his desk, writing furiously. The next morning he left for work at the usual time but returned home at 11:00 A.M., his car overflowing with aquariums and other equipment for tropical fish. He had quit his job, then withdrawn all the money from the family's savings account and spent it on tropical fish equipment. Wayne reported that the previous night he had worked out a way to modify existing equipment so that fish "won't die anymore. We'll be millionaires." After unloading the paraphernalia, Wayne set off to canvass the neighborhood for possible buyers, going door-to-door and talking to anyone who would listen.

Wayne reported that no one in his family had been treated for bipolar disorder, but his mother had gone through periods when she would stop sleeping and become extremely adventurous. For the most part, the family had regarded these episodes as unproblematic, but during one period she had set off across the country without the children and had returned only after spending a major amount of money.

The following bit of conversation indicates Wayne's incorrigible optimism and provocativeness:

Therapist: *Well, you seem pretty happy today.*
Wayne: *Happy! Happy! You certainly are a master of understatement, you rogue! [Shouting, literally jumping out of his seat.] Why, I'm ecstatic! I'm leaving for the West Coast today, on my daughter's bicycle. Only 3,100 miles. That's nothing, you know. I could probably walk, but I want to get there by next week. And along the way I plan to contact a lot of people about investing in my fish equipment. I'll get to know more people that way—you know, Doc, "know" in the biblical sense. Oh, God, how good it feels.*

of full-blown manic or depressive episodes, people with the disorder and those close to them typically notice the ups and downs. During the lows, a person may be sad, feel inadequate, withdraw from people, and sleep for 10 hours a night. During the highs, a person may be boisterous, overly confident, socially uninhibited and gregarious, and need little sleep.

Epidemiology and Consequences of Bipolar Disorders Bipolar I disorder is much rarer than MDD. In an epidemiological study that involved diagnostic interviews with 61,392 people across 11 countries, about 6 out of 1,000 (0.6 percent) people met the criteria for bipolar I disorder (Merikangas, Jin, He, et al., 2011). Rates of bipolar disorder appear to be higher in the United States than in other countries that have been studied. For example, in the United States, about 1 percent of people experience bipolar I disorder (Merikangas, Akiskal, Angst, et al., 2007). It is hard to interpret the findings regarding the relatively high prevalence of bipolar disorder in the United States. In one study, researchers asked psychiatrists from the United States, India, and the United Kingdom to watch the same videotaped interviews and rate the severity of manic symptoms. Psychiatrists from the United States and from India tended to see symptoms as more severe than did those from the United Kingdom—culture may shape tendencies to label behaviors as manic symptoms (Mackin, Targum, Kalali, et al., 2006).

It is extremely hard to estimate the prevalence of milder forms of bipolar disorder, because some of the most commonly used diagnostic interviews are not reliable. When researchers have reinterviewed people who met diagnostic criteria for bipolar II disorder using structured clinical interviews, the initial diagnosis of bipolar II disorder was confirmed for less than half of people (Kessler, Akiskal, Angst, et al., 2006). (Many of those were diagnosed with other forms of bipolar disorder.) As you might expect given the low reliability, the prevalence estimates then vary, with large-scale epidemiological studies suggesting that bipolar II disorder affects somewhere between 0.4 percent to 2 percent of people (Merikangas et al., 2007, 2011). It is estimated that about 4 percent of people experience cyclothymic disorder (Regeer, Ten Have, Rosso, et al., 2004).

More than half of those with bipolar spectrum disorders report onset before age 25 (Merikangas et al., 2011), but these conditions are being seen with increasing frequency among children and adolescents (Kessler et al., 2005). Bipolar disorders occur equally often in men and women, but women experience more episodes of depression than do men (Altshuler, Kupka, Hellemann, et al., 2010). About two-thirds of people diagnosed with bipolar disorder meet diagnostic criteria for a comorbid anxiety disorder, and more than a third report a history of substance abuse.

Bipolar I disorder is among the most severe forms of mental illnesses. One-third of people remain unemployed a full year after hospitalization for mania (Harrow, Goldberg, Grossman, et al., 1990). It has been estimated that people with bipolar disorders are unable to work about 25 percent of the time (Kessler et al., 2006). Suicide rates are high for both bipolar I and bipolar II disorders (Angst, Stassen, Clayton, et al., 2002). One in every four persons with bipolar I disorder and one in every five of those with bipolar II disorder report a history of suicide attempts (Merikangas et al., 2011). People with bipolar disorders are at high risk for a range of other medical conditions, including cardiovascular disease, diabetes mellitus, obesity, and thyroid disease (Kupfer, 2005). Not only are medical problems present, they are often quite severe. People who have been hospitalized for bipolar I disorder are twice as likely to die from medical illnesses in a given year as are people without mood disorders (Osby, Brandt, Correia, et al., 2001). These sad consequences of bipolar disorders are not offset by evidence that hypomania is associated with creativity and achievement (see Focus on Discovery 5.4).

People with cyclothymia are at elevated risk for developing episodes of mania and major depression. Even if full-blown manic episodes do not emerge, the chronicity of cyclothymic symptoms takes a toll.

FOCUS ON DISCOVERY 5.4

Creativity and Mood Disorders

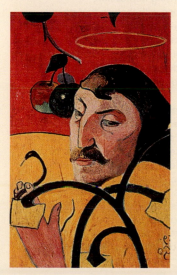

Noted psychologist Kay Redfield Jamison, shown here in 1993, has written extensively about creativity and mood disorders. (Time & Life Pictures/ Getty Images, Inc.)

In her book *Touched with Fire: Manic-Depressive Illness and the Artistic Temperament* (1992), Kay Jamison, an expert on bipolar disorders and herself a longtime sufferer from bipolar I disorder, assembled much evidence linking mood disorders, especially bipolar disorder, to artistic creativity. Of course, most people with mood disorders are not particularly creative, and most creative people do not have mood disorders—but the list of visual artists, composers, and writers who seem to have experienced mood disorders is impressive, including Michelangelo, van Gogh, Tchaikovsky, Schumann, Gauguin, Tennyson, Shelley, Faulkner, Hemingway, (F. Scott) Fitzgerald, and Whitman, among others. In recent years, many actors and actresses have also spoken out about their history of mania, including Stephen Frye, Carrie Fisher, and Linda Hamilton.

Many people assume that the manic state itself fosters creativity through elated mood, increased energy, rapid thoughts, and a heightened ability

Self-portrait by Paul Gauguin. He is one of the many artists and writers who apparently suffered from a mood disorder. (Paul Gauguin/SUPERSTOCK.)

to make connections among seemingly unrelated events. Extreme mania, however, lowers creative output, and even if people produce more work during a manic period, the quality of that work might suffer, as seems to have been the case for the composer Robert Schumann (Weisberg, 1994). Moreover, studies have shown that people who have experienced episodes of mania tend to be less creative than those who have had the milder episodes of hypomania, and both groups tend to produce less creative output than do non-ill family members (Richards, Kinney, Lunde, et al., 1988). These findings are important because many people with bipolar disorder worry that taking medications may limit their creativity. Rather, reducing manic symptoms should help, rather than hurt, creativity.

Frank Sinatra is quoted as having said this about himself: "Being an 18-karat manic depressive, and having lived a life of violent emotional contradictions, I have an over-acute capacity for sadness as well as elation." (p. 218, Summers, A. & Swan, R. (2006). Sinatra: The Life, NY, NY: Vintage Books.) (Getty Images, Inc.)

Mood disorders are common among artists and writers. Tchaikovsky was affected. (Photo Researchers, Inc.)

Check Your Knowledge 5.1 (Answers are at the end of the chapter.)

Fill in the blanks.

1. Major depressive disorder is diagnosed based on at least _____ symptoms lasting at least _____ weeks.
2. Approximately _____ percent of people will experience major depressive disorder during their lifetime.
3. Among adults, depressive symptoms must last for at least _____ years to qualify for a DSM-5 diagnosis of dysthymia.
4. Worldwide, approximately _____ out of every 1,000 people will experience a manic episode during their lifetime.
5. Bipolar I disorder is diagnosed on the basis of _____ episodes, and bipolar II disorder is diagnosed on the basis of _____ episodes.

Subtypes of Depressive Disorders and Bipolar Disorders

The mood disorders are highly heterogeneous—that is, people who have been diagnosed with the same disorder may show very different symptoms. The proposed DSM-5 deals with this by providing criteria for dividing MDD and bipolar disorders into a number of subtypes, based on either specific symptoms or the pattern of symptoms over time (see Table 5.2 for a list of subtypes and their definitions). **Rapid cycling** (see Figure 5.3) and seasonal subtypes refer to the overall pattern of episodes over time, whereas other subtypes describe the current episode of major depression or mania. All of the subtypes can be applied to either major depressive disorder or bipolar disorders, with the exception of rapid cycling, which is diagnosed only for bipolar disorder. Most of the episode subtypes can be applied to both depressed and manic episodes, but the term **melancholic** is used only for episodes of depression.

In addition to subtypes, DSM-5 proposes specifiers for the severity of each disorder. An example of severity ratings for depression is included in Figure 3.5 (p. 72).

Table 5.2 Subtypes of Major Depressive Disorder and Bipolar Disorders

Subtype	Applicable to MDD?	Applicable to bipolar disorder?	Definition
Seasonal pattern	Yes	Yes	Episodes happen regularly at a particular time of the year
Rapid cycling	No	Yes	At least four episodes within the past year
Mood-congruent psychotic features	Yes	Yes	Delusions or hallucinations with themes that are consistent with the mood state (e.g., guilt, disease, or death themes accompanying depression)
Mood-incongruent psychotic features	Yes	Yes	Delusions or hallucinations with themes that do not match the valence of the depressive or manic episode
Mixed features	Yes	Yes	At least three manic symptoms are present during a depressive episode, or at least three depressive symptoms are present during a manic episode
Catatonic features	Yes	Yes	Extreme physical immobility or excessive peculiar physical movement
Melancholic features	Yes	Yes (for depressive episodes)	Lack of pleasure in any activity, inability to gain relief from positive events, and at least three other symptoms of depression, such as a distinct quality of mood, depressive symptoms that are worse in the morning than at other times of day, waking at least 2 hours too early, loss of appetite, psychomotor retardation or agitation, or guilt
Atypical features	Yes	Yes	Symptoms that are unusual for depressive or manic episodes are present
Postpartum onset	Yes	Yes	Onset within 4 weeks postpartum
With anxiety	Yes	Yes	Symptoms of anxiety are present
Suicide risk severity	Yes	Yes	Suicidal ideation, plans, or other risk indicators are present

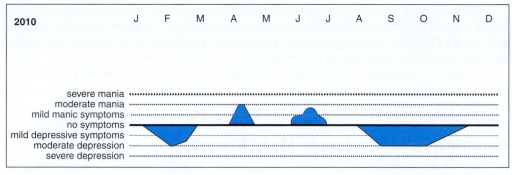

Figure 5.3 The rapid cycling subtype of bipolar disorder is defined by at least four mood episodes per year, as shown in this case.

The seasonal subtype of major depressive disorder has achieved a fair amount of support (see Focus on Discovery 5.2 for discussion), but many of the other subtypes have not been well validated. For example, although about 14 percent of women meet diagnostic criteria for postpartum depression (O'Hara & Swain, 1996), many of these women had experienced at least some symptoms before the birth, and the prevalence of depression postpartum is not drastically elevated compared to other periods in life. Similarly, problems exist with the rapid cycling subtype. In a longitudinal study, 95 percent of persons with rapid cycling bipolar disorder at baseline were no longer experiencing rapid cycling 1 year later (Schneck, Miklowitz, Miyahara, et al., 2008). As a third example of problems with subtypes, MDD with melancholic features may just be a more severe type of depression—that is, people with melancholic features have more comorbidity (e.g., with anxiety disorders), more frequent episodes of depression, and more impairment in everyday activities (Kendler, 1997). Although most subtypes are not related to distinct causes or to long-term prognosis, the subtypes may suggest targets to consider in treatment planning.

Mike Wallace, an internationally recognized reporter, has talked openly about his struggles with major depressive disorder. (© AP/Wide World Photos.)

Quick Summary

The proposed DSM-5 contains two broad types of mood disorders: depressive disorders and bipolar disorders. Depressive disorders include major depressive disorder and dysthymia as well as three new disorders: mixed anxiety/depressive disorder, premenstrual dysphoric disorder, and disruptive mood dysregulation disorder. Bipolar disorders include bipolar I disorder, bipolar II disorder, and cyclothymic disorder. Major depression is characterized by severe episodes lasting at least 2 weeks, whereas dysthymia is characterized by milder symptoms that last at least 2 years.

Bipolar I disorder is diagnosed on the basis of a single lifetime manic episode, and bipolar II disorder is diagnosed on the basis of hypomania and major depression. Cyclothymia is defined by frequent shifts between mild depressive and manic symptoms that last at least 2 years.

Subtypes of mood disorders are used to differentiate patterns of symptoms. Seasonal and rapid cycling subtypes are defined by the pattern of episodes over time; other subtypes are used to label the features of the current episode, including mood-congruent or mood-incongruent psychotic features, mixed features, catatonic features, postpartum onset, anxious features, suicide risk severity, and, for depression, melancholia.

MDD is one of the most common psychological disorders, whereas bipolar I disorder affects 1 percent or less of the population. MDD affects twice as many women as men. Most people with MDD will experience another episode. Bipolar disorder is even more recurrent than MDD—about 50 percent of people with bipolar I disorder experience four or more episodes.

Etiology of Mood Disorders

When we think of the profound extremes embodied in the mood disorders, it is natural to ask why these happen. How can we explain Lily sinking into the depths of depression? What factors combined to drive Wayne into his frenzied state of unrealistic ambitions? Studies of etiology focus on why these disorders unfold. No single cause can explain mood disorders. A number of different factors combine to explain their onset.

While the diagnostic criteria specify several different depressive disorders and bipolar disorders, the research on etiology and treatment has tended to focus on major depressive disorder and bipolar I disorder. For simplicity, we refer to these conditions as depression and bipolar disorder through the remainder of this chapter.

We begin by discussing neurobiological factors involved in depression and bipolar disorder. After describing these neurobiological factors, we discuss psychosocial predictors of depression, then turn to psychosocial models of bipolar disorder.

Neurobiological Factors in Mood Disorders

As Table 5.3 shows, there are many different approaches to understanding the neurobiological factors involved in mood disorders. Here, we will discuss genetic, neurotransmitter, brain-imaging, and neuroendocrine research.

Genetic Factors   The more careful studies of MZ (identical) and DZ (fraternal) twins yield heritability estimates of 37 percent for MDD (Sullivan, Neale, & Kendler, 2000). That is, about 37 percent of the variance in depression is explained by genes. Heritability estimates are higher when researchers study more severe samples (e.g., when the people in the study are recruited in inpatient hospitals rather than outpatient clinics). Beyond the twin studies, one small adoption study also supports the modest heritability of MDD (Wender, Kety, Rosenthal, et al., 1986).

Bipolar disorder is among the most heritable of disorders. Much of the evidence for this comes from studies of twins. The most careful twin studies involve community studies where a representative sample is interviewed (rather than focusing only on people who seek treatment, who may have more severe cases of the disorder than those who are not treated). A Finnish community-based twin sample that used structured interviews to verify diagnoses obtained a heritability estimate of 93 percent (Kieseppa, Partonen, Haukka, et al., 2004). Adoption studies also confirm the importance of heritability in bipolar disorder (e.g., Wender et al., 1986). Bipolar II disorder is also highly heritable (Edvardsen, Torgersen, Roysamb, et al., 2008). Genetic models, however, do not explain the timing of manic symptoms. Other factors likely serve as the immediate triggers of symptoms.

There is a huge amount of interest in finding the specific genes involved in mood disorders through molecular genetics research (see Chapters 2 and 4 for a review of these methods). You should be aware of the large number of nonreplications within this field. For example, in a meta-analysis of bipolar disorder and MDD, Kato (2007) identified 166 genetic loci (i.e., locations on specific chromosomes) that had been linked with bipolar disorder and with MDD in initial studies. Of those 166 loci, only 6 have been studied multiple times and replicated in more than 75 percent of relevant studies.

These inconsistencies are even more troubling because positive results are much more likely to be published than null findings. Segurado and colleagues (2003) took an extra step to avoid these publication biases. Whereas previous analyses had compiled only published data, they gathered 18 original data sets, each with more than 20 probands affected by bipolar disorder, to be able to analyze even the negative, unpublished findings for genetic regions associated with bipolar disorder. Their meta-analysis provided the strongest support for three out of 120 regions implicated in bipolar disorder: 9p22.3–21.1, 10g11.21–22.1, and 14q24.1–32.12.

Table 5.3 Summary of Neurobiological Hypotheses about Major Depression and Bipolar Disorder		
Neurobiological Hypothesis	**Major Depression**	**Bipolar Disorder**
Genetic contribution	Moderate	High
Serotonin and dopamine receptor dysfunction	Present	Present
Cortisol dysregulation	Present	Present
Changes in activation of emotion-relevant regions in the brain	Present	Present
Increased activity of the striatum	Not present	Present during mania
Changes in cell membranes and receptors	Not present	Present

Even these three regions have not been replicated in more than 10 of the 18 studies. Positive findings should be taken with a grain of salt, as disconfirmation appears to be the rule rather than the exception.

Despite the complexities of this area, there are some consistent patterns emerging across studies. We will discuss findings below that suggest that a polymorphism of the serotonin transporter gene may influence vulnerability to depression when life stress occurs. In addition, there is evidence that a gene that influences dopamine function, the DRD4.2, is related to MDD, in that a meta-analysis of 917 patients and 1,164 controls revealed that MDD was more common among people with a polymorphism in the DRD4.2 gene (Lopez Leon, Croes, Sayed-Tabatabaei, et al., 2005). These findings help provide an understanding of how the neurotransmitter deficits associated with mood disorders might develop.

Because the mood disorders are characterized by so many different symptoms, most researchers think that these disorders will eventually be related to a set of genes rather than to any single gene. Even if we can identify the genes involved in mood disorders, many questions still remain about how they work. It is unlikely that genes simply control whether or not a person develops depression. Rather, as we will discuss later, genes may guide the way people regulate emotions or respond to life stressors (Kendler, Gatz, Gardner, et al., 2006). As such, they may set the stage for mood disorders to occur when other conditions are present.

Neurotransmitters Three neurotransmitters have been studied the most in terms of their possible role in mood disorders: norepinephrine, dopamine, and serotonin. Each of these neurotransmitters is present in many different areas of the brain. Figure 5.4 illustrates how widespread serotonin and dopamine pathways are in the brain.

Researchers initially believed that mood disorders would be explained by absolute levels of neurotransmitters in the synaptic cleft that were either too high or too low. For example, depression would be tied to low norepinephrine and dopamine levels, and mania would be tied to high norepinephrine and dopamine levels. Mania and depression were also both posited to be tied to low serotonin levels (Thase, Jindal, & Howland, 2002). Evidence, however, did not support the idea that absolute levels of neurotransmitters were important in the mood disorders.

Studies of antidepressants were one source of contradictory evidence. On the one hand, these studies do suggest that depression is related in some way to these neurotransmitters. For example, effective antidepressants promote an immediate increase in levels of serotonin, norepinephrine, and/or dopamine. See Figure 5.5 for an overview of these immediate effects. But when researchers studied the time course of how antidepressants change neurotransmitter levels, they began to realize that depression could not be explained just by the absolute level of the neurotransmitters. Antidepressants take 7 to 14 days to relieve depression; by that time, the neurotransmitter levels have already returned to their previous state. It would seem, then, that a simple change in norepinephrine, dopamine, or serotonin levels is not a good explanation for why the drugs alleviate depression.

Other evidence also indicates that absolute levels of neurotransmitters do not tell the whole story. For decades, researchers studied the metabolites of neurotransmitters as an index of how much of a neurotransmitter was being released into the synaptic cleft. Recall that after a neurotransmitter is released into the synaptic cleft, enzymes begin to break down the neurotransmitter that is not reabsorbed by the cell. Metabolite studies, then, assess how much neurotransmitter has been broken down and carried into the cerebrospinal fluid, the blood, or the urine. Findings from metabolite studies were not consistent, suggesting that many people with depression did not have disturbances in the absolute levels of neurotransmitters; similarly, many people with mania did not have disturbances in the absolute levels of neurotransmitters (Placidi, Oquendo, Malone, et al., 2001; Ressler & Nemeroff, 1999).

Given this inconsistent evidence, researchers began to focus on the idea that mood disorders might be related to the sensitivity of postsynaptic receptors that respond to the presence of neurotransmitter in the synaptic cleft. How can researchers test models of high or low receptor sensitivity? If receptors are more or less sensitive, one might expect people to react differently to drugs that influence

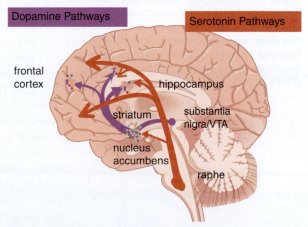

Figure 5.4 Serotonin and dopamine pathways are widespread in the brain.

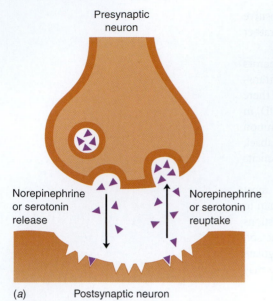

Presynaptic neuron

Norepinephrine or serotonin release

Norepinephrine or serotonin reuptake

(a)   Postsynaptic neuron

Presynaptic neuron

Tricyclic or second-generation antidepressant

(b)   Postsynaptic neuron

Figure 5.5 (a) When neurotransmitters are released into a synapse, a pumplike reuptake mechanism begins to recapture some of the neurotransmitter before it reaches the postsynaptic neuron. (b) Tricyclic drugs block this reuptake process so that more neurotransmitter reaches the receptor. Selective serotonin reuptake inhibitors act more selectively on serotonin. Adapted from Snyder (1986), p. 106.

the level of a given neurotransmitter. For example, receptors that are overly sensitive may respond to even the smallest amount of a neurotransmitter in the synaptic cleft. If receptors are insensitive, a person may show a more pronounced response to a drop in neurotransmitter levels. Researchers have focused more on dopamine and serotonin in these studies than on norepinephrine.

People with depression are less responsive than other people are to drugs that increase dopamine levels, and it is thought that the functioning of the dopamine might be lowered in depression (Naranjo, Tremblay, & Busto, 2001). Dopamine plays a major role in the sensitivity of the **reward system** in the brain, which is believed to guide pleasure, motivation, and energy in the context of opportunities to obtain rewards (Depue & Iacono, 1989). Some research suggests that diminished function of the dopamine system could help explain the deficits in pleasure, motivation, and energy in major depressive disorder (Treadway & Zald, 2011).

Among people with bipolar disorder, several different drugs that increase dopamine levels have been found to trigger manic symptoms. One possibility is that dopamine receptors may be overly sensitive in bipolar disorder (Anand, Verhoeff, Seneca, et al., 2000; Strakowski, Sax, Setters, et al., 1997).

In addition to dopamine, studies have also focused on the sensitivity of serotonin receptors. Researchers have conducted a set of studies that involve experimentally lowering serotonin levels. A person who has insensitive receptors is expected to experience depressive symptoms as levels drop. To lower serotonin levels, researchers deplete levels of **tryptophan**, the major precursor of serotonin. Tryptophan can be depleted with a drink that contains high levels of 15 amino acids but no tryptophan. Within hours, serotonin levels are lowered, an effect that lasts for several hours. As a control condition, people can be given a similar-tasting drink that has no effect on tryptophan. Studies show that depleting tryptophan (and so lowering serotonin levels) causes temporary depressive symptoms among people with a history of depression or a family history of depression (Benkelfat, Ellenbogen, Dean, et al., 1994; Neumeister, Konstantinidis, Stastny, et al., 2002). This effect is not observed among people with no personal or family history of depression. Current thinking is that people who are vulnerable to depression may have less sensitive serotonin receptors, causing them to respond more dramatically to lower levels of serotonin.

Researchers have also examined the effects of tryptophan depletion in bipolar disorder. These studies have focused on those who are vulnerable but do not have the diagnosis—family members of people with bipolar disorder. Like people diagnosed with MDD and their family members, relatives of those with bipolar disorder demonstrate stronger mood reactions to tryptophan depletion compared to matched controls (Sobczak, Honig, Nicolson, et al., 2002). As with depression, it would appear that bipolar disorder may be related to diminished sensitivity of the serotonin receptors.

Brain-Imaging Studies Two different types of brain-imaging studies are commonly used in research on mood disorders. *Structural studies* focus on whether a brain region is smaller or larger among people with a disorder compared to control participants. *Functional activation studies* focus on whether there is a change in the activity of a brain region. Functional studies are used to gain information on how people use the cells they have, inferred based on blood flow to different areas of the brain. Many of the structural changes in MDD are seen only among people who have had multiple episodes of depression (Gotlib & Hamilton, 2008; Sheline, 2000). Here, then, we focus on functional activation studies.

Functional brain-imaging studies suggest that episodes of MDD are associated with changes in many of the brain systems that are involved in experiencing and regulating emotion (Davidson, Pizzagalli, & Nitschke, 2002; Phillips, Ladouceur, & Drevets, 2008a). Table 5.4 summarizes four primary brain structures that have been most studied in depression: the amygdala, the **subgenual anterior cingulate**, the hippocampus, and the **dorsolateral prefrontal cortex** (see also Figure 5.6). We will discuss each of these regions, beginning with the amygdala.

Table 5.4 Brain Structures Involved in Emotion Responses in Major Depression

Brain Structure	Levels of Activity among People with Mood Disorders as Shown in Functional Activation Studies
Amygdala	Elevated
Subgenual anterior cingulate	Elevated
Dorsolateral prefrontal cortex	Diminished during emotion regulation
Hippocampus	Diminished

The amygdala helps a person to assess how emotionally important a stimulus is. For example, animals with damage to the amygdala fail to react with fear to threatening stimuli and also fail to respond positively to food. In humans, the amygdala has been shown to respond when people are shown pictures of threatening stimuli. Functional brain activation studies show elevated activity of the amygdala among people with MDD. For example, when shown negative words or pictures of sad or angry faces, people with current MDD have a more intense and sustained reaction in the amygdala than do people with no MDD (Sheline et al., 2001). This pattern of amygdala overreactivity to emotional stimuli does not look like a medication effect or even a consequence of being in a depressed state, because it can be shown even when people are not taking medications (Siegle, Thompson, Carter, et al., 2007) and among relatives of people with depression who have no personal history of MDD (Van Der Veen, Evers, Deutz, et al., 2007). These findings suggest that amygdala hyperreactivity to emotional stimuli in depression might be part of the vulnerability to depression rather than just the aftermath of being depressed.

The other regions involved in depression (the subgenual anterior cingulate, the hippocampus, and the dorsolateral prefrontal cortex) appear to be particularly important to emotion regulation (Phillips et al., 2008a). MDD is associated with greater activation of the subgenual anterior cingulate (Gotlib & Hamilton, 2008). Helen Mayberg and her colleagues have studied this region using deep brain stimulation, a technique that involves implanting electrodes into the brain. They implanted electrodes into an area next to the subgenual anterior cingulate cortex of six people whose severe depression had not responded to treatment (Mayberg, Lozano, Voon, et al., 2005). By applying a small current to the electrodes, they were able to decrease activity in the subgenual anterior cingulate cortex temporarily. Four of the six people reported immediate relief from their depressive symptoms. Although it is too early to consider this as a treatment, the findings provide support for the idea that this part of the brain plays an important role in depression.

Finally, people with depression demonstrate diminished activation of the hippocampus during exposure to emotional stimuli (Davidson et al., 2002; Schaefer, Putnam, Benca, et al., 2006) and of the dorsolateral prefrontal cortex when asked to regulate their emotions (Fales, Barch, Rundle, et al., 2008). Difficulty activating these regions is believed to interfere with effective emotion regulation.

How might these findings fit together? One theory is that the overactivity in the amygdala during depression causes oversensitivity to emotionally relevant stimuli. At the same time, systems involved in regulating emotions are compromised (the subgenual anterior cingulate, the hippocampus, and the dorsolateral prefrontal cortex).

Many of the brain structures implicated in MDD also appear to be involved in bipolar disorder. In functional studies, bipolar I disorder is associated with elevated responsiveness in the amygdala, increased activity of the anterior cingulate during emotion regulation tasks, and diminished activity of the hippocampus and dorsolateral prefrontal cortex (Houenou, Frommberger, Carde, et al., 2011; Phillips, Ladouceur, & Drevets, 2008b).

To date, brain-imaging research tells us little about what differentiates people with bipolar disorder from those with MDD. Many of the neuroimaging findings for

A) Dorsolateral prefrontal cortex (blue)

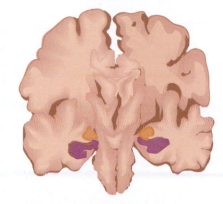

B) Hippocampus (purple) and amygdala (orange)

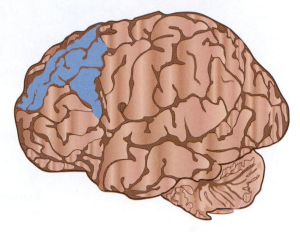

C) Anterior cingulate cortex (yellow) and subgenual anterior cingulate (brown)

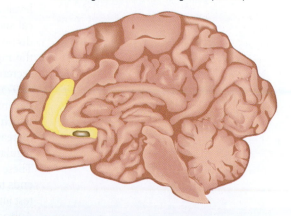

Figure 5.6 Key brain regions involved in mood disorders. Adapted from the *Annual Review of Psychology*, 53, copyright 2002 by Annual Reviews, www.annualreviews.org. Reprinted with permission from the publisher.

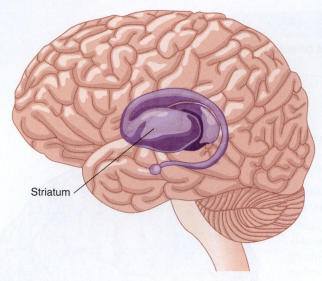

Figure 5. 7 The striatum appears to be overly active during mania.

bipolar disorder are very similar to those seen among patients with MDD. One clue might emerge from studying what happens in the brain during manic periods. Many of the brain patterns that are shown during mania are very similar to those shown during depression. On the other hand, one difference emerges. During mania, but not depression, a brain region called the striatum (see Figure 5.7), which is implicated in reactions to reward, is overly active (Marchand & Yurgelun-Todd, 2010). These findings, though, are tentative. Knowing that the striatum is more active during a manic episode does not tell us whether this is a cause of the condition.

Another set of promising findings suggest that MDD and bipolar disorder might be differentiated by changes in the way that neurons throughout the brain function. People with bipolar disorder often have deficits in the membranes of their neurons (Looney & El-Mallakh, 1997). These deficits seem to operate across the brain, and they influence how readily neurons can be activated. These cellular membrane deficits are not seen in people with MDD (Thiruvengadam & Chandrasekaran, 2007). Similar research is focused on a protein involved in the functioning of many aspects of the neuron, protein kinase C. Protein kinase C has a major role in the function of receptors and cell membranes of neurons throughout the brain. Protein kinase C activity appears to be abnormally high among people with mania (Yildiz, Guleryuz, Ankerst, et al., 2008). Although these findings for neuronal function are less well established than are other brain findings, they suggest intriguing differences between bipolar disorder and MDD.

The Neuroendocrine System: Cortisol Dysregulation The HPA axis (hypothalamic–pituitary–adrenocortical axis; see Figure 2.12), the biological system that manages reactivity to stress, may be overly active during episodes of MDD. As described above, there is evidence that the amygdala is overly reactive among people with MDD, and the amygdala sends signals that activate the HPA axis. The HPA axis triggers the release of cortisol, the main stress hormone. Cortisol is secreted at times of stress and increases activity of the immune system to help the body prepare for threats.

Various findings link depression to high cortisol levels. For example, people with **Cushing's syndrome**, which causes oversecretion of cortisol, frequently experience depressive symptoms. A second line of research with animals has shown that when chemicals that trigger cortisol release are injected into the brain, many of the classic symptoms of depression are produced, including decreased interest in sex, decreased appetite, and sleep disturbance (Gutman & Nemeroff, 2003). In animals and humans, then, too much cortisol seems to produce depressive symptoms.

Even among people who are depressed but do not have Cushing's syndrome, cortisol levels are often poorly regulated—that is, the system does not seem to respond well to biological signals to decrease cortisol levels (Garbutt, Mayo, Little, et al., 1994). Among people who do not have a mood disorder, dexamethasone suppresses cortisol secretion over the course of the night. In contrast, for some those with MDD, dexamethasone does not suppress cortisol secretion, particularly among those with psychotic symptoms of depression (Nelson & Davis, 1997). This lack of cortisol suppression is seen as a sign of poor regulation of the HPA axis. The dexamethasone suppression test (dex/CRH) is an even more sensitive test of the HPA system in which researchers administer both dexamethasone and corticotropin-releasing hormone (which increases cortisol levels). About 80 percent of people hospitalized for depression show poor regulation of the HPA system on the dex/CRH test (Heuser, Yassouridis, & Holsboer, 1994). These abnormal responses to dexamethasone, though, normalize when the depressive episode ends for most people. People who continue to show elevated cortisol responses to the dex/CRH test after recovery from a depressive episode are more likely to relapse within the next year (e.g., Aubry, Gervasoni, Osiek, et al., 2007).

Although cortisol helps mobilize beneficial short-term stress responses, prolonged high levels of cortisol can cause harm to body systems. For example, long-term excesses of cortisol have been linked to damage to the hippocampus—studies have found smaller-than-normal hippocampus volume among people who have experienced depression for years (e.g., Videbech & Ravnkilde, 2004).

Like people with MDD, people with bipolar disorder fail to demonstrate the typical suppression of cortisol after the dex/CRH test. This suggests that bipolar disorder is also characterized by a poorly regulated cortisol system (Watson, Thompson, Ritchie, et al., 2006). Like those with MDD, people with bipolar disorder who continue to show abnormal responses to cortisol challenge tests after their episode clears are at high risk for more episodes in the future (Vieta, Martinez-DeOsaba, Colom, et al., 1999).

In sum, both bipolar disorder and MDD are characterized by problems in the regulation of cortisol levels. Dysregulation in cortisol levels also predicts a worse course of illness for bipolar disorder and MDD.

Quick Summary

Bipolar disorder is highly heritable, and major depression is modestly heritable.

Neurotransmitter models focus on serotonin, dopamine, and norepinephrine. Current research focuses on receptor sensitivity rather than absolute levels of neurotransmitters. Receptor sensitivity is often tested by manipulating the levels of neurotransmitters. Tryptophan depletion studies indicate that deficits in serotonin receptors are associated with depression and bipolar disorder. It also appears that depression may be related to diminished dopamine receptor sensitivity and mania may be related to enhanced dopamine receptor sensitivity.

Neuroimaging studies suggest that depression and bipolar disorder are both associated with changes in regions of the brain that are involved in emotion. These changes seem consistent with a greater emotional reactivity (heightened activity of the amygdala) but less ability to regulate emotion (diminished activity of the dorsolateral prefrontal cortex and hippocampus, and greater activity of the subgenual anterior cingulate).

Major depressive disorder and bipolar disorder are both related to poor regulation of cortisol when assessed using the dex/CRH test. Cortisol dysregulation also predicts a more severe course of mood symptoms over time.

As noted, major depressive disorder and bipolar disorder seem similar on many of these biological variables. Compared to major depressive disorder, bipolar disorder may be uniquely related to increased sensitivity of the dopamine receptors, increased activity in a region of the brain called the striatum, and changes in protein kinase C, which influences the receptors and the membranes of neurons throughout the brain.

Check Your Knowledge 5.2

Answer the questions.

1. Estimates of heritability are approximately _____ percent for MDD and _____ percent for bipolar I disorder.
   a. 60, 93
   b. 20, 100
   c. 37, 93
   d. 10, 59
2. Depression and mania involve diminished receptor sensitivity of which of the following neurotransmitter systems?
   a. acetylcholine
   b. serotonin
   c. dopamine
   d. norepinephrine
3. Recent models suggest that depression is:
   a. related to absolute levels of neurotransmitters
   b. related to changes in receptor sensitivity for neurotransmitters
   c. unrelated to neurotransmitter systems
4. In depression, dysregulation of the HPA axis is shown by:
   a. hypersensitivity of the pituitary gland
   b. failure to suppress cortisol by dexamethasone
   c. too little cortisol
   d. elevated parasympathetic nervous system activity
5. One brain region that appears to be overly active among people with mood disorders is the:
   a. hippocampus
   b. dorsolateral prefrontal cortex
   c. cerebellum
   d. amygdala

Social Factors in Depression: Life Events and Interpersonal Difficulties

Data indicate that neurobiological factors influence whether or not a person develops a mood disorder. Does this mean that social and psychological theories are useless? Not in the least. For example, neurobiological theories are consistent with increased emotional reactivity to life events among people with mood disorders. Neurobiological factors, then, may be diatheses (p. 58) that increase risk for mood disorders in the context of other triggers or stressors.

The role of stressful life events in triggering episodes of depression is well established. A great deal of research has focused on cause–effect relationships: do life events cause depression, or does depression cause life events? Prospective studies have been particularly important, because they have shown that life events typically happen before the depressive episode begins. Even with a prospective study, though, it remains possible that some life events are caused by early symptoms of depression that have not yet developed into a full-blown disorder.

Even when researchers exclude stressful life events caused by mild depressive symptoms, there is much evidence that stress can cause major depressive disorder. In careful prospective studies, 42 to 67 percent of people report that they experienced a very serious life event (that was not caused by symptoms) in the year before their depression began. Common events include losing a job, a key friendship, or a romantic relationship. These findings have been replicated in at least 12 studies, conducted in six different countries (Brown & Harris, 1989a). Certain types of life events, such as loss and humiliation, appear particularly likely to trigger depressive episodes (Kendler, Hettema, Butera, et al., 2003). Above and beyond the people who report stressful life events that happened suddenly, many people with depression report that they had been experiencing long-term chronic stressors before the depression, such as poverty (Brown & Harris, 1989b). Life events appear to be particularly important in the first episode of depression but less likely to be involved in later episodes (Monroe & Harkness, 2005; Stroud, Davila, Hammen, et al., 2011).

Why do some people, but not others, become depressed after stressful life events? The obvious answer is that some people must be more vulnerable to stress than others. In the previous section, we described neurobiological systems involved in depression; many of these systems could be involved in reactivity to stress. Psychological and cognitive vulnerabilities also appear to be important. The most common models, then, are diathesis–stress models—that is, models that consider both preexisting vulnerabilities (diatheses) and stressors. Diatheses could be biological, social, or psychological.

One diathesis may be a lack of social support. People who are depressed tend to have sparse social networks and to regard those networks as providing little support (Keltner & Kring, 1998). Low social support may lessen a person's ability to handle stressful life events. One study showed that women experiencing a severely stressful life event without support from a confidant had a 40 percent risk of developing depression, whereas those with a confidant's support had only a 4 percent risk (Brown & Andrews, 1986). Social support, then, seems to buffer against the effects of severe stressors.

There is also some evidence that interpersonal problems within the family are particularly likely to trigger depression. A long line of research has focused on **expressed emotion (EE)**, defined as a family member's critical or hostile comments toward or emotional overinvolvement with the person with depression. High EE strongly predicts relapse in depression. Indeed, one review of six studies found that 69.5 percent of patients in families with high EE relapsed within 1 year, compared to 30.5 percent of patient in families with low EE (Butzlaff & Hooley, 1998). In a community study, marital discord also predicted the onset of depression (Whisman & Bruce, 1999).

Clearly, interpersonal problems can trigger the onset of depressive symptoms, but it is also important to consider the flip side of the coin. Once depressive symptoms emerge, they can create interpersonal problems—that is, depressive symptoms seem to elicit negative reactions from others (Coyne, 1976). For example, roommates of college students with depression rated social contacts with them as less enjoyable, and they reported feeling hostility toward them (Joiner, Alfano, & Metalsky, 1992).

Other research has explored the interpersonal effects of constant reassurance seeking (Joiner, 1995). More than most, people who are depressed seek reassurance that others truly care about them. But even when others express support, they are only temporarily satisfied. Their negative self-concept causes them to doubt the positive feedback, and their constant efforts to obtain reassurance come to irritate others. People experiencing depression actually elicit negative feedback (e.g., by asking questions like "How do you truly feel about me?" after the other person has already given support); eventually, other people's responses can confirm the person's negative self-concept. Ultimately, the person's excessive reassurance seeking can lead to rejection (Joiner & Metalsky, 1995).

Many of the negative social behaviors, such as excessive reassurance seeking, could be the result of depression. If some of these same social problems are present before symptoms appear, can the problems increase the risk for depression? Research suggests that the answer is yes. Among a group of undergraduates who were not initially depressed, those who were high in reassurance seeking were more likely to develop depressive symptoms over a 10-week period (Joiner & Metalsky, 2001). Similarly, research using high-risk samples, identified before the onset of depression, suggests that interpersonal problems may precede depression. For example, the behavior of elementary school children of parents with depression was rated negatively by both peers and teachers (Weintraub, Prinz, & Neale, 1978); low social competence predicted the onset of depression among elementary school children (Cole, Martin, Powers, et al., 1990); and poor interpersonal problem-solving skills predicted increases in depression among adolescents (Davila, Hammen, Burge, et al., 1995). Interpersonal problems are one risk factor for depression.

Psychological Factors in Depression

Many different psychological factors may play a role in depressive disorders. In this section, we discuss personality and cognitive factors. Personality and cognitive theories describe different diatheses that might increase the risk of responding to negative life events with a depressive episode.

Neuroticism   Several longitudinal studies suggest that **neuroticism**, a personality trait that involves the tendency to react to events with greater-than-average negative affect, predicts the onset of depression (Jorm, Christensen, Henderson, et al., 2000). A large study of twins suggests that neuroticism explains at least part of the genetic vulnerability to depression (Fanous, Prescott, & Kendler, 2004). As you would expect, neuroticism is associated with anxiety as well as dysthymia (Kotov, Gamez, Schmidt, et al., 2010). We discuss the overlap of anxiety and depression in Focus on Discovery 5.5.

Cognitive Theories   In cognitive theories, negative thoughts and beliefs are seen as major causes of depression. Pessimistic and self-critical thoughts can torture the person with depression. We will describe three cognitive theories. Beck's theory and hopelessness theory both emphasize these types of negative thoughts, although the theories differ in some important ways. Rumination theory emphasizes the tendency to dwell on negative moods and thoughts.

Beck's Theory   Aaron Beck (1967) argued that depression is associated with a **negative triad**: negative views of the self, the world, and the future (see Figure 5.9). The "world" part of the depressive triad refers to the person's own corner of the world—the situations he or she faces. For example, people might think "I cannot possibly cope with all these demands and responsibilities" as opposed to worrying about problems in the broader world outside of their life.

According to this model, in childhood, people with depression acquired negative schema through experiences such as loss of a parent, the social rejection of peers, or the depressive attitude of a parent. Schemas are different from conscious thoughts—they are an underlying set of beliefs that operate outside of a person's awareness to shape the way a person makes sense of his or her experiences. The negative schema is activated whenever the person encounters situations similar to those that originally caused the schema to form.

Proposed DSM-5 Criteria for Mixed Anxiety/ Depressive Disorder

- Three or four of the symptoms of major depression
- Depressed mood or absence of pleasure
- Anxious distress as evidenced by at least two of the following: irrational worry, preoccupation with worries, trouble relaxing, motor tension, or fear that something awful might happen
- Symptoms are present for at least 2 weeks
- No other DSM diagnosis of anxiety or depression is present

FOCUS ON DISCOVERY 5.5

Understanding the Overlap in Anxiety and Depression

One idea proposed for DSM-5 was to consider whether anxiety disorders and depressive disorders are distinct. There are several reasons to question whether anxiety disorders should be considered to be separable from depressive disorders. Chief among these reasons is the high rate of comorbidity. At least 60 percent of people with an anxiety disorder will experience major depressive disorder during their lifetime, and vice versa—about 60 percent of those with depression will experience an anxiety disorder (Kessler et al., 2003a; Moffitt, Caspi, Harrington, et al., 2007).

Certain anxiety disorders overlap with depressive disorders more than do others. Depression appears to be particularly likely to co-occur with generalized anxiety disorder (GAD; see p. 181) and posttraumatic stress disorder (PTSD; p. 216) (Watson, 2009). Indeed, GAD is more correlated with depression than it is with other anxiety disorders (Watson, 2005). Beyond patterns of comorbidity, the etiology of GAD, PTSD, and depression overlaps. The genetic risk for GAD and depression overlaps substantially (Kendler et al., 2003). Neuroticism is a robust risk factor for each of these conditions as well (Watson, 2005). Major depression, dysthymia, GAD, and PTSD each involve a propensity toward unhappiness and distress, whereas other anxiety disorders involve a propensity toward fear.

In response to this overlap, one group of researchers recommended that mood and anxiety disorders be subsumed into one larger chapter in the DSM-5 (Watson, O'Hara, & Stuart, 2008). Within that larger chapter, they recommended differentiating distress disorders: major depressive disorder, dysthymia, generalized anxiety disorder, and PTSD; fear disorders: panic, agoraphobia, social phobia, and specific phobia; and bipolar disorders (see Figure 5.8). Although this categorization was based on strong evidence from the epidemiological and genetic data, the crafters of DSM-5 decided not to make such a drastic change.

Rather than reorganizing in such a major way, the DSM-5 will likely include a diagnostic criteria for **mixed anxiety/depressive disorder** (MADD; see diagnostic criteria). The MADD diagnosis is designed to capture people who experience a blend of anxiety and depressive symptoms that lead to substantial distress or impairment, even though they do not have enough symptoms to be diagnosed with one of the other anxiety or depressive disorders. When outpatients were interviewed about current symptoms, MADD was reported as commonly as either a depressive or an anxiety disorder (Zinbarg, Barlow, Liebowitz, et al., 1994). About 8 percent of people met diagnostic criteria for current MADD, and they reported as much functional impairment as those with depressive or anxiety disorders. The new diagnosis appears well justified based on the data on prevalence and severity.

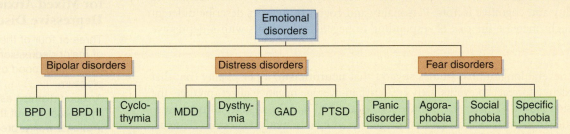

Figure 5.8 A proposed revision of the emotional disorders. Adapted from Watson, D. (2005). *Journal of Abnormal Psychology, 114*(4), 522–536.

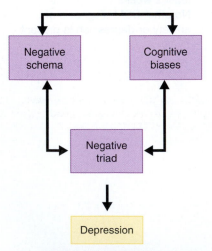

Figure 5.9 The interrelationships among different kinds of cognitions in Beck's theory of depression.

Once activated, negative schemas are believed to cause **cognitive biases**, or tendencies to process information in certain negative ways (Kendall & Ingram, 1989). That is, Beck suggested that people with depression might be overly attentive to negative feedback about themselves. They might have overly persistent memories of that negative feedback. Likewise, they might fail to notice or to remember positive feedback about themselves. People with a schema of ineptness might readily notice signs that they are inept and remember feedback that they are inept. Signs that they are competent, though, are not noted or remembered. Overall, people who are depressed make certain cognitive errors to arrive at biased conclusions. Their conclusions are consistent with the underlying schema, which then maintains the schema (a vicious circle).

How has Beck's theory been tested? One widely used instrument in studies of Beck's theory is a self-report scale called the Dysfunctional Attitudes Scale (DAS), which includes items concerning whether people would consider themselves worthwhile or lovable. Hundreds of studies have shown that people demonstrate negative thinking on scales like the DAS during depression (Haaga, Dyck, & Ernst, 1991).

In studies of how people process information, depression is associated with a tendency to stay focused on negative information once it is initially noticed (Gotlib & Joormann, 2010). For example, if shown pictures of negative and positive facial expressions, those with depression tend to look at the negative pictures for longer than they look at the positive pictures.

People with depression also tend to remember more negative than positive information. In a meta-analysis of 25 studies, Mathews and MacLeod (2002) described evidence that most people who are not depressed will remember more positive than negative information. For example, if presented with a list of self-descriptive adjectives containing 20 negative and 20 positive words, most people will remember more of the positive than the negative words when queried later in a session. People with major depression, though, tend to remember about 10 percent more negative words than positive words. While nondepressed people seem to wear rose-colored glasses, those with depression tend to have a negative bias in the way that they attend to and recall information.

Despite the clear evidence that thinking is negative during a depressive episode, the greatest challenge for cognitive theories of depression is to resolve questions of cause and effect. That is, can certain cognitive styles cause depression, or do depressive symptoms cause those cognitive styles? Some studies suggest that people with negative cognitive styles are at elevated risk for developing depression. For example, in a study of 1,507 adolescents, very high scores on the DAS in combination with negative life events predicted the onset of MDD (Lewinsohn, Joiner, & Rohde, 2001). Other researchers found that high scores on the DAS predicted relapse for several years after treatment for depression (Segal et al., 2006). On the other hand, in a study of 770 women followed for 3 years, the DAS did not predict first episodes of depression, nor did the DAS scores predict recurrent episodes of depression once history of depression was controlled (Otto, Teachman, Cohen, et al., 2007). Hence, findings are not consistent regarding the DAS.

Other studies have examined related cognitive variables as a way to predict depression. For example, cognitive biases in the way people process positive and negative information were found to predict depression over a 12- to 18-month period in a large sample of undergraduate students (Rude, Valdez, Odom, et al., 2003).

Hopelessness Theory   According to **hopelessness theory** (see Figure 5.10; Abramson, Metalsky, & Alloy, 1989), the most important trigger of depression is hopelessness, which is defined as an expectation that (1) desirable outcomes will not occur and that (2) the person has no responses available to change this situation. Within this model, hopelessness is hypothesized to contribute to only one type of depression (hopelessness depression), which is defined by symptoms of decreased motivation, sadness, suicidality, decreased energy, psychomotor retardation, sleep disturbances, poor concentration, and negative cognitions.

Hopelessness is believed to be triggered by life events that have important consequences for the person and/or the person's self-evaluations. The model places emphasis on two key dimensions of **attributions**—the explanations a person forms about why a stressor has occurred (Weiner, Frieze, Kukla, et al., 1971):

- Stable (permanent) versus unstable (temporary) causes
- Global (relevant to many life domains) versus specific (limited to one area) causes

Table 5.5 illustrates these dimensions by considering how different people might explain their low score on the Graduate Record

Being rejected by peers may lead to the development of the negative schema that, according to Beck's theory, plays a key role in depression. (© Monkey Business Images/Shutterstock.)

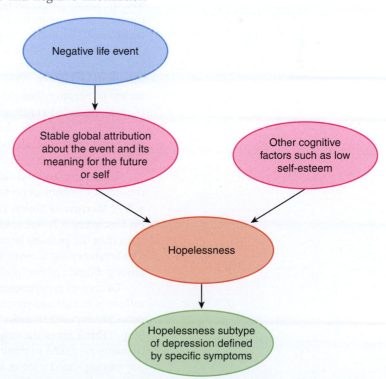

Figure 5.10 Major elements of the hopelessness theory of depression.

Table 5.5 An Example of Attributions: Why I Failed My GRE Math Exam		
	Stable	Unstable
Global	I lack intelligence.	I am exhausted.
Specific	I lack mathematical ability.	I am fed up with math.

Examination (GRE). People whose **attributional style** leads them to believe that negative life events are due to stable and global causes are likely to become hopeless, and this hopelessness will set the stage for depression. Within this model, it is acknowledged that negative attributions are accurate sometimes—a person may genuinely be facing a stressful situation that will be chronic and influence many aspects of his or her life. For some, low self-esteem promotes hopelessness by undermining their confidence that they can cope with life's challenges.

Gerald Metalsky and colleagues conducted the first test of hopelessness theory. Early in the semester, college students completed the Attributional Style Questionnaire (ASQ), as well as questionnaires to assess their grade aspirations, depressive symptoms, hopelessness, and self-esteem. These measures were used to predict depressive symptoms after a test among the students whose grades were below their expectations. Those who attributed poor grades to global and stable factors experienced more hopelessness, but this pattern was found only among students whose self-esteem was low. Hopelessness predicted depressive symptoms. Clearly, these results support the hopelessness theory. A similar study conducted with children in the sixth and seventh grades yielded almost identical results (Robinson, Garber, & Hillsman, 1995).

One study has assessed several different aspects of cognitive theories of depression. In the Temple-Wisconsin Cognitive Vulnerability to Depression study, the DAS, a measure used to test Beck's theory, and the ASQ, the measure used in tests of the hopelessness theory, were used to define the high-risk and low-risk groups of students. The 173 students in the upper 25 percent of the distributions for both measures were classified as high risk; the 176 students in the bottom 25 percent of the distributions were classified as low risk. Both groups were followed for $2\frac{1}{2}$ years to predict the development of first episodes of MDD, recurrent episodes of MDD, and also the hopelessness subtype of MDD. Findings from this study provided support for cognitive theories: students in the high-risk group were more likely to develop first episodes of MDD, recurrent MDD, and the hopelessness subtype of MDD than were students in the low-risk group (Alloy, Abramson, Whitehouse, et al., 2006).

Rumination Theory While Beck's theory and the hopelessness model tend to focus on the nature of negative thoughts, Susan Nolen-Hoeksema (1991) has suggested that a specific way of thinking called **rumination** may increase the risk of depression. Rumination is defined as a tendency to repetitively dwell on sad experiences and thoughts, or to chew on material again and again. The most detrimental form of rumination may be a tendency to brood or to regretfully ponder why an episode happened (Treynor, Gonzalez, & Nolen-Hoeksema, 2003).

Tendencies to ruminate, as measured using self-report scales, have been found to predict the onset of major depressive episodes among initially nondepressed persons (Just & Alloy, 1997; Morrow & Nolen-Hoeksema, 1990; Nolen-Hoeksema, 2000). As described in Focus on Discovery 5.1, one interesting aspect of this theory is that women tend to ruminate more than men do, perhaps because of sociocultural norms about emotion and emotion expression. The tendency for women to ruminate more may help explain the higher rates of depression among women as compared to men (Nolen-Hoeksema, 2000).

Dozens of experimental studies have been conducted to see how inducing rumination can influence moods and problem solving. Typically, in the rumination-induction condition, participants are exposed to stress and then asked to dwell on their current feelings and on themselves (e.g., "Think about the way you feel inside"), whereas in a distraction (control) condition, participants are asked to think about topics unrelated to their self or feelings (e.g., "Think about a fire darting round a log in a fire place") (Watkins, 2008). Findings of these experimental studies indicate that rumination interferes with problem solving and increases negative moods, particularly when people focus on negative aspects of their mood and their self (Watkins, 2008).

Fitting Together the Etiological Factors in Depressive Disorders

Research integrating the neurobiological and psychosocial etiology of depressive disorders is increasingly common. One example of this integration is the growing attention to the serotonin transporter gene. In rhesus monkeys, the presence of a polymorphism (at least one short allele) in this gene is associated with poor serotonergic function. A study found that people with this polymorphism were at greater risk for depression after a stressful life event than those without the polymorphism (Caspi, Sugden, Moffitt, et al., 2003). That is, having at least one short allele was associated with elevated reactivity to stress (see Figure 5.11). Thus, some people seem to inherit a propensity for a weaker serotonin system, which is then expressed as a greater likelihood to experience depression after a severe stressor. This finding has been replicated in other large-scale studies, particularly when the studies involved careful measurement of life stressors (Uher & McGuffin, 2010). Thus genetic vulnerability could set the stage for depressive disorder after major negative life events. Intriguingly, a polymorphism in the serotonin transporter gene has also been related to elevated activity of the amygdala (Hariri, Drabant, Munoz, et al., 2005). This type of work, drawing together genetic and neurobiological risk factors with social and psychological variables, is increasingly common. By considering the set of variables together, researchers can begin to develop more precise models of who is likely to become depressed under what circumstances.

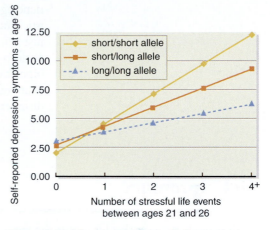

Figure 5.11 Life events interact with the serotonin transporter gene to predict symptoms of depression. Adapted from Caspi et al. (2002). *Science, 301,* 387, AAAS.

Social and Psychological Factors in Bipolar Disorder

Most people who experience a manic episode during their life will also experience a major depressive episode, but not everyone will. Given this, researchers often study the triggers of manic and depressive episodes separately within bipolar disorder.

Depression in Bipolar Disorder The triggers of depressive episodes in bipolar disorder appear similar to the triggers of major depressive episodes (Johnson, Cuellar, & Miller, 2010). As in MDD, negative life events appear important in precipitating depressive episodes in bipolar disorder. Similarly, neuroticism, negative cognitive styles (Reilly-Harrington, Alloy, Fresco, et al., 1999), expressed emotion (Yan, Hammen, Cohen, et al., 2004), and lack of social support predict depressive symptoms in bipolar disorder.

Predictors of Mania Two types of factors have been found to predict increases in manic symptoms over time: reward sensitivity and sleep deprivation. Both of these models integrate psychological and biological facets of vulnerability to mania.

Reward Sensitivity The first model suggests that mania reflects a disturbance in the reward system of the brain (Depue, Collins, & Luciano, 1996). Researchers have demonstrated that people with bipolar disorder describe themselves as highly responsive to rewards on a self-report measure (Meyer, Johnson, & Winters, 2001). Being highly reward sensitive has also been shown to predict the onset of bipolar disorder (Alloy, Abramson, Walshaw, et al., 2008, 2009) and a more severe course of mania after onset (Meyer et al., 2001). In addition, a particular kind of life event predicts increases in manic symptoms among people with bipolar I disorder (Johnson, Cuellar, Ruggero, et al.,

2008; 2000)—specifically, life events that involve attaining goals, such as gaining acceptance to graduate school or getting married. How could successes like these promote increases in symptoms? Researchers have proposed that life events involving success may trigger cognitive changes in confidence, which then spiral into excessive goal pursuit (Johnson, 2005). This excessive goal pursuit may help trigger manic symptoms among people with bipolar disorder.

Sleep Disruption. Researchers using a range of approaches have documented that mania is intricately tied to disruptions in sleep and circadian (daily) rhythms (Murray & Harvey, 2010). Experimental studies indicate that sleep deprivation can precede the onset of manic episodes. In one study, participants who were experiencing bipolar depression were asked to stay at a sleep center, where they were kept awake all night. By the next morning, about 10 percent were experiencing at least mild symptoms of mania (Colombo, Benedetti, Barbini, et al., 1999). In naturalistic studies, people often report that they had experienced a life event that disrupted their sleep just before the onset of manic episodes (Malkoff-Schwartz, Frank, Anderson, et al., 2000). Just as sleep deprivation can trigger manic symptoms, protecting sleep can help reduce symptoms of bipolar disorder (Frank, Swartz, & Kupfer, 2000). See Focus on Discovery 4.1 for a case study of an intervention that increased time spent in bed as a way of diminishing symptoms of bipolar disorder. Sleep and circadian rhythm disruption appear to be important aspects of mania risk.

Quick Summary

Research strongly suggests that life events can trigger MDD. Because many people do not become depressed after a life event, researchers have studied diatheses that could explain vulnerability to life events.

Interpersonal research highlights the role of low social support, high expressed emotion, high need for reassurance, and poor social skills as risk factors for depression. Once a person becomes depressed, increases in reassurance seeking may lead to rejection from other people, potentially worsening depression.

Beyond social factors, psychological risk factors can help explain why some people become depressed. Evidence suggests that neuroticism, which involves high negative affect, predicts the onset of depression. Cognitive factors include a negative schema; negative beliefs about the self, world, and future; biases to attend to and recall negative rather than positive information; stable and global attributions for stressors that lead to hopelessness; and tendencies to ruminate. Prospective evidence supports each of these cognitive models.

Less psychological research is available on bipolar disorder. Nonetheless, many of the variables that predict MDD also appear to predict depressive symptoms within bipolar disorder. Mania appears to be predicted by sleep disruption and by life events involving goal attainment.

Treatment of Mood Disorders

Most episodes of depression end after a few months, but the time may seem immeasurably longer to people with depression and to those close to them. With mania, even a few days of acute symptoms can create troubles for relationships and jobs. Moreover, suicide is a risk for people with mood disorders. Thus, it is important to treat mood disorders. Indeed, recent research suggests that it pays to treat depression. In one study, researchers ran a program at 16 large U.S. companies to identify depression, provide referrals for people with depression, and even offer therapy by phone (Wang, Simon, Avorn, et al., 2007). Although the program cost several hundred dollars per worker, it saved about $1,800 per employee in lost time at work, employee turnover, and other costs.

An important public health goal is to increase the number of people who receive adequate treatment. Certainly, many people try to obtain treatment; more than 180,000,000 prescriptions per year are filled for antidepressants in the United States (IMS Health, 2006). Despite this, surveys suggest that half of people who meet diagnostic criteria for major depression do not receive care for their symptoms (Gonzalez et al., 2010).

In this section, we cover psychological treatments of depressive disorders and bipolar disorder. Then we turn to biological treatments of depressive disorders and bipolar disorder.

Psychological Treatment of Depression

Several different forms of psychological treatment have been shown to help relieve depression. As with studies of etiology, most of the research has focused on MDD. We note when treatments have been shown to be effective in the treatment of dysthymia.

Interpersonal Psychotherapy A treatment known as interpersonal psychotherapy (IPT) has fared well in clinical trials. As we described in Chapter 2, IPT builds on the idea that depression is closely tied to interpersonal problems (Klerman, Weissman, Rounsaville, & Chevron, 1984). The core of the therapy is to examine major interpersonal problems, such as role transitions, interpersonal conflicts, bereavement, and interpersonal isolation. Typically, the therapist and the patient focus on one or two such issues, with the goal of helping the person identify his or her feelings about these issues, make important decisions, and make changes to resolve problems related to these issues. Like cognitive behavioral treatments, IPT is typically brief (e.g., 16 sessions). Techniques include discussing interpersonal problems, exploring negative feelings and encouraging their expression, improving both verbal and nonverbal communications, problem solving, and suggesting new and more satisfying modes of behavior.

Several studies have found that IPT is effective in relieving MDD (Elkin, Shea, Watkins, et al., 1989) and that it prevents relapse when continued after recovery (Frank, Kupfer, Perel, et al., 1990). In addition, studies indicate that IPT can be effective in treating MDD among adolescents (Mufson, Weissman, Moreau, et al., 1999) and postpartum women (O'Hara, Stuart, Gorman, et al., 2000; Zlotnick, Johnson, Miller, et al., 2001). In a study among villagers in Uganda, group sessions of IPT provided relief from depressive symptoms (Bolton, Bass, Neugebauer, et al., 2003). IPT has also been found to be effective in the treatment of dysthymia (Markowitz, 1994). For many different groups, then, IPT appears to be helpful in relieving depression.

Cognitive Therapy In keeping with their theory that depression is caused by negative schema and cognitive biases, Beck and associates devised a cognitive therapy (CT) aimed at altering maladaptive thought patterns. The therapist tries to help the person with depression to change his or her opinions about the self. When a person states that he or she is worthless because "nothing goes right, and everything I try to do ends in a disaster," the therapist helps the person look for evidence that contradicts this overgeneralization, such as abilities that the person is overlooking or discounting. The therapist also teaches the person to monitor self-talk and to identify thought patterns that contribute to depression. The therapist then teaches the person to challenge negative beliefs and to learn strategies that promote making realistic and positive assumptions. Often, the client is asked to monitor their thoughts each day and to practice challenging overly negative thoughts (see Table 5.6 for an example of a thought monitoring homework assignment). Beck's emphasis is on cognitive restructuring (i.e., persuading the person to think less negatively).

Beck also includes a behavioral technique in his therapy called behavioral activation (BA), in which people are encouraged to engage in pleasant activities that might bolster positive thoughts about one's self and life. For example, the therapist encourages patients to schedule positive events such as going for a walk and talking with friends.

More than 75 randomized controlled trials have been conducted on CT for depression (Gloaguen, Cottraux, Cucherat, et al., 1998). Many studies have demonstrated the efficacy of cognitive therapy for relieving symptoms of MDD (Hollon, Haman, & Brown, 2002). With modifications, CT is promising in the treatment of dysthymia (Hollon, Haman, Brown, 2002). The strategies that clients learn in CT help diminish the risk of relapse even after therapy ends, an important issue given how common relapse is in MDD (Vittengl, Clark, Dunn, et al., 2007). CT is particularly helpful in preventing relapse for those who need this protection the most—people with at least five episodes of previous depression gain protection from relapse through CT (Bockting, Schene, Spinhoven, et al., 2005).

Table 5.6 An Example of Daily Thought Monitoring, a Strategy Commonly Used in Cognitive Therapy

Date & Time	Situation *What was happening?*	Negative emotion *Note type of emotion (e.g., sad, nervous, angry) and the intensity of the emotion (0–100)*	Automatic negative thought	How much did you believe this initial thought (0–100)?	Alternative thought *Is there another view of the situation?*	Re-rate your belief in the initial thought	Outcome *Note type of emotion felt and emotion intensity (0-100) after considering the alternative*
Tuesday morning	I made a mistake on a report at work.	Sad—90 Embarrassed-80	I always mess things up. I'm never going to be good at anything.	90	My boss didn't give me enough time to prepare the report. I could have done a better job with more time.	50	Relief-30 Sad-30
Wednesday dinner	Eating dinner at a restaurant. An old friend from high school was at the next table and didn't recognize me.	Sad-95	I'm a nobody.	100	I've changed my hair drastically since then. Many people don't recognize me, but maybe she would have been happy to see me if I had reminded her of who I was.	25	Sad-25
Thursday breakfast	My husband left for work without saying goodbye to me.	Sad-90	Even the people I love don't seem to notice me.	100	I know that he had a huge presentation and he gets stressed.	20	Sad-20

Clinical Case: An Example of Challenging a Negative Thought in Cognitive Therapy

The following dialogue is an example of one way that a therapist might begin to challenge a person's negative thoughts in CT, although it would take several sessions to help a client learn the cognitive model and to identify overly negative thoughts.

> Therapist: *You said that you are a "loser" because you and Roger got divorced. Now we already defined what it is to be a loser—not to achieve anything.*
> Patient: *Right. That sounds really extreme.*
> Therapist: *OK. Let's look at the evidence for and against the thought that you have achieved something. Draw a line down the center of the page. On the top I'd like you to write, "I have achieved some things."*
> Patient: *[draws line and writes statement]*
> Therapist: *What is the evidence that you have achieved some things?*
> Patient: *I graduated from college, I raised my son, I worked at the office, I have some friends, and I exercise. I am reliable. I care about my friends.*
> Therapist: *OK. Let's write all of that down. Now in the right column let's write down evidence*

> *against the thought that you have achieved some things.*
> Patient: *Well, maybe it's irrational, but I would have to write down that I got divorced.*
> Therapist: *OK. Now in looking at the evidence for and against your thought that you have achieved some things, how do you weigh it out? 50–50? Differently than 50–50?*
> Patient: *I'd have to say it's 95% in favor of the positive thought.*
> Therapist: *So, how much do you believe now that you have achieved some things?*
> Patient: *100%.*
> Therapist: *And how much do you believe that you are a failure because you got divorced?*
> Patient: *Maybe I'm not a failure, but the marriage failed. I'd give myself about 10%.*
> (quoted from p. 46, Leahy, 2003)

Note: As is typical, this dialogue challenges some, but not all, negative thoughts. Future sessions are likely to examine other negative thoughts.

Computer-administered versions of CT have been developed. Typically, these interventions include at least brief contact with a therapist to guide the initial assessment, to answer questions, and to provide support and encouragement with the homework. Several randomized controlled trials provide evidence that computer-based CT is effective compared to treatment as usual in which patients were instructed to seek help from other sources, as they normally would (Andrews, Hobbs, Borkovec, et al., 2010). Because computer-based programs have varied in their effectiveness, it will be important to ensure that consumers gain access to well-tested versions of computerized CT (Spek, Cuijpers, Nyklicek, et al., 2007).

An adaptation of CT called **mindfulness-based cognitive therapy (MBCT)** focuses on relapse prevention after successful treatment for recurrent episodes of major depression (Segal, Williams, & Teasdale, 2001). MBCT is based on the assumption that a person becomes vulnerable to relapse because of repeated associations between sad mood and patterns of self-devaluative, hopeless thinking during major depressive episodes. As a result, when people who have recovered from depression become sad, they begin to think as negatively as they had when they were severely depressed. These reactivated patterns of thinking in turn intensify the sadness (Teasdale, 1988). Thus, in people with a history of major depression, sadness is more likely to escalate, which may contribute to the onset of new episodes of depression.

The goal of MBCT is to teach people to recognize when they start to become depressed and to try adopting what can be called a "decentered" perspective, viewing their thoughts merely as "mental events" rather than as core aspects of the self or as accurate reflections of reality. For example, the person might say to himself or herself such things as "thoughts are not facts" and "I am not my thoughts" (Teasdale, Segal, Williams, et al., 2000, p. 616). In other words, using a wide array of strategies, including meditation, the person is taught over time to develop a detached relationship to depression-related thoughts and feelings. This perspective, it is believed, can prevent the escalation of negative thinking patterns that may cause depression.

In one multisite study (Teasdale et al., 2000) people who formerly had depression were randomly assigned to MBCT or to "treatment as usual". Results of this study showed that MBCT was more effective than "treatment as usual" in reducing the risk of relapse among people with three or more previous major depressive episodes. MBCT does not appear to protect against relapse among people with only one or two previous major depressive episodes (Ma & Teasdale, 2004). This treatment, then, shows promise for patients with highly recurrent major depression.

Behavioral Activation (BA) Therapy Above we mentioned that BA is one component of Beck's therapy. BA was originally developed as a stand-alone treatment (Lewinsohn, 1974). This treatment was based on the idea that many of the risk factors for depression can result in low levels of positive reinforcement. That is, life events, low social support, marital distress, poverty, and individual differences in social skill, personality, and coping may all lead to low levels of positive reinforcement. As depression begins to unfold, inactivity, withdrawal, and inertia are common symptoms, and these symptoms will diminish the already low levels of positive reinforcement even further (Lewinsohn, 1974). Consequently, the goal of BA is to increase participation in positively reinforcing activities so as to disrupt the spiral of depression, withdrawal, and avoidance (Martell, Addis, & Jacobson, 2001).

BA has received a great deal of attention after positive findings in a study designed to identify the most effective ingredients in Beck's therapy (Jacobson & Gortner, 2000). Findings suggested that the BA component of CT performs as well as the full package does in relieving MDD and preventing relapse over a 2-year follow-up period (Dobson, Hollon, Dimidjian, et al., 2008). A replication study provided support for the efficacy of BA in a study of 214 patients with MDD (Dimidjian, Hollon, Dobson, et al., 2006). Group versions of behavioral therapy also appear to be effective (Oei & Dingle, 2008), and the treatment has now been successfully applied in many different settings for clients from a diverse range of backgrounds (Dimidjian, Barrera, Martell, et al., 2011). These findings challenge the notion that people must directly modify their negative thinking to alleviate depression and suggest instead that engaging in rewarding activities may be enough.

Behavioral Couples Therapy As described above, depression is often tied to relationship problems, including marital and family distress. Drawing on these findings, researchers have studied behavioral couples therapy as a treatment for depression. In this approach, researchers work with both members of a couple to improve communication and relationship satisfaction. Findings indicate that when a person with depression is also experiencing marital distress, **behavioral couples therapy** is as effective in relieving depression as individual CT (Jacobson, Dobson, Fruzzetti, et al., 1991) or antidepressant medication (Barbato & D'avanzo, 2008). As you might expect, marital therapy has the advantage of relieving relationship distress more than does individual therapy.

Psychological Treatment of Bipolar Disorder

Medication is a necessary part of treatment for bipolar disorder, but psychological treatments can supplement medications to help address many of its associated social and psychological problems. These psychotherapies can also help reduce depressive symptoms in bipolar disorder.

Educating people about their illness is a common component of treating many disorders, including bipolar disorder and schizophrenia. **Psychoeducational approaches** typically help people learn about the symptoms of the disorder, the expected time course of symptoms, the biological and psychological triggers for symptoms, and treatment strategies. Studies confirm that careful education about bipolar disorder can help people adhere to treatment with medications such as lithium (Colom, Vieta, Reinares, et al., 2003). This is an important goal, because as many as half of people being treated for bipolar disorder do not take medication consistently (Regier, Narrow, Rae, et al., 1993). A friend of one of the authors put it like this: "Lithium cuts out the highs as well as the lows. I don't miss the lows, but I gotta admit that there were some aspects of the highs that I do miss. It took me a while to accept that I had to give up those highs. Wanting to keep my job and my marriage helped!" A drug alone does not address this kind of concern. Beyond helping people be more consistent about their medications, psychoeducational programs have been shown to help people avoid hospitalization (Morriss, Faizal, Jones, et al., 2007).

Several other types of therapy are designed to help build skills and reduce symptoms for those with bipolar disorder. Both CT and family-focused therapy (FFT) have received particularly strong support (Lam, Bright, Jones, et al., 2000). CT draws on many of the types of techniques that are used in major depressive disorder, with some additional content designed to address the early signs of manic episodes. FFT aims to educate the family about the illness, enhance family communication, and develop problem-solving skills (Miklowitz & Goldstein, 1997).

In a major study of therapy for bipolar disorder, researchers studied people who had bipolar disorder and who were depressed at the time they sought treatment (Miklowitz, Otto, Frank, et al., 2007). To make sure that findings would generalize to different types of treatment centers, patients were recruited from 14 widely different treatment clinics across the United States. All of the patients in the trial received intensive medication treatment, because researchers were interested in whether adding psychotherapy to medication treatment for bipolar disorder is helpful. Patients were randomly assigned to receive either psychotherapy or a control treatment called collaborative care. The 130 patients assigned to collaborative care were offered three supportive sessions with a treatment provider. The 163 patients in the psychotherapy condition were further assigned to receive either CT, FFT, or IPT. Psychotherapy was offered for up to 9 months. Each type of psychotherapy helped relieve depression more than the collaborative care condition did. There was no evidence that CT, FFT, or IPT differed in their effects on depression. These findings suggest that it is important for people with bipolar disorder to receive psychotherapy when they are experiencing depression and that several types of therapy can be helpful.

Biological Treatment of Mood Disorders

A variety of biological therapies are used to treat depression and mania. The two major biological treatments are electroconvulsive therapy and drugs.

Electroconvulsive Therapy for Depression Perhaps the most dramatic and controversial treatment for MDD is electroconvulsive therapy (ECT). For the most part now, ECT is only used to treat MDD that has not responded to medication. ECT entails deliberately inducing a momentary seizure and unconsciousness by passing a 70- to 130-volt current through the patient's brain. Formerly, electrodes were placed on each side of the forehead, a method known as bilateral ECT. Today, *unilateral ECT*, in which the current passes only through the nondominant (typically the right) cerebral hemisphere, is often used because side effects are less pronounced (McCall, Reboussin, Weiner, et al., 2000). In the past, the patient was usually awake until the current triggered the seizure, and the electric shock often created frightening contortions of the body, sometimes even causing bone fractures. Now the patient is given a muscle relaxant before the current is applied. The convulsive spasms of muscles are barely perceptible, and the patient awakens a few minutes later remembering nothing about the treatment. Typically, patients receive between 6 and 12 treatments, spaced several days apart.

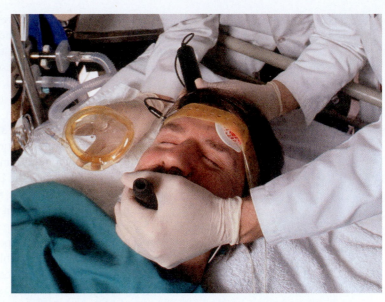

Electroconvulsive therapy is an effective treatment for depression that has not responded to medication. Using unilateral shock and muscle relaxants has reduced undesirable side effects. (Will & Deni McIntyre/Photo Researchers, Inc.)

Even with these improvements in procedures, inducing a seizure is drastic treatment. Why should anyone agree to undergo such radical therapy? The answer is simple. ECT is more powerful than antidepressant medications for the treatment of depression (Pagnin, De Querioz, Pini, et al., 2004; UK ECT Review Group, 2003), particularly when psychotic features are present (Sackeim & Lisanby, 2001), even though we don't know why it works. Most professionals acknowledge that people undergoing ECT face some risks of short-term confusion and memory loss. It is fairly common for patients to have no memory of the period during which they received ECT and sometimes for the weeks surrounding the procedure. Unilateral ECT produces fewer cognitive side effects than bilateral ECT does (Sackeim & Lisanby, 2001). Nonetheless, even unilateral ECT is associated with deficits in cognitive functioning 6 months after treatment (Sackeim, Prudic, Fuller, et al., 2007). In any case, clinicians typically resort to ECT only if less drastic treatments have failed. Given that suicide is a real possibility among people who are depressed, many experts regard the use of ECT after other treatments have failed as a responsible approach.

Medications for Depressive Disorders Drugs are the most commonly used and best-researched treatments—biological or otherwise—for depressive disorders (and, as we will see, for bipolar disorders as well). As shown in Table 5.7, there are three major categories of **antidepressant** drugs: **monoamine oxidase inhibitors (MAOIs), tricyclic antidepressants,**

Table 5.7 Medications for Treating Mood Disorders

Category	Generic Name	Trade Name	Side Effects
MAO antidepressants	tranylcypromine	Parnate	Possibly fatal hypertension if taken with certain foods or medications, dry mouth, dizziness, nausea, headaches
Tricyclic antidepressants	imipramine amitriptyline	Tofranil Elavil	Heart attack, stroke, hypotension, blurred vision, anxiety, tiredness, dry mouth, constipation, gastric disorders, erectile dysfunction, weight gain
Selective serotonin reuptake inhibitor (SSRI) antidepressants	fluoxetine sertraline	Prozac Zoloft	Nervousness, fatigue, gastrointestinal complaints, dizziness, headaches, insomnia, suicidality
Mood stabilizers	lithium	Lithium	Tremors, gastric distress, lack of coordination, dizziness, cardiac arrhythmia, blurred vision, fatigue, death from overdose in rare cases
Anticonvulsants	divalproex sodium	Depakote	Pancreatitis
Antipsychotics	olanzapine	Zyprexa	Hyperglycemia, diabetes, tardive dyskinesia, and, in elderly patients, cardiovascular problems, neuroleptic malignant syndrome

and **selective serotonin reuptake inhibitors (SSRIs)**. The clinical effectiveness of all three classes of drugs is about the same (Depression Guidelines Panel, 1993). A number of double-blind studies have shown these medications to be effective in treating depressive disorders, with 50–70 percent of people who complete treatment showing major improvement (Depression Guidelines Panel, 1993; Nemeroff & Schatzberg, 1998). These medications have been found to be effective in treating dysthymia as well as major depression (Hollon, Thase, & Markowitz, 2002).

One report, however, suggests that these published studies may overestimate how many people respond well to antidepressant medications. When pharmaceutical companies conduct studies to apply for either initial approval to market a medication or to support a change in the use of a medication in the US, the data must be filed with the Food and Drug Administration (FDA). One research team recently examined what happened to the data from antidepressant studies conducted between 1987 and 2004 (Turner, Matthews, Linardatos, et al., 2008). The FDA files included data on 74 studies. Of these 74 studies, 51 percent were rated as having positive findings (i.e., supported the use of the antidepressant). All but one of the studies with positive findings were published. Of the studies with negative findings, less than half were published, and even in those reports, the published reports described the findings as positive even though the FDA had rated them as neutral or negative. Overall, then, published findings may be biased to be positive. In the face of discouraging reports such as this, one strategy is to conduct very large-scale trials to help understand who does and does not respond to antidepressants and what to do when a person does not gain relief.

In an attempt to study antidepressant medication in the real world using a large sample, the STAR-D trial examined antidepressant response among 3,671 patients across 41 sites, including 18 primary care facilities (Rush, Trivedi, Wisniewski, et al., 2006). Many previous treatment studies have screened for patients with "pure" depression (i.e., no other comorbid disorders) and offered treatment in specialized university clinics. In sharp contrast to the types of clean, non-comorbid depression histories reported in most medication trials, most of the patients enrolled in STAR-D suffered from chronic or recurrent depression, had comorbid psychiatric conditions, and had already received some (unsuccessful) treatment for the current episode. Rather than assessing whether antidepressant medication or psychotherapy was more helpful than a placebo treatment, the goal of the study was to consider the types of practical questions that physicians face in daily practice. For example, if initial treatment does not work, will switching to a second antidepressant work or should two antidepressants be given at the same time? What is the best treatment option if this second stage of treatment fails? Patients were all started on citalopram (Celexa), an SSRI. If they did not respond to citalopram, they were offered (1) a choice of a different medication to replace the citalopram, (2) a chance to add a second medication to the citalopram, or (3) CT if they were willing to pay part of the cost.

Findings were generally sobering. Only about one-third of patients achieved full symptom relief when treated with citalopram (Trivedi, Rush, Wisniewski, et al., 2006). Among those who did not respond, very few wanted to pay for CT. Among patients who did not respond to citalopram and were switched to a second round of medication treatment, about 30.6 percent achieved remission, regardless of which type of medication treatment they received. Among patients who did not respond well to either the first or second round of treatment, few responded to a third antidepressant (13.7 percent), and even fewer responded to a fourth antidepressant (13 percent). Even among those who achieved remission at one of these steps, relapse rates were high, so that even with the complex array of treatments offered, only 43 percent of people achieved sustained recovery (Nelson, 2006). Findings from this study highlight a number of important gaps in our science. First, there is a need for more careful testing of treatments in the real world, as findings may differ from those obtained in specialty clinics. Second, there is a need for new treatments for those who do not respond well to currently available treatments.

The concerns raised by this trial and by other research have led to an intensive focus on understanding why antidepressants work better for some people than for others. Findings of two separate meta-analyses suggest that antidepressants are more effective than placebo for those with severe depression but not for those with mild depression (Fournier, Derubeis, Hollon, et al.,

2010; Kirsch, Deacon, Huedo-Medina, et al., 2008). Although these findings have led to substantial debate, it is important to consider that many medication trials focus on patients with very serious depression (Derubeis, 2011), and yet prescriptions are sometimes offered to those with very minor symptoms.

Among patients who are prescribed an antidepressant, 40 percent stop taking the medication within the first month (Olfson, Blanco, Liu, et al., 2006), most commonly because they find the side effects unpleasant (see Table 5.7) (Thase & Rush, 1997). The MAOIs are the least used antidepressants because of their potentially life-threatening side effects if combined with certain foods or beverages. The SSRIs have become the most commonly prescribed antidepressants because they tend to produce fewer side effects than the other classes of antidepressants (Enserink, 1999). In March 2004, however, the FDA asked manufacturers to include packaging information warning people that there have been case reports of suicidality associated with SSRIs, particularly during the early phases of treatment or after increases in dosage. There is specific concern about the potential for suicidality in children, adolescents, and young adults, and researchers continue to look at this important issue, as findings have been controversial (see Chapter 13). Such effects seem very rare, but the FDA approach is designed to protect against risk, even if that risk is faced by only a small number of people.

Although the various antidepressants hasten recovery from an episode of depression, relapse is common after the drugs are withdrawn (Reimherr, Strong, Marchant, et al., 2001). This is not to dismiss the advantages of temporary relief, given the potential for interpersonal problems, suicide, and hospitalization as depression continues. Results from one meta-analysis of 31 different drug trials suggest that continuing antidepressants after remission lowers the risk of recurrence from approximately 40 percent to about 20 percent (Geddes, Carney, Davies, et al., 2003). Treatment guidelines recommend continuing antidepressant medications for at least 6 months after a depressive episode ends—and longer if a person has experienced several episodes. To prevent recurrence, medication doses should be as high as those offered during acute treatment.

Research Comparing Treatments for Major Depressive Disorder Combining psychotherapy and antidepressant medications bolsters the odds of recovery by more than 10–20 percent above either psychotherapy or medications alone for most people with depression (Hollon, Thase, et al., 2002). One study found that even offering CT by telephone for those beginning antidepressants could improve outcomes compared to medication alone (Simon, 2009). Each treatment offers unique advantages. Antidepressants work more quickly than psychotherapy, thus providing immediate relief. Psychotherapy may take longer but may help people learn skills that they can use after treatment is finished to protect against recurrent depressive episodes.

Many patients are interested in knowing whether medications or therapy will be more effective in relieving symptoms. In four initial studies, CT performed as well as medication in relieving acute symptoms of depression (Derubeis, Gelfand, Tang, et al., 1999), but in another major study CT did not provide as much symptom relief as did medication for severe depression (Elkin, Shea, & Shaw, 1996). To address controversy over these mixed findings, researchers designed a trial to compare CT versus antidepressants in the treatment of severe depression (Hollon & Derubeis, 2003). Researchers randomly assigned 240 patients with severe depression to receive antidepressant medication, CT, or a placebo for 4 months. Those who recovered were followed for another 12 months. CT was as effective as antidepressant medication for severe depression, and both treatments were more effective than placebo. CT had two advantages: it was less expensive than medication, and over the long term it helped protect against relapse once treatment was finished (Hollon, Derubeis, Shelton, et al., 2005).

Medications for Bipolar Disorder Medications that reduce manic symptoms are called *mood-stabilizing medications*. **Lithium**, a naturally occurring chemical element, was the first mood stabilizer identified. Up to 80 percent of people with bipolar I disorder experience at least mild benefit from taking this drug (Prien & Potter, 1993). Even though symptoms may become milder with medications, most patients continue to experience at least mild manic and depressive symptoms. One meta-analysis combined the findings of five trials including 770 patients randomly assigned to receive lithium or placebo and followed for at least 1 year. The results indicated that 40 percent of people relapsed while taking lithium as compared to 60 percent while taking placebo (Geddes, Burgess, Hawton, et al., 2004).

Because of possibly serious side effects, lithium has to be prescribed and used very carefully. Lithium levels that are too high can be toxic, so patients taking lithium must have regular blood tests. It is recommended that lithium be used continually for the person's entire life (Maj, Pirozzi, Magliano, et al., 1998).

Two classes of medications other than lithium (Bowden, Lecrubier, Bauer, et al., 2000) have been approved by the FDA for the treatment of acute mania: anticonvulsant (antiseizure) medications such as divalproex sodium (Depakote) and antipsychotic medications such as olanzapine (Zyprexa). Lithium is still recommended as the first choice, but these other treatments are recommended for people who are unable to tolerate lithium's side effects. Like lithium, these medications help reduce mania and, to some extent, depression. Unfortunately, even these medications have serious side effects. Anticonvulsants have been found to be related to a small increase in suicidal ideation compared to rates for placebo (Food and Drug Administration, January 31, 2008). Beyond anticonvulsant and antipsychotic medications, several other medications show promising early results (Stahl, 2006).

Typically, lithium is used in combination with other medications. Because lithium takes effect gradually, therapy for acute mania typically begins with both lithium and an antipsychotic medication, such as olanzapine, which has an immediate calming effect (Scherk, Pajonk, & Leucht, 2007).

The mood-stabilizing medications used to treat mania also help relieve depression (Young, Goey, Minassian, et al., 2010). Nonetheless, many people continue to experience depression even when taking a mood-stabilizing medication like lithium. For these people, an antidepressant medication is often added to the regimen (Sachs & Thase, 2000), but there are two potential issues with this practice. First, it is not clear whether antidepressants actually help reduce depression among persons who are already taking a mood stabilizer (the first type of treatment provided in bipolar disorder) (Sachs, Nierenberg, Calabrese, et al., 2007). Second, among people with bipolar disorder, antidepressants are related to a modest increase in the risk of a manic episode (Tondo, Vazquez, & Baldessarini, 2010).

Clinical Case: Treatment Decisions for Lily

Lily, the woman described earlier in this chapter, reported increasing problems because of her depression. She was prescribed Prozac (fluoxetine) with the hope this would quickly relieve her symptoms. But after 4 weeks, finding the side effects of fatigue and sickness uncomfortable, medication was discontinued.

With so many different types of treatment available, deciding on the best therapy for each client can be a challenge. Sometimes this decision reflects the personal preferences of the doctor or therapist. Ideally, it incorporates the treatment preferences of the client as well.

Lily had experienced lots of changes in her life suggesting that *person-centred therapy* might fit. But she was blaming herself for being a "bad mother and a bad wife" indicating that *cognitive behavioral therapy* might help as well. The couple's marital conflict also suggested *integrated behavioral couples therapy* could be appropriate.

Person Centred Therapy (PCT)
The focus of PCT is to create a comfortable, non-judgmental environment by demonstrating congruence (genuineness),

empathy, and unconditional positive regard toward clients while using a non-directive approach. This aids patients in finding own solutions to their problems.

Cognitive Behavioral Therapy (CBT)
CBT aims to solve problems concerning dysfunctional emotions, behaviors and cognitions through a goal-oriented, systematic procedure in the present. To aid the therapeutic process, clients may be asked to keep a diary of significant events and associated feelings, thoughts and behaviors. During therapy, clients are encouraged to question their assumptions and beliefs about themselves and others, and identify those which might be disadvantageous and unrealistic.

Integrated Behavioral Couples Therapy (IBCT)
IBCT is based around the idea that *doing* something about your problems (rather than thinking or talking about them) is what makes the difference. This is translated into the therapeutic process by getting couple to identify and change disadvantageous behavioral patterns and develop new ways to compromise and resolve problems.

Depression and Primary Care

About half of all antidepressant prescriptions are written by primary care physicians. Research has shown that primary care doctors, perhaps because of time pressure, often fail to diagnose episodes of depression, and even when they offer treatment, these treatments tend to be too short, medication doses tend to be too small, and opportunities for psychotherapy tend to be limited. One group of researchers studied antidepressant treatment at a health maintenance organization (HMO) and found that only about half of the patients received an adequate regimen of drug therapy (Simon, Von Korff, Rutter, et al., 2001).

Researchers are studying how to improve the quality of care offered by primary care physicians or within HMOs. Simply telling doctors to diagnose and treat depression does not work very well; studies of written treatment guidelines and workshops for doctors do not show much effect on treatment practices (Gilbody, Whitty, Grimshaw, et al., 2003). More intensive programs, however, do seem to help. For example, promising results have been obtained with telephone follow-ups, increased nursing care, or specific guidelines that help physicians identify patients who should receive more intensive care (Gilbody et al., 2003). Similar programs, involving more nursing support and more patient psychoeducation, have been shown to be helpful in bipolar disorder (Simon, Ludman, Bauer, et al., 2006).

A Final Note on Treatment

Some of the most exciting research today is focused on how treatments work. Researchers have shown that successful treatments, whether with psychotherapy, medications, or ECT, change activity in the brain regions related to depression (Brody, Saxena, Stoessel, et al., 2001; Goldapple, Segal, Garson, et al., 2004; Nobler, Oquendo, Kegeles, et al., 2001). Intriguingly, antidepressant medications and ECT both stimulate growth of neurons in the hippocampus in rats (Duman, Malberg, & Nakagawa, 2001), and the effects of antidepressants, at least in animals, appear to depend on whether these neurons grow (Santarelli, Saxe, Gross, et al., 2003). Understanding more about how psychological and medication treatments change underlying neurobiological processes may help us refine treatments for the future.

Researchers are also beginning to study how medications influence receptor sensitivity. These types of studies are being conducted for both mania and depression. For example, one line of research is examining whether antidepressants alter chemical messengers called second messengers (see Figure 2.7), which then adjust postsynaptic receptor sensitivity. Another area of current research focuses on **G-proteins** (guanine nucleotide-binding proteins), which play an important role in modulating activity in the postsynaptic cell. High levels of G-proteins have been found in patients with mania and low levels in patients with depression (Avissar, Nechamkin, Barki-Harrington, et al., 1997; Avissar, Schreiber, Nechamkin, et al., 1999). Some have argued that the therapeutic effects of lithium, the most effective pharmacological treatment for mania, may result from its ability to regulate G-proteins (Manji, Chen, Shimon, et al., 1995).

Quick Summary

Many different treatments are available for depression. Cognitive therapy (CT), interpersonal psychotherapy (IPT), behavioral activation (BA) treatment, and behavioral couples therapy have received support. The three forms of antidepressants have been found to be similarly effective; SSRIs have become more popular because they have fewer side effects than MAOIs and tricyclic antidepressants. Although findings are not entirely consistent, most research has found that CT is as effective as antidepressant medication even in the treatment of severe MDD.

Medication treatment is the first line of defense against bipolar disorder. The best-researched mood stabilizer is lithium, but anticonvulsants and antipsychotic medications are also effective mood stabilizers. Recent findings cast doubt on whether antidepressant medication is helpful in bipolar disorder. Some psychological treatments may help when offered as supplements to medications for the treatment of bipolar disorder. The best-validated approaches include psychoeducational approaches, CT, and family therapy (FFT). IPT has fared well in one large trial as well. These treatments appear particularly helpful in improving adherence to medication regimens and relieving depressive symptoms within bipolar disorder.

Check Your Knowledge 5.4

Circle all answers that apply.
1. Which of the following psychotherapies have obtained support in the treatment of MDD?
   a. interpersonal psychotherapy
   b. behavioral activation
   c. psychoanalytic therapy
   d. cognitive therapy
2. The most effective treatment for MDD with psychotic features is:
   a. Prozac
   b. any antidepressant medication
   c. ECT
   d. psychotherapy
3. Selective serotonin reuptake inhibitors (SSRIs) are more popular than other antidepressants because they:
   a. are more effective
   b. have fewer side effects
   c. are cheaper

Clinical Case: Dan

Dan had attended a barbeque at his neighbor's house. He brought a rice salad and had helped cook the sausages. He even played football with the children who were running around until they all had to go inside to escape the rain. Two days later, Dan drove his car out of the garage, walked back in, shut the door, suspended a rope from the ceiling, stood on a chair, tied the rope round his neck and stepped off the chair.

His former girlfriend reported that he had been upset about the breakup of their three-year relationship and her growing attachment to a colleague who had recently joined her department at work. Still, all those who knew him were deeply shocked as he had not indicated by his behavior that he felt so bad.

Suicide

Writers who killed themselves, such as Sylvia Plath, have provided insights into the causes of suicide. (Corbis-Bettmann.)

No other kind of death leaves friends and relatives with such long-lasting feelings of distress, shame, guilt, and puzzlement as does suicide (Gallo & Pfeffer, 2003). Survivors have an especially high mortality rate in the year after the suicide of a loved one.

We will focus on quantitative research on suicide, but those who study suicide learn from many different sources. Many philosophers have written searchingly on the topic, including Descartes, Voltaire, Kant, Heidegger, and Camus. In addition, novelists such as Herman Melville and Leo Tolstoy have provided insights on suicide, as have writers who have killed themselves, such as Virginia Woolf and Sylvia Plath.

It is important to begin by defining terms (see Table 5.8). Suicidal ideation refers to thoughts of killing oneself and is much more common than attempted or completed suicide. Suicide attempts involve behaviors that are intended to cause death but do not result in death. **Suicide** involves behaviors that are intended to cause death and actually do so. **Non-suicide self-injury** involves behaviors that are meant to cause immediate bodily harm but are not intended to cause death (see Focus on Discovery 5.6).

Table 5.8 Key Terms in the Study of Suicidality

Suicide ideation: thoughts of killing oneself
Suicide attempt: behavior intended to kill oneself
Suicide: death from deliberate self-injury
Non-suicidal self-injury: behaviors intended to injure oneself without intent to kill oneself

FOCUS ON DISCOVERY 5.6

Non-Suicidal Self-Injury

Researchers are quickly learning that non-suicidal self-injury (NSSI), is more common than previously thought (Nock, 2010), and contrary to previous thinking, it is practiced by many who do not have borderline personality disorder (Nock, Kazdin, Hiripi, et al., 2006). Here we describe how this behavior is defined and some reasons it occurs.

There are two key issues to consider in defining NSSI. The first is that the person did not intend to cause death. The second is that the behavior is designed to immediately cause injury. Most commonly, people cut, hit, or burn their body (Franklin, Hessel, Aaron, et al., 2010). When surveyed, anywhere from 13 to 45 percent of adolescents report having engaged in NSSI, but the higher estimates may be due to overly broad definitions. For example, some studies will include "scratching to the point of bleeding," without ruling out poison ivy or other reasons people might be scratching. Without a doubt, though, there is a group of people who engage in serious attempts to hurt themselves. The modal profile is of a person who tries NSSI infrequently (less than 10 times) during early adolescence and then stops (Nock, 2009). A subset of people seem to persist in self-injury, sometimes reporting more than 50 incidents of self-injury per year, and it is this profile of persistent NSSI that researchers are working to understand (Nock & Prinstein, 2004).

Why would someone hurt themself again and again? A fair amount of research suggests that self-injury often occurs when people are acutely distressed, but that doesn't provide a

In an interview with the BBC, Princess Diana described reaching a point of such pain that she engaged in non-suicidal self-injury. (WireImage/Getty Images, Inc.)

very satisfying answer—most people do not respond to emotional distress by hurting themselves. In a comprehensive review, Nock and colleagues (2010) argue that there are many different reasons that people will hurt themselves. For some, the injury seems to help quell other negative emotions, such as anger. Some report feeling satisfied after self-injury because they have given themselves punishment that they believe they deserved. The behavior can also be reinforcing interpersonally—others may respond by increasing support or by reducing aggression. Several studies provide evidence that those who are prone to self-injury do seem to experience more intense emotions than others do, believe that they deserve to be punished, and report difficulty managing relationships constructively. Not only do they report intense emotionality, but they also show greater psychophysiological reactivity during a challenging laboratory task compared to control participants (Nock & Mendes, 2008). In one study, people who engaged in NSSI were asked to record feelings, events, and NSSI incidents daily over time. Feelings of self-hatred and of being rejected were common just before incidents of self-injury (Nock, Prinstein, & Sterba, 2009). Taken together, findings suggest that NSSI may be reinforcing both psychologically (by relieving feelings of self-hatred and anger) and socially (by eliciting more supportive reactions from others). It is likely to require integrated social, emotional, and cognitive research to fully understand this complex behavioral pattern.

Epidemiology of Suicide and Suicide Attempts

Suicide rates may be grossly underestimated because some deaths are ambiguous—for example, a seemingly accidental death may have involved suicidal intentions. Nonetheless, it has been estimated that, on average, every 20 minutes someone in the United States dies from suicide (Arias, Anderson, Kung, et al., 2003).

Studies on the epidemiology of suicidality suggest the following:

- The overall suicide rate in the United States is about 1 per 10,000 in a given year (Centers for Disease Control and Prevention, 2006). In the United States, it is estimated that approximately 1 in 20 suicide attempts results in death (Moscicki, 1995).

- Worldwide, about 9 percent of people report suicidal ideation at least once in their lives, and 2.5 percent have made at least one suicide attempt (Nock & Mendes, 2008).

- Men are four times more likely than women to kill themselves (Arias et al., 2003).

- Women are more likely than men are to make suicide attempts that do not result in death (Nock & Mendes, 2008).

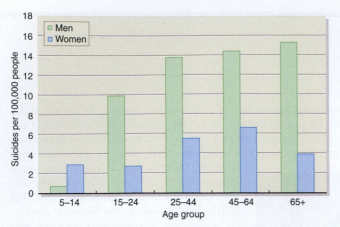

Figure 5.12 Annual deaths due to suicides per 100,000 people. From Arias et al. (2003).

- Guns are by far the most common means of suicide in the United States (Arias et al., 2003), accounting for about 60 percent of all suicides. Men usually choose to shoot or hang themselves; women are more likely to use pills, a less lethal method, which may account for their lower rate of completed suicide.

- The suicide rate increases in old age. The highest rates of suicide in the United States are for white males over age 50.

- The rates of suicide for adolescents and children in the United States are increasing dramatically but are still far below the rates of adults (see Figure 5.12). Some estimates suggest that at least 40 percent of children and adolescents experience suicidal ideation at least once. Because young people are less likely to die from other causes, suicide ranks as the third leading cause of death among those aged 10 to 24.

- Being divorced or widowed elevates suicide risk four- or fivefold.

Models of Suicide

Suicide is such a complex and multifaceted act that no single model can hope to explain it. Myths about suicide abound, highlighting the need for careful research (see Table 5.9). The study of suicide involves many different ethical questions and forces people to consider their own views on life and death.

Psychological Disorders Suicide is discussed in this chapter because many persons with mood disorders have suicidal thoughts and some engage in suicidal behaviors. More than half of those who try to kill themselves are depressed at the time of the act (Centers for Disease Control and Prevention, 2006), and as many as 15 percent of people who have been hospitalized with depression ultimately die from suicide (Angst et al., 2002). Other mental illnesses also are important in understanding suicide: as many as 90 percent of people who attempt suicide are suffering from a mental illness. Among people hospitalized for schizophrenia, bipolar I disorder, or bipolar II disorder, 10–12 percent die from suicide eventually (Angst et al., 2002; Roy, 1982). Impulse control disorders, substance use disorders, and borderline personality disorder are also each related to a higher risk of suicidal actions (Linehan, 1997; Nock & Mendes, 2008). Even less severe mental disorders, such as panic disorder and eating disorders, are associated with elevated risk of suicide (Linehan, 1997; Schmidt, Woolaway-Bickel, & Bates, 2000). With most of these disorders, though, suicides are most likely when a person is experiencing comorbid depression (Angst et al., 2002; Schmidt et al., 2000). Although understanding suicide within the context of mental disorders is extremely important, most people with mental illnesses do not die from suicide.

Table 5.9 Myths about Suicide

Common Myth	Contrary Evidence
People who discuss suicide will not actually commit suicide.	Up to three-quarters of those who take their own lives communicate their intention beforehand.
Suicide is committed without warning.	People usually give many warnings, such as saying that the world would be better off without them or making unexpected and inexplicable gifts of highly valued possessions.
Suicidal people want to die.	Most people are thankful after suicide is prevented.
People who attempt suicide by low lethal means are not serious about killing themselves.	Many people are not well informed about pill dosages or human anatomy. Because of this, people who really want to die sometimes make nonlethal attempts.

Sources: Drawn from Fremouw, De Perzel, & Ellis (1990); Shneidman (1973).

Neurobiological Models Twin studies suggest that heritability is about 48 percent for suicide attempts (Joiner, Brown, & Wingate, 2005). Adoption studies also support the heritability of suicidality.

Just as low levels of serotonin appear related to depression, there is a connection between serotonin and suicide (Mann, Huang, Underwood, et al., 2000). Low levels of serotonin's major metabolite, 5-HIAA, have been found among people who committed suicide (Van Praag, Plutchik, & Apter, 1990). Serotonin dysfunction appears particularly relevant for understanding violent suicide. That is, violent forms of suicide have been found to be related to particularly low 5-HIAA levels in postmortem assays (Roy, 1994; Winchel, Stanley, & Stanley, 1990) and to a polymorphism of the serotonin transporter gene (5-HTTLPR) (Bondy, Buettner, & Zill, 2006). These findings suggest that serotonin dysfunction may increase the risk of violent suicide.

Beyond the serotonin system, other research has found that among patients with MDD, those who had an abnormal dexamethasone suppression test response had a 14-fold increase in the risk of suicide over the next 14 years (Coryell & Schlesser, 2001).

Social Factors Economic and social events have been shown to influence suicide rates. As one example, across the past 100 years, suicide rates have been shown to increase modestly during economic recessions (Luo, Florence, Quispe-Agnoli, et al., 2011). Some of the strongest evidence for the role of the social environment in suicide comes from the major effects of media reports of suicide. In one example of these effects, suicides rose 12 percent in the month after Marilyn Monroe's death (Phillips, 1985). A review of 293 studies found that media coverage of a celebrity suicide is much more likely to spark an increase in suicidality than coverage of a noncelebrity suicide (Stack, 2000). Media reports of natural deaths of famous people are not followed by increases in suicide, suggesting that it is not grief per se that is the influential factor (Phillips, 1974). These statistics suggest that sociocultural factors matter.

Social factors that are more directly relevant to the individual are also powerful predictors of suicidality. In a comprehensive review, Van Orden and colleagues (2010) argue that social isolation and a lack of social belonging are among the most powerful predictors of suicidal ideation and behavior. They argue that the sensation of being alone, without others to turn to, is a major factor in the development of suicidality.

Psychological Models Suicide may have many different meanings. It may be intended to induce guilt in others, to force love from others, to make amends for wrongs, to rid oneself of unacceptable feelings, to rejoin a dead loved one, or to escape from emotional pain or an emotional vacuum. Undoubtedly, the psychological variables involved in suicide vary across people, but many researchers have attempted to identify risk factors that operate across people.

Several researchers relate suicide to poor problem solving (Linehan & Shearin, 1988). Problem-solving deficits do predict suicide attempts prospectively (Dieserud, Roysamb, Braverman, et al., 2003). Problem-solving deficits also relate to the seriousness of previous suicide attempts, even after controlling for depression severity, age, and intellectual functioning (Keilp, Sackeim, Brodsky, et al., 2001).

One might expect that a person who has trouble resolving problems would be more vulnerable to hopelessness. Hopelessness, which can be defined as the expectation that life will be no better in the future than it is now, is strongly tied to suicidality. High levels of hopelessness are associated with a fourfold elevation in the risk of suicide (Brown, Beck, Steer, et al., 2000), and hopelessness is important even after controlling for depression levels (Beck, Kovacs, & Weissman, 1975).

Beyond these negative characteristics (e.g., poor problem solving, hopelessness), positive qualities may motivate a person to live and help a clinician build a

On March 28, 1941, at the age of 59, Virginia Woolf drowned herself in the river near her Sussex home. Two suicide notes were found in the house, similar in content; one may have been written 10 days earlier, and it is possible that she may have made an unsuccessful attempt then, for she returned from a walk soaking wet, saying that she had fallen. The first was addressed to her sister Vanessa and the second to her husband, Leonard. To him, she wrote:

Dearest, I feel certain I am going mad again. I feel we can't go through another of those terrible times. And I shan't recover this time. I begin to hear voices, and I can't concentrate. So I am doing what seems the best thing to do. You have given me the greatest possible happiness. You have been in every way all that anyone could be. I don't think two people could have been happier till this terrible disease came. I can't fight it any longer. I know that I am spoiling your life, that without me you could work. And you will I know. You see I can't even write this properly. I can't read. What I want to say is I owe all the happiness of my life to you. You have been entirely patient with me and incredibly good. I want to say that—everybody knows it. If anybody could have saved me it would have been you. Everything has gone from me but the certainty of your goodness. I can't go on spoiling your life any longer I don't think two people could have been happier than we have been. V.

Quoted from pp. 400–401, Briggs, J. (2005). Virginia Woolf: An Inner Life. Orlando, Fl: Harcourt, Inc.

English novelist and critic Virginia Woolf (1882–1941). (Photo by George C. Beresford/Getty Images.)

case for choosing life (Malone, Oquendo, Haas, et al., 2000). One line of research builds on the Reasons for Living Inventory (Linehan, Goodstein, Nielsen, et al., 1983). Items on this inventory tap into what is important to the person, such as responsibility to family and concerns about children. People with more reasons to live tend to be less suicidal than those with few reasons to live (Ivanoff, Jang, Smyth, et al., 1994).

While many people think about suicide, relatively few engage in suicidal actions. Additional variables seem to predict the switch from thinking about suicide to acting on those thoughts (Van Orden, Witte, Gordon, et al., 2008). Among people who are experiencing suicidal thoughts, hundreds of studies document that people who are more impulsive are more likely to attempt suicide or to die from suicide (Brezo, Paris, & Turecki, 2006). While intense distress and hopelessness might set off thoughts about suicide, suicidal actions might be driven by other factors, such as impulsivity.

Preventing Suicide

Many people worry that talking about suicide will make it more likely to happen. Rather, clinicians have learned that it is helpful to talk about suicide openly and matter-of-factly. Giving a person permission to talk about suicide may relieve a sense of isolation.

Sadly, some colleges seem to be creating policies that keep students from talking about suicidal ideas. About 10 percent of college students report that they thought about suicide in the past year. Even though suicide rates remain relatively low (about 7.5 per 100,000 students), colleges have increasingly encouraged students who endorse suicidality to withdraw (Appelbaum, 2006). More progressive schools have implemented outreach programs to allow students a chance to discuss these thoughts. Some offer web-based counseling to allow students to remain anonymous.

Most people are ambivalent about their suicidal intentions, and they will communicate their intentions in some way. "The prototypical suicidal state is one in which a person cuts his or her throat, cries for help at the same time, and is genuine in both of these acts. . . . Individuals would be happy not to do it, if they didn't have to" (Shneidman, 1987, p. 170). Among those who attempt suicide but do not die, 80 percent report within the next 2 days that they are either glad to be alive or ambivalent about whether they want to die (Henriques, Wenzel, Brown, et al., 2005). This ambivalence gives the clinician an important foothold.

Treating the Associated Psychological Disorder   One approach to suicide prevention builds on our knowledge that most people who kill themselves are suffering from a psychological disorder. Thus when Beck's cognitive approach successfully lessens a patient's depression, that patient's suicidal risk is also reduced. Marsha Linehan's dialectical behavior therapy with borderline patients provides another example of a treatment that is designed for a specific disorder but also provides protection from suicide (see Chapter 15).

Studies have found that medications for mood disorders reduce the risk of suicidality three- to fourfold (Angst et al., 2002). Specifically, lithium appears effective in suicide prevention for people with bipolar disorder (Cipriani, Pretty, Hawton, et al., 2005). Among people who have been diagnosed with depressive disorders, ECT (Kellner, Fink, Knapp, et al., 2005) and antidepressants (Bruce, Ten Have, Reynolds III et al., 2004) reduce suicidality. Risperidone (Clozapine), an antipsychotic medication, also appears to reduce the risk of suicide attempts among people with schizophrenia (Meltzer, 2003).

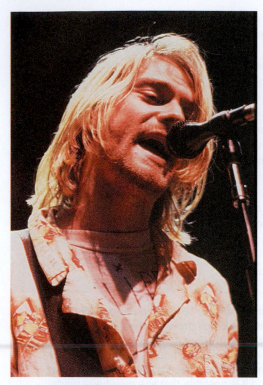

The suicide of Nirvana's lead singer, Kurt Cobain, triggered an increase in suicide among teenagers. (Kevin Estrada/Retna.)

After a broken engagement at age 31, Abraham Lincoln developed symptoms of depression that were so severe that his friends feared he would hurt himself, and they removed any sharp objects from his room. "I am now the most miserable man living," he confessed. "Whether I shall ever be better I cannot tell; I awfully forebode I shall not. To remain as I am is impossible; I must die or be better." (Cited in Goodwin, 2003.) (Granger Collection.)

Treating Suicidality Directly Cognitive behavioral approaches appear to be the most promising therapies for reducing suicidality (Van Der Sande, Buskens, Allart, et al., 1997). These programs have been found to reduce the risk of a future attempt among suicide attempters by 50 percent compared to treatment as usually offered in the community (Brown, Ten Have, Henriques, et al., 2005). They have also been found to reduce suicidal ideation (Joiner, Voelz, & Rudd, 2001). In a meta-analysis of 28 treatment trials, adults who received cognitive behavioral treatment were found to report less hopelessness, suicidal ideation, and suicidal behavior than those who received no treatment or other forms of treatment (Tarrier, Taylor, & Gooding, 2008).

Cognitive behavioral treatments include a set of strategies to prevent suicide (Brown, Henriques, Ratto, et al., 2002). Therapists help clients understand the emotions and thoughts that trigger urges to commit suicide. Therapists work with clients to challenge their negative thoughts and to provide new ways to tolerate emotional distress. They also help clients problem-solve about the life situations they are facing. The goal is to improve problem solving and social support and thereby to reduce the feelings of hopelessness that often precede these episodes.

Professional organizations such as the American Psychiatric Association, the National Association of Social Workers, and the American Psychological Association charge their members with protecting people from suicide even if doing so requires breaking the confidentiality of the therapist–patient relationship. Therapists are expected to take reasonable precautions when they learn a patient is suicidal (Roy, 1995). One approach to keeping such patients alive is to hospitalize them as a short-term means of keeping them safe until they can begin to consider ways of improving their life.

Some have argued against involuntary hospitalizations and other efforts to keep people from killing themselves. Boldly and controversially, Thomas Szasz (1999) argues that it is impractical and immoral to prevent suicide. It is impractical because people who are determined to die will be able to do so (even hospitalized patients manage to take their own lives). In his view, it is immoral because people should be free to make choices. In our view, his principal omissions are that treatment and hospitalization often do deter people from suicide, and most people who are prevented from killing themselves are grateful afterward for another chance at life. There are no easy answers here, but it is important to raise the questions.

Suicide Prevention There are more than 200 **suicide prevention centers** in the United States, plus others abroad (Lester, 1995). These centers typically aim to provide 24-hour phone hotline support to people in suicidal crises. It is exceedingly difficult to do controlled research on suicide prevention since the base rates are so low and the ability to track suicide in a large population is limited.

One approach to this issue has been to study suicide prevention within the military, where rates of suicide are elevated, programs can be offered to the entire community, and outcomes can be tracked carefully. In one study, researchers examined rates of suicide in the Air Force before and after implementation of a comprehensive suicide prevention program. The program provided training for military leaders and for soldiers to encourage and destigmatize help seeking, to normalize the experience of distress, and to promote effective coping with distress. Implementation of the program led to a 25 percent drop in rates of completed suicide (Knox, Pflanz, Talcott, et al., 2010). These findings provide strong evidence that prevention efforts can reduce rates of suicide.

Community mental health centers often provide a 24-hour-a-day hotline for people who are considering suicide. (Mark Antman/The Image Works.)

Check Your Knowledge 5.5

True or false?
1. Men have higher rates of suicide than women.
2. Men have higher rates of suicide attempts than women.
3. Adolescents have higher rates of suicide than older adults do.
4. Dopamine dysfunction is implicated in suicidality.
5. Most people with MDD will make a suicide attempt.

Summary

Clinical Descriptions and Epidemiology

- There are two broad types of mood disorders: depressive disorders and bipolar disorders.
- Depressive disorders include major depression and dysthymia, along with the new diagnoses of mixed anxiety/depressive disorder, premenstrual dysphoric disorder, and disruptive mood dysregulation disorder. Bipolar disorders include bipolar I disorder, bipolar II disorder, and cyclothymia.
- Bipolar I disorder is defined by mania. Bipolar II disorder is defined by hypomania and episodes of depression. Major depressive disorder, bipolar I disorder, and bipolar II disorder are episodic. Recurrence is very common in these disorders.
- Dysthymia and cyclothymia are characterized by low levels of symptoms that last for at least 2 years.
- Major depression is one of the most common psychiatric disorders, affecting 16.2 percent of people during their lifetime. Rates of depression are twice as high in women as in men. Bipolar I disorder is much rarer, affecting 1 percent or less of the population.

Etiology

- Genetic studies provide evidence that bipolar disorder is strongly heritable and that depression is somewhat heritable.
- Neurobiological research has focused on the sensitivity of receptors rather than on the amount of various transmitters, with the strongest evidence for diminished sensitivity of the serotonin receptors in depression and mania. There is some evidence that mania is related to heightened sensitivity of the dopamine receptors and that depression is related to diminished sensitivity of dopamine receptors.
- Bipolar and unipolar disorders seem tied to elevated activity of the amygdala and the subgenual anterior cingulate and to diminished activity in the dorsolateral prefrontal cortex and hippocampus during tasks that involve emotion and emotion regulation. During mania, greater levels of activation of the striatum have been observed. Mania also may involve elevations in protein kinase C.
- Overactivity of the hypothalamic–pituitary–adrenal axis (HPA), as indexed by poor suppression of cortisol by dexamethasone, is related to severe forms of depression and to bipolar disorder.
- Socioenvironmental models focus on the role of negative life events, lack of social support, and family criticism as triggers for episodes but also consider ways in which a person with depression may elicit negative responses from others. People with less social skill and those who tend to seek excessive reassurance are at elevated risk for the development of depression.
- The personality trait that appears most related to depression is neuroticism. Neuroticism predicts the onset of depression.
- Influential cognitive theories include Beck's cognitive theory, hopelessness theory, and rumination theory. All argue that depression can be caused by cognitive factors, but the nature of the cognitive factors differs across theories. Beck's theory focuses on the cognitive triad, negative schemas, and cognitive biases. According to hopelessness theory, low self-esteem or beliefs that a life event will have long-term meaningful consequences can instill a sense of hopelessness, which is expressed in a specific set of depressive symptoms called hopelessness depression. Rumination theory focuses on the negative effects of repetitively dwelling on the reasons for a sad mood. Cross-sectional and prospective evidence is available for each model.
- Psychological theories of depression in bipolar disorder are similar to those proposed for unipolar depression. Some researchers have proposed that manic symptoms arise because of dysregulation in the reward system in the brain. Mania can be triggered by life events involving goal attainment. Mania also can be triggered by sleep deprivation.

Treatment

- Several psychological therapies are effective for depression, including interpersonal psychotherapy, cognitive therapy, behavioral activation therapy, and behavioral couples therapy.
- The major approaches that have been found to help as adjuncts to medication for bipolar disorder include psychoeducation, family therapy, and cognitive therapy.
- Electroconvulsive shock and several antidepressant drugs (tricyclics, selective serotonin reuptake inhibitors, and MAOIs) have proved their worth in lifting depression. Lithium is the best-researched treatment for bipolar disorder, but antipsychotic and anticonvulsant medications also help decrease manic symptoms. Antidepressant medications have become controversial in the treatment of bipolar disorder.

Suicide

- Men, elderly people, and people who are divorced or widowed are at elevated risk for suicide. Most people who commit suicide meet diagnostic criteria for psychiatric disorders, with more than half experiencing depression. Suicide is at least partially heritable, and neurobiological models focus on serotonin and overactivity in the HPA. Environmental factors are also important: sociocultural events such as celebrity suicides and economic recessions can influence rates of suicide in the population, and social isolation is a robust predictor of suicide. Psychological vulnerability factors for suicidal ideation include poor problem solving, hopelessness, and lack of reasons to live; among those with suicidal ideation, suicidal action appears related to impulsivity.
- Several approaches have been taken to suicide prevention. For people with a mental illness, psychological treatments and medications to quell symptoms help reduce suicidality. Many people believe it is important to address suicidality more directly, though. CBT can help reduce suicidal ideation and behavior. Suicide hotlines are found in most cities, and some research suggests that suicide prevention can work.

Answers to Check Your Knowledge Questions

5.1 1. five (including mood), two; 2. 16–17; 3. two; 4. six; 5. manic, hypomanic

5.2 1. c; 2. b; 3. b; 4. b; 5. d

5.3 1. T; 2. F; 3. T; 4. T

5.4 1. a, b, d; 2. c; 3. b

5.5 1. T; 2. F; 3. F; 4. F; 5. F

Key Terms

antidepressant
attribution
attributional style
behavioral couples therapy
bipolar I disorder
bipolar II disorder
cognitive biases
Cushing's syndrome
cyclothymic disorder
dorsolateral prefrontal cortex
dysthymic disorder
episodic disorder

expressed emotion (EE)
flight of ideas
G-proteins
hopelessness theory
hypomania
lithium
major depressive disorder
   (MDD)
mania
melancholic
mindfulness-based cognitive
   therapy (MBCT)

mixed anxiety/depressive
   disorder
monoamine oxidase inhibitors
   (MAOIs)
mood disorders
negative triad
neuroticism
non-suicidal self-injury (NSSI)
postpartum onset
psychoeducational approaches
psychomotor agitation
psychomotor retardation

rapid cycling
reward system
rumination
seasonal affective disorder
selective serotonin reuptake
   inhibitors (SSRIs)
subgenual anterior cingulate
suicide
suicide prevention centers
tricyclic antidepressants
tryptophan

6 Anxiety Disorders

LEARNING GOALS

1. Be able to describe the clinical features of the anxiety disorders.
2. Be able to describe how the anxiety disorders tend to co-occur with each other, and be able to understand how gender and culture influence the prevalence of anxiety disorders.
3. Be able to recognize commonalities in etiology across the anxiety disorders, as well as the factors that shape the expression of specific anxiety disorders.
4. Be able to describe treatment approaches that are common across the anxiety disorders and how treatment approaches are modified for the specific anxiety disorders.

Clinical Case: James

James was a 23-year-old student completing his first year of medical school. The year had been a hard one, not only because of the long hours and academic challenges of medical school, but also because his mother had developed cancer. One day, while attending rounds, James found himself feeling light-headed and dizzy. During rounds, the consultant would ask students to diagnose and explain a given case, and on that day James became extremely worried about whether he would be able to answer these questions when his turn came. As he thought about this, his heart began to pound, his breathing became rapid and shallow, his palms began to sweat and his mouth was dry. Overwhelmed by a sudden sensation of smothering, which was accompanied by a deep sense of fear that something was horribly wrong, James abruptly fled the room without explaining his departure. Later in the day, he thought about how to explain himself, but could not think about how to describe the situation to the consultant. That night, he could not sleep, worrying about if it would happen again. James was also concerned about how this would affect his ability to do his job properly, such as leading a small research group and meeting with other medical staff and patients. One week later while driving to the hospital, he experienced a sudden attack of similar symptoms, which forced him to stop at the side of the road. He took the day off from medical school. Over the next few months, James became anxious when he traveled away from home because he feared being humiliated by the return of these symptoms. He avoided going out with friends, and he turned down opportunities for training that involved public interviews of patients. Despite his withdrawal, he experienced three more attacks, each in unexpected situations. He also began to experience gastrointestinal problems, suffering intermittently from cramping and diarrhea. James began to think that maybe medical school was a poor choice for him, because he had such deep fears about experiencing another attack during ward rounds. After he read about panic disorder in one of his textbooks, he decided to visit a psychologist. The psychologist confirmed that he was experiencing an anxiety disorder called panic disorder, and they started cognitive behavioral treatment.

VERY FEW OF US go through even a week of our lives without experiencing anxiety or fear. In this chapter, we focus on a group of disorders called **anxiety disorders**. Both anxiety and fear play a significant role in these disorders, so it is important to understand some of the similarities and differences between these two emotions.

Anxiety is defined as apprehension over an anticipated problem. In contrast, **fear** is defined as a reaction to immediate danger. Psychologists focus on the "immediate" aspect of fear versus the "anticipated" aspect of anxiety—fear tends to be about a threat that's happening now, whereas anxiety tends to be about a future threat. Thus, a person facing a bear experiences fear, whereas a college student concerned about the possibility of unemployment after graduation experiences anxiety.

Both anxiety and fear can involve arousal, or sympathetic nervous system activity. Anxiety often involves moderate arousal, and fear involves higher arousal. At the low end, a person experiencing anxiety may feel no more than restless energy and physiological tension; at the high end, a person experiencing fear may sweat profusely, breathe rapidly, and feel an overpowering urge to run.

Anxiety and fear are not necessarily "bad"—in fact, both are adaptive. Fear is fundamental for "fight-or-flight" reactions—that is, fear triggers rapid changes in the sympathetic nervous system that prepare the body for escape or fighting. In the right circumstance, fear saves lives. (Imagine a person who faces a bear and experiences no impulse to flee, no surge in energy, and no marshaling of that energy to run quickly!) In some anxiety disorders, though, the fear system seems to misfire—a person experiences fear at a time when there is no danger in the environment (see the discussion of panic attacks later in this chapter).

Anxiety is adaptive in helping us notice and plan for future threats—that is, to increase our preparedness, to help people avoid potentially dangerous situations, and to think through potential problems before they happen. In laboratory studies first conducted 100 years ago and since verified many times over, a small degree of anxiety has been found to improve performance on laboratory tasks (Yerkes & Dodson, 1908). Ask anyone with extreme test anxiety, though, and they will tell you that too much anxiety interferes with performance. Anxiety, then, provides a classic example of a **U**-shaped curve with performance—an absence of anxiety is a problem, a little anxiety is adaptive, and a lot of anxiety is detrimental.

In this chapter, we examine the anxiety disorders included in DSM-5: specific phobias, social anxiety disorder, panic disorder, agoraphobia, and generalized anxiety disorder. We will cover the anxiety disorders of obsessive-compulsive disorder and trauma-related disorders (posttraumatic stress disorder and acute stress disorder) in the next chapter, even though these are included as anxiety disorders in the DSM-IV-TR. Obsessive-compulsive disorder and trauma-related disorders share a good deal in common with the anxiety disorders but are also distinct in some important ways. To recognize those distinctions, the proposed DSM-5 places these conditions in new chapters next to anxiety disorders. See Figure 6.1 for an overview of how DSM-IV-TR and DSM-5 organize the various anxiety disorders into chapters.

Anxiety disorders as a group are the most common type of psychiatric diagnosis. For example, in one study of over 8,000 adults in the United States, approximately 28 percent of people reported having experienced symptoms at some point during their life that met the DSM-IV-TR criteria for diagnosis of an anxiety disorder (Kessler, Berglund, Demler, et al., 2005). Phobias are particularly common. As a group, anxiety disorders are very costly to society and to people with the disorders. These disorders are associated with twice the average rate of medical costs (Simon, Ormel, VonKroff, et al., 1995), higher risk of cardiovascular disease and other medical conditions (Roy-Byrne, Davidson, Kessler, et al., 2008; Smoller, Pollack, Wassertheil-Smoller, et al., 2007), twice the risk of suicidal ideation and attempts compared to people without a psychiatric diagnosis (Sareen et al., 2005), difficulties in employment (American Psychiatric Association, 2000), and serious interpersonal concerns (Zatzick, Marmer, Weiss, et al., 1997). All of the anxiety disorders are associated with substantial decrements in the quality of life (Olatunji, Cisler, & Tolin, 2007).

We begin by defining the symptoms of the anxiety disorders before turning to the common themes in the etiology for the anxiety disorders as a group. We then describe specific etiological factors that shape whether a specific anxiety disorder develops. Like most disorders, many different paradigms have helped shed light on the anxiety disorders. Hence, throughout our discussions of etiology we look at issues from various perspectives, with particular focus on genetic, neurobiological, personality, cognitive, and behavioral research. Finally, we consider the treatment of the

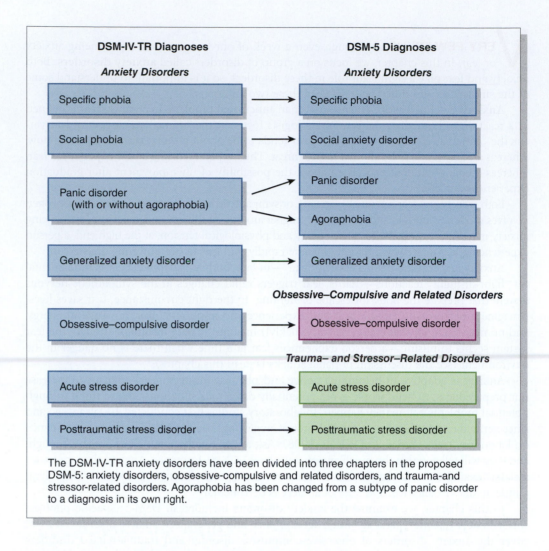

The DSM-IV-TR anxiety disorders have been divided into three chapters in the proposed DSM-5: anxiety disorders, obsessive-compulsive and related disorders, and trauma-and stressor-related disorders. Agoraphobia has been changed from a subtype of panic disorder to a diagnosis in its own right.

Figure 6.1 Diagnoses of anxiety disorders.

anxiety disorders. We describe commonalities in the psychological treatment of the various anxiety disorders, and then we describe how these general treatment principles are modified to address specific anxiety disorders. Finally, we discuss biological treatments of the anxiety disorders.

Clinical Descriptions of the Anxiety Disorders

There is a lot of overlap in the way the various anxiety disorders are defined. All share excessively high or frequent anxiety. Except for generalized anxiety disorder, the anxiety disorders we discuss in this chapter also involve tendencies to experience unusually intense fear (Cox, Clara, & Enns, 2002). For each, several criteria must be met for a DSM-5 diagnosis to be made:

- Symptoms must interfere with important areas of functioning or cause marked distress.
- Symptoms are not caused by a drug or a medical condition.
- The fears and anxieties are distinct from the symptoms of another anxiety disorder.

Each disorder, though, is defined by a different set of symptoms related to anxiety or fear (see Table 6.1 for a brief summary).

Specific Phobias

A **specific phobia** is a disproportionate fear caused by a specific object or situation, such as fear of flying, fear of snakes, and fear of heights. The person recognizes that the fear is excessive but still goes to great lengths to avoid the feared object or situation. The names for these fears consist of a Greek word for the feared object or situation followed by the suffix -*phobia* (derived from the

Proposed DSM-5 Criteria for Specific Phobia

- Marked and disproportionate fear consistently triggered by specific objects or situations
- The object or situation is avoided or else endured with intense anxiety
- Symptoms persist for at least 6 months.

Note: The DSM-IV-TR criterion that the person recognizes that the fear is unrealistic is not included in DSM-5. DSM-IV-TR includes the duration criterion only for those under age 18.

Table 6.1 Anxiety Disorders Covered in This Chapter		
Disorder	**Description**	**Likely Key Changes in DSM-5**
Specific phobia	Fear of objects or situations that is out of proportion to any real danger	Duration criteria specified for adults Person need not perceive fear as unrealistic
Social anxiety disorder	Fear of unfamiliar people or social scrutiny	Name changed from social phobia Duration criteria specified for adults
Panic disorder	Anxiety about recurrent panic attacks	
Agoraphobia	Anxiety about being in places where escaping or getting help would be difficult if anxiety symptoms occurred	New disorder (formerly a subtype of panic disorder)
Generalized anxiety disorder	Uncontrollable worry for at least 3 months	Minimum duration reduced from 6 to 3 months Behavioral outcomes of worry are specified as part of criteria

Table 6.2 Names of Highly Unlikely Phobias	
Fear	**Phobia**
Anything new	Neophobia
Asymmetrical things	Asymmetriphobia
Books	Bibliophobia
Children	Pedophobia
Dancing	Chorophobia
Englishness	Anglophobia
Garlic	Alliumphobia
Peanut butter sticking to the roof of the mouth	Arachibutyrophobia
Technology	Technophobia
Mice	Musophobia
Pseudoscientific terms	Hellenophobia

Source: Drawn from www.phobialist.com.

name of the Greek god Phobos, who frightened his enemies). Two of the more familiar phobias are claustrophobia (fear of closed spaces) and acrophobia (fear of heights). Table 6.2 describes potential names of some highly unlikely phobias. Despite this array of possible phobias, in reality, specific phobias tend to cluster around a small number of feared objects and situations. The DSM categorizes specific phobias according to these sources of fear (see Table 6.3). A person with one type of specific phobia is very likely to have another type of specific phobia as well—that is, there is high comorbidity of specific phobias (Kendler, Myers, Prescott, et al., 2001). The Clinical Case of Joe provides a glimpse of how specific phobias can interfere with important life goals.

Social Anxiety Disorder

Social anxiety disorder is a persistent, unrealistically intense fear of social situations that might involve being scrutinized by, or even just exposed to, unfamiliar people. Although this disorder is labeled social phobia in the DSM-IV-TR, the term *social anxiety disorder* is proposed in the DSM-5 because the problems caused by it tend to be much more pervasive and to interfere much more with normal activities than the problems caused by other phobias (Liebowitz, Heimberg, Fresco, et al., 2000). People with social anxiety disorder, like Maureen in the Clinical Case, usually try to avoid situations in which they might be evaluated, show signs of anxiety, or behave in embarrassing ways. The most common fears include public speaking, speaking up in meetings or classes, meeting new people, and talking to people in authority (Ruscio et al., 2008). Although this may sound like shyness, people with social anxiety disorder avoid more social situations, feel more discomfort socially,

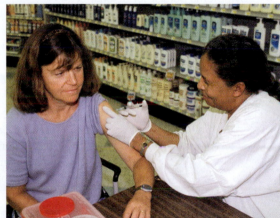

One form of specific phobia is an intense fear of blood, injection, or injuries. (David Young-Wolf/PhotoEdit.)

Table 6.3 Types of Specific Phobias		
Type of Phobia	**Examples of the Feared Object**	**Associated Characteristics**
Animal	Snakes, insects	Generally begins during childhood
Natural environment	Storms, heights, water	Generally begins during childhood
Blood, injection, injury	Blood, injury, injections, or other invasive medical procedures	Clearly runs in families; profile of heart rate slowing and possible fainting when facing feared stimulus (LeBeau et al., 2010)
Situational	Public transportation, tunnels, bridges, elevators, flying, driving, closed spaces	Tends to begin either in childhood or in mid-20s.
Other	Fear of choking, fear of contracting an illness, etc.; children's fears of loud sounds, clowns, etc.	

Clinical Case: Joe

Joe was a 22-year-old man whose friends invited him on a backpacking trip to Australia. He was worried about the trip because he knew that Australia is known for large spiders. For as long as he could remember, Joe had been afraid of spiders. It had begun after sleeping in a tent when he was young, and a spider had run over his face. Before deciding on whether to go or not, Joe decided to see a therapist.

He mentioned avoiding certain films that feature spiders, and avoiding cleaning under the beds or behind cupboards in case he disturbed a spider. The idea of being in a country with large spiders had greatly increased his anxiety. He was prescribed a course of selective serotonin reuptake inhibitors and put on a waiting list of for cognitive-behavioral treatment.

● Proposed DSM-5 Criteria for Social Anxiety Disorder

- Marked and disproportionate fear consistently triggered by exposure to potential social scrutiny
- Exposure to the trigger leads to intense anxiety about being evaluated negatively
- Trigger situations are avoided or else endured with intense anxiety
- Symptoms persist for at least 6 months.

Note: DSM-IV-TR labels this disorder as social phobia. The DSM-IV-TR but not DSM-5 specifies that the person recognizes the fear is unrealistic. DSM-IV-TR includes the duration criterion only for those under age 18.

Acrophobia, or phobia of heights, is common. Other specific phobias include fears of animals, injections, and enclosed spaces. (Bill Aron/PhotoEdit.)

Social anxiety disorder typically begins in adolescence and interferes with developing friendships. (Spencer Grant/PhotoEdit.)

and experience these symptoms for longer periods of their life than people who are shy (Turner, Beidel, & Townsley, 1990). They often fear that they will blush or sweat excessively. Speaking or performing in public, eating in public, using public restrooms, or engaging in virtually any activity in the presence of others can cause extreme anxiety. People with social anxiety disorder often work in occupations far below their talents because of their extreme social fears. Many would rather work in an unrewarding job with limited social demand than deal with social situations every day.

Among people with social anxiety disorder, at least a third also meet the DSM-IV-TR criteria for a diagnosis of avoidant personality disorder (Chavira, Stein, & Malcarne, 2002). The symptoms of the two conditions overlap a great deal, and there is overlap in the genetic vulnerability for the two conditions (Reichborn-Kjennerud, Czajkowski, Torgerson, et al., 2007). Avoidant personality disorder, though, is a more severe disorder with an earlier onset and more pervasive symptoms. See Chapter 15 for more discussion of avoidant personality disorder.

Social anxiety disorder generally begins during adolescence, when social interactions become more important. For some, though, the symptoms first emerge during childhood. Without treatment, social anxiety disorder tends to be chronic.

Social anxiety disorder can range in severity from a relatively few specific fears to a more generalized host of fears. For example, some people might be anxious about speaking in public but not other social situations. In contrast, others report fearing most social situations. The number of fears experienced is related to more comorbidity with other disorders, such as depression and alcohol abuse, and more negative effects on the person's social and occupational activities (Acarturk, de Graaf, van Straten, et al., 2008).

Clinical Case: Maureen

Maureen, a 30-year-old accountant, sought psychotherapy after reading a newspaper notice advertising group therapy for people with difficulties in social situations. Maureen appeared nervous during the interview and described deep distress over the amount of anxiety she experienced in conversations with others. She described the problem as becoming worse over the years, to the point where she no longer interacted socially with anyone other than her husband. She would not even go to the supermarket for fear of having to interact with people. Maureen explained that she was afraid of social interactions because she would feel extreme shame if others thought that she was stupid or could not express herself well. This fear made Maureen so nervous that she would often stammer or forget what she was going to say while talking to others, thus adding to her apprehension that others would see her as stupid and creating a vicious circle of ever-increasing fear.

Panic Disorder

Panic disorder is characterized by frequent panic attacks that are unrelated to specific situations and by worry about having more panic attacks (see the Clinical Case of James at the beginning of this chapter). A **panic attack** is a sudden attack of intense apprehension, terror, and feelings of impending doom, accompanied by at least four other symptoms. Physical symptoms can include labored breathing, heart palpitations, nausea, upset stomach, chest pain, feelings of choking and smothering, dizziness, lightheadedness, sweating, chills, heat sensations, and trembling. Other symptoms that may occur during a panic attack include **depersonalization** (a feeling of being outside one's body); **derealization** (a feeling of the world's not being real); and fears of losing control, of going crazy, or even of dying. Not surprisingly, people often report that they have an intense urge to flee whatever situation they are in when a panic attack occurs. The symptoms tend to come on very rapidly and reach a peak of intensity within 10 minutes.

We can think about a panic attack as a misfire of the fear system—physiologically, the person experiences a level of sympathetic nervous system arousal matching what most people might experience when faced with an immediate threat to life. Because the symptoms are inexplicable, the person tries to make sense of the experience. A person who begins to think that he or she is dying, losing control, or going crazy is likely to feel even more fear. Among people with panic disorder, 90 percent report just these types of beliefs when panic attacks occur.

Panic attacks that occur unexpectedly are called *uncued* attacks. Panic attacks that are clearly triggered by specific situations, such as seeing a snake, are referred to as *cued* panic attacks. People who only have cued attacks are most likely to suffer from a phobia. According to the DSM criteria, for a diagnosis of panic disorder, a person must experience recurrent uncued panic attacks. They also must worry about the attacks or change their behavior because of the attacks for at least 1 month—hence, the response to panic attacks is as important as the attacks themselves in making this diagnosis.

Remember that the criteria for panic disorder specify that panic attacks must be recurrent. But it is fairly common for people to experience a single panic attack—more than a quarter of people in the United States report that they have experienced at least one panic attack during their lifetime (Kessler, Chiu, Jin, et al., 2006), and 3–5 percent report a panic attack in the past year (G. R. Norton, Cox, & Malan, 1992). As Table 6.4 shows, though, many fewer people

Proposed DSM-5 Criteria for Panic Disorder

- Recurrent uncued panic attacks
- At least 1 month of concern about the possibility of more attacks, worry about the consequences of an attack, or maladaptive behavioral changes because of the attacks.

Table 6.4 Percent of People in the General Population Who Meet Diagnostic Criteria for Anxiety Disorders in the Past Year and in Their Lifetime

Anxiety Disorder	12-Month Prevalence			Lifetime Prevalence
	Male	Female	Total	Total
Panic disorder	1.7	3.0	2.3	6.0
Phobia or social anxiety disorder	7.5	17.7	12.6	n/a
Social anxiety disorder				12.10
Specific phobia				12.15
Generalized anxiety disorder	1.0	2.1	1.5	5.7

Sources: Past year estimates from Jacobi (2004). Lifetime estimates from Kessler, Berglund, et al. (2005).

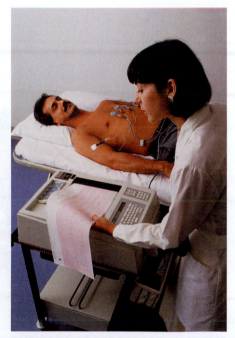

People with panic disorder often seek cardiac tests because they are frightened by changes in their heart rate. (MacNeal Hospital/David Joel/Stone/Getty Images.)

In agoraphobia, a person is afraid of being in shopping malls, crowds, and other public situations from which escape would be difficult if anxiety symptoms occurred; people with agoraphobia can become housebound. (Frank Siteman/Stone/Getty Images.)

develop full-blown panic disorder. Among those who develop panic disorder, the onset is typically in adolescence. Over time it can take a heavy toll; for example, as many as one-quarter of people with panic disorder report being unemployed for more than 5 years (Leon, Portera, & Weissman, 1995).

Agoraphobia

Agoraphobia (from the Greek *agora,* meaning "marketplace") is defined by anxiety about situations in which it would be embarrassing or difficult to escape if anxiety symptoms occurred. Commonly feared situations include crowds and crowded places such as grocery stores, malls, and churches. Sometimes the situations are those that are difficult to escape from, such as trains, bridges, or long road trips. Many people with agoraphobia are virtually unable to leave their house, and even those who can leave do so only with great distress.

In the DSM-IV-TR, agoraphobia is coded as a subtype of panic disorder. The proposed DSM-5 instead includes agoraphobia as a separate diagnosis. This change brings the DSM in line with the International Classification of Diseases (ICD) diagnostic system which has long recognized agoraphobia as a separate diagnosis. The new diagnosis also fits evidence from research studies. In one study of over 3,000 community participants, more than half of people who had symptoms of agoraphobia reported no symptoms of panic attacks or panic disorder (Wittchen, Nocon, Beesdo, et al., 2008). Indeed, five different large epidemiological studies suggest that at least half of people with agoraphobia symptoms do not experience panic attacks (Andrews, Charney, Sirovatka, et al., 2009). Those who do not experience panic attacks are concerned about what will happen if other anxiety symptoms develop.

Less is known about the epidemiology of agoraphobia because many of the U.S. studies have examined this only as a subtype of panic disorder. It is clear that agoraphobia is related to significant impairment in daily functioning. Several studies suggest that the effects of agoraphobia on quality of life are as severe as those observed for the other anxiety disorders (Wittchen, Gloster, Beesdo-Baum, et al., 2010).

A crowd is likely to be very distressing to people with agoraphobia because escape would be difficult if anxiety symptoms occurred. (© Rafael Ramirez Lee/Shutterstock.)

Generalized Anxiety Disorder

The central feature of **generalized anxiety disorder** (GAD) is worry. Like Stefan in the Clinical Case, people with GAD are persistently worried, often about minor things. The term *worry* refers to the cognitive tendency to chew on a problem and to be unable to let go of it (Mennin, Heimberg, & Turk, 2004). Often, worry continues because a person cannot settle on a solution to the problem. Most of us worry from time to time, but the worries of people with GAD are excessive, uncontrollable, and long-lasting. GAD is not diagnosed if a person worries only about concerns driven by another psychological disorder; for example, a person with claustrophobia who only worries about being in closed spaces would not meet the criteria for GAD. The worries of people with GAD are similar in focus to those of most people: they worry about relationships, health, finances, and daily hassles (Roemer, Molina, & Borkovec, 1997)—but they worry more about these issues, and these persistent worries interfere with daily life. Other symptoms of GAD include difficulty concentrating, tiring easily, restlessness, irritability, and muscle tension.

The proposed DSM-5 criteria require that symptoms must be present for at least 3 months to qualify for a diagnosis of GAD. This is a shift from the DSM-IV-TR criteria, which require symptoms to persist for at least 6 months for a person to qualify for the diagnosis. This change is made to enhance reliability, as many people have a difficult time recalling how anxious they were 6 months ago (Andrews, Cuijpers, Craske, et al., 2010). With this briefer duration requirement, the prevalence of the DSM-5 diagnosis of GAD will be higher than the prevalence documented for the DSM-IV-TR diagnosis of GAD.

GAD typically begins in adolescence, though many people who have GAD report having had a tendency to worry all their lives (Barlow, Blanchard, Vermilyea, et al., 1986). Once it develops, GAD is often chronic; in one study, about half of people with GAD reported ongoing symptoms 5 years after an initial interview (Yonkers, Dyck, Warshaw, & Keller, 2000).

Comorbidity in Anxiety Disorders

More than half of people with one anxiety disorder meet the criteria for another anxiety disorder during their life (Brown, Campbell, Lehman, et al., 2001). This comorbidity within the anxiety disorders is particularly pronounced for GAD, which is associated with a fourfold greater risk of developing another anxiety disorder compared to the rates in the general population (Beesdo, Pine, Lieb, & Wittchen, 2010). That is, more than 80 percent of people who meet the DSM-IV-TR diagnostic criteria for GAD will meet criteria for another anxiety disorder (Yonkers et al., 2000). Beyond high rates of diagnosable anxiety disorders, it is very common for people with one anxiety disorder to report **subthreshold symptoms** (symptoms that do not meet full diagnostic criteria) of other anxiety disorders (Barlow, 2004). Comorbidity within anxiety disorders arises for two primary reasons:

Proposed DSM-5 Criteria for Generalized Anxiety Disorder

- Excessive anxiety and worry at least 50 percent of days *about at least two life domains (e.g., family, health, finances, work, and school)*
- The worry is sustained for at least 3 months
- The anxiety and worry are associated with at least three of the following:
  - restlessness or feeling keyed up or on edge
  - being easily fatigued
  - difficulty concentrating or mind going blank
  - irritability
  - muscle tension
  - sleep disturbance
- *The anxiety and worry are associated with marked avoidance of situations in which negative outcomes could occur, marked time and effort preparing for situations that might have a negative outcome, marked procrastination, difficulty making decisions due to worries, or repeatedly seeking reassurance due to worries*

Note: Italics reflect changes introduced in DSM-5. The DSM-IV-TR criterion that the person finds it hard to control the worry is not included in DSM-5. The DSM-IV-TR criteria specify duration of 6 months rather than 3 months. DSM-IV-TR criteria specify that the anxiety was about a number of events or activities.

Clinical Case: Stefan

Stefan, a 31-year-old trainee accountant, was sent to a neurologist for investigations into feelings of dizziness and nausea during the day and difficulty falling asleep at night. A brain scan and various blood tests ruled out a brain tumor and various other conditions such as thyroid disease. Stefan was then referred for psychotherapy. He was quite visibly distressed during the entire initial interview, shaking, sweating, and continually fidgeting in his chair. Although he described only physical complaints, a picture of pervasive anxiety soon emerged. Stefan reported that he nearly always felt tense and frequently experienced periods of extended fear for no apparent reason.

Stefan seemed to worry about everything, and at work he was easily distracted, finding it difficult to give his full attention to the matter in hand. He spent much of the time worrying about his ability to form effective working and personal relationships. He described getting angry easily with other people, such as colleagues. As he put it, "Little things they do upset me too much. I just can't cope unless everything is going exactly right." Stefan reported that he had always been nervous, more so than friends and siblings, but that his anxiety had become much worse during his adolescence, and a series of short-lived relationships with women hadn't helped.

- The symptoms used to diagnose the various anxiety disorders overlap; for example, social anxiety and agoraphobia might both involve a fear of crowds.
- Some etiological factors, like certain neurobiological or personality characteristics, may increase risk for more than one anxiety disorder. (See the next section for discussion of some of these risk factors.)

Anxiety disorders are also highly comorbid with other disorders. Three-quarters of people with an anxiety disorder meet the diagnostic criteria for at least one other psychological disorder (Kessler, Crum, Warner, et al., 1997). More specifically, about 60 percent of people in treatment for anxiety disorders meet the diagnostic criteria for major depression (Brown et al., 2001). We discuss this overlap in Focus on Discovery 5.4. Other conditions commonly comorbid with anxiety disorders include substance abuse (Jacobsen, Southwick, & Kosten, 2001) and personality disorders (Johnson, Weissman, & Klerman, 1992). As with many disorders, comorbidity is associated with greater severity and poorer outcomes of the anxiety disorders (Newman, Moffitt, Caspi, & Silva, 1998; Newman, Schmitt, & Voss, 1997). Anxiety disorders also are often comorbid with medical disorders—for example, in one study of men, those with high levels of phobic symptoms were three times more likely to develop coronary heart disease than those with low levels of phobic symptoms (Kawachi, Colditz, Ascherio, et al., 1994).

Gender and Sociocultural Factors in the Anxiety Disorders

It is well known that gender and culture are closely tied to the risk for anxiety disorders and to the specific types of symptoms that a person develops. As you will see, there are still some puzzles about why these patterns exist.

Gender

Several studies suggest that women are at least twice as likely as men to be diagnosed with an anxiety disorder (de Graaf, Bijl, Ravelli, et al., 2002). Table 6.4 shows gender ratios that are observed for several of the anxiety disorders. There is a pretty clear consensus in the field that women are more vulnerable to anxiety disorders than are men.

There are many different theories about why women are more likely to develop anxiety disorders than men are. Women may be more likely to report their symptoms. Psychological differences also might help explain these gender gaps. For example, men may be raised to believe more in their personal control over situations, a variable we will discuss later as protective against anxiety disorders. Social factors, like gender roles, are also likely to play a role. For example, men may experience more social pressure than women to face fears—as you will see below, facing fears may be the basis for one of the most effective treatments available. Women may also experience different life circumstances than do men. For example, women are much more likely than men to be sexually assaulted during childhood and adulthood (Tolin & Foa, 2006). These traumatic events may interfere with developing a sense of control over one's environment, and, as we will see below, having less control over one's environment may set the stage for anxiety disorders. It also appears that women show more biological reactivity to stress than do men (Olff, Langeland, Draijer, & Gersons, 2007), perhaps as a result of these cultural and psychological influences. Although the gender gap is not fully understood, it is an important phenomenon.

Culture

People in every culture seem to experience problems with anxiety disorders. But the focus of these problems appears to vary by culture. For example, in Japan a syndrome called *taijin kyofusho* involves fear of displeasing or embarrassing others; people with this syndrome typically fear such things as making direct eye contact, blushing, having body odor, or having a bodily deformity. The symptoms of this disorder overlap with those of social anxiety disorder, but the focus on others' feelings is distinct. Perhaps this focus is related to characteristics of traditional Japanese culture that encourage extreme concern for the feelings of others and discourage the direct communication of one's own feelings (McNally, 1997).

Several other culturally specific syndromes provide examples of how culture and environment may shape the focus of an anxiety disorder. *Kayak-angst*, a disorder that is similar to panic disorder, occurs among the Inuit people of western Greenland; seal hunters who are alone at sea may experience intense fear, disorientation, and concerns about drowning. Other syndromes, such as *koro* (a sudden fear that one's genitals will recede into the body—reported in southern and eastern Asia), *shenkui* (intense anxiety and somatic symptoms attributed to the loss of semen, as through masturbation or excessive sexual activity—reported in China and similar to other syndromes reported in India and Sri Lanka), and *susto* (fright-illness, the belief that a severe fright has caused the soul to leave the body—reported in Latin America and among Latinos in the United States), also involve symptoms similar to those of the anxiety disorders defined in the DSM. As with the Japanese syndrome taijin kyofusho, the objects of anxiety and fear in these syndromes relate to environmental challenges as well as to attitudes that are prevalent in the cultures where the syndromes occur. In other words, culture influences what people come to fear (Kirmayer, 2001). (See p. 74 for more discussion of culturally specific syndromes.)

Beyond culturally specific syndromes, the prevalence of anxiety disorders varies across cultures. This is not surprising given that cultures differ with regard to factors such as attitudes toward mental illness, stress levels, the nature of family relationships, and the prevalence of poverty—all of which are known to play a role in the occurrence or reporting of anxiety disorders. For example, in Taiwan and Japan, the prevalence of anxiety disorders seems to be quite low; however, this may reflect a strong stigma associated with having mental problems, which could lead to underreporting in those countries (Kawakami, Shimizu, Haratani, et al., 2004). In Cambodia and among Cambodian refugees, very elevated rates of panic disorder (often diagnosed traditionally as *kyol goeu*, or "wind overload") have been reported, perhaps because of the extreme stress experienced by Cambodians over the past several decades (Hinton, Ba, Peou, & Um, 2000; Hinton, Um, & Ba, 2001).

When researchers consider the more specific symptoms that comprise the anxiety disorders, findings are more controversial. For some time, researchers have thought that people from different cultures express symptoms of psychological distress and anxiety in different ways, but new findings raise doubt about how major those cultural differences are. At one time, many researchers believed that somatic (physical) expressions of distress were more common in "collectivistic" cultures—that is, in cultures where, in some sense, the group is held to be more important than the individual (in contrast to "individualistic" Western cultures). It now seems, however, that this conclusion might reflect sampling problems—that is, researchers often studied anxiety and depression in psychological clinics in the United States but in medical clinics in other cultures. One can imagine that a person seeing a medical doctor might be likely to emphasize somatic concerns! Indeed, many people, regardless of culture, tend to describe anxiety and depression initially in terms of bodily sensations when visiting a medical clinic. When researchers interview people in similar settings and ask specifically about psychological concerns, the ratio of somatic to psychological expression of symptoms appears much more similar across cultures (Kirmayer, 2001). Nonetheless, some cross-cultural differences in symptom profiles continue to be documented even with these more careful assessments. For example, people from Latin American and Asian countries are more likely to report symptoms of ringing in the ears, neck soreness, and headaches during panic attacks. The proposed DSM-5 criteria for panic attack will note these potential cross-cultural differences (Lewis-Fernandez, Hinton, Lavia, et al., 2010). A sensation of rising heat in the head and neck is also commonly reported as a symptom of panic attacks

Disorders similar to panic attacks occur cross-culturally. Among the Inuit, kayak-angst is defined by intense fear in lone hunters. (B & C Alexander/Photo Researchers, Inc.)

among people from Latin American countries and Nigeria, and so the proposed DSM-5 criteria for panic attacks include "heat sensations" in place of the DSM-IV-TR criteria of "hot flashes" (Craske, Kircanski, Epstein, et al., 2010).

Quick Summary

As a group, anxiety disorders are the most common type of mental illness. As Table 6.1 shows, the specific anxiety disorders are each defined by a different type of key symptom. That is, a specific phobia is defined by an intense fear of an object or situation, social anxiety disorder by an intense fear of strangers or social scrutiny, panic disorder by anxiety about recurrent panic attacks, agoraphobia by a fear of places where escaping or getting help would be difficult if anxiety symptoms were to occur, and generalized anxiety disorder by worries lasting at least 3 months.

People with one anxiety disorder are very likely to experience a second anxiety disorder during their life. About 60 percent of people with anxiety disorders will experience an episode of major depression during their life. Women are much more likely than men to report an anxiety disorder. Culture influences the focus of fears, the ways that symptoms are expressed, and even the prevalence of different anxiety disorders.

Check Your Knowledge 6.1 (Answers are at the end of the chapter.)

For items 1–4, match the word to the definition.
1. fear
2. anxiety
3. worry
4. phobia
   a. an emotional response to immediate danger
   b. an excessive fear of a specific object or situation that causes distress or impairment
   c. a state of apprehension often accompanied by mild autonomic arousal
   d. thinking about potential problems, often without settling on a solution

Answer the questions.
5. GAD is defined by:
   a. worry
   b. panic attacks

   c. fear of situations in which escape would be hard
   d. obsessions and compulsions
6. A person with one anxiety disorder has about a _____ percent chance of developing a second disorder and about a _____ percent chance of developing major depressive disorder.
   a. 35, 25
   b. 55, 35
   c. 75, 60
   d. 90, 60
7. The odds that a person will develop an anxiety disorder sometime during his or her lifetime are at least:
   a. 1 in 10
   b. 1 in 5
   c. 1 in 4
   d. 1 in 2

Common Risk Factors across the Anxiety Disorders

In this section, we consider risk factors associated with anxiety disorders. We begin by describing a set of factors that seem to increase risk for all of the anxiety disorders. The existence of such risk factors may help explain why people with one anxiety disorder are likely to develop a second one—that is, some risk factors increase the odds of having more than one anxiety disorder. For example, the factors that increase risk for social anxiety disorder may also increase risk for panic disorder.

Unlike the way we have organized most of the other chapters in this book, we have chosen to begin with the behavioral model. We do this because classical conditioning of a fear response is at the heart of many anxiety disorders. Many of the other risk factors, including genes, neurobiological risk factors, personality traits, and cognition, can influence how readily a person can be conditioned to develop a new fear response. Taken together, the risk factors combine to create an increased sensitivity to threat (Craske, Rauch, Uisano, et al., 2009). Table 6.5 summarizes the general risk factors for anxiety disorders.

Fear Conditioning

Above, we mentioned that most anxiety disorders involve fears that are more frequent or intense than what most people experience. Where do these fears come from? Behavioral theory of anxiety disorders focuses on conditioning. **Mowrer's two-factor model** of anxiety disorders, published in 1947, continues to influence thinking in this area (see Figure 6.2). Mowrer's model suggests two steps in the development of an anxiety disorder (Mowrer, 1947):

1. Through *classical conditioning*, a person learns to fear a neutral stimulus (the CS) that is paired with an intrinsically aversive stimulus (the UCS).

2. Through *operant conditioning*, a person gains relief by avoiding the CS. This avoidant response is maintained because it is reinforcing (it reduces fear).

Consider an example. Imagine that a man is bitten by a dog and then develops a phobia of dogs. Through classical conditioning, he has learned to associate dogs (the CS) with painful bites (the UCS). This corresponds to step 1 above. In step 2, the man reduces his fear by avoiding dogs as much as possible; the avoidant behavior is reinforced by the reduction in fear. This second step explains why the phobia isn't extinguished. With repeated exposure to dogs that don't bite, the man would have lost his fear of dogs, but by avoiding dogs, the man gets little or no such exposure.

We should note that Mowrer's early version of the two-factor model does not actually fit the evidence very well; several extensions of this model, which we look at next, have been developed that fit the evidence better (Mineka & Zinbarg, 1998). One extension of the model has been to consider different ways in which classical conditioning could occur (Rachman, 1977). These include the following:

- It could occur by direct experience, like the conditioned fear of dogs in the example above.

- It could occur by seeing another person harmed or frightened by a stimulus (e.g., seeing a dog bite a man or watching a YouTube video of a vicious dog attack). This type of learning is called modeling (Fredrikson, Annas, & Wik, 1997). In one study, researchers showed participants a movie of a man who received shocks. Participants were told that they would receive shocks next. When watching the stranger receive shocks, participants demonstrated increased activity in the amygdala, just as they would if they had personally experienced the aversive stimulus (Olsson, Nearing, & Phelps, 2007).

- It could occur by verbal instruction—for example, by a parent warning a child that dogs are dangerous.

Beyond considering these different sources of classical conditioning, researchers have shown that people with anxiety disorders seem to acquire fears more readily through classical conditioning and to show a slower extinction of fears once they are acquired (Craske et al., 2009). Most studies of this phenomenon use carefully controlled tests in a laboratory setting. For example, in one study, researchers conditioned people to fear a neutral picture of a Rorschach card (see p. 88) by pairing the card with a shock six times (Michael, Blechert, Vriends, et al., 2007). After receiving six shocks, most of the people in the study learned to fear the Rorschach card, as measured using skin conductance responses to seeing the card—even those without an anxiety disorder developed this conditioned response. Those with and without an anxiety disorder differed in the extinction phase of the study, when the card was shown without any shock being provided. People who were not diagnosed with panic

Table 6.5 Factors That Increase Risk for More than One Anxiety Disorder
Behavioral conditioning (classical and operant conditioning)
Genetic vulnerability
Increased activity in the fear circuit of the brain
Decreased functioning of GABA and serotonin; increased norepinephrine activity
Behavioral inhibition
Neuroticism
Cognitive factors, including sustained negative beliefs, perceived lack of control, and attention to cues of threat

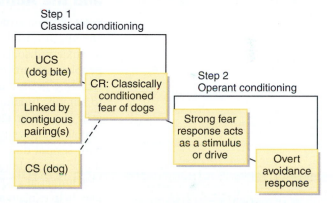

Figure 6.2 Two-factor model of conditioning as applied to dog phobia.

Susan Mineka's research showed that when monkeys observe another monkey display fear of a snake, they also acquire the fear. This indicates that modeling may play a role in the etiology of phobias. (Courtesy of Susan Mineka.)

disorder showed a quick drop in their fear responses during the extinction phase, but people with panic disorder showed very little drop in their fear response. Hence, people with panic disorder appear to sustain classically conditioned fears longer. Findings from a meta-analysis of 20 studies suggest that anxiety disorders are related to a greater propensity to develop fears through classical conditioning and to a slower extinction of those fears once they are acquired (Lissek, Powers, McClun, et al., 2005). Many of the risk factors we describe next could influence this sensitivity to fear conditioning.

Genetic Factors: Are Genes a Diathesis for Anxiety Disorders?

Twin studies suggest a heritability of 20–40 percent for specific phobias, social anxiety disorder, GAD and PTSD, and about 50 percent for panic disorder (Hettema, Neale, & Kendler, 2001; True, Rice, Eisen, et al., 1993). Some genes may elevate risk for several different types of anxiety disorder, while others may elevate risk for a specific type of anxiety disorder (Hettema, Prescott, Myers, et al., 2005). For example, having a family member with a phobia increases the risk of developing not only a phobia but also other anxiety disorders (Kendler et al., 2001).

Neurobiological Factors: The Fear Circuit and the Activity of Neurotransmitters

A set of brain structures called the **fear circuit** tend to be involved when people are feeling anxious or fearful (Malizia, 2003). The fear circuit, shown in Figure 6.3, appears to be related to anxiety disorders. One part of the fear circuit that seems particularly activated among people with anxiety disorders is the amygdala. The amygdala is a small, almond-shaped structure in the temporal lobe that appears to be involved in assigning emotional significance to stimuli. In animals, the amygdala has been shown to be critical for the conditioning of fear. The amygdala sends signals to a range of different brain structures involved in the fear circuit. Studies suggest that when shown pictures of angry faces (one signal of threat), people with several different anxiety disorders respond with greater activity in the amygdala than do people without anxiety disorders (Blair, Shaywitz, Smith, et al., 2008; Monk, Nelson, McClun, et al., 2006). Hence, elevated activity in the fear circuit, particularly the amygdala, may help explain many different anxiety disorders. **The medial prefrontal cortex** appears to be important in helping to regulate amygdala activity—it is involved in extinguishing fears as well as using emotion regulation strategies to control emotions (Indovina, Robbins, Nunez-Elizalde, et al., 2011; Kim, Loucks, Palmer, et al., 2011). Researchers have found that people who meet diagnostic criteria for anxiety disorders display less activity in the medial prefrontal cortex (Shin, Wright, Cannistraro, et al., 2005). New evidence suggests that the pathway, or connectivity, linking these two regions may be deficient among those with anxiety disorders (Kim et al., 2011). These deficits in connectivity between the medial prefrontal cortex and the amygdala may interfere with the effective regulation and extinction of anxiety (Yehuda & LeDoux, 2007). We will discuss other parts of the fear circuit, like the locus coeruleus, when we discuss specific anxiety disorders.

Many of the neurotransmitters involved in the fear circuit are involved in anxiety disorders. For instance, anxiety disorders seem to be related to poor functioning of the serotonin system (Chang, Cloak, & Ernst, 2003; M. B. Stein, 1998) and higher-than-normal levels of norepinephrine (Geracioti, Baker, Ekhator, et al., 2001). GABA appears to be involved in inhibiting activity throughout the brain, and one of its effects is decreased anxiety (Sinha, Mohlman, & Gorman, 2004). Poor GABA function, then, could contribute to anxiety.

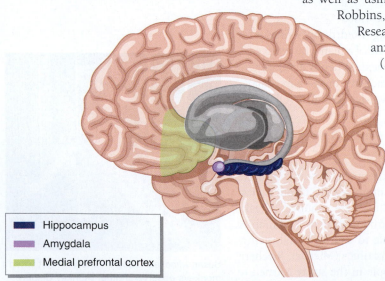

■ Hippocampus
■ Amygdala
■ Medial prefrontal cortex

Figure 6.3 Fear and anxiety appear to be related to a set of structures in the brain called the fear circuit. The amygdala and medial prefrontal cortex are particularly involved in anxiety disorders.

Personality: Behavioral Inhibition and Neuroticism

Some infants show the trait of **behavioral inhibition**, a tendency to become agitated and cry when faced with novel toys, people, or other stimuli. This behavioral pattern, which has been described in infants as young as 4 months old, may be inherited and may set the stage for the later development of anxiety disorders. One study followed infants from 14 months through 7.5 years; 45 percent of those who showed elevated behavioral inhibition levels at 14 months showed symptoms of anxiety at age 7.5, compared to only 15 percent of those who had shown low behavioral inhibition levels (Kagan & Snidman, 1999). Behavioral inhibition appears to be a particularly strong predictor of social anxiety disorder: 30 percent of infants showing elevated behavioral inhibition developed social anxiety disorder by adolescence (Biederman, Rosenbaum, Hirshfeld et al., 1990).

Neuroticism is a personality trait defined by the tendency to react to events with greater-than-average negative affect. How does neuroticism relate to anxiety disorders? In a sample of 7,076 adults, neuroticism predicted the onset of both anxiety disorders and depression (de Graaf et al., 2002). People with high levels of neuroticism were more than twice as likely to develop an anxiety disorder as those with low levels. In another study of 606 adults followed over 2 years, neuroticism was a major correlate and predictor of anxiety and depression (Brown, 2007).

Cognitive Factors

Researchers have focused on several separate cognitive aspects of anxiety disorders. Here, we focus on three: sustained negative beliefs about the future, a perceived lack of control, and attention to signs of threat.

Sustained Negative Beliefs about the Future

Sustained Negative Beliefs about the Future People with anxiety disorders often report believing that bad things are likely to happen. For example, people with panic disorder might believe that they will die when their heart begins to pound, whereas people with social anxiety disorder might believe that they will suffer humiliating rejection if they blush. As pointed out by David Clark and colleagues (Clark, Salkovskis, Hackmann, et al., 1999), the key issue is not why people think so negatively initially but, rather, how these beliefs are sustained. For example, by the time a person survives 100 panic attacks, you might expect the belief "this attack means I am about to die" would fade. One reason these beliefs might be sustained is that people think and act in ways that maintain these beliefs. That is, to protect against feared consequences, they engage in **safety behaviors**. For example, people who fear they will die from a fast heart rate stop all physical activity the minute they feel their heart race. They come to believe that only their safety behaviors have kept them alive. Hence, safety behaviors allow a person to maintain overly negative cognitions.

Perceived Control

Perceived Control People who think that they lack control over their environment appear to be at greater risk for a broad range of anxiety disorders than people who do not have that belief. For example, people with anxiety disorders report experiencing little sense of control over their surroundings (Mineka & Zinbarg, 1998). Childhood experiences, such as traumatic events (Hofmann, Levitt, Hoffman, et al., 2001), punitive and restrictive parenting (Chorpita, Brown, & Barlow, 1998), or abuse (Chaffin, Silovsky, & Vaughn, 2005), may promote a view that life is not controllable. Similarly, anxiety disorders often develop

Infants and toddlers showing behavioral inhibition—high anxiety about novel situations and people—are at greater risk of developing anxiety disorders during their lifetime. (David Young-Wolff/PhotoEdit.)

after serious life events that threaten the sense of control over one's life. Indeed, more than 70 percent of people report a severe life event before the onset of an anxiety disorder (Finlay-Jones, 1989). Other life experiences may shape the sense of control over the feared stimulus. For example, people who are used to dogs and feel comfortable about controlling dogs' behavior are much less likely to develop a phobia after a dog bite. On the whole, early and recent experiences of lack of control can influence whether a person develops an anxiety disorder (Mineka & Zinbarg, 2006).

Animal studies have illustrated that a lack of control over the environment can promote anxiety. For example, Insel and colleagues (Insel, Scanlan, Champoux, & Suomi, 1988) randomly assigned monkeys to one of two conditions. One group of monkeys grew up with the ability to choose whether and when they would receive treats. A second group of monkeys had no control over whether and when they received treats—that is, a given monkey in this second group was given a treat whenever a given monkey in the first group received a treat. The two groups of monkeys received the same number of treats. In the third year of life, monkeys who had grown up without control behaved in ways that looked anxious when facing new situations and interacting with other monkeys; monkeys who had grown up with control showed less anxiety. In sum, animal and human studies both point toward the importance of perceived lack of control in the development of anxiety disorders.

Attention to Threat People with anxiety disorders have been found to pay more attention to negative cues in their environment than do people without anxiety disorders (Williams, Watts, MacLeod et al., 1997). To test attention to threatening stimuli, researchers have used measures like the dot probe task (see Figure 6.4). In a meta-analysis of 172 studies, each of the specific anxiety disorders was associated with heightened attention to threatening stimuli on tasks like the dot probe task (Bar-Haim, Lamy, Pergamin, et al., 2007). For example, people with social anxiety disorder have been found to selectively attend to angry faces (Staugaard, 2010), whereas people with snake phobias selectively attend to cues related to snakes (McNally, Caspi, Riemann, et al., 1990; Öhman, Flykt, & Esteves, 2001). Researchers have also shown that this heightened attention to threatening stimuli happens automatically and very quickly—before people are even consciously aware of the stimuli (Öhman & Soares, 1994; Staugaard, 2010). In sum, anxiety disorders are associated with selective attention to signs of threat.

In one line of experimental research, investigators have examined whether attention to anxiety-related information can actually be created, and then whether this attention "bias" leads to more anxiety (Mathews & MacLeod, 2002). To train people to attend to threatening words, they used the dot probe task. To teach a negative bias, participants view hundreds of trials in which the dot is more likely to occur where the negative word was. For a control group, the dot randomly appears on the left or right side of the screen. People who were trained to attend to negative words reported a more anxious mood after training, especially when they were given a challenging task like an unsolvable puzzle to perform. The control group did not show an increase in anxious mood after training. The findings suggest that the way we focus our attention can foster an anxious mood.

Could these types of trained biases help us understand diagnosable levels of anxiety? Researchers have examined this by training people diagnosed with generalized anxiety disorder to attend to positive information (Amir, Beard, Burns, & Bomyea, 2009). To train a positive bias, the researchers used a version of the dot probe task in which dots appeared where the positive words had appeared. A control group completed an equivalent number of training sessions but used a version of the dot probe in which there was no systematic pattern to where the dot occurred. Training was conducted twice a week for 4 weeks, and during each session, participants completed 240 trials. Anxiety levels did not change over the course of the study in the control group. Participants in the positive-bias training condition obtained lower anxiety scores on self-report and interview measures post-training: 50 percent of the people who received positive-bias training no longer met the diagnostic criteria for GAD. Parallel benefits of attention training have been shown among people with social anxiety (Schmidt, Richey, Buckner et al., 2009).

First screen

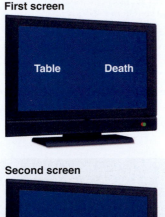

Second screen

Figure 6.4 The computerized dot probe task is used to test biases in attention and, in some studies, to train attentional biases. On the first screen of each trial, participants see one neutral word and one negative word. On the second screen, a dot appears in the location where one of the two words was. The participant is asked to press a button as quickly as possible to indicate whether the dot appears on the left or right side of the screen. In the case shown here, a person who was looking at the word *death* will see the dot and respond more quickly than a person who was looking at the word *table*.

Etiology of Specific Anxiety Disorders

Above, we discussed factors that might set the stage for development of anxiety disorders in general. Here, we turn to the question of how each of the specific anxiety disorders arise. That is, why does one person develop a specific phobia while another person develops generalized anxiety disorder? Keep in mind the common etiological factors already described and think about how these commonalities relate to and combine with the specifics described next.

Etiology of Specific Phobias

The dominant model of phobias is the two-factor model of behavioral conditioning, described above. Here we elaborate on how this model can be applied to understanding phobias. We'll describe some of the research evidence, as well as several refinements of the model.

Behavioral Factors: Conditioning of Specific Phobias

In the behavioral model, phobias are seen as a conditioned response that develops after a threatening experience and is sustained by avoidant behavior. In one of the first illustrations of this model, John Watson and his graduate student Rosalie Rayner published a case report in 1920 in which they demonstrated creating an intense fear of a rat (a phobia) in an infant, Little Albert, using classical conditioning. Little Albert was initially unafraid of the rat, but after repeatedly seeing the rat while a very loud noise was made, he began to cry when he saw the rat.

Little Albert, shown here with Watson and Rayner, was classically conditioned to develop a fear of a white rat. (Courtesy of Professor Benjamin Harris.)

As described above, behavioral theory suggests that phobias *could* be conditioned by direct trauma, modeling, or verbal instruction. But do most people with a phobia report one of these types of conditioning experiences? In one study, 1,937 people were asked whether they had had these types of conditioning experiences before the onset of their phobias (Kendler, Myers, & Prescott, 2002). Although conditioning experiences were common, about half of the people in the study could not remember any such experiences (see Table 6.6). Obviously, if many phobias start without a conditioning experience, this is a big problem for the behavioral model. But proponents of the behavioral model argue that people may forget conditioning experiences (Mineka & Öhman, 2002). Because of memory gaps, simple surveys of how many people remember a conditioning experience do not provide very accurate evidence about the behavioral model.

Table 6.6 Percent of People Reporting Conditioning Experiences before the Onset of a Phobia				
Type of Fear	Direct Trauma	Observed Trauma or Fear in Others	Taught Fear	No Memory of Conditioning Experience
Agoraphobia	27.0	3.4	4.6	65.1
Social	23.3	4.6	7.3	65.0
Animal	48.1	9.1	11.6	31.2
Situational	32.7	8.1	6.3	52.9
Blood/injection/injury	46.7	13.6	7.2	32.4

Source: From a survey of 1,937 people conducted by Kendler, Myers, and Prescott (2002).

Many people report that they develop a phobia after a traumatic event. Debate exists about why some people don't report that they had experienced a traumatic event before the onset of their phobia. (© Siamionau Pavel/Shutterstock.)

The notion of prepared learning suggests that we have evolved to pay special attention to signs of danger, including angry people, threatening animals, and dangerous natural environments. (Top to bottom: © devi/Shutterstock; © EcoPrint/Shutterstock; © Cheryl Ann Quigley/Shutterstock.)

Even among those who have had a threatening experience, many do not develop a phobia. How might we understand this? To begin, the risk factors described above, such as genetic vulnerability, neuroticism, negative cognition, and propensity toward fear conditioning, probably operate as diatheses—vulnerability factors that shape whether or not a phobia will develop in the context of a conditioning experience (Mineka & Sutton, 2006).

It is also believed that only certain kinds of stimuli and experiences will contribute to the development of a phobia. Mowrer's original two-factor model suggests that people could be conditioned to be afraid of all types of stimuli. But people with phobias tend to fear certain types of stimuli. Typically, people do not develop phobias of flowers, lambs, or lamp shades! But phobias of insects or other animals, natural environments, and blood are common. As many as half of women report a fear of snakes; moreover, many different types of animals also fear snakes (Öhman & Mineka, 2003). Researchers have suggested that during the evolution of our species, people learned to react strongly to stimuli that could be life-threatening, such as heights, snakes, and angry humans (Seligman, 1971). Perhaps our fear circuit has evolved to respond especially rapidly and automatically to these types of stimuli. That is, our fear circuit may have been "prepared" by evolution to learn fear of certain stimuli; hence, this type of learning is called **prepared learning**. As researchers have tested this model, some have discovered that people can be initially conditioned to fear many different types of stimuli (McNally, 1987). Fears of most types of stimuli fade quickly with ongoing exposure, though, whereas fears of naturally dangerous stimuli are sustained in most studies (Dawson, Schell, & Banis, 1986).

Prepared learning is also relevant to modeling, as indicated by a study involving four groups of rhesus monkeys (Cook & Mineka, 1989). Each group of monkeys was shown a videotape of a monkey exhibiting intense fear, but for each group, the videotape was edited to make the feared object appear to be different: a toy snake, a toy crocodile, flowers, or a toy rabbit. Only the monkeys exposed to the tapes showing a monkey who expressed fear of a toy snake or toy crocodile acquired fear of the object shown. These findings suggest that, with rhesus monkeys as with people, it is easier to condition fear of potentially life-threatening stimuli than of neutral stimuli.

Etiology of Social Anxiety Disorder

In this section, we review behavioral and cognitive factors related to social anxiety disorder. The trait of behavioral inhibition, discussed above, may also be important in the development of social anxiety disorder.

Behavioral Factors: Conditioning of Social Anxiety Disorder Behavioral perspectives on the causes of social anxiety disorder are similar to those on specific phobias, insofar as they are based on a two-factor conditioning model. That is, a person could have a negative social experience (directly, through modeling, or through verbal instruction) and become classically conditioned to fear similar situations, which the person then avoids. Through operant conditioning, this avoidance behavior is maintained because it reduces the fear the person experiences. There are few opportunities for the conditioned fear to be extinguished because the person tends to avoid social situations. Even when the person interacts with others, he or she may show avoidant behavior in smaller ways that have been labeled as safety behaviors. Examples of safety behaviors in social anxiety disorder include avoiding eye contact, disengaging from conversation, and standing apart from others. Although these behaviors are used to avoid negative feedback, they create other problems. Other people tend to disapprove of these types of avoidant behaviors, which then intensifies the problem (Wells, 1998). (Think about how you might respond if you were trying to talk to someone who looks at the floor, fails to answer your questions, and leaves the room in the middle of the conversation.)

Cognitive Factors: Too Much Focus on Negative Self-Evaluations Theory focuses on several different ways in which cognitive processes might intensify social anxiety (D. M. Clark & Wells, 1995). First, people with social anxiety disorders appear to have unrealistically negative beliefs about the consequences of their social behaviors—for example, they may believe that others will reject them if they blush or pause while speaking. Second, they attend more to how they are doing in social situations and their own internal sensations than other people do. Instead of attending to their conversation partner, they are often thinking about how others might perceive them (e.g., "He must think I'm an idiot"). They often form powerful negative visual images of how others will react to them (Hirsch & Clark, 2004). Of course, good conversation requires a focus on the other person, so too much thinking about inner feelings and evaluative cognitions can foster social awkwardness. The resultant anxiety interferes with their ability to perform well socially, creating a vicious circle—for example, the socially anxious person doesn't pay enough attention to others, who then perceive the person as not interested in them.

There is plenty of evidence that people with social anxiety disorder are overly negative in evaluating their social performance, even when they are not socially awkward (Stopa & Clark, 2000). For example, in one study, researchers assessed blushing in people with and without social anxiety disorder. Participants were asked to estimate how much they would blush during different tasks, such as singing a children's song. Then they were asked to engage in these different tasks. Participants with social anxiety disorder overestimated how much they would blush (Gerlach, Wilhelm, Gruber et al., 2001). Similarly, one research team asked people with social anxiety disorder to rate videos of their performance in giving a short speech. Socially anxious people rated their speeches more negatively than objective raters did, whereas people who were not socially anxious were not harsh in rating their own performance (Ashbaugh, Antony, McCabe et al., 2005). Therefore, people with social anxiety disorder may be unfairly harsh in their self-evaluations.

There is also evidence that social anxiety disorder is related to attention to internal cues rather than external (social) cues. For example, people with social anxiety disorder appear to spend more time than other people do monitoring for signs of their own anxiety. In one study, researchers gave participants a chance to watch their own heart rate displayed on a computer screen or to watch video material. People diagnosed with social anxiety disorder attended more closely to their own heart rate than did the people who were not diagnosed with social anxiety disorder (Pineles & Mineka, 2005). Hence, rather than focusing on external stimuli, people with this disorder tend to be busy monitoring their own anxiety levels.

How might all these risk variables fit together when we consider a person with social anxiety disorder, like Maureen? Maureen is likely to have inherited some tendency to be anxious when faced with new people. As she grew up, this may have interfered with her chances to acquire social skills and to gain self-confidence. Her fear of other people's opinions and her own negative thoughts about her social abilities create a vicious circle in which her intolerable anxiety leads her to avoid social situations, and then the avoidance leads to increased anxiety.

Etiology of Panic Disorder

In this section, we look at current thinking about the etiology of panic disorder, from neurobiological, behavioral, and cognitive perspectives. As you will see, all of these perspectives focus on how people respond to somatic (bodily) changes like increased heart rate.

Neurobiological Factors   Remember that a panic attack seems to reflect a misfire of the fear circuit, with a concomitant surge in activity in the sympathetic nervous system. We have seen that the fear circuit appears to play an important role in many of the anxiety disorders. Now we will see that a particular part of the fear circuit is especially important in panic disorder: the **locus coeruleus** (see Figure 6.5). The locus ceruleus is the major source of the neurotransmitter norepinephrine in the brain, and norepinephrine plays a major role in triggering sympathetic nervous system activity.

Kim Basinger, the Oscar-winning actress, describes her experiences of anxiety in the movie *Panic: A Film about Coping.* She is reported to have suffered from panic disorder, agoraphobia, and social anxiety disorder. (Matthew Simmons/Getty Images News and Sport Services.)

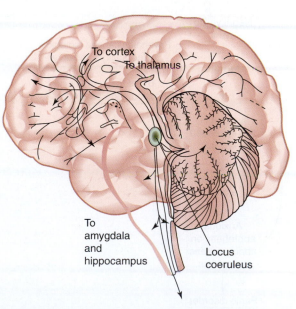

Figure 6.5 Locus coeruleus. Drawn from Martin, J. H. (1996). *Neuroanatomy Text and Atlas,* second edition.

Panic attacks can be experimentally triggered by a variety of agents that change bodily sensations, including drugs and even exercise. (Robin Nelson/PhotoEdit.)

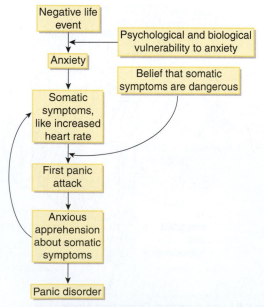

Figure 6.6 Interoceptive conditioning.

Monkeys exposed to feared stimuli, such as snakes, show high activity in the locus ceruleus. Further, when activity in the locus ceruleus is triggered using an electrical signal, monkeys behave as if they were having a panic attack (Redmond, 1977). In humans, drugs that increase activity in the locus ceruleus can trigger panic attacks, and drugs that decrease activity in the locus ceruleus, including clonidine and some antidepressants, decrease the risk of panic attacks.

Behavioral Factors: Classical Conditioning The behavioral perspective on the etiology of panic disorder focuses on classical conditioning. This model draws from an interesting pattern—panic attacks are often triggered by internal bodily sensations of arousal (Kenardy & Taylor, 1999). Theory suggests that panic attacks are classically conditioned responses to either the situations that trigger anxiety or the internal bodily sensations of arousal (Bouton, Mineka, & Barlow, 2001). Classical conditioning of panic attacks in response to bodily sensations has been called **interoceptive conditioning**: a person experiences somatic signs of anxiety, which are followed by the person's first panic attack; panic attacks then become a conditioned response to the somatic changes (see Figure 6.6).

Cognitive Factors in Panic Disorder Cognitive perspectives focus on catastrophic misinterpretations of somatic changes (D. M. Clark, 1996). According to this model, panic attacks develop when a person interprets bodily sensations as signs of impending doom (see Figure 6.7). For example, the person may interpret the sensation of an increase in heart rate as a sign of an impending heart attack. Obviously, such thoughts will increase the person's anxiety, which produces more physical sensations, creating a vicious circle.

The evidence that these cognitive factors can contribute to panic attacks is quite strong. To understand the evidence, it is important to know that panic attacks can be experimentally induced in the laboratory. Research has focused on triggering panic attacks experimentally for more than 75 years. These studies suggest an array of factors that create physiological sensations can trigger panic attacks among people with a history of panic attacks, including more than a dozen different medications (Swain, Koszycki, Shlik, & Bradwein, 2003). Even drugs that have opposite physiological effects can set off panic attacks (Lindemann & Finesinger, 1938). Exercise alone, simple relaxation, or the physical sensations caused by an illness such as inner-ear disease also can induce panic attacks (Asmundson, Larsen, & Stein, 1998). Another commonly used procedure involves exposing people to air with high levels of carbon dioxide; in response to the diminished oxygen, breathing rate increases, and for some people this induces panic. In short, many different bodily sensations can trigger panic attacks (Barlow, 2004). Cognitive researchers have focused on how to differentiate the people who do and do not develop a panic attack in these experimental studies. People who develop panic attacks after being exposed to these agents seem to differ from those who do not develop panic attacks on only one characteristic—the extent to which they are frightened by the bodily changes (Margraf, Ehlers, & Roth, 1986).

To show the role of cognitions as a predictor of panic attacks, researchers in one study used a paradigm described above, in which carbon dioxide levels are manipulated. Before breathing the carbon dioxide-manipulated air, some people were given a full explanation about the physical sensations they were likely to experience, and others were given no explanation. After breathing the air, those who had received a full explanation reported that they had fewer catastrophic interpretations of their bodily sensations, and they were much less likely to have a panic attack than those who did not receive an explanation (Rapee, Mattick, & Murrell, 1986). Catastrophic interpretations of bodily sensations, then, seem to be important in triggering panic attacks.

The propensity toward catastrophic interpretations can be detected before panic disorder develops. Many researchers have used a test called the **Anxiety Sensitivity Index**, which measures the extent to which people respond fearfully to their bodily sensations (Telch, Shermis, & Lucas, 1989). Sample items from this scale include "Unusual body sensations scare me" and "When I notice that my heart is beating rapidly, I worry that I might have a heart attack." In one study, college students with no history of panic attacks were divided into high and low scorers on the Anxiety Sensitivity Index (Telch & Harrington, 1992). Researchers then used the carbon dioxide manipulation described above to see who would develop panic attacks. As with the Rapee study, half of the participants were told that carbon dioxide would produce arousal symptoms, and half were not. When breathing carbon dioxide, panic attacks were most common among people who feared their bodily sensations, particularly if they were not warned about the physical effects of carbon dioxide on arousal. This result is exactly what the model predicts: unexplained physiological arousal in someone who is fearful of such sensations leads to panic attacks.

The Anxiety Sensitivity Index has also been shown to predict the onset of panic attacks in longer-term studies. In one study, researchers followed 1,296 Air Force recruits as they went through the stressful experiences of basic training (Schmidt, Lerew, & Jackson, 1999). Consistent with the model, recruits with initially high scores on the Anxiety Sensitivity Index were more likely to develop panic attacks during basic training than were those with low scores.

Etiology of Agoraphobia

Because agoraphobia was only recognized as a distinct disorder with the DSM-5, less is known about its etiology. As with other anxiety disorders, the development of agoraphobia appears related to genetic vulnerability and life events (Wittchen et al., 2010). Here we focus on a cognitive model of how these symptoms evolve.

Cognitive Factors: The Fear-of-Fear Hypothesis The principal cognitive model for the etiology of agoraphobia is the **fear-of-fear hypothesis** (Goldstein & Chambless, 1978), which suggests that agoraphobia is driven by negative thoughts about the consequences of experiencing anxiety in public. There is evidence that people with agoraphobia think the consequences of public anxiety would be horrible (D. A. Clark, 1997). They seem to have catastrophic beliefs that their anxiety will lead to socially unacceptable consequences (e.g., "I am going to go crazy") (Chambless, Caputo, Bright, & Gallagher, 1984).

Etiology of Generalized Anxiety Disorder

Generalized anxiety disorder (GAD) tends to co-occur with other anxiety disorders and with depression. Because the comorbidity is so high, researchers believe that many of the factors involved in predicting anxiety disorders in general are particularly important for understanding GAD. For example, deficits in the functioning of the GABA system, which are important for many anxiety disorders, appear to be involved in GAD (Tihonen, Kuikka, Rosanen, et al., 1997). Beyond these general risk factors, recent research has focused on cognitive factors.

Cognitive Factors: Why Do People Worry? Cognitive factors may help explain why some people worry more than others. Borkovec and colleagues focus on the main symptom of GAD—worry—in their cognitive model (Borkovec & Newman, 1998). Worry would seem so unpleasant that one might ask why anyone would worry a lot. Borkovec and colleagues have marshaled evidence that worry is actually reinforcing because it distracts people from more powerful negative emotions and images. The key to understanding this argument is to realize that worry does not involve powerful visual images and does not produce the physiological

Figure 6.7 An example of catastrophic misinterpretation of bodily cues. Drawn from Clark, D. M. (1997). Panic disorder and social anxiety disorder. In D. M. Clark & C. G. Fairburn (eds.), *Science and Practice of Cognitive Behaviour Therapy* (pp. 121–153). With permission, Oxford University Press.

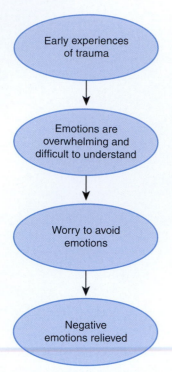

Figure 6.8 The excessive worry of GAD may be an attempt to avoid intense emotions.

changes that usually accompany emotion. Indeed, worrying actually decreases psychophysiological signs of arousal (Freeston, Dugas, & Ladoceur, 1996). Thus, by worrying, people with GAD may be avoiding unpleasant emotions that would be more powerful than worry. But as a consequence of this avoidance, their underlying anxiety about these images does not extinguish.

What kinds of anxiety-evoking images might people with GAD be avoiding? A possible answer comes from studies showing that many people with GAD report past traumas involving death, injury, or illness (Borkovec & Newman, 1998). In one study in which more than 1,000 participants were followed from age 3 to 32, researchers coded various forms of childhood maltreatment, including maternal rejection, harsh discipline, and childhood abuse. Maltreatment predicted a fourfold increase in the risk of developing GAD. It may be that worry distracts people with GAD from the distress of remembering these past traumas.

There is also support for the idea that people with GAD may be avoiding emotions. For example, people diagnosed with GAD report that it is harder to understand and label their feelings (Mennin, Heimberg, Turk, & Fresco, 2002) and to regulate their negative emotions (Roemer et al., 2009). See Figure 6.8 for an overview of how these processes might contribute to worry.

Some research suggests that people who have a hard time accepting ambiguity, that is, who find it intolerable to think that something bad *might* happen in the future, are more likely to worry and to develop GAD (Dugas, Marchand, & Ladouceur, 2005). This intolerance of uncertainty can predict increases in worry over time (Laugesen, Dugas, & Bukowski, 2003).

Quick Summary

Many risk factors set the stage for anxiety disorders generally, rather than for a specific anxiety disorder. Behavioral models of anxiety disorders build from Mowrer's two-factor model (classical conditioning followed by operant conditioning). These models have been extended to consider that the conditioning may be driven by direct exposure to an event, vicarious observation of someone else experiencing an event (modeling), or verbal instruction. Other risk factors may increase the propensity toward fear conditioning. Genes increase risk for anxiety disorders. Neurobiological research on anxiety focuses on elevated activity in the brain's fear circuit. Anxiety disorders also appear to involve poor functioning of the GABA and serotonin systems as well as high norepinephrine levels. The personality traits of behavioral inhibition and neuroticism are both related to the development of anxiety disorders. From the cognitive perspective, anxiety disorders are associated with negative expectations about the future, beliefs that life is uncontrollable, and a bias to attend to negative information.

Specific phobias are believed to reflect conditioning in response to a traumatic event. Many people report that they experienced traumatic conditioning experiences before developing specific phobias, but many people don't, perhaps because the conditioning experience has been forgotten. Prepared learning refers to the fact that people are likely to sustain conditioned responses to fear stimuli that have some evolutionary significance.

Social anxiety disorder appears related to conditioning and behavioral inhibition. Cognitive factors involved in social anxiety disorder include self-critical evaluations of social performance and tendencies to focus on internal thoughts and sensations.

Neurobiological research demonstrates that panic attacks are related to high activity in the locus ceruleus. Behavioral models emphasize the possibility that people could become classically conditioned to experience panic attacks in response to external situations or internal somatic signs of arousal. Conditioning to somatic signs is called interoceptive conditioning. Cognitive perspectives focus on catastrophic misinterpretations of somatic symptoms.

A cognitive model of agoraphobia focuses on "fear of fear," or overly negative beliefs about what will happen if one experiences anxiety.

Generalized anxiety disorder (GAD) has been related to deficits in the GABA system. One cognitive model emphasizes that worry might actually protect people from intensely disturbing emotional images. People with GAD also appear to be intolerant of ambiguity.

Check Your Knowledge 6.2

Choose the best answer for each item.

1. Research suggests that genes can explain _____ percent of the variance in anxiety disorders other than panic disorder.
   a. 0–20 percent
   b. 20–40 percent
   c. 40–60 percent
   d. 60–80 percent

2. _____ is a personality trait characterized by a tendency to react to events with intense negative affect.
   a. Extraversion
   b. Neurosis
   c. Neuroticism
   d. Psychosis

Circle all that apply.

3. Cognitive factors found to correlate with anxiety disorders include:
   a. low self-esteem
   b. attention to signs of threat
   c. hopelessness
   d. lack of perceived control

4. A key structure in the fear circuit is the:
   a. cerebellum
   b. amygdala

   c. occipital cortex
   d. inferior colliculi

Match the theory to the model of etiology:

5. Panic disorder
6. GAD
7. Specific phobias
   a. anxiety sensitivity
   b. overly sensitive cortisol receptors and small volume of the hippocampus
   c. prepared learning
   d. increased activity in the orbitofrontal cortex, caudate nucleus, and anterior cingulate
   e. avoidance of powerful negative emotions

Fill in the blanks.

8. The first step in Mowrer's two-factor model includes _____ conditioning, and the second step involves _____ conditioning.
   a. operant, operant
   b. classical, classical
   c. classical, operant
   d. operant, classical

Treatments of the Anxiety Disorders

Only a small proportion of people with anxiety disorders seek treatment. Although public awareness campaigns and pharmaceutical company advertising have increased treatment seeking, a community survey of 5,877 individuals suggested that fewer than 20 percent of people with anxiety disorders receive even minimally adequate treatment (Wang, Demler, & Kessler, 2002). One reason for the lack of treatment seeking may be the chronic nature of symptoms; a person suffering from an anxiety disorder might think "I'm just an anxious person" and not realize that treatment could help. Even when people do seek treatment, many will only visit a family doctor. Research has found that family physicians are less effective than psychiatrists in prescribing drugs that successfully treat anxiety disorders, mostly due to doses that are too low or treatments that are discontinued too quickly (Roy-Byrne, Katon, et al., 2001).

Commonalities across Psychological Treatments

Effective psychological treatments for anxiety disorders share a common focus: exposure— that is, the person must face what he or she deems too terrifying to face. Therapists from varying perspectives all agree that we must face up to the source of our fear or, as an ancient Chinese proverb puts it, "Go straight to the heart of danger, for there you will find safety." Even psychoanalysts, who believe that the unconscious sources of anxiety are buried in the past, eventually encourage confronting the source of fears (Zane, 1984). Although exposure is a core aspect of many cognitive behavioral treatments (CBT), these treatments differ in their strategies.

Systematic desensitization was the first widely used exposure treatment (Wolpe, 1958). In this treatment, the client is first taught relaxation skills. Then the client uses these skills to relax while undergoing exposure to a list of feared situations developed with the therapist—starting with the least feared and working up to the most feared (see p. 44 for a more detailed description). Although this technique is quite effective, researchers have now documented that exposure treatment works even if the relaxation component is not included (Marks, Lovell, Noshirvani, et al., 1998).

There have been more than 100 randomized controlled studies of CBT for anxiety disorders (Norton & Price, 2007), and dozens of these have compared CBT to a control treatment that involves some form of psychotherapy (Hofmann & Smits, 2008). Those studies suggest that CBT works well, even in comparison to other types of treatment. Exposure treatment is effective for 70–90 percent of clients.

The effects of CBT appear to endure when follow-up assessments are conducted 6 months after treatment (Hollon, Stewart, & Strunk, 2006). In the years after treatment, though, many people experience some return of their anxiety symptoms (Lipsitz, Mannuzza, Klein, et al., 1999). A couple of key principles appear important in protecting against relapse (Craske & Mystkowski, 2006). First, exposure should include as many features of the feared object as possible. For example, exposure for a person with a spider phobia might include a focus on the hairy legs, the beady eyes, and other features of spiders. Second, exposure should be conducted in as many different contexts as possible (Bouton & Waddell, 2007). As an example, it might be important to expose a person to a spider in an office but also outside in nature.

The behavioral view of exposure is that it works by extinguishing the fear response. A good deal of work has focused on how extinction works at a neurobiological level and how this information might be used to refine exposure treatment (Craske, Kircanski, Zelikowsky, et al., 2008). This work suggests that extinction does not work like an eraser. Let's take dog phobia as an example. Extinction will not erase the underlying fear of dogs altogether—the conditioned fear still resides deep inside the brain. Rather, extinction involves learning new associations to stimuli related to dogs. These newly learned associations inhibit activation of the fear. Thus, extinction involves learning, not forgetting.

A cognitive view of exposure treatment has also been proposed. According to this view, exposure helps people correct their mistaken beliefs that they are unable to cope with the stimulus. In this view, exposure relieves symptoms by allowing people to realize that, contrary to their beliefs, they can tolerate aversive situations without loss of control (Foa & Meadows, 1997). Cognitive approaches to treatment of anxiety disorders typically focus on challenging (1) a person's beliefs about the likelihood of negative outcomes if he or she faces an anxiety-provoking object or situation, and (2) the expectation that he or she will be unable to cope. Cognitive treatments typically then involve exposure, to help people learn that they can cope with these situations. Because both behavioral and cognitive treatments involve exposure and learning to cope differently with fears, it is not surprising that most studies suggest that adding a cognitive therapy component to exposure therapy for anxiety disorders does not bolster results (Deacon & Abramowitz, 2004). There are some very specific cognitive techniques that seem to help when added to exposure treatment, though, and we will describe some of these below.

Virtual reality is sometimes used to simulate feared situations such as flying, heights, and even social interactions. Exposure treatment using virtual reality appears to provide substantial relief from anxiety disorders (Parsons & Rizzo, 2008). Findings of several small randomized controlled trials indicate that exposure to these simulated situations appears to be as effective as in vivo (real life) exposure (Emmelkamp, Krijn, Hulsboch, et al., 2002; Klinger, Bouchard, Legeron, et al., 2005; Rothbaum, Anderson, Zimand, et al., 2006).

In addition to virtual reality programs, a series of computerized programs have been developed to guide clients in CBT for the anxiety disorders, and several of these programs are recommended in guidelines such as those published by the British government (Marks & Cavanagh, 2009). Computerized CBT programs for social phobia, panic disorder, and GAD achieve large effects compared to control conditions, and these effects appear to be sustained when clients are reassessed 6 months after they finish the program (Andrews et al., 2010). These programs seem to work best when at least some human contact is provided (Marks & Cavanagh, 2009). For example, therapists might conduct the initial screening to ensure that a person is enrolled in the right type of program, they might help a person develop the appropriate exposure hierarchy, or they might review homework assignments (Marks & Cavanagh, 2009). Even with this type of support, these programs substantially reduce the amount of professional contact time required to complete exposure treatment. As these programs become more widely distributed, it will be important to ensure that clients have access to the well-validated programs (Marks & Cavanagh, 2009).

Psychological Treatments of Specific Anxiety Disorders

Next, we look at how psychotherapy can be tailored to the specific anxiety disorders. Even though exposure treatment is used with each anxiety disorder, how can it be tailored to specific anxiety disorders?

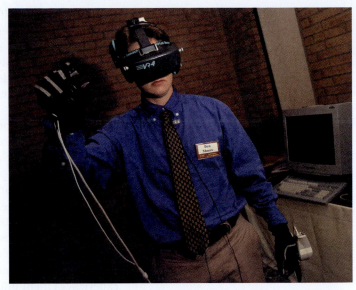

Virtual reality technology is sometimes used to facilitate exposure to feared stimuli. (Kim Kulish/Corbis Images.)

Psychological Treatment of Phobias Many different types of exposure treatments have been developed for phobias. Exposure treatments often include **in vivo** (real-life) **exposure** to feared objects. For phobias involving fear of animals, injections, or dental work, very brief treatments lasting only a couple of hours have been found to be highly effective—most people experience relief from phobic symptoms. Although systematic desensitization is effective (Barlow, Raffa, & Cohen, 2002), in vivo exposure is more effective than systematic desensitization (Choy, Fyer, & Lipsitz, 2007).

Psychological Treatment of Social Anxiety Disorder Exposure also appears to be an effective treatment for social anxiety disorder; such treatments often begin with role playing or practicing with the therapist or in small therapy groups before undergoing exposure in more public social situations (Marks, 1995). With prolonged exposure, anxiety typically extinguishes (Hope, Heimberg, & Bruch, 1995). Social skills training, in which a therapist might provide extensive modeling of behavior, can help people with social anxiety disorder who may not know what to do or say in social situations. Remember that safety behaviors, like avoiding eye contact, are believed to interfere with the extinction of social anxiety (Clark & Wells, 1995). Consistent with this idea, the effects of exposure treatment seem to be enhanced when people with social anxiety disorder are taught to stop using safety behaviors (Kim, 2005). That is, not only are people asked to engage in social activities but, while doing so, they are asked to make direct eye contact, to engage in conversation, and to be fully present. Doing so leads to immediate gains in how they are perceived by others, and it enhances the power of the exposure treatment (Taylor & Alden, 2011).

David Clark (1997) has developed a version of cognitive therapy for social anxiety disorder that expands on other treatments in a couple of ways. The therapist helps people learn not to focus their attention internally. The therapist also helps them combat their very negative images of how others will react to them. This cognitive therapy has been shown to be more effective than fluoxetine (Clark, Ehlers, McManus, et al., 2003) or than exposure treatment plus relaxation (Clark et al., 2006).

Social anxiety disorder is often treated in groups, which provide exposure to social threats and provide opportunities to practice new skills. (David Harry Stewart/Stone/Getty Images.)

Psychological Treatment of Panic Disorder A psychodynamic treatment for panic disorder has been developed. The treatment involves 24 sessions focused on identifying the emotions and meanings surrounding panic attacks. Therapists help clients gain insight into areas believed to relate to the panic attacks, such as issues involving separation, anger, and autonomy. In one randomized controlled trial, patients who were assigned to receive psychodynamic treatment achieved more symptom relief than those who were assigned to a control condition of relaxation training (Milrod, Leon, Busch, et al., 2007). In a separate trial, psychodynamic treatment for panic disorder was related to diminished rates of relapse when added as a supplement to antidepressant treatment (Wiborg & Dahl, 1996). More research is needed, though, because both of these studies were small.

Like the behavioral treatments for phobias already discussed, cognitive behavioral treatments for panic disorder focus on exposure (White & Barlow, 2004). One well-validated cognitive behavioral treatment approach called **panic control therapy (PCT)** is based on the tendency of people with panic disorder to overreact to the bodily sensations discussed above (Craske & Barlow, 2001). In PCT, the therapist uses exposure techniques—that is, he or she persuades the client to deliberately elicit the sensations associated with panic. For example, a person whose panic attacks begin with hyperventilation is asked to breathe rapidly for 3 minutes, or someone whose panic attacks are associated with dizziness might be requested to spin in a chair for several minutes. When sensations such as dizziness, dry mouth, lightheadedness, increased heart rate, and other signs of panic begin, the person experiences them under safe conditions; in addition, the person practices coping tactics for dealing with somatic symptoms (e.g., breathing from the diaphragm to avoid hyperventilation). With practice and encouragement from the therapist, the person learns to stop seeing internal sensations as signals of loss of control and to see them instead as intrinsically harmless sensations that can be controlled. The person's ability to create these physical sensations and then cope with them makes them seem more predictable and less frightening (Craske, Maidenberg, & Bystritsky, 1995).

In another version of cognitive treatment for panic disorder (Clark, 1996), the therapist helps the person identify and challenge the thoughts that make the physical sensations threatening (see Figure 6.7 for an example of one patient's thoughts). For example, if a person with panic disorder imagines that he or she will collapse, the therapist might help the person examine the evidence for this belief and develop a different image of the consequences of a panic attack. This treatment has been shown to work well in at least seven research studies, with specific evidence that this form of treatment is more helpful than pure exposure treatment and that few people drop out of treatment (Clark et al., 1999).

Psychological Treatment of Agoraphobia Cognitive behavioral treatments of agoraphobia also focus on exposure—specifically, on systematic exposure to feared situations. Exposure treatment of agoraphobia is more effective when the partner is involved (Cerny, Barlow, Craske, & Himadi, 1987). The partner without agoraphobia is encouraged to stop catering to the partner's avoidance of leaving home. There is also good support for self-guided treatment, in which those with agoraphobia use a manual to conduct their own step-by-step exposure treatment (Ghosh & Marks, 1987).

Psychological Treatment of Generalized Anxiety Disorder Almost all tested treatments for GAD include several cognitive or behavioral components (Roemer, Orsillo, & Barlow, 2004). The most widely used behavioral technique involves relaxation training to promote calmness (DeRubeis & Crits-Christoph, 1998). Relaxation techniques can involve relaxing muscle groups one-by-one or generating calming mental images. With practice, clients typically learn to relax rapidly. Studies suggest that relaxation training is more effective than nondirective treatment or no treatment. One form of cognitive therapy includes strategies to help people tolerate uncertainty, as people with GAD seem to be more distressed by uncertainty than are those without GAD (Ladoceur, Dugas, Freeston, et al., 2000). This treatment appears to be more helpful than relaxation therapy alone (Dugas, Brillon, Savard, et al., 2010). Borkovec and colleagues have also designed cognitive behavioral strategies to target worry, such as asking people to worry only during scheduled times, asking people to test whether worry "works" by keeping a diary of the outcomes of worrying, helping people focus their thoughts on the present moment instead of worrying, and helping people address core fears that they may be avoiding through worry (Borkovec, Alcaine, & Behar, 2004).

Quick Summary

Exposure treatment is the most well-validated psychological treatment for anxiety disorders. Cognitive treatments supplement exposure with interventions to challenge negative beliefs about what will happen when a person faces his or her fears.

For specific phobias, exposure treatments can work quite quickly. For social anxiety disorder, cognitive strategies, such as teaching a person to focus less on internal thoughts and sensations, are a helpful addition to exposure treatment. The most effective treatments for panic disorder include exposure to somatic sensations, along with cognitive techniques to challenge catastrophic misinterpretations of those symptoms. Exposure treatment for agoraphobia may be enhanced by including partners. Cognitive behavioral treatment of GAD can include relaxation training, strategies to help a person tolerate uncertainty and face core fears, and specific strategies to combat tendencies to worry.

Medications That Reduce Anxiety

Drugs that reduce anxiety are referred to as sedatives, minor tranquilizers, or **anxiolytics** (the suffix *-lytic* comes from a Greek word meaning "to loosen or dissolve"). Two types of medications are most commonly used for the treatment of anxiety disorders: **benzodiazepines** (e.g., Valium and Xanax) and antidepressants, including tricyclic antidepressants, selective serotonin reuptake inhibitors (SSRIs), and a newer class of agents called **serotonin–norepinephrine reuptake inhibitors (SNRIs)** (Hoffman & Mathew, 2008). Hundreds of studies have now confirmed that benzodiazepines and antidepressants provide more benefit than do placebos for anxiety disorders (Kapczinski, Lima, Souza, et al., 2002; Roemer et al., 2004; Stein, Ipser, & Balkom, 2004; Stein, Ipser, & Seedat, 2000). Beyond these medications that seem to help the range of anxiety disorders, certain drugs seem to be effective for specific anxiety disorders. For example, buspirone (BuSpar) has received approval from the Food and Drug Administration for generalized anxiety disorder (Hoffman & Mathew, 2008).

There are many effective treatments for anxiety. How does one decide which one to use? Generally, antidepressants are preferred over benzodiazepines. This is because people may experience severe withdrawal symptoms when they try to stop using benzodiazepines (Schweizer, Rickels, Case, & Greenblatt, 1990)—that is, they can be addictive.

Beyond this, the choice of drugs is often guided by concerns about side effects. All anxiolytics have side effects. Many people report being surprised by the extent of side effects and wishing they had known more about what to expect (Haslam, Brown, Atkinson et al., 2004). Benzodiazepines can have significant cognitive and motor side effects, such as memory lapses and difficulty driving. Antidepressants tend to have fewer side effects than benzodiazepines. Nonetheless, as many as half of people discontinue tricyclic antidepressants because of side effects like jitteriness, weight gain, elevated heart rate, and high blood pressure (cf. Taylor, Hayward, King, et al., 1990). Compared to tricyclic antidepressants, SSRIs tend to have fewer side effects. This has led to SSRIs being considered the first-line medications for treatment of most anxiety disorders. Some people, however, do experience side effects from SSRIs, including restlessness, insomnia, headache, and diminished sexual functioning (Bandelow, Zohar, Hollander, et al., 2008). Many people stop taking anxiolytic medications because of the side effects.

This leads us to the key problem: most people relapse once they stop taking medications. In other words, medications are only effective during the time when they are taken. Because of this, and the general effectiveness of exposure treatments, psychological treatments are

In an interview with Oprah Winfrey (September 24, 2009), Barbra Streisand described social anxiety so intense that she was unable to perform in public for 27 years. (Carlo Allegri/Getty Images.)

typically considered the preferred treatment of most anxiety disorders (Foa, Libowitz, Kozak, et al., 2005; Keane & Barlow, 2004; Kozak, Liebowitz, & Foa, 2000; McDonough & Kennedy, 2002), with the possible exception of GAD (Mitte, 2005).

Combining Medications with Psychological Treatment In general, adding anxiolytics to exposure treatment actually leads to worse long-term outcomes than exposure treatment without anxiolytics, perhaps because people do not get the same chance to face their fears (Hollon et al., 2006). One possible exception to this is the treatment of social anxiety disorder, where one carefully conducted study suggested that combination treatment of anxiolytics and cognitive-behavioral exposure achieved stronger results than either anxiolytics or cognitive-behavioral treatment alone (Blanco, Heimberg, Schneier, et al., 2010). For most anxiety disorders, though, adding anxiolytics to psychotherapy is not beneficial.

D-cycloserine (DCS), though, is a different type of drug, one that enhances learning. Researchers have examined it as a way to bolster exposure treatment (Ressler, Rothbaum, Tannenbaum, et al., 2004). In one study, 28 patients with acrophobia (fear of heights) were treated using two sessions of virtual reality exposure to heights. Half of the patients were randomly assigned to receive the medicine DCS while they completed the exposure sessions; the other half received placebo. The patients who received DCS were less afraid of heights at the end of treatment and 3 months later than were the patients who did not receive DCS. Similarly, DCS has been found to enhance the effects of exposure treatment for social anxiety disorder (Guastella, Richardson, Lovibond, et al., 2008; Hofmann, Meuret, Smits, et al., 2006) and for panic disorder (Otto, Tolin, Simon, et al., 2010). Hence, this learning-enhancement medication appears to bolster the effects of a psychotherapy based on conditioning principles.

Check Your Knowledge 6.3

True or False?
1. Anxiolytic medications work better than CBT.
2. Anxiety symptoms often return when a person stops taking anxiolytic medications.
3. Antidepressants are addictive.
4. Side effects are no longer a concern with modern anxiolytics.

Circle all that apply.
5. Which of the following are valid treatment approaches to anxiety disorders?
   a. supportive listening
   b. benzodiazepines
   c. antidepressants
   d. exposure
6. D-cycloserine:
   a. cannot be used with exposure treatment
   b. has no effect on the outcome of exposure treatment
   c. bolsters the effects of exposure treatment

Summary

Clinical Descriptions of the Anxiety Disorders

- As a group, anxiety disorders are the most common type of mental illness.
- The five major DSM-5 anxiety disorders include specific phobia, social anxiety disorder, panic disorder, agoraphobia, and generalized anxiety disorder. Anxiety is common to all the anxiety disorders, and fear is common in anxiety disorders other than generalized anxiety disorder.
- Phobias are intense, unreasonable fears that interfere with functioning. Specific phobias commonly include fears of animals; heights; enclosed spaces; and blood, injury, or injections.

- Social anxiety disorder is defined by intense fear of possible social scrutiny.
- Panic disorder is defined by recurrent attacks of intense fear that occur out of the blue. Panic attacks alone are not sufficient for the diagnosis; a person must be worried about the potential of having another attack.
- Agoraphobia is defined by fear and avoidance of being in situations where escaping or getting help would be hard if anxiety symptoms were to occur.
- In generalized anxiety disorder, the person is beset with virtually constant tension, apprehension, and worry that lasts for at least 3 months.

Gender and Sociocultural Factors in the Anxiety Disorders

- Anxiety disorders are much more common among women than men.
- The focus of anxiety, the prevalence of anxiety disorders, and the specific symptoms expressed may be shaped by culture.

Common Risk Factors across the Anxiety Disorders

- Mowrer's two-factor model suggests that anxiety disorders are related to two types of conditioning. The first stage involves classical conditioning, in which a formerly innocuous object is paired with a feared object. This can occur through direct exposure, modeling, or cognition. The second stage involves avoidance that is reinforced because it reduces anxiety. Many of the other risk factors may increase the propensity to develop and sustain these conditioned fears.
- Genes increase risk for a broad range of anxiety disorders. Beyond this general risk for anxiety disorders, there may be more specific heritability for certain anxiety disorders. Beyond genetic diatheses, other biological factors that are involved in a range of anxiety disorders include elevated activity in the fear circuit, poor functioning of the serotonin and GABA neurotransmitter systems, and increased norepinephrine activity.
- Cognitive factors include sustained negative beliefs about the future, lack of perceived control, and a heightened tendency to attend to signs of potential danger.
- Personality risk factors include behavioral inhibition and neuroticism.

Etiology of Specific Anxiety Disorders

- Behavioral models of specific phobias build on the two-factor model of conditioning. The evolutionary preparedness model suggests that fears of objects with evolutionary significance may be more sustained after conditioning.

Because not all people with negative experiences develop phobias, diatheses must be important.

- The behavioral model of social anxiety disorder expands the two-factor conditioning model to consider the role of safety behaviors. Other key risk factors include behavioral inhibition and cognitive variables such as excessively critical self-evaluations and a focus on internal sensations rather than social cues.
- Neurobiological models of panic disorder have focused on the locus ceruleus, the brain region responsible for norepinephrine release. Behavioral theories of panic attacks have posited that the attacks are classically conditioned to internal bodily sensations. Cognitive theories suggest that such sensations are more frightening due to catastrophic misinterpretation of somatic cues.
- Cognitive models of agoraphobia focus on "fear of fear"—overly negative beliefs about the negative consequences of anxiety.
- One model of GAD suggests that worry actually helps people avoid more intense emotions. People with GAD also seem to have difficulty tolerating ambiguity.

Psychological Treatment for the Anxiety Disorders

- Behavior therapists focus on exposure to what is feared. Systematic desensitization and modeling may be used as parts of exposure therapy. For some anxiety disorders, cognitive components may also be helpful in therapy.
- Exposure treatment for specific phobias tends to work quickly and well.
- Adding cognitive components to exposure treatment may help for social anxiety disorder.
- Treatment for panic disorder often involves exposure to physiological changes.
- Treatment for agoraphobia may be enhanced by including partners in the treatment process.
- Relaxation and cognitive behavioral approaches are helpful for GAD.

Medications to Relieve Anxiety

- Antidepressants and benzodiazepines are the most commonly used medications for anxiety disorders. There are concerns that benzodiazepines can be addictive.
- Discontinuing medications usually leads to relapse. For this reason, cognitive behavior therapy is considered a more helpful approach than medication treatment for most anxiety disorders.
- One new approach involves providing D-cycloserine during exposure treatment.

Answers to Check Your Knowledge Questions

6.1 1. a; 2. c; 3. d; 4. b; 5. a; 6. c; 7. c

6.2 1. b; 2. c; 3. b, d; 4. b; 5. a; 6. e; 7. c; 8. c

6.3 1. F, 2. T, 3. F, 4. F; 5. b, c, d; 6. c

Key Terms

agoraphobia
anxiety
anxiety disorders
Anxiety Sensitivity Index
anxiolytics
behavioral inhibition
benzodiazepines
D-cycloserine (DCS)

depersonalization
derealization
fear
fear circuit
fear-of-fear hypothesis
generalized anxiety disorder
  (GAD)
in vivo exposure

interoceptive conditioning
locus ceruleus
medial prefrontal cortex
Mowrer's two-factor model
panic attack
panic control therapy (PCT)
panic disorder
prepared learning

safety behaviors
serotonin–norepinephrine
  reuptake inhibitors (SNRIs)
social anxiety disorder
specific phobia
subthreshold symptoms

7 Obsessive-Compulsive-Related and Trauma-Related Disorders

LEARNING GOALS

1. Be able to define the symptoms and epidemiology of the obsessive-compulsive and related disorders and the trauma-related disorders.

2. Be able to describe the commonalities in the etiology of obsessive-compulsive and related disorders, as well as the factors that shape the expression of the specific disorders within this cluster.

3. Be able to summarize how the nature and severity of the trauma, as well as biological and psychological risk factors, contribute to whether trauma-related disorders develop.

4. Be able to describe the medication and psychological treatments for the obsessive-compulsive-related and trauma-related disorders.

Clinical Case: Alexandra

Alexandra was a 52-year-old woman who had obsessive-compulsive disorder. It had begun 17 years ago, shortly after a difficult divorce. Since then she had been up and down, but currently was as bad as ever. Alexandra was an only child. She recalls her childhood as essentially happy, although her mother constantly emphasized the virtues of cleanliness and neatness. She remembers having to tidy her room repeatedly, although as soon as her mother's back was turned she would revert back to her untidy ways. Her mother told her that this behavior would hurt her, but failed to explain how.

Alexandra was obsessed with a fear of contamination. Although she reported that she was afraid of touching nearly everything because germs could be anywhere, she was particularly afraid of touching newspapers, postal mail, door knobs, shiny paper, and silverware. She was unable to state why some of these particular objects were sources of possible contamination.

To try to reduce her discomfort, Alexandra engaged in a variety of compulsive rituals that recently had become a lot worse and were now taking up two to three hours every morning. In order not to be late for work, she now had to get up around 5am in order to spend a couple of hours in the bathroom, washing and rewashing herself. Alexandra realized that her repeated acts were unreasonable, but she believed that something terrible would happen if she didn't perform them.

IN THIS CHAPTER, WE examine obsessive-compulsive-related and trauma-related disorders. Obsessive-compulsive and related disorders are defined by repetitive thoughts and behaviors that are so extreme that they interfere with everyday life. The trauma-related disorders include posttraumatic stress disorder and acute stress disorder, two conditions that are triggered by exposure to severely traumatic events.

Obsessive-compulsive disorder and the trauma-related disorders are listed in the anxiety disorders chapter in the DSM-IV-TR. As you will see, people with these disorders report feeling anxious, and they often experience other anxiety disorders as well (Brakoulias, Starcevic, Sammut, et al., 2011). Many of the risk factors for other anxiety disorders contribute to these disorders, and the treatment approaches overlap a good deal as well. Nonetheless, these disorders also have some distinct causes compared to other anxiety disorders. To highlight those differences, the authors of DSM-5 created new chapters for obsessive-compulsive and related disorders and for trauma-related disorders (Phillips, Stein, Rauch, et al., 2010). They placed these chapters next to the anxiety disorder chapter to highlight that there is some overlap with anxiety disorders. As you read about these disorders, it is important to consider parallels with the diagnoses described in the anxiety disorders chapter.

Obsessive-Compulsive and Related Disorders

We will focus on three disorders in this section: obsessive-compulsive disorder (OCD), body dysmorphic disorder, and hoarding disorder (see Table 7.1). OCD, the prototypical disorder of this cluster, is defined by repetitive thoughts and urges (obsessions), as well as an irresistible need to engage in repetitive behaviors or mental acts (compulsions). Body dysmorphic disorder and hoarding disorder share symptoms of repetitive thoughts and behaviors. People with body dysmorphic disorder spend hours a day thinking about their appearance, and almost all engage in compulsive behaviors such as checking their appearance in the mirror. People with hoarding disorder spend a good deal of their time repetitively thinking about their current and potential future possessions. They also engage in intensive efforts to acquire new objects, and these efforts can resemble the compulsions observed in OCD. For all three conditions, the repetitive thoughts and behaviors are distressing, feel uncontrollable, and require a considerable amount of time. For the person with these conditions, the thoughts and behaviors feel unstoppable.

Beyond similarities in the symptoms, these syndromes often co-occur. For example, about a third of people with body dysmorphic disorders meet diagnostic criteria for OCD during their lifetime. Similarly, up to a quarter of people with hoarding disorder will meet diagnostic criteria for OCD. As we will see, there are many parallels in the etiology and treatment of these three conditions (Phillips, Stein, et al., 2010).

We will review the clinical features and epidemiology of these three disorders. Then we will describe research on the etiology. We end this section with a discussion of the biological and psychological treatment approaches to obsessive-compulsive and related disorders.

Table 7.1 Diagnoses of Obsessive-Compulsive and Related Disorders

DSM-5 Diagnoses	Key Features	Placement in DSM-IV-TR
Obsessive-compulsive disorder	• Repetitive, intrusive, uncontrollable thoughts or urges (obsessions) • Repetitive behaviors or mental acts that the person feels compelled to perform (compulsions)	• Anxiety disorder chapter
Body dysmorphic disorder	• Preoccupation with an imagined flaw in one's appearance • Excessive repetitive behaviors or acts regarding appearance (e.g., checking appearance, seeking reassurance)	• Somatoform disorder chapter
Hoarding disorder	• Acquiring an excessive number of objects • Inability to part with those objects	• New diagnosis proposed for DSM-5

Clinical Descriptions and Epidemiology of the Obsessive-Compulsive and Related Disorders

As mentioned, the obsessive-compulsive and related disorders all share a quality of repetitive thought as well as irresistible urges to engage repetitively in some behavior or mental act. As we will see next, though, the focus of thought and behavior takes a different form across the three conditions.

Obsessive-Compulsive Disorder Obsessive-compulsive disorder (OCD) is characterized by obsessions or compulsions. Of course, most of us have unwanted thoughts from time to time, like an advertising jingle that gets stuck in our mind. And most of us also have urges now and then to behave in ways that would be embarrassing or dangerous. But few of us have thoughts or urges that are persistent and intrusive enough to qualify us for a diagnosis of OCD.

Obsessions are intrusive and recurring thoughts, images, or impulses that are persistent and uncontrollable (i.e., the person cannot stop the thoughts) and that usually appear irrational to the person experiencing them. For Alexandra, described in the opening of the chapter, and others with OCD, obsessions have such force and frequency that they interfere with normal activities. The most frequent foci for obsessions include fears of contamination, sexual or aggressive impulses, body problems, religion, and symmetry or order (Bloch, Landeros-Weisenberger, Sen, et al., 2008). People with obsessions may also be prone to extreme doubts, procrastination, and indecision.

Compulsions are repetitive, clearly excessive behaviors or mental acts that the person feels driven to perform to reduce the anxiety caused by obsessive thoughts or to prevent some calamity from occurring. Alexandra's rituals regarding washing, described in the Clinical Case, fit this definition. Samuel Johnson, one of the most famous authors of the eighteenth century, has been described as suffering from multiple compulsions. For example, he felt compelled "to touch every post in a street or step exactly in the center of every paving stone. If he perceived one of these acts to be inaccurate, his friends were obliged to wait, dumbfounded, while he went back to fix it" (Stephen, 1900, cited in Szechtman, 2004). Even though rationally understanding that there is no need for this behavior, the person feels as though something dire will happen if the act is not performed. The sheer frequency with which compulsions are repeated may be staggering (for example, Alexandra spent at least two hours each morning washing and rewashing herself). Commonly reported compulsions include the following:

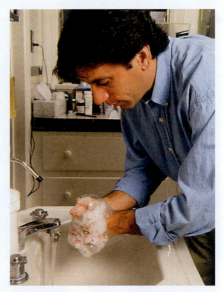

For people with obsessive-compulsive disorder, extreme fears of contamination can trigger abnormally frequent handwashing. (Bill Aron/PhotoEdit.)

- Pursuing cleanliness and orderliness, sometimes through elaborate rituals
- Performing repetitive, magically protective acts, such as counting or touching a body part
- Repetitive checking to ensure that certain acts are carried out—for example, returning seven or eight times in a row to see that lights, stove burners, or faucets were turned off, windows fastened, and doors locked

We often hear people described as compulsive gamblers, compulsive eaters, and compulsive drinkers. Even though people may report irresistible urges to gamble, eat, and drink, clinicians do not regard these behaviors as compulsions because they are often experienced as pleasurable. In one study, 78 percent of people with compulsions viewed their rituals as "rather silly or absurd" even though they were unable to stop performing them (Stern, 1978).

OCD tends to begin either before age 10 or else in late adolescence/early adulthood (Conceicao do Rosario-Campos, 2001). It has been described in children as young as age 2 (Rapoport, 1992). Among adults, about 1 percent meet diagnostic criteria in a given year (Jacobi, Wittchen, Holting, et al., 2004; Ruscio, Stein, Chiu, et al., 2010; Torres, Prince, Bebbington, et al., 2006), and about 2 percent meet diagnostic criteria during their lifetime (Ruscio et al., 2010). The disorder is slightly more common among women than men, with a gender ratio of about 1.5 (Jacobi et al., 2004; Torres et al., 2006). The pattern of symptoms appears to be similar across cultures (Seedat & Matsunaga, 2006). OCD is a chronic disorder— a 40-year follow-up study of people hospitalized for OCD in the 1950s showed that only 20 percent had recovered completely (Skoog & Skoog, 1999). More than three-quarters of people with OCD meet criteria for comorbid anxiety disorders during their lifetime, and about

Proposed DSM-5 Criteria for Obsessive-Compulsive Disorder

- Obsessions (recurrent, intrusive, persistent, *unwanted* thoughts, *urges*, or images that *the person tries to ignore, suppress, or neutralize*) or
- Compulsions (repetitive behaviors or thoughts that a person feels compelled to perform to prevent distress or a dreaded event *or in response to an obsession*)
- The obsessions or compulsions *are time consuming (e.g., require at least 1 hour per day)* or cause clinically significant distress or impairment

Note: Changes from the DSM-IV-TR criteria are italicized. DSM-IV-TR includes the criterion that the person understands the compulsions are excessive and will not prevent dreaded events.

two-thirds meet criteria for major depression during their lifetime. Substance use is also common (Ruscio et al., 2010). About one-third of people with OCD experience at least some symptoms of hoarding (Steketee & Frost, 2003).

Katharine Phillips has conducted extensive research on body dysmorphic disorder. (Courtesy Katharine A. Phillips, M. D., Professor of Psychiatry and Human Behavior, Director of Research for Adult Psychiatry, Director, Body Dismorphic Disorder Program, Rhode Island Hospital.)

Proposed DSM-5 Criteria for Body Dysmorphic Disorder

- Preoccupation with a *perceived* defect or in appearance
- *The person has performed repetitive behaviors or mental acts (e.g., mirror checking, seeking reassurance, or excessive grooming) in response to the appearance concerns*
- Preoccupation is not restricted to concerns about weight or body fat

Note: Changes from the DSM-IV-TR criteria are italicized.

Body Dysmorphic Disorder People with **body dysmorphic disorder** (BDD) are preoccupied with an imagined or exaggerated defect in their appearance. Although people with BDD may appear attractive to others, they perceive themselves as ugly or even "monstrous" in their appearance (Phillips, 2006a). Women tend to focus on their skin (like Lorraine in the Clinical Case on the next page), hips, breasts, and legs, whereas men are more likely to focus on their height, penis size, or body hair (Perugi, Akiskal, Giannotti, et al., 1997). Some men suffer from the preoccupation that their body is small or insufficiently muscular, even when others would not share this perception.

Like persons with OCD, people with BDD find it very hard to stop thinking about their concerns. On average, people with BDD think about their appearance for 3 to 8 hours per day (Phillips, Wilhelm, Koran, et al., 2010). Also like people with OCD, people with BDD find themselves compelled to engage in certain behaviors. In BDD, the most common compulsive behaviors include checking their appearance in the mirror, comparing their appearance to that of other people, asking others for reassurance about their appearance, or using strategies to change their appearance or camouflage disliked body areas (grooming, tanning, exercising, changing clothes, and applying makeup) (Phillips, Wilhelm, et al., 2010). While many spend hours a day checking their appearance, some try to avoid being reminded of their perceived flaws by avoiding mirrors, reflective surfaces, or bright lights (Albertini & Phillips, 1999). While most of us do things to feel better about our appearance, people with this disorder spend an inordinate amount of time and energy on these endeavors.

The symptoms are extremely distressing. About a third of patients with BDD describe delusions about their appearance, such as being convinced that others are laughing at them or staring at their flaws (Phillips, 2006), and as many as a quarter have plastic surgery (Phillips, et al., 2001). Unfortunately, plastic surgery does little to allay their concerns (Veale, 2000), and many people report wanting to sue or hurt their physicians after the surgery because they are so disappointed. As many as a fifth of people with this disorder have thought about committing suicide (Rief, Buhlmann, Wilhelm, et al., 2006).

The preoccupation with appearance can interfere with many aspects of occupational and social functioning. People with BDD often experience high levels of shame, anxiety, and depression about their appearance, and several behavioral responses to those powerful feelings are common. Some may avoid contact with others because they are so concerned about being evaluated for their appearance, and sometimes these fears are so overwhelming that the person becomes housebound. About 40 percent of people with the disorder are unable to work (Didie, Menard, Stern, et al., 2008).

BDD occurs slightly more often in women than in men, but even among women it is relatively rare, with a prevalence of less than 2 percent (Rief et al., 2006). Among women seeking plastic surgery, however, about 5 to 7 percent meet the diagnostic criteria for this disorder (Altamura, Paluello, Mundo, et al., 2001). BDD typically begins in late adolescence. As many as 90 percent of persons diagnosed with the disorder report symptoms 1 year after diagnosis (Phillips, 2006b), but over an 8-year period about three-quarters of people will recover from their symptoms (Bjornsson, Dyck, Moitra, et al., 2011).

Social and cultural factors surely play a role in how people decide whether they are attractive. Among college students, concerns about body appearance appear to be more common in America than in Europe—as many as 74 percent of American students report at least some concern about their body image, with women being more likely than men to report dissatisfaction (Bohne, 2002). Most of these concerns, though, are not extreme enough to be characterized as psychological disorders. People with BDD experience agonizing distress over their perceived physical flaws.

Case reports from around the world suggest that the symptoms and outcomes of BDD are similar across cultures (Phillips, 2005). The body part that becomes a focus of concern sometimes differs by culture, though. For example, eyelid concerns are more common in Japan than in Western countries. Japanese patients with BDD appear to be more concerned about offending others than are Western patients (Suzuki, Takei, Kawai, et al., 2003).

Nearly all people with BDD meet the diagnostic criteria for another disorder. The most common comorbid disorders include major depressive disorder, social anxiety disorder, obsessive-compulsive disorder, substance use disorders, and personality disorders (Gustad, 2003). Care should be taken to distinguish BDD from eating disorders. Most people with BDD are concerned about several different aspects of their appearance. When shape and weight concerns are the only foci, clinicians should consider whether the symptoms are better explained by an eating disorder.

Hoarding Disorder Collecting is a favorite hobby for many people. What distinguishes the common fascination with collections from the clinical disorder of hoarding? For people with **hoarding disorder,** the need to acquire is only part of the problem. The bigger problem is that they abhor parting with their objects, even when others cannot see any potential value in them. Most typically, as illustrated in the Clinical Case of Dena, the person has acquired a huge range of different kinds of objects—collections of clothes, tools, or antiques may be gathered along with old containers, bottle caps, and sandwich wrappers. About two-thirds of people who hoard seem to be unaware of the severity of their behavior (Steketee & Frost, 2003). People with hoarding disorder are extremely attached to their possessions, and they are very resistant to efforts to get rid of them.

About one-third of people with hoarding disorder, much more often women than men, also engage in animal hoarding (Patronek & Nathanson, 2009). People who engage in animal hoarding sometimes view themselves as animal rescuers, but those who witness the problem see it differently—the accumulating number of animals often outstrips the person's ability to provide adequate care, shelter, and food.

The consequences of hoarding can be quite severe. The accrual of objects often overwhelms the person's home. In one study, case workers for elder services agencies were asked to describe their clients who suffered from hoarding disorder. Although the sampling strategy likely focused on particularly severe cases, the findings were notable. The case workers reported that among their clients who had problems with hoarding, the hoarding led to extremely filthy homes for about a third of people, characterized by overpowering odors

Some people with body dysmorphic disorder may spend hours a day checking on their appearance, but others may avoid mirrors because they find it painful to consider their appearance. (© Poulsons Photography/ Shutterstock.)

Clinical Case: Lorraine

Lorraine was a 23-year-old woman who started psychotherapy four months after the death of her father from bowel cancer. At the first therapy session, she fidgeted a lot, refused to take her coat off despite the warmth of the clinic room, preferring to remain huddled inside it. She struggled to make eye contact with the therapist. Lorraine said that she had been taking long breaks at work because she was uncomfortable when customers were in the clothes store—she had the feeling they were staring at her. When asked why she thought that, she said that she knew they were looking at her stomach and bottom, which were far too large and wobbly. She was unable to look at herself in the mirror and felt excruciating pain if she caught a glimpse of her reflection in shop windows. She could only get dressed in the dark, which meant in the morning that she had to dress herself in the windowless shower room with the light off. She thought her body was "repulsively ugly." She said that these symptoms had come and gone since adolescence, but had become much worse over the last two years.

Proposed DSM-5 Criteria for Hoarding Disorder

- Persistent difficulty discarding or parting with possessions, regardless of the value others may attribute to these possessions
- Strong urges to save items and/or distress associated with discarding
- The symptoms result in the accumulation of a large number of possessions that clutter key areas the home or workplace to the extent that their intended use is no longer possible unless others intervene.

from rotten food or feces. More than 40 percent had accumulated so many items that they were no longer able to use their refrigerator, kitchen sink, or bathtub, and about 10 percent were unable to use their toilet (Kim, Steketee, & Frost, 2001). Respiratory conditions, poor hygiene, and difficulties with cooking can all contribute to poor physical health. Many family members sever relationships, unable to understand the attachment to the objects. About three-quarters of people with hoarding disorder engage in excessive buying (Frost, Tolin, Steketee, et al., 2009) and many are unable to work (Tolin, Frost, Steketee, et al., 2008), making poverty all too common among people with this condition (Samuels, Bienvenu III, Pinto, et al., 2007). As the problem escalates, health officials often become involved to try to address the safety and health concerns. About 10 percent of persons with hoarding disorder will be threatened with eviction at some point in their lives (Tolin et al., 2008). For some, the money spent on acquiring leads to homelessness. When animals are involved, animal protection agencies sometimes become involved.

No studies have used structured diagnostic interviews in community representative samples to estimate the prevalence of hoarding disorder. On self-report scales, about 2 percent of the population acknowledge moderate problems with hoarding symptoms (Iervolino, Rijsdijk, Cherkas, et al., 2011). Although hoarding is more common among men than among women (Samuels et al., 2007), very few men seek treatment (Steketee & Frost, 2003). Hoarding behavior usually begins in childhood or early adolescence (Grisham, Frost, Steketee, et al., 2006). These early symptoms may be kept under control by parents and by limited income, so severe impairment from the hoarding often does not surface until later in life. Animal hoarding often does not emerge until middle age or older (Patronek & Nathanson, 2009).

Hoarding was not recognized as a diagnosis until the DSM-5. There is some debate about whether hoarding disorder will be placed in the chapter on obsessive-compulsive and related disorders or will be placed in the appendix for further research. In the DSM-IV-TR, hoarding is described as a symptom that can accompany OCD. Although hoarding is often comorbid with OCD, it can also occur among those who do not have OCD symptoms (Bloch et al., 2008). Depression, generalized anxiety disorder, and social phobia are common among people diagnosed with hoarding (Mataix-Cols, Frost, Pertusa, et al., 2010). Occasionally, hoarding develops among people with schizophrenia or dementia (Hwang, Tsai, Yang, et al., 1998).

Clinical Case: Dena

Dena was referred for treatment after animal care officials received reports from neighbors. A home inspection revealed over 100 animals living in her 3-acre yard and inside her house, many of them suffering from malnutrition, overcrowding, and disease. When interviewed, she reported that she was running a rescue mission for animals and that she was "just a little behind" because donations had diminished with the bad economy.

When the therapist visited her home, it became clear that her collections extended far beyond her animals. The rooms of her small home were so crowded that two of the doors to the outside could no longer be reached. Heaps of clothes and fabric mixed with miscellaneous furniture parts brimmed to the ceiling of her living room. In the kitchen, a collection of theater memorabilia crowded out access to the stove and refrigerator. The dining room was

covered with assorted items—bags of trash, heaps of bills, old newspapers, and several sets of china she had purchased "at a bargain" at yard sales.

When the therapist tried to raise the idea that they could help her organize and neaten her home, Dena became enraged. She said that she had only allowed the therapist to visit to help her broker an arrangement with the animal control authorities and that she did not want to hear any comments about her home. She described years of fighting with her family over her housekeeping, and she said she had done everything in her power to escape from their uptight rules and regulations. She claimed no need for the stove, stating that she wasn't about to start cooking hot meals as a single woman living alone. After the initial unsuccessful home visit, she refused any further contact with the therapist.

Quick Summary

The obsessive-compulsive and related disorders include obsessive-compulsive disorder (OCD), body dysmorphic disorder (BDD), and hoarding disorder. OCD is defined by obsessions and/or compulsions. BDD is defined by a preoccupation with an imagined defect in appearance. Hoarding disorder, a new diagnosis in the DSM-5, is defined by excessive acquisition of objects and severe difficulties in discarding objects, even when they are objectively without value.

People with BDD and hoarding disorder often have a history of OCD. Beyond this, the obsessive-compulsive and related disorders are commonly comorbid with anxiety disorders and major depressive disorder.

Check Your Knowledge 7.1 (Answers are at the end of the chapter.)

For each vignette, name the disorder (if any) that best fits the symptoms.

1. Sam, a 15-year-old male, reports that he has had a really bad song stuck in his head for days. He is frustrated that he cannot seem to rid himself of the song, no matter what he does.
2. Jan, a 41-year-old woman, was referred by her husband. He was worried because she spent hours and hours in the bathroom each day, crying while looking in the mirror at her hairline. She was convinced that her face and hairline were horribly asymmetrical and that others would dislike her as a result. She had visited two doctors to inquire about getting hair implants along her forehead, but both doctors felt that this was not advisable, as they saw no evidence that her hairline was in any way atypical.
3. June, a 60-year-old woman, needs to sell her house for financial reasons. The realtor has told her she must get rid of her stuff for the house to sell. At this point, there is no place in the house to sit, as so many different collections fill every possible spot. Her children have stopped visiting as they became so frustrated by her excessive spending behavior and her all-consuming focus on her possessions. Although June understands that she must purge her house of these collections, she is unable to do so. Every time she tries to sort through what to keep or not, she is paralyzed with overwhelming anxiety.

Etiology of the Obsessive-Compulsive and Related Disorders

Obsessive-compulsive disorder, body dysmorphic disorder and hoarding disorder share some overlap in etiology. Current models suggest that this overlap might be due to genetic and neurobiological risk factors. For example, people with BDD and hoarding disorder often have a family history of OCD (Gustad, 2003; Taylor, Jang, & Asmundson, 2010). OCD and BDD seem to involve some of the same brain regions. Brain-imaging studies indicate that three closely related areas of the brain are unusually active in people with OCD (see Figure 7.1): the **orbitofrontal cortex** (an area of the medial prefrontal cortex located just above the eyes), the **caudate nucleus** (part of the basal ganglia), and the anterior cingulate (Menzies, Chamberlain, Laird, et al., 2008; Rotge, Guehl, Dilharreguy, et al., 2009). When people with OCD are shown objects that tend to provoke symptoms (such as a soiled glove for a person who fears contamination), activity in these three areas increases (McGuire, 1994).

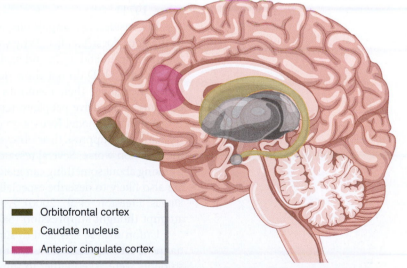

■ Orbitofrontal cortex
■ Caudate nucleus
■ Anterior cingulate cortex

Figure 7.1 Key brain regions in the obsessive-compulsive and related disorders: The orbitofrontal cortex, caudate nucleus, and anterior cingulate.

A similar pattern emerges when people with BDD view pictures of their own face. In those studies, BDD appears related to hyperactivity of the orbitofrontal cortex and the caudate nucleus (Feusner, Phillips, & Stein, 2010). Less is known about the neurobiology of hoarding disorder because this is a newly defined diagnosis.

While these genetic and neurobiological risk factors may set the stage for developing one of these disorders, why might one person develop OCD and another develop body dysmorphic disorder? Cognitive behavioral models focus on factors that might promote one disorder as compared to the other.

Etiology of Obsessive-Compulsive Disorder There is a moderate genetic contribution to OCD, with estimates of heritability ranging from 30 to 50 percent (Taylor et al., 2010). This would suggest that other variables also play a major role in the development of OCD, and we focus in particular on cognitive and behavioral contributions here.

At least 80 percent of people experience brief intrusive thoughts from time to time—a terrible song or image gets stuck in your head (Rachman, 1978). Because intrusive thoughts are so common, much of the psychological research has focused on why such thoughts persist, rather than on why such thoughts happen in the first place. After all, we don't diagnose OCD until intrusive thoughts are so persistent that they cause real distress or impairment.

Consider for a moment how we know to stop thinking about something, to stop cleaning, or to quit studying for a test or organizing our desk. There is no absolute signal from the environment. Rather, most of us stop when we have the sense of "that is enough." **Yedasentience** is defined as this subjective feeling of knowing (Woody & Szechtman, 2011). Just like you have a signal that you have eaten enough food, yedasentience is an intuitive signal that you have thought enough, cleaned enough, or in other ways done what you should to prevent chaos and danger. One theory suggests that people with OCD suffer from a deficit in yedasentience. Because they fail to gain the internal sense of completion, they have a hard time stopping their thoughts and behaviors. Objectively, they seem to know that there is no need to check the stove or wash their hands again, but they suffer from an anxious internal sense that things are not complete.

Other cognitive behavioral models tend to provide distinct explanations for compulsions versus obsessions. Behavioral models emphasize operant conditioning of compulsions. That is, compulsions are reinforced because they reduce anxiety (Meyer & Chesser, 1970). For example, compulsive handwashing would provide immediate relief from the anxiety associated with obsessions about germs. Similarly, checking the stove may provide immediate relief from the anxiety associated with the thought that the house will catch fire. Consistent with this view, after compulsive behavior, self-reported anxiety and even psychophysiological arousal drop (Carr, 1971).

In considering compulsions, a key question is why a single instance of checking the stove or the door doesn't suffice. Why would persons with OCD feel compelled to check the stove or the locks again and again and again? One theory is that they mistrust their memory. Although people with OCD do not show deficits in their memory, they often describe feeling a lack of confidence about their memories (Hermans, Engelen, Grouwels, et al., 2008). This lack of certainty could drive people to repeat rituals.

A different model focuses on obsessions. This model suggests that people with OCD may try harder to suppress their obsessions than other people and, in doing so, may actually make the situation worse. Several researchers have shown that people with OCD tend to believe that thinking about something can make it more likely to occur (Rachman, 1977). People with OCD are also likely to describe especially deep feelings of responsibility for what occurs (Ladoceur, Dugas, Freeston, et al., 2000). As a consequence of these two factors, they are more likely to attempt **thought suppression** (Salkovskis, 1996).

Unfortunately, it is hard to suppress thoughts. Consider the findings of one study of what happens when people are asked to suppress a thought (Wegner, 1987). Two groups of college students were asked either to think about a white bear or not to think about one; they were also told to ring a bell every time they thought about a white bear. The findings indicated that attempts to avoid thinking about the white bear did not work—students thought about the bear more than once a minute when trying not to do so. Beyond that, there was a rebound effect—after students tried to suppress thoughts about the bear for 5 minutes, they thought about the bear much more often during the next 5 minutes. Trying to suppress a thought may have the paradoxical effect of inducing preoccupation with it.

Most studies look at the effects of suppression over a matter of minutes, but the effects of trying to suppress a thought can continue for days. In one study, for example, people were asked to identify a recent intrusive thought and then were told to pay attention to the thought, were told to suppress the thought, or were given no instructions about the thought (Trinder, 1994). Participants recorded how often they had the intrusive thought and how uncomfortable the experience was for the next 4 days. People told to suppress the thought had more frequent intrusions of the thought and rated the intrusions as more uncomfortable over the 4-day period.

Beyond these studies of how hard it is to suppress thoughts, there is some evidence that thought suppression does actually play a role in OCD—namely, people with OCD tend to give more reasons why they should try to suppress thoughts than do people without OCD. For example, people who say they believe that bad things will happen if you think about them are more likely to try to suppress thoughts, and people who report more thought suppression also report more obsessive symptoms (Rassin, 2000).

Etiology of Body Dysmorphic Disorder Why would some people look in the mirror, see a nose that others see as perfectly reasonable, and respond with horror?

Cognitive models of BDD focus on what happens when a person with this syndrome looks at his or her body. People with BDD seem to be able to accurately see and process their physical features—the problem does not appear to be one of distortion of the physical features. Rather, those with BDD are more attuned to features that are important to attractiveness, such as facial symmetry, than are those without BDD (Lambrou, Veale, & Wilson, 2011).

When looking at visual stimuli, people with BDD appear to focus on details more than on the whole (Deckersbach, Savage, Phillips, et al., 2000). This influences how they look at facial features (Feusner et al., 2010). Rather than considering the gestalt, they examine one feature at a time, which makes it more likely that they will become engrossed in considering a small flaw. They also consider attractiveness to be vastly more important than do control participants (Lambrou et al., 2011). Indeed, many people with BDD seem to believe that their self-worth is exclusively dependent on their appearance (Veale, 2004).

Because of the importance of their appearance, people with BDD tend to spend a lot of time focusing on their appearance, to the exclusion of focusing on other, more positive stimuli. Their efforts to avoid situations in which their appearance might be judged can also interfere with important aspects of life.

Etiology of Hoarding Disorder In considering hoarding, many take an evolutionary perspective (Zohar & Felz, 2001). Imagine you were a caveman with no access to grocery stores to replenish food reserves and no clothing stores to find warm clothes when the weather got cold. In those situations, it would be adaptive to store any vital resources you could find. The question, though, is how these basic instincts become so uncontrollable for some people. The cognitive behavioral model suggests a number of factors that might be involved. According to the cognitive behavioral model, hoarding is related to poor organizational abilities, unusual beliefs about possessions, and avoidance behaviors (Steketee & Frost, 2003). Let's review each of these factors, considering how they might lead to excessive acquisition as well as difficulties getting rid of objects.

Several different types of cognitive problems interfere with organizational abilities among people with hoarding disorder. Many people with hoarding disorder demonstrate difficulties with attention (Hartl, Duffany, Allen, et al., 2005). They also find it difficult to categorize objects. When asked to sort objects into categories, hoarders tend to be slow, to generate many more categories than others do, and to find the process much more anxiety-provoking (Wincze, Steketee, & Frost, 2007). Many report that it is difficult for them to make decisions (Samuels et al., 2009). These difficulties attending to the task at hand, organizing objects, and making decisions influence almost every aspect of acquiring objects, organizing the home, and removing excessive acquisitions. Faced with decisions about which object is the better one to acquire, many will go ahead and get two, three, or more of the same type of object. Faced with decisions about how to store an object, many become overwhelmed. Health inspectors report that some homes are filled with unopened possessions still in the bag. Many patients find it excruciatingly hard to sort through their objects and figure out what to discard, even with a supportive therapist present (Frost & Steketee, 2010).

Beyond these difficulties with organizational skills, the cognitive model focuses on the unusual beliefs that people with hoarding disorder hold about their possessions. Almost by definition, hoarders demonstrate an extreme emotional attachment to their possessions. They report feeling comforted by their objects, being frightened by the idea of losing an object, and seeing the objects as core to their sense of self and identity. They perceive a sense of responsibility for taking care of those objects and are likely to resent it if others touch, borrow, or remove them (Steketee & Frost, 2003). These attachments may be even stronger when animals are involved. Animal hoarders often describe their animals as their closest confidants (Patronek & Nathanson, 2009). These beliefs about the importance of each and every object interfere with any attempts to tackle the clutter.

In the face of the anxiety of all these decisions, avoidance is common—many people with this disorder feel that it is better to pause than to make the wrong decision or to lose a valued object (Frost, Steketee, & Greene, 2003). Avoidance is considered one of the key factors that maintains the clutter.

Treatment of the Obsessive-Compulsive and Related Disorders

Treatments that work for obsessive-compulsive disorder, body dysmorphic disorder, and hoarding disorder are similar. Each of these disorders responds to serotonin reuptake inhibitors. The major psychological approach is exposure and response prevention, although this treatment is tailored for the specific conditions.

Medications Serotonin reuptake inhibitors (SRIs) are the most commonly used medications for the obsessive-compulsive and related disorders. SRIs were initially developed as antidepressants, but it is well established that they are effective in the treatment of OCD (Steketee & Barlow, 2004) and BDD (Hollander, Allen, Kwon, et al., 1999). The most commonly prescribed SRI for OCD is clomipramine (Anafranil; McDonough & Kennedy, 2002). In one multisite study, clomipramine led to an approximately 50 percent reduction in OCD symptoms (Mundo, 2000), and it is helpful for youth as well as adults (Franklin & Foa, 2011). Between 50 and 75 percent of people with BDD respond to treatment with SRIs (Hollander et al., 1999).

"Selective" serotonin reuptake inhibitors (SSRIs) are a newer class of SRIs that have fewer side effects. Although more studies are available for SRIs like clomipramine, SSRIs also appear to be effective in the treatment of OCD (Soomro, Altman, Rajagopal, et al., 2008) and BDD (Phillips, 2006).

There are no randomized controlled trials of medications for hoarding disorder. Much of our knowledge is based on studies of OCD patients who also have hoarding symptoms. Although most studies indicate that hoarding symptoms respond less to medication treatment than do other OCD symptoms (Steketee & Frost, 2003), findings of one study indicated that patients with hoarding disorder demonstrated as much of a response to the SSRI paroxetine (Paxil) as did those with OCD (Saxena, Brody, Maidment, et al., 2007). Although these findings are promising, there is a need for randomized controlled trials of medications for hoarding disorder.

Psychological Treatment The most widely used psychological treatment for the obsessive-compulsive and related disorders is **exposure and response prevention (ERP)**. This cognitive behavioral treatment was pioneered in England by Victor Meyer (1966) as an approach for OCD. Meyer developed ERP by tailoring the exposure treatment discussed in Chapter 6 to address the compulsive rituals that people with OCD use to reduce anxiety. We'll describe this treatment as it is applied to OCD, and then we will explain how it has been adapted for BDD and hoarding disorder.

Obsessive-Compulsive Disorder OCD sufferers often hold an almost magical belief that their compulsive behavior will prevent awful things from happening. In the response prevention component of ERP, people expose themselves to situations that elicit the compulsive act and then refrain from performing the compulsive ritual—for instance, the person touches a dirty dish and then refrains from washing his or her hands. The reasoning behind this approach goes like this:

1. Not performing the ritual exposes the person to the full force of the anxiety provoked by the stimulus.
2. The exposure results in the extinction of the conditioned response (the anxiety).

The first study of ERP as a treatment for OCD involved creating a controlled environment at Middlesex Hospital in London (Meyer, 1966). These days, the therapist guides exposure to feared stimuli in the home, often with help from family members (Foa & Franklin, 2001).

A meta-analysis of 19 studies comparing ERP to control treatments suggested that ERP was highly effective in reducing obsessions and compulsions (Rosa-Alcazar, Sanchez-Meca, Gomez-Conesa, et al., 2008). ERP appears to be more effective than clomipramine for the treatment of OCD (Foa, Libowitz, Kozak, et al., 2005), and it is effective for children and adolescents as well as adults (Franklin & Foa, 2011). ERP also appears to work well outside of academic settings and carefully controlled treatment trials—researchers have shown excellent outcomes for ERP offered by community therapists who do not specialize in OCD (Franklin & Foa, 2011). Even though most people experience a clinically significant reduction in symptoms with ERP, some mild symptoms are likely to remain (Steketee & Frost, 1998).

Exposure treatment for OCD can include confronting one's worst fears, such as contamination by dirty objects. (Copyright John Wiley & Sons, Inc.)

In the short term, refraining from performing a ritual is extremely unpleasant for people with OCD. (To get some idea of how unpleasant, try delaying for a minute or two before scratching an itch.) Typically, ERP involves refraining from performing rituals during sessions lasting upwards of 90 minutes, with 15 to 20 sessions within a 3-week period, and with instructions to practice between sessions as well. Given the intensity of treatment, it is not surprising that about 25 percent of clients refuse ERP treatment (Foa & Franklin, 2001). Clients with OCD tend to fear changes, and these tendencies create special problems for behavior therapy and medication approaches (Jenike, 1994).

Cognitive approaches to OCD focus on challenging people's beliefs about what will happen if they do not engage in rituals (Van Oppen, 1995). Eventually, to help test such beliefs, these approaches will use exposure. Several studies suggest that cognitive approaches perform as well as ERP (Derubeis & Crits-Christoph, 1998).

Body Dysmorphic Disorder The basic principles of ERP are tailored in several ways to address the symptoms of BDD. For example, to provide exposure to the most feared activities, clients might be asked to interact with people who could be critical of their looks. For response prevention, clients are asked to avoid the activities they use to reassure themselves about their appearance, such as looking in mirrors and other reflective surfaces. As illustrated in the Clinical Case of Paul, these behavioral techniques are supplemented with strategies to address the cognitive features of the disorder, such as the tendencies to attend to appearance while ignoring other stimuli, the excessively critical evaluations of one's physical features, and the belief that self-worth depends on one's appearance.

Several trials have shown that cognitive behavioral treatment (CBT) produces a major decrease in body dysmorphic symptoms compared to control conditions (Looper, 2002). It appears as though treatments that include a cognitive component are more powerful than those that address only behaviors (Williams, Hadjistavropoulos, & Sharpe, 2006), but both treatments produce lasting effects (Ipser, Sander, & Stein, 2009).

Clinical Case: Paul

Paul, a 33-year-old physical therapist, sought treatment at a clinic specializing in body dysmorphic disorder because of his deeply distressing preoccupation with his nose and jaw line. Although by objective standards he was an attractive man, he reported that his nose was "too long and bumpy" and that his jaw was "feminine and scrawny." He reported that checking and worrying about his appearance had taken over every aspect of his life.

Paul reported that he had been a shy child, who first began to be "horrified" by his appearance during puberty. During those years, he had noticed that his friends developed more square jaw lines, and he became distressed that his jaw remained "scrawny and young looking." Over the past two decades, his preoccupation with his appearance had interfered with dating, but he retained a few close friends. By the time he came for treatment, he was spending 4 hours or more per day thinking about his nose. He would spend hours staring into the mirror, sometimes measuring his nose and sometimes doing exercises he had developed in an attempt to add muscle to the regions around his nose. He had sought surgery, but the surgeon he consulted refused to operate on what seemed to be a flawless nose. He often avoided going out, and when he did so, he had to check on his appearance repeatedly throughout the evening. He had become worried that his clients were too focused on his physical flaws to pay attention to his instructions. Sometimes he was unable to go to work because he was overwhelmed by his anxiety.

Paul and his therapist agreed to use CBT to address his BDD (Wilhelm, Buhlmann, Hayward, et al., 2010). The first step in this treatment is psychoeducation. As part of this, he and the therapist reviewed childhood and current influences on his symptoms. Paul described his parents' extremely high standards for appearance, along with his father's obsessive and perfectionistic style. He had struggled throughout his life with the sense that he could not live up to their standards. He and the therapist identified several current cognitions (thoughts) that seemed to contribute to his anxiety, including the belief that others were noticing his appearance and evaluating it negatively. In response to his feelings of shame, anxiety, and depression, he had developed a series of avoidance behaviors that were interfering with building healthy social and work relationships.

The next step was to start addressing his negative cognitions about his appearance. Paul was asked to record his most negative thoughts each day. He was also taught ways to evaluate whether these thoughts might be overly harsh. He was able to identify thoughts like "Any flaw means I'm ugly" or "I know my client is thinking about how ugly my nose is," and he began to consider alternative ways of thinking.

As Paul developed more positive ways of thinking about his appearance, the therapist began to target his avoidant and ritualistic behaviors. Paul tended to avoid social events, bright lights, and even eye contact with others, and he understood that these behaviors were interfering with his life. Treatment consisted of exposure, in which Paul was gradually coached to engage in making eye contact, social activities, and even talking with others under bright light. His rituals included checking his appearance, engaging in facial exercises, studying others' noses, and surfing plastic surgery websites. These rituals were conducted in response to intense anxiety, but the therapist was able to help him understand that the rituals did not actually address his anxiety or relieve his concerns. Rituals were tackled using response prevention—Paul was asked to avoid conducting the rituals and to monitor his mood and anxiety as he did so.

After five sessions of treatment, Paul's therapist introduced perceptual retraining. As described previously, when people with BDD look at themselves in the mirror, they focus on small details of their worst feature, and they are overly evaluative. As a daily homework assignment, Paul was asked to spend time looking in the mirror but focusing on the whole of his appearance. He was also asked to describe his nose using nonevaluative, objective language. During the first several days, he found this extremely anxiety-provoking, but his anxiety in response to this exercise diminished rapidly within a week. Soon, he was able to appreciate some of his features that he had previously ignored—for example, he noticed that he had nice eyes.

It is common for people with body dysmorphic disorder to focus excessive attention on own appearance. Paul was trained to refocus his attention on people and events outside of himself. For example, when dining with a friend, he was coached to attend to the sound of his friend's voice, the flavor of the food, and the content of their conversation.

As Paul made gains in these areas, the therapist began to work on the more difficult and core aspects of cognitions—his deeply held negative beliefs about the meaning of his appearance. Paul described feeling that his physical flaws made him unlovable. The therapist helped him begin to consider his many positive qualities.

The tenth and final session consisted of reviewing the skills he had learned and discussing the strategies he would use if symptoms returned. Over the course of treatment, Paul's symptoms remitted such that by the time of the last session, he was no longer distressed about his nose. [Drawn from Wilhelm et al., 2010]

Hoarding Disorder Treatment for hoarding is based on the ERP therapy that is employed with OCD (Steketee & Frost, 2003). The exposure element of treatment focuses on the most feared situation for people with hoarding disorder—getting rid of their objects. Response prevention focuses on halting the rituals that they engage in to reduce their anxiety, such as counting or sorting their possessions.

Despite the common elements, treatment is tailored in many ways for hoarding. As illustrated in the case of Dena, many people with hoarding disorder don't recognize the gravity of problems created by their symptoms. Therapy cannot begin to address the hoarding symptoms until the person develops insight. To facilitate this, motivational strategies are used to help the person consider reasons to change. Once people decide to change, therapists help them make decisions about their objects, provide tools to help them get their clutter organized, and schedule sessions to work on "de-cluttering." The therapists supplement their office sessions with in-home visits. In the first randomized controlled trial of this approach, patients who received CBT demonstrated significantly more improvement than did those assigned to a waiting list (Steketee et al., 2010). With 26 weeks of treatment, about 70 percent of patients showed at least modest improvement in hoarding symptoms.

Early cognitive behavioral interventions focused on helping clients discard their objects as quickly as possible, hoping to avoid the quagmire of indecision and anxiety that might come from too much focus on evaluating possessions. Unfortunately, patients tended to drop out of treatment, and even those who did remain often showed little response (Abramowitz, Franklin, Schwartz, et al., 2003; Mataix-Cols, Marks, Greist, et al., 2002).

Family relationships are often profoundly damaged for those with hoarding disorder. Relatives usually try various approaches to helping people rid their life of clutter, only to become more and more frustrated and angry as those attempts fail. Many resort to coercive strategies, including removing the hoarder's possessions while the person is away—strategies that typically create mistrust and animosity. Family approaches to hoarding begin by building rapport around these difficult issues (Tompkins & Hartl, 2009). Rather than aiming for a total absence of clutter, family members are urged to identify the aspects of hoarding and clutter that are most dangerous for safety. They can use their concern regarding these issues to begin dialogue and set priorities with the person with hoarding disorder.

Despite the evidence that rapidly removing possessions tends to fail, the TV show *Hoarders* features many individuals who are faced with ridding themselves of objects under dire threat of eviction or other contingencies, and so are forced to discard their collections within days or weeks. (JOEL KOYAMA/MCT/Landov LLC.)

Quick Summary

OCD, BDD, and hoarding disorder are moderately heritable. People with BDD and hoarding disorder often report a family history of OCD. OCD and BDD are both characterized by high activity in the orbitofrontal cortex and the caudate nucleus, and OCD additionally involves high activity in the anterior cingulate.

OCD is moderately heritable. Psychologically, OCD appears to be characterized by a deficit in yedasentience. Behaviorists theorize that compulsions might be reinforced because they provide relief from anxiety. The repetition of compulsions may be related to a lack of confidence in memory. Cognitive models of obsessions focus on thought suppression.

People with BDD do not appear to have distorted visual perceptions of their body. Rather, the cognitive model of BDD focuses on a detail-oriented analytic style, tendencies to overvalue the

meaning of appearance for self-worth, and excessive attention to cues related to appearance. Behavioral factors include an excessive engagement in appearance-related activities, coupled with avoidance of situations that might involve to evaluations of their appearance.

Cognitive behavioral models of hoarding disorder focus on poor organizational abilities (difficulties with attention, categorization, and decision making), unusual beliefs about possessions, and avoidance behaviors.

SRIs are the most-studied medication treatment for the obsessive-compulsive and related disorders, but SSRIs have also received some support. The major psychological treatment approach for the obsessive-compulsive and related disorders is exposure and response prevention (ERP). Treatment for hoarding disorder often involves motivational strategies to enhance insight and willingness to consider change.

Check Your Knowledge 7.2

Answer the questions.
1. List three reasons to consider OCD, BDD, and hoarding as related conditions.
2. What type of medication has been most carefully tested for the treatment of obsessive-compulsive and related disorders?
3. What is the most commonly used psychological treatment for obsessive-compulsive and related disorders?

Posttraumatic Stress Disorder and Acute Stress Disorder

Rescue workers, such as this firefighter who was at the World Trade Center in the aftermath of the 9/11 terrorist attack, could be vulnerable to PTSD. (Marco Townsend/AFP/Getty Images, Inc.)

Posttraumatic stress disorder and acute stress disorder are diagnosed only when a person has experienced a traumatic event. As such, the criteria for these diagnoses incorporate the cause of symptoms, which is in sharp contrast to the rest of the DSM, where diagnoses are based entirely on symptoms.

Clinical Description and Epidemiology of Posttraumatic Stress Disorder and Acute Stress Disorder

Posttraumatic stress disorder (PTSD) entails an extreme response to a severe stressor, including increased anxiety, avoidance of stimuli associated with the trauma, and symptoms of increased arousal. Although people have known for many years that the stresses of combat can have powerful adverse effects on soldiers, the aftermath of the Vietnam War spurred the development of this diagnosis.

Diagnoses of these disorders are considered only in the context of serious traumas; the person must have experienced or witnessed an event that involved actual or threatened death, serious injury, or sexual violation. As noted above, war veterans have often been exposed to these sorts of severe traumas. For women, rape is the most common type of trauma preceding PTSD (Creamer, 2001), with at least one-third of women meeting criteria for PTSD after a rape (Breslau, Chilcoat, Kessler, et al., 1999).

In the proposed DSM-5, the symptoms for PTSD are grouped into four major categories:

- *Intrusively reexperiencing* the traumatic event. The person may have repetitive memories or nightmares of the event. The person may be intensely upset by or show marked physiological reactions to reminders of the event (e.g., helicopter sounds that remind a veteran of the battlefield; darkness that reminds a woman of a rape).

● Proposed DSM-5 Criteria for Posttraumatic Stress Disorder

A. The person was exposed to death or threatened death, actual or threatened serious injury, or *actual or threatened sexual violation, in one or more of the following ways: experiencing the event personally, witnessing the event, learning that a violent or accidental death or threat of death occurred to a close other, or experiencing repeated or extreme exposure to aversive details of the event(s)*

B. At least 1 of the following **intrusion** symptoms:
- Recurrent, involuntary, and intrusive distressing memories of the trauma, or in children, repetitive play regarding the trauma themes
- Recurrent distressing dreams related to the event(s)
- Dissociative reactions (e.g., flashbacks) in which the individual feels or acts as if the trauma(s) were recurring
- Intense or prolonged distress or physiological reactivity in response to reminders of the trauma(s)

C. At least 1 of the following **avoidance** symptoms:
- Avoids *internal reminders* of the trauma(s)
- Avoids *external reminders* of the trauma(s)

D. *At least 3 (or 2 in children) negative alterations in cognitions and mood that began or worsened after the trauma(s):*

- Inability to remember an important aspect of the trauma(s)
- *Persistent and exaggerated negative expectations about one's self, others, or the world*
- *Persistently excessive blame of self or others about the trauma(s)*
- *Pervasive negative emotional state*
- Markedly diminished interest or participation in significant activities
- Feeling of detachment or estrangement from others
- Persistent inability to experience positive emotions

E. At least 3 (or 2 in children) of the following **alterations in arousal and reactivity** that began or worsened after the trauma(s):
- Irritable or aggressive behavior
- *Reckless or self-destructive behavior*
- Hypervigilance
- Exaggerated startle response
- Problems with concentration
- Sleep disturbance

F. The *symptoms began or worsened after the trauma(s) and* continued for at least one month

---

Note: Changes from DSM-IV-TR criteria are noted in italics. DSM-IV-TR criteria specify that the person's response to the initial trauma involved intense fear, helplessness, or horror. Criterion D is new to DSM-IV-TR; the numbing symptoms noted in this category were formerly considered as evidence of avoidance.

- *Avoidance* of stimuli associated with the event. Some may try to avoid all reminders of the event. For example, a Turkish earthquake survivor stopped sleeping indoors after he was buried alive at night (McNally, 2003). Other people try to avoid thinking about the trauma; some may remember only disorganized fragments of the event. These symptoms may seem contradictory to reexperiencing symptoms; although the person is using avoidance to try to prevent reminders, the strategy often fails, and so reexperiencing occurs.

- Other signs of *mood and cognitive change* after the trauma. These can include inability to remember important aspects of the event, persistently negative cognition, blaming self or others for the event, pervasive negative emotions, lack of interest or involvement in significant activities, feeling detached from others, or inability to experience positive emotions.

- Symptoms of *increased arousal and reactivity.* These symptoms include irritable or aggressive behavior, reckless or self-destructive behavior, difficulty falling asleep or staying asleep, difficulty concentrating, hypervigilance, and an exaggerated startle response. Laboratory studies have confirmed that people with PTSD demonstrate heightened arousal, as measured by physiological responses to trauma-relevant images (Orr, 2003).

Once PTSD develops, symptoms are relatively chronic. In one study of people diagnosed with PTSD, about half continued to experience diagnosable symptoms when interviewed several years later (Perkonigg, 2005). Suicidal thoughts are common among people with PTSD (Bernal, Haro, Bernert, et al., 2007), as are incidents of nonsuicidal self-injury (Weierich & Nock, 2008). In a study of 15,288 army veterans followed for 30 years after their initial military service, PTSD was associated with a greater risk of early death from medical illness, accidents, and suicides (Boscarino, 2006).

The proposed DSM-5 criteria for PTSD differ from the DSM-IV-TR criteria in several ways. First, DSM-IV-TR requires that the person experienced extreme fear, helplessness, or horror at the time of the event. Many people with PTSD symptoms report feeling as though they were detached from their self or emotions at the time of the trauma. To reflect this, the

Proposed DSM-5 Criteria for Acute Stress Disorder

A. The person was exposed to death or threatened death, actual or threatened serious injury, or actual or threatened sexual violation, in one or more of the following ways: experiencing the event personally, witnessing the event, learning that a violent or accidental death or threat of death occurred to a close other, or experiencing repeated or extreme exposure to aversive details of the event(s)

B. At least 8 of the following symptoms began or worsened since the trauma and lasted 3 to 31 days:
   - Recurrent, involuntary, and intrusive distressing memories of the traumatic event
   - Recurrent distressing dreams related to the traumatic event
   - Dissociative reactions (e.g., flashbacks) in which the individual feels or acts as if the traumatic event were recurring
   - Intense or prolonged psychological distress or physiological reactivity at exposure to reminders of the traumatic event
   - Subjective sense of numbing, detachment from others, or reduced responsiveness to events
   - Altered sense of the reality of one's surroundings or oneself (e.g., seeing oneself from another's perspective, being in a daze)
   - Inability to remember at least one important aspect of the traumatic event
   - Avoids internal reminders of the trauma(s)
   - Avoids external reminders of the trauma(s)
   - Sleep disturbance
   - Hypervigilance
   - Irritable or aggressive behavior
   - Exaggerated startle response
   - Agitation or restlessness

DSM-IV-TR Criteria for Acute Stress Disorder

- Exposure to a traumatic event causing extreme fear, helplessness, or horror
- During or after the event, the person experiences dissociative symptoms
- The event is reexperienced intrusively in dreams, thoughts, or intense reactivity to reminders
- The person feels numb, detached, or unable to remember the event
- Increased arousal or anxiety
- Symptoms occur within the first month after the trauma

criterion that a person experience intense emotion at the time of the trauma is removed in the proposed DSM-5. Second, the DSM-IV-TR criterion for trauma has been criticized for being overly broad. Even vicarious exposure to trauma, which could include watching news reports about war and terrorism, qualifies as a PTSD-relevant form of trauma according to the DSM-IV-TR criteria (McNally, 2009). In the proposed DSM-5, criteria for defining traumatic events are narrower; for example, it is specified that exposure to media accounts does not qualify as trauma. Third, many of the symptoms described in the DSM-IV-TR criteria, such as difficulty concentrating, difficulty sleeping, and diminished interest in activities, are also criteria for major depressive disorder. The proposed DSM-5 criteria specify that these symptoms must begin after the trauma. Finally, for a diagnosis of PTSD, DSM-IV-TR requires the presence of either avoidance symptoms (such as avoiding reminders of the trauma) or numbing symptoms (such as decreased interest in others, a sense of estrangement from others, and an inability to feel positive emotions). Evidence suggests avoidance and numbing are distinct (Asmundson, Stapleton, & Taylor, 2004). DSM-5 criteria require avoidance symptoms to be present for a diagnosis of PTSD. Numbing symptoms are considered along with the many other possible signs of changes in cognition and mood.

In addition to PTSD, the DSM includes a diagnosis for **acute stress disorder (ASD)**. ASD is diagnosed when symptoms occur between 3 days and 1 month after a trauma. The symptoms of ASD are fairly similar to those of PTSD, but the duration is shorter. The DSM-IV-TR specified that dissociative symptoms must be present; because this was not empirically validated or parallel with the criteria for PTSD, this criterion is not included in the proposed DSM-5 criteria for ASD. On the whole, the ASD criteria have been changed to be much more similar to PTSD (see the ASD criteria boxes for DSM-IV-TR and DSM-5 to see these changes in more detail).

The ASD diagnosis is not as well accepted as the PTSD diagnosis. There are two major concerns about this diagnosis. First, some have criticized the ASD diagnosis because it could stigmatize short-term reactions to serious traumas, even though these are quite common (Harvey & Bryant, 2002). For example, after a rape, as many as 90 percent of women report at least some (subsyndromal) symptoms (Rothbaum, 1992), and among people who have been exposed to a mass shooting, approximately one-third develop symptoms of ASD (Classen, 1998). Second, most people who go on to meet diagnostic criteria for PTSD do not experience ASD in the first month after the trauma (Bryant, Creamer, O'Donnell, et al., 2008). As the DSM-5 criteria for ASD are so much more parallel with the PTSD criteria, one might expect that the DSM-5 ASD diagnosis will be more predictive of PTSD than the DSM-IV-TR diagnosis has been.

Because less is known about ASD, we will focus on PTSD as we discuss epidemiology and etiology. One reason to consider this diagnosis, though, is that ASD does predict a higher risk of developing PTSD within 2 years (Harvey & Bryant, 2002). When we consider treatments, we will review evidence that treating ASD may help prevent the development of PTSD.

Clinical Case: Graham

Graham is a 34-year-old man who was referred for specialist psychiatric treatment by his military physician. Graham had recently separated from his wife, and reported having no close friends. He felt haunted by images of his time in Afghanistan ever since he had returned from a tour of duty two years before. Graham reported that he frequently experienced recurring and intrusive recollections during the day, and recurrent distressing nightmares of particular scenes and events in the hills in Afghanistan. He tried to avoid reminders of the war, including newspaper and TV coverage, political conversations, and even seeing helicopters, but he often stumbled into reminders unexpectedly. When Graham did, he found that he was quickly overwhelmed by intense fear, helplessness and physical shakiness. On a more day-to-day basis, Graham reported difficulty in falling asleep, angry outbursts and a pervasive feeling of hopelessness.

He had an ongoing difficult relationship with his wife, and when he visited his two children she would often complain bitterly about him leaving her and the children and not 'caring anymore.' When asked if he wanted to get back together with her, he said he wasn't sure what he felt about her and that he had not really felt emotionally engaged with her or anyone else since the war.

PTSD tends to be highly comorbid with other conditions. In one study of a representative community sample, researchers conducted diagnostic assessments repeatedly from ages 3 until age 26. Among people who had developed PTSD by age 26, almost all (93 percent) had been diagnosed with another psychological disorder before age 21. The most common disorders are other anxiety disorders, major depression, substance abuse, and conduct disorder (Koenen, Moffitt, Poulton, et al., 2007). Two-thirds of those with PTSD at age 26 had experienced another anxiety disorder by age 21.

Among people exposed to a trauma, women are twice as likely to develop PTSD as are men (Breslau et al., 1999). This is consistent with the gender ratio observed for most anxiety disorders. Women may also face different life circumstances than do men. For example, women are much more likely than men to be sexually assaulted during childhood and adulthood (Tolin & Foa, 2006). In studies that control for a history of sexual abuse and assault, men and women have comparable rates of PTSD (Tolin & Foa, 2006).

Culture may shape the risk for PTSD in several ways. Some cultural groups may be exposed to higher rates of trauma and, as a consequence, manifest higher rates of PTSD. This seems to be the case for Latinos living in the United States, perhaps related to the frequent exposure to political violence they experienced in their native countries (Pole, 2008), and for minority populations in the United States (Ritsher, 2002). Culture also may shape the types of symptoms observed in PTSD. *Ataque de nervios,* originally identified in Puerto Rico, involves physical symptoms and fears of going crazy in the aftermath of severe stress and thus is similar to PTSD.

Etiology of Posttraumatic Stress Disorder

Above, we mentioned that two-thirds of people who develop PTSD have a history of another anxiety disorder. Not surprisingly, then, many of the risk factors for PTSD overlap with the risk factors for other anxiety disorder that we described in Chapter 6 (see Table 6.5). For example, PTSD appears related to genetic risk for anxiety disorders (Tambs, Czajkowsky, Roysamb, et al., 2009), high levels of activity in areas of the fear circuit such as the amygdala (Rauch, 2000), childhood exposure to trauma (Breslau, 1995), and tendencies to attend selectively to cues of threat (Bar-Haim, 2007). As with other anxiety disorders, neuroticism and negative affectivity predict the onset of PTSD (Pole, Neylan, Otte, et al., 2009; Rademaker, Van Zuiden, Vermetten, et al., 2011).

Also parallel with other anxiety disorders, PTSD has been related to the two-factor model of conditioning. In this model, the initial fear in PTSD is assumed to arise from classical conditioning (Keane, 1985). For example, a woman may come to fear walking in the neighborhood (the conditioned stimulus) where she was raped (the unconditioned stimulus). This classically conditioned fear is so intense that the woman avoids the neighborhood as much as possible. Operant conditioning contributes to the maintenance of this avoidance behavior; the avoidance is reinforced by the reduction of fear that comes from not being in the presence of the conditioned stimulus. This avoidant behavior interferes with chances for the fear to extinguish.

Keeping these parallels in mind, in this section we focus on factors that are uniquely associated with PTSD. We begin by describing a large body of evidence that suggests that certain kinds of traumas may be more likely to trigger PTSD than other types. Even among people who experience traumas, though, not everyone develops PTSD. Thus, a great deal of research has been conducted on neurobiological and coping variables that help predict the onset of PTSD.

Nature of the Trauma: Severity and the Type of Trauma Matter

The severity of the trauma influences whether or not a person will develop PTSD. Consider the case of people who are exposed to war. About 20 percent of American fighters wounded in Vietnam developed PTSD, contrasted with 50 percent of those who were prisoners of war there (Engdahl, 1997). During Operation Desert Storm (in the 1990–1991 conflict following the Iraqi invasion of Kuwait), among those assigned to collect, tag, and bury scattered body parts of the dead, 65 percent developed PTSD (Sutker, 1994). As shown in Figure 7.2, the number of World War II soldiers admitted for psychiatric care was closely related to how many casualties occurred in their battalions (Jones & Wessely, 2001). During World War II, doctors believed that 98

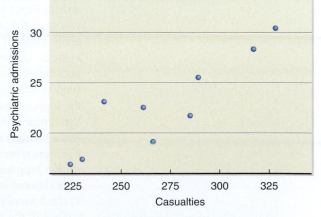

Figure 7.2 Percent of Canadian soldiers admitted for psychiatric care as a function of the number of casualties in their battalion during World War II. Drawn from Jones & Wessely, 2001.

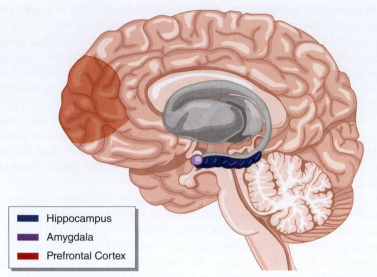

Hippocampus
Amygdala
Prefrontal Cortex

Figure 7.3 A smaller hippocampus may be related to the risk of developing PTSD.

percent of men would develop psychiatric problems with 60 days of continuous combat (Grossman, 1995).

The occurrence of PTSD among residents of New York City after the terrorist attack on the World Trade Center on September 11, 2001 showed a similar correspondence with the severity of the trauma. Based on a telephone survey after the attack, researchers determined that 7 percent of the adults living south of 110th Street in New York City (but well north of the World Trade Center) reported symptoms that would have warranted a diagnosis of PTSD, but 20 percent of those living south of Canal Street (close to the disaster site) reported such symptoms (Galea, 2002). In short, among people who have been exposed to traumas, those exposed to the most severe traumas seem most likely to develop PTSD.

Beyond severity, the nature of the trauma matters. Traumas caused by humans are more likely to cause PTSD than are natural disasters (Charuvastra, 2008). For example, rapes, combat experience, abuse, and assault all are associated with higher risk than are natural disasters. It may be that these events are seen as more distressing because they challenge ideas about humans as benevolent.

Neurobiological Factors: Hippocampus and Hormones As with other anxiety disorders, PTSD appears to be related to greater activation of the amygdala and diminished activation of the medial prefrontal cortex (Shin, Rauch, & Pitman, 2006), regions that are integrally involved in learning and extinguishing fears. Although these two regions seem involved in many of the anxiety disorders, PTSD appears uniquely related to the function of the hippocampus. The hippocampus is known for its role in memory, particularly for memories related to emotions (see Figure 7.3). Brain-imaging studies show that among people with PTSD, the hippocampus has a smaller volume than among people who do not have PTSD (Bremner, Vythilingam, Vermetten, et al., 2003). A study of multiple pairs of identical twins, one of whom was a Vietnam veteran and the other not, is especially revealing of how hippocampal volume and PTSD are related (Gilbertson, Shenton, Ciszewski, et al., 2002). As in previous studies of veterans, smaller hippocampal volume was associated with PTSD symptoms, but this study went on to find an additional important pattern. That is, there was a relationship between hippocampal volume in the nonveteran twins and the likelihood of PTSD in the veteran twins. Smaller hippocampal volume of the nonveteran twin was related to greater likelihood that the veteran twin would develop PTSD after military service. This suggests that smaller-than-average hippocampal volume probably precedes the onset of disorder. See Focus on Discovery 7.1 for more perspectives on how these findings regarding the hippocampus can be integrated with cognitive models to understand memory complaints in PTSD.

Coping When faced with a traumatic event, some people seem to rise to the challenge and show extraordinary resilience. It is clear that how a person copes during the trauma and afterwards helps predict whether PTSD will develop (Brewin & Holmes, 2003).

Survivors of natural disasters, such as the Japanese earthquake in 2011, are at risk for PTSD, but their risk may not be as high as those who experience traumas caused by humans, such as assaults. (Left: Flying Colours Ltd/Getty Images, Inc.; Right: AFP/ Getty Images.)

Several types of studies suggest that people who cope with a trauma by trying to avoid thinking about it are more likely than others to develop PTSD (Sharkansky, King, King, et al., 2000). Much of this work focuses on symptoms of **dissociation** (such as feeling removed from one's body or emotions, or being unable to remember the event). We discuss dissociation in more detail in Chapter 8. Dissociation and memory suppression may keep the person from confronting memories of the trauma. People who have symptoms of dissociation during and immediately after the trauma are more likely to develop PTSD, as are people who try to suppress memories of the trauma (Ehlers, Mayou, & Bryant, 1998). The correlation between dissociation and PTSD has been confirmed in a meta-analysis of 16 studies involving 3,534 participants (Ozer, Best, Lipsey, et al., 2003). A range of studies now show that symptoms of dissociation shortly after being raped predict the development of PTSD (Brewin & Holmes, 2003). Moreover, people who continue to use dissociation in the years after the trauma are at risk for ongoing PTSD symptoms (Briere, Scott, & Weathers, 2005). A compelling study of dissociation assessed rape victims within 2 weeks of the assault (Griffin, Resick, & Mechanic, 1997). Women were asked questions about dissociation during the rape (e.g., "Did you feel numb?" and "Did you have moments of losing track of what was going on?"), and based on their responses, they were divided into a high-dissociation group and a low-dissociation group. Women in the high-dissociation group were much more likely to have PTSD symptoms than women in the low-dissociation group. The authors also used psychophysiological measures to understand more about how dissociation worked. For this part of the study, women talked about the rape and about neutral topics. While talking, the women reported when they felt stress and they were measured for psychophysiological arousal. Even though the women in the high-dissociation group reported emotional stress while talking about being raped, they actually showed less physiological arousal than did the women in the low-dissociation group.

Other protective factors may help a person cope with severe traumas more adaptively. Two that seem particularly important include high intelligence (Breslau, Lucia, & Alvarado, 2006; Kremen, Koenen, Boake, et al., 2007) and strong social support (Brewin, Andrews, & Valentine, 2000). Having better intellectual ability to make sense of horrifying events, and more friends and family members to help with that process, helps people avoid symptoms after traumatic events.

One line of research focuses on people who report growth in the context of a traumatic experience. For some, trauma awakens an increased appreciation of life, renews a focus on life priorities, and provides an opportunity to understand one's strengths in overcoming adversity (Bonanno, 2004; Tedeschi, Park, & Calhoun, 1998). Hence, despite the challenges of trauma, some people may learn better coping skills and develop improved resourcefulness.

FOCUS ON DISCOVERY 7.1

Perspectives on Memory: Integrating Neurobiology and Cognition

People with post-traumatic stress disorder seem to have frequent intrusions of traumatic memories. This is consistent with findings that surges of norepinephrine and cortisol, which are typically present during periods of extreme stress, lead to stronger memory formation particularly for the central aspects of a threatening experience. Key brain structures involved in this "overconsolidation" are the amygdala and the ventromedial prefrontal cortex.

Research shows that blockade of norepinephrine sites in the rodent lateral amygdala following reactivation of fear memory disrupts memory reconsolidation and lastingly impairs fear memory (Dębiec, Bush & LeDoux, 2011). So, whilst the amygdala appears to mediates the acquisition and expression of conditioned fear and the enhancement of emotional memory, the ventromedial prefrontal cortexis involved in the extinction of conditioned fear and the volitional regulation of negative emotion. It has been theorized that the ventromedial prefrontal cortex exerts inhibition on the amygdala, and that a defect in this inhibition could account for the symptoms of post-traumatic stress disorder (Koenigs & Grafman, 2009). This theory is supported by functional imaging studies of post-traumatic stress disorder patients, who exhibit hypoactivity in the ventromedial prefrontal cortex but hyperactivity in the amygdala. A recent study of brain-injured and trauma-exposed combat veterans by Koenigs and colleagues in 2008, confirmed that amygdala damage reduces the likelihood of developing PTSD. What is not entirely clear, however, is the neurocognitive mechanism by which the amygdala mediates PTSD. Human and non-human data demonstrate that the amygdala is critically involved in the expression of negative affect and emotion-related behavior such as conditioned fear responses, which implicates at least 3 possible (but not mutually exclusive) mechanisms:

- Amygdala damage could confer resistance to post traumatic stress disorder through the diminished expression of fear- or anxiety-related responses;
- The amygdala could underlie post-traumatic stress disorder by virtue of its role in the consolidation of emotional memories. Research shows that emotionally arousing stimuli are more readily retrieved than emotionally neutral stimuli, and that the amygdala is responsible for this emotional memory enhancement (McGaugh 2004). In some sense, post-traumatic stress disorder can be conceived as a disorder of extreme emotional memory enhancement, in which emotionally traumatic events are consolidated and recalled to an excessive, pathological degree. Perhaps amygdala damage impairs the obtrusive recall of emotionally traumatic events that defines the disorder.
- The amygdala's role in post-traumatic stress disorder is related to its function in the detection and evaluation of biologically relevant stimuli, such as threat.

Dębiec, J. Bush, D.E.A., & LeDoux, J.E. (2011) Noradrenergic enhancement of reconsolidation in the amygdala impairs extinction of conditioned fear in rats—a possible mechanism for the persistence of traumatic memories in PTSD. Depression and Anxiety 28:186–193, 2011.

Michael Koenigs[1] and Jordan Grafman: Post-traumatic stress disorder: The role of medial prefrontal cortex and amygdala. *Neuroscientist*. 2009 October; 15(5): 540–548.

Koenigs M., Huey ED., Raymont V., Cheon B., Solomon J., Wassermann EM. Focal brain damage protects against post-traumatic stress disorder in combat veterans. *Nat Neurosci*. 2008;11:232–237.

Quick Summary

Posttraumatic stress disorder (PTSD) and acute stress disorder (ASD) are both severe reactions to trauma; ASD occurs in the first 4 weeks after a trauma, and PTSD lasts for more than 4 weeks after a trauma. PTSD and ASD can be diagnosed only among people who have experienced a severe trauma.

Some of the general risk factors for anxiety disorders appear to be involved in the development of PTSD. These general risk factors include genetic vulnerability, amygdala hyperactivity, neuroticism, childhood trauma exposure, and tendencies to attend to cues of threat in the environment. PTSD has also been related to Mowrer's two-factor model of anxiety.

Even among people who have been traumatized, though, the likelihood that a person will develop PTSD depends on the severity of the trauma. Neurobiological research has found that people with small hippocampal volume are more likely to develop PTSD. After exposure to trauma, people who rely on dissociative coping strategies (i.e., who avoid thinking about the trauma) seem more likely to develop PTSD than people who rely on other strategies. Other resources that might promote adaptive coping, such as higher IQ and stronger social support, can protect against the development of PTSD.

Treatment of Posttraumatic Stress Disorder and Acute Stress Disorder

A good deal of work has focused on treatment of PTSD using medication and psychological treatments. Less research is available on ASD.

Medications Dozens of randomized controlled trials have been conducted to examine medication treatments of PTSD (Stein, Ipser, & Seedat, 2000). One class of antidepressant, the selective serotonergic reuptake inhibitors (SSRIs), has received strong support as a treatment for PTSD. Relapse is common if medications are discontinued.

Psychological Treatment of Posttraumatic Stress Disorder In Chapter 6, we described exposure treatment, which is the primary psychological approach to treating anxiety disorders. With the support of a therapist, the person is asked to face his or her worst fears, most typically by working up an exposure hierarchy from less intense fears to the most intense fears. The goal of treatment is to extinguish the fear response, particularly the overgeneralized fear response, but also to help challenge the idea that the person could not cope with the anxiety and fear generated by those stimuli. As clients learn that they can cope with their anxiety, avoidance responses can be reduced.

In PTSD, the focus of exposure treatment is on memories and reminders of the original trauma, with the person being encouraged to confront the trauma to gain mastery and extinguish the anxiety. Where possible, the person is directly exposed to reminders of the trauma in vivo—for example, by returning to the scene of the event. In other cases, **imaginal exposure** is used—the person deliberately remembers the event (Keane, Fairbank, Caddell, et al., 1989). Evidence indicates that exposure treatment that focuses on trauma-related events, either in imagination or directly, is more effective in treating PTSD than medication or supportive unstructured psychotherapy (Bradley, Greene, Russ, et al., 2005). Exposure treatment has been used successfully with a broad range of people. For example, the approach was found to work well in a study of Sudanese refugees (Neuner, Schauer, Klaschik, et al., 2004). Despite the success of this approach, there has been a great deal of controversy over another treatment of PTSD. See Focus on Discovery 7.2 for more discussion of these controversies.

Therapists have also used virtual reality (VR) technology to treat PTSD, because this technology can provide more vivid exposure than some clients may be able to generate in their imaginations. In one study, Vietnam veterans with PTSD benefited from taking a VR helicopter trip replete with the sounds of battle (Rothbaum, Hodges, Alarcon, et al., 1999).

Exposure therapy is hard for both the patient and the therapist because it requires such intense contact with traumatizing events. For example, women who have developed PTSD after rape might be asked to relive the fearsome events of the attack, imagining them in vivid detail (Rothbaum & Foa, 1993). The patient's symptoms may even increase temporarily in the initial stages of therapy (Keane, Gerardi, Quinn, et al., 1992). Treatment is likely to be particularly hard and to require more time when the client has experienced recurrent traumas, which is often the case with child abuse.

FOCUS ON DISCOVERY 7.2

Eye Movement Desensitization and Reprocessing

In 1989, Francine Shapiro began to promulgate an approach to trauma treatment called eye movement desensitization and reprocessing (EMDR). In this procedure, the person imagines a situation related to the trauma, such as seeing a horrible automobile accident. Keeping the image in mind, the person visually tracks the therapist's fingers as the therapist moves them back and forth about a foot in front of the person's eyes. This process continues for a minute or so, or until the person reports that the image is becoming less painful. At this point, the therapist tells the person to say whatever negative thoughts he or she is having, while continuing to track the therapist's fingers. Finally, the therapist tells the person to think a positive thought (e.g., "I can deal with this") and to hold this thought in mind, still tracking the therapist's fingers. This treatment, then, consists of classic imaginal exposure techniques, along with the extra technique of eye movement. Studies in which EMDR was used to treat people with PTSD have reported dramatically rapid symptom relief (van der Kolk, Spinazzola, Blaustein, et al., 2007). EMDR proponents argue that the eye movements promote rapid extinction of the conditioned fear and correction of mistaken beliefs about fear-provoking stimuli (Shapiro, 1999). The claims of dramatic efficacy have extended to disorders other than PTSD, including attention-deficit/hyperactivity disorder, dissociative disorders, panic disorder, public-speaking fears, test anxiety, and specific phobias (Lohr, Tolin, & Lilienfeld, 1998).

Despite the remarkable claims about this approach, several studies have indicated that the eye movement component of treatment is not necessary. For example, one researcher developed a version of EMDR that included all its techniques except eye movement and then conducted a study in which people were randomly assigned to receive either a version without eye movement or a version with eye movement (Pitman, Orr, Altman, et al., 1996). The two groups achieved similar symptom relief. Since the time of this study, findings from a series of studies have found that this therapy is no more effective than traditional cognitive behavioral treatment of PTSD (Seidler & Wagner, 2006). Some have argued that EMDR should not be offered as a treatment because the eye movement component is not supported either by studies or by adequate theoretical explanations (Goldstein, de Beurs, Chambless, et al., 2000).

Several cognitive strategies have been used to supplement exposure treatment for PTSD. Interventions designed to bolster people's beliefs in their ability to cope with the initial trauma have been shown to fare well in a series of studies (Keane, Marshall, & Taft, 2006), even when patients are experiencing comorbid conditions (Gillespie, Duffy, Hackmann, et al., 2002). Cognitive processing therapy is designed to help victims of rape and childhood sexual abuse dispute tendencies toward self-blame. This approach has also received empirical support (Chard, 2005; Resick, Nishith, Weaver, et al., 2002) and appears to be particularly helpful in reducing guilt (Resick, Nishith, & Griffin, 2003). Research has been mixed about whether cognitive therapy provides benefit above and beyond exposure treatment for addressing other symptoms of PTSD (Foa, Cahill, Boscarino, et al., 2005).

Psychological Treatment of Acute Stress Disorder Is it possible to prevent the development of PTSD by offering treatment to people who have developed acute stress disorder (ASD)? Short-term (five or six session) cognitive behavioral approaches that include exposure appear to do so. For example, Richard Bryant and colleagues (1999) found that early intervention decreased the risk that ASD would develop into PTSD. The success of this approach has now been replicated across five studies. Findings of a meta-analysis indicate that risk of PTSD among those who received exposure therapy was reduced to 32 percent, as compared to 58 percent for those who were assigned to a control condition (Kornør, Winje, Ekeberg, et al., 2008).

The positive effects of these early interventions appear to last for years. Researchers examined the effect of treatment on symptoms over a 5 year period among adolescents who had survived a devastating earthquake. Even 5 years after the earthquake, adolescents who had received cognitive behavioral intervention reported less severe PTSD symptoms than did those who had not received treatment (Goenjian, Walling, Steinberg, et al., 2005).

Exposure treatment appears to be more effective than cognitive restructuring in preventing the development of PTSD (Bryant, Mastrodomenico, Felmingham, et al., 2008). Unfortunately, not all approaches to prevention seem to work as well as exposure treatment (see Focus on Discovery 7.3).

FOCUS ON DISCOVERY 7.3

Critical Incident Stress Debriefing

Critical incident stress debriefing (CISD) involves immediate treatment of trauma victims within 72 hours of the traumatic event (Mitchell & Everly, 2000). Unlike cognitive behavioral treatment, the therapy is usually limited to one long session and is given regardless of whether the person has developed symptoms. Therapists encourage people to remember the details of the trauma and to express their feelings as fully as they can. Therapists who practice this approach often visit disaster sites immediately after events—sometimes invited by local authorities (as in the aftermath of the World Trade Center attack) and sometimes not; they offer therapy both to victims and to their families.

Like EMDR, CISD is highly controversial. A review of six studies, all of which included randomly assigning clients to receive CISD or no treatment, found that those who received CISD tended to fare worse (Litz, Gray, Bryant, et al., 2002). No one is certain why harmful effects occur, but remember that many people who experience a trauma do not develop PTSD. Many experts are dubious about the idea of providing therapy for people who have not developed a disorder. Some researchers raise the objection to CISD that a person's natural coping strategies may work better than those recommended by someone else (Bonanno, Wortman, Lehman, et al., 2002).

Check Your Knowledge 7.3

Answer the questions.

1. List two major risk factors that contribute specifically to PTSD (as opposed to increasing general risk for anxiety disorders).
2. In conducting exposure treatment for PTSD, ___exposure is sometimes used because _____ exposure cannot be conducted for experiences as horrific as war and rape.

3. Cognitive therapy when added to exposure for PTSD is particularly helpful in addressing (choose the answer that best fits):
   a. suicidal tendencies
   b. risk of relapse
   c. depersonalization
   d. guilt

Summary

Obsessive-Compulsive and Related Disorders

- People with obsessive-compulsive disorder (OCD) have intrusive, unwanted thoughts and feel pressure to engage in rituals to avoid overwhelming anxiety. People with body dysmorphic disorder (BDD) experience persistent and severe thoughts that they have a flawed appearance. Hoarding disorder is characterized by tendencies to acquire an excessive number of objects and extreme difficulties in ridding oneself of those objects.
- Family history studies suggest that there may be some shared genetic risk across these three disorders. OCD has been robustly linked to activity in the orbitofrontal cortex, the caudate nucleus, and the anterior cingulate. BDD also involves hyperactivity in regions of the orbitofrontal cortex and the caudate nucleus.
- OCD is moderately heritable. Tendencies toward repetitive thought and behavior in OCD may be intensified by a lack of yedasentience. In behavioral accounts, compulsions are considered avoidance responses that are reinforced because they provide relief from anxiety. Compulsions are repeated in part because the person doubts his or her memory of checking. Obsessions may be intensified by attempts to suppress unwanted thoughts, in part because people with OCD seem to feel that thinking about something is as bad as doing it.
- The cognitive model relates BDD to a detail-oriented analytic style, an overvaluing of the importance of appearance to self-worth, and too much attention to cues related to appearance. Behavioral factors include an excessive engagement in appearance-related activities, coupled with avoidance of situations that might expose people to evaluations of their appearance.
- Cognitive behavioral risk factors for hoarding include poor organizational abilities, unusual beliefs about the importance of possessions and responsibility for those possessions, and avoidance behaviors.
- ERP is a well-validated approach for the treatment of OCD that involves exposure, along with strategies to prevent engaging in compulsive behaviors. ERP has been adapted for the treatment of BDD and hoarding. For the treatment of BDD, ERP is supplemented with cognitive strategies to challenge people's overly negative views of their appearance, their excessive focus on their appearance, and their beliefs that self-worth depends on their appearance. For hoarding disorder, ERP is supplemented with strategies to increase insight and motivation.
- SRIs are the most tested medications for OCD, body dysmorphic disorder, and hoarding disorder. SSRIs also appear helpful, but less research is available. No randomized controlled trial has been conducted to examine treatment for hoarding disorder.

Trauma-Related Disorders

- Posttraumatic stress disorder (PTDS) is diagnosed only after a traumatic event. It is marked by symptoms of reexperiencing the trauma, arousal, and avoidance or emotional numbing. Acute stress disorder (ASD) is defined by similar symptoms, but dissociative symptoms must be present and the symptoms last less than one month.
- Many of the risk factors involved in anxiety disorders are related to the development of PTSD, such as genetic vulnerability, hyperactivity of the amygdala, childhood trauma exposure, neuroticism, attention to negative cues in the environment, and behavioral conditioning. Research and theory on the causes that are specific to PTSD focus on risk factors such as small hippocampal volume, the severity and nature of the traumatic event, dissociation, and other factors that may influence the ability to cope with stress, such as social support and intelligence.
- SSRIs are the most supported medication approach for PTSD.
- Psychological treatment of PTSD involves exposure, but often imaginal exposure is used. Psychological interventions for ASD can reduce the risk that PTSD will develop.

Answers to Check Your Knowledge Questions

7.1. 1. no diagnosis (because symptoms do not lead to impairment); 2. body dysmorphic disorder; 3. hoarding disorder

7.2. 1. any three of these: (a) all share symptoms of uncontrollable repetitive thoughts and behavior; (b) the syndromes often co-occur; (c) people with BDD and hoarding disorder often have a family history of OCD; (d) all three conditions respond to SRIs; (e) all three conditions respond to exposure and response prevention; 2. clomipramine; 3. exposure and response prevention

7.3. 1. any two of the following: small volume of the hippocampus; coping strategies that prevent processing the trauma, such as dissociation; low IQ; poor social support; 2. imaginal, in vivo; 3. d

Key Terms

8 Dissociative Disorders and Somatic Symptom Disorders

1. Be able to define the symptoms of the dissociative and somatic symptom disorders.
2. Be able to summarize current debate regarding the etiology of dissociative identity disorder.
3. Be able to explain the etiological models of the somatic symptom disorders.
4. Be able to describe the available treatments for dissociative and somatic symptom disorders.

Clinical Case: Gina

In December 1965, Dr. Robert Jeans was consulted by a woman named Gina Rinaldi, who had been referred to him by her friends. Gina, single and 31 years old, lived with another single woman and was working successfully as a writer at a large educational publishing firm. She was considered to be efficient, businesslike, and productive, but her friends had observed that she was becoming forgetful and sometimes acted out of character. The youngest of nine siblings, Gina reported that she had been sleepwalking since her early teens; her present roommate had told her that she sometimes screamed in her sleep.

Gina described her 74-year-old mother as the most domineering woman she had ever known. She reported that as a child she had been a fearful and obedient daughter. At age 28 she had an "affair," her first, with a former Jesuit priest, although it was apparently not sexual in nature. Then she became involved with T.C., a married man who assured her he would get a divorce and marry her. She indicated that she had been faithful to him since the start of their relationship. T.C., however, fell out of her favor as he did not come through with his promised divorce and stopped seeing Gina regularly.

After several sessions with Gina, Dr. Jeans began to notice a second personality emerging. Mary Sunshine, as she came to be called by Jeans and Gina, was quite different from Gina. She seemed more childlike, more traditionally feminine, ebullient, and seductive. Gina felt that she walked like a coal miner, but Mary certainly did not. Some concrete incidents indicated Mary's existence. Sometimes while cleaning her home, Gina found cups that had had hot chocolate in them—neither Gina nor her roommate liked hot chocolate. There were large withdrawals from Gina's bank account that she could not remember making. She even discovered herself ordering a sewing machine on the telephone, although she disliked sewing; some weeks later, she arrived at her therapy session wearing a new dress that Mary had sewn. At work, Gina reported, people were finding her more pleasant, and her colleagues took to consulting her on how to encourage people to work better with one another. All these phenomena were entirely alien to Gina. Jeans and Gina came to realize that sometimes Gina was transformed into Mary.

More and more often, Jeans witnessed Gina turning into Mary in the consulting room. T.C. accompanied Gina to a session during which her posture and demeanor became more relaxed, her tone of voice warmer. At another session Mary was upset and, as Jeans put it, chewed off Gina's fingernails. Then the two of them started having conversations with each other in front of Jeans.

A year after the start of therapy, an apparent synthesis of Gina and Mary began to emerge. At first it seemed that Gina had taken over entirely, but then Jeans noticed that Gina was not as serious as before, particularly about "getting the job done," that is, working extremely hard on the therapy. Jeans encouraged Gina to talk with Mary. The following is that conversation:

I was lying in bed trying to go to sleep. Someone started to cry about T.C. I was sure that it was Mary. I started to talk to her. The person told me that she didn't have a name. Later she said that Mary called her Evelyn. I was suspicious at first that it was Mary pretending to be Evelyn. I changed my mind, however, because the person I talked to had too much sense to be Mary. She said that she realized that T.C. was unreliable but she still loved him and was very lonely. She agreed that it would be best to find a reliable man. She told me that she comes out once a day for a very short time to get used to the world. She promised that she will come out to see you [Jeans] sometime when she is stronger. (Jeans, 1976, pp. 254–255)

Throughout January, Evelyn appeared more and more often, and Jeans felt that his patient was improving rapidly. Within a few months, she seemed to be Evelyn all the time; soon thereafter, this woman married a physician. Now, years later, she has had no recurrences of the other personalities. (Drawn from "The Three Faces of Evelyn," which appeared in 1976 in the *Journal of Abnormal Psychology*.)

IN THIS CHAPTER, WE discuss the dissociative disorders and the somatic symptom disorders. In early versions of the DSM, these disorders and the anxiety disorders were all classified together as neuroses, because anxiety was considered the predominant cause of these symptoms. Signs of anxiety, however, are not always observable in the dissociative and somatic symptom disorders, whereas anxiety is always clearly present in the anxiety disorders. Starting with DSM-III, in which classification is based on observable symptoms instead of presumed etiology, the diagnostic category of neurosis was abandoned, and somatic symptom disorders (formerly called somatoform disorders) and dissociative disorders became diagnostic categories separate from each other and from the anxiety disorders.

We cover dissociative disorders and somatic symptom disorders together in this chapter because both types of disorders are hypothesized to be related to some stressful experience, yet symptoms do not involve direct expressions of anxiety. In the dissociative disorders, the person experiences disruptions of consciousness—he or she loses track of self-awareness, memory, and identity. In the somatic symptom disorders, the person complains of bodily symptoms that suggest a physical defect or dysfunction, sometimes dramatic in nature. For some of these, no physiological basis can be found, and for others, the psychological reaction to the symptoms appears excessive.

Beyond the idea that both types of disorders are related to stress, it is worth noting that dissociative and somatic symptom disorders tend to be comorbid. Patients with dissociative disorders often meet criteria for somatic symptom disorders, and vice versa—those with somatic symptom disorders often meet the diagnostic criteria for dissociative disorders (Brown, Cardena, Nijenhuis, et al., 2007).

Dissociative Disorders

The proposed DSM-5 includes three major **dissociative disorders**: dissociative amnesia, depersonalization/derealization disorder, and dissociative identity disorder (formerly known as multiple personality disorder). Table 8.1 summarizes the key clinical features of the DSM-5 dissociative disorders and the major changes in the DSM-5 diagnoses of those disorders. Figure 8.1 shows the correspondence between DSM-IV-TR and DSM-5 disorders. The dissociative disorders are all presumed to be caused by a common mechanism, dissociation, which results in some aspects of cognition or experience being inaccessible consciously. Thus, dissociation involves the failure of consciousness to perform its usual role of integrating our cognitions, emotions, motivations, and other aspects of experience in our awareness. Some mild dissociative states are very common—in one example of a loss of self-awareness, a preoccupied person may miss a turn on the road home when thinking about problems. In contrast to common dissociative experiences like these, dissociative disorders are thought to result from extremely high levels of dissociation. Both psychodynamic and behavioral theorists consider pathological dissociation to be an avoidance response that protects the person from consciously experiencing stressful events. Among people undergoing very intense stressors, such as advanced military survival training, many report brief moments of mild dissociation (Morgan, Hazlett, Wang, et al., 2001).

Researchers know less about dissociative disorders compared to other disorders, and there is a great deal of controversy about the risk factors for these disorders, as well as the best treatments. To some, this controversy may seem daunting. We believe, however, that issues like this make a fascinating focus, as researchers strive to untangle a complex puzzle. Because so little is known about dissociative disorders, though, we will focus on one of these disorders in more depth: dissociative identity disorder.

Few high-quality studies have been done of the prevalence of the dissociative disorders; perhaps the best study to date found lifetime prevalence rates of 7.0 percent and 2.4 percent for dissociative amnesia and depersonalization disorder, respectively (Ross, 1991). Other studies, though, have obtained much lower estimates of the prevalence of this diagnosis in clinical practice. In a study involving less-structured diagnostic interviews of more than 11,000 psychiatric outpatients, about one in a thousand patients was diagnosed with a dissociative disorder (Mezzich, Fabrega, Coffman, et al., 1989).

Table 8.1 Diagnoses of Dissociative Disorders

DSM-5 Diagnosis	Description	Likely Key Changes in DSM-5
Dissociative amnesia	• Lack of conscious access to memory, typically of a stressful experience. The fugue subtype involves loss of memory for one's entire past or identity.	• Fugue is now a subtype of dissociative amnesia, rather than a separate diagnosis
Depersonalization/ derealization disorder	• Alteration in the experience of the self and reality	• Derealization added as a symptom
Dissociative identity disorder	• At least two distinct personalities that act independently of each other	• Wording of criteria changed to be more specific • Added criterion that symptoms are not part of a broadly recognized cultural or religious practice

Dissociation and Memory

Dissociative disorders raise fundamental questions about how memory works under stress. Psychodynamic theory suggests that in dissociative disorders, traumatic events are repressed. In this model, memories are forgotten (i.e., dissociated) because they are so aversive. There is considerable debate about whether repression occurs. Cognitive scientists have questioned how this could happen, because research shows that extreme stress usually enhances rather than impairs memory (Shobe & Kihlstrom, 1997). For example, children who go through extremely painful medical procedures have accurate, detailed memories of the experience. The nature of attention and memory, however, does change during periods of intense stress. Memory for emotionally relevant stimuli is enhanced by stress, while memory for neutral

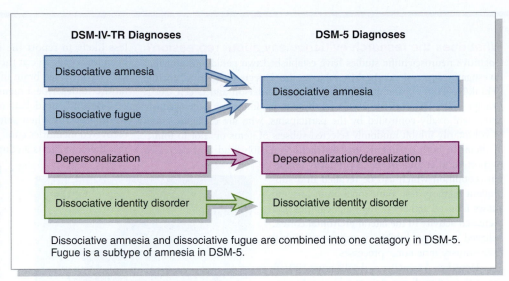

Figure 8.1 Diagnoses of dissociative disorders.

stimuli is impaired (Jelicic, Geraerts, Merckelbach, et al., 2004). People under stress tend to focus on the central features of the threatening situation and to stop paying attention to peripheral features (McNally, 2003). For example, people might remember every detail about a gun that was trained on them yet be unable to remember the face of the person who held the gun. On recall, then, they are likely to be unable to connect all aspects of the stressful situation into a coherent whole.

Given that the usual response to trauma is enhanced memory of the central features of the threat, how does the stress-related memory loss arise that we seem to see in the dissociative disorders? One answer might be that dissociative disorders involve unusual ways of responding to stress—for example, extremely high levels of stress hormones could interfere with memory formation (Andreano & Cahill, 2006). Some theorists believe that severe dissociation could interfere with memory. That is, in the face of severe trauma, memories may be stored in such a way that they are not accessible to awareness later when the person has returned to a more normal state (Kihlstrom, Tataryn, & Holt, 1993). Dissociative disorders are considered an extreme outcome of this process. Debate continues about how to understand memory in the context of trauma and dissociation (see Focus on Discovery 8.1).

FOCUS ON DISCOVERY 8.1

Debates about Repression: Memories of Abuse in Childhood

A history of severe abuse in childhood is thought to be an important cause of dissociative disorders. About 13.5% of women and 2.5% of men report that they have experienced some form of childhood sexual abuse (CSA; (Molnar, Buka, & Kessler, 2001)) and more have experienced other forms of abuse. Almost all people diagnosed with dissociative identity disorder report a history of abuse. There is no debate that abuse happens all too often, and that it can have profound effects on mental health and well-being.

Here, we focus on recovered memories of childhood abuse—that is, on cases in which a person has no memory of being abused as a child but then "recovers" the memories. Few issues are more hotly debated in psychology than whether these recovered memories are real. On one side, some argue that these recovered memories provide evidence for repression. Repression, as initially defined by Freud, involves suppressing unacceptably painful memories from consciousness. Although individuals

are unable to consciously recollect these memories, they continue to exert an unconscious effect which dramatically influences subsequent life in the form of, for example, by uncontrollable dissociative flashbacks, panic attacks, or psychosomatic symptoms.

Dissociation, on the other hand, is the process by which aspects of a traumatic event(s) are stored in an "unconscious" memory system. The mechanism by which this happens goes something like this: when experiences of childhood abuse involving extremely negative emotions cannot be integrated within a self-referential process and a coherent narrative can't be built, traumatic memories become dissociated and stored in a system with no direct verbal access. Brewin (2001, 2003) uses the term "situationally accessible memory" to denote the memory system where such dissociated elements are stored. Verbal memories of the traumatic event are often vague and include gaps.

What does the research evidence say about repression?

Cognitive neuroscientific studies have established two paradigms aimed at investigating repression in healthy subjects, the "Directed forgetting" and the "Think/No-Think" paradigm (Johnson, 1994; Anderson and Green, 2001; Erdelyi, 2006; Depue et al., 2007). In these tasks, forgetting is consciously and intentionally controlled by the participants, who are explicitly asked to voluntarily inhibit randomly selected subsets of items or "not to think" of them. In both paradigms, the instructions reliably lead to a decreased proportion of stimuli in the "voluntarily forgotten" condition which can be recalled in a subsequent memory test. Functional brain imaging shows reduced activity in the hippocampus and increased activity in the lateral prefrontal cortex, believed to reflect inhibitory executive control over primary mnemonic processes.

However, Axmacher and colleagues (2010) argue these paradigms do not adequately capture the clinical process of repression:

- Repression occurs specifically in situations which overload the executive processing capacities. During real repression, voluntary control is lacking; a person represses an experience because this experience induces an unbearable conflict. Therefore, attempting to induce repression by a recruitment of executive control processes is paradoxical. By this token, the process investigated using these paradigms should more precisely be termed the voluntary forgetting of unwanted content.

- If the mechanism of repression is considered in isolation, it appears as if the contents of repression are only secondary. However, repression doesn't occur with regard to random situations or stimuli, but only if an intense negative emotion is evoked. Thus, repression should be automatically induced by the experimental stimuli.

- A repression paradigm should not only reduce conscious access to "repressed" stimuli, but also exclude the possibility that these stimuli are just forgotten and show that unconscious memory for these items is enhanced.

Studying traumas outside the lab

To understand more about memories for highly painful events, some researchers have studied memory for traumas that occurred outside of the laboratory setting. In one study of whether memories of abuse can be forgotten, 94% of people with documented abuse still reported a memory of the abuse when they were asked about it almost 15 years later (Goodman, Ghetti, Quas et al., 2003). On the other hand, 6% of people reported that they had no memory of abuse. Even for those 6% of people, the lack of reported recall might reflect many processes other than repression. People might not want to discuss such distressing events during an interview. Some people might have been too young at the time of the abuse to be able to remember the events—people were

less likely to report the memory at the 15-year follow-up if they had been under age five at the time the abuse occurred. Some of the traumas may have caused brain injury that could cause gaps in memory. Thus, a failure to describe a memory may not be the same thing as repression.

Beyond the debate about whether repression occurs, how should we interpret it when someone develops a new memory? Where could recovered memories come from, if not from actual experiences? A leading researcher suggests a couple possibilities (Loftus, 1993):

Studies of memory show that recall of even a major event such as the terrorist attacks on 9/11/2001 can be considerably distorted. (© Robert Essel NYC/©Corbis.)

- **Popular writings.** The Courage to Heal (Bass & Davis, 1994) is an extremely popular guide for victims of CSA. It repeatedly suggests to readers that they were probably abused and offers as signs of abuse low self-esteem, feeling different from others, substance abuse, sexual dysfunction, and depression. The problem is that symptoms such as these can result from many factors other than CSA.

- **Therapists' suggestions.** By their own accounts (Poole, Lindsay, Memon et al., 1995), many therapists who genuinely believe that adult disorders result from abuse will suggest to their clients that they were probably sexually abused as children; sometimes the therapist does this with the assistance of hypnotic age regression and guided imagery (Poole et al., 1995).

Not only do memory distortions occur, but once they do, they hold emotional power. In one study, researchers interviewed people who reported having been abducted by space aliens (a presumably false memory). While participants talked about the experience, the researchers recorded heart rate, sweating, and other signs of arousal. People describing their abduction demonstrated just as much arousal as others did when they recounted experiences of war or trauma (McNally, Lasko, Clancy et al., 2004). Even false memories, then, can be associated with a lot of pain!

There is little doubt that abuse occurs. But we must be wary of uncritically accepting reports of abuse. This is an important issue, because recovered memories of abuse have been used in many court cases (Pope, 1998). In a typical scenario, a woman recovers a memory during psychotherapy, accuses one of her parents of having abused her during childhood, and brings charges against the parent. The repressed memory concept came into wider public awareness in the 1980s, but by the late 1990s, the tide had turned, and many courts refused to allow testimony based on recovered memories after a series of scandals and lawsuits (Piper, Pope, & Borowiecki J. J., 2000). One such example is the case of former nun Nora Wall. On the 16th of December 2005 the Irish Court of Criminal Appeal issued a certificate confirming a Miscarriage of Justice for Nora Wall's 1999 conviction for child rape, which was partly based on repressed memory evidence. The judgement stated that: "There was no scientific evidence of any sort adduced to explain the phenomenon of 'flashbacks' and/or 'retrieved memory', nor was the applicant in any position to meet such a case in the absence of prior notification thereof."

Dissociative Amnesia

As illustrated in the clinical case of Burt/Gene described on the next page, the person with **dissociative amnesia** is unable to recall important personal information, usually information about some traumatic experience. The holes in memory are too extensive to be explained by ordinary forgetfulness. The information is not permanently lost, but it cannot be retrieved during the episode of amnesia, which may last for as short a period as several hours or as long as several years. The amnesia usually disappears as suddenly as it began, with complete recovery and only a small chance of recurrence.

Most often the memory loss involves information about some part of a traumatic experience, such as witnessing the sudden death of a loved one. More rarely the amnesia is for entire events during a circumscribed period of distress. During the period of amnesia the person's behavior is otherwise unremarkable, except that the memory loss may cause some disorientation.

In a more severe subtype of amnesia called **fugue** (from the Latin *fugere*, "to flee"), the memory loss is more extensive. As in the Clinical Case of Burt/Gene below, the person not only becomes totally amnesic but suddenly leaves home and work and assumes a new identity. Sometimes the person takes on a new name, a new home, a new job, and even a new set of personality characteristics. The person may even succeed in establishing a fairly complex social life. More often, however, the new life does not crystallize to this extent, and the fugue is of relatively brief duration, consisting for the most part of limited but apparently purposeful travel, during which social contacts are minimal or absent. As in other forms of amnesia, recovery is usually complete, although it takes varying amounts of time; after recovery, people are fully able to remember the details of their life and experiences, except for those events that took place during the fugue. The first documented case of dissociative fugue appeared in the medical literature in 1887 in France. The case received widespread attention at medical conferences, and a small epidemic of fugue cases were reported throughout Europe in the years that followed (Hacking, 1998).

The pattern of memory deficits in dissociative amnesia highlights an important distinction. Typically, dissociative disorders involve deficits in explicit memory but not implicit memory. **Explicit memory** involves the *conscious* recall of experiences—for example, explicit memory would be involved in describing a bicycle you had as a child. **Implicit memory** involves learning based on experiences that are not consciously recalled—for example, implicit memory of how to ride a bike underlies the behavior of actually riding one. There are numerous examples of patients with dissociative disorders whose implicit memory remained intact (Kihlstrom, 1994). One woman, for example, became amnesic after being victimized by a practical joke. She had no explicit memory of the event, but she became terrified when passing the location of the incident (implicit memory). We will discuss some intriguing tests of implicit memory when we discuss the etiology of dissociative identity disorder.

In diagnosing dissociative amnesia, it is important to rule out other common causes of memory loss, such as dementia and substance abuse. Dementia can be fairly easily distinguished from dissociative amnesia. In dementia, memory fails slowly over time, is not linked to stress, and is accompanied by other cognitive deficits, such as an inability to learn new information. Memory loss after a brain injury or substance abuse can be linked to the time of the injury or substance use.

Amnesia can occur after a person has experienced some severe stress, such as marital discord, personal rejection, financial or occupational difficulties, war service, or a natural disaster,

---

Proposed DSM-5 Criteria for Dissociative Amnesia

- Inability to remember important personal information, usually of a traumatic or stressful nature, that is too extensive to be ordinary forgetfulness
- The amnesia is not explained by substances, or by other medical or psychological conditions
- *Specify dissociative fugue subtype if:*
  - *the amnesia includes inability to recall one's past, confusion about identity, or assumption of a new identity, and*
  - *sudden, unexpected travel away from home or work*

Note: Changes from DSM-IV-TR are italicized.

Clinical Case: Burt/Gene

A 42-year-old male was brought to the emergency room by the police after he was involved in a fight at the diner where he worked. The patient had given his name as Burt Tate, but when the police arrived he was unable to provide any identification. Several weeks before the fight, Burt had arrived in town and begun working as a short-order cook. He had no memory of where he had worked or lived before he had arrived in town.

At the emergency room, Burt could answer questions about the date and his location but could not remember anything about his previous life. He was not concerned by his memory gaps. There was no evidence that alcohol, drugs, head trauma, or any medical condition could explain the gaps in his memory. A missing person search revealed that he fit the description of a man named Gene who had disappeared a month before from a city about 200 miles away. Gene's wife was contacted, and she was able to confirm that "Burt" was her husband. Gene's wife explained that he had been experiencing considerable stress in his job as a manager at a manufacturing plant for 18 months leading up to his disappearance. Two days before his disappearance, Gene had a violent fight with his adolescent son, who called him a failure and moved out of the home. Gene claimed not to recognize his wife. [Adapted from Spitzer et al. (1994).]

In *Spellbound*, Gregory Peck played a man with amnesia. Dissociative amnesia is typically triggered by a stressful event, as it was in the film. (Springer/Corbis-Bettmann.)

but not all amnesias seem to immediately follow trauma (Hacking, 1998). It should also be noted that even among people who have experienced intense trauma, such as imprisonment in a concentration camp, dissociative amnesia and fugue are rare (Merckelbach, Dekkers, Wessel, et al., 2003).

Depersonalization/Derealization Disorder

In **depersonalization/derealization disorder,** the person's perception of the self or surroundings is disconcertingly and disruptively altered. The altered perceptions are usually triggered by stress. Unlike the other dissociative disorders in DSM-IV-TR, it involves no disturbance of memory. In depersonalization episodes, people rather suddenly lose their sense of self. This involves unusual sensory experiences. For example, their limbs may seem drastically changed in size or their voices may sound strange to them. They may have the impression that they are outside their bodies, viewing themselves from a distance. Sometimes they feel mechanical, as though they and others are robots.

Although the DSM-IV-TR diagnostic criteria included only one symptom to define this disorder—depersonalization—the proposed DSM-5 criteria include depersonalization, derealization, or both. Derealization refers to the sensation that the world has become unreal. The change in the DSM-5 criteria is based on the evidence that most people who experience depersonalization also experience derealization and that the course of symptoms is similar for both symptoms (Simeon, 2009).

The following quote, drawn from a 1953 medical textbook, captures some of the experience of this disorder:

> . . . the world appears strange, peculiar, foreign, dream-like. Objects appear at times strangely diminished in size, at times flat. Sounds appear to come from a distance. . . . The emotions likewise undergo marked alteration. Patients complain that they are capable of experiencing neither pain nor pleasure; love and hate have perished with them. They experience a fundamental change in their personality, and the climax is reached with their complaints that they have become strangers to themselves. It is as though they were dead, lifeless, mere automatons . . .
>
> (Schilder, 1953, p. 304–305)

Depersonalization/derealization disorder usually begins in adolescence, and it can start either abruptly or more insidiously. Once it begins, it has a chronic course—that is, it lasts a long time. Comorbid personality disorders are frequent, and during their lifetime, about two-thirds of people with this disorder will experience anxiety disorders and depression (Simeon, Gross, Guralnik, et al., 1997). As in the case of Mrs. A., described below, childhood trauma is often reported (Simeon, Guralnik, Schmeidler, et al., 2001).

The proposed DSM-5 diagnostic criteria for depersonalization/derealization disorder specify that the symptoms can co-occur with other disorders but should not be entirely explained by those disorders. It is important to rule out disorders that commonly involve these symptoms, including schizophrenia, posttraumatic stress disorder, and borderline personality disorder (Maldonado, Butler, & Spiegel, 1998). Depersonalization also can be triggered by hyperventilation, a common symptom of panic attacks.

Proposed DSM-5 Criteria for Depersonalization/ *Derealization* Disorder

- **Depersonalization:** Persistent or recurrent experiences of detachment from one's mental processes or body, as though one is in a dream, despite intact reality testing, or
- ***Derealization: persistent or recurrent experiences of unreality of surroundings***
- Symptoms are not explained by substances, another dissociative disorder, another psychological disorder, or by a medical condition

Note: Changes from DSM-IV-TR are italicized.

Clinical Case: Mrs. A.

Mrs. A was a 43-year-old woman who lived with her mother and son and worked in a clerical job. She had experienced symptoms of depersonalization several times per year for as long as she could remember. "It's as if the real me is taken out and put on a shelf or stored somewhere inside of me. Whatever makes me me is not there. It is like an opaque curtain . . . like going through the motions and having to exert discipline to keep the unit together." She had found these symptoms to be extremely distressing. She had experienced panic attacks for one year when she was 35. She described a childhood trauma history that included nightly genital fondling and frequent enemas by her mother from earliest memory to age 10. (Simeon et al., 1997, p. 1109)

Dissociative Identity Disorder

Consider what it would be like to have dissociative identity disorder (DID), as did Gina, the woman described at the opening of this chapter. People tell you about things you have done that seem out of character and interactions of which you have no memory. How can you explain these events?

Clinical Description of DID   According to the proposed DSM-5, a diagnosis of **dissociative identity disorder (DID)** requires that a person have at least two separate personalities, or alters—different modes of being, thinking, feeling, and acting that exist independently of one another and that emerge at different times. Each determines the person's nature and activities when it is in command. The primary alter may be totally unaware that the other alters exist and may have no memory of what those other alters do and experience when they are in control. Sometimes there is one primary personality, and this is typically the alter that seeks treatment. Usually, there are two to four alters at the time a diagnosis is made, but over the course of treatment others may emerge. The diagnosis also requires that the existence of different alters be chronic; it cannot be a temporary change resulting from the ingestion of a drug, for example.

Each alter may be quite complex, with its own behavior patterns, memories, and relationships. Usually the personalities of the different alters are quite different from one another, even polar opposites. Case reports have described alters who have different handedness, wear glasses with different prescriptions, like different foods, and have allergies to different substances. The alters are all aware of lost periods of time, and the voices of the others may sometimes echo in an alter's consciousness, even though the alter does not know to whom these voices belong.

DID usually begins in childhood, but it is rarely diagnosed until adulthood. It is more severe and extensive than the other dissociative disorders, and recovery may be less complete. It is much more common in women than in men. Other diagnoses are often present, including posttraumatic stress disorder, major depressive disorder, and somatic symptom disorders (Rodewald et al., 2011). DID is commonly accompanied by other symptoms such as headaches, hallucinations, suicide attempts, and self-injurious behavior, as well as by other dissociative symptoms such as amnesia and depersonalization (Scroppo, Drob, Weinberger, et al., 1998).

Cases of dissociative identity disorder are sometimes mislabeled in the popular press as schizophrenia (see Chapter 9), which derives part of its name from the Greek root *schizo*, which means "splitting away from"—hence the confusion. A split into two or more fairly separate and coherent personalities that exist alternately in the same person is entirely different from the symptoms of schizophrenia. People with DID do not show the thought disorder and behavioral disorganization characteristic of schizophrenia.

The inclusion of DID as a diagnosis in DSM is a matter of some controversy. For example, in a survey of board-certified psychiatrists, two-thirds reported reservations about the presence of DID in the DSM (Pope, Oliva, Hudson, et al., 1999). Students and the public often ask, "Does DID exist?" Clinicians can describe DID reliably; it "exists" in this sense. As we will discuss later, though, controversy swirls about the reasons these symptoms occur.

Proposed DSM-5 Criteria for Dissociative Identity Disorder

A. *Disruption of identity characterized by two or more distinct personality states (alters) or an experience of possession, as evidenced by discontinuities in sense of self, cognition, behavior, affect, perceptions, and/or memories. This disruption may be observed by others or reported by the patient.*

B. At least two of the alters recurrently take control of behavior

C. Inability of at least one of the alters to recall important personal information

D. *Symptoms are not part of a broadly accepted cultural or religious practice,* and are not due to drugs or a medical condition

Note: The DSM-IV-TR criterion A is less detailed. It specifies the presence of two or more identities or personality states (each with its own relatively enduring pattern of perceiving, relating to, and thinking about the environment and self). Other changes from DSM-IV-TR are italicized.

Check Your Knowledge 8.1 (Answers are at the end of the chapter.)

Answer the questions.

1. Dissociative amnesia fugue subtype is defined by:
   a. poor performance on neuropsychological tests
   b. assumption of a new identity
   c. symptoms of early dementia
   d. an acute confusion brought on by drug use
2. Most typically, dissociative amnesia involves being unable to remember:
   a. the entire life
   b. childhood

   c. a trauma
   d. life up until a trauma
3. In the context of dissociative identity disorder, *alter* refers to:
   a. extreme splitting
   b. a distinct personality
   c. the host personality
   d. the bridge between different personalities

In the film version of *Sybil,* about a famous case of dissociative identity disorder, the title role was played by Sally Field. (NBC/Photofest © NBC.)

The Epidemiology of DID: Increases over Time Although descriptions of anxiety, depression, and psychosis have abounded in literature from ancient times through today, there were no identified reports of DID or dissociative amnesia before 1800 (Pope, Poliakoff, Parker, et al., 2006). Reports of DID were relatively frequent between 1890 and 1920, with 77 case reports appearing in the literature during that time (Sutcliffe & Jones, 1962). After 1920, reports of DID declined until the 1970s, when they increased markedly, not only in the United States but also in countries such as Japan (Uchinuma & Sekine, 2000). In the 1990s, prevalence estimates were obtained in formal studies of 1.3 percent in Winnipeg, Canada and 0.4 percent in Sivas, Turkey (Akyuez, Dogan, Sar, et al., 1999; Ross, 1991). These figures are quite high comparatively—prevalence was earlier thought to be about one in a million.

What has caused the vast increases in the rates of the DID diagnosis over time? It is possible that more people began to experience symptoms of DID. But there are other possible explanations for the increase. DSM-III, which was published in 1980, defined the diagnosis of DID for the first time (Putnam, 1996). The popular 1973 book *Sybil* presented a dramatic case with 16 personalities (Schreiber, 1973). A series of other case reports were published in the 1970s as well. The case of Eve White, popularized in the book *The Three Faces of Eve* as well as a movie, provided a highly detailed report of DID. The diagnostic criteria and growing literature may have increased detection and recognition of symptoms. Indeed, in countries like China, where DID is not officially recognized as a diagnosis, rates of the disorder (per structured interview with patients being seen in clinics) are less than one-tenth what they are in countries like Canada where the diagnosis is officially recognized (Ross, 2008). Some critics hypothesize that the heightened diagnostic and media attention to this diagnosis led some therapists to suggest strongly to clients that they had DID, sometimes using hypnosis to probe for alters. It has even been claimed that in Sybil's case, the alters were created by a therapist who gave substance to Sybil's different emotional states by giving them names (Borch-Jacobsen, 1997). There has been significant controversy about *The Three Faces of Eve* as well.

Etiology of DID Almost all patients with DID report severe childhood abuse. There is also evidence that children who are abused are at risk for developing dissociative symptoms, although whether these symptoms reach diagnosable levels is not clear (Chu, 2000).

There are two major theories of DID: the **posttraumatic model** and the **sociocognitive model**. Despite their confusing names, both theories actually suggest that severe physical or sexual abuse during childhood sets the stage for DID. Since few people who are abused develop DID, both models focus on why some people do develop DID after abuse. As we will see, there is considerable debate between proponents of these two approaches regarding this issue.

The posttraumatic model proposes that some people are particularly likely to use dissociation to cope with trauma, and this is seen as a key factor in causing people to develop alters after trauma (Gleaves, 1996). There is evidence that children who dissociate are more likely to develop psychological symptoms after trauma (Kisiel & Lyons, 2001). But because DID is so rare, no prospective studies have focused on dissociative coping styles and the development of DID.

The other theory, the sociocognitive model, considers DID to be the result of learning to enact social roles. According to this model, alters appear in response to suggestions by therapists, exposure to media reports of DID, or other cultural influences (Lilienfeld, Lynn, Kirsch, et al., 1999; Spanos, 1994). An important implication of this model, then, is that DID could be created within therapy. This does not mean, however, that DID is viewed as conscious deception; the issue is not whether DID is real but how it develops.

A leading advocate of the idea that DID is basically a role-play suggests that people with histories of trauma may be particularly likely to have a rich fantasy life, to have had considerable practice at imagining they are other people, and to have a deep desire to please others (Spanos, 1994). Lilienfeld and colleagues (1999) note that many of the therapeutic techniques being used with DID reinforce clients for identifying different alters; this researcher argues that repeated probing and reinforcement for describing alters may promote these symptoms in vulnerable people. The clinical case of Elizabeth provides an extreme example of a therapist who unwittingly encourages her client to adopt a diagnosis of DID when it isn't justified by the symptoms. All of the symptoms

Clinical Case: Elizabeth, an Example of Unwarranted Diagnosis

In one book, a personal account was provided of a person who received a false diagnosis of DID. Elizabeth Carlson, a 35-year-old married woman, was referred to a psychiatrist after being hospitalized for severe depression. Elizabeth reported that soon after treatment began, her psychiatrist suggested to her that perhaps her problem was the elusive, often undiagnosed condition of multiple personality disorder [MPD, now referred to as DID]. Her psychiatrist reviewed "certain telltale signs of MPD. Did Carlson ever 'zone out' while driving and arrive at her destination without remembering how she got there? Why

yes, Carlson said. Well, that was an alter taking over the driving and then vanishing again, leaving her, the 'host' personality, to account for the blackout. Another sign of MPD [the psychiatrist said,] was 'voices in the head.' Did Carlson ever have internal arguments—for example, telling herself, 'Turn right' and then 'No, turn left'? Yes, Carlson replied, that happened sometimes. Well, that was the alters fighting with each other inside her head. Carlson was amazed and embarrassed. All these years, she had done these things, never realizing that they were symptoms of a severe mental disorder." (Acocella, 1999, p. 1)

that Elizabeth described are common experiences; indeed, none of the symptoms listed are actual diagnostic criteria for DID. According to this theory, people adopt the DID role when given suggestions by a therapist.

We will never have experimental evidence for either the posttraumatic model or the sociocognitive model, since it would be unethical to intentionally reinforce dissociative symptoms. Given this, what kinds of evidence have been raised in this debate?

DID Symptoms Can Be Role-Played It has been established that people are capable of role-playing the symptoms of DID. One relevant study was conducted in the 1980s after the trial of a serial murderer in California known as the Hillside strangler (Spanos, Weekes, & Bertrand, 1985). The accused murderer, Ken Bianchi, unsuccessfully pled not guilty by reason of insanity, claiming that the murders had been committed by an alter, Steve. (For a discussion of the insanity defense, see Chapter 16.)

In the study, undergraduate students were told that they would play the role of an accused murderer and that despite much evidence of guilt, a plea of not guilty had been entered. They were also told that they were to participate in a simulated psychiatric interview that might involve hypnosis. Then the students were taken to another room and introduced to the "psychiatrist," actually an experimental assistant. After a number of standard questions, the students were assigned to one of three experimental conditions. In the most important of these, the Bianchi condition, students were hypnotized and instructed to let a second personality come forward, just as had happened when Bianchi had been hypnotized. After the experimental manipulations, the possible existence of a second personality was probed directly by the "psychiatrist." In addition, students were asked questions about the facts of the murders. Finally, in a second session, those who acknowledged another personality were asked to take personality tests twice—once for each of their two personalities. Eighty-one percent of the students in the Bianchi condition adopted a new name, and many of these admitted guilt for the murders. Even the personality test results of the two personalities differed considerably.

Clearly, then, when the situation demands, people can adopt a second personality. However, this demonstration illustrates only that such role-playing is possible; it in no way demonstrates that DID results from role-playing.

Alters Share Memories, Even When They Report Amnesia One of the defining features of DID is the inability to recall information experienced by one alter when a different alter is present. Several studies suggest that even though different alters report being unable to share memories, they actually do share memories. Studies that demonstrate this use subtle tests of memory.

One group of researchers tested people with DID on implicit tests of memory (Huntjen, Postma, Peters, et al., 2003). In explicit memory

Roseanne Barr, a famous actress and comedian, talked about overcoming her history of dissociative identity disorder during an interview on the Larry King show (March 2, 2006). (Frederick M. Brown/Getty ImagesNews and Sport Services.)

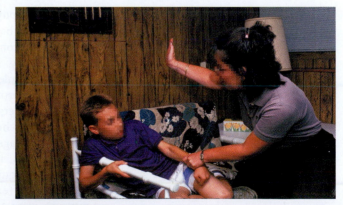

Physical or sexual abuse in childhood is regarded as a major factor in the development of dissociative disorders. (Robert Brenner/PhotoEdit.)

Ken Bianchi, a serial killer known as the Hillside strangler, unsuccessfully attempted an insanity defense. The jury decided that he was faking the symptoms of DID. (© AP/ Wide World Photos.)

tests, a person is taught a word list and then asked to recall the words at a second session. In implicit memory tests, experimenters determine if the word lists have subtler effects on performance. For example, if the first word list included the word *lullaby*, people might be quicker to identify *lullaby* as the word that fills in the puzzle l_l_a_y. Thirty-one people with DID were taught the initial word list and then asked to complete the implicit memory test when they returned to the second session as a different alter. The researchers focused analyses on the 21 participants who claimed at the second testing session that they had no memory of the first session. These 21 people performed comparably to people without DID on tests of implicit memory. That is, memories seemed to be transferred between alters.

Some authors have criticized this research, suggesting that DID might involve only deficits in explicit memories. In one study, researchers found evidence that alters also share explicit memories. Seven participants with DID who reported amnesia between alters were tested. At the first session, one alter was asked to listen to a set of words (list A) and to describe whether the words contained more than one syllable. At a second session with a different alter present, they were asked to state whether a second set of words contained more than one syllable (list B). Healthy controls also completed two sessions. All participants were then shown a series of words drawn from list A, list B, and new words, and asked to indicate whether or not each word had been present on list B. Most people will make errors on this test—shown a word from list A, they might mistakenly believe it was present on list B. If someone had no explicit memory of list A, then the words from list A shouldn't interfere like this. All of the participants diagnosed with DID reported that they had no memory of list A. Nonetheless, persons with DID demonstrated just as much interference from list A as did the control participants (Kong, Allen, & Glisky, 2008). The findings are supportive of a role-playing explanation of DID—people with DID demonstrated more accurate memories than they had acknowledged.

The Detection of DID Differs by Clinician A small number of clinicians contribute most of the diagnoses of DID within a time period. For example, a survey conducted in Switzerland found that 66 percent of the diagnoses of DID were made by fewer than 10 percent of the psychiatrists who responded (Modestin, 1992). In many centers, the diagnosis is not detected; in one study of initial diagnostic interviews of more than 11,000 outpatients at a major psychiatric center, DID was not diagnosed in a single case (Mezzich et al., 1989). Therapists who are most likely to diagnose DID tend to use hypnosis, to urge clients to try to unbury unremembered abuse experiences, or to name different alters. Proponents of the sociocognitive model argue that the extremes in diagnostic rates support the idea that certain clinicians are likely to elicit DID in their patients. Proponents of the posttraumatic model, however, point out that people with DID may be referred to clinicians who specialize in treating this condition (Gleaves, 1996). Once again, the data are inconclusive.

Many DID Symptoms Emerge after Treatment Starts Studies have shown that when patients with DID enter therapy, they are usually unaware of having alters. But as treatment progresses, they tend to become aware of alters, and they report a rapid increase in the number of alters they can identify. This pattern is consistent with the idea that treatment is evoking the DID symptoms (Lilienfeld et al., 1999). Proponents of posttraumatic theory, however, explain this pattern by suggesting that most alters began their existence during childhood and that therapy just allows the person to become aware of and describe alters.

One study, however, has provided evidence regarding childhood onset in cases of DID (Lewis, Yeager, Swica, et al., 1997). The study, which was conducted over a period of two decades, involved detailed examination of 150 convicted murderers. Fourteen of them were found to have DID. Eight of the 14 people had experienced trances during childhood (experiences that are frequently reported by people with DID). These symptoms were corroborated by at least three outside sources (e.g., by interviews with family members, teachers, and parole officers). Furthermore, several of the people with

Check Your Knowledge 8.2

True or false?
1. Prevalence of DID is currently at an all-time high.
2. Most people with DID report childhood abuse.

Fill in the blanks.
3. The _____ model of DID emphasizes role enactment, and the _____ model of DID emphasizes dissocation.

DID had shown distinctly different handwriting styles (consistent with the existence of alters) well before committing their crimes. The results of this study, then, support the idea that some symptoms begin in childhood for at least some people who are diagnosed with DID during adulthood. It is not clear, though, that the early symptoms included the presence of alters.

Treatment of DID There seems to be widespread agreement on several principles in the treatment of dissociative identity disorder, whatever the clinician's orientation (Kluft, 1994; Ross, 1989). These include an empathic and gentle stance, with the goal of helping the client function as one wholly integrated person. The goal of treatment should be to convince the person that splitting into different personalities is no longer necessary to deal with traumas. In addition, as DID is conceptualized as a means of escaping from severe stress, treatment can help teach the person more effective ways to cope with stress. Often, people with DID are hospitalized to help them avoid self-harm and to begin the treatment in a more intensive fashion.

Despite these common principles across treatment, there are important discrepancies across approaches. Psychodynamic treatment is probably used more for DID and the other dissociative disorders than for any other psychological disorders. The goal of this treatment is to overcome repressions (MacGregor, 1996), as DID is believed to arise from traumatic events that the person is trying to block from consciousness.

Unfortunately, some practitioners, particularly those who are drawing from a psychodynamic conceptualization, use hypnosis as a means of helping patients diagnosed with dissociative disorders to gain access to repressed material (Putnam, 1993). DID patients are unusually hypnotizable (Butler, Duran, Jasiukaitis, et al., 1996). Typically, the person is hypnotized and encouraged to go back in his or her mind to traumatic events in childhood—a technique called *age regression*. The hope is that accessing these traumatic memories will allow the person to realize that childhood threats are no longer present and that adult life need not be governed by these ghosts from the past (Grinker & Spiegel, 1944). Treatment involving age regression and recovered memories, though, can actually worsen DID symptoms (Fetkewicz, Sharma, & Merskey, 2000; Lilienfeld, 2007; Powell & Gee, 2000).

Because of the rarity of diagnosed cases of DID, there are no controlled studies of the results of treatment. Most of the reports come from the clinical observations of one highly experienced therapist, Richard Kluft (1994). The greater the number of alters, the longer the treatment lasted (Putnam, Guroff, Silberman, et al., 1986). In general, therapy took almost 2 years and upwards of 500 hours per patient. Years after treatment started, Kluft (1994) reported that 84 percent of an original 123 patients had achieved stable integration of alters and another 10 percent were at least functioning better. In a different follow-up study of 12 patients, 6 patients achieved full integration of their alters within a 10-year period (Coons & Bowman, 2001).

DID is often comorbid with anxiety and depression, which can sometimes be lessened with antidepressant medications. These medications have no effect on the DID itself, however (Simon, 1998).

Quick Summary

Dissociative disorders are defined on the basis of disruptions in consciousness, in which memories, self-awareness, or other aspects of cognition become inaccessible to the conscious mind. Dissociative amnesia is diagnosed based on the inability to recall important personal experience(s), usually of a traumatic nature. Dissociative fugue is a severe subtype of amnesia, in which the person not only has an inability to recall important information but also moves and assumes a new identity. In depersonalization/derealization disorder, the person's perception of the self and surroundings is altered; he or she may experience being outside the body or may perceive the world as being unreal. The person with dissociative identity disorder has two or more distinct personalities, each with unique memories, behavior patterns, and relationships.

Little research is available concerning the causes of these disorders. It is clear that DID is related to severe abuse, but considerable debate exists about the other causes of this disorder. The posttraumatic model suggests that DID is the result of using dissociation as a coping strategy to deal with the abuse. The sociocognitive model suggests that DID is caused by role-playing of symptoms among patients with a history of abuse and a deep need to satisfy authority figures like therapists. Proponents of the sociocognitive model note the dramatic shifts in diagnosis over time, the differences between clinicians in recognition of the disorder, the evidence that people can role-play symptoms of DID, the indications on subtle memory tests of alters sharing information that they deny awareness of, the findings that many people develop symptoms after treatment begins, and the indications that a small proportion of mental health providers provide most of the diagnoses of this condition.

Some mental health specialists have proposed strategies for treating DID that are reminiscent of the strategies used in treating PTSD. For example, in the safe, supportive context of therapy, patients are encouraged to think back to the traumatic events that are believed to have triggered their problems and to view those events with the expectation that they can come to terms with the horrible things that happened to them. Hypnosis and age regression techniques to recover memories are contra-indicated for DID.

Somatic Symptom Disorders

Somatic symptom disorders are defined by excessive concerns about physical symptoms or health. In DSM-IV-TR, these disorders were defined by physical symptoms that had no known physical cause, and they were labeled "somatoform" to capture the fact that the symptoms took the form of bodily (soma) sensations. Over time, it has become clear that it is close to impossible to distinguish whether some symptoms are biologically caused. Doctors often disagree on whether a symptom has a medical cause (Rief & Broadbent, 2007). Some people might have a condition that defies diagnosis because of limits in medical knowledge and technology. Indeed, most people experience at least one mild unexplained physical symptom at some point in their lifetime (Simon, Von Korff, Piccinelli, et al., 1999). The framers of DSM-5 took the bold step of removing the requirement that these symptoms be medically unexplained for some of these disorders. In the proposed DSM-5, complex somatic symptom disorder includes somatic symptoms regardless of whether they can be explained medically. To reflect this change, this set of disorders is called somatic symptom disorders in the proposed DSM-5.

As shown in Table 8.2, the proposed DSM-5 includes three major somatic symptom disorders: complex somatic symptom disorder, illness anxiety disorder, and functional neurological syndrome. Figure 8.3 shows the correspondence between DSM-IV-TR somatoform disorders and the proposed DSM-5 somatic symptom disorders. Complex somatic symptom disorder involves major distress or energy expenditure regarding a somatic symptom or symptoms. Illness anxiety disorder involves fears about having a major medical illness in the absence of somatic symptoms. Functional neurological syndrome involves neurological symptoms that are medically unexplained. Table 8.2 also lists malingering and factitious disorder, related disorders that we discuss in Focus on Discovery 8.2.

People with somatic symptom disorders tend to seek frequent medical treatment, sometimes at great expense. They often see several different physicians for a given health concern, and they may try many different medications. Hospitalization and even surgery are common. It has been estimated that somatic symptom disorders lead to medical expenditures of $256 billion per year in the United States (Barsky, Orav, & Bates, 2005). Although people with these disorders are the most frequent consumers of medical care, they are often dissatisfied with their medical care. For many, no medical explanation or cure can be identified. They often view their physicians as incompetent and uncaring (Persing, Stuart, Noyes, et al., 2000). Despite this, they will often continue extensive treatment seeking, visiting new doctors and demanding new tests. Many patients become unable to work because of the severity of their concerns.

Even though there is clear reason for concern about these syndromes, somatic symptom disorders have been criticized for several reasons:

- There is incredible diversity among people diagnosed with these conditions. For example, some people develop somatic symptoms in the context of anxiety and depressive disorders, whereas others do not (Lieb, Meinlschmidt, & Araya, 2007). Some may have medical conditions that provoke the symptoms; others may not.

- Complex somatic symptom disorder and illness anxiety disorder are defined by health concerns that are a cause of excessive anxiety or involve too much expenditure of time and energy. These are very subjective criteria. What is the threshold for too much concern or too much energy expenditure?

- The diagnoses of somatic symptom disorders are often considered stigmatizing by patients and by clinicians. Perhaps because of these concerns, the DSM-IV-TR diagnoses of somatoform disorders were rarely applied, even when the symptoms seemed to fit the diagnostic criteria. The DSM-5 committee on somatic symptom disorders made two changes in hopes of addressing stigma: they removed the criterion that symptoms be medically unexplained from complex somatic symptom disorder and they changed the name of this set of disorders from somatoform to somatic symptom disorders. It is too soon to tell whether the DSM-5 diagnoses will be adopted in clinical practice.

Table 8.2 Diagnoses of Somatic Symptom and Related Disorders

Proposed DSM-5 Diagnosis	Description	Likely Key Changes in DSM-5
Complex somatic symptom disorder	Somatic symptom(s) Excessive thoughts, feelings, and behaviors related to somatic symptoms	• Symptoms do not have to be medically unexplained • Pain is now a specifier, not a separate diagnosis
Illness anxiety disorder	Unwarranted fears about a serious illness despite absence of any significant somatic symptoms	• New diagnosis
Functional neurological disorder	Neurological symptom(s) that cannot be explained by medical disease or culturally sanctioned behavior	• Name of disorder changed from conversion disorder • Removed criterion that the clinician establish that the patient is not feigning symptoms • Removed criterion that psychological risk factors be apparent • Emphasized the importance of neurological testing
Malingering	Intentionally faking psychological or somatic symptoms to gain from those symptoms	
Factitious disorder	Falsification of psychological or physical symptoms, without evidence of gains from those symptoms	

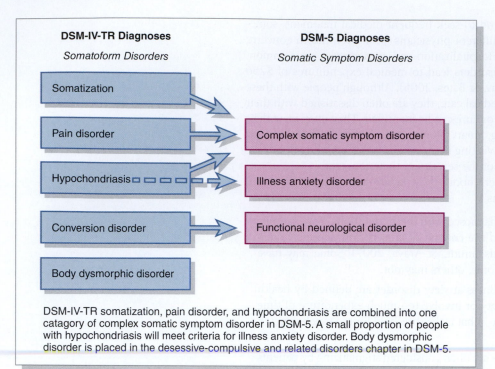

DSM-IV-TR somatization, pain disorder, and hypochondriasis are combined into one catagory of complex somatic symptom disorder in DSM-5. A small proportion of people with hypochondriasis will meet criteria for illness anxiety disorder. Body dysmorphic disorder is placed in the desessive-compulsive and related disorders chapter in DSM-5.

Figure 8.3 Diagnoses of somatic symptom disorders.

Because these disorders are so newly defined, we don't have good epidemiological evidence about the specific disorders. Extrapolating from what we know about DSM-IV-TR diagnoses, though, concerns about somatic symptoms and illness anxiety tend to develop early in adulthood (Cloninger, Martin, Guze, et al., 1986). Although many will experience these concerns throughout their life, the symptoms may wax and wane, and for some, recovery occurs naturally. In one study only a third of patients with DSM-IV-TR somatization disorder still reported multiple somatic concerns 12 months later (Simon & Gureje, 1999). Distress over health concerns is more persistent (Barsky, Fama, Bailey, et al., 1998). Somatic symptom disorders tend to co-occur with anxiety disorders, mood disorders, substance use disorders, and personality disorders (Golding, Smith, & Kashner, 1991; Kirmayer, Robbins, & Paris, 1994).

<table>
<tr><td>

Proposed DSM-5 Criteria for Complex Somatic Symptom Disorder

- At least one somatic symptom that is distressing or disrupts daily life
- Excessive thoughts, feelings, and behaviors related to somatic symptom(s) or health concerns, as indicated by at least two of the following: health-related anxiety, disproportionate are concerns about the medical seriousness of symptoms, and excessive time and energy devoted to health concerns
- Duration of at least 6 months
- Specify: predominant somatic complaints, predominant health anxiety, or predominant pain

Note: Changes from DSM-IV-TR are italicized

</td></tr>
</table>

Clinical Description of Complex Somatic Symptom Disorder

There are three core criteria for **complex somatic symptom disorder:** (1) one or more somatic symptoms that are distressing or result in significant disruption in daily life, (2) excessive anxiety, concern, or time and energy devoted to the somatic concern, and (3) duration of at least 6 months. The somatic symptoms can vary substantially—as illustrated by the case of Bettina, some might experience a multitude of symptoms from many different body systems. Others experience pain as the major concern.

The somatic symptoms may begin or intensify after some conflict or stress. To an outside observer, it may seem that the person is using the somatic symptom to avoid some unpleasant activity or to get attention and sympathy, but people with complex somatic symptom disorder have no sense of this—they experience their symptoms as completely physical. For patients for whom pain is the central concern, dependency on painkillers is a risk. Understanding psychological aspects of pain is important, because millions of Americans experience chronic pain, accounting for billions of dollars of lost work time and incalculable personal and familial suffering (Turk, 2001).

The proposed DSM-5 includes many changes in the way that these symptoms are diagnosed. As shown in Figure 8.3, DSM-IV-TR separates the diagnoses of pain disorder (in which the primary symptom involves pain) and somatization disorder (which involves multiple somatic symptoms from various body systems). Because these conditions often overlap, the proposed DSM-5 merges these two diagnoses into complex somatic symptom disorder. Compared to the DSM-IV-TR, the proposed DSM-5 system places more emphasis on the distress and behavior accompanying somatic symptoms, rather than the number or range of somatic symptoms.

Clinical Description of Illness Anxiety Disorder

The main feature of **illness anxiety disorder** is a preoccupation with fears of having a serious disease despite having no significant somatic symptoms. To meet the DSM criteria for diagnosis, these fears must lead to excessive care seeking or maladaptive avoidance behaviors that persist for at least 6 months.

Clinical Case: Bettina

Bettina, a 31-year-old woman, was referred to a psychologist by her local doctor. Over a period of about six months, she had seen her doctor around 18 times. Bettina had complained of rather vague complaints—general aches and pains, bouts of nausea, fatigue, irregular menstruation, and dizziness. But various tests had not revealed any physical illness.

Bettina was reluctant to see a therapist but when the therapist asked her to describe the history of her physical problems, she quickly warmed to the task. According to Bettina, she had always been sick. As a child she had had episodes of high fever, frequent respiratory infections, convulsions, and her first two operations, an appendectomy and a tonsillectomy.

Bettina's younger sister had died from leukaemia following a long illness, during which time she had mostly been cared for at home by their devoted mother. Bettina's mother was overcome by the death of her daughter, becoming increasingly depressed over the following 12 months, and finally taking her own life on the anniversary of her daughter's death. Her mother died at the age of 36, when Bettina was just 10 years old.

As she continued her account, Bettina's descriptions of her problems became more and more colorful. She provided graphic descriptions of problems with vomiting during her 20s, how the sight of food would make her vomit. At this time, Bettina had gone from one doctor to another. She had seen several gynecologists for her menstrual irregularity and pain during intercourse, and she had undergone dilation and curettage (scraping the lining of the uterus). She had been referred to neurologists for her headaches, dizziness, and fainting spells, and they had performed EEGs, spinal taps, and even a CT scan. Other physicians had ordered X-rays to look for the possible causes of her abdominal pain and EKGs for her chest pains. Doctors responding to her desperate pleas for a cure had performed rectal and gallbladder surgery.

When the interview shifted away from Bettina's medical history, it became apparent that she was highly anxious in many situations, particularly those in which she thought she might be evaluated by other people. Indeed, some of her physical complaints could be regarded as consequences of anxiety.

Illness anxiety disorder sounds somewhat parallel to the DSM-IV-TR diagnosis of hypochondriasis, which was defined by an unfounded fear about serious illness. Hypochondriasis is not the same as illness anxiety disorder, though—illness anxiety disorder is only diagnosed when a person has minimal or no somatic symptoms. Most people diagnosed with the DSM-IV-TR disorder of hypochondriasis experience somatic symptoms that are a focus of their concerns. When fears about a serious disease are accompanied by somatic symptoms, the appropriate DSM-5 diagnosis is complex somatic symptom disorder. Because so few people with hypochondriasis are free of somatic symptoms, very few people are expected to meet criteria for illness anxiety disorder.

Illness anxiety disorder often co-occurs with anxiety and mood disorders (Noyes, 1999). The framers of DSM-5 had some debate about whether this condition should be considered a somatic symptom disorder or an anxiety disorder. Because the focus of the condition is on health, it is currently considered a somatic symptom disorder.

Clinical Description of Functional Neurological Disorder

In **functional neurological disorder** (labeled as conversion disorder in DSM-IV-TR), the person suddenly develops neurological symptoms, such as blindness or paralysis. The symptoms suggest an illness related to neurological damage, but medical tests indicate that the bodily organs and nervous system are fine. People may experience partial or complete paralysis of arms or legs; seizures and coordination disturbances; a sensation of prickling, tingling, or creeping on the skin; insensitivity to pain; or anesthesia—the loss of sensation. Vision may be seriously impaired; the person may become partially or completely blind or have *tunnel vision*, in which the visual field is constricted as it would be if the person were peering through a tube. *Aphonia*, loss of the voice other than whispered speech, and *anosmia*, loss of the sense of smell, can also occur. Some people with functional neurological disorder seem complacent or even serene, are not particularly eager to part with their symptoms, and do not connect their symptoms with their stressful situations.

This disorder has a long history, dating back to the earliest writings on mental disorders. *Hysteria* was the term originally used to describe the disorder, which the Greek physician

---

Proposed DSM-5 Criteria for Illness Anxiety Disorder

- Preoccupation with and *high level of anxiety about* having or acquiring a serious disease
- *Excessive illness behavior (e.g., checking for signs of illness, seeking reassurance) or maladaptive avoidance (e.g., avoiding medical care or ill relatives)*
- *No more than mild somatic symptoms are present*
- *Not explained by other psychological disorders*
- Preoccupation lasts at least 6 months

Note: Illness anxiety disorder is a new diagnosis in the DSM-5, but it has some parallels with the DSM-IV-TR diagnosis of hypochondriasis. Criteria that differ from the DSM-IV-TR diagnosis of hypochondriasis are italicized. The DSM-IV-TR criteria for hypochondriasis specify that the preoccupation must continue despite medical reassurance.

Hippocrates considered to be an affliction limited to women and brought on by the wandering of the uterus through the body. (The Greek word *hystera* means "womb"; the wandering uterus symbolized the longing of the woman's body for the production of a child.) The term *conversion* originated with Sigmund Freud, who thought that anxiety and psychological conflict were converted into physical symptoms (see the Clinical Case of Anna O., an influential case for his theory).

The proposed DSM-5 includes several changes in this diagnosis. The DSM-IV-TR name of conversion theory has been changed because it harkened back to Freud's theory, which is a controversial model. The new diagnostic label uses the word *functional,* a common medical term for describing symptoms that are not explained by a medical disorder. The DSM-IV-TR diagnostic criteria specify that symptoms are associated with psychological stressors and that the patient is not feigning illness. Neither of these criteria can be reliably assessed, and so both are likely to be removed in DSM-5.

When a patient reports a neurological symptom, it is important to assess whether that symptom has a true neurological basis. Sometimes behavioral tests can help make this distinction. For example, arm tremors might disappear when the person is asked to move the arm rhythmically. Leg weakness might not be consistent when tested with resistance (Stone, Lafrance, Levenson, et al., 2010). In one form of functional neurological disorder, people report tunnel vision, which is incompatible with the biology of the visual system. In another example, people might show a seizurelike event at the same time that a normal EEG pattern is recorded (Stone et al., 2010).

Although some diagnostic distinctions are easy, the clinician still has to be careful in making this diagnosis. Consider, for instance, the classic example of "glove anesthesia," in which the person experiences little or no sensation in the part of the hand and lower arm that would be covered by a glove. For years this was considered a textbook illustration of anatomical nonsense because the nerves run continuously from the hand up the arm. Yet now it appears that carpal tunnel syndrome, a recognized medical condition, can produce symptoms similar to those of glove anesthesia. Nerves in the wrist run through a tunnel formed by the wrist bones and membranes. The tunnel can become swollen and may pinch the nerves, leading to tingling, numbness, and pain in the hand. People who use computer keyboards for many hours a day seem to be at risk for this condition. To enhance the reliability of functional neurological disorder, the proposed DSM-5 provides more guidance to clinicians about how to assess whether symptoms might be medically unexplained.

Symptoms of functional neurological disorder usually develop in adolescence or early adulthood, typically after a major life stressor. An episode may end abruptly, but sooner or later the disorder is likely to return, either in its original form or with a different symptom. The prevalence of functional neurological disorder is less than 1 percent, and more women than men are given the diagnosis (Faravelli, Salvatori, Galassi, et al., 1997). The disorder is more common among patients visiting neurology clinics, where as many as 3 percent meet criteria for DSM-IV-TR conversion disorder (Fink, Hansen, & Sondergaard, 2005). Patients with functional neurological disorder are highly likely to meet criteria for another somatic symptom disorder (Brown et al., 2007), and about half meet criteria for a dissociative disorder (Sar, Akyuz, Kundakci, et al., 2004). Other common comorbid disorders include major depressive disorder, substance use disorders, and personality disorders (Brown et al., 2007).

Proposed DSM-5 Criteria for *Functional Neurological Disorder*

- One or more *neurologic* symptoms affecting voluntary motor function, sensory function, *cognition, or seizure-like episodes*
- The physical signs or diagnostic findings *are internally inconsistent or incongruent with recognized neurological disorder*
- Symptoms cannot be explained by a medical condition
- Symptoms cause significant distress or functional impairment or warrant medical evaluation

Note: DSM-IV-TR criteria for conversion disorder specify that symptoms are related to conflict or stress and are not intentionally produced. Other changes from DSM-IV-TR are italicized.

Clinical Case: Anna O.

As described in the initial case report, Anna O. was sitting at the bedside of her seriously ill father when she dropped off into a waking dream. She saw a black snake come toward her sick father to bite him. She tried to ward it off, but her arm had gone to sleep. When she looked at her hand, her fingers seemed to turn into little snakes with death's heads.

The next day, when a bent branch recalled her hallucination of the snake, her right arm became rigidly extended. After that, whenever some object revived her hallucination, her arm responded in the same way—with rigid extension. Later, her symptoms extended to paralysis and anesthesia of her entire right side. [Drawn from Breuer & Freud (1895/1982)]

FOCUS ON DISCOVERY 8.2

Malingering and Factitious Disorder

In evaluating somatic symptoms, clinicians need to be aware of the potential for factitious disorder and malingering. Neither of these conditions are somatic symptom disorders, but we discuss them here because they can involve somatic symptoms.

Factitious and malingering disorders are conditions in which a person intentionally fakes an illness by deliberately producing, feigning, or exaggerating symptoms in order to avoid a responsibility, such as work, or to achieve some goal, such as being awarded an insurance settlement. In factitious disorder by proxy, a person deliberately produces, feigns, or exaggerates symptoms in a person who is in their care. Often, malingering has a clear potential for reward; this is in contrast to factitious disorder, where the sole goal often seems to be to adopt the patient role.

The modern history of factitious disorder began in 1951 when Dr Asher, a clinician, described case reports of patients who habitually migrate from hospital to hospital, seeking admission through feigned symptoms while embellishing their personal history (Galvin, Newton & Vandeven, 2005). He assigned the name Munchausen syndrome to this condition after Baron von Munchausen, a well-respected, retired German cavalry officer who had tales of his life stolen and parodied in a booklet in 1785. Persons with Munchausen syndrome were said to typically (1) exhibit numerous surgical scars, especially in the abdomen, (2) display a truculent or evasive manner, (3) provide a dramatic medical history of questionable veracity, and (4) attempt to conceal such documents as hospital discharge forms or insurance claims. Asher distinguished abdominal, hemorrhagic, and neurologic subtypes.

Since the publication of Asher's original paper, numerous reports of patients producing or falsifying almost every conceivable kind of illness have appeared in the literature. The type of patient described by Asher is

Kathleen Bush is was charged with child abuse and fraud for deliberately causing her child's illnesses. (Alan Diaz/ASSOCIATED PRESS/© AP/Wide World Photos.)

now thought to represent a minority of cases of factitious disorder. The term Munchausen syndrome most appropriately refers to the subset of patients who have a chronic variant of factitious disorder with predominantly physical signs and symptoms. In practice, however, many still use the term Munchausen syndrome interchangeably with factitious disorder.

In 1977, Roy Meadow introduced the term "Munchausen by proxy" which describes cases where an individual artificially produces illness in another person; typically a mother who produces illness in a young child. Professor Meadow's theory appeared to be vindicated in 1993 when his testimony was used in the case of Beverly Allitt. Allitt — nicknamed the Angel of Death — was convicted of killing four children and injuring nine more on the ward at Grantham Hospital in the UK. Her main method of murder was to inject the child with potassium chloride (to cause cardiac arrest), or with insulin (to induce lethal hypoglycemia). Although no-one ever established a motive for her actions, Alitt was ruled to be a prime example of Munchausen by proxy and was given 13 life sentences (reported in The *Times, Feb 16th, 2006*).

To distinguish between malingering and a functional neurological disorder or conversion disorder, clinicians try to determine whether the symptoms have been consciously or unconsciously adopted. In malingering, the symptoms are under voluntary control, which is not thought to be the case in a conversion disorder, where patients may present with symptoms such as numbness, blindness, paralysis, or fits without a neurological cause. Conversion disorder is unique in DSM-IV in explicitly requiring the exclusion of deliberate feigning. Unfortunately, this is only likely to be demonstrable where the patient confesses, or is "caught out" in a broader deception, such as a false identity.

Check Your Knowledge 8.3

Match the case description to the disorder. Assume that the symptoms cause significant distress or impairment.

1. Paula, a 24-year-old librarian, sought psychological help on the advice of her sister because of her deep fears about medical conditions. In daily phone calls with her sister, she would describe worries that she had cancer or a brain tumor. She had no somatic symptoms or signs of these conditions, but every time she saw an Internet report, a TV program, or a newspaper article on some new serious condition, she became worried she might have it. She had seen doctors several times per month for years, but when they identified no disease, she became annoyed with them, criticized the insensitivity of their medical tests, and sought a new consultant.

2. John, a 35-year-old man, was referred for psychological treatment by his surgeon because he seemed to be excessively nervous about his health. In the past 5 years, John had sought a stunning array of medical treatments

and tests for stomach distress, itching, frequent urination, and any number of other complaints. By the time he was referred, he had received 10 MRIs and too many X-rays to count, and he had seen 15 different specialists. Each test had been negative. He genuinely seemed to experience these symptoms, and there was no reason that he stood to gain from a medical diagnosis.

3. Thomas, a 50-year-old man, was referred for psychological treatment by an ophthalmologist. He reported that 2 weeks before, he had suddenly developed tunnel vision. Medical tests failed to reveal any reason for his tunnel vision.

   a. complex somatic symptom disorder
   b. Ilness anxiety disorder
   c. malingering
   d. functional neurological disorder

Etiology of Somatic Symptom Disorders

Although one might expect that somatic symptom disorders would be heritable, studies so far indicate there is no concordance among twins for somatic symptom disorders (Torgersen, 1986) or functional neurological disorder (Slater, 1961). These disorders do not appear to be heritable.

In considering research on the etiology of somatic symptom disorders, one challenge is that the DSM-5 diagnoses differ from the DSM-IV-TR diagnoses that have been used in most studies. The major features of complex somatic symptom disorder and illness anxiety disorder, though, include excessive attention to somatic symptoms and disproportionate anxiety about one's health. Neurobiological and cognitive behavioral models have focused on understanding these two tendencies, and we describe those models here. After discussing that research, we consider dominant models of functional neurological disorder, which include a psychodynamic theory as well as social and cultural influences.

Neurobiological Factors That Increase Awareness of and Distress over Somatic Symptoms

Everyone experiences occasional somatic symptoms. For example, we may feel muscle pain after a tough workout, small signs of an impending cold, or physiological responses of our body as we exercise. In understanding somatic symptom disorders, then, the key issue might not be whether people have some bodily sensation, but rather why some people are more keenly aware of and distressed by these sensations.

Neurobiological models of somatic symptom disorders focus on brain regions activated by unpleasant body sensations. Pain and uncomfortable physical sensations, such as heat, increase activity in regions of the brain called the anterior insula and the anterior cingulate (Price, Craggs, Zhou, et al., 2009). These regions have strong connections with the somatosensory cortex, a region of the brain involved with processing bodily sensations (see Figure 8.4). Heightened activity in these regions is related to greater propensity for somatic symptoms (Landgrebe, Barta, Rosengarth, et al., 2008) and more intense ratings of the unpleasantness of a standardized painful stimulus (Mayer, Berman, Suyenobu, et al., 2005). Some people, then, may have hyperactive brain regions that are involved in evaluating the unpleasantness of body sensations, which would help explain why they are more vulnerable to experiencing and noticing somatic symptoms and pain.

It is well known that pain and somatic symptoms can be increased by anxiety, depression, and stress hormones (Gatchel, Peng, Peters, et al., 2007). Depression and anxiety are also directly related to activity in the anterior cingulate (Wiech & Tracey, 2009). Experiences of

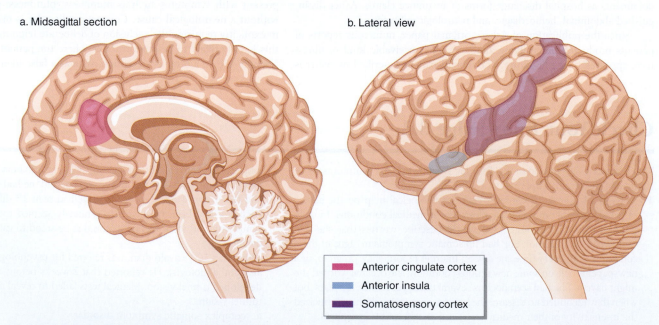

a. Midsagittal section   b. Lateral view

Anterior cingulate cortex
Anterior insula
Somatosensory cortex

Figure 8.4 People with somatic symptom disorders appear to have increased activity in brain regions implicated in evaluating the unpleasantness of body sensations: the anterior insula, the anterior cingulate, and the somatosensory cortex. The anterior cingulate is also involved in depression.

emotional pain, such as remembering a relationship breakup, can also activate the anterior cingulate and the anterior insula. The involvement of these regions in experiences of physical and emotional pain may help explain why emotions and depression can intensify experiences of pain (Villemure & Bushnell, 2009).

Cognitive Behavioral Factors That Increase Awareness of and Distress over Somatic Symptoms Like the neurobiological models of somatic symptom disorders, cognitive behavioral models focus on the mechanisms that could contribute to the excessive focus on and anxiety over health concerns. Figure 8.5 illustrates one model of how these cognitive and behavioral risk factors could fit together. The pink boxes are relevant to understanding how a person might initially develop a somatic symptom. The blue boxes are relevant for understanding reactions to a somatic symptom. Once a somatic symptom develops, two cognitive variables appear important: attention to body sensations and interpretation of those sensations (attributions).

To study attention to health cues, researchers have used a version of the emotion Stroop task (see p. 46). Patients with the DSM-IV-TR diagnoses of somatoform disorder, major depressive disorder, or panic disorder (Lim & Kim, 2005) were asked to name the color of words as quickly as possible, while ignoring the actual words. Many of the words were related to physical health and illness. Patients with somatoform disorder had more difficulty ignoring words that were related to physical health than other words, whereas other patients did not. Hence, people with excessive distress about their somatic symptoms may automatically focus on cues of physical health problems.

People prone to worries about their health also demonstrate an attributional style that involves interpreting physical symptoms in the worst possible way. (An attribution is a person's idea about why something is happening.) The specific attributions might vary. For example, one person might interpret a red blotch on the skin as a sign of cancer (Marcus et al., 2007). Another person might overestimate the odds that a symptom is a sign of a disease (Rief et al., 2006). The exact form of the cognitive bias may vary, but once these negative thoughts begin, the resultant elevations of anxiety and cortisol may exacerbate somatic symptoms and distress over those symptoms (Rief & Auer, 2001).

In Chapter 6, we described a very similar cognitive process as part of panic disorder. That is, people with panic disorder are likely to overreact to physiological symptoms. In panic disorder, the person often believes that the symptoms are a sign of an immediate threat (e.g., a heart attack), whereas in somatic symptom disorders, the person believes the symptoms are a sign of an underlying long-term disease (e.g., cancer or AIDS). The types of physical cues that a person focuses on also differ for people with panic disorder compared to somatic symptom disorders. The person with panic disorder often focuses on symptoms that will actually become worse as they become more anxious—for example, a fast heart rate, shortness of breath, or sweaty palms. In contrast, a patient with somatic symptom disorders cannot, for example, increase the size of a spot on the skin by misconstruing it as cancer.

The tendency to be overly concerned about one's health may have evolved from early experiences of medical symptoms or from family attitudes to physical illness. Consistent with these childhood influences on cognitive biases, people with somatic symptom disorders report that as children they often missed school because of illness (Barsky et al., 1995).

Fear that a bodily sensation signifies illness is likely to have two behavioral consequences. First, the person may assume the role of being sick and avoid work and social tasks, and this can intensify symptoms by limiting exercise and other healthy behaviors. Second, the person may seek reassurance from doctors and from family members, and this help-seeking behavior may be reinforced if it results in the person getting attention or sympathy. Often, people with these disorders tend to have trouble eliciting socially reinforcing interactions in other ways. For example, people with somatic symptom disorders often have trouble identifying their emotions and describing them directly (Bankier, Aigner, & Bach, 2001), so they may find attention and sympathy for health concerns particularly reinforcing. Beyond the attention, people may receive other types of behavioral reinforcers for somatic symptoms—for example, people receive disability payments based on how much symptoms interfere with their daily activities.

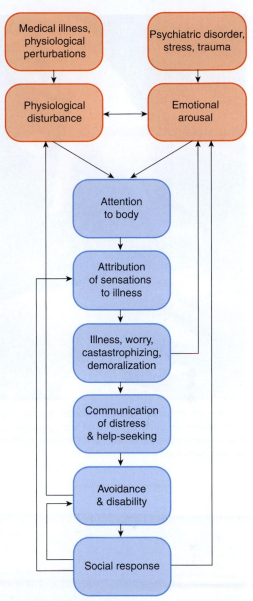

Figure 8.5 Mechanisms involved in somatic symptom disorders. From Looper and Kirmayer (2002).

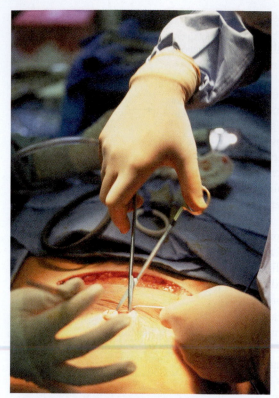

People with somatic symptom disorder may undergo unnecessary surgeries in hopes of finding a cure for their medical symptoms. (Michelle Del Guercio/Photo Researchers, Inc.)

Etiology of Functional Neurological Disorder Models of functional neurological disorder are fairly distinct from the models that have developed for the other somatic symptom disorders. In this section, we begin by discussing psychodynamic views of functional neurological disorder and then consider sociocultural factors.

Psychodynamic Perspective on Functional Neurological Disorder Functional neurological disorder occupies a central place in psychodynamic theories because the symptoms provide a clear example of the role of the unconscious. Consider trying to diagnose a woman who says that she awoke one morning with a paralyzed left arm. Assume that a series of neurological tests reveal no neurological disorder. Perhaps she has decided to fake paralysis to achieve some end—this would be an example of malingering (see Focus on Discovery 8.2). But what if you believe her? You would almost be forced to conclude that unconscious processes were operating. On a conscious level, she is telling the truth; she believes that her arm is paralyzed. On an unconscious level, some psychological factor is at work, making her unable to move her arm despite the absence of any physical cause.

One psychodynamic interpretation of functional neurological disorder is based on two case studies of hysterically blind adolescent women (Sackeim, Nordlie, & Gur, 1979). In one case, a young woman who reported being blind performed more poorly on a vision test than would a person who was actually blind (i.e., she performed below chance levels). In the other case, a teenage girl reported that she could not see to read, but tests showed that she could readily identify objects of various sizes and shapes and count fingers at a distance of 15 feet.

Drawing on these cases, Sackeim and colleagues (1979) proposed a two-stage model to account for the discrepancies between the women's vision tests and their reports of blindness. The first stage focuses on the idea that people can process visual information outside of their conscious awareness. The key is that the vision system consists of a set of modules within the brain. If these modules are not coordinated in an overarching conscious fashion, the brain may process some visual input such that the person can do well on certain visual tests. Despite these abilities, they may not be consciously aware of this visual input (the well-documented condition of **blindsight** provides one example of some visual modules remaining intact while the person lacks conscious awareness of visual cues). So it is possible for people truthfully to claim that they cannot see, even when tests suggest that they can. More generally, many different studies show that perceptions formed outside of consciousness can influence behavior (see Focus on Discovery 8.3). Hence, because some perceptual abilities may be unconscious (outside of awareness), hysterically blind persons are able to genuinely say that they cannot see, even when visual stimuli clearly influence their behavior. That is, one way to understand functional neurological disorder is that there is a disruption in consciousness, such that the person fails to have an explicit awareness of sensory and motor information (Kihlstrom, 1994).

Some psychoanalysts believe that the high frequency of functional neurological disorder in nineteenth-century Europe was due to the repressive sexual attitudes of the time. (Hulton Archive/Stone/Getty Images.)

The second stage of this model focuses on motivation—that is, some people, perhaps because of their personality, are motivated to appear blind. Such people would be expected to perform below chance levels on visual tests. Support for the importance of motivation comes from a study in which a man with hysterical blindness had his vision tested over a large number of sessions. He was given different motivational instructions in different sessions, and motivation was found to influence performance (Bryant & McConkey, 1989). The degree to which people need to be considered blind (their motivation) will shape how much they show signs of being able to see.

In sum, recent psychodynamic models of functional neurological disorder focus on the idea that people could be unconscious of certain perceptions and be motivated to have certain symptoms. Unfortunately, despite the fact that case studies set the stage for further empirical work, this work has not yet been done.

Social and Cultural Factors in Functional Neurological Disorder Over the past century, there has been an apparent decrease in the incidence of functional neurological disorder, which suggests a possible role for social and cultural factors. During the nineteenth century, Freud and his colleague Charcot seemed to have an abundance of female patients with this disorder, but contemporary clinicians rarely see anyone with such problems. Studies show that the diagnosis has declined in Western societies such as the United States and England (Hare, 1969) but has remained more common in countries that may place less emphasis on "psychologizing" distress, such as Libya (Pu et al., 1986), China, and India (Tseng, 2001). During World War I, a large number of men in combat developed symptoms resembling those of functional neurological disorder (Ziegler, Imboden, & Meyer, 1960), but by World War II the syndrome was less common among soldiers (Marlowe, 2001). Support for the role of social and cultural factors also comes from studies showing that symptoms of functional neurological disorder are more common among people from rural areas and people of lower socioeconomic status (Binzer & Kullgren, 1996).

Several hypotheses have been proposed to explain the cultural and historical patterns in diagnostic rates. Psychodynamic therapists point out that in the second half of the nineteenth century, when the incidence of these problems was apparently high in France and Austria, repressive sexual attitudes may have contributed to the increased prevalence of the disorder. The decrease in the incidence of such symptoms might reflect the greater psychological and medical sophistication of contemporary culture, which is more tolerant of anxiety than it is of dysfunctions that do not make physiological sense. An alternate explanation is that medical diagnostic practices vary from country to country, producing the different rates. A cross-national study is needed, in which diagnosticians trained to follow the same procedures interview participants in different countries.

FOCUS ON DISCOVERY 8.3

Evidence for the Unconscious

We are unaware of much that goes on in our minds—that is, much of the working of the mind proceeds outside consciousness (awareness). We can find a good deal of support for this idea in studies by cognitive psychologists. Consider these examples.

- In one study, participants were presented with different shapes for 1 millisecond (one-thousandth of a second) (Kunst-Wilson & Zajonc, 1980). Later they showed virtually no ability to recognize the shapes they had seen, but when they rated how much they liked these shapes, they preferred the ones they had been shown to other ones. It is known that familiarity affects judgments of stimuli; people tend to like familiar stimuli more than unfamiliar ones. This indicates that some aspects of the stimuli must have been absorbed, even though participants said that they did not recognize the shapes.
- Similarly, when people are presented with pictures of fearful faces for 33 milliseconds, they report no awareness of seeing the faces but show increased activity in the amygdala, a brain region involved in responding to emotionally relevant stimuli (Whalen 1998).

These experiments, and others like them, document that humans do have an unconscious. But the modern cognitive perspective understands the unconscious processes in a different way from psychoanalysis. Freud postulated that the unconscious was a repository of instinctual energy and repressed impulses. Contemporary researchers reject the notions of an energy reservoir and of repression, holding more simply that we are not aware of everything in our mind. While the original psychoanalytic view of the unconscious emphasized aggressive and sexual motivations, the newer cognitive perspective focuses on the brain as a highly efficient machine, in which some tasks are conducted automatically without entering consciousness.

A child participates in a dichotic listening experiment. He attends to information presented to only one ear, and later he will have difficulty consciously remembering the information presented to the unattended ear. Nonetheless, the information reaching the unattended ear can affect behavior. (Phanie/Photo Researchers, Inc.)

Quick Summary

The common feature of somatic symptom disorders is the excessive focus on physical symptoms. The nature of the concern, though, varies by disorder. The major somatic symptom disorders in the proposed DSM-5 include complex somatic symptom disorder, illness anxiety disorder, and functional neurological disorder. Complex somatic symptom disorder is defined by recurrent somatic symptoms that cause unwarranted anxiety or require too much time or energy. Illness anxiety disorder is defined by belief in a severe disease in the absence of somatic symptoms. Functional neurological disorder is characterized by sensory and motor dysfunctions that cannot be explained by medical tests. Somatic symptom disorders may arise suddenly in stressful situations.

Neurobiological models suggest that some people may have a propensity toward hyperactivity in regions of the brain involved in evaluating the unpleasantness of somatic sensations including the anterior cingulate and the anterior insula. These brain regions are also implicated in negative emotions and depression. Cognitive behavioral models of somatic symptom disorders focus on attention to and interpretation of somatic symptoms as a way of understanding why some people experience such intense anxiety about their health. Behavioral responses to these health concerns can include disengagement and isolation, as well as excessive help-seeking behavior.

Psychodynamic theories of functional neurological disorder have focused on the idea that people can be unaware of their perceptions and may be motivated to have symptoms.

Check Your Knowledge 8.4

True or false?
1. Functional neurological disorder is highly heritable.
2. The two-stage psychodynamic model of functional neurological disorder emphasizes unconscious perceptions and motivation for having symptoms.
3. Complex somatic symptom disorder involves hyperactivation of the cerebellum.

Treatment of Somatic Symptom Disorders

One of the major obstacles to treatment is that most people with somatic symptom disorders do not want to consult mental health professionals. It is not a good idea for a provider to try to convince patients that their symptoms are caused by psychological factors. Most somatic and pain concerns have both physical and psychological components, and so it is meaningless for the physician to debate the source of these symptoms with the patient. Patients may resent referrals from their physician because they interpret such a referral as a sign that the doctor thinks the illness is "all in their head." Rather than trying to refer patients, many innovative programs involve coaching general practitioners and their treatment teams to provide care for people with somatic symptom disorders. The goal is to establish a strong relationship that allows the person to have a sense of trust and comfort, so that the patient will feel more reassured about their health. In one study, patients with distressing and medically unexplained gastrointestinal symptoms were randomly assigned to receive high or low levels of warmth, attention, and reassurance from doctors. Those who received high levels of support showed more improvement in symptoms and quality of life over the next 6 weeks compared to those who received low levels of support (Kaptchuk et al., 2008). It is better to work with patients on ways to improve their lives than on debating them about the source of their symptoms.

Other health care system interventions involve informing physicians when a patient appears to be an intensive user of health care services so that they can minimize the use of diagnostic tests and medications. These types of interventions with physicians can reduce the frequency of health care services (Rost, Kashner, & Smith, 1994).

There are no randomized controlled trials for treatment of functional neurological disorder. In studies with no control group, traditional long-term psychoanalysis, psychodynamic psychotherapy, and hypnosis have not been demonstrated to be useful with functional neurological disorder (Kroenke, 2007; Simon, 1998).

Here, then, we focus on treatments for the other somatic symptom disorders. In studies with no control group, psychodynamic treatment has been found to be effective in alleviating the physical symptoms of somatic symptom disorders in the short term, but findings have been mixed when participants were followed for 9 months (Abass et al., 2009). Cognitive behavioral strategies have been developed to address the recurrent somatic symptoms and distress observed in somatic symptom disorders. After describing cognitive behavioral treatment, we summarize evidence that antidepressants can reduce the pain symptoms of complex somatic symptom disorder.

Cognitive Behavioral Treatment Cognitive behavioral therapists have applied many different techniques to help people with somatic symptom disorders. As illustrated with the clinical case of Louis described below, these include helping people (1) identify and change the emotions that trigger their somatic concerns, (2) change their cognitions regarding their somatic symptoms, and (3) change their behaviors so they stop playing the role of a sick person and gain more reinforcement for engaging in other types of social interactions (Looper & Kirmayer, 2002).

The negative emotions that accompany anxiety and depressive disorders often trigger physiological symptoms and intensify the distress about those somatic symptoms (Simon, Goreje, & Fullerton, 2001). Indeed, as shown in Chapters 5 and 6, physical health concerns are common among people suffering from anxiety or depression. It should therefore come as no surprise that treating anxiety and depression often reduces somatic symptom disorders (Phillips, Lì, & Zhang, 2002; Smith, 1992). Psychoeducation programs can help patients recognize links between their negative moods and somatic symptoms (Morley, 1997). Techniques such as relaxation training and various forms of cognitive behavioral treatment have proven useful in reducing depression and anxiety, and the reductions in depression and anxiety lead to reductions in somatic symptoms (Payne & Blanchard, 1995).

Many different cognitive strategies are used in the treatment of somatic symptom disorders. Some involve training people to pay less attention to their body. Alternatively, cognitive strategies might help people identify and challenge negative thoughts about their bodies (Warwick & Salkovskis, 2001). In another type of cognitive intervention, patients may learn to reframe their experience of a somatic symptom, such as pain, as illustrated by the following:

> The patient may be encouraged to alter the focus of their attention to the pain without switching attention directly away from the pain. In this instance, the subject may be asked to focus on the sensory qualities of the pain and transform it to a less threatening quality. For example, a young man with a severe "shooting" pain was able to reinterpret the sensory quality into an image which included him shooting a goal in a soccer match. As a result of this transformation, the impact of the pain was greatly reduced. (Morley, 1997, p. 236)

Behavioral techniques might help people resume healthy activities and rebuild a lifestyle that has been damaged by too much focus on illness-related concerns (Warwick & Salkovskis, 2001). Bettina, the woman described earlier, revealed that she was extremely anxious about her shaky marriage and about situations in which other people might judge her. Techniques such as exposure and cognitive restructuring could address her interpersonal fears, which might help lessen her somatic complaints. Assertiveness training and social skills training—for example, coaching Bettina in effective ways to approach and talk to people, to maintain eye contact, to give compliments, to accept criticism, and to make requests—could be useful in helping her to develop healthier interpersonal interactions. In general, it is advisable to focus less on what patients cannot do because of their pain and somatic symptoms and more on encouraging them to re-engage in satisfying activities and to gain a greater sense of control.

Behavioral and family approaches could help change Bettina's reliance on playing the role of a sick person (Warwick & Salkovskis, 2001). If the people who live with Bettina have adjusted to her illness by reinforcing her avoidance of normal adult responsibilities, family therapy might help. Bettina and the members of her family might be able to change relationships to support her movement away from a focus on physical complaints. A therapist might use operant conditioning approaches with family or friends to reduce the amount of attention they give the person's somatic symptoms.

Cognitive behavioral approaches have proven effective in reducing health concerns, symptoms of depression and anxiety, and health care utilization compared to no treatment conditions (Thomson & Page, 2007) and to usual medical care (Hollon et al., 2006). Several studies have found that cognitive behavioral treatment can reduce somatic symptoms compared to control conditions, but these effects have tended to be small (Deary et al., 2007). That is, these interventions may do more to reduce the *distress* about somatic symptoms than they do to reduce the actual somatic symptoms (Barksy & Ahern, 2004). In one study, cognitive behavioral treatment was as effective as an antidepressant in reducing illness anxiety symptoms (Greeven et al., 2007).

Antidepressant Treatment for Somatic Symptom Disorders with Pain   Antidepressants are likely to be helpful when pain is a dominant symptom of somatic symptom disorder. There is evidence from a number of double-blind experiments that low doses of some antidepressant drugs, most especially imipramine (Tofranil), are superior to a placebo in reducing chronic pain and related distress (Fishbain et al., 2000). Interestingly, these antidepressants reduce pain even when given in dosages too low to alleviate the associated depression (Simon, 1998). Antidepressants are preferred over opioid medications, which are highly addictive (Streltzer & Johansen, 2006).

Clinical Case: Louis

Louis was a 66-year-old man who was referred to a psychiatrist by his cardiologist because of concerns about anxiety. Although Louis acknowledged years of depressive and anxiety symptoms, he reported being much more concerned about his potential for heart problems. Several years before, he had developed intermittent symptoms of heart palpitations and chest pressure. Although extensive medical tests were within the normal range, he continued to seek additional tests and to monitor the results carefully. He had gathered a thick file of articles on cardiovascular conditions, had adopted strenuous diet and exercise routines, and had stopped all activities that might be too exciting and therefore challenging to his heart, such as travel and sex. He had even retired early from running his restaurant. By the time he sought treatment, he was measuring his blood pressure four times a day using two machines to average readings, and he was keeping extensive logs of his blood pressure readings.

   Before treatment could begin, Louis had to understand that the way he was thinking about his physical symptoms was intensifying those physical symptoms as well as creating emotional distress. His therapist taught him a model of symptom amplification, in which initial physical symptoms are intensified by negative thoughts and emotions. The therapist used statements

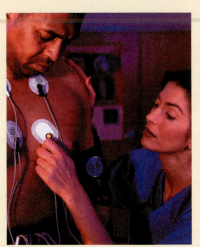

People with health anxiety are not easily reassured that they are well, even when extensive medical tests indicate no problems. (Dynamich GraphicsValue/SUPERSTOCK.)

such as "A headache you believe is due to a brain tumor hurts much more than a headache you believe is due to eye strain." Once Louis understood that his thoughts and behavior might be increasing his medical concerns, treatment focused on four goals. First, Louis was coached to identify one doctor with whom to routinely discuss health concerns and to stop seeking multiple medical opinions. Second, Louis was taught to reduce the time spent engaging in excessive illness-related behaviors, such as logging his blood pressure. His therapist showed him that these behaviors were actually increasing his anxiety rather than providing relief. Third, Louis was taught to consider the thoughts he had in response to his symptoms, which tended to be very negative and pessimistic. For example, the therapist and Louis identified ways in which he tended to catastrophize harmless physical sensations by viewing them as evidence for heart disease. Louis was taught to consider more benign reasons for his physical symptoms. Finally, Louis was encouraged to build other aspects of his life in order to diminish the focus on physical symptoms. Louis began to consult for restaurants. Taken together, these interventions helped Louis reduce his anxiety, diminish his focus on and concern about his health, and begin to lead a more enjoyable life. [Adapted from Barsky (2006).]

Quick Summary

Little is known about the treatment of functional neurological disorder. Cognitive behavioral treatments reduce the excessive focus on and distress over somatic symptoms that are defining features of illness anxiety disorder and complex somatic symptom disorders. One problem in treating somatic symptom disorders is that few people want to see a mental health provider for their physical symptoms. Physicians can reduce health care utilization by minimizing the use of diagnostic tests and instead by providing warm reassurance regarding patient concerns. Cognitive behavioral techniques have been found to be helpful for somatic symptom disorders. Strategies are designed to reduce depression and anxiety, to change cognitive responses to physical symptoms, to rebuild rewarding and engaging lifestyles, and to help patients shift from the sick role. Low doses of antidepressant medication may help relieve pain.

Summary

Dissociative Disorders

- Dissociative disorders are defined by disruptions of consciousness, memory, and identity.
- As described in Table 8.1, the proposed DSM-5 dissociative disorders include dissociative amnesia, depersonalization/derealization disorder, and dissociative identity disorder.
- Most of the writing about the causes of dissociative disorders focuses on dissociative identity disorder. People with dissociative identity disorder very often report severe physical or sexual abuse during childhood. One model, the posttraumatic model, suggests that extensive reliance on dissociation to fend off overwhelming feelings from abuse puts people at risk for developing dissociative identity disorder. The sociocognitive model, though, proposes that these symptoms are elicited by treatment. Proponents of the sociocognitive model point out that abuse in childhood may result in heightened suggestibility, that some therapists use strategies that suggest such symptoms to people, and that most people do not recognize the presence of any alters until after they see a therapist. Although one of the defining features of DID is the lack of shared memories between alters, evidence suggests that alters may share more memories than they report.
- Regardless of theoretical orientation, all clinicians focus their treatment efforts on helping clients cope with anxiety, face fears more directly, and operate in a manner that integrates their memory and consciousness.
- Psychodynamic treatment is perhaps the most commonly used treatment for dissociative disorders, but some of the techniques involved, such as hypnosis and age regression, may make symptoms worse.

Somatic Symptom Disorders

- Somatic symptom disorders share a common focus on physical symptoms. As shown in Table 8.2, the major somatic symptom disorders include complex somatic symptom disorder, illness anxiety disorder, and functional neurological disorder.
- The somatic symptom disorders do not appear to be heritable.
- Neurobiological models suggest that key brain regions involved in processing the unpleasantness of bodily sensations may be hyperactive among people with complex somatic symptom disorder. These regions include the anterior cingulate and the anterior insula. Cognitive variables are also important: some people are overly attentive to physical concerns and make overly negative interpretations about these symptoms and their implications. Behavioral reinforcement may maintain help-seeking behavior.
- Sackeim has proposed a two-stage psychodynamic model of functional neurological disorder that focuses on lack of conscious awareness of perceptions as well as motivation for symptoms.
- People with somatic symptom disorders often resent being referred for mental health care. Programs that involve primary care physicians in addressing these symptoms by providing warmth and reassurance while limiting medical tests have been shown to be helpful. Cognitive behavioral treatments of somatic symptom disorders, which have received a great deal of support for addressing the distress over somatic symptoms, try to relieve depressive and anxious symptoms, to reduce the excessive attention to bodily cues, to address the overly negative interpretations of physical symptoms, and to reinforce behavior that is not consistent with the sick role. Antidepressants have been shown to help relieve pain.

Answers to Check Your Knowledge Questions

8.1 1. b; 2. c; 3. b
8.2 1. T; 2. T; 3. sociocognitive, posttraumatic

8.3 1. b; 2. a; 3. d
8.4 1. F; 2. T; 3. F

Key Terms

blindsight
complex somatic symptom disorder
depersonalization/derealization disorder

dissociative amnesia
dissociative disorders
dissociative identity disorder (DID)
explicit memory

factitious disorder
fugue subtype
functional neurological disorder
illness anxiety disorder
implicit memory

malingering
posttraumatic model of DID
sociocognitive model of DID
somatic symptom disorders

9 Schizophrenia

All of a sudden things weren't going so well. I began to lose control of my life and, most of all, myself. I couldn't concentrate on my schoolwork, I couldn't sleep, and when I did sleep, I had dreams about dying. I was afraid to go to class, imagined that people were talking about me, and on top of that I heard voices. I called my mother in Pittsburgh and asked for her advice. She told me to move off campus into an apartment with my sister.

After I moved in with my sister, things got worse. I was afraid to go outside and when I looked out of the window, it seemed that everyone outside was yelling, "Kill her, kill her." My sister forced me to go to school. I would go out of the house until I knew she had gone to work; then I would return home. Things continued to get worse. I imagined that I had a foul body odor and I sometimes took up to 6 showers a day. I recall going to the grocery store one day, and I imagined that the people in the store were saying, "Get saved, Jesus is the answer." Things worsened—I couldn't remember a thing. I had a notebook full of reminders telling me what to do on that particular day. I couldn't remember my schoolwork, and I would study from 6:00 P.M. until 4:00 A.M. but never had the courage to go to class on the following day. I tried to tell my sister about it, but she didn't understand. She suggested that I see a psychiatrist, but I was afraid to go out of the house to see him.

One day I decided that I couldn't take this trauma anymore, so I took an overdose of 35 Darvon pills. At the same moment, a voice inside me said, "What did you do that for? Now you won't go to heaven." At that instant, I realized that I didn't really want to die. I wanted to live, and I was afraid. I got on the phone and called the psychiatrist whom my sister had recommended. I told him I had taken an overdose of Darvon and that I was afraid. He told me to take a taxi to the hospital. When I arrived at the hospital, I began vomiting, but I didn't pass out. Somehow, I just couldn't accept the fact that I was really going to see a psychiatrist. I thought that psychiatrists were only for crazy people, and I definitely didn't think I was crazy. As a result, I did not admit myself right away. As a matter of fact, I left the hospital and ended up meeting my sister on the way home. She told me to turn right back around because I was definitely going to be admitted. We then called my mother, and she said she would fly down the following day. (quoted in O'Neal, 1984, pp. 109–110)

THE YOUNG WOMAN DESCRIBED in this case study was diagnosed with schizophrenia. **Schizophrenia** is a disorder characterized by disturbances in thought, emotion, and behavior—disordered thinking, in which ideas are not logically related; faulty perception and attention; a lack of emotional expressiveness or, at times, inappropriate expressions; and disturbances in movement and behavior, such as a disheveled appearance. People with schizophrenia may withdraw from other people and from everyday reality, often into a life of odd beliefs (delusions) and hallucinations. Given that schizophrenia is associated with such widespread disruptions in a person's life, it has been difficult to uncover the causes of the disorder and develop effective methods to treat it. We still have a long way to go before we fully understand the multiple factors that trigger schizophrenia and have treatments that are both effective and free of unpleasant side effects.

The symptoms of schizophrenia invade every aspect of a person: the way someone thinks, feels, and behaves. Not surprisingly then, these symptoms can interfere with maintaining stable employment, living independently, having close relationships with other people. They can also provoke ridicule and persecution from other people. Substance abuse rates are high (Fowler, Carr, Carter, & Lewin, 1998), perhaps reflecting an attempt to achieve some relief from the symptoms (Blanchard, Squires, Henry, et al., 1999). On top of this grim picture, the suicide rate among people with schizophrenia is high. Indeed, people with schizophrenia are 12 times more likely to die of suicide than people in the general population. Not only are people with schizophrenia more likely to die from suicide than people in the general population, they are also more likely to die from any cause (Saha, Chant, & McGrath, 2007).

The lifetime prevalence of schizophrenia is slightly less than 1 percent, and it affects men slightly more often than women (Kirkbride, Fearon, Morgan, et al., 2006; Walker, Kestler, Bollini, Huchman, 2004). Schizophrenia is diagnosed more frequently among some groups, such as African Americans, though it remains unclear whether this reflects an actual difference among groups or bias among clinicians (Kirkbride et al., 2006; U.S. Department of Health and Human Services, 2001). Schizophrenia sometimes begins in childhood, but it usually appears in late adolescence or early adulthood, and usually somewhat earlier in men than in women. People with schizophrenia typically have a number of acute episodes of their symptoms and less severe but still debilitating symptoms between episodes.

Clinical Descriptions of Schizophrenia

The range of symptoms in the diagnosis of schizophrenia is extensive, although people with schizophrenia typically have only some of these problems at any given time. No single essential symptom must be present for a diagnosis of schizophrenia (see the proposed DSM-5 criteria box). Thus, people with schizophrenia can differ from one another quite a bit.

About 30 years ago, researchers divided symptoms into two domains called positive and negative (Crow, 1980; Strauss, Carpenter, & Bartko, 1974). Subsequently, the original domain of positive symptoms was divided into two—positive (hallucinations and delusions) and disorganized (disorganized speech and behavior) (Lenzenweger, Dworkin, & Wethington, 1991). The distinction among positive, negative, and disorganized symptoms has been very useful in research on etiology and treatment of schizophrenia—Table 9.1 shows the symptoms that comprise these domains.

In the following sections, we describe in some detail the individual symptoms that make up the positive, negative, and disorganized domains. We also describe motor abnormalities—symptoms that do not fit neatly into these three domains but are a part of the DSM diagnosis for schizophrenia.

Positive Symptoms

Positive symptoms comprise excesses and distortions, such as hallucinations and delusions. For the most part, acute episodes of schizophrenia are characterized by positive symptoms.

Delusions No doubt all of us at one time or another have been concerned because we believed that others thought ill of us. Some of the time this belief may be justified. After all, who is universally loved? Consider, though, the anguish you would feel if you were firmly convinced that many people did not like you—indeed, that they disliked you so much that they were plotting against you. Imagine that your persecutors have sophisticated listening devices that let them tune in on your most private conversations and gather evidence in a plot to discredit you. Those around you, including your loved ones, are unable to reassure you that people are not spying on you. Even your closest friends are gradually joining forces with your tormentor. Anxious and angry, you begin taking counteractions against the persecutors. You carefully check any new room you enter for listening devices. When you meet people for the first time, you question them at great length to determine whether they are part of the plot against you.

Such **delusions**, which are beliefs contrary to reality and firmly held in spite of disconfirming evidence, are common positive symptoms of schizophrenia. Persecutory delusions such as those just described were found in 65 percent of a large, cross-national sample of people diagnosed with schizophrenia (Sartorius, Shapiro, & Jablonksy, 1974). Delusions may take several other forms as well, including the following:

- A person may believe that thoughts that are not his or her own have been placed in his or her mind by an external source; this is called *thought insertion*. For example, a woman may believe that the government has inserted a computer chip in her brain so that thoughts can be inserted into her head.

- A person may believe that his or her thoughts are broadcast or transmitted, so that others know what he or she is thinking; this is called *thought broadcasting*. When walking down the street, a man may look suspiciously at passersby, thinking that they are able to hear what he is thinking even though he is not saying anything out loud.

- A person may believe that an external force controls his or her feelings or behaviors. For example, a person may believe that his or her behavior is being controlled by the signals emitted from cell phone towers.

- A person may have **grandiose delusions,** an exaggerated sense of his or her own importance, power, knowledge, or identity. For example, a woman may believe that she can cause the wind to change direction just by moving her hands.

- A person may have **ideas of reference**, incorporating unimportant events within a delusional framework and reading personal significance into the trivial activities of others. For instance, people with this symptom might think that overheard segments of conversations are about them, that the frequent appearance of the same person on a street where they customarily walk means that they are being watched, and that what they see on television or read in magazines somehow refers to them.

Believing that others are taking special notice is a common paranoid delusion. (James Lauritz/Getty Images, Inc.)

Table 9.1 Summary of the Major Symptom Domains in Schizophrenia

Positive Symptoms	Negative Symptoms	Disorganized Symptoms
Delusions, hallucinations	Avolition, alogia, anhedonia, blunted affect, asociality	Disorganized behavior, disorganized speech

Although delusions are found among more than half of people with schizophrenia, they are also found among people with other diagnoses, including bipolar disorder, depression with psychotic features, and delusional disorder.

Hallucinations and Other Disturbances of Perception   People with schizophrenia frequently report that the world seems somehow different or even unreal to them. As in the Clinical Case at the beginning of this chapter, some people report difficulties in paying attention to what is happening around them:

> I can't concentrate on television because I can't watch the screen and listen to what is being said at the same time. I can't seem to take in two things like this at the same time especially when one of them means watching and the other means listening. On the other hand I seem to be always taking in too much at the one time, and then I can't handle it and can't make sense of it. (quoted in McGhie & Chapman, 1961, p. 106)

The most dramatic distortions of perception are **hallucinations**, sensory experiences in the absence of any relevant stimulation from the environment. They are more often auditory than visual; 74 percent of one sample of people with schizophrenia reported having auditory hallucinations (Sartorius et al., 1974).

Some people with schizophrenia report hearing their own thoughts spoken by another voice. Other people may claim that they hear voices arguing, and others hear voices commenting on their behavior. Many people with schizophrenia experience their hallucinations as frightening or annoying. In one study of nearly 200 people with schizophrenia, those who had hallucinations that were longer, louder, more frequent, and experienced in the third person found them unpleasant. Hallucinations that were believed to come from a known person were experienced more positively (Copolov, Mackinnon, & Trauer, 2004).

Some theorists propose that people who have auditory hallucinations misattribute their own voice as being someone else's voice. Behavioral studies have shown that people with hallucinations are more likely to misattribute recordings of their own speech to a different source than are people without hallucinations or healthy controls (Allen, Johns, Fu, et al., 2004). Neuroimaging studies have examined what happens in the brain during auditory hallucinations. For example, studies using fMRI have found greater activity in Broca's area, the productive language area of the brain, when people with schizophrenia report hearing voices (McGuire, Shah, & Murray, 1993). Why might people make this misattribution? There may be a problem in the connections between the frontal lobe areas that enable the production of speech and the temporal lobe areas that enable the understanding of speech. A recent meta-analysis of 10 brain imaging studies found strongest activation in areas of the brain associated with speech production (e.g., Broca's area) but also found activation in areas associated with speech processing and understanding in the temporal lobes (Jardri, Pouchet, Pins, & Thomas, 2011). Other studies using both psychophysiological (Ford, Mathalon, Whitfield, et al., 2002) and brain-imaging methods (McGuire, Silbersweig, & Frith, 1996; Shergill, Brammer, Williams, et al., 2000) also support this idea.

Negative Symptoms

The **negative symptoms** of schizophrenia consist of behavioral deficits; they include avolition, asociality, anhedonia, blunted affect, and alogia (Kirkpatrick, Fenton, Carpenter, & Marder, 2006), all of which we describe below. These symptoms tend to endure beyond an acute episode and have profound effects on the lives of people with schizophrenia. They are also important prognostically; the presence of many negative symptoms is a strong predictor of a poor quality of life (e.g., occupational impairment, few friends) 2 years following hospitalization (Ho, Nopoulis, Flaum, et al., 1998).

Avolition   Apathy, or **avolition**, refers to a lack of motivation and a seeming absence of interest in or an inability to persist in what are usually routine activities, including work or school, hobbies, or social activities. For example, people with avolition may not be motivated to watch TV or hang out with friends.They may have difficulty persisting at work, school, or household chores and may spend much of their time sitting around doing nothing.

People with schizophrenia who have blunted affect may not outwardly show happiness, but they will feel it as strongly as people who smile. (Top: Blend Images/SuperStock, Inc.; Bottom: ThinkStock/SUPERSTOCK.)

Asociality Some people with schizophrenia have severe impairments in social relationships, referred to as **asociality.** They may have few friends, poor social skills, and very little interest in being with other people. They may not desire close relationships with family, friends, or romantic partners. Instead, they may wish to spend much of their time alone. When around others, people with this symptom may interact only superficially and briefly and appear aloof or indifferent to the social interaction.

Anhedonia A loss of interest in or a reported lessening of the experience of pleasure is called **anhedonia.** There are two types of pleasure experiences in the anhedonia construct. The first, called **consummatory pleasure,** refers to the amount of pleasure experienced in-the-moment or in the presence of something pleasurable. For example, the amount of pleasure you experience as you are eating a good meal is consummatory pleasure. The second type of pleasure, called **anticipatory pleasure,** refers to the amount of expected or anticipated pleasure from future events or activities. For example, the amount of pleasure you expect to receive after graduating from college is anticipatory pleasure. People with schizophrenia appear to have a deficit in anticipatory pleasure but not consummatory pleasure (Gard, Kring, Germans, Gard, et al., 2007; Kring, 1999; Kring & Caponigro, 2010). That is, when asked about expected future situations or activities that are pleasurable for most people (e.g., good food, recreational activities, social interactions) on an anhedonia questionnaire, people with schizophrenia report that they derive less pleasure from these sorts of activities than do people without schizophrenia (Gard et al., 2007; Horan, Kring, & Blanchard, 2006). However, when presented with actual pleasant activities, such as amusing films or tasty beverages, people with schizophrenia report experiencing as much pleasure as do people without schizophrenia (Gard et al., 2007). Thus, the anhedonia deficit in schizophrenia appears to be in anticipating pleasure, not experiencing pleasure in-the-moment or in the presence of pleasurable things.

Blunted Affect **Blunted affect** refers to a lack of outward expression of emotion. A person with this symptom may stare vacantly, the muscles of the face motionless, the eyes lifeless. When spoken to, the person may answer in a flat and toneless voice and not look at his or her conversational partner. Blunted affect was found in 66 percent of a large sample of people with schizophrenia (Sartorius et al., 1974).

The concept of blunted affect refers only to the outward expression of emotion, not to the patient's inner experience, which is not impoverished at all. Over 20 different studies have shown that people with schizophrenia are much less facially expressive than are people without schizophrenia, and this is true in daily life or in laboratory studies when emotionally evocative stimuli (films, pictures, foods) are presented. However, people with schizophrenia report experiencing the same amount or *even more* emotion than people without schizophrenia (Kring & Moran, 2008).

Alogia **Alogia** refers to a significant reduction in the amount of speech. Simply put, people with this symptom do not talk much. A person may answer a question with one or two words and will not be likely to elaborate on an answer with additional detail. For example, if you ask a person with alogia to describe a happy life experience, the person might respond "getting married" and then fail to elaborate even when asked for additional information.

Although we have just described five different negative symptoms, research suggests these symptoms can be understood more simply as representing two domains (Blanchard & Cohen, 2006; Horan, Kring, Gur, et al., 2011; Messinger, Tremeau, Antonius, et al., 2011). The first domain, involving motivation, emotional experience, and sociality, is sometimes referred to as the *experience* domain. The second domain, involving outward expression of emotion and vocalization, is referred to as the *expression* domain.

Disorganized Symptoms

Disorganized symptoms include disorganized speech and disorganized behavior.

Disorganized Speech Also known as *formal thought disorder,* **disorganized speech** refers to problems in organizing ideas and in speaking so that a listener can understand. The following excerpt illustrates the incoherence sometimes found in the conversation of people with schizophrenia as an interviewer tries to ask John, a person with schizophrenia, several questions.

Interviewer: Have you been nervous or tense lately?
John: No, I got a head of lettuce.
Interviewer: You got a head of lettuce? I don't understand.
John: Well, it's just a head of lettuce.
Interviewer: Tell me about lettuce. What do you mean?
John: Well … lettuce is a transformation of a dead cougar that suffered a relapse on the lion's toe. And he swallowed the lion and something happened. The … see, the. … . Gloria and Tommy, they're two heads and they're not whales. But they escaped with herds of vomit, and things like that.
Interviewer: Who are Tommy and Gloria?
John: Uh, … there's Joe DiMaggio, Tommy Henrich, Bill Dickey, Phil Rizzuto, John Esclavera, Del Crandell, Ted Williams, Mickey Mantle, Roy Mande, Ray Mantle, Bob Chance …
Interviewer: Who are they? Who are those people?
John: Dead people …they want to be fucked … by this outlaw.
Interviewer: What does all that mean?
John: Well, you see, I have to leave the hospital. I'm supposed to have an operation on my legs, you know. And it comes to be pretty sickly that I don't want to keep my legs. That's why I wish I could have an operation.
Interviewer: You want to have your legs taken off?
John: It's possible, you know.
Interviewer: Why would you want to do that?
John: I didn't have any legs to begin with. So I would imagine that if I was a fast runner, I'd be scared to be a wife, because I had a splinter inside of my head of lettuce. (Neale & Oltmanns, 1980, pp. 103-104)

Although John may make repeated references to central ideas or themes, the images and fragments of thought are not connected; it is difficult to understand what he is trying to tell the interviewer.

Speech may also be disorganized by what are called **loose associations,** or **derailment**, in which case the person may be more successful in communicating with a listener but has difficulty sticking to one topic. Steve Lopez, a reporter for the *Los Angeles Times,* befriended a man with schizophrenia named Nathaniel in the LA area who was a gifted musician (and also homeless). Lopez wrote about their friendship in the book *The Soloist* (S. Lopez, 2008). Nathaniel often exhibited loose associations. For example, in response to a question about Beethoven, Nathaniel replied:

Cleveland doesn't have the Beethoven statue. That's a military-oriented city, occupied, preoccupied, with all the military figures of American history, the great soldiers and generals, but you don't see the musicians on parade, although you do have Severance Hall, Cleveland Music School Settlement, Ohio University Bobcats, Buckeyes of Ohio State. All the great soldiers are there from the United States Military, World War Two, Korean War, whereas in Los Angeles you have the LAPD, Los Angeles County Jail, Los Angeles Times, Mr. Steve Lopez. That's an army, right? (quote in Lopez, 2008, pp. 23-24)

As this quote illustrates, a person with this symptom seems to drift off on a train of associations evoked by an idea from the past. People with schizophrenia have also described what it is like to experience disorganized speech.

My thoughts get all jumbled up. I start thinking or talking about something but I never get there. Instead, I wander off in the wrong direction and get caught up with all sorts of different things that may be connected with things I want to say but in a way I can't explain. People listening to me get more lost than I do. My trouble is that I've got too many thoughts. You might think about something, let's say that ashtray and just think, oh yes, that's for putting my cigarette in, but I would think of it and then I would think of a dozen different things connected with it at the same time. (quoted in McGhie & Chapman, 1961, p. 108)

It would seem logical to expect disorganized speech to be associated with problems in language production, but this does not appear to be the case. Instead, disorganized speech is associated with problems in what is called executive functioning—problem solving, planning, and making associations between thinking and feeling. Disorganized speech is also related to the ability to perceive semantic information (i.e., the meaning of words) (Kerns & Berenbaum, 2002, 2003).

Disorganized Behavior **Disorganized behavior** takes many forms. People with this symptom may go into inexplicable bouts of agitation, dress in unusual clothes, act in a childlike or silly manner, hoard food, or collect garbage. They seem to lose the ability to organize their behavior and make it conform to community standards. They also have difficulty performing the tasks of everyday living.

Catatonia includes several movement problems such as maintaining an unusual posture for long periods of time. (Grunnitus Studio/Photo Researchers, Inc.)

Movement Symptoms

One other symptom of schizophrenia does not fit neatly into the categories we have just presented, but it is a part of the DSM criteria. Grossly abnormal psychomotor behavior refers to disturbances in movement behavior. Catatonia is the prime example of this symptom.

Several motor abnormalities define **catatonia.** People with this symptom may gesture repeatedly, using peculiar and sometimes complex sequences of finger, hand, and arm movements, which often seem to be purposeful. Some people manifest an unusual increase in their overall level of activity, including much excitement, wild flailing of the limbs, and great expenditure of energy similar to that seen in mania. At the other end of the spectrum is **catatonic immobility:** people adopt unusual postures and maintain them for very long periods of time. Catatonia can also involve *waxy flexibility*—another person can move the patient's limbs into positions that the patient will then maintain for long periods of time.

FOCUS ON DISCOVERY 9.1

History of the Concept of Schizophrenia

Two European psychiatrists, Emil Kraepelin and Eugen Bleuler, initially formulated the concept of schizophrenia. Kraepelin first described **dementia praecox**, his term for what we now call schizophrenia, in 1898. Dementia praecox included several diagnostic subtypes—dementia paranoides, catatonia, and hebephrenia—that had been regarded as distinct entities by clinicians in the previous few decades. Although these disorders were symptomatically diverse, Kraepelin believed that they shared a common core, and the term dementia praecox reflected what he believed was that core—an early onset (praecox) and a progressive, inevitable intellectual deterioration (dementia). The dementia in dementia praecox is not the same as the dementias we discuss in the chapter on neurocognitive disorders (Chapter 14), which are defined principally by severe memory impairments. Kraepelin's term referred to a general "mental enfeeblement."

Bleuler broke with Kraepelin's description on two major points: he believed that the disorder did not necessarily have an early onset, and he believed that it did not inevitably progress toward dementia. Thus the label "dementia praecox" was no longer appropriate, and in 1908 Bleuler proposed his own term, *schizophrenia,* from the Greek words *schizein* ("to split") and *phren* ("mind"), capturing what he viewed as the essential nature of the condition.

With age of onset and deteriorating course no longer considered defining features of the disorder, Bleuler faced a conceptual problem. The symptoms of schizophrenia could vary widely among people, so he had to provide some justification for putting them into a single diagnostic category. That is, he needed to specify some common denominator, or essential property, that

Emil Kraepelin (1856–1926), a German psychiatrist, articulated descriptions of schizophrenia (then called dementia praecox) that have proved remarkably durable in the light of contemporary research. (Hueton Archive Getty Images.)

would link the various disturbances. The metaphorical concept that he adopted for this purpose was the "breaking of associative threads."

For Bleuler, associative threads joined not only words but also thoughts. Thus, goal-directed, efficient thinking and communication were possible only when these hypothetical structures were intact. The notion that associative threads were disrupted in people with schizophrenia could then be used to account for the range of other disturbances. Bleuler viewed attentional difficulties, for example, as resulting from a loss of purposeful direction in thought, in turn causing passive responses to objects and people in the immediate surroundings.

Kraepelin had recognized that a small percentage of people with symptoms of dementia praecox did not deteriorate, but he preferred to limit this diagnostic category to people who had a poor prognosis. Bleuler's work, in contrast, led to a broader concept of the disorder. He diagnosed some people with a good prognosis as having schizophrenia, and he also diagnosed schizophrenia in many people who would have received different diagnoses from other clinicians.

Eugen Bleuler (1857–1939), a Swiss psychiatrist, contributed to our conceptions of schizophrenia and coined the term. (Corbis-Bettmann.)

Catatonia is seldom seen today, perhaps because medications work effectively on these disturbed motor processes. Alternatively, Boyle (1991) has argued that the apparent high prevalence of catatonia during the early part of the twentieth century reflected misdiagnosis. Specifically, the similarities between encephalitis lethargica (sleeping sickness) and catatonia suggest that many cases of the former were misdiagnosed as the latter. This idea was portrayed in the film *Awakenings,* which was based on the career and writings of Oliver Sacks. See Focus on Discovery 9.1 for more on the history of schizophrenia and its symptoms.

Schizophrenia and the DSM-5

The DSM-5 criteria for schizophrenia will likely differ in some ways from the DSM-IV-TR criteria (summarized in Table 9.2 and in the proposed DSM-5 criteria box on p. 254). Like DSM-IV-TR, the DSM-5 will likely require that the symptoms last for at least 6 months for the diagnosis. The 6-month period must include at least 1 month of an acute episode, or active phase, defined by the presence of at least two of the following symptoms: delusions, hallucinations, disorganized speech, abnormal psychomotor behavior, such as catatonia, and negative symptoms. The remaining time required for the diagnosis can occur either before the active phase or after the active phase. This time criterion eliminates people who have a brief psychotic episode and then recover quickly.

DSM-5 will likely remove the subtypes of schizophrenia that were part of the DSM-IV-TR (i.e., paranoid, disorganized, catatonic, undifferentiated). The reason they are likely to be removed is due to their questionable usefulness, poor reliability, considerable overlap between subtypes, and poor predictive validity; that is, the diagnosis of one or another type of schizophrenia provided little information helpful in either treating the disorder or predicting its course.

Schizophrenia will be part of the chapter likely entitled "Schizophrenia Spectrum and other Psychotic Disorders." There are a number of other disorders in this group, which are listed in Table 9.2.

Two brief psychotic disorders are **schizophreniform disorder** and **brief psychotic disorder.** The symptoms of schizophreniform disorder are the same as those of schizophrenia

Table 9.2 Diagnoses of Schizophrenia Spectrum and other Psychotic Disorders

DSM-5 Diagnoses	Likely Key Changes
Schizophrenia	• No subtypes
	• Negative symptoms are described in more detail
	• Removal of criterion that one of the symptoms must be hallucinations, delusions, or disorganized speech
	• Removal of requirement that only one symptom be present if delusion is bizarre
Schizoaffective disorder	• Delusions or hallucinations for at least 2 weeks in absence of symptoms meeting mood disorder criteria (instead of "prominent mood symptoms")
	• Symptoms of a major mood episode present for over 30 percent of the lifetime duration of the illness
Delusional disorder	• No changes likely in DSM-5
Schizophreniform disorder	• No changes likely in DSM-5
Brief psychotic disorder	• No changes likely in DSM-5
Attenuated psychosis syndrome	• New category proposed for DSM-5
	• Less severe presentation of delusions, hallucinations, or disorganized speech in past month occurring at least once/week

but last only from 1 to 6 months. Brief psychotic disorder lasts from 1 day to 1 month and is often brought on by extreme stress, such as bereavement. These two disorders will not likely change in DSM-5. **Schizoaffective disorder** comprises a mixture of symptoms of schizophrenia and mood disorders. The DSM-5 will likely require either a depressive or manic episode rather than simply mood disorder symptoms as was done in DSM-IV-TR.

A person with **delusional disorder** is troubled by persistent delusions of persecution or by delusional jealousy, the unfounded conviction that a spouse or lover is unfaithful. Other delusions seen in this disorder include delusions of being followed, delusions of erotomania (believing that one is loved by some other person, usually a complete stranger with a higher social status), and delusions of having a general medical condition (e.g., having cancer). This category will not likely change in DSM-5.

The DSM-5 may include a new category called *attenuated psychosis syndrome.* We discuss this in more detail in Focus on Discovery 9.2.

FOCUS ON DISCOVERY 9.2

Attenuated Psychosis Syndrome: A New Category for DSM-5?

DSM-5 may include a new disorder in the "Schizophrenia Spectrum and Other Psychotic Disorders" chapter called attenuated psychosis syndrome (APS). This proposal has generated a good deal of discussion and debate in the field. After describing the proposed disorder, we briefly consider the pros and cons of including this new diagnostic category in the next DSM.

The idea for such a new category came from research over the past two decades that has sought to identify young people who are at risk for developing schizophrenia. These types of studies are called *clinical high-risk* studies (discussed more on p. 275), and the starting point for these prospective, longitudinal studies is the reliable identification of youth who present with mild positive symptoms that might later develop into schizophrenia (Miller, McGlashan, Rasen, et al., 2002). Research using the Structured Interview for Prodromal Syndromes (SIPS) has identified groups of young people who differ from people without these mild symptoms and from people who have a family history of schizophrenia (people studied in *familial high-risk* studies, discussed on p. 263). Such people have been referred to as prodromal; the word *prodrome* refers to the early signs of a disease. Young people meeting prodromal criteria on the SIPS differ from young people who do not meet prodromal criteria in a number of domains, including their everyday functioning and their rate of conversion to schizophrenia spectrum disorders (Woods, Addington, Cadenhead, et al., 2009). Between 10 and 30 percent of people meeting prodromal criteria develop a schizophrenia spectrum disorder compared with only 0.2 percent of the general population (Carpenter & van Os, 2011).

The proposed DSM-5 criteria for APS were based in part on these findings. To meet the diagnosis, someone must exhibit all six of the following:

1. At least one of: delusions, hallucinations, or disorganized speech in attenuated form, serious enough that it cannot be ignored.
2. The symptom(s) occur(s) at least once a week for one month.
3. The symptom(s) started or got worse in the past year.
4. The symptom(s) is/are upsetting or disabling.
5. The symptom(s) can't be explained by another disorder.
6. Person has never been diagnosed with another DSM-5 psychotic disorder.

What are some of the arguments in favor of adding this new category to DSM-5? First, identifying APS may help people get treatment that otherwise would go unnoticed by mental health professionals. Unfortunately, under the current health insurance system in the United States, people often cannot get treatment unless they have an official diagnosis. Second, the hope is that the identification and treatment of people with APS might prevent them from developing schizophrenia or other schizophrenia spectrum disorders.

However, there are a number of arguments against adding this new category (Yung, Nelson, Thompson, & Wood, 2010). First, it is not clear if the category itself has enough reliability and validity to support its inclusion in the DSM. Second, there is a high level of comorbidity with prodromal symptoms: over 60 percent of young people meeting the prodromal criteria have a history of depression, raising the possibility that APS is really part of a mood disorder, not a schizophrenia spectrum disorder. Third, there is concern that applying a new diagnostic label, particularly to young people, might be stigmatizing or lead to discrimination. Because not all people with APS will develop schizophrenia, it may unnecessarily alarm young people and their families. Finally, while providing treatment for people with distressing or disabling attenuated positive symptoms is a laudable goal, there is concern that the treatment will too closely resemble that for schizophrenia, further blurring the line between the two conditions. Indeed, there is not yet an effective treatment for APS (Carpenter & van Os, 2011).

With the publication of DSM-5 scheduled for May 2013, it will be interesting to see if APS is added as a new category or is instead added to the Appendix as a category in need of further study.

Quick Summary

Schizophrenia is a very heterogeneous disorder. It affects men slightly more than women and typically begins in late adolescence or early adulthood. Symptoms can be distinguished as positive, negative, and disorganized. Positive symptoms include hallucinations and delusions. Negative symptoms include avolition, alogia, blunted affect, anhedonia, and asociality. Together, the negative symptoms represent two domains: experience and expression. Disorganized symptoms include disorganized speech and disorganized behavior. No one of these symptoms is critical for the diagnosis of schizophrenia. The DSM-5 will likely no longer include schizophrenia subtypes because they do not have a good deal of validity and are not that useful. Other psychotic disorders include schizophreniform disorder and brief psychotic disorder, which differ from schizophrenia in duration. Schizoaffective disorder involves symptoms of both schizophrenia and mood disorders. Delusional disorder involves delusions but no other symptoms of schizophrenia, and the delusions are less bizarre than those in schizophrenia. A new category proposed for DSM-5, attenuated psychosis syndrome, involves positive symptoms in attenuated form that cause distress and have worsened in the past year.

Check Your Knowledge 9.1 (Answers are at the end of the chapter.)

List the symptom that each clinical vignette describes.

1. Charlie enjoyed going to movies. He particularly liked to see horror movies because they made him feel really scared. His sister was surprised to learn this, because when she went to movies with Charlie, he didn't gasp out loud or show fear on his face.
2. Marlene was convinced that Christian Bale was sending her messages. In his movie *The Dark Knight,* his battles with the Joker were a signal that he was prepared to fight for them to be together. That he signed autographs at his movie opening also told her that he was trying to get in touch with her.

3. Sophia didn't want to go out to dinner with her family. She reasoned that these dinners were always the same food and conversation, so why bother? Later in the week, her mother mentioned that Sophia was not doing much around the house. Sophia said that nothing she could think of to do would be fun.
4. Jevon was talking with his doctor about the side effects of his medication. He talked about having dry mouth and then immediately began talking about cottonmouth snakes and jungle safaris and how hiking was good for your health but that Barack Obama was in better shape than George Bush.

Etiology of Schizophrenia

What can explain the scattering and disconnection of thoughts, lack of emotion expression, odd delusions, and bewildering hallucinations of people with schizophrenia? As we will see, there are a number of factors contributing to the cause of this complex disorder.

Genetic Factors

A good deal of research supports the idea that schizophrenia has a genetic component, as we discuss in the sections below on behavior genetics and molecular genetics research. The evidence is somewhat more convincing from behavior genetics studies, largely because they have been well replicated. Current evidence indicates that schizophrenia is genetically heterogeneous—that is, genetic factors may vary from case to case—mirroring the fact, noted earlier, that schizophrenia is certainly symptomatically heterogeneous. As with the case of any gene or genes, they do their work via the environment, so gene–environment interaction studies are likely to help more clearly pinpoint the nature of the genetic contribution to schizophrenia (Walker & Tessner, 2008).

Behavior Genetics Research   Family, twin, and adoption studies support the idea that genetic factors play a role in schizophrenia. Many behavior genetic studies of schizophrenia

Table 9.3 Summary of Major Family and Twin Studies of the Genetics of Schizophrenia

Relation to Proband	Percentage with Schizophrenia
Spouse	1.00
Grandchildren	2.84
Nieces/nephews	2.65
Children	9.35
Siblings	7.30
DZ twins	12.08
MZ twins	44.30

Source: After Gottesman, McGuffin, & Farmer (1987).

were conducted when the definition of schizophrenia was considerably broader than it is now. However, behavior genetics investigators collected extensive descriptive data on their samples, allowing the results to be reanalyzed later using newer diagnostic criteria.

Family Studies   Table 9.3 presents a summary of the risk for schizophrenia in various relatives of index cases with schizophrenia. (In evaluating the figures, keep in mind that the risk for schizophrenia in the general population is a little less than 1 percent.) Quite clearly, relatives of people with schizophrenia are at increased risk, and the risk increases as the genetic relationship between proband and relative becomes closer (Kendler, Karkowski-Shuman, & Walsh, 1996). Other studies have found that people with schizophrenia in their family histories have more negative symptoms than those whose families are free of schizophrenia (Malaspina Goetz, Yale, et al., 2000), suggesting that negative symptoms may have a stronger genetic component.

A recent family study examined over 2 million people from Denmark from the Danish Civil Registration System (Gottesman, Laursen, Bertelsen & Mortensen, 2010). This system records all inpatient and outpatient admissions for health-related issues, including mental disorders. The researchers examined the cumulative incidence of schizophrenia and bipolar disorder among people with one, two, or no biological parents who had been admitted for treatment for schizophrenia or bipolar disorder. They also examined the incidence of these disorders among children who had one parent admitted for schizophrenia and one parent admitted for bipolar disorder. The findings are presented in Table 9.4. As you might expect, the incidence of schizophrenia was highest for children who had two parents admitted for schizophrenia. The incidence of schizophrenia was higher for people with one parent admitted for schizophrenia and one parent admitted for bipolar disorder compared to those people who had just one parent admitted for schizophrenia. These findings suggest that there may be some shared genetic vulnerability between schizophrenia and bipolar disorder, something that has also been suggested by molecular genetics studies, which we turn to shortly.

The results of family studies suggest that genes play a role in schizophrenia, but of course the relatives of a person with schizophrenia share not only genes but also common experiences. Recall from Chapter 2 that genes do much of their work via the environment. Therefore, the influence of the environment cannot be discounted in explaining the higher risks among relatives.

Behavior genetics studies often study twins or more rarely, triplets and quadruplets. In one rare case, all of the Genain quadruplet girls (not pictured) developed schizophrenia. (© UK History/Alamy.)

Twin Studies   Table 9.3 also shows the risk for identical (MZ) and fraternal (DZ) twins of people with schizophrenia. The risk for MZ twins (44.3 percent), although greater than that for DZ twins (12.08 percent), is still much less than 100 percent. Similar results have been obtained in more recent studies (Cannon, Kaprio, Lonngvist, et al., 1998; Cardno, Marshall, Coid, et al., 1999). The less-than-100-percent concordance in MZ twins is important: if genetic transmission alone accounted for schizophrenia and one identical twin had schizophrenia, the other twin would also have schizophrenia. Twin study research also suggests that negative symptoms may have a stronger genetic component than do positive symptoms (Dworkin & Lenzenwenger, 1984; Dworkin, Lenzenwenger, & Moldin, 1987).

Table 9.4 Summary of Gottesman and Colleagues (2010) Family Study

Psychopathology in Parents	Incidence of Schizophrenia
Both parents with schizophrenia	27.3%
One parent with schizophrenia	7.0%
No parent with schizophrenia	0.86%
One parent with schizophrenia and one parent with bipolar disorder	15.6%

As with family studies, of course, there is a critical problem in interpreting the results of twin studies. A common environment rather than common genetic factors could account for some portion of the increased risk. By common environment, we mean not only similar shared and nonshared environmental factors, such as child-rearing practices or peer relationships, but also a more similar intrauterine environment, for MZ twins are more likely than DZ twins to share a single blood supply.

A clever analysis supporting a genetic interpretation of the high risk found for identical twins was performed by Fischer (1971). She reasoned that if these rates indeed reflected a genetic effect, the twins without schizophrenia would presumably carry risk genes for schizophrenia, even though it was not expressed behaviorally, and thus might pass along an increased risk for the disorder to their children. Indeed, the rate of schizophrenia and schizophrenia-like psychoses in the children of the MZ twins without schizophrenia was 9.4 percent, while the rate among the children of the twins with schizophrenia was only slightly and nonsignificantly higher, 12.3 percent. Both rates are substantially higher than the 1 percent prevalence found in the general population, which lends further support to the importance of genetic factors in schizophrenia.

Adoption Studies The study of children whose biological mothers had schizophrenia but who were reared from early infancy by adoptive parents without schizophrenia is another useful behavior genetics study method. Such studies eliminate the possible effects of being reared in an environment where a parent has schizophrenia.

In a now-classic study, Heston (1966) followed up 47 people born between 1915 and 1945 to women with schizophrenia. The infants were put up for adoption at birth and raised by adoptive parents. Fifty control participants were selected from the same adoption agency that had placed the children of the women with schizophrenia. The follow-up assessment revealed that none of the controls was diagnosed with schizophrenia, versus 16.6 percent (five) of the offspring of women with schizophrenia.

Another large study of adopted offspring of mothers with schizophrenia found similar results. In this study, the risk for developing schizophrenia among the 164 adoptees who had a biological mother with schizophrenia was 8.1 percent; the risk for the 197 control adoptees who did not have a biological parent with schizophrenia was significantly lower at 2.3 percent. The risk for other disorders, such as schizoaffective disorder or schizophreniform disorder, was also greater among the adoptees with a biological parent with schizophrenia than among the control adoptees (Tienari, Wynne, Moring, et al., 2000).

A different type of adoption study was carried out in Denmark (Kety, Rosenthal, Wender, et al., 1976, 1994), where researchers examined the records of children who had been adopted at a young age. All adoptees who had later been diagnosed with schizophrenia were selected as the index cases. From the remaining cases, the investigators chose a control group of people who did not have schizophrenia but were similar to the index group on such variables as sex and age. Both the adoptive and the biological families of the two groups were then identified, and a search was made to determine who among them had a psychiatric history. As might be expected if genetic factors figure in schizophrenia, the biological relatives of the group with schizophrenia were diagnosed with schizophrenia more often than were members of the general population; the adoptive relatives were not.

Familial High-Risk Studies A different type of family study is called the **familial high-risk study.** This type of study begins with one or two biological parents with schizophrenia and follows their offspring longitudinally in order to identify how many of these children may develop schizophrenia and what types of childhood neurobiological and behavioral factors may predict the disorder's onset. The first familial high-risk study of schizophrenia was begun in the 1960s (Mednick & Schulsinger, 1968). The researchers chose Denmark because Danish registries make it possible to keep track of people for long periods of time. The high-risk participants were 207 young people whose mothers had schizophrenia. (The researchers decided that the mother should be the parent with the disorder because paternity is not always easy to determine.) Then 104 low-risk participants, people whose mothers did not have schizophrenia, were matched to the high-risk subjects on variables such as sex, age, father's occupation, rural

Sarnoff Mednick, a psychologist at the University of Southern California, pioneered the use of the familial high-risk method for studying schizophrenia. He has also contributed to the hypothesis that a maternal viral infection is implicated in this disorder. (Courtesy Sarnoff A. Mednick.)

or urban residence, years of education, and institutional upbringing versus rearing by the family. In 1972 the now-grown men and women were followed up with a number of measures, including a battery of diagnostic tests. Fifteen of the high-risk participants were diagnosed with schizophrenia; none of the control participants were so diagnosed.

Additional analyses of the group of participants who were diagnosed with schizophrenia suggested that positive and negative symptoms of schizophrenia may have different etiologies (Cannon, Mednick, & Parnas, 1990). People with predominantly negative symptoms had a history of pregnancy and birth complications and a failure to show electrodermal responses to simple stimuli. By contrast, people with predominantly positive symptoms had a history of family instability, such as separation from parents and placement in foster homes or institutions for periods of time.

In the wake of this pioneering study, other high-risk investigations were undertaken, some of which have also yielded information concerning the possible causes of adult psychopathology, but not necessarily schizophrenia specifically. The New York High-Risk Study found that a composite measure of attentional dysfunction predicted behavioral disturbance at follow-up (Cornblatt & Erlenmeyer-Kimling, 1985).

Furthermore, low IQ was a characteristic of the first high-risk children to be hospitalized (Erlenmeyer-Kimling & Cornblatt, 1987). In an Israeli study, poor neurobehavioral functioning (poor concentration, poor verbal ability, lack of motor control and coordination) predicted schizophrenia spectrum outcomes, as did earlier interpersonal problems (Marcus, Hans, Nagier, et al., 1987). The New England Family Study found that children of a parent (mother or father) with a schizophrenia spectrum disorder were six times more likely to develop schizophrenia spectrum disorder by age 40 than children without a parent with schizophrenia (Goldstein, Buka, Seidman, & Tsuang, 2010). This study also included a group of parents who had what they called "affective psychosis," including bipolar disorder or major depressive disorder with psychotic features. Children of parents with affective psychosis were not at greater risk for developing a schizophrenia spectrum disorder, but they were 14 times more likely to develop an affective psychosis than children of parents without any psychosis.

Molecular Genetics Research Knowing that schizophrenia has a genetic component is in many ways just the starting point for research. Understanding exactly what constitutes the genetic predisposition is the challenge faced by molecular genetics researchers. As with nearly all of the disorders we cover in this book, the predisposition for schizophrenia is not transmitted by a single gene.

Association studies try to narrow in on specific genes associated with schizophrenia. Recall from Chapter 4 that the goal of an association study is to establish how often a specific gene or genes and a particular trait or behavior (i.e., phenotype) co-occur. Research was initially focused on genes associated with the dopamine D2 receptor because, as we discuss later in the chapter, this receptor is associated with the effectiveness of some medications used to treat schizophrenia. Although there are some positive findings (Glatt, Faraone, & Tsuang, 2003), a number of other studies are negative (Owen, Williams, & O'Donovan, 2004).

Four candidate genes have received some support from association studies. Two of these genes have been associated with schizophrenia (DTNBP1 and NGR1) and two have been associated with the cognitive deficits associated with schizophrenia (COMT and BDNF). The gene called *DTNBP1* encodes a protein called dysbindin that is expressed throughout the brain, but the function of either the gene or the protein is not yet entirely clear. It appears to impact the dopamine and glutamate neurotransmitter systems throughout the brain (MacDonald & Chafee, 2006), and these systems are implicated in schizophrenia, as we discuss later on. In addition, a postmortem study has shown that compared to people without schizophrenia, the brains of people with schizophrenia had less dysbindin in a number of brain areas, including the frontal cortex, temporal cortex, hippocampus, and limbic system structures (Weickert, Straub, McClintock, et al., 2004). Another gene, *NGR1*, which has been linked to the neurotransmitter glutamate's NMDA (*N*-methyl-*D*-aspartate) receptor and is helpful with the process of myelination (i.e., producing the protective insulating sheath of myelin around neurons), has also been found to be associated with schizophrenia.

Other research has found that a gene called *COMT* is associated with executive functions that rely on the **prefrontal cortex** (reviewed by Goldberg & Weinberger, 2004). A number of studies have demonstrated that people with schizophrenia have deficits in executive functions, which include planning, working memory, and problem solving, and other studies have shown problems in the prefrontal cortex. A few association studies have implicated the COMT gene in schizophrenia (Harrison & Weinberger, 2004; Owen et al., 2004). The *BDNF* gene has been studied and linked with cognitive function in people with and without schizophrenia. This gene has a polymorphism called Val66Met, whereby a person can have two Val alleles (Val/Val), two Met alleles (Met/Met), or one Val and one Met allele (Val/Met). In a large study of people with and without schizophrenia, verbal memory was better for people who had two Val alleles (Val/Val) compared to people who had either one or two Met alleles (Val/Met or Met/Met) (Ho, Milev, O'Leary, et al., 2006).

Although there have been some replications of studies with these four genes, there have also been failures to replicate the association between these genes and schizophrenia. In addition, these four genes do not appear in genome-wide association studies. This may reflect the tremendous genetic heterogeneity associated with schizophrenia (Kim, Zerwas, Trace, & Sullivan, 2011).

Genome-wide association (GWAS) studies have also been applied to the study of schizophrenia. Recall from Chapter 2 that this technique allows researchers to identify rare mutations, such as CNVs (copy number variations), in genes rather than just known gene loci. Mutations are changes in a gene that occur randomly and for unknown reasons. A CNV refers to an abnormal copy (a deletion or a duplication) of one or more sections of DNA in a gene (see p. 33). As an example, one GWAS found over 50 rare CNV mutations that were three times more common among people with schizophrenia than in people without schizophrenia across two different samples of people (Walsh, McClellan, McCarthy, et al., 2008). Some of the identified gene mutations are known to be associated with other presumed risk factors in the etiology of schizophrenia, including the neurotransmitter glutamate and proteins that promote the proper placement of neurons in the brain during brain development. Furthermore, even though the identified mutations were more common in people with schizophrenia than people without schizophrenia, they were identified only in about 20 percent of the people with schizophrenia. Thus, other genetic factors await discovery in future studies.

Two recent reviews of GWAS studies in schizophrenia concluded that three CNV deletions (22q11.21, 15q13.3, 1q21.1; see Figure 9.1 for how to decode these tangles of letters and numbers) had met the stringent replication requirements of modern-day genetics research (Bassett, Scherer, & Brzustowicz, 2010; Kim et al., 2011). An additional deletion involving the NRXN1 gene and one CNV duplication (16p11.2) have also been replicated in more than one study, but the findings are not quite as strong.

GWAS studies of the sequence of genes have also been conducted. These studies seek to identify single nucleotide polymorphisms (SNPs; see p. 32) that are associated with schizophrenia. The findings of these studies have not been as well replicated as the GWAS studies of CNVs,

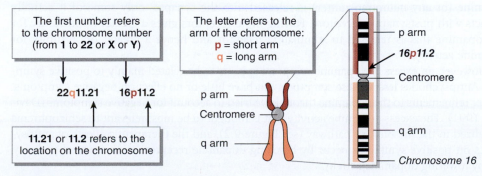

Figure 9.1 Decoding the language of genes.

but one of the intriguing findings to emerge is that the SNPs associated with schizophrenia are also associated with bipolar disorder, suggesting that there may be a common genetic vulnerability for both of these disorders (Owen, Craddock, & O'Donovan, 2010).

There are three important points about these mutations: (1) they are all very rare; (2) only a small number of people with these rare mutations have schizophrenia; (3) they are not specific to schizophrenia. Given that these are so rare, does this mean that these researchers are on the wrong track to finding genetic vulnerability to schizophrenia? Not necessarily. These findings confirm the genetic heterogeneity of schizophrenia and the idea that people with the same disorder (schizophrenia) may not necessarily have the same genetic factors contributing to the disorder. Current genetics research supports the idea that the genetic vulnerability to schizophrenia may be made up of many rare mutations.

The Role of Neurotransmitters

Present research is examining several different neurotransmitters, such as serotonin and glutamate, to see what role they might play in the etiology of schizophrenia. The first neurotransmitter to receive substantial research attention was dopamine. We trace the history of this research here, highlighting how it has both helped and hindered efforts to identify causes and treatments for schizophrenia.

Dopamine Theory The theory that schizophrenia is related to excess activity of the neurotransmitter dopamine is based principally on the knowledge that drugs effective in treating schizophrenia reduce dopamine activity. Researchers noted that antipsychotic drugs, in addition to being useful in treating some symptoms of schizophrenia, produce side effects resembling the symptoms of Parkinson's disease. Parkinson's disease is known to be caused in part by low levels of dopamine in a particular nerve tract of the brain. It was subsequently confirmed that antipsychotic drugs fit into and thereby block a particular type of postsynaptic dopamine receptors, called D2 receptors. From this knowledge about the action of the drugs that help people with schizophrenia, it was natural to conjecture that schizophrenia resulted from excess activity in dopamine nerve tracts. Further indirect support for this **dopamine theory** of schizophrenia came from the literature on *amphetamine psychosis*. Amphetamines can produce a state that closely resembles schizophrenia in people who do not have the disorder, and they can exacerbate the symptoms of people with schizophrenia (Angrist, Lee, & Gershon, 1974).

Based on the evidence just reviewed, researchers at first assumed that an excess of dopamine caused schizophrenia. But as other studies progressed, this assumption turned out to be too simple to account for the wide range of symptoms of schizophrenia. Some evidence supports the idea that people with schizophrenia have an excess number of dopamine receptors or oversensitive dopamine receptors. For example, postmortem studies of brains of people who had schizophrenia, as well as PET scans of living people with schizophrenia, have revealed that dopamine receptors are greater in number or are hypersensitive in some people with schizophrenia (Hietala, Syvalahti, Vuorio, et al., 1994; Tune, Wong, Pearlson, et al., 1993; Wong, Wagner, Tune, et al., 1986). Having too many dopamine receptors would be functionally akin to having an overactive dopamine system. The reason is that when dopamine (or any neurotransmitter) is released into the synapse, only some of it actually interacts with postsynaptic receptors. Having more receptors gives a greater opportunity for the dopamine that is released to stimulate a receptor and hence a greater opportunity for dopamine activity.

However, an excess of dopamine receptors appears to be related mainly to positive symptoms. Antipsychotics lessen these symptoms but have little or no effect on negative symptoms. Further refinements to the dopamine theory have tried to account for negative symptoms (Davis et al., 1991). The excess dopamine activity that is thought to be most relevant to schizophrenia is localized in the mesolimbic pathway (see Figure 9.2), and the therapeutic effects of antipsychotics on positive symptoms occur by blocking dopamine receptors in this neural pathway, thereby lowering dopamine activity.

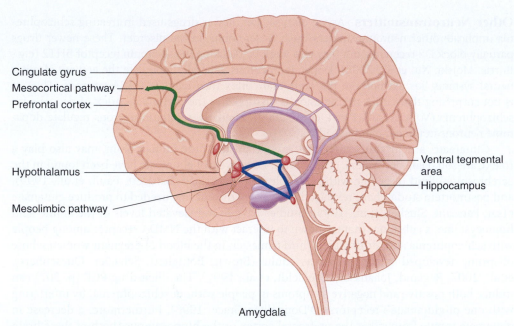

Cingulate gyrus
Mesocortical pathway
Prefrontal cortex

Hypothalamus

Mesolimbic pathway

Ventral tegmental area
Hippocampus

Amygdala

Figure 9.2 The brain and schizophrenia. The mesocortical pathway (in green) begins in the ventral tegmental area and projects to the prefrontal cortex. The mesolimbic pathway (in blue) also begins in the ventral tegmental area but projects to the hypothalamus, amygdala, hippocampus, and nucleus accumbens.

The mesocortical pathway is another scene of dopamine activity. It begins in the same brain region as the mesolimbic pathway but projects to the prefrontal cortex. The prefrontal cortex also projects to other brain areas that are innervated by dopamine. The dopamine neurons in the prefrontal cortex may be underactive and thus fail to exert inhibitory control over the dopamine neurons in the subcortical brain areas, such as the amygdala, with the result that there is dopamine overactivity in the pathways. Because the prefrontal cortex is thought to be especially relevant to the negative symptoms of schizophrenia, the underactivity of the dopamine neurons in this part of the brain may contribute to the negative symptoms of schizophrenia (see Figure 9.3). This proposal has the advantage of accounting for the simultaneous presence of positive and negative symptoms in the same person with schizophrenia. Furthermore, because antipsychotics do not have major effects on the dopamine neurons in the prefrontal cortex, we would expect them to be relatively ineffective as treatments for negative symptoms, and they are. When we examine research on structural abnormalities in the brains of people with schizophrenia, we will see some close connections between these two domains.

Despite the positive evidence we have reviewed, the dopamine theory is not a complete theory of schizophrenia. For example, it takes several weeks for antipsychotics to begin lessening the positive symptoms of schizophrenia, although they begin blocking dopamine receptors rapidly (Davis, 1978). This disjunction between the behavioral and pharmacological effects of antipsychotics is difficult to understand within the context of the theory. One possibility is that although antipsychotics do indeed block D2 receptors, their ultimate therapeutic effect may result from the effect this blockade has on other brain areas and other neurotransmitter systems (R.M. Cohen, Nordahl, Semple, et al., 1997).

Schizophrenia is a disorder with widespread symptoms covering perception, emotion, cognition, motor activity, and social behavior. It is unlikely that a single neurotransmitter could account for all of them. Thus, schizophrenia researchers have cast a broader neurotransmitter net, moving away from an emphasis on dopamine.

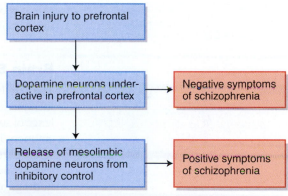

Brain injury to prefrontal cortex

Dopamine neurons underactive in prefrontal cortex → Negative symptoms of schizophrenia

Release of mesolimbic dopamine neurons from inhibitory control → Positive symptoms of schizophrenia

Figure 9.3 Dopamine theory of schizophrenia.

Other Neurotransmitters As we discuss later, newer drugs used in treating schizophrenia implicate other neurotransmitters, such as serotonin, in the disorder. These newer drugs partially block D2 receptors, but they also work by blocking the serotonin receptor 5HT2 (e.g., Burris, Molski, Xu, et al., 2002). Dopamine neurons generally modulate the activity of other neural systems; for example, in the prefrontal cortex they regulate GABA neurons. Thus, it is not surprising that GABA transmission is disrupted in the prefrontal cortex of people with schizophrenia (Volk, Austin, Pierri, et al., 2000). Similarly, serotonin neurons regulate dopamine neurons in the mesolimbic pathway.

Glutamate, a neurotransmitter that is widespread in the human brain, may also play a role (Carlsson, Hanson, Waters, et al., 1999). Low levels of glutamate have been found in the cerebrospinal fluid of people with schizophrenia (Faustman, Bardgett, Faull, et al., 1999), and postmortem studies have revealed low levels of the enzyme needed to produce glutamate (Tsai, Parssani, Slusher, et al., 1995). Studies have found elevated levels of the amino acid homocysteine, a substance that is known to interact with the NMDA receptor among people with schizophrenia and, during their third trimester, in the blood of pregnant women whose offspring developed schizophrenia as adults (Brown, Bottiglieri, Schaefer, Quesenberry, et al., 2007; Regland, Johansson, Grenfeldt, et al., 1995). The illicit drug PCP (p. 307) can induce both positive and negative symptoms in people without schizophrenia, by interfering with one of glutamate's receptors (O'Donnell & Grace, 1998). Furthermore, a decrease in glutamate inputs from either the prefrontal cortex or the hippocampus (both of these brain structures are implicated in schizophrenia) to the corpus striatum (a temporal lobe structure) could result in increased dopamine activity (O'Donnell & Grace, 1998). Additional evidence suggests that cognitive deficits in schizophrenia supported by the prefrontal cortex as well as symptoms of disorganization may be connected to deficits involving NMDA (MacDonald & Chafee, 2006). A new medication that targets glutamate receptors is currently being tested, and the early results are promising, both with respect to reducing symptoms and with respect to not promoting weight gain, which is a troubling side effect associated with many medications used to treat schizophrenia (Patil, Zhang, Martenyi, et al., 2007).

Brain Structure and Function

The search for a brain abnormality that causes schizophrenia began as early as the syndrome was identified, but studies did not begin to yield consistent findings until fairly recently. The challenge of such a task is indeed daunting. Because schizophrenia affects so many domains (thought, emotion, behavior), it is unlikely that a single type of brain abnormality can account for all of schizophrenia's symptoms. In the last two decades, however, spurred by a number of technological advances, research has yielded some promising results. Among the most well replicated findings of brain abnormalities in schizophrenia are enlargement of the ventricles, dysfunction in the prefrontal cortex, and dysfunction in the temporal cortex and surrounding brain regions.

Enlarged Ventricles Postmortem studies of the brains of people with schizophrenia consistently reveal enlarged ventricles. The brain has four ventricles, which are spaces in the brain filled with cerebrospinal fluid. Having larger fluid-filled spaces implies a loss of brain cells. Meta-analyses of several neuroimaging studies have most consistently revealed that some people with schizophrenia, even very early in the course of the illness and across the course of the illness, have enlarged ventricles (Kempton, Stahl, Williams, et al., 2010; Wright, Rabe-Hesketh, Woodruff, et al., 2000). Further evidence concerning enlarged ventricles comes from two MRI studies of pairs of MZ twins, only one of whom had schizophrenia (McNeil, Cantor-Graae, & Weinberger, 2000; Suddath, Christison, Torrey, et al., 1990). In both studies the ill twin had larger ventricles than the well twin, and in one of the studies most of the twins with schizophrenia could be identified by simple visual inspection of the scan. Because the twins were genetically identical in these studies, these results suggest that the origin of these brain abnormalities may not be genetic. Two recent meta-analyses of longitudinal studies suggest that the enlarged ventricles may increase over the course of the illness, above and beyond what occurs in typical aging (Kempton et al., 2010; Olabi, Ellison-Wright, McIntosh, et al., 2011). This suggests that aspects of brain abnormalities in schizophrenia progress (get worse) over time.

Large ventricles in people with schizophrenia are correlated with impaired performance on neuropsychological tests, poor functioning prior to the onset of the disorder, and poor response to drug treatment (Andreasen, Olsen, Dennert, et al., 1982; Weinberger, Cannon-Spoor, Potkin, et al., 1980). The extent to which the ventricles are enlarged, however, is modest, and many people with schizophrenia do not differ from people without schizophrenia in this respect. Furthermore, enlarged ventricles are not specific to schizophrenia, as they are also evident in the CT scans of people with other disorders, such as bipolar disorder with psychotic features (Rieder, Mann, Weinberger, et al., 1983). People with these disorders can show ventricular enlargement almost as great as that seen in schizophrenia (Elkis, Friedman, Wise, et al., 1995)[1].

Factors Involving the Prefrontal Cortex A variety of evidence suggests that the prefrontal cortex is of particular importance in schizophrenia.

- The prefrontal cortex is known to play a role in behaviors such as speech, decision making, emotion, and goal-directed behavior, which are disrupted in schizophrenia.

- MRI studies have shown reductions in gray matter in the prefrontal cortex (Buchanan, Vladar, Barta, et al.,1998).

- People with schizophrenia perform more poorly on neuropsychological tests designed to tap functions promoted by the prefrontal region, including working memory or the ability to hold bits of information in memory (Barch, Csernansky, Conturo, et al., 2002, 2003; Heinrichs & Zakzanis, 1998).

- In a type of functional imaging in which glucose metabolism is studied in various brain regions while people perform psychological tests, people with schizophrenia have shown low metabolic rates in the prefrontal cortex (Buchsbaum, Kessler, King, et al., 1984). Glucose metabolism in the prefrontal cortex has also been studied while people with schizophrenia are performing neuropsychological tests of prefrontal function. Because the tests place demands on the prefrontal cortex, glucose metabolism normally goes up as energy is used. People with schizophrenia, especially those with prominent negative symptoms, do poorly on the tests and also fail to show activation in the prefrontal region (Potkin, Alva, Fleming, et al., 2002; Weinberger, Berman, & Illowsky, 1988). Failure to show frontal activation has also been found using fMRI (Barch, Carter, Braver, et al., 2001; MacDonald & Carter, 2003).

- Finally, failure to show frontal activation is related to the severity of negative symptoms (O'Donnell & Grace, 1998) and thus parallels the work on dopamine underactivity in the frontal cortex already discussed.

Despite the reduced volume of the gray matter in the prefrontal cortex (and also the temporal cortex), the number of neurons in this area does not appear to be reduced. More detailed studies indicate that what is lost may be what are called "dendritic spines" (Goldman-Rakic & Selemon, 1997; McGlashan & Hoffman, 2000). Dendritic spines are small projections on the shafts of dendrites where nerve impulses are received from other neurons at the synapse (see Figure 9.4). The loss of these dendritic spines means that communication among neurons (i.e., functioning of the synapses) is disrupted, resulting in what some have termed a "disconnection syndrome." One possible result of the failure of neural systems to communicate could be the speech and behavioral disorganization seen in schizophrenia. Current research is linking these abnormalities in dendritic spines with the candidate genes and CNVs identified in schizophrenia, discussed in the earlier section on genetic factors (Penzes, Cahill, Jones, et al., 2011).

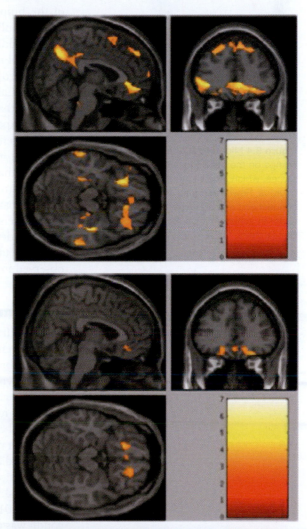

The pictures show brain activation from an fMRI study that involved maintaining pleasant emotional experience over a 12-second delay. The control group showed greater activation in areas of the frontal lobes compared to the schizophrenia group. Adapted from Ursu et al. (2011), *American Journal of Psychiatry, 168*, 276-285. (Courtesy of Ann Kring.)

---

[1]Other findings also suggest that the schizophrenia and psychotic mood disorders should not perhaps be totally separate diagnostic categories. The disorders share some symptoms (notably, delusions) and some possible etiological factors (e.g., genetic factors, increased dopamine activity), and they respond similarly to medications. An important implication is that researchers would be well served to focus some of their efforts on psychotic symptoms in other disorders as well as in schizophrenia.

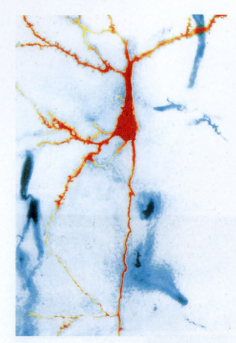

Figure 9.4 Micrograph of a neuron. The bumps on the dendrites are dendritic spines, which receive inputs from other neurons. Fewer dendritic spines may impair connections among neurons and may be a factor in schizophrenia. (BSIP/Sercomi/Photo Researchers, Inc.)

Problems in the Temporal Cortex and Surrounding Regions Additional research has found that people with schizophrenia have structural and functional abnormalities in the temporal cortex, including areas such as the temporal gyrus, hippocampus, amygdala, and anterior cingulate. For example, research also shows a reduction in cortical gray matter in temporal as well as frontal brain regions (Gur, Turetsky, Cowell, et al., 2000) and reduced volume in the basal ganglia (e.g., the caudate nucleus), hippocampus, and limbic structures (Chua & McKenna, 1995; Gur & Pearlson, 1993; Keshavan, Rosenberg, Sweeney, et al., 1998; Lim, Adalsteinssom, Spielman, et al., 1998; Nelson, Saykin, Flashman, et al., 1998; Velakoulis, Pantelis, McGorry, et al., 1999; Walker, Mittal, Tessner, et al., 2008). A twin study found reduced hippocampus volume among twins with schizophrenia, but not among the twins without schizophrenia (van Erp, Saleh, Huttunen, et al., 2004). A meta-analysis of MRI studies conducted with people during their first episode of schizophrenia concluded that the volume of the hippocampus was significantly reduced compared to people without schizophrenia (Steen, Mull, McClure, et al., 2006).

An additional interesting piece of evidence regarding the hippocampus comes from a meta-analysis of nine studies assessing the brain volume of over 400 first-degree relatives of people with schizophrenia and over 600 first-degree relatives of people without schizophrenia (Boos, Aleman, Cahn, et al., 2007). Relatives of people with schizophrenia had smaller hippocampal volumes than relatives of people without schizophrenia. These findings suggest that reduced hippocampal volume in people with schizophrenia may reflect a combination of genetic and environmental factors.

What makes these findings about the hippocampus all the more intriguing is the fact that the hypothalamic–pituitary–adrenal (HPA) axis is closely connected to this area of the brain. Chronic stress is associated with reductions in hippocampal volume in other disorders, such as posttraumatic stress disorder. Although people with schizophrenia do not necessarily experience more stress compared to people without schizophrenia, they are more reactive to stress. Other evidence indicates that the HPA axis is disrupted in schizophrenia. Taken together, stress reactivity and a disrupted HPA axis likely contribute to the reductions in hippocampal volume observed in people with schizophrenia (Walker et al., 2008).

Environmental Factors Influencing the Developing Brain

Several different environmental factors have been studied as possible contributing factors to schizophrenia (Brown, 2011; van Os, Kenis, & Rutten, 2010). A possible cause of some of the observed brain abnormalities in schizophrenia is damage during gestation or birth. Many studies have shown high rates of delivery complications in people with schizophrenia (Brown, 2011; Walker et al., 2004); such complications could have resulted in a reduced supply of oxygen to the brain, resulting in loss of cortical gray matter (Cannon, van Erp, Rosso, et al., 2002). These obstetrical complications do not raise the risk schizophrenia in everyone who experiences them; rather, the risk for schizophrenia is increased in those who experience complications and have a genetic diathesis (Cannon & Mednick, 1993).

Additional research suggests that maternal infections during pregnancy are associated with greater risk of their children developing schizophrenia when they become adults (Brown & Derkits, 2010). For example, one study found that maternal exposure to the parasite toxoplasma gondii was associated with a nearly 2.5 times greater risk of schizophrenia among the mothers' children when they became adults (A. S. Brown, Schaeffeer, Quesenberry, et al., 2005). This is a common parasite, carried by many people with no ill effects.

The most widely studied prenatal infection has been influenza. Studies have examined rates of schizophrenia among adults who had likely been exposed to the flu virus during their mothers' pregnancies (Mednick, Huttonen, & Machon, 1994; Mednick, Machon, Huttunen, et al., 1988). During the 1957 Helsinki influenza epidemic, people who had been exposed to the flu virus during the second trimester of pregnancy had much higher rates of schizophrenia than those who had been exposed in either of the other trimesters and much higher rates than nonexposed control adults. This finding was replicated in only half of nearly 30 later studies, calling it into question. And a more recent study found evidence that mothers' exposure to the flu during *first* trimester of pregnancy, as directly measured by the presence of flu antibodies in the blood, was associated with a sevenfold increase in the risk for schizophrenia among their children (Brown, Begg, Gravenstein, et al., 2004). Though the increase in risk sounds large, the difference from the control group was not quite statistically different, suggesting it is a small effect.

If, as the findings we have just reviewed suggest, the development of the brains of people with schizophrenia goes awry very early, why does the disorder begin many years later, in adolescence or early adulthood? The prefrontal cortex is a brain structure that matures late, typically in adolescence or early adulthood. Thus a problem in this area, even one that begins early in the course of development, may not show itself in the person's behavior until the period of development when the prefrontal cortex begins to play a larger role in behavior (Weinberger, 1987). Notably, dopamine activity also peaks in adolescence, which may further set the stage for the onset of schizophrenia symptoms (Walker et al., 2008). Adolescence is also typically a developmental period that is fraught with stress. Recall from our discussions in Chapter 2 that stress activates the HPA axis (see p. 40), causing cortisol to be secreted. Research in the past 10 years has demonstrated that cortisol increases dopamine activity, particularly in the mesolimbic pathway, perhaps increasing the likelihood of the development of schizophrenia symptoms (Walker et al., 2008).

Another proposed explanation is that the development of symptoms in adolescence could reflect a loss of synapses due to excessive pruning, the elimination of synaptic connections. Pruning is a normal part of brain development that occurs at different rates in different areas of the brain. It is mostly complete in sensory areas by about 2 years of age but continues in the prefrontal cortex until mid-adolescence. If too extensive, pruning would result in the loss of necessary communication among neurons (McGlashan & Hoffman, 2000).

An additional environmental factor that has been studied as a risk factor for schizophrenia among adolescents is cannabis (marijuana) use. Among people already diagnosed with schizophrenia, cannabis use is associated with a worsening of symptoms (Foti, Kotov, Guey, et al., 2010). But does cannabis use contribute to the onset of schizophrenia? A meta-analysis of studies examining the prospective relationship between cannabis use in adolescence and the onset of schizophrenia in adolescence or adulthood indicated that the risk of developing schizophrenia was greater among those who used cannabis compared to those who did not (Arseneault, Cannon, Poulton, et al., 2002). Although the studies were prospective, the findings are still correlational, and you will recall from Chapter 4 that correlation does not mean causation! Other studies suggest that the linkage between cannabis use and risk of developing schizophrenia is observed only among those who are genetically vulnerable to schizophrenia. For example, Caspi and colleagues (2005) found a gene–environment interaction between a particular polymorphism in the COMT gene (discussed earlier) and cannabis use. The combination of cannabis use and one COMT polymorphism were associated with increased risk of schizophrenia, but neither alone was associated with increased risk for schizophrenia.

Psychological Factors

People with schizophrenia do not appear to experience more stress in daily life than people without schizophrenia (Phillips, Francey, Edwards, et al., 2007; Walker et al., 2008). However, people with schizophrenia appear to be very reactive to the stressors we all encounter in daily living. In one study, people with psychotic disorders (92 percent with schizophrenia), their first-degree relatives, and people without any psychiatric disorder participated in a 6-day ecological momentary assessment study in which they recorded stress and mood several times each day. Daily life stress predicted greater decreases in positive moods in both people with schizophrenia and their relatives compared with controls. Stress also predicted greater increases in negative moods in the people with schizophrenia compared with both relatives and controls (Myin-Germeys, van Os, Schwartz, et al., 2001). Thus, people with schizophrenia were particularly vulnerable to daily stress. Research also shows that, as with many of the disorders we have discussed in this book, increases in life stress increase the likelihood of a relapse (Ventura, Neuchterlein, Lukoff, et al., 1989; Walker et al., 2008).

Additional research on psychological factors in the development and relapse of schizophrenia has focused on socioeconomic status and the family.

Socioeconomic Status and Urban Living For many years we have known that the highest rates of schizophrenia are found in urban areas inhabited by people of the lowest socioeconomic status (SES) in several countries, including the United States, Denmark, Norway, and the United Kingdom (Hollingshead & Redlich, 1958; Kohn, 1968). The relationship between SES and schizophrenia is not such that the prevalence of schizophrenia goes up as SES goes down. Rather, there is a sharp upturn in the prevalence of schizophrenia in people of the lowest socioeconomic status.

The correlation between SES and schizophrenia is consistent but difficult to interpret in causal terms. Is it that stressors associated with SES and urban living may contribute to the development of schizophrenia—the **sociogenic hypothesis?** Degrading treatment by others of higher status, low levels of education, and lack of rewards and opportunities may, taken together, make very low SES so stressful that people who are predisposed to develop schizophrenia readily develop the disorder. In addition, these stressors could have neurobiological effects; for example, children of mothers whose nutrition during pregnancy was poor are at increased risk for schizophrenia (Susser, Neugebauer, Hoek, et al., 1996).

Or is it the case that during the course of their developing illness, people with schizophrenia drift into poor neighborhoods because their illness impairs their earning power and they cannot afford to live elsewhere—the **social selection hypothesis**?

A study in Israel evaluated the two hypotheses by investigating both SES and ethnic background (Dohrenwend, Levav, Schwartz, et al., 1992). The rates of schizophrenia were examined in Israeli Jews of European ethnic background and in more recent immigrants to Israel from North Africa and the Middle East. The latter group experienced considerable racial prejudice and discrimination in Israel. The sociogenic hypothesis would predict that because they experienced high levels of stress regardless of socioeconomic status, the members of the disadvantaged ethnic group should have consistently higher rates of schizophrenia regardless of status. However, this pattern did not emerge, supporting the social selection hypothesis. Thus, research results are more supportive of the social selection hypothesis than of the sociogenic hypothesis.

Family-Related Factors Early theorists regarded family relationships, especially those between a mother and her son, as crucial in the development of schizophrenia. At one time the view was so prevalent that the term *schizophrenogenic mother* was coined for the supposedly cold and dominant, conflict-inducing parent who was said to produce schizophrenia in her offspring (Fromm-Reichmann, 1948). These mothers were characterized as rejecting, overprotective, self-sacrificing, impervious to the feelings of others, rigid and moralistic about sex, and fearful of intimacy. Controlled studies evaluating the schizophrenogenic-mother theory have not supported it. The damage done to families by this theory, however, was significant. For generations, parents blamed themselves for their child's illness, and until the 1970s, psychiatrists often joined in this blame game.

How Do Families Influence Schizophrenia? Other studies continued to explore the possibility that the family plays some role in the etiology of schizophrenia. For the most part, the findings are only suggestive, not conclusive. For example, a few studies of families of people with schizophrenia have found that they communicate more vaguely with one another and have higher levels of conflict than families of people without schizophrenia. It is plausible, though, that the conflict and unclear communication are a response to having a young family member with schizophrenia.

Further evidence favoring some role for the family comes from the Finnish adoption study described above (Tienari et al., 2000). Various aspects of family life in the adoptive families were extensively studied and then related to the adjustment of the children (Tienari, Wynne, Moring, et al., 1994). The families were categorized into levels of maladjustment based on material from clinical interviews and psychological tests. More serious psychopathology was found among the adoptees reared in a disturbed family environment. Furthermore, among children reared in a disturbed family environment, those having a biological parent with schizophrenia showed more psychopathology than did the control participants. Although it is tempting to conclude that both a genetic predisposition and a noxious family environment are necessary to increase risk for psychopathology, a problem in interpretation remains: the disturbed family environment could be a response to a disturbed child. Thus we cannot firmly conclude that an etiological role for the family has been established.

Families and Relapse A series of studies initiated in London indicate that the family can have an important impact on the adjustment of people with schizophrenia after they leave the hospital. In one study, investigators conducted a 9-month follow-up study of a sample of people with schizophrenia who returned to live with their families after being discharged from the hospital (Brown, Bone, Dalison, et al., 1966). Interviews were conducted with parents or spouses before discharge and rated for the number of critical comments made about the patient and for expressions of hostility toward the patient and emotional overinvolvement with the patient. The following is an example of a critical comment made by a father remarking on his daughter's behavior, in which he is expressing the idea that his daughter is deliberately symptomatic to avoid housework: "My view is that Maria acts this way so my wife doesn't give her any responsibilities around the house" (quote in Weisman, Neuchterlein, Goldstein, et al., 1998). Combining these three characteristics—critical comments, hostility, and emotional overinvolvement—led to the creation of the construct called **expressed emotion (EE)**. Families in the original study were divided into two groups: those revealing a great deal of expressed emotion (high-EE families) and those revealing little (low-EE families). At the end of the follow-up period, only 10 percent of the patients returning to low-EE homes had relapsed, but 58 percent of the patients returning to high-EE homes had gone back to the hospital.

This research, which has since been replicated (see Butzlaff & Hooley, 1998, for a meta-analysis), indicates that the environment to which people with schizophrenia are discharged has great bearing on how soon they are rehospitalized. Researchers have also found that negative symptoms of schizophrenia are most likely to elicit critical comments, as in the example presented in the previous paragraph, and that the relatives who make the most critical comments are the most likely to view people with schizophrenia as being able to control their symptoms (Lopez, Nelson, Snyder, et al., 1999; Weisman et al., 1998).

There are also important cultural differences in EE. Lopez and colleagues (2009) found that Anglo American caregivers were higher in EE than recently immigrated Mexican American caregivers, and this was true for all aspects of EE (i.e., critical comments, hostility, and emotional overinvolvement). Nearly three-quarters of Anglo American caregivers designated as high EE were so designated due to high hostility and critical comments; only 8 percent were designated as high EE based on emotional overinvolvement. By contrast, the Mexican American caregivers high in EE were fairly evenly divided between those who were high in hostility and critical comments and those who were high in emotional overinvolvement. These findings have important implications for developing and providing family interventions for schizophrenia, which we review a bit later in the chapter. Another study found that emotional overinvolvement specifically predicted relapse in Mexican Americans with schizophrenia, and that the linkage between EE and relapse was highest among Mexican Americans who had acculturated more to the ways of the United States (Aguilera, Lopez, Breitborde, et al., 2010).

What is not yet clear is exactly how to interpret the effects of EE. Is EE causal, or does it reflect a reaction to the ill relative's behavior? For example, if the condition of a person with schizophrenia begins to deteriorate, family concern and involvement may increase. Indeed, disorganized or dangerous behavior by the patient might seem to warrant limit setting and other familial efforts that could increase the level of EE. Research indicates that both interpretations of the operation of EE may be correct. Recently discharged people with schizophrenia and their high- or low-EE families were observed as they engaged in a discussion of a family problem. Two key findings emerged (Rosenfarb, Goldstein, Mintz, & Neuchterlein, 1994).

Expressed emotion, which includes hostility, critical comments, and emotional overinvolvement, has been linked with relapse in schizophrenia. (Lisette Le Bon/SUPERSTOCK.)

1. The expression of unusual thoughts by the people with schizophrenia ("If that kid bites you, you'll get rabies") elicited a greater number of critical comments by family members who had previously been characterized as high in EE than by those characterized as low in EE.

2. In high-EE families, critical comments by family members led to increased expression of unusual thoughts by the people with schizophrenia.

Thus, this study found a bidirectional relationship in high-EE families: critical comments by family members elicited more unusual thoughts by relatives with schizophrenia, and unusual thoughts expressed by the relatives with schizophrenia led to increased critical comments.

How does stress, such as a high level of EE, increase the symptoms of schizophrenia and precipitate relapses? One answer to this question relates the effects of stress on the HPA axis and its link to dopamine (Walker et al., 2008). Stress activates the HPA axis, causing cortisol to be secreted, which can then increase dopamine activity (Walker et al., 2008). Furthermore, heightened dopamine activity itself can increase HPA activation, which may make a person overly sensitive to stress. Thus, there is a bidirectional relationship between HPA activation and dopamine activity.

Developmental Factors

What are people who develop schizophrenia like before their symptoms begin? This question has been addressed using retrospective and prospective studies. The retrospective studies are sometimes referred to as "follow-back" studies because the starting point is a group of adults with schizophrenia that researchers then follow back to childhood to unearth records and tests from childhood.

Elaine Walker has conducted many studies of the development of schizophrenia.
(Courtesy Elaine F. Walker, Emory University.)

Retrospective Studies In the 1960s, researchers found that children who later developed schizophrenia had lower IQs and were more often delinquent and withdrawn than members of various control groups, usually comprising siblings and neighborhood peers (Albee, Lane, & Reuter, 1964; Berry, 1967; Lane & Albee, 1965). Other studies found that boys who later developed schizophrenia were rated by teachers as disagreeable, whereas girls who later developed schizophrenia were rated as passive (Watt, 1974; Watt, Stolorow, Lubensky, et al., 1970).

More recently, researchers have examined emotional and cognitive deficits that were present before the onset of schizophrenia. In one very clever study, Elaine Walker and colleagues analyzed the home movies of children who later developed schizophrenia. The movies were made as part of normal family life and were made before the onset of schizophrenia (Walker, Davis, & Savoie, 1994; Walker, Grimes, Davis, et al., 1993). Compared with their siblings who did not later develop schizophrenia, the children who later developed schizophrenia as young adults showed poorer motor skills and more expressions of negative emotions. Other studies have examined past childhood assessments of the cognition and intellectual functioning of adults who had schizophrenia. These studies found that adults with schizophrenia scored lower on IQ and other cognitive tests as children compared to adults without schizophrenia (Davis, Malmberg, Brandt, et al., 1997; Woodbury, Giuliano, & Seidman, 2008).

As intriguing as these findings are, these studies were not necessarily designed with the intention of predicting the development of schizophrenia from childhood behavior. Rather, they began with an adult sample of people with schizophrenia and then looked back at records and data collected from their childhoods to see if there were characteristics that distinguished them as young children.

Prospective Studies A more recent prospective study identified childhood characteristics that were associated with the development of schizophrenia in early adulthood (Reichenberg, Aushalom, Harrington, et al., 2010). In this study, a large sample of people from Dunedin, New Zealand, were assessed several times between the ages of 7 and 32. IQ tests were administered at ages 7, 9, 11, and 13; diagnostic assessments were conducted at ages 21, 26, and 32. The researchers found that lower scores on the IQ test in childhood predicted the onset of schizophrenia in young adulthood, even after they controlled for low socioeconomic status (which is associated with lower IQ scores; see Chapter 3). The children who later developed schizophrenia showed stable deficits in several of the verbal IQ subtests compared to children who did not develop schizophrenia. Thus, children who developed schizophrenia as adults had signs of a cognitive deficit beginning at age 7 that remained stable through adolescence.

These findings are broadly consistent with the idea that something goes awry in development that is associated with the onset of schizophrenia in late adolescence or early adulthood. Nevertheless, more specific information is required if developmental histories are to provide clear evidence regarding the etiology of schizophrenia.

One of the difficulties with the familial high-risk studies that we discussed earlier has to do with the large sample sizes that are required. As shown in Table 9.3, the percentage of children with a biological parent who has schizophrenia who go on to themselves develop schizophrenia is around 10 percent. If a study begins with 200 high-risk children, only about 20 of them may go on to develop schizophrenia. In addition, it is not particularly easy to locate a large sample of women or men with schizophrenia who have had their own children.

Because of these difficulties, the **clinical high-risk study** has been used in recent research. A clinical high-risk study is a design that identifies people with early, attenuated signs of schizophrenia, most often milder forms of hallucinations, delusions, or disorganization that nonetheless cause impairment (see Focus on Discovery 9.2 for a possible new DSM-5 category that has been informed by these types of studies). One such study has been ongoing in Australia for the past several years, following people between the ages of 14 and 30 who were referred to a mental health clinic in the mid-1990s (Yung, McGorry, McFarlane, et al., 1995). None of the participants had schizophrenia when they entered the study, but many later exhibited varying degrees of schizophrenia symptoms and some, but not all, had a biological relative with a psychotic disorder. These participants were deemed to be at "ultra-high risk" of developing schizophrenia or psychotic disorders. Since the study began, 41 of the original 104 participants have developed some type of psychotic disorder (Yung, Phillips, Hok, et al., 2004). An MRI study of 75 of the 104 participants found that those people who later developed a psychotic disorder had lower gray matter volumes than those who had not developed a psychotic disorder (Pantelis, Velakoulis, McGorry, et al., 2003). Recall that reduced gray matter volume has been found in people with schizophrenia; this study suggests that this characteristic may predate the onset of schizophrenia and other psychotic disorders.

A similar longitudinal study, the North American Prodrome Longitudinal Study (NAPLS), is being carried out at eight different centers in the United States and Canada. Participants were identified as clinical high-risk based on the Structured Interview for Prodromal Syndromes (see also Focus on Discovery 9.2). In this study, 82 of the 291 clinical high-risk (CHR) participants who also had a family history of schizophrenia (familial high risk, or FHR) had developed schizophrenia or some type of psychotic disorder (Cannon, Cadenhead, Cornblatt, et al., 2008). The researchers identified a number of factors that predicted a greater likelihood of developing a psychotic disorder, including having a biological relative with schizophrenia, a recent decline in functioning, high levels of positive symptoms, and high levels of social impairment.

Quick Summary

Given its complexity, a number of causal factors are likely to contribute to schizophrenia. The genetic evidence is strong, with much of it coming from family, twin, and adoption studies. Familial high-risk studies have found that children with a biological parent with schizophrenia are more likely to develop adult psychopathology, including schizophrenia, and have difficulties with attention and motor control, among other things. Molecular genetics studies include association studies and genome-wide association (GWAS) studies. Promising genes from association studies include DTNBP1, NGR1, BDNF, and COMT, but replication is also needed here. GWAS studies have pointed to copy number variations (CNVs) that are associated with genetic vulnerability to schizophrenia.

Neurotransmitters play a role in schizophrenia. For years, dopamine was the focus of study, but later findings led investigators to conclude that this one neurotransmitter could not fully account for schizophrenia. Other neurotransmitters are also the focus of study, such as serotonin, GABA, and glutamate. A number of different brain areas have been implicated in schizophrenia. One of the most widely replicated findings is of enlarged ventricles. Other research supports the role of the prefrontal cortex, particularly reduced activation of this area, in schizophrenia. Dysfunction in the temporal cortex has also been documented.

Environmental factors, such as obstetric complications and prenatal infections, may impact the developing brain and increase the risk of schizophrenia. Cannabis use among adolescents has been associated with greater risk of schizophrenia, particularly among those who are genetically vulnerable to the disorder.

Research has examined the role of socioeconomic status in schizophrenia, and generally this work supports the social selection hypothesis more than the sociogenic hypothesis. Early theories blamed families, particularly mothers, for causing schizophrenia, but research does not support this view. Communication in families is

important and could perhaps constitute the stress in the diathesis–stress theory of schizophrenia. Expressed emotion has also been found to predict relapse in schizophrenia, though there are important cultural differences in expressed emotion.

Retrospective developmental studies looked back at the childhood records of adults with schizophrenia and found that some adults with schizophrenia had lower IQs and were withdrawn and delinquent as children. Other studies found that adults who later developed schizophrenia expressed a lot of negative emotion and had poor motor skills. A prospective study confirmed that lower IQ in childhood is a predictor of the later onset of schizophrenia and that the IQ deficits are stable across childhood. Clinical high-risk studies identify people who are showing early signs of schizophrenia.

Check Your Knowledge 9.2

Fill in the blanks.
1. _____ and _____ studies do not do such a good job of teasing out genetic and environmental effects: _____ studies do a better job.
2. _____ and _____ are two genes that have been associated with schizophrenia; _____ and _____ are two genes that have been associated with cognitive deficits seen in schizophrenia.

3. Some studies showing the _____ area of the brain to be disrupted in schizophrenia also show that people with schizophrenia do poorly on tasks that rely on this area, such as planning and problem solving.
4. _____, _____, and _____ are the three components of expressed emotion.

Treatment of Schizophrenia

Treatments for schizophrenia most often include a combination of short-term hospital stays (during the acute phases of the illness), medication, and psychosocial treatment. A problem with any kind of treatment for schizophrenia is that some people with schizophrenia lack insight into their impaired condition and refuse any treatment at all (Amador, Flaum, Andreasen, et al., 1994). Results from one study suggest that gender (female) and age (older) are predictors of better insight among people in their first episode of the illness (McEvoy, Johnson, Perkins, et al., 2006), and this may help account for why women with schizophrenia tend to respond better to treatment (Salem & Kring, 1998). Those who lack insight, and thus don't believe they have an illness, don't see the need for professional help, particularly when it includes hospitalization or drugs. Family members therefore face a major challenge in getting their relatives into treatment, which is one reason they sometimes turn to involuntary hospitalization via civil commitment.

Medications

Prior to the 1950s, there were very few viable treatment options for people with schizophrenia. In the 1950s, several medications collectively referred to as **antipsychotic drugs,** also referred to as *neuroleptics* because they produce side effects similar to the symptoms of a neurological disease, were found to help with some of the symptoms of schizophrenia. For the first time, many people with schizophrenia did not need to stay in a hospital for long periods of time and could instead go home with a prescription. Focus on Discovery 9.3 presents a brief history of the development of these drugs. As we discussed in Chapter 1 and return to in Chapter 16,

FOCUS ON DISCOVERY 9.3

Stumbling Toward a Cure: The Development of Antipsychotic Medications

The history of antipsychotic drug development has been long and torturous, often based on chance findings that bear little relationship to the science behind the investigations. In 1891, Ehrlich observed the antimalarial effects of methylene blue, a phenothiazine derivative. Later, the phenothiazines were developed for their antihistaminergic properties. In 1951, Laborit and Huguenard administered a phenothiazine called chlorpromazine to patients for its potential calming effects during surgery. Shortly thereafter, its use was extended to treatment in psychiatric patients which, serendipitously, uncovered chlorpromazine's antipsychotic properties. However, chlorpromazine can also cause extrapyramidal symptoms (EPS), such as neck and eye spasms, and feelings of motor restlessness, which can have a major impact on medication compliance.

Between 1954 and 1975, about 40 antipsychotic drugs were brought to market. Thereafter, there was a hiatus in the development until the introduction of clozapine in 1990 which heralded the era of "atypical" antipsychotic drugs. Compared to the phenothiazines, atypical antipsychotics show a reduced potential to induce EPS, they also have an increased efficacy for the negative symptoms of schizophrenia, and can be beneficial in some patients previously regarded as treatment-resistant (López-Muñoz, et al., 2005).

the zeal to discharge people with schizophrenia from hospitals did not match the needs of all people with the disorder. Some people did and still do need treatment in a hospital, even if for a short time. Unfortunately, it is difficult to receive such treatment today due to the cost and limited availability of hospital beds for people with schizophrenia and other severe mental disorders. Nevertheless, medications have made it possible for some people with schizophrenia to lead lives outside of a hospital. As well will see, however, medications have their own sets of problems.

First-Generation Antipsychotic Drugs and Their Side Effects The discovery of the phenothiazines, including the drug Thorazine, led to a complete change in the treatment of schizophrenia. Just 20 years after their discovery, these drugs were the primary form of treatment for schizophrenia. Other types of antipsychotics that are used to treat schizophrenia include the butyrophenones (e.g., haloperidol, trade name Haldol) and the thioxanthenes (e.g., thiothixene, trade name Navane). Both types seem generally as effective as the phenothiazines and work in similar ways. These classes of drugs can reduce the positive and disorganized symptoms of schizophrenia but have little or no effect on the negative symptoms, perhaps because their primary mechanism of action involves blocking dopamine D2 receptors. Recall from our discussion earlier that the dopamine theory helps account for positive symptoms, but not negative symptoms. Together, these drugs are referred to as first-generation antipsychotics because they came out of the first "wave" of significant research discoveries of effective medication treatments for schizophrenia. The second wave produced a group of drugs referred to as second-generation antipsychotics, a class of drugs we will discuss in more detail later. Despite the enthusiasm with which these drugs are prescribed, they are not a cure. About 30 percent of people with schizophrenia do not respond favorably to the first-generation antipsychotics, and about half the people who take any antipsychotic drug quit after 1 year and up to three-quarters quit before 2 years because the side effects are so unpleasant (Harvard Mental Health Letter, 1995; Lieberman, Stroup, et al., 2005).

People who respond positively to the antipsychotics are typically kept on so-called maintenance doses of the drug, just enough to continue the therapeutic effect. One large randomized controlled trial found that people who were on maintenance doses of the drug risperidone for 1 year after beginning treatment had lower relapse rates than people who had dose reductions at either 4 or 26 weeks after the beginning of treatment (Wang, Xiang, Cai, et al., 2010). Some people who are maintained on medication may make only marginal adjustment to the community, however. For example, they may be unable to live unsupervised or to hold down the kind of job for which they would otherwise be qualified, and their social relationships may be sparse. In short, some symptoms may go away, but lives are still not fulfilling for many people with schizophrenia.

Commonly reported side effects of all antipsychotics include sedation, dizziness, blurred vision, restlessness, and sexual dysfunction. In addition, some particularly disturbing side effects, termed *extrapyramidal side effects,* resemble the symptoms of Parkinson's disease. People taking antipsychotics may develop tremors of the fingers, a shuffling gait, and drooling. Other side effects include dystonia, a state of muscular rigidity, and dyskinesia, an abnormal motion of voluntary and involuntary muscles, producing chewing movements as well as other movements of the lips, fingers, and legs; together they cause arching of the back and a twisted posture of the neck and body. Another side effect is akasthesia, an inability to remain still; people pace constantly and fidget.

In a rare muscular disturbance called *tardive dyskinesia,* the mouth muscles involuntarily make sucking, lip-smacking, and chin-wagging motions. In more severe cases, the whole body can be subject to involuntary motor movements. This syndrome is observed mainly in older people with schizophrenia who had been treated with first-generation medications before drugs were developed to prevent tardive dyskinesia from developing. It affects about 10 to 20 percent of these older people treated with first-generation antipsychotics for a long period of time and is not responsive to any known treatment (Sweet, Mulsant, Gupta, et al., 1995). Finally, a side effect called *neuroleptic malignant syndrome* occurs in about 1 percent of cases. In this condition, which can sometimes be fatal, severe muscular rigidity develops, accompanied by fever. The heart races, blood pressure increases, and the person may lapse into a coma.

Because of these serious side effects, some clinicians believe it is unwise to prescribe high doses of antipsychotics for extended periods of time. Current clinical practice guidelines from the American Psychiatric Association call for treating people with the smallest possible doses of drugs (APA, 2004). The clinician is put in a bind by this situation: if medication is reduced, the chance of relapse increases, but if medication is continued, serious and untreatable side effects may develop.

Second-Generation Antipsychotic Drugs and Their Side Effects In the decades following the introduction of the first-generation antipsychotic drugs, there appeared to be little interest in developing new drugs to treat schizophrenia. This situation changed about 25 years ago, with the introduction of clozapine (trade name Clozaril) in the United States. Although the precise mechanism of the therapeutic effects of clozapine is not yet completely understood, we do know that it has an impact on serotonin receptors. Early studies of this drug suggested it could produce therapeutic gains in people with schizophrenia who did not respond well to first-generation antipsychotics (Kane, Honigfeld, Singer, et al., 1988). Later studies suggested that this drug worked better than older drugs with fewer side effects and less relapse and treatment noncompliance (Conley, Love, Kelly, et al., 1999; Kane, Marder, Schooler, et al., 2001; Rosenheck, Cramer, Allan, et al., 1999; Wahlbeck, Chelne, Essali, et al., 1999).

However, researchers and clinicians soon learned that clozapine had its own set of serious side effects. It can impair the functioning of the immune system in a small percentage of people (about 1 percent) by lowering the number of white blood cells, a condition called agranulocytosis, which makes people vulnerable to infection and even death. For this reason, people taking clozapine have to be carefully monitored with routine blood tests. It also can produce seizures and other side effects, such as dizziness, fatigue, drooling, and weight gain (Meltzer, Cola, & Way, 1993).

Nevertheless, the apparent success of clozapine stimulated drug companies to begin a more earnest search for other drugs that might be more effective than first-generation antipsychotics. These drugs, including clozapine, are referred to as the **second-generation antipsychotic drugs** because their mechanism of action is not like that of the typical or first-generation antipsychotic medications. Two second-generation antipsychotics developed after clozapine are olanzapine (trade name Zyprexa) and risperidone (trade name Risperdal). Early studies of these two drugs indicated that they produced fewer of the side effects that first-generation antipsychotics produce, suggesting people were somewhat less likely to discontinue treatment (Dolder, Lacro, Dunn, et al., 2002), but later studies have not always replicated this (Lieberman, 2006). According to a recent meta-analysis comparing the second-generation drugs with one another, all of them work about the same, with some advantage in reducing positive symptoms observed for clozapine and olanzapine (Leucht, Komossa, Rummel-Kluge, et al., 2009). See Table 9.5 for a summary of major drugs used to treat schizophrenia.

The second-generation antipsychotics appear to be equally as effective as first-generation antipsychotics in reducing positive and disorganized symptoms (Conley & Mahmoud, 2001), particularly for people who have not responded to at least two other medications (Lewis, Barnes, Davies, et al., 2006). A meta-analysis of 124 studies comparing first- and second-generation antipsychotic drugs found that some, but not all, second-generation drugs were modestly more effective than the first-generation drugs in reducing negative symptoms and improving cognitive deficits (Davis, Chen, & Glick, 2003).

However, the news is not all good. A comprehensive randomized controlled clinical trial (called Clinical Antipsychotic Trials of Intervention Effectiveness, or CATIE) compared four second-generation drugs (olanzapine, risperidone, ziprasidone, and quetiapine) and one first-generation drug (perphenazine) against one another (Lieberman et al., 2005). Close to 1,500 people from all over the United States were in the study. What set this study apart from others included in the meta-analyses mentioned above was that it was not sponsored by one of the drug companies that makes the drugs. Among the many findings from this study, three stand out. First, the second-generation drugs were not more effective than the older, first-generation drug. Second, the second-generation drugs did not produce fewer unpleasant side effects. And third, nearly three-quarters of the people stopped taking the medications before the 18 months of the study design had ended. Similar results have been found in another large study (Jones, Barnes, Davies, et al., 2006). Despite the early promise of second-generation drugs, more work is needed to develop better treatments for schizophrenia.

In addition, other studies suggest that second-generation antipsychotics may have serious side effects of their own (Freedman, 2003). First, these drugs can and do also produce extrapyramidal side effects (Miller, Caroff, Davis, et al., 2008; Rummel-Kluge, Komossa, Schwarz, Hunger, Schmid, Kissling, et al., 2010). Second, other second-generation drugs besides clozapine also cause weight gain (Rummel-Kluge, Komossa, Schwarz, Hunger, Schmid, Lobos, et al., 2010). One study found that nearly half of patients taking these medications had significant weight gain (Young, Niv, Cohen, et al., 2010). In addition to being unpleasant, weight gain is associated with other serious health problems, such as increased cholesterol and increases in blood glucose, which can cause type 2 diabetes. For example, clozapine and olanzapine have been related to the development of type 2 diabetes (Leslie & Rosenheck, 2004); however, it is not clear whether the medicine itself increases this risk, perhaps via the side effect of weight gain, or whether people taking the medications were predisposed to developing diabetes independent of their medication usage. Other evidence suggests that these drugs may increase the risk for pancreatitis (Koller, Cross, Doraiswamy, et al., 2003). In 2005, the drug company that produces olanzapine, Eli Lilly, agreed to settle a series of lawsuits, paying out over $700 million to patients taking the drug. The company was sued for failing to adequately warn patients of these serious side effects. The drug's label now contains warnings about possible side effects, including weight gain, elevated blood sugar, and elevated cholesterol levels.

Another disturbing aspect of the second-generation antipsychotic medications is that they tend not to be used among people of color. Two different studies have found that African Americans were more likely to be prescribed the first-generation antipsychotics and less likely to be prescribed the second-generation antipsychotics (Kreyenbuhl, Zito, Buchanan, et al., 2003; Valenti, Narendran, & Pristach, 2003). This is unfortunate for a number of reasons, but particularly since there is some evidence that African Americans may experience more side effects than whites in response to the first-generation medications (Frackiewicz, Sramek, Herrera, et al., 1997). More broadly, these results echo the findings of the Surgeon General's supplement to his landmark report on mental health in 2001 that elucidated a number of disparities in mental health treatment among members of ethnic minority groups (USDHHS, 2001). Compared with other disorders reviewed in this book, there has been relatively less research on schizophrenia across different ethnic groups. This must be a focus of future research.

Table 9.5 Summary of Major Drugs Used in Treating Schizophrenia		
Drug Category	**Generic Name**	**Trade Name**
First-generation drugs	Chlorpromazine	Thorazine
	Fluphenazine decanoate	Prolixin
	Haloperidol	Haldol
	Thiothixene	Navane
	Trifluoperazine	Stelazine
Second–generation drugs	Clozapine	Clozaril
	Aripiprazole	Abilify
	Olanzapine	Zyprexa
	Risperidone	Risperdal
	Ziprasidone	Geodon
	Quetiapine	Seroquel

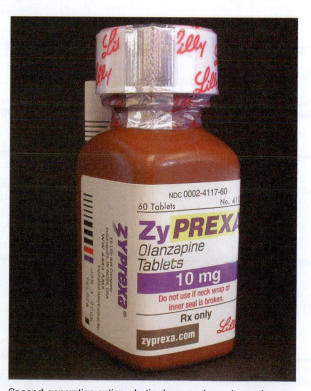

Second-generation antipsychotic drugs such as olanzapine may have fewer side effects than first-generation antipsychotic drugs, but they still have side effects. (Copyright Eli Lilly and Company. All Rights Reserved. Used with permission. ®ZYPREXA is a registered trademark of Ely Lilly and Company.)

Other research suggests that the second-generation antipsychotics are also effective in improving aspects of cognition, such as attention and memory, that are known to be deficient in many people with schizophrenia (Heinrichs & Zakzanis, 1998) and are associated with poor social functioning (Green, 1996). A number of studies suggest that these medications may be more effective than the first-generation drugs at improving cognitive functioning (P.D. Harvey, Green, Keefe, et al., 2004; Harvey, Green, McGurk, 2003; Keefe, Bilder, Davis, et al., 2007). More generally, the second-generation antipsychotics may thus make possible more thoroughgoing changes in schizophrenia and its behavioral consequences than do drugs that do not help with these cognitive abilities. However, other evidence suggests that psychological treatments (reviewed below) are also effective, perhaps more so, at alleviating cognitive deficits.

Evaluation of Drug Treatments Antipsychotic drugs are an indispensable part of treatment for schizophrenia and will undoubtedly continue to be an important component. Furthermore, the limited success of clozapine, olanzapine, and risperidone has stimulated a continued effort to find new and more effective drug therapies for schizophrenia. Many other drugs are currently being evaluated, so we may be on the verge of a new era in the treatment of schizophrenia.

Psychological Treatments

Our growing knowledge about neurobiological factors in schizophrenia and the continuing improvement in antipsychotic medications should not lead us to neglect the importance of psychosocial factors in both the etiology and treatment of schizophrenia. This is made clear in the following excerpt from a review of empirically supported psychological treatments for schizophrenia:

> For veteran practitioners who have long considered only biological treatments as effective in protecting schizophrenic individuals from stress-induced relapse and disability . . . evidence [on reducing expressed emotion in families, reviewed later] that supports the protective value of psychosocial treatments . . . may serve as an antidote to the insidious biological reductionism that often characterizes the field of schizophrenia research and treatment. . . . It is essential to view treatments of schizophrenia in their biopsychosocial matrix—leaving out any of the three components . . . will diminish the impact and efficacy of treatment. (Kopelowicz & Liberman, 1998, p. 192)

Neglecting the psychological and social aspect of schizophrenia compromises efforts to help people and their families who are struggling with this illness. Indeed, the current treatment recommendations for schizophrenia as compiled by the schizophrenia Patient Outcomes Research Team (PORT) are medications plus psychosocial interventions (Lehman, Kreyenbuhl, Buchanan, et al., 2004). The 2004 PORT recommendations were based on extensive reviews of treatment research. In addition a review of 37 prospective studies of people after their first episode of schizophrenia found that the combination of medication and psychosocial treatment predicted the best outcome (Menezes, Arenovich, & Zipursky, 2006).

An example of the positive effects that come from combination treatments is found in a recent and large (over 1,200 people) randomized controlled trial conducted in China that compared medication alone with medication plus a comprehensive psychosocial intervention that included family therapy, cognitive behavior therapy, psychoeducation, and skills training. People in both groups had a similar reduction in schizophrenia symptoms. However, people who received the combined treatment had lower rates of relapse and treatment discontinuation, as well as greater improvements in functioning (Guo, Zhai, Liu, et al., 2010). See Focus on Discovery 9.4 for another example of a successful combination treatment approach.

In 2009, new PORT recommendations were issued to specifically address different types of psychosocial treatments. Based on a careful literature review, a number of psychosocial interventions, including skills training, cognitive behavior therapy, and family-based treatments, have a solid evidence base to support their use as an adjunctive treatment to medications (Dixon, Dickerson, Bellack, et al., 2010). Other treatments, such as cognitive remediation approaches, have a growing evidence base and are the focus of much current research. We turn to these psychosocial treatments next.

Social Skills Training Social skills training is designed to teach people with schizophrenia how to successfully manage a wide variety of interpersonal situations—discussing their medications with their psychiatrist, ordering meals in a restaurant, filling out job applications, interviewing for jobs, saying no to drug dealers on the street, and reading bus schedules.

FOCUS ON DISCOVERY 9.4

Living with Schizophrenia

A heartening example of one woman's struggles with and triumphs over schizophrenia is found in the 2007 book *The Center Cannot Hold: My Journey through Madness.* This book was written by Elyn Saks, an endowed professor of law at the University of Southern California who also happens to have schizophrenia (Saks, 2007). In the book, she describes her lifelong experience with this illness. Prior to the publication of the book, only a few of Professor Saks's close friends even knew that she had schizophrenia. Why did she keep it a secret? Certainly stigma is part of the reason. As we have discussed throughout this book, stigma toward people with mental illness is very much alive in the twenty-first century and can have seriously negative consequences for people with illnesses like schizophrenia.

What makes Professor Saks's life story particularly encouraging is that she has achieved exceptional professional and personal success in her life despite having such a serious mental illness. She grew up in a loving and supportive family, earned a bachelor's degree from Vanderbilt University, graduating as her class valedictorian, earned a prestigious Marshall fellowship to study philosophy at Oxford in the United Kingdom, graduated from Yale Law School as editor of the prestigious *Yale Law Review,* and is a tenured professor of law at a major university. How did she do it?

She believes that a combination of treatments (including psychoanalysis and medications), social support from family and friends, hard work, and acknowledging that she has a serious illness have all helped her cope with schizophrenia and its sometimes unpredictable and frightening symp-

Elyn Saks, a law professor at USC, has schizophrenia. (Damian Dovarganes/ © ASSOCIATED PRESS/Wide World Photos.)

toms. Although psychoanalysis does not have a good deal of empirical support for its efficacy with schizophrenia, it was and remains a central part of Professor Saks's treatment regimen. This illustrates nicely the fact that even though some treatments may not be effective for a group of people, they can nonetheless be effective for individuals. One of the things that appears to have been helpful for Professor Saks, from her early days in psychoanalysis as a Marshall scholar at Oxford University until the present, has been her

ability to "be psychotic" when she is with her psychoanalyst. So much of her energy was spent trying to hide her symptoms and keep them from interfering with her life; psychoanalysis became a safe place for her to let these symptoms more fully out into the open. The different analysts she has had over the year were also among the chief proponents of adding antipsychotic medication to her treatment, something that Professor Saks resisted for many years. Having the unwavering support of close friends and her husband has also been a tremendous help, particularly during her more symptomatic periods. Her loved ones would not turn and run the other way when she was psychotic. Instead, they would support her and help her get additional treatment if it was needed.

She still experiences symptoms, sometimes every day. Her symptoms include paranoid delusions, which she describes as very frightening (e.g., believing that her thoughts have killed people). She also experiences disorganization symptoms, which she eloquently describes in the book:

Consciousness gradually loses its coherence. One's center gives way. The center cannot hold. The "me" becomes a haze, and the solid center from which one experiences reality breaks up like a bad radio signal. There is no longer a sturdy vantage point from which to look out, take things in, assess what's happening. No core holds things together, providing the lens through which to see the world, to make judgments and comprehend risk. (Saks, 2007, p. 13)

Even though she still experiences symptoms, she has been able to come to terms with the fact that schizophrenia is a part of her life. Would she prefer not to have the illness? Sure. But she also recognizes that she has a wonderful life filled with friends, loved ones, and meaningful work. She is not defined by her illness, and she importantly notes that "the humanity we all share is more important than the mental illness we may not" (Saks, 2007, p. 336). Her life is an inspiration to all, not just those with mental illness. Her story reminds us that life is difficult, more so for some than others, but that it can be lived, and lived to the fullest.

Most of us take these skills for granted and give little thought to them in our daily lives, but people with schizophrenia cannot take them for granted—they need to work hard to acquire or reacquire such skills (Heinssen, Liberman, & Kopelowicz, 2000; Liberman, Eckman, Kopelowicz, et al., 2000). Social skills training typically involves role-playing and other group exercises to practice skills, both in a therapy group and in actual social situations.

Research has shown that people with schizophrenia can be taught new social behaviors that help them achieve fewer relapses, better social functioning, and a higher quality of life (Kopelowicz, Liberman, & Zarate, 2002). Some of the studies are noteworthy in demonstrating benefits over a period of 2 years following treatment (Liberman, Wallace, Blackwell, et al., 1998; Marder, Wirshing, Glynn, et al., 1999), though not all results are positive (Pilling, Bebbington, Kuipers, et al., 2002). Social skills training is usually a component of treatments for schizophrenia that go beyond the use of medications alone, including family therapies for lowering expressed emotion, which we discuss next. For example, social skills training that included family therapy was found to be more effective than treatment as usual (medication plus a 20-minute monthly meeting with a psychiatrist) in a randomized controlled trial conducted in Mexico (Valencia, Racon, Juarez, et al., 2007).

Family Therapies Many people with schizophrenia who are discharged from hospitals go home to their families. Earlier we discussed research showing that high levels of expressed emotion (EE) within the family, including being hostile, hypercritical, and overprotective, have been linked to relapse and rehospitalization. Based on this finding, a number of family therapies have been developed. These therapies may differ in length, setting, and specific techniques, but they have several features in common:

- *Education about schizophrenia—specifically about the genetic or neurobiological factors that predispose some people to the illness, the cognitive problems associated with schizophrenia, the symptoms of schizophrenia, and the signs of impending relapse.* High-EE families are typically not well informed about schizophrenia, and giving them some basic information helps them be less critical of the relative with schizophrenia. Knowing, for example, that neurobiology has a lot to do with having schizophrenia and that the illness involves problems in thinking clearly and rationally might help family members be more accepting and understanding of their relative's inappropriate or ineffectual actions. Therapists encourage family members to lower their expectations of their relative with schizophrenia, and they make clear to family and the person with schizophrenia alike that proper medication and therapy can reduce stress on the patient and prevent deterioration.

- *Information about antipsychotic medication.* Therapists impress on both the family and the ill relative the importance of taking antipsychotic medication, becoming better informed about the intended effects and the side effects of the medication, taking responsibility for monitoring response to medication, and seeking medical consultation rather than just discontinuing the medication if adverse side effects occur.

- *Blame avoidance and reduction.* Therapists encourage family members to blame neither themselves nor their relative for the illness and for the difficulties all are having in coping with it.

- *Communication and problem-solving skills within the family.* Therapists focus on teaching the family ways to express both positive and negative feelings in a constructive, empathic, nondemanding manner rather than in a finger-pointing, critical, or overprotective way. They focus as well on making personal conflicts less stressful by teaching family members ways to work together to solve everyday problems.

- *Social network expansion.* Therapists encourage people with schizophrenia and their families to expand their social contacts, especially their support networks.

- *Hope.* Therapists instill hope that things can improve, including the hope that the person with schizophrenia may not have to return to the hospital.

Therapists use various techniques to implement these strategies. Examples include identifying stressors that could cause relapse, training families in communication skills and problem solving, and having high-EE family members watch videotapes of interactions of low-EE families (Penn & Mueser, 1996). Compared with standard treatments (usually just medication), family therapy plus medication has typically lowered relapse over periods of 1 to 2 years. This positive finding is evident particularly in studies in which the treatment lasted for at least 9 months (Falloon, Boyd, McGill, et al., 1982, 1985; Hogarty, Anderson, Reiss, et al., 1986, 1991; Kopelowicz & Liberman, 1998; McFarlane, Lukens, Link, et al., 1995; Penn & Mueser, 1996).

Cognitive Behavior Therapy At one time, researchers assumed that it was futile to try to alter the cognitive distortions, including delusions, of people with schizophrenia.

Family therapy can help educate people with schizophrenia and their families about schizophrenia and reduce expressed emotion. (Bruce Ayres/Stone/Getty Images.)

Now, however, a growing body of evidence demonstrates that the maladaptive beliefs of some people with schizophrenia can in fact benefit from cognitive behavior therapy (CBT) (Garety, Fowler, & Kuipers, 2000; Wykes, Steel, Everitt, & Tarrier, 2008).

People with schizophrenia can be encouraged to test out their delusional beliefs in much the same way as people without schizophrenia do. Through collaborative discussions (and in the context of other modes of treatment, including antipsychotic drugs), some people with schizophrenia have been helped to attach a nonpsychotic meaning to paranoid symptoms and thereby reduce their intensity and aversive nature, similar to what is done for depression and panic disorder (Beck & Rector, 2000; Drury, Birchwood, Cochrane, & Macmillan, 1996; Haddock, Tarrier, Spaulding, et al., 1998). Researchers have found that CBT can also reduce negative symptoms, for example, by challenging belief structures tied to low expectations for success (avolition) and low expectations for pleasure (anticipatory pleasure deficit in anhedonia) (Beck, Rector, & Stolar, 2004; Rector, Beck, & Stolar, 2005; Wykes et al., 2008).

Findings from the first few randomized controlled trials of CBT in schizophrenia suggest that this treatment, along with medication, can help reduce hallucinations and delusions (Bustillo, Lauriello, Horan, et al., 2001). A more recent meta-analysis of 34 studies of close to 2,000 people with schizophrenia across eight countries found small to moderate effect sizes for positive symptoms, negative symptoms, mood, and general life functioning (Wykes et al., 2008). CBT has been used as an adjunctive treatment for schizophrenia in Great Britain for over 10 years, and the results have been positive, even in community settings (Sensky, Turkington, Kingdom, et al., 2000; Turkington, Kingdom, & Turner, 2002; Wykes et al., 2008). One study has found that stress management training was effective in reducing stress among people with schizophrenia—a noteworthy outcome indeed, given the link between stress and relapse (Norman, Malla, McLean, et al., 2002).

Cognitive Remediation Therapies In recent years, researchers have been attending to fundamental aspects of cognition that are disordered in schizophrenia in an attempt to improve these functions and thereby favorably affect behavior. The fact that positive clinical outcomes from risperidone are associated with improvements in certain kinds of memory (Green, Marshall, Wirshing, et al., 1997) lends support to the more general notion that therapies directed at basic cognitive processes—the kind that nonclinical cognitive scientists study—hold promise for improving the social and emotional lives of people with schizophrenia. This general approach concentrates on trying to normalize such functions as attention and memory, which are known to be deficient in many people with schizophrenia and are associated with poor social adaptation (Green, Kern, Braff, & Mintz, 2000).

Recently developed treatments that seek to enhance basic cognitive functions such as verbal learning ability are referred to as **cognitive remediation training** or **cognitive enhancement therapy (CET)** or *cognitive training*. A 2-year randomized controlled clinical trial compared group-based CET with enriched supportive therapy (EST). CET consisted of nearly 80 hours of computer-based training in attention, memory, and problem solving. Groups also worked on such routine social-cognitive skills as reading and understanding newspaper editorials, solving social problems, and starting and maintaining conversations. EST included supportive and educational elements. All people were also taking medications. At the 1- and 2-year follow-up assessments, CET was more effective than EST in improving cognitive abilities in problem solving, attention, social cognition, and social adjustment, while symptom reduction was the same for both treatments (Hogarty, Flesher, Ulrich, et al., 2004). People who received CET were also rated as being more ready for employment and, in fact, tended to be employed at the end of 2 years, largely driven by the fact that these people were more likely to be in volunteer positions than those in the EST group. A more recent study compared CET with supportive therapy and found that CET was associated with improvements in social functioning that remained 1 year after the treatment ended (Eack, Greenwald, Hogarty, & Keshaven, 2010). Thus, CET is effective at reducing symptoms and improving cognitive abilities, and it appears to be linked to good functional outcomes, such as employment and social functioning.

A review of 17 other randomized trials of cognitive remediation therapies found that these interventions, for the most part, improve cognitive abilities, whether the treatments focus on specific tasks (e.g., a memory test) or on broader strategies (e.g., problem solving) or whether done via computer-based training (Twamley, Jeste, & Bellack, 2003). Only a few of these studies included measures of symptoms and functional outcomes, such as employment or general functioning, but those that did generally found that cognitive training improved symptoms and functional outcomes. As promising as these findings are, nearly all of the studies have been with white men; thus, their generalizability remains to be established. And not all studies yield positive results (Pilling et al., 2002).

Two recent meta-analyses of 26 (McGurk, Twamley, Sitzer, et al., 2007) and 40 studies (Wykes, Huddy, Cellard, et al., 2011) found small to medium effect sizes for overall cognitive functioning and specific cognitive domains, including attention, verbal memory, problem solving, verbal working memory, processing speed, and social cognition. Cognitive remediation was also associated with a reduction in symptoms and an improvement in everyday functioning, though the effect sizes for these two domains were small. Cognitive remediation was more likely to be associated with an improvement in functioning if there was also another type of psychosocial treatment, such as social skills training, added to the treatment program.

A somewhat different cognitive remediation program has also shown promising results. This treatment also involves intensive (50 hours) computer training, but the task was developed based on neuroscience research showing that improving basic cognitive and perceptual processes (e.g., discriminating simple sounds) can then impact higher-order cognitive processes (e.g., memory and problem solving). The cognitive remediation task in this training is an auditory task that gets progressively more difficult as people get better at it. They perform a series of tasks that require them to discriminate between complex speech sounds. In a recent randomized controlled trial, people with schizophrenia who received the intensive auditory computer training showed greater improvement in overall cognition as well as in specific domains (memory, attention, processing speed, working memory, and problem solving) compared to participants who played computer games for the same amount of time (Fisher, Holland, Merzenich, & Vinogradov, 2009).

Psychoeducation As we discussed in Chapter 5 for bipolar disorder, psychoeducation is an approach that seeks to educate people about their illness, including the symptoms of the disorder, the expected time course of symptoms, the biological and psychological triggers for symptoms, and treatment strategies. A recent meta-analysis of 44 studies of psychoeducation in schizophrenia found that it was effective, in combination with medication, at reducing relapse and rehospitalization and increasing medication compliance (Xia, Merinder, & Belgamwar, 2011).

Case Management After large numbers of people were discharged from hospitals (referred to as deinstitutionalization) in the 1960s, many people with schizophrenia no longer resided in hospitals and thus had to fend for themselves in securing needed services. Lacking the centralized hospital as the site where most services were delivered, the mental health system became more complex. In 1977, fearing that many people with schizophrenia were not accessing services, the National Institute of Mental Health established a program giving grants to states to help people with schizophrenia cope with the mental health system. Out of this program, a new mental health specialty, the case manager, was created.

Initially, case managers were basically brokers of services; because they were familiar with the system, they were able to get people with schizophrenia into contact with providers of whatever services they required. As the years passed, different models of case management developed. The major innovation was the recognition that case managers often needed to provide direct clinical services and that services might best be delivered by a team rather than brokered out. The Assertive Community Treatment model (Stein & Test, 1980) and the Intensive Case Management model (Surles, Blanch, Shern & Donahue, 1992) both entail a multidisciplinary team that provides services in the community, such as medication, treatment for substance abuse, help in dealing with stressors people with schizophrenia face regularly (such as managing money), psychotherapy, vocational training, and assistance in obtaining housing and employment. Case managers hold together and coordinate the range of medical and psychological services that people with schizophrenia need to keep functioning outside of institutions with some degree of independence and peace of mind (Kopelowicz et al., 2002). Both of these models continue to be part of the PORT recommendations for psychosocial treatments, with established evidence of their effectiveness (Dixon et al., 2010).

Indications are that this more intensive treatment is superior to less intensive methods in reducing time spent in the hospital, improving housing stability, and ameliorating symptoms (Mueser, Bond, Drake, & Resnick, 1998). However, more intensive case management has not shown positive effects in other domains, such as improvement in social functioning.

In order for this approach to be effective, there have to be enough case managers for people with schizophrenia. Too often, the caseloads of these mental health professionals are much too high.

Residential Treatment   Residential treatment homes, or "halfway houses," are sometimes good alternatives for people who do not need to be in the hospital but are not quite well enough to live on their own or even with their family. These are protected living units, typically located in large, formerly private residences. Here people discharged from the hospital live, take their meals, and gradually return to ordinary community life by holding a part-time job or going to school. As part of what is called *vocational rehabilitation,* residents learn marketable skills that can help them secure employment and thereby increase their chances of remaining in the community. Living arrangements may be relatively unstructured; some houses set up moneymaking enterprises that help train and support the residents.

Depending on how well funded the residential treatment facility is, the staff may include psychiatrists or clinical psychologists or both. The frontline staff members are often undergraduate psychology majors or graduate students in clinical psychology or social work, who live at the facility and act both as administrators and as friends to the residents. Group meetings, at which residents talk out their frustrations and learn to relate to others in honest and constructive ways, are often part of the routine. There are many such programs across the United States that have helped thousands of people with schizophrenia make enough of a social adaptation to be able to remain out of the hospital.

The need in the United States for effective residential treatment cannot be underestimated, especially in light of the deinstitutionalization that has seen tens of thousands of people discharged from hospitals. People with schizophrenia almost always need follow-up community-based services, and these are scarce. Indeed, today a large percentage of homeless people in the United States are mentally ill, including many people with schizophrenia. Social Security benefits are available to those with schizophrenia, but if they do not have an address, they often do not receive all the benefits to which they are entitled. Though there are good residential treatment programs available, there are not enough of them.

Integrating therapy with gainful employment is important in keeping people with schizophrenia out of hospitals (Kopelowicz & Liberman, 1998; Kopelowicz et al., 2002). For example, the U.S. government has begun to recognize the importance of employment by allowing people with schizophrenia to continue receiving Social Security disablity benefits for up to 2 years while they are earning money from (low-paying) jobs that can increase their chances of living independently or at least outside of the hospital. This welcome change in policy (from one that terminated such benefits once the person began earning money) represents a recognition of the harmful effects of not working and not being able to live in a reasonably independent manner.

Still, obtaining employment can pose a major challenge because of bias and stigma against people with schizophrenia. Although the Americans with Disabilities Act of 1990 prohibits employers from asking applicants if they have a history of serious mental illness, people with schizophrenia still have a difficult time obtaining regular employment because their symptoms make negatively biased employers fearful of hiring them. Also a factor is how much leeway employers are willing to give people whose thinking, emotions, and behavior can be unconventional to some degree.

Despite these difficulties, the trend seems to be to do whatever is necessary to assist people in working and living in as autonomous a manner as their physical and mental condition will allow (Kopelowicz & Liberman, 1998). Additional funding will be needed to create more residential treatment facilities with the hope of reducing the number of people with schizophrenia who are without treatment.

Check Your Knowledge 9.3

True or false?

1. First-generation antipsychotics include medications like Haldol or Prolixin; second-generation antipsychotics include clozapine and olanzapine.
2. Second-generation antipsychotics produce more motor side effects than first-generation antipsychotics.
3. Cognitive behavior therapy, but not cognitive enhancement therapy, is effective for schizophrenia, if given along with medications.
4. One important focus of residential treatment programs is to help people with schizophrenia become employed.

Summary

Clinical Description

- The symptoms of schizophrenia involve disturbances in several areas, including thought, perception, and attention; motor behavior; emotion; and life functioning. Symptoms are typically divided into positive, negative, and disorganized categories. Positive symptoms include excesses and distortions, such as delusions and hallucinations. Negative symptoms are behavioral deficits, which include avolition, asociality, anhedonia, blunted affect, and alogia. Disorganized symptoms include disorganized speech and behavior. Motor symptoms include catatonia.

- The DSM-5 will likely remove the old subtypes of schizophrenia because they have little predictive validity and clinical usefulness.

- Other schizophrenia spectrum disorders in DSM-5 include schizophreniform disorder, brief psychotic disorder, schizoaffective disorder, and delusional disorder. A new category called attenuated psychosis syndrome may be added to DSM-5; there are arguments for and against adding this new disorder.

Etiology

- The evidence for genetic transmission of schizophrenia is impressive. Family and twin studies suggest a genetic component; adoption studies show a strong relationship between having a parent with schizophrenia and the likelihood of developing the disorder, typically in early adulthood. Familial high-risk studies have longitudinally studied the offspring of a parent with schizophrenia to determine if problems in childhood might predict the onset of the disorder. Association studies indicate genes such as DTNBP1, NGR1, and COMT, and BDNF are associated with schizophrenia. Genome-wide association studies (GWAS) have found rare genetic mutations called copy number variations (CNVs) to be associated with schizophrenia.

- The genetic predisposition to develop schizophrenia may involve neurotransmitters. It appears that increased sensitivity of dopamine receptors in the brain is related to the positive symptoms of schizophrenia. The negative symptoms may be due to dopamine underactivity in the prefrontal cortex. Other neurotransmitters, such as serotonin, glutamate, and GABA, are also involved.

- The brains of some people with schizophrenia have enlarged ventricles, problems with the prefrontal cortex, and problems with the temporal cortex and surrounding regions. Some of these structural abnormalities could result from maternal viral infection during the first trimester of pregnancy or from damage sustained during a difficult birth. The combination of brain development during adolescence, stress, and the HPA axis are important for understanding why symptoms typically emerge during late adolescence, even if a brain disturbance has been in place since gestation. Cannabis use in adolescence has been linked to a higher risk for developing schizophrenia, primarily for those who are genetically vulnerable to schizophrenia.

- The diagnosis of schizophrenia is most frequently applied to people of the lowest socioeconomic status, apparently because of downward social mobility created by the disorder. High levels of expressed emotion in families, as well as increases in general life stress, have been shown to be important determinants of relapse. Retrospective developmental studies have identified problems in childhood that were there prior to the onset of schizophrenia, but these studies were not designed to predict schizophrenia, so it is difficult to interpret the findings. Clinical high-risk studies have identified young people with mild symptoms who are at higher risk for developing schizophrenia spectrum disorders.

Treatment

- Antipsychotic drugs, especially the phenothiazines, have been widely used to treat schizophrenia since the 1950s. These first-generation drugs are somewhat effective, but they can also produce serious side effects. Second-generation antipsychotic drugs, such as clozapine and risperidone, are equally as effective as first-generation drugs, and they have their own set of side effects. Drugs alone are not a completely effective treatment, though, as people with schizophrenia need to be (re)taught ways of dealing with the challenges of everyday life.

- Family therapy aimed at reducing high levels of expressed emotion has been shown to be valuable in preventing relapse. In addition, social skills training and various cognitive behavioral therapies have helped people with schizophrenia meet the inevitable stresses of family and community living. Recent efforts to change the thinking of people with schizophrenia with cognitive behavior therapy are showing promise as well. Cognitive remediation therapies focus on improving cognitive skills. These are effective at helping with things such as memory, attention, and problem solving and are also associated with an improvement in daily functioning.

Answers to Check Your Knowledge Questions

9.1 1. blunted affect; 2. delusion or ideas of reference; 3. anhedonia (anticipatory); 4. disorganized thinking or derailment.

9.2 1. Family, twin, adoption; 2. DTNBP1, NGRl, COMT, BDNF; 3. prefrontal; 4. Hostility, critical comments, emotional overinvolvement

9.3 l. T; 2. F; 3. F; 4. T

Key Terms

alogia	clinical high-risk study	disorganized symptoms	prefrontal cortex
anhedonia	cognitive enhancement	dopamine theory	schizoaffective disorder
anticipatory pleasure	therapy (CET) (cognitive	expressed emotion (EE)	schizophrenia
antipsychotic drugs	remediation training)	familial high-risk study	schizophreniform disorder
asociality	consummatory pleasure	grandiose delusions	second-generation
avolition	delusional disorder	hallucinations	antipsychotic drugs
blunted affect	delusions	ideas of reference	social selection hypothesis
brief psychotic disorder	dementia praecox	loose associations (derailment)	social skills training
catatonia	disorganized behavior	negative symptoms	sociogenic hypothesis
catatonic immobility	disorganized speech	positive symptoms	

10 Substance Use Disorders

With Contributions by Dora Brown

PEOPLE HAVE USED VARIOUS substances in the hope of reducing physical pain or altering states of consciousness for centuries. Around the world, almost all people use one or more substances that affect the central nervous system, relieving physical and mental anguish or producing euphoria. Despite the often devastating consequences of taking such substances into the body, their initial effects are usually pleasing, a factor that is perhaps at the root of substance use disorders.

Clinical Descriptions, Prevalence, and Effects of Substance Use Disorders

The world is witness to many forms of drug cultures. People all over the world use drugs to wake up (coffee or tea), to stay awake (cigarettes), to relax (alcohol), and to reduce pain (aspirin). The widespread availability and frequent use of various drugs sets the stage for the potential abuse of drugs, the topic of this chapter.

In the UK, it is estimated that in 2002/03 there were around 140,900 problem drug misusers in treatment at drug treatment agencies and general practitioners in England, compared to around 128,200 in 2001/02 (an increase of 10%).

Equally, a "census" of problem drug misusers in treatment estimated that there were around 118,500 people in treatment in 2000/01. The estimated increase between 2000/01 and 2001/02 was 8%. (All statistics provided by the National Drug Treatment Monitoring System in England, 2001/02 and 2002/03, Department of Health, 2007). Similarly, and using more recent data from the US, presented in Table 10.1, the frequency of use of several drugs, legal and illegal, can be noted. These figures do not represent the frequency of substance use disorders but simply provide an indication of the pervasiveness of drug use in the US.

Interestingly, in the UK, a study undertaken by the NHS Information Centre (2010), shows that drug misuse among *young people* is on the decline. This survey is the latest in a series designed to monitor smoking, drinking and drug use among secondary school pupils aged 11 to 15.

Prior to DSM-5, the pathological use of substances fell into two categories: substance abuse and substance dependence. However, reviews of the research literature in preparation

Table 10.1 Percentage of U.S. Population Reporting Drug Use in Past Month (2009)

Substance	Percentage Reporting Use
Alcohol	51.9
Cigarettes	27.7
Marijuana	6.6
Nonmedical psychotherapeutics	2.8
Cocaine	0.7
Hallucinogens	0.5
Inhalants	0.01

Data are percentages of people in the United States age 12 and over. Nonmedical psychotherapeutics refers to the use of pain medicines (2.1%), tranquilizers (0.8%), stimulants (0.5%), or sedatives (0.1%) for a nonmedical, nonprescribed use.
Source: SAMHSA (2010).

for DSM-5 pointed to several problems with this two-category distinction. First, the reliability of the substance abuse category was poor (see Chapter 3 for the importance of diagnostic category reliability). Second, most people who meet criteria for abuse (particularly for alcohol) do not go on to develop dependence, as was originally believed (Schuckit, Smith, Danko, et al., 2001). Third, analyses of the DSM criteria indicated that they represent one and not two distinct categories. Thus, DSM-5 will likely have one category called **substance use disorder** instead of two categories. The differences between DSM-IV-TR and DSM-5 are depicted in Figure 10.1.

As in DSM-IV-TR, the DSM-5 will likely contain substance use disorder categories for specific substances, including alcohol, amphetamines, cannabis, cocaine, hallucinogens, inhalants, opioids, phencyclidine, sedatives/hypnotics/anxiolytics, and tobacco.

The term **addiction** typically refers to a more severe substance use disorder that is characterized by having more symptoms, tolerance, and withdrawal, by using more of the substance than intended, by trying unsuccessfully to stop, by having physical or psychological problems made worse by the drug, and by experiencing problems at work or with friends. In the DSM-5, meeting four or more of the diagnostic criteria will likely be considered severe substance use disorder. In addition, if a person has either tolerance or withdrawal, the substance use disorder will meet the proposed diagnostic category specifier "with physiological dependence." If there is no tolerance or withdrawal, the proposed specifier "without physiological dependence" will apply.

Tolerance is indicated by either (1) larger doses of the substance being needed to produce the desired effect or (2) the effects of the drug becoming markedly less if the usual amount is taken. **Withdrawal** refers to the negative physical and psychological effects that develop when a person stops taking the substance or reduces the amount. Substance withdrawal symptoms can include muscle pains and twitching, sweats, vomiting, diarrhea, and insomnia. In general, being physiologically dependent on a drug is associated with more severe problems (Schuckit, Daeppen, Tipp, et al., 1998).

Proposed DSM-5 Criteria for Substance Use Disorder

Problematic pattern of use that impairs functioning. Two or more symptoms within a 1-year period:

- Failure to meet obligations
- Repeated use in situations where it is physically dangerous
- Repeated relationship problems
- Continued use despite problems caused by the substance
- Tolerance
- Withdrawal
- Substance taken for a longer time or in greater amounts than intended
- Efforts to reduce or control use do not work
- Much time spent trying to obtain the substance
- Social, hobbies, or work activities given up or reduced
- Continued use despite knowing problems caused by substance
- Craving to use the substance is strong

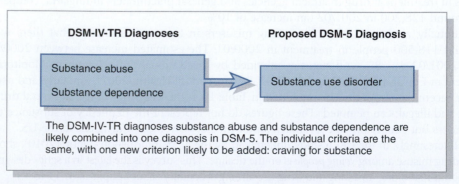

The DSM-IV-TR diagnoses substance abuse and substance dependence are likely combined into one diagnosis in DSM-5. The individual criteria are the same, with one new criterion likely to be added: craving for substance

Figure 10.1 Diagnoses of Substance Use and Addictive Disorders.

Clinical Case: Charlotte

Charlotte was 38 years old and an unmarried chemistry teacher who had always been "the life and soul of the party". However, a series of incidents had recently brought the effects of her drinking into sharp focus. Three weeks ago she had a bad fall while drunk at a party. Last week, following a very late night, she arrived at work smelling of alcohol and incapable of teaching her lab class. Her head of department took her to one side and told her to go home and not come back in until she was sober. This finally got her to admit that something was wrong.

Underneath Charlotte's superficial jocularity, a deepening depression was developing. Increasingly she would find herself overcome by a sense of hopeless and tears would well up in her eyes. She now began each day with a drink of vodka (as it didn't make her breath smell). During weekends, she was usually intoxicated by the afternoon. The sudden death of her cat, which was run over outside her house 12 months earlier had triggered a quick increase in her drinking, and within six months she had slipped into a pattern of severe alcohol dependence.

In 2009/10, in England, there were 5,809 admissions to hospital with a primary diagnosis of a drug-related mental health and behavioral disorder. This number is 2.5% more than in 2008/09 when there were 5,668 admissions. There were more male than female admissions (4,184 and 1,618 respectively) (The Information Centre, NHS, 2010).

Drug and alcohol use disorders are among the most stigmatized of disorders. Terms such as *addict* or *alcoholic* are tossed about carelessly, as if these words capture the essence of people, not the disorder that they suffer from. Historically, drug and alcohol problems have been viewed as moral lapses rather than as conditions in need of treatment. Unfortunately, such attitudes persist today. Yet there is convincing evidence that becoming physiologically dependent on drugs or alcohol is not, in fact, only a matter of personal choice. True, people make decisions about whether or not to try alcohol or drugs, but the ways in which these decisions and the substances involved interact with an individual's neurobiology, social setting, culture, and other environmental factors all conspire to create dependence. Such factors put some people at higher risk for substance dependence than others; it is a mistake to consider substance use disorders as somehow solely the result of moral failing or personal choice. But it is also a mistake to consider those dependent on drugs or alcohol as being without recourse to change the course of their disorder. Treatment and behavioral change can work in this sphere in much the same way they can work for diseases such as diabetes, where people can change the course of their disease with insulin and diet control.

We turn now to an overview of some of the major substance use disorders, those involving alcohol, tobacco, marijuana, opiates, stimulants, and hallucinogens.

Alcohol Use Disorder

The term *alcoholic* is familiar to most people, yet it does not have a precise meaning. People who are physiologically dependent on alcohol generally have more severe symptoms, such as tolerance or withdrawal, than do people without tolerance or withdrawal symptoms (Schuckit et al., 1998). The effects of the abrupt withdrawal of alcohol in a heavy user may be rather dramatic because the body has become accustomed to alcohol. Specifically, a person may feel anxious, depressed, weak, restless, and unable to sleep. He or she may have muscle tremors, especially of the fingers, face, eyelids, lips, and tongue, and pulse, blood pressure, and temperature may be elevated.

An etching showing the vivid portrayal of delirium tremens in a scene in a play. (Culver Pictures, Inc.)

Polydrug abuse involves the abuse of multiple drugs. Alcohol and nicotine are a frequent combination, although most people who smoke and drink in social situations do not have problems with these substances. (© Emely/©Corbis.)

In relatively rare cases, a person who has been drinking heavily for a number of years may also experience **delirium tremens (DTs)** when the level of alcohol in the blood drops suddenly. The person becomes delirious as well as tremulous and has hallucinations that are primarily visual but may be tactile as well. Unpleasant and very active creatures—snakes, cockroaches, spiders, and the like—may appear to be crawling up the wall or over the person's body or to be filling the room. Feverish, disoriented, and terrified, the person may claw frantically at his or her skin to get rid of the creatures.

Although changes in the liver enzymes that metabolize alcohol can account to a small extent for tolerance, research suggests that the central nervous system is responsible as well. Some research suggests that tolerance results from changes in the number or sensitivity of GABA or glutamate receptors (Tsai, Ragan, Chang, et al., 1998). Withdrawal may result because some neural pathways increase their activation to compensate for alcohol's inhibitory effects in the brain.

Alcohol use disorder is often part of what is called **polydrug abuse,** abusing more than one drug at a time. It is estimated, for example, that 80 to 85 percent of people who abuse alcohol are smokers. This very high comorbidity may occur because alcohol and nicotine are cross-tolerant; that is, nicotine can induce tolerance for the rewarding effects of alcohol and vice versa. Thus, consumption of both drugs may be increased to maintain their rewarding effects (Rose, Brauer, Behm, et al., 2004).

Prevalence and Cost of Alcohol Abuse and Dependence As an example, the following statistics give a picture of current prevalence of alcohol use and abuse in the UK. In a recent adults and children study in England (2009, Statistics on Alcohol, The Information Centre, NHS, 2011) 69% of men and 55% of women (aged 16 and over) reported drinking an alcoholic drink on at least one day in the week prior to interview. 10% of men and 6% of women reported drinking on every day in the previous week.

In the week prior to interview, 37% of men drank over 4 units on at least one day and 29% of women drank more than 3 units on at least one day. Also, 20% of men reported drinking over 8 units and 13% of women reported drinking over 6 units on at least one day. The average weekly alcohol consumption was 16.4 units for men and 8.0 units for women. 26% of men reported drinking more than 21 units in an average week. For women, 18% reported drinking more than 14 units in an average week.

As with patterns of drug use, young people present a different picture with 18% of secondary school pupils aged 11 to 15 reported drinking alcohol in the week prior to interview compared with 26% in 2001. Around half of pupils had ever had an alcoholic drink (51%), compared with 61% in 2003.

In 2009/10, there were 1,057,000 alcohol related admissions to hospital. This is an increase of 12% on the 2008/09 figure (945,500) and more than twice as many as in 2002/03 (510,800).

Alcohol is often implicated in vehicular accidents. (© Mark E.Gibson/ CORBIS/©Corbis.)

In 2010, there were 160,181 prescription items for drugs for the treatment of alcohol dependency prescribed in primary care settings or NHS hospitals and dispensed in the community. This is an increase of 6% on the 2009 figure (150,445) and an increase of 56% on the 2003 figure (102,741).

More men than women have problems with alcohol, though the gender difference has decreased over the past 20 years, perhaps due to shifting attitudes toward women and drinking. That is, there is no longer a taboo against women drinking alcohol. Women begin drinking at a later age than men, but they can become physiologically dependent as quickly as men do (Keyes, Martins, Blanco, & Hasin, 2010).

The prevalence of alcohol problems differs by ethnicity and education level as well. White and Hispanic adolescents and adults are more likely to binge drink than African American adolescents and adults. Binge and heavy-use drinking are lowest among Asian Americans (SAMHSA, 2010). Using DSM-IV-TR categories, alcohol dependence was most prevalent among Native Americans and Hispanics and least prevalent among Asian Americans and African Americans (Smith, Stinson, Dawson, et al., 2006).

Alcohol use disorders are comorbid with several personality disorders, mood disorders, schizophrenia, and anxiety disorders as well as with other drug use (Kessler, Crum, Warner, et al., 1997; Langen-bucher, Labouvie, Morgenstern, et al., 1997; Skinstad & Swain, 2001).

Expenditures on health care for people dependent on alcohol in the United States were estimated to be over $26 billion annually over 10 years ago (NIAAA, 2001); the costs are likely higher now. Alcohol-related traffic fatalities are a serious problem, and the highest-risk drivers are young men.

Short-Term Effects of Alcohol How does alcohol produce its short-term effects? After being swallowed and reaching the stomach, alcohol begins to be metabolized by enzymes. Most of it goes into the small intestine, and from there is absorbed into the blood. It is then broken down, primarily in the liver, which can metabolize about 1 ounce of 100-proof (50 percent alcohol) liquor per hour. Quantities in excess of this amount remain in the bloodstream. Whereas absorption of alcohol can be very quick, removal is always slow.

Although Figure 10.2 shows mean blood alcohol levels based on a person's weight and amount of alcohol consumption, the effects of alcohol vary with its concentration in

Blood Alcohol Concentration Calculator									
# OF DRINKS CONSUMED/SEX		**WEIGHT**							
		100	120	140	160	180	200	220	240
1	Male	.04	.04	.03	.03	.02	.02	.02	.02
	Female	.05	.04	.04	.03	.03	.03	.02	.02
2	Male	.09	.07	.06	.05	.05	.04	.04	.04
	Female	.10	.08	.07	.06	.06	.05	.05	.04
3	Male	.13	.11	.09	.08	.07	.07	.06	.05
	Female	.15	.13	.11	.10	.08	.08	.07	.06
4	Male	.17	.15	.13	.11	.10	.09	.08	.07
	Female	.20	.17	.15	.13	.11	.10	.09	.09
5	Male	.22	.18	.16	.14	.12	.11	.10	.09
	Female	.25	.21	.18	.16	.14	.13	.12	.11
6	Male	.26	.22	.19	.16	.15	.13	.12	.11
	Female	.30	.26	.22	.19	.17	.15	.14	.13
7	Male	.30	.25	.22	.19	.17	.15	.14	.13
	Female	.36	.30	.26	.22	.20	.18	.16	.15
8	Male	.35	.29	.25	.22	.19	.17	.16	.15
	Female	.41	.33	.29	.26	.23	.20	.18	.16
9	Male	.39	.35	.28	.25	.22	.20	.18	.16
	Female	.46	.38	.33	.29	.26	.23	.21	.19
10	Male	.39	.35	.28	.25	.22	.20	.18	.16
	Female	.51	.42	.36	.32	.28	.25	.23	.21
11	Male	.48	.40	.34	.30	.26	.24	.22	.20
	Female	.56	.46	.40	.35	.31	.27	.25	.23
12	Male	.53	.43	.37	.32	.29	.26	.24	.21
	Female	.61	.50	.43	.37	.33	.30	.28	.25
13	Male	.57	.47	.40	.35	.31	.29	.26	.23
	Female	.66	.55	.47	.40	.36	.32	.30	.27
14	Male	.62	.50	.43	.37	.34	.31	.28	.25
	Female	.71	.59	.51	.43	.39	.35	.32	.29
15	Male	.66	.54	.47	.40	.36	.34	.30	.27
	Female	.76	.63	.55	.46	.42	.37	.35	.32

Figure 10.2 Blood alcohol concentration calculator. Note that values are just estimates. An actual BAC will vary depending on metabolism and amount of food in the stomach.

the bloodstream. Levels in the bloodstream depend on the amount ingested in a particular period of time, the presence of food in the stomach (food retains the alcohol and reduces its absorption rate), the weight and body fat of the person drinking, and the efficiency of the liver. Two ounces of alcohol will thus have a different effect on a 180-pound man who has just eaten than on a 110-pound woman with an empty stomach. However, women achieve higher blood alcohol concentrations even after adjustment for differences in body weight, perhaps due to differences in body water content between men and women.

It is also important to consider the question: what counts as a drink? A 12-ounce glass of beer, a 5-ounce glass of wine, and 1.5 ounces of "hard liquor" (like a shot of tequila) are all considered one drink. The size of the drink is not what matters. Rather, it is the alcohol content of the particular beverage. See the website Rethinking Drinking for more on this (http://rethinkingdrinking.niaaa.nih.gov).

Alcohol produces its effects through its interactions with several neural systems in the brain. It stimulates GABA receptors, which may account for its ability to reduce tension. (GABA is a major inhibitory neurotransmitter; the benzodiazepines, such as Xanax, have an effect on GABA receptors similar to that of alcohol.) Alcohol also increases levels of serotonin and dopamine, which may be the source of its ability to produce pleasurable effects. Finally, alcohol inhibits glutamate receptors, which may cause the cognitive effects of alcohol intoxication, such as slowed thinking and memory loss.

A novel study examined the effects of alcohol on both the brain and behavior. Participants were given different doses of alcohol while in an fMRI scanner performing a simulated driving test (Calhoun, Pekar, & Pearlson, 2004). The low dose (.04 blood alcohol content) led to just a small impairment in motor functioning, but the high dose (.08 blood alcohol content) led to more significant motor impairment that interfered with driving ability. Furthermore, the effects of the alcohol in the brain were in areas associated with monitoring errors and making decisions (the anterior cingulate and orbitofrontal cortex), which suggested to the researchers that people at the legal limit of alcohol may make poor decisions about driving and not realize they are making mistakes.

Long-Term Effects of Prolonged Alcohol Abuse Almost every tissue and organ of the body is adversely affected by prolonged consumption of alcohol. For example, alcohol provides so many calories—a pint of 80-proof spirits supplies about half a day's caloric requirements—that drinkers often reduce their intake of food. But the calories provided by alcohol are empty; they do not supply the nutrients essential for health, and the result can be severe malnutrition. Alcohol also contributes directly to malnutrition by impairing the digestion of food and absorption of vitamins. In older people who have chronically abused alcohol, a deficiency of B-complex vitamins can cause amnestic syndrome, a severe loss of memory for both recent and long-past events. These memory gaps are often filled in by reporting imaginary events (confabulation).

Prolonged alcohol use plus reduction in the intake of proteins contributes to the development of cirrhosis of the liver, a disease in which some liver cells become engorged with fat and protein, impeding their function; some cells die, triggering an inflammatory process, and when scar tissue develops, blood flow is obstructed. The World Health Organization report (WHO, 2002) indicated that 4% of the burden of disease and 3.2% of all deaths globally were attributed to alcohol, and that alcohol was the foremost risk to health in low-mortality developing countries and the third in developed countries.

Other common changes to the body due to drinking include damage to the endocrine glands and pancreas, heart failure, erectile dysfunction, hypertension, stroke, and capillary hemorrhages, which are responsible for the swelling and redness in the face, especially the nose, of people who chronically abuse alcohol. Chronic heavy drinking is associated with damage to many areas of the brain, many of which are implicated in memory functions.

Heavy alcohol consumption by a woman during pregnancy is the leading known cause of intellectual developmental disorder among children. The growth of the fetus is slowed, and cranial, facial, and limb anomalies can be produced, a condition known as **fetal alcohol syndrome (FAS)**. Even moderate drinking can produce undesirable, if less severe, effects on the fetus, leading the WHO to counsel total abstention during pregnancy as the safest course. Research with children who did not have FAS but whose mothers drank moderately (i.e., about one drink per day) during the first trimester revealed that these children had impairments in learning and memory (Willford, Richardson, Leech, et al., 2004) and exhibited growth deficits (such as smaller head size and lower height and weight) at age 14 (Day, Leech, Richardson, et al., 2004). Research is beginning to solve the puzzle of why some fetuses exposed to alcohol will not develop any problems, whereas others will have profound problems. For example, by 6 months of age, infants exposed to alcohol prenatally may exhibit problems in attention that can then contribute to the development of other cognitive problems later in childhood (Kable & Coles, 2004). The news is not all bad. Animal research has shown that some of the problems associated with prenatal alcohol exposure, such as deficits in learning and memory, can be turned around (Klintsova, Scamra, Hoffman, et al., 2002). In addition, research suggests that growth deficits associated with prenatal alcohol exposure can be mitigated if children are raised in a more stable and healthy environment, indicating that the biological effects of early alcohol exposure are sensitive to environmental conditions (Day & Richardson, 2004).

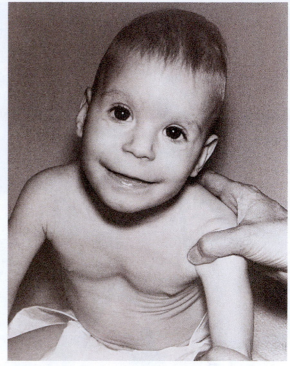

Heavy drinking during pregnancy can cause fetal alcohol syndrome. Children with this disorder can have facial abnormalities and intellectual developmental disorder. (Courtesy of James W. Hanson.)

Although it is appropriate and accurate to pay attention to the negative effects of alcohol, other evidence points to the positive health benefits for some people. Light drinking has been related to lower risk for coronary heart disease and stroke (Kloner & Rezkalla, 2007; Sacco, Elkind, Boden-Albala, et al., 1999; Theobald, Bygren, Carstensen, et al., 2000). If alcohol does have a beneficial effect, it could be due to physiological (e.g., acetate, a metabolite of alcohol, increases coronary blood flow) or psychological (a less-driven lifestyle and diminished hostility) factors, or, most likely, the interaction between the two factors. Indirect evidence suggests that consumption of low to moderate amounts of red wine may lower the so-called bad cholesterol (i.e., LDL) and raise the so-called good cholesterol (HDL) levels (Kloner & Rezkalla, 2007; Powers, Saultz, & Hamilton, 2007).

Check Your Knowledge 10.1 (Answers are at the end of the chapter.)

True or false?

1. The diagnosis of a substance use disorder requires both tolerance and withdrawal.

2. Research suggests that nicotine can enhance the rewarding properties of alcohol.

3. Even moderate drinking by pregnant women can cause learning and attention problems in their children.

Tobacco Use Disorder

Not long after Columbus's first commerce with Native Americans, sailors and merchants began to imitate the Native Americans' smoking of rolled leaves of tobacco, with the result that they, too, began to crave it. When not smoked, tobacco was—and is—chewed or ground into small

California's Tobacco Education Media Campaign parodies tobacco ads to illustrate health risks associated with smoking and to attack pro-tobacco influences. (California Tobacco Control Program.)

pieces and inhaled as snuff. **Nicotine** is the addicting agent of tobacco. The neural pathways that become activated stimulate the dopamine neurons in the mesolimbic area that seem to be involved in producing the reinforcing effects of most drugs (Stein, Pankiewicz, Harsch, et al., 1998).

Prevalence and Health Consequences of Smoking The threat to health posed by smoking has been documented convincingly, for example, by the Information Centre for Health and Social care in England (NHS, 2011). In 2009, 21% of adults reported smoking, the same as in 2007 and 2008 but lower than 39% in 1980. In 2009, those aged 16–19 and 20–24 reported the highest prevalence of cigarette smoking (27% and 28% respectively), while those aged 60 and over reported the lowest prevalence (14%).

Prevalence of cigarette smoking continues to be higher among men than women with 22% of men and 20% of women reporting smoking. This compares with 42% of men and 36% of women in 1980.

The overall decrease in smoking prevalence seems to be mainly due to the increase in people who have never smoked or only occasionally smoked. The proportion of adults who have never smoked or only occasionally smoked has been rising steadily, from 43% in 1982 to 53% in 2009.

Women are more likely to never or occasionally smoke then men, however the increase in the percentage of 'never or only occasionally' smokers is larger among men than women; the proportion of men increased from 32% in 1982 to 49% in 2009, whereas for women the increase was from 51% to 57%. By comparison, the proportion of adults who were ex-regular smokers increased by 3 percentage points from 23% in 1982 to 26% in 2009.

In 2009, current smokers smoked an average of 13.1 cigarettes a day. Men smoked a slightly higher number of cigarettes a day than women, with men smoking on average 13.9 cigarettes a day, compared with 12.4 for women. The number of cigarettes smoked per day was similar among smokers from the three different socio-economic groups (routine and manual, intermediate and managerial and professional).

Among some of the medical problems associated with, and almost certainly caused or exacerbated by, long-term cigarette smoking are emphysema; cancers of the larynx and of the esophagus, pancreas, bladder, cervix, and stomach; complications during pregnancy; sudden infant death syndrome; periodontitis; and a number of cardiovascular disorders. The most probable harmful components in the smoke from burning tobacco are nicotine, carbon monoxide, and tar, which consist primarily of certain hydrocarbons, many of which are known carcinogens (Jaffe, 1985).

For England as a whole it is estimated that, on average, each year 86,500 deaths were caused by smoking over the period 1998–2002. This represents an average of over 1,663 deaths per week, 237 deaths every day, and nearly 10 deaths an hour. Of the total number of smoking-attributable deaths, just over 62% (53,800) are among males and 38% are among women (32,700). In contrast, 900 male deaths and 500 female deaths caused by Parkinson's disease are estimated to have been prevented through smoking. Furthermore, 200 deaths from endometrial cancer are estimated to have been prevented among women. Ironically, this is one of the little known positive side-effects of smoking!

The net overall figure for smoking-attributable mortality is therefore given as 84,900. In terms of cause of death, the greatest attributable proportion is given for lung cancer. Just over nine in ten male lung cancer deaths, and eight in ten female lung cancer deaths, are estimated to be smoking-attributable. Over 70% of mortality due to cancer of the oesophagus is estimated to be smoking-attributable, and over three quarters of male upper respiratory cancer deaths are due to smoking.

Research demonstrates the significance of ethnicity in nicotine addiction as well as the intricate interplay among behavioral, social, and neurobiological factors (Leischow, Ranger-Moore, & Lawrence, 2000). It has been known for

Parental smoking greatly increases the chances that children will begin to smoke. (© Elena Kouptsova-Vasic/Shutterstock.)

years that African American cigarette smokers are less likely to quit and are more likely, if they continue to smoke, to get lung cancer. Why? It turns out that they retain nicotine in their blood longer than do whites, that is, they metabolize it more slowly (Mustonen, Spencer, Hoskinson, et al., 2005). Another reason has to do with the type of cigarette smoked. African Americans are more likely to smoke menthol cigarettes, and research shows that people who smoke menthol inhale more deeply and hold the smoke in for longer, thus providing more opportunity for deleterious effects (Celebucki, Wayne, Connolly, et al., 2005).

Research has found that Chinese Americans metabolize less nicotine from cigarettes than either white or Latino smokers (Benowitz, Pérez-Stable, Herrera, et al., 2002). In general, lung cancer rates are lower among Asians than among whites or Latinos. The relatively lower metabolism of nicotine among Chinese Americans may help explain why lung cancer rates are lower in this group.

Health Consequences of Secondhand Smoke   As we have known for many years, the health hazards of smoking are not restricted to those who smoke. The smoke coming from the burning end of a cigarette, so-called **secondhand smoke**, or environmental tobacco smoke (ETS), contains higher concentrations of ammonia, carbon monoxide, nicotine, and tar than does the smoke actually inhaled by the smoker. According to a report by WHO in 2010, secondhand smoke is estimated to have caused about 603,000 premature deaths in 2004. These include 16,600 deaths from lower respiratory infections and 1,100 from asthma in children, and 21,000 deaths from lung cancer, 3,500 deaths from asthma and 379,000 deaths from ischaemic heart disease (IHD) in adults. This disease burden amounts in total to about 10.9 million disability-adjusted life years (DALys). Of all deaths attributable to SHS, 28% occur in children, and 47% in women. The main sources of uncertainty include the estimation of exposure.

A report on Tobacco by the WHO (2011) states that there is no safe level of exposure to secondhand tobacco smoke. Every person should be able to breathe smoke-free air. Smoke-free laws protecting the health of non-smokers are popular, as they do not harm business and encourage smokers to quit. However, while the number of people protected from secondhand smoke more than doubled to 739 million in 2010, from 354 million in 2008:

Children of mothers who smoke are at increased risk for respiratory infections, bronchitis, and inner-ear infections. (Getty Images/Custom Medical Stock Photo RM/ Getty Images, Inc.)

- Only nearly 11% of people are protected by comprehensive national smoke-free laws.
- Of the 100 most populous cities, only 22 are smoke free.
- Almost half of children regularly breathe air polluted by tobacco smoke.
- Over 40% of children have at least one smoking parent.
- Secondhand smoke causes more than 600,000 premature deaths per year.
- In 2004, children accounted for 28% of the deaths attributable to secondhand smoke.
- There are more than 4,000 chemicals in tobacco smoke, of which at least 250 are known to be harmful and more than 50 are known to cause cancer.
- In adults, secondhand smoke causes serious cardiovascular and respiratory diseases, including coronary heart disease and lung cancer. In infants, it causes sudden death. In pregnant women, it causes low birth weight.

Marijuana

Marijuana consists of the dried and crushed leaves and flowering tops of the hemp plant, *Cannabis sativa*. It is most often smoked, but it may be chewed, prepared as a tea, or eaten in baked goods. **Hashish**, much stronger than marijuana, is produced by removing and drying the resin exudate of the tops of cannabis plants. In DSM-5, cannabis use disorder will likely be the category name that includes marijuana.

Originally the hemp plant was extensively cultivated in the United States not for smoking but for its fibers, which were used in the manufacture of cloth and rope. By the nineteenth century, the medicinal properties of cannabis resin had been noted, and it was marketed by several drug companies as a treatment for rheumatism, gout, depression, cholera, and neuralgia. It was also smoked for

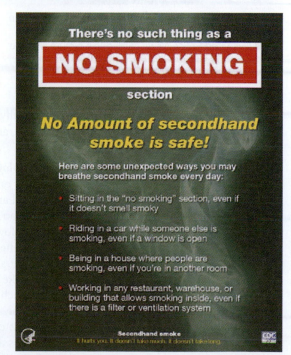

There's no such thing as a

NO SMOKING

section

No Amount of secondhand smoke is safe!

Here are some unexpected ways you may breathe secondhand smoke every day:

- Sitting in the "no smoking" section, even if it doesn't smell smoky
- Riding in a car while someone else is smoking, even if a window is open
- Being in a house where people are smoking, even if you're in another room
- Working in any restaurant, warehouse, or building that allows smoking inside, even if there is a filter or ventilation system

Secondhand smoke
It hurts you. It doesn't take much. It doesn't take long.

The Surgeon General's report from 2006 noted that no amount of secondhand smoke is safe. (Courtesy Centers for Disease Control.)

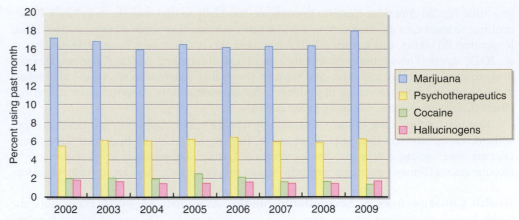

Figure 10.3 Trends in drug use among young people age 18–25. *Source:* SAMHSA, 2010.

Recreational use of hashish in a fashionable apartment in New York City in the nineteenth century. An 1876 issue of the *Illustrated Police News* carried this picture with the title "Secret Dissipation of New York Belles: Interior of a Hasheesh Hell on Fifth Avenue." (Culver Pictures, Inc.)

pleasure, though this was little seen in the United States until 1920. At that time, the passage of the Eighteenth Amendment prohibiting the sale of alcohol prompted some people to begin smoking marijuana brought across the border from Mexico. Unfavorable reports in the press attributing crimes to marijuana use led to the enactment of a federal law against the sale of the drug in 1937. Today marijuana use is illegal in most countries.

Prevalence of Marijuana Use   Marijuana is the most frequently used illicit drug. In a report by Atha (2005) for the Independent Drug Monitoring Unit Ltd, it is noted that the Home Office in the UK conducts British Crime Survey every 2 years, including questions on whether people have ever used a range of drugs, and if so whether they have done so in the past year or past month. The prevalence of marijuana use has been rising in these surveys since they were first conducted in the early 1980's. In the UK, around 15 million people would now admit having tried marijuana or as it is also known, cannabis, with 2 to 5 million regular users. Marijuana use is higher in the 16–29 age-group, although the rise in use is sharpest amongst older adults.

Effects of Marijuana   As with most other drugs, marijuana use has its risks. Generally, the more we learn about a drug, the less benign it turns out to be, at least for some people, and marijuana is no exception (see Focus on Discovery 10.1).

Psychological Effects   The intoxicating effects of marijuana, like those of most drugs, depend in part on its potency and the size of the dose. Smokers of marijuana find it makes them feel relaxed and sociable. Large doses have been reported to bring rapid shifts in emotion, to dull attention, to fragment thoughts, to impair memory, and to give the sense that time is moving more slowly. Extremely heavy doses have sometimes been found to induce hallucinations and other effects similar to those of LSD, including extreme panic, sometimes arising from the belief that a frightening experience will never end. Dosage can be difficult to regulate because it may take up to half an hour after smoking marijuana for its effects to appear; many users thus get much higher than intended.

The major active chemical in marijuana is delta-9-tetrahydrocannabinol (THC). The amount of THC in marijuana is variable, but marijuana is more potent now than it was two decades ago (Zimmer & Morgan, 1995). In addition, users smoke more now than in the past (e.g., a "blunt" contains more cannabis than a joint).

FOCUS ON DISCOVERY 10.1

Is Marijuana a Gateway Drug?

The so-called stepping-stone, or gateway, theory of marijuana use has been around for a long time. According to this view, marijuana is dangerous not only in itself but also because it is a first step for young people on the path to becoming addicted to other drugs, such as heroin.

Studies have established several specific dangers from using marijuana, as described in the text. But is marijuana a gateway to more serious substance abuse or dependence? First of all, there is little evidence to suggest that this theory applies to African Americans. Furthermore, about 40 percent of regular marijuana users do not go on to use such drugs as heroin and cocaine (Stephens, Roffman, & Simpson, 1993). So if by *gateway* we mean that escalation to a more serious drug is inevitable, then marijuana is not a gateway drug. However, we do know that many, but far from all, who use heroin and cocaine began their drug experimentation

Most people who use marijuana do not go on to use heroin, but many heroin users do begin their drug use with marijuana. (© Couperfield/Shutterstock.)

with marijuana. And at least in the United States and New Zealand, users of marijuana are more likely than nonusers to experiment later with heroin and cocaine (Fergusson & Horwood, 2000; Kandel, 2002; Miller & Volk, 1996).

Thus, even though marijuana use often precedes other drug use, it does not appear to *cause* later drug use, as the term *gateway* implies. Rather, it may be that marijuana is the first drug to be tried because it is more socially acceptable than other drugs.

An abundance of scientific evidence indicates that marijuana can interfere with a wide range of cognitive functions. Of special significance are findings that show an impact on short-term memory. One prospective study assessed IQ scores at multiple time points among users between the ages of 17 and 23 and found a decline of about 4 points in current, regular users (Fried, Watkinson, James, et al., 2002).

Several studies have demonstrated that being high on marijuana impairs complex psychomotor skills necessary for driving. Poor performance after smoking one or two marijuana cigarettes containing 2 percent THC can persist for up to 8 hours after a person believes he or she is no longer high, creating the danger that people will drive when they are not functioning adequately.

Does chronic use of marijuana affect intellectual functioning even when the person is not using the drug? Unfortunately, not many well-controlled studies have been conducted to address this question. Collectively, current evidence suggests that long-term users may exhibit a slight impairment in learning and memory, but there is not strong evidence to suggest such impairments persist after discontinuation of use (Rey et al., 2004).

Physical Consequences The short-term effects of marijuana include bloodshot and itchy eyes, dry mouth and throat, increased appetite, reduced pressure within the eye, and somewhat raised blood pressure.

We know that the long-term use of marijuana seriously impairs lung structure and function (Grinspoon & Bakalar, 1995). Even though marijuana users smoke far fewer cigarettes than do tobacco smokers, most inhale marijuana smoke more deeply and retain it in their lungs for much longer periods of time. Since marijuana has some of the same carcinogens found in tobacco, its harmful effects are greater than would be expected were only the absolute number of cigarettes or pipefuls considered. For example, one marijuana cigarette smoked in the typical way is the equivalent of five tobacco cigarettes in carbon monoxide intake, four in tar intake, and ten in terms of damage to cells lining the airways (Sussman, Stacy, Dent, et al., 1996).

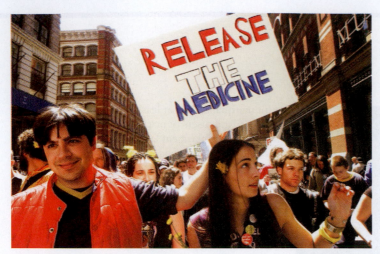

Demonstrators in New York advocate the legalization of marijuana for medical purposes. (Spencer Platt/Getty Images, Inc.)

How does marijuana affect the brain? In the early 1990s, researchers identified two cannabinoid brain receptors, called CB1 and CB2 (Matsuda, Lolait, Brownstein, et al., 1990; Munro, Thomas, Abu-Shaar, et al., 1993). CB1 receptors are found throughout the body and the brain, with a particularly high number in the hippocampus, an important region of the brain for learning and memory. Based on accumulating evidence, researchers have concluded that the well-documented short-term memory problems associated with marijuana use are linked to the effects of marijuana on these receptors in the hippocampus (e.g., Sullivan, 2000).

In addition, a PET study found that smoking marijuana was associated with increased blood flow to regions in the brain often associated with emotion, including the amygdala and the anterior cingulate. Decreased blood flow was observed in regions of the temporal lobe that have been associated with auditory attention, and participants in this study who were high on marijuana performed poorly on a listening task (O'Leary, Block, Flaum, et al., 2000). These findings might help explain some of the psychological effects associated with marijuana use, including changes in emotion and attentional capabilities.

Is marijuana addictive? Contrary to widespread earlier belief, it may be. Controlled observations have confirmed that habitual use of marijuana does produce tolerance (Compton, Dewey, & Martin, 1990). Whether long-term users experience withdrawal when accustomed amounts of marijuana are not available is less clear, though surveys and laboratory studies conducted in the past 10 years suggest that withdrawal symptoms, such as restlessness, anxiety, tension, stomach pains, and insomnia, do occur (Rey et al., 2004).

Therapeutic Effects Ironically, therapeutic uses of marijuana came to light just as the negative effects of regular and heavy usage of the drug were being uncovered. In the 1970s several double-blind studies showed that THC and related drugs could reduce the nausea and loss of appetite that accompany chemotherapy for some people with cancer (e.g., Salan, Zinberg, & Frei, 1975). Later findings confirmed this result (Grinspoon & Bakalar, 1995). Marijuana often appears to reduce nausea when other antinausea agents fail. Marijuana is also an effective treatment for the discomfort of AIDS (Sussman et al., 1996), glaucoma, chronic pain, muscle spasms, and seizures.

The potential benefits of smoking marijuana were confirmed in reports by a panel of experts to the National Institutes of Health (NIH, 1997) and a committee of the Institute of Medicine, a branch of the National Academy of Sciences (Institute of Medicine, 1999). These reports suggested that these benefits be taken more seriously by medical researchers and clinicians. The NIH agreed to fund research on the subject, including research on whether the benefits from taking THC in pill form are comparable to what people report from smoking marijuana. (Most people report more beneficial effects from smoking than from swallowing THC in capsule form; this may be due to other compounds than THC in marijuana leaves that are separate from THC.) The Institute of Medicine report recommended that people with "debilitating symptoms" or terminal illnesses be allowed to smoke marijuana under close medical supervision for up to 6 months; the rationale for smoking was based on the just-mentioned findings that THC swallowed by mouth does not provide the same relief. But the Institute of Medicine report also emphasized the dangers of smoking per se and urged the development of alternative delivery systems, such as inhalers.

The recommendations of medical experts represent sharp disagreement with governments. The use of marijuana represents a criminal offence to this day in the UK and most European countries. However, in the UK, for example, there is a move by politicians towards decriminalization and public opinion is also moving towards support of drug law reform and some form of liberalization (Atha, 2005).

Quick Summary

Alcohol and drug use is common all over the world. The DSM-5 will likely list substance use disorder as the major category, with severity determined by the number of symptoms present and a specifier for physiological dependence, which means that either tolerance or withdrawal is present.

Withdrawal from alcohol can involve hallucinations and delirium tremens. People who use or are addicted to alcohol may use other drugs, particularly nicotine. Alcohol use is particularly high among college students; men are more likely to drink alcohol than women, and differences in use, abuse, and dependence by ethnicity have been observed. Even light or moderate drinking during pregnancy can be associated with later problems in learning for the child.

Smoking remains prevalent, though it has been on the decline. Cigarette smoking causes a number of illnesses, including several cancers, heart disease, and other lung diseases. Although more men smoke than women, the rates are the same among adolescent boys and girls. The ill effects of tobacco are greater for African Americans. Secondhand smoke, also called environmental tobacco smoke, is also linked to a number of serious health problems.

Marijuana makes people feel relaxed and sociable, but it can also interfere with attention, memory, and thinking. In addition, it has been linked to lung-related problems. It remains the most prevalently used drug, particularly among younger people. Men use it more than women. Users can develop tolerance to marijuana; it is less clear whether withdrawal symptoms occur after users stop smoking it. Marijuana also has therapeutic benefits, including for those suffering from the side effects of chemotherapy and for those with AIDS, glaucoma, seizures, chronic pain, and muscle spasms.

Check Your Knowledge 10.2

Fill in the blanks.
1. List three types of cancer that are caused by smoking.
2. Marijuana can have _____ effects on learning and memory; it is less clear if there are _____ effects.

3. List three of the therapeutic benefits of marijuana.

Opiates

The **opiates** include opium and its derivatives morphine, heroin, and codeine. They are considered sedatives, but in the DSM-5, opiate use disorder will likely be in a category distinct from sedative/hypnotic/anxiolytic use disorder.

The opiates are a group of addictive drugs that in moderate doses relieve pain and induce sleep. Foremost among them is **opium,** originally the principal drug of illegal international traffic; it was known to the people of the Sumerian civilization, dating as far back as 7000 B.C. They gave the poppy that supplied this drug the name opium, meaning "the plant of joy."

In 1806 the alkaloid **morphine,** named after Morpheus, the Greek god of dreams, was separated from raw opium. This bitter-tasting powder proved to be a powerful sedative and pain reliever. Before its addictive properties were noted, it was commonly used in medicines. In the middle of the nineteenth century, when the hypodermic needle was introduced in the United States, morphine began to be injected directly into the veins to relieve pain.

Concerned about administering a drug that could disturb the lives of people, scientists began studying morphine. In 1874 they found that morphine could be converted into another powerful pain-relieving drug, which they named **heroin.** Used initially as a cure for morphine addiction, heroin was substituted for morphine in cough syrups and other patent medicines. So many maladies were treated with heroin that it came to be known as G.O.M., or "God's own medicine" (Brecher, 1972). However, heroin proved to be even more addictive and more potent than morphine. Today, heroin is most often injected, though it can also be smoked, snorted, or taken orally.

An opium poppy. Opium is harvested by slitting the seed capsule, which allows the raw opium to seep out. (Dr. Jeremy Burgess/Photo Researchers, Inc.)

More recently, opiates legally prescribed as pain medications, including **hydrocodone** and **oxycodone,** have become drugs of abuse. Hydrocodone is most often combined with other drugs, such as acetaminophen (the active agent in Tylenol), to create prescription pain medicines such as Vicodin, Zydone, or Lortab. Oxycodone is found in medicines such as Percodan, Tylox, and OxyContin. Vicodin is one of the most commonly abused drugs containing hydrocodone, and OxyContin is one of the most commonly abused drugs containing oxycodone.

Prevalence of Opiate Abuse and Dependence. There are enormous difficulties in gathering data in this area, but a report from the National Treatment Agency for Substance Misuse (2011) states that, in total, there were an estimated 306,150 opiate and/or crack cocaine users aged 15 to 64 in England in 2009/10. This converts to 8.93 per thousand population aged 15 to 64. The estimated prevalence of opiate use was 7.70 per thousand population aged 15 to 64 and the estimated prevalence of crack cocaine use was 5.37 per thousand. The estimated prevalence of drug injecting was 3.01 per thousand population aged 15 to 64. Nationally, there was a decrease in prevalence of opiate and/or crack cocaine use between 2008/09 and 2009/10; this decrease was statistically significant. There was a slight increase in the prevalence of opiate use from 262,428 in 2008/09 to 264,072 in 2008/10. The estimates for the period 2009/10 also show a decrease in the levels of crack cocaine use, but this was not statistically significant.

Non-medical use of opiates was not an offence in the UK until after the First World War but doctors were still allowed to prescribe them (mainly morphine) to people who had become dependent. Not many people used morphine or heroin, and most who did, obtained it from doctors. Diversion of heroin from doctors saw the number of users increase in the 1960s and all but a few specialist doctors were stopped from prescribing it.

The mid 1970s saw the beginnings of a significant market in imported illegally manufactured 'chinese' heroin from Hong Kong. In the mid 1980s the number of users of heroin and other opiates increased dramatically, particularly in inner city deprived areas. This heroin came from the so called golden crescent countries of Iran, Pakistan and Turkey. This type of heroin was originally produced for smoking rather than injecting and followed the rise in Iranian refugees to the UK after the fall of the Shah in 1979.

The British government responded by developing new community based drug services and running anti-heroin media campaigns as well as needle exchange schemes to reduce needle sharing and the incidence of HIV.

Today street heroin usually comes as an off white or brown powder. For medical use heroin usually comes as tablets or an injectable liquid. A number of synthetic opiates (called opioids) are also manufactured for medical use and have similar effects to heroin. These include dihydrocodeine

Clinical Case: Franck

Franck was a 27-year-old man who had been addicted to heroin for six years. He first tried heroin during his time at university. He had experimented with marijuana at school, and was introduced to heroin at a late-night party during his first semester. Unable to control his habit, Franck dropped out of university a year later. He tried moving back with his family for a short time, but after repeatedly stealing money from his mother's purse, Franck's dad felt he had no alternative but to ask him to leave home. Franck said he would move in with some friends, but in reality, he began living in a derelict building, and alternated between begging for money and petty theft to support his habit. This remained the pattern of Franck's life for the next five years. Over this time, he lost a tremendous amount of weight and became quite malnourished. He was over 1.8 metres tall,

but he weighed only 68 kilograms. Food wasn't a priority on most days, though he was usually able to gather a meal of scraps from the local cafe. Franck tried to get into several rehabilitation programs, but they required that Franck remain free of heroin for at least a week before he could be admitted. He was able to resist for a day or two, but then withdrawal symptoms would begin, making it too painful to continue without the drug. A friend from the streets, formerly addicted to heroin, had recently helped Franck get to a methadone clinic. He tolerated the methadone really well, and continued to attend the clinic for a further three months. He re-established contact with his parents and, with continued support from the clinic, he started getting job training as a support worker at the treatment centre. He was hopeful that he would shake his habit for good.

(DF 118s), pethidine (often used in childbirth), Diconal, Palfium, Temgesic and methadone, a drug which is often prescribed as a substitute drug in the treatment of heroin addiction.

Heroin can be smoked ('chasing the dragon'), snorted or prepared for injection. Opioids made for medical use may be used for non-medical reasons, especially by heroin users who cannot get hold of heroin. Methadone is usually prescribed as a syrup which is drunk.

Psychological and Physical Effects Opiates produce euphoria, drowsiness, and sometimes a lack of coordination. Heroin and opiates also produce a "rush," a feeling of warm, suffusing ecstasy immediately after an intravenous injection. The user sheds worries and fears and has great self-confidence for 4 to 6 hours. However, the user then experiences a severe letdown, bordering on stupor.

Opiates produce their effects by stimulating neural receptors of the body's own opioid system (the body naturally produces opioids, called endorphins and enkephalins). Heroin, for example, is converted into morphine in the brain and then binds to opioid receptors, which are located throughout the brain. Some evidence suggests that a link between these receptors and the dopamine system is responsible for opiates' pleasurable effects. However, evidence from animal studies suggests that opiates may achieve their pleasurable effects via their action in the area of the brain called the nucleus accumbens, perhaps independently from the dopamine system (Koob, Caine, Hyytia, et al., 1999).

Heroin was synthesized from opium in 1874 and was soon being added to a variety of medicines that could be purchased without prescription. This ad shows a teething remedy containing heroin. It probably worked. (National Library of Medicine/ Photo Researchers, Inc.)

Opiates are clearly addicting, for users develop tolerance and show withdrawal symptoms. Withdrawal from heroin may begin within 8 hours of the last injection, at least after high tolerance has built up. During the next few hours after withdrawal begins, the person typically experiences muscle pain, sneezing, and sweating; becomes tearful; and yawns a great deal. The symptoms resemble those of influenza. Within 36 hours, the withdrawal symptoms become more severe. There may be uncontrollable muscle twitching, cramps, chills alternating with excessive flushing and sweating, and a rise in heart rate and blood pressure. The person is unable to sleep, vomits, and has diarrhea. These symptoms typically persist for about 72 hours and then diminish gradually over a 5- to 10-day period.

People who abuse opiates face serious problems. In a 29-year follow-up of 500 people addicted to heroin, about 28 percent had died by age 40; half of these deaths were from homicide, suicide, or accident, and one-third were from overdose (Hser, Anglin, & Powers, 1993). The social consequences of using an illegal drug are also serious. The drug itself and the process of obtaining it become the center of the person's existence, governing all activities and social relationships. The high cost of drugs—users must often spend upwards of $200 per day for opiates—often drives users into acquiring money through illegal activities, such as theft, prostitution, or selling drugs.

An additional problem associated with intravenous drug use is exposure, through sharing needles, to infectious agents such as the human immunodeficiency virus (HIV), which causes AIDS. Notably, there is good consensus among scientists that the free distribution of needles and syringes, so-called needle exchange programs, reduces needle sharing and the spread of infectious agents associated with intravenous drug use (Gibson, 2001; Yoast, Williams, Deitchman, et al., 2001). Contrary to some political rhetoric, such programs in combination with methadone treatment (discussed later in this chapter) do not lead to an increase in either initial or continued use of drugs. In the UK, heroin and other opiates are controlled under the **Misuse of Drugs Act** making it illegal to possess them or to supply them to other people without a prescription. Heroin is treated as a Class A drug where the maximum penalties are 7 years imprisonment and a fine for possession and life imprisonment and a fine for supply.

Morphine, opium, methadone, pethidine and Diconal are also Class A drugs under the Act. Codeine and dihydrocodeine (DF118) are Class B drugs and Temgesic and Distalgesic are Class C drugs.

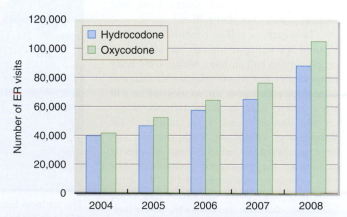

Figure 10.4 Emergency room visits after overdoses of hydrocodone and oxycodone continue to increase. In 2002, the numbers for hydrocodone and oxycodone were 25,000 and 21,000 respectively (SAMHSA, 2011).

Stimulants

Stimulants act on the brain and the sympathetic nervous system to increase alertness and motor activity. Amphetamines are synthetic stimulants; cocaine is a natural stimulant extracted from the coca leaf. Focus on Discovery 10.2 discusses a less risky and more prevalent stimulant, caffeine.

Amphetamines　The first **amphetamine**, benzedrine, was synthesized in 1927, and other amphetamines were synthesized soon afterwords. Almost as soon as benzedrine became commercially available in the early 1930s as an inhalant to relieve stuffy noses, the public discovered its stimulating effects, and physicians soon began to prescribe it and the other amphetamines to control mild depression and appetite. During World War II, soldiers on both sides were supplied with amphetamines to ward off fatigue.

Amphetamines such as benzedrine, dexedrine, and methedrine produce their effects by causing the release of norepinephrine and dopamine and blocking the reuptake of these neurotransmitters. Amphetamines are taken orally or intravenously and can be addicting. Wakefulness is heightened, intestinal functions are inhibited, and appetite is reduced—hence their use in dieting. The heart rate quickens, and blood vessels in the skin and mucous membranes constrict. The person becomes alert, euphoric, and outgoing and is possessed of seemingly boundless energy and sell-confidence. Larger doses can make a person nervous, agitated, and confused; other symptoms include palpitations, headaches, dizziness, and sleeplessness. Sometimes heavy users become extremely suspicious and hostile, to the extent that they can be dangerous to others. Large doses taken over a period of time can induce a state quite similar to the paranoia sometimes seen with schizophrenia.

FOCUS ON DISCOVERY 10.2

Our Tastiest Addiction—Caffeine

What may be the world's most popular drug is seldom viewed as a drug at all, and yet it has strong effects, produces tolerance in people, and even subjects habitual users to withdrawal (Hughes, Higgins, Bickel, et al., 1991). Users and nonusers joke about it, and most readers of this book have probably had some this very day. We are, of course, referring to **caffeine**, a substance found in coffee, tea, cocoa, cola and other soft drinks, some cold remedies, and some diet pills.

Two cups of coffee, containing between 150 and 300 milligrams of caffeine, affect most people within half an hour. Metabolism, body temperature, and blood pressure all increase; urine production goes up, as most of us will attest; there may be hand tremors, appetite can diminish, and, most familiar of all, sleepiness is warded off. Panic disorder can be exacerbated by caffeine, not surprising in light of the heightened sympathetic nervous system arousal occasioned by the drug. Extremely large doses of caffeine can cause headache, diarrhea, nervousness, severe agitation, even convulsions and death. Death, though, is virtually impossible unless the

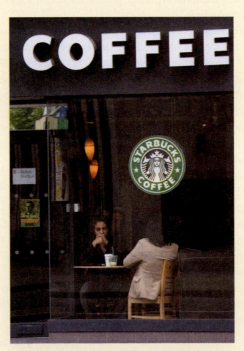

The caffeine found in coffee, tea, and soft drinks is probably the world's favorite drug. (Bloomberg via Getty Images.)

person grossly overuses tablets containing caffeine, because the drug is excreted by the kidneys without any appreciable accumulation.

Although it has long been recognized that drinkers of very large amounts of regular (caffeinated) coffee daily can experience withdrawal symptoms when consumption ceases, people who drink no more than two cups of regular coffee a day can suffer from headaches, fatigue, and anxiety if caffeine is withdrawn from their daily diet (Silverman, Evans, Strain, et al., 1992), and these symptoms can interfere with social and occupational functioning. These findings are disturbing because more than three-quarters of Americans consume a little more than two cups of regular coffee a day (Roan, 1992). And although parents usually deny their children access to coffee and tea, they often do allow them to imbibe caffeine-laden soft drinks, hot chocolate, and cocoa, and to eat chocolate candy and chocolate and coffee ice cream. Thus, our addiction to caffeine can begin to develop as early as 6 months of age, the form of it changing as we move from childhood to adulthood.

Clinical Case: Liz

Liz, a 40-year-old mother of two teenage girls, had just been arrested for stealing clothes from a designer clothes shop. She was under the influence of several prescription drugs and alcohol. Two months earlier, she had received a caution for causing a public disturbance whilst on a night out drinking and dancing with several girlfriends. Liz was determined to pull herself together for the sake of her girls, but her cravings for the painkillers were so intense that she was frequently unable to resist. She had been using prescription drugs on a fairly regular basis since she was 36 years old following a period of marital problems with her husband.

Tolerance to amphetamines develops rapidly, so more and more of the drug is required to produce the stimulating effect. One study demonstrated tolerance after just 6 days of repeated use (Comer, Hart, Ward, et al., 2001). As tolerance increases, some users may stop taking pills and start injecting methedrine, one of the strongest of the amphetamines, directly into the veins. Users may give themselves repeated injections of the drug and maintain intense and euphoric activity for a few days, without eating or sleeping, after which, exhausted and depressed, they sleep, or crash, for several days. Then the cycle starts again. After several repetitions of this pattern, the physical and social functioning of the person deteriorates considerably. Behavior becomes erratic and hostile, and users may become dangerous to themselves and others.

Methamphetamine Abuse of an amphetamine derivative called methamphetamine skyrocketed in the 1990s. Methamphetamine (crystal meth) is a central nervous system stimulant with a high potential for misuse and dependence. A synthetic drug, it is closely related chemically to amphetamine but produces greater effects on the central nervous system. The drug is also known by the street names of 'crystal meth', 'crank', 'tina' or 'ice'. Its euphoric effects are similar to but more intense and longer lasting than those of cocaine. Methamphetamine takes the form of a white odorless and bitter tasting crystalline powder, readily soluble in water or alcohol, and can also be produced in tablet or powder form. It can be smoked, injected, snorted or consumed orally.

Methamphetamine was first synthesized in 1887 (Feldman et al.,1997), but went unnoticed until it became the alternative to ephedrine, a drug commonly used to treat asthma. Medically produced amphetamines (including methamphetamine) were used in Japan, Britain, Germany and the US during the Second World War to enable soldiers to stay awake, alert and compulsively focused. As a consequence of the return home of soldiers who had been using it regularly and a simultaneous flood into the local market of methamphetamine, Japan suffered a meth epidemic after the War (1945-1957) (Suwaki, et al., 1997 Methamphetamine abuse in Japan: its 45 year history and the current situation.) From 1942, the Nazi leader Adolf Hitler received daily injections of methamphetamine from his personal physician, Dr Theodor Morell (Heston and Heston, 1979).

Amphetamines were used for medicinal purposes in the UK until the late 1960's. The sale of methamphetamine products from retail pharmacists was banned in the UK in 1968. In the USA the drug is available in pharmaceutical form for the treatment of Attention Deficit Hyperactivity Disorder (ADHD) and narcolepsy.

Methamphetamine use and its spread is of concern in several countries, particularly in South East Asia (Thailand and Japan), the USA, Australia and the Czech Republic. It is relatively uncommon in the UK although the drug's widespread use abroad and its appearance on the UK dance scene have led to fears of it becoming more popular.

Like other amphetamines, methamphetamine can be taken orally or intravenously. It can also be taken intranasally (i.e., by snorting). In a clear crystal form, the drug is often referred to as "crystal meth" or "ice." Craving for methamphetamine is particularly strong, often lasting several years after use of the drug is discontinued. Craving is also a reliable predictor of later use (Hartz, Frederick-Osborne, & Galloway, 2001). Like other amphetamines, users get an immediate high, or rush, that can last for hours. This includes feelings of euphoria as well as changes to

Hippocampal volumes

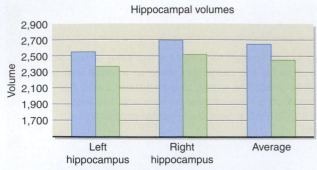

Figure 10.5 Results from an fMRI study showing that those who abused methamphetamine (green bars) had smaller hippocampal volume (size) than those in the control group (blue bars) who did not abuse methamphetamine. Adapted from Thompson et al. (2004).

the body, such as increases in blood flow to the heart and other organs and an increase in body temperature. The high eventually levels off (the "shoulder") and then it comes crashing down ("tweaking"). Not only do the good feelings crash, but the person also becomes very agitated. Physiological dependence on methamphetamine often includes both tolerance and withdrawal.

Several animal studies have indicated that chronic use of methamphetamine causes damage to the brain, affecting both the dopamine and the serotonin systems (Frost & Cadet, 2000). Neuroimaging studies have found similar effects in the human brain, particularly in the dopamine system. For example, one study of chronic meth users who met DSM diagnostic criteria for dependence found a number of users with damage to the hippocampus (see Figure 10.5). The volume of the hippocampus was smaller among chronic meth users, which correlated with poorer performance on a memory test (Thompson, Hayashi, Simon, et al., 2004). Another study reported that people who abused methamphetamine but were currently clean of the substance, some for as long as 11 months, had a significant reduction in a dopamine transporter gene (a transporter gene is a gene that either lets a drug enter a cell or prevents a drug from entering a cell) (Volkow, Chang, Wang, et al., 2001). In fact, in 3 of the 15 people studied, the reduction in dopamine reuptake was similar to that seen in the less severe stages of Parkinson's disease. Moreover, those with a history of methamphetamine abuse performed more slowly than a comparison group on several motor tasks, a finding similar to that seen with people with Parkinson's disease.

In a different study, men who were in treatment for methamphetamine dependence participated in a laboratory task of decision making while having their brains scanned with fMRI (Paulus, Tapert, & Schuckit, 2005). The researchers found that lower activation in several brain areas (dorsolateral prefrontal cortex, insula, and areas of the temporal and parietal lobes) during the decision-making task predicted relapse to methamphetamine abuse 1 year after treatment. It seems obvious that poor decision making might put one at higher risk for relapse. What this study also showed was that the brain areas that contribute to sound decision making are disrupted in some people who are dependent on methamphetamine. What is less clear is whether the methamphetamine damaged these areas or whether these areas were damaged before methamphetamine use began.

A caveat should be noted here. One difficulty with conducting these types of studies is finding participants who use only the drug of interest (in this case, methamphetamine) so that any observed effects can be linked to that drug and not others. However, it is difficult to find meth users who have not at some point used other substances, particularly alcohol and nicotine. For example, in one of the studies described above, the meth users did not differ from the control group in alcohol consumption, but they did smoke more (Thompson et al., 2004). Nevertheless, it seems clear that the deleterious effects of methamphetamine are many and serious.

The drug is relatively cheap and easy to manufacture although methods may involve inflammable chemicals and the release of toxic fumes. The chemicals needed to manufacture the drug (e.g. ephedrine, red phosphorous and iodine) are readily available. Some chemicals used to make methamphetamine are highly volatile and dangerous to breathe, causing damage ranging from eye irritation and nausea to coma and death.

Cocaine The alkaloid **cocaine** was first extracted from the leaves of the coca shrub in the mid-1800s and has been used since then as a local anesthetic. In the mid-1980s a new form of cocaine, called **crack,** appeared on the streets. Crack comes in a rock-crystal form that is then heated, melted, and smoked. The name *crack* comes from the crackling sound the rock makes when being heated. The presence of crack brought about an increase in the number of users of cocaine and in casualties. Because it was available in small, relatively inexpensive doses ($10 for about 100 milligrams versus $100 per gram of cocaine), younger and less affluent buyers began to experiment with the drug and to become addicted (Kozel & Adams, 1986). Crack is now most often used in poorer urban areas.

Cocaine prevalence has steadily climbed in the 1990's and 2000's and though recent indications suggest that the trend has stabilised, use in the UK, along with Spain, remains

A coca plant. The leaves contain about I percent cocaine. (Dr. Morley Read/Photo Researchers, Inc.)

the highest in Europe. In 1996 0.6% of 16 to 59 year olds had tried the drug in the last year. This peaked at 3% in 2008/09 though fell to 2.5%, or around 800,000 people, in 2009/10. Like on the continent, cocaine is the UK's second most used illicit substance after cannabis and like with cannabis, there is a considerable diversity among its users. This includes occasional recreational use as well as dependent and marginalised users.

In 2009/10, cocaine powder was estimated to have been used by around 800,000 individuals aged 16–59 and 300,000 aged 16–24. The proportion of 16–24 year olds decreased slightly from 12.2% in 2009 to 11.6%. The Home Office has estimated that there are around 181,000 crack cocaine users in England (all figures from DrugScope, 2010).

Cocaine has other effects in addition to reducing pain. It acts rapidly on the brain, blocking the reuptake of dopamine in mesolimbic areas. Cocaine yields pleasurable states because dopamine left in the synapse facilitates neural transmission. Self-reports of pleasure induced by cocaine are strongly related to the extent to which cocaine has blocked dopamine reuptake (Volkow, Wang, Fischman, et al., 1997). Cocaine can increase sexual desire and produce feelings of self-confidence, well-being, and indefatigability. An overdose may bring on chills, nausea, and insomnia, as well as strong paranoid feelings and terrifying hallucinations of insects crawling beneath the skin. Chronic use can lead to heightened irritability, impaired social relationships, paranoid thinking, and disturbances in eating and sleeping. Some, but not all, users develop tolerance to cocaine, requiring a large dose to achieve the same effect. Other users may become more sensitive to cocaine's effects, which are believed to be a contributing factor in deaths after a fairly small dosage. Stopping cocaine use appears to cause severe withdrawal symptoms.

Cocaine is a vasoconstrictor, causing the blood vessels to narrow. As users take larger and larger doses of the purer forms of cocaine now available, they are more often rushed to emergency rooms and may die of an overdose, often from a heart attack [DrugScope, 2011]. Cocaine also increases a person's risk for stroke and causes cognitive impairments, such as difficulty paying attention and remembering. Because of its strong vasoconstricting properties, cocaine poses special dangers in pregnancy, for the blood supply to the developing fetus may be compromised.

Cocaine can be sniffed (snorted), smoked in pipes or cigarettes, swallowed, or even injected into the veins; some heroin users mix the two drugs. Cocaine powder is often cut up into short lines and then sniffed up the nose through a rolled up banknote or straw. A typical weekend user might use one-quarter a gram or so over the weekend while more regular users could consume up to one or two grams a day. Because the effects can wear off quite quickly, heavy users can get through several grams in a relatively short period of time. When purified by this chemical process, the cocaine base—or freebase—produces very powerful effects because it is absorbed so rapidly. Like most drugs, the faster it is absorbed, the quicker and more intense the high. Freebase is usually smoked in a water pipe or sprinkled on a tobacco or marijuana cigarette. It is rapidly absorbed into the lungs and carried to the brain in a few seconds, where it induces an intense 2-minute high, followed by restlessness and discomfort.

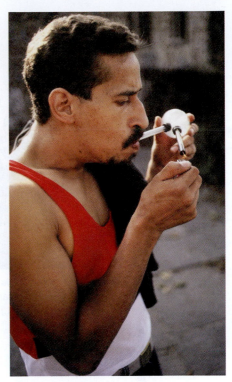

Crack use is highest in urban areas. (Wesley Bocxe/Photo Researchers, Inc.)

Hallucinogens, Ecstasy, and PCP

LSD and Other Hallucinogens   In 1938 the Swiss chemist Albert Hofmann manufactured a few milligrams of *d*-lysergic acid diethylamide into a drug known today as **LSD**. The term *psychedelic*, from the Greek words for "soul" and "to make manifest," was applied to emphasize the subjectively experienced expansion of consciousness reported by users of LSD and often referred to by them as a "trip." The term in current use for LSD and other drugs with similar effects is **hallucinogen**, which refers to the main effects of such drugs, hallucinations. Unlike the hallucinations in schizophrenia, however, these are usually recognized by the person as being caused by the drug.

The use of LSD and other hallucinogens peaked in the 1960s; by the 1980s, only 1 or 2 percent of people could be classified as regular users. Although thought of as a sixties' drug, LSD is very much part of the current UK drug scene. It is very difficult to know exactly how many young people have tried LSD or use it on any regular basis because in surveys it is often lumped together with other drugs like amphetamine and ecstasy.

Cocaine can be smoked, swallowed, injected, or snorted as shown here. (Mark Antman/The Image Works.)

Mescaline, obtained from the peyote cactus, is used in certain religious rites of Native American people of the American Southwest and northern Mexico. (Kal Muller/Woodfin Camp/Photoshot.)

However, in one 1998 survey in England in Wales, 11 percent of those aged 16-29 said they had tried it at least once, two percent said they had tried it during the year preceding the survey (DrugScope, 2004).

One survey of club goers listed LSD as their fourth favourite drug to take behind cannabis, ecstasy and amphetamines and that is probably a fair reflection of a more general UK league table of illicit drug use, although nitrites or poppers would be also be high up the list.

In addition to hallucinations, LSD can alter a person's sense of time (it seems to go slowly). A person using LSD may have sharp mood swings but can also experience an expanded consciousness such that he or she seems to appreciate sights and sounds like never before.

The effects of hallucinogens depend on a number of psychological variables in addition to the dose itself. A person's set—that is, attitudes, expectancies, and motivations with regard to taking drugs—is widely held to be an important determinant of his or her reactions to hallucinogens. The context in which the drug is experienced is also important.

Many users experience intense anxiety after taking LSD, in part because the perceptual experiences and hallucinations can provoke fears that they are "going crazy." For some, these anxieties unfold into full-blown panic attacks. The anxiety usually subsides as the drug is metabolized. A minority of people, however, go into a psychotic state that can require hospitalization and extended treatment.

Flashbacks (also referred to as hallucinogen persisting perception disorder, or HPPD) are visual recurrences of psychedelic experiences after the physiological effects of the drug have worn off. They occur in some people who have used LSD, most frequently in times of stress, illness, or fatigue. Flashbacks seem to have a force of their own; they may come to haunt people weeks and months after they have taken the drug and are very upsetting for those who experience them.

Other hallucinogens include mescaline and psilocybin, whose effects are thought to be due to stimulating serotonin receptors. **Mescaline,** an alkaloid and the active ingredient of peyote, was isolated in 1896 from small, disklike growths of the top of the peyote cactus. The drug has been used for centuries in the religious rites of Native American people living in the U.S. Southwest and northern Mexico. **Psilocybin** is a crystalline powder that Hofmann isolated from the mushroom *Psilocybe mexicana* in 1958.

Ecstasy and PCP   The hallucinogen-like substance **Ecstasy** became illegal in the US in 1985. Ecstasy is made from both MDA (methylenedioxyamphetamine) and MDMA (methylenedioxymethamphetamine). **MDMA** was first synthesized in the early 1900s, and it was used as an appetite suppressant for World War I soldiers. Chemical precursors to MDMA are found in several commonly used spices, such as nutmeg, dill, saffron, and sassafras. Not until the 1970s were the psychoactive properties of MDMA reported in the scientific literature.

Ecstasy contains compounds from both the hallucinogen and amphetamine families, but its effects are sufficiently different from either that some have suggested putting it in its own

Clinical Case: Antonia

University is a time when much learning takes place, and for Antonia this included Ecstasy (X). She went to a club, and a friend gave her a pill, she didn't know what it was but felt pressured by her friends to swallow it. They seemed to be having such a great time, and had so much energy. Within a short period of time, Antonia began to feel almost magical, as if she was seeing everything around her in a new light. It made her feel much loved and that she had many good friends who really cared about her. She talked passionately and intimately to friends and strangers alike. The next time she tried X, she felt more subdued, even anxious, and the slight headache and feelings of being "spaced out" the morning after the first time seemed to last longer. After several more times using X, she noticed that despite her enthusiasm and even craving for the effects, she found instead that she felt a little depressed and anxious, even several days after taking the drug.

FOCUS ON DISCOVERY 10.3

Nitrous Oxide—Not a Laughing Matter

Nitrous oxide is a colorless gas that has been available since the nineteenth century. Within seconds, it induces lightheadedness and a state of euphoria in most people; for some, important insights seem to flood the mind. Many people find otherwise mundane events and thoughts irresistibly funny, hence the nickname *laughing gas*.

Many people have received nitrous oxide at a dentist's office to facilitate relaxation and otherwise make a potentially uncomfortable and intimidating dental procedure more palatable. A major advantage of nitrous oxide over other analgesics and relaxants is that a person can return to a normal waking state within minutes of breathing enriched oxygen or normal air.

Nitrous oxide fits in the broader category of inhalants and has been used recreationally since it first became available, although it has been illegal for many years in most states except as administered by appropriate health professionals. As with the other drugs examined in this chapter, illegality has not prevented unsupervised use. It is one of the most prevalently used inhalants among teens (sniffing glue, gasoline, and paint are more prevalent), with rates of use as high as 22 percent among those who use inhalants (Wu, Pilowsky, & Schlenger, 2004).

Sometimes called "hippie crack" or "whippets," nitrous oxide balloons are often combined with the use of Ecstasy and other drugs at parties with bright laser lights and loud dance music (i.e., at raves).

Nitrous oxide is no laughing matter. (BananaStock/ SUPERSTOCK.)

category, called the "entactogens" (Morgan, 2000). Ecstasy remains a popular drug, particularly among those who are into the clubbing/dance scene, although there are indications that use may be decreasing. Findings from the 2007/08 British Crime Survey show that 1.5% of 16 to 59 year olds and 3.9% of 16 to 24 year olds reported using ecstasy in the last year. Based on the survey's findings, it is estimated that 2.39 million people in the 16-59 age group have used ecstasy at least once in their lifetime with 470,000 having used the drug in the last year (Home Office, 2008).

When compared with data from the previous five years, the 2007/08 figures mark the lowest reported levels of ecstasy use. For example, findings from the 2003/04 British Crime Survey showed that 2% of 16 to 59 year olds and 5.3% of 16 to 24 year olds reported using ecstasy in the last year. Based on those results, it was estimated that 614,000 16 to 59 year olds had used ecstasy at some point in the last year in 2003/04.

There have been over 200 reported deaths in the UK linked to ecstasy use over the last 5 years. Figures from the National Programme on Substance Abuse Deaths (np-SAD) show that, in 2007, ecstasy-type drugs were associated with 10 deaths where ecstasy was the only drug involved and 45 deaths ecstasy was implicated along with other drugs (Druglink, 2005).

Why this particular group of people died when so many others have also taken the drug is unknown, but we do know something about the medical circumstances surrounding their deaths.

Ecstasy acts primarily by contributing to both the release and the subsequent reuptake of serotonin (Huether, Zhou, & Ruther, 1997; Liechti, Baumann, Gamma, et al., 2000; Morgan, 2000). It was believed at one time that the use of Ecstasy was relatively harmless, but accumulating scientific evidence suggests that it may have neurotoxic effects on the serotonin system (De Souza, Battaglia, & Insel, 1990; Gerra, Zaimovic, Ferri, et al., 2000). It is difficult to say whether these toxic effects are directly due to drug use, since no studies in humans to date have assessed serotonin functioning both before and after Ecstasy use. Studies with animals, however, have shown that a single dose of Ecstasy causes serotonin depletion and that prolonged use can damage serotonin axons and nerve terminals (Harkin, Connor, Malrooney, et al., 2001; Morgan, 2000).

Users report that Ecstasy enhances intimacy and insight, improves interpersonal relationships, elevates mood and self-confidence, and promotes aesthetic awareness. It can also cause muscle tension, rapid eye movements, jaw clenching, nausea, faintness, chills or sweating,

Ecstasy is a popular party drug but, like many drugs, is not free of ill effects. (David Seed Photography/Getty Images, Inc.)

anxiety, depression, depersonalization, and confusion. Some evidence suggests that the subjective and physiological effects of Ecstasy, both pleasurable and adverse, may be stronger for women than men (Liechti et al., 2000).

PCP, phencyclidine, often called *angel dust,* is another drug that is not easy to classify. Developed as a tranquilizer for horses and other large animals, it generally causes serious negative reactions, including severe paranoia and violence. Coma and death are also possible. PCP affects multiple neurotransmitters in the brain, and chronic use is associated with a variety of neuropsychological deficits. People who abuse PCP are likely to have used other drugs either before or concurrently with PCP, so it is difficult to sort out whether neuropsychological impairments are due solely to PCP, to other drugs, or to the combination.

Quick Summary

Opiates include heroin and other pain medications like hydrocodone and oxycodone. Abuse of prescription pain medications has risen dramatically, and overdoses are common. Initial effects of opiates include euphoria; later, users experience a letdown. Death by overdose from opiates is a severe problem. Other problems include exposure to HIV and other infectious agents through the use of shared needles. Withdrawal is severe for opiates.

Amphetamines are stimulants that produce wakefulness, alertness, and euphoria. Men and women use these equally. Tolerance develops quickly. Methamphetamine is a synthesized amphetamine, and use has increased dramatically since the 1990s. Men use it more than women and whites more than other ethnic groups. Methamphetamine can damage the brain, including the hippo-

campus. Cocaine and crack remain serious problems. Cocaine can increase sexual desire, feelings of well-being, and alertness, but chronic use is associated with problems in relationships, paranoia, and trouble sleeping, among other things. The faster crack or cocaine is absorbed, the more quickly and intensely the person becomes high.

LSD was a popular hallucinogen in the 1960s and 1970s, often billed as a mind-expanding drug. The mind-expanding drug of the 1990s became Ecstasy. Although these drugs do not typically elicit withdrawal symptoms, tolerance can develop. Though Ecstasy use peaked in 2001, it is once again on the rise. PCP remains a problem in urban areas. This drug can cause severe paranoia and violence.

Check Your Knowledge 10.3

True or false?
1. Withdrawal from heroin begins slowly, days after use has been discontinued.
2. The use of OxyContin began in urban areas but quickly spread to rural areas.

3. Methamphetamine is a less potent form of amphetamine, less likely to be associated with brain impairment.
4. Ecstasy contains compounds associated with hallucinogens and amphetamines.

Etiology of Substance Use Disorders

Becoming physiologically dependent on a substance is a developmental process for some people. That is, for some people, they begin with a positive attitude toward a substance, then begin to experiment with using it, then begin using it regularly, then use it heavily, and finally become dependent on it (see Figure 10.6).

It appears that the factors that contribute to substance use disorders may depend on the point in the process that is being considered. For example, developing a positive attitude toward smoking and beginning to experiment with tobacco are strongly related to smoking by other family members (Robinson, Klesges, Zbikowski, et al., 1997). In contrast, becoming a regular smoker is more strongly related to smoking by peers and being able to acquire cigarettes readily (Robinson et al., 1997; Wang, Fitzhugh, Eddy, et al., 1997).

More generally, adopting a developmental approach to understanding the etiology of substance use disorders requires the study of persons across time, beginning at the earliest sign of substance use. Studies of the trajectories of substance use problems among adolescents suggest, not surprisingly, that different adolescents follow different trajectories (Jackson, Sher, & Wood, 2000; Wills, Sandy, Shinar, et al., 1999). For example, one study identified two typical trajectories toward alcohol abuse in adolescence: (1) a group that began drinking early in adolescence and continued to increase their drinking throughout high school and (2) a group that started drinking a lesser amount in early adolescence and increased drinking at two peak points, one in middle school and another later in high school. Boys were more likely to follow the trajectory of the first group; girls were more likely to follow the trajectory of the second group, with even steeper trajectories in drinking than the boys (Li, Duncan, & Hops, 2001).

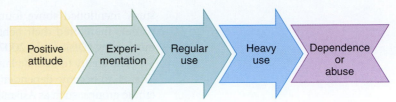

Figure 10.6 The process by which some people become dependent on a drug.

Other views incorporate what we know about the developing brain, particularly in adolescence. A review of the literature points to the fact that the area of the brain linked to judgment and decision making, novelty seeking, and impulse control—that is, the frontal cortex—is still developing at the time when adolescents are beginning to experiment with drugs and alcohol (Chambers, Taylor, & Potenza, 2003). The neural systems believed to be important for reward, including dopaminergic, serotonergic, and glutamatergic pathways, all pass through the developing frontal cortex.

Although applicable in many cases, a developmental approach does not account for all cases of substance abuse or dependence. For example, there are documented cases in which heavy use of tobacco or heroin did not result in dependence. Furthermore, we are not talking about an inevitable progression through stages. Some people have periods of heavy use of a substance—for example, alcohol—and then return to moderate use. Other people do not need a period of heavy use to become dependent on the substance, as in the case of methamphetamine. In the following sections, we discuss genetic, neurobiological, psychological, and sociocultural factors associated with substance use disorders. Keep in mind that these factors are likely to be differently related to different substances. Genetic factors, for example, may play some role in alcohol use disorder but be less important in hallucinogen use disorder.

Genetic Factors

Much research has addressed the possibility that there is a genetic contribution to drug and alcohol use disorders. Several studies have shown that relatives and children of problem drinkers have higher-than-expected rates of alcohol abuse or dependence (e.g., Chassin, Pitts, Delucia, et al., 1999). Stronger evidence for genetic factors comes from twin studies, which have revealed greater concordance in identical twins than in fraternal twins for alcohol use disorder (McGue, Pickens, & Svikis, 1992), smoking (True, Xiam, Scherrer, et al., 1999), heavy use of marijuana (Kendler & Prescott, 1998), and drug use disorders in general (Tsuang, Lyons, Meyer, et al., 1998). Behavioral genetics studies indicate that the genetic and shared environmental risk factors (see Chapter 2) for illicit drug use disorders may be rather nonspecific (Karkowski, Prescott, & Kendler, 2000; Kendler, Jacobsen, Prescott, et al., 2003). That is, genetic and shared environmental risk factors appear to be the same no matter what the drug (marijuana, cocaine, opiates, hallucinogens, sedatives, stimulants), and this appears to be true for both men and women (Kendler, Prescott, Myers, et al., 2003).

Of course, genes do their work via the environment, and research has uncovered gene–environment interactions in alcohol and drug use disorders. Among adolescents, peers and parents appear to be particularly important environmental variables. For example, a large twin study in Finland found that heritability for alcohol problems among adolescents was higher among those teens who had a large number of peers who drank compared to those who had a smaller number of peers who drank (Dick, Pagan, Viken, et al., 2007). The environment in this case was peer group drinking behavior. Another study found that heritability for both alcohol and smoking among adolescents was higher for those teens whose best friend also smoked and drank (Harden, Hill, Turkheimer, & Emery, 2008). In this case, the environment was best friend behavior. Another study found that heritability for smoking was greater for teens who went to schools where the "popular crowd" smoked compared to schools where the popular students did not smoke (Boardman, Saint Onge, Haberstick, et al., 2008). The Finnish twin study mentioned above found that heritability for smoking was higher among teens whose parents monitored their behavior less compared to teens who had a higher level of parental monitoring (Dick et al., 2007).

The ability to tolerate large quantities of alcohol may be inherited for alcohol use disorder. That is, to become dependent on alcohol, a person usually has to be able to drink a lot. Some ethnic groups, such as Asians, may have a low rate of alcohol problems because of physiological intolerance, which is caused by an inherited deficiency in enzymes involved in alcohol metabolism, called *alcohol dehydrogenases* or ADH. Mutations in genes called ADH2 and ADH3 code proteins for the ADH enzymes, and these genes have been linked with alcohol use disorders generally as well as among some Asian populations specifically (Edenberg, Xuie, Chen, et al., 2006; Sher, Grekin, & Williams, 2005). About three-quarters of Asians experience unpleasant effects like flushing (blood flow to the face) from small quantities of alcohol, which may protect them from becoming dependent on alcohol.

Research has also emerged on the mechanism through which genetics plays a role in smoking. Like most drugs, nicotine appears to stimulate dopamine release and inhibit its reuptake, and people who are more sensitive to these effects of nicotine are more likely to become regular smokers (Pomerleau, Collins, Shiffman, et al., 1993). Research has examined a link between smoking and a gene that regulates the reuptake of dopamine called SLC6A3. One form of this gene has been related to a lower likelihood of smoking (Lerman, Caporaso, Audrain, et al., 1999) and a greater likelihood of quitting (Sabo, Nelson, Fisher, et al., 1999). Research has also found that genes, such as CYP2A6, contribute to the body's ability to metabolize nicotine, with some people able to do this quickly and others more slowly. Slower nicotine metabolism means that nicotine stays in the brain longer. A longitudinal study of 12–13 year olds showed that those adolescents who had genes linked with slower nicotine metabolism were more likely to become dependent on it 5 years later (O'Loughlin, Paradis, Kim, et al., 2005). Other evidence has found that people with reduced activity in the CYP2A6 gene smoke fewer cigarettes and are less likely to become dependent on nicotine (Audrain-McGovern & Tercyak, 2011; Rao, Hoffmann, Zia, et al., 2000). This is an interesting example of a gene polymorphism serving a protective function.

Neurobiological Factors

You may have noticed that in our discussions of specific drugs, the neurotransmitter dopamine has almost always been mentioned. This is not surprising given that dopamine pathways in the brain are importantly linked to pleasure and reward. Drug use typically results in rewarding or pleasurable feelings, and it is via the dopamine system that these feelings are produced. In short, people take drugs to feel good. Research with both humans and animals shows that nearly all drugs, including alcohol, stimulate the dopamine systems in the brain (see Figure 10.7), particularly

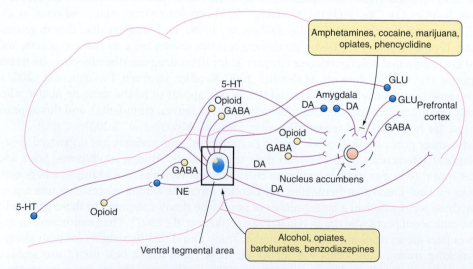

Figure 10.7 Reward pathways in the brain that are affected by different drugs. DA = dopamine; GABA = gamma-aminobutyric acid; GLU = glutamate; 5-HT = serotonin; NE = norepinephrine. Adapted from Camí & Farré (2003).

the mesolimbic pathway (Camí & Farré, 2003; Koob, 2008). Researchers have wondered, then, if problems in the dopamine pathways in the brain might somehow account for why certain people become dependent on drugs. Some evidence suggests that people dependent on drugs or alcohol have a deficiency in the dopamine receptor DRD2 (Noble, 2003).

One of the difficult issues to resolve is whether problems in the dopamine system may increase the vulnerability of some people to become dependent on a substance, sometimes called the "vulnerability model," or whether problems in the dopamine system are the consequence of taking substances (the "toxic effect model"). For drugs such as cocaine, there is currently research support for both views. Thus, this remains an important area to work out in future research.

People take drugs not only to feel good. They also take them to feel less bad. This is particularly true once a person becomes dependent on a substance, such as alcohol, methamphetamine, or heroin, whose withdrawal symptoms are excruciatingly unpleasant. In other words, people continue to take drugs to avoid the bad feelings associated with withdrawal. A substantial body of research with animals supports this motivation for drug-taking behavior (Koob & Le Moal, 2008), and this research helps to explain why relapse is so common.

Investigators have proposed a neurobiological theory, referred to as the *incentive-sensitization theory*, which considers both the craving ("wanting") for drugs and the pleasure that comes with taking the drug ("liking") (Robinson & Berridge, 1993, 2003). According to this theory, the dopamine system linked to pleasure, or liking, becomes supersensitive not just to the direct effects of drugs but also to the cues associated with drugs (e.g., needles, spoons, rolling paper). This sensitivity to cues induces craving, or wanting, and people go to extreme lengths to seek out and obtain drugs. Over time, the liking of drugs decreases, but the wanting remains very intense. These investigators argue that the transition from liking to powerful wanting, accomplished by the drug's effects on brain pathways involving dopamine, is what maintains the addiction.

Many researchers study the neurobiology of wanting or craving. A number of laboratory studies have shown that cues for a particular drug can elicit responses not altogether unlike those associated with actual use of the drug. For example, those who were dependent on cocaine showed changes in physiological arousal, increases in cravings and "high" feelings, and increases in negative emotions in response to cues of cocaine, which consisted of audio- and videotapes of people preparing to inject or snort cocaine, compared to people not dependent on cocaine (e.g., Roberts, Kuncel, Shiner, et al., 2000). Brain imaging studies have shown that cues for a drug, such as a needle or a cigarette, activate the reward and pleasure areas of the brain implicated in drug use.

What about the psychology of craving? Do people who crave a substance more actually use it more, even if they are trying to quit? An experience sampling study of people who were trying to quit smoking showed that they do (Berkman, Falk, & Lieberman, 2011). People who had just started a smoking-cessation program were given text messages 8 times a day for 21 consecutive days. At each text prompt, they reported how many cigarettes they had smoked, how much they were craving a cigarette, and how they were feeling. Reports of more craving predicted a greater likelihood of smoking when the participants received their next text. These investigators also examined participants' brain activation using fMRI during a task called the "go/no-go task." In this task, people are presented with letters one a time on a screen and are instructed to press a button when they see certain letters (e.g., L, V, T, N; the "go" part) but refrain from pressing the button when they see another letter (X; the "no-go" part). There are many more "go" trials than "no-go" trials, and thus it is challenging to keep from pressing the button during a "no-go" trial because people get into the habit of pressing the button many times in a row on the "go" trials. Areas of the brain that showed greater activation during "no-go" trials compared to "go" trials included the basal ganglia, inferofrontal gyrus, and pre-motor areas. People who showed greater activation in these areas during the task were better able to inhibit their button pressing, suggesting that their brain was doing a better job of providing the support for inhibiting a response when needed. In addition, greater activation in these brain regions was associated with less linkage between craving and smoking. That is, people who showed greater brain activation when inhibiting a button press were less likely to act on their cravings and begin to smoke again.

A large prospective study of heavy and light drinkers examined how wanting and liking during a lab session predicted actual drinking 2 years later. Heavy drinkers were people who had between 10 and 40 drinks a week and had more than one binge-drinking episode in most weeks; light drinkers were people who had between 1 and 5 drinks a week and had less than five binge drinking episodes a year. The participants came to three lab sessions where they were given different amounts of alcohol and then rated wanting, liking, and sedation feelings. The researchers assessed participants' real-world drinking behavior 2 years later. Perhaps not surprisingly, they found that the heavy drinkers reported greater wanting and liking of alcohol during the laboratory sessions than did the light drinkers. By contrast, the light drinkers reported greater feelings of sedation than the heavy drinkers during the lab sessions. At follow-up, the heavy drinkers who reported greater wanting and liking of alcohol during the laboratory sessions were drinking more than the heavy drinkers who reported less liking and wanting during the lab sessions (King, de Wit, McNamara, & Cao, 2011). Thus, even self-reports of wanting and liking are important for predicting drinking behavior.

Of course, neurobiological, genetic, and environmental factors do not operate in isolation. The most comprehensive explanations for substance use disorders will be those that consider how environmental factors enable genetic or neurobiological factors to have their effects. Research with animals shows this quite clearly. For example, studies of mice that were separated from their mothers at birth (a very stressful occurrence, even for mice!) responded to injections of amphetamine or cocaine later in life very differently from mice that had not been separated but had experienced stress early in life (a lot of handling by humans). The investigators showed that these two types of early stress differently impacted the way in which the dopamine system developed in these animals, which then contributed to their drug responses (Meaney, Brake, & Gratton, 2002).

Psychological Factors

In this section, we look at three types of psychological factors that may contribute to the etiology of substance use disorders. First, we consider the effects of drugs (particularly alcohol and nicotine) on mood; we examine the situations in which a tension-reducing effect occurs and the role of cognition in this process. Second, we consider people's expectancies about the effects of substances on behavior, including beliefs about the prevalence with which a drug is used and about the health risks associated with using that drug. Third, we consider personality traits that may make it more likely for some people to use drugs heavily.

Mood Alteration It is generally assumed that one of the main psychological motives for using drugs is to alter mood—that is, drug use is reinforced because it enhances positive moods or diminishes negative ones. For example, most people believe that an increase in tension (e.g., because of a bad day at work) leads to increased alcohol consumption. It has also been argued that stress might cause increases in smoking, at least the initiation of smoking and relapse after quitting smoking (Kassel, Stroud, & Paronis, 2003; Shiffman & Waters, 2004).

Longitudinal studies of stress and consumption have provided some support for this idea. For example, a longitudinal study of adolescent smokers found that increases in negative affect and negative life events were associated with increases in smoking (Wills, Sandy, & Yaeger, 2002). Other studies found that life stress precedes alcohol-related relapses (e.g., Brown, Beck, Steer, et al., 1990). But other longitudinal research did not find that alcohol consumption increased after reports of greater life stress (Brennan, Schutte, & Moos, 1999). Because so many third variables may relate to stress and substance consumption, most would agree that laboratory experimental studies are important in this area. Findings from those studies are complex and suggest that if tension reduction works, it does so only in certain contexts for certain people. In addition, substances can reduce more than just tension. For example, research has found that alcohol lessens negative emotions, but it also lessens positive emotions in response to anxiety-provoking situations (Curtin, Lang, Patrick, et al., 1998; Stritzke, Patrick, & Lang, 1995).

Studies of the tension-reducing properties of nicotine have also yielded mixed findings, with some studies showing that nicotine reduces tension and others not finding this effect (Kassel et al., 2003). The reasons for the mixed findings may have to do with a failure to consider where people are in their smoking behavior. Did they just start smoking? Are they a regular smoker? Have they tried to quit and failed? Research suggests that people experience a greater reduction of tension and negative affect more when starting to smoke than when regularly smoking or when in relapse after treatment (Kassel et al., 2003). Why might this be? A recent experimental study examined the types of situations that were associated with a reduction in negative affect after smoking (Perkins, Karelitz, Conklin, et al., 2010). Participants, who were regular smokers, had to give a speech, play a difficult computer game, abstain from smoking for 12 hours, and view disturbing pictures. The researchers found that people experienced the greatest reduction in negative affect after the abstinence condition. That is, smoking, after not being able to smoke, provided more relief from negative affect than it did after other stressful situations, suggesting that the situation is important to consider when thinking about whether smoking reduces negative affect.

However, it may not be nicotine that is associated with a reduction in negative affect, but rather the sensory aspects of smoking (i.e., inhaling). In the study just described, participants experienced a reduction in negative affect whether they were smoking cigarettes with or without nicotine (Perkins et al., 2010). Another experimental study randomly assigned smokers to have cigarettes with or without nicotine (indistinguishable by participants) after a negative or positive mood was induced (Perkins, Ciccocioppo, Conklin, et al., 2008). The researchers also manipulated smokers' expectancies. That is, some smokers expected and received a cigarette with nicotine, others expected nicotine but didn't get it, others expected no nicotine and didn't get it, and others expected no nicotine but received it anyway. Smoking reduced negative affect after both mood inductions, but this was true for smokers regardless of what they expected and actually received to smoke (i.e., a cigarette with or without nicotine). Instead, the effects of inhaling, whether there was nicotine or not, had the greatest association with reducing negative affect.

Subsequent research to examine the reasons for these inconsistent results has focused on the situation in which alcohol or nicotine is consumed—specifically, a situation in which distraction is present. Findings indicate that alcohol may reduce tension by altering cognition and perception (Curtin et al., 1998; Josephs & Steele, 1990; Steele & Josephs, 1988). Alcohol impairs cognitive processing and narrows attention to the most immediately available cues, resulting in "alcohol myopia" (Steele & Josephs, 1990). In other words, the intoxicated person has less cognitive capacity and tends to use that capacity to focus on an immediate distraction, if available, rather than on tension-producing thoughts, with a resultant decrease in anxiety. Experimental studies have also shown that cognitive distraction can also reduce aggressive behavior in people who are intoxicated (Giancola & Corman, 2007).

The benefits of distraction have also been documented for nicotine. Specifically, smokers who smoked in the presence of a distracting activity had a reduction in anxiety, whereas smokers who smoked without a distracting activity did not experience a reduction in anxiety (Kassel & Shiffman, 1997; Kassel & Unrod, 2000). However, alcohol and nicotine may increase tension when no distractions are present. For example, a person drinking alone may focus all his or her limited cognitive capacity on unpleasant thoughts, begin brooding, and become increasingly tense and anxious, a situation reflected in the expression "crying in one's beer."

In sum, the few available experimental studies suggest that there are important limits to when and how substances may reduce tension. Much more experimental research is needed (Kassel et al., 2003).

Tension reduction is only one aspect of the possible effects of drugs on mood. Some people may use drugs to reduce negative affect, whereas others may use drugs to increase positive affect when they are bored (Cooper, Frone, Russell, et al., 1995). In this case, increased drug use results from a high need for stimulation combined with expectancies that drugs will promote increased positive affect. These patterns have been confirmed among people who abuse alcohol and cocaine (Cooper et al., 1995; Hussong, Hicks, Levy, et al., 2001).

Expectancies about Alcohol and Drug Effects If it is true that alcohol does not reduce stress when consumed after the fact, why do so many people who drink believe that it helps them unwind? Expectation may play a role here—that is, people may drink after stress not because it actually reduces tension but because they expect it to do so. In support of this idea, studies have shown that people who expect alcohol to reduce stress and anxiety are those likely

Expectations about alcohol influence whether people will drink. (Michael Blann/Getty Images, Inc.)

to be frequent users (Rather, Goldman, Roehrich, et al., 1992; Sher, Walitzer, Wood, et al., 1991; Tran, Haaga, & Chambless, 1997). Furthermore, drinking amount and positive expectancies about alcohol appear to influence each other. The expectation that drinking will reduce anxiety increases drinking, which in turn makes the positive expectancies even stronger (Smith, Goldman, Greenbaum et al., 1995).

Other research has shown that expectancies about a drug's effects—for example, the beliefs that a drug will stimulate aggression and increase sexual responsiveness—predict increased drug use in general (Stacy, Newcomb, & Bentler, 1991). Similarly, people who believe (falsely) that alcohol will make them seem more socially skilled are likely to drink more heavily than those who accurately perceive that alcohol can interfere with social interactions. In now-classic experiments demonstrating the power of expectancies, participants who believe they are consuming a quantity of alcohol when they are actually consuming an alcohol-free beverage subsequently become more aggressive (Lang, Goeckner, Adessor, et al., 1975). Alcohol consumption is associated with increased aggression, but expectancies about alcohol's effects can also play a role (Bushman & Cooper, 1990; Ito, Miller, & Pollock, 1996). Thus, as we have seen in other contexts, cognitions can have a powerful effect on behavior. Research also suggests a reciprocal relationship between expectancies and alcohol use: positive expectancies predict alcohol use, and alcohol use helps to maintain and strengthen positive expectancies (e.g., Sher, Wood, Wood, et al., 1996).

The extent to which a person believes a drug is harmful and the perceived prevalence of use by others are also factors related to use. In general, the greater the perceived risk of a drug, the less likely it will be used. So, in general, positively perceived effects of drug use (e.g., enhanced mood, perceptual and aesthetic components) need to be sufficiently salient and more frequently experienced than negative effects (e.g., criminality, anxiety, 'hangover effects', effect on education, work, financial state and relationships) for use to be maintained (Van Etten et al., 1998). However, people often continue to take drugs despite knowledge or experience of negative effects or the potential risks involved (Cottler et al., 2001). Users may accept these negative effects and symptoms as part of the overall drug experience and so not be unduly worried by them. Similarly, many smokers do not believe that they are at increased risk for cancer or cardiovascular disease (Ayanian & Cleary, 1999). Furthermore, alcohol and tobacco are used more frequently among people who overestimate the frequency with which these substances are used by others (Jackson, 1997).

Personality Factors Personality factors may help to explain why certain people are more likely to abuse or become dependent on drugs and alcohol. Personality factors that appear to be important in predicting the later onset of substance use disorders include high levels of negative affect, sometimes called *negative emotionality;* a persistent desire for arousal along with increased positive affect; and constraint, which refers to cautious behavior, harm avoidance, and conservative moral standards. One longitudinal study found that 18-year-olds who were low in constraint but high in negative emotionality were more likely to develop a substance use disorder as young adults (Krueger, 1999).

Another prospective longitudinal study investigated whether personality factors could predict the onset of substance use disorders in over 1,000 male and female adolescents at age 17 and then again at age 20 (Elkins, King, McGue, et al., 2006). Low constraint and high negative emotionality predicted the onset of alcohol, nicotine, and illicit drug use disorders for both men and women.

Increasing evidence indicates that certain childhood problems and personality traits, such as attention deficit behaviors and sensation seeking/impulsivity, are associated with an increased risk of experimenting with controlled drugs and developing drug use disorders in later life (Giancola et al., 1996; Lynskey and Hall 2001; Tapert and Brown 2000). However, these are associated risk factors, and do not represent medicalisation of young peoples' drug use, i.e., drug use as a disease state.

Sociocultural Factors

Sociocultural factors play a widely varying role in substance use disorders. People's interest in and access to drugs are influenced by peers, parents, the media, and cultural norms about acceptable behavior.

At the broadest level, for example, we can look at great cross-national variation in substance consumption. Some research suggests that there are commonalities in substance use across countries. For example, a cross-national study of alcohol and drug use among high school students in 36 countries found that alcohol was the most common substance used across countries, despite great variation in the proportions of students who consumed alcohol, ranging from 32 percent in Zimbabwe to 99 percent in Wales (Smart & Ogburne, 2000). In all but two of the countries studied, marijuana was the next most commonly used drug. In those countries where marijuana was used most often (with more than 15 percent of high school students having ever used marijuana), there were also higher rates of use of amphetamines, Ecstasy, and cocaine.

Alcohol dependence is more prevalent in countries in which alcohol use is heavy. (© Realimage/Alamy Limited.)

Despite the commonalities across countries, other research documents striking cross-national differences in alcohol consumption. For example, the highest consumption rates have typically been found in wine-drinking societies, such as France, Spain, and Italy, where drinking alcohol regularly is widely accepted (deLint, 1978). Cultural attitudes and patterns of drinking thus influence the likelihood of drinking heavily and therefore of abusing alcohol. One finding that seems quite similar across different cultures is that men consume more alcohol than women. An analysis conducted by the International Research Group on Gender and Alcohol found that men drank more than women in Australia, Canada, the Czech Republic, Estonia, Finland, Israel, the Netherlands, Russia, Sweden, and the United States. Despite this consistency in gender differences, there was a large disparity across countries in the extent to which men drank more than women. For example, men drank three times more than women in Israel but only one and a half times more than women in the Netherlands (Wilsnack, Vogeltanz, Wilsnack, et al., 2000). These findings suggest that cultural prescriptions about drinking by men and women are important to consider.

Ready availability of the substance is also a factor. For example, in wine-drinking societies, wine is present in many settings, even in university cafeterias. Also, rates of alcohol use disorder are high among bartenders and liquor store owners, people for whom alcohol is readily available (Fillmore & Caetano, 1980). In 2003, drug use among youths who had been approached by drug dealers was 35 percent, compared to just under 7 percent among youths who had not been approached (SAMHSA, 2004). With regard to smoking, if cigarettes are perceived as being easy to get and affordable, the rate of smoking increases (Robinson et al., 1997). This is one of the reasons states raise taxes on alcohol and cigarettes so frequently. Of course, this tactic disproportionately affects the poor, which is not only unfair but does not necessarily target all who would benefit from substances being less available.

Family factors are important as well. For example, exposure to alcohol use by parents increases children's likelihood of drinking (Hawkins, Graham, Maguin, et al., 1997). Unhappy marriages predicted the onset of alcohol use disorder in a study of nearly 2,000 married couples (Whisman & Uebelacker, 2006). Acculturation into American society may interact with family factors for people of other cultural and ethnic backgrounds. For example, a study of middle school Hispanic students in New York found that children who spoke English with their parents were more likely to smoke marijuana than children who spoke Spanish (Epstein, Botvin, & Diaz, 2001). Psychiatric, marital, or legal problems in the family are also related to drug abuse, and a lack of emotional support from parents is linked to increased use of cigarettes, marijuana, and alcohol (Cadoret, Yates, Troughton, et al., 1995; Wills, DuHamel, & Vaccaro, 1995). Finally, longitudinal studies have shown that a lack of parental monitoring leads to increased association with drug-abusing peers and subsequent higher use of drugs (Chassin, Curran, Hussong, et al., 1996; Thomas, Reifman, Barnes, et al., 2000).

Advertising is one way that expectancies develop. (Bill Aron/PhotoEdit.)

Advertising is an important factor in stimulating drug use. The Joe Camel campaign greatly increased Camel's share of the market among elementary and high school students. (© Joel W. Rogers/©Corbis.)

The social setting in which a person operates can also affect substance use. For example, studies of smokers in daily life show that they are more likely to smoke with other smokers than with nonsmokers. In addition, smoking was more likely to occur in or outside bars and restaurants, or at home, rather than in the workplace or in others' homes (Shiffman, Gwaltney, Balabanis, et al., 2002; Shiffman, Paty, Gwaltney, et al., 2004). Other studies showed that having friends who smoke predicts smoking (Killen et al., 1997). In longitudinal studies, peer-group identification in the seventh grade predicted smoking in the eighth grade (Sussman, Dent, McAdams, et al., 1994) and increased drug use over a 3-year period (Chassin et al., 1996). Peer influences are also important in promoting alcohol and marijuana use (Hussong et al., 2001; Stice, Barrera, & Chassin, 1998; Wills & Cleary, 1999).

These findings support the idea that social networks influence a person's drug or alcohol behavior. However, other evidence indicates that people who are inclined to develop substance use disorders may actually select social networks that conform to their own drinking or drug use patterns. Thus, we have two broad explanations for how the social environment is related to substance use disorders: a social influence model and a social selection model. A longitudinal study of over 1,200 adults designed to test which model best accounted for drinking behavior found support for both models (Bullers, Cooper, & Russell, 2001). A person's social network predicted individual drinking, but individual drinking also predicted subsequent social network drinking. In fact, the social selection effects were stronger, indicating that people often choose social networks with drinking patterns similar to their own. No doubt the selected networks then support or reinforce their drinking.

Another variable to be considered is the media. Television commercials associate beer with athletic-looking males, bikini-clad women, and good times. Billboards equate cigarettes with excitement, relaxation, and being in style. Alcohol advertising in magazines has increased in recent years, and it seems that these ads are reaching girls more than boys. For example, between 2001 and 2002, exposure to alcohol ads for girls increased 216 percent, whereas exposure to such ads increased 46 percent for boys (Jernigan, Ostroff, Ross, et al., 2004). A review of studies found that tobacco billboards were over two times more common in primarily African American neighborhoods than they were in primarily European American neighborhoods (Primack, Bost, Land, et al., 2007). It is clear that advertising for drinking targets girls and advertising for smoking targets African Americans, but does advertising change smoking or drinking patterns?

The evidence indicates that it does. An analysis of consumption in 17 countries between 1970 and 1983 supports the role of advertising in promoting alcohol use. Those countries that banned ads for alcohol had 16 percent less consumption than those that did not (Saffer, 1991). In a longitudinal study of nonsmoking adolescents, those who had a favorite cigarette ad were twice as likely subsequently to begin smoking or to be willing to do so (Pierce, Choi, Gilpin, et al., 1998). A particularly striking example of this was the Joe Camel campaign for Camel cigarettes. Camel launched its campaign in 1988 with the Joe Camel character, which was modeled after either James Bond or the character played by Don Johnson in the television program *Miami Vice,* a popular show of the time. Before the campaign, in the period from 1976 to 1988, Camel was the preferred brand of less than 0.5 percent of seventh through twelfth graders. By 1991, Camel's share of this illegal market had increased to 33 percent (DiFranza, Richards, Paulman, et al., 1991)!

As part of a settlement in a class-action lawsuit, which included 46 states, that charged U.S. tobacco companies with manipulating nicotine levels to keep smokers addicted, several companies agreed to stop marketing efforts aimed at children. The American Legacy Foundation was formed as part of the settlement that followed this lawsuit (www.americanlegacy.org). The goals of this group are to prevent smoking among young people and to make sure information about smoking and how to stop smoking is accessible to everyone. We will discuss the important efforts of this group later in the chapter when we discuss prevention.

Despite these promises by tobacco companies, an analysis of internal documents of several tobacco companies (made public thanks to the lawsuit mentioned above) by researchers at the Harvard School of Public Health revealed that tobacco companies were still targeting their advertising toward young people (Kreslake, Wayne, Alpert, et al., 2008). Some tobacco companies, such as R.J. Reynolds, still advertise, and all magazine ads in 2005 were for menthol brands. The researchers found that tobacco companies' own research had found that cigarettes with lower levels of menthol appealed more to young people and that efforts were then made to market these milder menthol brands to young people. In 2005, nearly half of adolescent smokers chose menthol cigarettes.

Quick Summary

A number of etiological factors have been proposed to account for alcohol and drug dependence, and some have more support than others. Genetic factors play a role in alcohol dependence and perhaps also nicotine dependence. The ability to tolerate alcohol and metabolize nicotine may be what is heritable. Genes that are important for the operation of the dopamine system may be an important factor in explaining how genes influence substance dependence. Several studies show how genes interact with the environment for smoking and alcohol problems. The most-studied neurobiological factors are brain systems associated with dopamine pathways—the major reward pathways in the brain. The incentive-sensitization theory describes brain pathways involved in liking drugs and wanting (i.e., craving) drugs.

Psychological factors have also been evaluated, and there is support for the idea that tension reduction plays a role, but only under certain circumstances, such as when distractions are present. Expectancies about the effects of drugs, such as reducing tension, increasing aggression, and increasing sexual prowess, have been shown to predict drug and alcohol use. Expectancies about the effects of drugs are also powerful; the greater the perceived risk of a drug, the less likely it will be used. Studies of personality factors also help us understand why some people may be more prone to abuse drugs and alcohol.

Sociocultural factors play a role, including the culture, availability of a substance, family factors, social settings and networks, and advertising. There is support for both a social influence model and a social selection model.

Check Your Knowledge 10.4

1. Which of the following is *not* one of the sociocultural factors implicated in the etiology of substance abuse or dependence?
   a. the media
   b. gender
   c. availability of a substance
   d. social networks
2. Which of the following statements best captures the link between wanting, liking, and drinking according to a prospective study?
   a. Wanting, but not liking, predicted more drinking among heavy drinkers.

   b. Wanting predicted more drinking for heavy drinkers; liking predicted more drinking for light drinkers.
   c. Wanting and liking predicted more drinking among heavy drinkers.
   d. Sedation predicted less drinking for all types of drinking.
3. Genetic research on substance dependence indicates that:
   a. Genetic factors may be the same for many drugs.
   b. Additional studies need to be done to determine heritability.
   c. The dopamine receptor DRD1 may be faulty.
   d. Twin studies show that the environment is just as important as genes.

Treatment of Substance Use Disorders

The chronicity of addiction is really a kind of fatalism writ large. If an addict knows in his heart he is going to use again, why not today? But if a thin reed of hope appears, the possibility that it will not always be so, things change. You live another day and then get up and do it again. Hope is oxygen to someone who is suffocating on despair. (Carr, 2008)

The challenges in treating people who are dependent on substances are great, as illustrated by the quote above. Substance use disorders are typically chronic, and relapse occurs often. In view of these challenges, the field is constantly working to develop new and effective treatments, many of which we review in this section. The author of the quote, David Carr, was formerly addicted to cocaine, crack, and alcohol. Currently, he is a media columnist for the *New York Times*. For him, residential treatment was successful.

Many who work with those with alcohol or drug use disorders suggest that the first step to successful treatment is admitting there is a problem. To a certain extent, this makes sense. Why would someone get treatment for something that is not deemed a problem? Unfortunately, a number of treatment programs require people not only to admit a problem but also to demonstrate their commitment to treatment by stopping their use of alcohol or drugs before beginning treatment. This requirement can exclude many who desire and need treatment. For example, Franck (in the Clinical Case presented earlier) might not have been admitted to a residential program had he not been free of heroin for a week before trying to gain admission. Imagine if people with lung cancer were told they had to demonstrate their commitment to treatment by stopping smoking before the cancer could be treated. In the next sections, we review treatments for alcohol, nicotine, and other drug use disorders.

Treatment of Alcohol Use Disorder

The physical harm related to alcohol has been increasing in the UK in the past three decades. Deaths from alcoholic liver disease have doubled since 1980 (Leon & McCambridge, 2006) compared with a decrease in many other European countries. Alcohol related hospital admissions increased by 85% between 2002/03 and 2008/09, accounting for 945,000 admissions with a primary or secondary diagnosis wholly or partly related to alcohol in 2006/07 and comprising 7% of all hospital admissions (North West Public Health Observatory, 2010).

Inpatient Hospital Treatment The primary role of specialist treatment is to assist the individual to reduce or stop drinking alcohol in a safe manner (National Treatment Agency for Substance Misuse, 2010). At the initial stages of engagement with specialist services, service users may be ambivalent about changing their drinking behavior or dealing with their problems. At this stage, work on enhancing the service user's motivation towards making changes and engagement with treatment will be particularly important.

For most people who are alcohol dependent the most appropriate goal in terms of alcohol consumption should be to aim for complete abstinence. With an increasing level of alcohol dependence a return to moderate or 'controlled' drinking becomes increasingly difficult (Edwards & Gross, 1976; Schuckit, 2009). Further, for people with significant psychiatric or physical comorbidity (for example, depressive disorder or alcoholic liver disease), abstinence is the appropriate goal. However, hazardous and harmful drinkers, and those with a low level of alcohol dependence, may be able to achieve a goal of moderate alcohol consumption (Raistrick et al., 2006). Where a client has a goal of moderation but the clinician believes there are considerable risks in doing so, the clinician should provide strong advice that abstinence is most appropriate but should not deny the client treatment if the advice is unheeded (Raistrick et al., 2006).

For people who are alcohol dependent, the next stage of treatment may require medically-assisted alcohol withdrawal, if necessary with medication to control the symptoms and complications of withdrawal. For people with severe alcohol dependence and/or significant physical or psychiatric comorbidity, this may require assisted alcohol withdrawal in an inpatient or

Detoxification is often the first step in treatment for alcohol use disorder. (© Angela Hampton Picture Library/Alamy Limited.)

residential setting, such as a specialist NHS inpatient addiction treatment unit (Specialist Clinical Addiction Network, 2006). For the majority, however, alcohol withdrawal can be managed in the community either as part of shared care with the patient's GP or in an outpatient or home-based assisted alcohol withdrawal programme, with appropriate professional and family support (Raistrick et al., 2006).

Treatment of alcohol withdrawal is, however, only the beginning of rehabilitation and, for many, a necessary precursor to a longer-term treatment process. Withdrawal management should therefore not be seen as a standalone treatment. People who are alcohol dependent and who have recently stopped drinking are vulnerable to relapse, and often have many unresolved co-occurring problems that alcohol dependence and harmful alcohol use predispose to relapse (for example, psychiatric comorbidity and social problems) (Marlatt & Gordon, 1985). In this phase, the primary role of treatment is the prevention of relapse. This should include interventions aimed primarily at the drinking behavior, including psychosocial and pharmacological interventions, and interventions aimed at dealing with co-occurring problems. Interventions aimed at preventing relapse include individual therapy (for example, motivational enhancement therapy (MET), cognitive behavioral therapy (CBT), group and family based therapies, community-based and residential rehabilitation programmes, medications to attenuate drinking or promote abstinence (for example, naltrexone, acamprosate or disulfiram) and interventions promoting social support and integration (for example, social behavior and network therapy (SBNT) or 12-step facilitation (TSF) (Raistrick et al., 2006).

Alcoholics Anonymous The largest and most widely known self-help group in the world is Alcoholics Anonymous (AA), founded in 1935 by two recovering alcoholics. It has over 100,000 chapters and a membership numbering more than 2 million people in the United States and in more than 100 other countries. In 2009, over half of the people who received treatment for alcohol or drug use disorders did so through a self-help program like AA (SAMHSA, 2010).

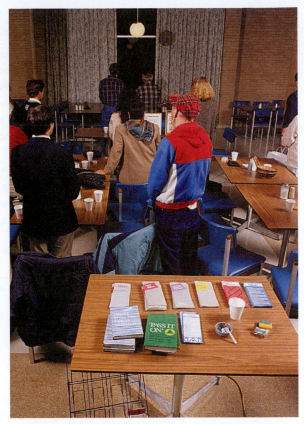

Alcoholics Anonymous is the largest self-help group in the world. At their regular meetings, newcomers rise to announce their addiction and receive advice and support from others. (Hank Morgan/Photo Researchers, Inc.)

Each AA chapter runs regular and frequent meetings at which newcomers rise to announce that they are alcoholics and older, sober members give testimonials, relating the stories of their problems with alcohol and indicating how their lives are better now. The group provides emotional support, understanding, and close counseling as well as a social network. Members are urged to call on one another around the clock when they need companionship and encouragement not to relapse. Programs modeled after AA are available for other substances, for example, Cocaine Anonymous and Marijuana Anonymous.

The AA program tries to instill in each member the belief that alcohol dependence is a disease that can never be cured and that continuing vigilance is necessary to resist taking even a single drink, lest uncontrollable drinking begin all over again. Even if the person has not consumed any alcohol for 15 years or more, the designation "alcoholic" is still necessary according to the tenets of AA, since the person is always an alcoholic, always carrying the disease, even if it is currently under control.

The spiritual aspect of AA is apparent in the 12 steps of AA, shown in Table 10.2, and there is evidence that belief in this philosophy is linked with achieving abstinence (Fiorentine & Hillhouse, 2000; Tonigan, Miller, & Connors, 2000). Other self-help groups do not have the religious overtones of AA, relying instead on social support, reassurance, encouragement, and suggestions for leading a life without alcohol. One such approach, termed *Rational Recovery,* focuses on promoting renewed self-reliance rather than reliance on a higher power (Trimpey, Velten, & Dain, 1993).

Noncontrolled trials show that AA provides significant benefit to participants (Moos & Moos, 2006; Ouimette, Finney, & Moos, 1997; Timko, Moos, Finney, et al., 2001). A large prospective study of over 2,000 men with alcohol dependence found that participation in AA predicted a better outcome 2 years later (McKeller, Stewart, & Humphreys, 2003). A 16-year prospective study of over 400 people seeking treatment for the first time found that of the people who stayed in AA for at least 27 weeks of the first year in the program,

Table 10.2 The 12 Steps of Alcoholics Anonymous

1. We admitted we were powerless over alcohol—that our lives had become unmanageable.
2. Came to believe that a power greater than ourselves could restore us to sanity.
3. Made a decision to turn our will and our lives over to the care of God as we understood Him.
4. Made a searching and fearless moral inventory of ourselves.
5. Admitted to God, to ourselves, and to another human being the exact nature of our wrongs.
6. Were entirely ready to have God remove all these defects of character.
7. Humbly asked Him to remove our shortcomings.
8. Made a list of all persons we had harmed, and became willing to make amends to them all.
9. Made direct amends to such people wherever possible, except when to do so would injure them or others.
10. Continued to take personal inventory and, when we were wrong, promptly admitted it.
11. Sought through prayer and meditation to improve our conscious contact with God as we understood Him, praying only for knowledge of His will for us and the power to carry that out.
12. Having had a spiritual awakening as the result of these steps, we tried to carry this message to alcoholics and to practice these principles in all our affairs.

Source: The Twelve Steps and Twelve Traditions. Copyright © 1952 by Alcoholics Anonymous World Services, Inc. Reprinted with permission of Alcoholics Anonymous World Services, Inc.

two-thirds were abstinent at the 16-year follow-up. Of the people who stayed in AA for fewer than 27 weeks, only one-third were abstinent at follow-up (Moos & Moos, 2006). In addition, becoming an AA member early in treatment and staying involved for a longer period of time is associated with a better outcome 8 years after treatment began (Moos & Humphreys, 2004).

All of this sounds like good news for people participating in AA. However, a review of the eight randomized controlled clinical trials found little benefit of AA over other types of treatment, including motivational enhancement, inpatient treatment, couples therapy, or cognitive behavior therapy (Ferri, Amato, & Davoli, 2008). In addition, AA has high dropout rates, and the dropouts are not always factored into the results of studies. There have been no controlled studies testing the efficacy of Rational Recovery, though two findings from preliminary studies suggest that it may be effective (Schmidt, Carns, & Chandler, 2001).

Couples Therapy Behaviorally oriented marital or couples therapy (O'Farrell & Fals Stewart, 2000) has been found to achieve some reductions in problem drinking, even a year after treatment has stopped, as well as some improvement in couples' distress generally (McCrady & Epstein, 1995).

Cognitive and Behavioral Treatments Contingency management therapy is a cognitive behavior treatment for alcohol and drug use disorders that involves teaching people and those close to them to reinforce behaviors inconsistent with drinking—for example, taking the drug Antabuse (discussed later in the chapter) and avoiding situations that were associated with drinking in the past. It is based on the belief that environmental contingencies can play an important role in encouraging or discouraging drinking. Vouchers are provided for not using a substance (alcohol, cocaine, heroin, marijuana; verified by urine samples), and the tokens are exchangeable for things that the person would like to have more of (Dallery, Silverman, Chutuape, et al., 2001; Katz, Gruber, Chutuape, et al., 2001; Silverman, Higgins, Brooner, et al., 1996). This therapy also includes teaching job-hunting and social skills, as well as assertiveness training for refusing drinks. For socially isolated people, assistance and encouragement are provided to establish contacts with other people who are not associated with drinking.

Relapse prevention is another cognitive behavioral treatment that has been effective with alcohol and drug use disorders. It can be a stand-alone treatment or a part of other interventions. Broadly, the goal is to help people avoid relapsing back into drinking or drug use once they have stopped. Focus on Discovery 10.4 discusses this important treatment in more detail.

FOCUS ON DISCOVERY 10.4

Relapse Prevention

Relapse prevention is an important part of any treatment for drug or alcohol use disorders. Mark Twain quipped that stopping smoking was easy—he'd done it hundreds of times! Marlatt and Gordon (1985) developed an approach to treatment called relapse prevention specifically to prevent relapse in substance abuse. In this approach, people dependent on alcohol are encouraged to believe that a lapse will not inevitably precipitate a total relapse and should be regarded as a learning experience rather than as a sign that the battle is lost, a marked contrast from the AA perspective (Marlatt & Gordon, 1985). This noncatastrophizing approach to relapse after therapy—falling off the wagon—is important because the overwhelming majority of people who are dependent on alcohol who become abstinent experience one or more relapses over a 4-year period (Polich, Armor, & Braiker, 1980). People dependent on alcohol examine sources of stress in their work, family, and relationships so that they can become active and responsible in anticipating and resisting situations that might lead them into excessive drinking (Marlatt, 1983; L. C. Sobell, Toneatto, & Sobell, 1990). The sources of stress that precipitate a relapse in alcohol use disorder may be different for men and women. For women, marital stress is a predictor of relapse. For men, however, marriage seems to protect them from relapse (Walitzer & Dearing, 2006).

Relapse prevention treatment appears to be more effective with some substances than with others. A meta-analysis of 26 randomized controlled clinical trials found that relapse prevention was most effective for alcohol and drug use disorders and least effective for nicotine use disorder (Irvin, Bowers, Dunn, et al., 1999). Most smokers relapse within a year of stopping, regardless of the means used to stop. In a pattern we have already seen, people who smoked the most—and are presumably more addicted to nicotine—relapse more often and more quickly than moderate or light smokers. Frequent slips, intense cravings and withdrawal symptoms, low tolerance for distress, younger age, physiological dependence on nicotine, low self-efficacy, stressful life events, observations of other smokers, weight concerns, and previous quitting attempts are all predictors of relapse (McCarthy, Piasecki, Fiore, et al., 2006; Ockene, Mermelstein, Bonollo, et al., 2000; Piasecki, 2006). One very detailed analysis, using experience sampling of smokers' thoughts, feelings, and symptoms both before and after they quit smoking, revealed that many smokers experience high levels of negative affect before their target quit day and that this anticipatory negative affect predicted a greater likelihood of relapse (McCarthy et al., 2006). Despite these difficulties, there is some encouraging evidence that self-help relapse prevention programs can be effective in reducing smoking relapse (Brandon, Vidrine, & Litvin, 2007). In these programs, smokers receive booklets in the mail describing the relapse prevention approach. These brochures appear to be effective up to 1 year after smoking was stopped.

What factors contribute to success? Research results (and common sense) tell us that ex-smokers who do not live with a smoker do better at follow-up than those who do live with a smoker (McIntyre-Kingsolver, Lichtenstein, & Mermelstein, 1986). So-called booster or maintenance sessions help, but in a very real sense they represent a continuation of treatment; when they stop, relapse is the rule (Brandon, Zelman, & Baker, 1987). Intensive interventions, such as a telephone counseling (Brandon, Collins, Juliano, et al., 2000), also help; however, they reach relatively few smokers. Brief relapse prevention interventions during medical visits are cost-effective and could potentially reach most smokers but are not consistently delivered (Ockene et al., 2000). On a positive note, there is considerably more social support for not smoking than there was 10 years ago, at least in the United States. Perhaps as time goes on, societal sanctions against smoking will help those who have succeeded in quitting remain abstinent.

Motivational Interventions As we described earlier, heavy drinking is particularly common among college students. One team of investigators designed a brief intervention to try to curb such heavy drinking in college (Carey, Carey, Maisto, et al., 2006). The intervention contained two parts: (1) a comprehensive assessment that included the Timeline Follow Back (TLFB) interview (Sobell & Sobell, 1996), which carefully assesses drinking in the past 3 months, and (2) a brief motivational treatment that included individualized feedback about a person's drinking in relation to community and national averages, education about the effects of alcohol, and tips for reducing harm and moderating drinking. Results from the study showed that the TLFB alone decreased drinking behavior, but that the combination of the TLFB and motivational intervention was associated with a longer-lasting reduction in drinking behavior, up to 1 year after the interview and intervention.

Moderation in Drinking At least since the advent of Alcoholics Anonymous, many have believed that people with alcohol use disorder had to abstain completely if they were to be successfully treated, for they were assumed to have no control over drinking once they had taken that first drink. This continues to be the belief of Alcoholics Anonymous, but research mentioned earlier, indicating that drinkers' beliefs about themselves and alcohol may be as important as the addiction to the drug itself, has called this assumption

Mark and Linda Sobell introduced controlled drinking approaches to the treatment of alcohol abuse. (Top: Courtesy of Mark Sobell; Bottom: Courtesy of Linda Sobell.)

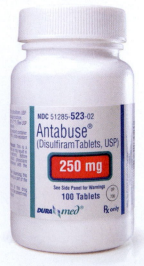

Antabuse is used to treat alcohol dependence. (Courtesy Teva Pharmaceuticals.)

into question. Considering the social difficulty of avoiding alcohol altogether, it may be preferable to teach a person who does not use alcohol in an extreme fashion to drink with moderation.

The term **controlled drinking** was introduced into the domain of alcohol treatment by Mark and Linda Sobell (Sobell & Sobell, 1993). It refers to a pattern of alcohol consumption that is moderate, avoiding the extremes of total abstinence and inebriation. Findings of one well-known treatment program suggested that people with less severe alcohol problems can learn to control their drinking and improve other aspects of their lives as well (Sobell & Sobell, 1976).

The Sobells' current approach to teaching moderation to people with alcohol use disorder is called *guided self-change*. The basic assumption is that people have more potential control over their immoderate drinking than they typically believe and that heightened awareness of the costs of drinking to excess as well as of the benefits of abstaining or cutting down can be of material help. For example, getting the person to delay 20 minutes before taking a second or third drink can help him or her reflect on the costs versus the benefits of drinking to excess. Evidence supports the effectiveness of this approach in helping people moderate their intake and otherwise improve their lives (Sobell & Sobell, 1993). A recent randomized controlled clinical trial demonstrated that guided self-change was equally effective as an individual or group treatment (Sobell, Sobell, & Agrawal, 2009).

Medications Some people who are in treatment for alcohol use disorder, inpatient or outpatient, take disulfiram, or **Antabuse,** a drug that discourages drinking by causing violent vomiting if alcohol is ingested. As one can imagine, adherence to an Antabuse regimen can be a problem.

For it to be effective, a person must already be strongly committed to change. However, in a large, multicenter study, Antabuse was not shown to have any benefit, and dropout rates were as high as 80 percent (Fuller, 1988).

Naltrexone is a narcotic antagonist which blocks the activity of endorphins that are stimulated by alcohol, thus reducing the craving for it. Evidence is mixed regarding whether this drug is more effective than a placebo in reducing drinking when it is the only treatment (Kryslal, Cramer, Krol, et al., 2001). But it does appear to add to overall treatment effectiveness when combined with cognitive behavioral therapy (Pettinati, Oslin, Kampman, et al., 2010; Streeton & Whelan, 2001; Volpicelli, Rhines, Rhines, et al., 1997; Volpicelli, Watson, King, et al., 1995).

Acamprosate, which has been in regular use in Europe for nearly 20 years under the brand name Campral, was approved by the FDA in 2004. Although its action is not completely understood, researchers believe that it impacts the glutamate and GABA neurotransmitter systems and thereby reduces the cravings associated with withdrawal. A review of data from all published double-blind, placebo-controlled clinical trials of acamprosate for people dependent on alcohol suggests that it is highly effective (Mason, 2001). A meta-analysis comparing the effectiveness of acamprosate and naltrexone found them equally effective (Kranzler & Van Kirk, 2001). There is, of course, the more general question of whether treating a substance abuse problem by giving another drug is necessarily a prudent strategy if one believes that some people come to rely on drugs in part because they are looking for a chemical solution to problems in their lives. Nevertheless, to the extent that medications are an effective treatment for alcohol dependence, disallowing them due to a concern over substituting one drug for another seems misguided.

Treatments for Smoking

The numerous laws that currently prohibit smoking in restaurants, trains, airplanes, and public buildings are part of a social context that provides incentives and support to stop smoking. In addition, people are more likely to quit smoking if other people around them quit. A longitudinal study of over 12,000 people documented that if people in one's social network quit smoking (spouses, siblings, friends, co-workers), the odds that a person will

Quick Summary

Inpatient hospital treatment for alcohol dependence is not as common today as it was in earlier years, primarily due to the cost. Detoxification from alcohol does often take place in hospitals, but treatment after this is more commonly done in outpatient settings.

Alcoholics Anonymous is the most common form of treatment for alcohol use disorder. It is a group-based self-help treatment that instills the notion of alcohol dependence as disease. Though not widely studied, available research suggests that AA is an effective treatment. There is some evidence that behavioral couples therapy is an effective treatment. Contingency management therapy, which involves teaching people and those close to them to reinforce

behaviors inconsistent with drinking, has shown some promise. Controlled drinking refers to a pattern of alcohol consumption that is moderate, avoiding the extremes of total abstinence and inebriation. The guided self-change treatment approach emphasizes control over moderate drinking, the costs of drinking to excess, and the benefits of abstaining.

Medications for alcohol use disorder treatment include Antabuse, naltrexone, and acamprosate. Antabuse is not an effective treatment in the long run. Noncompliance is a big problem. It is not clear that other medications are effective on their own, but they do seem to be beneficial in combination with cognitive behavior therapy.

---

quit smoking are much greater (Christakis & Fowler, 2008). For example, if a person's spouse stopped smoking, his or her chances of continued smoking decreased by nearly 70 percent. In short, peer pressure to quit smoking appears to be as effective as peer pressure to start smoking once was.

Some smokers who want to quit attend smoking clinics or consult with professionals for other specialized smoking-reduction programs. Even so, it is estimated that only about half of those who go through smoking-cessation programs succeed in abstaining by the time the program is over; only about 20 percent of those who have succeeded in the short term actually remain nonsmoking after a year. The greatest success overall is found among smokers who are better educated, older, or have acute health problems (USDHHS, 1998).

Psychological Treatments Probably the most widespread psychological treatment consists of a physician telling the person to stop smoking. Each year millions of smokers are given this counsel—because of hypertension, heart disease, lung disease, or diabetes, or on general grounds of preserving or improving health. Indeed, by age 65, most smokers have managed to quit (USDHHS, 1998). There is some evidence that a physician's advice can get some people to stop smoking, at least for a while, especially when the person also chews nicotine gum (Law & Tang, 1995). But much more needs to be learned about the nature of the advice, the manner in which it is given, its timing, and other factors that must surely play a role in determining whether smokers are prepared and able to alter their behavior primarily on a physician's say-so (USDHHS, 1998).

Another treatment approach that seems to work is called scheduled smoking (Compas, Haaga, Keefe, et al., 1998). The strategy is to reduce nicotine intake gradually over a period of a few weeks by getting smokers to agree to increase the time between cigarettes. For example, during the first week of treatment, a one-pack-a-day smoker would be put on a schedule allowing only 10 cigarettes per day; during the second week, only 5 cigarettes a day would be allowed; and during the third week, the person would taper off to zero. The cigarettes would have to be smoked on a schedule provided by the treatment team, not when the smoker feels an intense craving. In this way, the person's smoking behavior is controlled by

Laws that have banned smoking in many places have probably increased the frequency of quitting. (Digital Vision/SuperStock, Inc.)

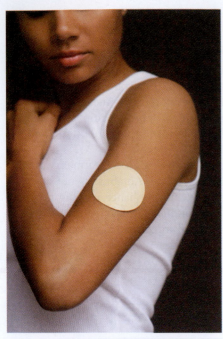

Nicotine patches are available over the counter to help relieve withdrawal symptoms. (©moodboard/©Corbis.)

the passage of time rather than by urges, mood states, or situations. Smokers who are able to stay with the agreed-upon schedule showed a 44 percent abstinence rate after 1 year, a very impressive outcome (Cinciripini, Lapitsky, Wallfisch, et al., 1994).

By age 18, about two-thirds of cigarette smokers regret having started smoking, one-half have already made an attempt to quit, and nearly 40 percent show interest in obtaining treatment for their dependence (Henningfield, Michaelides, & Sussman, 2000). Thus, targeting smoking-cessation programs toward teens would likely be a beneficial approach. One school-based program called Project EX includes training in coping skills and a psychoeducational component about the harmful effects of smoking. Two studies have found this program to be effective, both in the United States (Sussman, Dent, & Lichtman, 2001) and in China (Zheng, Sussman, Chen, et al., 2004), where the program was adapted to fit Chinese culture and language. Other smoking-cessation approaches for teens, including cognitive behavior therapy and motivational approaches, have been shown to be effective at getting adolescents to quit smoking. Cognitive behavioral approaches focus on problem solving and coping skills (Curry, Mermelstein, & Sporer, 2009).

Nicotine Replacement Treatments and Medications Reducing a smoker's craving for nicotine by providing it in a different way is the goal of nicotine replacement treatments. Attention to nicotine dependence is clearly important because the more cigarettes people smoke daily, the less successful they are at quitting. Nicotine may be supplied in gum, patches, inhalers, or electronic cigarettes. The idea is to help smokers endure the nicotine withdrawal that accompanies any effort to stop smoking. Although nicotine replacement alleviates withdrawal symptoms—which justifies its use in gum and in the nicotine patches to be described next—the severity of withdrawal is only minimally related to success in stopping smoking (Ferguson, Shiffman, & Gwaltney, 2006; Hughes, Higgins, Hatsukami, et al., 1990).

Gum containing nicotine is available over the counter in most western countries. The nicotine in gum is absorbed much more slowly and steadily than that in tobacco. The long-term goal is for the former smoker to be able to cut back on the use of the gum as well, eventually eliminating reliance on nicotine altogether.

This treatment involves some controversy, however. Ex-smokers can become dependent on the gum. Moreover, in doses that deliver an amount of nicotine equivalent to smoking one cigarette an hour, the gum causes cardiovascular changes, such as increased blood pressure, that can be dangerous to people with cardiovascular diseases. Nevertheless, some experts believe that even prolonged, continued use of the gum is healthier than obtaining nicotine by smoking, because at least the poisons in the smoke are avoided (de Wit & Zacny, 2000).

Nicotine patches are also available in most western countries. A polyethylene patch taped to the arm serves as a transdermal (through the skin) nicotine delivery system that slowly and steadily releases the drug into the bloodstream and thence to the brain. An advantage of the patch over nicotine gum is that the person need only apply one patch each day and not remove it until applying the next patch, making compliance easier. Treatment can be effective after 8 weeks of use for most smokers (Stead, Perera, Bullen, et al., 2008), with smaller and smaller patches used as treatment progresses. A drawback is that people who continue smoking while wearing the patch risk increasing the amount of nicotine in their body to dangerous levels.

Evidence suggests that the nicotine patch is superior to the use of a placebo patch in terms of both abstinence and subjective craving (Hughes et al., 1990). A meta-analysis of 111 trials of all types of nicotine replacement treatments (NRT,: patch, gum, nasal spray, inhaler, tablets) found that NRT was more effective than placebo in smoking cessation (Stead et al., 2008). However, NRT is not a panacea. Abstinence rates are only about 50 percent at 12-month follow-ups. The manufacturers state that the patch is to be used only as part of a psychological smoking-cessation program and then for not more than 3 months at a time. In addition, these types of nicotine replacement treatments are not effective with adolescents (Curry et al., 2009).

Combining the antidepressant medication buproprion (trade name Wellbutrin) and nicotine patches yielded a 12-month abstinence rate of 35 percent in one study (Jorenby, Leischow,

Nides, et al., 1999) but less promising results in others (Hughes, Stead, & Lancaster, 2004; Killen, Fortmann, Murphy, et al., 2006). Other promising non-nicotine pharmacotherapy for smoking cessation has included the drug clonidine and silver acetate (Benowitz & Peng, 2000). The FDA approved the prescription drug varenicline in 2006 for treatment of nicotine dependence, and early results suggest that this medication is effective in combination with behavioral treatment and that it is more effective than buproprion (Cahill, Stead, & Lancaster, 2007; Tonstad, Tonnesen, Hajek, et al., 2006).

Treatment of Drug Use Disorders

Central to the treatment of people who use illegal drugs such as heroin and cocaine is detoxification—withdrawal from the drug itself. Heroin withdrawal reactions range from relatively mild bouts of anxiety, nausea, and restlessness for several days to more severe and frightening bouts of delirium and panic. The type of reaction depends primarily on the purity of the heroin that the person has been using.

Detoxification is the first way in which therapists try to help a person dependent on a drug, and it may be the easiest part of the rehabilitation process. Enabling the drug user to function without drugs after detoxification is extremely difficult—typically, both therapist and client experience more disappointment and sadness than success in this process. The cravings for the substance often remain even after the substance has been removed via detoxification. A variety of approaches to this task are available, including psychological treatments, drug substitution treatments, and medications.

Psychological Treatments In the first direct comparison in a controlled study, the antidepressant medication desipramine (trade name Norpramine) and cognitive behavioral therapy (CBT) were both found to be somewhat effective in reducing cocaine use as well as in improving a person's family, social, and general psychological functioning (Carroll, Rounsaville, Gordon, et al., 1994; Carroll, Rounsaville, Nich, et al., 1995). In this 12-week study, desipramine was better than a placebo for people with a low degree of dependence on cocaine, whereas CBT was better for people with a high degree of dependence. This finding illustrates the significance of the psychological aspects of substance use.

In this study, people receiving CBT learned how to avoid high-risk situations (e.g., being around people using cocaine), recognize the lure of the drug for them, and develop alternatives to using cocaine (e.g., recreational activities with nonusers). People who abused cocaine in this study also learned strategies for coping with the craving and for resisting the tendency to regard a slip as a catastrophe (relapse prevention training; see Focus on Discovery 10.4). A more recent study testing the effectiveness of CBT for drug abuse in a community setting found that there was no difference in outcomes between CBT and standard substance abuse counseling (Morgenstern, Blanchard, Morgan, et al., 2001). We have a ways to go in order to make our treatments more effective in community settings.

Contingency management with vouchers has shown promise for cocaine, heroin, and marijuana use disorders (Dallery et al., 2001; Katz et al., 2001; Petry, Alessi, Marx, et al., 2005; Silverman et al., 1996). For example, a randomized treatment trial for people with marijuana use disorder compared a voucher treatment, CBT, and CBT plus vouchers (Budney, Moore, Rocha, et al., 2006). During the treatment, people who received the voucher treatment were more likely to remain abstinent than those in the CBT treatment or in the CBT plus vouchers

Group therapy in residential settings is frequently used to treat heroin addiction. (David M. Grossman/Photo Researchers, Inc.)

treatment. After treatment was over, however, people who received CBT plus vouchers were most likely to remain abstinent. Thus, vouchers appear to work in the short term, but CBT appears to be an effective component of treatment for marijuana use disorder in the long term with respect to maintaining abstinence after treatment is over.

Studies of contingency management for cocaine use disorder find that it is associated not only with a greater likelihood of abstinence but also with a better quality of life (Petry, Alessi, & Hanson, 2007). In an analysis that looked at four different studies of contingency management treatment for cocaine use disorder, the researchers found that people who received contingency management treatment were more likely to remain abstinent than people who received treatment as usual and that the duration of their abstinence during treatment was related to a higher quality of life after treatment. A meta-analysis of four randomized controlled clinical trials comparing contingency management, day treatment, or both treatments (combined condition) for cocaine use among homeless people found that the combined treatment and contingency management were both more effective than day treatment alone (Schumacher, Milby, Wallace, et al., 2007).

A treatment called *motivational interviewing* or *enhancement* therapy has also shown great promise. This treatment involves a combination of CBT techniques and techniques associated with helping clients generate solutions that work for themselves. A meta-analysis of this treatment found that it was effective for both alcohol and drug use disorders (Burke, Arkowitz, & Menchola, 2003). Another study found that motivational enhancement combined with CBT and contingency management was an effective treatment package for young people (ages 18–25) who were dependent on marijuana (Carroll, Easton, Nich, et al., 2006).

Self-help residential homes or communities are another psychological approach to treating heroin and other types of drug abuse and dependence. Drug-rehabilitation homes share the following features:

- Separation of people from previous social contacts, on the assumption that these relationships have been instrumental in maintaining the drug use disorder
- A comprehensive environment in which drugs are not available and continuing support is offered to ease the transition from regular drug use to a drug-free existence
- The presence of charismatic role models, people formerly dependent on drugs who appear to be meeting life's challenges without drugs
- Direct, often intense, confrontation in group therapy, in which people are goaded into accepting responsibility for their problems and for their drug habits and are urged to take charge of their lives
- A setting in which people are respected as human beings rather than stigmatized as failures or criminals

There are several obstacles to evaluating the efficacy of residential drug-treatment programs. Because the dropout rate is high, those who remain cannot be regarded as representative of the population of people addicted to illegal drugs; their motivation to stop using drugs is probably much stronger than that of people who don't volunteer for treatment or people who drop out. Any improvement participants in these programs make may reflect their uncommonly strong desire to rid themselves of the habit more than the specific qualities of the treatment program. Such self-regulating residential communities do, however, appear to help a large number of those who remain in them for a year or so (Institute of Medicine, 1990; Jaffe, 1985).

A new report published in 2010 by the Centre for Social Justice, proposes a series of reforms of the drug and alcohol treatment and criminal justice systems in the UK.

The Centre's Green Paper on Criminal Justice and Addiction accuses the previous government of taking a "fatalistic approach" to tackle addiction in community and prison settings. The report criticises an "overinvestment" in methadone prescribing programmes as a treatment for heroin dependency and advocates a "significant expansion" in the provision of abstinence-based residential rehabilitation services.

However, the Green Paper also acknowledges that 'harm reduction' approaches, including methadone programmes, often play "an important step in an individual's recovery". It argues that a failure to effectively address the underlying causes of substance misuse—such as poverty, unemployment, and a lack of stable accommodation, can condemn methadone maintenance programmes to 'failure'.

Other recommendations relating to community-based drug treatment include:

- The National Treatment Agency for Substance Misuse (NTA), established by the previous government in 2001 to oversee drug treatment in England, should be replaced by an Addiction Recovery Board (ARB). The ARB would be chaired by a minister and have responsibility for drug and alcohol policy;

- The current system of monitoring drug treatment 'success' against the number of clients accessing and maintained in treatment should be replaced by new outcome measures including abstinence, improved mental health and employment and housing status;

- Financial power at local levels for commissioning drug and alcohol treatment services should rest with local authorities rather than Primary Care Trusts (PCTs). The CSJ argues that the current PCT-led arrangement has contributed to an "overinvestment" in substitute prescribing services.

The report's proposed reforms of the criminal justice system include a recommendation that courts should be able to sentence offenders with substance misuse problems to secure residential drug rehabilitation centres as an alternative to prison. It also proposes that short prison sentences should be abolished and argues that these often preclude offenders with substance misuse problems accessing rehabilitation programmes while in prison.

Drug Replacement Treatments and Medications Two widely used programs for heroin use disorder involve the administration of *heroin substitutes*, drugs chemically similar to heroin that can replace the body's craving for it, or *opiate antagonists*, drugs that prevent the user from experiencing the heroin high. Recall from Chapter 2(p. 38) that an antagonist is a drug that dampens the activity of neurotransmitters, and an agonist is a drug that stimulates neurotransmitters. The first category includes **methadone**, levomethadyl acetate, and bupreophine, synthetic narcotics designed to take the place of heroin. Since these drugs are themselves addicting, successful treatment essentially converts the person's dependence on heroin into dependence on a different substance. This conversion occurs because these synthetic narcotics are **cross-dependent** with heroin; that is, by acting on the same central nervous system receptors, they become a substitute for the original dependency. Abrupt discontinuation of methadone results in its own pattern of withdrawal reactions, but because these reactions are less severe than those of heroin, methadone has potential for weaning heroin users altogether from drug dependence (Strain, Bigelow, Liebson, et al., 1999).

Treatment with the opiate antagonists involves a drug called naltrexone. First, people are gradually weaned from heroin. Then they receive increasing dosages of naltrexone, which prevents them from experiencing any high should they later take heroin. This drug works because it has great affinity for the receptors to which opiates usually bind; their molecules occupy the receptors without stimulating them. This leaves heroin molecules with no place to go, and therefore heroin does not have its usual effect on the user. As with methadone, however, treatment with naltrexone involves frequent (daily) and regular visits to a clinic, which requires motivation. In addition, people may not lose the craving for heroin for some time. Both clinical effectiveness and treatment compliance can be increased by adding a contingency management component to the therapy (Carroll, Ball, Nich, et al., 2001). Giving people vouchers that they can exchange for food and clothing in return for taking naltrexone and having drug-free urine samples

Methadone is a synthetic heroin substitute. People formerly addicted to heroin come to clinics each day and swallow their dose. (© SacramentoBee/ZUMApress.com/NewsCom.)

markedly improves effectiveness. One study compared two different naltrexone treatments: the daily pill naltrexone and surgically implanted naltrexone that was slowly released into the body over 30 days. People with implanted naltrexone used opioids less and reported less craving compared to those who received oral dose naltrexone (Hulse, Ngo, & Tait, 2010).

Treatment with a heroin substitute usually involves going to a drug-treatment clinic and swallowing the drug in the presence of a staff member, once a day for methadone and three times a week for levomethadyl acetate and bupreophine. There is some evidence that methadone maintenance can be carried out more simply and just as effectively by weekly visits to a physician (Fiellen, O'Connor, Chawarski, et al., 2001). The effectiveness of methadone treatment is improved if a high (80- to 100-milligram) dose is used as opposed to the more typical 40- to 50-milligram dose (Strain et al., 1999) and if it is combined with regular psychological counseling (Ball & Ross, 1991). Drug treatment experts generally believe that treatment with heroin substitutes is best conducted in the context of a supportive social interaction, not merely as a medical encounter (Lilly, Quirk, Rhodes, et al., 2000).

Since methadone does not provide a euphoric high, many people will return to heroin if it becomes available to them. In an effort to improve outcomes, researchers have tried adding contingency management to the usual treatment at methadone clinics. In one randomized controlled trial (Pierce, Petry, Stitzer, et al., 2006), people receiving methadone from a clinic could draw for prizes each time they submitted a (carefully supervised and obtained) urine sample that had no trace of illegal drugs or alcohol. Prizes ranged from praise to televisions. People who were in the contingency management group were more likely to remain drug-free than those people who received only usual care from the methadone clinic. Of course, it remains to be seen whether such abstinence gains can be maintained after treatment ends and therapists are no longer providing such incentives.

Unfortunately, many people drop out of methadone programs, in part because of side effects such as insomnia, constipation, excessive sweating, and diminished sexual functioning. The stigma associated with going to methadone clinics is also linked to dropout rates, as illustrated in the Clinical Case of Franck described earlier. Age of entry into treatment may be important —the older the person, the greater the likelihood that he or she will stick with the treatment regimen (Friedmann, Lemon, & Stein, 2001).

Given the limitations of heroin substitutes such as methadone and other opiate antagonists, researchers have been searching for alternative medications. In 2003, a new prescription drug was introduced for the treatment of heroin dependence. Buprenorphine (Suboxone) is a medication that actually contains two agents: buprenorphine and naloxone. Buprenorphine is a partial opiate agonist, which means it does not have the same powerfully addicting properties as heroin, which is a full agonist. Naloxone is an opiate antagonist, often used in emergency rooms for opiate or heroin overdoses. This unique combination in Suboxone does not produce an intense high, is only mildly addictive, and lasts for as long as 3 days. Heroin users do not need to go to a clinic to receive this medication since it can be prescribed to individuals. Thus, this treatment avoids the stigma associated with visiting methadone clinics. Suboxone is effective at relieving withdrawal symptoms, and because it lasts longer than methadone, researchers are hopeful that relapse will be less likely. Still, some users may miss the more euphoric high associated with heroin, thus hastening a relapse.

Drug replacement does not appear to be an effective treatment for cocaine abuse and dependence. A meta-analysis of nine randomized controlled clinical trials of stimulant medication as a treatment for cocaine abuse revealed little evidence that this type of medication is effective (Castells, Casas, Vidal, et al., 2007). Two double-blind experiments found poor results for the antidepressant desipramine (Arndt, Dorozynsky, Woody, et al., 1992; Kosten, Morgan, Falcione, et al., 1992).

Researchers recently developed a vaccine to prevent the high associated with cocaine use. The vaccine contains tiny amounts of cocaine attached to otherwise harmless pathogens. The body's immune system responds to this invasion by developing antibodies that then squelch the cocaine. It is hoped that with repeated exposure, the antibodies will be able to keep a good deal of the cocaine from reaching the brain. However, a randomized controlled clinical trial with over 100 people addicted to cocaine was not particularly promising (Martell, Orson, Poling, et al., 2009). First, for the vaccine to be effective, people needed to receive five shots, and only half of the sample followed through with this. Second, just over a third of people receiving all shots developed enough antibodies to keep cocaine from reaching the brain. And finally, although about half of the sample used cocaine less, the vaccine did not help stave off cravings for cocaine. Clearly, additional work needs to be done.

Developing effective treatments for methamphetamine dependence remains a challenge for the field. People like Liz, described in the Clinical Case earlier, do not have many places to turn for treatment. The largest effort to date is a randomized controlled clinical trial conducted across eight different sites referred to as the Methamphetamine Treatment Project (Rawson, Martinelli-Casey, Anglin, et al., 2004). This study compared a multifaceted treatment called Matrix with treatment as usual. The Matrix treatment consisted of 16 cognitive behavior therapy group sessions, 12 family education sessions, 4 individual therapy sessions, and 4 social support group sessions. Treatment as usual (TAU) consisted of the best available treatment currently offered at the eight outpatient clinics. This varied quite a bit across the sites, with some offering individual counseling and others offering group counseling; some offering 4 weeks of treatment and others offering 16 weeks. Results of the study are somewhat supportive of the Matrix treatment. Compared to those in TAU, those people receiving Matrix stayed in treatment longer and were less likely to use methamphetamine during treatment (confirmed with urine analysis). Unfortunately, at the end of treatment and at the 6-month follow-up, people who received Matrix were no less likely to have used methamphetamine than those in TAU. The good news is that all participants were less likely to use methamphetamine after 6 months, regardless of whether they received Matrix or TAU. Although these results are promising, additional work is clearly needed to develop effective treatments for methamphetamine abuse and dependence.

Quick Summary

Psychological treatments have not been all that effective for smoking cessation. Scheduled smoking, which involves reducing nicotine intake gradually over a period of a few weeks, has shown some promise. Nicotine gum appears to be somewhat effective, though users can become dependent on the gum. Nicotine patches are more effective than placebo patches, but 9 months after the treatment, abstinence differences between these receiving the drug and those receiving a placebo disappear. Adding buprioprion or therapy along with nicotine patches may be effective, but not for adolescents.

Detoxification is usually the first step in treatment for drug use disorders. There is some evidence that CBT is an effective treatment for cocaine dependence. Motivational interviewing has shown promise for the treatment of alcohol and other drug use disorders. Residential treatment homes have not been adequately evaluated for their efficacy, though they are a common form of treatment.

The use of heroin substitutes, such as methadone or naltrexone, is an effective treatment for heroin use disorder. Methadone can only be administered in a special clinic, and there is stigma associated with this type of treatment. A prescription drug called buprenorphine can be taken at home. Treating methamphetamine dependence remains a challenge.

Check Your Knowledge 10.5

Match the treatment approach to the type of substance(s).

Treatment	Substance
1. Suboxone	**a.** alcohol
2. AA	**b.** heroin
3. couples therapy	**c.** cocaine
4. opiate antagonist	**d.** nicotine
5. antidepressant	**e.** methamphetamine
6. patch	
7. Matrix	

Prevention of Substance Use Disorders

Many prevention efforts have been aimed at adolescents because substance use disorders in adulthood often follow experimentation in the teens and earlier. Programs, usually conducted in schools, have been directed at enhancing young adolescents' self-esteem, teaching social skills, and encouraging young people to say no to peer pressure. The results are mixed (Hansen, 1993; Jansen, Glynn, & Howard, 1996). Self-esteem enhancement has not been shown to be effective. In contrast, social skills training and resistance training (learning to say no) have shown some positive results, particularly with girls. There are several drug prevention interventions in schools, based on different approaches, theories or models (see Botvin 1999, 2000).

Children and young people who smoke become addicted to nicotine very quickly. They also tend to continue the habit into adulthood. Around two-thirds of people who have smoked took up the habit before the age of 18 (The Information Centre, 2006). Because the risk of disease is related to the length of time a person has smoked, people who take up smoking before the age of 18 face a greater than-average risk of developing lung cancer or heart disease (Royal College of Physicians, 1992).

The measures that hold promise for persuading young people to resist smoking may also be useful in dissuading them from trying illicit drugs and alcohol. Brief family interventions show such promise. Teacher interventions may also help. Gerry McElwee (Ulster Cancer Foundation) described his own experience of training over 100 teachers to run small group interventions to help reduce smoking in young people in Northern Ireland. This involved an intensive 2-day course and was met with considerable enthusiasm and good attendance by the teachers involved. Other evidence suggests that the longer alcohol use is delayed, the less likely alcohol dependence will develop (Grant & Dawson, 1997), suggesting that preventive interventions can play a big role in keeping the prevalence of alcohol dependence down.

Worldwide comprehensive tobacco control programs, which include increasing taxes on cigarettes, restricting tobacco advertising, conducting public education campaigns, and creating smoke-free environments, appear to be an effective strategy for reducing teenage smoking (WHO, 2000). In 2012, the Food and Drugs Administration in the US hopes to require new health warnings for cigarette packages that contain graphic images of the ill effects on health that smoking can have, although lawsuits to prevent this are underway. In addition, scores of school-based programs aimed at preventing young people from starting to use tobacco have been implemented. By and large, such programs have succeeded in delaying the onset of smoking (Sussman, Dent, Simon, et al., 1995). These programs share some common components, not all of them shown to be effective (Evans, 2001; Hansen, 1992; Sussman, 1996):

Examples of the new health warnings for cigarette packages proposed by the FDA to begin in 2012. (AFP PHOTO/NewsCom.)

- *Peer-pressure resistance training.* Students learn about the nature of peer pressure and ways to say no. Overall, programs based on peer-pressure resistance training appear to be effective in reducing the onset and level of tobacco use, as well as illegal drug use, in young people (Tobler, Roona, Ochshorn, et al., 2000).

- *Correction of beliefs and expectations.* Many young people believe that cigarette smoking is more prevalent (and by implication, more okay) than it actually is. Changing beliefs about the prevalence of smoking has been shown to be an effective strategy, perhaps because young people are so sensitive to what others their age do and believe. Establishing that it is not standard behavior to smoke cigarettes (or drink alcohol or use marijuana) appears to be significantly more effective than resistance training (Hansen & Graham, 1991).

- *Inoculation against mass media messages.* Some prevention programs try to counter the positive images of smokers that have been put forward in the media (e.g., the Joe Camel ads mentioned earlier). Sophisticated mass media campaigns, similar to the ones that have made tobacco a profitable consumer product, can be successful in discouraging smoking. For example, the *truth* campaign, instituted by the American Legacy Foundation, developed websites (www.thetruth.com and www.fairenough.com) and radio and television ads to tell youth about the health and social consequences of smoking and the ways in which the tobacco industry targets them so that they can make informed choices about whether to smoke. This campaign has been well received among young people, and one study found that awareness of and agreement with the *truth* messages were associated with less smoking among teens (Niederdeppe, Farrelly, & Haviland, 2004). These findings are particularly encouraging since we know that teenagers' receptivity to tobacco marketing is strongly related to whether or not they will actually smoke (Unger, Boley Cruz, Schuster, et al., 2001).

- *Peer leadership.* Most smoking and other drug prevention programs involve peers of recognized status, which adds to the impact of the messages being conveyed.

Summary

Clinical Descriptions

- DSM-5 will likely include substance use disorder instead of separate categories for substance abuse and substance dependence. Substance use disorders can be specified with or without physiological dependence, and the number of symptoms present determines severity. Physiological dependence requires the presence of either tolerance or withdrawal.

- Alcohol has a variety of short-term and long-term effects on individuals, ranging from poor judgment and impaired motor coordination to chronic health problems.

- People can become physiologically dependent on nicotine, most often via smoking cigarettes. Despite somberly phrased warnings from public health officials, tobacco continues to be used. Medical problems associated with long-term cigarette smoking include many cancers, emphysema, and cardiovascular disease. Moreover, the health hazards of smoking are not restricted to those who smoke, for secondhand (environmental) smoke can also cause lung damage and other problems.

- When used regularly, marijuana can damage the lungs and cardiovascular system and lead to cognitive impairments. Tolerance to marijuana can develop. Ironically, just as the possible dangers of marijuana began to be uncovered, it was found to have therapeutic effects, easing the nausea of people undergoing chemotherapy and easing discomfort associated with AIDS, glaucoma, chronic pain, seizures, and muscle spasms.

- Opiates slow the activities of the body and, in moderate doses, are used to relieve pain and induce sleep. Heroin has been a focus of concern because

usage is up and stronger varieties have become available. Dependence on prescription pain medication has skyrocketed in the past 20 years.

- Stimulants, which include amphetamines and cocaine, act on the brain and the sympathetic nervous system to increase alertness and motor activity. Tolerance and withdrawal are associated with all these drugs. Abuse of methamphetamine, a derivative of amphetamine, has risen dramatically since the 1990s.

- The hallucinogens—LSD, mescaline, and psilocybin—alter or expand consciousness. Use of the hallucinogen-like drug Ecstasy has dramatically risen, and it is also considered a threat to health. PCP use often leads to violence.

Etiology

- Several factors are related to the etiology of substance use disorders. Genetic factors have been studied most often with alcohol and tobacco use disorders. Specific genes have been identified, but the interaction of these genes with the environment is key for understanding genetic contributions. Neurobiological factors involving the brain's reward pathways appear to play a role in the use of some substances. Many substances are used to alter mood (e.g., to reduce tension or increase positive affect), and people with certain personality traits, such as those high in negative affect or constraint, are especially likely to use drugs. Cognitive variables, such as the expectation that the drug will yield positive effects, are also important. Finally, sociocultural variables, such as attitudes toward the substance, peer pressure, and how the media portray the substance, are all related to how frequently a substance is used.

Treatment

• Treatments of all kinds have been used to help people refrain from the use of both legal drugs (e.g., alcohol and tobacco) and illegal drugs (e.g., heroin and cocaine). Biological treatments have attempted to release users from their dependency, often by substituting another drug. Some benefits have been observed for treatments using such drugs as naltrexone, suboxone, and methadone. Current medications seek to damp down cravings. Nicotine replacement via gum, patches, or inhalers has met with some success in reducing cigarette smoking. None of these approaches appear to lead to enduring change, however, unless accompanied by psychological treatments with such goals as helping people resist pressures to indulge, cope with normal life stress, control emotions without relying on chemicals, and make use of social supports, such as Alcoholics Anonymous.

• Since it is easier never to begin using drugs than to stop using them, considerable effort has been expended to prevent substance abuse by implementing educational and social programs to equip young people to develop their lives without a reliance on drugs.

Answers to Check Your Knowledge Questions

10.1 1. F; 2. T; 3. T

10.2 1. lung, larynx, esophagus, pancreas, bladder, cervix, stomach; 2. short-term, long-term; 3. pain relief, reduction of nausea, increased appetite, relief from the discomfort from AIDS

10.3 l. F; 2. F; 3. F; 4. T

10.4 l. b; 2. c; 3. a

10.5 1. b; 2. a; 3. a; 4. b; 5. a, c, d; 6. d; 7. e

Key Terms

addiction
amphetamines
Antabuse
caffeine
cocaine
controlled drinking
crack
cross-dependent
delirium tremens (DTs)
detoxification

Ecstasy
fetal alcohol syndrome (FAS)
flashback
hallucinogen
hashish
heroin
hydrocodone
LSD
marijuana
MDMA

mescaline
methadone
methamphetamine
morphine
nicotine
nitrous oxide
opiates
opium
oxycodone
PCP

polydrug abuse
psilocybin
secondhand smoke
stimulants
substance use disorders
tolerance
withdrawal

11 Eating Disorders

Clinical Case: Sarah

Sarah was 16 when referred to the Child and Adolescent Mental Health Team by her GP. Her mother had made the initial appointment with the doctor after finding out Sarah had missed her last 4 periods. At the beginning of the new school year, Sarah decided to lose 10kg. Her plan was to walk to school, visit the gym twice a week, and cut out confectionary and fizzy drinks. Everything was going well. Sarah loved her slim body and enjoyed being told how good she looked. Then one afternoon in mid-December, Sarah was attacked. A man tried to pull her into a side street, but Sarah put up a fight and the man ran off. Everyone said what a lucky escape she'd had. And for a period of time, Sarah felt the same. But as the months passed, she couldn't help thinking that it wouldn't if she'd been a couple of years younger. Sarah was now 52kg, but she complained her thighs were too large and her cheeks were chubby. She weighed out her food meticulously, and argued with her parents for refusing to eat carbohydrates. Sarah drank water to stave off feelings of hunger and make sure she didn't "overeat" at meal times.

MANY CULTURES ARE PREOCCUPIED with food. In the United States today, new restaurants abound, and numerous magazines, websites, and television shows are devoted to food preparation. At the same time, many people are overweight. Dieting to lose weight is common, and the desire of many people, especially women, to be thinner has created a multibillion-dollar-a-year business. Given this intense interest in food and eating, it is not surprising that this aspect of human behavior is subject to disorder.

Although clinical descriptions of eating disorders can be traced back many years, particularly for anorexia nervosa, these disorders appeared in the DSM for the first time in 1980 as one subcategory of disorders beginning in childhood or adolescence. Eating disorders became a distinct category in DSM-IV, reflecting the increased attention they had received from clinicians and researchers. In DSM-5, eating disorders will likely be in a category called "Feeding and Eating Disorders" that also includes childhood disorders such as pica (eating nonfood substances for extended periods) and rumination disorders (repeated regurgitation of foods).

Unfortunately, eating disorders are also likely to be stigmatized. In one recent study, college students were presented vignettes depicting fictional women with different disorders and were then asked to rate these fictional women on a number of dimensions (Wingfield et al., 2011). Participants rated the women depicted with eating disorders as self-destructive and responsible for their conditions. Men in the study were particularly likely to believe that eating disorders were easy to overcome. In another study (Roehrig & McLean, 2010), participants were randomly assigned to read a vignette about a woman with an eating disorder or a woman with depression. Participants who read about the woman with the eating disorder viewed her as more responsible, more fragile, and more likely to be trying to get attention with her disorder compared to participants who read about the woman with depression. These types of attitudes and beliefs are not consistent with the current research on eating disorders.

Clinical Descriptions of Eating Disorders

We begin by describing anorexia nervosa and bulimia nervosa. The diagnoses of these two disorders share several clinical features. We then discuss binge eating disorder, which is proposed as a new diagnostic category in the DSM-5 rather than a condition in need of further study as it was in the DSM-IV-TR. Table 11.1 presents the likely key changes in these DSM-5 categories.

Anorexia Nervosa

Sarah, the woman just described, had **anorexia nervosa.** The term *anorexia* refers to loss of appetite, and *nervosa* indicates that the loss is due to emotional reasons. The term is something of a misnomer because most people with anorexia nervosa actually do not lose their appetite or interest in food. On the contrary, while starving themselves, most people with the disorder become preoccupied with food; they may read cookbooks constantly and prepare gourmet meals for their families.

Sarah met all three features required for the diagnosis:

1. *Restriction of behaviors that promote healthy body weight.* This is usually taken to mean that the person weighs much less than is considered normal [e.g., body mass index (BMI; see Table 11.3) less than 18.5 for adults] for that person's age and height. Weight loss is typically achieved through dieting, although purging (self-induced vomiting, heavy use of laxatives or diuretics) and excessive exercise can also be part of the picture.

2. *Intense fear of gaining weight and being fat.* This fear is not reduced by weight loss. There is no such thing as "too thin."

3. *Distorted body image or sense of body shape.* Even when emaciated, those with anorexia nervosa maintain that they are overweight and that certain parts of their bodies, particularly the abdomen, hips, and thighs, are too fat. To check on their body size, they typically weigh themselves frequently, measure the size of different parts of the body, and gaze critically at their reflections in mirrors. Their self-esteem is closely linked to maintaining thinness.

Prior to DSM-5, *amenorrhea (loss of menstrual period)* was one of the diagnostic criteria for anorexia nervosa. It is likely to be removed, however, in DSM-5 because there are many reasons why women can stop having their menstrual period that do not have anything to do with

Despite being thin, women with anorexia believe that parts of their bodies are too fat and spend a lot of time critically examining themselves in front of mirrors. (Susan Rosenberg/Photo Researchers, Inc.)

Table 11.1 Diagnoses of Eating Disorders

DSM-5 Diagnoses	Likely Key Changes
Anorexia Nervosa	Restriction of behaviors that promote healthy weight rather than "refusal to eat" as a criterion
	A focus on behaviors that interfere with weight gain
	Loss of menstrual period no longer required for diagnosis
	Subtypes specified for past 3 months rather than just current episode
Bulimia Nervosa	Minimum frequency of bingeing/purging to be once/week instead of twice/week for at least 3 months
	Non-purging subtype likely to be removed
Binge Eating Disorder	New category in DSM-5
	This was in the Appendix in DSM-IV-TR as a category in need of further study; additional research supports its addition to the DSM-5

Proposed DSM-5 Criteria for Anorexia Nervosa

- Restriction of food to promote healthy weight; body weight is significantly below normal
- Intense fear of weight gain
- Body image disturbance

weight loss. In addition, few differences have been found between women who have amenorrhea and the other three features of anorexia nervosa and those women who have the other three features but do not have amenorrhea (Attia & Roberto, 2009; Garfinkel et al., 1996). A summary of the diagnostic criteria for anorexia nervosa appears in the margin.

The distorted body image that accompanies anorexia nervosa has been assessed in several ways, most frequently by a questionnaire such as the Eating Disorders Inventory (Garner, Olmsted, & Polivy, 1983). Some of the items on this questionnaire are presented in Table 11.2. In another type of assessment, people with anorexia nervosa are shown line drawings of women with varying body weights and asked to pick the one closest to their own and the one that represents their ideal shape (see Figure 11.1). People with anorexia overestimate their own body size and choose a thin figure as their ideal. Despite this distortion in body size, people with anorexia nervosa are fairly accurate when reporting their actual weight (McCabe et al., 2001), perhaps because they weigh themselves frequently.

One interesting study found a slightly different pattern for men with eating disorders. Men with eating disorders didn't differ from men without eating disorders when pointing to their ideal male body type. However, the men with eating disorders overestimated their own body size considerably, thus demonstrating a distortion in their own body images (Mangweth et al., 2004).

DSM-5 will likely distinguish two types of anorexia nervosa, even though recent research calls into question the validity of these types. In the *restricting type*, weight loss is achieved by severely limiting food intake; in the *binge-eating/purging type*, the person has also regularly engaged in binge eating and purging. Initial research indicated a number of differences between these two subtypes, thus supporting the validity of this distinction. For example, studies have shown that people with the binge-eating/purging subtype exhibit more personality disorders, impulsive behavior, stealing, alcohol and drug abuse, social withdrawal, and suicide attempts than do people with the restricting type of anorexia (e.g., Herzog et al., 2000; Pryor, Wiederman, & McGilley, 1996). Longitudinal research, however, suggests the distinction between subtypes may not be all that useful (Eddy et al., 2002). Nearly two-thirds of women who initially met criteria for the restricting subtype had switched over to the binge-eating/purging type 8 years later. Furthermore, this study found few differences in substance abuse or personality disturbances between the two subtypes. A review of the subtype literature for the preparation of DSM-5 concluded that the subtypes had limited predictive validity even though clinicians found them useful (Peat et al., 2009).

Table 11.2 Subscales and Illustrative Items from the Eating Disorders Inventory

Drive for thinness	I think about dieting.
	I feel extremely guilty after overeating.
	I am preoccupied with the desire to be thinner.
Bulimia	I stuff myself with food.
	I have gone on eating binges where I have felt that I could not stop.
	I have the thought of trying to vomit in order to lose weight.
Body dissatisfaction	I think that my thighs are too large.
	I think that my buttocks are too large.
	I think that my hips are too big.
Ineffectiveness	I feel inadequate.
	I have a low opinion of myself.
	I feel empty inside (emotionally).
Perfectionism	Only outstanding performance is good enough in my family.
	As a child, I tried hard to avoid disappointing my parents and teachers.
	I hate being less than best at things.
Interpersonal distrust	I have trouble expressing my emotions to others.
	I need to keep people at a certain distance (feel uncomfortable if someone tries to get too close).
Interoceptive awareness	I get confused about what emotion I am feeling.
	I don't know what's going on inside me.
	I get confused as to whether or not I am hungry.
Maturity fears	I wish that I could return to the security of childhood.
	I feel that people are happiest when they are children.
	The demands of adulthood are too great.

Source: From Garner et al. (1983).

Note: Responses use a six-point scale ranging from "always" to "never."

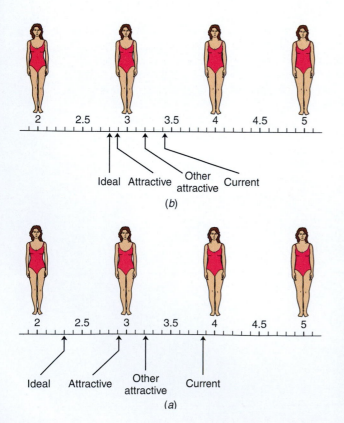

Anorexia nervosa typically begins in the early to middle teenage years, often after an episode of dieting and the occurrence of a life stress. Lifetime prevalence of anorexia is less than 1 percent, and it is at least 10 times more frequent in women than in men (Hoek & van Hoeken, 2003). When anorexia nervosa does occur in men, symptomatology and other characteristics, such as reports of family conflict, are generally similar to those reported by women with the disorder (Olivardia et al., 1995). As we discuss more fully later, the gender difference in the prevalence of anorexia most likely reflects the greater cultural emphasis on women's beauty, which has promoted a thin shape as the ideal over the past several decades.

Women with anorexia nervosa are frequently diagnosed with depression, obsessive-compulsive disorder, phobias, panic disorder, substance use disorders, and various personality disorders (Baker et al., 2010; Godart et al., 2000; Ivarsson et al., 2000; Root et al., 2010). Men with anorexia nervosa are also likely to have a diagnosis of a mood disorder, schizophrenia, or substance use

Figure 11.1 In this assessment of body image, respondents indicate their current shape, their ideal shape, and the shape they think is most attractive to the opposite sex. The figure actually rated as most attractive by members of the opposite sex is shown in both panels. Ratings of women who scored high on a measure of distorted attitudes toward eating are shown in (a); ratings of women who scored low are shown in (b). The high scorers overestimated their current size and ideally would be very thin. From Zellner, Harner, & Adler (1989).

disorder (Striegel-Moore et al., 1999). Suicide rates are quite high for people with anorexia, with as many as 5 percent completing suicide and 20 percent attempting suicide (Franko & Keel, 2006).

Physical Consequences of Anorexia Nervosa Self-starvation and use of laxatives produce numerous undesirable biological consequences in people with anorexia nervosa. Blood pressure often falls, heart rate slows, kidney and gastrointestinal problems develop, bone mass declines, the skin dries out, nails become brittle, hormone levels change, and mild anemia may occur. Some people lose hair from the scalp, and they may develop lanugo—a fine, soft hair—on their bodies. Levels of electrolytes, such as potassium and sodium, are altered. These ionized salts, present in various bodily fluids, are essential to neural transmission, and lowered levels can lead to tiredness, weakness, cardiac arrhythmias, and even sudden death.

Prognosis Between 50 and 70 percent of people with anorexia eventually recover. (Keel & Brown, 2010). However, recovery often takes 6 or 7 years, and relapses are common before a stable pattern of eating and weight maintenance is achieved (Strober, Freeman, & Morrell, 1997). As we discuss later, changing peoples' distorted views of themselves is very difficult, particularly in cultures that value thinness.

Anorexia nervosa is a life-threatening illness; death rates are 10 times higher among people with the disorder than among the general population and twice as high as among people with other psychological disorders. Mortality rates among women with anorexia range from 3 to 5 percent (Crow et al., 2009; Keel & Brown, 2010). Death most often results from physical complications of the illness—for example, congestive heart failure—and from suicide (Herzog et al., 2000; Sullivan, 1995).

Anorexia nervosa can be a life-threatening condition. It is especially prevalent among young women who are under intense pressure to keep their weight low. Brazilian model Ana Carolina Reston died from the condition in 2006 at age 21. (Reuters/Landov.)

Clinical Case: Harriet

Harriet was the middle of 3 children, born to professional parents. Both of her brothers loved sport, and showed little aptitude for school work. Harriet, on the hand, picked up reading and writing very quickly, and her parents hoped she would become a doctor or lawyer. At aged 4, Harriet was reading books written for 8 to 10 year olds. By the time she was 9, Harriet was sent to a high-achievers boarding-school where her academic abilities could be "hot housed". Over the next few years, Harriet performed well and her parents' aspirations grew. But as she approached her 15th birthday, Harriet lost interest in becoming a doctor and wanted to be a wildlife photographer. This brought her into conflict with her parents, which made her feel incredibly guilty. Harriet began to restrict her food intake, but found that after several days of semi-starvation she would lose control and go on an eating binge. This pattern of dieting and bingeing lasted for several months, and Harriet's fear of becoming fat seemed to increase during that time. At age 16, she hit on the solution of self-induced vomiting and fell into a pattern of bingeing and vomiting three or four times per week. Although she maintained this pattern in secret for a while, eventually Harriet's house mistress at school caught on and initiated treatment for her.

Bulimia Nervosa

Harriet's behavior illustrates the features of **bulimia nervosa**. *Bulimia* is from a Greek word meaning "ox hunger." This disorder involves episodes of rapid consumption of a large amount of food, followed by compensatory behavior, such as vomiting, fasting, or excessive exercise, to prevent weight gain. The DSM defines a *binge* as having two characteristics. First it involves eating an excessive amount of food, that is, much more than most people would eat, within a short period of time (e.g., 2 hours). Second, it involves a feeling of losing control over eating—as if one cannot stop. Bulimia nervosa is not diagnosed if the bingeing and purging occur only in the context of anorexia nervosa and its extreme weight loss; the diagnosis in such a case is anorexia nervosa, binge-eating/purging type. The key difference between anorexia and bulimia is weight loss: people with anorexia nervosa lose a tremendous amount of weight, whereas people with bulimia nervosa do not.

In bulimia, binges typically occur in secret; they may be triggered by stress and the negative emotions they arouse, and they continue until the person is uncomfortably full (Grilo, Shiffman, & Carter-Campbell, 1994). In the case of Harriet, she was likely to binge after periods of stress. Foods that can be rapidly consumed, especially sweets such as ice cream and cake, are usually part of a binge. One study found that women with bulimia nervosa were more likely to binge while alone and during the morning or afternoon. In addition, avoiding a craved food on one day was associated with a binge episode the next morning (Waters, Hill, & Waller, 2001). Other studies show that a binge is likely to occur after a negative social interaction—or at least the perception of a negative social exchange (Steiger et al., 1999).

Research suggests that people with bulimia nervosa sometimes ingest enormous quantities of food during binges, often more than what a person eats in an entire day; however, binges are not always as large as the DSM implies, and there is wide variation in the caloric content consumed by people with bulimia nervosa during binges (e.g., Rossiter & Agras, 1990). People report that they lose control during a binge, even to the point of experiencing something akin to a trancelike state, perhaps losing awareness of their behavior or feeling that it is not really they who are bingeing. They are usually ashamed of their binges and try to conceal them.

After the binge is over, feelings of discomfort, disgust, and fear of weight gain lead to the second step of bulimia nervosa—purging to attempt to undo the caloric effects of the binge. People with bulimia most often stick fingers down their throats to cause gagging, but after a time many can induce vomiting at will without gagging themselves. Laxative and diuretic abuse (which do little to reduce body weight) as well as fasting and excessive exercise are also used to prevent weight gain.

Although many people binge occasionally and some people also purge, the DSM-5 diagnosis of bulimia nervosa will likely require that the episodes of bingeing and purging occur at least once a week for 3 months. Is once a week a well-established cutoff point? Probably not. But the frequency will likely be changed from twice a week in DSM-IV-TR to once a week in DSM-5 because few differences were found between people who binge twice a week and those who do so less frequently. (Garfinkel, Kennedy, & Kaplan, 1995; Wilson & Sysko, 2009).

Like those with anorexia nervosa, people with bulimia nervosa are afraid of gaining weight, and their self-esteem depends heavily on maintaining normal weight. Whereas people without eating disorders typically underreport their weight and say they are taller than they actually are, people with bulimia nervosa are more accurate in their reports (Doll & Fairburn, 1998; McCabe et al., 2001). Yet people with bulimia nervosa are also likely to be highly dissatisfied with their bodies.

Two subtypes of bulimia nervosa are distinguished: in DSM-IV-TR: a *purging type* and a *nonpurging type* in which the compensatory behaviors are fasting or excessive exercise. And, as with anorexia, evidence for the validity of this distinction is mixed. In some studies, people diagnosed with nonpurging bulimia were heavier, binged less frequently, and showed less psychopathology than did people with purging-type bulimia (e.g., Mitchell, 1992). But in other research, few differences emerged between the two types (e.g., Tobin, Griffing, & Griffing, 1997). It is also difficult to distinguish the nonpurging bulimia type from binge eating disorder. The nonpurging type is likely to be removed from DSM-5 (van Hoeken et al., 2009).

Bulimia nervosa typically begins in late adolescence or early adulthood. About 90 percent of cases are women, and prevalence among women is thought to be about 1 to 2 percent of the population (Hoek & van Hoeken, 2003). Many people with bulimia nervosa were somewhat overweight before the onset of the disorder, and the binge eating often started during an episode of dieting. Although both anorexia nervosa and bulimia nervosa among women begin in adolescence, they can persist into adulthood and middle age (Keel et al., 2010; Slevec & Tiggemann, 2011).

Bulimia nervosa is comorbid with numerous other diagnoses, notably depression, personality disorders, anxiety disorders, substance use disorders, and conduct disorder (Baker et al., 2010; Godart et al., 2000, 2002; Root et al., 2010; Stice, Burton, & Shaw, 2004). Men with bulimia are also likely to be diagnosed with a mood disorder or substance use disorder (Striegel-Moore et al., 1999). Suicide rates are higher among people with bulimia nervosa than in the general population (Favaro & Santonastaso, 1997) but substantially lower than among people with anorexia (Franko & Keel, 2006).

Proposed DSM-5 Criteria for Bulimia Nervosa

- Recurrent episodes of binge eating
- Recurrent compensatory behaviors to prevent weight gain, for example, vomiting
- Body shape and weight are extremely important for self-evaluation

Which comes first, bulimia nervosa or the comorbid disorders? A prospective study examined the relationship between bulimia and depression symptoms among adolescent girls (Stice et al., 2004). This study found that bulimia symptoms predicted the onset of depression symptoms. However, the converse was also true; depression symptoms predicted the onset of bulimia symptoms. Thus, it appears each disorder increases the risk for the other. With respect to substance use disorders, another prospective study of over 1,200 twin pairs found that bulimia symptoms came before substance use disorder symptoms (Baker et al., 2010).

Physical Consequences of Bulimia Nervosa Like anorexia, bulimia is associated with several physical side effects. Although less common than in anorexia, menstrual irregularities, including amenorrhea, can occur, even though people with bulimia typically have a normal **body mass index (BMI)** (Gendall et al., 2000). The BMI is calculated by dividing weight in kilograms by height in meters squared and is considered a more valid estimate of body fat than many others. For women, a normal BMI is between 20 and 25. To calculate your own BMI, see Table 11.3. Bulimia nervosa, like anorexia, is a serious disorder with many unfortunate medical consequences (Mehler, 2011). For example, frequent purging can cause potassium depletion. Heavy use of laxatives induces diarrhea, which can also lead to changes in electrolytes and cause irregularities in the heartbeat. Recurrent vomiting has been linked to menstrual problems and may lead to tearing of tissue in the stomach and throat and to loss of dental enamel as stomach acids eat away at the teeth, which become ragged. The salivary glands may become swollen. Death from bulimia nervosa was once thought to be less common than from anorexia nervosa (Herzog et al., 2000; Keel & Brown, 2010; Keel & Mitchell, 1997), but a recent study of nearly 1000 women with bulimia nervosa found the mortality rate to be nearly 4 percent (Crow et al., 2009).

Prognosis Long-term follow-ups of people with bulimia nervosa reveal that close to 75 percent recover, although about 10 to 20 percent remain fully symptomatic (Keel et al., 1999; 2010; Reas et al., 2000; Steinhausen & Weber, 2009). Intervening soon after a diagnosis is made (i.e., within the first few years) is linked with an even better prognosis (Reas et al., 2000). People with bulimia nervosa who binge and vomit more and who have comorbid substance use or a history of depression have a poorer prognosis than people without these factors (Wilson et al., 1999).

Table 11.3 Computing Your Body Mass Index (BMI)

WEIGHT lbs	100	105	110	115	120	125	130	135	140	145	150	155	160	165	170	175	180	185	190	195	200	205	210	215
kgs	45.5	47.7	50.0	52.3	54.5	56.8	59.1	61.4	63.6	65.9	68.2	70.5	72.7	75.0	77.3	79.5	81.8	84.1	86.4	88.6	90.9	93.2	95.5	97.7
HEIGHT in/cm — ☐ Underweight ☐ Healthy ☐ Overweight ☐ Obese ☐ Extremely obese																								
5'0" - 152.4	19	20	21	22	23	24	25	26	27	28	29	30	31	32	33	34	35	36	37	38	39	40	41	42
5'1" - 154.9	18	19	20	21	22	23	24	25	26	27	28	29	30	31	32	33	34	35	36	36	37	38	39	40
5'2" - 157.4	18	19	20	21	22	22	23	24	25	26	27	28	29	30	31	32	33	33	34	35	36	37	38	39
5'3" - 160.0	17	18	19	20	21	22	23	24	24	25	26	27	28	29	30	31	32	32	33	34	35	36	37	38
5'4" - 162.5	17	18	18	19	20	21	22	23	24	24	25	26	27	28	29	30	31	31	32	33	34	35	36	37
5'5" - 165.1	16	17	18	19	20	20	21	22	23	24	25	25	26	27	28	29	30	30	31	32	33	34	35	35
5'6" - 167.6	16	17	17	18	19	20	21	21	22	23	24	25	25	26	27	28	29	29	30	31	32	33	34	34
5'7" - 170.1	15	16	17	18	18	19	20	21	22	22	23	24	25	25	26	27	28	29	29	30	31	32	33	33
5'8" - 172.7	15	16	16	17	18	19	19	20	21	22	22	23	24	25	25	26	27	28	28	29	30	31	32	32
5'9" - 175.2	14	15	16	17	17	18	19	20	20	21	22	22	23	24	25	25	26	27	28	28	29	30	31	31
5'10" - 177.8	14	15	15	16	17	18	18	19	20	20	21	22	23	23	24	25	25	26	27	28	28	29	30	30
5'11" - 180.3	14	14	15	16	16	17	18	18	19	20	21	21	22	23	23	24	25	25	26	27	28	28	29	30
6'0" - 182.8	13	14	14	15	16	17	17	18	19	19	20	21	21	22	23	23	24	25	25	26	27	27	28	29
6'1" - 185.4	13	13	14	15	15	16	17	17	18	19	19	20	21	21	22	23	23	24	25	25	26	27	27	28
6'2" - 187.9	12	13	14	14	15	16	16	17	18	18	19	19	20	21	21	22	23	23	24	25	25	26	27	27
6'3" - 190.5	12	13	13	14	15	15	16	16	17	18	18	19	20	20	21	21	22	23	23	24	25	25	26	26
6'4" - 193.0	12	12	13	14	14	15	15	16	17	17	18	18	19	20	20	21	22	22	23	23	24	25	25	26

Clinical Case: Amelia

"Yes, I'm obese. It's such an ugly word. It's hard for me to say it. I prefer overweight, but by definition, since the doctor says I weigh 20% more than I should, obese is the correct word. At 1.7m I should weigh about 57kg. So at 96kg I'm obese. I am a health conscious person. I do not smoke, and drink lightly. And I'm always busy. How did this ever happen to me? My mum was overweight for as long as I can remember. I felt so sorry for her. When we use to go shopping together, trying on clothes was a major ordeal. Mum never looked good in anything. Back in those days I don't think she realized that the fried bacon and egg breakfasts,

chips for tea were responsible for both her weight problem and the beginnings of my bad eating habits. By the time she died at the age of 52, she weighed about 98kg. At school my nickname was "Miss Piggy", and I was always the last to be picked for teams during games lessons. I just laughed it off."

Amelia has a couple of bingeing episodes a week. These episodes aren't sparked by feeling hungry, and even when she feels extremely full, she can't stop eating. Afterwards, Amelia describes feeling ashamed and angry at herself for having eaten so much.

Proposed DSM-5 Criteria for Binge Eating Disorder

- Reported binge eating episodes
- Binge eating episodes include at least three of the following: eating more quickly than usual eating until over full eating large amounts even if not hungry eating alone due to embarrassment about large food quantity feeling bad (e.g., disgusted, guilty, or depressed) after the binge
- No compensatory behavior is present

Binge Eating Disorder

In DSM-5, **binge eating disorder** will likely be included as a diagnosis (it was considered a diagnosis in need of further study in DSM-IV-TR). This disorder includes recurrent binges (one time per week for at least 3 months), lack of control during the bingeing episode, and distress about bingeing, as well as other characteristics, such as rapid eating and eating alone. It is distinguished from anorexia nervosa by the absence of weight loss and from bulimia nervosa by the absence of compensatory behaviors (purging, fasting, or excessive exercise). Most often, people with binge eating disorder are **obese**. A person with a BMI greater than 30 is considered obese. With the current explosion in the prevalence of obesity in the United States, it is perhaps not surprising that research on binge eating disorder continues to increase (Yanovski, 2003). It is important to point out, however, that not all obese people meet criteria for binge eating disorder. Indeed, only those who have binge episodes and report feeling a loss of control over their eating will qualify, which amounts to anywhere from 2 to 25 percent of obese people (Yanovski, 2003). For further discussion of obesity, see Focus on Discovery 11.1.

Its likely inclusion in DSM-5 reflects the current research on binge eating disorder that supports its validity, and the bulk of evidence supports its inclusion in DSM-5 (Striegel-Moore & Franco, 2008; Wonderlich et al., 2009). It can be reliably defined and measured (Striegel-Moore & Franco, 2003). It is associated with obesity and a history of dieting (Kinzl et al., 1999; Pike et al., 2001). It is linked to impaired work and social functioning, depression, low self-esteem, substance use disorders, and dissatisfaction with body shape (Spitzer et al., 1993; Striegel-Moore et al., 1998, 2001). Risk factors for developing binge eating disorder include childhood obesity, critical comments regarding being overweight, weight-loss attempts in childhood, low self-concept, depression, and childhood physical or sexual abuse (Fairburn et al., 1998; Rubinstein et al., 2010). One behavior genetics study (Hudson et al., 2006) found that relatives of obese people with binge eating disorder were more likely to have binge eating disorder themselves (20 percent) than were relatives of obese people without binge eating disorder (9 percent).

Binge eating disorder appears to be more prevalent than either anorexia nervosa or bulimia nervosa (Hudson et al., 2007). In the National Comorbidity Survey—Replication study, the prevalence was 3.5 percent for women and 2 percent for men. Research suggests that binge eating disorder is more common in women than men, although the gender difference is not as great as it is in anorexia or bulimia. Though only a few epidemiological studies have been done, binge eating disorder appears to be equally prevalent among European, African, Asian, and Hispanic Americans (Striegel-Moore & Franco, 2008). Binge eating disorder is comorbid with depression and anxiety disorders (Wonderlich et al., 2009).

Physical Consequences of Binge Eating Disorder Like the other eating disorders, there are physical consequences of binge eating disorder. Many of the physical consequences are likely a function of associated obesity, including increased risk of type 2 diabetes, cardiovascular problems, breathing problems, insomnia, and joint/muscle problems. However, research shows that a number of physical problems are present among people with binge eating disorder that are independent from co-occurring obesity, including sleep problems, anxiety, depression, irritable bowel syndrome, and, for women, early onset of menstruation (Bulik &. Reichborn-Kjennerud, 2003).

Prognosis Perhaps because it is a relatively new diagnosis, fewer studies have assessed the prognosis of binge eating disorder. Research so far suggests that between 25 and 82 percent of people recover (Keel & Brown, 2010; Striegel-Moore & Franco, 2008). One retrospective study found that people reported having their binge eating disorder for an average of 14.4 years, which is much longer than people with anorexia or bulimia report having their disorders (Pope et al., 2006).

Quick Summary

Anorexia nervosa has three characteristics: restriction of behaviors to promote a healthy body weight, an intense fear of gaining weight and being fat, and a distorted body image. Anorexia usually begins in the early teen years and is more common in women than men. Bodily changes that can occur after severe weight loss can be serious and life threatening. About 70 percent of women with anorexia eventually recover, but it can take many years.

Bulimia nervosa involves both bingeing and purging. Bingeing often involves sweet foods and is more likely to occur when someone is alone, after a negative social encounter, and in the morning or afternoon. One striking difference between anorexia and bulimia is weight loss: people with anorexia nervosa lose a tremendous amount of weight, whereas people with bulimia nervosa do not. Bulimia typically begins in late adolescence and is more common in women than men. Depression often co-occurs with bulimia, and each condition appears to be a risk factor for the other. Dangerous changes to the body can also occur as a result of bulimia, such as menstrual problems, tearing in the stomach and throat, and swelling of the salivary glands.

Binge eating disorder is characterized by several binges, and most (but not all) people who suffer from it are obese (defined as having a BMI greater than 30). Not all obese people meet criteria for binge eating disorder—only those who have binge episodes and report feeling a loss of control over their eating qualify. Binge eating disorder is more common than anorexia and bulimia and is more common in women than men, though the gender difference is not as great as it is in anorexia and bulimia. Changes to the body occur with binge eating disorder, and not all of these are due to the co-occurrence of obesity. About 60 percent of people with binge eating disorder recover, but it takes even longer than recovery for anorexia or bulimia.

FOCUS ON DISCOVERY 11.1

Obesity: A Twenty-First Century Epidemic?

Overweight and obesity occur when excess fat accumulates in the human body, posing a risk to health. Current definitions are based on both the body mass index and the waist circumference. As height is important, the body mass index (BMI) is an indicator of fat storage independent of height. It is calculated as body weight divided by height squared. Waist circumference has more recently been included in efforts to classify obesity, as the distribution of body fat has been found to be important and carrying it around the abdomen has been found to be especially unhealthy. Abdominal obesity is classified as a waist circumference of more than 88 cm in women and more than 102 cm in men.

Obesity is not an eating disorder, though it is an increasing public health problem. The World Health Organization estimates that in 2005 (the latest year available) approximately 1.6 billion adults were overweight, of which at least 400 million were obese. Once considered only a problem in high-income countries, overweight and obesity are on the rise in developing countries. In the 53 countries of the WHO European Region, experts estimate that 150 million adults and 15 million children will be obese by 2010. WHO projects that by 2015, the ranks of the overweight will grow to about 2.3 billion adults and that more than 700 million of them will be obese.

Countries which have very low levels of childhood obesity include Japan, Korea, and Switzerland.

% Population Obese	
Japan	2.9
Korea	3.2
Switzerland	7.7
Norway	8.3
Italy	8.6
Denmark	9.5
Netherlands	10.0
Sweden	10.4
Belgium	11.7
Finland	11.8

Source: www.vexen.co.uk/countries/best.html#Obesity

Health risks of obesity

The consequences of obesity are serious and risk increases progressively as BMI rises. Obesity is among the most important risk factors for type 2 diabetes, heart disease, stroke and some forms of cancer, making it one of the leading preventable causes of death worldwide and one of the most significant public health challenges of the 21st century. More and more diseases are being linked to obesity, including asthma, osteoarthritis and sleep apnoea.

Abdominal obesity, characterized by increased fat under the skin of the belly and between the abdominal organs (visceral obesity), is considered especially harmful, as it is particularly powerful in increasing the risk of heart disease and diabetes. It is increasingly clear that disturbed functioning of adipose tissue may be an important factor in obesity-related health risks. As people get fatter and their fat cells expand, the adipose tissue becomes less able to store fat and the body starts storing it in other tissues, such as muscle and liver, which may disturb cell function and lead to disease. Also, it has become clear that adipose tissue is a very active organ, secreting hormonal signals that may affect metabolism in other organs.

Why are the numbers of obese people on the increase?

Genetic factors You are more likely to be obese if one of your parents is obese, or both of your parents are obese. This may partly be due to learning bad eating habits from your parents. But, some people actually inherit a tendency in their genes that makes them prone to overeat. So, for some people, part of the problem is genetic.

It is not fully understood how this genetic factor works. Although research is beginning to unravel the secrets. Naturally occurring mutant mice with a brilliant yellow coat known as Ay, or yellow agouti, originally bred in China for mouse fanciers, turned out to be one of five mutant strains of mice that were obese because of a single gene mutation. In addition to Ay, the other mutant strains were *obese (ob)*, *diabetes (db)*, *fat*, and *tubby*, and they proved essential to genetic studies on metabolism and weight maintenance. Both the *ob* (or *obese*) and the *db* (or *diabetes*) mice typically weigh three times what a normal mouse weighs and accumulate five times the normal amount of body fat. During nearly eight

Obesity has become quite prevalent, particularly in the United States, in the past 30 years. (Bourreau/Photo Researchers, Inc.)

years of complicated genetic experimentation, Friedman and his colleagues provided the first glimpse of the biological system that controls the intake of food and the metabolism of fat and showed that the *ob* and *db* mice reflect two aspects of the same biological system. The researchers discovered that *ob* mice become fat because they lack a single gene, *ob*. This gene, normally active in fat cells, produces a protein that travels through the bloodstream to the brain and tells it, in effect, "I'm full." Friedman named the missing gene's product leptin, after the Greek word for thin (*leptos*). It then turned out that *db* mice lack a gene containing the instructions for making the leptin receptor—the biochemical antenna that receives the leptin signal from the fat cells. In other words, the brain of *db* mice is unable to receive the message "I'm full" dispatched by the fat cells. Finding these mouse genes enabled researchers to discover the same genes in humans. Although the biology of the system is extremely complex and still being worked out, leptin appears to play a critical role in day-to-day biology. "If the fat mass falls," Friedman says, "the level of leptin falls, and the urge to eat goes up. After an eating binge, the level of leptin rises, which is a signal to eat less. In addition to modulating food intake and energy expenditure, leptin has an effect on fertility, temperature maintenance, and fat and glucose metabolism."

Environmental Factors

Along with genetics, environmental factors play a role in obesity. Today's children, ages 8 to 18, consume multiple types of media (often simultaneously) and spend more time (44.5 hours per week) in front of computer, television, and game screens than any other activity in their lives except sleeping. Research has found strong associations between increases in advertising for non-nutritious foods and rates of childhood obesity. So, not only are children burning up *fewer* calories than ever before, they are also *consuming* more calories than ever before.

Most children under age 6 cannot distinguish between programming and advertising and children under age 8 do not understand the persuasive intent of advertising. Advertising directed at children this young is by its very nature exploitative. For example, the advertising budget for Coke and Pepsi combined was 21 billion euros in 2001 (Brownell & Horgen, 2003). Compare this to the 1.4 million Euros advertising campaign by the National Cancer Institute to promote eating more fruits and vegetables (Nestle, 2002).

Children are particularly susceptible to advertising. Children have a remarkable ability to recall content from the ads to which they have been exposed. Product preference has been shown to occur with as little as a single commercial exposure and to strengthen with repeated exposures. Product preferences affect children's product purchase requests and these requests influence parents' purchasing decisions. In a study conducted in 2004, Halford et al, examined the effect of TV advertisements for foods on food consumption in children's eating behavior. They compared the ability to recognize 8 food and 8 non-food related adverts in 3 groups of children: lean, over-weight and obese. Their consumption of sweet and savoury, high and low fat snack foods were also measured after the experiments. There were no differences in the number of non-food adverts recognized by the lean and obese children, but the obese children recognized significantly more of the food adverts. The ability to recognize the food adverts also correlated with the amount of food eaten after exposure to them. The overall snack food intake of the obese and overweight children was significantly higher than the lean children in the non-food advert (control) condition. The consumption of all the food increased post-food advert with the exception of the low-fat savoury snack. These findings show obese children have a heightened alertness to food-related cues, moreover, exposure to such cues increased food intake in all children. As already suggested, these data suggest the relationship between TV viewing and childhood obesity appears not merely to be a matter of excessive inactivity, but exposure to food adverts promotes consumption.

Living with the stigma of obesity

There is clear evidence of weight stigma and bias in multiple aspects of daily life for obese individuals. Multiple forms of weight stigmatization also occur in educational settings. Obese students face numerous obstacles, ranging from harassment and rejection from peers at school, to biased attitudes from teachers, lower college acceptances and wrongful dismissals from college. Negative perceptions of obese persons exist in employment settings where obese employees are viewed as less competent, lazy and lacking in self-discipline by their co-workers and employers. These attitudes can have a negative impact on wages, promotions and decisions about employment status for obese employees. Weight stigma also exists in healthcare settings. Negative attitudes about overweight patients have been reported by physicians, nurses, dietitians, psychologists, and medical students. Research shows that even healthcare professionals who specialize in the treatment of obesity hold negative attitudes.

Etiology of Eating Disorders

As with other disorders, a single factor is unlikely to cause an eating disorder. Several areas of current research—genetics, neurobiology, sociocultural pressures to be thin, personality, the role of the family, and the role of environmental stress—suggest that eating disorders result when several influences converge in a person's life.

Genetic Factors

Both anorexia nervosa and bulimia nervosa run in families. First-degree relatives of young women with anorexia nervosa are more than ten times more likely than average to have the disorder themselves (e.g., Strober et al., 2000). Similar results are found for bulimia nervosa, where first-degree relatives of women with bulimia nervosa are about four times more likely than average to have the disorder (e.g., Kassett et al., 1989; Strober et al., 2000). Furthermore, first-degree relatives of women with eating disorders appear to be at higher risk for anorexia or bulimia (Lilenfeld et al., 1998; Strober et al., 1990, 2000). Although eating disorders are quite rare among men, one study found that first-degree relatives of men with anorexia nervosa were at greater risk for having anorexia nervosa (though not bulimia) than relatives of men without anorexia (Strober et al., 2001). Finally, relatives of people with eating disorders are more likely than average to have symptoms of eating disorders that do not meet the complete criteria for a diagnosis (Lilenfeld et al., 1998; Strober et al., 2000).

Twin studies of eating disorders also suggest a genetic influence. Most studies of both anorexia and bulimia report higher MZ than DZ concordance rates (Bulik, Wade, & Kendler, 2000) and that genes account for a portion of the variance among twins with eating disorders (Wade et al., 2000). On the other hand, research has shown that nonshared/ unique environmental factors (see p. 31), like different interactions with parents or different peer groups, also contribute to the development of eating disorders (Klump, McGue, & Iacono, 2002). For example, a study of more than 1,200 twin pairs found that 42 percent of the variance in bulimia symptoms was attributable to genetic factors but 58 percent of the variance was attributable to unique environmental factors (Baker et al., 2010). Research also suggests that key features of the eating disorders, such as dissatisfaction with one's body, a strong desire to be thin, binge eating, and preoccupation with weight, are heritable (Klump, McGue, & Iacono, 2000). Additional evidence suggests that common genetic factors may account for the relationship between certain personality characteristics, such as negative emotionality and constraint, and eating disorders (Klump, McGue, & Iacono, 2002). The results of these studies are consistent with the possibility that genes play a role in eating disorders, but studies showing how genetic factors interact with the environment are needed.

Neurobiological Factors

The hypothalamus is a key brain center for regulating hunger and eating. Research on animals with lesions to the lateral hypothalamus indicates that they lose weight and have no appetite (Hoebel & Teitelbaum, 1966). Thus, it is not surprising that the hypothalamus has been proposed to play a role in anorexia. The level of some hormones regulated by the hypothalamus, such as cortisol, is indeed abnormal in people with anorexia. Rather than causing the disorder, however, these hormonal abnormalities occur as a result of self-starvation, and levels return to normal after weight gain (Doerr et al., 1980; Stoving et al., 1999). Furthermore, the weight loss of animals with hypothalamic lesions does not parallel what we know about anorexia. These animals appear to have no hunger and to become indifferent to food, whereas people with anorexia continue to starve themselves despite being hungry and having an interest in food. Nor does the hypothalamic model account for body-image disturbance or fear of becoming fat. A dysfunctional hypothalamus thus does not seem highly likely as a factor in anorexia nervosa.

Endogenous opioids are substances produced by the body that reduce pain sensations, enhance mood, and suppress appetite. Opioids are released during starvation and have been hypothesized to play a role in both anorexia and bulimia. Starvation among people with anorexia may increase the levels of endogenous opioids, resulting in a positively reinforcing euphoric state (Marrazzi & Luby, 1986). Furthermore, the excessive exercise seen among some people with eating disorders would increase opioids and thus be reinforcing (Davis, 1996; Epling & Pierce, 1992).

Some research supports the theory that endogenous opioids play a role in eating disorders, at least in bulimia. For example, two studies found low levels of the endogenous opioid beta-endorphin (see Figure 11.2) in people with bulimia (Brewerton et al., 1992; Waller et al., 1986). In one of these studies, the researchers observed that the people with more severe cases of bulimia had the lowest levels of beta-endorphin (Waller et al., 1986). It is important to note, however, that these findings demonstrate that low levels of opioids are seen concurrently with bulimia, not that such levels are seen before the onset of the disorder. In other words, we don't know if the low levels of opioids are a cause of bulimia or an effect of changes in food intake or purging.

Finally, some research has focused on neurotransmitters related to eating and satiety (feeling full). Animal research has shown that serotonin promotes satiety. Therefore, it could be that the binges of people with bulimia result from a serotonin deficit that causes them not to feel satiated as they eat. Animal research has also shown that food restriction interferes with serotonin synthesis in the brain. Thus, among people with anorexia, the severe food intake restrictions could interfere with the serotonin system.

Researchers have examined levels of serotonin metabolites among people with anorexia and bulimia. Several studies have reported low levels of serotonin metabolites among people with anorexia (e.g., Kaye et al., 1984) and bulimia (e.g., Carrasco et al., 2000; Jimerson et al., 1992; Kaye et al., 1998). Lower levels of a neurotransmitter's metabolites are one indicator that the neurotransmitter activity is underactive. In addition, people with anorexia who have not been restored to a healthy weight show a poorer response to serotonin agonists (i.e., drugs that stimulate serotonin receptors) than those people who have regained a good portion of their weight, again suggesting an underactive serotonin system (Attia et al., 1998; Ferguson et al., 1999). People with bulimia also show smaller responses to serotonin agonists (Jimerson et al., 1997; Levitan et al., 1997). The antidepressant drugs that are often effective treatments for anorexia and bulimia (discussed

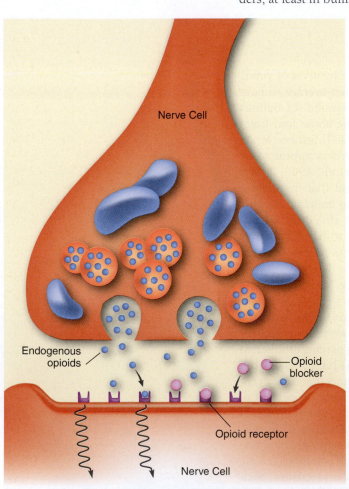

Figure 11.2 Endogenous opioid systems in the brain.

later) are known to increase serotonin activity, adding to the possible importance of serotonin. Serotonin, though, could also be linked to the comorbid depression often found in anorexia and bulimia.

More recently, researchers have examined the role of the neurotransmitter dopamine in eating behavior. Studies with animals have shown that dopamine is linked to the pleasurable aspects of food that compel an animal to go after food (e.g., Szczypka et al., 2001), and brain imaging studies in humans have shown how dopamine is linked to the motivation to obtain food and other pleasurable or rewarding things. In one study with healthy people, participants were presented with smells and tastes of food while undergoing a PET scan (Volkow et al., 2002). The participants also filled out a measure of dietary restraint (see Table 11.4). People who scored higher on dietary restraint exhibited greater dopamine activity in the dorsal striatum area of the brain during the presentation of food. This finding suggests that restrained eaters may be more sensitive to food cues, since one of the functions of dopamine is to signal the salience of particular stimuli. Whether or not these findings will be relevant to people with eating disorders remains to be seen.

A small fMRI study of 14 women with anorexia nervosa and 14 women without an eating disorder found that women with anorexia reported feeling more positively about pictures of underweight women compared to pictures of normal or overweight women (Fladung et al., 2010). The women without anorexia felt more positively when viewing pictures of normal-weight women. Brain activation matched these ratings of feelings: women with anorexia showed greater activation in the ventral striatum, an area of the brain linked to dopamine and reward (see Chapter 5), than women without anorexia when viewing pictures of underweight women.

Another study found that women with either anorexia nervosa or bulimia nervosa had greater expression of the dopamine transporter gene DAT (Frieling et al., 2010). Recall from Chapter 2 that a gene is "turned on," or expressed, as it interacts with different aspects of the environment. The expression of DAT influences the release of a protein that regulates the reuptake of dopamine back into the synapse. This study also found that women with either eating disorder exhibited less expression of another dopamine gene called DRD_2. Other studies have found disturbances in the DRD_2 gene only among women with anorexia (Bergen et al., 2005). These findings point to the role of dopamine in eating disorders and will need to be replicated in future studies.

Though we can expect further neurotransmitter research in the future, keep in mind that much of this work focuses on brain mechanisms relevant to hunger, eating, and satiety but does little to account for other key features of both disorders, in particular the intense fear of

---

Table 11.4 The Restraint Scale

1. How often are you dieting? Never; rarely; sometimes; often; always.

2. What is the maximum amount of weight (in pounds) you have ever lost within 1 month? 0–4; 5–9; 10–14; 15–19; 20+.

3. What is your maximum weight gain within a week? 0–1; 1.1–2; 2.1–3; 3.1–5; 5.1+.

4. In a typical week, how much does your weight fluctuate? 0–1; 1.1–2; 2.1–3; 3.1–5; 5.1+.

5. Would a weight fluctuation of 5 pounds affect the way you live your life? Not at all; slightly; moderately; very much.

6. Do you eat sensibly in front of others and splurge alone? Never; rarely; often; always.

7. Do you give too much time and thought to food? Never; rarely; often; always.

8. Do you have feelings of guilt after overeating? Never; rarely; often; always.

9. How conscious are you of what you are eating? Not at all; slightly; moderately; extremely.

10. How many pounds over your desired weight were you at your maximum weight? 0–1; 1–5; 6–10; 11–20; 21+.

Source: From Polivy, Herman, & Howard (1980).

becoming fat. Furthermore, as suggested, the evidence so far does not show that brain changes predate the onset of eating disorders. Thus, we know that brain activity or gene expression of certain dopamine genes is correlated with eating disorders, not that these things cause eating disorders.

Cognitive Behavioral Factors

Cognitive behavioral theories of eating disorders focus on understanding the thoughts, feelings, and behaviors that contribute to distorted body image, fear of fat, and loss of control over eating. People with eating disorders may have maladaptive schemata that narrow their attention toward thoughts and images related to weight, body shape, and food (Fairburn, Shafran, & Cooper, 1999).

The fear of being fat, which is so important in eating disorders, is partly based on society's negative stereotypes about overweight people. (SERGIO MORAES/Reuters/Landov LLC.)

Anorexia Nervosa Cognitive behavioral theories of anorexia nervosa emphasize fear of fatness and body-image disturbance as the motivating factors that powerfully reinforce weight loss. Many who develop anorexia symptoms report that the onset followed a period of weight loss and dieting. Behaviors that achieve or maintain thinness are negatively reinforced by the reduction of anxiety about becoming fat. Furthermore, dieting and weight loss may be positively reinforced by the sense of mastery or self-control they create (Fairburn et al., 1999; Garner, Vitousek, & Pike, 1997). Some theories also include personality and sociocultural variables in an attempt to explain how fear of fatness and body-image disturbances develop. For example, perfectionism and a sense of personal inadequacy may lead a person to become especially concerned with his or her appearance, making dieting a potent reinforcer. Similarly, seeing portrayals in the media of thinness as an ideal, being overweight, and tending to compare oneself with especially attractive others all contribute to dissatisfaction with one's body (Stormer & Thompson, 1996).

Another important factor in producing a strong drive for thinness and a disturbed body image is criticism from peers and parents about being overweight (Paxton et al., 1999). In one study supporting this conclusion, adolescent girls aged 10 to 15 were evaluated twice, with a 3-year interval between assessments. Obesity at the first assessment was related to being teased by peers and at the second assessment was linked to dissatisfaction with their bodies. Dissatisfaction was in turn related to symptoms of an eating disorder.

It is known that bingeing frequently results when diets are broken (Polivy & Herman, 1985). Thus, when a lapse occurs in the strict dieting of a person with anorexia nervosa, the lapse is likely to escalate into a binge. The purging after an episode of binge eating can again be seen as motivated by the fear of weight gain that the binge elicited. People with anorexia who do not have episodes of bingeing and purging may have a more intense preoccupation with and fear of weight gain (Schlundt & Johnson, 1990) or may be more able to exercise self-control.

Bulimia Nervosa and Binge Eating Disorder People with bulimia nervosa are also thought to be overconcerned with weight gain and body appearance; indeed, they judge their self-worth mainly by their weight and shape. They also have low self-esteem, and because weight and shape are somewhat more controllable than are other features of the self, they tend to focus on weight and shape, hoping their efforts in this area will make them feel better generally. They try to follow a pattern of restrictive eating that is very rigid, with strict rules

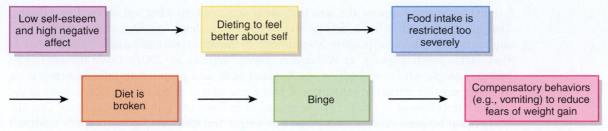

Figure 11.3 Schematic of cognitive behavioral theory of bulimia nervosa.

regarding how much to eat, what kinds of food to eat, and when to eat. These strict rules are inevitably broken, and the lapse escalates into a binge. After the binge, feelings of disgust and fear of becoming fat build up, leading to compensatory actions such as vomiting (Fairburn, 1997). Although purging temporarily reduces the anxiety from having eaten too much, this cycle lowers the person's self-esteem, which triggers still more bingeing and purging, a vicious circle that maintains desired body weight but has serious medical consequences (see Figure 11.3 for a summary of this theory).

One group of researchers developed the Restraint Scale (see Table 11.4), a questionnaire measure of concerns about dieting and overeating (Polivy et al., 1980). These researchers have conducted a series of laboratory studies on people with high scores on this measure. These studies are generally conducted under the guise of being taste tests. One such study was described as an assessment of the effects of temperature on taste (Polivy, Heatherton, & Herman, 1988). To achieve a "cold" condition, some participants first drank a 15-ounce chocolate milk shake (termed a *preload* by the investigators) and were then given three bowls of ice cream to taste and rate for flavor. Participants were told that once they had completed their ratings, they could eat as much of the ice cream as they wanted. The researchers then measured the amount of ice cream eaten.

In laboratory studies following this general design, people who scored high on the Restraint Scale ate more than nondieters after a fattening preload, even when the preload was perceived as fattening but was actually low in calories (e.g., Polivy, 1976) and even when the food was relatively unpalatable (Polivy, Herman, & McFarlane, 1994). Thus, people who score high on the Restraint Scale show a pattern similar to that of people with bulimia nervosa, albeit at a much less intense level.

Several additional conditions have been found to further increase the eating of restrained eaters after a preload, most notably various negative mood states, such as anxiety and depression (e.g., Herman et al., 1987). The increased consumption of restrained eaters is especially pronounced when their self-image is threatened (Heatherton, Herman, & Polivy, 1991) and if they have low self-esteem (Polivy et al., 1988). Finally, when restrained eaters are given false feedback indicating that their weight is high, they respond with increases in negative emotion and increased food consumption (McFarlane, Polivy, & Herman, 1998).

The eating pattern of people with bulimia or binge eating disorder is similar to, but more extreme than, the behavior highlighted in the studies of restrained eaters. People with bulimia nervosa or binge eating disorder typically binge when they encounter stress and experience negative affect, as has been shown in several studies. In ecological momentary assessment (EMA; see Chapter 3 p. 91), the investigators are able to show how specific binge-and-purge events are linked to changes in emotions and stress in the course of daily life (Smyth et al., 2007). A meta-analysis of 82 EMA studies found that negative affect preceded the onset of a binge among people with bulimia or binge eating disorder, but the effect sizes (see p. 127) were stronger for binge eating disorder (Haedt-Matt & Keel, 2011). The binge may therefore function as a means of regulating negative affect (Smyth et al., 2007; Stice & Agras, 1999). However, the meta-analysis of EMA studies also showed that people with bulimia or binge eating disorder experienced *more* negative affect after the binge, so the use of bingeing as a way to regulate affect appears not to be very successful.

Evidence also supports the idea that stress and negative affect are relieved by purging. That is, negative affect levels decline and positive affect levels increase after a purge event, supporting the idea that purging is reinforced by negative affect reduction (Haedt-Matt & Keel, 2011; Jarrell, Johnson, & Williamson, 1986; Smyth et al., 2007). Given the similarities between people who score high on the Restraint Scale and people with bulimia nervosa, we might expect that restrained eating would play a central role in bulimia. In fact, a study of the naturalistic course of bulimia (i.e., the course of bulimia left untreated) has found that the relationship between concern over shape and weight and binge eating was partially mediated by restrained eating (Fairburn et al., 2003). In other words, concerns about body shape and weight predicted restrained eating, which in turn predicted an increase in binge eating across 5 years of follow-up assessments. Other studies have failed to find this relationship (Burne & McLean, 2002), however, and thus additional research will need to sort out the ways in which restraint is linked with the symptoms of bulimia.

Research methods from cognitive science have been used to study how attention, memory, and problem solving are impacted in people with eating disorders. Using cognitive tasks such as the Stroop task (see p. 46 in Chapter 2) and the dot probe test, research shows that people with anorexia and bulimia focus their attention on food-related words or images more than other images (Brooks et al., 2011). People with anorexia nervosa and people who score high on restrained eating remember food words better when they are full but not when they are hungry (Brooks et al., 2011). Other studies have found that college women with eating disorder symptoms pay attention to and better remember images depicting other people's body size more than images depicting emotion (Treat & Viken, 2010). Thus, women with eating disorders pay greater attention not only to their own bodies, food, and weight but also to other women's bodies, food, and shapes. This bias toward food and body image may make it harder for women with eating disorders to change their thinking patterns. As we shall see later, cognitive behavior therapy devotes a good bit of time to teaching people with eating disorders to alter these memory and attention biases.

Sociocultural factors appear to play a role in the faulty perceptions and eating habits of those with eating disorders. We turn to these influences next.

Quick Summary

Genetic factors appear to play a role in both anorexia and bulimia. Both disorders tend to run in families, and twin studies support the role of genetics in the actual disorders and particular characteristics of the disorders, such as body dissatisfaction, preoccupation with thinness, and binge eating. The hypothalamus does not appear to be directly involved in eating disorders, and low levels of endogenous opioids are seen concurrently with bulimia, but not before the onset of the disorder. Thus, changes in food intake could affect the opioid system instead of changes in the opioid system affecting food intake. Research findings on the role of serotonin in anorexia are mixed. Serotonin may play a role in bulimia, with studies finding a decrease in serotonin metabolites and smaller responses to serotonin agonists. Newer research suggests dopamine may play a role in restrained eating, a characteristic that is found in people with eating disorders. The neurobiological factors do not do a particularly good

job of accounting for some key features of anorexia and bulimia, in particular the intense fear of becoming fat.

Cognitive behavioral theories focus on body dissatisfaction, preoccupation with thinness, and attention and memory. The Restraint Scale measures concerns about dieting and overeating, and high scores are linked to binge eating among people without eating disorders. The eating pattern of people with bulimia and binge eating disorder is similar to, but more extreme than, the behavior highlighted in the studies of restrained eaters. Studies have found that concerns about body shape and weight predicted restrained eating, which in turn predicted an increase in binge eating. People with eating disorders pay greater attention to food and body-image-related things, and they tend to remember these better as well, suggesting that their attention and memory may be biased toward food and body image.

Sociocultural Factors

Throughout history, the standards societies have set for the ideal body—especially the ideal female body—have varied greatly. Think of the famous nudes painted by Rubens in the seventeenth century: according to modern standards, these women are chubby. Over the past 50 years, the American cultural ideal has progressed steadily toward increasing thinness. *Playboy* centerfolds became thinner between 1959 and 1978, for example (Garner et al., 1980), and beauty pageant contestants also became thinner through 1988. A study that calculated the body mass index (BMI) of *Playboy* centerfolds from 1985 to 1997 (Owen & Laurel-Seller, 2000) found that all but one of the centerfolds had a BMI of less than 20, which is considered to be a low weight, and almost half of the centerfolds had a BMI of less than 18, which is considered to be underweight.

For men, the situation appears somewhat different. In a study parallel to the studies examining *Playboy* centerfolds, researchers analyzed the BMI of *Playgirl* male centerfolds from 1973 to 1997 (Leit, Pope, & Gray, 2001). They found that the centerfolds' BMI *increased* over the period and that their muscularity, assessed using a fat-to-muscle estimate, increased even more. Thus for men, magazines focus attention on the masculine ideal of normal body weight or on increased muscle mass (Mishkind et al., 1986).

Somewhat paradoxically, as cultural standards were moving in the direction of thinness over the later part of the twentieth century, more and more people were becoming overweight. The prevalence of obesity has doubled since 1900 (see Focus on Discovery 11.1). Currently, over two-thirds of Americans are overweight (and over a third are obese), setting the stage for greater conflict between the cultural ideal and reality.

As society has become more health and fat conscious, dieting to lose weight has become more common; the number of dieters increased from 7 percent of men and 14 percent of women in 1950 to 29 percent of men and 44 percent of women in 1999 (Serdula et al., 1999). The focus on cutting carbohydrates, so widespread during the past few years, added yet another craze to dieting. For example, the sale of low-carb foods yielded nearly $30 billion in 2004; more than 1,500 new low-carb foods were introduced in a 2-year period; the number of low-carb diet books increased from 15

Cultural standards regarding the ideal feminine shape have changed over time. Even in the 1950s and 1960s, the feminine ideal was considerably heavier than what it has become in the 1970s through today.
(Top: ©SuperStock/SuperStock; Left: Photo by Lambert/Getty Images, Inc.; Right: Photo by Frazer Harrison/Getty Images for Mercedes-Benz Fashion Week/Getty Images, Inc.)

to 194 between 1999 and 2004; and 26 million people in the United States were on a diet that severely limited carbohydrate consumption in 2004 (Kadlic et al., 2004). Like many diet fads, the low-carb craze has quieted since 2004. In fact, a 2009 study in the *New England Journal of Medicine* reported that diets were equally effective, whether carbs, fat, or protein is cut, as long as the total number of calories is reduced (Sacks et al., 2009). Surgeries such as liposuction (vacuuming out fat deposits just under the skin) and gastroplasty (surgically changing the stomach so it cannot digest as much food) are becoming more common despite their risk (Brownell & Horgen, 2003).

The percentages above indicate that women are more likely than men to be dieters. The onset of eating disorders is typically preceded by dieting and other concerns about weight, supporting the idea that social standards stressing the importance of thinness play a role in the development of these disorders (Killen et al., 1994; Rubinstein et al., 2010; Stice, 2001).

It is likely that women who either are actually overweight or fear being fat are also dissatisfied with their bodies. Not surprisingly, studies have found that people with both a high BMI and body dissatisfaction are at higher risk for developing eating disorders (Fairburn et al., 1997; Killen et al., 1996). Body dissatisfaction is also a robust predictor of the development of eating disorders among adolescent girls (Killen et al., 1996). In addition, preoccupation with

Al Roker, the weatherperson on NBC's *Today Show*, had gastric bypass surgery to accomplish weight loss. (Evan Agostini/Getty Images News and Sport Services.)

Celebrities such as Christina Ricci have publicly discussed their struggles with eating disorders. (Allstar Picture Library/Alamy.)

being thin or feeling pressure to be thin predicts an increase in body dissatisfaction among adolescent girls, which in turn predicts more dieting and negative emotions. Preoccupation with thinness and body dissatisfaction both predict greater eating disorder pathology (Stice, 2001), and these factors were operating in the case of Harriet, presented earlier. Finally, exposure to media portrayals of unrealistically thin models can influence reports of body dissatisfaction. One study reviewed results from 25 experiments that presented images of thin models to women and then asked the women to report on their body satisfaction. Perhaps not surprisingly, results from these studies showed that women reported a decline in body satisfaction after viewing these images (Groesz, Levine, & Murnen, 2002). Another study found that men's body dissatisfaction, as indexed by a greater discrepancy between the muscularity of the actual and ideal self, increased after viewing images of muscular men (Leit, Gray, & Pope, 2002).

The sociocultural ideal of thinness is a likely vehicle through which people learn to fear being or even feeling fat. In addition to creating an undesired physical shape, being fat has negative connotations, such as being unsuccessful and having little self-control. Obese people are viewed by others as less smart and are stereotyped as lonely, shy, and greedy for the affection of others (DeJong & Kleck, 1986). Even more disturbing, health professionals who specialize in obesity have also exhibited beliefs that obese people are lazy, stupid, or worthless (Schwartz et al., 2003). Reducing the stigma associated with being overweight will be beneficial to those with eating disorders as well as those who are obese.

Not only does the fear of being fat contribute to eating pathology, but more recently the celebration of extreme thinness via websites, blogs, and magazines may also play a role. Websites that are "pro-ana" (short for anorexia) or "pro-mia" (short for bulimia) and other "thinsperation" websites and blogs have developed a following of women who seek support and encouragement for losing weight, often to a dangerously low level. These sites often post photos of female celebrities who are extremely thin as inspiration (hence, the term *thinsperation*). Some of these women have publicly discussed their struggles with eating disorders (e.g., the actress Christina Ricci), but others have not.

A recent review of the impact of these "pro–eating disorder" websites noted that the evidence suggests that women who visited these sites were more dissatisfied with their bodies, had more eating disorder symptoms, and had more prior hospitalizations for eating disorders (Rouleau & von Ranson, 2011). To tease apart causation from correlation, researchers have randomly assigned healthy women to view either pro–eating disorder or other health-related or tourist websites (Jett, La Perte, & Wanchism, 2010), supposedly as part of a website evaluation survey. Women completed food diaries for one week before and one week after viewing these websites. Women assigned to the pro–eating disorder website condition restricted their eating more the following week than did the women assigned to the other website conditions. These results suggest that viewing these websites has the potential to cause unhealthful changes in eating behavior.

Gender Influences We have discussed the fact that eating disorders are more common in women than in men. One primary reason for the greater prevalence of eating disorders among women is likely due to the fact that Western cultural standards about thinness have changed over the past 50 years, today reinforcing the desirability of being thin for women more than for men.

Another sociocultural factor, though, has remained remarkably resilient to change—namely, the objectification of women's bodies. Women's bodies are often viewed through a sexual lens; in effect, women are defined by their bodies, whereas men are esteemed more for their accomplishments. According to objectification theory (Fredrickson & Roberts, 1997), the prevalence of objectification messages in Western culture (in television, advertisements, and so forth) has led some women to "self-objectify," which means that they see their own bodies through the eyes of others. Research has shown that self-objectification causes women to feel more shame about their bodies. Shame is most often elicited in situations where an individual's ideal falls short of a cultural ideal or standard. Thus, women likely experience body shame when they observe a mismatch between their ideal self and the cultural (objectified) view of women. Research has also shown that both self-objectification and body shame are associated with disordered eating (Fredrickson et al., 1998; McKinley & Hyde, 1996; Noll & Fredrickson, 1998). The risk for eating disorders among groups of women who might be expected to be particularly concerned with their weight—for example, models, dancers, and gymnasts—appears to be especially high (Garner et al., 1980).

Do eating disorders and weight concerns go away as women get older? A large, 20-year prospective study of over 600 men and women reported important differences in dieting and other eating disorder risk factors for men and women (Keel et al., 2007). The men and women were first surveyed about dieting, BMI, weight, body image, and eating disorder symptoms when they were in college. Follow-up surveys were completed 10 and 20 years after college. Thus, the men and women were around age 40 at the 20-year follow-up assessment. The researchers found that after 20 years, women dieted less and were less concerned about their weight and body image compared to when they were in college, even though they actually weighed more. In addition, eating disorder symptoms decreased over the 20 years for women, as did the risk factors for eating disorders (concern about body image frequency of dieting). Changes in life roles—having a life partner, having a child—were also associated with decreases in eating disorder symptoms for women. By contrast, men were more concerned about their weight and were dieting more. Like women, they weighed more in their early forties than when they were in college. Decreases in risk factors such as concern about body image and dieting frequency were also associated with decreases in eating disorder symptoms for men.

Cross-Cultural Studies Evidence for eating disorders across cultures depends on the disorder. Anorexia has been observed in a number of cultures and countries besides the United States; for example, in Hong Kong, China, Taiwan, England, Korea, Japan, Denmark, Nigeria, South Africa, Zimbabwe, Ethiopia, Iran, Malaysia, India, Pakistan, Australia, the Netherlands, and Egypt (Keel & Klump, 2003). Furthermore, cases of anorexia have been documented in cultures with very little Western cultural influence. An important caveat must be made, however. The anorexia observed in these diverse cultures does not always include the intense fear of gaining weight or being fat that is part of the DSM criteria, at least initially. Thus, intense fear of fat likely reflects an ideal more widely espoused in more Westernized cultures. For example, Lee (1991) described a disorder similar to anorexia nervosa in Hong Kong that involved severe emaciation, food refusal, and amenorrhea, but not a fear of becoming fat. Is this a cultural variant of anorexia or a different disorder, such as depression? This question is but one of the challenges that face cross-cultural researchers (Lee et al., 2001). Indeed, in some other cultures, higher weight among women is especially valued and considered a sign of fertility and healthiness (Nasser, 1988). The variation in the clinical presentation of anorexia across cultures provides a window into the importance of culture in establishing realistic versus potentially disordered views of one's body. However, there is also evidence that cultural variation is diminishing when it comes to eating disorders. A 20-year study of eating disorders in Hong Kong found evidence of Western influence in both the prevalence and presentation of eating disorders (Lee et al., 2010). First, both anorexia and bulimia were twice as common in 2007 than they were in 1987. Second, 25 percent more women reported body dissatisfaction and fear of fat in 2007 than in 1987. Thus, in a fairly short period of time, eating disorders in Hong Kong appear to have become more Western.

Another feature of eating disorders that may be heavily influenced by Western ideals of beauty and thinness is body image. In a study supporting the notion of cross-cultural differences in body-image perception, Ugandan and British college students rated the attractiveness of drawings of nudes ranging from very emaciated to very obese (Furnham & Baguma, 1994). Ugandan students rated the obese females as more attractive than did the British students.

Bulimia nervosa appears to be more common in industrialized societies, such as the United States, Canada, Japan, Australia, and Europe, than in nonindustrialized nations. However, as cultures undergo social changes associated with adopting the practices of more Westernized cultures, particularly the United States (Watters, 2010), the incidence of bulimia appears to increase (Abou-Saleh, Younis, & Karim, 1998; Lee et al., 2010; Nasser, 1997). A comprehensive review of research on culture and eating disorders conducted nearly 10 years ago could not find evidence of bulimia outside of a Westernized culture (Keel & Klump, 2003). It will be interesting to see if this changes in the next 10 years.

Jessica Alba has spoken openly about her eating disorder. (FilmMagic/Getty Images, Inc.)

Ethnic Differences In the United States, it was reported at one time that the incidence of anorexia was eight times greater in white women than in women of color (Dolan, 1991). More recent studies do not support this contention. Indeed there is a somewhat greater incidence of eating disturbances and body dissatisfaction among white women than black women (Grabe & Hyde, 2006; Perez & Joiner, 2003), but differences in actual eating disorders, particularly bulimia, do not appear to be as great (Wildes, Emery, & Simons, 2001). In addition, the greatest differences between white and black women in eating disorder pathology appear to be most pronounced in college student samples; fewer differences are observed in either high school or nonclinical community samples (Wildes et al., 2001). Finally, a meta-analysis found more similarities than differences in body dissatisfaction among ethnic groups in the United States (Grabe & Hyde, 2006). White women and Hispanic women reported greater body dissatisfaction than African American women, but no other ethnic differences were reliably found.

Differences have been observed in the United States in some areas, however. Studies show that white teenage girls diet more frequently than do African American teenage girls and are more likely to be dissatisfied with their bodies (Fitzgibbons et al., 1998; Striegel-Moore et al., 2000). The relationship between BMI and body dissatisfaction also differs by ethnicity. Compared with African American adolescents, white adolescents become more dissatisfied with their bodies as their BMI rises (Striegel-Moore et al., 2000). As already noted, both dieting and body dissatisfaction are related to an increased risk for developing an eating disorder. Indeed, one study found that white women with binge eating disorder were more dissatisfied with their bodies than African American women with binge eating disorder, and the white women were more likely to have a history of bulimia nervosa than the African American women (Pike et al., 2001).

Socioeconomic status is also important to consider (Caldwell, Brownell, & Wilfley, 1997; French et al., 1997). The emphasis on thinness and dieting has spread beyond white women of upper and middle socioeconomic status to women of lower socioeconomic status, as has the prevalence of eating disorder pathology (e.g., Story et al., 1995; Striegel-Moore et al., 2000). In addition, acculturation, the extent to which someone assimilates their own culture with a new culture, may be another important variable to consider. This process can at times be quite stressful. A recent study found that the relationship between body dissatisfaction and bulimia symptoms was stronger for African American and Hispanic college students who reported higher levels of acculturative stress compared to those students who reported lower levels of this type of stress (Perez et al., 2002).

Finally, very little is known about the prevalence of eating disorders among Latina or Native American women, and this remains a much-needed research focus. Data from a recent epidemiological study of Latina women age 18 or older found that binge eating disorder was more prevalent than bulimia nervosa but that the prevalence rates for both disorders were comparable to prevalence rates in Caucasian women (Alegria et al., 2007). The diagnosis of bulimia was more likely for women who had lived in the United States for several years than for women who had recently immigrated, indicating that acculturation may play a role. In contrast to other eating disorders, anorexia nervosa was very rare among Latina women (only 2 out of over 2,500 women had a lifetime history of anorexia).

Beyond the study of racial or ethnic differences in eating disorders, attention should also be paid to stereotyped beliefs about race and eating disorders. One study found that college students who read a fictional case study about a woman with eating disorder symptoms were more likely to ascribe an eating disorder to the woman if her race was presented as Caucasian rather than African American or Hispanic (Gordon, Perez, & Joiner, 2002). In other words, the symptoms were rated as clinically significant only for the white case presentation, not for the African American or Hispanic ones, even though the details were identical. Although it remains to be seen whether mental health

Standards of beauty vary cross-culturally, as shown by Gaugain's painting of Tahitian women. (Musée d'Orsay, Paris/Lauris-Giraudon, Paris/SUPERSTOCK.)

professionals would also exhibit the same stereotypes when making clinical judgments, it suggests that symptoms may be more easily overlooked among non-Caucasian women.

Other Factors Contributing to the Etiology of Eating Disorders

Personality Influences   We have already seen that neurobiological changes occur as a result of an eating disorder. It is also important to keep in mind that an eating disorder itself can affect personality. A study of semistarvation in male conscientious objectors conducted in the late 1940s supports the idea that the personality of people with eating disorders, particularly those with anorexia, is affected by their weight loss (Keys et al., 1950). For a period of 6 weeks, the men were given two meals a day, totaling 1,500 calories, to simulate the meals in a concentration camp. On average, the men lost 25 percent of their body weight. They all soon became preoccupied with food; they also reported increased fatigue, poor concentration, lack of sexual interest, irritability, moodiness, and insomnia. Four became depressed, and one developed bipolar disorder. This research shows vividly how severe restriction of food intake can have powerful effects on personality and behavior, which we need to consider when evaluating the personalities of people with anorexia and bulimia.

In part as a response to the findings just mentioned, some researchers have collected retrospective reports of personality before the onset of an eating disorder. This research describes people with anorexia as having been perfectionistic, shy, and compliant before the onset of the disorder. The description of people with bulimia includes the additional characteristics of histrionic features, affective instability, and an outgoing social disposition (Vitousek & Manke, 1994). It is important to remember, however, that retrospective reports in which people with an eating disorder and their families recall what the person was like before diagnosis can be inaccurate and biased by awareness of the person's current problem.

Prospective studies examine personality characteristics before an eating disorder is present. In one study, more than 2,000 students in a suburban Minneapolis school district completed a variety of tests for 3 consecutive years. Among the measures were assessments of personality characteristics as well as an index of the risk for developing an eating disorder based on the Eating Disorders Inventory. During year 1 of the study, cross-sectional predictors of disordered eating included body dissatisfaction; poor interoceptive awareness, which is the extent to which people can distinguish different biological states of their bodies (see Table 11.2 for items that assess interoceptive awareness); and a propensity to experience negative emotions (Leon et al., 1995). At year 3, these same variables were found to have prospectively predicted disordered eating (Leon et al., 1999). An additional study found that perfectionism prospectively predicted the onset of anorexia in young adult women (Tyrka et al., 2002).

Additional research has taken a closer look at the link between perfectionism and anorexia. Perfectionism is multifaceted and may be self-oriented (setting high standards for oneself), other-oriented (setting high standards for others), or socially oriented (trying to conform to the high standards imposed by others). A recent review of many studies concludes that perfectionism, no matter how it is measured, is higher among girls with anorexia than girls without anorexia and that perfectionism remains high even after successful treatment for anorexia (Bardone-Cone et al., 2007). A multinational study found that people with anorexia scored higher on self- and other-oriented types of perfectionism than people without anorexia (Halmi et al., 2000). Finally, mothers of girls with anorexia scored higher on perfectionism than mothers of girls without anorexia (Woodside et al., 2002). This intriguing finding needs to be replicated, but it suggests that what is genetically transmitted in anorexia could be a personality characteristic, such as perfectionism, that increases the vulnerability for the disorder rather than the disorder per se.

Characteristics of Families   Studies of the characteristics of families of people with eating disorders have yielded variable results. Some of the variation stems, in part, from the different methods used to collect the data and from the sources of the information. For example, self-reports of people with eating disorders consistently

Severe food restriction can have profound effects on behavior and personality, as illustrated by the Keys study. (Wallace Kirkland/Time & Life Pictures/Getty Images, Inc.)

People with eating disorders consistently report that their family life was high in conflict. (Penny Tweedie/Stone/Getty Images.)

reveal high levels of conflict in the family (e.g., Bulik, Sullivan, et al., 2000; Hodges, Cochrane, & Brewerton, 1998). Reports of parents, however, do not necessarily indicate high levels of family problems.

Family characteristics may contribute to the risk for developing an eating disorder; however, eating disorders also likely have an impact on family functioning. One study assessed both people with eating disorders and their parents on tests designed to measure rigidity, closeness, emotional overinvolvement, critical comments, and hostility (Dare et al., 1994). The families showed considerable variation in whether parents were overinvolved with their children; the families were also quite low in conflict (low levels of criticism and hostility). A family study in which assessments were conducted before and after treatment of the patient found that ratings of family functioning improved after treatment (Woodside et al., 1995). Finally, one study examined identical twins discordant for bulimia (i.e., one twin had the disorder; the other didn't). The twin who developed bulimia reported greater family discord than the twin who did not develop the disorder. Because these studies rely on retrospective self-reports, it remains unclear whether the family discord was a contributory factor or consequence of the eating disorder.

To better understand the role of family functioning, it will be necessary to study these families directly by observational measures rather than by self-reports alone. Although an adolescent's perception of his or her family's characteristics is important, we also need to know how much of reported family discord is perceived and how much is consistent with others' perceptions. In one of the few observational studies conducted thus far, parents of children with eating disorders did not appear to be very different from control parents. The two groups did not differ in the frequency of positive and negative messages given to their children, and the parents of children with eating disorders were more self-disclosing than were the controls. The parents of children with eating disorders did lack some communication skills, however, such as the ability to request clarification of vague statements (van den Broucke, Vandereycken, & Vertommen, 1995). Observational studies such as this, coupled with data on perceived family characteristics, would help determine whether actual or perceived family characteristics are related to eating disorders.

Child Abuse and Eating Disorders   Some studies have indicated that self-reports of childhood sexual abuse are higher among people with eating disorders than among people without eating disorders, especially those with bulimia nervosa (Deep et al., 1999; Webster & Palmer, 2000). Since, as discussed in Chapter 8, some research indicates that memories of abuse may be created in therapy, it is notable that high rates of sexual abuse have been found among people with eating disorders who have not been in treatment as well as those who have (Romans et al., 2001; Wonderlich et al., 1996, 2001). Still, the role of childhood sexual abuse in the etiology of eating disorders remains uncertain. Furthermore, high rates of childhood sexual abuse are found among people with different diagnoses, so if it plays some role, it may not be highly specific to eating disorders (Fairburn, Cooper, et al., 1999; Romans et al., 2001).

Research has also found higher rates of childhood physical abuse among people with eating disorders. These data suggest that future studies should focus on a broad range of abusive experiences. Furthermore, it has been suggested that the presence or absence of abuse may be too general a variable. Abuse at a very early age, involving force and by a family member, may bear a stronger relationship to eating disorders than abuse of any other type (Everill & Waller, 1995).

Quick Summary

Sociocultural factors, including society's preoccupation with thinness, may play a role in eating disorders. This preoccupation is linked to dieting efforts, and dieting precedes the development of eating disorders among many people. In addition, the preoccupation with thinness, as well as media portrayals of thin models, predicts an increase in body dissatisfaction, which also precedes the development of eating disorders. Stigma associated with being overweight also contributes. Women are more likely to have eating disorders than men, and the ways in which women's bodies are objectified may lead some women to see their bodies as others do (self-objectify), which in turn may increase body dissatisfaction and eating pathology. Anorexia appears to occur in many cultures; bulimia appears to be more common in industrialized and Westernized societies. Eating disorders are slightly more common among white women than women of color, with the difference being most pronounced in college student samples. Eating disorders used to be more common among women of higher socioeconomic status, but this is less true today.

Research on personality characteristics finds that perfectionism may play a role. Other personality characteristics that predicted disordered eating across 3 years include body dissatisfaction, the extent to which people can distinguish different biological states of their bodies, and a propensity to experience negative emotions. Troubled family relationships are fairly common among people with eating disorders, but this could be a result of the eating disorder, not necessarily a cause of it. High rates of sexual and physical abuse are found among people with eating disorders, but these are not risk factors specific to the development of eating disorders.

Check Your Knowledge 11.2

True or false?
1. The brain structure linked to the cause of eating disorders is the hypothalamus.
2. Prospective studies of personality and eating disorders indicate that the tendency to experience negative emotions is related to disordered eating.
3. Anorexia appears to be specific to Western culture; bulimia is seen all over the world and is thus not culture specific.
4. Child abuse appears to be a specific causal factor for eating disorders.
5. Cognitive behavioral views of bulimia suggest that women judge their self-worth by their weight and shape.

Treatment of Eating Disorders

Hospitalization is frequently required to treat people with anorexia so that their ingestion of food can be gradually increased and carefully monitored. Weight loss can be so severe that intravenous feeding is necessary to save the person's life. The medical complications of anorexia, such as electrolyte imbalances, also require treatment. For both anorexia and bulimia, both medications and psychological treatments have been used.

Medications

Because bulimia nervosa is often comorbid with depression, it has been treated with various antidepressants, such as fluoxetine (Prozac). In one multicenter study, 387 women with bulimia were treated as outpatients for 8 weeks. Fluoxetine was shown to be superior to a placebo in reducing binge eating and vomiting; it also decreased depression and lessened distorted attitudes toward food and eating. Findings from most studies, including double-blind studies with placebo controls, confirm the efficacy of a variety of antidepressants in reducing purging and binge eating, even among people who had not responded to prior psychological treatment (Walsh et al., 2000; Wilson & Fairburn, 1998; Wilson & Pike, 2001).

On the negative side, many people with bulimia drop out of drug treatment (Fairburn, Agras, & Wilson, 1992). In the multicenter fluoxetine study cited, almost one-third of the women dropped out before the end of the 8-week treatment, primarily because of the side effects of the medication. In contrast, fewer than 5 percent of women dropped out of cognitive behavior therapy (Agras et al., 1992). Moreover, most people relapse when various kinds of antidepressant medication are withdrawn (Wilson & Pike, 2001), as is the case with many psychoactive drugs. There is some evidence that this tendency to relapse is reduced if antidepressants are given in the context of cognitive behavior therapy (Agras et al., 1994).

Medications have also been used to treat anorexia nervosa. Unfortunately, they have not been very successful in improving weight or other core features of anorexia (Attia et al., 1998; Johnson, Tsoh, & Varnado, 1996). Medication treatment for binge eating disorder has not been as well studied. Limited evidence suggests that antidepressant medications are not effective in reducing binges or weight loss (Grilo, 2007). Recent trials of antiobesity drugs, such as sibutramine and atomoxetine, show some promise in binge eating disorder, but additional clinical trials are needed.

Psychological Treatment of Anorexia Nervosa

Little in the way of controlled research exists on psychological treatments for anorexia nervosa, but we will present what appear to be the most promising of the psychotherapeutic approaches to this life-threatening disorder.

Therapy for anorexia is generally believed to be a two-tiered process. The immediate goal is to help the person gain weight in order to avoid medical complications and the possibility of death. The person is often so weak and physiological functioning so disturbed that hospital treatment is medically imperative (in addition to being needed to ensure that the patient ingests some food). Operant conditioning behavior therapy programs (e.g., providing reinforcers for weight gain) have been somewhat successful in achieving weight gain in the short term (Hsu, 1990). However, the second goal of treatment—long-term maintenance of weight gain—remains a challenge for the field.

Beyond immediate weight gain, psychological treatment for anorexia can also involve cognitive behavior therapy (CBT). One study that combined hospital treatment with CBT found that reductions in many anorexia symptoms persisted up to 1 year after treatment (Bowers & Ansher, 2008).

Family therapy is the principal form of psychological treatment for anorexia, based on the notion that interactions among members of the patient's family can play a role in treating the disorder (Le Grange & Lock, 2005). In one kind of family therapy, anorexia is cast as an interpersonal rather than an individual issue, and attempts are made to bring the family conflict to the fore. How is this accomplished? The therapist holds family lunch sessions, since conflicts related to anorexia are believed to be most evident at mealtime. These lunch sessions have three major goals:

Family therapy is a main form of treatment for anorexia nervosa. (Michael Newman/PhotoEdit.)

1. Changing the patient role of the person with anorexia

2. Redefining the eating problem as an interpersonal problem

3. Preventing the parents from using their child's anorexia as a means of avoiding conflict

One strategy is to instruct each parent to try individually to force the child to eat. The other parent may leave the room. The individual efforts are expected to fail. But because of this failure and frustration, the mother and father may now work together to persuade the child to eat. Thus, rather than being a focus of conflict, the child's eating will produce cooperation and increase parental effectiveness in dealing with the child (Rosman, Minuchin, & Liebman, 1975). One early study of 50 girls being treated for anorexia with this type of family therapy suggested that as many as 86 percent of the girls were still functioning well when assessed at times ranging from 3 months to 4 years after treatment (Rosman, Minuchin, & Liebman, 1976).

In a newer family-based therapy (FBT) developed in England, the focus is on helping parents work on restoring their daughter to a healthy weight while at the same time building up family functioning in the context of adolescent development (Lock & Le Grange, 2001; Lock et al., 2001; Loeb et al., 2007). A recent randomized controlled clinical trial compared FBT with individual therapy and found that both treatments were equally effective at the end of the 24-session treatment. However, more girls receiving FBT were in full remission (49 percent) 1 year after treatment than girls receiving individual therapy (23 percent) (Lock et al., 2011). Another study of FBT found that the girls who had gained weight by session 4 were more likely to be in full remission at the end of treatment (Doyle et al., 2010). Thus, early weight gain may be an important predictor of a good outcome. Although the findings are promising, additional work needs to be done to improve the outcomes for anorexia.

Psychological Treatment of Bulimia Nervosa

Cognitive behavior therapy (CBT) is the best-validated and most current standard for the treatment of bulimia (Fairburn, 1985; Fairburn et al., 2009; Fairburn, Marcus, & Wilson, 1993). In CBT, people with bulimia are encouraged to question society's standards for physical attractiveness. People with bulimia must also uncover and then change beliefs that encourage them to starve themselves to avoid becoming overweight. They must be helped to see that normal body weight can be maintained without severe dieting and that unrealistic restriction of food intake can often trigger a binge. They are taught that all is not lost with just one bite of high-calorie food and that snacking need not trigger a binge, which will be followed by induced vomiting or taking laxatives, which in turn will lead to still lower self-esteem and depression. Altering this all-or-nothing thinking can help people begin to eat more moderately. They also learn assertiveness skills, which help them cope with unreasonable demands placed on them by others, as well as more satisfying ways of relating to people.

The overall goal of treatment in bulimia nervosa is to develop normal eating patterns. People with bulimia need to learn to eat three meals a day and even some snacks between meals without sliding back into bingeing and purging. Regular meals control hunger and thereby, it is hoped, the urge to eat enormous amounts of food, the effects of which are counteracted by purging. To help people with bulimia develop less extreme beliefs about themselves, the cognitive behavior therapist gently but firmly challenges such irrational beliefs as "No one will respect me if I am a few pounds heavier than I am now" or "Eric loves me only because I weigh 112 pounds and would surely reject me if I ballooned to 120 pounds." A generalized assumption underlying these and related cognitions for women might be that a woman has value only if she is a few pounds underweight—a belief that is presented in the media and advertisements.

One intervention that is sometimes used in the cognitive behavioral treatment approach has the patient bring small amounts of forbidden food to eat in the session. Relaxation is employed to control the urge to induce vomiting. Unrealistic demands and other cognitive distortions—such as the belief that eating a small amount of high-calorie food means that the patient is an utter failure and doomed never to improve—are continually challenged. The therapist and patient work together to identify events, thoughts, and feelings that trigger an urge to binge and then to learn more adaptive ways to cope with these situations. In the case of Harriet, she and her therapist discovered that bingeing often took place after she was criticized by her parents. Therapy included the following:

- Encouraging Harriet to assert herself if the criticism is unwarranted
- Desensitizing her to social evaluation and encouraging her to question society's standards for ideal weight and the pressures on women to be thin—not an easy task by any means
- Teaching her that it is not a catastrophe to make a mistake and it is not necessary to be perfect, even if the parents' criticism is valid

The outcomes of cognitive behavioral therapies are rather promising, both in the short term and over time. A meta-analysis showed that CBT yielded better results than antidepressant drug treatments (Whittal, Agras, & Gould, 1999), and therapeutic gains were maintained at 1-year

Actress Mary-Kate Olsen has been treated for an eating disorder. (Peter Kramer/Getty Images News and Sport Services.)

follow-up (Agras et al., 2000), nearly 6 years later (Fairburn et al., 1995), and 10 years later (Keel et al., 2002). But there are limitations to these positive outcomes, as we will see.

Findings from a number of studies indicate that CBT often results in less frequent bingeing and purging, with reductions ranging from 70 to more than 90 percent. Extreme dietary restraint is also reduced significantly, and there is improvement in attitudes toward body shape and weight (Compas et al., 1998; Richards et al., 2000). However, if we focus on the people themselves rather than on numbers of binges and purges across people, we find that at least half of those treated with CBT improve very little (Wilson, 1995; Wilson & Pike, 1993). Clearly, while CBT may be the most effective treatment available for bulimia, it still has room for improvement.

Some studies have examined whether adding exposure and ritual prevention (ERP) to CBT for bulimia might boost the treatment effects of CBT (recall that ERP is an aspect of the cognitive behavioral treatment of obsessive-compulsive disorder in Chapter 6). This ERP component involves discouraging the person from purging after eating foods that usually elicit an urge to vomit. In one study, the combination of ERP and CBT was more effective than CBT without ERP, at least in the short term (e.g., Fairburn et al., 1995). ERP may not continue to be an advantage over the long term, however. One study examined outcome 3 years after treatment for people with bulimia who had received CBT either with or without ERP. It found similar outcomes for the two groups (Carter et al., 2003). That is, 85 percent of people with bulimia did not meet criteria for bulimia 3 years after treatment, regardless of which treatment they had received.

People with bulimia who are successful in overcoming their urge to binge and purge also improve in associated problem areas such as depression and low self-esteem. This result is not surprising. People who are able to achieve normal eating patterns after having viewed bulimia as an uncontrollable problem can be expected to feel less depressed and to feel generally better about themselves.

CBT alone is more effective than any available drug treatment (Compas et al., 1998; Walsh et al., 1997). But are outcomes better when antidepressant medication is added to CBT? Evidence on this front is mixed. Adding antidepressant drugs, however, may be useful in alleviating the depression that often occurs with bulimia (Keel et al., 2002; Wilson & Fairburn, 1998).

Another form of CBT, called guided self-help CBT, has also shown promise for some people. In this type of treatment, people receive self-help books on topics like perfectionism, body image, negative thinking, and food and health. Patients meet for a small number of sessions with a therapist who helps guide them through the self-help material. Preliminary results suggest that this is an effective treatment compared to a wait-list control group and to traditional CBT for bulimia. In addition, greater confidence in one's ability to change is associated with better outcomes (Steele, Bergin, & Wade, 2011).

In several other studies (Fairburn et al., 1991; Fairburn, Jones, et al., 1993), interpersonal therapy (IPT) fared well in comparisons with CBT, though it did not produce results as quickly. The two modes of intervention were equivalent at 1-year follow-up in effecting change across all four of the specific aspects of bulimia: binge eating, purging, dietary restraint, and maladaptive attitudes about body shape and weight (Wilson, 1995). This pattern—CBT superior to IPT immediately after treatment but IPT catching up at follow-up—was replicated in a later study (Agras et al., 2000).

Family therapy is also effective for bulimia, though it has been studied less frequently than either CBT or IPT. A recent randomized clinical trial demonstrated that family-based therapy was superior to supportive psychotherapy for adolescents with bulimia with respect to decreasing bingeing and purging up to 6 months after treatment was completed (Le Grange et al., 2007).

Psychological Treatment of Binge Eating Disorder

Although not as extensively studied as with bulimia nervosa, cognitive behavior therapy has been shown to be effective for binge eating disorder in several studies (Grilo, 2007). CBT for binge eating disorder targets binges as well as restrained eating by emphasizing self-monitoring, self-control, and problem solving as regards eating. Gains from CBT appear to last for up to 1 year after treatment. CBT also appears to be more effective than treatment with fluoxetine (Grilo, 2007). Randomized controlled clinical trial has shown that interpersonal therapy (IPT) is equally effective as CBT and guided self-help CBT for binge eating disorder (Wilfley et al., 2002; Wilson et al., 2010). These three treatments are more effective than behavioral weight-loss programs, which are often used to treat obesity. More specifically, CBT and IPT reduce binge eating (but not necessarily weight), whereas behavioral weight-loss programs may promote weight loss but do not curb binge eating.

One recent study compared three treatments for binge eating disorder: (1) therapist-led group CBT, (2) therapist-assisted group CBT, and (3) structured self-help group CBT with no therapist. Results showed that people in the therapist-led group CBT had the greatest reduction in binge eating at 6-month and 12-month follow-ups but that all groups had a greater reduction in binges than a group of people assigned to a wait-list control group (Peterson et al., 2009). Fewer people dropped out of the therapist-led group as well. Thus, having a therapist lead a CBT group may help keep people in treatment and help reduce binges, but, importantly, people in the therapist-assisted and "therapist-free" groups also showed reductions in binges. Given that therapist cost and/or availability may limit treatment for some people, having options such as these available is promising.

Quick Summary

Antidepressant medications have shown some benefit in the treatment of bulimia, but not anorexia. However, people with bulimia are more likely to discontinue the medication than to discontinue therapy. Psychological treatment of anorexia must first focus on weight gain. Family therapy is common for anorexia, but studies are needed to demonstrate whether this is effective. The most effective psychological treatment for bulimia is cognitive behavior therapy. CBT involves changing a patient's beliefs and thinking about thinness, being overweight, dieting, and restriction of food, with the overall goal being to reestablish normal eating patterns. CBT alone is more effective than medication treatment, though antidepressants can help lessen comorbid depression. CBT is also effective for binge eating disorder.

Preventive Interventions for Eating Disorders

A different approach to treating eating disorders involves prevention. Intervening with children or adolescents before the onset of eating disorders may help to prevent these disorders from ever developing. Broadly speaking, three different types of preventive interventions have been developed and implemented:

1. *Psychoeducational approaches.* The focus is on educating children and adolescents about eating disorders in order to prevent them from developing the symptoms.

2. *Deemphasizing sociocultural influences.* The focus here is on helping children and adolescents resist or reject sociocultural pressures to be thin.

3. *Risk factor approach.* The focus here is on identifying people with known risk factors for developing eating disorders (e.g., weight and body-image concern, dietary restraint) and intervening to alter these factors.

Stice, Shaw, and Marti (2007) conducted a meta-analysis of all such prevention studies conducted between 1980 and 2006, and they found modest support for some of these prevention approaches. The most effective prevention programs are those that are interactive rather than didactic, include adolescents age 15 or older, include girls only, and involve multiple sessions rather than just one session. Some effects appear to last as long as two years.

One recent randomized trial found that two types of preventive interventions show promise for reducing eating disorder symptoms among adolescent girls (average age of 17). One program, called the dissonance reduction intervention, focused on deemphasizing sociocultural influences; the other, called the healthy weight intervention, targeted risk

Prevention programs that are interactive have been effective for girls with eating disorders. (Tony Freeman/PhotoEdit.)

factors (Stice et al., 2008). Both programs included just one 3-hour session. Specifically, girls in the dissonance reduction intervention talked, wrote, and role-played with one another to challenge society's notions of beauty (i.e., the thin-ideal). Girls in the healthy weight intervention worked together on developing healthy weight and exercise programs for themselves. Participation in either program was associated with less negative affect, less body dissatisfaction, lower thin-ideal internalization, and lower risk of developing eating disorder symptoms 2 to 3 years after the session compared to girls who did not participate in a session. These findings point to the importance of continuing to develop and implement prevention programs.

Check Your Knowledge 11.3

Fill in the blanks.

1. Research suggests that _____ therapy is an effective treatment for bulimia, both in the short and long term.
2. For anorexia, _____ may be required to get the patient to gain weight. There are not many _____ that have been shown to be effective. The most common type of therapy used to treat anorexia is _____.
3. Research on prevention programs has shown that two programs show promise up to 3 years after the intervention: _____ intervention and _____ intervention.

Summary

Clinical Descriptions

- Two eating disorders are anorexia nervosa and bulimia nervosa. A third disorder, binge eating disorder, will likely be included in DSM-5. The symptoms of anorexia nervosa include refusal to maintain normal body weight, an intense fear of being fat, and a distorted sense of body shape. Anorexia typically begins in adolescence, is 10 times more frequent in women than in men, and is comorbid with several other disorders, notably depression. Its course is not favorable, and it can be life threatening. The symptoms of bulimia nervosa include episodes of binge eating followed by purging, fear of being fat, and a distorted body image. Like anorexia, bulimia begins in adolescence, is much more frequent in women than in men, and is comorbid with other diagnoses, such as depression. Prognosis is somewhat more favorable than for anorexia. The symptoms of binge eating disorder include episodes of bingeing but no compensatory purging. People with binge eating disorder are often obese, but not all obese people have binge eating disorder.

Etiology

- Research in the eating disorders has examined genetics and brain mechanisms. Evidence is consistent with a possible genetic diathesis. Endogenous opioids and serotonin, both of which play a role in mediating hunger and satiety, have been examined in eating disorders. Low levels of both these brain chemicals have been found in people with eating disorders, but evidence that these cause eating disorders is limited. Dopamine is also involved with eating, but its role in eating disorders is less well studied.

- On a psychological level, several factors play important roles. Cognitive behavioral theories of eating disorders propose that fear of being fat and body-image distortion make weight loss a powerful reinforcer. Among people with bulimia nervosa, negative affect and stress precipitate binges that create anxiety, which is then relieved by purging.

- As sociocultural standards changed to favor a thinner shape as the ideal for women, the frequency of eating disorders increased. The objectification of women's bodies also exerts pressure on women to see themselves through a sociocultural lens. The prevalence of eating disorders is higher in industrialized countries, where the cultural pressure to be thin is strongest. White women tend to have more body dissatisfaction and general eating disturbances than African American women, though the prevalence rates for actual eating disorders are not markedly different between these two ethnic groups.

- Research on characteristics of families with an eating-disordered child have yielded different data depending on how the data were collected. Reports of people with eating disorders show high levels of conflict, but actual observations of the families do not find them especially troubled. Studies of personality have found that people with eating disorders are high in negative emotion and perfectionism and low in interoceptive awareness. Many women with eating disorders report being abused as children, but early abuse does not appear to be a specific risk factor for eating disorders.

Treatment

- The main neurobiological treatment for eating disorders is the use of antidepressants. Although they are somewhat effective, dropout rates from drug-treatment programs are high and relapse is common when people stop taking the medication. Treatment of anorexia often requires hospitalization to reduce the medical complications of the disorder. Providing reinforcers for weight gain has been somewhat successful, but no treatment has yet been shown to produce long-term maintenance of weight gain. Family-based treatments show the most promise for anorexia.

- Cognitive behavioral treatment for bulimia focuses on questioning society's standards for physical attractiveness, challenging beliefs that encourage severe food restriction, and developing normal eating patterns. Outcomes are good, both in the short and long term. Cognitive behavioral treatment for binge eating disorder focuses on reducing binges, and early indications suggest that it is effective.

- Prevention programs show promise, particularly those programs that include girls age 15 or older, involve more than one session, and are interactive rather than didactic (i.e., lecture format). Outcomes appear promising up to 3 years after the prevention programs are instituted.

Answers to Check Your Knowledge Questions

11.1 1. c; 2. b; 3. d

11.2 1. F; 2. T; 3. F; 4. F; 5. T

11.3 1. cognitive behavior; 2. hospitalization, medications, family therapy; 3. dissonance reduction, healthy weight

Key Terms

anorexia nervosa

binge eating disorder

body mass index (BMI)

bulimia nervosa

obese

12 Sexual Disorders

SEXUALITY IS ONE of the most personal areas of life. Each of us is a sexual being with preferences and fantasies that may surprise or even shock us from time to time. Usually these are part of normal sexual functioning. But when our fantasies or desires begin to affect us or others in unwanted or harmful ways, they begin to qualify as abnormal. In this chapter we consider the range of human sexual thoughts, feelings, and actions that are listed in DSM-5 as sexual dysfunctions and paraphilias (see Table 12.1).

For perspective, we begin by briefly describing norms and healthy sexual behavior. Then we consider two forms of sexual problems: sexual dysfunctions and paraphilias. Sexual dysfunctions are defined by persistent disruptions in the ability to experience sexual arousal, desire, or orgasm, or by pain associated with intercourse. Paraphilias are defined by persistent and troubling attractions to unusual sexual activities or objects.

Sexual Norms and Behavior

Definitions of what is normal or desirable in human sexual behavior vary with time and place. Consider contemporary Western worldviews that *inhibition* of sexual expression causes problems. Contrast this with nineteenth- and early-twentieth-century views that *excess* was the culprit; in particular, excessive masturbation in childhood was widely believed to lead to sexual problems in adulthood. Von Krafft-Ebing (1902) postulated that early masturbation damaged the sexual organs and exhausted a finite reservoir of sexual energy, resulting in diminished ability to function sexually in adulthood. Even in adulthood, excessive sexual activity was thought to underlie problems such as erectile failure. The general Victorian view was that sexual appetite was dangerous and therefore had to be restrained. For example, to discourage handling of the genitals by children, metal mittens were promoted; to distract adults from too much sex, outdoor exercise and a bland diet were recommended. In fact, Kellogg's Corn Flakes and graham crackers were developed as foods that would lessen sexual interest. They didn't.

Other changes over time have influenced people's attitudes and experiences of sexuality. For example, technology has changed sexual experiences, as the number of people accessing sexual content on the Internet increased dramatically over the past decade. Even as the accessibility of sexual content increased so dramatically, AIDS

Norms about sexuality have fluctuated a great deal over time. In the early twentieth century, corn flakes were promoted as part of a bland diet to reduce sexual desire. (Corbis Images.)

and other sexually transmitted diseases changed the risks associated with sexual behavior. In the United States more than 19 million sexually transmitted infections are estimated to occur each year (Centers for Disease Control and Prevention, 2009b), and one in four women is infected with a sexually transmitted infection by age 19 (Forhan, Gottlieb, Sternberg, et al., 2009). See Figure 12.1 for recent HIV statistics. Other changes are influencing sexual norms as well. As the population of the United States ages, a newfound emphasis on the right to a good sex life until the day of death has emerged, supported by an increasing array of medications (Tiefer, 2003).

Aside from changes over time and across generations, culture influences attitudes and beliefs about sexuality. In some cultures, sexuality is viewed as an important part of well-being and pleasure, whereas in others, sexuality is viewed as relevant only for procreation (Bhugra, Popelyuk, & McMullen, 2010). Cultures also vary in their acceptance of variations in sexual behavior. For example, among Sambians living in Papua New Guinea, Herdt wrote in 1984 about rituals in which pubescent males engage in oral sex with older men as a way of learning about their sexuality. In other cultures it is common to stigmatize same-gender sexual behavior. Clearly, we must keep varying cultural norms in mind as we study human sexual behavior. See Focus on Discovery 12.1 for a look at the complicated path taken by health professionals in response to changing attitudes toward sexual orientation.

What are the norms in our culture today? To answer this question, it is important to gather samples that are representative of the population in terms of age, gender, ethnicity, socioeconomic status, and other key characteristics. We will discuss various representative surveys involving thousands of participants throughout this chapter. See Table 12.2 for data from one of these large representative surveys. Sometimes participants in these studies are asked to respond to written questions, as people may feel more comfortable describing their behavior in writing than in discussion with an interviewer. In the most recent large-scale representative study (Herbenick, Reece, Schick, et al., 2010b), researchers gathered data over the Internet, as it seemed that participants might feel most comfortable with this format. Even with sensitivity to participant comfort, it remains difficult to gather data on how common certain sexual behaviors are. We will discuss this issue more when we discuss paraphilias later.

Gender and Sexuality

Few topics raise as much political debate or personal turmoil as gender differences in sexuality. Across a wide range of indices, men report more engagement in sexual thought and behavior than do women. Of course, these are averages, there are going to be exceptions, and most of these differences are small (Andersen, Cyranowski, & Aarestad, 2000). But compared to women, men report thinking about sex, masturbating, and desiring sex more often, as well as desiring more sexual partners and having more partners (Baumeister, Catanese, & Vohs, 2001; Herbenick, Reece, Schick, et al., 2010a).

Beyond these differences in sex drive, Peplau (2003) has described several other ways in which the genders tend to differ in sexuality. Women tend to be more ashamed of any flaws in their appearance than do men, and this shame can interfere with sexual satisfaction (Sanchez & Kiefer, 2007). For women, sexuality appears more closely tied to relationship status and social norms than for men (Baumeister, 2000). For example, women tend to report less sexual drive and masturbation when they are not in a relationship; men don't experience the same shift when a relationship ends. Some argue that the DSM pays too little attention to the relational components of human sexuality in describing sexual dysfunction, especially for women. Some propose that there should be a more women-centered definition that includes "discontent or dissatisfaction with any emotional, physical, or relational aspect of sexual experience" (Tiefer, Hall, & Tavris, 2002, pp. 228–229). Among women with sexual symptoms, more than half believe their symptoms are caused by relationship problems (Nicholls, 2008). Men are more likely to think about their sexuality in terms of power than are women (Andersen, Cyranowski, & Espindle, 1999).

Of course, there are many parallels in men's and women's sexuality. For example, in a survey of more than 1,000 women, many reported

Table 12.1 Diagnoses of the Sexual Disorders in the Proposed DSM-5

Sexual dysfunctions
  Sexual interest, desire, and arousal disorders
    Sexual interest/arousal disorder in women
    Hypoactive sexual desire disorder in men
    Erectile disorder
  Orgasmic disorders
    Female orgasmic disorder
    Early ejaculation
    Delayed ejaculation
  Sexual pain disorders
    Genito-pelvic pain/penetration disorder
Paraphilias
  Fetishistic disorder
  Transvestic disorder
  Pedohebephilic disorder
  Exhibitionistic disorder
  Voyeuristic disorder
  Frotteuristic disorder
  Sexual masochism disorder
  Sexual sadism disorder
  Paraphilia not otherwise specified (e.g., coprophilia, necrophilia)

Source: APA, 2011.

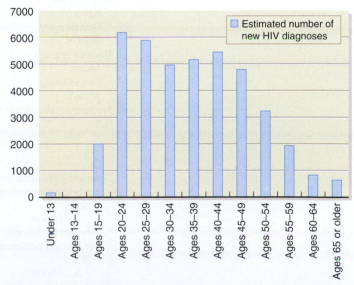

Figure 12.1 Estimated number of new diagnoses of HIV in the United States by age group in 2009 (Drawn from CDC, 2011).

FOCUS ON DISCOVERY 12.1

Learning from History

There has been a long history of debate over the medical approach to **sexual orientation**—the preference for a same-sex partner and to **gender identity**—the sense of self as male or female. Gender identity is distinct from sexual orientation. Many have argued that the DSM approach has fostered stigma.

In 1973, under pressure from various groups, the DSM category "homosexuality" as a sexual disorder was replaced by "sexual orientation disturbance." This new diagnosis was to be applied to gay men and lesbians "disturbed by, in conflict with, or wish to change their sexual orientation." The change was approved, but not without protests from some convinced that homosexuality reflects a fixation at an early stage of psychosexual development and is therefore inherently abnormal.

Included in the DSM-III was a new category called *ego-dystonic homosexuality*, which referred to a person who is homosexually aroused, is persistently distressed by this arousal, and wishes to become heterosexual. But in the years following its publication in the DSM-III, clinicians made little use of the diagnosis of ego-dystonic homosexuality. With subsequent versions of the DSM (DSM IV, DSM IV-TR), the category of ego-dystonic homosexuality was dropped, and replaced with broader category of "sexual disorder not otherwise specified," which refers to "persistent and marked distress about one's sexual orientation." This new category doesn't specify

Harris was born a male, but after sex-reassignment surgery at age 23 she became an extremely successful model and pop star in South Korea. (Sean Gallup/Gelly Images, Inc.)

a sexual orientation but can be applied when a person is distressed over a heterosexual or homosexual orientation.

Recent developments in how same-sex attraction and behavior is now conceived has lead to debate about whether people who request reorientation therapy should receive these services. The question is, should clients who are distressed by their experiences of same-sex attraction receive services to ameliorate their distress in a manner consistent with their beliefs and values? The key arguments for and against reorientation therapy are discussed by Yarhouse and Throckmorton (2002), and can be summarised as follows. Those who support a ban on reorientation therapy do so on the basis of the belief that homosexuality is no longer considered a mental illness; and therefore, those who request reorientation therapy do so because of internalized homophobia, and sexual orientation is immutable.

But on the other side of the ethical debate, reorientation therapy should be offered to (any) persons who report distress on the basis of respect for the autonomy and self-determination of person; a respect for valuative frameworks, creeds, and religious beliefs and values regarding the moral status of same-sex behavior; and service provision in response to a clinical problem based on the available scientific research.

Table 12.2 Participation in Selected Sexual Behaviors in the Past Year by Gender		
Behavior	Male (%)	Female (%)
Give oral sex		
Never	30.0	35.2
Occasionally	49.3	53.0
Always	20.7	11.8
Receive oral sex		
Never	30.5	33.2
Occasionally	50.5	52.2
Always	19.0	14.6
Number of sex partners		
0	9.9	13.6
1	66.7	74.7
2–4	18.3	10.0
5+	5.1	1.7
Frequency of sexual intercourse		
For unmarried participants		
None	22.2	30.6
< 3 × /month	38.9	36.6
At least 1 × /week	38.9	32.8
For married participants		
None	1.3	2.6
< 3 × /month	31.4	33.9
At least 1 × /week	67.3	63.5

Source: Laumann, Gagnon, Michael, et al., 1994.

that their primary motivation for having sex was sexual attraction and physical gratification (Meston & Buss, 2009). It would be an exaggeration to claim that the sole reason women are having sex is to promote relationship closeness. It is important to acknowledge commonalities as well as differences across genders.

Nonetheless, given that some gender differences are apparent, debate continues about the reasons for these gender differences. Are they based on cultural prohibitions regarding women's sexuality? Are they based on biological differences? Are they tied to women's greater investment in parenting? It is hard to design research to tease apart cultural and biological influences on sexuality. Intriguingly, though, at least some research suggests that some gender differences seem to be remarkably consistent across cultures. In one study of more than 16,000 people (albeit mostly college students), men in 52 different countries reported that they wanted more partners over the course of a lifetime than did women (Schmitt, Alcalay, Allik, et al., 2003). These findings suggest that biology may shape men's desire for many lifetime partners more than culture does. We know less about the basis for other gender differences in sexuality. There must be some reason for these differences, though. As Baumeister (2000) points out, in a perfect world, wouldn't men and women be well matched on their sexual preferences?

We will see throughout this chapter that gender shapes sexual disorders in a number of ways. Women are much more likely to report symptoms of sexual dysfunction than are men, but men are much more likely to meet diagnostic criteria for paraphilias. A better understanding of gender differences in sexuality is needed to understand why there are such major gender differences in sexual diagnoses.

The Sexual Response Cycle

Many researchers have focused on understanding the **sexual response cycle.** The Kinsey group made breakthroughs in the 1940s by interviewing people about their sexuality (Kinsey, Pomeroy, & Martin, 1948). Masters and Johnson created another revolution in research on human sexuality 50 years ago when they began to gather direct observations and physiological measurements of people masturbating and having sexual intercourse. Most contemporary conceptualizations distill proposals by Masters and Johnson (1966) and Kaplan (1974). Kaplan identified four phases in the human sexual response cycle.

As portrayed in the movie *Kinsey*, Alfred Kinsey shocked people when he began to interview people to understand more about norms in sexual behavior. (Gamma-Keystone via Getty Images.)

1. **Desire phase.** A concept introduced by Kaplan (1974), this stage refers to sexual interest or desire, often associated with sexually arousing fantasies or thoughts.

2. **Excitement phase.** During this phase, men and women experience pleasure and increased blood flow to the genitalia (see Figure 12.2 for the sexual anatomy of men and women). In men, this flow of blood into tissues produces an erection of the penis. In women, blood flow creates enlargement of the breasts and changes in the vagina, such as increased lubrication.

3. **Orgasm phase.** In this phase, sexual pleasure peaks in ways that have fascinated poets and the rest of us ordinary people for thousands of years. In men, ejaculation feels inevitable and indeed almost always occurs (in rare instances, men have an orgasm without ejaculating, and vice versa). In women, the outer walls of the vagina contract. In both sexes, there is general muscle tension.

4. **Resolution phase.** This last stage refers to the relaxation and sense of well-being that usually follow an orgasm. In men there is an associated refractory period during which further erection is not possible. The duration of the refractory period varies across men and even in the same man across occasions. Women are often able to respond again with sexual excitement almost immediately, a capability that permits multiple orgasms.

Newer data calls into question the validity of distinguishing the desire and excitement phases for women. That is, the distinction between the desire and excitement phase is not clear for many women (Graham et al., 2010). Further, desire seems to arise in response to physiological arousal for about a third of women (Carvalheira, Brotto, & Leal, 2010).

There is also some question about the way in which Kaplan defined the excitement stage by relying on biological changes. Subjective excitement may not mirror biological excitement for women. Some of the research on this topic has used a device called a **vaginal plethysmograph** to measure women's physiological arousal (see Figure 12.3). When blood flow is measured by the vaginal plethysmograph, most women experience a rapid, automatic response to erotic stimuli. But the amount of blood flow to the vagina has little correlation with women's subjective level of desire or excitement (Basson, Brotto, Laan, et al., 2005). Indeed, many women report no or low subjective excitement when those biological changes happen (Everaerd, Laan, Both, et al., 2000). Biological and subjective excitement need to be considered separately for women, even though they tend to be highly correlated for men.

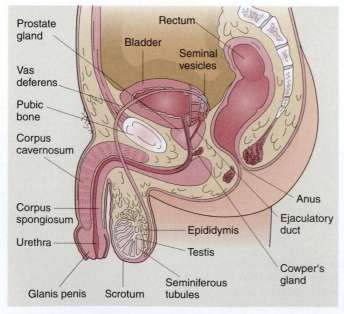
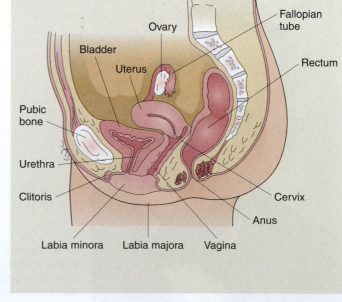

Figure 12.2 The male and female sexual anatomy.

Quick Summary

Sexuality is profoundly shaped by culture and experience, so it is important to be aware of subjective biases in thinking about diagnoses. Gender also shapes sexuality: for example, men report more frequent sexual thoughts and behaviors than do women.

Kaplan described four phases of the sexual response cycle: desire, excitement, orgasm, and resolution. Over time, researchers have learned that the Kaplan phases do not fit the data for women in two ways: the desire and excitement phase may not be distinct, and the Kaplan definition of the excitement phase may be overly biological.

Check Your Knowledge 12.1 (Answers are at the end of the chapter.)

True or false?
1. Men report more sex drive than women do.
2. Women's sexuality is more closely tied to relationship status than is men's sexuality.
3. Men describe their sexuality as more related to power than women do.
4. Men are able to have more orgasms during a given sexual experience than are women.
5. The applicability of Kaplan's model of the human sexual response cycle to women has been criticized because the desire and excitement phase may not be as distinct for women compared to men.

6. Gender differences in the desired number of lifetime partners are observed only in Western cultures.

Choose the best answer for the following question.
7. Which of the following is not a phase in Kaplan's model of the sexual response cycle?
   a. desire
   b. ejaculation
   c. excitement
   d. resolution

Sexual Dysfunctions

Sexuality usually occurs in the context of an intimate personal relationship. At its best, it provides a forum for closeness and connection. For better or for worse, our sexuality shapes at least part of our self-concept. Do we please the people we love, or, more simply, are we able to enjoy fulfillment from a pleasurable sexual experience? When sexual problems emerge, they can wreak havoc on our self-esteem and relationships. Partnerships are likely to suffer if sexual dysfunctions become so severe that the intense satisfaction and tenderness of sexual activity are lost.

We turn now to sexual problems that interfere with sexual enjoyment for many people at some time during their life. We begin by describing the different types of sexual dysfunctions described in the proposed DSM-5. Then we discuss etiology and treatments for these problems.

Clinical Descriptions of Sexual Dysfunctions

The proposed DSM-5 divides **sexual dysfunctions** into three categories: those involving sexual desire, arousal, and interest; orgasmic disorders; and sexual pain disorders. Separate diagnoses are provided for men and women. The diagnostic criteria for all sexual dysfunctions specify that dysfunction should be persistent and recurrent and should cause clinically significant distress or problems with functioning. A diagnosis of sexual dysfunction is not made if the problem is believed to be due entirely to a medical illness (such as advanced diabetes, which can cause erectile problems in men) or to another psychological disorder (such as major depression). Figure 12.4 shows the correspondence of DSM-IV-TR diagnoses and proposed DSM-5 diagnoses of sexual dysfunction.

One might not expect people to report problems as personal as sexual dysfunction in community surveys. But many people do report these symptoms—the prevalence of occasional symptoms of sexual dysfunctions is actually quite high. Table 12.3 presents data from a survey

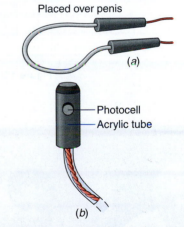

Figure 12.3 Behavioral researchers use two genital devices for measuring sexual arousal. Both are sensitive indicators of blood flow into the genitalia, a key physiological process in sexual arousal. (*a*) For men, the penile plethysmograph measures changes in the circumference of the penis by means of a strain gauge, consisting of a very thin rubber tube filled with mercury. As the penis enlarges with blood, the tube stretches, changing its electrical resistance. (*b*) For women, biological sexual arousal can be measured by a vaginal plethysmography. Shaped like a tampon, this apparatus can be inserted into the vagina to measure increases in blood flow. Biological arousal may not be associated with subjective arousal or desire for women.

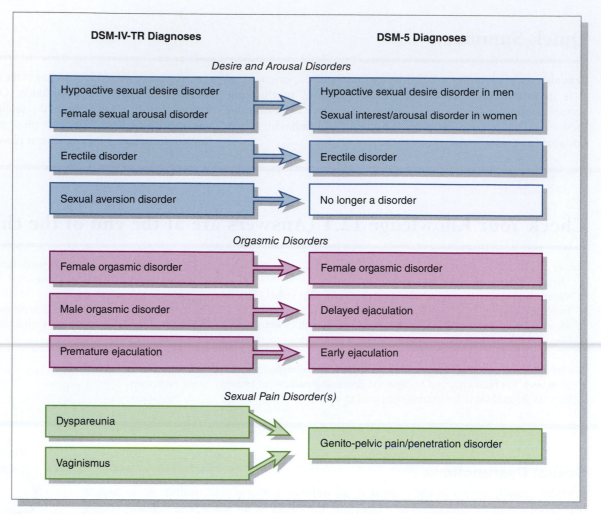

DSM-IV-TR Diagnoses		DSM-5 Diagnoses
Desire and Arousal Disorders		
Hypoactive sexual desire disorder	→	Hypoactive sexual desire disorder in men
Female sexual arousal disorder		Sexual interest/arousal disorder in women
Erectile disorder	→	Erectile disorder
Sexual aversion disorder	→	No longer a disorder
Orgasmic Disorders		
Female orgasmic disorder	→	Female orgasmic disorder
Male orgasmic disorder	→	Delayed ejaculation
Premature ejaculation	→	Early ejaculation
Sexual Pain Disorder(s)		
Dyspareunia	→	Genito-pelvic pain/penetration disorder
Vaginismus	→	

Figure 12.4 Diagnoses of sexual dysfunctions.

The pioneering work of the sex therapists William H. Masters and Virginia Johnson helped launch a candid and scientific appraisal of human sexuality. (Time & Life Pictures/Getty Images, Inc.)

of more than 20,000 men and women who were asked whether they had experienced various symptoms of sexual dysfunction for at least 2 of the past 12 months (Laumann, Nicolosi, Glasser, et al., 2005). More women (43 percent) than men (31 percent) reported symptoms of sexual dysfunction (Laumann, Paik, & Rosen, 1999).

Although a lot of people acknowledged symptoms, clinical diagnoses are not made unless a person experiences distress or impairment from symptoms; distress or impairment were not assessed in the Laumann survey. Two other studies have reported a very similar percentage (about 44 percent) of women who reported symptoms of sexual dysfunction (Bancroft, Loftus, & Long, 2003; Shifren, Monz, Russo, et al., 2008). But when women are asked whether they are distressed by these symptoms, only a quarter to a half of the women with symptoms acknowledge distress—11 to 23 percent of women report experiencing both sexual symptoms and distress over those symptoms. To be sure, these are high prevalence rates, but most women experiencing a symptom do not meet criteria for a clinical diagnosis. Unfortunately, we have almost no data on how many men have experienced sexual dysfunctions at a diagnosable level (American Psychiatric Association, 2000).

Although the diagnostic system for sexual dysfunction reflects the stages in the sexual cycle, the problems often don't break out so cleanly in real life. Many people with problems in one phase of a sexual cycle will report problems in another phase (Segraves & Segraves, 1991). Some of this may just be a vicious circle. For example, men who develop early ejaculation may begin to worry about sex and then experience problems with sexual desire or sexual arousal (Rowland, Cooper, & Slob, 1996). Beyond the consequences for the

Table 12.3 Self-Reported Rates of Experiencing Symptoms of Sexual Dysfunction for 2 of the Past 12 Months by Region among 20,000 Sexually Active Adults Ages 40 to 80

	Lacked Interest in Sex	Inability to Reach Orgasm	Orgasm Reached Too Quickly	Pain During Sex	Sex Not Pleasurable	Trouble Lubricating	Trouble Maintaining or Achieving an Erection
Women							
Northern Europe	25.6	17.7	7.7	9.0	17.1	18.4	NA
Southern Europe	29.6	24.2	11.5	11.9	22.1	16.1	NA
Non-European West	32.9	25.2	10.5	14.0	21.5	27.1	NA
Central/South America	28.1	22.4	18.3	16.6	19.5	22.5	NA
Middle East	43.4	23.0	10.0	21.0	31.0	23.0	NA
East Asia	34.8	32.3	17.6	31.6	29.7	37.9	NA
Southeast Asia	43.3	41.2	26.3	29.2	35.9	34.2	NA
Men							
Northern Europe	12.5	9.1	20.7	2.9	7.7	NA	13.3
Southern Europe	13.0	12.2	21.5	4.4	9.1	NA	12.9
Non-European West	17.6	14.5	27.4	3.6	12.1	NA	20.6
Central/South America	12.6	13.6	28.3	4.7	9.0	NA	13.7
Middle East	21.6	13.2	12.4	10.2	14.3	NA	14.1
East Asia	19.6	17.2	29.1	5.8	12.2	NA	27.1
Southeast Asia	28.0	21.1	30.5	12.0	17.4	NA	28.1

Note: Non-European West includes Australia, Canada, New Zealand, South Africa, and the United States.
Source: After Laumann et al. (2005).

individual, sexual problems in one person may lead to sexual problems in the partner. This potential for co-occurence of diagnoses is worth keeping in mind as we review the specific sexual dysfunction disorders defined in the proposed DSM-5.

Disorders Involving Sexual Interest, Desire, and Arousal The proposed DSM-5 includes three disorders relevant to sexual interest, desire, and arousal. **Sexual interest/arousal disorder in women** refers to persistent deficits in sexual interest (sexual fantasies or urges), biological arousal, or subjective arousal (see p. 371 for diagnostic criteria). For men, the proposed DSM-5 diagnoses consider sexual interest and arousal separately. **Hypoactive sexual desire disorder in men** refers to deficient or absent sexual fantasies and urges, and **erectile disorder** refers to failure to attain or maintain an erection through completion of the sexual activity. The clinical case of Robert provides an illustration of hypoactive sexual desire disorder, and the clinical case of Paul and Petula (see p. 371) provides an illustration of erectile disorder. It is important to rule out biological explanations for these symptoms for both men and women. For example, laboratory tests of hormone levels are a routine part of assessment for postmenopausal women (Bartlik & Goldberg, 2000).

Among people seeking treatment for sexual dysfunctions, more than half complain of low desire. Diagnoses related to low sexual desire became more common among men and women seeking treatment from the 1970s to the 1990s (Beck, 1995). As Table 12.3 shows, women are more likely than men to report at least occasional concerns about their level of sexual desire. Postmenopausal women are two to four times as likely as women in their 20s are to report low sexual desire. On the other hand, older women are less likely to be distressed over this low sexual desire (Derogatis & Burnett, 2008). Occasional symptoms of erectile disorder are the most common sexual concern among men, with rates ranging from 13 to 28 percent, depending on the country (Laumann et al., 2005). Male erectile disorder increases greatly with age, with as many as 15 percent of men in their 70s reporting erectile disorder (Feldman, Goldstein, Hatzichristou, et al., 1994) and as many as 70 percent reporting occasional erectile dysfunction (Kim & Lipshultz, 1997).

Of all the proposed DSM-5 diagnoses, the sexual desire disorders, often colloquially referred to as low sex drive, seem the most subjective. How often should a person want sex?

Proposed DSM-5 Criteria for Hypoactive Sexual Desire Disorder in Men

- Persistently deficient or absent sexual fantasies and desires, as judged by the clinician

Note: DSM-IV-TR does not provide separate diagnoses for men and women with hypoactive sexual desire.

Proposed DSM-5 Criteria for Erectile Disorder

On at least 75 percent of sexual occasions for 6 months:

- Inability to attain or maintain an erection for completion of sexual activity, or
- *Marked decrease in erectile rigidity interferes with penetration or pleasure*

Note: Changes from DSM-IV-TR criteria are italicized.

And with what intensity? Often, partners are the ones who encourage a person to see a clinician. The hypoactive desire category may owe its existence to the high expectations some people have about being sexual. Data attest to the significance of subjective and cultural factors in defining low sex drive; for example, hypoactive sexual desire disorder is reported more often by American men than by British (Hawton, Catalan, Martin, et al., 1986) or German men (Arentewicz & Schmidt, 1983) despite similar levels of sexual activity across these cultures. Cultural norms seem to influence perceptions of how much sex a person "should" want.

The proposed DSM-5 criteria for these disorders include many changes from DSM-IV-TR, as summarized in Table 12.4. As shown in Figure 12.4, DSM-IV-TR distinguishes sexual desire disorder from sexual arousal disorder in women. The decision to combine these disorders into

Table 12.4 Diagnoses of Sexual Dysfunction in the Proposed DSM-5

Proposed DSM-5 Diagnoses	Key Changes in DSM-5
Sexual interest/arousal disorder in women	• Interest disorder and arousal disorder are no longer considered distinct for women, as these often overlap. • Rather than a single-symptom approach, six criteria will be included. • Duration and severity criteria are added.
Hypoactive sexual desire disorder in men	• Changes may be recommended once field trials are concluded.
Female orgasmic disorder	• Duration and severity criteria are added.
Erectile disorder	• Duration and severity criteria are added.
Early ejaculation	• Duration and severity criteria are added.
Delayed ejaculation	• Duration and severity criteria are added.
Genito-pelvic pain/penetration disorder	• New diagnosis that merges the DSM-IV-TR diagnoses of vaginismus and dyspareunia.

Clinical Case: Robert

Robert was a highly intelligent 25-year-old graduate student in physics at a leading East Coast university when he sought treatment for what he called "sexual diffidence." He was engaged to a young woman, and he said he loved his fiancée very much and felt compatible with her in every conceivable way except in bed. There, try as he might, and with apparent understanding from his fiancée, he found himself uninterested in responding to or initiating sexual contact. Both parties had attributed these problems to the academic pressures he had faced for the past 2 years, but a discussion with the therapist revealed that Robert had had little interest in sex—either with men or with women—for as far back as he could remember, even when work pressures decreased. He asserted that he found his fiancée very attractive and appealing, but as with other women he had known, his feelings were not passionate.

He had masturbated very rarely in adolescence and did not begin dating until late in college, though he had had many female acquaintances. His general approach to life, including sex, was analytical and intellectual, and he described his problems in a very dispassionate and detached way to the therapist. He freely admitted that he would not have contacted a therapist at all were it not for the quietly stated wishes of his fiancée, who worried that his lack of interest in sex would interfere with their future marital relationship.

After a few individual sessions, the therapist asked the young man to invite his fiancée to a therapy session, which the client readily agreed to do. During a joint session, the couple appeared to be very much in love and looking forward to a life together, though the woman expressed concern about her fiancé's lack of sexual interest.

one diagnosis in the proposed DSM-5 is based on the evidence we described earlier about desire and arousal being hard to distinguish for many women. Indeed, almost all women who seek treatment for sexual arousal disorder also report low desire (Segraves & Segraves, 1991). The DSM-5 categories are designed to fit with these changes in understanding of sexual dysfunctions.

In DSM-IV-TR, female sexual arousal disorder is based on inadequate genital arousal. This is not ideal because it is increasingly clear that biological and subjective arousal don't always correspond in women, and women seeking treatment are usually concerned by a lack of subjective, rather than biological, arousal (Basson, Althof, Davis, et al., 2004). When laboratory studies are conducted using a vaginal plethysmograph, women who are concerned by a lack of subjective arousal often have normal biological responses to erotic stimuli (Graham, 2010). To build from this knowledge, proposed DSM-5 criteria for sexual interest/arousal disorder in women include biologically or subjectively low arousal.

Other DSM-5 changes are suggested to address concerns that the DSM-IV-TR criteria for sexual dysfunctions are too vague regarding duration. It is pretty common for people to have sexual symptoms for a month, and for most people, these symptoms will remit naturally over time. For example, about 6 percent of men report erectile dysfunction symptoms lasting for 1 month in a given year, but less than 1 percent report that those symptoms continued for 6 months or more (Mercer, Fenton, Johnson, et al., 2003). About 40 percent of women report that they experienced a loss of desire for at least a month in a given year, but only 10 percent report that the loss of desire persisted for a full 6 months. As shown in the diagnostic boxes throughout this chapter, the proposed DSM-5 criteria for sexual dysfunctions are specific in requiring symptoms to persist for 6 months.

Proposed DSM-5 Criteria for Sexual Interest/Arousal Disorder in Women

Diminished, absent, or reduced frequency of at least three of the following for 6 months or more:

- Interest in sexual activity
- Sexual thoughts or fantasies
- Initiation of sexual activity and responsiveness to partner's attempts to initiate
- Sexual excitement/pleasure during 75 percent of sexual encounters
- Sexual interest/arousal elicited by any internal or external erotic cues
- Genital or nongenital sensations during 75 percent of sexual encounters

Note: DSM-IV-TR criteria define arousal disorder as persistent inability to attain or maintain sexual excitement (lubrication and swelling of the genitalia) adequate for completion of sexual activity

---

Clinical Case: Paul and Petula

When Paul and Petula sought treatment at a sex therapy clinic, they were a young couple who had been living together for 6 months and were engaged to be married. Petula reported that Paul "hasn't been able to keep his erection after he enters me" for the past 2 months. Paul would experience initial sexual arousal but then lose his erection almost immediately after entering Petula. Although they enjoyed sexual intercourse during the beginning of their relationship, the erectile problems started after they moved in together. During the interview, the psychiatrist learned that they had considerable conflict over the amount of time they spent together and over commitment, and at times Petula has been violent toward Paul. Neither person described depression, and no medical problems appeared to be involved. (Drawn from Spitzer, Gibbon, Skodol, et al., 1994.)

Orgasmic Disorders As with other sexual dysfunctions, the DSM-5 includes separate diagnoses for problems in achieving orgasm for women and men. **Female orgasmic disorder** refers to the persistent absence of orgasm after sexual excitement. Women have different thresholds for orgasm. Although some have orgasms quickly and without much clitoral stimulation, others need prolonged clitoral stimulation. Given this, it is not surprising that about one-third of women report that they do not consistently experience orgasms with their partners (Laumann et al., 2005). Female orgasmic disorder is not diagnosed unless the absence of orgasms is persistent and troubling. About two-thirds of women report that they have faked an orgasm, and most say that they did so to try to protect their partner's feelings (Muehlenhard & Shippee, 2010). Many men are unaware (or at least don't report) that their partners don't achieve orgasms (Herbenick et al., 2010a).

Women's problems reaching orgasm are distinct from problems with sexual arousal. Many women achieve arousal during sexual activity but then do not reach orgasm. Indeed, laboratory research has shown that arousal levels while viewing erotic stimuli do not distinguish women with orgasmic disorder from those without orgasmic disorder (Meston & Gorzalka, 1995).

The proposed DSM-5 includes two orgasmic disorders of men: **early ejaculation**, defined by ejaculation that occurs too quickly, and **delayed ejaculation disorder**, defined by persistent difficulty in ejaculating. Although researchers do not know how many men meet formal diagnostic criteria, 20 to 30 percent of men reported early ejaculation and 10 to 20 percent of men reported that they had trouble reaching orgasm for at least a couple of months in the past year in the Laumann survey (2005). Although brief periods of symptoms may be fairly common, less than 3 percent of men acknowledged symptoms of early ejaculation lasting for 6 months or more (Segraves, 2010).

As with other sexual dysfunctions, the proposed DSM-5 diagnoses of orgasmic disorders will include more specific duration and severity criteria than the DSM-IV-TR (Segraves, 2010). The criteria for early ejaculation are drawn from diagnostic criteria used by the International Society for Sexual Medicine (McMahon, Althof, Waldinger, et al., 2008).

Sexual Pain Disorders In the proposed DSM-5, **genito-pelvic pain/penetration disorder** is defined by persistent or recurrent pain during intercourse. Some women report that the pain starts at entry, whereas others report pain only after penetration (Meana, Binik, Khalife, et al., 1997). A first step in making this diagnosis is ensuring that the pain is not caused by a medical problem, such as an infection (McCormick, 1999), or, in women, by a lack of vaginal lubrication due to low desire or postmenopausal changes. Although sexual pain disorders can be diagnosed in both men and women, we focus on women because it is extremely rare for men to seek treatment for these concerns.

Most women with this sexual pain disorder experience sexual arousal and can have orgasms from manual or oral stimulation that does not involve penetration. Women who experience pain when attempting sexual intercourse show normative sexual arousal to films of oral sex, but, not surprisingly, their arousal declines when they watch a depiction of intercourse (Wouda, Hartman, Bakker, et al., 1998).

Prevalence rates for occasional symptoms of pain during intercourse among women have been estimated to range from 10 to 30 percent (Laumann et al., 2005). This is a very common complaint seen by gynecologists (Leiblum, 1997).

As shown in Figure 12.4, the DSM-IV-TR distinguished two pain disorders: dyspareunia and vaginismus. Dyspareunia is defined by persistent or recurrent pain during sexual intercourse. Vaginismus is defined by involuntary muscle spasms of the outer third of the vagina to a degree that makes intercourse impossible. These disorders are combined in the proposed DSM-5 because it has become clear that they typically co-occur. In research that directly measures muscle tension of the vagina, women with dyspareunia and vaginismus demonstrate comparable levels of muscle tension (Binik, 2010). Given that dyspareunia and vaginismus are virtually impossible to discriminate in practice, combining them seems to be a good idea.

Etiology of Sexual Dysfunctions

In their widely acclaimed book *Human Sexual Inadequacy,* Masters and Johnson (1970) drew on their case studies to publish a theory of why sexual dysfunctions develop. Masters and Johnson used a two-tier model of immediate and distal causes to conceptualize the etiology of

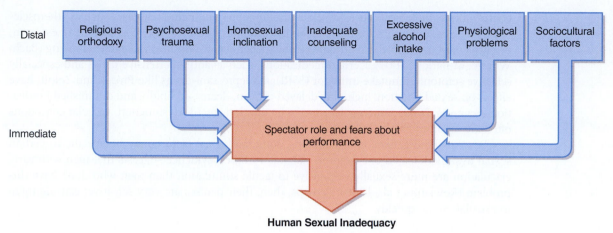

Figure 12.5 Distal and immediate causes of human sexual inadequacies, according to Masters and Johnson.

human sexual inadequacy (see Figure 12.5). The immediate causes can be distilled down to two: fears about performance and the adoption of a **spectator role.** Fears about performance involve concerns with how one is "performing" during sex. Spectator role refers to being an observer rather than a participant in a sexual experience. Both involve a focus on sexual performance that impedes the natural sexual responses. These immediate causes of sexual dysfunctions were hypothesized to have one or more historical antecedents, such as sociocultural influences, biological causes, sexual traumas, or homosexual preferences. Masters and Johnson's work set the stage for researchers to begin systematically studying risk factors for sexual dysfunction. We turn now to research on the causes of sexual dysfunctions. Figure 12.6 summarizes factors related to sexual dysfunctions. One thing is clear—sexual functioning is complex and multifaceted.

Biological Factors As noted above, a first step in making a diagnosis of sexual dysfunction is to rule out medical diseases as the cause. The proposed DSM-5 includes separate diagnoses for sexual dysfunctions that are caused by medical illnesses. Some have criticized this division in the diagnoses because sexual dysfunctions often have some biological and some psychological

Proposed DSM-5 Criteria for Genito-Pelvic Pain/Penetration Disorder

Persistent or recurrent difficulties for at least 6 months with at least one of the following:
- Inability to have vaginal intercourse/penetration
- Marked vulvovaginal or pelvic pain during vaginal penetration or intercourse attempts
- Marked fear or anxiety about pain or penetration
- Marked tensing of the pelvic floor muscles during attempted vaginal penetration

	Successful sexual functioning	Poor sexual functioning
Psychological factors	Good emotional health Attraction toward partner Positive attitude toward partner Positive sexual attitude	Depression or anxiety disorders Focus on performance Too much routine Poor self-esteem Uncomfortable environment for sex Rigid, narrow attitude toward sex Negative thoughts about sex
Physical factors	Good physical health Regular appropriate exercise Good nutrition	Smoking Heavy drinking Cardiovascular problems Diabetes Neurological diseases Low physiological arousal SSRI medications Antihypertensive medication Other drugs
Social and sexual history factors	Positive sexual experiences in past Good relationship with partner Sexual knowledge and skills	Rape or sexual abuse Relationship problems, such as anger or poor communication Long periods of abstinence History of hurried sex

Figure 12.6 Predictors of sexual functioning. Adapted from Wincze & Barlow (1997).

contributions. Biological causes of sexual dysfunctions can include diseases such as atherosclerosis, diabetes, multiple sclerosis, and spinal cord injury; low levels of testosterone or estrogen; heavy alcohol use before sex; chronic alcohol dependence; and heavy cigarette smoking (Bach, Wincze, & Barlow, 2001). Certain medications, such as antihypertensive drugs and especially selective serotonin reuptake inhibitor (SSRI) antidepressant drugs like Prozac and Zoloft, have effects on sexual function, including delayed orgasm, decreased libido, and diminished lubrication (Segraves, 2003). Among older men who develop erectile dysfunction, vascular conditions often are involved (Wylie & MacInnes, 2005).

Beyond these general considerations, some biological factors may be specific to certain sexual dysfunctions. As one example, laboratory-based evidence suggests that men with early ejaculation are more sexually responsive to tactile stimulation than men who don't have this problem (Rowland et al., 1996). Perhaps, then, their penises are very sensitive, causing them to ejaculate more quickly.

Psychosocial Factors Some sexual dysfunctions can be traced to rape, childhood sexual abuse, or other degrading encounters. Sexual abuse during childhood is associated with diminished arousal and desire, and, among men, with double the rate of early ejaculation (Laumann et al., 1999). See Focus on Discovery 12.3, later in this chapter, for a discussion of childhood sexual abuse and its repercussions. Beyond the role of traumatic experiences, it is important to consider the benefits of positive experiences—many people with sexual problems lack knowledge and skill because they have not had opportunities to learn about their sexuality (Lopiccolo & Hogan, 1979).

Broader relationship problems often interfere with sexual arousal and pleasure (Bach et al., 2001). For women, concerns about a partner's affection appear particularly correlated with sexual satisfaction (Nobre & Pinto-Gouveia, 2008). For people who tend to be anxious about their relationships, sexual problems may exacerbate underlying worries about relationship security (Birnbaum, Reis, Mikulincer, et al., 2006). As one might expect, people who are angry with their partners are less likely to want sex (Beck & Bozman, 1995). Even in couples who are satisfied in other realms of the relationship, poor communication can contribute to sexual dysfunction. For any number of reasons, including embarrassment, worry about the partner's feelings, or fear, one lover may not tell the other about preferences even if a partner is engaging in unstimulating or even aversive behaviors.

Depression and anxiety increase the risk of sexual dysfunctions (Hayes, Dennerstein, Bennett, et al., 2008). People who are depressed are more than twice as likely as nondepressed people (62 percent to 26 percent) to have a sexual dysfunction (Angst, 1998). People with panic disorder, who are often fearful of physical sensations like rapid heart rate and sweating, are also at risk for sexual dysfunction (Sbrocco, Weisberg, Barlow, et al., 1997). Anxiety and depression are particularly comorbid with sexual pain (Meana, Binik, Khalife, et al., 1998) and with disorders involving low sexual desire and arousal (Araujo, Durante, Feldman, et al., 1998; Hartmann, Heiser, Ruffer-Hesse, et al., 2002).

Beyond evidence that depression and anxiety are detrimental, several studies suggest that low general physiological arousal can interfere with specific sexual arousal. Meston and Gorzalka (1995) examined the role of arousal by assigning women to exercise or no-exercise conditions, and then asking women to watch erotic films. Consistent with the positive role of higher arousal, exercise facilitated sexual arousal. No wonder, then, that exhausted couples, turning to sex after a full day of work, parenting, socializing, and other roles, can encounter problems with sexuality. Too much stress and exhaustion clearly impede sexual functioning (Morokoff & Gilliland, 1993).

Negative cognitions, such as worries about pregnancy or AIDS, negative attitudes about sex, or concerns about the partner, interfere with sexual functioning (Reissing, Binik, & Khalife, 1999). But as Masters and Johnson first suggested, cognitions concerning sexual performance are particularly important (Carvalho & Nobre, 2010). Consider the idea that variability in sexual performance is common; a stressful day, a distracting context, a relationship concern, or any number of other issues may diminish sexual responsiveness. The key issue may be how people think about their diminished physical response when it happens. One theory is that people who blame themselves for decreased sexual performance will be more likely to develop recurrent problems.

In a test of the role of self-blame and erectile dysfunction, Weisberg and colleagues (2001) asked 52 male participants to watch erotic videos. During the videos, their sexual arousal (penile circumference) was measured using a **penile plethysmograph** (see Figure 12.3). Regardless of their actual arousal, the men were given false feedback that the size of their erection was smaller than that typically measured among aroused men. Men were randomly assigned to receive two different explanations for this false feedback. In the first, they were told that the films did not seem to be working for most men (external explanation). In the second, they were told that the pattern of their responses on questionnaires about sexuality might help explain the low arousal (internal explanation). After receiving this feedback, the men were asked to watch one more film. The men who were given an internal explanation reported less arousal and also showed less physiological evidence of arousal during this film than those given an external explanation. These results, then, support the idea that people who blame themselves when their body doesn't perform will experience diminished subsequent arousal. Needless to say, men in this study were carefully debriefed after the experiment!

Whereas men may worry about their erection, women can suffer from intrusive thoughts about their attractiveness. Many women struggle with negative intrusive thoughts about their weight or appearance during sex (Pujols, Seal, & Meston, 2010).

Beyond concerns about performance and attractiveness, Masters and Johnson found that many of their sexually dysfunctional patients had learned negative views of sexuality from their social and cultural surroundings. For example, some religions and cultures may discourage sexuality for the sake of pleasure, particularly outside marriage. Other cultures may disapprove of sexual initiative or behavior among women, other than for the sake of procreation. One female patient suffering from a lack of sexual desire, for example, had been taught as she was growing up not to look at herself naked in the mirror and that intercourse was reserved for marriage and then only to be endured for purposes of having children. Guilt about engaging in sexual behavior appears to vary by cultural group and can inhibit sexual desire (Woo, Brotto, & Gorzalka, 2011).

Quick Summary

In the proposed DSM-5, the sexual dysfunction disorders are divided into the following:

- Sexual interest, desire, and arousal disorders (sexual interest/arousal disorder in women, hypoactive sexual desire disorder and erectile disorder in men)
- Orgasmic disorders (female orgasmic disorder, delayed ejaculation, early ejaculation)
- Sexual pain disorders (primarily genito-pelvic pain/penetration disorder)

Although there are no good estimates of how many people meet full diagnostic criteria for sexual dysfunction disorders, in one major survey, 43 percent of women and 31 percent of men reported at least some symptoms of sexual dysfunction. People who experience one sexual dysfunction disorder often experience a comorbid sexual dysfunction disorder; for example, a man who is experiencing early ejaculation may develop hypoactive sexual desire disorder. Before diagnosing sexual dysfunction, it is important to rule out medical explanations for a symptom. The key etiological variables involved in sexual dysfunctions appear to be previous sexual abuse, relationship problems, lack of sexual knowledge, psychological disorders like depression, anxiety or alcohol abuse, low arousal and exhaustion, and negative cognitions and attitudes about sexuality. For early ejaculation, one possible cause is an overly sensitive penis.

Treatments of Sexual Dysfunctions

The pioneering work of Masters and Johnson (1970) in the treatment of sexual dysfunctions is described in Focus on Discovery 12.2. Over the past decades, therapists and researchers have elaborated on this work and created new procedures, several of which we will describe. A therapist may choose only one technique for a given case, but the multifaceted nature of sexual dysfunctions often requires the use of a combination of techniques. These approaches are generally suitable for treating sexual dysfunctions in homosexual as well as heterosexual clients.

FOCUS ON DISCOVERY 12.2

Masters and Johnson's Therapy for Sexual Dysfunctions

In their book *Human Sexual Inadequacy,* Masters and Johnson (1970) reported on the successful results of one of the first sex therapy programs, which they had carried out with almost 800 clients. Each couple had traveled to St. Louis and spent 2 weeks participating in intensive therapy during the day and completing sexual homework in a hotel at night.

Couples were always seen by one male and one female therapist. For several days, couples completed an assessment of social history, sexual history, sexual values, and medical concerns. During the assessment and first few days of treatment, sexual intercourse was forbidden. Sometimes the couple discussed sex for the first time at the clinic.

On the third day, the therapists began to offer interpretations about the sources of problems. If a person had negative attitudes toward sex, this would be addressed. But the basic emphasis was on relationship problems, rather than the individual difficulties of either partner. A premise of the therapy was that "there is no such thing as an uninvolved partner in any marriage in which there is some form of sexual inadequacy" (Masters & Johnson, 1970, p. 2). Whatever the problem, the couple was encouraged to see it as their mutual responsibility. At the same time, the clients were introduced to the idea of the spectator role. They were told, for example, that a male with erectile problems—and often his partner as well—usually worries about how well he is doing and that this pattern of observing the state of the erection, although totally understandable, blocks his natural responses and interferes with sexual enjoyment.

At the end of the third day, the couple was asked to engage in sensate focus. The couple was instructed to choose a time when both partners felt a sense of warmth and compatibility. During sensate-focus exercises, the couple was instructed not to have intercourse. Indeed, initially they were instructed not to touch each other's genitalia. Rather, they were to undress and give each other pleasure by touching each other's bodies. The co-therapists appointed one marital partner to do the first pleasuring; the partner who was "getting" was simply to be allowed to enjoy being touched. The one being touched was not required to feel a sexual response and was responsible for immediately telling the partner if something became uncomfortable. Then the roles were to be switched. The sensate-focus assignment usually promoted contact, constituting a first step toward reestablishing sexual intimacy.

Most of the time, partners began to realize that their physical encounters could be intimate and pleasurable without necessarily being a prelude to sexual intercourse. On the next evening, the partner being pleasured was instructed to give specific direction by guiding his or her partner's hand to regulate pressure and rate of stroking. Touching of genitals and breasts was now allowed, but still no intercourse. After two days of sensate focus, treatment began to be tailored to specific problems. To illustrate the process, we will outline the therapy for female orgasmic disorder.

After the sensate-focus exercises increased comfort, the woman was encouraged to focus on maximizing her own sexual stimulation without trying to have an orgasm. Her sexual excitement usually increased as a result. The therapists gave her partner explicit instructions about generally effective means of manually stroking the female genital area, although the female partner was encouraged to make decisions and express her wishes to her partner in the moment. At this stage it was emphasized that having orgasms was not the focus.

After the woman began to enjoy being pleasured by manual stimulation, she was told to place herself on top of the man, gently insert the penis, and simply attend to her feelings. When she felt inclined, she could begin to move her pelvis slowly. She was encouraged to regard the penis as something for her to play with, something that could provide her with pleasure. The male could begin to thrust slowly. At all times, however, the woman was to decide what should happen next. When the couple was able to maintain this exploration for minutes at a time without the man thrusting forcefully toward orgasm, a major change had usually taken place in their sexual interactions: for many couples, this was the first time that the woman had taken charge of planning their sexual interactions to enhance her own pleasure. In their subsequent encounters, most couples began to have mutually satisfying intercourse.

Many therapists continue to use the Masters and Johnson techniques, although success rates have tended to be lower than those originally reported (Segraves & Althof, 1998). Some believe that the lower success rates may be attributed to the couples who are seeking treatment these days rather than to the therapy itself; as sex therapy has become more popular, treatment-seeking couples today often have poorer marital relationships than did those who sought treatment in the early years of sex therapy.

Anxiety Reduction Well before the publication of the Masters and Johnson therapy program, behavior therapists appreciated that many clients with sexual dysfunctions needed gradual and systematic exposure to anxiety-provoking aspects of the sexual situation. Systematic desensitization and in vivo (real-life) desensitization have been employed with some success (Wolpe, 1958), especially when combined with skills training. For example, a woman with genito-pelvic pain/penetration disorder might first receive psychoeducation about her body, be trained in relaxation, and then practice inserting her fingers or dilators into her vagina, starting with small insertions and working up to larger ones (Leibium, 1997). Such programs have been shown to be helpful for many women with sexual pain disorders (Jung & Reidenberg, 2006).

Simple psychoeducation programs about sexuality also do a great deal to reduce anxiety. Accordingly, several studies have now shown that psychoeducation can be as effective as systematic desensitization for male erectile disorder and for women with low arousal or orgasmic disorder (Emmelkamp, 2004).

For the treatment of early ejaculation, anxiety-reduction techniques sometimes have a different focus. Anxiety about ejaculating too soon may be a natural result of an overemphasis on intercourse as a sole focus of sexual behavior. Sex therapists advise couples to expand their repertoire of activities to include techniques not requiring an erect penis, such as oral or manual manipulation, so that gratification of the partner is possible after the man has climaxed. When the exclusive focus on penile insertion is removed, a couple's anxieties about sex often diminish enough to permit greater ejaculatory control.

Directed Masturbation   Directed masturbation was devised by LoPiccolo and Lobitz (1972) to enhance women's comfort with and enjoyment of their sexuality. The first step is for the woman to carefully examine her nude body, including her genitals, and to identify various areas with the aid of diagrams. Next, she is instructed to touch her genitals and to find areas that produce pleasure. Then she increases the intensity of masturbation using erotic fantasies. If orgasm is not achieved, she is to use a vibrator in her masturbation. Finally, her partner enters the picture, first watching her masturbate, then doing for her what she has been doing for herself, and finally having intercourse in a position that allows him to stimulate the woman's genitals manually or with a vibrator. Directed masturbation has been shown to be helpful in the treatment of orgasmic disorder (O'Donohue, Dopke, & Swingen, 1997), particularly when women have a lifelong inability to experience orgasm, with success rates of 90 percent for that subgroup (Riley & Riley, 1978). It is also helpful in the treatment of sexual desire disorder (Renshaw, 2001).

Procedures to Change Attitudes and Thoughts   In one cognitive approach, clients are encouraged to focus on the pleasant sensations that accompany even incipient sexual arousal. The sensate-focus exercises described in Focus on Discovery 12.2, for example, are a way of helping the person be more aware of and comfortable with sexual feelings. The focus on physical sensations may counter the destructive tendency to think about one's performance or attractiveness during sex. Other cognitive interventions are designed to challenge the self-demanding, perfectionistic thoughts that often cause problems for people with sexual dysfunctions. A therapist might try to reduce the pressure a man with erectile dysfunction feels by challenging his belief that intercourse is the only true form of sexual activity. Kaplan (1997) recommends several procedures to try to increase the attractiveness of sex. She has clients engage in erotic fantasies and gives them courtship and dating assignments, such as getting away for a weekend.

Skills and Communication Training   To improve sexual skill and communication, therapists assign written materials and show clients explicit videos demonstrating sexual techniques (McMullen & Rosen, 1979). Encouraging partners to communicate their likes and dislikes to each other has been shown to be helpful for a range of sexual dysfunctions (Rosen, Leiblum, & Spector, 1994). Taken together, skills and communication training also exposes partners to potentially anxiety-provoking material, such as expressing sexual preferences, which allows for a desensitizing effect. Telling a partner one's preferences in sex is often made more difficult by tensions that go beyond the sexual relationship, which leads us to the next strategy.

Couples Therapy   Sexual dysfunctions are often embedded in a distressed relationship. Sex therapists often work from a systems perspective in which a sexual problem is viewed as one aspect of a complex network of relationship factors (Wylie, 1997). Troubled couples usually need training in nonsexual communication skills (Rosen, 2000). Some therapists focus on nonsexual issues, such as difficulties with in-laws or with child rearing—either in addition to or instead of interventions directly focused on sex. For women with sexual dysfunctions occurring in the context of relationship distress, behavioral couples therapy has been found to improve many aspects of sexual functioning (Zimmer, 1987).

Medications and Physical Treatment   As we consider medical treatments, it is worth noting that some have argued that many sexual problems are inherently interpersonal and so should not be addressed with a strictly medical approach (Rosen & Leiblum, 1995).

In the movie *Something's Gotta Give,* Jack Nicholson portrays a man whose use of Viagra complicates his cardiovascular treatment. (The Kobal Collection/Art Resource.)

For women in particular, sexuality has strong links with relationship satisfaction (Tiefer, 2001). Despite these caveats, medical treatments for sexual dysfunction are popular.

There has been a huge increase in pharmacological approaches to sexual dysfunctions. Antidepressant drugs have been found to be helpful when depression appears to contribute to diminished sex drive. A complicating factor, though, is that some of these psychoactive drugs themselves interfere with sexual responsiveness. Sometimes a second medication may be used to counteract the sexual side effects of the first; for example, buproprion (Wellbutrin) has been shown to help address the libido problems caused by SSRI medications (Segraves, 2003).

Early Ejaculation For the treatment of early ejaculation, the squeeze technique is often used, in which a partner is trained to squeeze the penis in the area where the head and shaft meet to rapidly reduce arousal. This technique is practiced without insertion, and then during insertion, the penis is withdrawn and the squeeze is repeated as needed. Success rates initially tend to be high (60 to 90 percent), but there is some relapse over time (Polonsky, 2000). Antidepressant drugs, particularly SSRIs, have been found to be helpful in a series of studies over the past 15 years (Althof, Abdo, Dean, et al., 2010). Dapoxetine (Priligy), a short-acting SSRI, has been approved for the treatment of early ejaculation in several European countries based on evidence from a series of randomized controlled trials (McMahon, Althof, Kaufman, et al., 2011) but remains under review by the U.S. Food and Drug Administration.

Erectile Disorder The most common intervention for erectile disorder is a phosphodiesterase type 5 (PDE-5) inhibitor, such as sildenafil (Viagra), tadafil (Cialis), or vardenafil (Levitra). PDE-5 inhibitors relax smooth muscles and thereby allow blood to flow into the penis, creating an erection during sexual stimulation but not in its absence. PDE-5 inhibitors are taken 1 hour before sex, and the effects last for about 4 hours. Although these medications can produce side effects such as headaches and indigestion, most men will tolerate them to gain relief from their sexual symptoms. Indeed, it is estimated that worldwide sales of PDE-5 medications reached 5 billion dollars in 2010 (Wilson, 2011). PDE-5 inhibitors may be dangerous for men with cardiovascular disease, and this is a concern since many of the older men who experience erectile dysfunction are at risk for hypertension and coronary artery disease.

In a summary of 27 treatment studies comparing Viagra to placebo, about 83 percent of men who took sildenafil were able to successfully have intercourse compared to about 45 percent of men who were assigned to a placebo condition (Fink, MacDonald, Rutks, et al., 2002). Some men continue to experience intermittent erectile dysfunction on Viagra, and so many men are not satisfied with Viagra alone. Sex therapy appears to be a helpful addition to Viagra treatment (Melnik, Soares, & Nasello, 2008). Several trials of Viagra and related medicines have been conducted with women, but the results are not promising (Laan, Everaerd, & Both, 2005).

Quick Summary

Psychological treatments for sexual dysfunction include techniques to reduce anxiety, to increase knowledge and awareness of the body, to reduce negative thoughts about sexuality, to improve couples' communication, and to reduce performance anxiety.

Medical treatments are increasingly popular, despite some criticism. Medications such as Viagra and Cialis are commonly used to treat erectile dysfunction. Antidepressant drugs can be helpful in the treatment of early ejaculation.

The Paraphilias

In DSM-5 the **paraphilias** are a group of disorders defined by recurrent sexual attraction to unusual objects or sexual activities lasting at least 6 months. In other words, there is a deviation (*para*) in what the person is attracted to (*philia*). DSM differentiates the paraphilias based on the source of arousal, for example, providing one diagnostic category for people whose sexual attractions are focused on inanimate objects and another diagnostic category for people whose attractions are focused on children (see Table 12.5). Surveys have shown that many people occasionally fantasize about some of the activities we will be describing. For example, 50 percent of men report voyeuristic fantasies of peeping at unsuspecting naked women (Hanson & Harris, 1997). In a large group of people who volunteered for a study of sexuality and health, 7.7 percent reported that they had been aroused by spying on others having sex, and 3.1 percent reported that they had been aroused by exposing their genitalia to a stranger at least once during their lifetime (Langstrom & Seto, 2006). By 2007, there were 381 Yahoo groups with a name related to sexual fetishes (Scorolli, Ghirlanda, Enquist, et al., 2007).

As some of these behaviors become more common, considerable debate has emerged about whether it is appropriate to diagnose some of the paraphilias. In 2009, the Swedish National Board of Health and Welfare decided to remove some of the paraphilias. Fetishistic disorder, sexual sadism disorder, sexual masochism disorder, and transvestic disorder are no longer included in their psychiatric classification system (Langstrom, 2010). The board reasoned that many people practice variant sexual behaviors safely with consenting adult partners and do not experience any distress or impairment as a result (Richters, De Visser, Rissel, et al., 2008). The American Psychiatric Association's Sexual and Gender Identity Disorders Work Group has recommended retaining these disorders in DSM-5 but notes that these should be diagnosed only when they cause marked distress or impairment or when the person engages in sexual activities with a nonconsenting person.

Table 12.5 Paraphilias Included in DSM

DSM-IV-TR Diagnosis	Object of Sexual Attraction	Proposed DSM-5 Diagnosis
Fetishism	An inanimate object or nongenital body part	Fetishistic disorder
Transvestic fetishism	Cross-dressing	Transvestic disorder
Pedophilia	Children	Pedohebephilic disorder
Voyeurism	Watching unsuspecting others undress or have sex	Voyeuristic disorder
Exhibitionism	Exposing one's genitals to an unwilling stranger	Exhibitionistic disorder
Frotteurism	Sexual touching of an unsuspecting person	Frotteuristic disorder
Sexual sadism	Inflicting pain	Sexual sadism disorder
Sexual masochism	Receiving pain	Sexual masochism disorder

Clinical Case: William

William was a twenty-eight-year-old computer programmer when he sought treatment after being arrested for voyeuristic behavior. William grew up as the second of four children in a conservative, religious family living in a rural area. He began to masturbate at age fifteen, and he did so while watching his sister urinate in their outhouse. Despite feeling very guilty, he continued to masturbate several times a week while having voyeuristic fantasies. A couple of times, he had masturbated while watching strangers undress.

As an adult, William was a timid, shy, and lonely man. He lived alone, and 6 months before the arrest, he had been rejected in a long-term relationship. In response, he withdrew from other social relationships and began drinking more alcohol. As his self-esteem deteriorated, his voyeuristic fantasies became more and more urgent.

One summer night, William had been feeling lonely and depressed, and he had been drinking heavily at a lounge with a topless dancer. After leaving the bar, he had been driving through a suburban neighborhood when he noticed someone in an upstairs window. Without thinking much, he had parked, erected a ladder he found near the house, and climbed up to the window to peep. The residents called the police when they heard him, and William was arrested. He was very shocked at the arrest, but he knew that his behavior was destructive, and he was motivated to change. [Rosen & Rosen (1981), pp. 452–453. Reprinted by permission of McGraw-Hill Book Company].

Impairment and engagement of nonconsenting others are important boundaries between normative and problematic sexual behavior. For some sexual behaviors, though, these dimensions rarely apply. For example, transvestic disorder does not typically involve nonconsenting others, and it rarely leads to impairment; the diagnosis of this disorder typically rests on the presence of distress. In Focus on Discovery 12.1, we noted that diagnostic systems that rely on distress are illogical. The person who cross-dresses for sexual gratification and accepts the behavior won't meet diagnostic criteria. In contrast, the person who feels guilty and ashamed because he or she has internalized stigma about this behavior is diagnosable. Because transvestic behavior so rarely leads to impairment or involves nonconsenting others, we do not discuss transvestic disorder further here.

Accurate prevalence statistics are not available for the paraphilias. Research is limited by the lack of structured diagnostic interviews to reliably assess these conditions (Krueger, 2010b) and by the reticence of many people with paraphilias to reveal their proclivities. Because some persons with paraphilias seek nonconsenting partners or otherwise violate people's rights in offensive ways (as we will see in exhibitionistic and pedohebephilic disorders), these disorders can have legal consequences. But statistics on arrests are likely to be underestimates because many crimes go unreported and some paraphilias (e.g., voyeuristic disorder) involve an unsuspecting victim. The data do indicate, though, that most people with paraphilias are male and heterosexual; even with masochism disorder and pedohebephilia, which occur in noticeable numbers of women, men vastly outnumber women.

Here we provide a clinical description of the paraphilias. As we describe the symptoms, we describe the epidemiology of these disorders. Most people with paraphilias meet criteria for other paraphilias (Abel, Becker, Cunningham-Rathner, et al., 1988) and for other DSM-IV-TR diagnoses such as mood and anxiety disorders (Kafka & Hennen, 2002), and we'll discuss some of these profiles of comorbidity as we discuss the specific paraphilias. After summarizing clinical descriptions of the paraphilias, we will discuss models of the etiology and treatment of these disorders.

Fetishistic Disorder

Fetishistic disorder is defined by a reliance on an inanimate object or a nongenital part of the body for sexual arousal. A fetish refers to the object of these sexual urges, such as women's shoes or feet. The person with fetishistic disorder, almost always a man, has recurrent and intense sexual urges toward these fetishes, and the presence of the fetish is strongly preferred or even necessary for sexual arousal.

Clothing (especially underwear), leather, and articles related to feet (stockings, women's shoes) are common fetishes. Beyond nonliving objects, some people focus on nonsexual body parts, such as hair, nails, hands, or feet, for sexual arousal. Because there is no evidence to suggest that there is a difference in the etiology or consequences of a boot fetish compared to a foot fetish, the proposed DSM-5 includes a reliance on nonsexual body parts for sexual arousal under the diagnosis of fetishistic disorder.

Proposed DSM-5 Criteria for Fetishistic Disorder

- For at least 6 months, recurrent and intense sexually arousing fantasies, urges, or behaviors involving the use of nonliving objects *or nongenital body parts*
- Causes significant distress or impairment in functioning
- The sexually arousing objects are not limited to articles of female clothing used in cross-dressing or to devices designed to provide tactile genital stimulation, such as a vibrator

Note: Changes from the DSM-IV-TR criteria are italicized.

Clinical Case: Ruben

Ruben is a single, 32-year-old male photographer who sought treatment for his "abnormal sex drive." He reported that he was particularly concerned that he was more attracted to women's underwear than to the women themselves. Ruben reported that he remembered being excited by pictures of women in their underwear at age 7. At age 13 he reached orgasm by masturbating while imagining women in their underwear. He began to steal underwear from his sister to use while masturbating. As he grew older, he would take opportunities to sneak into other women's rooms and steal their underwear. He began to have intercourse at age 18, and his preferred partner was a prostitute that he asked to wear underwear with the crotch removed while they had sex. He found that he preferred masturbating into stolen underwear more than sexual intercourse. He avoided dating "nice women," as he feared they would not understand his sexual behavior, and he also avoided friends who might encourage him to date such women. He had begun to experience significant depression over the ways in which his sexual behavior was limiting his social life. [Adapted from Spitzer et al. (1994).]

Some carry on their fetishism by themselves in secret by fondling, kissing, smelling, sucking, placing in their rectum, or merely gazing at the adored object as they masturbate. Others need their partner to don the fetish as a stimulant for intercourse. For many, a fetish may never reach a diagnosable level. As examples of diagnosable impairment, though, some become interested in acquiring a collection of the desired objects, and they may even commit burglary week after week to add to their hoard.

The person with fetishistic disorder feels a compulsive attraction to the object; the attraction is experienced as involuntary and irresistible. It is the degree of the erotic focus—the exclusive and very special status the object occupies as a sexual stimulant—that distinguishes fetishistic disorder from the ordinary attraction that, for example, high heels may hold for heterosexual men in Western cultures. The person with a boot fetish must see or touch a boot to become aroused, and the arousal is overwhelmingly strong when a boot is present.

The disorder usually begins in adolescence, although the fetish may have acquired special significance even earlier, during childhood. People with fetishistic disorder often have other paraphilias, such as pedohebephilic, sadism and masochism disorders (Mason, 1997).

Many people experiment with sadomasochism and fetishes. Paraphilias are not diagnosed unless the sexual interests cause marked distress or impairment. (Cindy Charles/PhotoEdit.)

Pedohebephilic Disorder and Incest

According to the DSM, **pedohebephilic disorder** (*pedes* is Greek for "child", *hebe* is Greek for "pubescence," and *philia* is Greek for "attraction") is diagnosed when adults derive sexual gratification through sexual contact with prepubertal or pubescent children, or when they experience recurrent, intense, and distressing desires for sexual contact with prepubertal or pubescent children. DSM-5 requires that the offender be at least 18 years old and at least 5 years older than the child (see diagnostic criteria on p. 382). Most men who acknowledge pedohebephilic disorder report that they use child pornography (Riegel, 2004), and so the DSM-5 includes use of child pornography as one part of the criteria. As in most paraphilias, a strong subjective attraction impels the behavior. Sometimes a man with pedohebephilic disorder is content to stroke the child's hair, but he may also manipulate the child's genitalia, encourage the child to manipulate his, and, less often, attempt penile insertion. The molestations may be repeated over a period of weeks, months, or years if they are not discovered by other adults or if the child does not protest. Some people with pedohebephilic disorder intentionally frighten the child by, for example, killing a pet and threatening further harm if the youngster tells his or her parents.

People with pedohebephilic disorder generally molest children that they know, such as neighbors or friends of the family. Sadly, incidents abound involving scoutmasters, camp counselors, and clergy. Most with pedohebephilic disorder do not engage in violence other than the sexual act, although when they do, it is often a focus of lurid stories in the media. Because overt physical force is seldom used in pedohebephilic disorder, the child molester often denies that he is actually forcing himself on his victim. Despite molesters' distorted beliefs, child sexual abuse inherently involves a betrayal of trust and other serious negative consequences (see Focus on Discovery 12.3 for a discussion of these consequences).

In one meta-analysis of 61 follow-up studies involving 28,972 sexual offenders, sexual arousal in response to pictures of young children as measured by penile plethysmograph

FOCUS ON DISCOVERY 12.3

The Effects of Pedohebephilic Disorder: Outcomes After Childhood Sexual Abuse

Pedophilia is a paraphilia that involves an abnormal interest in children and *Hebephilia* is the sexual attraction to adolescents.

Criteria for *Pedohebephilic Disorder*, according to DSM V, is the presence of one or both of the following in a person who is at least aged 18 years, and is at least five years older his/her victims.

1. Fantasies, urges, or behaviors relating to the recurrent and intense sexual arousal from prepubescent or pubescent children.

2. Equal or greater arousal from such children than from physically mature individuals, over a period of at least six months.

Symptoms associated with the condition include:

- The presence of significant distress or impairment in important areas of functioning from sexual attraction to children;
- The person has sought sexual stimulation, on separate occasions, from either of the following:
  - Repeated use of, and greater arousal from, pornography depicting prepubescent or pubescent children than from pornography depicting physically mature persons, for a period of six months or longer

But what about the child-victims of sexual abuse?

In one major community survey, 13.5 percent of women and 2.5 percent of men reported experiencing some form of childhood sexual abuse (Molnar, Buka, & Kessler, 2001). A child abuser is usually not a stranger. He may be a father, an uncle, a brother, a teacher, a coach, a neighbour, or even a cleric. The abuser is often an adult whom the child knows and trusts. When the abuser is someone close to the child, the child is likely to be torn by allegiance to the abuser on the one hand and, on the other hand, by fear, revulsion, and the knowledge that what is happening is wrong. The betrayal of this trust makes the crime more abhorrent than it would be if no prior relationship existed between abuser and child. As with childhood incest, molestation or sexual harassment by an authority figure violates trust and respect. The victim, whatever his or her age, cannot give meaningful consent. The power differential is just too great.

How does the all-too-common experience of childhood sexual abuse affect mental health during childhood and beyond? What can be done to protect children and to help children heal from childhood sexual abuse?

Effects on the Child

For recovery from the emotional trauma associated with childhood sexual abuse, prognosis varies depending on a number of abuse-specific and individual and environmental factors. These factors include the following:

- The child's inherent coping mechanisms and response to trauma and its aftermath
- Response evident in the child's environment to the victimization
- Age when the abuse occurred
- Relationship of the perpetrator to the child
- Length of time over which the abuse occurred
- Pattern of the abuse

The response within the caregiving environment to the victimization appears to have an important impact on the ability of the child to work through the difficult issues raised by the sexual abuse.

Looking at children 5 years after presentation for sexual abuse and comparing them to a similarly aged group of children who were not abused, one study found that the children who were sexually abused displayed the following:

- More disturbed behavior
- Lower self-esteem
- Increased tendency for depression
- Increased tendency for anxiety

Proposed DSM-5 Criteria for Pedohebephilic Disorder

- For at least 6 months, recurrent and intense, sexually arousing fantasies, urges, or behaviors involving sexual contact with a prepubescent *or pubescent* child
- Arousal is as strong or stronger for children than for adults
- Person has acted on these urges *with prepubescent or pubescent children, has repeatedly gained more arousal from child pornography than from pornography depicting mature persons for at least 6 months,* or the urges and fantasies cause clinically significant distress or interpersonal problems
- Person is at least *18* years old and 5 years older than the child

Note: Changes from the DSM-IV-TR criteria are italicized. DSM-IV-TR criteria specify an age of 16 or older.

was one of the strongest predictors of repeated sexual offenses (Hanson & Bussiere, 1998). Nonetheless, arousal in response to pictures of children is not a perfect predictor of pedohebephilic disorder. Many men who are conventional in their sexual interests and behavior can be sexually aroused by erotic pictures of children. In a study using both self-report and penile plethysmographic measures, one-quarter of men drawn from a community sample showed or reported arousal when viewing sexually provocative pictures of children (Hall, Hirschman, & Oliver, 1995). Indeed, across studies, 3 to 9 percent of men describe having experienced at least one sexual fantasy involving a child (Seto, 2009). Although these findings might seem disturbing, they highlight the importance of the distinction made by the DSM and by health professionals between fantasy and behavior. Pedohebephilic disorder is diagnosed only when adults either act on their sexual urges toward children or are distressed by the urges.

Incest is listed as a subtype of pedohebephilic disorder. **Incest** refers to sexual relations between close relatives for whom marriage is forbidden. It is most common between brother and sister. The next most common form, which is considered more pathological, is between father and daughter.

The taboo against incest is virtually universal in human societies (Ford & Beach, 1951), with the notable exception of Egyptian pharaohs, who could marry their sisters or other females of their immediate families. In Egypt, it was believed that the royal blood should not be contaminated by that of outsiders. The incest taboo makes sense according to present-day scientific knowledge. The offspring from a father–daughter or a brother–sister union have a greater probability of inheriting a pair of recessive genes, one from each parent. For the most part, recessive genes have negative biological effects, such as serious birth defects. The incest taboo, then, has adaptive evolutionary significance.

Retrospective studies of adults with severe personality disorders characterized by dissociation, impaired interpersonal relationships, and self-mutilation have found a high and significant correlation with histories of childhood sexual abuse. Prognosis related to any physical injury or infection resulting from the sexual abuse is expected to follow a typical healing course and respond to standard medical interventions. Paolucci et al's meta-analysis of 37 studies involving 25,367 individuals reported no universal response to childhood sexual abuse; however, they did confirm that the experience is negative and that clear evidence shows a link between childhood sexual abuse and subsequent negative short-term and long-term developmental effects. Paolucci et al conclude that, rather than thinking about a single, specific childhood sexual abuse response syndrome such as posttraumatic stress disorder, depression, suicide, sexual promiscuity, victim-perpetrator cycle, and poor academic performance, a multifaceted model of traumatization is more appropriate. According to this view, childhood sexual abuse produces multifaceted effects and that distinct mechanisms and processes may operate to account for the variety of outcomes.

Prevention

Childhood sexual abuse prevention efforts have focused on primary schools. Common elements include teaching children to recognize inappropriate adult behavior, resist inducements, leave the situation quickly, and report the incident to an appropriate adult (Wolfe, 1990). Children are taught to say "no" in a firm, assertive way when an adult talks to or touches them in a manner that makes them feel uncomfortable. Instructors may use comic books, films, and descriptions of risky situations to teach about sexual abuse and how children can protect themselves.

Evaluations of school programs suggest that they do increase awareness of sexual abuse. Researchers do not know whether children are able to translate what they have learned into overt behavior that reduces the problem (Wolfe, 1990).

Dealing with the Problem

When they suspect that something is awry, parents must raise the issue with their children; unfortunately, many adults are uncomfortable doing so. Physicians also need to be sensitive to signs of sexual abuse. Sexual and nonsexual forms of abuse are reportable offenses; professionals who suspect abuse are required by law to report their suspicions to the police or child protective agencies. For a child, reporting sexual abuse can be extremely difficult. We tend to forget how helpless and dependent the child feels, and it is difficult to imagine how frightening it would be to tell one's parents that one had been fondled by a brother or grandfather.

Most cases of sexual abuse do not leave any physical evidence, such as torn vaginal tissue. Furthermore, there is no behavioral pattern, such as anxiety, depression, or increased sexual activity that unequivocally indicates that abuse has occurred (Kuehnle, 1998). Therefore, the child's own report is the primary source of information about whether childhood sexual abuse has occurred. The problem is that leading questions can produce some false reports. Great skill is required in questioning a child about possible sexual abuse to avoid biasing the youngster one way or the other. Some jurisdictions use innovative procedures to reduce the stress on the child while protecting the rights of the accused adult, for example, videotaped testimony, closed-courtroom trials, closed-circuit televised testimony, and special coaching sessions to explain what to expect in the courtroom (Wolfe, 1990). Having the child play with anatomically correct dolls can be useful in getting at the truth, but it should be only one part of an assessment, because many nonabused children portray such dolls having sexual intercourse (Jampole & Weber, 1987).

Many children need treatment (Litrownik & Castillo-Canez, 2000). As with adult survivors of rape, post traumatic stress disorder can be a consequence. Many interventions are similar to those used for post traumatic stress disorder in adults; the emphasis is on exposure to memories of the trauma through discussion in a safe and supportive therapeutic atmosphere (Johnson, 1987). It is also important for children to learn that healthy human sexuality is not about power and fear (McCarthy, 1986). As with rape, it is important to change the person's attribution of responsibility from "I was bad" to "He/she was bad." As yet there has been no controlled research on these various interventions, but uncontrolled studies are encouraging (Arnold, Kirk, Roberts et al., 2003).

There is evidence that families in which incest occurs are unusually patriarchal, especially with respect to the subservient position of women to men (Alexander & Lupfer, 1987). Parents in these families also tend to be more neglectful and emotionally distant from their children (Madonna, Van Scoyk, & Jones, 1991).

Typically, men who commit incest abuse their pubescent daughters, whereas men with nonincestual pedohebephilic disorder are usually interested in prepubertal children. Consistent with this difference in the age of victims, men who molest children within their families show greater penile arousal (as measured by penile plethysmography) to adult heterosexual cues than do men who molest unrelated children (Marshall, Barbaree, & Christophe, 1986).

What are the demographic characteristics of people who engage in pedohebephilic disorder and incest? People with pedohebephilic disorder can be straight or gay, though most are heterosexual. Up to half of all child molestations, including those that take place within the family, are committed by adolescent males (Morenz & Becker, 1995). Academic problems are common, as are other criminal behaviors (Becker & Hunter, 1997). Most older heterosexual men with pedohebephilic disorder are or have been married. Psychologically, men with pedohebephilic disorder demonstrate elevated impulsivity and psychopathy compared to the general population (Ridenour, Miller, Joy, et al., 1997). These men often meet criteria for comorbid conduct disorder and substance abuse, and molestations are more likely to occur when the person with pedohebephilic disorder is intoxicated. As with other paraphilias, depression and anxiety disorders are also common (Galli, McElroy, Soutullo, et al., 1999). Evidence also suggests that men with pedohebephilic disorder have sexual fantasies about children when their mood is negative, perhaps as a way to cope with their unhappiness; however, having the fantasy appears to increase negative affect. This downward spiral may then contribute to the urge to molest a child (Looman, 1995).

Voyeuristic Disorder

Voyeuristic fantasies are quite common in men but do not by themselves warrant a diagnosis (Hanson & Harris, 1997). **Voyeuristic disorder** involves an intense and recurrent desire to obtain sexual gratification by watching unsuspecting others in a state of undress or having sexual relations. For some men with this disorder, voyeurism is their only sexual activity; for others, it is preferred but not absolutely essential for sexual arousal (Kaplan & Kreuger, 1997). As in the case of William earlier in this chapter, the looking, often called peeping, helps the person become sexually aroused and is sometimes essential for arousal. People with voyeuristic disorder achieve orgasm by masturbation, either while watching or later while remembering the peeping. Sometimes the person with voyeuristic disorder fantasizes about having sexual contact with the observed person, but it remains a fantasy; he or she seldom contacts the observed person. A true voyeur, almost always a man, does not find it particularly exciting to watch a woman who is undressing for his benefit. The element of risk seems important, for the voyeur is excited by the anticipation of how the woman would react if she knew he was watching.

The prevalence is difficult to assess since most incidents are not reported to the police. Indeed, people with voyeuristic disorder are most often charged with loitering rather than with peeping itself (Kaplan & Kreuger, 1997).

Voyeuristic disorder typically begins in adolescence. People who meet diagnostic criteria for voyeuristic disorder often have other paraphilias, but they do not tend to have elevated rates of other mental disorders.

Exhibitionistic Disorder

Exhibitionistic disorder is a recurrent, intense desire to obtain sexual gratification by exposing one's genitals to an unwilling stranger, sometimes a child. It typically begins in adolescence. As with voyeuristic disorder, there is seldom an attempt to have actual contact with the stranger. In one study, persons diagnosed with exhibitionistic disorder reported that they had been arrested for only 1 out of every 150 incidents (Abel, Becker, Mittelman, et al., 1987). Many exhibitionists masturbate during the exposure. In most cases there is a desire to shock or embarrass the observer.

The urge to expose seems overwhelming and virtually uncontrollable to the exhibitionist and is apparently triggered by anxiety and restlessness as well as by sexual arousal. Because of the compulsive nature of the urge, the exposures may be repeated often and even in the same place and at the same time of day. At the time of the act, the social and legal consequences are far from exhibitionists' minds (Stevenson & Jones, 1972). In the desperation and tension of the moment, they may experience headaches and palpitations and have a sense of unreality. After exposing themselves, exhibitionists tend to flee and feel remorseful. Other paraphilias are very common in exhibitionists, notably voyeuristic and frotteuristic disorders (see the next section) (Freund, 1990).

Frotteuristic Disorder

Frotteuristic disorder involves the sexually oriented touching of an unsuspecting person. The frotteur may rub his penis against a woman's thighs or buttocks or fondle her breasts or genitals. These attacks typically occur in places such as a crowded bus or sidewalk that provide an easy means of escape. Frotteuristic disorder has not been studied very extensively. It typically occurs along with other paraphilias (Langstrom, 2010). Most men who engage in frotteurism report doing so dozens of times (Abel et al., 1987).

Sexual Sadism and Masochism Disorders

Sexual sadism disorder is defined by an intense and recurrent desire to obtain or increase sexual gratification by inflicting pain or psychological suffering (such as humiliation) on another. **Sexual masochism disorder** is defined by an intense and recurrent desire to obtain

---

Proposed DSM-5 Criteria for Voyeuristic Disorder

- For at least 6 months, recurrent and intense sexually arousing fantasies, urges, or behaviors involving the observation of unsuspecting others who are naked, disrobing, or engaged in sexual activity
- Person has acted on these urges *with at least three unsuspecting persons on separate occasions*, or the urges and fantasies cause marked distress or interpersonal problems

Note: Changes from the DSM-IV-TR criteria are italicized.

Proposed DSM-5 Criteria for Exhibitionistic Disorder

- For at least 6 months, recurrent, intense, and sexually arousing fantasies, urges, or behaviors involving showing one's genitals to an unsuspecting stranger
- Person has acted on these urges *to at least three strangers on separate occasions*, or the urges and fantasies cause clinically significant distress or interpersonal problems

Note: Changes from the DSM-IV-TR are italicized.

Proposed DSM-5 Criteria for Frotteuristic Disorder

- For at least 6 months, recurrent and intense and sexually arousing fantasies, urges, or behaviors involving touching or rubbing against a nonconsenting person
- Person has acted on these urges *with at least three nonconsenting persons on separate occasions*, or the urges and fantasies cause clinically significant distress or problems

Note: Changes from the DSM-IV-TR criteria are italicized.

or increase sexual gratification through being subjected to pain or humiliation. Some sadists achieve orgasm by inflicting pain, and some masochists achieve orgasm by being subjected to pain. For others, though, the sadistic and masochistic practices, such as spanking, are just one aspect of sexual activity.

The manifestations of sexual masochism disorder are varied. Examples include physical bondage, blindfolding, spanking, whipping, electric shocks, cutting, humiliation (e.g., being urinated or defecated on, being forced to wear a collar and bark like a dog, or being put on display naked), and taking the role of slave and submitting to orders and commands. Most sadists establish relationships with masochists to derive mutual sexual gratification. Although many people are able to take both dominant and submissive roles, masochists outnumber sadists.

Sadistic and masochistic behaviors have become more accepted over time: 5 to 10 percent of the population have tried some form of sadomasochistic activity, such as blindfolding one's partner (Baumeister & Butler, 1997). In major cities, clubs cater to members seeking sadomasochistic partnerships. Most people who engage in sadomasochistic behaviors are relatively comfortable with their sexual practices (Spengler, 1977).

As sadomasochistic practices have become more common and more openly practiced, there has been some debate about whether these diagnoses should be retained in DSM-5. Many people who engage in sadomasochism appear to be free of distress or impairment and so would not meet criteria for diagnosis (Krueger, 2010a). These diagnostic labels were retained because some sadistic and masochistic practices can be dangerous. One particularly dangerous form of masochism, called asphyxiophilia, can result in death or brain damage; it involves sexual arousal by restricting breathing, which can be achieved using a noose, a plastic bag, or chest compression.

There is also some concern that the diagnosis of sexual sadism disorder is rarely applied in clinical settings. In an unpublished review of over 500 million visits to psychiatrists, gynecologists, urologists, and other physicians, no doctor recorded a diagnosis of sexual sadism disorder (Narrow, 2008, cited in Krueger, 2010b). Doctors in clinical settings may not use the diagnosis even when symptoms are present because of worries over stigma. The diagnosis, then, seems to be applied almost entirely within forensic settings (Krueger, 2010b).

Sexual sadism and masochism disorders seem to begin by early adulthood. Both these disorders are found in straight and gay relationships. Surveys have found that 20 to 30 percent of the members of sadomasochistic clubs are female (Moser & Levitt, 1987), and it has been assumed that a similar gender ratio might be true of diagnosable sadism and masochism. Most sadists and masochists lead otherwise conventional lives, and there is some evidence that they are above average in income and educational status (Moser & Levitt, 1987). Alcohol abuse is common among sadists (Allnutt, Bradford, Greenberg, et al., 1996).

Etiology of the Paraphilias

Of the many theories about the etiology of the paraphilias, the principal ones come from biological and behavioral perspectives. Because many people do not want to talk about their paraphilias, researchers have few opportunities to understand their causes. Indeed, research in this area is so difficult to conduct that most studies rely on small, nonrepresentative samples. As an example, only four studies were published between 1990 and 2009 that included more than 25 participants diagnosed with fetishistic disorder (Kafka, 2010).

Neurobiological Factors Because the overwhelming majority of people with paraphilias are men, there has been speculation that androgens (hormones like testosterone) play a role. Androgens regulate sexual desire, and sexual desire appears to be atypically high among people with paraphilias (Kafka, 1997). Nonetheless, men with paraphilias do not appear to have high levels of testosterone or other androgens (Thibaut, De La Barra, Gordon, et al., 2010). If biology turns out to be important, it most likely will be but one factor in a complex network of causes that includes experience as a major player (Meyer, 1995).

Psychological Factors Most psychological theories of the paraphilias involve a set of risk factors. Dominant models emphasize conditioning experiences, relationship histories, abuse, and cognition.

Proposed DSM-5 Criteria for Sexual Sadism Disorder

- For at least 6 months, recurrent, intense, and sexually arousing fantasies, urges, or behaviors involving the physical or psychological suffering of another person
- Causes clinically significant distress or impairment in functioning or the person has acted on these urges with *at least two* nonconsenting others *on separate occasions*

Note: Changes from the DSM-IV-TR are italicized.

Proposed DSM-5 Criteria for Sexual Masochism Disorder

- For at least 6 months, recurrent, intense, and sexually arousing fantasies, urges, or behaviors involving the act of being humiliated, beaten, bound, or made to suffer
- Causes marked distress or impairment in functioning

Check Your Knowledge 12.3

Choose the diagnostic category that best fits each vignette. If not diagnosable, state so.

1. Joe is able to obtain sexual arousal only by rubbing his body against strangers. He has worked out a set of rituals to engage in this behavior; he knows which bus routes and times will be most crowded, chooses a bus that tends to have many women, and times his attacks so that he can leave the bus at a stop along with many other people.

2. Sam and Terry enjoy a good sexual relationship. They have mutually satisfying sex at least weekly. Occasionally, Terry likes to be tied down before sex, but she is able to enjoy sex without bondage as well. Most of their sex life involves no hint of pain or bondage.

3. Matt feels aroused only when he is able to cause pain to someone as part of engaging in sex. Most of the time, he indulges in these activities at a sadomasochism club. He has not been able to sustain a relationship with any of the women he has met in clubs. He is deeply distressed by his inability to enjoy other forms of sexuality.

4. Barry is a 40-year-old single man who has never had a sustained dating relationship or sexual partner. Several times a week, Barry parks his car at the beach, masturbates, and then finds a way to lure a woman to his car, usually by asking for directions. He is unable to have an orgasm unless the woman notices his erection. He has been arrested three times for this behavior.

Some behavioral theorists view the cause of paraphilias as classical conditioning that by chance has linked sexual arousal with unusual or inappropriate stimuli (Kinsey et al., 1948). For example, a young man may masturbate to images of women dressed in black leather boots. According to this theory, repetitions of these experiences make boots sexually arousing. Similar proposals have been made for pedohebephilic, voyeuristic, and exhibitionistic disorders. Although there is some minor support (Rachman, 1966), research has not supported most components of the classical conditioning hypothesis (O'Donohue & Plaud, 1994). As described later, however, some therapeutic strategies have been developed based on these ideas.

From an operant conditioning perspective, some paraphilias, such as exhibitionistic disorder and pedohebephilic disorder, are considered an outcome of inadequate social skills. Evidence does indicate that men with pedohebephilic disorder often have poor social skills (Dreznick, 2003). These paraphilias may thus be activities that substitute for more conventional relationships and sexual activity. On the other hand, the fact that many pedophiles and exhibitionists have conventional social and sexual relationships indicates that the issue is more complex than a simple absence of nondeviant sexual outlets (Maletzky, 2000).

The childhood histories of people with paraphilias reveal that often they were exposed to physical abuse, sexual abuse, and poor parent–child relationships (Mason, 1997). In studies of adult offenders, rates of sexual abuse are more than threefold higher among sexual offenders compared to those charged with nonsexual offenses (Jespersen, Lalumiere, & Seto, 2009), and are particularly high among those charged with sexual offenses against children (Jespersen et al., 2009). But this cannot be the whole story—at least a third of people who commit sexual offenses against children do not report a history of sexual abuse (Jespersen et al., 2009), and only a small percentage of sexually abused children develop pedohebephilic disorder as adults. In a long-term follow-up of 908 children with histories of sexual abuse, only 3.9 percent were charged with any type of sexual offense as adults (Salter, McMillan, Richards, et al., 2003). In a follow-up of 224 boys who were sexually abused over 7–12 years, about 12 percent committed sexual offenses, and most were toward children. The offenses were most likely to occur when the abused boys reached adolescence and were particularly likely to occur if there was neglect, family violence, or lack of supervision and if the abuse had been perpetrated by a woman.

Cognitive distortions and attitudes also play a role in the paraphilias. Men who engage in paraphilias that involve nonconsenting women may have hostile attitudes and a lack of empathy toward women. Others may have distortions in the ways they think about their sexual behavior. For example, a voyeur may believe that a woman who left her blinds up while undressing wanted someone to look at her (Kaplan & Kreuger, 1997). A person with pedohebephilic disorder may believe that children want to have sex with adults (Marshall, 1997). Table 12.6 contains examples of the kinds of unwarranted beliefs that may be associated with pedohebephilic disorder and exhibitionistic disorder. Rape is also included in the table. See Focus on Discovery 12.4 for a discussion of rape.

Some research suggests that alcohol and negative affect are often the immediate triggers of incidents of pedohebephilic disorder, voyeuristic disorder, and exhibitionistic disorder. This is

Table 12.6 Examples of Cognitive Distortions and Justifications in Sexual Paraphilias and Rape

Category	Pedohebephilic Disorder	Exhibitionistic Disorder	Rape
Misattributing blame	"She started it by being too cuddly."	"The way she was dressed, she was asking for it."	"She was saying no, but her body said yes."
Denying sexual intent	"I was just teaching her about sex . . . better from her father than from someone else."	"I was just looking for a place to pee."	"I was just trying to teach her a lesson; she deserved it."
Debasing the victim	"She was such a bad kid, she was bound to get herself in trouble."	"She was just a slut anyway."	"The way she came on to me at the party, she deserved it."
Minimizing consequences	"She was messed up even before it happened."	"I never touched her, so I couldn't have hurt her."	"She'd had sex with hundreds of guys before. It was no big deal."
Deflecting censure	"This happened years ago. Why can't everyone forget about it?"	"It's not like I raped anyone."	"I only did it once."
Justifying the cause	"If I wasn't molested as a kid, I'd never have done this."	"If I knew how to get dates, I wouldn't have to expose."	"If my girlfriend gave me what I want, I wouldn't be forced to rape."

Source: Maletzky (2002).

consistent with evidence that alcohol decreases inhibition. Deviant sexual activity, like alcohol use, may be a means of escaping from negative affect (Baumeister & Butler, 1997).

Treatments for the Paraphilias

Because many of the behaviors involved in paraphilias are illegal, some people diagnosed with them are imprisoned and court-ordered into treatment. Much of the available research on treatment focuses on men who have been charged with sexual offenses. Men who are arrested, though, may be a more severe subset of those with paraphilias.

Outcomes for incarcerated juvenile and adult sex offenders are highly variable across studies (Becker & Hunter, 1997; Maletzky, 2002). Data on treatment are hard to interpret for several reasons. First, most researchers avoid using control groups who receive no treatment—many researchers consider it unethical to withhold treatment when the consequences of sexual offenses are so severe. Second, it is difficult to compare findings because the patients enrolled in different studies vary greatly. Some programs select the most problematic prisoners for treatment, whereas others treat those with the most promising prognoses. Third, many studies do not evaluate whether treatment successes are sustained over time, even though recidivism increases as the years go by, especially when 2 years have passed since termination of treatment (Maletzky, 2002). Despite these concerns, there is evidence that treatment—whether biological or psychological—does help. In a meta-analysis of 12 studies of men arrested for sexual offenses, those who received treatment of some form—either biological or psychological—were about a third less likely to have repeat offenses than those who did not receive treatment (Hall et al., 1995). With these issues as background, we now describe cognitive behavioral and biological treatments for the paraphilias. Then we consider legal efforts to protect the public from sex offenders.

Strategies to Enhance Motivation   Sex offenders often lack motivation to change their illegal behavior. They may deny their problem, minimize the seriousness of their problem, and feel confident that they can control their behavior without professional assistance. Some blame the victim, even a child, for being overly seductive. Many drop out of treatment. For these reasons, such people are often judged to be inappropriate for treatment programs (Dougher, 1988). To enhance motivation for treatment, a therapist can do the following (Miller & Rollnick, 1991):

1. Empathize with the offender's reluctance to admit that he is an offender and to seek treatment, thereby reducing defensiveness and hostility

2. Point out that treatment might help him control his behavior better

3. Emphasize the negative consequences of refusing treatment (e.g., transfer to a less attractive incarceration setting if the person is already in custody) and of offending again (e.g., stiffer legal penalties)

FOCUS ON DISCOVERY 12.4

Rape

It has been estimated that 20 to 25 percent of American women will be raped during their lifetimes (Crowell & Burgess, 1996). Rape is an important issue on college campuses. A discouraging 30 percent of female college students report that they have experienced the use of physical force, threats, or harm after they refused sexual contact with a person, with 8.7 percent reporting that they had experienced physical harm (Struckman-Johnson, 1988). Rape occurs far too often.

The specifics of rape cases vary widely. Although men can be victims of sexual assault, our discussion focuses on women, because more than 90 percent of rapes are committed by men against women (Crowell & Burgess, 1996). Younger women and girls are much more likely to be victims of rape than are older women (see Figure A). About 70 percent of rapes are committed by someone known to the woman (National Center for Justice, 2003). Up to 70 percent of rapes are associated with intoxication (Crowell & Burgess, 1996). Very rarely, rapists murder their victims.

Most women who are raped will experience symptoms of anxiety in the weeks after an attack (Rothbaum & Foa, 1993), and at least a third will develop PTSD (Breslau, Chilcoat, Kessler, et al., 1999). More detail on PTSD and its treatment is provided in Chapter 7.

The Rapist: Understanding the Etiology of Rape

Is the rapist primarily someone who seeks the thrill of dominating and humiliating a woman through intimidation and assault? Is he an ordinarily unassertive man with a fragile ego who, feeling inadequate after disappointment and rejection in work or love, takes out his frustrations on an unwilling stranger? What types of characteristics distinguish rapists?

There is no DSM diagnosis to capture a tendency to rape, but the DSM-5 sexual and gender identity work group is considering including paraphilic coercive disorder in the appendix for further study. There are several traits that appear elevated among rapists. Sexually aggressive men tend to show

antisocial and impulsive personality traits (Crowell & Burgess, 1996). Many rapists have unusually high hostility toward women (Malamuth, 1998). More specific to sexual interactions, other studies have found that rapists tend to respond with more sexual arousal than nonsexual offenders to images of coercive sexual activity (Lalumiere & Quinsey, 1994). They may also have cognitive distortions in the way they evaluate the consequences of their behavior (see Table 12.6). Some rapists seem to have problems distinguishing friendliness from seductiveness and in accurately reading cues from a woman indicating that she wants intimacies to cease (Malamuth & Brown, 1994). In one major community survey, men who had assaulted women sexually were 3.5 times more likely to report erectile dysfunction than those who had

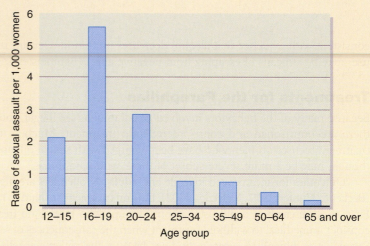

Figure A Annual rates of sexual assault victimization among women by age group. From National Center for Justice (2003).

4. Explain that the psychophysiological assessment of the patient's sexual arousal will make it harder to deny sexual proclivities to the authorities (Garland & Dougher, 1991)

Cognitive Behavioral Treatment   In the earliest years of behavioral treatment, paraphilias were narrowly viewed as attractions to inappropriate objects and activities. Looking to behavioral psychology for ways to reduce these attractions, researchers fixed on aversion therapy. Thus, a person with a boot fetish would be given a shock on the hands or a drug that produces nausea when looking at a boot, a person with pedohebephilic disorder when gazing at a photograph of a nude child, and so on. A variation of aversion therapy based on imagery is covert sensitization, whereby the person imagines situations he finds inappropriately arousing and also imagines feeling sick or ashamed for feeling and acting this way. Versions of covert sensitization have been developed that pair the aversive imagery with a foul odor (Maletzky, 2000). Studies of covert sensitization have shown that it reduces deviant arousal, but little evidence is available that these techniques alone actually change the behavior (Maletzky, 2000).

Cognitive procedures are often used to counter the distorted thinking of people with paraphilias. Table 12.6 contains examples of cognitive distortions that would be targets for modification. For example, an exhibitionist might claim that the girls he exposes himself to are too young to be harmed by it. The therapist would counter this distortion by pointing out that the younger the victim, the worse the harm will be (Maletzky, 1997).

not (Laumann et al., 1999). Rapists also appear to have a high sex drive (as measured by frequency of sexual outlets) (Kafka, 1997).

There is also data to suggest that observing exposure to violence against women, even in films, can lead men to view violence as more acceptable. In a controlled experiment, undergraduate men who stated that they regarded rape as unacceptable were aroused by video portrayals of rape if the woman was depicted as having an orgasm during the assault (Malamuth & Check, 1983). Since the time this study was conducted, eight experiments have been conducted in which men are asked to watch videos that contain either sexual activities with violence or sexual activities without violence. A meta-analysis of these studies suggested that after watching the videos that contained violence, men

This famous scene from *Gone with the Wind* illustrates one of the myths about rape—that despite initial resistance, women like to be "taken." (Everett Collection, Inc.)

were significantly more likely to report that violence toward women was acceptable (Allen, D'Alessio, & Brezgel, 1995). This research suggests that rape may be encouraged by pornography that depicts women enjoying violent sexual relations.

Psychological Treatment for Rapists

Treatment programs for rapists rely on the general approaches we describe for paraphilias. These include motivational strategies, a range of cognitive behavioral techniques, and pharmacological treatments. As with the research on treatment for paraphilias, the evidence regarding the effectiveness of these approaches is remarkably slim. Only one study has randomly assigned men who are sexual offenders to cognitive behavioral treatment or to no treatment (Marques et al., 2005). That study found that among 24 rapists, 20 percent of men in the treatment group committed an offense during the 5-year follow-up period, compared to 29 percent in the no-treatment group. Although these findings might seem discouraging, any gain is important with such a difficult problem.

Reforming the Legal System

Estimates are that less than half of rapes are reported (National Center for Victims of Violent Crime, 2004). Interviews with half a million women indicated three reasons for reluctance to report rape:

1. Considering the rape a private matter
2. Fearing reprisals from the rapist or his family or friends
3. Believing that police would be ineffective or insensitive (Wright, 1991)

Several legal reforms have been enacted to address these types of concerns. For example, all states now allow for prosecution of rapes that occur within marriages; the laws in most states consider the likely absence of witnesses for such a private act; and, perhaps most importantly, information about the victim's previous sexual behavior and history is no longer admissible in court. Despite these changes, trials remain very stressful, and only a very small percentage of rapists are ultimately convicted of their crimes.

In general, cognitive and behavioral approaches have become more sophisticated and broader in scope since the 1960s, when the paraphilias were addressed almost exclusively through aversive conditioning and cognitive interventions. Current approaches supplement these traditional approaches with techniques such as social skills training and sexual impulse control training (Maletzky, 2002). Training in empathy toward others is another increasingly common cognitive technique; teaching the sex offender to consider how his or her behavior would affect someone else may lessen the tendency to engage in such activities. Relapse prevention, modeled after the work on substance abuse described in Chapter 10, is also an important component of many broader treatment programs. A therapist who uses relapse prevention techniques would help a person identify situations and emotions that might trigger symptomatic behavior. Interventions that combine cognitive interventions with behavioral interventions appear to be more successful than those that are strictly behavioral (Hall et al., 1995).

Most of the available evidence for these interventions is based on studies with no control group. Without a control group, it seemed as though interventions were helping relieve symptoms—many people reported diminished symptoms of paraphilia after treatment (Maletzky, 2002). Unfortunately, when compared to a control group that did not receive treatment, cognitive behavioral therapy did not appear to reduce legal recidivism (Marques, Wiederanders, Day, et al., 2005). Although these findings are discouraging, efforts to provide treatment, even if only minimally effective, stand the chance of protecting others after the person is released from prison (Prentky, 1990). This remains an important area for ongoing research.

Biological Treatment A variety of biological interventions have been tried on sex offenders. Castration, or removal of the testes, was used a great deal until hormonal treatments (described next) became available. Although no controlled trials are available, about 3 percent of men who underwent surgical castration reoffended during follow-up periods lasting about 11 years—a rate far lower than one might expect without castration (Wille & Boulanger, 1984). Surgical castration is not a common treatment today due to major ethical concerns.

On the other hand, several medications have been used to treat paraphilias, particularly among sex offenders. Typically, these medications are used as a supplement to psychological treatment. Among men, sexual drive and functioning are regulated by androgens (testosterone and dihydrotestosterone). Hence, hormonal agents that reduce androgens have been used to treat paraphilias, including medroxyprogesterone acetate (MPA, trade name Depo-Provera), cyproterone acetate (CPA, Gyrostat), and luteinizing hormone–releasing hormone (LHRH) agents. There is evidence from randomized controlled trials that these agents reduce arousal to deviant objects, as measured using the penile plethysmograph (Thibaut et al., 2010). Despite the promising findings, many ethical issues are raised about the indefinite use of hormonal agents. Long-term use of hormonal agents is associated with a number of negative side effects, including infertility, liver problems, osteoporosis, and diabetes (Gunn, 1993). Informed consent concerning these risks must be obtained, and many patients will not agree to use these drugs long term (Hill, Briken, Kraus, et al., 2003).

Beyond drugs that influence hormones, SSRI antidepressants are commonly used. Although pre–post measures suggest that SSRIs reduce arousal to deviant objects, researchers have not conducted randomized controlled trials of SSRIs to consider how these medications compare to a control condition, and so the quality of the research evidence is poor (Thibaut et al., 2010).

Efforts to Protect the Public: Megan's Law The rates of recidivism after prison release have led to public pressure to forbid sexual offenders from returning to the locales where they were arrested. A further trend is exemplified in laws that allow police to publicize the whereabouts of registered sex offenders if they are considered to be a potential danger. These laws also permit citizens to use computerized police records to determine whether sex offenders are living in their neighborhoods (Kempster, 1996).

Referred to by some as Megan's law, this statute and others like it across the United States arose from public outrage at the brutal murder of a second grader in New Jersey who was kidnapped while walking home from school. The person convicted of this crime was a twice-convicted child molester. Sadly, some neighborhoods have responded with vigilantism when residents become aware of sex offenders in their neighborhoods (Younglove & Vitello, 2003). It should come as no surprise that civil liberties groups are challenging these laws.

Quick Summary

Paraphilias are defined by a sexual attraction to an unusual sexual object or activity that lasts at least 6 months and causes significant distress or impairment. The DSM diagnostic criteria for paraphilias are distinguished based on the object of sexual attraction. The major DSM-5 diagnoses of paraphilias include fetishistic disorder, pedohebephilic disorder, voyeuristic disorder, exhibitionistic disorder, frotteuristic disorder, sexual sadism disorder, sexual masochism disorder, and transvestic disorder. The latter diagnosis was not discussed here.

Researchers do not know the prevalence of these disorders, nor is much research available on the causes of paraphilias. Neurobiological theory has focused on excessively high levels of male hormones (testosterone), but the theory has not received strong support. Psychological theories focus on conditioning to inappropriate sexual objects, histories of physical and sexual abuse, poor parenting, social skill deficits, hostility toward women and cognitive distortions. Alcohol use and negative affect are often immediate triggers of inappropriate sexual behaviors.

The research evidence regarding treatments for paraphilias is limited. Treatment approaches must begin with a focus on engaging and motivating the client, which is often difficult to do. Early cognitive behavioral approaches focused on aversion therapy (including covert sensitization) and cognitive techniques to challenge distorted beliefs about the consequences of sexual behaviors. Over time, cognitive behavioral therapists have also begun to use techniques to improve social skills, to help people control impulses, to increase empathy for potential victims, and to identify potential high-risk situations for the return of symptoms. The most common medication treatments involve antidepressants or medications that reduce male hormone levels, but the research on antidepressants is poor and the hormonal medications have serious side effects. Laws have been passed that allow the public to access information about where sexual offenders live, but civil liberties groups are opposed to some aspects of these laws.

Check Your Knowledge 12.4

Answer the questions.
1. Which of the following has not been related to paraphilias?
   a. childhood abuse
   b. cognitive distortions
   c. negative affect
   d. all of the above have been related to paraphilias
2. The most commonly used biological treatments to reduce sexual desire and paraphilic behaviors are:

   a. surgical castration
   b. hormonal agents and antidepressants
   c. antianxiety medications
   d. none of the above
3. Name three cognitive behavioral interventions used in the treatment of paraphilias: _____, _____, _____.

Summary

Sexual Norms

- Sexual behavior and attitudes are heavily influenced by culture, so any discussion of disorders in sexuality must be sensitive to the idea that norms are likely to change over time and place. Currently, a great deal of research is focused on gender differences in sexuality.
- Kaplan identified four phases in the sexual response cycle: desire, excitement, orgasm, and resolution. The applicability of the Kaplan model for women has been criticized.

Sexual Dysfunctions

- The proposed DSM-5 includes the following sexual dysfunction diagnoses: sexual interest/arousal disorder in women, hypoactive sexual desire disorder in men, erectile disorder, female orgasmic disorder, early ejaculation, delayed ejaculation, and genito-pelvic pain/penetration disorder. Many people experience brief sexual symptoms, but these are not diagnosable unless they are recurrent, cause either distress or impairment, and are not explained by medical conditions.
- Research on the etiology of sexual dysfunctions is difficult to conduct, as surveys may be inaccurate and laboratory measures may be difficult to gather. Researchers have identified many different variables that can contribute to sexual dysfunctions, including biological variables, previous sexual experiences, relationship issues, psychopathology, negative affect and low arousal, and negative cognitions.
- Many effective interventions for sexual dysfunctions are available, most of them cognitive behavioral. Sex therapy, aimed at reversing old habits and teaching new skills, was propelled into public consciousness by the Masters and Johnson work. Their method hinges on gradual, nonthreatening exposure to increasingly intimate sexual encounters. Sex therapists also aim to educate patients in sexual anatomy and physiology, reduce anxiety, teach communication skills, and improve attitudes and thoughts about sexuality.

Couples therapy is sometimes appropriate as well. Biological treatments such as Viagra may be used for the treatment of erectile dysfunction.

Paraphilias

- In the paraphilias, unusual imagery and acts are persistent and necessary for sexual gratification. The principal paraphilias in the proposed DSM-5 are fetishistic disorder, pedohebephilic disorder, voyeuristic disorder, exhibitionistic disorder, frotteuristic disorder, sexual sadism disorder, sexual masochism disorder, and transvestic disorder. (We do not discuss transvestic disorder because there is no evidence that the behavior causes impairment.)
- Efforts have also been made to detect hormonal abnormalities in people with paraphilias, but the findings are inconclusive.
- The behavioral view of paraphilias emphasizes classical conditioning as well as deficiencies in social skills that make it difficult for the person to interact normally with other adults. There is limited support for behavioral risk factors. Exposure to childhood sexual abuse may be a risk factor. Alcohol use may increase the odds of acting on sexual urges. Cognitive distortions appear to be involved.
- The most promising treatments for the paraphilias are cognitive behavioral. One conditioning procedure is to pair the inappropriate sexual object with aversive stimuli. Cognitive methods focus on the cognitive distortions of the person with a paraphilia. Approaches to improve social skills, empathy, and impulse control, and to avoid relapse triggers, are common. Studies suggest that psychological treatments do reduce rates of legal offenses. Drugs that reduce testosterone levels have been found to reduce both sex drive and deviant sexual behaviors, but because of the side effects, there are ethical issues involved in the long-term use of these drugs. SSRI antidepressants are commonly prescribed to reduce sexual drive of men with paraphilias, but the quality of the research evidence is poor.

Answers to Check Your Knowledge Questions

12.1 1. T; 2. T; 3. T; 4. F; 5. T; 6. F; 7. b
12.2 1. F (unless the problem is recurrent and leads to distress or impairment, it cannot be diagnosed); 2. F; 3. T; 4. T
12.3 1. frotteuristic disorder; 2. not a diagnosable disorder (because there is no evidence of distress or impairment); 3. sexual sadism disorder; 4. exhibitionistic disorder

12.4 1. d; 2. b; 3. any three of the following: cognitive interventions to reduce distorted thinking, aversion therapy (including covert sensitization), social skills training, interventions to improve sexual impulse control, empathy training, relapse prevention

Key Terms

delayed ejaculation
desire phase
early ejaculation
erectile disorder
excitement phase
exhibitionistic disorder
female orgasmic disorder
fetishistic disorder

frotteuristic disorder
genito-pelvic pain/penetration
   disorder
hypoactive sexual desire
   disorder in men
incest
orgasm phase
paraphilias

pedohebephilic disorder
penile plethysmograph
resolution phase
sexual dysfunctions
sexual interest/arousal disorder
   in women
sexual masochism disorder
sexual response cycle

sexual sadism disorder
spectator role
vaginal plethysmograph
voyeuristic disorder

13 Disorders of Childhood

1. Be able to describe the issues in the diagnosis of psychopathology in children.
2. Be able to discuss the description, etiology, and treatments for externalizing problems, including ADHD and conduct disorder, and for internalizing problems, including depression and anxiety disorders.
3. Be able to understand the learning disabilities dyslexia and dyscalculia as well as our current understanding of the causes and treatments for dyslexia.
4. Be able to describe the description and diagnosis of intellectual developmental disorder and the current research on causes and treatments.
5. Be able to describe the symptoms, causes, and treatments for autism spectrum disorders.

Clinical Case: Zach

Zach is 12 years old, the second of three children. His problems began in nursery school with bad behavior in the play room which had persisted into primary school. As an infant he cried frequently, he didn't eat well and his sleep was frequently fitful and restless. Verbal reprimands, which had been effective in controlling his siblings' behavior, had no effect on him. Until a late age if Zach was stopped from doing something, he would still have a temper tantrum which included throwing himself on the ground (or throwing anything he could get hold of). Zach's relationships with his siblings at home and peers at school were poor. He had been through phases of biting his younger brother, and delighted in getting classmates into trouble. At his new secondary school, he had already been warned about stirring up trouble and not paying attention. In class, he was rarely prepared to answer when the teacher called on him, and he usually forgot to write down the homework assignments.

Zach loved football, and his local team had just been promoted to the premiership. That week's fixture was against Manchester United—and his father had managed to get tickets but said that Zach could only go if he had finished all of his homework before the game started. On the afternoon of the match, Zach was incredibly excited. He only had a couple of pages of maths to do. Thirty minutes later, his father came in from the garden to find Zach playing a computer game; the maths homework was half done. Zach's father couldn't believe it and told Zach that he had let him down. He then left for the game without him. Zach was extremely upset and disappointed and in frustration broke a model rocket he had spent several weeks making at school.

At bedtime, annoyed and discouraged, Zach was unable to sleep. He often lay awake for what seemed like hours, reviewing the disappointments of the day and berating himself for his failures. On this night, he ruminated about his lack of friends, the frustration of his teachers, and his parents' exhortations to pay attention and "get it together."

Zach's parents and the school decided to contact a psychologist to discuss the problems he was having, both academically and socially. At the first visit, the psychologist spent the first part of the session discussing Zach's early childhood, behavioral problems at school and home. The psychologist then spent time alone with Zach. Zach initially maintained that he didn't understand why he was there, but later conceded that he was having some problems at school and agreed that it would be a good idea to try and do something about his behavior. His parents were then called back into the clinic room, and the psychologist explained Zach's problem in an operant-conditioning framework. Although a biological basis may be a contributory factor in Zach's behavior, the psychologist proposed a structured program of positive and negative reinforcement would help.

MOST THEORIES OF CHILDHOOD disorders, whether behavioral, cognitive, or neurobiological, consider childhood experience and development critically important to adult mental health. Most theories also regard children as better able to change than adults and thus as particularly suitable for treatment. The number of children diagnosed with and treated for different psychological disorders has dramatically increased in recent years, but not without controversy (see Focus on Discovery 13.4 later in the chapter). Also controversial is the tremendous increase in the number of medication prescriptions given to children. For example, antipsychotic medications prescribed for children increased fivefold between 1993 and 2002, with over 1 million such prescriptions written in 2002 (Olfson, Blanco, Liu, et al., 2006).

In this chapter we discuss several of the disorders that are most likely to arise in childhood and adolescence. We first consider disorders involving inattention, impulsivity, and disruptive behavior, followed by depression and anxiety disorders. Finally, we discuss disorders in which the acquisition of cognitive, language, motor, or social skills is disturbed. These include learning disorder as well as the most severe of developmental disorders, intellectual developmental disorder and autism spectrum disorder, which are usually chronic, persisting into adulthood.

Classification and Diagnosis of Childhood Disorders

Before making a diagnosis of a particular disorder in children, clinicians must first consider what is typical for a particular age. The diagnosis of children who lie on the floor kicking and screaming when they don't get their way would be assessed differently at age 2 than at age 7. The field of **developmental psychopathology** focuses on the disorders of childhood within the context of life-span development, enabling us to identify behaviors that are considered appropriate at one stage but disturbed at another.

Some childhood disorders, such as separation anxiety disorder, are unique to children. Others, such as attention-deficit/hyperactivity disorder, have been conceptualized primarily as childhood disorders but may continue into adulthood. Still others, such as depression, may begin in childhood but are common in adulthood as well. Although eating disorders typically begin in adolescence, they are presented separately in Chapter 11.

There will likely be several changes to the childhood disorders in DSM-5. As shown in Figure 13.1, even the organization of the disorders is changing a bit. In DSM-IV-TR, all

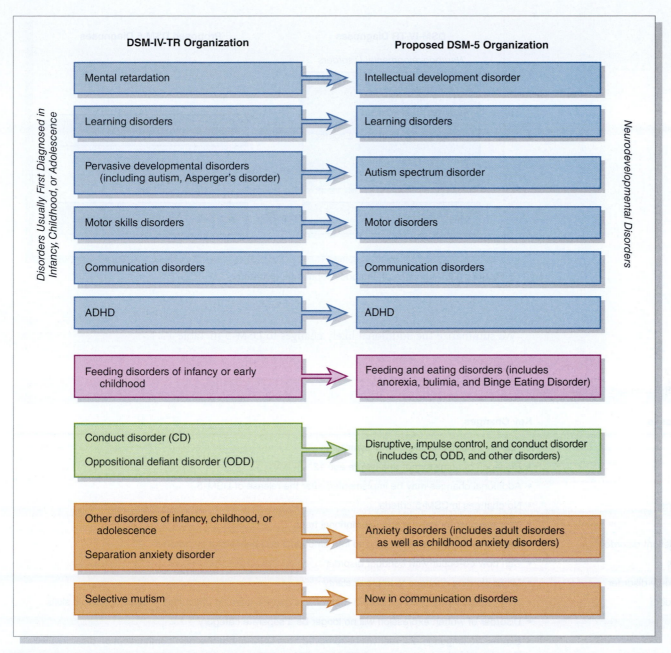

Figure 13.1 Organization of childhood disorders in DSM-IV-TR and DSM-5.

the childhood disorders were in one chapter. In DSM-5, there are two proposed chapters: "Neurodevelopmental Disorders" and "Disruptive, Impulse Control, and Conduct Disorder." Other disorders, such as separation anxiety disorder, will be in the chapter for adult anxiety disorders.

Other likely changes in DSM-5 will involve new names for disorders (see Figure 13.2). For example, what was formerly called mental retardation will be called intellectual developmental disorder to be consistent with the approach of the American Association on Intellectual and Developmental Disabilities (AAIDD). Another proposed change is the combination of three disorders from DSM-IV-TR (autistic disorder, Asperger's disorder, and pervasive developmental disorder not otherwise specified) into one DSM-5 disorder called autism spectrum disorder.

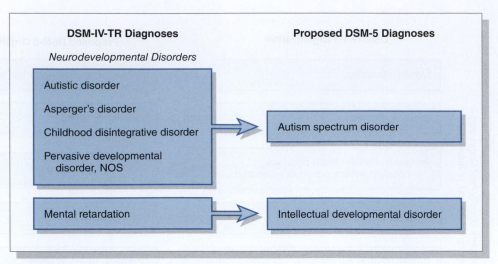

Figure 13.2 Diagnoses of neurodevelopmental disorders.

We summarize the additional likely changes to DSM-5 in Table 13.1.

Table 13.1 Diagnoses of Childhood Disorders

DSM-5 Diagnoses	Key Changes
ADHD	• Four new additional impulsivity symptoms • Presence of some symptoms before age 12 • Additional changes may be implemented after the release of DSM-5
Conduct disorder	• No changes in DSM-5 criteria • New specifier for callous and unemotional traits
Oppositional defiant disorder	• Criteria are the same but organized into emotional and behavioral symptoms • Can now co-occur with conduct disorder
Separation anxiety disorder	• Minor wording changes to improve clarity
Learning disorders	• New category proposed for DSM-5 that reflects general learning difficulties in basic academic skills • Disorder of written expression will no longer be a separate category • Expressive language disorder will be removed from DSM-5, but five new communication disorders will likely be added
Dyslexia	• Formerly named reading disorder • Reading achievement and comprehension removed and replaced with accuracy and fluency
Dyscalculia	• Formerly named mathematics disorder • Criteria broadened to include problems with numeracy skills, not just mathematics
Intellectual developmental disorder	• Formerly named mental retardation • Broader specification of functional and adaptive impairments • Types no longer specified based on IQ scores
Autism spectrum disorder	• Formerly named autistic disorder • Combines autism, Asperger's, PDD NOS, and childhood disintegrative disorder • Communication and social interaction domains are combined into one broad domain given their overlap • Language delay not required for diagnosis • Must be present from early childhood

The more prevalent childhood disorders are often divided into two broad domains, externalizing disorders and internalizing disorders. **Externalizing disorders** are characterized by more outward-directed behaviors, such as aggressiveness, noncompliance, overactivity, and impulsiveness; the category includes attention-deficit/hyperactivity disorder, conduct disorder, and oppositional defiant disorder. **Internalizing disorders** are characterized by more inward-focused experiences and behaviors, such as depression, social withdrawal, and anxiety; the category includes childhood anxiety and mood disorders. Children and adolescents may exhibit symptoms from both domains, as described in the Clinical Case of Zach.

The behaviors that comprise externalizing and internalizing disorders are prevalent across many countries, such as Switzerland (Steinhausen & Metzke, 1998), Australia (Achenbach, Hensley, Phares, et al., 1990), Puerto Rico (Achenbach et al., 1990), Kenya (Weisz, Sigman, Weiss, et al., 1993), and Greece (MacDonald, Tsiantis, Achenbach, et al., 1995). Across cultures, externalizing behaviors are consistently found more often among boys and internalizing behaviors more often among girls, at least in adolescence (Weisz, Suwanlert, Wanchai, et al., 1987). Focus on Discovery 13.1 discusses the possible role of culture in the prevalence of these problem behaviors in children.

As we will see, childhood disorders involve an interaction of genetic, neurobiological, and psychological factors. In Focus on Discovery 13.2, we consider another disorder that adversely impacts children: asthma.

FOCUS ON DISCOVERY 13.1

The Role of Culture in Internalizing and Externalizing Behavior Problems

The values and mores of a culture may play a role in whether a certain pattern of child behavior develops or is considered a problem. One study found that in Thailand, children with internalizing behavior problems, such as fearfulness, were the ones most likely to be seen in clinics, whereas in the United States, those with externalizing behavior problems, such as aggressiveness and hyperactivity, were more commonly seen (Weisz et al., 1987). The researchers attributed these differences to the fact that Buddhism, which disapproves of and discourages aggression, is widely practiced in Thailand. In other words, cultural sanctions against acting out in aggressive ways may have kept these behaviors from developing at the rate that they do in the United States. One of the issues in this study was that the researchers only used assessment measures that were normed on U.S. samples, leaving open the possibility that behavior differences between the two cultures were missed because they were not validly assessed for both cultures (see Chapter 3 for more on the issue of culture and assessment).

Indeed, findings from a follow-up study suggest that the behavior problems described in the same terms may not really be exactly the same across Thai and U.S. cultures (Weisz, Weiss, Suwanlert, et al., 2003). The researchers compared specific behavior problems (e.g., somatic complaints, aggressive behavior) and broad domains (internalizing, externalizing) using U.S. and Thai assessment measures. The broad domains of internalizing and externalizing behaviors were found to be the same in Thai and U.S. children, but more specific categories within those domains were not. Among boys, somatic complaints were seen consistently across cultures, but shyness was seen less consistently. Among girls, shyness was seen consistently across cultures but verbal aggressive behavior was not.

These studies point to the importance of studying psychopathology across cultures. It is dangerous to assume that the measures we develop to assess psychopathology in the United States will work equally well across cultures. As the investigators cited above point out, our theories about the causes of psychopathology need to be able to account for cultural variation in such factors as parenting practices, beliefs and values, and the ways in which parents report on their child's behavior problems. This remains an urgent and important challenge for our field.

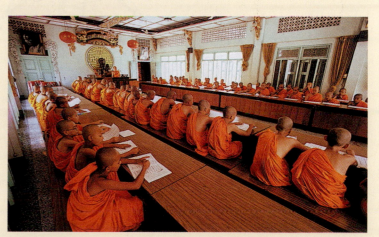

Thai teenagers serving as novices in a Buddhist temple. Buddhist culture may contribute to the relatively low prevalence of externalizing disorders in Thailand. (Paul Chesley/Stone/Getty Images.)

FOCUS ON DISCOVERY 13.2

Asthma

Asthma, a disorder of the respiratory system (see Figure A), afflicts 23 million people in the United States, including 7 million children. The prevalence rates of asthma are highest for children ages 5–14 and 15–19 (NHBLI, 2010). In California, children with asthma missed an average of 1 week of school in 2005 (Meng, Babey, Hastert, et al., 2008). During childhood, asthma is more common among boys than among girls, but by adulthood, it is more common among women than among men (NHBLI, 2009).

In an asthma attack, the air passages in the lungs become narrowed, causing extremely labored and wheezy breathing. In addition, activity of the immune system during asthma attacks leads to inflammation of lung tissue, resulting in an increase in mucus secretion and edema (accumulation of fluid in the tissues) (Moran, 1991).

Most often, asthma attacks begin suddenly. A severe attack is a frightening experience and may cause a panic attack (Carr, 1998, 1999), which exacerbates the asthma. People with asthma have immense difficulty getting air into and out of the lungs and feel as though they are suffocating; the gasping, wheezing, and coughing can compound the fear. After an attack, a person may become exhausted by the exertion and fall asleep as soon as breathing is more normal.

Asthma attacks occur intermittently, sometimes almost daily and sometimes separated by weeks or months, and vary in severity.

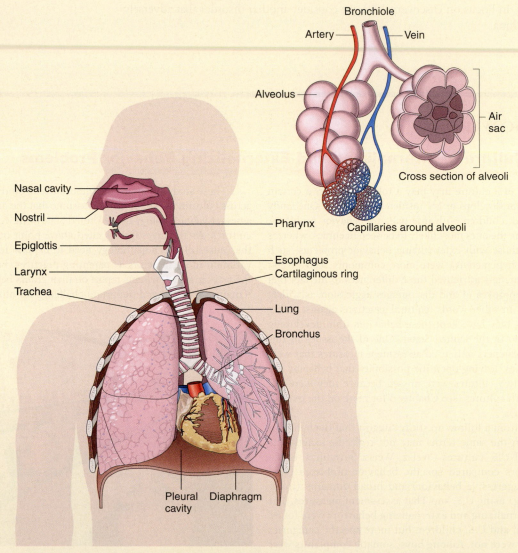

Figure A Major structures of the respiratory system—trachea, lungs, bronchi, bronchioles, and alveoli—and the ancillary organs. In asthma, the air passages, especially the bronchioles, become constricted and fluid and mucus build up in the lungs.

The frequency of attacks may increase seasonally, when certain pollens are present. Symptoms may last an hour or may continue for several hours or sometimes even for days.

For people with exercise-induced asthma, the attacks follow strenuous exercise. Although some athletes are debilitated by the attacks, others are able to perform at the highest level despite their asthma—for example, Jackie Joyner-Kersee, a six-time Olympic medalist in track and field.

What Causes Asthma?

Asthma attacks seem to be brought on by a very wide variety of factors, including allergens, exercise, cold temperature, viral infections, and environmental toxins such as secondhand smoke and air pollution. Stress or negative emotions can exacerbate the impact of environmental toxins on asthma.

Biological Factors

When asthma is caused primarily by allergens, the cells in the respiratory tract are especially sensitive to one or more substances (allergens), such as pollen, molds, fur, air pollution, smoke, and dust mites, which bring on an attack. People whose asthma is primarily allergic may have an inherited hypersensitivity of the respiratory mucosa, which then overresponds to one or more of such usually harmless substances. Asthma runs in families, which is consistent with genetic factors playing a role (Eder, Ege, & von Mutius, et al., 2006). Studies are narrowing in on how genes may interact with environmental factors to produce asthma (e.g., Cookson & Moffatt, 1997, 2000).

Stressful Life Events and Negative Emotions

Even when asthma is originally induced by an infection or allergy, psychological stress

Olympic medalist Jackie Joyner-Kersee suffers from exercise-induced asthma. (© AP/Wide World Photos.)

can precipitate an attack. Because of the link between the autonomic nervous system (ANS) and the constriction and dilation of the airways, and the connection between the ANS and emotions, research has focused on heightened experience and expression of negative emotions.

Negative emotions have also been found to be directly related to reports of asthma symptoms and to peak expiratory flow, which is an assessment of airway obstruction obtained by taking a deep breath and then exhaling as hard as possible into a device that measures the force of the air expelled. A prospective study asked children ages 6 to 13 and their parents to keep daily records of asthma symptom reports and peak expiratory flow for 18 months (Sandberg, Jävenpää, Paton, et al., 2004). The parents and children were also interviewed about stressful life events during the period of the study. The investigators found that the children were nearly five times as likely to have an asthma attack if they experienced a stressful life event 1 or 2 days before the attack. In addition, the children who experienced stressful life events were more likely to have another attack 5 to 7 weeks later.

Treating Asthma

Asthma is most often treated with medications. First, quick-acting corticosteroid inhalers are used when an asthma attack occurs. These can stop the symptoms and bring relief quickly. Second, anti-inflammatory medications are taken more regularly, such as cromolyn sodium, to reduce inflammation of the airways.

Behavioral interventions can also be helpful for adults and children with asthma. The focus of these interventions is on managing triggers of attacks, including allergens, pollen, dust, pollution, secondhand smoke, and stress. Interventions aimed at regulating negative emotions can also be helpful.

Attention-Deficit/Hyperactivity Disorder

The term *hyperactive* is familiar to most people, especially parents and teachers. The child who is constantly in motion—tapping fingers, jiggling legs, poking others for no apparent reason, talking out of turn, and fidgeting—is often called hyperactive. Often, these children also have difficulty concentrating on the task at hand for an appropriate period of time. When such problems are severe and persistent enough, these children may meet the criteria for diagnosis of **attention-deficit/hyperactivity disorder (ADHD)**. Recognizing the impact of ADHD on children and families, the U.S. Congress created a National ADHD Awareness Day, with the first such day being on September 7, 2004.

Clinical Descriptions, Prevalence, and Prognosis of ADHD

What distinguishes the typical range of hyperactive behaviors from a diagnosable disorder? When these behaviors are extreme for a particular developmental period, persistent across different situations, and linked to significant impairments in functioning, the diagnosis of ADHD may be appropriate. The ADHD diagnosis does not properly apply to children who are rambunctious, active, or slightly distractible, for in the early school years children are often so (Whalen, 1983). Using the label simply because a child is more lively and more difficult to control than a parent or teacher would like is a serious mistake. The diagnosis of ADHD should be reserved for truly severe and persistent cases.

Children with ADHD seem to have particular difficulty controlling their activity in situations that call for sitting still, such as in the classroom or at mealtimes. When told to be quiet, they appear unable to stop moving or talking. Their activities and movements seem haphazard. They may quickly wear out their shoes and clothing, smash their toys, and exhaust their families and teachers.

Many children with ADHD have inordinate difficulty getting along with peers and establishing friendships (Blachman & Hinshaw, 2002; Hinshaw & Melnick, 1995), perhaps because their behavior is often aggressive and intrusive. Although these children are usually friendly and talkative, they often miss subtle social cues, such as noticing when other children are tiring of their constant jiggling. Unfortunately, children with ADHD often overestimate their ability to navigate social situations with peers (Hoza, Murray-Close, Arnold, et al., 2010). A recent longitudinal study of children with and without ADHD who were followed up every year for 6 years found that poor social skills, aggressive behavior, and self-overestimation of performance in social situations all predicted problems with peers up to 6 years later. The researchers also found what they called "vicious cycles" with these three domains—poor social skills, aggressive behavior, and overestimation of one's social abilities—all in turn predicted a decline in these abilities at the next follow-up, which in turn predicted greater problems with peers at the next follow-up (Murray-Close, Hoza, Hinshaw, et al., 2010).

In another study, children were asked to instant-message (IM) other children in what appeared to be an online chat room (Mikami, Huang-Pollack, Pfiffner, et al., 2007). Actually, children were interacting with four simulated peers on the computer, and thus all children got the same IMs from the simulated peers. The researchers coded the messages and the participants' reported experiences of the chat elicited in subsequent interviews. Children with ADHD were more likely to IM statements that were hostile and off the topic than were children without ADHD, and children's chat room experiences were related to other measures of social skills difficulties, suggesting that this common way of "interacting" with peers, even though not face-to-face, is also impaired among children with ADHD.

Children with ADHD can know what the socially correct action is in hypothetical situations but be unable to translate this knowledge into appropriate behavior in real-life social interactions (Whalen & Henker, 1985, 1991). Children with ADHD are often singled out very quickly and rejected or neglected by their peers. For example, in a study of previously unacquainted boys at a summer camp, boys with ADHD who exhibited a number of externalizing behaviors, such as overt aggression and noncompliance, were regarded quite negatively by their peers during the first day of camp, and these impressions remained unchanged throughout the 6-week camp period (Erhardt & Hinshaw, 1994; Hinshaw, Zupan, Simmel, et al., 1997).

The DSM-IV-TR includes three subtypes, but these may be removed from DSM-5:

1. Predominantly inattentive type: children whose problems are primarily those of poor attention

2. Predominantly hyperactive-impulsive type: children whose difficulties result primarily from hyperactive/impulsive behavior

3. Combined type: children who have both sets of problems

The combined type comprises the majority of children with ADHD. These children are more likely than those with other subtypes to develop conduct problems and oppositional behavior, to be placed in special classes for children with behavior problems, and to have difficulties interacting with their peers (Faraone, Biederman, Weber, et al., 1998). Because most children with ADHD have the combined type and because many children "switch" subtypes over time as their symptoms change, the DSM-5 may eliminate the three subtypes and instead add codes within the ADHD diagnosis to indicate whether particular symptom types predominate. Children with

Proposed DSM-5 Criteria for Attention-Deficit/ Hyperactivity Disorder

- Either A or B:
  A. Six or more manifestations of inattention present for at least 6 months to a maladaptive degree and greater than what would be expected given a person's developmental level, e.g., careless mistakes, not listening well, not following instructions, easily distracted, forgetful in daily activities.
  B. Six or more manifestations of hyperactivity-impulsivity present for at least 6 months to a maladaptive degree and greater than what would be expected given a person's developmental level, e.g., fidgeting, running about inappropriately (in adults, restlessness), acting as if "driven by a motor," interrupting or intruding, incessant talking.
- Some of the above present before age 12
- Present in two or more settings, e.g., at home, school, or, work
- Significant impairment in social, academic, or occupational functioning
- For people age 17 or older, only four signs of inattention and/ or four signs of hyperactivity-impulsivity are needed to meet the diagnosis

attentional problems but with otherwise developmentally appropriate activity levels appear to have more difficulties with focused attention or speed of information processing (Barkley, Grodzinsky, & DuPaul, 1992), perhaps associated with problems involving the neurotransmitter dopamine and certain areas of the brain, including the prefrontal cortex (Krause, Dresel, Krause, et al., 2003), topics which we turn to below.

A difficult differential diagnosis is between ADHD and conduct disorder, which involves gross violation of social norms. These two disorders frequently co-occur and share some features in common (Beauchaine, Hinshaw, & Pang, 2010; Hinshaw, 1987). There are some differences, however. ADHD is associated more with off-task behavior in school, cognitive and achievement deficits, and a better long-term prognosis. Children with ADHD act out less in school and elsewhere and are less likely to be aggressive and to have antisocial parents. Their home life is also usually marked by less family hostility, and they are at less risk for delinquency and substance abuse in adolescence compared to children with conduct disorder (Faraone, Biederman, Jetton, et al., 1997; Hinshaw, 1987; Jensen, Martin, & Cantwell, 1997).

When these two disorders occur in the same child, the worst features of each are manifest. Such children exhibit the most serious antisocial behavior, are most likely to be rejected by their peers, have the worst academic achievement, and have the poorest prognosis (Hinshaw & Lee, 2003). Girls with both ADHD and conduct disorder exhibit more antisocial behavior, other psychopathology, and risky sexual behavior than girls with only ADHD (Monuteaux, Faraone, Gross, et al., 2007).

Stephen Hinshaw, a renowned developmental psychopathology researcher and expert on mental illness stigma, is conducting one of the largest ongoing studies of girls with ADHD. (Courtesy Stephen Hinshaw, Ph.D.)

Internalizing disorders, such as anxiety and depression, also frequently co-occur with ADHD. Recent estimates suggest that as many as 30 percent of children with ADHD may have comorbid internalizing disorders (e.g., Jensen et al., 1997; MTA Cooperative Group, 1999b). In addition, about 15 to 30 percent of children with ADHD have a learning disorder (Barkley, DuPaul, & McMurray, 1990; Casey, Rourke, & Del Dotto, 1996), and many children with ADHD are placed in special educational programs because of their difficulty in adjusting to a typical classroom environment (Barkley et al., 1990).

Although having both ADHD and conduct disorder is associated with substance use, a prospective study found that the hyperactive symptoms of ADHD predicted subsequent substance (nicotine, alcohol, illicit drugs) use at age 14 and substance use disorder at age 18 even after controlling for symptoms of conduct disorder, and this was equally true for boys and girls (Elkins, McGue, & Iacono, 2007).

The consensus on prevalence estimates is that about 3 to 7 percent of school-age children worldwide currently have ADHD (American Psychiatric Association, 2000). When similar criteria for ADHD are used across countries as diverse as the United States, Kenya, China, and Thailand, the prevalence rates are similar (Anderson, 1996); however, using the same criteria may not adequately capture cultural differences in ADHD (see Focus on Discovery 13.1).

Much evidence indicates that ADHD is more common in boys than in girls, but exact figures depend on whether the sample is taken from clinic referrals or from the general population. Boys are more likely to be referred to clinics because of a higher likelihood of aggressive and antisocial behavior. Until recently, very few carefully controlled studies of girls with ADHD were conducted. Two groups of researchers have conducted large, careful studies of ADHD in girls (Biederman & Faraone, 2004; Hinshaw, 2002). Here are some of key findings at the initial assessment and then again 5 years later (Hinshaw, Carte, Sami, et al., 2002; Hinshaw, Owens, Sami, et al., 2006) or 11 years later (Biederman et al., 2010):

- Girls with the combined type were more likely to have a comorbid diagnosis of conduct disorder or oppositional defiant disorder than girls without ADHD, and this difference remained 5 years after initial diagnosis.

- Girls with the combined type were viewed more negatively by peers than girls with the inattentive type and girls without ADHD; girls with the inattentive type were also viewed more negatively than girls without ADHD.

- Girls with ADHD were likely to be more anxious and depressed than were girls without ADHD, and this remained true 5 years after initial diagnosis.

Aggression is not uncommon among boys with ADHD, and it contributes to their being rejected by peers. (© Lisa F. Young/Shutterstock.)

- Girls with ADHD exhibited a number of neuropsychological deficits, particularly in executive functioning (e.g., planning, solving problems), compared with girls without ADHD, replicating other findings (Castellanos, Marvasti, Ducharme, et al., 2010).

- By adolescence, girls with ADHD were more likely to have symptoms of an eating disorder and substance abuse than girls without ADHD (Mikami, Hinshaw, Arnold, et al., 2010).

- By young adulthood (age 22), the lifetime and past year prevalence rates of mood disorders, anxiety disorders, and substance use disorders were higher for girls with ADHD than girls without ADHD (Biederman, Petty, Monuteaux, et al., 2010).

At one time it was thought that ADHD simply went away by adolescence. However, this belief has been challenged by numerous longitudinal studies (Barkley, Fischer, Smallish, et al., 2002; Biederman, Faraone, Milberger, et al., 1996; Hinshaw et al., 2006; Lee, Lahey, Owens, et al., 2008; Weiss & Hechtman, 1993). Although some children show reduced severity of symptoms in adolescence, 65 to 80 percent of children with ADHD still meet criteria for the disorder in adolescence (Biederman, Monuteaux, Mick, et al., 2006; Hart, Lahey, Loeber, et al., 1995; Hinshaw et al., 2006). Table 13.2 provides a catalogue of behaviors that are found more often among adolescents with ADHD than among adolescents without it. Many children with ADHD do not appear to take a "hit" with respect to academic achievement, however—many studies indicate that achievement is within the average range for both adolescent boys (Lee et al., 2008) and girls (Hinshaw et al., 2006).

In adulthood, most people with ADHD are employed and financially independent, but some studies have found that adults with ADHD are generally at a lower socioeconomic level and change jobs more frequently than is typical (Mannuzza, Klein, Bonagura, et al., 1991; Weiss & Hechtman, 1993). Findings from a review of the studies that have assessed ADHD

Table 13.2 Behaviors in Adolescents with and without ADHD

Behavior	Percentage of Adolescents Who Show This Behavior	
	With ADHD	**Without ADHD**
Blurts out answers	65.0	10.6
Distracted easily	82.1	15.2
Doesn't complete tasks before moving to another	77.2	16.7
Doesn't sustain attention	79.7	16.7
Doesn't follow instructions	83.7	12.1
Doesn't listen to others well	80.5	15.2
Engages in physically dangerous activities	37.4	3.0
Fidgets	73.2	10.6
Finds it hard to play quietly	39.8	7.6
Gets out of seat often	60.2	3.0
Interrupts others	65.9	10.6
Loses things needed for tasks	62.6	12.1
Talks a lot	43.9	6.1

Source: Adapted from Barkley et al. (1990).

longitudinally into adulthood indicate that up to 15 percent of people continued to meet DSM criteria as 25-year-old adults. Even more people—close to 60 percent—continued to meet DSM criteria for ADHD in partial remission as adults (Faraone, Biederman, & Mick, 2005). Thus, ADHD symptoms may decline with age, but they do not entirely go away for many people.

Etiology of ADHD

Genetic Factors Substantial evidence indicates that genetic factors play a role in ADHD (Thapar, Langley, Owen, et al., 2007). Adoption studies (e.g., Sprich, Biederman, Crawford, et al., 2000) and numerous large-scale twin studies (e.g., Levy, Hay, McStephen, et al., 1997; Sherman, Iacono, & McGue, 1997) indicate a genetic component to ADHD, with heritability estimates as high as 70 to 80 percent (Tannock, 1998). Molecular genetics studies that seek to identify genes linked to ADHD are under way. Some of the more promising findings involve genes associated with the neurotransmitter dopamine. Specifically, two different dopamine genes have been implicated in ADHD: a dopamine receptor gene called DRD4 (e.g., Faraone, Doyle, Mick, et al., 2001) and a dopamine transporter gene called DAT1 (Krause et al., 2003; Waldman, Rowe, Abramowitz, et al., 1998). The evidence in support of DRD4's association with ADHD is stronger at this point, as several different studies have consistently found a relationship between this gene and ADHD. Findings for DAT1 are more mixed, with some studies finding a link and others not finding a link with ADHD (Thapar et al., 2007). Even with these promising findings, most investigators agree that a single gene will not ultimately be found to account for ADHD. Rather, several genes interacting with environmental factors will provide the most complete picture of the role of genes in ADHD. For example, recent studies have found that the DRD4 or DAT1 genes are associated with increased risk of ADHD only among those who also had particular environmental factors—namely, prenatal maternal nicotine or alcohol use (Brookes, Mill, Guindalini, et al., 2006; Neuman, Lobos, Reich, et al., 2007). Additional gene–environment studies are under way, and if these findings are replicated, we will have a clearer picture of how genes and environments contribute to ADHD.

Michael Phelps, who won eight gold medals in swimming at the 2008 Olympics, also struggled with ADHD as a child. (Heinz Kluetmeier/Sports illustrated/Getty Images, Inc.)

Neurobiological Factors Studies suggest that brain structure and function differ in children with and without ADHD, particularly in areas of the brain linked to the neurotransmitter dopamine. For example, studies of brain structure have found that dopaminergic areas of the brain, such as the caudate nucleus, globus pallidus, and frontal lobes, are smaller in children with ADHD than children without ADHD (Castellanos, Lee, Sharp, et al., 2002; Swanson et al., 2007). Studies of brain function have found that children with ADHD exhibit less activation in frontal areas of the brain while performing different cognitive tasks (Casey & Durston, 2006; Nigg & Casey, 2005; Rubia, Overmeyer, Taylor, et al., 1999). Moreover, children with ADHD perform poorly on neuropsychological tests that rely on the frontal lobes (such as inhibiting behavioral responses), providing further support for the theory that a basic deficit in this part of the brain may be related to the disorder (Barkley, 1997; Nigg, 2001; Nigg & Casey, 2005; Tannock, 1998).

Perinatal and Prenatal Factors Other neurobiological risk factors for ADHD include a number of perinatal and prenatal complications. Low birth weight, for example, is a predictor of the development of ADHD (e.g., Bhutta, Cleves, Casey, et al., 2002; Breslau, Brown, Del Dotto, et al., 1996; Whitaker, van Rossen, Feldman, et al., 1997). However, the impact of low birth weight on later symptoms of ADHD can be mitigated by greater maternal warmth (Tully, Arseneault, Caspi, et al., 2004). Other complications associated with childbirth, as well as mothers' use of substances such as tobacco (discussed below) and alcohol, are also predictive of ADHD symptoms (Tannock, 1998).

Environmental Toxins Early theories of ADHD in the 1970s involved the role of environmental toxins in the development of hyperactivity. One theory of hyperactivity enjoyed much attention in the popular press for many years. Feingold (1973) proposed that additives and artificial colors in foods upset the central nervous systems of children who were hyperactive, and he prescribed a diet free of them. However, well-controlled studies of the so-called Feingold diet have found that very few children with ADHD respond positively to it (Goyette & Conners, 1977). Even though these early findings did not support Feingold's theory, researchers continue to examine how different elements of the diet, particularly additives, may influence hyperactive behavior. These later studies use more sophisticated research designs, such as placebo-controlled, double-blind studies, but the results remain modest. For example, a meta-analysis of 15 studies found a small effect size for artificial food coloring on hyperactive behavior among children with ADHD (Schnab & Trinh, 2004). A recent study found a similarly small effect of food additives and artificial food coloring on hyperactive behavior among children in the community (McCann, Barrett, Cooper, et al. 2007). Thus, there is limited evidence that food additives impact hyperactive behavior. The popular view that refined sugar can cause ADHD has not been supported by careful research (Wolraich, Wilson, & White, 1995).

Lead is another environmental toxin that has been studied. Some evidence suggests that higher blood levels of lead may be associated to a small degree with symptoms of hyperactivity and attentional problems (Braun, Kahn, Froelich, et al., 2006; Thompson, Raab, Hepburn, et al., 1989), as well as with the diagnosis of ADHD (Nigg, Knotterus, Martel, et al., 2008; Nigg, Nikolas, Knotterus, 2010). However, most children with higher blood levels of lead do not develop ADHD, and most children with ADHD do not show such elevated blood levels. Nevertheless, given the unfortunate frequency with which children are exposed to low levels of lead, investigators continue to examine how lead exposure might play a role, perhaps by influencing other cognitive abilities. One recent study found that blood levels of lead were associated with both deficits in cognitive control (e.g., the ability to inhibit a response or switch attention elsewhere) and with the hyperactivity symptoms of ADHD (Nigg et al., 2008).

Nicotine—specifically, maternal smoking—is an environmental toxin that may play a role in the development of ADHD. One study found that 22 percent of mothers of children with ADHD reported smoking a pack of cigarettes per day during pregnancy, compared with 8 percent of mothers whose children did not develop ADHD (Milberger, Biederman, Faraone, et al., 1996). This effect remained even after controlling for maternal depression and alcohol use (Chabrol, Peresson, Milberger, et al., 1997). A twin study found that maternal smoking predicted ADHD symptoms even after controlling for genetic influences and other environmental risk factors (Thapar, Fowler, Rice, et al., 2003). Finally, a review of 24 studies examining the association between maternal smoking and ADHD found that exposure to tobacco in utero was associated with ADHD symptoms (Linnet, Dalsgaard, Obel, et al., 2003). Several animal studies conducted since the 1980s indicate that chronic exposure to nicotine increases dopamine release in the brain and causes hyperactivity (e.g., Fung & Lau, 1989; Vaglenova, Birru, Pandiella, et al., 2004). Furthermore, withdrawal from nicotine is associated with decreases in dopamine release in the brain and causes irritability. On the basis of these data, researchers hypothesize that maternal smoking can affect the dopaminergic system of the developing fetus, increasing the risk of developing behavioral disinhibition and ADHD.

Psychological Factors in ADHD Psychological factors are also important in ADHD, particularly in their interaction with neurobiological factors. For example, the parent–child relationship interacts with neurobiological factors in a complex way to contribute to ADHD symptom expression (Hinshaw et al., 1997). Just as parents of children with ADHD may give them more commands and have negative interactions with them (Anderson, Hinshaw, & Simmel, 1994; Heller, Baker, Henker, et al., 1996), so these children have been found to be less compliant and more negative in interactions with their parents (Barkley, Karlsson, & Pollard, 1985; Tallmadge & Barkley, 1983). Certainly, it must be difficult to parent a child who is impulsive, aggressive, noncompliant, and unable to follow instructions. As we will discuss shortly, stimulant medication has been shown to reduce hyperactivity and increase compliance in some children with ADHD. Significantly, when such medication is used, either alone or in combination with behavioral treatment, the parents' commands, negative behavior, and ineffective parenting also decrease (Barkley, 1990; Wells, Epstein, Hinshaw, et al., 2000), suggesting that the child's behavior has at least some negative effect on the parents' behavior.

It is also important to consider a parent's own history of ADHD. As noted above, there appears to be a substantial genetic component to ADHD. Thus, it is not surprising that

Children born to mothers who smoked cigarettes during pregnancy have an increased risk for ADHD. (© Monkey Business Images/Shutterstock.)

many parents of children with ADHD have ADHD themselves. In one study that examined couples' parenting practices with their ADHD children, fathers who had a diagnosis of ADHD were less effective parents, suggesting that parental psychopathology may make parenting all the more difficult (Arnold, O'Leary, & Edwards, 1997). Family characteristics thus may well contribute to maintaining or exacerbating the symptoms and consequences of ADHD; however, there is little evidence to suggest that families actually cause ADHD (Johnston & Marsh, 2001).

Treatment of ADHD

We now turn to treatments. ADHD is typically treated with medication and with behavioral therapies based on operant conditioning.

Stimulant Medications   Stimulant medications, such as methylphenidate, or Ritalin, have been prescribed for ADHD since the early 1960s. Other medications approved by the Food and Drug Administration (FDA) to treat ADHD include Adderall, Concerta, and Strattera. In 2006, an estimated 2.5 million children in the United States were taking stimulant medication (National Survey on Children's Health, 2003), including almost 10 percent of all 10-year-old boys. The prescription of these medications has sometimes continued into adolescence and adulthood in light of the accumulating evidence that the symptoms of ADHD do not usually disappear with the passage of time.

The drugs used to treat ADHD reduce disruptive behavior and improve ability to concentrate. Numerous controlled studies comparing stimulants with placebos in double-blind designs have shown short-term improvements in concentration, goal-directed activity, classroom behavior, and social interactions with parents, teachers, and peers, as well as reductions in aggressiveness and impulsivity in about 75 percent of children with ADHD (Spencer, Biederman, Wilens, et al., 1996; Swanson, McBurnett, Christian, et al., 1995).

The best designed randomized controlled trial of treatments for ADHD was the Multimodal Treatment of Children with ADHD (MTA) study. Conducted at six different sites for 14 months with nearly 600 children with ADHD, the study compared standard community-based care and three other treatments: (1) medication alone, (2) medication plus intensive behavioral treatment, involving both parents and teachers, and (3) intensive behavioral treatment alone. Across the 14-month period, children receiving medication alone had fewer ADHD symptoms than children receiving intensive behavioral treatment alone. The combined treatment was slightly superior to the medication alone and had the advantage of not requiring as high a dosage of Ritalin to reduce ADHD symptoms. In addition, the combined treatment yielded improved functioning in areas such as social skills more than did the medication alone. The medication alone and the combined treatment were superior to community-based care, though the behavioral treatment alone was not (MTA Cooperative Group, 1999a, 1999b).

Other analyses from the MTA study revealed that the combined treatment was associated with fewer behavioral problems at school, perhaps linked to a decrease in negative and ineffective parenting (Hinshaw, Owens, Wells, et al., 2000). In addition, white, African American, and Latino children benefited equally from treatment, particularly from the combined treatment (Arnold, Elliott, Sachs, et al., 2003).

Despite the initially promising findings from the MTA study, additional follow-ups from this study have not been quite as encouraging, at least where medication is concerned. Importantly, all the children maintained the gains made during the 14-month treatment, even as they all returned to receiving standard community care, and this was true at the 3-, 6-, and 8-year follow-ups. However, children in the medication alone or the combined treatment groups were no longer doing better than children who received the intensive behavioral treatment or standard community care at the 3-year follow-up (Jensen, Arnold, Swanson, et al., 2007) or the 6- and 8-year follow-ups (Molina, Hinshaw, Swanson, et el., 2009). In other words, the relatively superior effects of medication that were observed in the combined treatment and medication alone groups did not persist beyond the study, at least for some of the children (Swanson, Hinshaw, et al., 2007).

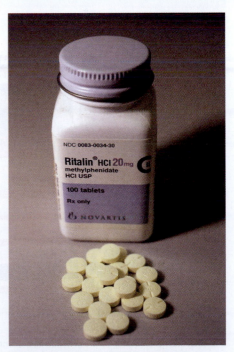

Ritalin is a commonly prescribed and effective drug treatment for ADHD. (Allan Tannenbaum/The Image Works.)

Does this mean that medication does not work? Not necessarily. The MTA study demonstrated that carefully prescribed and managed stimulant medication is effective for children with ADHD. However, medication as it is administered in the community does not appear to offer any benefits above and beyond other forms of treatment according to these MTA follow-up studies as well as other studies (Weiss & Hechtman, 1993; Whalen & Henker, 1991).

These findings are important in light of the side effects that stimulant medication can have, such as transient loss of appetite, weight loss, stomach pain, and sleep problems. In May 2006, the FDA recommended but did not mandate that a "black box" warning, the strongest possible safety warning the FDA can issue for medications, about cardiovascular risks (e.g., heart attack) be added to stimulant medications. In February 2007, the FDA mandated that drug makers develop patient medication guides to describe these risks to consumers.

Psychological Treatment Other promising treatments for ADHD involve parent training and changes in classroom management (Chronis, Jones, & Raggi, 2006). These programs have demonstrated at least short-term success in improving both social and academic behavior. In these treatments, children's behavior is monitored at home and in school, and they are reinforced for behaving appropriately—for example, for remaining in their seats and working on assignments. Point systems and daily report cards (DRCs) are typical components of these programs. Children earn points or stars for behaving in certain ways; the children can then spend their earnings for rewards. The DRC also allows parents to see how their child is doing in school. The focus of these programs is on improving academic work, completing household tasks, or learning specific social skills, rather than on reducing signs of hyperactivity, such as running around and jiggling. Accumulating evidence supports the efficacy of parent-training programs, although it is unclear whether they improve children's behavior beyond the effects of treatment with medication (Abikoff & Hechtman, 1996; Anastopoulos, Shelton, DuPaul, et al., 1993; MTA Cooperative Group, 1999a, 1999b).

School interventions for children with ADHD include training teachers to understand the unique needs of these children and to apply operant techniques in the classroom (Welsh, Burcham, DeMoss, et al., 1997), providing peer tutoring in academic skills (DuPaul & Henningson, 1993), and having teachers provide daily reports to parents about in-school behavior, which are followed up with rewards at home (Kelley, 1990). Research has demonstrated that certain classroom structures can help children with ADHD. Ideally, teachers vary the presentation format and materials used for tasks, keep assignments brief and provide immediate feedback on whether they have been done correctly, have an enthusiastic and task-focused style, provide breaks for physical exercise, and schedule academic work during the morning hours. Such environmental changes are designed to accommodate the limitations imposed by this disorder rather than to change the disorder itself.

Findings from the MTA study indicate that intensive behavioral therapies can be very helpful to children with ADHD. In that study, some of the children participated in an intensive 8-week summer program that included a number of validated behavioral treatments. At the end of the summer program, children receiving the combined treatment had very few significant improvements over children receiving the intensive behavioral treatment alone (Arnold et al., 2003; Pelham, Gnagy, Greiner, et al., 2000). This finding suggests that intensive behavioral therapy may be as effective as Ritalin combined with a less intensive behavioral therapy.

Point systems and star charts, which are common in classrooms, are particularly useful in the treatment of ADHD. (Lew Merrim/Photo Researchers, Inc.)

Check Your Knowledge 13.1 (Answers are at the end of the chapter.)

True or false?
1. The two broad domains of childhood psychopathology are internalizing disorders and externalizing disorders.
2. Girls with the combined type of ADHD have more severe problems than girls with the predominantly inattentive type, similar to findings with boys.

3. Dopamine has been investigated in ADHD, particularly genes for the DRD4 receptors.
4. The most effective treatment for ADHD is behavioral treatment without medication.

Conduct Disorder

Conduct disorder is another externalizing disorder. The DSM-5 criteria for conduct disorder focus on behaviors that violate the basic rights of others and violate major societal norms. Nearly all such behavior is also illegal. The symptoms of conduct disorder must be frequent and severe enough to go beyond the mischief and pranks common among children and adolescents. These behaviors include aggression and cruelty toward people or animals, damaging property, lying, and stealing. Often the behavior is marked by callousness, viciousness, and lack of remorse. DSM-5 will likely include a "callous and unemotional trait" diagnostic specifier for children who show these types of characteristics since these traits are associated with more individual and family problems. A recent longitudinal study found that children with high levels of conduct problems and high levels of callous and unemotional traits had more problems with symptoms, peers, and families compared to children with conduct problems but low levels of callous and unemotional traits (Fontaine, McCrory, Boivin, et al., 2011).

A related but less well understood externalizing disorder in the DSM-IV-TR is **oppositional defiant disorder** (ODD). There is some debate as to whether ODD is distinct from conduct disorder, a precursor to it, or an earlier and milder manifestation of it (Hinshaw & Lee, 2003; Lahey, McBurnett, & Loeber, 2000). ODD is diagnosed if a child does not meet the criteria for conduct disorder—most especially, extreme physical aggressiveness—but exhibits such behaviors as losing his or her temper, arguing with adults, repeatedly refusing to comply with requests from adults, deliberately doing things to annoy others, and being angry, spiteful, touchy, or vindictive.

Commonly comorbid with ODD are ADHD, learning disorders, and communication disorders, but ODD is different from ADHD in that the defiant behavior is not thought to arise from attentional deficits or sheer impulsiveness. One manifestation of difference is that children with ODD are more deliberate in their unruly behavior than children with ADHD. Although conduct disorder is three to four times more common among boys than among girls, research suggests that boys are only slightly more likely to have ODD, and some studies find no difference in prevalence rates for ODD between boys and girls (Loeber, Burke, Lahey, et al., 2000). Because less is known about ODD, we will focus here on the more serious diagnosis of conduct disorder.

Clinical Description, Prevalence, and Prognosis of Conduct Disorder

Perhaps more than any other childhood disorder, conduct disorder is defined by the impact of the child's behavior on people and surroundings. Schools, parents, peers, and the criminal justice system usually determine which externalizing behaviors constitute unacceptable conduct.

Conduct disorder is diagnosed among those who are aggressive, steal, lie, and vandalize property. (Ken Lax/Photo Researchers, Inc.)

Proposed DSM-5 Criteria for Conduct Disorder

- Repetitive and persistent behavior pattern that violates the basic rights of others or conventional social norms as manifested by the presence of three or more of the following in the previous 12 months and at least one of them in the previous 6 months:

  A. Aggression to people and animals, e.g., bullying, initiating physical fights, physically cruel to people or animals, forcing someone into sexual activity

  B. Destruction of property, e.g., fire-setting, vandalism

  C. Deceitfulness or theft, e.g., breaking into another's house or car, conning, shoplifting

  D. Serious violation of rules, e.g., staying out at night before age 13 in defiance of parental rules, truancy before age 13

- Significant impairment in social, academic, or occupational functioning

Many children with conduct disorder display other problems, such as substance abuse and internalizing disorders. The Pittsburgh Youth Study, a longitudinal investigation of conduct disorder in boys, found a strong association between substance use and delinquent acts (van Kammen, Loeber, & Stouthamer-Loeber, 1991). For example, among seventh graders who reported having tried marijuana, more than 30 percent had attacked someone with a weapon and 43 percent admitted breaking and entering; fewer than 5 percent of children who reported no substance use had committed these acts. Some research suggests that conduct disorder precedes substance use problems (Nock, Kazdin, Hiripi, et al., 2006), but other findings suggest that conduct disorder and substance use occur concomitantly, with the two conditions exacerbating each other (Loeber et al., 2000). Further, some evidence indicates that comorbid conduct disorder and substance use portend a more severe outcome for boys than for girls (Whitmore, Mikulich, Thompson, et al., 1997).

Anxiety and depression are common among children with conduct disorder, with comorbidity estimates varying from 15 to 45 percent (Loeber & Keenan, 1994; Loeber et al., 2000). Evidence suggests that conduct disorder precedes depression and most anxiety disorders, with the exceptions of specific and social phobias, which appear to precede conduct disorder (Nock et al., 2006). Girls with conduct disorder may be at higher risk for developing comorbid disorders, including anxiety, depression, substance abuse, and ADHD, than are boys with conduct disorder (Loeber & Keenan, 1994).

Recent estimates suggest that conduct disorder is fairly common, with a prevalence rate of 9.5 percent (Nock et al., 2006). A review of epidemiological studies suggests the prevalence rates range from 4 to 16 percent for boys and 1.2 to 9 percent for girls (Loeber et al., 2000). As shown in Figure 13.3, both the incidence and the prevalence of serious lawbreaking peak sharply at around age 17 and drop precipitously in young adulthood (Moffitt, 1993). Not all the criminal acts represented in Figure 13.3 are marked by the viciousness and callousness that are often a part of conduct disorder, but the figure illustrates the problem of antisocial behavior in children and adolescents.

Moffitt (1993) theorized that two different courses of conduct problems should be distinguished. Some people seem to show a life-course-persistent pattern of antisocial behavior, beginning to show conduct problems by age 3 and continuing to commit serious transgressions into adulthood. Others are adolescence-limited—they have typical childhoods, engage in high levels of antisocial behavior during adolescence, and have typical, nonproblematic adulthoods. Moffitt proposed that the adolescence-limited form of antisocial behavior is the result of a maturity gap between the adolescent's physical maturation and his or her opportunity to assume adult responsibilities and obtain the rewards usually accorded such behavior. The life-course-persistent type is more common among boys (10.5%) than girls (7.5%); the adolescence-limited type is also more common among boys (19.6%) than girls (17.4%) (Odgers, Moffitt, Broadbent, et al., 2008).

Cumulative evidence supports this distinction (Moffitt, 2007). The original sample from which Moffitt and colleagues made the life-course-persistent and adolescence-limited distinction was a sample of over 1,000 people from Dunedin, New Zealand, who were assessed every 2 or 3 years from age 3 to 32. Both boys and girls with the life-course-persistent form of conduct disorder had an early onset of antisocial behavior that persisted through adolescence and into adulthood. As children they had a number of other problems, such as academic underachievement, neuropsychological deficits, and comorbid ADHD (Moffitt & Caspi, 2001). Other evidence supports the notion that children with the life-course-persistent type have more severe neuropsychological deficits and family psychopathology, and these findings have been replicated across cultures (Hinshaw & Lee, 2003).

Those who were classified as life-course-persistent continued to have the most severe problems, including psychopathology, poorer physical health, lower socioeconomic status, lower levels of education, partner and child abuse, and violent behavior at age 32; this was true for men and women (Odgers et al., 2008). Interestingly, those classified as adolescence-limited, who were expected to "grow out" of their aggressive and antisocial behavior, continued

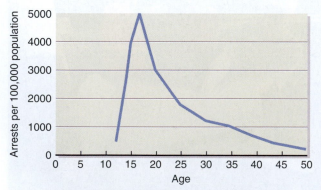

Figure 13.3 Arrest rates across ages for the crimes of homicide, rape, robbery, aggravated assault, and auto theft. Adapted from Blumstein, A., Cohen, J., & Farrington, D. P. *Criminology, 26*, 11. Copyright © 1988. The American Society of Criminology.

to have troubles with substance use, impulsivity, crime, and overall mental health in their mid-20s (Moffitt, Caspi, Harrington, et al., 2002). Moffitt and colleagues have since suggested that *adolescent onset* is the more appropriate term for this group of people, as the conduct problems are not entirely limited to adolescence (Odgers, Caspi, Broadbent, et al., 2007). By age 32, women with the adolescent-onset type were not having difficulties with violent behavior, but men still were. However, both men and women continued to have substance use problems, economic problems, and physical health problems (Odgers et al, 2008).

The prognosis for children diagnosed as having conduct disorder is mixed. The results just described show that men and women with the life-course-persistent type of conduct disorder will likely continue to have all sorts of problems in adulthood, including violent and antisocial behavior. However, conduct disorder in childhood does not inevitably lead to antisocial behavior in adulthood. For example, another longitudinal study indicated that although about half of boys with conduct disorder did not fully meet the criteria for the diagnosis at a later assessment (1 to 4 years later), almost all of them continued to demonstrate some conduct problems (Lahey, Loeber, Burke, et al., 1995).

Children with the life-course-persistent type of conduct disorder continue to have trouble with the law into their mid-20s. (The Image Works.)

Etiology of Conduct Disorder

It seems clear that multiple factors are involved in the etiology of conduct disorder, including genetic, neurobiological, psychological, and social factors that interact in a complex manner (Figure 13.4). A review concluded that the evidence favors an etiology that includes heritable temperamental characteristics that interact with other neurobiological difficulties (e.g., neuropsychological deficits) as well as with a whole host of environmental factors (e.g., parenting, school performance, peer influences) (Hinshaw & Lee, 2003).

Genetic Factors The evidence for genetic influences in conduct disorder is mixed, although heritability likely plays a part. For example, a study of over 3,000 twin pairs indicated only a modest genetic influence on childhood antisocial behavior; family–environment influences were more significant (Lyons, True, Eisen, et al., 1995). However, a study of over 2,600 twin pairs in Australia found a substantial genetic influence and almost no family–environment influence for childhood symptoms of conduct disorder (Slutske, Heath, Dinwiddie, et al., 1997). The authors of the latter study point out that differences in the samples may have accounted for the different findings.

Three large-scale adoption studies, in Sweden, Denmark, and the United States, have been conducted, but two of them focused on the heritability of criminal behavior rather than conduct disorder (Simonoff, 2001). As with most traits, these studies indicate that criminal and antisocial behavior is accounted for by both genetic and environmental factors. Interestingly, despite different prevalence rates for boys and girls, the evidence favoring genetic and environmental contributions to conduct disorder and antisocial behavior does not differ between boys and girls. A meta-analysis of twin and adoption studies of antisocial behavior indicated that 40 to 50 percent of antisocial behavior was heritable (Rhee & Waldman, 2002).

Distinguishing types of conduct problems may help to clarify findings on the heritability of conduct disorder. Evidence from twin studies indicates that aggressive behavior (e.g., cruelty to animals, fighting,

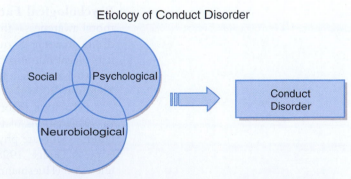

Figure 13.4 Neurobiological, psychological, and social factors all play a role in conduct disorder.

destroying property) is clearly heritable, whereas other delinquent behavior (e.g., stealing, running away, truancy) may not be (Edelbrock, Rende, Plomin, et al., 1995; Rhee & Waldman, 2002). Other evidence suggests that the time when antisocial and aggressive behavior problems begin is related to heritability. For example, aggressive and antisocial behaviors that begin in childhood, as in the case of Moffitt's life-course-persistent type, are more heritable than similar behaviors that begin in adolescence (Taylor, Iacono, & McGue, 2000).

One elegant study examined the interaction between genetic and environmental factors in predicting later adult antisocial behavior (Caspi, McClay, Moffitt, et al., 2002). It examined the MAOA gene, which is located on the X chromosome and releases an MAO enzyme, which metabolizes a number of neurotransmitters, including dopamine, serotonin, and norepinephrine. This gene varies in its activity, with some people having high MAOA activity and others having low MAOA activity. Using a large sample of over 1,000 children from Dunedin, New Zealand (the same sample that was the basis for Moffitt's characterization of the life-course-persistent and adolescence-limited types of conduct disorder), the researchers measured MAOA activity and assessed the extent to which the children had been maltreated. Being maltreated as a child was not enough to predict later conduct disorder, nor was the presence of low MAOA activity. Rather, those children who were both maltreated and had low MAOA activity were more likely to develop conduct disorder than either children who were maltreated but had high MAOA activity or children who were not maltreated but had low MAOA activity. Thus, both environment and genes mattered. A meta-analysis of several such studies confirms these findings: being maltreated was linked to later antisocial behavior only via genetics (Taylor & Kim-Cohen, 2007).

Neuropsychological Factors and the Autonomic Nervous System Neuropsychological deficits have been implicated in the childhood profiles of children with conduct disorder (Lynam & Henry, 2001; Moffitt, Lynam, & Silvia, 1994). These deficits include poor verbal skills, difficulty with executive functioning (the ability to anticipate, plan, use self-control, and solve problems), and problems with memory. In addition, children who develop conduct disorder at an earlier age (i.e., life-course-persistent type) have an IQ score of 1 standard deviation below age-matched peers without conduct disorder, and this IQ deficit is apparently not attributable to lower socioeconomic status or school failure (Lynam, Moffitt, & Stouthamer-Loeber, 1993; Moffitt & Silvia, 1988).

Other studies indicate that autonomic nervous system abnormalities are associated with antisocial behavior in adolescents. Specifically, lower levels of resting skin conductance and heart rate are found among adolescents with conduct disorder, suggesting that they have lower arousal levels than adolescents without conduct disorder (Ortiz & Raine, 2004; Raine, Venebales, & Williams, 1990). Why does low arousal matter? Similar to findings on adult antisocial personality traits (Chapter 15), these studies suggest that adolescents who exhibit antisocial behavior may not fear punishment as much as adolescents who don't exhibit such behavior. Thus, these children may be more likely to behave in antisocial ways without the fear that they will get caught. The fear of getting caught keeps most children from breaking the law.

Psychological Factors An important part of typical child development is the growth of moral awareness—the acquisition of a sense of what is right and wrong and the ability, even desire, to abide by rules and norms. Most people refrain from hurting others not only because it is illegal but also because it would make them feel guilty. Children with conduct disorder seem to be deficient in this moral awareness, lacking remorse for their wrongdoing (Cimbora & McIntosh, 2003).

Behavioral theories that look to both modeling and operant conditioning provide useful explanations of the development and maintenance of conduct problems. For example, children who are physically abused by parents are likely to be aggressive when they grow up (Coie & Dodge, 1998). Children may also imitate aggressive acts seen elsewhere, such as on television (Huesmann & Miller, 1994). Since aggression is often an effective, albeit unpleasant, means of achieving a goal, it is likely to be reinforced. Thus, aggressive behavior is likely to be maintained. Modeling may help explain the onset of delinquent behavior among adolescents who had not previously shown conduct problems. Perhaps these adolescents imitate the behavior of persistently antisocial peers who are seen as enjoying high-status possessions and sexual opportunities (Moffitt, 1993).

In addition, parenting characteristics such as harsh and inconsistent discipline and lack of monitoring are consistently associated with conduct problems in children. Perhaps children who do not experience negative consequences for early misbehavior later develop more serious conduct problems (Coie & Dodge, 1998).

A social-cognitive perspective on aggressive behavior (and, by extension, conduct disorder) comes from the work of Kenneth Dodge and associates. Dodge has constructed a social information processing theory of child behavior that focuses on how children process information about their world and how these cognitions markedly affect their behavior (Crick & Dodge, 1994). In one of his early studies (Dodge & Frame, 1982), Dodge found that the cognitive processes of aggressive children had a particular bias; these children interpreted ambiguous acts, such as being bumped in line, as evidence of hostile intent. Such perceptions may lead these children to retaliate aggressively for actions that may not have been intended as provocative. This can create a vicious cycle: their peers, remembering these aggressive behaviors, may tend to be aggressive more often against them, further angering the already aggressive children (see Figure 13.5). Deficits in social information processing also predict antisocial behavior among adolescents (Crozier, Dodge, Griffith, et al., 2008). More recently, Dodge and colleagues have linked deficits in social information processing to heart rate among adolescents who exhibit antisocial behavior. Specifically, low heart rate predicted antisocial behavior among male adolescents independent from social information processing deficits, a finding consistent with studies reviewed earlier on low arousal and conduct problems. However, the link between high heart rate and antisocial behavior was accounted for by social information processing deficits for both male and female adolescents (Crozier et al., 2008).

Peer Influences Investigations of how peers influence aggressive and antisocial behavior in children have focused on two broad areas: (1) acceptance or rejection by peers and (2) affiliation with deviant peers. Studies have shown that being rejected by peers is causally related to aggressive behavior, particularly in combination with ADHD (Hinshaw & Melnick, 1995). Other studies have shown that being rejected by peers can predict later aggressive behavior, even after controlling for prior levels of aggressive behavior (Coie & Dodge, 1998). Associating with other deviant peers also increases the likelihood of delinquent behavior (Capaldi & Patterson, 1994).

Do children with conduct disorder choose to associate with like-minded peers, thus continuing on their path of antisocial behavior (i.e., a social selection view), or does simply being around deviant peers help initiate antisocial behavior (i.e., a social influence view)? Recent studies examining gene–environment interactions have shed light on this question, and the answer appears to be that both views are correct. That is, as we reviewed earlier, we know that genetic factors are at play in conduct disorder, and these factors in turn play a role in encouraging children with conduct disorder to select more deviant peers to associate with. However, environmental influence, particularly neighborhood (e.g., poverty in the neighborhood) and family (e.g., parental monitoring) factors play a role in whether children associate with deviant peers, and this in turns influences and exacerbates conduct disorder (Kendler, Jacobson, Myers, et al., 2008).

Sociocultural Factors Poverty and urban living are associated with higher levels of delinquency. Unemployment, poor educational facilities, disrupted family life, and a subculture that deems delinquency acceptable are all contributing factors (Lahey, Miller, Gordon, et al., 1999; Loeber & Farrington, 1998). The combination of early antisocial behavior in the child and socioeconomic disadvantage in the family predicts early criminal arrests (Patterson, Crosby, & Vuchinich, 1992).

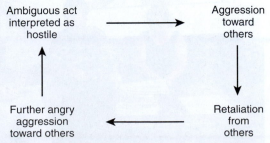

Figure 13.5 Dodge's cognitive theory of aggression. The interpretation of ambiguous acts as hostile is part of a vicious cycle that includes aggression toward and from others.

A study of African American and white youths drawn from the Pittsburgh Youth Study indicates that the greater severity of delinquent acts commonly found among African Americans appears to be linked to their living in poorer neighborhoods, not to their race (Peeples & Loeber, 1994). The researchers designated neighborhoods as "underclass" or "non-underclass" based on factors such as family poverty, families with no one employed, and male joblessness. In the total sample—ignoring differences in socioeconomic status—African American youths were more likely than white youths to have committed serious delinquent acts (e.g., car theft, breaking and entering, aggravated assault). But African American youths who were not living in underclass neighborhoods did not differ from white youths in serious delinquent behavior. Social factors matter. The strongest correlates of delinquency other than neighborhood were hyperactivity and lack of parental supervision; once these factors were controlled, residence in underclass neighborhoods was significantly related to delinquent behavior, whereas ethnicity was not.

Treatment of Conduct Disorder

The treatment of conduct disorder appears to be most effective when it addresses the multiple systems involved in the life of a child (family, peers, school, neighborhood).

Family Interventions Some of the most promising approaches to treating conduct disorder involve intervening with the parents and families of the child. In addition, evidence suggests that intervening early, if even just briefly, can make an impact. In a randomized controlled trial (Shaw, Dishion, Supplee, et al., 2006), researchers compared what is called the family checkup (FCU) treatment to no treatment. FCU involves three meetings to get to know, assess, and provide feedback to parents regarding their children and parenting practices. In this study, FCU was offered to families with toddlers who were at high risk of developing conduct problems (based on the presence of conduct or substance abuse problems in parents or early signs of conduct behavior in the children). This brief, three-session intervention was associated with less disruptive behavior compared to no treatment, even 2 years after the intervention.

Gerald Patterson and colleagues have worked for over four decades developing and testing a behavioral program called **parent management training (PMT)**, in which parents are taught to modify their responses to their children so that prosocial rather than antisocial behavior is consistently rewarded. Parents are taught to use techniques such as positive reinforcement when the child exhibits positive behaviors and time-out and loss of privileges for aggressive or antisocial behaviors.

This treatment has been modified by others, but, in general, it is the most efficacious intervention for children with conduct disorder and oppositional defiant disorder. Both parents' and teachers' reports of children's behavior and direct observation of behavior at home and at school support the program's effectiveness (Kazdin, 2005; Patterson, 1982). PMT has been shown to alter parent–child interactions, which in turn is associated with a decrease in antisocial and aggressive behavior (Dishion & Andrews, 1995; Dishion, Patterson, & Kavanagh, 1992). PMT has also been shown to improve the behavior of siblings and reduce depression in mothers involved in the program (Kazdin, 1985). PMT has been adapted for Latino families and has been shown to be effective in modifying parent and child behaviors (Martinez & Eddy, 2005).

Longer-term follow-ups suggest that the beneficial effects of PMT persist for 1 to 3 years (Brestan & Eyberg, 1998; Long, Forehand, Wierson, et al., 1994). Parent and teacher training approaches have been incorporated into larger community-based programs such as Head Start and have been shown to reduce childhood conduct problems and increase positive parenting behaviors (Webster-Stratton, 1998; Webster-Stratton, Reid, & Hammond, 2001). (See Focus on Discovery 13.3 for more on Head Start.)

Parent management training can be effective in treating conduct disorder. (Michael Newman/PhotoEdit.)

FOCUS ON DISCOVERY 13.3

Early Childhood Education and Care in Europe: Tackling Social and Cultural Inequalities

Research shows that children from low-income families, ethnic minorities, immigrant families and single-parent families tend to perform less well at school and, as a result, see their chances of successful careers jeopardized.

In order to achieve equity, but also for social and economic reasons, it is important to reduce the gap in outcomes between different sections our community and to this effect, the development of high-quality education and care services for young children provides a promising route.

It is within this context that the European Commission has published its first *Communication on Early Childhood Education and Care*, a paper that highlights the need for a universal system that fully integrates educational and care services from birth, in order to lay solid foundations in the early years for more effective learning in later life. The *Communication on Early Childhood Education and Care* paper rejects the option of targeting services and providing benefits to vulnerable groups because of the difficulty in identifying groups and also amid fears that it could lead to stigma and segregation later in life, and offers, instead, a framework to cover all early childhood services across members states of European Union.

According to the calculations, 17.2% of European households with one child under the age of 6 are living below the poverty line. This European average hides significant disparities and there is particular cause for concern in countries where more than 20% of households with a child under the age of 6 are living below this line. These include:

Estonia (22.2%), Italy (21.1%), Lithuania (22.8%), Luxembourg (20.1%), Poland (25%), Portugal (21%) and the United Kingdom (22.6%). Looking at the wider picture, in all European countries, apart from Sweden and Norway, 10% of households with a young child under the age of 6 are living below the poverty line. This indicator is particularly important as, according to the most relevant research, the poverty factor overrides all other risk factors. The 'winning formula' consists in combining care and education of the young child in a formal setting with support for parents. Research still needs to identify the precise nature and characteristics of the parental support which should be provided in European countries. Doubtless, it should involve work on the beliefs of parents and their understanding of what the education of young children should be. Although the research results do not provide a completely consistent picture, there does appear to be a promising way forward. Researchers have identified two main belief systems: 'traditional collectivist' and 'modern individualist' (see Palacios et al., 1992; Triandis, 1997; as cited by Leseman in Chapter 1). Parents who adhere to 'traditional collectivist' beliefs, that is to say a pattern of understanding which is characterized *by 'the fact that the interests of the individual child are subordinated to the interests of the greater social unit of the (extended) family and local community'* seem to offer less stimulating development opportunities than parents who hold the opposite view. However, there is still much to discover regarding the type of parental support needed and how it should be targeted in European countries.

Multisystemic Treatment   Another promising treatment for serious juvenile offenders is **multisystemic treatment (MST)** (Borduin, Mann, Cone, et al., 1995). MST involves delivering intensive and comprehensive therapy services in the community, targeting the adolescent, the family, the school, and, in some cases, the peer group (Figure 13.6). The treatment is based on the view that conduct problems are influenced by multiple factors within the family as well as between the family and other social systems.

The strategies used by MST therapists are varied, incorporating behavioral, cognitive, family-systems, and case-management techniques. The therapy's uniqueness lies in emphasizing individual and family strengths, identifying the social context for the conduct problems, using present-focused and action-oriented interventions, and using interventions that require daily or weekly efforts by family members. Treatment is provided in "ecologically valid" settings, such as the home, school, or local recreational center, to maximize the chances that improvement will carry through into the regular daily lives of children and their families. MST has been shown to be effective in a number of studies (Henggeler, Schoenwald, Borduin, et al., 1998; Ogden & Halliday-Boykins, 2004).

In comparison with adolescents who received an equivalent number of sessions (about 25) of traditional individual therapy in an office setting, adolescents who received MST displayed fewer behavior problems and experienced far fewer arrests over the following 4 years. For example, whereas more than 70 percent of the adolescents receiving traditional therapy were arrested in the 4 years after treatment, only 22 percent of those completing MST were arrested. In addition, assessment of other family members indicated that parents involved in MST had fewer psychiatric symptoms, and families were more supportive and showed less conflict and hostility in videotaped interactions. In contrast, the quality of interactions in the

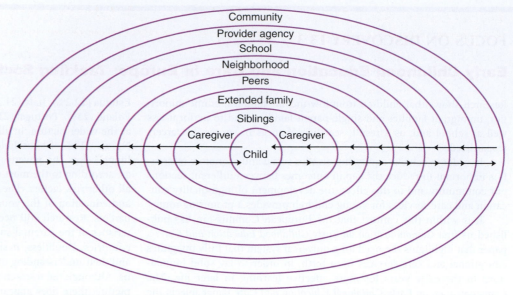

Figure 13.6 Multisystemic treatment (MST) includes consideration of many different factors when developing a child's treatment, including family, school, community, and peers.

families of the adolescents receiving traditional individual therapy deteriorated after treatment. Even the adolescents receiving MST who dropped out of treatment within 4 sessions were arrested significantly less than adolescents who completed the full course of traditional individual therapy.

Quick Summary

ADHD and conduct disorder are referred to as externalizing disorders. They appear across cultures, although there are also differences in the manifestation of externalizing symptoms in different cultures. Both disorders are more common in boys than girls. A number of factors work together to cause ADHD and conduct disorder. Genetic factors play a particularly important role in ADHD but are also implicated in conduct disorder. Neurobiological research has implicated areas of the brain and neurotransmitters such as dopamine in

ADHD; neuropsychological deficits are seen in both disorders. Other risk factors for ADHD include low birth weight and maternal smoking. Family and peer variables are also important factors to consider, especially in how they interact with genetic and neurobiological vulnerabilities. The most effective treatment for ADHD is a combination of medication, such as Adderall, and behavioral therapy. For conduct disorder, family-based treatments, such as PMT, are effective, as are treatments that include multiple points for intervention, as in MST.

Check Your Knowledge 13.2

Fill in the blanks.

1. Moffitt and colleagues have provided a good deal of evidence for two types of conduct disorder. The _____ type is associated with an early age of onset and continued problems into adolescence and adulthood. The _____ type begins in the teenage years and is hypothesized to remit by adulthood, though a recent follow-up study has not supported the idea that this type remits.

2. Comorbidity is common in conduct disorder. Other problems that co-occur with conduct disorder include: _____, _____, _____, and _____.

3. A successful treatment for conduct disorder that involves the family is called _____. Another successful community-focused treatment that works with the child, parents, peers, and schools is _____.

Depression and Anxiety in Children and Adolescents

So far, we have discussed disorders that are specific to children. The internalizing disorders, which include depression and anxiety disorders, first begin in childhood or adolescence but are quite common in adults as well. Much richer descriptions of these disorders are presented in Chapter 5 (mood disorders) and Chapters 6 and 7 (anxiety disorders). Here, we describe the ways in which the symptoms, etiology, and treatment of these disorders differ in children as compared to adults.

Depression and anxiety disorders commonly co-occur with ADHD and conduct disorder, as we have already noted. Furthermore, depression and anxiety disorders commonly co-occur with each other among children, as they do among adults. Although early research indicated that depression and anxiety can be distinguished in children and adolescents in much the same way as among adults—that is, children with depression show low levels of positive affect and high levels of negative affect, and children with anxiety show high levels of negative affect but do not show low levels of positive affect (Lonigan, Phillips, & Hooe, 2003)—more recent research calls this into question (Anderson & Hope, 2008). Next, we consider in more detail some of the etiological factors and treatment considerations for childhood depression and anxiety.

Depression

Clinical Descriptions and Prevalence of Depression in Childhood and Adolescence

There are both similarities and differences in the symptomatology of children and adults with major depressive disorder (Garber & Flynn, 2001). Children and adolescents ages 7 to 17 and adults both tend to show the following symptoms: depressed mood, inability to experience pleasure, fatigue, concentration problems, and suicidal ideation. Children and adolescents differ from adults in showing more guilt but lower rates of early-morning wakefulness, early-morning depression, loss of appetite, and weight loss. As in adults, depression in children is recurrent. Longitudinal studies have demonstrated that both children and adolescents with major depression are likely to continue to exhibit significant depressive symptoms when assessed even 4 to 8 years later (Garber, Kelly, & Martin, 2002; Lewinsohn, Rohde, Seeley, et al., 2000).

In general, depression occurs in less than 1 percent of preschoolers (Kashani & Carlson, 1987; Kashani, Holcomb, & Orvaschel, 1986) and in 2 to 3 percent of school-age children (Cohen, Cohen, Kasen, et al., 1993; Costello, Costello, Edelbrock, et al., 1988). By adolescence, rates of depression are around 6 percent for girls and 4 percent for boys (Costello et al., 2006).

The prevalence among adolescent girls is almost twice that among adolescent boys, just as we have seen with adult depression (see Focus on Discovery 5.1). Although adolescent girls experience depression more often than adolescent boys, there are few differences in the types of symptoms they experience (Lewinsohn, Petit, Joiner, et al., 2003). Interestingly, the gender difference does not occur before age 12; the full gender difference does not emerge until adolescence (Hankin, Abramson, Moffitt, et al., 1998).

Etiology of Depression in Childhood and Adolescence

What causes a young person to become depressed? As with adults, evidence suggests that genetic factors play a role (Klein, Lewinsohn, Seeley, et al., 2001). Indeed, the results of genetic studies with adults (see Chapter 5) apply to children and adolescents also, since genetic influences are present from birth, though they may not be expressed right away. A child with a depressed parent has four times the risk of developing depression as a child without a depressed parent (Hammen & Brennan, 2001). Of course, having a depressed parent likely confers risk via both genes and environment.

Indeed, studies of depression in children have also focused on family and other relationships as sources of stress that might interact with genetic factors. As with adults, early adversity and negative life events also play a role (Garber, 2006). One recent study found that early adversity (e.g., financial hardship, maternal depression, chronic illness as a child) predicted depression between ages 15 and 20, particularly among adolescents who had experienced a number of negative life events by age 15 (Hazel, Hamman, Brennan, et al., 2008).

Many of the symptoms of childhood depression are the same as adult depression, including sad mood. (Christian JACQUET/ Getty Images.)

Having a mother or father who is depressed increases the chances of being depressed as a child or adolescent; less is known about the reasons for this increased risk (Garber et al., 2002; Kane & Garber, 2004; Lewinsohn et al., 2000). We know that depression in either or both spouses is often associated with marital conflict; we should expect, therefore, that parental depression will have negative effects on their children, and it does (Hammen, 1997). Rejection by parents is modestly associated with depression in childhood, as confirmed by a meta-analysis of 45 studies (McLeod, Wood, & Weisz, 2007). The effect size for parental rejection was considered small across the studies, suggesting that factors other than parental rejection play a larger role in causing depression in childhood.

Other interpersonal factors are associated with depression in children, including negative interactions with partners (Chiariello & Orvaschel, 1995) and impaired relationships with siblings, friends, and romantic partners (Beevers, Rohde, Stice, et al., 2007; Lewinsohn, Roberts, Seeley, et al., 1994; Shih, Eberhart, Hammen, et al., 2006). Unfortunately, children with depression are often rejected by peers because they are not enjoyable to be around (Kennedy, Spence, & Hensley, 1989). These negative interactions in turn may aggravate the negative self-image and sense of worth that the depressed child already has. That is, interpersonal problems are probably not just a consequence of depression, but also probably intensify and maintain the depression. These types of interpersonal factors seem to be particularly important predicting the development of depression among adolescent girls (Hammen, 2009).

Consistent with both Beck's theory and the hopelessness theory of depression (see Chapter 5), cognitive distortions and negative attributional styles are associated with depression in children and adolescents in ways similar to what has been found with adults (Garber et al., 2002; Lewinsohn et al., 2000). For example, cognitive research with children with depression indicates that their outlooks are more negative than are those of children without depression and resemble those of adults with depression (Prieto, Cole, & Tageson, 1992). Negative thoughts and hopelessness also predict a slower time to recovery from depression among adolescents (Rhode, Seeley, Kaufman, et al., 2006). As with interpersonal functioning, it is important to remember that depression can make children think more negatively (Cole, Martin, Peeke, et al., 1998). Hence, it is important to consider longitudinal research.

A key question in the study of children with depression is: when do children actually develop stable attributional styles? That is, can young children have a stable way of thinking about themselves in the midst of such profound cognitive development? Recall from Chapter 5 that attributions can vary in whether they are stable (things will always be bad), internal (it is my fault that things are bad), and global (all aspects of life are bad) negative thoughts. A longitudinal study examined the development of attributional style in children (Cole, Ciesla, Dallaire, et al., 2008). Specifically, the researchers prospectively studied three groups of children for 4 years each. At year 1 of the study, the three groups were (1) children in second grade, (2) children in fourth grade, and (3) children in sixth grade. These three groups were followed yearly until the children were in grades 5, 7, and 9, respectively. Participants completed child and adolescent versions of an attributional style questionnaire along with measures of depression. The results of the study revealed a number of key findings. First, all children could complete the attributional style measure and do so in a manner that was reliable and consistent. However, children's attributional style changed over the course of development. Specifically, attributions became more stable but not more internal or global as children got older. In addition, attributional style didn't appear to be a stable style until children were early adolescents. Finally and importantly, attributional style did not interact with negative life events to predict depression (i.e., it was not a cognitive diathesis) for young children. It wasn't until the children were in eighth or ninth grade that support for attributional style as a cognitive diathesis emerged. Thus, results of this study suggest that attributional style becomes style-like by early adolescence and serves as a cognitive diathesis for depression by the middle school years.

Treatment of Childhood and Adolescent Depression   Research on the safety and efficacy of medications for childhood and adolescent depression has lagged behind analogous research with adults (Emslie & Mayes, 2001), but there are nonetheless safety concerns about the use of antidepressants among children and adolescents (see Focus on Discovery 13.4). The side effects experienced by some children taking antidepressants include diarrhea, nausea, sleep problems, and agitation (Barber, 2008). Some studies have shown that antidepressant drugs are no better than placebos in children and adolescents (Geller, Cooper, Graham, et al., 1992;

Keller, Ryan, Strober, et al., 2001); however, a recent major trial provided some support for the efficacy of antidepressants. That is, a randomized controlled trial comparing Prozac, cognitive behavioral therapy (CBT), and both combined for adolescents with depression called the Treatment for Adolescents with Depression Study (TADS) found that the combined treatment was the most effective through 12 weeks and that there were modest advantages of Prozac compared to cognitive behavior therapy (March, Silva, Petrycki, et al., 2004). This pattern of results remained true after 36 weeks (TADS team, 2007). A meta-analysis of 27 randomized controlled trials of antidepressant medication treatment for depression and anxiety disorders in children found that the medications were most effective for anxiety disorders other than obsessive compulsive disorder (OCD) and less effective for OCD and depression (Bridge, Iyengar, Salary, et al., 2007).

Several concerns have been raised about antidepressants, though. A first concern is the potential for side effects. More importantly, concerns with respect to suicidality prompted a series of hearings in the United States and the United Kingdom about the safety of antidepressants for children. In the study cited above (March et al., 2004), 7 out of 439 adolescents attempted suicide, of whom 6 were in the Prozac group and 1 was in the CBT group. (See Focus on Discovery 13.4 for more on this complex issue.) Evidence is controversial, though, and suicide effects likely occur early in treatment. In the major meta-analysis described above, researchers looked at suicidality rates in the studies of depression (Bridge et al., 2007). The risk of suicidal ideation was 3 percent for those children taking antidepressants and 2 percent for those taking placebo. It is important to note that this analysis shows that children taking medication were at risk for suicidal ideation, not that medication caused the suicide thoughts or attempts. There were no completed suicides in any of the 27 studies reviewed.

Another issue has to do with how long the treatment effects last. A naturalistic follow-up of just under half the adolescents in the TADS study found that although most (96 percent) had recovered 2 years after the study, close to half of those who recovered by the end of treatment had a recurrent episode of depression 5 years later (Curry, Silva, Rohde, et al., 2011). Girls were more likely to have a recurrence than boys, as were adolescents who had a comorbid anxiety disorder. However, the rate of recurrence did not differ depending on the kind of treatment the adolescents received during the TADS study. In other words, the modest benefits of Prozac over cognitive behavior therapy reported in the TADS study did not seem to protect this group of adolescents from having a future episode of depression 5 years later.

Most psychosocial interventions are modeled after treatments developed for adults. Several innovations have been made to adapt these treatments, though. For example, interpersonal therapy has been modified for use with depressed adolescents by focusing on issues of concern to adolescents, such as peer pressure, the stress inherent in the transition from childhood to adulthood, and the conflict between dependency on parents (and parental figures, like teachers) and the drive to be independent (Moreau, Mufson, Weissman, et al., 1992). Cognitive behavioral therapy in school settings appears to be effective and is associated with more rapid reduction of symptoms than family or supportive therapy (Curry, 2001). About 63 percent of adolescents with depression treated with CBT show significant improvement at the end of treatment (Lewinsohn &

Clinical Case: Nicole

Nicole was 15 years old when she attended her first therapeutic session with a child psychologist. Her presentation was marked by low mood and she was tired and thin. Discussions with the therapist revealed recurrent insomnia, hypervigilance and recurrent thoughts about suicide. Nicole's mood was particularly low in the mornings, lifting slightly as the day proceeded. A course of Prozac had been successful in lifting her "blackness" as she described it but her suicidal thoughts, if anything, seemed to be getting worse. Her parents and her doctor did not want her to stay on the medication for too long and wanted to combine it with interpersonal psychotherapy (IPP), which aims to promote more effective inter-personal relationships, and cognitive-behavioral therapy (CBT). After six weekly sessions, Nicole realized the

benefits. Learning how to manage her relationships with her family and her friends increased her feelings of self-worth and confidence, whilst the CBT provided her with insight into how her behavior, thoughts and beliefs affected her mood. It became clear that both Nicole and her parents had extremely high standards for evaluating her academic performance. The therapist began to identify with Nicole those situations in which her perfectionism worked for her and when and how it might work against her. She became increasingly comfortable with this perspective and decided she wanted to continue to set high standards regarding her performance in mathematical course work (which was a clear area of strength), but she did not need to be so demanding of herself regarding art or physical education.

Clarke, 1999). A study designed to identify what types of adolescents might benefit the most from CBT found that it was most beneficial for Caucasian adolescents, those adolescents with good coping skills at pretreatment, and adolescents with recurrent depression (Rhode et al., 2006). The Clinical Case of Nicole illustrates CBT techniques with an adolescent. If these findings hold up, it suggests that other types of interventions may be effective for ethnic minority adolescents and for those who are experiencing their first episode of depression.

A meta-analysis of 35 studies of psychotherapy for depression in children and adolescents found that therapy had a modest effect (Weisz, McCarty, & Valeri, 2006) and that cognitive therapy was no better than other types of therapy. Though therapy was effective in the short term, the long-term effects were not as robust. Thus, although psychotherapy is effective, we need to devise more effective treatments.

A good deal of work has focused on how to prevent the onset of depression in adolescents and children. A meta-analysis examined two types of preventive interventions for depression: selective and universal (Horowitz & Garber, 2006). Selective prevention programs target particular youth based on family risk factors (e.g., parents with depression), environmental factors (e.g., poverty), or personal factors (e.g., hopelessness). Universal programs are targeted toward large groups, typically in schools, and seek to provide education and information about depression. Results of the meta-analysis indicated that selective prevention programs were more effective than universal programs in preventing depression symptoms among adolescents.

A recent, large randomized control clinical trial of a selective prevention program for at-risk adolescents, defined as having at least one parent with depression, showed promising results (Garber, Clarke, Weersing, et al., 2009). Adolescents were randomly assigned to a group CBT intervention that focused on problem solving skills and changing negative thoughts or to a usual care group (i.e., any mental health care they sought out on their own). The incidence of depression episodes was lower for adolescents in the CBT group than those in the usual care group, suggesting that the treatment had an effective preventative effect.

Anxiety

Just about every child experiences fears and worries as part of the normal course of development. Common fears, most of which are outgrown, include fear of the dark and of imaginary creatures (in children under 5) and fear of being separated from parents (in children under 10). In general, as with adults, fears are reported more often for girls than for boys (Lichenstein & Annas, 2000), though this sex difference may be due at least in part to social pressures on boys that make them reluctant to admit that they are afraid of things.

The seriousness of some childhood anxiety problems should not be underestimated. Not only do children suffer, as do adults, from the aversiveness of being anxious—simply put, anxiety doesn't feel good—but their anxiety may also work against their acquisition of skills appropriate to various stages of their development. For example, a child who is painfully shy and finds interacting with peers virtually intolerable is unlikely to learn important social skills. This deficit may persist as the child grows into adolescence and will form the foundation of still further social difficulties. Then, whether in the workplace or at college, the adolescent's worst fear—"people will dislike and reject me"—is likely to be realized as his or her awkward, even off-putting, behavior toward others produces rejecting and avoiding responses.

Clinical Descriptions and Prevalence of Anxiety in Childhood and Adolescence

For fears and worries to be classified as disorders according to DSM criteria, children's functioning must be impaired; unlike adults, however, children need not regard their fear as excessive or unreasonable, because children sometimes are unable to make such judgments. Based on these criteria, about 3 to 5 percent of children and adolescents would be diagnosed as having an anxiety disorder (Rapee, Schniering, & Hudson, 2009). Although most unrealistic childhood fears dissipate over time, it is also the case that most anxious adults can trace their anxiety back to childhood.

Anxiety disorders in childhood and adolescence can interfere with other aspects of development. (VOISIN/PHANIE/Photo Researchers, Inc.)

FOCUS ON DISCOVERY 13.4

Controversies in the Diagnosis and Treatment of Children with Psychopathology

In recent years, the number of children diagnosed with psychological disorders has risen, sometimes dramatically, as has the number of children taking psychoactive medications. But are medications safe for children?

Antidepressant Medications

Children are prescribed antidepressant drugs, although the evidence for the effectiveness and safety of pharmacological treatment of depression and other disorders in children and adolescents is scant (Hazell, 2003) and widely debated (Ramchandani, 2004)—particularly for selective serotonin reuptake inhibitors (Moynihan, 2004; Committee on Safety of Medicines, 2004). It's been reported that between 1994 and 2000, paediatric use of selective serotonin reuptake inhibitors (SSRI) increased by 50%, leading to more than one million children per year receiving one or more prescriptions for fluoxetine (Prozac), sertraline (Zoloft), paroxetine (Paxil) and other drugs in the SSRI class. Most of that use has been for depression, which is known as Major Depressive Disorder or MDD in the medical literature (Leslie, 2003).

This massive increase in pediatric use has been almost entirely "off-label," that is, without specific regulatory approval. Only one drug in this class—fluoxetine—has been approved by the Food and Drug Administration (FDA) in the US for use in children and adolescents. And this approval only came in 2003, more than 10 years *after* the drug had first been used. The FDA's approval of fluoxetine for children was based on two studies whose outcomes were controversial.

In one drug trial, the treatment effect of fluoxetine compared to placebo was "non-significant" but trended in the direction of favouring the drug in one trial of 96 patients. Even that trend was based on what was considered to be a low threshold for measuring relief from the symptoms of depression. A second trial involving 210 youths "did not win on the protocol specified endpoint." However, other measures of psychic well-being indicated that about 70% of patients improved compared to 60% on placebo (Statistical Reviews, Application Number 18-936/SE5-064,").

Since 2004, selective serotonin reuptake inhibitors (SSRIs) have carried a black-box warning from the Food and Drug Administration (FDA) about the increased risk for suicide in paediatric patients taking the drugs. More recently, the FDA expanded the warning for young adults ages 18 to 24. The FDA has stopped short of banning antidepressants for these age groups and in fact the warning label states that "depression and other serious psychiatric disorders are themselves associated with increases in the risk of suicide." "The new black-box warning is clearly an attempt to balance the small risk posed by antidepressants against their well-documented benefits," a June 7, 2007, editorial in the New England Journal of Medicine states. "But this new label has the potential to confuse both patients and physicians."

Risk/Benefit Analysis

After the 2004 warning, antidepressant usage among children declined, and for the first time in years the Centers for Disease Control and Prevention noted a slight increase in suicide among youth. A 2007 study, funded in large part by pharmaceutical manufacturer Eli Lilly and Company, found that the FDA's 2004 advisory is associated with a significant reduction in diagnosis and treatment of pediatric depression. According to the study, which appeared in the June 2007 American Journal of Psychiatry, prescriptions for SSRIs for children fell nearly 30 percent after the black-box warnings were implemented.

A new comprehensive study conducted by researchers at the University of Pittsburgh Medical Center concluded that the benefits of SSRIs outweigh the risks of youth suicides. Their findings appeared in the April 18, 2007, issue of JAMA (Journal of the American Medical Association). The researchers analyzed data on 5,310 children and teenagers from 27 trials of pediatric major-depressive, obsessive-compulsive and non-OCD anxiety disorders. Their research included several recent studies that weren't part of the 2004 FDA analysis. The studies were randomized and placebo controlled. The antidepressants included Prozac®, Paxil®, Zoloft®, Celexa®, Lexapro®, Effexor®, Serzone® (no longer available in the United States), and Remeron®.

Suicidal Thoughts or Behaviors

The effectiveness of the drugs was measured using rating scales. Like the FDA, the Pittsburgh researchers looked for evidence of increased suicidal thoughts, preparatory actions toward imminent suicidal behavior and actual suicide attempts. There were no suicides in any of the studies. They found a slight increase—less than 1 percent—in suicidal behaviors or attempts associated with antidepressant treatment. The FDA found a 2 percent increase. Another FDA study, released May 2, 2007, used a much more comprehensive set of data—nearly 100,000 participants age 18 to 24 in 372 randomized trials. The agency found a less than 2 percent increase in suicidal thoughts and behaviors among those taking SSRIs. "Some may argue that any risk of suicidal ideation/suicide attempt cannot possibly justify treatment with antidepressants for children and adolescents," the authors of the Pittsburgh study stated. "Instead, we believe that the strength of evidence presented here supports the cautious and well-monitored use of antidepressant medications as one of the first-line treatment options."

Where Antidepressants Work Best

According to their findings, antidepressants have the greatest efficacy for children and teens when used to treat anxiety. They are somewhat useful in the treatment of obsessive-compulsive disorders but less effective in treating depression, particularly in young children. Other significant findings were these:

- Teens respond better than children to treatment for depression and anxiety. Among depressed children younger than 12, Prozac was the only antidepressant that worked better than a placebo.
- On antidepressants, 61 percent of patients studied improved compared to 50 percent who improved taking a placebo.
- On antidepressants, 52 percent of the young patients with obsessive-compulsive disorders improved compared to 32 percent on placebos.
- On antidepressants, 69 percent of those suffering anxiety disorders improved compared to 39 percent who improved on the placebo.

Study Limitations

None of the studies analyzed by the FDA or the University of Pittsburgh examined suicidal thoughts or behaviors as an outcome. Careful screening excluded patients at risk for suicide. The data come from trials to assess the short-term efficacy of antidepressants, not the long-term safety. Additionally, other adverse effects of the drugs such as mania, irritability or agitation were not assessed.

What's Happening in the UK?

In 2003, the Medicines and Healthcare products Regulatory Agency (MHRA), the British equivalent of the FDA, effectively banned the use of these drugs, except for Prozac/fluoxetine, in children and adolescents under 18 years of age. Although it is possible that, in common with the other SSRIs, Prozac/fluoxetine is associated with a small increased risk of self-harm and suicidal thoughts. Overall, the balance of risks and benefits for Prozac/fluoxetine in the treatment of depressive illness in under-18s is judged to be favourable.

Stimulant Medications

In 1937, Dr. Charles Bradley became the first doctor to prescribe the psychostimulant medication benzedrine to treat hyperactive children. Methylphenidate, better known as Ritalin, was approved to treat hyperactivity in children in the 1957. At this time, the disorder was known as "minimal brain dysfunction." The term was eventually changed to "hyperkinetic disorder" in the 1960s. In 1996, the brand name of an amphetamine known as Obetrol was changed to Adderall when it was approved as a treatment for ADHD. Before that time, it had been used to treat obesity.

Despite ample evidence concerning the short-term benefits of medication (principally stimulants) and behavioral therapy, uncertainty has continued among providers and researchers as to the relative merits of behavioral and medication treatments and their combination, particularly concerning treatment effects after the acute 2- to 3-month span of most studies. Few studies have subjected these two major forms of evidence-based treatment to head-to-head comparative trials and before the Multimodal Treatment Study of Children with ADHD. As a consequence, critical questions such as *what treatment works best, and for whom, and for how long?*

In 1992, one of the largest studies of treatment for ADHD, the Multimodal Treatment began. Five hundred seventy-nine children were randomly assigned to either routine community care or one of three study-delivered treatments, all lasting 14 months. The 3 treatment conditions consisted of medication only (usually Ritalin), intensive CBT only, or a combination of the 2. Children were assessed at four time points with multiple outcome measures. Results indicated that medication alone was more effective than psychosocial treatments alone. However, the most effective treatment was one that combined both medication and psychosocial treatments. For other functioning domains (social skills, academic, parent-child relations, oppositional behavior, anxiety/depression), results suggested slight advantages of medication plus CBT over single treatments (medication, CBT) and community care (Jensen et al., 2001).

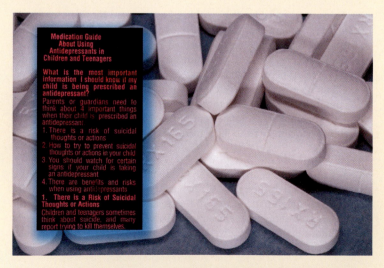

The FDA required that black box warnings be put on antidepressants for use with adolescents. (Scott Camazine/Phototake.)

Autism Spectrum Disorder (ASD): Diagnosis and Causes

The number of cases of ASD has increased dramatically over the past 10 years. For example, a 11-state study conducted by the Centers for Disease Control and Prevention (CDC) reported the prevalence rate of autism-spectrum disorders in the United States (autism, Asperger's disorder) to be 0.9 percent (1 in 110 children), up from earlier reports of about 1 in 500 (CDC, 2009). A large study in Korea found the prevalence rate to be even higher, over 2% (1 in every 38 children; Kim et al., 2011). Why has there been such an increase? Are there that many more children with ASD, or is the increase simply a reflection of increased awareness of ASD amongst mental health professionals?

ASD wasn't formally recognized in the DSM until 1980, and the diagnostic criteria have broadened quite a bit between the publication of DSM-III in 1980 and the release of DSM-IV in 1994 (Asperger's disorder was first formally recognized in DSM-IV). More children met the criteria for a diagnosis of autism under the broader criteria of DSM-IV than they did under the more narrow criteria of DSM-III (Gernsbacher, Dawson, & Goldsmith, 2005). Additionally, there is greater public awareness of ASD, and this may spur families to seek out mental health professionals for a formal psychological assessment. Some children with ASD may have been diagnosed with intellectual developmental disorder in years past; it is likely that more children are now being correctly diagnosed. Also, the delay in or lack of language acquisition has become a widely recognized warning sign among parents and mental health professionals that autism may be a consideration.

Although the rise in ASD may be accounted for in large part by better diagnosis, awareness, and mandated services, most experts agree that there are actually more cases today than there were 30 years ago.

With the increase in ASD has come an increase in parents and families advocating for their children. Parents have been particularly worried that ASD may be caused by vaccines routinely given to toddlers.

Claims of a connection between the MMR vaccine and ASD were raised by Andrew Wakefield and colleagues. In their paper, published in the Lancet in 1998, Wakefield claimed was that the MMR vaccine causes a series of events that include intestinal inflammation, loss of intestinal barrier function, entrance into the bloodstream of encephalopathic proteins, and consequent development of autism. In support of his hypothesis, Dr. Wakefield described 12 children with neurodevelopmental delay (8 with autism). All of these children had gastrointestinal complaints and developed autism within 1 month of receiving MMR.

An investigation by the *Sunday Times* revealed that Andrew Wakefield had many undeclared conflicts of interest and had fraudulently manipulated the data (Deer, 2009). The 1998 paper was retracted, and Wakefield was found guilty by the UK General Medical Council of serious professional misconduct in 2010 and struck off the Medical Register. The scientific consensus is that there is no credible evidence linking the MMR vaccine to the development of ASD, and that the vaccine's benefits greatly outweigh its risks. Some of the critical flaws with Wakefield's study include the following:

1. About 90 percent of children in England received MMR at the time this paper was written. Because MMR is administered at a time when many children are diagnosed with autism, it would be expected that most children with autism would have received an MMR vaccine, and that many would have received the vaccine recently. The observation that some children with autism recently received MMR is, therefore, expected. However, determination of whether MMR causes autism is best made by studying the incidence of autism in both vaccinated and unvaccinated children. This wasn't done.

2. Although the authors claim that autism is a consequence of gastro-intestinal inflammation, gastrointestinal symptoms were observed after, not before, symptoms of autism in all 8 cases.

3. Children with autism were claimed to have low levels of circulating immunoglobulin A (IgA). However, levels reported were within the normal range for that age group.

4. Intestinal nodular hyperplasia (like enlarged tonsils in young children) is considered to be a variant of normal.

Separation anxiety disorder is characterized by constant worry that some harm will befall their parents or themselves when they are away from their parents. When at home, such children shadow one or both of their parents. Since the beginning of school is often the first circumstance that requires lengthy and frequent separations of children from their parents, separation anxiety is often first observed when children begin school.

Another anxiety disorder among children and adolescents is social anxiety disorder (called social phobia in DSM-IV-TR). Most classrooms include at least one or two children who are extremely quiet and shy. Often these children will play only with family members or familiar peers, avoiding strangers both young and old. Their shyness may prevent them from acquiring skills and participating in a variety of activities enjoyed by most of their peers, for they avoid playgrounds and stay out of games played by other children. Extremely shy children may refuse to speak at all in unfamiliar social circumstances, a condition called *selective mutism*. In crowded rooms, they cling and whisper to their parents, hide behind the furniture, cower in corners, and may even throw tantrums. At home, they ask their parents endless questions about situations that worry them. Withdrawn children usually have warm and satisfying relationships with family members and family friends, and they show a desire for affection and acceptance.

Prevalence estimates for social anxiety disorder among children and adolescents is around 1 percent (Kashani & Orvaschel, 1990; Rapee et al., 2009), and it is more of a problem with adolescents, who have a more acute concern about the opinions of others than younger children do.

Children who are exposed to traumas such as chronic abuse, community violence, and natural disasters may experience symptoms of posttraumatic stress disorder (PTSD) similar to those experienced by adults. As with adults, these symptoms fall into four broad categories: (1) intrusions or reexperiencing the traumatic event, as in nightmares, flashbacks, or intrusive thoughts; (2) avoiding trauma-related situations or information and experiencing a general numbing of responses, as in feelings of detachment or anhedonia; (3) negative changes in cognitions or mood related to the traumatic event; and (4) hyperarousal, which can include irritability, sleep problems, and hypervigilance (Davis & Siegal, 2000). Some symptoms in children differ from those in adults; for example, children may exhibit signs of agitation instead of extreme fear or hopelessness. DSM-5 may include a new category called PTSD in preschool children with slightly different criteria that are appropriate for children age 6 and younger.

Obsessive compulsive disorder is also found among children and adolescents, with prevalence estimates ranging from less than 1 to 4 percent (Flament, Whitaker, Rapoport, et al., 1988; Heyman, Fombonne, Simmons, et al., 2003; Rapee et al., 2009). The symptoms in childhood are similar to symptoms in adulthood: both obsessions and compulsions are involved. The most common obsessions in childhood involve dirt or contamination as well as aggression; recurrent thoughts about sex or religion become more common in adolescence (Turner, 2006). OCD in children is more common in boys than girls, but this sex difference does not remain in adolescence or adulthood.

Etiology of Anxiety Disorders in Childhood and Adolescence

As with adults, genetics plays a role in anxiety among children, with heritability estimates ranging from 29 to 50 percent in one study (Lau, Gregory, Goldwin, et al., 2007). However, genes do their work via the environment, with genetics playing a stronger role in separation anxiety in the context of more negative life events experienced by a child (Lau et al., 2007).

Parenting practices play a small role in childhood anxiety. Specifically, parental control and overprotectiveness, more than parental rejection, is associated with childhood anxiety. However, parental control accounted for only 4 percent of the variance in childhood anxiety according to a

> ### ● Proposed DSM-5 Criteria for Separation Anxiety Disorder
>
> Excessive anxiety that is not developmentally appropriate about being away from home and parents or other attachment figures, with at least three symptoms that last for at least 4 weeks. Onset is before age 18:
>
> - Recurrent and excessive distress when separated
> - Excessive worry that something bad will happen to parent or attachment figure
> - Refusal or reluctance to go to school without parent
> - Refusal or reluctance to sleep without parent
> - Nightmares about separation
> - Repeated physical complaints (e.g., headache, stomachache) when separated

Separation anxiety disorder involves an intense fear of being away from parents or other attachment figures. (Sean Justice/Getty Images.)

meta-analysis of 47 studies (McCleod, Weisz, & Wood, 2007). Thus, 96 percent of the variance is accounted for by other factors. Other psychological factors that predict anxiety symptoms among children and adolescents include emotion-regulation problems and insecure attachment in infancy (Bosquet & Egeland, 2006).

Theories of the etiology of social anxiety in children are generally similar to theories of social anxiety in adults. For example, research has shown that children with anxiety disorders overestimate the danger in many situations and underestimate their ability to cope with them (Boegels & Zigterman, 2000). The anxiety created by these cognitions then interferes with social interaction, causing the child to avoid social situations and thus not to get much practice at social skills. In adolescence, peer relationships are important. Specifically, a longitudinal study found that adolescents who perceived that they were not accepted by their peers were more likely to be socially anxious (Teachman & Allen, 2007). Other research points to behavioral inhibition as an important risk factor for the development of social anxiety (also discussed in Chapter 6). Children who had high levels of behavioral inhibition at age 4 were 10 times as likely as children with lower levels to have social anxiety disorder by age 9 (Essex et al., 2010).

Theories about the causes of PTSD in children are similar to the theories for adults. There must be exposure to a trauma, either experienced or witnessed. Like adults, children who have a propensity to experience anxiety may be at more risk for developing PTSD after exposure to trauma. Specific risk factors for children may include level of family stress, coping styles of the family, and past experiences with trauma (Martini, Ryan, Nakayama, et al., 1990). Some theorists suggest that parental reactions to trauma can help to lessen children's distress; specifically, if parents appear in control and calm in the face of stress, a child's reaction may be less severe (Davis & Siegal, 2000).

Treatment of Anxiety in Childhood and Adolescence How are childhood fears overcome? Many simply dissipate with time and maturation. For the most part, treatment of such fears is similar to that employed with adults, with suitable modifications to accommodate the different abilities and circumstances of childhood. The major focus of these treatments is on exposure to the feared object. Millions of parents help children overcome fears by exposing them gradually to feared objects, often while acting simultaneously to inhibit their anxiety. If a little girl fears school, a parent takes her by the hand and walks her slowly toward the building. Offering rewards for moving closer to a feared object or situation can also be encouraging to a child who is afraid. Compared to exposure treatments for adults, treatments may be modified for children by including more modeling (seeing an adult approach the feared object) and more reinforcement.

Evidence indicates that cognitive behavior therapy can be helpful to many children with anxiety disorders (Compton, March, Brent, et al., 2004; Davis & Whiting, 2011; Kendall, Safford, Flannery-Schroeder, et al., 2004). This type of treatment typically involves working with both children and parents. Beyond exposure, the treatment includes psychoeducation, cognitive restructuring, modeling, skills training, and relapse prevention (Kendall, Aschenbrand, & Hudson, 2003; Velting, Setzer, & Albano, 2004). One of the more widely used treatments is called the Coping Cat (Kendall et al., 2003). This treatment is used with children between the ages of 7 and 13; it focuses on confronting fears, developing new ways to think about fears, exposure to feared situations, practice, and relapse prevention. Parents are also included in a couple of sessions. At least two randomized controlled clinical trials have shown this treatment to be effective (Kendall, Flannery-Schroeder, Panichelli-Mindel, et al., 1997; Kendall et al., 2004). A follow-up study of children who received this treatment found that after 7 years, most children were still anxiety-free. Furthermore, the children who remained anxiety-free after 7 years were less likely to have used drugs such as alcohol or marijuana than children for whom the treatment was less effective (Kendall et al., 2004).

Philip Kendall and colleagues conducted a randomized controlled trial comparing individual CBT, family CBT, and family psychoeducation for the treatment of childhood anxiety. Both individual and family CBT included the Coping Cat workbook, both were more effective than family psychoeducation at reducing anxiety (Kendall, Hudson, Gosch, et al., 2008), and the effects lasted 1 year after treatment. The family CBT was more effective than individual CBT when both parents had an anxiety disorder. This study points to the importance of considering not only the child's anxiety but also levels of parental anxiety when deciding on a treatment for childhood anxiety. Another study examined the Coping Cat treatment alone and in combination with sertraline (Zoloft) for children with separation anxiety, general anxiety, and social anxiety and found that the combination treatment was more effective than either the Coping Cat or medication alone (Walkup, Albano, Piacentini, et al., 2008). Given the high comorbidity in this sample, it may be that a combination treatment works well for children with more severe anxiety problems. It will be important to replicate this finding in another study.

Behavior therapy and group cognitive behavior therapy have been found to be effective for social anxiety disorder in children (Davis & Whiting, 2011). Only a few studies have examined the efficacy of cognitive behavior therapy for OCD in children and adolescents, with only four randomized controlled clinical trials published thus far. Two recent reviews suggest that CBT is an effective treatment for children and adolescents (Davis & Whiting, 2011; Freeman, Choate-Summers, Moore, et al., 2007). CBT appears to be equally as effective as medication, and CBT plus medication is more effective than medication alone but not more than CBT alone (O'Kearney, Anstey, & von Sanden, et al., 2006). However, for children and adolescents with severe OCD, a combination of CBT and sertraline (Zoloft) was more effective than CBT alone [Pediatric OCD treatment study (POTS) team, 2004]. CBT does not appear to be as effective for very young children (e.g., ages 3 or 4). Other methods of providing treatment, including "bibliotherapy" and computer-assisted therapy, have shown promise as well. In bibliotherapy, parents are given written materials and are the "therapist" with their children. Although this is effective at reducing childhood anxiety, it does not appear to be as effective as CBT group treatments (Rapee, Abbott, & Lyneham, 2006).

Only a few studies have evaluated the efficacy of treatment of PTSD among children and adolescents, but the available research suggests that cognitive behavioral treatments, whether individual or group, are effective for children and adolescents with PTSD (Davis & Whiting, 2011).

Quick Summary

Anxiety disorders and depression in children are referred to as internalizing disorders. Depression in childhood and adolescence looks similar to depression in adulthood, although there are notable differences. In childhood, depression affects boys and girls equally, but in adolescence girls are affected almost twice as often as boys. Genetics and stressful life events play a role in depression in childhood. Research on cognitive factors in childhood depression supports the notion that attributional style also plays a role; however, this work must consider the developmental stage of the child. Treatment for depression among children is facing a good deal of controversy, at least where medication is concerned. A randomized controlled trial found that a combination of medication and CBT was the most effective treatment. Concerns about the effect of medications on suicide risk need to be addressed.

Anxiety and fear are typical in childhood. When fears interfere with functioning, such as keeping a child from school, intervention is warranted. Theories about the causes of anxiety disorders in children are similar to theories about their causes in adulthood, though less research has been done with children on, for example, cognitive factors. Cognitive behavioral therapy is an effective intervention for a number of different anxiety disorders in childhood. Other problems, such as PTSD in childhood, require additional study.

Learning Disabilities

Clinical Case: Tim

Several years ago, Tim was a student in one of our undergraduate courses who showed an unusual pattern of strengths and weaknesses. His comments in class were exemplary, but his handwriting was sometimes indecipherable and his spelling was very poor. After the instructor had noted these problems on his midterm examination, Tim came to see him and explained that he was dyslexic and that it took him a long time to complete the weekly reading assignments and to write papers and exams. The instructor decided to give Tim extra time for written work because he was obviously of superior intelligence and highly motivated to excel. Given this chance, he earned an A in the course and when he graduated, he was admitted to a leading law school.

A **learning disability** is a condition in which a person shows a problem in a specific area of academic, language, speech, or motor skills that is not due to intellectual developmental disorder or deficient educational opportunities. Children with a learning disability are usually of average or above-average intelligence but have difficulty learning some specific skill in the affected area (e.g., arithmetic or reading), and thus their progress in school is impeded.

Clinical Descriptions

The term *learning disabilities* is not used by DSM but is used by most mental health professionals to group together three categories of disorders that do appear in DSM: learning disorders, communication disorders, and motor disorders. These disorders are described briefly in Table 13.3. Any of these disorders may apply to a child who fails to develop to the degree appropriate to his or her intellectual level in a specific academic, language, or motor skill area. Learning disabilities are often identified and treated within the school system rather than through mental health clinics. An older study suggested that the disorders are only slightly more common in boys (Shaywitz, Shaywitz, Fletcher, et al., 1990), but a recent study of four large epidemiological samples indicates that reading disorders, at least, are far more common in boys than in girls (Rutter, Caspi, Fergusson, et al., 2004). The prevalence rates for dyslexia and dyscalculia are about the same, ranging from 4 to 7 percent of children (Landerl, Fussenegger, Moll, et al., 2009).

Etiology of Learning Disabilities

Most research on learning disabilities concerns dyslexia, perhaps because it is the most prevalent of this group of disorders: it affects 5 to 10 percent of school-age children. Research has advanced more slowly on dyscalculia.

Keira Knightly, a highly successful actress, suffers from dyslexia. (DAVE M. BENETT/ Getty Images, Inc.)

Table 13.3 Learning, Communication, and Motor Disorders Likely to Be in DSM-5

Learning disorders include:

- **Dyslexia** (formerly called reading disorder) involves significant difficulty with word recognition, reading comprehension, and typically written spelling as well.
- **Dyscalculia** (formerly called mathematics disorder) involves difficulty in producing or understanding numbers, quantities, or basic arithmetic operations.

Communication disorders include:

- **Speech sounds disorder** (formerly called phonological disorder) involves correct comprehension and sufficient vocabulary use, but unclear speech and improper articulation. For example, *blue* comes out *bu*, and *rabbit* sounds like *wabbit*. With speech therapy, complete recovery occurs in almost all cases, and milder cases may recover spontaneously by age 8.
- **Childhood onset fluency disorder** (formerly called stuttering) is a disturbance in verbal fluency that is characterized by one or more of the following speech patterns: frequent repetitions or prolongations of sounds, long pauses between words, substituting easy words for those that are difficult to articulate (e.g., words beginning with certain consonants), and repeating whole words (e.g., saying "go-go-go-go" instead of just a single "go"). DSM-IV-TR estimates that up to 80 percent of people with stuttering recover, most of them without professional intervention, before the age of 16.

Five new communication disorders are proposed for DSM-5: *language impairment disorder, late language emergence disorder, specific language impairment disorder, social communication disorder, and voice disorder.*

Motor disorders include:

- **Tourette's disorder** involves one or more vocal and multiple motor tics (sudden, rapid movement or vocalization) that start before the age of 18.
- **Developmental coordination disorder** (formerly called motor skills disorder involves marked impairment in the development of motor coordination that is not explainable by intellectual developmental disorder or a disorder such as cerebral palsy.

Etiology of Dyslexia Family and twin studies confirm that there is a heritable component to dyslexia (Pennington, 1995; Raskind, 2001). Furthermore, the genes that are associated with dyslexia are the same genes associated with typical reading abilities (Plomin & Kovas, 2005). These so-called generalist genes are thus important for understanding normal as well as abnormal reading abilities. Research has also examined gene–environment interactions in dyslexia, and here the evidence so far suggests that heritability of reading problems varies depending on parental education. Genes play a bigger role in dyslexia among children whose parents have more education compared to children whose parents have less education (Friend, DeFries, Olson, et al., 2009; Kremen, Jacobson, Xian, et al., 2005). Homes with high parental education likely emphasize reading and provide a lot of opportunity for children to read. In this type of environment, then, a child's risk for developing dyslexia is more driven by heritable combinations of genes.

There is fairly good consensus among investigators that the core deficits in dyslexia include problems in language processing. Evidence from psychological, neuropsychological, and neuroimaging studies supports this contention. Research points to one or more problems in language processing that might underlie dyslexia, including perception of speech and analysis of the sounds of spoken language and their relation to printed words (Mann & Brady, 1988), difficulty recognizing rhyme and alliteration (Bradley & Bryant, 1985), problems with rapidly naming familiar objects (Scarborough, 1990; Wolf, Bally, & Morris, 1986), and delays in learning syntactic rules (Scarborough, 1990). Many of these processes fall under what is called *phonological awareness*, which is believed to be critical to the development of reading skills (Anthony & Lonigan, 2004).

Studies using various brain-imaging techniques support the idea that children with dyslexia have a problem in phonological awareness. These studies show that areas in the left temporal, parietal, and occipital regions of the brain are important for phonological awareness, and these same regions are centrally involved in dyslexia (see Figure 13.7).

For example, a study using fMRI found that, compared with children without dyslexia, children with dyslexia failed to activate the temporoparietal area during a phonological processing task (Temple, Poldrack, Salidas, et al., 2001). A larger study using fMRI found that compared to children without dyslexia, children with dyslexia showed less activation in the left temporoparietal and occipitotemporal areas while doing a number of reading-relevant tasks, such as identifying letters and sounding out words (Shaywitz, Shaywitz, Pugh et al., 2002). A treatment study showed that after a year of intensive treatment for reading problems, children with dyslexia were better readers and also showed greater activation in the left temporoparietal and occipitotemporal areas while completing a reading task, compared to a group of children who received a less intensive treatment (Shaywitz, Shaywitz, Blachman, et al., 2004).

Similar findings using fMRI have been found among adults with dyslexia (Horwitz, Rumsey, & Donahue, 1998; Klingberg, Hedehus, Temple, et al., 2000). An fMRI study with adults examined three different types of readers (Shaywitz, Shaywitz, Fulbright, et al., 2003). The first group was called persistently poor readers (PPR)—they had trouble reading early in school (second grade) and later in school (ninth or tenth grade). The second group was called accuracy improved (AI)—they had trouble reading early in school but not later in school. The third group was called nonimpaired readers (NI)—they had no trouble with reading either early or late in school. On behavioral reading tasks completed outside the scanner, the PPR group performed more poorly than the AI and NI groups. On many tests, the AI group performed as well as the NI group, suggesting they had compensated for their early reading problems. However, the brain-imaging results told a different story. Specifically, the NI group activated the traditional areas of the brain linked to reading: the left temporal-parietal-occipital regions. However, the AI group did not show as much activation in these areas but did show activation in areas on the right

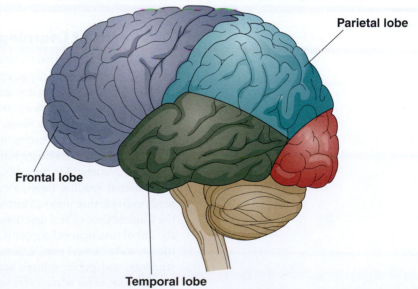

Parietal lobe

Frontal lobe

Temporal lobe

Figure 13.7 Areas of the brain implicated in dyslexia include parts of the frontal, parietal, and temporal lobes, at least for Western languages.

Recent interventions for dyslexia have improved children's reading. (© Eduard Titov/Shutterstock.)

side of the brain, suggesting that their compensation for early reading problems relied on areas of the brain not traditionally involved in reading. Paradoxically, the PPR group also activated the left side of the brain linked with reading. However, this group of poor readers also activated other areas of the brain associated with memory, suggesting that they were trying to rely on memorization of words to read rather than on language areas more efficiently used in reading.

It should be noted that the fMRI studies discussed above were done with children and adults in the United States who spoke English. A study examining Chinese children with dyslexia failed to find a problem with the temporoparietal area of the brain during reading tasks; instead, the left middle frontal gyrus showed less activation (Siok, Perfetti, Lin, et al., 2004). The investigators speculate that the differences between the English and Chinese languages may account for the different brain regions involved. Reading English requires putting together letters that represent sounds. Reading Chinese, in contrast, requires putting together symbols that represent meanings. Indeed, reading Chinese requires mastery of nearly 6,000 different symbols. Thus, Chinese relies more on visual processing, while English relies more on sound processing.

Etiology of Dyscalculia There is evidence of some genetic influence on individual variations in math skills. In particular, the type of math disability that involves poor semantic memory is most likely to be heritable. A study of over 250 twin pairs conducted through the Colorado Learning Disabilities Research Center suggested that common genetic factors underlie both reading and math deficits in children with both disorders (Gillis & DeFries, 1991; Plomin & Kovas, 2005). Furthermore, the evidence suggests that any genes associated with dyscalculia are also associated with mathematics ability (Plomin & Kovas, 2005).

Functional brain imaging studies of people with dyscalculia suggest that areas of the parietal lobe are less active during tasks requiring mathematics. Specifically, an area called the intraparietal sulcus has been implicated in dyscalculia (Wilson & Dehaene, 2007).

Researchers have investigated whether dyscalculia might be linked to dyslexia in terms of the cognitive deficits that are associated with both of these learning disorders. That is, children who have problems with phonological awareness might have problems not only with reading but also with the symbols and numbers in mathematics. The evidence suggests, however, that these two learning disorders are somewhat independent (Jordan, 2007). If anything, having dyslexia may make dyscalculia worse, but they seem to have some different cognitive deficits at their core. Children with both dyslexia and dyscalculia have deficits in phonological awareness, but children with only dyscalculia do not. Children with dyscalculia have trouble with tasks requiring manipulation of numbers, whether with actual numbers or with the use of calculations, as in estimating size, but children with dyslexia do not (Landerl et al., 2009).

Treatment of Learning Disabilities

Several strategies are used to treat learning disabilities, both in school programs and in private tutoring. Traditional linguistic approaches, used primarily in cases of reading and writing difficulties, focus on instruction in listening, speaking, reading, and writing skills in a logical, sequential, and multisensory manner, such as reading out loud under close supervision. In young children, readiness skills, such as letter discrimination, phonetic analysis, and learning letter–sound correspondences, may need to be taught before explicit instruction in reading is attempted. Phonics instruction involves helping children master the task of converting sounds to words (National Institute of Child Health and Human Development, 2000). Findings from the National Reading Panel, a comprehensive review of the research on teaching children to read, indicate that phonics instruction is beneficial for children with reading difficulties. Like the Clinical Case of Tim described earlier, people with dyslexia can often succeed in college with the aid of instructional supports, such as podcast or webcast lectures that can be re-reviewed, tutors, and untimed tests. Colleges are required by law to provide special services to help such students, and public schools are now required to provide transitional vocational and career planning for older adolescents with learning disabilities.

One promising development in treating communication disorders (Merzenich, Jenkins, Johnson, et al., 1996; Tallal, Miller, Bedi, et al., 1996) is based on previous findings that children with such disorders have difficulty discriminating certain sounds. Researchers developed special computer games and audiotapes that slow speech sounds. After intensive training with these modified speech stimuli for 1 month, children with severe language disorders were able to improve their language skills to the point at which they were functioning as typically developing children do. Similar training using unmodified speech stimuli resulted in very little progress.

Based on their promising initial findings, these investigators expanded the treatment, now called Fast ForWord, and conducted a larger study including 500 children from the United States and Canada. Children received daily training for 6 to 8 weeks, and results again indicated that the intervention was effective. Children improved in speech, language, and auditory processing skills by about $1\frac{1}{2}$ years of ability (Tallal, Merzenich, Miller, et al., 1998). The researchers speculate that this training method may even help prevent dyslexia, since many reading-disordered children had difficulties understanding language as young children.

Most children with learning disabilities have probably experienced a great deal of frustration and failure, eroding their motivation and confidence. Whatever their design, treatment programs should provide opportunities for children to experience feelings of mastery and self-confidence. Rewarding small steps can be useful in increasing the child's motivation, helping the child focus attention on the learning task, and reducing behavioral problems caused by frustration.

Intellectual Developmental Disorder

In DSM-IV-TR, mental retardation was the name of the disorder that will likely be called **intellectual developmental disorder** in DSM-5. Why the change? After all, many people are familiar with the term *mental retardation*. However, this is not the term that most mental health professionals use or prefer, perhaps due to the stigma associated with this older term. Indeed, most mental health professionals follow the guidelines of the American Association on Intellectual and Developmental Disabilities (AAIDD) more than the DSM criteria.

The AAIDD is an organization whose mission is to "promote progressive policies, sound research, effective practices, and universal human rights for people with intellectual disabilities" (AAIDD: www.aaidd.org). The group changed its own name in 2006 (it was formerly known as the American Association of Mental Retardation) in large part to acknowledge that *intellectual disability* is now the preferred term over *mental retardation* (Schalock, Luckasson, Shogren, et al., 2007). AAIDD has been in existence since 1876 and has routinely published guidelines for classifying and defining intellectual disabilities that are less focused on the severity of disability and more on determining what steps are necessary to facilitate higher functioning.

The 11th edition of the AAIDD guidelines for defining intellectual disability was published in 2010; the key difference between the 2010 guidelines and the guidelines published in 2002 is the name change. That is, the term *intellectual disability* is now used instead of *mental retardation*. The current AAIDD guidelines are summarized in Table 13.4.

Table 13.4 The AAIDD Definition of Intellectual Disability

Intellectual disability is characterized by significant limitations both in intellectual functioning and in adaptive behavior as expressed in conceptual, social, and practical adaptive skills.

This disability begins before age 18.

Five Assumptions Essential to the Application of the Definition

1. Limitations in present functioning must be considered within the context of community environments typical of the individual's age, peers, and culture.
2. Valid assessment considers cultural and linguistic diversity as well as differences in communication, sensory, motor, and behavioral factors.
3. Within an individual, limitations often coexist with strengths.
4. An important purpose of describing limitations is to develop a profile of needed supports.
5. With appropriate personalized supports over a sustained period, the life functioning of the person with intellectual disability generally will improve.

Source: © 2002 American Association on Intellectual and Developmental Disabilities, from http://www.aaidd.org/intellectualdisabilitybook/content_2678.cfm?navID=282

Diagnosis and Assessment of Intellectual Developmental Disorder

The DSM-5 diagnostic criteria for intellectual developmental disorder will likely continue to include three criteria: (1) significantly below average intellectual functioning, (2) deficits in adaptive behavior, and (3) an onset prior to age 18.

However, changes in the first two criteria are also proposed to make the DSM-5 more consistent with the approach of the AAIDD. First, there will likely be explicit recognition that an IQ score must be considered within a person's cultural context. Second, adaptive functioning will also likely be assessed and considered in light of the person's age and cultural group. Finally, the DSM-5 will likely no longer distinguish between mild, moderate, and severe intellectual disability based on IQ scores alone was done in DSM-IV-TR.

Even with these DSM-5 changes, the AAIDD approach still does a better job of encouraging the identification of an individual's strengths and weaknesses on psychological, physical, and environmental dimensions with a view toward determining the kinds and degrees of support needed to enhance the person's functioning in different domains. Consider Roger, a 24-year-old man with an IQ of 45 who has attended a special program for people with intellectual disability since he was 6. From the DSM, he would not be expected to be able to live independently, get around on his own, or progress beyond second grade. The AAIDD approach, however, would emphasize what is needed to maximize Roger's functioning. Thus, a clinician might discover that Roger can use the bus system if he takes a route familiar to him, and thus he might be able to go to a movie by himself from time to time. And although he cannot prepare complicated meals, he might be able to learn to prepare frozen entrées in a microwave oven. The assumption is that by building on what he can do, Roger will make more progress.

In the schools, an individualized educational program (IEP) is based on the person's strengths and weaknesses and on the amount of instruction needed. Students are identified by the classroom environment they are judged to need. This approach can lessen the stigmatizing effects of having intellectual developmental disorder and may also encourage a focus on what can be done to improve the student's learning.

Etiology of Intellectual Developmental Disorder

At this time, the primary cause of intellectual developmental disorder can be identified in only 25 percent of the people affected. The causes that can be identified are typically neurobiological.

When assessing adaptive behavior, the cultural environment must be considered. A person living in a rural community may not need the same skills as those needed by someone living in New York City, and vice versa. (Left: Simon Clay/Getty Images, Inc.; Right: Dan Bigelow/The Image Bank/ Getty Images, Inc.)

Genetic or Chromosomal Abnormalities One chromosomal abnormality that has been linked with intellectual developmental disorder is *trisomy 21*, which refers to having an extra copy (i.e., three instead of two) of chromosome 21. This is also known as **Down syndrome**. Estimates of the prevalence of Down syndrome suggest it occurs in about 1 out of every 850 live births in the United States (Shin, Besser, Kucik, et al., 2009).

People with Down syndrome may have intellectual developmental disorder as well as some distinctive physical signs, such as short and stocky stature; oval, upward-slanting eyes; a prolongation of the fold of the upper eyelid over the inner corner of the eye; sparse, fine, straight hair; a wide and flat nasal bridge; square-shaped ears; a large, furrowed tongue, which may protrude because the mouth is small and its roof low; and short, broad hands.

Another chromosomal abnormality that can cause intellectual developmental disorder is **fragile X syndrome**, which involves a mutation in the fMR1 gene on the X chromosome (National Fragile X Foundation: www.fragilex.org). Physical symptoms associated with fragile X include large, underdeveloped ears and a long, thin face. Many people with fragile X syndrome have intellectual developmental disorder. Others may not have intellectual developmental disorder but nonetheless have learning disabilities, difficulties on neuropsychological tests, and mood swings. About a third of children with fragile X syndrome also exhibit autism spectrum behaviors, suggesting that the fMR1 gene may be one of the many genes that contribute to autism (Hagerman, 2006).

Recessive-Gene Diseases Several hundred recessive-gene diseases have been identified, and many of them can cause intellectual developmental disorder. Here we discuss one recessive-gene disease, phenylketonuria.

In **phenylketonuria (PKU)**, the infant, born without obvious signs of difficulty, soon begins to suffer from a deficiency of a liver enzyme, phenylalanine hydroxylase. This enzyme is needed to convert phenylalanine, an amino acid contained in protein, to tyrosine, an amino acid that is essential for the production of certain hormones, such as epinephrine. Because of this enzyme deficiency, phenylalanine and its derivative, phenylpyruvic acid, are not broken down and instead build up in the body's fluids. This buildup eventually damages the brain because the unmetabolized amino acid interferes with the process of myelination, the sheathing of neuron axons, which is essential for neuronal function. Myelination supports the rapid transmittal of neuronal impulses. The neurons of the frontal lobes, the site of many important cognitive functions, such as decision making, are particularly affected, and intellectual disabilities can be profound.

Although PKU is rare, with an incidence of about 1 in 15,000 live births, it is estimated that 1 person in 70 is a carrier of the recessive gene. A blood test is available for prospective parents who have reason to suspect that they might be carriers. Pregnant women who carry the recessive gene must monitor their diet closely so that the fetus will not be exposed to toxic levels of phenylalanine (Baumeister & Baumeister, 1995). State laws require testing newborns for PKU. After the newborn with PKU has consumed milk for several days, an excess amount of unconverted phenylalanine can be detected in the blood. If the test is positive, the parents are taught to provide the infant a diet low in phenylalanine.

Parents are encouraged to introduce the special diet as early as possible and to maintain it indefinitely. Studies have indicated that children whose dietary restrictions stop at age 5–7 begin to show subtle declines in functioning, particularly in IQ, reading, and spelling (Fishler, Azen, Henderson, et al., 1987; Legido, Tonyes, Carter, et al., 1993). Even among children with PKU who maintain the diet, however, deficits in perceptual, memory, and attentional abilities have been observed (Banich, Passarotti, White, et al., 2000; Huijbregts, de Sonneville, Licht, et al., 2002).

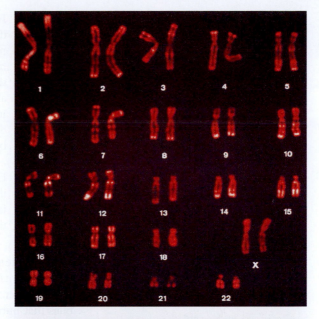

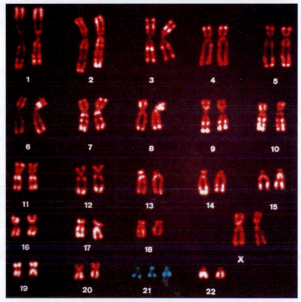

(Top) The normal complement of chromosomes is 23 pairs. (Bottom) In Down syndrome, there are three copies (a trisomy) of chromosome 21. (Kunkel/Phototake.)

Child with Down syndrome. (Rhea Anna/Getty Images, Inc.)

Infectious Diseases While in utero the fetus is at increased risk of intellectual disabilities resulting from maternal infectious diseases such as rubella (German measles). The consequences of these diseases are most serious during the first trimester of pregnancy, when the fetus has no detectable immunological response, that is, its immune system is not developed enough to ward off infection. Cytomegalovirus, toxoplasmosis, rubella, herpes simplex, HIV, and syphilis are all maternal infections that can cause both physical deformities and intellectual developmental disorder. The mother may experience slight or no symptoms from the infection, but the effects on the developing fetus can be devastating.

Infectious diseases can also affect a child's developing brain after birth. Encephalitis and meningococcal meningitis may cause brain damage and even death if contracted in infancy or early childhood. In adulthood, these infections are usually far less serious. There are several forms of childhood meningitis, a disease in which the protective membranes of the brain are acutely inflamed and fever is very high.

Environmental Hazards Several environmental pollutants are implicated in intellectual developmental disorder. One such pollutant is mercury, which may be ingested by eating affected fish. Another is lead, which is found in lead-based paints, smog, and the exhaust from automobiles that burn leaded gasoline. Lead poisoning can cause kidney and brain damage as well as anemia, intellectual disabilities, seizures, and death. Lead-based paint is now prohibited in the United States, but it is still found in older homes, where children may eat pieces that flake off.

Treatment of Intellectual Developmental Disorder

Residential Treatment Since the 1960s, there have been serious and systematic attempts to educate children with intellectual developmental disorder as fully as possible. Although many people can acquire the competence needed to function effectively in the community, some people need the extra support of a residential treatment program.

Since 1975, people with intellectual developmental disorder have had a legal right to appropriate treatment in the least restrictive setting (for more on these legal and ethical issues, see Chapter 16). Ideally, adults with intellectual developmental disorder live in small to medium-sized residences that are integrated into the community. Medical care is provided, and trained, live-in supervisors and aides help with residents' special needs around the clock. Residents are encouraged to participate in household routines to the best of their abilities. Many adults with intellectual developmental disorder have jobs and are able to live independently in their own apartments. Others live semi-independently in apartments housing three to four adults; generally, a counselor provides aid in the evening.

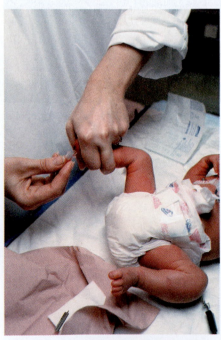

States require that newborns be tested for PKU. If excess phenylalanine is found in the blood, a special diet is recommended for the baby. (Garo/Photo Researchers, Inc.)

Behavioral Treatments Early-intervention programs using behavioral techniques have been developed to improve the level of functioning of people with intellectual developmental disorder. Specific behavioral objectives are defined, and children are taught skills in small, sequential steps (Reid, Wilson, & Faw, 1991).

Children with more severe intellectual developmental disorder usually need intensive instruction to be able to feed, toilet, and groom themselves. To teach a child a particular routine, the therapist usually begins by dividing the targeted behavior, such as eating, into smaller components: pick up spoon, scoop food from plate onto spoon, bring spoon to mouth, remove food with lips, chew, and swallow food. Operant conditioning principles are then applied to teach the child these components of eating. For example, the child may be reinforced for successive approximations to picking up the spoon until he or she is able to do so. This operant approach, sometimes called *applied behavior analysis*, is also used to reduce inappropriate and self-injurious behavior. Reinforcing substitute behaviors can often reduce these behaviors.

Studies of these programs indicate consistent improvements in fine motor skills, acceptance by others, and self-help skills. However, the programs appear to have little effect on gross motor skills and linguistic abilities, and no long-term improvements in IQ or school performance have been demonstrated.

Cognitive Treatments Many children with intellectual developmental disorder fail to use strategies in solving problems, and when they do use strategies, they often do not use them effectively. Self-instructional training teaches these children to guide their problem-solving efforts through speech.

For example, one group of researchers taught high school students with intellectual developmental disorder to make their own buttered toast and clean up after themselves (Hughes, Hugo, & Blatt, 1996). A teacher would demonstrate and verbalize the steps involved in solving a problem, such as the toaster's being upside down or unplugged. The young people learned to talk themselves through the steps using simple verbal or signed instructions. For example, when the toaster was presented upside down, the person would be taught to first state the problem ("Won't go in"), then to state the response ("Turn it"), self-evaluate ("Fixed it"), and self-reinforce ("Good"). They were rewarded with praise and high-fives when they verbalized and solved the problem correctly. Several studies have demonstrated that even people with severe intellectual developmental disorder can learn self-instructional approaches to problem solving and then generalize the strategy to new tasks, including taking lunch orders at a cafeteria and performing janitorial duties (Hughes & Agran, 1993).

Although lead-based paint is now illegal, it can still be found in older homes. Eating these paint chips can cause lead poisoning, which can cause intellectual developmental disorder. (Time & Life Pictures/ Getty Images.)

Computer-Assisted Instruction Computer-assisted instruction is increasingly found in educational and treatment settings of all kinds; it may be especially well suited to the education of people with intellectual developmental disorder. The visual and auditory components of computers can help to maintain the attention of distractible students; the level of the material can be geared to the individual, ensuring successful experiences; and the computer can meet the need for numerous repetitions of material without becoming bored or impatient, as a human teacher might. For example, computers have been used to help people with intellectual developmental disorder learn to use an ATM (Davies, Stock, & Wehmeyer, 2003). Smartphones can be enormously helpful by serving as aids for reminders, directions, instructions, and daily tasks.

Computer-assisted instruction is well suited for applications in the treatment of intellectual developmental disorder. (Robin Nelson/ PhotoEdit.)

Quick Summary

Learning disorders, communication disorders, and motor disorders are all referred to by mental health professionals as learning disabilities. Most research has been conducted on learning disorders, particularly dyslexia. Children with dyslexia have significant difficulty with word recognition, reading comprehension, and typically written spelling as well. Research has uncovered how the brain is involved in dyslexia, particularly areas of the brain that support language, including the temporoparietal and occipitotemporal areas. However, important cultural differences have been noted, suggesting that there may not be one universal mechanism to account for dyslexia. The ways in which the brain supports different languages will be an important part of future research. Interventions for dyslexia involve intensive work on reading and language skills. Not only are these interventions successful, but they may also promote changes in the brain that could contribute to the longer-term success of the treatment.

The DSM-5 will likely use the term *intellectual developmental disorder* rather than *mental retardation* and emphasize the importance of assessing intellectual ability and adaptive functioning within a person's cultural group, consistent with the approach of the AAIDD. Categories based on IQ scores will no longer be used. The approach of the AAIDD stresses the importance of identifying an individual's strengths and weaknesses. There are a number of known causes of intellectual developmental disorder, including genetic abnormalities, infections, and toxins.

Check Your Knowledge 13.3

Answer the questions.

1. Which of the following is *not* considered a learning disability?
   a. dyscalculia
   b. dyslexia
   c. intellectual developmental disorder
   d. developmental coordination disorder

2. A study examining children with dyslexia who spoke either Chinese or English found:
   a. The left middle frontal gyrus showed less activation during reading among Chinese-speaking children with dyslexia.
   b. The left temporoparietal cortex showed less activation during reading among Chinese-speaking children with dyslexia.
   c. The left middle frontal gyrus showed less activation during reading among English-speaking children with dyslexia.

   d. The left temporoparietal cortex showed more activation during reading among English-speaking children with dyslexia.

3. Which of the following has not been established as a cause for intellectual developmental disorder?
   a. chromosomal abnormalities such as trisomy 21
   b. PKU
   c. lead poisoning
   d. All the above have been found to cause intellectual developmental disorder.

4. Which of the following has been studied as possible causes for dyscalculia?
   a. gene–environment interactions
   b. the frontal lobes of the brain
   c. dyslexia
   d. All the above have been found to cause dyscalculia.

Autism Spectrum Disorder

Imagine that you are in a special education classroom for children. You are taking a course on child disabilities, and one of the requirements is to volunteer some time in this class. One of the children in the room is standing in front of a fish tank. You notice his graceful, deft movements, his dreamy smile, and the remote look in his eyes. You start talking to him about the fish, but instead of acknowledging your comment, or even your presence, he begins rocking back and forth while continuing to smile, as if enjoying a private joke. Later, you ask the teacher about the boy, and she tells you that he has autism.

Clinical Descriptions, Prevalence, and Prognosis of Autism Spectrum Disorder

Although autism was first described about 70 years ago (see Focus on Discovery 13.5 for the history of autism), it was not formally included in the DSM until the third edition, published in 1980. Over the past 30 years, the diagnosis and definition have changed quite a bit (see Focus on Discovery 13.4), and another significant change is likely to take place in DSM-5. Specifically, a number of separate diagnostic categories from DSM-IV-TR—autistic disorder, Asperger's disorder, pervasive developmental disorder not otherwise specified, and childhood disintegrative disorder—are likely to be combined into one category called **autism spectrum disorder.** Why the change? Research conducted on the different DSM-IV-TR categories did not support the distinctive categories. In other words, these disorders all share similar clinical features and etiologies and seem to vary only in severity. Thus, DSM-5 will likely have the one disorder category, autism spectrum disorder (ASD), which will include different clinical specifiers relating to severity and the extent of language impairment. Because mental health professionals have been using the term *autism spectrum* for many years, we also adopt the term here in our discussions of this disorder.

The proposed DSM-5 criteria for ASD are presented in the nearby box. In the next sections, we describe the clinical features, focusing on problems in social and emotional interactions and in communication as well as on repetitive or ritualistic behaviors.

Social and Emotional Disturbances Children with ASD can have profound problems with the social world (Dawson, Toth, Abbott, et al., 2004). They may rarely approach others and may look through or past people or turn their backs on them. For example, one study found that children with ASD rarely offered a spontaneous greeting or farewell (either verbally

FOCUS ON DISCOVERY 13.5

A Brief History of Autism Spectrum Disorder

Autism was identified in 1943 by a psychiatrist at Johns Hopkins, Leo Kanner, who, in the course of his clinical work, noted 11 disturbed children who behaved in ways that were not common in children with intellectual developmental disorder or schizophrenia. He named the syndrome *early infantile autism* because he observed that "there is from the start an extreme autistic aloneness that, whenever possible, disregards, ignores, shuts out anything that comes to the child from the outside" (Kanner, 1943).

Kanner considered autistic aloneness the most fundamental symptom. He also learned that these 11 children had been unable from the beginning of life to relate to people in the ordinary way. They were severely limited in language and had a strong, obsessive desire for everything about them to remain unchanged. Despite its early description by Kanner and others (Rimland, 1964), the disorder was not accepted into official diagnostic nomenclature until the publication of DSM-III in 1980, where it was called autistic disorder.

Asperger's disorder was named after Hans Asperger, who in 1944 described the syndrome as being less severe and with fewer communication deficits than autism. It was first introduced to the DSM in 1994 in DSM-IV. Social relationships are poor and stereotyped behavior is intense and rigid, but language and intelligence are intact. Because research suggests that Asperger's disorder does not differ qualitatively from autistic disorder, these two categories will likely be combined in DSM-5. Nevertheless, more research has been conducted in the last 10 years on Asperger's disorder, perhaps due to the recognition of this condition among adults who for years wondered why they were different from others. Adults with the DSM-IV-TR diagnosis Asperger's disorder are now more frequently recognized and treated by mental health professionals (Gaus, 2007).

It remains to be seen if these same people will continue to seek and receive the support and help they need when the category is subsumed under the autism spectrum disorder category in DSM-5. On the one hand, some worry that stigma associated with the name *autism* might keep people from seeking help (see Focus on Discovery 3.3 on the underreporting of stigmatized behavior). On the other hand, some states, like California and Texas, mandate services for children with autism, but not Asperger's, and thus more people might get help.

Researchers, clinicians, and families have referred to the "autism spectrum" for years, so, in some ways, this change might not be so difficult to accommodate, at least in terms of the name. The removal of Asperger's disorder as a diagnostic category may be more difficult. People who have finally understood what is wrong with them will now have to think differently about what disorder they have. Time will tell what this change brings.

or through smiling, making eye contact, or gesturing) when meeting or departing from an adult (Hobson & Lee, 1998). Another study found that 1-year-old children with ASD attended to other people's faces far less often at their birthday parties than did children without autism (Osterling & Dawson, 1994). Few children with ASD initiate play with other children, and they are usually unresponsive to anyone who approaches them. Children with ASD sometimes make eye contact, but their gaze may have an unusual quality. Typically, children gaze to gain someone's attention or to direct the other person's attention to an object; children with ASD generally do not (Dawson et al., 2004). This is often referred to as a problem in **joint attention**. That is, interactions that require two people to pay attention to each other, whether speaking or communicating emotion nonverbally, are impaired in children with autism.

Proposed DSM-5 Criteria for Autism Spectrum Disorder

A total of six or more items from A, B, and C below, with at least two from A and one each from B and C:

A. Deficits in social communication and social interactions as manifested by all of the following:
- Deficits in nonverbal behaviors such as eye contact, facial expression, body language
- Deficit in development of peer relationships appropriate to developmental level
- Deficits in social or emotional reciprocity such as not approaching others, not having a back-and-forth conversation, reduced sharing of interests and emotions

B. Restricted, repetitive behavior patterns, interests, or activities manifested by at least two of the following:
- Stereotyped or repetitive speech, motor movements, or use of objects
- Excessive adherence to routines, rituals in verbal or nonverbal behavior, or extreme resistance to change
- Very restricted interests that are abnormal in focus, such as preoccupation with parts of objects
- Hyper- or hyporeactivity to sensory input or unusual interest in sensory environment, such as fascination with lights or spinning objects

C. Onset in early childhood

D. Symptoms limit and impair functioning

Heather Kuzmich, a finalist on the television show *America's Next Top Model,* has what was called Asperger's disorder in DSM-IV-TR but will likely be called autism spectrum disorder in DSM-5. (© Circe Hamilton/CameraPress/Retna.)

A study with adults found that people with ASD pay attention to different parts of faces than do people without ASD (Spezio, Adolphs, Hurley, et al., 2007). In order to figure out what type of emotion someone's face is displaying, the other person typically needs to look at the upper and lower face. Some emotions are reflected in the eyes (e.g., anger, happiness). In the study, adults with ASD focused their gaze mostly on the mouth region and almost entirely neglected the eye region. This relative neglect likely contributes to their difficulties in perceiving emotion in other people.

Consistent with the findings showing that children with ASD do not pay attention to other people's faces or capture their gaze, fMRI studies have found that people with ASD do not show activation in the fusiform gyrus, other regions in the temporal lobes, and the amygdala, the areas of the brain most often associated with identifying faces and emotion, when completing face perception or identity tasks (Critchley, Daly, Bullmore, et al., 2001; Pierce, Haist, Sedaghadt, et al., 2004; Pierce, Muller, Ambrose, et al., 2001). Instead, other areas of the brain show activation during these tasks, suggesting perhaps a less efficient system for identifying faces.

When someone else initiates play, children with ASD may be compliant and engage in the activity for a period of time. Physical play, such as tickling and wrestling, may not be enjoyable to children with ASD. Observations of their spontaneous play in an unstructured setting reveal that children with ASD spend much less of their time engaged in symbolic play, such as making a doll drive to the store or pretending that a block is a car, than do either children with intellectual developmental disorder or typically developing children of comparable mental age (Sigman, Ungerer, Mundy, et al., 1987).

Some researchers have proposed that children with ASD have a deficient "theory of mind" and that this is their core deficit, leading to the kinds of social dysfunctions we have described here (Gopnik, Capps, & Meltzoff, 2000; Sigman, 1994). *Theory of mind* refers to a person's understanding that other people have desires, beliefs, intentions, and emotions that may be different from one's own. This ability is crucial for understanding and successfully engaging in social interactions. Theory of mind typically develops between $2\frac{1}{2}$ and 5 years of age. Children with ASD seem not to undergo this developmental milestone and thus seem unable to understand others' perspectives and emotional reactions. Research has also shown that people with ASD (and those with Asperger's disorder) have disturbances in areas of the brain linked to the abilities needed to form a theory of mind (Castelli, Frith, Happe, et al., 2002).

Although some children with ASD can learn to understand emotional experiences, they "answer questions about . . . emotional experiences like normal children answer difficult arithmetic questions" (Sigman, 1994, p. 151), with concentrated effort. Laboratory studies of children with ASD have found that they may recognize others' emotions without really understanding them (Capps, Rasco, Losh, et al., 1999; Capps, Yirmiya, & Sigman, 1992). For example, when asked to explain why someone was angry, a child with ASD responded "because he was yelling" (Capps, Losh, & Thurber, 2000).

Communication Deficits Even before they acquire language, some children with ASD show deficits in communication. Babbling, a term describing the utterances of infants before they begin to use words, is less frequent in infants with ASD and conveys less information than it does in other infants (Ricks, 1972). By 2 years of age, most typically developing children use words to represent objects in their surroundings and construct one- and two-word sentences to express more complex thoughts, such as "Mommy go" or "Me juice." In contrast, children with ASD lag well behind in these abilities and often show other language disturbances.

One such feature associated with ASD is echolalia, in which the child echoes, usually with remarkable fidelity, what he or she has

Children with ASD do not often play or socially interact with other children. (Ruth Jenkinson/Getty Images.)

heard another person say. The teacher may ask a child with ASD, "Do you want a cookie?" The child's response may be, "Do you want a cookie?" This is immediate echolalia. In delayed echolalia, the child may be in a room with the television on and appear to be completely uninterested. Several hours later or even the next day, the child may echo a word or phrase from the television program.

Another language abnormality common in the speech of children with ASD is **pronoun reversal**, in which children refer to themselves as "he," "she," or "you" (or even by their own name). For example:

Parent: What are you doing, Johnny?
Child: He's here.
Parent: Are you having a good time?
Child: He knows it.

Pronoun reversal is closely linked to echolalia—when children with ASD use echolalic speech, they refer to themselves as they have heard others speak of them and misapply pronouns. Children with ASD are very literal in their use of words. If a father provided positive reinforcement by putting his daughter on his shoulders when she learned to say the word *yes*, then the child might say *yes* to mean she wants to be lifted onto her father's shoulders. Or a child may say "do not drop the cat" to mean "no," because a parent had used these emphatic words when the child was about to drop the family feline.

Repetitive and Ritualistic Acts   Children with ASD can become extremely upset over changes in their daily routines and surroundings. An offer of milk in a different drinking cup or a rearrangement of furniture may make them cry or precipitate a temper tantrum.

An obsessional quality may pervade the behavior of children with ASD. In their play, they may continually line up toys or construct intricate patterns with household objects. As they grow older, they may become preoccupied with train schedules, subway routes, and number sequences. Children with ASD are also likely to perform a more limited number of behaviors than children without ASD and are less likely to explore new surroundings.

Children with ASD may also display stereotypical behavior, peculiar ritualistic hand movements, and other rhythmic movements, such as endless body rocking, hand flapping, and walking on tiptoe. They may spin and twirl string, crayons, sticks, and plates, twiddle their fingers in front of their eyes, and stare at fans and other spinning things. Researchers often describe these as self-stimulatory activities. The children may become preoccupied with manipulating an object and may become very upset when interrupted.

Some children with ASD can become preoccupied with and form strong attachments to simple inanimate objects (e.g., keys, rocks, a wire-mesh basket, light switches, a large blanket) and to more complex mechanical objects (e.g., refrigerators and vacuum cleaners). If the object is something they can carry, they may walk around with it in their hands, and this may interfere with their learning to do more useful things.

Comorbidity and ASD   Many children with ASD score below 70 on standardized intelligence tests, which can make it difficult to distinguish between ASD and intellectual developmental disorder. There are important differences, however. Children with intellectual developmental disorder usually score poorly on all parts of an intelligence test, but children with ASD may score poorly on those subtests related to language, such as tasks requiring abstract thought, symbolism, or sequential logic (Carpentieri & Morgan, 1994). Children with ASD usually obtain better scores on items requiring visual-spatial skills, such as matching designs in block-design tests and putting together disassembled objects (Rutter, 1983). Sensorimotor development is the area of greatest relative strength among children with ASD. These children, who may show severe and profound deficits in cognitive abilities, can be quite graceful and adept at swinging, climbing, or balancing, whereas children with intellectual developmental disorder have far more difficulty in areas of gross motor development, such as learning to walk. Sometimes children with ASD may have isolated skills that reflect great talent, such as the ability to multiply two four-digit numbers rapidly in their heads. They may also have exceptional long-term memory, being able to recall the exact words of a song heard years earlier.

People with ASD frequently engage in stereotyped behavior, such as ritualistic hand movements. (Nancy Pierce/Photo Researchers, Inc.)

ASD is also comorbid with learning disorders, with one study reporting over a third of the children with ASD also having a learning disorder (Lichtenstein, Carlstrom, Ramstam, et al., 2010). In addition, ASD is also comorbid with anxiety, with between 11 and 84 percent of children with ASD also experiencing clinically significant anxiety, including separation anxiety, social anxiety, general anxiety, and specific phobias (White, Oswald, Ollendick, Scahill, 2009).

Prevalence of Autism Spectrum Disorder ASD begins in early childhood and can be evident in the first months of life. It affects about 1 of every 110 children (CDC, 2009a). Studies show that about four times more boys than girls have ASD (Volkmar, Szatmari, & Sparrow, 1993). There has been a large increase in the number of ASD diagnoses over the past 25 years—close to a 300 percent increase in California, for example (Maugh, 2002) (see Focus on Discovery 13.4 for more on this). ASD is found in all socioeconomic, ethnic, and racial groups. The diagnosis of ASD is remarkably stable. In one recent study, only 1 out of 84 children diagnosed with ASD at age 2 no longer met the diagnostic criteria at age 9 (Lord, Risi, DiLavore, et al., 2006).

Prognosis for Autism Spectrum Disorder What happens to children with ASD when they reach adulthood? Kanner (1973) reported on the adult status of nine of the eleven children described in his original paper first describing autism. Two had developed epileptic seizures;

FOCUS ON DISCOVERY 13.6

The Story of a Woman Living with Autism Spectrum Disorder

Temple Grandin is a woman with autism spectrum disorder. She also has a Ph.D. in animal science, runs her own business designing machinery for use with farm animals, and is on the faculty at Colorado State University. Three autobiographical books (Grandin, 1986, 1995, 2008) and a profile by neurologist Oliver Sacks (1995) provide a moving and revealing portrait of the mysteries of ASD. A highly acclaimed and awarded HBO movie based on Grandin's 1995 book *Thinking in Pictures* was released in 2010 and starred Clare Danes as Temple. Grandin has also written other books about her professional work with animals.

Lacking understanding of the complexities and subtleties of human social discourse, deficient in the ability to empathize with others, Grandin sums up her relationship to the nonautistic world saying, "Much of the time I feel like an anthropologist on Mars" (Sacks, 1995, p. 259).

Grandin recalls from her childhood sudden impulsive behavior and violent rages as well as hyperfocused attention, "a selectivity so intense that it could create a world of its own, a place of calm and order in the chaos and tumult" (Sacks, 1995, p. 254). She describes "sensations heightened, sometimes to an excruciating degree [and] she speaks of her ears, at the age of 2 or 3, as helpless microphones, transmitting everything, irrespective of relevance, at full, overwhelming volume" (Sacks, 1995, p. 254).

Grandin was diagnosed with autism in 1950 at age 3. She had no speech at all, and doctors predicted that institutionalization would be her fate. However, with the help of a therapeutic nursery school and speech therapy and with the support of her family, she learned to speak by age 6 and began to make more contact with others. Still, as an adolescent observing other children interact, Grandin "sometimes wondered if they were all telepathic" (Sacks, 1995, p. 272), so mysterious did she find the ability of normal children to understand each other's needs and wishes, to empathize, to communicate.

Visiting her one day at her university, Sacks made several observations that convey the autistic flavor of this uncommon person:

She sat me down [in her office] with little ceremony, no preliminaries, no social niceties, no small talk about my trip or how I liked

Colorado. She plunged straight into talking of her work, speaking of her early interests in psychology and animal behavior, how they were connected with self-observation and a sense of her own needs as an autistic person, and how this had joined with the [highly developed] visualizing and engineering part of her mind to point her towards the special field she had made her own: the design of farms, feedlots, corrals, slaughterhouses—systems of many sorts for animal management.

She spoke well and clearly, but with a certain unstoppable impetus and fixity. A sentence, a paragraph, once started, had to be completed; nothing left implicit, hanging in the air. (Sacks, 1995, pp. 256–257)

In her own writings, Grandin points out that many people with ASD are great fans of *Star Trek*, especially the characters of Spock and Data, the former a member of the Vulcan race, purely intellectual, logical beings who eschew any consideration of the emotional side of life, and the latter an android, a highly sophisticated computer housed in a human body and, like Spock, lacking in emotion. (One of the dramatic themes involving both characters was, of course, their flirtation with the experience of human emotion, portrayed with particular poignancy by Data. This is a theme in Grandin's life as well.) As Grandin (1995) wrote at age 47:

All my life I have been an observer, and I have always felt like someone who watches from the outside. I could not participate in the social interactions of high school life.

Even today, personal relationships are something I don't really understand. I've remained celibate because doing so helps me avoid the many complicated situations that are too difficult for me to handle. [M]en who want to date often don't understand how to relate to a woman. They [and I myself] remind me of Data, the android on Star Trek. In one episode, Data's attempts at dating were a disaster. When he tried to be romantic [by effecting a change in a subroutine of his computer program], he complimented his date by using scientific terminology. Even very able adults with autism have such problems. (pp. 132–133) one of these had died, and the other was in a state hospital. Four others had spent most of their lives in hospitals. Of the remaining three, one was still mute but was working on a farm and as an orderly in a nursing home. The other two had made satisfactory recoveries; although both still lived with their parents and had little social life, they were gainfully employed and had developed some recreational interests.

Similar outcomes have been found in more recent population-based, follow-up studies (Gillberg, 1991; Nordin & Gillberg, 1998; Von Knorring & Hagloff, 1993). Generally, children with higher IQs who learn to speak before age 6 have the best outcomes, and a few of these function fairly well in adulthood. For example, one longitudinal study of children with ASD from preschool to early adulthood found that IQs over 70 predicted more strengths and fewer weaknesses in adaptive functioning as they grew older (McGovern & Sigman, 2005), and outcomes were better for those who had interacted and engaged more with their peers. Other studies of people with ASD who have higher IQ scores have indicated that most do not require residential care and some are able to attend college and support themselves through employment (Yirmiya & Sigman, 1991). Still, many independently functioning adults with ASD continue to show impairment in social relationships (Howlin, Goode, Hutton, & Rutter, 2004; Howlin, Mawhood, & Rutter, 2000). Focus on Discovery 13.6 describes a woman with ASD whose adult life is remarkable for its professional distinction blended with the social and emotional deficits that are part of ASD.

Some of the deficiencies of people with ASD make them charmingly honest and trustworthy. "Lying," wrote Grandin, "is very anxiety-provoking because it requires rapid interpretations of subtle social cues [of which I am incapable] to determine whether the other person is really being deceived" (Grandin, 1995, p. 135).

Grandin's professional career is impressive. She uses her remarkable powers of visualization and her empathy for farm animals to design machines such as a chute leading cows to slaughter that takes them on a circular route, protecting them from awareness of their fate until the moment of death. She has also designed and built a "squeeze machine," a device that provides comforting hugs without the need for human contact. It has "two heavy, slanting wooden sides, perhaps four by three feet each, pleasantly upholstered with a thick, soft padding. They [are] joined by hinges to a long, narrow bottom board to create a V-shaped, body-sized trough. There [is] a complex control box at one end, with heavy-duty tubes leading off to another device, in a closet. [An] industrial compressor exerts a firm but comfortable pressure on the body, from the shoulders to the knees" (Sacks, 1995, pp. 262–263). Her explanation of the rationale behind this contraption is that as a little girl she longed to be hugged but was also very fearful of physical contact with another person. When a favorite, large-bodied aunt hugged her, she felt both overwhelmed and comforted. Terror commingled with pleasure.

She started to have daydreams—she was just five at the time—of a magic machine that could squeeze her powerfully but gently, in a huglike way, and in a way entirely commanded and controlled by her. Years later, as an adolescent, she had seen a picture of a squeeze chute designed to hold or restrain calves and realized that that was it: a little modification to make it suitable for human use, and it could be her magic machine. (Sacks, 1995, p. 263)

After watching her demonstrate the machine and trying it himself, Sacks observed:

It is not just pleasure or relaxation that Temple gets from the machine but, she maintains, a feeling for others. As she lies in her machine, she says, her thoughts often turn to her mother, her favorite aunt, her teachers. She feels their love for her, and hers for them. She feels that the machine opens a door into an otherwise closed emotional world and allows her, almost teaches her, to feel empathy for others. (Sacks, 1995, p. 264)

Sacks has great admiration for Grandin's professional success and for the interesting and productive life she has made for herself, but when it comes to human interactions, it is clear that she does not get it. "I was struck by the enormous difference, the gulf, between Temple's immediate, intuitive recognition of animal moods and signs and her extraordinary difficulties understanding human beings, their codes and signals, the way they conduct themselves" (Sacks, 1995, p. 269).

Accounts such as those of Grandin and Sacks can provide insight into how people adapt to their own idiosyncrasies, using the sometimes peculiar gifts they have been given and working around the deficiencies with which they have been saddled. "Autism, while it may be pathologized as a syndrome, must also be seen as a whole mode of being, a deeply different mode or identity, one that needs to be conscious (and proud) of itself," wrote Sacks (1995, p. 277). "At a public lecture, Temple ended by saying, 'If I could snap my fingers and be nonautistic, I would not—because then I wouldn't be me. Autism is part of who I am'" (Sacks, 1995, p. 291).

Temple Grandin, Ph.D., was diagnosed with autism in early childhood but has had a successful academic career. (John Epperson/Associated Press/AP/Wide World Photos.)

Etiology of Autism Spectrum Disorder

The earliest theory about the etiology of ASD was that psychological factors such as bad parenting were responsible for its development. This narrow and faulty perspective has been replaced in recent years by theories based on evidence that genetic and neurological factors are important in the etiology of this puzzling syndrome. Despite the lack of empirical support for early psychological theories, they gained enough recognition to place a tremendous emotional burden on parents who were told that they were at fault for their child's ASD.

Genetic Factors Evidence suggests a genetic component for ASD, with heritability estimates of around .80 (Lichtenstein et al., 2010). The risk of ASD or language delay among siblings of people with the disorder is much higher than it is among siblings of people who do not have ASD (Constantino, Zhang, Frazier, et al., 2010; McBride, Anderson, & Shapiro, 1996). Even stronger evidence for genetic transmission of ASD comes from twin studies, which have found between 47 and 90 percent concordance for ASD between identical twins, compared with concordance rates of 0 to 20 percent between fraternal twins (Bailey, LeCouteur, Gottesman, et al., 1995; Le Couteur, Bailey, Goode, et al., 1996; Lichtenstein et al., 2010). However, this does not rule out environmental effects. Remember that genes do their work via the environment. In addition, another recent twin study called the California Autism Twin Study used the most current and well-validated method for diagnosing ASD rather than relying solely on medical records or parental reports as other studies have done. Contrary to other studies, this study found that shared environmental factors (e.g., common experiences in a family; see Chapter 2) accounted for over half of the risk for developed autism (Hallmayer, Cleveland, Torres, et al., 2011).

A series of studies following twins and families with a member with ASD suggest that ASD is linked genetically to a broader spectrum of deficits in communication and social interaction (Bailey et al., 1995; Bolton, MacDonald, Pickles, et al., 1994; Constantino et al., 2010; Folstein & Rutter, 1977a, 1977b). For example, most of the identical twins without ASD displayed communication deficits, such as delayed development of language abilities or reading impairments, as well as severe social deficits, including no social contacts outside the family, lack of responsiveness to social cues or conventions, and little or no spontaneous affection shown toward caregivers. In contrast, fraternal twins of children with ASD are almost always normal in their social and language development and live independently in adulthood (Le Couteur et al., 1996). In families where more than one child had ASD or language delay, unaffected siblings also exhibited deficits in social communication and interactions (Constantino et al., 2010). Taken together, the evidence from family and twin studies supports a genetic contribution to ASD.

Molecular genetics studies try to pinpoint areas of the genome that may confer risk for ASD. Recall from Chapter 2 that genome-wide association studies (GWAS) look for differences in gene sequence (single nucleotide polymorphisms; SNPs) and gene structure (copy number variations; CNVs). One research group studying CNVs found that a deletion on chromosome 16 was associated with ASD in three different samples (Weiss, Shen, Korn, et al., 2008). The deletion represents a genetic flaw—it was not supposed to be deleted—and the researchers suggest that although it is not clear why the flaw occurs, it is nonetheless associated with an increased risk of developing ASD. Other GWAS studies have identified SNPs between two genes on chromosome 5 that have been replicated in two independent samples of people with ASD (Wang, Zhang, Ma, et al., 2009) and one sample of people without ASD but who had communication and social-emotional difficulties (St. Pourcain, Wang, Glessner, et al., 2010).

Neurobiological Factors More and more research is linking the language, social, and emotional deficits in ASD to the brain. A number of studies examining the brain in ASD have been well replicated, allowing for a clearer picture of what may go wrong in the brain among people with ASD. What remains to be figured out is why the brain goes awry early in development.

Studies using magnetic resonance imaging (MRI) found that, overall, the brains of adults and children with ASD are larger than the brains of adults and children without ASD (Courchesne, Carnes, & Davis, 2001; Piven, Arndt, Bailey, et al., 1995, 1996). This same finding has been supported by studies using the measurement of head circumference as an indicator of brain size (Courchesne, Carper, & Akshoomoff, 2003). What makes these findings more interesting and puzzling is that most children with ASD are born with brains of a relatively normal size; however, between the ages of 2 and 4, the brains of children with ASD become significantly larger

(Courchesne, 2004). One longitudinal study assessed brain size using MRI when children with and without autism were 2 years old and again when they were 4 or 5 years old. The researchers found that the children with autism had larger brain size at age 2 but that it did not continue to increase at ages 4 or 5, thus suggesting that the brain growth does not continue past the first few years of life (Hazlett, Poe, Gerig, et al., 2011). Having a larger-than-normal brain is not necessarily a good thing, as it might indicate that neurons are not being pruned correctly. The pruning of neurons is an important part of brain maturation; older children have fewer connections between neurons than do babies. Adding further to this puzzle, brain growth in ASD appears to slow abnormally in later childhood. It will be important for investigators to figure out how this pattern of brain growth is linked to the signs and symptoms of ASD. It is worth noting that the areas of the brain that are "overgrown" in ASD include the frontal, temporal, and cerebellar, which have been linked with language, social, and emotional functions.

Other areas of the brain are implicated in ASD as well. Sixteen MRI and autopsy studies from nine independent research groups all found abnormalities in the cerebellum of children with ASD (Haas, Townsend, Courchèsne, et al., 1996), and more recent studies have confirmed this finding (e.g., Hardan, Minshew, Harenski, et al., 2001). Another study found that the commonly observed tendency of children with ASD to explore their surroundings less than other children do is correlated with a larger-than-normal cerebellum (Pierce & Courchesne, 2001). Neurological abnormalities in people with ASD suggest that in the course of development, their brain cells fail to align properly and do not form the network of connections found in normal brains.

Two studies examined the size of the amygdalae among children and adults with ASD. Given that ASD is associated with social and emotional difficulties, and that the amygdalae are associated with social and emotional behavior, it stands to reason that the amygdalae might be involved in ASD. One study found that the amygdalae were larger among children with ASD (Munson, Dawson, Abbott, et al., 2006) and that larger amygdalae at ages 3 or 4 predicted more difficulties in social behavior and communication at age 6. This finding is consistent with studies showing overgrowth of other brain areas. However, the other study found that *small* amygdalae size in ASD was correlated with difficulties in emotional face perception and less gaze in the eye region of faces during the perception task (Nacewicz, Dalton, Johnstone, et al., 2006). How can we make sense of the seemingly different findings? Participants in the study by Nacewicz and colleagues were older, suggesting that the brain changes that continue throughout in development may be differentially related to social and emotional impairments.

Treatment of Autism Spectrum Disorder

The most promising efforts at treatment of ASD are psychological. Various treatments that combine psychological treatment and drugs have been studied as well, but with few positive results. Treatments for children with ASD are usually aimed at reducing their unusual behavior and improving their communication and social skills. In most cases, the earlier the intervention begins, the better the outcome. Identifying ASD early is a key priority for the field. In a promising longitudinal study, children at high risk for developing ASD (parent or sibling with an ASD) were studied beginning at age 14 months. Even though these children did not yet have language, the researchers were able to identify deficits in joint attention and communication that allowed for an early provisional diagnosis of ASD (Landa, Holman, & Garrett-Mayer, 2007).

It is important to note that even though genetic and neurological factors in the etiology of ASD have much more empirical support than psychological factors, it is the psychological treatments that currently show the most promise, not medications. The lesson is that a neurological defect may well be treatable psychologically.

Behavioral Treatment In the late 1980s, Ivar Lovaas conducted an intensive operant conditioning–based program of behavioral treatment with young (under 4 years old) children with ASD (Lovaas, 1987). Therapy encompassed all aspects of the children's lives for more than 40 hours a week over more than 2 years. Parents were trained extensively so that treatment could continue during almost all the children's waking hours. Nineteen children receiving this intensive treatment were compared with 40 children who received a similar treatment for less than 10 hours per week. Both groups of children were rewarded for being less aggressive, more compliant, and more socially appropriate—for example, talking and playing with other

Ivar Lovaas, a behavior therapist, was noted for his operant conditioning treatment of children with autism. (Lovaas Institute.)

children. The goal of the program was to mainstream the children, the assumption being that children with ASD, as they improve, benefit more from being with typically developing peers than from remaining by themselves or with other seriously disturbed children.

The results of this landmark study were dramatic and encouraging. The IQs for the intensive-therapy group averaged 83 in first grade (after about 2 years in the intensive therapy) compared with about 55 for the other group; 12 of the 19 reached the normal range, compared with only 2 (of 40) of the others. Furthermore, 9 of the 19 in the intensive-therapy group were promoted to second grade in a regular public school, whereas only 1 of the much larger group achieved this level of functioning. A follow-up of these children 4 years later indicated that the intensive-treatment group maintained their gains in IQ, adaptive behavior, and grade promotions in school (McEachin, Smith, & Lovaas, 1993). Although critics have pointed out weaknesses in the study's methodology and outcome measures (Shopler, Short, & Mesibov, 1989), this ambitious program confirms the benefits of intensive therapy with the heavy involvement of both professionals and parents in dealing with the challenges of ASD.

One of the weaknesses of the study was that it was not a randomized, controlled clinical trial. There has been only one randomized controlled clinical trial to examine the efficacy of intensive behavioral treatment on a broader scale. This study compared an intensive behavioral treatment (about 25 hours a week, instead of 40) to a treatment that consisted of parent training only (Smith, Groen, & Wynn, 2000). Although the behavioral treatment was more effective than parent training alone, the children in this study did not show the same gains as in the study discussed above, perhaps due to the fact that the treatment was implemented for fewer hours.

A recent meta-analysis of 22 studies using intensive behavioral treatments, either in a clinic setting or with parents as the primary point of intervention, reported a number of noteworthy results. First, the average quality of these studies, rated on a 1 to 5 scale with 5 being the best, was only 2.5. Few were randomized clinical trials, and many had very small sample sizes. With these limitations in mind, the overall effect sizes (see Chapter 4) were large for changes in IQ, language skills, overall communication, socialization, and daily living skills (Virués-Ortega, 2010). These results are encouraging, but it remains important to conduct more rigorous studies of these types of treatments.

Other research also suggests that education provided by parents is beneficial. Parents are present in many different situations and thus can help children generalize the gains they make. For example, one group of researchers demonstrated that 25 to 30 hours of parent training was as effective as 200 hours of direct clinic treatment in improving the behavior of children with ASD (Koegel, Schreibman, Britten, et al., 1982). This research group has also focused on comparing different strategies for behavioral parent training, with interesting discoveries. They found that parents could be more effective when taught to focus on increasing their children's general motivation and responsiveness rather than being taught to focus on changing individually targeted problem behaviors in a sequential manner (Koegel, Bimbela, & Schreibman, 1996). For example, allowing the child to choose the teaching materials, providing natural reinforcers (e.g., play and social praise) rather than edible reinforcers, and reinforcing attempts to respond as well as correct responses all led to improved family interactions and more positive communication between parents and their children with ASD. This more focused approach to treatment is called *pivotal response treatment* (PRT), a term based on the notion that intervening in a key, or pivotal, area may lead to changes in other areas. At least 10 studies have found PRT to be effective (reviewed in Koegel, Koegel, & Brookman, 2003).

Other interventions seek to improve children's problems in joint attention and communication. In a randomized controlled clinical trial, children ages 3 and 4 with ASD were randomly assigned to a joint attention (JA) intervention, a symbolic play (SP) intervention, or a control group (Kasari, Freeman, & Paparella, 2006). All children were already part of an early-intervention program; the JA and SP interventions were additional interventions provided to the children in 30-minute daily blocks for 6 weeks. Children in the JA and SP treatments showed more improvement than children in the control group, and at 6 and 12 months after the treatment, children in the JA and SP groups had greater expressive language skills than children in the control group (Kasari, Paparella, Freeman, & Jahromi, 2008).

Drug Treatment   The most commonly used medication for treating problem behaviors in children with ASD is haloperidol (trade name Haldol), an antipsychotic medication used in the treatment of schizophrenia. Some controlled studies have shown that this drug reduces social withdrawal, stereotyped motor behavior, and such maladaptive behaviors as self-mutilation and aggression (Anderson, Campbell, Adams, et al., 1989; McBride et al., 1996; Perry, Campbell, Adams, et al., 1989). Many children do not respond positively to the drug, however, and it has not shown any positive effects on other aspects of ASD, such as social functioning and language impairments (Holm & Varley, 1989). Haloperidol also has serious side effects (Posey & McDougle, 2000). In a longitudinal study, over 30 percent of children with ASD developed drug-related dyskinesias, or jerky muscle disturbances, although most went away after the drug was withdrawn (Campbell, Armenteros, Malone, et al., 1997).

Evidence that children with ASD may have elevated blood levels of serotonin (Anderson & Hoshino, 1987) encouraged research on medications that reduce the action of serotonin. There was an initial flurry of enthusiastic claims that the drug fenfluramine, known to lower serotonin levels in rats and monkeys, was associated with dramatic improvement in the behavior and thought processes of children with ASD (Ritvo, Freeman, Geller, et al., 1983), but later studies delivered much more modest findings (Leventhal, Cook, Morford, et al., 1993; Rapin, 1997). Although fenfluramine may work with some children with ASD to slightly improve their social adjustment, attention span, activity level, and stereotyped behavior, no consistent effect has been shown on cognitive measures such as IQ or language functioning.

Researchers have also studied naltrexone, an opioid receptor antagonist, and found that this drug reduces hyperactivity in children with ASD and produces a moderate improvement in the initiation of social interactions (Aman & Langworthy, 2000; Willemsen-Swinkels, Buitelaar, & van Engeland, 1996; Williams, Allard, Spears, et al., 2001). One controlled study suggested mild improvements in the initiation of communication as well (Kolmen, Feldman, Handen, et al., 1995), but others found no changes in communication or social behavior (Feldman, Kolmen, & Gonzaga, 1999; Willemsen-Swinkels et al., 1996; Willemsen-Swinkels, Buitelaar, Weijnen, et al., 1995). The drug does not appear to affect the core symptoms of ASD, and some evidence suggests that at some doses it may increase self-injurious behavior (Anderson, Hanson, Malecha, et al., 1997).

In sum, pharmacological treatment of ASD is, at this point, less effective than behavioral treatments.

Check Your Knowledge 13.4

True or false?
1. All children with ASD also have intellectual developmental disorder.

2. Children with ASD have difficulty recognizing emotions in others.
3. Medication is an effective treatment for ASD.

Summary

Clinical Descriptions

• Childhood disorders are often organized into two domains: externalizing disorders and internalizing disorders. Externalizing disorders are characterized by such behaviors as aggressiveness, noncompliance, overactivity, and impulsiveness; they include attention-deficit/hyperactivity disorder, conduct disorder, and oppositional defiant disorder. Internalizing disorders are characterized by such behaviors as depression, social withdrawal, and anxiety; they include childhood anxiety and mood disorders.

• Attention-deficit/hyperactivity disorder (ADHD) is a persistent pattern of inattention and/or hyperactivity and impulsivity that is more frequent and more severe than what is typically observed in children of a given age. Conduct disorder is characterized by high and widespread levels of aggression, lying, theft, vandalism, cruelty to other people and to animals, and other acts that violate laws and social norms.

• Mood and anxiety disorders in children share similarities with the adult forms of these disorders. However, differences that reflect different stages of development are also important.

- Learning disorders are diagnosed when a child fails to develop to the degree expected for his or her intellectual level in a specific academic, language, or motor skill area. These disorders are often identified and treated within the school system rather than through mental health clinics. Evidence suggests that gene–environment interactions are operating for dyscalculia. fMRI studies point to different areas of the brain being implicated in dyslexia and dyscalculia.

- The likely DSM-5 diagnostic criteria for intellectual developmental disorder include deficits in intellectual functioning and adaptive behavior, with onset before the age of 18. Most professionals focus more on the strengths of people with intellectual developmental disorder. This shift in emphasis is associated with increased efforts to design psychological and educational interventions that make the most of individuals' abilities. The term *mental retardation* will likely no longer be used in DSM-5.

- Autism spectrum disorder begins early in life, and the number of children with this diagnosis has risen in recent years. The major symptoms are a failure to relate to other people; communication problems, consisting of either a failure to learn any language or speech irregularities, such as echolalia and pronoun reversal; and theory of mind problems.

Etiology

- There is strong evidence for genetic and neurobiological factors in the etiology of ADHD. Low birth weight and maternal smoking are also risk factors. Family factors interact with these genetic vulnerabilities.

- Among the apparent etiological and risk factors for conduct disorder are a genetic predisposition, inadequate learning of moral awareness, modeling and direct reinforcement of antisocial behavior, negative peer influences, and living in impoverished and crime-ridden areas.

- Etiological factors for mood and anxiety disorders in children are believed to be largely the same as in adulthood, though additional research is needed.

- There is mounting evidence that the most widely studied of the learning disorders, dyslexia, has genetic and other neurobiological components.

- Some forms of intellectual developmental disorder have a neurological basis, such as the chromosomal trisomy that causes Down syndrome. Certain infectious diseases in the pregnant mother, such as HIV, rubella, and syphilis, as well as illnesses that affect the child directly, such as encephalitis, can interfere with cognitive and social development. Environmental factors such as lead paint can also cause intellectual developmental disorder.

- Family and twin studies give compelling evidence for genetic factors in ASD, but the environment also plays a role. Abnormalities have been found in the brains of children with ASD, including an overgrowth of the brain by age 2 and abnormalities in the cerebellum.

Treatment

- A combined treatment including stimulant drugs, such as Adderall or Ritalin, and reinforcement for staying on task has shown effectiveness in reducing the symptoms of ADHD.

- The most promising approach to treating young people with conduct disorder involves intensive intervention in multiple systems, including the family, school, and peer systems.

- The most effective intervention for mood and anxiety disorders is cognitive behavioral therapy. Medication is effective for depression among adolescents, though its use is not without controversy.

- The most widespread interventions for dyslexia and dyscalculia are educational.

- Applied behavioral analysis, self-instructional training, and modeling, have been used to successfully treat many of the behavioral problems of people with intellectual developmental disorder and to improve their problem-solving skills.

- The most promising treatments for ASD are psychological, involving intensive behavioral interventions and work with parents. Various drug treatments have been used but have proved less effective than behavioral interventions.

Answers to Check Your Knowledge Questions

13.1 1. T; 2. T; 3. T; 4. F

13.2 1. life-course-persistent, adolescent-onset; 2. ADHD, substance abuse, depression, anxiety; 3. parent management training, multisystemic treatment.

13.3 1. c; 2. a; 3. d; 4. a

13.4 1. F; 2. T; 3. F

Key Terms

attention-deficit/hyperactivity disorder (ADHD)
Asperger's disorder
autism spectrum disorder
child onset fluency disorder (stuttering)
communication disorders
conduct disorder

developmental psychopathology
Down syndrome
dyscalculia
dyslexia
externalizing disorders
fragile X syndrome
intellectual developmental disorder

internalizing disorders
joint attention
learning disabilities
learning disorders
motor disorders
multisystemic treatment (MST)
oppositional defiant disorder

parent management training (PMT)
phenylketonuria (PKU)
pronoun reversal
separation anxiety disorder
speech sounds disorder

14 Late Life and Neurocognitive Disorders

LEARNING GOALS

LEARNING GOALS

1. Be able to describe common misconceptions about age-related changes and to understand genuine age-related changes.
2. Be able to discuss issues involved in conducting research on aging.
3. Be able to describe the prevalence of psychological disorders in the elderly and issues involved in estimating the prevalence.
4. Be able to explain the symptoms, etiology, and treatment of the major forms of dementia.
5. Be able to discuss the symptoms, causes and treatment of delirium.

Clinical Case: Simon

Simon, a 68-year-old retired company executive was hospitalized for a hip replacement. Although Simon got through a bottle of whiskey a week, his drinking was limited to a couple of (large) shots in the evening, and it was not disruptive or problematic to his family life. Simon's hip replacement surgery went well, he made a good recovery from anesthesia and his pain was well controlled. However, during the third postoperative night, Simon became quite restless and could not sleep. The next day he was visibly fatigued and had lost his appetite. The next night his restlessness became more pronounced, and he became fearful—calling out for the nurse, but then when she appeared he wouldn't explain what he wanted. It later transpired that at this time, Simon thought his nurses had been replaced by visually similar imposters and that the contents of his wash bag had been replaced by less expensive and inferior items. In the morning Simon was very frightened and paranoid. He knew who he was, but a quick examination of current levels of cognitive function revealed that he didn't know the year, let along the day, he couldn't remember why he was in hospital, or the name of the hospital. At this point, psychiatric consultation was obtained.

The consultant diagnosed Simon with delirium, probably due to the interaction of sleep deprivation, alcohol withdrawal, use of strong analgesics, and the stress of the operation. The treatment consisted of a reduction in pain medications, along with 50 mg of chlorpromazine (Thorazine) three times daily and 500 mg of chloral hydrate at bedtime. It reversed his confusion within two days, and he was able to return home in a week with no symptoms. [Adapted from Strub & Black, 1981, pp. 89–90].

IN THIS CHAPTER, we focus on psychological disorders in late life. The elderly are most vulnerable to the neurocognitive disorders of dementia and delirium, and we consider these topics in detail. We begin by reviewing some general topics relevant to understanding late life. We describe common myths about aging, challenges faced by the elderly, and some remarkable strengths that come with growing older. Conducting research on these topics, though, is complicated by a few key methodological issues, and we discuss some of the ways these issues can influence findings. We describe evidence that the prevalence of psychological disorders such as depression, anxiety, and substance abuse in the elderly is quite low. With this information as backdrop, we turn to dementia and delirium, the main topics of this chapter.

Aging: Issues and Methods

As we age, physiological changes are inevitable, and there may be emotional and mental changes as well. Many of these may influence social interactions. In contrast to the esteem in which they are held in most Asian countries, older adults are generally not treated well in the United States. The process of growing old is feared by many, even abhorred. Perhaps our lack of regard for older adults stems from our own deep-seated fear of growing old. The old person with serious infirmities is an unwelcome reminder that we all may one day walk with an unsteady gait, see less clearly, taste food less keenly, and experience more physical illness.

The social problems of aging may be especially severe for women. Even with the consciousness-raising of the past decades, our society does not readily accept women with wrinkles and sagging bodies. Although men with gray hair at the temples are often seen as distinguished, signs of aging in women are not valued in the United States and many other countries. The cosmetics and plastic surgery industries make billions of dollars each year exploiting the fear inculcated in women about looking their age.[1] According to some experts, however, being female confers certain mental health benefits as people age.

The old are usually defined as those over the age of 65, an arbitrary point set largely by social policies rather than any physiological process. To have some rough demarcation points, gerontologists usually divide people over age 65 into three groups: the young-old, those aged 65 to 74; the old-old, those aged 75 to 84; and the oldest-old, those over age 85.

People spend billions of dollars per year on cosmetics and plastic surgery to reduce signs of aging. (©Inspirestock/©Corbis.)

---

[1]We should point out, though, that increasing numbers of men are undergoing plastic surgery in an effort to look younger than their years.

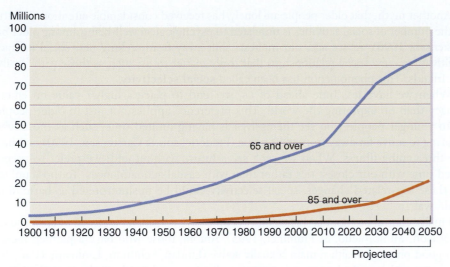

Figure 14.1 The number of old and old-old U.S. citizens is on the rise. Number of people age 65 and over, by decade of birth, 1900–2000 and projected 2010–2050. From U.S. Census Bureau, Decennial Census and Projections.

Edna Parker died in 2008 at the age of 115. The number of centenarians (people who live to be more than 100 years old) in the United States is expected to grow 10-fold by 2050. (©AP/Wide World Photos.)

At the time of the last census, people 65 and older comprised 12.4 percent (35 million) of the U.S. population. Figure 14.1 shows the dramatic increase in the number of older Americans over time. As of 2009, there were 50,000 Americans at least 100 years old (U. S. Bureau of the Census, 2010); by 2050, that number is expected to grow more than 10-fold to over 800,000 (U.S. Bureau of the Census, 1999).

Given these statistics, it is not surprising that 69 percent of practicing psychologists conduct clinical work with older adults (Qualls, Segal, Norman, et al., 2002). A major concern, though, is that fewer than 30 percent of psychologists report receiving any formal training about late-life issues (Qualls et al., 2002).

Myths about Late Life

APA ethical principles state that it is important for psychologists working with the elderly to examine their stereotypes about late life (American Psychiatric Association, 2004). Most people in the United States have certain assumptions about old age. Common myths include the idea that we will become doddering and befuddled. We worry that we will be unhappy, cope poorly with troubles, and become focused on our poor health. We worry that we will become lonely and that our sex lives will become unsatisfying.

Each of these myths has been debunked. As we will see, severe cognitive problems do not occur for most people in late life, though a mild decline in cognitive functioning is common (Langa, Larson, Karlawish, et al., 2008). Elderly people (age 60 and older) actually experience less negative emotion than do young people (age 18–30 years) (Lawton, Kleban, Dean, et al., 1992). Although some might suspect that these findings are artifacts of a reluctance of older individuals to describe negative feelings to researchers, laboratory studies verify that the elderly are actually more skilled at regulating their emotions. For example, when older people are asked to think or talk about emotionally charged topics, they display less physiological reactivity than do younger people (Kisley, Wood, & Burrows, 2007; Levenson, Carstensen, & Gottman, 1994). When viewing positive images, they show more robust brain activation in key emotion regions than do younger people (Mather, Canli, English, et al., 2004). Many older people underreport somatic symptoms, perhaps because of beliefs that aches and pains are an inevitable part of late life. People in late life are no more likely to meet criteria for somatic symptom disorders than are the young (Regier, Boyd, Burke, et al., 1988; Siegler & Costa, 1985).

Contrary to stereotypes, many older people maintain an active interest in sex. Studies indicate that the frequency of sexual activity among healthy couples in their 70s remains high. (© Losevsky Pavel/Shutterstock.)

The quality of sleep diminishes as people age. (Corbis Digital Stock.)

As illustrated by John Glenn's space flight at age 77, advancing age need not lead to a curtailment of activities. (ROBERTO SCHMIDT/AFP/Getty Images, Inc.)

Another myth, that older people are lonely, has received considerable attention. The truth is that the number of social activities is unrelated to psychological well-being among older people (Carstensen, 1996). As we age, our interests shift away from seeking new social interactions to cultivating a few social relationships that really matter to us, such as those with family and close friends. This phenomenon has been called **social selectivity.**

When we have less time ahead of us, we tend to place a higher value on emotional intimacy than on exploring the world. This preference applies not just to older people but also to younger people who see themselves as having limited time, such as those who are preparing to move far away from their home (Frederickson & Carstensen, 1990) or who have a life-threatening illness. When we can't see a future without end, we prefer to spend our limited time with our closest ties rather than with casual acquaintances. To those unfamiliar with these age-related changes, social selectivity could be misinterpreted as harmful social withdrawal.

Finally, contrary to popular belief, older people have considerable sexual interest and capacity (Deacon, Minicchiello, & Plummer, 1995). Among those who have a partner, most who are in good physical health remain sexually active (Lindau, Schumm, Laumann, et al., 2007).

In sum, older adults have many coping mechanisms and much wisdom on which to draw. Many stereotypes we hold about the elderly are false. Beyond questioning assumptions, it is important to recognize the diversity of older people. Not only are older people different from one another, but they are more different from one another than are people in any other age group. People tend to become less alike as they grow older. That all old people are alike is a prejudice held by many people. A moment's honest reflection may reveal that certain traits come to mind when we hear that a person is age, say, 67. But to know that a person is 67 years old is actually to know very little about him or her. Each older person brings to late life a developmental history that makes his or her reactions to common problems unique.

The Problems Experienced in Late Life

We know that mental health is tied to the physical and social problems in a person's life. As a group, no other people have more of these problems than the elderly. They have them all—physical decline and disabilities, sensory and neurological deficits, loss of loved ones, the cumulative effects of a lifetime of many unfortunate experiences, and social stresses such as stigmatizing attitudes toward the elderly. Eighty percent of elderly people have at least one major medical condition (National Academy on an Aging Society, 1999). As described by one author, "Late life would qualify as the Olympics of coping" (Fisher, 2011, p. 145).

One facet of aging deserves particular attention. As people age, the quality and depth of sleep declines, so that by age 65, 25 percent of people report insomnia (Mellinger, Balter, & Uhlenhuth, 1985). Rates of sleep apnea, a disorder in which a person stops breathing for seconds to minutes during the night, also increase with age (Prechter & Shepard, 1990). Insomnia is often caused by medication side effects (Rodin, McAvay, & Timko, 1988) or by pain from medical problems (Prinz & Raskind, 1978). Untreated and chronic sleep deficits can worsen physical, psychological, and cognitive problems and can even increase risk of mortality (Ancoli, Kripke, Klauber, et al., 1996). Fortunately, psychological treatment has been shown to reduce insomnia among the elderly (McCurry, Logsdon, Teri, et al., 2007).

Several problems are evident in the medical treatment available during late life. One of the main difficulties is that the chronic health problems of older people seldom diminish; physicians focused on identifying cures can become frustrated when none are available (Zarit, 1980). Other problems result from the time pressure of the health care system. All too often, doctors do not check to see if the person is taking other medications or seeing other doctors. *Polypharmacy,* the prescribing of multiple drugs to a person, can result. About one-third of elderly persons are prescribed at least five medications (Qato, Alexander, Conti, et al., 2008). This increases the risk of adverse drug reactions that may cause numerous side effects, toxicity, and allergic reactions. Often, physicians then prescribe more medications to combat the side effects, thus continuing the vicious circle.

Further complicating the picture is the fact that most psychoactive drugs are tested on younger people; gauging the appropriate dose for the less efficient metabolism of the kidneys and liver of the older person represents a challenge for the medical practitioner—side effects and toxicity are much more common (Gallo & Lebowitz, 1999). The increased sensitivity to side effects is a particular problem with psychiatric medications. One review of medical charts of more than 750,000 elderly patients found that more than one-fifth had filled a prescription for a medication deemed inappropriate for people over the age of 65 due to serious side effects (Curtis, Ostbye, Sendersky, et al., 2004). Therefore, it is important that the primary care physician of elderly people keep track of all prescribed medications taken, discontinue nonessential drugs, and prescribe only the minimum dosages needed.

Research Methods in the Study of Aging

Research on aging requires an understanding of several special issues. Chronological age is not as simple a variable in psychological research as it might seem. Because other factors associated with age may influence findings, we must be cautious when we attribute differences between age groups solely to the effects of aging. In the field of aging, as in studies of childhood development, a distinction is made among three kinds of effects (see Table 14.1):

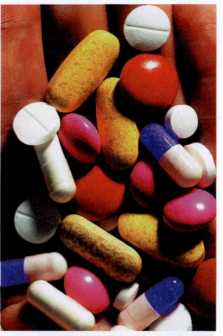

Polypharmacy is all too common in late life (Tony Why/Phototake.)

- **Age effects** are the consequences of being a certain chronological age.
- **Cohort effects** are the consequences of growing up during a particular time period with its unique challenges and opportunities. For example, experiences like the Great Depression, a world war, or 9/11 each shape experiences and attitudes. Similarly, the expectations for marriage have changed drastically in the past century, at least in Western societies, from a focus on stability to a focus on happiness and personal fulfillment.
- **Time-of-measurement effects** are confounds that arise because events at a particular point in time can have a specific effect on a variable that is being studied (Schaie & Hertzog, 1982). For example, people tested right after Hurricane Katrina in New Orleans might demonstrate elevated levels of anxiety.

Two major research designs are used to assess developmental change: cross-sectional and longitudinal. In cross-sectional studies, the investigator compares different age groups at the same moment in time on the variable of interest. Suppose that in 1995 we took a poll in the United States and found that many interviewees over age 80 spoke with a European accent, whereas those in their 40s and 50s did not. Could we conclude that as people grow older, they develop European accents? Hardly! Cross-sectional studies do not examine the same people over time; consequently, they do not provide clear information about how people change as they age.

In longitudinal studies, the researcher periodically retests one group of people using the same measure over a number of years or decades. For example, the Baltimore Longitudinal Study of Aging is one of the longest-running studies of aging. Since 1958, researchers have been following 1,400 men and women to see how their lifestyles, medical conditions, and psychological health change over time. In this study, a great deal has been learned about mental health and aging. For example, researchers were able to combat myths that people become more unhappy over time. Rather, people who were happy at age 30 tended to be

Table 14.1 Age, Cohort, and Time-of-Measurement Effects		
Age Effects	**Cohort Effects**	**Time-of-Measurement Effects**
The effects of being a certain age; e.g., being old enough to receive Social Security	The effects of having grown up during a particular time period; e.g., frugality may be increased among those who lived through the Great Depression of the 1930s	The effects of testing people at a particular time in history; e.g., people became more frank during the 1990s to surveys about their sexual behavior, as media discussion of sexuality increased

happy as they moved into late life (Costa, Metter, & McCrae, 1994). In general, longitudinal designs allow us to trace individual patterns of consistency or change over time. Although longitudinal studies offer fundamental advantages, results can be biased by attrition, in which participants drop out of the study due to death, immobility, or lack of interest. When people are no longer available for follow-up because of death, this is called **selective mortality.** The tendency for less healthy individuals to die more quickly can lead to biased samples in long-term follow-up studies. Selective mortality results in a particular form of bias, in that results obtained with the remaining sample are more relevant to drawing conclusions about relatively healthy people than about unhealthy people. Beyond attrition due to death, people with the most problems are likely to drop out from a study, whereas the people who remain are usually healthier than the general population. Later in this chapter, we will discuss how these issues of cohort effects and selective mortality might influence estimates of the prevalence of psychological disorder (Kiecolt-Glaser & Glaser, 2002).

Cohort effects refer to the fact that people of the same chronological age may differ considerably depending on when they were born. (Top: Liaison/Getty Images, Inc.; Bottom: Marc Romanelli/Getty Images.)

Check Your Knowledge 14.1 (Answers are at the end of the chapter.)

True or false?
1. Most people develop major memory problems in late life.
2. Sexual interest typically declines as people age.

3. Side effects of medications are of less concern as people age because most people adjust to them over time.
4. Most people become unhappier as they age.

Psychological Disorders in Late Life

The DSM criteria are the same for older and younger adults. The process of diagnosis, though, must be considered with care. DSM criteria specify that a psychological disorder should not be diagnosed if the symptoms can be accounted for by a medical condition or medication side effects. Because medical conditions are more common in the elderly, it is particularly important to rule out such explanations. Medical problems such as thyroid problems, Addison's disease, Cushing's disease, Parkinson's disease, Alzheimer's disease, hypoglycemia, anemia, and vitamin deficiencies can produce symptoms that mimic schizophrenia, depression, or anxiety. Medical problems can also worsen the course of depression (see Focus on Discovery 5.3 for one example of how complex these relationships can be). Angina, congestive heart failure, and excessive caffeine consumption may all cause a faster heart rate, which can be mistaken as a symptom of anxiety (Fisher & Noll, 1996). Age-related deterioration in the vestibular system (inner-ear control of one's sense of balance) can account for panic symptoms such as severe dizziness. Antihypertensive medication, hormones, corticosteroids, and antiparkinson medications may contribute to depression or anxiety. Clinicians must be extremely careful to consider the interactions between physical and psychological health. With this in mind, we consider how common it is for older people to have mental disorders.

Estimating the Prevalence of Psychological Disorders in Late Life

The prevalence estimates for psychological disorders defy stereotypes of unhappiness and anxiety in late life. Findings indicate that persons over age 65 have the lowest overall prevalence of mental disorders of all age groups. Table 14.2 provides 12-month estimates from the National Comorbidity Survey–Replication (NCS–R) study, which involved a community representative sample of 9,282 people living in the United States who completed extensive diagnostic interviews (Gum, King-Kallimanis, & Kohn, 2009). As shown, every single disorder was less common in the elderly than in younger adults. None of those aged 65 and older met criteria for a drug abuse or dependency disorder. Although not covered in the NCS–R study, rates of schizophrenia are also low among the elderly (U.S. Department of Health and Human Services, 1999). Overall, only about 8.5 percent reported symptoms that were severe enough to be diagnosed. Most people 65 years of age and older are free from serious psychopathology.

Beyond examining the prevalence rates of disorder, it is important to consider the incidence rates, or how many people are experiencing the onset of a new disorder. Most people who have an episode of a psychological disorder late in life are experiencing a recurrence of a disorder that started earlier in life rather than an initial onset. For example, 97 percent of older adults with generalized anxiety disorder report that their anxiety symptoms began before the age of 65 (Alwahhabi, 2003), and 94 percent of older adults with major depressive disorder report depressive episodes earlier in life (Norton, Skoog, Toone, et al., 2006). Late onset is also extremely rare for schizophrenia (Karon & VandenBos, 1998). In contrast, late onset is more common for alcohol dependence among older adults with drinking problems (Liberto, Oslin, & Ruskin, 1996). It appears, though, that most people with psychological disorders in late life are experiencing a continuation of symptoms that began earlier.

Table 14.2 One-Year Prevalence Estimates for Psychological Disorders by Age Group

	18–44 Years	60–64 Years	65 Years and Older
Anxiety disorders			
Panic disorder	3.2 (0.3)	2.8 (0.4)	0.7 (0.2)
Agoraphobia without panic	0.8 (0.2)	1.1 (0.3)	0.4 (0.2)
Specific phobia	9.7 (0.5)	9.2 (0.7)	4.7 (0.6)
Social phobia	8.6 (0.5)	6.1 (0.5)	2.3 (0.4)
Generalized anxiety	2.8 (0.2)	3.2 (0.3)	1.2 (0.3)
Posttraumatic stress[a]	3.7 (0.4)	5.1 (0.6)	0.4 (0.1)
Any anxiety disorder[a]	20.7 (0.7)	18.7 (1.3)	7.0 (0.8)
Mood disorders			
Major depressive disorders	8.2 (0.4)	6.5 (0.5)	2.3 (0.3)
Dysthymia	1.5 (0.2)	1.9 (0.4)	0.5 (0.2)
Bipolar I and bipolar II disorders	1.9 (0.2)	1.2 (0.3)	0.2 (0.1)
Any mood disorder	10.2 (0.4)	8.0 (0.6)	2.6 (0.4)
Substance disorders[a]			
Alcohol abuse	2.6 (0.2)	0.9 (0.2)	0
Drug abuse	1.5 (0.2)	0.2 (0.01)	0
Any substance disorder	3.6 (0.3)	1.0 (0.2)	0
Any disorder[a]			
At least one disorder	27.6 (0.8)	22.4 (1.5)	8.5 (0.9)

[a]5,692 people completed interviews regarding these diagnoses.
Drawn from the NCS–R study [Gum, King-Kallimanis; Kohn (2009)].

Why are rates of psychopathology so low in late life? There are several completely different answers to this question. Some have argued that methodological issues might be leading us to underestimate the prevalence of psychological disorders in late life. It also appears that there may be some processes related to aging that promote better mental health.

Methodological Issues in Estimating the Prevalence of Psychopathology

Methodologically, older adults may be more uncomfortable acknowledging and discussing mental health or drug use problems compared to younger people. In one study, elderly people were interviewed about depressive symptoms, and then a family member was interviewed about whether that elderly person was experiencing depressive symptoms. Among those elderly whom family members described as meeting criteria for major depressive disorder, about one-quarter did not disclose depressive symptoms to the interviewer (Davison, McCabe, & Mellor, 2009). Discomfort discussing symptoms may minimize prevalence estimates.

In addition to reporting bias, there may be cohort effects. For example, many people who reached adulthood during the drug-oriented era of the 1960s continue to use drugs as they age. Their generation is more likely to have problems with substance abuse in late life than are previous generations. Although the 50-and-older age group accounted for only 6.6 percent of substance abuse admissions in the United States in 1992, by 2008 the same age group accounted for 12.2 percent of such admissions.

Beyond these explanations, people with mental illness are at risk for dying earlier—before age 65—for several different reasons. Among heavy drinkers, the peak years for death from cirrhosis are between 55 and 64 years of age, and cardiovascular disease is also common (Shaper, 1990). Cardiovascular disease is also more common among people with a history of anxiety disorders, depressive disorders, and bipolar disorder (Kubzansky, 2007). Even milder psychological disorders compromise immune function, and as people age, they become particularly sensitive to these immune effects (Kiecolt-Glaser & Glaser, 2001). This may lead to worse outcomes for many medical conditions that are more common as people age. Psychological disorders are associated with increased mortality (Angst, Stassen, Clayton, et al., 2002). For example, Frojdh and colleagues (2003) conducted surveys with over 1,200 elderly people living in Sweden. Compared to those with low scores, those who obtained high scores on a self-report measure of depression were 2.5 times as likely to die within the next 6 years. Because people with psychological disorders may die earlier, studies on aging may suffer from the issue of selective mortality.

These three methodological issues—response biases, cohort effects, and selective mortality—could help explain the low rates of psychological disorders in late life. Most researchers, though, believe that aging is also genuinely related to better mental health. Above, we described findings that emotional coping improves as people age. This should translate into a decrease in psychological disorders. Some longitudinal studies suggest that many people who experience psychological disorders early in life seem to grow out of those symptoms. For example, longitudinal studies indicate that heavy drinkers tend to drink less as they enter late life (Fillmore, 1987). Findings like these suggest that enhanced coping abilities developed across the life course may help protect people from mental illness during late life.

Quick Summary

As the number of older people in the United States burgeons, more and more mental health professionals are working with this population. Unfortunately, even mental health professionals tend to hold certain stereotypes about late life. It is important to recognize that, as they age, most people tend to become more effective at regulating emotions, to remain interested in sex, to downplay medical symptoms, and to focus on core relationships over superficial social acquaintances and activities. The challenges of late life do include insomnia and declining health for many people. As increasing numbers of chronic health problems emerge, polypharmacy becomes an issue for many.

Compounding the hazards of polypharmacy, people become more sensitive to medication side effects and toxicity as they age.

In research on aging, it is difficult to disentangle age effects, cohort effects, and time-of-measurement effects. Cross-sectional studies do not help distinguish age and cohort effects. Longitudinal studies provide more clarity about age and cohort effects, but the validity of findings can be challenged by attrition. One form of attrition, selective mortality, is particularly important to consider in studies of aging.

When the elderly present with psychological disorders, it is critically important to evaluate potential medical causes. The elderly are particularly susceptible to negative effects of medical conditions and medications, and these effects may mimic psychological conditions.

Studies suggest lower rates of mental illness among the elderly compared to other age groups. Although some methodological issues (cohort effects, selective mortality, and lack of disclosure) might explain part of this effect, it is also possible that some people become more psychologically healthy as they age.

Neurocognitive Disorders in Late Life

Most elderly people do not have cognitive disorders. Indeed, the prevalence of cognitive impairment has declined among people over the age of 70 in the United States in the last 15 years, perhaps because of improvements in diet, medical care, and education levels over time (Langa et al., 2008). Nonetheless, cognitive disorders account for more hospital admissions and inpatient days than any other geriatric condition (Zarit & Zarit, 1998). We will examine two principal types of cognitive disorders: dementia, a deterioration of cognitive abilities, and delirium, a state of mental confusion. For each, we will consider the clinical description as well as causal factors and treatment.

Dementia

Dementia is a descriptive term for the deterioration of cognitive abilities to the point that functioning becomes impaired. As we will discuss, there are many different causes for dementia. Difficulty remembering things, especially recent events, is the most common symptom of dementia. People may leave tasks unfinished because they forget to return to them after an interruption. The person who had started to fill a teapot at the sink leaves the water running. As the dementia progresses, a parent is unable to remember the name of a daughter or son and later may not even recall that he or she has children or recognize them when they come to visit. Hygiene may become poor because the person forgets to bathe or dress adequately. People with dementia also may get lost, even in familiar surroundings. Judgment may become faulty, and the person may have difficulty comprehending situations and making plans or decisions. People with dementia may lose control of their impulses; they may use coarse language, tell inappropriate jokes, shoplift, and make sexual advances to strangers. The ability to deal with abstract ideas deteriorates, and disturbances in emotions are common, including symptoms of depression, flatness of affect, and sporadic emotional outbursts. Delusions and hallucinations can occur (American Psychiatric Association, 2000). People with dementia are likely to show language disturbances as well, such as vague patterns of speech. Despite intact sensory functioning, they may also have trouble recognizing familiar surroundings or naming common objects. Episodes of delirium, a state of mental confusion (discussed in detail later), may also occur.

The course of dementia may be progressive, static, or remitting, depending on the cause. Many people with progressive dementia eventually become withdrawn and apathetic. In the terminal phase of the illness, personality loses its sparkle and integrity. Relatives and friends say that the person is just not himself or herself anymore. Social involvement with others keeps narrowing. Finally, the person is oblivious to his or her surroundings.

Most dementias develop very slowly over a period of years; subtle cognitive and behavioral deficits can be detected well before the person shows any noticeable impairment (Small, Fratiglioni, Viitanen, et al., 2000). The early signs of decline noted before functional impairment is present have been labeled as mild cognitive impairment.

Diagnostic criteria for dementia and mild cognitive impairment have been developed by a consensus panel of leading experts with support from the National Institute of Aging and the Alzheimer's Association (Albert, Dekosky, Dickson, et al., 2011; McKhann, Knopman, Chertkow, et al., 2011). The proposed DSM-5 system also provides parallel diagnoses like those for mild cognitive impairment as well as for dementia. See Table 14.3 for an overview of the proposed DSM-5 diagnoses. DSM mild neurocognitive disorders are similar to mild cognitive impairment, whereas DSM major neurocognitive disorders are similar to a diagnosis of dementia. Throughout this chapter, we use the terms *dementia* (rather than *major neurocognitive disorder*) and *mild cognitive impairment* (rather than *mild neurocognitive disorder*).

There is some debate about where to draw the line between mild cognitive impairment and dementia, as well as how early to diagnose mild cognitive impairment. The proposed DSM-5 distinguishes between mild and major neurocognitive disorder based on whether symptoms interfere with the ability to live independently. The proposed DSM-5 criteria for mild neurocognitive disorder require a low score on only one cognitive test. It has been shown that this may lead to a high rate of diagnosis for mild neurocognitive disorder; requiring low scores on at least two different cognitive tests could drastically decrease the base rates of diagnosis (Jak, Bondi, Delano-Wood, et al., 2009).

There is reason to be cautious about diagnosing these early signs of decline. Not all people with mild cognitive symptoms develop dementia. Among adults with mild cognitive impairment, about 10 percent per year will develop dementia; among adults without mild cognitive impairment, about 1 percent per year will develop dementia (Bischkopf, Busse, & Angermeyer, 2002). It is important to provide careful psychoeducation regarding these diagnoses so that patients and family members do not assume that symptoms will necessarily progress.

Worldwide prevalence estimates of dementia in 2000 were over 25 million, which represented about 0.4 percent of the world population (Wimo, Winblad, Aguero-Torres, et al., 2003). The prevalence of dementia increases with advancing age. Across international studies, the prevalence of dementia has been found to be 1 to 2 percent in people aged 60 to 69 but increases progressively to more than 20 percent in those 85 or older (Ferri, Prince, Brayne, et al., 2005).

There are many different types of dementia. Here we discuss four types of dementia: Alzheimer's disease, the most researched form; frontotemporal dementia, defined by the areas of the brain that are most affected; vascular dementia, caused by cerebrovascular disease; and dementia with Lewy bodies, defined by the presence of Lewy bodies (abnormal deposits on neurons). After discussing these four, we briefly describe other causes of dementia. By far, the most common form of dementia is Alzheimer's disease, which accounts for about 80 percent of dementias (Terry, 2006).

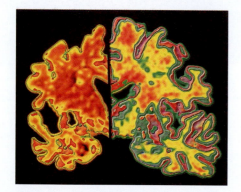

Computer-generated images of a brain of a person with Alzheimer's disease and a healthy brain. Note that the diseased brain (left) has shrunk considerably owing to the loss of nerve cells. (Alfred Pasieka/Photo Researchers, Inc.)

Alzheimer's Disease In **Alzheimer's disease**, initially described by the German neurologist Alois Alzheimer in 1906, the brain tissue irreversibly deteriorates, and death usually occurs within 12 years after the onset of symptoms. Over 50,000 Americans die each year from this disease, and in 2000, it was the seventh leading cause of death among men and women over the age of 65 (NCHS, 2004). The illness may begin with absentmindedness and difficulties in

Clinical Case: Winifred

Winifred was a 75-year-old mother of three and grand-mother of six. She had been married twice and talked a lot about her second husband Jonathan. They had traveled with his job all around the world. Sadly Jonathan died when Winifred was 66. She carried on living alone for a further five years. At the beginning, the manifestations of Alzheimer's disease were very subtle. Sometimes, when talking to one of her children on the phone, she would say "cat" when talking about her pet dog, or she would say "men" instead of "pen." Her family just put this down to old age, but when she started sending birthday presents to her grandchildren at the wrong time of year, and phoning up at strange times in the night, her family became increasingly concerned. After one visit, when her son found her sitting in soiled clothes, and the house looked as if it hadn't been cleaned for weeks, the family decided that Winifred was no longer capable of looking after herself.

Winifred was placed in a residential nursing home near her daughter. Winifred's forgetfulness has increased: she rarely remembers the events of one day to the next, and, although she recognizes her children, the grandchildren rarely visit now as she doesn't seem to know them at all.

Table 14.3 Proposed DSM-5 Neurocognitive Disorders

Delirium

Neurocognitive disorder: Specify mild or major

    Neurocognitive disorder associated with Alzheimer's disease

    Neurocognitive disorder associated with fronto-temporal lobar degeneration

    Neurocognitive disorder associated with vascular disease

    Neurocognitive disorder associated with traumatic brain injury

    Neurocognitive disorder associated with Lewy body disease

    Neurocognitive disorder associated with Parkinson's disease

    Neurocognitive disorder associated with HIV infection

    Neurocognitive disorder associated with substance use

    Neurocognitive disorder associated with Huntington's disease

    Neurocognitive disorder associated with prion disease

    Other specified neurocognitive disorder

concentration and in memory for new material, as described in the Clinical Case of Mary Ann. These shortcomings may be overlooked for several years but eventually interfere with daily living. As the disease develops, problems with language skills and word finding intensify. Visual-spatial abilities decline, which can be manifested in **disorientation** (confusion with respect to time, place, or identity) and trouble copying figures. People with the disorder are typically unaware of their cognitive problems initially, and they may blame others for lost objects even to the point of developing delusions of being persecuted. Memory continues to deteriorate, and the person becomes increasingly disoriented and agitated. As the disorder progresses, the person may no longer recognize friends or family and may need help to eat, dress, and bathe. Apathy is common even before the cognitive symptoms become noticeable (Balsis, Carpenter, & Storandt, 2005), and about a third of people develop full-blown depression as the illness worsens (Strauss & Ogrocki, 1996).

People with Alzheimer's disease have more **plaques** (small, round beta-amyloid protein deposits that are outside the neurons) and **neurofibrillary tangles** (twisted protein filaments composed largely of the protein tau in the axons of neurons) than would be expected for the person's age. Some people produce excessive amounts of beta-amyloid, whereas others seem to have deficiencies in the mechanisms for clearing beta-amyloid from the brain (Jack, Albert, Knopman, et al., 2011). (The beta-amyloid plaques are most densely present in the frontal cortex (Klunk, Engler, Nordberg, et al., 2004), and they may be present for 10 to 20 years before the cognitive symptoms become noticeable.) Plaques can be measured using a specialized type of PET scan. Tangles are most often measured in cerebrospinal fluid, although they can be measured using a PET scan as well. Tangles are most densely present in the hippocampus, an area that is important for memory. Over time, as the disease progresses, plaques and tangles spread through more of the brain (Klunk et al., 2004; Sperling, Aisen, Beckett, et al., 2011).

As shown in Figure 14.2, these plaques and tangles appear related to a host of brain changes over time. At early stages, there seems to be a loss of synapses for acetylcholinergic (ACh) and glutamatergic neurons (Selkoe, 2002). Neurons also begin to die: As neurons die, the cerebral cortex, the entorhinal cortex, and the hippocampus shrink, and later the frontal, temporal, and parietal lobes shrink. As this happens, the ventricles become enlarged. The cerebellum, spinal cord, and motor and sensory areas of the cortex are less affected, which is why people with Alzheimer's do not appear to have anything physically wrong with them until late in the disease process. For some time people with Alzheimer's are able to walk around normally, and their overlearned habits, such as making small talk, remain intact, so that in short encounters strangers may not notice anything amiss. About 25 percent of people with Alzheimer's disease eventually develop brain deterioration that leads to motor deficits.

Proposed DSM-5 Criteria for Mild Neurocognitive Disorder

- Minor cognitive decline from previous levels in one or more domains based on both of the following:
  - Concerns of the patient, a close other, or a clinician
  - Neurocognitive performance below appropriate norms (i.e., between the 3rd and 16th percentile) on formal testing or equivalent clinical evaluation
- The cognitive deficits do not interfere with independence (i.e., tasks such as paying bills or managing medications), even though greater effort, compensatory strategies, or accommodation may be required to maintain independence.
- The cognitive deficits do not occur exclusively in the context of delirium and are not due to another psychological disorder.

Proposed DSM-5 Criteria for Major Neurocognitive Disorder

- Significant cognitive decline from previous levels in one or more domains based on both of the following:
  - Concerns of the patient, a close other, or a clinician
  - Neurocognitive performance below the 3rd percentile on formal testing or equivalent clinical evaluation
- The cognitive deficits interfere with independence.
- The cognitive deficits do not occur exclusively in the context of a delirium and are not due to another psychological disorder.

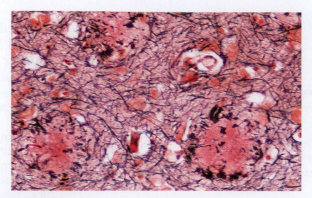
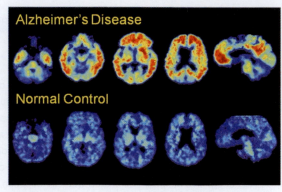

Positron Emission Tomography (PET) images of the brain after administration of Pittsburgh Compound B (PIB) in a woman with Alzheimer's disease shows high levels of amyloid plaque. In contrast, low levels of amyloid plaque are seen in the PET images of a woman with no Alzheimer's symptoms. (Left: Martin Rotker/Phototake; Right: Images courtesy of Gil Rabinovici (University of California San Francisco) and William Jagust (University of California Berkeley.)

In the largest twin study of Alzheimer's disease, a heritability estimate of 79 percent was reported. That is, about 79 percent of the variance in onset of Alzheimer's disease appears related to genes, and about 21 percent of the variance appears related to environmental factors (Gatz, Reynolds, Fratiglioni, et al., 2006).

Some cases of Alzheimer's disease exhibit a particular form of a gene on chromosome 19, called the apolipoprotein ε4 or ApoE-4 allele. Having one E4 allele increases the risk of Alzheimer's disease to about 20 percent but having two E4 alleles brings the risk substantially higher. Researchers are beginning to understand some of the ways that the E4 may increase risk of the disorder: people with two of the E4 alleles show overproduction of beta-amyloid plaques, loss of neurons in the hippocampus, and low glucose metabolism in several regions of the cerebral cortex even before they develop symptoms of Alzheimer's disease (Bookheimer

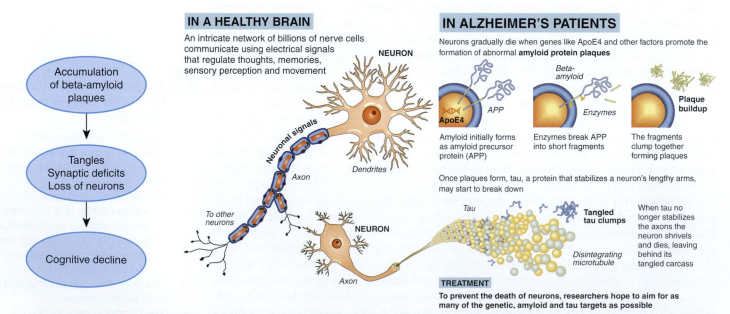

Figure 14.2 In Alzheimer's disease, risk factors such as the gene ApoE-4 increase production of precursors to amyloid. Beta-amyloid plaques build up outside of the neurons 10 to 20 years before the cognitive symptoms are diagnosable. Neurofibrillary tangles of tau form, and the neurons die.

& Burggren, 2009). One other gene that seems to be involved in Alzheimer's disease is GAB2. Researchers are working to identify other specific genes that increase risk for Alzheimer's disease, but it has been hard to replicate findings across studies (Bertram & Tanzi, 2009).

Beyond genes, lifestyle variables may play a role in Alzheimer's. For example, smoking, being single, depression, and low social support are related to a greater risk of Alzheimer's disease, while a Mediterranean diet, exercise, education, and cognitive engagement predict a lower risk (Williams, Plassman, Burke, et al., 2010). In one study, these effects were studied in 2,509 elderly who were enrolled in the study during their 70s and followed for 8 years. Those with a high school education who exercised at least once a week, remained socially active, and did not smoke sustained their cognitive functioning without decline throughout the 8 years (Yaffe, Fiocco, Lindquist, et al., 2009). Of the various lifestyle factors, the effects for exercise, cognitive engagement, and depression have received a good deal of study, and so we focus on those here.

Several studies suggest that exercise may ward off memory problems. A meta-analysis of 16 studies that had followed 163,797 participants over time indicated that exercise is strongly related to a decreased risk of developing Alzheimer's disease (Hamer & Chida, 2009). Regular exercise predicts less decline in executive functions, such as coordinating and planning (Erickson & Kramer, 2009). We will return to the benefits of exercise as we discuss interventions.

Engagement in intellectual activities also appears helpful, with some proposing a "use it or lose it" model of Alzheimer's. For example, regular reading of a newspaper is related to lower risk (Wilson, Scherr, Schneider, et al., 2007). Findings of a meta-analysis including 29,000 persons drawn from 22 representative community samples suggested that frequent cognitive activity (for example, reading and puzzle solving) is related to a 46 percent decrease in risk of Alzheimer's disease compared to infrequent cognitive activity (Valenzuela & Sachdev, 2006). One concern is that it is hard to know from naturalistic studies whether the people who choose to engage in cognitive activities differ in some important way (on characteristics relevant to disease) from those who do not engage in these activities. Intervention studies that randomly assign people to take part in cognitive training can help address this methodological issue. In intervention studies, cognitive training programs that focus on improving memory, reasoning, or cognitive processing speed have been shown to have modest benefits for elderly persons over a 5-year period. These benefits seem to be primarily in the area involved in the training—for example, memory training might help enhance memory but doesn't seem to help reasoning abilities (Willis, Tennstedt, Marsiske, et al., 2006).

One intriguing finding is that among people with similar levels of plaques and tangles in their brain, those with higher levels of cognitive activity show fewer cognitive symptoms. That is, cognitive activity seems to protect against the expression of underlying neurobiological disease (Wilson et al., 2007). This type of work has led to the concept of **cognitive reserve,** or the idea that some people may be able to compensate for the disease by using alternative brain networks or cognitive strategies such that cognitive symptoms are less pronounced.

We mentioned above that depression can be a consequence of dementia (Vinkers, Gussekloo, Stek, et al., 2004). The opposite direction of effects seems to occur as well: a lifetime history of depression predicts more decline in cognitive functioning (Ganguli, Du, Dodge, et al., 2006); greater risk for Alzheimer's disease and other forms of dementia (Saczynski, Beiser, Seshadri, et al., 2010); and, among those who develop Alzheimer's disease, a faster progression of the illness (Rapp, Schneider-Beeri, Grossman, et al., 2006). These effects seem to be present even when baseline cognitive impairment and other medical issues are controlled (Goveas, Espeland, Woods, et al., 2011).

The frequency of Alzheimer's disease increases with advanced age. (© Abel Mitja Varela/iStockphoto.)

Clinical Case: Mary Ann

I was diagnosed three years ago at age 62 with early-stage Alzheimer's disease. I have a master's degree in social work from the University of Chicago, and I worked as a family therapist. The majority of my career was spent in end-stage hospice work, which I dearly loved. All of a sudden—but it wasn't all of a sudden, of course—I began to realize that I wasn't the gal I used to be. It was different inside my head.

It was the very simple things. I would be talking with someone on the telephone, then hang up and ask myself, "Who was that? What did we talk about?" My husband

John says he knew something serious was going on when we returned from a vacation together and I told him, "I really had a great time in California. I'm so sorry you couldn't make it."

My message to people with Alzheimer's is this: Be gentle with yourself. This disease requires that you lower your expectations of yourself. That's a hard thing for most of us to do. The fear is losing yourself, knowing that you won't bring this self to the end stage of your life.

(Quoted from Mary Ellen Becklenberg, *Time* magazine, October 2010, p. 59)

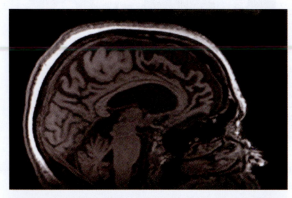

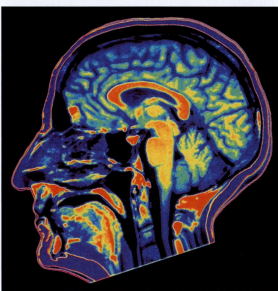

The image on the top is an MRI scan of a person with frontal temporal dementia (FTD). The image on the bottom is an MRI scan of a healthy person. The scan of the person on the top shows the atrophy, or loss of brain volume, in the frontal region. FTD is also characterized by atrophy in the temporal regions. (Top: Courtesy of Dr. Murray Grossman, Univeristy of Pennsylvania; Bottom: Scott Camazine/Photo Researchers, Inc.)

Frontotemporal Dementia As suggested by the name, **frontotemporal dementia (FTD)** is caused by a loss of neurons in frontal and temporal regions of the brain. The neuronal deterioration of FTD occurs predominantly in the anterior temporal lobes and prefrontal cortex (Miller, Ikonte, Ponton, et al., 1997). FTD typically begins in the mid- to late 50s, and it progresses rapidly; death usually occurs within 5–10 years of the diagnosis (Hu, Seelaar, Josephs, et al., 2009).

Unlike Alzheimer's disease, memory is not severely impaired in FTD. The diagnostic criteria for FTD recently developed by an international consortium include deterioration in at least three of the following areas at a level that leads to functional impairment: empathy, executive function (cognitive capacity to plan and organize), ability to inhibit behavior, compulsive or perseverative behavior, hyperorality (tendencies to put nonfood objects in the mouth), and apathy (Rascovsky, in press). In early stages, significant others may notice changes in personality and judgment. For example, the successful and savvy businessman may begin to make terrible investments (Levenson & Miller, 2007).

The disorder strikes emotional processes in a more profound manner than Alzheimer's disease does, and in doing so, it can damage social relationships. Particular deficits seem to emerge in the ability to regulate emotions (Goodkind, Gyurak, McCarthy, et al., 2010). Even though this may lead to atypical behaviors, people with FTD may not realize they are violating social conventions (Mendez, Lauterbach, & Sampson, 2008). In one innovative study relevant to this, persons with FTD, those with Alzheimer's disease, and healthy controls were asked to sing along with the Temptations song "My Girl." In the next stage of the experiment, they were asked to watch an audiovisual recording of their singing without the accompaniment present (they were not warned in advance that this was going to happen). Most of us would feel some embarrassment as we listened to our faltering, out-of-tune performance, and indeed, persons with Alzheimer's disease and healthy controls showed facial and psychophysiological signs of embarrassment. Those with FTD, though, failed to show embarrassment in their facial expressions or their psychophysiological responses. As you might imagine, the changes in personality and emotion, together with a lack of insight (Mendez et al., 2008), would influence relationships. Marital satisfaction is more affected by FTD than by Alzheimer's disease (Ascher, Sturm, Seider, et al., 2010).

It is increasingly clear that FTD can be caused by many different molecular processes (Mackenzie, Neumann, Bigio, et al., 2009). One of these is Pick's disease, characterized by the presence of Pick bodies (spherical inclusions) within neurons, but many other diseases or pathological processes can result in FTD. Some people with FTD show high levels of tau, the protein filaments that contribute to the neurofibrillary tangles observed in Alzheimer's disease, but others do not

(Josephs, 2008). FTD has a strong genetic component, although there may be multiple genetic pathways involved (Cruts, Gijselinck, van der Zee, et al., 2006).

Vascular Dementia **Vascular dementia** is diagnosed when dementia is a consequence of cerebrovascular disease. Most commonly, the person had a series of strokes in which a clot formed, impairing circulation and causing cell death. About 7 percent of people will develop dementia in the year after a first stroke, and the risk of dementia increases with recurrent strokes (Pendlebury & Rothwell, 2009). Risk for vascular dementia involves the same risk factors as those for cardiovascular disease in general—for example, a high level of "bad" (LDL) cholesterol, cigarette smoking, and elevated blood pressure (Moroney, Tang, Berglund, et al., 1999). Strokes and vascular dementias are more common in African Americans than Caucasians (Froehlich, Bogardus, & Inouye, 2001). Because strokes and cardiovascular disease can strike different regions of the brain, the symptoms of vascular dementia can vary a good deal. The onset of symptoms is usually more rapid in vascular dementia than in other forms of dementia. Vascular dementia can co-occur with Alzheimer's disorder.

Dementia with Lewy Bodies **Dementia with Lewy bodies (DLB)** can be divided into two subtypes, depending on whether or not it occurs in the context of Parkinson's disease. About 80 percent of people with Parkinson's disease will develop DLB, but some people without Parkinson's will develop DLB as well.

The symptoms associated with this type of dementia are often hard to distinguish from the symptoms of Parkinson's (such as the shuffling gait) and Alzheimer's disease (such as loss of memory). DLB is more likely than Alzheimer's disease to include prominent visual hallucinations and fluctuating cognitive symptoms (American Psychiatric Association, 2004). People with DLB are often extremely sensitive to the physical side effects of antipsychotic medications. Another distinct symptom of DLB is that people often experience intense dreams accompanied by levels of movement and vocalizing that may make them seem as though they are "acting out their dreams" (McKeith, Dickson, Lowe, et al., 2005).

Dementias Caused by Disease and Injury A number of other medical conditions can produce dementia. Encephalitis, a generic term for any inflammation of brain tissue, is caused by viruses that enter the brain. Meningitis, an inflammation of the membranes covering the outer brain, is usually caused by a bacterial infection. Both encephalitis and meningitis can cause dementia. The organism that produces the venereal disease syphilis (*Treponema pallidum*) can invade the brain and cause dementia. HIV, head traumas, brain tumors, nutritional deficiencies (especially of B-complex vitamins), kidney or liver failure, and endocrine problems such as hyperthyroidism can result in dementia. Exposure to toxins (such as lead or mercury) and chronic substance use are both additional causes.

Prevention and Treatment of Dementia A few drugs, as described below, may provide modest protection against cognitive decline, but the effects are slim. Despite intensive efforts, there is no cure for dementia, and most efforts to develop treatments have failed entirely. Likewise, most efforts at prevention of Alzheimer's disease have failed (Williams et al., 2011), despite early-heralded reports about Vitamin E, statins, and nonsteroidal anti-inflammatory drugs. Similarly, attempts to help people reminisce about key memories or to provide additional sensory stimulation have shown effects that are minuscule

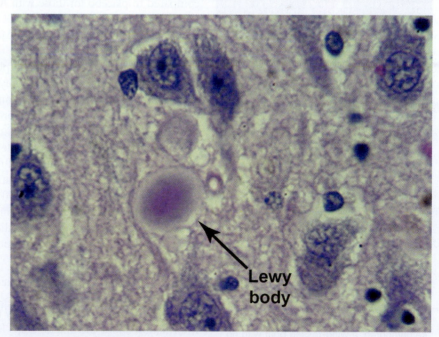

Dementia with Lewy bodies is defined by the presence of abnormal deposits called Lewy bodies. The Lewy bodies are found throughout the brain. (Courtesy Kondi Wong, Armed Forces Institute of Pathology website address: http://www.genome.gov/press-Display.cfm?photoID=10004.)

Although depression is less common among older adults than younger ones, older adults often experience more severe cognitive impairments from their depression than do younger adults. (© Yuri Arcurs/Shutterstock.)

at best (American Psychiatric Association, 2007; Chung & Lai, 2009). For treatment providers and family members, the desire for prevention and cures is intense.

Some of the disappointments in developing treatments have led to new ways of thinking about these disorders. For example, for some time, researchers were striving to find ways to remove beta-amyloid plaques from the brains of people with Alzheimer's disease. Surprisingly, when researchers developed a medication that removed plaques, they found that cognitive deficits continued and even worsened after the plaques were removed (Holmes, Boche, Wilkinson, et al., 2008). Remember, though, that beta-amyloid plaques accumulate in the brain for years before symptoms are observed among people with Alzheimer's disease. By the time people had been diagnosed and had begun to receive the intervention, biological disease processes had already been occurring for years. Findings like these have led people to focus more on prevention. One way to do this is to study factors that reduce the chances that mild cognitive impairment will develop into full-blown dementia. Another way is to study people who have early biological markers indicating risk for Alzheimer's disease. In a joint initiative of the National Institute of Aging and the Alzheimer's Association, conventions were established recently for classifying biological markers of disease before symptoms emerge in order to facilitate prevention research. Of importance, markers will include signs of plaques, tangles, and neuronal death so as to encourage researchers to consider each potential target (Sperling et al., 2011). The next generation of work inspired by this approach is eagerly awaited.

We will begin by describing medications used to treat dementia and related syndromes. Then we will describe evidence for psychological and lifestyle approaches, including promising findings for exercise programs.

Medications No medications have been shown to address the cognitive symptoms of FTD (Caselli & Yaari, 2008). Here, then, we focus on interventions for the other forms of dementia. Much more is known about treatments for Alzheimer's disease than for the other forms of dementia.

Medications may help slow decline, but they do not restore memory function to previous levels. The most commonly used medications for dementia are the cholinesterase inhibitors (drugs that interfere with the breakdown of acetylcholine), including donepezil (Aricept) and rivastigmine (Exelon). Cholinesterase inhibitors have a slight effect in slowing memory decline compared to placebo for those with Alzheimer's (Birks, 2006) and dementia with Lewy bodies (Maidment, Fox, & Boustani, 2006). Unfortunately, many people discontinue these drugs due to aversive side effects such as nausea (Maidment et al., 2006). In addition to cholinesterase inhibitors, memantine (Namenda), a drug that affects glutamate receptors believed to be involved in memory, has shown small effects in placebo-controlled trials for Alzheimer's disease.

Medical treatments are commonly used to address psychological symptoms, such as depression, apathy, and agitation, that commonly co-occur with dementia. For example, antidepressants can help relieve comorbid depressive symptoms in Alzheimer's disease (Modrego, 2010) and FTD (Mendez et al., 2008). Because depression produces more cognitive impairment in the elderly than it does in younger people (Lockwood, Alexopoulos, Kakuma, et al., 2000), treating depressive symptoms can often lead to improvements in cognitive symptoms.

Although antipsychotic medications can provide modest relief for aggressive agitation (Lonergan, Britton, Luxenberg, 2007), they also increase the risk of death among elderly people with dementia (Food and Drug Administration, 2005; Gill, Bronskill, Normand, et al., 2007). Despite the risks, antipsychotic medications are all too commonly prescribed for people with dementia when behavioral interventions could be effective without the same risks.

Former president Ronald Reagan died from Alzheimer's disease. His daughter wrote the following about his disease: ". . . the past is like the rudder of a ship. It keeps you moving through the present, steers you into the future. Without it, without memory, you are unmoored, a wind-tossed boat with no anchor. You learn this by watching someone you love drift away" (Davis, 2002). (Nick Ut/ ASSOCIATED PRESS/AP/Wide World Photos.)

Psychological and Lifestyle Treatments Supportive psychotherapy can help families and patients deal with the effects of the disease. Generally, the therapist allows opportunities for the person with dementia and the family to discuss the illness. The therapist also provides accurate information about the illness, helps family members care for the person in the home, and encourages a realistic rather than a catastrophic attitude in dealing with the many specific challenges that this cognitive disorder presents (Knight, 1996). See Focus on Discovery 14.1 for more detail on treatments offered to support caregivers.

Exercise also appears to have modest benefits in improving cognitive function. In a meta-analysis of 12 studies including 824 people exercise programs were shown to improve cognitive functioning for those with mild to moderate cognitive deficits (Heyn, Abreu, & Ottenbacher, 2004). Exercise programs have also been shown to improve cognitive functioning among those already diagnosed with Alzheimer's disease (Cott, Dawson, Sidani, et al., 2002).

Behavioral approaches have been shown to help compensate for memory loss and to reduce depression and disruptive behavior among people with early stages of Alzheimer's disease. For example, external memory aids such as shopping lists, calendars, phone lists, and labels can help when placed prominently as visual reminders (Buchanan, Christenson, Houlihan, et al., 2011). Pleasant and engaging activities can be increased as a way of diminishing depression (Logsdon, McCurry, & Teri, 2007). Triggers for disruptive behavior can be identified and changed. Music may help reduce agitation and disruptive behavior while it is being played (Livingston, Johnston, Katona, et al., 2005). These behavioral interventions can provide important alternatives to medication approaches.

Providing memory aids is one way of compensating for memory loss. (RubberBall/SuperStock, Inc.)

Check Your Knowledge 14.2

Answer the questions.

1. A plaque is:
   a. a small, round beta-amyloid protein deposit
   b. a protein filament composed of the protein tau
   c. a buildup of the myelin sheath surrounding neurons in the hippocampus
   d. a small white spot on a brain scan
2. A neurofibrillary tangle is:
   a. a small, round beta-amyloid protein deposit
   b. a protein filament composed of the protein tau
   c. a buildup of the myelin sheath surrounding neurons in the hippocampus
   d. a small white spot on a brain scan
3. Which neurotransmitter is most involved in Alzheimer's disease?
   a. dopamine
   b. serotonin
   c. GABA
   d. acetylcholine
4. FTD involves profound changes in:
   a. memory
   b. social and emotional behavior
   c. motor control
   d. attention

FOCUS ON DISCOVERY 14.1

Support for Caregivers

For every person with a severely disabling dementia living in an institution, there are at least two living in the community, usually supported by a family (especially wives and daughters). Caregiving for dementia requires much more time than caregiving for most other disorders (Ory, Hoffman, Yee, et al., 1999) and has been shown to be extremely stressful across a number of cultures (Torti, Gwyther, Reed, et al., 2004). Caregivers are at risk for clinical depression and anxiety (Dura, Stukenberg, & Kiecolt-Glaser, 1991), physical illness (Vitaliano, Zhang, & Scanlan, 2003), and decreased immune functioning (Kiecolt-Glaser, Dura, Speicher, et al., 1991) compared to noncaregivers. Further, for some caregivers, depression and loneliness persist long after their ill spouse has died (Robinson-Whelan, Tada, McCallum, et al., 2001).

Families can be helped, however, to cope better with the daily stress of having a family member with Alzheimer's. For example, because people with Alzheimer's have great difficulty placing new information into memory, they can engage in a reasonable conversation but forget a few minutes later what has been discussed. A caregiver may become impatient unless he or she understands that this impairment is to be expected because of the brain damage. Family members can learn communication strategies to adapt to the memory loss. For example, families can ask questions that embed the answer. For example, it is much easier to respond to "Was the person you just spoke to on the phone Harry or Tom?" than to "Who just called?"

It is also useful for caregivers to understand that patients do not always recognize their limitations and may try to engage in activities beyond their abilities, sometimes dangerously so. Caregivers must set limits regarding dangerous activities. For example, caregivers often need to tell a relative with Alzheimer's disease that driving is off-limits (and then remove the car keys, as they can assume that the relative will forget the new rule).

Programs that teach coping strategies for the caregivers (e.g., increasing pleasant activities, exercise, or social support) as well as individual behavioral therapy programs have been shown to relieve caregiver burden (Selwood, Johnson, Katona,

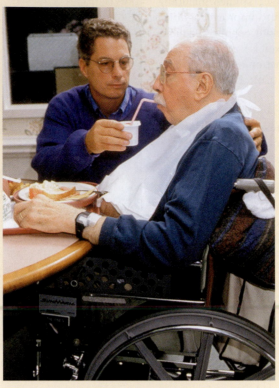

Caring for a relative with Alzheimer's disease is a source of severe stress. (David Young-Wolff/PhotoEdit.)

et al., 2007) and depression (Mittelman, Brodaty, Wallen, et al., 2008). Programs lasting at least 6 weeks (Selwood et al., 2007) or offering multiple components (e.g., psychoeducation about dementia, case-management services, and cognitive behavioral strategies) more consistently reduce caregivers' distress (Acton & Kang, 2001). Because family caregivers are so powerfully affected, it is recommended that they be given respites from their task. To accomplish this, sometimes the person with dementia is admitted to the hospital briefly or enrolled in an adult day-care center; sometimes a health care worker takes over long enough for the family to take a holiday. Caregiver support programs have been found to improve the immune function of caregivers (Garand, Buckwalter, Lubaroff, et al., 2002), decrease the medical costs of the person with dementia, and slow the timing of institutionalization (Teri, Gibbons, McCurry, et al., 2003).

New research is examining the best ways to integrate caregiver programs into the medical system. Researchers have shown that these programs can be offered effectively in HMO settings, improving the ease of access (Toseland, McCallion, Smith, et al., 2004). One study found that providing social work consultation to caregivers improved the quality of medical treatment provided to people with Alzheimer's disease (Vickrey, Mittman, Connor, et al., 2006).

Delirium

The term **delirium** is derived from the Latin words *de,* meaning "out of," and *lira,* meaning "track." The term implies being off-track or deviating from the usual state (Wells & Duncan, 1980). As illustrated in the Clinical Case of Simon at the beginning of this chapter, delirium is typically described as a clouded state of consciousness. The two most common symptoms are extreme trouble focusing attention and profound disturbances in the sleep/wake cycle (Meagher, 2007). Patients, sometimes rather suddenly, have so much trouble focusing attention that they cannot maintain a coherent stream of thought. As the sleep/wake cycle becomes disturbed, patients become drowsy during the day yet awake and agitated at night. Vivid dreams and nightmares are common. People with delirium may be impossible to engage in conversation because of their wandering attention and fragmented thinking. In severe delirium, speech is rambling and incoherent. Bewildered and confused, some people with delirium may become so disoriented that they are unclear about what day it is, where they are, and even who they are. Memory impairment, especially for recent events, is common.

In the course of a 24-hour period, people with delirium have lucid intervals in which they become alert and coherent. They are usually worse during sleepless nights. These daily fluctuations help distinguish delirium from other syndromes, especially Alzheimer's disease.

Perceptual disturbances are frequent in delirium. People mistake the unfamiliar for the familiar; for example, they may state that they are at home instead of in a hospital. Although visual hallucinations are common, they are not always present. Delusions—beliefs contrary to

Proposed DSM-5 Criteria for Delirium

- Disturbance in attention and awareness
- A change in cognition, such as disturbance in orientation, language, memory, perception, and planning, not better accounted for by a dementia
- Rapid onset (usually within hours or days) during the course of a day
- Symptoms are caused by a medical condition
- Fluctuation

reality—have been noted in about 25 percent of older adults with delirium (Camus, Burtin, Simeone, et al., 2000). These delusions tend to be poorly worked out, fleeting, and changeable.

Swings in activity and mood accompany these disordered thoughts and perceptions. People with delirium can be erratic, ripping their clothes one moment and sitting lethargically the next. They may also shift rapidly from one emotion to another—depression, anxiety, fright, anger, euphoria, and irritability. Fever, flushed face, dilated pupils, tremors, rapid heartbeat, elevated blood pressure, and incontinence of urine and feces are common. If delirium worsens, the person may become stuporous and lethargic (Webster & Holroyd, 2000).

Unfortunately, delirium is often misdiagnosed (Knight, 1996). For example, among 77 hospitalized older adults who had clear symptoms of delirium, about 60 percent had no notation of delirium in their hospital chart (Lauril, Pitkala, Strandberg, et al., 2004). Physicians are particularly unlikely to detect delirium when lethargy is present (Cole, 2004).

People of any age are subject to delirium, but it is more common among children and older adults. Among older adults, it is particularly common in nursing homes and hospitals. One study found that 6 to 12 percent of nursing home residents developed delirium in the course of 1 year (Katz, Parmelee, & Brubaker, 1991), and rates much higher than this have been found in elderly hospital patients (Meagher, 2001).

Delirium is often misdiagnosed when a person has dementia. Table 14.4 compares the features of dementia and delirium. Knight (l996) offers a useful suggestion for distinguishing delirium from dementia:

> The clinical "feel" of talking with a person with delirium is rather like talking to someone who is acutely intoxicated or in an acute psychotic episode. Whereas the demented patient may not remember the name of the place where she or he is, the delirious patient may believe it is a different sort of place altogether, perhaps mistaking a psychiatric ward for a used car lot. (pp. 96–97)

Detecting and treating delirium is of fundamental importance. Untreated, the mortality rate for delirium is high; more than one-third of people with the condition die within a year (McCusker, Cole, & Abrahamowicz, 2002). Beyond the risk of death, elderly adults who develop delirium in the hospital are at an increased risk of further cognitive decline (Jackson, Gordon, Hart, et al., 2004) and of being transferred to a nursing home (Witlox, Eurelings, de Jonghe, et al., 2010). It is not clear why delirium predicts such bad outcomes; some believe that delirium may be an indicator of an underlying frailty that becomes apparent in the face of medical conditions.

Etiology of Delirium As noted in the diagnostic criteria, delirium is caused by medical conditions. Several causes of delirium have been identified: drug intoxications and drug-withdrawal reactions, metabolic and nutritional imbalances (as in uncontrolled diabetes, thyroid dysfunction, kidney or liver failure, congestive heart failure, or malnutrition), infections or fevers (like pneumonia or urinary tract infections), neurological disorders (like head trauma or seizures),

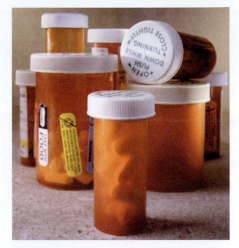

Medication misuse, whether deliberate or inadvertent, can be a serious problem among older people and can cause delirium. (Eric Kamp/Phototake.)

Table 14.4 Comparative Features of Dementia and Delirium

Dementia	Delirium
Gradual deterioration of abilities	Rapid onset
Deficits in memory for recent events	Trouble concentrating and staying with a train of thought
Caused by disease processes that are directly influencing the brain	Secondary to another medical condition
Usually progressive and nonreversible	Fluctuations over the course of a day
Treatment offers only minimal benefit	Usually reversible by treating underlying condition, but potentially fatal if cause—e.g., infection or malnutrition—not treated
Prevalence increases with age	Prevalence is highest in the very young as well as the old

and the stress of major surgery (Knight, 1996; Zarit & Zarit, 1998). One of the most common triggers of delirium is hip surgery (Marcantonio, Flacker, Wright, et al., 2001). As in the case of Simon at the start of this chapter, however, delirium usually has more than one cause.

Why are older adults so vulnerable to delirium? Many explanations have been offered: the physical declines of late life, the increased susceptibility to chronic diseases, the many medications prescribed for older people, and the greater sensitivity to drugs. Brain damage and dementia also greatly increase the risk of delirium (Purdie, Honigman, & Rosen, 1981).

Treatment of Delirium Complete recovery from delirium is possible if the underlying cause is treated promptly and effectively. The patient must be examined thoroughly for all possible reversible causes of the disorder, such as drug intoxication, infections, fever, and malnutrition, and then treated accordingly. Beyond treating the underlying medical conditions, the most common treatment is atypical antipsychotic medication (Lonergan, Britton, Luxenberg, et al., 2007). It usually takes 1 to 4 weeks for the condition to clear; it takes longer in older people than in younger people.

Because of the high rates of delirium in hospitalized older adults, preventive strategies are recommended to prevent delirium from beginning. In one study of such strategies, researchers randomly assigned 852 elderly hospitalized patients to receive either standard medical care only or standard medical care along with an intervention designed to prevent delirium. This intervention addressed common risk factors for delirium within the hospital setting, such as sleep deprivation, immobility, dehydration, and visual and hearing impairment. Among other strategies, medical tests and rounds were scheduled later in the morning to avoid waking patients, patients were helped to resume walking soon after surgery, glasses and hearing aids were returned as soon as possible after medical procedures, and care was given to help patients consume enough liquid and calories. The patients who received the intervention were less likely to develop delirium, and those who did develop delirium recovered more quickly compared to patients who received standard medical care (Inouye, Bogardus, Charpentier, et al., 1999).

The high risk of delirium among people with dementia raises another set of prevention issues. The family of a person with dementia should learn the symptoms of delirium and know about its reversible nature so that they do not interpret the onset of delirium as a new stage of a progressive dementia. With proper diagnosis and treatment, the person can usually return to the earlier state.

Quick Summary

Dementia is a broad term to capture cognitive decline, most commonly a decline in memory for recent events. As cognitive deficits become more widespread and profound, social and occupational functioning becomes more and more disturbed. Dementia affects approximately 1 to 2 percent of people in their 60s but more than 20 percent of people over the age of 85. There are many types of dementia, including Alzheimer's, frontotemporal, vascular, dementia with Lewy bodies, and dementia from other medical causes.

Alzheimer's disease is characterized by plaques and tangles in the brain. Risk of developing the disease is higher among those with at least one ApoE-4 allele. The expression of genetic vulnerability, though, is influenced by lifestyle and psychological factors, such as depression, exercise, and cognitive engagement.

Frontotemporal dementia (FTD) is characterized by neuronal deterioration in the frontal and temporal lobes. Pick's disease is one form of FTD. The primary symptoms of FTD include marked changes in social and emotional behavior, including problems with empathy, executive function, disinhibition, compulsive behavior, hyperorality, and apathy.

Vascular dementia often occurs after a stroke. Genetic factors do not play a direct role in vascular dementia.

Dementia with Lewy bodies is characterized by visual hallucinations, fluctuations in cognitive functioning, supersensitivity to side effects of antipsychotic medications, and intense dreams during which the person moves and talks. It is common among people diagnosed with Parkinson's disease.

The cholinesterase inhibitors and memantine are the major medical treatments for dementia, but these medications offer modest effects. Exercise appears to improve cognitive functioning for people with mild cognitive impairment as well as those with Alzheimer's disease. Antidepressants and behavioral treatments can help relieve comorbid symptoms of depression. Antipsychotic medications can reduce agitation for those with dementia but also increase the risk of death; behavioral treatments can be used safely to reduce agitation. Caregivers of people with Alzheimer's are at high risk for depression and anxiety. Multimodal interventions that address a range of caregiver issues, including periods of respite from caretaking, offer some protection against psychological symptoms.

Delirium is a neurocognitive disorder characterized by clouded consciousness. The person can seem unaware of and unable to attend to the environment. Symptoms tend to come on acutely and vary throughout the day. Delirium is most likely to affect children and older adults; among the elderly, it is particularly common in hospitals and nursing homes. By definition, delirium is secondary to an underlying medical condition. If the underlying medical condition is treated, full recovery from delirium can be expected. Delirium is often not detected, though, and the risk of further cognitive decline and even death is quite high when symptoms are not addressed.

Check Your Knowledge 14.3

Answer the questions.

1. Dementia is most commonly characterized by:
   a. anxiety
   b. memory loss
   c. frank disorganization
   d. sad mood
2. Delirium is characterized by:
   a. anxiety
   b. memory loss
   c. frank disorganization
   d. sad mood
3. Mary, a 70-year-old woman, was hospitalized for hip surgery. Although there were no immediate complications from the surgery, her son became concerned when he visited her that night because she was not making any sense. She thanked him for checking her into the Ritz Carlton and laughed giddily when he told her that she was in the hospital. Half an hour later, she began sobbing. Although she seemed fine the next morning, symptoms of acute confusion reemerged by lunchtime. Which diagnosis is most likely for Mary?
   a. Alzheimer's disease
   b. frontotemporal dementia
   c. mania
   d. delirium

Summary

Aging: Issues and Methods

- As life expectancy continues to improve, it will become even more important to learn about the disorders suffered by some older people and the most effective means of treating them.
- Several stereotypes about aging are false. Generally, people in late life report low levels of negative emotion, are not inappropriately concerned with their health, and are not lonely. Elderly couples report active sex lives as long as health problems do not interfere. On the other hand, poverty, stigma, bereavement, and physical disease are common challenges for people as they age.
- In research studies, differences between a younger and an older group could reflect either cohort effects or effects of chronological age. Longitudinal studies are more helpful for making this distinction than cross-sectional studies are.

Psychological Disorders in Late Life

- Data indicate that persons over age 65 have the lowest overall rates of psychological disorders of all age groups. When older people experience psychological disorders, the symptoms are often a recurrence of a disorder that first emerged earlier in life. It is important to rule out medical causes of psychological symptoms occurring during late life.

Neurocognitive Disorders in Late Life

- Serious cognitive disorders affect a small minority of older people. Two principal disorders have been distinguished: dementia and delirium.
- In dementia, the person's intellectual functioning declines and memory, abstract thinking, and judgment deteriorate. As the dementia progresses, the person may become oblivious to his or her surroundings. A variety of diseases can cause this deterioration. The most common is Alzheimer's disease. Genes play a major role in the etiology of Alzheimer's disease. A history of depression is a risk factor, and exercise and cognitive engagement appear to be protective.
- Other forms of dementia include frontotemporal dementia, vascular dementia, dementia with Lewy bodies, and dementia due to other medical conditions.
- Dementia usually responds only minimally to medication treatment, but the person and the family affected by the disease can be counseled on how to make the remaining time manageable and even rewarding. Exercise programs for people with dementia may help improve cognitive functioning.

• Delirium is defined by a sudden onset of difficulties with attention and awareness. The person may show a sudden clouding of consciousness, as well as other symptoms such as fragmented and undirected thought, incoherent speech, inability to sustain attention, hallucinations, illusions, disorientation, lethargy or hyperactivity, and mood swings. The condition is reversible, provided that the underlying cause is adequately treated. Causes include overmedication, infection of brain tissue, high fevers, malnutrition, dehydration, endocrine disorders, head trauma, cerebrovascular problems, and surgery.

Answers to Check Your Knowledge Questions

14.1 1. F; 2. F; 3. F; 4. F
14.2 1. a; 2. b; 3. d; 4. b

14.3 1. b; 2. c; 3. d

Key Terms

age effects
Alzheimer's disease
cognitive reserve
cohort effects

delirium
dementia
dementia with Lewy bodies (DLB)
disorientation

frontotemporal dementia (FTD)
neurofibrillary tangles
plaques
selective mortality

social selectivity
time-of-measurement effects
vascular dementia

15 Personality and Personality Disorders

LEARNING GOALS

1. Be able to explain the differences between the DSM-IV-TR and the proposed DSM-5 approaches to personality and personality disorders.

2. Be able to describe the personality trait domains in the proposed DSM-5 and to define the key features of each of the DSM-5 personality disorder types.

3. Be able to describe the genetic, neurobiological, social, and psychological risk factors for the DSM-5 personality disorder types.

4. Be able to describe the available medication and psychological treatments of the DSM-5 personality disorder types.

Clinical Case: Justine

Justine was 24 years old when she was first admitted to a psychiatric hospital, following the breakup of a short-lived relationship with a man she had formed a passionate attachment to. She feared being alone more than anything in her life, and the breakup led to an escalation in her recurrent thoughts of cutting, burning, and killing herself. She had been in outpatient treatment with a psychologist for several months already, before the breakup, but the concern over a possible suicide attempt led her therapist to conclude that she could no longer be managed as an outpatient. Justine's first experience with psychotherapy occurred when she was an adolescent. Her parents first noticed that she was pulling her eyelashes out, but then when a bald spot gradually appeared near her crown, they didn't know how to deal with it without making Justine feel self-conscious. Family therapy was started, and it seemed to go well at first. Justine was enthusiastic about the therapist and asked for additional, private sessions with him. During the private sessions, Justine revealed she smoked marijuana fairly regularly at a friend's house, and had engaged in unprotected sex with her friend's brother. Her relationships with the other kids at school were changeable. There was a constant parade of new friends, whom Justine at first thought to be the greatest ever but who soon disappointed her and were cast aside, often in very unpleasant ways. Except for the one friend she smoked with, Justine said that she had few friends to hang round with at weekends.

After several weeks of family therapy, Justine's parents noticed that she was angry and abusive toward the therapist. After a few more weeks had passed, Justine refused to attend further sessions. In a subsequent conversation with the therapist, Justine's mother learned that she had behaved seductively toward the therapist during their private sessions and that her changed attitude coincided with his rejection of her advances, despite the therapist's attempt to mix firmness with warmth and empathy. Justine left secondary school at 16 and had a series of low-paying jobs. Most of them didn't last long, as her relationships with co-workers paralleled her relationships with her peers in school. When Justine started a new job she would find someone she really liked, but something would come between them, and the relationship would end angrily. She was often suspicious of her co-workers and reported that she heard them plotting how to prevent her from getting ahead on the job. She was quick to find hidden meanings in their behavior, as when she interpreted being the last person asked to sign a birthday card to mean that she was the least liked person in the office. She indicated that she "got vibes" from others and could tell when they really didn't like her even in the absence of any direct evidence. Justine's frequent mood swings, with periods of depression, feelings of emptiness and extreme irritability, led her to seek therapy several times. But after initial enthusiasm, her relationships with therapists always deteriorated, resulting in premature termination of therapy. By the time of her hospitalization, she had seen six therapists.

THE PERSONALITY DISORDERS ARE a heterogeneous group of disorders defined by problems with forming a stably positive sense of self and with sustaining close and constructive relationships. From time to time, we all behave, think, and feel in ways that look similar to symptoms of personality disorders, but an actual personality disorder is defined by the extreme, inflexible, and maladaptive ways in which these traits are expressed. People with **personality disorders** experience difficulties with their identity and their relationships in multiple domains of life, and these problems are sustained for years. The symptoms of personality disorders are pervasive and persistent.

The changes in the DSM-5 are more profound for personality diagnosis than for any other aspect of diagnosis. In this chapter, we begin by describing differences between DSM-IV-TR and DSM-5, with an eye toward helping you understand some of the goals the DSM-5 Workgroup on Personality and Personality Disorders hoped to achieve in making such major changes. We then provide a more detailed overview of the proposed DSM-5 system for assessing personality. With an understanding of the steps in diagnosis as background, we then consider the personality disorder types included in the DSM-5. For each, we review the clinical description, the epidemiology, and the available research on etiology. We end with a discussion of the available treatment options for personality disorders.

Comparing Personality Assessment in the DSM-IV-TR and the Proposed DSM-5

DSM-IV-TR includes ten personality disorders, each defined by a unique set of symptoms (see Table 15.1). The system includes specific criteria for defining each of the disorders, and clinicians are urged to consider whether personality disorders are present for all clients, regardless of whether they are seeking treatment for another condition. The diagnoses have been shown to have relatively strong interrater reliability when structured diagnostic interviews are used (Zanarini, Skodol, Bender, et al., 2000), and some of the personality disorders have become major foci of research. Presence of a personality disorder has been found to robustly predict a poorer treatment outcome for many different conditions (Crits-Christoph & Barber, 2002).

Table 15.1 Key Features of the DSM-IV-TR Personality Disorders

Included in the Proposed DSM-5

Obsessive-compulsive	Preoccupation with order, perfection, and control
Narcissistic	Grandiosity, need for admiration, and lack of empathy
Schizotypal	Cognitive distortions, disorganized and eccentric behavior, and lack of capacity for close relationships
Avoidant	Social inhibition, feelings of inadequacy, and hypersensitivity to negative evaluation
Antisocial	Disregard for and violation of the rights of others
Borderline	Instability of interpersonal relationships, self-image, and affect, as well as marked impulsivity

Not Included in the Proposed DSM-5

Paranoid	Distrust and suspiciousness of others
Schizoid	Detachment from social relationships and restricted range of emotional expression
Histrionic	Excessive emotionality and attention seeking
Dependent	Submissive behavior, fears of separation, and excessive need to be taken care of

In contrast to the DSM-IV-TR, the proposed DSM-5 includes only six personality disorder types (see Table 15.1 to see which personality disorder types are maintained in the proposed DSM-5 system). To supplement these personality disorder diagnoses, the DSM-5 system includes personality trait dimensions (e.g., ratings of antagonism, negative affectivity, or other dimensions). When people with a personality disorder take a personality inventory, they acknowledge more extreme personality traits than those seen in the general population (Clark & Livesley, 2002). Many studies show that personality disorders are characterized by extremes of personality trait dimensions (Samuel & Widiger, 2008), so the DSM-5 proposes a way to integrate personality assessment with research on those traits.

The change in the number of personality disorder types and the inclusion of personality trait dimensions are meant to address a set of concerns with DSM-IV-TR. Let's review these concerns and consider how the new system might address them.

- About half of people who meet criteria for one DSM-IV-TR personality disorder meet diagnostic criteria for another personality disorder (Lenzenweger, Lane, Loranger, et al., 2007). By limiting the number of diagnostic categories, overlap should be reduced. Comorbidity is also not a concern with dimensional personality scores; we expect people to have a profile of low and high scores across various dimensions.

- Some of the DSM-IV-TR personality diagnoses are rare in community settings, and even in most clinical settings, the disorders are present for less than 2 percent of patients (Crawford, Cohen, Johnson, et al., 2005; Samuels, Eaton, Bienvenu, et al., 2002; Zimmerman, Rothschild, & Chelminski, 2005). As shown in Table 15.2, most of the personality disorder types retained in the proposed DSM-5 are relatively common, particularly in treatment settings.

- Many people who seem to have serious personality problems don't fit any of the personality disorder diagnoses. The proposed DSM-5 personality trait dimensions can be used even if a person does not meet diagnostic criteria for a personality disorder.

- Those who qualify for a given personality disorder can vary a good deal from one another in the nature of their personality traits and the severity of their condition. By using the personality trait dimension system, clinicians can further specify which personality traits are of most concern for a given client.

Table 15.2 Rates of Personality Disorders in the Community and in Treatment Settings

Disorder	Prevalence in the Community (%)	Prevalence in Treatment Settings (%)	Gender Ratio
Obsessive compulsive	1.9	8.7	Females > males
Narcissistic	1.0	2.3	Males > females
Schizotypal	0.6	0.6	Males > females
Avoidant	1.2	14.7	Females > males
Antisocial	3.8	3.6	Males > females
Borderline	2.7	9.3	Females > males

Source: Prevalence estimates for community settings are drawn from Trull, Jahng, Tomko, et al. (2010); Samuels et al. (2002). Prevalence estimates for treatment settings are drawn from Zimmerman et al. (2005). Diagnoses were made using DSM-IV-TR criteria.

• Although the very definition of personality disorders suggests that they should be stable over time, Figure 15.1 shows that about half of the people diagnosed with a personality disorder at one point in time did not receive the same diagnosis when they were interviewed 2 years later. Many of those who no longer met diagnostic criteria still had some symptoms at the second interview, just not at the levels required for diagnosis. Because these subsyndromal symptoms can be captured in a dimensional system, personality trait ratings tend to be more stable over time than are personality disorder diagnoses (McGlashan, Grilo, Sanislow, et al., 2005).

Beyond addressing those more specific concerns, including a dimensional approach in the DSM-5 integrates the diagnostic system with a large literature showing that personality trait dimensions are related to many aspects of psychological adjustment and even physical outcomes. For example, many psychological disorders such as anxiety, depression, and somatic symptom disorder can be related to elevations of personality traits like neuroticism (Kotov, Gamez, Schmidt, et al., 2010). Personality dimensions also robustly predict important interpersonal outcomes such as the quality of friendships, the risk of divorce, and the level of psychosocial functioning (Hopwood & Zanarini, 2010; Ozer & Benet-Martinez, 2006; Roberts, Kuncel, Shiner, et al., 2007). Hence there is a lot known about these personality dimensions.

Reading over this section, some of you may begin to wonder if a dimensional approach could replace the personality disorder diagnoses. It is worth noting that personality disorders have been in use for decades, and the diagnostic approach has some important advantages. Researchers and clinicians want to be able to communicate with one another and their clients when a set of problems seems severe enough to warrant treatment, and it is not entirely clear when dimensions become sufficiently extreme to be considered pathological. Even if one can denote a pathological range on personality dimensions, certain personality disorders seem to be more than the sum of the parts, as you will see as we discuss the specific personality disorder types later in this chapter. Borderline personality disorder, for example, involves a complex combination of many different traits (First, 2010). So there are some clear advantages to using personality disorder diagnoses along with dimensional scores. Because there are major advantages to dimensional and diagnostic approaches to personality, the DSM-5 includes both. We turn now to describing the proposed DSM-5 system for evaluating personality and personality disorders. Although the new system includes many improvements, there is still considerable debate about personality disorder diagnoses. See Focus on Discovery 15.1 for discussion of two issues in this area.

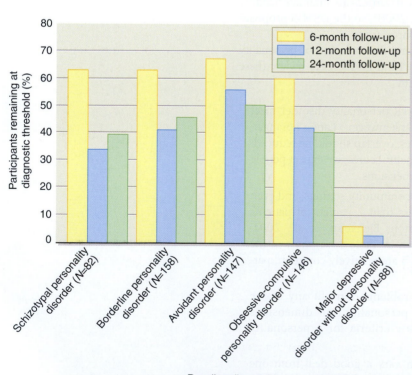

Figure 15.1 Test–retest stability for personality disorders and major depressive disorder across 6-, 12-, and 24-month follow-up interviews. Drawn from Grilo, Shea, Sanislow, et al. (2004); Shea, Stout, Gunderson, et al. (2002).

FOCUS ON DISCOVERY 15.1

Issues in Assessing Personality and Personality Disorders

The proposed DSM-5 addresses many of the problems that were inherent in the DSM-IV-TR approach to diagnosing personality disorders. Despite the gains, there are still some issues worth keeping in mind as we discuss personality disorders.

Can People Describe Their Own Personalities Accurately?

It is not clear that people can always accurately describe their own personalities. When people's own reports of their personality disorder symptoms are compared to the reports of friends and families, agreement tends to be low (Klonsky, Oltmanns, & Turkheimer, 2002). Intriguingly, it is not the case that people always downplay their difficulties; sometimes clients are more harsh than are their friends and family members, and sometimes they are less harsh in describing their personality symptoms. Nonetheless, having more than one perspective on personality disorders is important. Interviews with people who know the patient well can improve the accuracy of personality evaluations (Connelly & Ones, 2010). However, published studies of personality disorders rarely gather data from people other than the person being diagnosed (Bornstein, 2003).

Gender and Personality Disorders

For many personality disorders, prevalence varies a great deal by gender (see Table 15.2). For example, women are more likely than men to be diagnosed with borderline personality disorders, and men are more likely than women to be diagnosed with antisocial, narcissistic, and obsessive-compulsive personality disorders. Research has suggested that clinicians are biased by gender stereotypes in the way they diagnose personality disorders. For example, clinicians might focus on different behaviors, depending on whether they are diagnosing a man or a woman. In a typical test of this issue, two different vignettes are written involving people with personality disorders. The versions are identical except that in one, the person in the vignette is named Joan, and in the other, the person is named John. Clinicians read the vignettes and provide the most likely diagnosis. In these types of studies, clinicians are more likely to diagnose the person as having borderline personality disorder if the vignette is about a woman and more likely to diagnose the person as having antisocial personality disorder if the vignette is about a man (Garb, 1997). These findings highlight how important it is for clinicians to be aware of biases.

The Steps of Personality Assessment in the Proposed DSM-5

The DSM-5 approach to personality is complex. It integrates personality dimensions and diagnoses, multiple steps in assessment, and many different rating scales. More specifically, the proposed DSM-5 includes three types of personality ratings (Skodol, Clark, Bender, et al., 2011):

- Levels of personality functioning scale
- Six personality disorder types
- Five personality trait domain ratings as well as 25 facet ratings to describe the more specific dimensions within each of the five domains

The system is designed to be flexible. A clinician who does not have the time to rate 25 specific facets of personality could still provide a single score to indicate the degree of impairment in personality functioning and could record whether some form of personality disorder appears to be present. Those who are using personality dimensions to refine their treatment or research can use the full approach. For someone using the full approach, the sequence of steps in assessing personality is described in Figure 15.2. Let's take these steps in order.

Levels of Personality Functioning

For decades, researchers have developed various scales to assess personality functioning. To define levels of personality functioning for the proposed DSM-5, Bender and colleagues (2011) conducted a search for these various assessment tools. They then considered the topics that were most commonly covered and could be reliably rated across scale. Their review of the literature suggested two broad types of impairment that were important to consider: disturbances in one's sense of self or identity and chronic interpersonal disturbances. Items reflecting problems in those two areas appear to correlate with personality disorder diagnoses

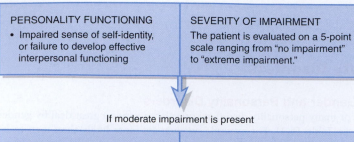

Figure 15.2 Steps in evaluating personality and personality disorders in the proposed DSM-5. Adapted from Carey, B (Feb. 10, 2010) the *New York Times*.

across a range of studies and scales (Morey, Berghuis, Bender, et al., 2011). Those are pretty broad areas, though, and as you might imagine, there are a host of ways that people could have trouble with their identity or relationships. The authors further narrowed in on a set of themes that seemed to occur again and again across scales, and they used this to create a rating scale for self and interpersonal functioning (see Table 15.3).

Personality Disorder Types

If at least moderate impairment is present on the levels of functioning scale, the next step is to evaluate whether those problems fit with one of the six DSM-5 **personality disorder types** described in Table 15.1. For those who seem to have a personality disorder but don't match one of the types, the label "personality disorder trait specified" is used, and then the specific maladaptive traits are noted. This category can be used to diagnose someone who met criteria for a DSM-IV-TR personality disorder that is no longer included in the DSM-5, such as paranoid personality disorder. In the proposed DSM-5, this person might be diagnosed with personality disorder trait specified, and it would be noted that he or she showed high suspiciousness.

The six personality disorder types in the proposed DSM-5 are each drawn from the DSM-IV-TR, but the definitions of these types have changed. In the DSM-IV-TR, personality disorders are diagnosed based on whether a person met a specific number of diagnostic criteria. For example, borderline personality disorder is diagnosed if a person demonstrated at least five out of eight criteria (see criteria for borderline personality disorder on p. 484). In the proposed DSM-5, each personality disorder type is defined using a list of the personality domains and facets. Throughout this chapter, we include the DSM-IV-TR criteria and the proposed DSM-5 criteria so that you can compare the two systems.

Table 15.3 Proposed Rating for Levels of Personality Functioning in the DSM-5
Self
Identity: Experience of oneself as unique, with clear boundaries between self and others; stability of self-esteem and accuracy of self-appraisal; capacity for, and ability to regulate, a range of emotional experience
Self-direction: Pursuit of coherent and meaningful short-term and life goals; utilization of constructive and prosocial internal standards of behavior; ability to self-reflect productively
Interpersonal
Empathy: Comprehension and appreciation of others' experiences and motivations; tolerance of differing perspectives; understanding of the effects of own behavior on others
Intimacy: Depth and duration of positive connections with others; desire and capacity for closeness: mutuality of regard reflected in interpersonal behavior
Rate the overall degree of impairment in self and interpersonal functioning: _____
0 No impairment
1 Mild impairment
2 Moderate impairment
3 Serious impairment
4 Extreme impairment
Source: Quoted from Bender et al. (2011), p. 344.

Even if a person seems to have impairments in self and interpersonal functioning and at least one pathological trait, the clinician is asked to consider several issues before assigning a personality disorder type. These issues are captured in the criteria for personality disorder. First, clinicians are expected to consider cultural context. As with all diagnoses, only those symptoms that are unusual for a person's cultural context should be considered in making a diagnosis. Second, only stable personality characteristics are to be considered. Many people may struggle with their relationships or self-image during an acute life crisis or a severe episode of depression; these are not the types of personality concerns this system is designed to capture. Finally, the goal is to consider pervasive problems—those that seem to occur across settings, such as in family relationships, occupational domains, and close friendships.

Personality Trait Domains and Facets

The proposed DSM-5 includes two types of dimensional scores: 5 **personality trait domains** and 25 more specific **personality trait facets**, as shown in Table 15.4. Each dimension can be

> ### Proposed DSM-5 Criteria for Personality Disorder
> - Significant impairments in self and interpersonal functioning
> - At least one pathological personality trait domain or facet
> - Personality impairments are persistent and pervasive
> - Personality impairments are not explained by developmental stage, sociocultural environment, substance abuse, another psychological condition, or a medical condition.

Table 15.4 The 5 Personality Trait Domains and 25 Facets in the Proposed DSM-5

I. Negative Affectivity

1.	Anxiousness	I worry a lot about terrible things that might happen.
2.	Emotional lability	I never know where my emotion will go from moment to moment.
3.	Hostility	I'm nasty and short to anybody who deserves it.
4.	Perseveration	I get fixated on certain things and can't stop
5.	(Lack of) restricted affectivity	I don't react much to things that seem to make others emotional.
6.	Separation insecurity	I dread being without someone to love me.
7.	Submissiveness	I do what other people tell me to do.

II. Detachment

8.	Anhedonia	I almost never enjoy life.
9.	Depressivity	The future looks really hopeless to me.
10.	Intimacy avoidance	I steer clear of romantic relationships.
11.	Suspiciousness	Plenty of people are out to get me.
12.	Withdrawal	I don't like spending time with others.

III. Antagonism

13.	Attention seeking	I do things to make sure people notice me.
14.	Callousness	I don't care about other people's problems.
15.	Deceitfulness	I don't hesitate to cheat if it gets me ahead.
16.	Grandiosity	To be honest, I'm just more important than other people.
17.	Manipulativeness	It is easy for me to take advantage of others.

IV. Disinhibition

18.	Distractibility	I can't concentrate on anything.
19.	Impulsivity	I always do things on the spur of the moment.
20.	Irresponsibility	I make promises that I don't really intend to keep.
21.	(Lack of) rigid perfectionism	If something I do isn't absolutely perfect, it's simply not acceptable.
22.	Risk taking	I have no limits when it comes to doing dangerous things.

V. Psychoticism

23.	Eccentricity	Other people seem to think my behavior is weird.
24.	Perceptual dysregulation	Things around me often feel unreal or more real than usual.
25.	Unusual beliefs and experiences	Sometimes I can influence other people just by sending my thoughts to them.

From Krueger et al. (2011).

FOCUS ON DISCOVERY 15.2

Comparing the Proposed DSM-5 Trait Domains and Facets to the Five-Factor Model

The DSM-5 personality trait domains and facets are closely related to a very influential model of personality called the **five-factor model** (McCrae & Costa, 1990). The five-factor model was designed to understand normative personality patterns—the traits that distinguish healthy individuals from one another—but the DSM-5 Task Force on Personality and Personality Disorders aimed to cover those traits that are most related to psychological dysfunction. Some of the dimensions in the five-factor model relate well to psychological disorder, such as neuroticism (Kotov et al., 2010). On the other hand, some changes were made to keep the DSM-5 system related to the types of personality disturbances most commonly seen in clinical settings (Krueger et al., 2011). As one example, the five-factor model trait of Openness to Experience does not relate well to psychopathologies; depression, anxiety, and substance abuse are not related to whether a person will have high or low scores on

Openness to Experience. As shown in Table A, the proposed DSM-5 trait system does not include Openness to Experience. Rather, it includes one dimension that is not defined as part of the five-factor model: psychoticism, defined by unusual and bizarre thinking and behavior. The DSM-5 domains have also been labeled using terms that are most commonly used by clinicians, which often relate to the more pathological end of the continuum.

In the five-factor model, each of the five factors has six facets, or components; for example, the extraversion factor includes the facets of warmth, gregariousness, assertiveness, activity, excitement seeking, and positive emotionality. The proposed DSM-5 includes facet ratings as well, but some of the facets differ. As with the trait domains, the DSM-5 includes only those facets that seem most relevant for understanding psychological disturbance (see Table 15.4).

Table A Five-Factor Personality Traits and Corresponding DSM-5 Domain Traits

Five-Factor Personality Trait	DSM-5 Domain
Neuroticism	Negative affectivity
Extraversion/introversion	Detachment
Openness to experience	Not included
Agreeableness/antagonism	Antagonism
Conscientiousness	Disinhibition
Not included	Psychoticism (schizotypy)

rated on a scale of 0 ("very little or not at all descriptive") to 3 ("extremely descriptive"). These ratings can be used whenever personality is relevant for treatment planning, even if the person does not match any of the personality disorder types and even if his or her pathological personality traits are not severe enough to warrant a personality disorder diagnosis. The dimensional scores provide a richer sense of detail than do the personality disorder types.

The dimensional system can be flexibly adapted to the setting. Clinicians can make their own ratings based on an interview, but the DSM-5 Workgroup on Personality and Personality Disorders is also creating a self-report scale that can be used to assess these dimensions (Krueger, Eaton, Derringer, et al., 2011). Clinicians can also choose how much of the dimensional system to use. For those who just want a quick summary, the personality trait domain scores can be rated, but for those who want more detail, the facet ratings can be used. The DSM-5 criteria highlight key facets that are most closely related to each personality disorder type. In sum, clinicians decide whether they want to use personality trait domains, more specific trait facets, or just those facets related to a given personality disorder type, as well as whether they want to use self-report scales or clinical interviews to make those ratings.

Most of the trait domains and facets proposed for DSM-5 were chosen from an extensive body of work on five-factor model of personality, but as we discuss in Focus on Discovery 15.2, some modifications were made to adapt this model to understanding psychopathology. Because some of the proposed DSM-5 trait domains and facets are new, changes are expected for this system over time as research evolves.

Returning to Justine, described in our opening Clinical Case, we can now consider how her diagnosis might look within the proposed DSM-5 system. As shown, clinicians can record notes for each of the steps in the assessment process.

Clinical Case: DSM-5 Personality Diagnosis for Justine

Levels of Personality Functioning: 3 serious impairment
Personality Disorder Type: Borderline
Clinically Significant Traits:
Trait domains: Negative emotionality, antagonism, disinhibition, schizotypy
Trait facets: Emotional lability, self-harm, separation insecurity, hostility, impulsivity, unusual perceptions

Quick Summary

Personality disorders are defined by long-standing and pervasive ways of being that cause distress and impairment through their influence on identity and relationships. People with personality disorders often experience other comorbid conditions, including mood, anxiety, substance abuse, and other personality disorders. The DSM-IV-TR includes ten personality disorders. The proposed DSM-5 includes only six personality disorder types: schizotypal, antisocial, borderline, narcissistic, avoidant, and obsessive-compulsive personality disorder. The proposed DSM-5 also includes a dimensional system for evaluating personality trait domains and more specific personality facets. The changes were made to address concerns about high levels of comorbidity between the different personality disorder types; low prevalence for some of the personality disorder types, and correspondingly limited research; heterogeneity among those diagnosed with a given personality disorder type; generally low stability of personality disorders over time; and evidence that personality traits can correlate with psychological disorders, interpersonal functioning, and treatment outcome, even after considering the role of personality disorders.

The DSM-5 system includes three types of personality ratings: levels of personality functioning, personality disorder types, and personality trait and facet ratings. The proposed DSM-5 personality trait domains and facets largely overlap with the five-factor model personality dimensions, but some changes were made to ensure that the DSM-5 system relates well to psychological disorders.

Check Your Knowledge 15.1 (Answers are at the end of the chapter.)

True or false?
1. Most of the DSM-IV-TR personality disorders can be diagnosed with good interrater reliability if structured diagnostic interviews are used.
2. Most people diagnosed with a personality disorder will still show that personality disorder 2 years later.

3. Most studies of personality disorders include informants.

Answer the following question.
4. List three ways in which the proposed DSM-5 approach to personality differs from DSM-IV-TR.

Personality Disorder Types

In this section, we'll describe the clinical characteristics, epidemiology, and etiological models for each of the six DSM-5 personality disorder types. Of course, available research is based on the DSM-IV-TR definitions, so some findings may change as the DSM-5 approach to diagnosing personality disorder becomes more widely used in research.

For the person with obsessive-compulsive personality disorder, the overly perfectionistic quest for order may interfere with being productive. (Dan Saelinger/Getty Images, Inc.)

We will begin by describing obsessive-compulsive, narcissistic, schizotypal, and avoidant personality disorders, and then we will discuss two personality disorders that have been the focus of much more extensive research: antisocial and borderline personality disorder types.

Obsessive-Compulsive Personality Disorder

The person with **obsessive-compulsive personality disorder** is a perfectionist, preoccupied with details, rules, and schedules. People with this disorder often pay so much attention to detail that they fail to finish projects. They are more oriented toward work than pleasure. They have inordinate difficulty making decisions (lest they err) and allocating time (lest they focus on the wrong thing). Their interpersonal relationships are often troubled because they demand that everything be done the right way—their way. They often become known as "control freaks." Generally, they are serious, rigid, formal, and inflexible, especially regarding moral issues. They are unable to discard worn-out and useless objects, even those with no sentimental value, and they are likely to be excessively frugal to a level that causes concern among those around them.

Obsessive-compulsive personality disorder is distinct from obsessive-compulsive disorder (OCD), despite the similarity in names. The personality disorder does not include the obsessions and compulsions that define the latter. Nonetheless, the two conditions often co-occur (Skodol, Oldham, Hyler, et al., 1995). Of the personality disorders, the one that is most frequently comorbid with obsessive-compulsive personality disorder is avoidant personality disorder.

Very little research has been conducted to examine the etiology of obsessive-compulsive personality disorder. Two available twin studies provided conflicting heritability estimates (Reichborn-Kjennerud, Czajkowski, Neale, et al., 2007; Torgersen, Lygren, Øien, et al., 2000). There is some indication that the genetic vulnerability of obsessive-compulsive personality disorder might overlap with that of obsessive-compulsive disorder; family members of those with obsessive-compulsive disorder tend to have high levels of the traits involved in obsessive-compulsive personality disorder, such as perfectionism (Calvo, Lázaro, Castro-Fornieles, et al., 2009).

● DSM-IV-TR Criteria for Obsessive-Compulsive Personality Disorder

Intense need for order and control, as shown by the presence of at least four of the following beginning by early adulthood and evidenced in many contexts:
- Preoccupation with rules, details, and organization to the extent that the point of an activity is lost
- Extreme perfectionism interferes with task completion
- Excessive devotion to work to the exclusion of leisure and friendships
- Inflexibility about morals and values
- Difficulty discarding worthless items
- Reluctance to delegate unless others conform to one's standards
- Miserliness
- Rigidity and stubbornness

● Proposed DSM-5 Criteria for Obsessive-Compulsive Personality Disorder

Pathological **personality traits** in the following domains and facets:
1. **Compulsivity**, characterized by **rigid perfectionism**
2. **Negative affectivity**, characterized by **perseveration**

The person meets criteria for a personality disorder.

Note: Facets are printed in blue.

Narcissistic Personality Disorder

People with **narcissistic personality disorder** have a grandiose view of their abilities and are preoccupied with fantasies of great success (as demonstrated by Bob in the Clinical Case). They are more than a little self-centered—they require almost constant attention and excessive admiration. Their interpersonal relationships are disturbed by their lack of empathy, by their arrogance coupled with feelings of envy, by their habit of taking advantage of others, and by their feelings of entitlement—they expect others to do special favors for them. People with this disorder are extremely sensitive to criticism and might become enraged when others do not admire them. They tend to seek out high-status partners whom they idealize, but when, inevitably, these partners fall short of their unrealistic expectations, they become angry and rejecting (like those with borderline personality disorder). They are also likely to change partners if given an opportunity to be with a person of higher status. This disorder most often co-occurs with borderline personality disorder (Morey, 1988).

Etiology of Narcissistic Personality Disorder In this section, we discuss the two most influential models of the etiology of this disorder: the self-psychology model and the social-cognitive model. Both theories are attempts to understand how a person develops these traits.

Self-Psychology Model Heinz Kohut established a variant of psychoanalysis known as *self-psychology*, which he described in his two books, *The Analysis of the Self* (1971) and *The Restoration of the Self* (1977). Kohut noted that the person with narcissistic personality disorder projects remarkable self-importance, self-absorption, and fantasies of limitless success on the surface. But Kohut theorized that these characteristics mask a very fragile self-esteem. People with narcissistic personality disorder strive to bolster their sense of self-worth through unending quests for respect from others.

Kohut described parenting styles that might contribute to the development of narcissism. When parents respond to a child with respect, warmth, and empathy, they endow the youngster with a normal sense of self-worth. Parental coldness may contribute to an insecure sense of self. Beyond this, Kohut described a pattern in which the child is valued as a means of fostering the parents' self-esteem and the child's talents and abilities are overly emphasized. The child will experience a deep sense of shame over any of his or her shortcomings. Hence, Kohut hypothesized that two parenting dimensions would increase risk of narcissism: emotional coldness and an overemphasis on the child's achievements. Recent research indicates that people with high levels of narcissism report experiencing both of these parenting issues when they were children (Otway & Vignoles, 2006).

Social-Cognitive Model A model of narcissistic personality disorder developed by Carolyn Morf and Frederick Rhodewalt (2001) is built around two basic ideas: (1) people with this disorder have fragile self-esteem, in part because they are trying to maintain the belief that they are special, and (2) interpersonal interactions are important to them for bolstering self-esteem, rather than for gaining closeness or warmth. In other words, they are captive to the goal of maintaining a grand vision of themselves, and this goal pervades their experiences. The work of Morf and Rhodewalt is impressive in that they have designed laboratory research studies aimed at elucidating the cognitive, emotional, and interpersonal processes associated with narcissistic personality disorder.

DSM-IV-TR Criteria for Narcissistic Personality Disorder

Presence of five or more of the following shown by early adulthood in many contexts:
- Grandiose view of one's importance
- Preoccupation with one's success, brilliance, beauty
- Belief that one is special and can be understood only by other high-status people
- Extreme need for admiration
- Strong sense of entitlement
- Tendency to exploit others
- Lack of empathy
- Envious of others
- Arrogant behavior or attitudes

Proposed DSM-5 Criteria for Narcissistic Personality Disorder

Pathological **personality traits** in the following domain and facets:
1. Antagonism, characterized by **grandiosity** and **attention seeking**

The person meets criteria for a personality disorder.

Clinical Case: Bob

Bob, a 50-year-old college professor, sought treatment only after urging from his wife. During the interview, Bob's wife noted that he seemed so focused on himself and his own advancement that he often belittled others. Bob was dismissive of these concerns, stating that he had never been the sort of person to tolerate fools, and he could see no reason why he should begin offering such tolerance now—in rapid fire, he described his supervisor, his students, his parents, and a set of former friends as lacking the intelligence to merit his friendship. He willingly acknowledged working long hours but stated that his research had the potential to change life for people and that other activities could not be allowed to interfere with his success.

Narcissistic personality disorder draws its name from the Greek mythological figure Narcissus, who fell in love with his own reflection, was consumed by his own desire, and was transformed into a flower. (Museum Bojimans Van Beuningen, Rotterdam, Netherlands/Bridgeman Art Library/SuperStock, Inc.)

To assess the idea that people with narcissistic personality disorder are trying to maintain grandiose beliefs about themselves, they examine biases in how people with this disorder rate themselves in various settings. For example, in laboratory studies, people with narcissistic personality disorder overestimate their attractiveness to others and their contributions to group activities. ("Others must be jealous of me; I've been responsible for the lion-share of our progress here today.") In some studies, researchers have provided people with feedback that they were successful on a task (regardless of their actual performance), then asked participants to rate the reasons why they were successful. In these types of studies, people with narcissistic personality disorder attribute successes to their abilities rather than chance or luck. So a set of studies suggest that people with narcissistic personality disorder show cognitive biases that would help maintain grandiose beliefs about the self.

To assess whether people with narcissistic personality disorder have fragile self-esteem, Morf and Rhodewalt review studies of how much self-esteem depends on external feedback. For example, when falsely told they have done poorly on an IQ test, they show much more reactivity than others do; similarly, they show more reactivity to being told they have succeeded at something. Morf and Rhodewalt argue that this vulnerability of self-esteem to external feedback arises from the attempt to maintain an inflated self-view.

According to this theory, when people with narcissistic personality disorder interact with others, their primary goal is to bolster their own self-esteem. This goal influences how they act toward others in several ways. First, they tend to brag a lot; this often works well initially, but over time, repeated bragging comes to be perceived negatively by others (Paulhus, 1998). Second, when someone else performs better than they do on a task that is relevant to self-esteem, they will denigrate the other person, even if they have to do so to that person's face. That is, it is more important for them to be admired or to achieve competitive success than it is to be close to others. This framework makes it easy to understand why people with narcissistic personality disorder do things that alienate others; their sense of self depends on "winning," not in gaining or maintaining closeness (Campbell, 2007).

Schizotypal Personality Disorder

Schizotypal personality disorder is defined by unusual and eccentric thoughts and behavior (psychoticism), interpersonal detachment, and suspiciousness. People with this disorder might have odd beliefs or magical thinking—for instance, the belief that they can read other people's minds and see into the future. It is also common for them to have ideas of reference (the belief that events have a particular and unusual meaning for them personally) and to show suspiciousness and paranoid ideation. They might also have recurrent illusions (inaccurate sensory perceptions), such as sensing the presence of a force or a person that is not actually there. In their speech, they might use words in an unusual and unclear fashion—for example, they might say "not a very talkable person" to mean a person who is not easy to talk to. Their behavior and appearance might also be eccentric—for example, they might talk to themselves or wear dirty and disheveled clothing. Their affect appears constricted and flat, and they tend to be aloof from others. A study of the relative importance of these symptoms for diagnosis found that paranoid ideation, ideas of reference, and illusions were most telling (Widiger, Frances, & Trull, 1987).

The symptoms of schizotypal personality disorder are similar to those seen in schizophrenia, but they tend to be much milder versions of those symptoms. Although most do not develop schizophrenia, some people diagnosed with schizotypal personality disorder develop more severe psychotic symptoms over time, and a small proportion do develop schizophrenia over time (Raine, 2006). It is common for people with schizotypal personality disorder to meet criteria for avoidant personality disorder, perhaps because both involve interpersonal detachment (McGlashan, Grilo, Skodol, et al., 2000).

DSM-IV-TR Criteria for Schizotypal Personality Disorder

Presence of five or more of the following in many contexts beginning in early adulthood:

- Ideas of reference
- Peculiar beliefs or magical thinking, e.g., belief in extrasensory perception
- Unusual perceptions, e.g., distorted feelings about one's body
- Peculiar patterns of thought and speech
- Suspiciousness or paranoia
- Inappropriate or restricted affect
- Odd or eccentric behavior or appearance
- Lack of close friends
- Anxiety around other people, which does not diminish with familiarity

Proposed DSM-5 Criteria for Schizotypal Personality Disorder

Pathological **personality traits** in the following domains and facets:

1. **Psychoticism**, characterized by **eccentricity, cognitive and perceptual dysregulation,** and **unusual beliefs and experiences**
2. **Detachment**, characterized by **restricted affectivity** and **withdrawal**
3. **Negative affectivity**, characterized by **suspiciousness**

The person meets criteria for a personality disorder.

Note: Facets are printed in blue.

What causes the odd thinking, bizarre behavior, and interpersonal difficulties that appear in this personality disorder? Schizotypal personality disorder appears to be highly heritable; heritability has been estimated to be about 61 percent (Torgersen et al., 2000). Moreover, the genetic vulnerability for schizotypal personality disorder appears to overlap with the genetic vulnerability for schizophrenia (Siever & Davis, 2004). That is, family studies and adoption studies have shown that the relatives of people with schizophrenia are at increased risk for schizotypal personality disorder (Nigg & Goldsmith, 1994; Tienari, Wynne, Laksy, et al., 2003). Studies have consistently shown that people with schizotypal personality disorder have deficits in cognitive and neuropsychological functioning that are similar to but milder than those seen in schizophrenia (McClure, Barch, Flory, et al., 2008; Raine, 2006). Furthermore, and again paralleling findings from schizophrenia research, people with schizotypal personality disorder have enlarged ventricles and less temporal lobe gray matter (Dickey, McCarley, & Shenton, 2002).

Despite this strong overlap with schizophrenia, some people with schizotypal personality disorder have no family history of schizophrenia. Among this subgroup, early trauma and adversity are commonly reported (Raine, 2006).

Avoidant Personality Disorder

People with **avoidant personality disorder** are so fearful of criticism, rejection, and disapproval that they will avoid jobs or relationships to protect themselves from negative feedback. In social situations they are restrained because of an extreme fear of saying something foolish, being embarrassed, blushing, or showing other signs of anxiety. They believe they are incompetent and inferior to others and are reluctant to take risks or try new activities.

Avoidant personality disorder often co-occurs with social anxiety disorder (see p. 177), probably a result of the fact that the diagnostic criteria for these two disorders are so similar (Skodol et al., 1995). Some have argued that avoidant personality disorder might actually be a more chronic variant of social anxiety disorder (Alden, Laposa, Taylor, et al., 2002). Both avoidant personality disorder and social anxiety disorder are related to a syndrome called taijin kyofusho that occurs in Japan (*taijin* means "interpersonal" and *kyofusho* means "fear"). Like people with avoidant personality disorder and social anxiety disorder, those with taijin kyofusho are overly sensitive in interpersonal situations and avoid interpersonal contact. But what they fear is somewhat different from the usual fears of those with the DSM diagnoses. People with taijin kyofusho tend to be anxious or ashamed about how they affect or appear to others—for example, they fear that they are ugly or have body odor (Ono, Yoshimura, Sueoka, et al., 1996).

As with those with social anxiety disorders, several other types of disorders are often comorbid with avoidant personality disorder. About 80 percent of people with avoidant personality disorder have comorbid major depression, like Leon in the Clinical Case. Other common comorbid conditions include borderline personality disorder, schizotypal personality disorder, and alcohol abuse (McGlashan et al., 2000).

Little is known about why avoidant personality disorder develops, perhaps because many with these symptoms find it so uncomfortable to be interviewed for research. The heritability of this personality disorder appears to be about 27 to 35 percent (Reichborn-Kjennerud, Czajkowski, Neale, et al., 2007; Torgersen et al., 2000). The genetic vulnerability for avoidant personality disorder appears to overlap with the genetic vulnerability to social anxiety disorder (Reichborn-Kjennerud, Czajkowski, Torgersen, et al., 2007).

DSM-IV-TR Criteria for Avoidant Personality Disorder

A pervasive pattern of social inhibition, feelings of inadequacy, and hypersensitivity to criticism as shown by four or more of the following starting in early adulthood in many contexts:
- Avoidance of occupational activities that involve significant interpersonal contact, because of fears of criticism or disapproval
- Unwilling to get involved with people unless certain of being liked
- Restrained in intimate relationships because of the fear of being shamed or ridiculed
- Preoccupation with being criticized or rejected
- Inhibited in new interpersonal situations because of feelings of inadequacy
- Views self as socially inept or inferior
- Unusually reluctant to try new activities because they may prove embarrassing

Proposed DSM-5 Criteria for Avoidant Personality Disorder

Pathological **personality traits** in the following domains and facets:
1. **Detachment**, characterized by **withdrawal, intimacy avoidance,** and **anhedonia**
2. **Negative affectivity**, characterized by **anxiousness**

The person meets criteria for a personality disorder.

Note: Facets are printed in blue.

Clinical Case: Leon

Leon was a 45-year-old man who sought treatment for depression, which he claimed to have experienced almost continuously since the first grade. During the interview, Leon described feeling uncomfortable socially for as long as he could remember. By age 5, he would experience intense anxiety with other children, and his mind would "go blank" if he had to speak in front of others. He grew up dreading birthday parties, teachers' classroom questions, and meeting new children. Although he was able to play with some of the children in his neighborhood, he had never developed a "best friend," and he had never been able to go out on a date. Although he did well academically through high school, his grades worsened during college. He took a job at the post office after graduation because it involved little social interaction. [Adapted from Spitzer, Gibbon, Skodol, et al. (1994).]

Antisocial Personality Disorder and Psychopathy

Informally, the terms *antisocial personality disorder* and *psychopathy* (sometimes referred to as *sociopathy*) often are used interchangeably. Antisocial behavior, such as breaking laws, is an important component of both, but there are important differences between the two disorders. One difference is that antisocial personality disorder is included in the DSM, whereas psychopathy is not. In this section, we will review the definitions of these two highly related constructs and then discuss research on the etiology of these syndromes.

Antisocial Personality Disorder: Clinical Description

Antisocial personality disorder (APD) involves a pervasive pattern of disregard for the rights of others. The person with APD is distinguished by aggressive, impulsive, and callous traits. DSM-IV-TR criteria specify the presence of conduct disorder; although this is not a criterion in the proposed DSM-5, people with APD often report a history of such symptoms as truancy, running away from home, frequent lying, theft, arson, and deliberate destruction of property by early adolescence. People with APD show irresponsible behavior such as working inconsistently, breaking laws, being irritable and physically aggressive, defaulting on debts, being reckless and impulsive, and neglecting to plan ahead. They show little regard for truth and little remorse for their misdeeds.

People with avoidant personality disorder often avoid interpersonal interactions, as they find them to be so stressful. (© F1online digitale Bildagentur GmbH/Alamy.)

APD is observed much more frequently among men than women. Rates are also higher among younger than among older adults, and some people seem to mature out of the symptoms. In one study, people who had been hospitalized for APD were followed up 16 to 45 years later. About one-quarter of them no longer had APD, and another one-third had improved (Black, Baumgard, & Bell, 1995). About three-quarters of people with APD meet the diagnostic criteria for another disorder, with substance abuse being the most common comorbid disorder (Newman, Moffitt, Caspi, et al., 1998). Not surprisingly, then, high rates of APD are observed in drug and alcohol rehabilitation facilities (Sutker & Adams, 2001). About three-quarters of convicted felons meet diagnostic criteria for APD.

Psychopathy: Clinical Description

The concept of **psychopathy** predates the DSM diagnosis of antisocial personality disorder. In his classic book *The Mask of Sanity*, Hervey Cleckley (1976) drew on his clinical experience to formulate diagnostic criteria for psychopathy. Cleckley's criteria for psychopathy focus on the person's thoughts and feelings. In Cleckley's

Clinical Case

A 19-year-old man with irregular breathing, a rapid pulse, and dilated pupils was brought to the hospital by a friend, who eventually admitted that they had been using a lot of cocaine before the symptoms began. The men didn't want to identify themselves, but eventually the medical team was able to get enough information to contact the patient's mother, who arrived at the hospital distraught and smelling of alcohol. When interviewed, she reported that her son had a long history of disobedience and disengagement from family activities. When she attempted to set rules, he became violently argumentative; he often stayed out all night. She said that the father was not present to help with parenting. She believed that her son was a good student and a star basketball player, but both of these beliefs turned out to be false. Later research revealed, though, that her son was deeply involved in drugs and in drag racing, and he bragged that he typically consumed a case of beer per day. He used various schemes to get money for drugs, including stealing car radios and taking money from his mother. He denied that he had any problems and ended his first interview with a therapist early. [Adapted from Spitzer et al. (1994).]

> ### DSM-IV-TR Criteria for Antisocial Personality Disorder
>
> - Age at least 18
> - Evidence of conduct disorder before age 15
> - Pervasive pattern of disregard for the rights of others since the age of 15 as shown by at least three of the following:
>   1. Repeated lawbreaking
>   2. Deceitfulness, lying
>   3. Impulsivity
>   4. Irritability and aggressiveness
>   5. Reckless disregard for own safety and that of others
>   6. Irresponsibility as seen in unreliable employment or financial history
>   7. Lack of remorse
>
> ### Proposed DSM-5 Criteria for Antisocial Personality Disorder
>
> Pathological **personality traits** in the following domains and facets:
>   1. **Antagonism**, characterized by **manipulativeness, deceitfulness, callousness, hostility**
>   2. **Disinhibition**, characterized by **irresponsibility, impulsivity,** and **risk taking**
>
> The person meets criteria for a personality disorder.
>
> *Note:* Facets are printed in blue.

description, one of the key characteristics of psychopathy is poverty of emotions, both positive and negative: Psychopathic people have no sense of shame, and their seemingly positive feelings for others are merely an act. They are superficially charming and use that charm to manipulate others for personal gain. Their lack of anxiety might make it impossible for them to learn from their mistakes, and their lack of remorse leads them to behave irresponsibly and often cruelly toward others. Another key point in Cleckley's description is that the antisocial behavior of a person with psychopathy is performed impulsively, as much for thrills as for a reason such as financial gain.

The most commonly used scale to assess psychopathy is the Psychopathy Checklist–Revised (Hare, 2003). Raters using this scale conduct an extensive interview but also gather information from other sources, such as criminal records and social worker reports. Some of the 20 items overlap with the criteria for APD, including juvenile delinquency, criminality, impulsivity, irresponsibility, superficial charm, pathological lying, and manipulativeness. The scale also includes affective symptoms such as lack of remorse, shallow affect, and lack of empathy (Hare & Neumann, 2006).

The DSM-IV-TR criteria differ from psychopathy criteria in important ways, including the requirement that a person develop symptoms before age 15. This has led to a considerable divergence between the two syndromes; only 20 percent of people diagnosed with DSM-IV-TR APD obtained high scores on the Psychopathy Checklist (Rutherford, Cacciola, & Alterman, 1999). The proposed DSM-5 guidelines for diagnosing APD are more parallel with the criteria for psychopathy. That is, the DSM-5 guidelines do not specify an age of onset. The changes in DSM-5 should enhance the concordance of APD and psychopathy diagnoses.

Etiology of Antisocial Personality Disorder and Psychopathy In this section, we consider the etiology of APD and psychopathy. As we review the research in this area, keep in mind two issues that make findings a little hard to integrate. First, research has been conducted on persons diagnosed in different ways—some with DSM-IV-TR APD and some with psychopathy. Second, most research on APD and psychopathy has been conducted on persons who have been convicted as criminals. Thus, the results of this research might not be applicable to psychopaths who are not criminals or who avoid arrest. Indeed, on cognitive and psychophysiological measures, psychopaths who have been convicted show more deficits than those who have not been caught (Ishikawa, Raine, Lencz, et al., 2001).

We describe a series of theories of etiology. We begin by reviewing genetic evidence and then discuss evidence that the family environment and poverty influence the risk of developing these symptoms. We then discuss psychological models, but in doing so, we deviate from our organizational approach in other sections of the book, where we tend to separate neurobiological and psychological models. Here we consider psychological and neurobiological evidence together, because brain imaging is an increasingly common way of testing psychological models of antisocial personality disorder and psychopathy.

Three-quarters of convicted felons meet the DSM-IV-TR criteria for antisocial personality disorder. (Chris Steele-Perkins/Magnum Photos. Inc.)

Genetic Factors Adoption studies reveal a higher-than-normal prevalence of antisocial behavior in adopted children of biological parents with APD and substance abuse (Cadoret, Yates, Troughton, et al., 1995; Ge, Conger, Cadoret, et al., 1996). Older studies suggested that criminality (Gottesman & Goldsmith, 1994), psychopathy (Taylor, Loney, Bobadilla, et al., 2003), and APD (Eley, Lichtenstein, & Moffitt, 2003) are moderately heritable, with heritability estimates of 40 to 50 percent. Across studies, heritability appears to be higher when aggressive forms of antisocial behavior are studied (65 percent) as compared to forms that involve only rule breaking (48 percent) (Burt & Donnellan, 2009).

Remember, though, that poor reliability will limit validity and that test–retest and multiple informant reliability estimates for personality disorders can be low. Some studies have addressed this by gathering repeated measures of symptoms (Burt, 2009), by gathering multiple indices of psychopathy (Larsson, Andershed, & Lichtenstein, 2006), or by gathering reports of antisocial symptoms from teachers, parents, and children (Baker, Jacobson, Raine, et al., 2007). By combining multiple measures, one can obtain an index of psychopathy or antisocial behavior that is much more reliable. Each study using this type of approach has found higher heritability estimates.

Genetic risk for APD, psychopathy, conduct disorder, and substance abuse appear to be related. A person might inherit a general vulnerability for these types of symptoms, and then environmental factors might shape which of the symptoms evolve (Kendler, Prescott, Myers, et al., 2003; Larsson, Tuvblad, Rijsdijk, et al., 2007). Some genetic risk, however, is very specific—for example, some genes might influence aggressive behavior within APD (Eley et al., 2003).

Adoption research has also shown that genetic, behavioral, and family influences are very hard to disentangle (Ge et al., 1996). That is, the genetically influenced antisocial behavior of the child can provoke harsh discipline and lack of warmth, even in adoptive parents, and these parental characteristics in turn exacerbate the child's antisocial tendencies.

Social Factors: Family Environment and Poverty Since much psychopathic behavior violates social norms, many investigators focus on the primary agent of socialization, the family, in their search for the explanation of such behavior. High negativity, low warmth, and parental inconsistency predict antisocial behavior (Marshall & Cooke, 1999; Reiss, Heatherington, Plomin, et al., 1995). The family environment might be particularly important when a child has an inherited tendency toward antisocial behavior. For example, in the adoption study referred to above (Cadoret et al., 1995), an adverse environment in the adoptive home (such as marital problems and substance abuse) was related to the development of APD, particularly when the biological parents had APD.

Outside of twin studies, there is substantial prospective research to show that social factors, including poverty and exposure to violence, predict antisocial behavior in children (Loeber & Hay, 1997), even when children are not genetically at risk for APD (Jaffee, Moffitt, Caspi, et al., 2002). Among adolescents with conduct disorder, those who are impoverished are twice as likely to develop APD as are those from higher socioeconomic status backgrounds (Lahey, Loeber, Burke, et al., 2005).

Fearlessness There is a large body of work relating psychopathy to deficits in the experience of fear and threat. In defining the psychopathic syndrome, Cleckley noted the inability of people with psychopathy to profit from experience or even from punishment; they seem to be unable to avoid the negative consequences of social misbehavior. Many are chronic lawbreakers despite their experiences with jail sentences. They seem immune to the anxiety or pangs of conscience that keep most of us from breaking the law, lying, or injuring others, and they have difficulty curbing their impulses. Cleckley argued that psychopaths might not learn to avoid certain behaviors because they are unresponsive to punishments for their antisocial behavior. The behavioral model draws from this idea to suggest that the rule-breaking behavior of psychopaths stems from deficits in developing conditioned fear responses.

A classic study tested the idea that people with psychopathy fail to learn from punishment because they are fearless (Lykken, 1957). Lykken assessed how well people with psychopathy learned to avoid shock. Consistent with theory, people with psychopathy were poorer than controls at learning to avoid shock.

Studies of the activity of the autonomic nervous system have also supported the idea that psychopaths are less responsive to fear-eliciting stimuli than are other people. At rest, people with psychopathy have lower-than-normal levels of skin conductance, and their skin conductance is less reactive when they are confronted with or anticipate an aversive stimulus (Lorber, 2004). In one study, low skin conductance reactivity to aversive stimuli (loud tones) at age 3 was found to predict psychopathy scores at age 28 (Glenn, Raine, Venables, et al., 2007). In an interesting extension of this theory, researchers used brain activity as a way to examine what happens with classical conditioning in which an unconditioned stimulus (painful pressure) was repeatedly paired with neutral pictures (the conditioned stimuli). To measure responses to the conditioned stimulus after these repeated pairings, the researchers measured activity of the amgydala and other brain regions involved in emotion (Birbaumer, Veit, Lotze, et al., 2005). After conditioning, healthy control participants showed increases in amygdala activity when viewing the neutral pictures. People with psychopathy, though, did not show this expected increase in amygdala activity. These findings suggest that the people with psychopathy fail to show classical conditioning to aversive stimuli at a very basic level.

Impulsivity Above we have been focused on how people with psychopathy respond to threats. One related theory, though, considers impulsivity, which has been defined as a lack of response to threats when pursuing potential rewards. The idea is that the lack of response to threat might be particularly severe when a person with psychopathy is trying to gain a reward, such as money or other resources.

People with psychopathy do show impulsivity when presented with a task designed to test the ability to modify responses depending on success or failure (Patterson & Newman, 1993). In one study demonstrating this phenomenon, participants played a computerized card game (Newman, Patterson, & Kosson, 1987). If a face card appeared, the participant won 5¢; if a nonface card appeared, the participant lost 5¢. After each trial, the participant had the opportunity to continue or stop the game. The probability of losing was controlled by the experimenter and started at 10 percent. Thereafter, the probability of losing increased by 10 percent for every 10 cards played until it reached 100 percent. People with psychopathy continued to play the game much longer than did people without psychopathy. Nine of twelve people in the psychopathy group never quit, even though they had lost money on 19 of the last 20 trials. That is, the psychopaths did not quit pursuing reward even though they were being punished.

A card-guessing task that manipulates the odds of winning and losing was used to demonstrate impulsivity among psychopaths (Newman, Patterson, & Kosson, 1987). (Courtesy Joseph Newman.)

In an interesting extension of this research, researchers then showed that people with high levels of psychopathy can respond appropriately to threat if they pause to attend to negative feedback. The same game was played again with one variation—a 5-second waiting period was imposed after feedback, thus delaying the decision about whether to play again. This dramatically reduced the number of trials played by people with psychopathy. It seems that enforcing a delay might lead people with psychopathy to reflect on negative feedback and behave less impulsively (Newman, Schmitt, & Voss, 1997).

On the whole, these findings suggest that people with psychopathy may be unresponsive to threats when they are pursuing rewards. Part of this deficit might be overcome by slowing the person down so that he or she attend to the signals of threat.

Neurobiological research also supports the idea that psychopathy is related to impulsivity. Remember that the prefrontal cortex is involved in inhibiting impulsivity. People with psychopathy have less gray matter in the prefrontal cortex than do people without psychopathy (Raine & Yang, 2007).

Deficits in Empathy Driving Unresponsiveness to Others' Victimization The research we have described so far has been based on the idea that punishment does not arouse strong emotions in people with psychopathy and thus does not inhibit antisocial behavior. But some researchers believe that empathy, not punishment, is the critical agent of socialization. Empathy means being in tune with the emotional reactions of others; thus, empathizing with someone's distress could inhibit the tendency toward callous exploitation. From this perspective, one could argue that some features of psychopathy arise from a lack of empathy.

Several types of research provide support for this theory. When asked to identify the emotion conveyed in pictures of various strangers, men with psychopathy do very poorly in recognizing others' fear, even though they recognize other emotions well (Marsh & Blair, 2008). To test whether lack of empathy creates an insensitivity to watching someone be victimized, researchers have shown pictures of victimization events (e.g., a break-in, a physical attack) to persons with psychopathy and to control participants. People with psychopathy show less of a psychophysiological response to pictures of victimization than do those without psychopathy (Levenston, Patrick, Bradley, et al., 2000). Parallel findings have emerged from a brain-imaging study. Whereas participants without psychopathy showed activation of the ventromedial prefrontal cortex when they viewed a moral violation, those with psychopathy failed to show this response (Harenski, Harenski, Shane, et al., 2010).

Check Your Knowledge 15.2

You are the director of human resources for a large corporation. You are asked to review a set of situations in which employees had interpersonal and task-focused problems that were severe and persistent enough to raise concerns in the workplace. Name the most likely personality disorder for each of the following.

1. Mariana refuses to meet with customers. She states that she is terrified that they will see that she does not know much. It turns out that she has called in sick the last three times her boss scheduled an appointment with her, and her colleagues barely know her name. When asked, she says that meeting with any of these people makes her feel horribly nervous about potential rejection of her ideas. She asks for a position that would involve little social contact.

2. Sheila has had three subordinate employees request transfers from her department. They each stated that she was too controlling, picked on small mistakes, and would not listen to any new ideas for solving problems. At the interview, she brought in a typed, 15-page chart of the goals she would like to execute for the company. Despite having an inordinate number of goals, she has failed to complete a single project during her first year with the company.

3. Police contact you to let you know that they have arrested Sam, one of your employees. He was caught at a bank trying to cash a $10,000 company check on which he had forged the signature. You learn that Sam had previously defrauded three other companies. When you meet with Sam, he laughs about how easy it was to get access to the checkbook, and he does not seem the least bit sorry.

Borderline Personality Disorder

Borderline personality disorder (BPD) has been a major focus of interest for several reasons. Among these reasons, BPD is very common in clinical settings, very hard to treat, and associated with suicidality.

Clinical Description of Borderline Personality Disorder

The core features of **borderline personality disorder** are impulsivity and instability in relationships and mood. For example, attitudes and feelings toward other people might change drastically, inexplicably, and very quickly, particularly from passionate idealization to contemptuous anger. In an experience sampling study, BPD was characterized by more abrupt, large, and unexpected changes in negative moods than was major depressive disorder (Trull, Solhan, Tragesser, et al., 2008). As in the Clinical Case of Justine, which opened this chapter, the intense anger of people with BPD often damages relationships. People with BPD are overly sensitive to small signs of emotions in others (Lynch, Rosenthal, Kosson, et al., 2006). Their unpredictable, impulsive, and potentially self-damaging behavior might include gambling, reckless spending, indiscriminate sexual activity, and substance abuse. People with BPD often have not developed a clear and coherent sense of self—they sometimes experience major swings in such basic aspects of identity as their values, loyalties, and career choices. They cannot bear to be alone, have fears of abandonment, demand attention, and experience chronic feelings of depression and emptiness. They may experience transient psychotic and dissociative symptoms when stressed.

Suicidal behavior is a particular concern in BPD. One study found that over a 20-year period, approximately 7.5 percent of people with BPD committed suicide (Linehan & Heard, 1999). In a study of 621 people with BPD, 15.5 percent were found to have engaged in at least one suicidal behavior within the previous year (Yen, Shea, Pagano, et al., 2003). People with BPD are also particularly likely to engage in non-suicidal self-injury (see Focus on Discovery 5.6). For example, they might slice their legs with a razor blade or burn their arms with cigarettes—behaviors that are harmful but unlikely to cause death. At least two-thirds of people with BPD will engage in self-mutilation at some point during their lives (Stone, 1993).

● DSM-IV-TR Criteria for Borderline Personality Disorder

Presence of five or more of the following in many contexts beginning in early adulthood:
- Frantic efforts to avoid abandonment
- Unstable interpersonal relationships in which others are either idealized or devalued
- Unstable sense of self
- Self-damaging, impulsive behaviors in at least two areas, such as spending, sex, substance abuse, reckless driving, binge eating
- Recurrent suicidal behavior, gestures, or self-injurious behavior (e.g., cutting self)
- Chronic feelings of emptiness
- Recurrent bouts of intense or poorly controlled anger
- During stress, a tendency to experience transient paranoid thoughts and dissociative symptoms

● Proposed DSM-5 Criteria for Borderline Personality Disorder

Pathological **personality traits** in the following domains and facets:
1. **Negative affectivity,** characterized by **emotional lability, anxiousness, separation insecurity,** and **depressivity**
2. **Disinhibition,** characterized by **impulsivity** and **risk taking**
3. **Antagonism,** characterized by **hostility**

The person meets criteria for a personality disorder.

Note: Facets are printed in blue.

Over a 10- or 15-year period, about three-quarters of people with BPD stabilize and so no longer meet diagnostic criteria (Zanarini, Frankenburg, Hennen, et al., 2006). Most people no longer meet the diagnostic criteria by age 40 (Paris, 2002). Symptoms of self-harm and suicidality diminish more quickly than do other symptoms, such as tendencies toward anger and impulsivity (Zanarini et al., 2006).

People with BPD are highly likely to have comorbid posttraumatic stress disorder or mood disorders (McGlashan et al., 2000). They are also at risk for comorbid substance-related disorders and eating disorders, as well as for schizotypal personality disorder (McGlashan et al., 2000). When present, comorbid conditions predict greater likelihood that BPD symptoms will be sustained over a 6-year period (Zanarini, Frankenburg, Hennen, et al., 2004).

A colorful account by Jonathan Kellerman, a clinical psychologist and successful mystery writer, gives a good sense of what people with BPD are like.

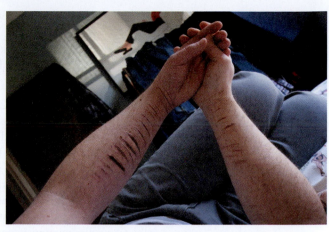

People with borderline personality disorder often engage in self-injurious behavior. (© Janine Wiedel Photolibrary/Alamy.)

> *They're the chronically depressed, the determinedly addictive, the compulsively divorced, living from one emotional disaster to the next. Bed hoppers, stomach pumpers, freeway jumpers, and sad-eyed bench-sitters with arms stitched up like footballs and psychic wounds that can never be sutured. Their egos are as fragile as spun sugar, their psyches irretrievably fragmented, like a jigsaw puzzle with crucial pieces missing. They play roles with alacrity, excel at being anyone but themselves, crave intimacy but repel it when they find it. Some of them gravitate toward stage or screen; others do their acting in more subtle ways. . . . Borderlines go from therapist to therapist, hoping to find a magic bullet for the crushing feelings of emptiness. They turn to chemical bullets, gobble tranquilizers and antidepressants, alcohol and cocaine. (Kellerman, 1989, pp. 113–114)*

Fortunately, research on new treatments for BPD, discussed later in the chapter, supports a more positive outlook than Kellerman offers.

Etiology of Borderline Personality Disorder   BPD is a complex syndrome, and accordingly, many different risk factors may contribute to its development. We discuss neurobiological factors, social factors, and Linehan's diathesis–stress theory, which integrates neurobiological and social factors.

Neurobiological Factors   Biological factors seem to be quite important to the development of BPD. Genes account for more than 60 percent of the variance in the development of this disorder. People with BPD also demonstrate lower serotonin function than do controls (Soloff, Meltzer, Greer, el al., 2000). Other vulnerabilities may contribute to the components of emotion dysregulation or impulsivity, rather than to the disorder as a whole (Siever, 2000).

Several studies suggest that biological factors may contribute to the emotional dysregulation. Parents of people with BPD have elevated rates of mood disorders (Shachnow, Clarkin, DiPalma, et al., 1997). More direct evidence comes from studies of the amygdala in BPD. The amygdala is a brain region that is strongly implicated in emotion reactivity (see Figure 6.3) and activity of the amygdala has been found to be heightened in several disorders that involve intense emotionality, including mood disorders and anxiety disorders. People with BPD show increased activation of the amygdala (Herpetz, Dietrich, Wenning, et al., 2001; Silbersweig, Clarkin, Goldstein, et al., 2007). Amygdala activation seems relevant for understanding the emotion dysregulation of BPD.

There is some indication that genetic and neurobiological vulnerability may contribute to the impulsive features of BPD as well. First degree relatives of patients with BPD have high rates of disorders related to impulsivity, such as substance abuse and antisocial personality disorder (White, Gunderson, Zanarini, et al., 2003). Regarding neurobiology, the prefrontal cortex is thought to help control impulsiveness, and in some studies, people with BPD show low levels of activity and structural changes in the prefrontal cortex (van Elst, 2003; van Elst, Thiel, Hesslinger, et al., 2001) and, more specifically, in the anterior cingulate cortex (Minzenberg, Fan, New, et al., 2007, 2008). Connectivity between the prefrontal cortex and the amygdala also seems to be disrupted (New, Hazlett, Buchsbaum, et al., 2007). Taken together, findings suggest that neurobiological factors may contribute to the impulsive features of BPD.

Social Factors: Childhood Abuse   People with BPD are much more likely to report a history of parental separation, verbal abuse, and emotional abuse during childhood than are people diagnosed with other personality disorders (Reich & Zanarini, 2001). Indeed, such abuse is believed to be more frequent among people with BPD than among people diagnosed with most other disorders (Herman, Perry, & van der Kolk, 1989), with the exception of dissociative identity disorder (see Chapter 8), which is also characterized by very high rates of childhood abuse. Given the frequency of dissociative symptoms in people with BPD, we can speculate that BPD and dissociative identity disorder might be related and that, in both, dissociation is caused by the extreme stress of child abuse. Indeed, one study found that people who dissociated after child abuse were more likely to develop symptoms of BPD (Ross, Waller, Tyson, et al., 1998). One major psychological model builds on these high rates of reported abuse to explain how a person might come to develop the symptoms of BPD. We review this theory next.

Linehan's Diathesis–Stress Theory   Marsha Linehan proposes that BPD develops when people who have difficulty controlling their emotions because of a biological diathesis (possibly genetic) are raised in a family environment that is invalidating. That is, a diathesis of emotional dysregulation interacts with experiences of invalidation to promote the development of BPD. In an invalidation environment, the person's feelings are discounted and disrespected—that is, the person's efforts to communicate feelings are disregarded or even punished. An extreme form of invalidation is child abuse, either sexual or nonsexual, where the abusive parent claims to love the child and yet hurts the child.

The two main hypothesized factors—emotional dysregulation and invalidation—interact with each other in a dynamic fashion (see Figure 15.3). For example, the emotionally dysregulated child makes enormous demands on his or her family. The exasperated parents ignore or even punish the child's outbursts, which leads the child to suppress his or her emotions. The suppressed emotions build up to an explosion, which then gets the attention of the parents. Thus, the parents end up reinforcing the very behaviors that they find aversive. Many other patterns are possible, of course, but what they have in common is a vicious circle, a constant back-and-forth between dysregulation and invalidation.

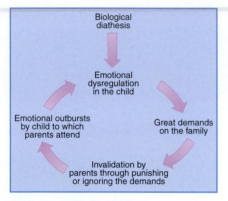

Figure 15.3 Marsha Linehan's diathesis–stress theory of borderline personality disorder.

Quick Summary

People with obsessive-compulsive personality disorder are meticulous perfectionists who desire order and control to an excessive degree. Although the personality disorder can be distinguished from obsessive-compulsive disorder in that obsessions and compulsions are not present, the two conditions tend to co-occur. Obsessive-compulsive personality disorder is modestly heritable, and there is some research suggesting that the genetic vulnerability may be related to obsessive-compulsive disorder.

People with narcissistic personality disorder overtly demonstrate a highly inflated self-esteem but also harbor a deep need for admiration. According to the self-psychology theory of narcissistic personality disorder, parents who are inconsistent and focused on their own worth fail to help the child develop a stable sense of

self-worth. Social-cognitive theory proposes that the behavior of the person with narcissistic personality disorder is shaped by the goal of maintaining specialness and the belief that the purpose of interpersonal interactions is to bolster self-esteem.

People with schizotypal personality disorder are eccentric in their thoughts and behavior. Genetic and neurobiological studies indicate that schizotypal personality disorder and schizophrenia are related.

People with avoidant personality disorder are extremely uncomfortable in social situations because of fears that they will be perceived negatively. They struggle with feeling inadequate and, as a consequence, will avoid many interpersonal situations. The disorder often co-occurs with social anxiety disorder, and some have even argued that it is a more severe variant of social anxiety disorder.

Antisocial personality disorder is defined by violation of rules and a disregard for others' feelings and social norms. Psychopathy is related to antisocial personality disorder but is not defined in the DSM. Psychopathy criteria focus on internal experiences. The proposed DSM-5 definition of antisocial personality disorder is more aligned with psychopathy criteria than the DSM-IV-TR definition is.

When carefully measured, antisocial personality disorder and psychopathy are both highly heritable. Beyond genes, family environment and poverty seem to play a role in the development of this disorder.

People with psychopathy are relatively fearless, which may contribute to a failure to learn from punishment. The diminished response to punishment seems particularly pronounced when they are pursuing reward, and so this can be seen as a form of impulsivity. Their callous treatment of others might also be linked to their lack of empathy. Biological research supports fearlessness (lack of response to punishment), impulsivity, and lack of empathy.

The key features of borderline personality disorder include intense emotionality, unstable identity, and impulsivity. There is evidence that BPD is inherited and that serotonin function is diminished. Other biological risk factors seem particularly related to emotional dysregulation and impulsivity. Consistent with the greater emotionality, people with BPD have also been found to demonstrate increased activity in the amygdala and to have high rates of mood disorders among first-degree relatives. Consistent with the symptoms of impulsivity, research indicates diminished activity in the prefrontal cortex among people with BPD and high rates of disorders involving impulsivity among first-degree relatives.

People with BPD report elevated rates of abuse. Linehan's model builds on the high rates of abuse and parental invalidation reported by people with BPD and also emphasizes the biological diathesis for emotional dysregulation.

Check Your Knowledge 15.3

Answer the questions.

1. Which personality disorder type is most related to schizophrenia in family history studies?
   a. schizoid
   b. schizotypal
   c. antisocial
   d. borderline

2. Which of the following factors play a central role in Linehan's model of BPD (choose all that apply)?
   a. emotional dysregulation
   b. parental invalidation
   c. conflicts between introjected values and current needs
   d. splitting as a defense mechanism

3. Which of these personality disorders is most common in clinical settings?
   a. obsessive-compulsive
   b. schizotypal
   c. antisocial
   d. borderline

4. Which personality disorder types have been related to impulsivity (choose all that apply)?
   a. schizotypal
   b. avoidant
   c. obsessive-compulsive
   d. antisocial
   e. borderline

Treatment of Personality Disorders

It is important to bear in mind that many people with personality disorders enter treatment for a condition other than their personality disorder. For example, a person with antisocial personality disorder might seek treatment of substance abuse; a person with avoidant personality disorder might seek treatment for social phobia; a patient with obsessive-compulsive personality disorder might seek help for depression. Clinicians are encouraged to consider whether personality disorders are present because personality disorders predict slower improvement in psychotherapy (Crits-Christoph & Barber, 2002; Hollon & DeRubeis, 2003). Here we consider treatments to address the symptoms of personality disorders. We begin by describing approaches that are relevant across the various personality disorder types and then discuss treatments designed for specific personality disorders.

General Approaches to the Treatment of Personality Disorders

A review of 15 studies suggested that 52 percent of clients recover from personality disorders within about 15 months of treatment (Perry, Banon, & Ianni, 1999). Most of these studies of the effectiveness of either day treatment or psychotherapy, though, do not include a control group but rather compare clients to those receiving standard care. This is of concern—remember that half of personality disorders seem to dissipate over time naturally (see Figure 15.1). Given this, psychotherapy studies comparing active treatment to a control treatment are needed.

People with serious symptoms of personality disorders might attend a day treatment program that offers psychotherapy, in both group and individual formats, for several hours per day. Typically, psychotherapy sessions are interspersed with social and occupational therapy. The length of such programs varies, but some last several months. Programs tend to vary in their treatment approaches, with some offering psychodynamic approaches, others offering supportive approaches, and still others offering cognitive behavioral treatments. Beyond day treatment programs, many clients are seen in individual outpatient psychological treatment.

Psychodynamic therapists aim to alter the patient's present-day views of the childhood problems assumed to underlie the personality disorder. For example, they might guide a man with obsessive-compulsive personality disorder to the realization that his childhood quest to win his parents' love by being perfect does not need be carried into adulthood—that he does not need to be perfect to win the approval of others and that it is possible to make mistakes without being abandoned by those whose love he seeks. Studies of psychodynamic treatment often include a broad range of different personality disorders.

In cognitive therapy for personality disorders, Aaron Beck and colleagues (1990) apply the same kind of analysis used in the treatment of depression (see p. 157). Each disorder is analyzed in terms of negative cognitive beliefs that could help explain the pattern of symptoms (see Table 15.5). For example, cognitive therapy for a perfectionistic person with obsessive-compulsive personality disorder entails first persuading the patient to accept the essence of the cognitive model—that feelings and behaviors are primarily a function of thoughts. Biases in thinking are then explored, such as when the patient concludes that he or she cannot do anything right because of a small failure in one particular endeavor. The therapist also looks for dysfunctional assumptions or schemas that might underlie the person's thoughts and feelings—for example, the belief that it is critical for every decision to be correct. Beyond challenging cognitions, Beck's approach to personality disorders incorporates a variety of other cognitive behavioral techniques.

The traits that characterize the personality disorders are probably too ingrained to change thoroughly. Instead, the therapist—regardless of theoretical orientation—might find it more realistic to change a disorder into a style or a more adaptive way of approaching life (Millon, 1996).

In the next sections, we will describe specific treatment options for the DSM-5 personality disorder types. Because there are no randomized controlled trials for obsessive-compulsive personality disorder or for narcissistic personality disorder, we focus on the other personality disorders here. Because relatively little is known, we review treatment of schizotypal personality disorder, avoidant personality disorder, and psychopathy only briefly before focusing on the larger literature on the treatment of borderline personality disorder.

Table 15.5 Examples of Maladaptive Cognitions Hypothesized to Be Associated with Each Personality Disorder

Personality Disorder	Maladaptive Cognitions
Avoidant	If people know the real me, they will reject me.
Obsessive-compulsive	I know what's best.
	People should do better and try harder.
Narcissistic	Since I am special, I deserve special rules.
	I am better than others.
Antisocial	I am entitled to break rules.
	Others are exploitative.

Source: Beck & Freeman (1990).

Treatment of Schizotypal Personality Disorder, Avoidant Personality Disorder, and Psychopathy

Treatments for schizotypal personality disorder draw on the connections of this disorder with schizophrenia. More specifically, antipsychotic drugs (e.g., risperidone, trade name Risperdal) have shown effectiveness with schizotypal personality disorder (Raine, 2006). These medications seem particularly helpful for reducing the unusual thinking. Antidepressants can also be helpful with some of the symptoms of schizotypal personality disorder. Little research is available on psychological approaches to the treatment of schizotypal personality disorder.

Avoidant personality disorder appears to respond to the same treatments that are effective for those with social anxiety disorder. That is, antidepressant medications as well as cognitive behavioral treatment can be helpful (Reich, 2000). A person diagnosed as having an avoidant personality disorder is extremely sensitive to criticism. This sensitivity might be treated by social skills training in how to address criticism, by systematic desensitization, or by cognitive therapy (Renneberg, Goldstein, Phillips, et al., 1990). Group versions of cognitive behavioral treatment have been found to be helpful and may offer chances to practice constructive social interactions in a safe environment (Alden, 1989). Avoidant personality disorder may require more intensive and long-lasting treatment than does social anxiety disorder.

Despite early pessimistic views on whether psychopathy could be treated (e.g., Cleckley, 1976), a comprehensive meta-analysis of 42 studies of the psychological treatment of psychopathy suggests that treatment can be helpful (Salekin, 2002). These studies had many methodological problems, but 17 of them, involving 88 people with psychopathy, found that psychoanalytic psychotherapy was very helpful in domains such as improving interpersonal relationships, increasing the capacity for feeling remorse and empathy, reducing the amount of lying, being released from probation, and holding down a job. Similar positive therapeutic effects were found in five studies employing cognitive behavioral techniques with 246 people with psychopathy. Therapy was more beneficial for younger clients. To be at all effective, treatment had to be quite intensive: four times a week for at least a year—a very heavy dose of psychosocial treatment whatever one's theoretical orientation. These are remarkably positive findings given the widely held belief that psychopathy is basically untreatable. The author of the meta-analysis, though, cautions at the end of his article that ". . . research needs to make some attempt to determine whether clients are 'faking good' in treatment studies or whether the changes are genuine" (Salekin, 2002 p. 107).

Treatment of Borderline Personality Disorder

Few clients pose a greater challenge to treatment than do those with borderline personality disorder (BPD), regardless of the type of treatment being used. Clients with BPD tend to show their interpersonal problems in the therapeutic relationship as much as they do in other relationships. Because these clients find it inordinately difficult to trust others, therapists find it challenging to develop and maintain the therapeutic relationship. Patients alternately idealize and vilify the therapist, demanding special attention and consideration one moment—such as therapy sessions at odd hours and countless phone calls during periods of particular crisis—and refusing to keep appointments the next; they beg the therapist for understanding and support but insist that certain topics are off-limits.

Suicide is always a serious risk, but it is often difficult for the therapist to judge whether a frantic phone call at 2:00 A.M. is a call for help or a manipulative gesture designed to test how special the patient is to the therapist and to what lengths the therapist will go to meet the patient's needs at the moment. As in the case of Justine (see the Clinical Case at the beginning of this chapter), hospitalization is often necessary to protect against the threat of suicide. Seeing such clients is so stressful that it is common for therapists to regularly consult with another therapist for advice and for support in dealing with their own emotions as they cope with the extraordinary challenges of helping these clients.

Antidepressants and mood stabilizers have been tried as ways of quelling the mood symptoms and the impulsivity of BPD. There is some evidence that antidepressants can decrease the aggressiveness and depression often found in these clients (Rinne, van den Brink, Wouters, et al., 2002) and that the mood stabilizer lithium can reduce some of the irritability, anger, and suicidality (Links, Steiner, Boiago, et al., 1990). Despite some positive findings for each medication approach, most medications have been tested in only one study; much more research is needed (Toffers, Völlm, Rücker, et al., 2010).

Dialectical Behavior Therapy of Borderline Personality Disorder Marsha Linehan (1987) introduced an approach that she called **dialectical behavior therapy** (DBT), combining client-centered empathy and acceptance with cognitive behavioral problem solving, emotion-regulation techniques, and social skills training. The concept of dialectics comes from the work of German philosopher Georg Wilhelm Friedrich Hegel (1770–1831). It refers to a constant tension between any phenomenon (any idea, event, etc., called the *thesis*) and its opposite (the *antithesis),* which is resolved by the creation of a new phenomenon (the *synthesis).* In DBT, the term *dialectical* is used in two main ways:

- In one sense, it refers to the seemingly opposite strategies that the therapist must use when treating people with BPD—accepting them as they are and yet helping them change. (For a closer look at the dialectic between acceptance and change, see Focus on Discovery 15.3.)

- In the other sense, it refers to the patient's realization that splitting the world into good and bad is not necessary; instead, one can achieve a synthesis of these apparent opposites. For example, instead of seeing a friend as either all bad (thesis) or all good (antithesis), the friend can be seen as having both kinds of qualities (synthesis).

Hence, the therapist and the client in DBT are both encouraged to adopt a dialectical view of the world.

FOCUS ON DISCOVERY 15.3

Drawing from Personal Experience to Promote Acceptance and Change

As described earlier, Marsha Linehan has developed one of the leading theories of why BPD occurs, and the treatment she pioneered, dialectical behavior therapy, is one of the best-validated approaches for this condition. In a brave move, Linehan recently decided to speak publically about her own experiences of BPD (Carey, 2011). Hospitalized at age 17 for her severe suicidality, she found ways to injure herself even when the staff confined her to a seclusion chamber—left alone with no objects, she banged her head against the wall and floor. She remained hospitalized for 26 months. Failed treatments continued for several years, until she found a way out of the struggles on her own—through radical acceptance. She earned a Ph.D. in clinical psychology, and she drew on her own personal experiences to help others, in the process becoming one of the most productive researchers in the field of clinical psychology.

Linehan (1987) argues that a therapist treating clients with BPD has to adopt a posture that might seem inconsistent to the Western mind. The therapist must work for change while at the same time accepting the real possibility that no changes are going to occur. Linehan's notions of acceptance are drawn from Zen philosophy and from Rogerian approaches to psychotherapy.

Linehan's reasoning is that people with BPD are so sensitive to rejection and criticism that even gentle encouragement to behave or think differently can be misinterpreted as a serious rebuke, leading to extreme emotional reactions. When this happens, the therapist, who may have been revered a moment earlier, is suddenly vilified. Thus, while observing limits—"I would be

Marsha Linehan created dialectical behavior therapy, which combines cognitive behavioral therapy with acceptance. (Courtesy of Marsha M. Linehan.)

very sad if you killed yourself, so I hope very much that you won't"—the therapist must convey to the patient that he or she is fully accepted. This is hard to do if the patient is threatening suicide, showing uncontrolled anger, or railing against imagined rebukes from the therapist.

Completely accepting the patient does not mean approving of everything the patient does; rather, it means that the therapist must accept the situation for what it is. And this acceptance, argues Linehan, must be real: the therapist must truly accept clients as they are; acceptance should not be in the service of change, an indirect way of encouraging clients to behave differently. "Acceptance can transform but if you accept in order to transform, it is not acceptance. It is like loving. Love seeks no reward but when given freely comes back a hundredfold. He who loses his life finds it. He who accepts, changes" (Linehan, personal communication, November 16, 1992). Full acceptance does not, in Linehan's view, preclude change. Indeed, she proposes the opposite—that it is the refusal to accept that precludes change.

Linehan's approach also emphasizes that clients, too, must accept who they are and what they have been through. Clients are asked to accept that their childhood is now unchangeable, that their behaviors might have caused relationships to end, and that they feel emotions more intensely than others do. This approach, it is hoped, will provide a basis for understanding the self.

The cognitive behavioral aspect of DBT, conducted both individually and in groups, involves four stages. In the first stage, dangerously impulsive behaviors are addressed, with the goal of promoting greater control. In the second stage, the focus is on learning to modulate the extreme emotionality. This phase might involve coaching to help a person learn to tolerate emotional distress. Stage three focuses on improving relationships and self-esteem. Stage four is designed to promote connectedness and happiness. Throughout, clients learn more effective and socially acceptable ways of handling their day-to-day problems. Basically, DBT involves cognitive behavioral therapy combined with interventions to provide validation and acceptance to the client.

Linehan and colleagues conducted a trial in which clients were randomly assigned either to DBT or to treatment as usual, meaning any therapy available in the community. After 1 year of treatment and again 6 and 12 months later, clients in the two groups were compared on a variety of measures (Linehan, Heard, & Armstrong, 1993). The findings immediately after treatment revealed that DBT was superior to treatment as usual—clients showed less intentional self-injurious behavior, including fewer suicide attempts; dropped out of treatment less; and spent fewer days in the hospital. There were, however, no differences in self-reported depression and feelings of hopelessness between the two treatment groups. At the follow-up assessments, the superiority of DBT was maintained. In addition, DBT clients had better work records, reported less anger, and were judged as better adjusted than the comparison therapy clients. But most clients were still feeling quite miserable at the 1-year follow-up, underscoring the extreme difficulty of treating such clients. Since that time, many others have tested the efficacy of DBT, with good results. In a meta-analysis of 16 studies, DBT was found to have moderate positive effects in reducing self-injury and suicidality compared to control conditions (Kliem, Kröger, & Kosfelder, 2010).

Mentalization-Based Therapy of Borderline Personality Disorder **Mentalization-based therapy** is a form of psychodynamic treatment that was developed for BPD. The theory behind this treatment emphasizes that people with BPD fail to engage in *mentalization*—thinking about their own and others' feelings. It is argued that early insecurity in relationships, coupled with intense trauma, leads the person to defensively avoid thinking about feelings and relationships. Because the person does not carefully consider these issues, expectations for relationships based on early experiences continue to pervade current relationships. The therapist's goal is to foster a more active, thoughtful approach to relationships and feelings. Treatment involves weekly individual psychotherapy, as well as group sessions held a couple times per week, for up to 3 years.

To study the efficacy of this program, researchers enrolled 44 people diagnosed with BPD who were attending a day hospital program. Patients were randomly assigned to receive the mentalization-based treatment for up to 3 years as a supplement to their usual care or to continue with their usual care (Bateman & Fonagy, 2004). Initial findings were positive, and at an 8-year follow-up, rates of suicide attempts remained lower among those who had received the mentalization-based treatment.

In one study, researchers compared a similar psychodynamic treatment and DBT to a supportive therapy control group. Although psychodynamic treatment and DBT both led to lower depression and anxiety scores, psychodynamic therapy appeared more effective than DBT in reducing anger (Clarkin, Levy, Lenzenweger, et al., 2007).

Schema-Focused Cognitive Therapy of Borderline Personality Disorder **Schema-focused cognitive therapy** enriches traditional cognitive therapy with a broader focus on how early childhood antecedents and parenting shape current cognitive patterns. In schema-focused therapy, the therapist and the patient work to identify the maladaptive assumptions (schema) that a client holds about relationships from his or her early experiences. It is assumed that the person also has a schema for healthy relationships, and the goal of therapy is to increase the use of this healthy schema, rather than automatic behaviors reflecting the problematic relationship schema. Similar to some psychodynamic approaches, the therapist is working to change internalized representations of relationships drawn from early difficult experiences. Similar to other cognitive therapies, though, the therapist might place emphasis on how these patterns are being expressed in current life and might use homework assignments to try to change these patterns. Because the treatment is designed to address more lifelong issues, this particular form of cognitive therapy can require 3 years. Although traditionally offered as individual therapy, a group version of CT has shown encouraging results when used as a supplement to standard therapy for the treatment of BPD (Blum, John, Pfohl, et al., 2008). In one study, schema-focused therapy led to more reduction of symptoms than did psychodynamic therapy (Giesen-Bloo, van Dyck, Spinhoven, et al., 2006).

Summary

- Personality disorders are defined as enduring patterns of behavior and inner experience that disrupt functioning.
- The DSM-IV-TR includes ten personality disorder types; the proposed DSM-5 includes six personality types, along with dimensional personality domain and facet ratings. Changes were made to reduce comorbidity among the personality disorders and to provide a richer means of describing variations for those with and without personality disorders. Personality dimensions have the advantage of showing more stability over time than do personality disorders, and personality dimensions have been an extensive focus of research on psychological and physical disorders, social adjustment, and treatment outcome.

Personality Disorder Types

- The DSM-5 personality disorder types include obsessive-compulsive, narcissistic, schizotypal, avoidant, antisocial, and borderline personality disorders.
- Obsessive-compulsive personality disorder is defined by a perfectionistic, detail-oriented style. The etiology of obsessive-compulsive personality disorder might be related to obsessive-compulsive disorder.
- Narcissistic personality disorder is defined by inflated self-esteem and a deep need for admiration. The self-psychology model and the social-cognitive model both focus on how the need for admiration develops and how it then shapes behavior.
- Schizotypal personality disorder is defined by unusual thought and behavior and by social aloofness. Genetic research supports the idea that schizotypal personality disorder is related to schizophrenia.
- The major symptom of avoidant personality disorder is fear of rejection or criticism. Avoidant personality disorder is modestly heritable. Avoidant personality disorder is often comorbid with social anxiety disorder, and it is believed that the etiology of these two conditions might be related.
- Antisocial personality disorder and psychopathy overlap a great deal but are not equivalent. The DSM-IV-TR diagnosis of antisocial personality focuses on behavior, whereas that of psychopathy emphasizes emotional deficits. The proposed DSM-5 prototype description for antisocial personality disorder is more closely aligned with the criteria for psychopathy.
- When designs involving repeated measurements or multiple informants are used to bolster the reliability of pathology measures, antisocial personality

disorder and psychopathy appear to be highly heritable. Psychopathy and antisocial behavior also appear to be related to family environment and poverty. Psychological models of psychopathy emphasize a lack of response to punishment (fearlessness), poor empathy, and elevated impulsivity.

- Borderline personality disorder is defined by a highly changeable sense of self-identity, emotional dysregulation, impulsivity, and unstable relationships.
- There is evidence that much of the vulnerability to borderline personality disorder is inherited, and there are also findings regarding deficits in frontal lobe functioning and regarding greater amygdala activation. People with borderline personality disorder report extremely high rates of child abuse and parental separation compared to the general population. Linehan's cognitive behavioral theory of borderline personality disorder proposes an interaction between emotional dysregulation and an invalidating family environment.

Treatment of Personality Disorders

- Personality disorders are usually comorbid with other disorders such as depression and anxiety disorders, and they tend to predict poorer outcomes for these disorders.
- Psychodynamic, cognitive behavioral, and pharmacological treatments are all used for personality disorders. Research on day treatment programs is promising. Relatively little research has been conducted regarding the treatment of personality disorders, and the gap in knowledge is particularly severe for obsessive-compulsive and narcissistic personality disorders.
- Treatment of schizotypal personality disorder is parallel with the treatment of schizophrenia; antipsychotic medication, and sometimes antidepressant medication, can be helpful.
- Treatment of avoidant personality disorder is parallel with the treatment of social anxiety disorder; antidepressants and cognitive behavioral treatment can be helpful.
- Psychopathy, formerly considered virtually untreatable, might respond to long-term psychoanalytic treatment.
- Some promising evidence is emerging for the utility of dialectical behavior therapy, mentalization-based therapy, and schema-focused therapy for borderline personality disorder.

Answers to Check Your Knowledge Questions

15.1 1. T; 2. F; 3. F; 4. Any three of the following: six personality disorder types instead of ten; inclusion of personality trait domains and facets (dimensional scores); inclusion of levels of functioning scale

15.2 1. avoidant personality disorder type; 2. obsessive-compulsive personality disorder type; 3. antisocial personality disorder type

15.3 1. b; 2. a, b; 3. d; 4. d, e

Key Terms

antisocial personality disorder
avoidant personality disorder
borderline personality disorder
dialectical behavior therapy
five-factor model

mentalization-based treatment
narcissistic personality disorder
obsessive-compulsive
    personality disorder
personality disorder

personality disorder types
personality trait domains
personality trait facets
psychopathy

schema-focused cognitive
    therapy
schizotypal personality disorder

16 Legal and Ethical Issues
With Contributions from Nicky Edelstyn

LEARNING GOALS

1. Be able to differentiate the legal concepts of insanity and the various standards for the insanity defense.
2. Be able to describe the issues surrounding competency to stand trial.
3. Be able to delineate the conditions under which a person can be committed to a hospital under civil law.
4. Be able to discuss the difficulties associated with predicting dangerousness and the issues surrounding the rights to receive and refuse treatment.
5. Be able to describe the ethics surrounding psychological research and therapy.

THE UNITED STATES BILL OF RIGHTS was drawn up in the late 18th century to protect the rights of U.S. citizens and others residing in the U.S. It consists of 10 amendments which reflect the philosophical ideal of the U.S. government to allow citizens the maximum degree of liberty consistent with preserving order in the community at large. For example, the first amendment is designed to protect citizens' rights to religious freedom, freedom of expression, a free press, and the right to free association. The fifth and sixth amendments are probably the ones viewers of U.S. TV crime shows are most familiar with. The fifth amendment states that no one can be tried for a serious crime unless indicted (accused) by a grand jury. No one can be forced to testify against herself or himself. No one can be punished without due process of law. The right of people to a speedy trial, to legal counsel, and to confront their accusers is contained within the sixth amendment.

European citizens can look to the **Convention for the Protection of Human Rights and Fundamental Freedoms, 1953** (commonly known as the European Convention on Human Rights) to protect their human rights and fundamental freedoms. It was drafted by the Council of Europe after World War II in 1948 in partial response to the most serious human rights violations which had occurred during the Second World War (most notably, the Holocaust) and to put in place legislature that prevented similar violations of human rights occurring in the future. The Convention incorporates a traditional civil liberties approach to securing "effective political democracy", from the strongest traditions of the English Bill of Rights, the United States Bill of Rights, the French Declaration of the Rights of Man and German Basic Law. The Convention contains "articles" which enshrine the right of citizens to, for example, a fair trial (article 6) "… including the right to a public hearing before an independent and impartial tribunal within reasonable time, the presumption of innocence, and other minimum rights for those charged with a criminal offence (adequate time and facilities to prepare their defense, access to legal representation, right to examine witnesses against them or have them examined, right to the free assistance of an interpreter)."

We open our final chapter in this way because the legal and mental health systems collaborate continually, although often subtly, to deny some individuals their basic civil rights. With the best of intentions, judges, hospitals, legal associations, and professional mental health groups have worked over the years to protect society at large from the actions of people regarded as mentally ill and considered dangerous to themselves or to others. But in so doing they have denied many thousands of people their basic civil rights.

People with mental illness who have broken the law or who are alleged to have done so are subject to **criminal commitment**, a procedure that confines a person in a mental hospital either for determination of competency to stand trial or after acquittal by reason of insanity, as in the clinical case of David (presented later in the chapter).

Civil commitment is a set of procedures by which a person who is deemed mentally ill and dangerous but who has not broken a law can be deprived of liberty and placed in a psychiatric hospital. In this chapter we look at legal and forensic psychology in depth before turning to an examination of some important ethical issues as they relate to therapy and research.

Before discussing issues around the insanity defense and criminal commitment, we examine first the role of psychiatry and psychology in the criminal justice system.

Psychology and Law

Legal psychology involves empirical research of the law, legal institutions, and people who come into contact with the law. Legal psychologists typically take basic social and cognitive principles and apply them to issues in the legal system such as eyewitness memory and jury decision-making. The term "legal psychology" has only recently come into usage, primarily as a way to differentiate the experimental focus of legal psychology from the clinically oriented forensic psychology.

Together, legal psychology and forensic psychology form the field more generally recognized as "psychology and law". Following earlier efforts by psychologists to address legal issues, psychology and law became a field of study in the 1960s as part of an effort to enhance justice (Fox, 1999).

FOCUS ON LEGAL PSYCHOLOGY AND EYE-WITNESS TESTIMONY

Elizabeth Loftus is the highest-ranking female in the list of top 100 psychologists. She's gained worldwide renown for her experiments showing that memory, far from being an accurate record, is influenced by subsequent exposure to information and events and is re-constituted according to the biases these create. The application to the legal system is explored below.

Loftus's research, which began in the 1970s, revealed two important findings for the legal system. First, that witness reports of the same incident varied according to the wording used by the questioner. Second, false memories can be planted. Her 'Lost in the Mall' and 'Bugs Bunny' studies proved that she could—in 30% of subjects—make them believe something that had never happened was part of their childhood history.

Reconstruction of Automobile Destruction

In this seminal 1974 study, Loftus and Palmer showed that memory is not a factual recording of an event and that memories can become distorted by other information which occurs after the event. Many research studies have shown how difficult it is for people to estimate temporal and spatial information relating to time, speed and distance. It seems that judgment of speed is especially difficult, with witnesses of traffic accidents varying in their estimations as to how fast a vehicle was actually travelling.

The Loftus and Palmer study consists of two laboratory experiments. In the first, 45 U.S. college students were each shown seven film clips of traffic accidents. The clips were short excerpts from safety films made for driver education, and ranged from 5 to 30 seconds long. Following each clip, the students were asked to write an account of the accident they had just seen. They were also asked to answer some specific questions but the critical question was to do with the speed of the vehicles involved in the collision. There were five conditions in the experiment which varied only in terms of how the questions were worded.

For Example:

Condition 1: 'About how fast were the cars going when they smashed into each other?'

Condition 2: 'About how fast were the cars going when they collided into each other?'

Condition 3: 'About how fast were the cars going when they bumped into each other?'

Condition 4: 'About how fast were the cars going when they hit each other?'

Condition 5: 'About how fast were the cars going when they contacted each other?'

The basic question was therefore 'About how fast were the cars going when they ***** each other?'. In each condition, a different word or phrase was used to fill in the blank.

These words were: *smashed, collided, bumped, hit, contacted.*

Forensic Psychologists perform a wide range of tasks within the criminal justice system. This requires forensic psychologists to have a firm grasp of the legal system and the law, in addition to their expertise in psychology.

In preparing for court, forensic psychologists are involved in integrating evidence from psychological and mental status exams, background materials, such as police reports, prior psychiatric or psychological evaluations, medical records and other available pertinent information.

The European Association of Psychology and Law (EAPL) is a relatively new organization coming into being in 1990, with the aim of building bridges between practitioners, researchers and teachers at the interface between psychology and law in all its diverse aspects. If offending is conceptualized from a developmental perspective, members of the association are concerned with offenders—and their victims—across the life span. Psychology is relevant to the offending pathway, from early risk factors in childhood and early intervention approaches, to the process of detection and identification after a crime is committed, to the collection of evidence and its presentation in court. Psychology is also relevant after conviction in terms of the treatment of those convicted, and of their victims. The multidisciplinary American Psychological Association's Division operates along similar lines in the United States.

Legal and forensic psychologists may be requested to testify in court as expert witnesses, where it is necessary to communicate psychological findings into the legal language of the courtroom in a way that can be understood. Reflecting their different perspectives and qualifications, a legal psychologist may be requested to testify about issues associated with the validity of eyewitness memory, for example, whereas a forensic psychologist may be called upon to comment on the defendant's mental capacity and therefore competency to stand trial.

Their results revealed that the phrasing of the question brought about a change in their participants' estimate of the speed the car was travelling. The descriptor "*smashed*" elicited the highest speed estimate (40.8 miles per hour) compared to the others (*collided*: 39.1 mph; *bumped*: 38.1 mph; *hit*: 34 mph and *contacted*: 31.8 mph).

Loftus and Palmer provided two explanations of their findings. Firstly, they suggested that the results could be due to a distortion in the memory of the participant. The memory of how fast the cars were travelling could have been distorted by the verbal label which had been used to characterize the intensity of the crash. Their second interpretation was that the results could be due to response-bias factors, in which case the participant is not sure of the exact speed and therefore adjusts his or her estimate to fit in with the expectations of the questioner.

In their second experiment, Loftus and Palmer wanted to find out if the participants memories really had been distorted by the verbal label. They used a similar procedure in which 3 groups of (50) college students viewed the same one minute film containing a 4-second scene of a multiple car accident, and were then questioned about it. Two groups were each asked a different question:

'How fast were the cars going when they hit each other?'
'How fast were the cars going when they smashed into each other?'

The third "control" group were not questioned about the speed of the vehicles.

One week later, the participants returned and, without viewing the film again, they answered a series of questions about the accident. The critical question was 'Did you see any broken glass?' The critical question was part of a longer series of questions and was placed in a random position on each participants question paper. There was in fact no broken glass in the film.

The results showed that having the verb "smashed" in the question made participants twice as likely to recall seeing broken glass. On the basis of these findings, Loftus and Palmer developed the reconstructive hypothesis.

According to the reconstructive hypothesis two kinds of information go into a person's memory of an event. The first is the information obtained from perceiving an event (e.g. witnessing a video of a car accident), and the second is the other information supplied to us after the event (e.g. the question containing hit or smashed). Over time, the information from these two sources may be integrated in such a way that we are unable to tell from which source some specific detail is recalled. All we have is one 'memory'.

The main strength of Loftus' argument is its wider implications. Based on evidence like that of Loftus's, the Devlin Report (1976) recommended that the trial judge be required to instruct the jury that it is not safe to convict on a single eyewitness testimony alone, except in exceptional circumstances or when there is substantial corroborative evidence.

Loftus's reconstructive hypothesis has also meant that the police and lawyers are urged to use as few leading questions as possible (i.e. questions suggesting to the witness the desired answer), although in reality this practice is still widely carried out.

References

Loftus, E.F. & Palmer, J.C. (1974) Reconstruction of auto-mobile destruction: An example of the interaction between language and memory. Journal of Verbal Learning and Verbal Behaviour, 13, 585–89.

Clinical Case: David

David had been hearing voices for several days. Unable to drown them out with music or talking, he became more and more troubled. The voices were telling him that he was the one chosen by God to rid the world of evil. David went to the emergency room of the local hospital seeking relief. Instead of being admitted, David was given a prescription for Haldol and sent on his way. Two days later, David took a loaded gun into the busy train station and began shooting. He killed two people and injured four others. When he was arrested, David told the police he was answering to God. His speaking was disorganized and hard to follow, and he expressed a number of paranoid beliefs.

David was found competent to stand trial because he understood that he was charged with murder and he was able to help his attorney with his defense. At trial, David entered a plea of "not guilty by reason of insanity" (NGRI). His defense lawyer arranged for David to be evaluated by a psychologist. The psychologist concluded that David had schizophrenia, and that at the time of the crime he was unable to discern right from wrong (he thought his behavior was the right thing to do since God was directing him) and unable to conform his behavior to the requirements of the law. The prosecution did not dispute these findings, and the case was

settled before going to trial. David was committed to the local forensic hospital for an indeterminate period of time. He was to remain there until he was no longer dangerous and mentally ill. Periodic evaluations would be conducted to see if David could be transferred to a less secure hospital.

After seven years in the hospital, David had done very well. He took his prescribed medication (Zyprexa), was never in a physical altercation with other patients, participated in individual and group therapy, worked in the hospital machine shop, and served as a team leader for the unit he was living in. David felt horribly remorseful for the crimes he had committed, and he recognized that he had schizophrenia that would require treatment for the rest of his life. The treatment team on the unit all agreed that David was no longer dangerous and that his schizophrenia was under control with the medication. They recommended that he be transferred to a less secure psychiatric hospital. David's attorney presented the case before a judge in the courtroom that was part of the hospital. The attorneys for the state objected to David's release, arguing that David could stop taking his medications and become violent again. The judge agreed that release was premature at this time and ordered that David remain in the forensic hospital for another year before being evaluated again.

In forensic assessments, it is of critical importance that the forensic psychologist *doesn't* attempt to empathize with the client's point of view. Their responsibility is to assess the consistency of factual information across multiple sources. Forensic psychologists must be able to provide the evidence or source on which any information is based.

Unlike the more traditional clinical assessments undertaken by clinical psychologists where obtaining informed consent from the client is a routine procedure, informed consent is not required when the assessment is ordered by the court (for a more detailed discussion of informed consent see later section *Ethical Dilemmas in Therapy and Research*). Instead, the defendant simply needs to be notified about the purpose of the evaluation and the fact that he or she will have no control over how the information obtained is used. While psychologists infrequently have to be concerned about malingering or feigning illness in a non-criminal clinical setting, a forensic psychologist must be able to recognize exaggerated or faked symptoms.

Malingering

An overriding issue in any type of forensic psychological assessment is the issue of malingering and deception. Malingering exists on a continuum so the forensic psychologist must be skilled in recognizing varying degrees of feigned symptoms. A defendant may be intentionally faking a mental illness or may be exaggerating the degree of symptomatology. It is important if malingering is suspected to observe the defendant in other settings as it is difficult to maintain false symptoms consistently over time.

In some cases, the court views malingering or feigning illness as obstruction of justice and sentences the defendant accordingly. In United States v. Binion, malingering or feigning illness during a competency evaluation was held to be obstruction of justice and led to an enhanced sentence. As such, fabricating mental illness in a competency-to-stand-trial assessment now can be raised to enhance the sentencing level following a guilty plea (http://federal-circuits.vlex. com/vid/usa-v-dammeon-binion-19469412)

Summary of the forensic psychologist's interactions with and ethical responsibilities to their client

- **Scope.** Rather than the broad set of issues a psychologist addresses in a clinical setting, a forensic psychologist addresses a narrowly defined set of events or interactions of a nonclinical nature.

- **Importance of client's perspective.** A clinician places primary importance on understanding the client's unique point of view, while the forensic psychologist is interested in accuracy, and the client's viewpoint is secondary.

- **Voluntariness.** Usually in a clinical setting a psychologist is dealing with a voluntary client. A forensic psychologist evaluates clients by order of a judge or at the behest of an attorney.

- **Autonomy.** Voluntary clients have more latitude and autonomy regarding the assessment's objectives. Any assessment usually takes their concerns into account. The objectives of a forensic examination are confined by the applicable statutes or common law elements that pertain to the legal issue in question.

- **Threats to validity.** While the client and therapist are working toward a common goal, although unconscious distortion may occur, in the forensic context there is a substantially greater likelihood of intentional and conscious distortion.

- **Relationship and dynamics.** Therapeutic interactions work toward developing a trusting, empathic therapeutic alliance, a forensic psychologist may not ethically nurture the client or act in a "helping" role, as the forensic evaluator had divided loyalties and there are substantial limits on confidentiality he can guarantee the client. A forensic evaluator must always be aware of manipulation in the adversary context of a legal setting. These concerns mandate an emotional distance that is unlike a therapeutic interaction.

- **Pace and setting.** Unlike therapeutic interactions which may be guided by many factors, the forensic setting with its court schedules, limited resources, and other external factors, place great time constraints on the evaluation without opportunities for reevaluation. The forensic examiner focuses on the importance of accuracy and the finality of legal dispositions.

The Concept of Insanity

Almost as early as the concept of mens rea, or "guilty mind," and the rule "No crime without an evil intent" had begun to be accepted in English common law, the concept of *insanity* was taken into consideration. Broadly speaking, insanity refers to a disordered mind, and a disordered mind may be regarded as unable to formulate and carry out a criminal purpose (S. J. Morse, 1992). In other words, a disordered mind cannot be a guilty mind, and only a guilty mind can engender culpable actions.

It is important to note that insanity is a legal concept, not a psychological one. The **insanity defense** is where the defendant claims that because of mental health problems they were not responsible for their actions and therefore, are exempt from full criminal punishment. As such, its definition comes from court proceedings.

In the United Kingdom, Ireland and the United States, use of the insanity defense is rare, although since the Criminal Procedure (Insanity and Fitness to Plead) Act 1991 insanity pleas have steadily increased in the UK.

In today's courts, judges and lawyers call on psychiatrists and clinical psychologists for assistance in dealing with criminal acts thought to result from the accused person's disordered mental state. Although the insanity defense was developed to protect people's rights, in practice, the insanity defense often results in a greater denial of liberties than they would otherwise experience.

The Insanity Defense

The **insanity defense** is the legal argument that a defendant should not be held responsible for an illegal act if it is attributable to mental illness or intellectual disability that interferes with rationality or that results from some other excusing circumstance, such as not knowing right from wrong. A staggering amount of material has been written on the insanity defense, even though it is pleaded in less than 1 percent of all cases that reach trial and even when pleaded, it is rarely successful (Morse, 1982; Steadman, 1979; Steadman et al., 1993).

Because an insanity defense is based on the accused's mental condition at the time the crime was committed, retrospective, often speculative, judgment on the part of attorneys, judges, jurors, and mental health professionals is required. Often, disagreement between defense and prosecution psychiatrists and psychologists is the rule.

Mental illness and crime do not go hand in hand. A person can be diagnosed as mentally ill and be held responsible for a crime. However, someone who has no mental illness at all can commit the most heinous or bizarre crime, despite our tendency to think someone must have been "crazy" to commit such a crime. Indeed, decades of social psychological research tell us that otherwise normal people can do horrendous, criminal acts under the right circumstances or contexts (Aronson, 2004).

Where did the insanity defense come from? Some type of insanity defense, loosely defined, has been around since the 7th century B.C. (Robinson, 1996). However, we will consider more recent legal precedents that set the stage for our current definitions of insanity and have shaped the development of the two main insanity pleas used today.

History of the Insanity Defense

The concept of defense by insanity has existed since ancient Greece and Rome. However, in colonial America a delusional Dorothy Talbye was hanged in 1638 for murdering her daughter, as at the time common law made no distinction between insanity and criminal behavior. Edward III, under English Common law, declared that a person was insane if their mental capacity was no more than that of a "wild beast" (in the sense of a dumb animal, rather than being frenzied). The first complete transcript of an insanity trial dates to 1724. It is likely that the insane, like those under 14, were spared ordeal by trial. When jury by trial replaced this, the jury were expected to find the insane guilty but then refer the case to the King for a Royal Pardon.

From 1500 onwards juries could acquit the insane, and detention required a separate civil procedure (Walker, 1985). The Criminal Lunatics Act 1800, passed with retrospective effect following the acquittal of James Hadfield, mandated detention at his or her majesty's pleasure (indefinitely) even for those who although insane at the time of the offence were now sane.

The insanity defense has its origins in the M'Naghten Rules of 1843 (see later section on Landmark Cases and Laws) which recognises the fact that severe mental illness may render a defendant unable to appreciate the nature of his or her actions during the commission of the crime and therefore cannot be held accountable.

Diminished Responsibility

Lesser degrees of mental impairment may be reflected in sentencing or the partial defense of diminished responsibility, which results in a manslaughter rather than murder conviction. The insanity defense is available in most jurisdictions that respect human rights and have a rule of law although the extent to which it can be applied differs between jurisdictions.

The insanity defense is based on evaluations by forensic professionals that the defendant was incapable of distinguishing between (legal) right and wrong or appreciating the nature of his or her actions at the time of the offense. Some jurisdictions require the evaluation to address the defendant's ability to control his or her behavior at the time of the offense (the volitional limb). A defendant claiming insanity is pleading "**not guilty by reason of insanity**" (NGRI) or "**guilty but insane/mentally ill**" in some jurisdictions which, if successful, may result in the defendant being committed to a psychiatric facility for an indeterminate period.

Diminished responsibility or diminished capacity can be employed as a mitigating factor or partial defense to murder and in the U.S. is applicable to more circumstances than the insanity defense. For example, some jurisdictions accept inebriation or other drug intoxication as mitigating factors whilst intoxication is not accepted as an insanity defense on its own. If diminished responsibility or capacity is presented convincingly, the charges may be reduced to the lesser offense of manslaughter or the sentence may be more lenient.

Competency and Criminal Responsibility

The issue of competency is whether a defendant is able to adequately assist his attorney in preparing a defense, make informed decisions about trial strategy and whether or not to plead guilty or accept a plea agreement. This issue is dealt with in UK law as "fitness to plead". Criminal responsibility, however, deals with whether a defendant can be held legally responsible for his criminal behavior.

Competency largely deals with the defendant's present condition, while criminal responsibility addresses the condition at the time the crime was committed.

In the UK, the Crown Prosecution Service (CPS) is a Government department responsible for public prosecutions of people charged with criminal offences in England and Wales. The CPS uses the term "mentally disordered offender" to describe a person who has a disability or disorder of the mind and has committed or is suspected of committing a criminal offence. This term covers a range of offences, disabilities and disorders. A mental disorder may be relevant to the defendant's fitness to plead. The defendant is considered unfit to plead if s/he is unable to either:

- to comprehend the course of proceedings on the trial, so as to make a proper defense;
- to know that s/he might challenge any jurors to whom s/he may object;
- to comprehend the evidence; or
- to give proper instructions to her/his legal representatives.

Landmark Cases and Laws   Several court rulings and established principles bear on the problems of legal responsibility and mental illness. Table 16.1 summarizes these rulings and principles (for more on these issues, see Frederick, Mrad, & DeMier, 2007).

The irresistible impulse concept was formulated in 1834 in a case in Ohio. According to this concept, if a pathological impulse or uncontrollable drive compelled the person to commit the criminal act, an insanity defense is legitimate. The irresistible-impulse test was confirmed in two subsequent court cases, *Parsons v. State and Davis v. United States.*[1]

The M'Naghten rule was formulated in the aftermath of a murder trial in England in 1843. The defendant, Daniel M'Naghten, had set out to kill the British prime minister, Sir Robert Peel, but had mistaken Peel's secretary for Peel. M'Naghten claimed that he had been instructed to kill Lord Peel by the "voice of God." The judges ruled that

> *to establish a defense of insanity, it must be clearly proved that, at the time of the committing of the act, the party accused was labouring under such a defect of reason, from disease of the mind, as not to know the nature and quality of the act he was doing; or if he did know it, that he did not know he was doing what was wrong.*

American Law Institute Guidelines   In 1962 the American Law Institute (ALI) proposed its own guidelines, which were intended to be more specific and informative to lay jurors than were other tests. The **American Law Institute guidelines** state the following:

---

[1]*Parsons v. State*, 2 So. 854, 866–67 (Ala.1887); *Davis v. United States*, 165 U.S. 373, 378 (1897).

Table 16.1 Landmark Cases and Laws Regarding the Insanity Defense

Irresistible impulse (1834)	A pathological impulse or drive that the person could not control compelled that person to commit a criminal act.
M'Naghten rule (1843)	The person did not know the nature and quality of the criminal act in which he or she engaged, or, if the person did know it, the person did not know what he or she was doing was wrong.
American Law Institute guidelines (1962)	1. The person's criminal act is a result of "mental disease or defect" that results in the person's not appreciating the wrongfulness of the act or in the person's inability to behave according to the law (combination of M'Naghten rule and irresistible impulse).
	2. "[T]he terms 'mental disease or defect' do not include an abnormality manifested only by repeated criminal or otherwise antisocial conduct" (American Law Institute, 1962).
Insanity Defense Reform Act (1984)	1. The person's criminal act is a result of severe mental illness or defect that prevents the person from understanding Reform Act (1984) the nature of his or her crime.
	2. The burden of proof is shifted from the prosecution to the defense. The defense has to prove that the person is insane.
	3. The person is only released from the forensic or prison hospital after being judged to be no longer dangerous and to have recovered from mental illness. This could be longer than he or she would have been imprisoned if convicted.
Guilty but mentally ill (1975)	The person can be found legally guilty of a crime—thus maximizing the chances of incarceration—and the person's mental illness plays a role in how he or she is dealt with. Thus, even a seriously ill person can be held morally and legally responsible but can then be committed to a prison hospital or other suitable facility for psychiatric treatment rather than to a regular prison for punishment.

1. A person is not responsible for criminal conduct if at the time of such conduct as a result of mental disease or defect he lacks substantial capacity either to appreciate the criminality (wrongfulness) of his conduct or to conform his conduct to the requirements of law.

2. As used in the article, the terms "mental disease or defect" do not include an abnormality manifested only by repeated criminal or otherwise antisocial conduct (American Law Institute, 1962, p. 66).

The first ALI guideline combines the M'Naghten rule and the concept of irresistible impulse. The phrase "substantial capacity" in the first guideline is designed to limit an insanity defense to those with the most serious mental disorders. The second guideline concerns those who are repeatedly in trouble with the law; repetitive criminal behavior and psychopathy are not evidence for insanity.

Insanity Defense Reform Act In a highly publicized trial in March 1981, John Hinckley Jr. was found not guilty by reason of insanity (NGRI) for his assassination attempt against President Ronald Reagan. After the verdict, the court received a flood of mail from citizens outraged that a would-be assassin of a U.S. president had not been held criminally responsible and had only been committed to an indefinite stay in a mental hospital until deemed mentally healthy enough for release. Their outrage reflects the public misperceptions about the insanity defense. The public often believes that a person is "getting away" with a crime when found not guilty by reason of insanity and that he or she will be released from the hospital in short order. In reality, many people who are committed to a mental hospital stay there longer than they would have stayed in prison had they been given a sentence (as vividly illustrated in the clinical case below of Michael Jones). With respect to John Hinckley, he has been committed to St. Elizabeth's Hospital, a public mental hospital in Washington, D.C., for 29 years. Although he can be released whenever his mental health is deemed adequate, this has not yet happened. He has slowly won more freedoms: In 2003, a judge ruled that Hinckley could have six day-long unsupervised visits with his parents outside St. Elizabeth's hospital but only in the Washington, D.C., area. In 2005, a judge allowed Hinckley to have seven overnight visits with his parents at their home in Virginia, but he must carry a GPS enabled cellphone and he is not allowed to be without a parent or sibling. His internet access is also restricted. As of 2007, doctors need give four days advance notice to the Secret Service, instead of two weeks, when Hinckley visits his parents.

Because of the publicity surrounding the trial and the public outrage at the Hinckley verdict, the insanity defense became a target of vigorous criticism from many quarters. As Judge Parker, who presided at the trial, put it: "For many, the [Hinckley] defense was a clear manifestation of the failure of our criminal justice system to punish people who have clearly violated the law" (quoted in Simon & Aaronson, 1988, p. vii).

As a consequence of political pressures to "get tough" on criminals, Congress enacted the Insanity Defense Reform Act in October 1984, addressing the insanity defense for the first time at the federal level. This new law, which has been adopted in all federal courts, contains several provisions designed to make it more difficult to enter an insanity plea.

- It eliminates the irresistible-impulse component of the ALI rules. This volitional and behavioral aspect of the ALI guidelines had been strongly criticized because one could regard any criminal act as arising from an inability to stay within the limits of the law.

- It changes the ALI's "lacks substantial capacity . . . to appreciate" to "unable to appreciate." This alteration in the cognitive component of the law is intended to tighten the grounds for an insanity defense by making more stringent the criterion for impaired judgment.

- The act also stipulates that the mental disease or defect must be "severe," the intent being to exclude insanity defenses on the basis of disorders such as antisocial personality disorder. Also abolished by the act were defenses relying on "diminished capacity" or "diminished responsibility," based on such mitigating circumstances as extreme passion or "temporary insanity." Again, the purpose was to make it harder to mount an insanity defense.

- It shifts the burden of proof from the prosecution to the defense. Instead of the prosecution having to prove that the person was sane beyond a reasonable doubt at the time of the crime (the most stringent criterion, consistent with the constitutional requirement that people are considered innocent until proved guilty), the defense must prove that the defendant was not sane and must do so with "clear and convincing evidence" (a less stringent but still demanding standard of proof). Table 16.2 shows the different standards of proof used in U.S. courts. The heavier burden now placed on the defense is, like the other provisions, designed to make it more difficult to relieve a defendant of moral and legal responsibility.[2]

- Finally, the person may remain committed longer than the ordinary sentence. A person is only released when no longer dangerous and no longer mentally ill.

Table 16.2 Standards of Proof	
Standard	**Certainty Needed to Convict (%)**
Beyond a reasonable doubt	95
Clear and convincing evidence	75
Beyond a preponderance of the evidence	51

---

[2]According to Simon and Aaronson (1988), this provision arose in large measure from the inability of the prosecution to prove John Hinckley's sanity when he shot Reagan and three others. Several members of the jury testified after the trial to a subcommittee of the Senate Judiciary Committee that the judge's instructions on the burden of proof played a role in their verdict of NGRI. Even before the act, almost half the states required that the defendant must prove insanity, but only one, Arizona, had the "clear and convincing" standard. A majority of the states now place the burden of proof on the defense, albeit with the least exacting of legal standards of proof, "by a preponderance of the evidence."

Jeffrey Dahmer, who was tried for butchering, cannibalizing, and having sex with the corpses of 15 boys and young men, was found guilty but mentally ill. (Reuters/ Corbis images).

Guilty but Mentally Ill Some U.S. states have created what seems to be a compromise verdict—guilty but mentally ill (GBMI). A GBMI verdict allows the usual sentence to be imposed but also allows for the person to be treated for mental illness during incarceration, though treatment is not guaranteed. If the person is still considered to be dangerous or mentally ill after serving the imposed prison sentence, he or she may be committed to a mental hospital under civil law proceedings.

Critics of the GBMI verdict argue that it does not benefit criminal defendants with mental illness and does not result in appropriate treatment for those convicted (Woodmansee, 1996). A 1997 South Carolina Supreme Court case[3] found that South Carolina's GBMI statute did provide some benefit because it mandated that convicted people with mental illness receive mental health evaluations before being placed in the general prison population. Unfortunately, these assessments have not been shown to lead to better treatment. Other critics of the GBMI verdict note that the verdict is confusing and even deceiving to jurors. Jurors believe that GBMI is not as "tough" as a guilty verdict, but in reality people receiving a GBMI verdict often spend more time incarcerated than if they had been found guilty (Melville & Naimark, 2002).

One of the more famous cases involving the GBMI verdict was the 1992 conviction of Jeffrey Dahmer in Milwaukee, Wisconsin. He had been accused of and had admitted to butchering, cannibalizing, and having sex with the corpses of 15 boys and young men. Dahmer entered the insanity plea allowed in Wisconsin—guilty but mentally ill—and his sanity was the sole focus of an unusual trial that had jurors listening to conflicting testimony from mental health experts about the defendant's state of mind during the serial killings to which he had confessed. They had to decide whether he had had a mental disease that prevented him from knowing right from wrong or from being able to control his actions. Even though there was no disagreement that he was mentally ill, diagnosable as having some sort of paraphilia, Dahmer was deemed sane and therefore legally responsible for the grisly murders. The judge sentenced him to 15 consecutive life terms. Later, another inmate in prison killed him.

Current Insanity Pleas The two insanity pleas available in state and federal courts in the United States have been crafted from the legal definitions and precedents just reviewed. With the **not guilty by reason of insanity (NGRI)** plea, there is no dispute over whether the person actually committed the crime—both sides agree that the person committed the crime. However, due to the person's insanity at the time of the crime, the defense attorney argues that the person should not be held responsible for the crime and should thus be acquitted of the crime. The successful NGRI plea indicates the person is not held responsible for the crime due to his or her mental illness. People acquitted with the NGRI plea are committed indefinitely to a forensic hospital. That is, they are only released from forensic hospitals if they are deemed no longer dangerous and no longer mentally ill (we discuss the difficulties in making these determinations below).

A forensic hospital looks very much like a regular hospital except that the perimeter of the grounds is secured with gates, barbed wires, or electric fences. Inside the hospital, doors to the different units may be locked, and bars may be placed on windows on the lower floors. Patients do not stay in jail cells, however. They stay in either individual or shared rooms. Security professionals are on hand to keep patients safe. They typically do not carry weapons of any sort, and they may be dressed in regular clothing rather than uniforms.

The second insanity plea is **guilty but mentally ill (GBMI)**. As described earlier, this plea allows an accused person to be found legally guilty of a crime—thus maximizing the chances of incarceration—but allows for psychiatric judgment on how to deal with the convicted person if he or she is considered to have been mentally ill when the act was committed. Thus, even a seriously ill person can be held morally and legally responsible for a

---

[3]*South Carolina v. Hornsby*, 484 S.E.2d 869 (S.C. Sup. Ct. 1997).

Table 16.3 Comparing NGRI and GBMI

	NGRI	GBMI
Responsibility for crime	Not responsible	Responsible
Where committed	Forensic hospital	Prison
Given sentence?	No	Yes
When released	When no longer dangerous and mentally ill	End of sentence, but could then be committed civilly if dangerous and mentally ill
Treatment given?	Yes	Possibly

crime but can then, in theory, be committed to a prison hospital or other suitable facility for psychiatric treatment rather than to a regular prison for punishment. In reality, however, people judged GBMI are usually put in the general prison population, where they may or may not receive treatment.

Table 16.3 compares these two insanity pleas. Eleven states allow for some or all of the GBMI provisions; four states have both NGRI and GBMI available. Four states—Idaho, Montana, Kansas, and Utah—do not allow for any insanity defense. The remaining states have some version of NGRI available. Taking a cue from the Insanity Defense Reform Act, states vary as to whether the burden of proof rests with the state or the defendant.

In the case of Michael Jones, the court considered whether someone who was found NGRI could be kept in a hospital longer than the person might have spent in prison had he or she

Clinical Case: Michael Jones

To illustrate the predicament that a person can get into by raising insanity as a condition for a criminal act, we consider a celebrated—some would call it infamous—Supreme Court case.[4]

Michael Jones was arrested, unarmed, on September 19, 1975, for attempting to steal a jacket from a department store in Washington, D.C. He was charged the next day with attempted petty larceny, a misdemeanor punishable by a maximum prison sentence of 1 year. The court ordered that he be committed to St. Elizabeth's Hospital for a determination of his competency to stand trial.

On March 2, 1976, almost six months after the alleged crime, a hospital psychologist reported to the court that Jones was competent to stand trial, although he had "schizophrenia, paranoid type." The psychologist also reported that the alleged crime resulted from Jones's condition, his paranoid schizophrenia. This comment is noteworthy because the psychologist was not asked to offer an opinion on Jones's state of mind during the crime, only on whether Jones was competent to stand trial. Jones then pleaded not guilty by reason of insanity. Ten days later, on March 12, the court found him NGRI and formally

committed him to St. Elizabeth's Hospital for treatment of his mental disorder.

On May 25, 1976, a customary 50-day hearing was held to determine whether Jones should remain in the hospital any longer. A psychologist from the hospital testified that Jones still suffered from paranoid schizophrenia and was a danger to himself and to others. A second hearing was held on February 22, 1977, 17 months after Jones's commitment to St. Elizabeth's, for determination of competency. The defendant demanded release since he had already been hospitalized longer than the 1-year maximum sentence he would have served had he been found guilty of the theft of the jacket. The court denied the request and returned him to St. Elizabeth's.

In response to an appeal, the District of Columbia Court of Appeals agreed with the original court. Ultimately, in November 1982, more than seven years after his hospitalization, Jones's appeal to the Supreme Court was heard. On June 29, 1983, by a five-to-four decision, the Court affirmed the earlier decision: Jones was to remain at St. Elizabeth's. Jones was fully released from St. Elizabeth's in August 2004, 28 years after the crime!

---

[4]*Jones v. United States*, 463 U.S. 354 (1983).

been found guilty of the crime. Jones argued that he should be released; the Supreme Court disagreed. According to the court ruling, Jones could not be punished for the crime because his insanity left him legally blameless—this is the logic of the insanity defense. Jones would have been released from prison sooner had he pleaded guilty.

The Court was also concerned about Jones's dangerousness. Jones argued in his petition to the Supreme Court that his theft of the jacket was not dangerous because it was not a violent crime. The Court stated, however, that for there to be violence in a criminal act, the act itself need not be dangerous. It cited a previous decision that a nonviolent theft of an article such as a watch may frequently result in violence through the efforts of the criminal to escape, or of the victim to protect his or her property, or of the police to apprehend the fleeing thief.[5]

The dissenting justices of the Court commented that the longer someone such as Jones had to remain in the hospital, the harder it would be for him to demonstrate that he was no longer a dangerous person or mentally ill. Extended institutionalization would likely make it more difficult for him to afford medical experts other than those associated with the hospital and to behave like someone who was not mentally ill. Given that Jones remained in the hospital for 28 years, it would seem that the dissenting justices were correct.

A later case before the Supreme Court in 1992, ruled that someone found NGRI could not remain committed if no longer mentally ill, even if that person is still considered dangerous.[6]

Other cases have considered the impact of medication on a person entering the NGRI plea. If a defendant wishes, the effects of the medication must be explained to the jury, lest the jury conclude from the defendant's relatively rational drug-produced demeanor that he or she could not have been insane at the time of the crime.[7] This requirement acknowledges that juries form their judgments of legal responsibility or insanity at least in part based on how the defendant appears during the trial. If the defendant appears healthy, the jury may be less likely to believe that the crime was an act of a disturbed mental state rather than of free will—even though an insanity defense has to do with the defendant's state of mind during the crime, not his or her psychological state during the trial.

Quick Summary

Insanity is a legal term, not a mental health term. Meeting the legal definition is not necessarily the same thing as having a diagnosable mental illness and vice versa. The insanity defense is the legal argument that a defendant should not be held responsible for an illegal act if it is attributable to mental illness that interferes with rationality or that results from some other excusing circumstance, such as not knowing right from wrong.

The irresistible-impulse standard suggested that an impulse or drive that the person could not control compelled that person to commit the criminal act. The M'Naghten rule specified that a person could not distinguish right from wrong at the time of the crime because of the person's mental illness. The first part of the American Law Institute guidelines combines the M'Naghten rule and the concept of irresistible impulse. The second concerns those who are repeatedly in trouble with the law; they are not to be deemed mentally ill only because they keep committing crimes. The Insanity Defense Reform Act shifted the burden of proof from the prosecution to the defense, removed the irresistible impulse component, changed wording regarding substantial capacity, and specified that mental illness must be severe. The Jones case illustrates a number of the complexities associated with the insanity defense.

The not guilty by reason of insanity (NGRI) plea signifies that an accused person should not be held responsible for the crime due to his or her mental illness. The guilty but mentally ill (GBMI) plea signifies that an accused person is legally guilty of a crime but can then, in theory, be committed to a prison hospital or other suitable facility for psychiatric treatment rather than to a regular prison for punishment.

[5]*Overholser v. O'Beirne*, 302 F.2d 85, 861, (D.C. Cir. 1961).
[6]*Foucha v. Lousiana*, 504 U.S. 71 (1992).
[7]*State v. Jojola*, 553 F.2d 1296 (N.M. Ct. App. 1976).

Check Your Knowledge 16.1 (Answers are at the end of the chapter.)

Match the statement with the correct insanity standard.

1. can't control behavior
2. found guilty
3. doesn't know right from wrong
4. affirmative defense

   a. GBMI
   b. NGRI
   c. irresistible impulse
   d. M'Naghten rule

Clinical Case: Yolanda

Yolanda, a 51-year-old African American woman, was arrested after taking a box of doughnuts from the local QuickMart. At the time of her arrest, she claimed she needed the doughnuts to feed the seven babies growing inside her. She said that Malcolm X was the father of her soon-to-be-born children and that she would soon assume the position of Queen of the New Cities. When asked what the New Cities were, she responded this was a new world order that would be in place following the alignment of the clouds with the planets Jupiter, Saturn, and Venus. Yolanda's public defender immediately realized that Yolanda was not ready for trial; she asked for a competency hearing and arranged for a psychologist to conduct an evaluation. Yolanda was diagnosed with schizophrenia, disorganized type, and her thought disturbance was found to be so profound that she was not able to understand that she had been charged with a crime. Furthermore, she was unable to help her attorney prepare a defense. Instead, Yolanda viewed her attorney as a threat to her unborn babies (she was not pregnant) and feared the attorney would keep her from assuming her rightful position as queen. At her competency hearing, the judge declared that Yolanda was not competent to stand trial and that she be committed to the local forensic hospital for a period of three months, after which another competency evaluation would be held.

At the hospital, Yolanda was prescribed Olanzapine, and her thinking became more coherent and organized after 2 months. One of the unit's psychologists worked with Yolanda, teaching her about the criminal justice system. She worked to help Yolanda understand what the charge of theft meant and what a defense attorney, prosecuting attorney, judge, and jury were. At the end of three months, a different psychologist evaluated Yolanda and recommended that she now be considered competent to stand trial. Yolanda's public defender came to the hospital and met with her to discuss the case. Yolanda was able to help her attorney by telling her about her past hospitalizations and treatment history for schizophrenia. Yolanda realized she was not pregnant but still held onto beliefs about the New Cities. Still, Yolanda understood that she had stolen the doughnuts and this was why she had to go to court. At her next competency hearing, Yolanda was deemed competent to stand trial. Two months later, she went to court again. This time, she entered a plea of NGRI. After a short trial, the judge accepted her NGRI plea and she returned to the forensic hospital. The treatment goals were now focused on helping Yolanda recover from schizophrenia, not on restoring her competency to stand trial.

A 1972 Supreme Court case, Jackson v. Indiana,[8] forced the states to a speedier determination of incompetency. The case concerned a deaf and mute man with intellectual developmental disorder who was deemed not only incompetent to stand trial but unlikely ever to become competent. The Court ruled that the length of pretrial confinement must be limited to the time it takes to determine whether treatment during this detainment is likely to render the defendant competent to stand trial. If the defendant is unlikely ever to become competent, the state must, after this period, either institute civil commitment proceedings or release the defendant. Laws in most states define more precisely the minimal requirements for competency to stand trial, ending the latitude that has deprived thousands of people of their rights to due process (Fourteenth Amendment) and a speedy trial (Sixth Amendment). Defendants today cannot be committed for determination of competency for a period longer than the maximum possible sentence they face.[9] Today, most people are deemed competent to stand trial in about 6 months. People who have intellectual disabilities or serious mental illness such as schizophrenia that has required long-term hospitalization are least likely to ever be deemed competent to stand trial (Zapf & Roesch, 2011).

---

[8]Jackson v. Indiana, 406 **U.S.** 715 (1972).
[9]United States v. DeBellis, 649 F.2d 1 (1st Cir. 1981); State v. Moore, 467 N.W. 2d 201 (Wis. Ct. App. 1991).

FOCUS ON DISCOVERY 16.1

Another Look at Insanity versus Mental Illness

On June 20, 2001, believing that her five children, ranging in age from six months to seven years, were condemned to eternal damnation, 37-year-old Andrea Yates, who lived with her husband and children in Houston, Texas, systematically drowned each child in a bathtub. As recounted on the CNN website:

> . . . when the police reached [the] modest brick home on Beachcomber Lane in suburban Houston, they found Andrea drenched with bathwater, her flowery blouse and brown leather sandals soaking wet. She had turned on the bathroom faucet to fill the porcelain tub and moved aside the shaggy mat to give herself traction for kneeling on the floor. It took a bit of work for her to chase down the last of the children; toward the end, she had a scuffle in the family room, sliding around on wet tile.
> . . . She dripped watery footprints from the tub to her bedroom, where she straightened the blankets around the kids in their pajamas once she was done with them. She called 911 and then her husband. "It's time. I finally did it," she said before telling him to come home and hanging up.

The nation was horrified by her actions, and in the months following the murders, information became known about Yates's frequent bouts of depression, especially after giving birth, as well as her several suicide attempts and hospitalizations for severe depression.

Eight months later her trial was held. The defense argued that she was mentally ill at the time of the murders—and for many periods of time preceding the events—and that she was unable to distinguish right from wrong when she put her children to death. The prosecution argued that she had known right from wrong and therefore should be found guilty. On two things the defense and the prosecution agreed: (1) she had murdered her children, and (2) she was mentally ill at the time of the murder. Where they disagreed was on the crucial question as to whether her mental illness entailed not being able to distinguish right or wrong, the familiar M'Naghten principle of criminal responsibility.

This trial shows the difficulty of making a successful insanity defense and is a vivid example of the critical difference between mental illness and insanity. No one disagreed that she was severely depressed, probably psychotic, when she killed her

five small children. But, as we have seen, mental illness is not the same as legal insanity. Employing the right–wrong principle, the jury deliberated for only 3 hours and 40 minutes on March 12, 2002, and delivered a verdict of guilty. They had rejected the defense's contention that Ms. Yates could not distinguish right from wrong at the time of the crime. On March 15, the jury decided to spare her life and recommended to the presiding judge that she get life in prison, not being eligible for parole for 40 years.

The trial and the guilty verdict occasioned impassioned discussion in the media and among thousands of people. How could the jury not have considered her insane? If such a person is not insane, who could be judged to be so? Should the right–wrong M'Naghten principle be dropped from the laws of half the states in the United States? Didn't her phoning 911 to report what she had done prove that she knew she had done something very wrong? Didn't the careful and systematic way she killed her children reflect a mind that, despite her deep depression and delusional thinking, could formulate a complex plan and execute it successfully? Had she received proper treatment from psychiatrists, especially from the one who had recently taken her off the antidepressant medication that had been helping her and had sent her home without adequate follow-up?

As it turns out, these questions were addressed in the Yates case after all. In January 2005, an appeals court overturned Yates's murder conviction because the jury had heard false testimony from one of the expert witnesses that may have unduly influenced their decision. A prosecution witness testified that Yates's behavior may have been influenced by an episode of the television show *Law and Order* that showed a woman with depression drowning her children, suggesting she knew right from wrong. However, there was no such episode on this television show, so Yates could not have been so influenced. A new trial was conducted, and on July 26, 2006, after 3 days of deliberations, the new jury found Yates not guilty by reason of insanity. She was placed in a maximum-security forensic hospital in Texas. In 2007, she was transferred to a minimum-security hospital in Texas, and she is scheduled for a recommitment hearing in Fall 2011 that may result in her release to an outpatient facility if she is no longer deemed mentally ill and dangerous.

Andrea Yates, who drowned her five children, pled NGRI. Although she was suffering from mental illness, her initial plea was unsuccessful because she was judged capable of knowing right from wrong. After the initial verdict was thrown out, her NGRI plea was successful in the second trial. (©AP/Wide World Photos.)

Medication has had an impact on the competency issue. On the one hand, the concept of "synthetic sanity" (Schwitzgebel & Schwitzgebel, 1980) has been used to argue that if a drug, such as Zyprexa, temporarily produces a bit of rationality in an otherwise incompetent defendant, the trial may proceed. The likelihood that the defendant will again become incompetent to stand trial if the drug is withdrawn does not disqualify the person from going to court.[10] On the other hand, the individual rights of the defendant should be protected against forced medication, because there is no guarantee that such treatment would render the person competent to stand trial, and there is a chance that it might cause harm. A subsequent Supreme Court ruling[11] held that a criminal defendant generally couldn't be forced to take medication in an effort to render him or her competent to stand trial. Courts now require safeguards against the involuntary use of medications to ensure that the defendant's civil rights are protected, even when a drug might restore legal competency to stand trial.[12]

In 2003, the Supreme Court issued a new ruling such that forced medication to restore competency could be used only in very limited circumstances.[13] In this case, St. Louis dentist Charles Sell had been charged in 1997 with two different counts of fraud and with conspiring to kill a former employee and an FBI agent who arrested him. Sell was later diagnosed with delusional disorder and was found incompetent to stand trial. This was in essence a nonviolent crime, and the Supreme Court did not see that forced medication was justified in this case. The court ruled that forced medication could be used only if alternative treatments had failed; medication is likely to be effective; medication won't interfere with a person's right to defend him- or herself at trial, and there is an important government interest in trying the defendant for a serious crime.

It turns out the medications are the most effective means of restoring a person's competence to stand trial. Research has shown that the more medications reduce a person's symptoms, the more likely they are to be able to be deemed competent. Though more research is needed, education about the legal proceedings seems to help competency restoration, but it appears that education without medication is not as effective (Zapf & Roesch, 2011).

Even if a person with a mental disorder is found competent to stand trial, that person may not be able to serve as his or her own defense attorney. A 2008 U.S. Supreme Court decision[14] held that a judge might deny the right of self-representation if it is clear that the defendant would not receive a fair trial. Focus on Discovery 16.2 discusses the unusual challenge posed by dissociative identity disorder in criminal commitments.

Check Your Knowledge 16.2

True or false?
1. The *Jackson* case established that people who will not be restored to competency should be found NGRI.

2. To be competent to stand trial, a person must be able to understand the charges and assist his or her attorney.

---

[10]*State v. Hampton*, 218 So.2d 311 (La. 1969); *State v. Stacy*, no. 446 (*Crim. App.*, Knoxville, Tenn., August 4, 1977); *United States v. Hayes*, 589 F.2d 811 (1979).
[11]*Riggins v. Nevada*, 504 U.S. 127 (1992).
[12]*United States v. Waddell*, 687 F. Supp. 208 (1988).
[13]*Sell v. United States*, 539 U.S. 02-5664 (2003).
[14]*Indiana v. Edwards*, 554 U. S. 164 (2008).

FOCUS ON DISCOVERY 16.2

Dissociative Identity Disorder and the Insanity Defense

Imagine that as you are having a cup of coffee one morning, you hear pounding at the front door. You hurry to answer and find two police officers staring grimly at you. One of them asks, "Are you Jane Smith?" "Yes," you reply. "Well, ma'am, you are under arrest for grand theft and for the murder of John Doe." The officer then reads you your Miranda rights against self-incrimination, handcuffs you, and takes you to the police station, where you are allowed to call your lawyer.

This would be a scary situation for anybody. What is particularly frightening and puzzling to you and your lawyer is that you have absolutely no recollection of having committed the crime that a detective later describes to you. You are horrified that you cannot account for the time period when the murder was committed—in fact, your memory is startlingly blank for that entire time. And, as if this were not bizarre enough, the detective then shows you a tape in which you are clearly firing a gun at a bank teller during a holdup. "Is that you in the videotape?" asks the detective. You confer with your lawyer, saying that it certainly looks like you, including the clothes, but you are advised not to admit anything one way or the other.

Let's move forward in time now to your trial some months later. Witnesses have come forward and identified you beyond a reasonable doubt. There is no one you know who can testify that you were somewhere other than at the bank on the afternoon of the robbery and the murder. But did you murder the teller in the bank? You are able to assert honestly to yourself and to the jury that you did not. And yet even you have been persuaded that the person in the videotape is you—and that that person committed the robbery and the murder.

Because of the strange nature of the case, your lawyer arranged prior to the trial to have you interviewed by a psychiatrist and a clinical psychologist, both of them well-known experts in forensics. Through extensive questioning, they have decided that you have dissociative identity disorder (DID, formerly called multiple personality disorder) and that the crimes were committed not by you, Jane Smith, but by your rather violent alter, Laura. Indeed, during one of the interviews, Laura emerged and boasted about the crime, even chuckling over the fact that you, Jane, would be imprisoned for it.

Can DID be an excusing condition for a criminal act? Should Jane Smith be held responsible for a crime committed by her alter, Laura?

In reviews of the DID literature and of its forensic implications, Elyn Saks (1997) of the University of Southern California Law Center argued that DID should be regarded as a special case in mental health law and that a new legal principle should be established. Her argument takes issue with legal practice that would hold a

person with DID responsible for a crime as long as the personality acting at the time of the crime intended to commit it.

What is intriguing about Saks's argument is that she devotes a major portion of it to defining personhood. What is a person? Is a person the body we inhabit? Well, most of the time our sense of who we are as persons does not conflict with the bodies we have come to know as our own or rather, as us. But in DID there is a discrepancy. The body that committed the crimes at the bank was Jane Smith. But it was her alter, Laura, who committed the crimes. Saks argues that, peculiar as it may sound, the law should be interested in the body only as a container for the person. It is the person who may or may not be blameworthy, not the body. Nearly all the time they are one and the same, but in the case of DID they are not. In a sense, Laura committed the murder by using Jane's body.

Then is Jane blameworthy? The person Jane did not commit the crime; she did not even know about it. For the judge to sentence Jane—or more specifically, the body in the courtroom who usually goes by that name—would be unjust, argues Saks, for Jane is descriptively innocent. To be sure, sending Jane to prison would punish Laura, for whenever Laura would emerge, she would find herself imprisoned. But what of Jane? Saks concludes that it is unjust to imprison Jane because she is not blameworthy. Rather, we must find her not guilty by reason of dissociative identity disorder and remand her for treatment of the disorder.

Dissociative identity disorder would not, however, be a justification for a verdict of NGRI if the alter that did not commit the crime was aware of the other alter's criminal intent and did not do anything to prevent the criminal act. Under these circumstances, argues Saks, the first alter would

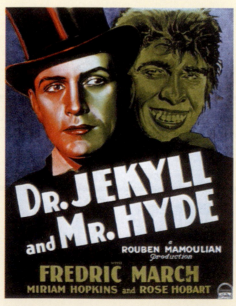

Poster for the classic film about Jekyll and Hyde. (Jerry Ohlinger's Movie Material Store)

be complicit in the crime and would therefore be somewhat blameworthy. A comparison Saks draws is to Robert Louis Stevenson's fictional character of Dr. Jekyll and Mr. Hyde. Jekyll made the potion that caused the emergence of Mr. Hyde, his alter, with the foreknowledge that Hyde would do evil. So even though Jekyll was not present when Hyde was in charge, he would nonetheless be blameworthy because of his prior knowledge of what Hyde would do—not to mention that he, Jekyll, had concocted the potion that created his alter, Hyde.

Saks is optimistic about the effectiveness of therapy for DID and believes that people like Jane/Laura can be integrated into one personality and then released to rejoin society. Saks goes so far as to argue that people with DID who are judged dangerous but who have not committed a crime should be subject to civil commitment, even though this would be tantamount to preventive detention. In this way, she suggests, future crimes might be avoided.

Civil Commitment

Historically, governments have had a duty to protect their citizens from harm. We take for granted the right and duty of government to set limits on our freedom for the sake of protecting us. Few drivers, for example, question the legitimacy of imposing limits on them by providing traffic signals that often make them stop when they would rather go. Government has a long-established right as well as an obligation to protect us both from ourselves—the *parens patriae*, "power of the state"—and from others—the police power of the state. Civil commitment is one further exercise of these powers.

In virtually all European countries (as well as those in the United States), a person can be committed to a psychiatric hospital against his or her will if a judgment is made that he or she is (1) mentally ill and (2) a danger to self—that is, the person is suicidal or unable to provide for the basic physical needs of food, clothing, and shelter—or to others (Perlin, 1994). At present, dangerousness to others is more often the principal criterion in court rulings that point to imminent dangerousness (e.g., the person is right on the verge of committing a violent act).[15] In some jurisdictions, a finding of imminent dangerousness must be evidenced by a recent overt act, attempt, or threat; however, there are some jurisdictions that do not require an overt act [*In Re: Albright*, 836 P.2d 1 (Kan. App. 1992)]. Such commitment is supposed to last for only as long as the person remains dangerous.[16]

Specific commitment procedures generally fit into one of two categories, formal and informal. Formal (or judicial) commitment is by order of a court. Any responsible citizen—usually the police, a relative, or a friend, can request it. If a judge believes that there is a good reason to pursue the matter, he or she will order a mental health examination. The person has the right to object to these attempts to "certify" him or her, and a court hearing can be scheduled to allow the person to present evidence against commitment.

Informal, emergency commitment of people with mental illness can be accomplished without initially involving the courts. For example, if a hospital administrative board believes that a voluntary patient requesting discharge is too mentally ill and dangerous to be released, it is able to detain the patient with a temporary, informal commitment order.

Involuntary Commitment or Civil Commitment is a legal process through which an individual with symptoms of severe mental illness is court-ordered into treatment in a hospital (inpatient) or in the community (outpatient).

The United Nations General Assembly (resolution 46/119 of 1991), "Principles for the Protection of Persons with Mental Illness and the Improvement of Mental Health Care" is a non-binding resolution advocating certain broadly-drawn procedures for the carrying out of involuntary commitment. These principles have been used in many countries where local laws have been revised or new ones implemented.

In Germany for example, there is a growing tendency to use the law on legal guardianship, instead of mental health law, to justify involuntary commitment or treatment. The ward's legal guardian decides if the individual must go into a hospital for treatment, and the police will then act on this decision.

In the United Kingdom, involuntary commitment is informally known as "sectioning," after the various *sections* of the Mental Health Act 1983 (covering England and Wales), the Mental Health (Northern Ireland) Order 1986 and the Mental Health (Care and Treatment) (Scotland) Act 2003 that provide its legal basis.

In England and Wales, Approved Mental Health Professionals have a lead role in coordinating Mental Health Act assessments, which they conduct in cooperation with usually two medical practitioners. Under the Mental Health Act, detention is determined by utility and purpose. Mentally ill individuals may be detained under Section 2 for a period of assessment lasting up to 28 days or Section 3 for a period of treatment lasting up to 6 months. Patients already on a ward may be detained under section 5(2) for up to 72 hours for the purposes of allowing an assessment to take place for section 2 or 3. Separate sections deal with mentally ill

---

[15]*Suzuki v. Yuen*, 617 F.2d 173 (9th Cir. 1980).
[16]*United States v. DeBellis*, 649 F.2d 1 (1st Cir. 1981).

criminal offenders. In all cases detention needs to be justified on the basis that the person has a mental disorder and poses a risk of harm to their own health, safety, or the safety of others.[21]

Under the amended Mental Health Act 2007, which came into force in November 2008, to be detained under Section 3 for treatment, appropriate treatment must be available in the place of detention.

Supervised Community Treatment orders means people can be discharged to the community on a conditional basis, remaining liable to recall to hospital if they break the conditions of the community treatment order.

Preventive Detention and Problems in the Prediction of Dangerousness

There is a widespread perception that people with mental illness are associated with violence and violent offending, particularly homicide. However, mental health advocacy groups and many mental health clinicians argue that it is a myth that people with mental health problems are more likely to commit a violent act compared to the general population. Several large, population-based studies have examined this disputed relationship, with some studies reporting no increased risk of violence among patients with schizophrenia compared with the general population, whereas other studies do report an association between violent offending and schizophrenia. In a recent review of the literature published in 2009, researchers from the UK and Sweden compared the risk of violence in people with schizophrenia and other psychoses and the risk of violence in the general population (Fazel, et al., 2009). Their work indicated that whilst schizophrenia and other psychoses are associated with violence, this association appear to be mediated (to a large extent) by substance abuse. Importantly, this increased risk for violence in patients co-morbid for schizophrenia and substance abuse was **similar** to that found in individuals with substance abuse and **without** psychosis. Suggesting that issues around substance abuse rather than schizophrenia per se are the main contributory factors. (**Seena Fazel**[1]*, **Gautam Gulati**[1], **Louise Linsell**[1], **John R. Geddes**[1], **Martin Grann**[2] Schizophrenia and Violence: Systematic Review and Meta-Analysis. Public Library of Science – Medicine 2009, http://www.plosmedicine.org/article/info%3Adoi%2F10.1371%2Fjournal.pmed.1000120).

The MacArthur Violence Risk Assessment Study, a large prospective study of violent behaviour among persons recently discharged from psychiatric hospitals, found that people with mental illness reported more violent thoughts while in the hospital compared to people not in the hospital (Grisso et al., 2000). However, these people were not necessarily more likely to actually be violent once they left the hospital. Actual violent behavior was found only among a subsample of people with mental illness (e.g., those with a diagnosis of substance abuse or those who had severe symptoms and persistent violent thoughts). A recent meta-analysis of violence and mental illness found that people with what they termed "major mental illness" (schizophrenia spectrum disorders, bipolar disorder, depression with psychotic features) were slightly more likely to be aggressive, but again, this was particularly true when a person had the positive or disorganization symptoms of schizophrenia (see Chapter 9) or was also abusing drugs (Douglas, Guy, & Hart, 2009). By and large, then, the general public is seldom affected by violence from people with mental illness, even though certain people with mental illness can and will be violent.

People with mental illness are not necessarily more likely to be violent than people without mental illness, contrary to the way movies often portray people with mental illness. (The Kobal Collection, Ltd.)

The Prediction of Dangerousness The likelihood of committing a dangerous act is central to civil commitment, but is dangerousness easily predicted? Early studies examining the accuracy of predictions that a person would commit a dangerous act found that mental health professionals were poor at making this judgment (e.g., Kozol, Boucher, & Garofalo, 1972; Monahan, 1973, 1976).

However, newer, empirically supported methods for assessing and predicting violence have been developed that identify and measure violence risk factors based on clinical judgment (e.g., Historical-Clinical-Risk Management- 20 or HCR-20; Webster et al., 1997) or a combination of clinical judgment and statistical algorithms (e.g., Violence Risk Appraisal Guide (VRAG; Quinsey et al., 2006). These measures seem to work equally well, but it remains a challenge to accurately predict future dangerousness (Skeem & Monahan, 2011).

Research suggests that violence prediction is most accurate under the following conditions (Campbell, Stefan, & Loder, 1994; Monahan, 1984; Monahan & Steadman, 1994; Steadman et al., 1998):

- If a person has been repeatedly violent in the recent past, it is reasonable to predict that he or she will be violent in the near future unless there have been major changes in the person's attitudes or environment.

- If violence is in the person's distant past, and if it was a single but very serious act, and if that person has been incarcerated for a period of time, then violence can be expected on release if there is reason to believe that the person's predetention personality and physical abilities have not changed and if the person is going to return to the same environment in which he or she was previously violent.

- Even with no history of violence, violence can be predicted if the person is judged to be on the brink of a violent act, for example, if the person is pointing a loaded gun at an occupied building.

Violence among people with mental illness is often associated with medication noncompliance (Monahan, 1992; Steadman et al., 1998). **Outpatient commitment** is one way of increasing medication compliance. It is an arrangement whereby a patient is allowed to leave the hospital but must live in a halfway house or other supervised setting and report to a mental health agency frequently. To the extent that outpatient commitment increases compliance with medication regimens and other mental health treatment—and evidence indicates that it does (Munetz et al., 1996)—we can expect violence to be reduced. Indeed, support services, such as halfway houses, can markedly reduce the chances that a person who might otherwise be prone to committing a violent act will actually commit one (Dvoskin & Steadman, 1994). For a discussion of therapists' responsibilities to predict dangerousness, see Focus on Discovery 16.3.

Toward Greater Protection of the Rights of People with Mental Illness

As previously discussed at the beginning of this chapter, The U.S. Constitution and the European Convention are remarkable documents. They lay down the basic duties of elected officials and guarantee a set of civil rights. But there is often some distance between the abstract delineation of a civil right and its day-to-day implementation. Moreover, the judiciary must interpret these documents as they bear on specific contemporary problems. Since nowhere in either the Constitution or the Convention is there specific mention of people with mental illness, lawyers and judges interpret various sections of these document to justify what they consider necessary in society's treatment of people whose mental health is in question. This is illustrated particularly clearly in relation to a series of court decisions made in the United States.

Beginning in the 1970s, a number of court decisions were rendered to protect people from being involuntarily hospitalized unless absolutely necessary. For example, a 1979 Supreme Court decision, *Addington v. Texas*,[17] further provides that the state must produce clear and convincing evidence that a person is mentally ill and dangerous before he or she can be involuntarily committed to a psychiatric hospital. In 1980, the Ninth Circuit Court of Appeals ruled that this danger must be imminent.[18]

---

[17]*Addington v. Texas*, 441 U.S. 418 (1979).
[18]*Suzuki v. Yuen*, 617 F.2d at 173.

FOCUS ON DISCOVERY 16.3

The *Tarasoff* Case—The Duty to Warn and to Protect

The client's right to privileged communication—the legal right of a client to require that what goes on in therapy remain confidential—is an important protection, but it is not absolute. Society has long stipulated certain conditions in which confidentiality in a relationship should not be maintained because of the harm that can befall others. A famous California court ruling in 1974[a] described circumstances in which a therapist not only may but *must* breach the sanctity of a client's communication. First, we describe the facts of the case.

Clinical Case

In the fall of 1968, Prosenjit Poddar, a graduate student from India studying at the University of California at Berkeley, met Tatiana (Tanya) Tarasoff at a folk dancing class. They saw each other weekly during the fall, and on New Year's Eve she kissed him. Poddar interpreted this act as a sign of formal engagement (as it might have been in India, where he was a member of the Harijan, or "untouchable," caste). But Tanya told him that she was involved with other men and indicated that she did not wish to have an intimate relationship with him.

Poddar was depressed as a result of the rebuff, but he saw Tanya a few times during the spring (occasionally tape-recording their conversations in an effort to understand why she did not love him). Tanya left for Brazil in the summer, and Poddar, at the urging of a friend, went to the student health facility, where a psychiatrist referred him to a psychologist for psychotherapy. When Tanya returned in October 1969, Poddar discontinued therapy. Based in part on Poddar's stated intention to purchase a gun, the psychologist notified the campus police, both orally and in writing, that Poddar was dangerous and should be taken to a community mental health center for psychiatric commitment.

The campus police interviewed Poddar, who seemed rational and promised to stay away from Tanya. They released him and notified the health service. No further efforts at commitment were made because the supervising psychiatrist apparently decided that there was no need and, as a matter of confidentiality, requested that the letter to the police as well as certain therapy records be destroyed.

On October 27, Poddar went to Tanya's home armed with a pellet gun and a kitchen knife. She refused to speak to him. He shot her with the pellet gun. She ran from the house; he pursued, caught, and repeatedly and fatally stabbed her. Poddar was found guilty of voluntary manslaughter rather than first- or second-degree murder. The defense established with the aid of the expert testimony of three psychiatrists that Poddar's diminished mental capacity, schizophrenia, precluded the malice necessary for first- or second-degree murder. After his prison term, he returned to India, where, according to his own report, he is happily married (Schwitzgebel & Schwitzgebel, 1980, p. 205).

Under the privileged communication statute of California, the counseling center psychologist properly breached the confidentiality of the professional relationship and took steps to have Poddar civilly committed, for he judged Poddar to be an imminent danger. Poddar had stated that he intended to purchase a gun, and by his other words and actions he had convinced the therapist that he was desperate enough to harm Tarasoff. What the psychologist did not do, and what the court decided he should have done, was to warn the likely victim, Tanya Tarasoff, that her former friend had bought a gun and might use it against her. As stated by the California Supreme Court in *Tarasoff*: "Once a therapist does in fact determine, or under applicable professional standards reasonably should have determined, that a patient poses a serious danger of violence to others, he bears a duty to exercise reasonable care to protect the foreseeable victims of that danger." The *Tarasoff* ruling requires clinicians, in deciding when to violate confidentiality, to use the very imperfect skill of predicting dangerousness. Since the original ruling, it has been extended in several ways.

Extending Protection to Foreseeable Victims

A subsequent California court ruling[b] held by a bare majority that foreseeable victims include those in close relationship to the identifiable victim. In this instance, a mother was hurt by a shotgun fired by the dangerous patient, and her 7-year-old son was present when the shooting took place. The boy later sued the psychologists for damages brought on by emotional trauma. Since a young child is likely to be in the company of his or her mother, the court concluded in *Hedlund* that the *Tarasoff* ruling extended to the boy.

Extending Protection Further to Potential Victims

A 1983 decision of a federal circuit court in California[c] ruled that Veterans Administration psychiatrists should earlier have warned the murdered lover of an outpatient, Phillip Jablonski, that she was a foreseeable victim, even though the patient had never made an explicit threat against her to the therapists. The reasoning was that Jablonski, having previously raped

---

[a]*Tarasoff v. Regents of the University of California,* 529 P.2d 553 (Cal. 1974), vacated, reheard in bank, and affirmed, 131 Cal. Rptr. 14, 551 P.2d 334 (1976). The 1976 California Supreme Court ruling was by a four-to-three majority.
[b]*Hedlund v. Superior Court,* 34 Cal.3d 695 (1983).
[c]*Jablonski by Pahls v. United States,* 712 F.2d 391 (1983).

Being hospitalized against one's wishes is less likely today, in large part due to changes in health care that emphasize outpatient care over inpatient care. In fact, it is increasingly difficult to hospitalize a patient today who is in real need of at least a short hospital stay. However, many rights of people with mental illness are still curtailed. An analysis of mental health–related bills introduced in state legislatures in 2002 (Corrigan et al., 2005) found that 75 percent of these contracted liberties of people with mental illness (e.g., allowing involuntary medication) and

and otherwise harmed his wife, would likely direct his continuing "violence . . . against women very close to him" (p. 392).

The court also found the hospital psychiatrists negligent in not obtaining Jablonski's earlier medical records. These records showed a history of harmful violent behavior, which, together with the threats his lover was complaining about, should have moved the hospital to institute emergency civil commitment. The court ruled that the failure to warn was a proximate or immediate cause of the woman's murder. Proper consideration of the medical records, said the judge, would have convinced the psychiatrists that Jablonski was a real danger to others and should be committed.

This broadening of the duty to warn and protect has placed mental health professionals in California in an even more difficult predicament, for the potentially violent patient need not even mention the specific person he or she may harm. It is up to the therapist to deduce who are possible victims, based on what he or she can learn of the patient's past and present circumstances.

Extending Protection to Potential Victims as Yet Unknown

Many courts have augmented the duty to warn and protect to foreseeable victims of child abuse and even to possible victims as yet unknown. In one such case,[d] a medical student underwent his own psychoanalysis as one of the requirements to become a psychoanalyst. During the therapy, he admitted that he was a pedophile. Later in his training, he saw a male child as a patient as part of his psychiatric residency and sexually assaulted the boy. The court decided that the training analyst, who was not only the student's therapist but also an instructor in the school, had reason to know that his patient-student "posed a specific threat to a specific group of persons, namely future minor patients, with whom [the student] would necessarily interact as part of his training" (p. 8). Even though the student did not have child patients at the time he revealed his pedophilia (and thus there were no specific people whom the instructor could warn and take steps to

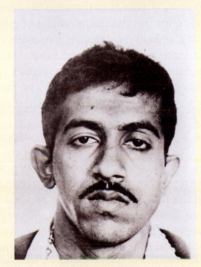

Prosenjit Poddar was convicted of manslaughter in the death of Tatiana Tarasoff. The court ruled that his therapist, who had become convinced Poddar might harm Tarasoff, should have warned her of the impending danger. (©AP/Wide World Photos.)

protect), the supervisor—as his instructor, not just his therapist—was judged to have sufficient control over the student's professional training and activities (specifically, the power to keep the student from pursuing his interests in working with children) for the *Tarasoff* ruling to be relevant.

Extending Protection Based on Families' Reports

In 2004, a California appeals court ruled that therapists have a duty to warn a possible victim if the threat is reported by a member of the patient's family.[e] In this case, a therapist learned about a threat not from his patient but from a family member of his patient. His patient revealed to his parents that he had thoughts of killing his ex-girlfriend's new boyfriend. The parents contacted the therapist about this threat. The therapist did not contact the new boyfriend, who was later killed by his patient. The parents of the boyfriend sued for wrongful death, saying the therapist should have warned their son. The court agreed and ruled that a close family member is in essence a part of the patient, and thus a therapist does have a duty to warn potential victims if notified by a close family member of a patient.

Extending Protection to Property

Tarasoff was further extended by a Vermont State Supreme Court ruling, *Peck v. Counseling Service of Addison County,*[f] which held that a mental health practitioner has a duty to warn a third party if there is a danger of damage to property. The case involved a 29-year-old male patient who, after a heated argument with his father, told his therapist that he wanted to get back at his father and indicated that he might do so by burning down his father's barn. He proceeded to do just that. No people or animals were harmed in the fire; the barn housed no animals and was located 130 feet away from the parents' home. The court's conclusion that the therapist had a duty to warn was based on reasoning that arson is a violent act and therefore a lethal threat to people who may be in the vicinity of the fire.

---

[d]*Almonte v. New York Medical College*, 851 F. Supp. 34, 40 (D. Conn. 1994) (denying motion for summary judgment).
[e]*Ewing v. Goldstein*, Cal. App. 4th B163112.2d. (2004).
[f]*Peck v. Counseling Service of Addison County*, 499 A.2d 422 (Vt. 1985).

---

33 percent contracted privacy rights (e.g., sharing mental health records in the interest of public safety) (see also Focus on Discovery 1.1 in Chapter 1).

We turn now to a discussion of several issues and trends that revolve around the protections provided to those with mental disorders: the principle of the least restrictive alternative; the right to treatment; the right to refuse treatment; and, finally, the way in which these several themes conflict in efforts to provide humane mental health treatment while respecting individual rights.

Least Restrictive Alternative As noted earlier, civil commitment rests on presumed dangerousness, a condition that may vary depending on the circumstances. A person may be deemed dangerous if living in an apartment by himself or herself, but not dangerous if living in a residential treatment home and taking prescribed medications every day under medical supervision. The **least restrictive alternative** to freedom is to be provided when treating people with mental disorders and protecting them from harming themselves and others. A number of court rulings require that only those people who cannot be adequately looked after in less restrictive settings be placed in hospitals.[19] In general terms, mental health professionals have to provide the treatment that restricts the patient's liberty to the least possible degree while remaining workable.[20] It is unconstitutional to confine a person with mental illness who is nondangerous and who is capable of living on his or her own or with the help of willing and responsible family or friends.[21] Of course, this principle has meaning only if society provides suitable residences and treatments, which unfortunately does not happen as much as it needs to.

Right to Treatment Another aspect of civil commitment that has come to the attention of the courts is the so-called right to treatment. If a person is deprived of liberty because he or she is mentally ill and is a danger to self or others, is the state not required to provide treatment to alleviate these problems?

The right to treatment was extended to all civilly committed patients in a landmark 1972 case, *Wyatt v. Stickney*.[22] In that case, an Alabama federal court ruled that treatment is the only justification for the civil commitment of people with mental illness to a psychiatric hospital. This ruling, upheld on appeal, is frequently cited as ensuring protection of people confined by civil commitment, at least to the extent that the state cannot simply put them away without meeting minimal standards of care. In fact, when people with intellectual developmental disorder (as opposed to those judged to be mentally ill) are released from an institution, health officials are not relieved of their constitutional duty to provide reasonable care and safety as well as appropriate training.[23]

The *Wyatt* ruling was significant, because previously the courts had asserted that it was beyond their competence to pass judgment on the care given to people with mental illness, and they had assumed that mental health professionals possessed special and exclusive knowledge about psychopathology and its treatment. Repeated reports of abuses, however, gradually prodded the judicial system to rule on what went on within the walls of psychiatric hospitals. The *Wyatt* decision set forth very specific requirements for psychiatric hospitals—for example, dayrooms of at least 40 square feet, curtains or screens for privacy in multi-patient bedrooms, and no physical restraints except in emergency situations. The ruling also specified how many mental health professionals ought to be working in the hospital. When the *Wyatt* action was taken, Alabama state psychiatric hospitals averaged one physician per 2,000 patients, an extreme situation. After *Wyatt*, there were to be at least two psychiatrists for every 250 patients.

The *Wyatt* ruling appeared to have been weakened by a later Supreme Court decision, *Youngberg v. Romeo*,[24] regarding the treatment of a boy with intellectual developmental disorder, Nicholas Romeo, who had been placed in physical restraints on occasion to keep him from hurting himself and others. While maintaining that people with mental illness have a right to reasonable care and safety, this 1982 decision deferred to the professional judgment of the mental health professionals responsible for the boy. However, later cases extended protections to people with intellectual developmental disorder,[25] and held that professional judgment is not the final word when it comes to constitutional protections of people with intellectual disabilities in public hospitals, a ruling more in line with *Wyatt*.[26]

---

[19]*Lake v. Cameron*, 267 F. Supp 155 (D.C. Cir. 1967); *Lessard*, 349 F. Supp. at 1078.

[20]*In Re: Tarpley*, 556 N.E.2d, superseded by 581 N.E.2d 1251 (1991).

[21]*Project Release v. Prevost*, 722 F.2d 960 (2d Cir. 1983).

[22]*Wyatt v. Stickney*, 325 F.Supp. 781 (M.D. Ala. 1971), enforced in 334 F.Supp. 1341 (M.D. Ala. 1971), 344 F.Supp. 373, 379 (M.D. Ala. 1972), *aff'd sub nom Wyatt v. Anderholt*, 503 F.2d 1305 (5th Cir. 1974).

[23]*Thomas S. v. Flaherty*, 902 F.2d 250, cert. denied, 111 S.Ct. 373 (1990).

[24]*Youngberg v. Romeo*, 102 S.Ct. 2452 (1982).

[25]*Feagley v. Waddill*, 868 F.2d 1437 (5th Cir. 1989).

[26]*Thomas S. v. Flaherty* 902 F.2d 250, 252 (4th Cir.1990).

In a celebrated case, *O'Connor v. Donaldson*,[27] that eventually went to the Supreme Court in 1975, a civilly committed man sued two state hospital doctors for his release and for monetary damages on the grounds that he had been kept against his will for 14 years without being treated and without being dangerous to himself or to others. In January 1957, at the age of 49, Kenneth Donaldson was committed to the Chattahoochee state hospital in Florida on petition of his father, who felt that his son was delusional. At a brief court hearing, a county judge found that Donaldson had schizophrenia and committed him for "care, maintenance, and treatment."

In 1971, Donaldson sued Dr. O'Connor, the hospital superintendent, and Dr. Gumanis, a hospital psychiatrist, for release. Testimony at the trial in a U.S. District Court in Florida made it clear that at no time during his hospitalization had Donaldson's conduct posed any real danger to others or to himself. Furthermore, just before his commitment in 1957 he had been earning a living and taking adequate care of himself. Nonetheless, O'Connor had repeatedly refused Donaldson's requests for release, feeling it was his duty to determine whether he could adapt successfully outside the hospital. His judgment was that Donaldson could not. In deciding the question of dangerousness on the basis of how well the patient could live outside the institution, O'Connor was applying a more restrictive standard than that required by most state laws.

Civil commitment supposedly requires that the person be dangerous. But in actual practice, the decision to commit can be based on a judgment of severe disability, as in the case of some people who are homeless. (Corbis Images.)

The evidence indicated that Donaldson received only custodial care during his hospitalization. No treatment that could conceivably alleviate his assumed mental illness was undertaken. The therapy that O'Connor claimed Donaldson was undergoing consisted of being kept in a large room with 60 other patients. Donaldson had been denied privileges to stroll around the hospital grounds or even to discuss his case with Dr. O'Connor. O'Connor also regarded as delusional Donaldson's expressed desire to write a book about his hospital experiences (which Donaldson did after his release; the book sold well).

The Supreme Court[28] ruled on June 26, 1975 that "a State cannot constitutionally confine . . . a nondangerous individual who is capable of surviving safely in freedom by himself or with the help of willing and responsible family members or friends." In 1977, Donaldson settled for $20,000 from Dr. Gumanis and from the estate of Dr. O'Connor, who had died during the appeals process.

Because of this decision, a civilly committed person's status must be periodically reviewed, for the grounds on which the person was committed cannot be assumed to continue in effect forever.

Right to Refuse Treatment Does a committed patient have the right to refuse treatment or a particular kind of treatment? The answer is yes, but with qualifications.

The right of committed people to refuse medication is hotly debated. Psychiatrist E. Fuller Torrey (1996) asserts that because many people with mental illness have no insight into their condition, they believe they do not need any treatment and thus subject themselves and their loved ones to sometimes desperate and frightening situations by refusing medication or other modes of therapy, most of which involve hospitalization. Torrey's arguments plead for consideration of the costs of untreated mental illness.

On the other hand, there are many arguments against forcing a person to take medications. The side effects of most antipsychotic drugs are often aversive and are sometimes harmful and irreversible in the long run. And, as many as one-third of people with mental illness who take medications do not benefit from them.

There is a trend toward granting even involuntarily committed people certain rights to refuse medication, based on the constitutional protections of freedom from physical invasion, freedom of thought, and the right to privacy. In an extension of the least-restrictive-treatment principle, the court ruled that the government cannot force antipsychotic drugs on a person

---

[27]*O'Connor v. Donaldson*, 95 S.Ct. 2486 (1975).
[28]*O'Connor v. Donaldson*, 422, U.S. 563 (1975)

only on the supposition that at some future time he or she might become dangerous.[29] The threat to the public safety has to be clear and imminent to justify the risks and restrictions that such medications pose, and it must be shown that less intrusive intervention will not likely reduce impending danger to others. In other words, forcible medication necessarily restricts liberty in addition to whatever physical risks it could bring; there has to be a very good reason to deprive a person of liberty and privacy via such intrusive measures. For example, a ruling in favor of forcible medication was made in a case of a person who had been threatening to assassinate the president of the United States. He posed a threat to his own safety, and he could be shown by clear and convincing evidence to be seriously mentally impaired.[30]

When someone already hospitalized is believed to be too impaired to give informed consent about a treatment, mental health law sometimes invokes the doctrine of substituted judgment, the decision that the patient would have made if he or she had been able or competent to make a decision.[31] This principle creates as many problems as it solves. Deciding when a patient is competent to refuse treatment is one of the most controversial topics in the mental health law literature (e.g., Appelbaum & Grisso, 1995; Grisso & Appelbaum, 1991; Winick, 1997).

Deinstitutionalization, Civil Liberties, and Mental Health

Court rulings such as *Wyatt v. Stickney* and *O'Connor v. Donaldson* put mental health professionals on notice to be careful about keeping people in psychiatric hospitals against their will and to attend more to the specific treatment needs of people with mental illness. Pressure was placed on state governments to upgrade the quality of care in hospitals. In view of the abuses that have been documented in hospital care, these are surely encouraging changes. But the picture is not all that rosy. For judges to declare that patient care must meet certain minimal standards does not automatically translate into realization of that praiseworthy goal. Money is not in unlimited supply, and the care of people with mental illness has not been among any government's high priorities.

Beginning in the 1960s, the United States and many European countries embarked on a policy referred to as *deinstitutionalization*, discharging as many patients as possible from mental hospitals and discouraging admissions. Indeed, civil commitment is more difficult to achieve now than it was in the 1950s and 1960s, despite the fact that some people with mental illness need short stays in a hospital.

Care in the Community was the name of the British policy of deinstitutionalization, and treating and caring for physically and mentally disabled people in their homes rather than in an institution.

As was the case in the United States, institutional care was the target of widespread concern and criticism in the UK during the 1960s and 1970s,[1] but it was not until the 1980s that the government of Margaret Thatcher adopted a new policy of care after the Audit Commission published a report called 'Making a Reality of Community Care'[2] which outlined the advantages of domiciled care.

The main aim of Thatcher's community care policy was to maintain individuals in their own homes wherever possible, and taking away the burden of the provision care from long-stay hospitals or residential establishment. There was wide spread support for this policy from a moral and humanitarian perspective. But it would be naive to think that there wasn't a strong financial driver behind it as well.

There were three key objectives of Community Care policy:

- The overriding objective was to cap public expenditure on independent sector residential and nursing home care. This was achieved in that local authorities became responsible for operating a needs-based yet cash-limited system.

[29]*United States v. Charters*, 863, F.2d 302
[30]*Dautremont v. Broadlawns Hospital*, 827 F.2d 291 (8th Cir. 1987).
[31]*Guardianship of Weedon*, 565 N.E. 2d 432, 409 Mass. 196 (1991).

- There was a clear agenda about developing a mixed economy of care, i.e. a variety of providers. The mixed economy provision in residential and nursing home care has been maintained despite the social security budget being capped. And there are now many independent organisations providing domiciliary care services.

- To redefine the boundaries between health and social care. Much of the continuing care of elderly and disabled people was provided by the NHS. Now much of that has been re-defined as social care and is the responsibility of local authorities.

The Griffiths Report: 'Community Care: Agenda for Action'

In 1988 Sir Roy Griffiths produced a report or a Green Paper called 'Community Care: Agenda for Action', also known as The Griffiths Report, in which he was basically saying that community care was not working because no one wanted to accept the responsibility for community care. In 1989 the government published its response to the Griffiths Report in the White Paper *Caring for People: Community Care in the next Decade and Beyond* and enacted in the National Health Service and Community Care Act 1990.

The community care reforms outlined in the 1990 Act have been in operation since April 1993. They have been evaluated but no clear conclusions have been reached. A number of authors have been highly critical of the reforms. For example, Hadley and Clough (1996) claim the reforms 'have created care in chaos' (Hadley and Clough 1996).

Under-resourcing of community-based treatment programs are also reported from the United States. Some effective programs were described in Chapter 9, but these are very much the exception, not the rule. The state of affairs in cities is an unrelenting crisis for the hundreds of thousands of people with mental illness who have been released since the 1960s without adequate community services to help them. Rates of homelessness have soared among the mentally ill, and homeless persons do not have fixed addresses and need help in establishing eligibility and residency for the purpose of receiving benefits. The state of homelessness undoubtedly exacerbates the emotional suffering of people with mental illness. People with mental illness are an especially defenseless segment of the homeless population.

Deinstitutionalization may be a misnomer. *Trans*institutionalization may be more apt, for declines in the census of psychiatric hospitals have occasioned increases in the presence of people with mental illness in nursing homes, the mental health departments of nonpsychiatric hospitals, and prisons (Cloud, 1999; Kiesler, 1991), and these settings are by and large not equipped to handle the particular needs of people with mental illness.

Indeed in some cases, prisons have become the new "hospitals" for the people with mental illness in the twenty-first century. Here are some disconcerting facts:

1. More than 70% of the prison population has two or more mental health disorders. (Social Exclusion Unit, 2004, quoting Psychiatric Morbidity Among Prisoners In England And Wales, 1998)

2. Male prisoners are 14 times more likely to have two or more disorders than men in general, and female prisoners are 35 times more likely than women in general. (Social Exclusion Unit, 2004, quoting Psychiatric Morbidity Among Prisoners In England And Wales, 1998)

3. The suicide rate in prisons is almost 15 times higher than in the general population: in 2002 the rate was 143 per 100,000 compared to 9 per 100,000 in the general population. (The National Service Framework For Mental Health: Five Years On, Department of Health, 2004; Samaritans Information Resource Pack, 2004)

Police officers are now called on to do the work of mental health professionals. They are often the first to come in contact with a person with mental illness and can make decisions as to whether a person should be taken to a hospital or jail. In several cities, mental health professionals have teamed up with police officers to form mobile crisis units (Lamb, Weinberger, & DeCuir, 2002). These units consist of trained mental health professionals who work in conjunction with local police to find the best option for a person with mental illness in the community. Because police officers are increasingly called on to work with people with mental illness, communities are recognizing the need for the police to receive proper training. New laws passed in the past decade including America's Law Enforcement and Mental Health Project Act (2000) and the later extension of this, called the Mentally Ill Offender Treatment and Crime Reduction Act (2004), provide funding for such training. These laws also provide funds to set up what are referred to as mental health courts in local communities. The idea is that people with mental illness who commit a crime may be better served by courts that can monitor treatment availability and adherence.

The approach of building partnerships between mental health professionals and law enforcement led to the creation of the Consensus Project (www.consensusproject.org). The Council of State Governments coordinated collaboration between criminal justice, mental health, and local and national lawmakers. A report entitled *Criminal Justice/Mental Health Consensus Project* was released in 2002, and it has been influential in increasing awareness of the large numbers of people with mental illness who are now housed in jails rather than in treatment facilities. The report outlines a number of policy ideas, all aimed at increasing cooperation between mental health and criminal justice and ultimately benefiting those with mental illness who are in the criminal justice system or who are at risk of becoming involved (e.g., sent to jail rather than treatment following a public outburst that reflects an exacerbation of illness).

Quick Summary

The legal standard for competency to stand trial requires that the accused understand the charges against him or her and be able to assist his or her attorney in the defense. Someone who is judged incompetent to stand trial receives treatment to restore competence and then returns to face the charges. The *Jackson* case specified that the pretrial period could be no longer than it takes to determine whether a person will ever become competent to stand trial. The use of medication to restore competency to stand trial can be used in limited circumstances.

A person can be civilly committed to a hospital against his or her wishes if the person is mentally ill and a danger to self or others. Formal commitment requires a court order; informal commitment does not. People with mental illness who are not substance abusers are not necessarily more likely to engage in violence than are non–mentally ill people who are not substance abusers.

Early studies on the prediction of dangerousness had a number of flaws. Later research has shown that repeated acts of violence, a single serious violent act, being on the brink of violence, and medication noncompliance can maximize accuracy in predictions.

Court cases have tried to balance a person's rights with the rights of society to be protected. The least restrictive alternative to freedom is to be provided when treating people with mental disorders and protecting them from harming themselves and others. A series of court cases have generally supported the notion that those people committed to a hospital have the right to receive treatment. People with mental illness have the right to refuse treatment as well, except when doing so poses a danger to self or others.

Beginning in the 1960s, large numbers of people were released from mental hospitals in what has been called deinstitutionalization. Unfortunately, there are not enough treatment options available in the community. Prisons are seen by some as the new "hospitals" for people with mental illness. Police officers are called on to do the work once reserved for mental health professionals. Partnerships between police, courts, and community mental health providers are promising for helping people with mental illness.

Check Your Knowledge 16.3

True or false?
1. People with schizophrenia who are co-morbid for substance abuse are more likely to be violent than those with substance abuse only.
2. Past violence is a predictor of future violence.
3. Court decisions have determined that hospitalized patients do not have a right to treatment unless they are dangerous.
4. People with mental illness can refuse treatment if they are found incompetent to stand trial after being charged with a nonviolent offense.

Ethical Dilemmas in Therapy and Research

The issues reviewed thus far place legal limits on the activities of mental health professionals. These legal constraints are important, for laws are one of society's strongest means of encouraging all of us to behave in certain ways. Mental health professionals also have to work within a set of ethical constraints. The most common way of defining "ethics" is to think about in terms of norms for conduct that distinguish between acceptable and unacceptable behavior. Ethical norms are so ubiquitous that one might be tempted to regard them as simple commonsense. On the other hand, if morality were nothing more than commonsense, then why are there so many ethical disputes and issues in our society? One explanation of these disagreements is that all people recognize some common ethical norms but different individuals interpret, apply, and balance these norms in different ways in light of their society's ideologies, their own values and life experiences. Although most societies use laws to enforce widely accepted moral standards and ethical and legal rules use similar concepts, it is important to remember that ethics and law are not the same. An action may be legal but unethical or illegal but ethical. Another way of defining 'ethics' focuses on the disciplines that study standards of conduct, such as philosophy, theology, law, psychology or criminology.

We examine now the ethics of making psychological inquiries and interventions into the lives of other human beings.

Ethical Constraints on Research

Instances of abuse carried out in the name of medical research appear throughout the 20th century. Practically everyone is aware of the terrible medical atrocities of the Nazis during World War II, many of which were perpetrated by a select group of German doctors and scientists motivated as much by medical curiosity as by Nazi ideology. The painful and frequently deadly experiments were carried out on thousands of concentration camp prisoners without their consent. Concentration camp prisoners were subjected to "freezing experiments" to find an effective treatment for hypothermia, injected with immunization compounds and sera for the prevention and treatment of contagious diseases, including malaria, typhus, tuberculosis, typhoid fever, yellow fever, and infectious hepatitis, and subjected to phosgene and mustard gas in order to test possible antidotes.

The most notorious medical experimentation sought to advance the racial and ideological tenets of the Nazi worldview, and implemented under the direction of Dr Josef Mengele at Auschwitz. Some of his medical experiments son Jews and Romany gypsies soughtto determine amongst other things how different "races" withstood various contagious diseases, and to develop an efficient and inexpensive procedure for the mass sterilization of groups Nazi leaders considered to be racially or genetically undesirable.

In the 1990s, the US President, Bill Clinton, offered an apology to the families of the families of those men involved in the infamous Tuskegee project. For forty years between 1932 and 1972, the U.S. Public Health Service conducted an experiment on 399 black men in the late stages of syphilis. These men, for the most part illiterate sharecroppers from one of the poorest counties in Alabama, were never told what disease they were suffering from, nor of its seriousness. (Mis)Informed that they were being treated for "bad blood,"[1] their doctors had no intention of curing them of syphilis at all. The data for the experiment was to be collected from autopsies of the men, and they were thus deliberately left to degenerate under the ravages of tertiary syphilis—which can include tumors, heart disease, paralysis, blindness, insanity, and death. "As I see it," one of the doctors involved explained, "we have no further interest in these patients until they die." By the end of the experiment, 28 of the men had died directly of syphilis, 100 were dead of related complications, 40 of their wives had been infected, and 19 of their children had been born with congenital syphilis.

Sadly, ethical abuse in the name of medical research isn't consigned to the 20th century. The beginning of the 21st century has witnessed international concern over the conduct of clinical trials of medicinal products in the developing world. Until 1995, clinical trials were mainly conducted in the USA, Europe, and Japan, but in the era of globalisation drug companies have been steadily outsourcing their research enterprises to the developing world (Glickman et al., 2009). On the one hand the globalisation of clinical research brings global benefits, enabling pharmaceutical companies to test new drugs more quickly and effectively than if trials were limited to the developed world (Medical Progress Today). Clinical trials also bring resources and expertise to resource-poor countries, and give trial participants access to treatment that they would otherwise be denied. The counter argument is, however, that these sorts of clinical trials exploit the poverty of ill people in the developing world, by taking advantage of their need for medical help in order to make the maximum profit from new drugs. There is a concern that powerful companies and research institutions cannot be held to account by the poor, illiterate, sick people who often become part of clinical trials, and that the pharmaceutical industry has used citizens of resource-poor countries as guinea pigs for drugs which have more relevance for the West than for the country hosting the trial.

In the 2005 film *The Constant Gardener*, based on a novel by John le Carré, the characters Tess and Justin come up against a drug corporation that is using Kenya's population for fraudulent testing of a tuberculosis drug ("dypraxa") with known harmful side effects and disregards the well-being of its poor African test subjects.

Until recently, a distinction was made between therapeutic research, focused on investigating work that may yield a direct health-related benefit, and non-therapeutic research where a participant may be a healthy volunteer providing baseline, control data, and / or a patient who is being investigated for a matter that is unrelated/or will offer little benefit to them. Whilst the specific issues raised by therapeutic and non-therapeutic research may differ, the fundamental ethical issues remain the same: participants need to be provided with information so that they can make a fully informed decision about taking part (or not), for consent to be freely given, participants need to feel free of coercion or inducement. Participants have the right to anonymity and confidentiality, and it is the duty of the researcher to make explicit those scenarios when anonymity and confidentiality may be breached, for example, in the presence of disclosures indicating harm may occur either to the participant him or herself, or to others.

International, national and professional body guidelines now govern the ethical conduct of research on human participants (for example, The World Health Organization http://www.efpa. eu/ethics/efpa-guidelines; the European Union Directive on Clinical Research (2001/20/CE)), and in the UK, research on patients is carefully monitored through the work of the National Research Ethics Service (NRES) and its local research ethics committees. However, the moral responsibility lies with those individuals (investigators) who design and implement the research. It is therefore of fundamental importance that these investigators understand the ethical issues that arise when carrying out research on human participants.

Informed Consent

The cornerstone of ethical research is informed consent. The researcher must provide enough information to enable potential participants to decide whether they want to be in a study. The study must be described in language that is accessible to these individuals, and outlines what will happen if they agree to take part in respect of activities, potential benefits and possible risks, how confidentiality and anonymity will be maintained (and any circumstances in which confidentiality will be breached). Also, how long the data will be stored, and who will have access to it. There must be no inducement or coercion (for example, providing patient-participants with better clinical care compared to those patients who decline to take part). Participants must also understand that they have the right not to take part in the study or to withdraw from the study at any point, without any fear of penalty. This is very important in educational establishments where, for example, students' are recruited in to a study run by a researcher who also has responsibility for student assessment and progression.

A central issue is that potential participants must be able to understand the study and associated risks. But what if the prospective participant is unable to understand fully what is being asked? Is it ethical to take away the opportunity for such individuals to take part in research if they wish? In clinical settings, researchers must ascertain that patients are not having trouble understanding the study.

The Mental Capacity Act (2005) aims to strike a balance between protecting and respecting the interests, wishes and feelings of those (aged 16 and over) who lack capacity, with the need for appropriate research. Such research is considered essential if knowledge of what causes a person to lack or lose capacity, and the treatment of people who lack capacity, is to be improved. The Act includes a range of safeguards, in particular the fundamental principle that the person's interests must be assumed to outweigh those of science and society. One of the ways in which this requirement applies to research, is that investigators must take reasonable steps to identify someone whom the potential participant can consult, and can act as an advocate for the individual. This person (the consultee) must have the best interests of the individual at heart, and may be engaged in caring for the person, or interested in his welfare, and willing to help. The consultee can be an attorney appointed under a registered Lasting Power of Attorney, or a deputy appointed by the Court of Protection. The Act also specifies who the consultee cannot be: a person working in a professional capacity, or a paid care worker. If there is no-one who can fulfil the role of consultee the researcher must nominate a person (who must not have any connection with the research project).

The issue of informed consent is of concern to researchers and clinicians who work with people with a psychotic illness like schizophrenia or a degenerative brain disease such as Alzheimer's disease. Having either a diagnosis of either schizophrenia or Alzheimer's disease does not necessarily mean a person cannot provide informed consent (Carpenter et al., 2000; Marson, Huthwaite, & Hebert, 2004; Wirshing et al., 1998). Measures have been developed to assess capacity for consent in these populations (Palmer, Dunn, Appelbaum, et al., 2005; Dunn, Milap, Mowrangi, et al., 2006), and these clinical populations will continue to be areas of active research, especially as the number of people over age 65 continues to increase (Marson, 2001).

These results point to the importance of examining each person individually for ability to give informed consent, rather than assuming that a person is unable to do so by virtue of being hospitalized for schizophrenia or Alzheimer's disease. Thus, having a mental disorder does not necessarily mean that a person cannot give informed consent.

Confidentiality and Privileged Communication

When people consult a psychiatrist or clinical psychologist, they are assured by professional ethics codes that what goes on in the session will remain confidential. Confidentiality means that nothing will be revealed to a third party except for other professionals and those intimately involved in the treatment, such as a nurse or medical secretary.

A privileged communication goes even further. It is communication between parties in a confidential relationship that is protected by law. The recipient of such a communication cannot legally be compelled to disclose it as a witness. The right of privileged communication is a major exception to the access courts have to evidence in judicial proceedings. Society believes that in the long term the interests of people are best served if communications to a spouse and to certain professionals remain off limits to the prying eyes and ears of the police, judges, and prosecutors. The privilege applies to such relationships as those between husband and wife, physician and patient, pastor and penitent, attorney and client, and psychologist and patient. The legal expression is that the patient or client "holds the privilege," which means that only he or she may release the other person to disclose confidential information in a legal proceeding.

There are important limits to a client's right of privileged communication, however. For example, this right is eliminated for any of the following reasons in some states:

- The client has accused the therapist of malpractice. In such a case, the therapist can divulge information about the therapy in order to defend himself or herself in any legal action initiated by the client.
- The client is less than 16 years old and the therapist has reason to believe that the child has been a victim of a crime such as child abuse. In fact, the psychologist is required to report to the police or to a child welfare agency within 36 hours any suspicion he

or she has that the child client has been physically abused, including any suspicion of sexual molestation.

- The client initiated therapy in hopes of evading the law for having committed a crime or for planning to do so.

- The therapist judges that the client is a danger to self or others and disclosure of information is necessary to ward off such danger (recall Focus on Discovery 16.3 on *Tarasoff*).

Who Is the Client or Patient?

Is it always clear to the clinician who the client is? In private therapy, when an adult pays a clinician a fee for help with a personal problem that has nothing to do with the legal system, the consulting individual is clearly the client. But an individual may be seen by a clinician for an evaluation of his or her competency to stand trial, or the clinician may be hired by an individual's family to assist in civil commitment proceedings. Perhaps the clinician is employed by a state mental hospital as a regular staff member and sees a particular patient about problems in controlling aggressive impulses.

It should be clear, although it sometimes is not, that in these instances the clinician is serving more than one client. In addition to the patient, he or she serves the family or the state, and it is incumbent on the mental health professional to inform the patient that this is so. This dual allegiance does not necessarily indicate that the patient's own interests will be sacrificed, but it does mean that discussions will not inevitably remain secret and that the clinician may in the future act in a way that displeases or even seriously compromises the interests of the patient.

Quick Summary

Ethical restraints on research are necessary to avoid the abuses that have occurred in the past. A number of ethical codes regarding psychological research have been developed. Research must be approved not just for scientific merit by research governance and funding bodies but also undergo review by ethical research committees. There is also a requirement for students and researchers in the behavioural and medical sciences to be informed and trained in research ethics, on the basis of special coursework and examinations, to make it less likely that research participants will be put at risk.

Special precautions must be taken to ensure that research participants with mental illness fully understand the risks and benefits of any research they are asked to participate in and that particular care is taken to make certain that they can decline or withdraw from research without feeling coerced. Informed consent procedures must include enough information about the research so that participants know about the risks and feel free to withdraw without penalty.

In therapy sessions, patients have the right to have what is discussed kept confidential (can't be disclosed to a third party), and this discussion is considered a privileged communication (information in confidential relationship protected by law). However, confidentiality and the privileged communication can be broken if an individual is a danger to self or others, is suing a therapist for malpractice, is a child under 16 who has been the victim of a crime or abuse, or is trying to evade the law for a crime committed or planned.

Summary

- Some civil liberties are rather routinely set aside when mental health professionals and the courts judge that mental illness has played a decisive role in determining an individual's behavior. This may occur through criminal or civil commitment.

- There is an important difference between mental illness and insanity. The latter is a legal concept. A person can be diagnosed as mentally ill and yet be deemed sane enough both to stand trial and to be found guilty of a crime.

- Criminal commitment sends a person to a hospital either before a trial for an alleged crime, because the person is deemed incompetent to stand trial, or after an acquittal by reason of insanity.

- A person who is considered mentally ill and dangerous to self and to others, although he or she has not broken a law, can be civilly committed to hospital or be allowed to live outside of a hospital but only under supervision and with restrictions placed on his or her activities.

- Several landmark cases and principles in law address the conditions under which a person who has committed a crime might be excused from legal responsibility for it—that is, not guilty by reason of insanity. These involve the presence of an irresistible impulse and the notion that some people may not be able to distinguish between right and wrong (the M'Naghten rule). The Insanity Defense Reform Act of 1984 made it harder for accused criminals to argue insanity as defense.

- Two insanity pleas used today include not guilty by reason of insanity and guilty but mentally ill. They differ from one another in terms of whether a person is responsible for his or her criminal actions, where they receive treatment, and how long they remain committed.

- Court rulings have provided greater protection to all committed people with mental illness, particularly those under civil commitment. They have the right to written notification, to counsel, to a jury decision concerning their commitment, and to Fifth Amendment protection against self-incrimination; the right to the least restrictive treatment setting; the right to be treated; and, in most circumstances, the right to refuse treatment, particularly any procedure that entails considerable risk.

- Ethical issues concerning research include restraints on what kinds of research are allowable and the duty of scientists to obtain informed consent from prospective human participants.

- In the area of therapy, ethical issues concern the right of clients to confidentiality and the question of who is the client (e.g., an individual or the hospital that is paying the clinician).

Answers to Check Your Knowledge Questions

16.1 1. c; 2. a; 3. d; 4. b
16.2 1. F; 2. T; 3. T

16.3 1. F; 2. T; 3. F; 4. T

Key Terms

American Law institute guidelines
civil commitment
competency to stand trial
confidentiality
criminal commitment
guilty but mentally ill (GBMI)
in absentia
informed consent
insanity defense
irresistible impulse
least restrictive alternative
M'Naghten rule
not guilty by reason of insanity (NGRI)
outpatient commitment
privileged communication

Glossary

ABAB design. An experimental design in which behavior is measured during a baseline period (A), during a period when a treatment is introduced (B), during the reinstatement of the conditions that prevailed in the baseline period (A), and finally during a reintroduction of the treatment (B); commonly used in operant research to isolate cause–effect relationships.

acute stress disorder. A short-lived anxiety reaction to a traumatic event; if it lasts more than a month, it is diagnosed as posttraumatic stress disorder.

addiction. Use of a drug that is accompanied by a physiological dependence on it, made evident by tolerance and withdrawal symptoms.

adoptees method. Research method that studies children who were adopted and reared completely apart from their parents, thereby eliminating the influence of being raised by disordered parents.

advanced directive. Legal document in which an individual—before becoming incapable of making such decisions—prescribes and proscribes certain courses of action to be taken to preserve his or her health or terminate life support.

age effects. The consequences of being a given chronological age. Compare *cohort effects*.

agonist. A drug that stimulates receptors normally specific to a particular neurotransmitter.

agoraphobia. Literally, fear of the marketplace. Anxiety disorder in which the person fears situations in which it would be embarrassing or difficult to escape if panic symptoms occurred; most commonly diagnosed in some individuals with panic disorder.

allele. Any of the various forms in which a particular gene is found.

alogia. A negative symptom in schizophrenia, marked by poverty of speech.

alternate-form reliability. See *reliability*.

Alzheimer's disease. A dementia involving a progressive atrophy of cortical tissue and marked by memory impairment, intellectual deterioration, and, in more extreme cases, involuntary movements of limbs, occasional convulsions, and psychotic behavior. See also *plaques* and *neurofibrillary tangles*.

American Law Institute guidelines. Rules proposing that insanity is a legitimate defense plea if, during criminal conduct, an individual could not judge right from wrong or control his or her behavior as required by law. Repetitive criminal acts are disavowed as a sole criterion. Compare *M'Naghten rule* and *irresistible impulse*.

amphetamines. A group of stimulating drugs that produce heightened levels of energy and, in large doses, nervousness, sleeplessness, and paranoid delusions.

amygdala. A subcortical structure of the temporal lobe involved in attention to emotionally salient stimuli and memory of emotionally relevant events.

anal stage. In psychoanalytic theory, the second psychosexual stage, which occurs during the second year of life when the anus is considered the principal erogenous zone.

analogue experiment. An experimental study of a phenomenon different from but related to the actual interests of the investigator; for example, animal research used to study human disorders or research on mild symptoms used as a bridge to clinical disorders.

analytical psychology. A variation of Freud's psychoanalysis introduced by Carl Jung, focusing less on biological drives and more on factors such as self-fulfillment, the collective unconscious, and religious symbolism.

anhedonia. A negative symptom in schizophrenia or a symptom in depression in which the individual experiences a loss of interest and pleasure. See also *anticipatory pleasure* and *consummatory pleasure*.

anorexia nervosa. A disorder in which a person refuses to maintain normal weight, has an intense fear of becoming obese, and feels fat even when emaciated.

Antabuse. A drug that makes the drinking of alcohol produce nausea and other unpleasant effects; trade name for disulfiram.

antagonist. A drug that dampens the effect of a neurotransmitter on its receptors; for example, many dopamine antagonists block dopamine receptors.

anterior cingulate. In the subcortical region of the brain, the anterior portion of the cingulate gyrus, stretching about the corpus callosum.

anterior insula. A region of the cerebral cortex involved in processing bodily sensations. Believed to be hyperactive to somatic sensations among people with somatic symptom disorders.

anticipatory pleasure. Expected or anticipated pleasure for events, people, or activities in the future. See also *consummatory pleasure*.

antidepressant. Any drug that alleviates depression; also widely used to treat anxiety disorders.

antipsychotic drugs. Psychoactive drugs, such as Thorazine, that reduce psychotic symptoms but have long-term side effects resembling symptoms of neurological diseases.

antisocial personality disorder type. Personality disorder defined by the absence of concern for others' feelings or social norms and a pervasive pattern of rule breaking.

anxiety. An unpleasant feeling of fear and apprehension accompanied by increased physiological arousal; in learning theory, considered a drive that mediates between a threatening situation and avoidance behavior. Anxiety can be assessed by self-report, by measuring physiological arousal, and by observing overt behavior.

anxiety disorders. Disorders in which fear or tension is overriding and the primary disturbance; include phobic disorders, panic disorder, generalized anxiety disorder, and agoraphobia. In DSM-IV-TR, these disorders also included obsessive-compulsive disorder, acute stress disorder, and posttraumatic stress disorder.

Anxiety Sensitivity Index (ASI). A test that measures the extent to which people respond fearfully to their bodily sensations; predicts the degree to which unexplained physiological arousal leads to panic attacks.

anxiolytics. Minor tranquilizers or benzodiazepines used to treat anxiety disorders.

asociality. A negative symptom of schizophrenia marked by an inability to form close relationships and to feel intimacy.

Asperger's disorder. A DSM-IV-TR disorder believed to be a mild form of DSM-IV-TR autism in which social relationships are poor and stereotyped behavior is intense and rigid, but language and intelligence are intact. Combined with autism in autism spectrum disorder category in DSM-5.

association study. A type of molecular genetics study where researchers examine the relationship between a specific allele of a gene and a trait or behavior in the population

asthma. A disorder characterized by narrowing of the airways and increased secretion of mucus, often causing extremely labored and wheezy breathing.

asylums. Refuges established in western Europe in the fifteenth century to confine and provide for the mentally ill; forerunners of the mental hospital.

attachment theory. The type or style of an infant's attachment to his or her caregivers can set the stage for psychological health or problems later in development

attention-deficit/hyperactivity disorder (ADHD). A disorder in children marked by difficulties in focusing adaptively on the task at hand, inappropriate fidgeting and antisocial behavior, and excessive non-goal-directed behavior.

attribution. The explanation a person has for why an event or behavior has occurred.

autism spectrum disorder. A disorder beginning in childhood that involves deficits in social communication and social interactions, restricted and repetitive behaviors, and in some cases severe deficits in speech. DSM-5 will likely combine Asperger's disorder, pervasive developmental disorder not otherwise specified, and childhood disintegrative disorder into the category autism spectrum disorder.

autonomic nervous system (ANS). The division of the nervous system that regulates involuntary functions; innervates endocrine glands, smooth muscle, and heart muscle; and initiates the physiological changes that are part of the expression of emotion. See also *sympathetic* and *parasympathetic nervous systems*; compare *somatic nervous system*.

avoidant personality disorder type. Personality disorder defined by aloofness and extreme sensitivity to potential rejection, despite an intense desire for affiliation and affection.

avolition. A negative symptom in schizophrenia in which the individual lacks interest and drive.

behavior genetics. The study of individual differences in behavior that are attributable to differences in genetic makeup.

behavior therapy. A branch of psychotherapy conceived narrowly as the application of classical and operant conditioning to the alteration of clinical problems but more broadly as applied experimental psychology in a clinical context.

behavioral activation (BA) therapy. Clinical approach to depression that seeks to increase participation in positively reinforcing activities.

behavioral assessment. A sampling of ongoing cognitions, feelings, and overt behavior in their situational context. Compare *projective test* and *personality inventory*.

behavioral couples therapy. Clinical approach to depression in which a couple works to improve communication and satisfaction; more likely to relieve relationship distress than individual cognitive therapy.

behavioral inhibition. The tendency to exhibit anxiety or to freeze when facing threat. In infants, it manifests as a tendency to become agitated and cry when faced with novel stimuli and may be a heritable predisposition for the development of anxiety disorders.

behavioral medicine. An interdisciplinary field concerned with integrating knowledge from medicine and behavioral science to understand health and illness and to prevent as well as treat psychophysiological disorders and other illnesses in which a person's psyche plays a role. See also *health psychology*.

behaviorism. The school of psychology originally associated with John B. Watson, who proposed that observable behavior, not consciousness, is the proper subject matter of psychology. Contemporary behaviorists do use mediational concepts, provided they are firmly anchored to observables.

benzodiazepines. Any of several drugs commonly used to treat anxiety, such as Valium and Xanax.

binge eating disorder. Included as a disorder in DSM-5; includes recurrent episodes of unrestrained eating.

bipolar I disorder. A diagnosis defined on the basis of at least one lifetime episode of mania. Most people with this disorder also experience episodes of major depression.

bipolar II disorder. A form of bipolar disorder, diagnosed in those who have experienced at least one major depressive episode and at least one episode of hypomania.

blindsight. Conversion disorder wherein patients have suffered lesions in the visual cortex and report themselves blind but can perform well on some specific visual tests.

blunted affect. A negative symptom of schizophrenia that involves a lack of outward expression of emotion.

body dysmorphic disorder. A somatoform disorder marked by preoccupation with an imagined or exaggerated defect in appearance—for example, facial wrinkles or excess facial or body hair.

body mass index (BMI). Measure of body fat calculated by dividing weight in kilograms by height in meters squared; considered a more valid estimate of body fat than many others.

BOLD (blood oxygenation level dependent). The signal detected by functional MRI studies of the brain; measures blood flow and thus neural activity in particular regions.

borderline personality disorder type. Personality disorder defined by impulsiveness and unpredictability, an uncertain self-image, intense and unstable social relationships, and extreme swings of mood.

brain stem. The part of the brain connecting the spinal cord with the cerebrum; contains the pons and medulla oblongata and functions as a neural relay station.

brief psychotic disorder. A disorder in which a person has a sudden onset of psychotic symptoms—incoherence, loose associations, delusions, hallucinations—immediately after a severely disturbing event; the symptoms last more than 1 day but no more than 1 month. Compare *schizophreniform disorder*.

brief therapy. Time-limited psychotherapy, usually ego-analytic in orientation and lasting no more than 25 sessions.

bulimia nervosa. A disorder characterized by episodic, uncontrollable eating binges followed by purging either by vomiting or by taking laxatives.

caffeine. Perhaps the world's most popular drug; a generalized stimulant of body systems, including the sympathetic nervous system. Though seldom viewed as a drug, caffeine is addictive, produces tolerance, and subjects habitual users to withdrawal.

cardiovascular disease. Medical problems involving the heart and the blood circulation system, such as hypertension or coronary heart disease.

case study. The collection of historical or biographical information on a single individual, often including experiences in therapy.

catatonia. Constellation of schizophrenic symptoms including repetitive, peculiar, complex gestures and, in some cases, an almost manic increase in overall activity level.

catatonic features. Immobility or excessive and peculiar physical movements characterizing a subtype of episodes of major depressive disorder or mania.

catatonic immobility. A fixity of posture, sometimes grotesque, maintained for long periods, with accompanying muscular rigidity, trancelike state of consciousness, and waxy flexibility.

categorical classification. An approach to assessment in which a person is or is not a member of a discrete grouping. Compare *dimensional classification*.

cathartic method. A therapeutic procedure to relieve emotional suffering introduced by Breuer and developed further by Freud in the late nineteenth century, whereby a patient recalls and relives an earlier emotional catastrophe and reexperiences the tension and unhappiness.

caudate nucleus. A nucleus within the basal ganglia involved in learning and memory that is implicated in body dysmorphic disorder and obsessive-compulsive disorder.

central nervous system. The part of the nervous system that in vertebrates consists of the brain and spinal cord, to which all sensory impulses are transmitted and from which motor impulses pass out; supervises and coordinates the activities of the entire nervous system.

cerebellum. An area of the hindbrain concerned with balance, posture, and motor coordination.

cerebral cortex. The thin outer covering of each of the cerebral hemispheres; highly convoluted and composed of nerve cell bodies that constitute the gray matter of the brain.

cerebrum. The two-lobed structure extending from the brain stem and constituting the anterior (frontal) part of the brain; the largest and most recently developed portion of the brain, responsible for coordinating sensory and motor activities and performing higher cognitive processes.

childhood onset fluency disorder (stuttering). Communication disorder of childhood marked by frequent and pronounced verbal dysfluencies, such as repetitions of certain sounds.

chromosomes. The threadlike bodies within the nucleus of the cell, composed primarily of DNA and bearing the genetic information of the organism.

civil commitment. A procedure whereby a person can be legally certified as mentally ill and hospitalized, even against his or her will. Compare *criminal commitment* and *outpatient commitment*.

classical conditioning. A basic form of learning, sometimes referred to as Pavlovian conditioning, in which a neutral stimulus is repeatedly paired with another stimulus (called the unconditioned stimulus, UCS) that naturally elicits a certain desired response (called the unconditioned response, UCR). After repeated trials, the neutral stimulus becomes a conditioned stimulus (CS) and evokes the same or a similar response, now called the conditioned response (CR). Compare *operant conditioning*.

clinical high-risk study. A study that identifies people who show subtle or early clinical signs of a disorder, such as schizophrenia, and then follows them over time to determine who might be at risk for developing the disorder.

clinical interview. General term for conversation between a clinician and a patient that is aimed at determining diagnosis, history, causes of problems, and possible treatment options.

clinical psychologist. An individual who has earned a Ph.D. degree in psychology or a Psy. D. and whose training has included an internship in a mental hospital or clinic.

clinical significance. The degree to which effect size is large enough to be meaningful in predicting or treating a clinical disorder. Compare *statistical significance*.

cocaine. A pain-reducing, stimulating, and addictive alkaloid obtained from coca leaves that increases mental powers, produces euphoria, heightens sexual desire, and in large doses causes paranoia and hallucinations.

cognition. The process of knowing; the thinking, judging, reasoning, and planning activities of the human mind. Behavior is now often explained as depending on these processes.

cognitive behavior therapy (CBT). Behavior therapy that incorporates theory and research on cognitive processes such as thoughts, perceptions, judgments, self-statements, and tacit assumptions; a blend of both the cognitive and behavioral paradigms.

cognitive behavioral paradigm. General view that people can best be understood by studying how they perceive and structure their experiences and how this influences behavior.

cognitive biases. Tendencies to perceive events in a negative manner, for example, by attending to or remembering negative information more than positive information; hypothesized to be driven by underlying negative schemas.

cognitive enhancement therapy (CET). Also known as cognitive training, treatment that seeks to improve basic cognitive functions such as verbal learning ability in people with schizophrenia, meanwhile reducing symptoms as well.

cognitive restructuring. Any behavior therapy procedure that attempts to alter the manner in which a client thinks about life so that he or she changes overt behavior and emotions.

cognitive therapy. See *cognitive restructuring*. See also *cognitive behavior therapy*.

cohort effects. The consequences of having been born in a given year and having grown up during a particular time period with its own unique pressures, problems, challenges, and opportunities. Compare *age effects*.

collective unconscious. Jung's concept that every human being carries within the wisdom, ideas, and strivings of those who have come before.

communication disorders. Learning disorders in a child who fails to develop to the degree expected by his or her intellectual level in a specific language skill area; include speech sounds disorder and child onset fluency disorder.

comorbidity. The co-occurrence of two disorders, as when a person has depression and social phobia.

competency to stand trial. A legal decision as to whether a person can participate meaningfully in his or her own defense.

complex somatic symptom disorder. A DSM-5 diagnosis defined by excessive concern and help seeking regarding physical symptoms.

compulsion. The irresistible impulse to repeat an irrational act or thought over and over again. Compare *obsession*.

concordance. As applied in behavior genetics, the similarity in psychiatric diagnosis or in other traits within a pair of twins.

concurrent validity. See *validity*.

conditioned response (CR). See *classical conditioning*.

conditioned stimulus (CS). See *classical conditioning*.

conduct disorder. Pattern of extreme disobedience in youngsters, including theft, vandalism, lying, and early drug use.

confidentiality. A principle observed by lawyers, doctors, pastors, psychologists, and psychiatrists which dictates that the contents of a professional and private relationship not be divulged to anyone else. See also *privileged communication*.

construct validity. The extent to which scores or ratings on an assessment instrument relate to other variables or behaviors according to some theory or hypothesis.

consummatory pleasure. Pleasure experienced in-the-moment or in the presence of a pleasurable stimulus. See also *anticipatory pleasure*.

content validity. See *validity*.

control group. Those for whom the active condition of the independent variable is not administered, thus forming a baseline against which the effects of the active condition of the independent variable can be evaluated.

controlled drinking. A pattern of alcohol consumption that is moderate, avoiding the extremes of total abstinence and of inebriation.

conversion disorder. A DSM-IV-TR disorder in which sensory or motor function is impaired, even though there is no detectable neurological explanation for the deficits. See also *functional neurological disorder*.

copy number variation (CNV). Refers to variation in gene structure involving copy number changes in a defined chromosomal region; could be in the form of a deletion where a copy is deleted or an addition (duplication) where an extra copy is added.

corpus callosum. The large band of nerve fibers connecting the two cerebral hemispheres.

correlation. The tendency for two variables, such as height and weight, to covary.

correlation coefficient. A statistic ranging in value from −1.00 to +1.00 that measures the degree to which two variables are related. The sign indicates whether the relationship is positive or negative, and the magnitude indicates the strength of the relationship.

correlational method. The research strategy used to establish whether two or more variables are related without manipulating the independent variable. Relationships may be positive—as values for one variable increase, those for the other do also—or negative—as values for one variable increase, those for the other decrease. Compare *experiment*.

cortisol. A "stress hormone" secreted by the adrenal cortices; helps the body prepare to face threats.

counseling psychologist. A doctoral-level mental health professional whose training is similar to that of a clinical psychologist, though usually with less emphasis on research and serious psychopathology.

crack. A rock-crystal form of cocaine that is heated, melted, and smoked; more often used in poorer urban areas than conventional cocaine.

criminal commitment. A procedure whereby a person is confined in a mental hospital either for determination of competency to stand trial or after acquittal by reason of insanity. Compare *civil commitment*.

criterion validity. See *validity*.

cross-dependent. Acting on the same neurotransmitter receptors, as methadone does with heroin.

cross-fostering. Research method that studies offspring who were adopted and reared completely apart from their biological parents, where the adoptive parent has a particular disorder but the biological parent does not, thereby introducing the influence of being raised by disordered parents.

cross-sectional design. Studies in which different age groups are compared at the same time. Compare *longitudinal design*.

CT or CAT scan. Refers to computerized axial tomography, a method of diagnosis in which X-rays are taken from different angles and then analyzed by computer to produce a representation of the part of the body in cross section.

cultural competence. The capacity of a therapist to understand the patient's cultural framework and its implications for therapeutic work.

Cushing's syndrome. An endocrine disorder usually affecting young women, produced by oversecretion of cortisone and marked by mood swings, irritability, agitation, and physical disfigurement.

cyclothymic disorder. A form of bipolar disorder characterized by swings between elation and depression over at least a 2-year period, but with moods not so severe as manic or major depressive episodes.

cytokines. Immune system molecules, released by activated macrophages, which help initiate such bodily responses to infection as fatigue, fever, and activation of the HPA axis.

D-cycloserine (DCS). A medication that enhances learning which has been found to enhance the effects of exposure therapy for several of the anxiety disorders.

defense mechanisms. In psychoanalytic theory, reality-distorting strategies unconsciously adopted to protect the ego from anxiety.

delayed ejaculation. A disorder in men involving delay in reaching orgasm or inability to reach orgasm.

delirium. A state of great mental confusion in which consciousness is clouded, attention cannot be sustained, and the stream of thought and speech is incoherent. The person is probably disoriented, emotionally erratic, restless or lethargic, and often has illusions, delusions, and hallucinations.

delirium tremens (DTs). One of the withdrawal symptoms that sometimes occurs when a period of heavy alcohol consumption is terminated; marked by fever, sweating, trembling, cognitive impairment, and hallucinations.

delusional disorder. A disorder in which the individual has persistent delusions and is very often contentious but has no disorganized thinking or hallucinations.

delusions. Beliefs contrary to reality, firmly held in spite of evidence to the contrary and common in paranoid disorders: of control, belief that one is being manipulated by some external force such as radar, television, or a creature from outer space; of grandeur, belief that one is an especially important or powerful person; of persecution, belief that one is being plotted against or oppressed by others.

dementia praecox. An older term for schizophrenia, believed then to be an incurable and progressive deterioration of mental functioning beginning in adolescence.

dementia. Deterioration of mental faculties—memory, judgment, abstract thought, control of impulses, intellectual ability—that impairs social and occupational functioning and eventually changes the personality. See *Alzheimer's disease*.

dementia with Lewy bodies (DLB). Form of dementia that often co-occurs with Parkinson's disease; characterized by shuffling gait, memory loss, and hallucinations and delusions.

demonology. The doctrine that a person's abnormal behavior is caused by an autonomous evil spirit.

dependent personality disorder. A DSM-IV-TR disorder in which people are overly concerned about maintaining relationships. People with this disorder often allow others to make decisions for them and are reticent to make demands that could challenge relationships.

dependent variable. In a psychological experiment, the behavior that is measured and is expected to change with manipulation of the independent variable.

depersonalization. An alteration in perception of the self in which the individual loses a sense of reality and feels estranged from the self and perhaps separated from the body; may be a temporary reaction to stress and fatigue or part of panic disorder, depersonalization disorder, or schizophrenia.

depersonalization/derealization disorder. A dissociative disorder in which the individual feels unreal and estranged from the self and surroundings enough to disrupt functioning. People with this disorder may feel that their extremities have changed in size or that they are watching themselves from a distance.

derealization. Loss of the sense that the surroundings are real; present in several psychological disorders, such as panic disorder, depersonalization disorder, and schizophrenia.

desire phase. The first stage of the sexual response cycle, characterized by sexual interest or desire, often associated with sexually arousing fantasies.

detoxification. The initial stage in weaning an addicted person from a drug; involves medical supervision of the sometimes painful withdrawal.

developmental psychopathology. The field that studies disorders of childhood within the context of normal life-span development.

diagnosis. The determination that the set of symptoms or problems of a patient indicates a particular disorder.

Diagnostic and Statistical Manual of Mental Disorders. See *DSM-5*.

dialectical behavior therapy. A therapeutic approach to borderline personality disorder that combines client-centered empathy and acceptance with behavioral problem solving, social skills training, and limit setting.

diathesis. Predisposition toward a disease or abnormality.

diathesis–stress. As applied in psychopathology, a view that assumes that individuals predisposed toward a particular mental disorder will be particularly affected by stress and will then manifest abnormal behavior.

dimensional classification. An approach to assessment in which a person is placed on a continuum. Compare *categorical classification*.

directionality problem. A difficulty that arises in the correlational method of research when it is known that two variables are related but it is unclear which is causing the other.

disorganized behavior. Symptom of schizophrenia that is marked by odd behaviors that do not appear organized, such as bouts of agitation, unusual dress, or childlike, silly behavior.

disorganized speech. Speech found in schizophrenia patients that is marked by poorly organized ideas and speech that is difficult for others to understand; also known as formal thought disorder.

disorganized symptoms. Broad category of symptoms in schizophrenia that includes disorganized speech, disorganized thinking, and disorganized behavior.

disorientation. A state of mental confusion with respect to time; place; and identity of self, other persons, and objects.

dissociation. A process whereby a group of mental processes is split off from the main stream of consciousness or behavior loses its relationship with the rest of the personality.

dissociative amnesia. A dissociative disorder in which the person suddenly becomes unable to recall important personal information to an extent that cannot be explained by ordinary forgetfulness.

dissociative disorders. Disorders in which the normal integration of consciousness, memory, or identity is suddenly and temporarily altered; include dissociative amnesia, dissociative identity disorder (multiple personality), and depersonalization/derealization disorder.

dissociative fugue. See *fugue subtype.*

dissociative identity disorder (DID). A rare dissociative disorder (formerly called multiple personality disorder, or MPD) in which two or more fairly distinct and separate personalities are present within the same individual, each with his or her own memories, relationships, and behavior patterns, with only one of them dominant at any given time.

dizygotic (DZ) twins. Birth partners who developed from separate fertilized eggs and who are only 50 percent alike genetically, just as siblings born from different pregnancies involving the same father; also called fraternal twins. Compare *monozygotic twins.*

dopamine. Central nervous system neurotransmitter, a catecholamine that is also a precursor of norepinephrine and apparently figures in schizophrenia and Parkinson's disease.

dopamine theory. The view that schizophrenia is linked to an increase in the number of dopamine receptors.

dorsolateral prefrontal cortex. A region of the prefrontal cortex involved in working memory, motor planning, organization, and regulation that is implicated in many psychopathologies.

double-blind procedure. A method for reducing the biasing effects of the expectations of research participant and experimenter; neither is allowed to know whether the independent variable of the experiment is being applied to the participant.

Down syndrome (trisomy 21). A form of intellectual developmental disorder caused by a third copy of a particular chromosome; involves an IQ usually less than 50 as well as distinctive physical characteristics.

DSM-5. The current *Diagnostic and Statistical Manual of Mental Disorders* of the American Psychiatric Association.

dyscalculia. Learning disorder characterized by difficulty recalling arithmetic facts, counting objects, and aligning numbers in columns.

dyslexia. A learning disorder involving significant difficulty with word recognition, reading comprehension, and (typically) spelling.

dyspareunia. DSM-IV-TR diagnosis for persistent or recurrent pain during sexual intercourse not attributable to a medical problem.

dysthymia (dysthymic disorder). Depressive symptoms that last for at least 2 years but do not meet criteria for the diagnosis of major depressive disorder.

early ejaculation. A sexual dysfunction disorder in which the man consistently ejaculates within 1 minute of partnered sexual activity.

ecological momentary assessment (EMA). Form of self-observation involving collection of data in real time (e.g., diaries) regarding thoughts, moods, and stressors.

Ecstasy. A relatively new hallucinogen, chemically similar to mescaline and the amphetamines.

effectiveness. How well a therapeutic treatment works in the real world in the hands of broader samples of non-academic, less supervised therapists. Compare *efficacy.*

efficacy. How well a therapeutic treatment works under rarified, academic research conditions. Compare *effectiveness.*

ego. In psychoanalytic theory, the predominantly conscious part of the personality, responsible for decision making and for dealing with reality.

electrocardiogram (EKG). A recording of the electrical activity of the heart, made with an electrocardiograph.

electroconvulsive therapy (ECT). A treatment that produces a convulsion by passing electric current through the brain; despite public concerns about this treatment, it can be useful in alleviating profound depression.

electrodermal responding. A recording of the minute electrical activity of the sweat glands on the skin, allowing inference of an emotional state.

electroencephalogram (EEG). A graphic recording of electrical activity of the brain, usually of the cerebral cortex, but sometimes of lower areas.

emotion. The expression, experience, and physiology that guide responses to problems and challenges in the environment.

empirically supported treatments (ESTs). Approaches whose efficacy has been demonstrated and documented through research that meets the APA's standards for research on psychotherapy.

endorphins. Opiates produced within the body; may have an important role in the processes by which the body builds up tolerance to drugs and is distressed by their withdrawal.

enzyme. A complex protein that acts as a catalyst in regulating metabolic activities.

epidemiology. The study of the frequency and distribution of illness in a population.

epigenetics. The study of changes in gene expression that are caused by something other than changes in the DNA (gene) sequence or structure, such as DNA methylation.

episodic disorder. A condition, such as major depressive disorder, whose symptoms dissipate but that tends to recur.

erectile disorder. A recurrent and persistent inability to attain an erection or maintain it until completion of sexual activity.

etiology. All the factors that contribute to the development of an illness or disorder.

excitement phase. As applied by Masters and Johnson, the second stage of the sexual response cycle, characterized by pleasure associated with increased blood flow to the genitalia.

executive functioning. The cognitive capacity to plan how to do a task, how to devise strategies, and how to monitor one's performance.

exhibitionistic disorder (exhibitionism). Marked preference for obtaining sexual gratification by exposing one's genitals to an unwilling observer.

exorcism. The casting out of evil spirits by ritualistic chanting or torture.

experiment. The most powerful research technique for determining causal relationships; involves the manipulation of an independent variable, the measurement of a dependent variable, and the random assignment of participants to the several different conditions being investigated. Compare *correlational method.*

experimental effect. A statistically significant difference between two groups experiencing different manipulations of the independent variable.

explicit memory. Memory involving the conscious recall of experiences; the area of deficits typically seen in dissociative amnesia. Compare *implicit memory.*

exposure. Real-life (in vivo) or imaginal confrontation of a feared object or situation, especially as a component of systematic desensitization. See also *imaginal exposure.*

exposure and response prevention (ERP). The most widely used and accepted treatment of obsessive-compulsive disorder, in which the sufferer is prevented from engaging in compulsive ritual activity and instead faces the anxiety provoked by the stimulus, leading eventually to extinction of the conditioned response (anxiety).

expressed emotion (EE). Hostility, criticism, and emotional overinvolvement directed from other people toward the patient, usually within a family.

external validity. The extent to which the results of a study can be considered generalizable.

externalizing disorders. Domain of childhood disorders characterized by outward-directed behaviors, such as aggressiveness, noncompliance, overactivity, and impulsiveness; the category includes attention-deficit/hyperactivity disorder, conduct disorder, and oppositional defiant disorder. Compare *internalizing disorders.*

extinction. The elimination of a classically conditioned response by the omission of the unconditioned stimulus. In operant conditioning, the elimination of the conditioned response by the omission of reinforcement.

extraversion. Personality trait associated with frequent experiences of positive affect and social engagement.

factitious disorder. Disorder in which the individual's physical or psychological symptoms appear under voluntary control and are adopted merely to assume the role of a sick person; called factitious disorder by proxy or Munchausen syndrome when a parent produces a physical illness in a child.

falsifiability. The extent to which a scientific assertion is amenable to systematic probes, any one of which could negate the scientist's expectations.

familial high-risk study. A study involving the offspring of people with a disorder, such as schizophrenia, who have a high probability of later developing a disorder.

family method. A research strategy in behavior genetics in which the frequency of a trait or of abnormal behavior is determined in relatives who have varying percentages of shared genetic background.

family-focused treatment (FFT). With the goal of reducing the likelihood of relapse of bipolar disorder or schizophrenia, treatment that aims to educate the person's family about illness, enhance communication, and develop problem-solving skills.

fear. A reaction to real or perceived immediate danger in the present; can involve arousal, or sympathetic nervous system activity.

fear circuit. Set of brain structures, including the amygdala, that tend to be activated when the individual is feeling anxious or fearful; especially active among people with anxiety disorders.

fear-of-fear hypothesis. A cognitive model for the etiology of agoraphobia; suggests the condition is driven by negative thoughts about the consequences of having a panic attack in public.

female orgasmic disorder. A recurrent and persistent delay or absence of orgasm in a woman during sexual activity adequate in focus, intensity, and duration; in many instances the woman may experience considerable sexual excitement.

female sexual arousal disorder. Formerly called frigidity, the inability of a female to reach or maintain the lubrication–swelling stage of sexual excitement or to enjoy a subjective sense of pleasure or excitement during sexual activity.

fetal alcohol syndrome (FAS). Retarded growth of the developing fetus and infant involving cranial, facial, and limb anomalies as well as intellectual disabilities; caused by heavy consumption of alcohol by the mother during pregnancy.

fetishistic disorder (fetishism). Reliance on an inanimate object for sexual arousal.

five-factor model. A personality theory that isolates five major dimensions of personality: neuroticism, extraversion, openness to experience, agreeableness, and conscientiousness.

fixation. In psychoanalytic theory, the arrest of psychosexual development at a particular stage through too much or too little gratification at that stage.

flashback. An unpredictable recurrence of experiences from an earlier drug high.

flight of ideas. A symptom of mania that involves a rapid shift in conversation from one subject to another with only superficial associative connections.

fragile X syndrome. Malformation (or even breakage) of the X chromosome, associated with intellectual developmental disorder; symptoms include large, underdeveloped ears; a long, thin face; a broad nasal root; enlarged testicles in males; and, in many cases, attention deficits and hyperactivity.

free association. A key psychoanalytic procedure in which the analysand is encouraged to give free rein to his or her thoughts and feelings, verbalizing whatever comes into the mind without monitoring its content. The assumption is that over time, repressed material will come forth for examination by both analysand and psychoanalyst.

frontal lobe. The anterior portion of each cerebral hemisphere, in front of the central sulcus; active in reasoning and other higher mental processes.

frontal-subcortical dementias. Dementias that involve impairment of both cognitive and motor functions; include Huntington's chorea, Parkinson's disease, normal-pressure hydrocephalus, and vascular dementia.

frontotemporal dementia (FTD). Dementia that begins typically in the mid to late 50s, characterized by deficits in executive functions such as planning, problem solving, and goal-directed behavior as well as recognition and comprehension of emotions in others. Compare *Alzheimer's disease*.

frotteuristic disorder (frotteurism). The sexually oriented touching of an unsuspecting person, typically in public places that provide an easy means of escape.

fugue subtype. Subtype of dissociative amnesia disorder in which the person experiences total amnesia, moves, and establishes a new identity.

functional magnetic resonance imaging (fMRI). Modification of magnetic resonance imaging (MRI) that allows researchers to take pictures of the brain so quickly that metabolic changes can be measured, resulting in a picture of the brain at work rather than of its structure alone.

functional neurological disorder. A DSM-5 disorder defined by neurological symptoms such as blindness or paralysis that cannot be explained medically.

gamma-aminobutyric acid (GABA). Inhibitory neurotransmitter that may be involved in the anxiety disorders.

gender identity. The ingrained sense a person has of being either a man or a woman.

gene. The smallest portion of DNA within a chromosome that functions as a piece of functional hereditary information.

gene expression. The switching on and off of the reading (transcription and translation) of genes into their products (usually proteins) and thus their associated phenotypes.

gene–environment interaction. The influence of genetics on an individual's sensitivity or reaction to an environmental event. Compare *reciprocal gene–environment interaction*.

general adaptation syndrome (GAS). Hans Selye's model to describe the biological reaction of an organism to sustained and unrelenting stress; the several stages culminate in death in extreme circumstances.

general paresis. Infection of the central nervous system by the spirochete *Treponema pallidum*, which destroys brain tissue; marked by eye disturbances, tremors, and disordered speech as well as severe intellectual deterioration and psychotic symptoms.

generalized anxiety disorder (GAD). Disorder characterized by anxiety so chronic, persistent, and pervasive that it seems free-floating. The individual is jittery and strained, distractible, and worried that something bad is about to happen. A pounding heart, fast pulse and breathing, sweating, flushing, muscle aches, a lump in the throat, and an upset gastrointestinal tract are some of the bodily indications.

genetic paradigm. The approach to human behavior that focuses on both heritability of traits and complex interactions between genes and environment.

genital stage. In psychoanalytic theory, the final psychosexual stage, reached in adulthood, in which heterosexual interests predominate.

genito-pelvic pain/penetration disorder. A disorder in which the woman persistently experiences pain or vaginal muscle spasms when intercourse is attempted.

genome–wide association studies (GWAS). Studies of variations in the entire human genome to identify associations between variations in genes and particular behaviors, traits, or disorders. Large sample sizes are needed for these types of studies.

genotype. An individual's unobservable, genetic constitution, that is, the totality of genes present in the cells of an individual; often applied to the genes contributing to a single trait. Compare *phenotype*.

glial cell. Cells in the brain that are not neurons. They support and protect neurons.

G-proteins. Guanine nucleotide-binding proteins that serve to modulate activity within the postsynaptic cell, are implicated in mania and depression, and are possibly the intracellular target of lithium.

grandiose delusions. Found in paranoid schizophrenia, delusional disorder, and mania, an exaggerated sense of one's importance, power, knowledge, or identity. See also *delusions*.

gray matter. The neural tissue—made up largely of nerve cell bodies—that constitutes the cortex covering the cerebral hemisphere, the nuclei in lower brain areas, columns of the spinal cord, and the ganglia of the autonomic nervous system. Compare *white matter*.

guilty but mentally ill (GBMI). Insanity plea in which a mentally ill person can be held morally and legally responsible for a crime but can then, in theory, be sent to a prison hospital or other suitable facility for psychiatric treatment rather than to a regular prison for punishment. In reality, however, people judged GBMI are usually put in the general prison population, where they may or may not receive treatment. Compare *not guilty by reason of insanity*.

hallucinations. Perceptions in any sensory modality without relevant and adequate external stimuli.

hallucinogen. A drug or chemical, such as LSD, psilocybin, or mescaline, whose effects include hallucinations; often called a psychedelic.

harmful dysfunction. Proposed definition of mental disorder that contains both a value judgment (harmful) and a putatively objective scientific component (dysfunction).

hashish. The dried resin of the cannabis plant, stronger in its effects than the dried leaves and stems that constitute marijuana.

health psychology. A branch of psychology dealing with the role of psychological factors in health and illness. See also *behavioral medicine*.

heritability. The extent to which variability in a particular behavior/disorder within a population can be attributed to genetic factors.

heroin. An extremely addictive narcotic drug derived from morphine.

high-risk method. A research technique involving the intensive examination of people, such as the offspring of people with schizophrenia, who have a high probability of later developing a disorder.

hippocampus. In the subcortical region of the brain, the long, tubelike structure that stretches from the septal area into the temporal lobe.

histrionic personality disorder. A DSM-IV-TR personality disorder defined by overly dramatic behavior, emotional excess, and sexually provocative behavior.

hoarding disorder. A disorder in which the person has a compulsive need to acquire objects and extreme difficulty in disposing of those objects.

hopelessness theory. Cognitive theory of depression that began with learned helplessness theory, was modified to incorporate attributions, and has been modified again to emphasize hopelessness—an expectation that desirable outcomes will not occur and that no available responses can change the situation.

HPA axis. The neuroendocrine connections among hypothalamus, pituitary gland, and adrenal cortex, central to the body's response to stress.

hydrocodone. An opiate combined with other drugs such as acetaminophen to produce prescription pain medications, including the commonly abused drug Vicodin. See also *oxycodone*.

hypnosis. A trancelike state or behavior resembling sleep, induced by suggestion, characterized primarily by increased suggestibility.

hypoactive sexual desire disorder. A sexual dysfunction disorder defined by absence of or deficiency in sexual fantasies and urges in men; for women, see sexual interest/arousal disorder.

hypochondriasis. A DSM-IV-TR disorder in which the person, misinterpreting rather ordinary physical sensations, is preoccupied with fears of having a serious disease.

hypomania. An extremely happy or irritable mood accompanied by symptoms like increased energy and decreased need for sleep, but without the significant functional impairment associated with mania.

hypothalamus. In the subcortical region of the brain, the structure that regulates many visceral processes, including metabolism, temperature, perspiration, blood pressure, sleeping, and appetite.

hypothesis. Specific expectation or prediction about what should occur or be found if a theory is true or valid.

id. In psychoanalytic theory, that part of the personality present at birth, comprising all the energy of the psyche and expressed as biological urges that strive continually for gratification.

ideas of reference. Delusional thinking that reads personal significance into seemingly trivial remarks or activities of others and completely unrelated events.

illness anxiety disorder. A disorder defined by excessive concern and help seeking about health concerns in the absence of major physical symptoms.

imaginal exposure. Treatment for anxiety disorders that involves visualizing feared scenes for extended periods of time. Frequently used in the treatment of posttraumatic stress disorder when in vivo exposure to the initial trauma cannot be conducted.

implicit memory. Memory that underlies behavior but is based on experiences that cannot be consciously recalled; typically not compromised in cases of dissociative amnesia. Compare *explicit memory.*

in absentia. Literally, "in one's absence." Courts are concerned that a person be able to participate personally and meaningfully in his or her own trial and not be tried in absentia because of a distracting mental disorder.

in vivo. As applied in psychology, taking place in a real-life situation.

inappropriate affect. Emotional responses that are out of context, such as laughter when hearing sad news.

incest. Sexual relations between close relatives, most often between daughter and father or between brother and sister.

incidence. In epidemiological studies of a particular disorder, the rate at which new cases occur in a given place at a given time. Compare *prevalence.*

independent variable. In a psychological experiment, the factor, experience, or treatment that is under the control of the experimenter and that is expected to have an effect on participants as assessed by changes in the dependent variable.

index case (proband). The person who in a genetic investigation bears the diagnosis or trait in which the investigator is interested.

individual psychology. A variation of Freud's psychoanalysis introduced by Alfred Adler, focusing less on biological drives and more on such factors as people's conscious beliefs and goals for self-betterment.

informed consent. The agreement of a person to serve as a research participant or to enter therapy after being told the possible outcomes, both benefits and risks.

insanity defense. The legal argument that a defendant should not be held responsible for an illegal act if the conduct is attributable to mental illness. See also *not guilty by reason of insanity* and *guilty but mentally ill.*

intellectual developmental disorder. A disorder characterized by below-average intellectual functioning associated with impairment in adaptive behavior and identified at an early age.

intelligence quotient (IQ). A standardized measure indicating how far an individual's raw score on an intelligence test is from the average raw score of his or her chronological age group.

intelligence test. A standardized means of assessing a person's current mental ability, for example, the Stanford–Binet test or the Wechsler Adult Intelligence Scale.

interleukin-6 (IL-6). A proinflammatory cytokine; elevated levels can result from stress as well as infection and have been linked to numerous diseases in older adults.

internal consistency reliability. See *reliability.*

internal validity. See *validity.*

internalizing disorders. Domain of childhood disorders characterized by inward-focused experiences and behaviors, such as depression, social withdrawal, and anxiety; the category includes childhood anxiety and mood disorders. Compare *externalizing disorders.*

interoceptive conditioning. Classical conditioning of panic attacks in response to internal bodily sensations of arousal (as opposed to the external situations that trigger anxiety).

interpersonal psychotherapy (IPT). A short-term, here-and-now focused psychological treatment initially developed for depression and influenced by the psychodynamic emphasis on relationships.

interpretation. In psychoanalysis, a key procedure in which the psychoanalyst points out to the analysand where resistance exists and what certain dreams and verbalizations reveal about impulses repressed in the unconscious; more generally, any statement by a therapist that construes the client's problem in a new way.

interrater reliability. See *reliability.*

irresistible impulse. The term used in an 1834 Ohio court ruling on criminal responsibility which determined that an insanity defense can be established by proving that the accused had an uncontrollable urge to perform the act.

joint attention. Interactions between two people require paying attention to each other, whether speaking or communicating emotion nonverbally. This is impaired in children with autism spectrum disorder.

latency period. In psychoanalytic theory, the years between ages 6 and 12, during which id impulses play a minor role in motivation.

law of effect. A principle of learning that holds that behavior is acquired by virtue of its consequences.

learning disabilities. General term for learning disorders, communication disorders, and motor skills disorder.

learning disorders. A set of developmental disorders encompassing dyslexia and dyscalculia; characterized by failure to develop in a specific academic area to the degree expected by the child's intellectual level.

least restrictive alternative. The legal principle according to which a hospitalized patient must be treated in a setting that imposes as few restrictions as possible on his or her freedom.

libido. Freudian term for the life-integrating instinct or force of the id; sometimes equated with sexual drive.

lithium. A drug useful in treating both mania and depression in bipolar disorder.

locus ceruleus. The brain region in the fear circuit that is especially important in panic disorder; the major source in the brain of norepinephrine, which helps trigger sympathetic nervous system activity.

longitudinal design. Investigation that collects information on the same individuals repeatedly over time, perhaps over many years, in an effort to determine how phenomena change. Compare *cross-sectional design.*

loose associations (derailment). In schizophrenia, an aspect of disorganized thinking wherein the patient has difficulty sticking to one topic and drifts off on a train of associations evoked by an idea from the past.

LSD. *d*-lysergic acid diethylamide, a drug synthesized in 1938 and discovered by accident to be a hallucinogen in 1943.

magnetic resonance imaging (MRI). A technique for measuring the structure (or, in the case of functional magnetic resonance imaging, the activity) of the living brain. The person is placed inside a large circular magnet that causes hydrogen atoms to move; the return of the atoms to their original positions when the current to the magnet is turned off is translated by a computer into pictures of brain tissue.

major depressive disorder (MDD). A disorder of individuals who have experienced episodes of depression but not of mania. Depression episodes are marked by sadness or loss of pleasure, accompanied by symptoms such as feelings of worthlessness and guilt; withdrawal from others; loss of sleep, appetite, or sexual desire; and either lethargy or agitation.

male orgasmic disorder. A recurrent and persistent delay or absence of ejaculation after an adequate phase of sexual excitement.

malingering. Faking a physical or psychological incapacity in order to avoid a responsibility or gain an end, where the goal is readily recognized from the individual's circumstances; distinct from conversion disorder, in which the incapacity is assumed to be beyond voluntary control.

mania. Intense elation or irritability, accompanied by symptoms such as excessive talkativeness, rapid thoughts, distractibility, grandiose plans, heightened activity, and insensitivity to the negative consequences of actions.

marijuana. A drug derived from the dried and ground leaves and stems of the female hemp plant *Cannabis sativa.*

marriage and family therapist. A mental health professional who specializes in treating couples and families and how these relationships impact mental health. Training can be at the master's or Ph.D. level, and some M.S.W. programs offer training in marriage and family therapy.

MDMA. Methylenedioxymethamphetamine, a chemical component of Ecstasy; initially used as an appetite suppressant for World War I soldiers and derived from precursors found in nutmeg, dill, saffron, and sassafras.

medial prefrontal cortex. A region of the cortex in the anterior frontal lobes involved in executive function and emotion regulation that is implicated in mood and anxiety disorders.

melancholic. Subtype of major depressive disorder in which the individual is unable to feel better even momentarily when something good happens, regularly feels worse in the morning and awakens early, and suffers a deepening of other symptoms of depression.

mental disorder. The DSM-IV-TR defines mental disorder as a clinically significant behavioral or psychological syndrome or patterns. The definition includes a number of key features, including distress, disability or impaired functioning, violation of social norms, and dysfunction.

mental retardation. DSM-IV-TR disorder characterized by below-average intellectual functioning associated with impairment in adaptive behavior and identified at an early age.

mentalization-based treatment. A structured form of psychodynamic therapy developed for borderline personality disorder in which the person is encouraged to focus on his or her emotions and relationships.

mescaline. A hallucinogen and alkaloid that is the active ingredient of peyote.

mesmerize. The first term for *hypnotize*, after Franz Anton Mesmer, an Austrian physician who in the late eighteenth century treated and cured hysterical or conversion disorders with what he considered the animal magnetism emanating from his body and permeating the universe.

meta-analysis. A quantitative method of analyzing the results of a set of studies on a topic, by standardizing the results.

metabolite. A chemical breakdown product of an endogenous molecule, such as a neurotransmitter, or of an exogenous drug; used to gauge current or recent level of its precursor.

metacognition. The knowledge people have about the way they know and learn about their world, for example, recognizing the usefulness of a map in finding their way in a new city.

methadone. A synthetic addictive heroin substitute for treating those addicted to heroin that eliminates its effects and the cravings.

methamphetamine. An amphetamine derivative whose abuse skyrocketed in the 1990s.

mindfulness-based cognitive therapy (MBCT). Recent adaptation of cognitive therapy/restructuring that focuses on relapse prevention after successful treatment for recurrent episodes of major depression; aims to "decenter" the person's perspective in order to break the cycle between sadness and thinking patterns.

Minnesota Multiphasic Personality Inventory (MMPI). A lengthy personality inventory that identifies individuals with states such as anxiety, depression, masculinity–femininity, and paranoia, through their true–false replies to groups of statements.

M'Naghten rule. An 1843 British court decision stating that an insanity defense can be established by proving that the defendant did not know what he or she was doing or did not realize that it was wrong.

modeling. Learning by observing and imitating the behavior of others or teaching by demonstrating and providing opportunities for imitation.

molecular genetics. Studies that seek to determine the components of a trait that are heritable by identifying relevant genes and their functions.

monoamine oxidase (MAO) inhibitors. A group of antidepressant drugs that prevent the enzyme monoamine oxidase from deactivating catecholamines and indolamines.

monozygotic (MZ) twins. Genetically identical twins who have developed from a single fertilized egg. Compare *dizygotic twins*.

mood disorders. Disorders, such as depressive disorders or mania, in which there are disabling disturbances in emotion.

moral treatment. A therapeutic regimen, introduced by Philippe Pinel during the French Revolution, whereby mentally ill patients were released from their restraints and were treated with compassion and dignity rather than with contempt and denigration.

morphine. An addictive narcotic alkaloid extracted from opium, used primarily as an analgesic and as a sedative.

motor disorder. A learning disorder characterized by marked impairment in the development of motor coordination that is not accounted for by a physical disorder such as cerebral palsy.

Mowrer's two-factor model. Mowrer's theory of avoidance learning according to which (1) fear is attached to a neutral stimulus by pairing it with a noxious unconditioned stimulus, and (2) a person learns to escape the fear elicited by the conditioned stimulus, thereby avoiding the unconditioned stimulus.

multiaxial classification system. Classification having several dimensions, all of which are employed in categorizing; DSM-IV-TR is an example.

multisystemic treatment (MST). Treatment for serious juvenile offenders that involves delivering intensive and comprehensive therapy services in the community, targeting the adolescent, the family, the school, and, in some cases, the peer group, in ecologically valid settings and using varied techniques.

narcissistic personality disorder type. Personality disorder defined by extreme selfishness and self-centeredness; a grandiose view of one's uniqueness, achievements, and talents; an insatiable craving for admiration and approval from others; willingness to exploit others to achieve goals; and expectation of much more from others than one is willing to give in return.

negative reinforcement. The strengthening of a tendency to exhibit desired behavior by rewarding responses in that situation with the removal of an aversive stimulus.

negative symptoms. Behavioral deficits in schizophrenia, which include flat affect, anhedonia, asociality, alogia, and avolition. Compare *positive symptoms*.

negative triad. In Beck's theory of depression, a person's negative views of the self, the world, and the future, in a reciprocal causal relationship with pessimistic assumptions (schemas) and cognitive biases such as selective abstraction.

nerve impulse. A wave of depolarization that propagates along the neuron and causes the release of neurotransmitter; action potential.

neurofibrillary tangles. Abnormal protein filaments present in the cell bodies of brain cells in patients with Alzheimer's disease.

neurologist. A physician who specializes in medical diseases that affect the nervous system, such as muscular dystrophy, cerebral palsy, or Alzheimer's disease.

neuron. A single nerve cell.

neuropsychological tests. Psychological tests, such as the Luria–Nebraska, that can detect impairment in different parts of the brain.

neuropsychologist. A psychologist who studies how brain dysfunction affects cognition, emotion, and behavior.

neuroscience paradigm. A broad theoretical view that holds that mental disorders are caused in part by some aberrant process directed by the brain.

neuroticism. The tendency to react to events with greater-than-average negative affect; a strong predictor of onset of anxiety disorders and depression.

neurotransmitters. Chemical substances important in transferring a nerve impulse from one neuron to another, for example, serotonin and norepinephrine.

nicotine. The principal alkaloid of tobacco (an addicting agent).

nitrous oxide. A gas that, when inhaled, produces euphoria and sometimes giddiness.

nonshared environment. Factors distinct among family members, such as relationships with friends or specific experiences unique to a person. Compare *shared environment*.

norepinephrine. A catecholamine neurotransmitter of the central nervous system, disturbances in the tracts of which apparently figure in depression and mania. It is also a sympathetic nervous system neurotransmitter, a hormone released in addition to epinephrine and similar in action, and a strong vasoconstrictor.

not guilty by reason of insanity (NGRI). Insanity plea that specifies an individual is not to be held legally responsible for the crime because the person had a mental illness at the time of the crime. Different states and federal law have different standards for defining mental illness and what must be demonstrated by the defense. In most cases, the defense must show that because of the mental illness, the accused person could not conform his or her behavior to the law and did not know right from wrong when the crime was committed. Compare *guilty but mentally ill*.

obese. Currently defined as exhibiting a body mass index (BMI) of greater than 30.

object relations theory. Variant of psychoanalytic theory that focuses on the way children internalize (*introject*) images of the people who are important to them (e.g., their parents), such that these internalized images (*object representations*) become part of the ego and influence how the person reacts to the world.

obsession. An intrusive and recurring thought that seems irrational and uncontrollable to the person experiencing it. Compare *compulsion*.

obsessive-compulsive disorder (OCD). An anxiety disorder in which the mind is flooded with persistent and uncontrollable thoughts or the individual is compelled to repeat certain acts again and again, causing significant distress and interference with everyday functioning.

obsessive-compulsive personality disorder type. Personality disorder defined by inordinate difficulty making decisions, hyperconcern with details and efficiency, and poor relations with others due to demands that things be done just so, as well as the person's unduly conventional, serious, formal, and stingy emotions.

occipital lobe. The posterior portion of each cerebral hemisphere, situated behind the parietal lobe and above the temporal lobes; responsible for reception and analysis of visual information and for some visual memory.

operant conditioning. The acquisition or elimination of a response as a function of the environmental contingencies of reinforcement and punishment. Compare *classical conditioning*.

opiates. A group of addictive sedatives that in moderate doses relieve pain and induce sleep.

opium. One of the opiates, the dried, milky juice obtained from the immature fruit of the opium poppy; an addictive narcotic that produces euphoria and drowsiness while reducing pain.

oppositional defiant disorder. An externalizing disorder of children marked by high levels of disobedience to authority but lacking the extremes of conduct disorder.

oral stage. In psychoanalytic theory, the first psychosexual stage, which extends into the second year; during it the mouth is the principal erogenous zone.

orbitofrontal cortex. The portion of the frontal lobe located just above the eyes; one of three closely related brain regions that are unusually active in individuals with obsessive-compulsive disorder.

orgasm phase. The third stage of the sexual response cycle, characterized by a peak of sexual pleasure, generally including ejaculation in men and contraction of the outer vaginal walls in women.

outcome research. Research on the efficacy of psychotherapy.

outpatient commitment. A form of civil commitment consistent with the principle of least restrictive alternative, whereby the person is not hospitalized but rather is allowed to remain free in the community under legal/medical constraints that ensure, for example, that prescribed medication is taken and other measures are observed.

oxycodone. An opiate combined with other drugs to produce prescription pain medications, including the commonly abused drug OxyContin. See also *hydrocodone*.

pain disorder. A somatoform disorder in which the person complains of severe and prolonged pain that is not fully explainable by organic pathology and is thus assumed to be caused or intensified by psychological factors.

panic attack. A sudden attack of intense apprehension, terror, and impending doom, accompanied by symptoms such as labored breathing, nausea, chest pain, feelings of choking and smothering, heart palpitations, dizziness, sweating, and trembling.

panic control therapy (PCT). A cognitive behavior treatment, based on the tendency of individuals with panic disorder to overreact to bodily stimuli, in which sensations are induced physically and coped with under safe conditions.

panic disorder. An anxiety disorder in which the individual has sudden, inexplicable, and frequent panic attacks; in DSM-IV-TR, diagnosed as with or without agoraphobia. See also *panic attack*.

paradigm. A set of basic assumptions that outlines the universe of scientific inquiry, specifying both the concepts regarded as legitimate and the methods to be used in collecting and interpreting data.

paranoia. The general term for delusions of persecution, of grandiosity, or both; found in several pathological conditions, delusional disorders, paranoid schizophrenia, and paranoid personality disorder but can also be produced by large doses of certain drugs, such as cocaine or alcohol.

paranoid personality disorder. DSM-IV-TR personality disorder defined by expectation of mistreatment at the hands of others, suspicion, secretiveness, jealousy, argumentativeness, unwillingness to accept blame, and cold and unemotional affect.

paraphilias. Sexual attraction to unusual objects and sexual activities unusual in nature.

parasympathetic nervous system. The division of the autonomic nervous system that is involved with maintenance; controls many of the internal organs and is active primarily when the organism is not aroused. Compare *sympathetic nervous system*.

parent management training (PMT). Behavioral program in which parents are taught to modify their responses to their children so that prosocial rather than antisocial behavior is consistently rewarded.

parietal lobe. The middle division of each cerebral hemisphere, situated behind the central sulcus and above the lateral sulcus; the receiving center for sensations of the skin and of bodily positions.

PCP. Phencyclidine, also known by street names such as angel dust, PeaCE Pill, and zombie; this very powerful and hazardous drug causes profound disorientation, agitated and often violent behavior, and even seizures, coma, and death.

pedohebophilia (pedophilia). A paraphilia defined by a marked preference for obtaining sexual gratification through contact with people defined legally as underage.

penile plethysmograph. A device for detecting blood flow and thus for recording changes in the size of the penis.

personality disorder types. A group of disorders involving long-standing, inflexible, and maladaptive personality traits that impair social and occupational functioning.

personality inventory. A self-report questionnaire comprised of statements assessing habitual behavioral and affective tendencies.

personality trait domains. Five personality dimensions included in the DSM-5 to help supplement diagnoses of personality disorders: negative affectivity, detachment, antagonism, disinhibition, and psychoticism.

personality trait facets. Twenty-five specific personality dimensions included in the DSM-5 to provide greater detail on the personality trait domains.

PET scan. Computer-generated picture of the living brain, created by analysis of emissions from radioactive isotopes injected into the bloodstream.

phallic stage. In psychoanalytic theory, the third psychosexual stage, extending from ages 3 to 5 or 6, during which maximal gratification is obtained from genital stimulation.

phenotype. The totality of physical characteristics and behavioral traits of an individual or a particular trait exhibited by an individual; the product of interactions between genetics and the environment over the course of development. Compare *genotype*.

phenylketonuria (PKU). A genetic deficiency in a liver enzyme, phenylalanine hydroxylase, that causes severe intellectual developmental disorder unless phenylalanine can be largely restricted from the diet.

phobia. An anxiety disorder in which there is intense fear and avoidance of specific objects and situations, recognized as irrational by the individual.

phonological disorder. DSM-IV-TR communication disorder in childhood in which some words sound like baby talk because the person is not able to make certain speech sounds. Renamed speech sounds disorder in DSM-5.

placebo. Any inactive therapy or chemical agent, or any attribute or component of such a therapy or chemical, that affects a person's behavior for reasons related to his or her expectation of change.

placebo effect. The action of a drug or psychological treatment that is not attributable to any specific operations of the agent. For example, a tranquilizer can reduce anxiety both because of its special biochemical action and because the recipient expects relief. See also *placebo*.

plaques. Small, round areas composed of remnants of lost neurons and beta-amyloid, a waxy protein deposit; present in the brains of patients with Alzheimer's disease.

pleasure principle. In psychoanalytic theory, the demanding manner by which the id operates, seeking immediate gratification of its needs.

polydrug abuse. The misuse of more than one drug at a time, such as drinking heavily and taking cocaine.

polygenic. As applied to psychopathology or any other trait, caused by multiple genes contributing their effects, typically during multiple stages of development.

polymorphism. Any specific difference in DNA sequence that exists within a population.

positive reinforcement. The strengthening of a tendency to exhibit desired behavior by rewarding responses in that situation with a desired reward.

positive symptoms. Behavioral excesses in schizophrenia, such as hallucinations and delusions. Compare *negative symptoms*.

postpartum onset. Onset within 4 weeks postpartum, characterizing a subtype of episodes of major depressive disorder or mania.

posttraumatic model (of DID). Etiological model of dissociative identity disorder that assumes the condition begins in childhood as a result of severe physical or sexual abuse. Compare *sociocognitive model (of DID)*.

posttraumatic stress disorder (PTSD). An anxiety disorder in which a particularly stressful event, such as military combat, rape, or a natural disaster, brings in its aftermath intrusive reexperiencing of the trauma, a numbing of responsiveness to the outside world, estrangement from others, and a tendency to be easily startled, as well as nightmares, recurrent dreams, and otherwise disturbed sleep.

predictive validity. See *validity*.

predisposition. An inclination or diathesis to respond in a certain way, either inborn or acquired; in abnormal psychology, a factor that lowers the ability to withstand stress and inclines the individual toward pathology.

prefrontal cortex. The region of the frontal lobe of the brain that helps maintain an image of threats and rewards faced, as well as maintain focus and plan relevant to those threats and rewards.

premature ejaculation. Inability of the male to inhibit his orgasm long enough for mutually satisfying sexual relations.

prepared learning. In classical conditioning theory, a biological predisposition to associate particular stimuli readily with the unconditioned stimulus.

prevalence. In epidemiological studies of a disorder, the percentage of a population that has the disorder at a given time. Compare *incidence*.

privileged communication. The communication between parties in a confidential relationship that is protected by statute, which a spouse, doctor, lawyer, pastor, psychologist, or psychiatrist thus cannot be forced to disclose, except under unusual circumstances.

probands. The sample of people who in a genetic investigation bears the diagnosis or trait in which the investigator is interested.

prognosis. A prediction of the likely course and outcome of an illness. Compare *diagnosis*.

projective hypothesis. The notion that standard but highly unstructured stimuli, as found in the Rorschach assessment's series of inkblots, are necessary to bypass defenses in order to reveal unconscious motives and conflicts.

projective test. A psychological assessment device, such as the Rorschach series of inkblots, employing a set of standard but vague stimuli, on the assumption that unstructured material will allow unconscious motivations and fears to be uncovered.

pronoun reversal. A speech problem in which the child refers to himself or herself as "he," "she," or "you" and uses "I" or "me" in referring to others; often found in the speech of children with autistic disorder.

pruning. In neural development, the selective loss of synaptic connections, especially in the fine-tuning of brain regions devoted to sensory processing.

psilocybin. A psychedelic drug extracted from the mushroom *Psilocybe mexicana*.

psyche. In psychoanalytic theory, the totality of the id, ego, and superego, including both conscious and unconscious components.

psychiatric nurse. A nurse, typically with a bachelor's degree, who receives specialized training in mental illness. A nurse practitioner may prescribe psychiatric medications.

psychiatrist. A physician (M.D.) who has taken specialized postdoctoral training, called a residency, in the diagnosis, treatment, and prevention of mental disorders.

psychoactive medications. Prescribed chemical compounds—for example, Prozac—having a psychological effect that alters mood or thought process.

psychoanalysis. Primarily the therapy procedures pioneered by Freud, entailing free association, dream analysis, and working through the transference neurosis. More recently the term has come to encompass the numerous variations on basic Freudian therapy.

psychoanalytic theory. Theory originating with Freud that psychopathology results from unconscious conflicts in the individual.

psychoeducational approaches. Especially with bipolar disorder and schizophrenia, the component of treatment that helps people learn about symptoms, expected time course, triggers for symptoms, and treatment strategies.

psychological tests. Standardized procedures designed to measure performance on a particular task or to assess personality.

psychomotor agitation. A symptom characterized by pacing, restlessness, and inability to sit still.

psychomotor retardation. A symptom commonly observed in major depressive disorder in which the person moves his or her limbs and body slowly.

psychoneuroimmunology. Field that studies how psychological factors (especially stressors) impact the immune system (adversely).

psychopathology. The field concerned with the nature and development of mental disorders.

psychopathy. A personality syndrome related to antisocial personality disorder but defined by an absence of emotion, impulsivity, manipulativeness, and irresponsibility.

psychophysiology. The discipline concerned with the bodily changes that accompany psychological events.

psychotherapy. A primarily verbal means of helping troubled individuals change their thoughts, feelings, and behavior to reduce distress and to achieve greater life satisfaction.

psychotic features. Delusions or hallucinations characterizing a subtype of episodes of major depressive disorder or mania. Also used to refer to positive symptoms of schizophrenia.

random assignment. A method of assigning people to groups by chance (e.g., using a flip of a coin). The procedure helps to ensure that groups are comparable before the experimental manipulation begins.

randomized controlled trials (RCTs). Studies in which clients are randomly assigned to receive either active treatment or a comparison (a placebo condition involving no treatment or an active-treatment control group that receives another treatment); experimental treatment studies, where the independent variable is the treatment type and the dependent variable is client outcome.

rapid cycling. Term applied to bipolar disorders if the person has experienced at least four episodes within the past year.

rational-emotive behavior therapy (REBT). A cognitive-restructuring behavior therapy introduced by Albert Ellis and based on the assumption that much disordered behavior is rooted in absolutistic, unrealistic demands and goals, such as, "I must be universally loved."

reactivity. The phenomenon wherein behavior changes because it is being observed.

reality principle. In psychoanalytic theory, the manner in which the ego delays gratification and otherwise deals with the environment in a planned, rational fashion.

receptor. A protein embedded in a neural cell membrane that interacts with one or more neurotransmitters. Nonneural receptor proteins include hormone receptors.

reciprocal gene–environment interaction. The genetic predisposition for an individual to seek out certain environments that increase the risk of developing a particular disorder. Compare *gene–environment interaction*.

reliability. The extent to which a test, measurement, or classification system produces the same scientific observation each time it is applied. Reliability types include test–retest, the relationship between the scores that a person achieves when he or she takes the same test twice; interrater, the relationship between the judgments that at least two raters make independently about a phenomenon; split-half, the relationship between two halves of an assessment instrument that have been determined to be equivalent; alternate-form, the relationship between scores achieved by people when they complete two versions of a test that are judged to be equivalent; and internal consistency, the degree to which different items of an assessment are related to one another.

resolution phase. The fourth and final stage of the sexual response cycle, characterized by an abatement of muscle tension, relaxation, and a sense of well-being.

reuptake. Cellular process by which released neurotransmitters are taken back into the presynaptic cell, terminating their present postsynaptic effect but making them available for subsequent modulation of nerve impulse transmission.

reversal (ABAB) designs. An experimental design in which behavior is measured during a baseline period (A), during a period when a treatment is introduced (B), during the reinstatement of the conditions that prevailed in the baseline period (A), and finally during a reintroduction of the treatment (B); commonly used in operant research to isolate cause–effect relationships.

reward system. System of brain structures involved in the motivation to pursue rewards. Believed to be involved in depression, mania, schizophrenia, and substance use disorders.

risk factor. A condition or variable that increases the likelihood of developing a disorder.

Rorschach Inkblot Test. A projective test in which the examinee is instructed to interpret a series of 10 inkblots reproduced on cards.

rumination. Repetitive thought about why a person is experiencing a negative mood.

safety behaviors. Behaviors used to avoid experiencing anxiety in feared situations, such as the tendency of people with social phobia to avoid looking at other people (so as to avoid perceiving negative feedback) or the tendency of people with panic disorder to avoid exercise (so as to avoid somatic arousal that could trigger a panic attack).

schema. A mental structure for organizing information about the world.

schizoaffective disorder. Diagnosis applied when a patient has symptoms of both mood disorder and either schizophreniform disorder or schizophrenia.

schizoid personality disorder. DSM-IV-TR personality disorder defined by emotional aloofness; indifference to the praise, criticism, and feelings of others; maintenance of few, if any, close friendships; and solitary interests.

schizophrenia. A disorder characterized by disturbances in thought, emotion, and behavior; disordered thinking in which ideas are not logically related; delusional beliefs; faulty perception, such as hallucinations; disturbances in attention; disturbances in motor activity; blunted expression of emotion; reduced desire for interpersonal relations and withdrawal from people; diminished motivation and anticipatory pleasure. See also *schizoaffective disorder*, *schizophreniform disorder*, and *brief psychotic disorder*.

schizophreniform disorder. Diagnosis given to people who have all the symptoms of schizophrenia for more than 2 weeks but less than 6 months. Compare *brief psychotic disorder*.

schizotypal personality disorder type. Personality disorder defined by eccentricity, oddities of thought and perception (magical thinking, illusions, depersonalization, derealization), digressive speech involving over-elaborations, and social isolation; under stress, behavior may appear psychotic.

seasonal affective disorder. A subtype of mood disorders in which episodes consistently occur at the same time of year; in the most common form, major depressive episodes consistently occur in the winter.

second messengers. Intracellular molecules whose levels are increased by sustained activity of neurotransmitter, for example, receptors, and which affect the resting states of ion channels or regulate gene expression of receptor molecules, thus modulating the cell's sensitivity to neurotransmitter.

second-generation antipsychotic drugs. Any of several drugs, such as clozapine, used to treat schizophrenia that produce fewer motor side effects than traditional antipsychotics while reducing positive and disorganized symptoms at least as effectively; may, however, be associated with increased and serious side effects of other varieties.

secondhand smoke. Also referred to as environmental tobacco smoke (ETS), the smoke from the burning end of a cigarette; contains higher concentrations of ammonia, carbon monoxide, nicotine, and tar than the smoke inhaled by the smoker.

sedatives. Drugs that slow bodily activities, especially those of the central nervous system; used to reduce pain and tension and to induce relaxation and sleep.

selective mortality. The tendency for less healthy individuals to die more quickly, which leads to biased samples in long-term follow-up studies.

selective serotonin reuptake inhibitors (SSRIs). A specific form of serotonin reuptake inhibitors (SRIs) with less effect on dopamine and norepinephrine levels; SSRIs inhibit the reuptake of serotonin into the presynaptic neuron, so that serotonin levels in the cleft are sustained for a longer period of time.

self-monitoring. In behavioral assessment, a procedure whereby the individual observes and reports certain aspects of his or her own behavior, thoughts, or emotions.

sensate focus. A term applied to exercises prescribed at the beginning of the Masters and Johnson sex therapy program, in which partners are instructed to fondle each other to give pleasure but to refrain from intercourse, thus reducing anxiety about sexual performance.

separation anxiety disorder. A disorder in which the child feels intense fear and distress when away from someone on whom he or she is very dependent.

septal area. In the subcortical region of the brain, the area anterior to the thalamus.

serotonin. A neurotransmitter of the central nervous system whose disturbances apparently figure in depression.

serotonin reuptake inhibitors (SRIs). Any of various drugs that inhibit the presynaptic reuptake of the neurotransmitter serotonin, thereby prolonging its effects on postsynaptic neurons.

serotonin transporter gene. A particular gene critical to the gene–environment interactions that apparently contribute to the development of depression.

serotonin–norepinephrine reuptake inhibitors (SNRIs). Any of various drugs that inhibit the presynaptic reuptake of serotonin and norepinephrine, such that both neurotransmitters will have more prolonged effects on postsynaptic neurons.

sex-reassignment surgery. An operation removing existing genitalia and constructing a substitute for the genitals of the opposite sex.

sexual aversion disorder. Avoidance of nearly all genital contact with other people. Compare *hypoactive sexual desire disorder*.

sexual dysfunctions. Dysfunctions in which the appetitive or psychophysiological changes of the normal sexual response cycle are inhibited. Compare *hypoactive sexual desire disorder*.

sexual interest/arousal disorder in women. A sexual dysfunction characterized by a loss of sexual interest (urges, fantasies or desires) or lack of physiological or subjective arousal to sexual cues.

sexual masochism. A marked preference for obtaining or increasing sexual gratification through subjection to pain or humiliation.

sexual orientation. An individual's emotional, romantic, or sexual attraction toward other people that is stable and enduring.

sexual response cycle. The general pattern of sexual physical processes and feelings, made up of four phases: appetitive interest, excitement, orgasm, and resolution.

sexual sadism. A marked preference for obtaining or increasing sexual gratification by inflicting pain or humiliation on another person.

shared environment. Factors that family members have in common, such as income level, child-rearing practices, and parental marital status and quality. Compare *nonshared environment*.

single nucleotide polymorphism (SNP). A variation in gene sequence. Specifically, differences between people in a single nucleotide (A, T, G, or C) in the DNA sequence of a particular gene.

single-case experimental design. A design for an experiment conducted with a single subject. Typically, behavior is measured within a baseline condition, then during an experimental or treatment condition, and finally within the baseline condition again.

social anxiety disorder (social phobia). A collection of fears linked to the presence of other people.

social selection hypothesis. An attempt to explain the correlation between social class and schizophrenia by arguing that people with schizophrenia tend to move downward in socioeconomic status. Compare *sociogenic hypothesis.*

social selectivity. The late-life shift in interest away from seeking new social interactions and toward cultivating those few social relationships that matter most, such as with family and close friends.

social skills training. Behavior therapy procedures, such as modeling and behavior rehearsal, for teaching individuals how to meet others, talk to them and maintain eye contact, give and receive criticism, offer and accept compliments, make requests and express feelings, and otherwise improve their relations with other people.

social worker. A mental health professional who holds a master of social work (M.S.W.) degree.

sociocognitive model (of DID). Etiological model of dissociative identity disorder that considers the condition to be the result of learning to enact social roles, though not through conscious deception, but in response to suggestion. Compare *posttraumatic model (of DID).*

sociogenic hypothesis. An idea that seeks causes in social conditions, for example, that being in a low social class can cause one to become schizophrenic. Compare *social selection hypothesis.*

somatic nervous system. The division of the nervous system that controls muscles under voluntary control. Compare *autonomic nervous system.*

somatic symptom disorders. A group of disorders defined by anxiety about health and excessive focus on physical symptoms.

somatization disorder. A DSM-IV-TR somatoform disorder, once called Briquet's syndrome, in which the person continually seeks medical help for recurrent and multiple physical symptoms that have no discoverable physical cause, despite a complicated medical history that is dramatically presented. Compare *hypochondriasis.*

somatoform disorders. DSM-IV-TR disorders in which symptoms suggest a physical problem but have no known physiological cause; believed to be linked to psychological conflicts and needs but not voluntarily assumed. See also *somatization disorder, functional neurological disorder, pain disorder,* and *hypochondriasis.*

somatosensory cortex. A region of the cortex along the lateral postcentral gyrus that is key in processing the sensation of touch.

specific phobia. An unwarranted fear and avoidance of a specific object or circumstance, for example, fear of nonpoisonous snakes or fear of heights.

spectator role. As applied by Masters and Johnson, a pattern of behavior in which the individual's focus on and concern with sexual performance causes him or her to be an observer rather than a participant and thus impedes natural sexual responses.

speech sounds disorder. Communication disorder in childhood in which some words sound like baby talk because the person is not able to make certain speech sounds.

standardization. The process of constructing a normed assessment procedure that meets the various psychometric criteria for reliability and validity.

statistical significance. A result that has a low probability of having occurred by chance alone and is by convention regarded as important. Compare *clinical significance.*

stigma. The pernicious beliefs and attitudes held by a society, ascribed to groups considered deviant in some manner, such as people with mental illness.

stimulant. A drug, such as cocaine, that increases alertness and motor activity and at the same time reduces fatigue, allowing an individual to remain awake for an extended period of time.

stress. State of an organism subjected to a stressor; can take the form of increased autonomic activity and in the long term can cause breakdown of an organ or development of a mental disorder.

structured interview. An interview in which the questions are set out in a prescribed fashion for the interviewer; assists professionals in making diagnostic decisions based on standardized criteria.

stuttering. DSM-IV-TR communication disorder of childhood marked by frequent and pronounced verbal dysfluencies, such as repetitions of certain sounds. See also *childhood onset fluency disorder.*

subgenual anterior cingulate. A region in the anterior cortex that is part of a network of structures involved in emotion processing; believed to be overly active in major depressive disorder.

substance use disorders. Disorders in which drugs such as alcohol and cocaine are abused to such an extent that behavior becomes maladaptive, social and occupational functioning are impaired, and control or abstinence becomes impossible. Dependence on the drug may be physiological and produce tolerance and withdrawal.

subthreshold symptoms. Symptoms of a disorder that are clinically significant but do not meet full diagnostic criteria.

suicide. The intentional taking of one's own life.

suicide prevention centers. Staffed primarily by paraprofessionals who are trained to be empathic and to encourage suicidal callers—assumed to be ambivalent—to consider nondestructive ways of dealing with what is bothering them.

superego. In psychoanalytic theory, the part of the personality that acts as the conscience and reflects society's moral standards as learned from parents and teachers.

sympathetic nervous system. The division of the autonomic nervous system that acts on bodily systems—for example, contracting the blood vessels, reducing activity of the intestines, and increasing the heartbeat—to prepare the organism for exertion, emotional stress, or extreme cold. Compare *parasympathetic nervous system.*

symptom. An observable physiological or psychological manifestation of a disease.

synapse. Small gap between two neurons where the nerve signal passes electrically or chemically from the axon of the first to the dendrites, cell body, or axon of the second.

systematic desensitization. A major behavior therapy procedure that has a fearful person, while deeply relaxed, imagine a series of progressively more fearsome situations, such that fear is dispelled as a response incompatible with relaxation; useful for treating psychological problems in which anxiety is the principal difficulty.

tardive dyskinesia. A muscular disturbance of patients who have taken phenothiazines for a very long time, marked by involuntary motor movements such as lip smacking and chin wagging.

temporal lobe. A large region of each cerebral hemisphere situated below the lateral sulcus and in front of the occipital lobe; contains primary auditory and general association areas.

test–retest reliability. See *reliability.*

thalamus. A major brain relay station consisting of two egg-shaped lobes; receives impulses from all sensory areas except the olfactory and transmits them to the cerebrum for higher processing.

Thematic Apperception Test (TAT). A projective test consisting of black-and-white pictures, each depicting a potentially emotion-laden situation, about each of which the examinee is instructed to make up a story. See also *projective hypothesis.*

theory. A formally stated and coherent set of propositions that explain and logically order a range of phenomena, generating testable predictions or hypotheses.

third-variable problem. The difficulty in the correlational method of research whereby the relationship between two variables may be attributable to a third factor.

thought suppression. Key feature of obsessive-compulsive disorder; has the paradoxical effect of inducing preoccupation with the object of thought.

time-of-measurement effects. A possible confound in longitudinal studies whereby conditions at a particular point in time can have a specific effect on a variable that is being studied over time.

time-out. An operant conditioning procedure in which, after bad behavior, the person is temporarily removed from a setting where reinforcers can be obtained and placed in a less desirable setting, for example, in a boring room.

token economy. A behavior therapy procedure, based on operant conditioning principles, in which hospitalized patients are given scrip rewards, such as poker chips, for socially constructive behavior. The tokens can be exchanged for desirable items and activities such as cigarettes and extra time away from the ward.

tolerance. A physiological process in which greater and greater amounts of an addictive drug are required to produce the same effect. See also *addiction.*

transcription. In genetics, the first step in gene expression. A section of DNA sequence is transcribed to RNA; a sequence of DNA synthesizes a copy of RNA.

transference. The venting of the analysand's emotions, either positive or negative, by treating the psychoanalyst as the symbolic representative of someone important in the past.

transvestic fetishism. The practice of dressing in the clothing of the opposite sex, for the purpose of sexual arousal.

treatment outcome research. Studies designed to assess whether medical or psychological approaches are efficacious in relieving symptoms of a disorder. See also *randomized controlled trials 5.*

tricyclic antidepressants. A group of antidepressants with molecular structures characterized by three fused rings; interfere with the reuptake of norepinephrine and serotonin.

tryptophan. Amino acid that is the major precursor of serotonin; experimental depletion has found that a lowered serotonin level causes temporary depressive symptoms in people with a personal or family history of depression.

twin method. Research strategy in behavior genetics in which concordance rates of monozygotic and dizygotic twins are compared.

unconditioned response (UCR). See *classical conditioning.*

unconditioned stimulus (UCS). See *classical conditioning.*

unconscious. A state of unawareness without sensation or thought; in psychoanalytic theory, the part of the personality, in particular the id impulses or energy, of which the ego is unaware.

vaginal plethysmograph. A device for measuring physiological signs of sexual arousal in women; the device is shaped like a tampon and is inserted into the vagina to measure increases in blood flow.

vaginismus. DSM-IV-TR diagnosis defined by painful, spasmodic contractions of the outer third of the vagina, making penetration impossible or extremely difficult.

validity. In research, includes internal, the extent to which results can be confidently attributed to the manipulation of the independent variable, and external, the extent to which results can be generalized to other populations and settings. Validity as applied to psychiatric diagnoses includes concurrent, the extent to which previously undiscovered features are found among patients with the same diagnosis, and predictive, the extent to which predictions can be made about the future behavior of patients with the same diagnosis. Validity as applied to psychological and psychiatric measures includes content validity, the extent to which a measure adequately samples the domain of interest, and criterion, the extent to which a measure is associated in an expected way with some other measure (the criterion). See also *construct validity*.

vascular dementia. A form of dementia caused by cerebrovascular disease, most commonly occurring after strokes. Because the areas of the brain affected by disease can vary, the symptoms of vascular dementia vary as well.

ventricles. Cavities deep within the brain, filled with cerebrospinal fluid, that connect to the spinal cord.

voyeuristic disorder (voyeurism). Marked preference for obtaining sexual gratification by watching others in a state of undress or having sexual relations.

white matter. Neural tissue, particularly of the brain and spinal cord, consisting of tracts or bundles of myelinated (sheathed) nerve fibers. Compare *gray matter*.

withdrawal. Negative physiological and psychological reactions evidenced when a person suddenly stops taking an addictive drug; cramps, restlessness, and even death are examples. See also *addiction*.

yedasentience. The subjective sense of knowing that one has achieved closure on an action or thought; theorized to be deficient among persons with obsessive-compulsive disorder.

References

Abbey, S. E., & Stewart, D. E. (2000). Gender and psychosomatic aspects of ischemic disease. *Journal of Psychosomatic Research, 48*, 417–423.

Abel, G. G., Becker, J. V., Cunningham-Rathner, J., Mittelman, M., & Rouleau, J. L. (1988). Multiple paraphilic diagnoses among sex offenders. *Bulletin of the American Academy of Psychiatry & the Law, 16*(2), 153–168.

Abel, G. G., Becker, J. V., Mittelman, M., Cunningham-Rathner, J., Rouleau, J. L., & Murphy, W. D. (1987). Self-reported sex crimes of nonincarcerated paraphiliacs. *Journal of Interpersonal Violence, 2*(1), 3–25. doi: 10.1177/088626087002001001

Abercrombie, H. C., Kalin, N. H., Thurow, M. E., Rosenkranz, M. A., & Davidson, R. J. (2003). Cortisol variation in humans affects memory for emotionally laden and neutral information. *Behavioral Neuroscience, 117*(3), 505–516. doi: 10.1037/0735-7044.117.3.505

Abikoff, H. B., & Hechtman, L. (1996). Multimodal therapy and stimulants in the treatment of children with attention-deficit hyperactivity disorder. In E. D. Hibbs & P. S. Jensen (Eds.), *Psychosocial treatments for child and adolescent disorders: Empirically based strategies for clinical practice* (pp. 341–369). Washington, DC: American Psychological Association.

Abou-Saleh, M. T., Younis, Y., & Karim, L. (1998). Anorexia nervosa in an Arab culture. *International Journal of Eating Disorders, 23*, 207–212.

Abramowitz, J. S., Franklin, M. E., Schwartz, S. A., & Furr, J. M. (2003). Symptom presentation and outcome of cognitive-behavioral therapy for obsessive-compulsive disorder. *Journal of Consulting and Clinical Psychology, 71*(6), 1049–1057. doi: 10.1037/0022-006X.71.6.1049

Abramson, L. Y., Metalsky, G. I., & Alloy, L. B. (1989). Hopelessness depression: A theory-based subtype of depression. *Psychological Review, 96*, 358–372.

Acarturk, C., de Graaf, R., van Straten, A., Have, M. T., & Cuijpers, P. (2008). Social phobia and number of social fears, and their association with comorbidity, health-related quality of life and help seeking: A population-based study. *Social Psychiatry and Psychiatric Epidemiology, 43*(4), 273–279.

Achenbach, T. M., Hensley, V. R., Phares, V., & Grayson, D. (1990). Problems and competencies reported by parents of Australian and American children. *Journal of Child Psychology and Psychiatry, 31*, 265–286.

Acocella, J. (1999). *Creating hysteria: Women and multiple personality disorder*. San Francisco: Jossey-Bass.

Acton, G. J., & Kang, J. (2001). Interventions to reduce the burden of caregiving for an adult with dementia: A meta-analysis. *Research in Nursing and Health, 24*, 349–360.

Adler, A. (1930). *Guiding the child on the principles of individual psychology*. New York: Greenberg.

Agras, W. S., Crow, S. J., Halmi, K. A., Mitchell, J. E., Wilson, G. T., & Kraemer, H. C. (2000). Outcome predictors for the cognitive-behavioral treatment of bulimia nervosa: Data from a multisite study. *American Journal of Psychiatry, 157*, 1302–1308.

Agras, W. S., Rossiter, E. M., Arnow, B., et al. (1994). One-year follow-up of psychosocial and pharmacologic treatments for bulimia nervosa. *Journal of Clinical Psychiatry, 55*, 179–183.

Agras, W. S., Rossiter, E. M., Arnow, B., Schneider, J. A., Telch, C. F., Raeburn, S. D., . . . Koran, L. M. (1992). Pharmacologic and cognitive-behavioral treatment for bulimia nervosa: A controlled comparison. *American Journal of Psychiatry, 149*, 82–87.

Aguilera, A., Lopez, S. R., Breitborde, N. J., Kopelowicz, A., & Zarate, R. (2010). Expressed emotion and sociocultural moderation in the course of schizophrenia. *Journal of Abnormal Psychology, 119*, 875–885.

Ainsworth, M. S., Blehar, M. C., Waters, E., & Wall, S. (1978). *Patterns of attachment: A psychological study of the strange situation*. Oxford, England: Erlbaum.

Akiskal, H. S., Hantouche, E. G., Bourgeois, M. L., Azorin, J. M., Sechter, D., Allilaire, J. F., et al. (2001). Toward a refined phenomenology of mania: Combining clinician-assessment and self-report in the French EPIMAN study. *Journal of Affective Disorders, 67*, 89–96.

Akyuez, G., Dogan, O., Sar, V., Yargic, L. I., & Tutkun, H. (1999). Frequency of dissociative disorder in the general population in Turkey. *Comprehensive Psychiatry, 40*, 151–159.

Alarcon, R. D., Becker, A. E., Lewis-Fernandez, R., Like, R. C., Desai, P., Foulks, E., et al. (2009). Issues for DSM-V: The role of culture in psychiatric diagnosis. *Journal of Nervous and Mental Disease, 197*, 559–560.

Albee, G. W., Lane, E. A., & Reuter, J. M. (1964). Childhood intelligence of future schizophrenics and neighborhood peers. *Journal of Psychology, 58*, 141–144.

Albert, M. S., Dekosky, S. T., Dickson, D., Dubois, B., Feldman, H. H., Fox, N. C., . . . Phelps, C. H. (2011). The diagnosis of mild cognitive impairment due to Alzheimer's disease: Recommendations from the National Institute on Aging–Alzheimer's Association workgroups on diagnostic guidelines for Alzheimer's disease. *Alzheimer's and Dementia : The Journal of the Alzheimer's Association, 7*(3), 270–279. doi: 10.1016/j.jalz.2011.03.008

Albertini, R. S., & Phillips, K. A. (1999). Thirty-three cases of body dysmorphic disorder in children and adolescents. *Journal of the American Academy of Child and Adolescent Psychiatry, 38*, 453–459.

Alden, L. E. (1989). Short-term structured treatment for avoidant personality disorder. *Journal of Consulting and Clinical Psychology, 57*, 756–764.

Alden, L. E., Laposa, J. M., Taylor, C. T., & Ryder, A. G. (2002). Avoidant personality disorder: Current status and future directions. *Journal of Personality Disorders, 16*, 1–29.

Alegria, M., Canino, G., Shrout, P. E., Woo, M., Duan, N., & Vila, D. (2008). Prevalence of mental illness in immigrant and non-immigrant U.S. Latino groups. *American Journal of Psychiatry, 165*, 359–369.

Alegria, M., Woo, M., Cao, Z., Torres, M., Meng, X. L., & Striegel-Moore, R. (2007). Prevalence and correlates of eating disorders among Latinos in the United States. *International Journal of Eating Disorders, 40*, s15–s21.

Alexander, P. C., & Lupfer, S. L. (1987). Family characteristics and long-term consequences associated with sexual abuse. *Archives of Sexual Behavior, 16*, 235–245.

Allan, C., Smith, I., & Mellin, M. (2000). Detoxification from alcohol: A comparison of home detoxification and hospital-based day patient care. *Alcohol & Alcoholism, 35*, 66–69.

Allderidge, P. (1979). Hospitals, mad houses, and asylums: Cycles in the care of the insane. *British Journal of Psychiatry, 134*, 321–324.

Allen, M., D'alessio, D., & Brezgel, K. (1995). A meta-analysis summarizing the effects of pornography: II. Aggression after exposure. *Human Communication Research, 22*, 258–283.

Allen, P., Johns, L. C., Fu, C. H. Y., Broome, M. R., Vythelingum, G. N., & McGuire, P. K. (2004). Misattribution of external speech in patients with hallucinations and delusions. *Schizophrenia Research, 69*, 277–287.

Allnutt, S. H., Bradford, J. M., Greenberg, D. M., & Curry, S. (1996). Co-morbidity of alcoholism and the paraphilias. *Journal of Forensic Science, 41*, 234–239.

Alloy, L. B., Abramson, L. Y., Walshaw, P. D., Cogswell, A., Grandin, L. D., Hughes, M. E., . . . Hogan, M. E. (2008). Behavioral approach system and behavioral inhibition system sensitivities and bipolar spectrum disorders: Prospective prediction of bipolar mood episodes. *Bipolar Disorders, 10*(2), 310–322.

Alloy, L. B., Abramson, L. Y., Walshaw, P. D., Gerstein, R. K., Keyser, J. D., Whitehouse, W. G., . . . Harmon-Jones, E. (2009). Behavioral approach system (BAS)-relevant cognitive styles and bipolar spectrum disorders: Concurrent and prospective associations. *Journal of Abnormal Psychology, 118*(3), 459–471. doi: 10.1037/a0016604

Alloy, L. B., Abramson, L. Y., Whitehouse, W. G., Hogan, M. E., Panzarella, C., & Rose, D. T. (2006). Prospective incidence of first onsets and recurrences of depression in individuals at high and low cognitive risk for depression. *Journal of Abnormal Psychology, 115*, 145–156.

Altamura, C., Paluello, M. M., Mundo, E., Medda, S., & Mannu, P. (2001). Clinical and subclinical body dysmorphic disorder. *European Archives of Psychiatry and Clinical Neuroscience, 251*(3), 105–108.

Althof, S. E., Abdo, C. H., Dean, J., Hackett, G., Mccabe, M., McMahon, C. G., . . . Tan, H. M. (2010). International Society for Sexual Medicine's guidelines for the diagnosis and treatment of premature ejaculation. *Journal of Sexual Medicine, 7*(9), 2947–2969. doi: 10.1111/j.1743-6109.2010.01975.x

Altshuler, L. L., Kupka, R. W., Hellemann, G., Frye, M. A., Sugar, C. A., McElroy, S. L., . . . Suppes, T. (2010). Gender and depressive symptoms in 711 patients with bipolar disorder evaluated prospectively in the Stanley Foundation Bipolar Treatment Outcome Network. *American Journal of Psychiatry, 167*(6), 708–715.

Alwahhabi, F. (2003). Anxiety symptoms and generalized anxiety disorder in the elderly: A review. *Harvard Review of Psychiatry, 11,* 180–193.

Amador, X. F., Flaum, M., Andrease, N. C., Strauss, D. H., Yale, S. A., et al. (1994). Awareness of illne schizophrenia and schizoaffective and mood disorder. *Archives of General Psychiatry, 51,* 826–836.

Aman, M. G., & Langworthy, K. (2000). Pharmacotherapy for hyperactivity in children with autism and other pervasive developmental disorders. *Journal of Autism and Developmental Disorders, 30,* 451–459.

American Law Institute. (1962). *Model penal code: Proposed official draft.* Philadelphia: Author.

American Lung Association. (2010). *State of tobacco control 2010.* American Lung Association, http://www.stateoftobaccocontrol.org.

American Psychiatric Association. (2000). *Diagnostic and statistical manual of mental disorders (DSM-IV-TR)* [4th (Text Revision) ed.]. Washington, DC: Author.

American Psychiatric Association. (2004). Practice guidelines for the treatment of patients with schizophrenia (2nd ed.). Retrieved from http://www.psych.org.

American Psychiatric Association. (2007). Treatment of patients with Alzheimer's disease and other dementias (2nd ed.). *APA Practice Guidelines.* http://www.psych.org.

American Psychiatric Association. *Diagnostic and statistical manual of mental disorders* (First edition, 1952; second edition, 1968; third edition, 1980; revised, 1987; fourth edition, 1994; revised 2000 ed.). Washington, DC: Author.

American Psychological Association. (2002). Ethical principles of psychologists and code of conduct. *American Psychologist, 57,* 1060–1073.

Amir, N., Beard, C., Burns, M., & Bomyea, J. (2009). Attention modification program in individuals with generalized anxiety disorder. *Journal of Abnormal Psychology, 118*(1), 28–33. doi: 10.1037/a0012589

Amir, N., Foa, E. B., & Coles, M. E. (1998). Negative interpretation bias in social phobia. *Behaviour Research and Therapy, 36,* 945–957.

Anand, A., Verhoeff, P., Seneca, N., Zoghbi, S. S., Seibyl, J. P., Charney, D. S., & Innis, R. B. (2000). Brain SPECT imaging of amphetamine-induced dopamine release in euthymic bipolar disorder patients. *American Journal of Psychiatry, 157,* 1109–1114.

Anastopoulos, A. D., Shelton, T., DuPaul, G. J., & Guevremont, D. C. (1993). Parent training for attention deficit hyperactivity disorder: Its impact on parent functioning. *Journal of Abnormal Child Psychology, 20,* 503–520.

Ancoli, I. S., Kripke, D. F., Klauber, M. R., Fell, R., Stepnowsky, C., Estline, E., . . . Chinn, A. (1996). Morbidity, mortality and sleep-disordered breathing in community dwelling elderly. *Sleep: Journal of Sleep Research and Sleep Medicine, 19,* 277–282.

Andersen, B. L., Cyranowski, J. M., & Aarestad, S. (2000). Beyond artificial, sex-linked distinctions to conceptualize female sexuality: Comment on Baumeister (2000). *Psychological Bulletin, 126*(3), 380–384.

Andersen, B. L., Cyranowski, J. M., & Espindle, D. (1999). Men's sexual self-schema. *Journal of Personality and Social Psychology, 76,* 645–661.

Andersen, S. M., & Chen, S. (2002). The relational self: An interpersonal social-cognitive theory. *Psychological Review, 109,* 619–645.

Andersen, S. M., Reznik, I., & Manzella, L. M. (1996). Eliciting transient affect, motivation, and expectancies in transference: Significant-other representations and the self in social relations. *Journal of Personality and Social Psychology, 71,* 1108–1129.

Anderson, C. A., Hinshaw, S. P., & Simmel, C. (1994). Mother-child interactions in ADHD and comparison boys: Relationships to overt and covert externalizing behavior. *Journal of Abnormal Child Psychology, 22,* 247–265.

Anderson, E. R., & Hope, D. A. (2008). A review of the tripartite model for understanding the link between anxiety and depression in youth. *Clinical Psychology Review, 28,* 275–287.

Anderson, G. M., & Hoshino, Y. (1987). Neurochemical studies of autism. In D. J. Cohen, A. M. Donnellan, & R. Paul (Eds.), *Handbook of autism and pervasive developmental disorders* (pp. 166–191). New York: Wiley.

Anderson, L. T., Campbell, M., Adams, P., Small, A. M., Perry, R., & Shell, J. (1989). The effects of haloperidol on discrimination learning and behavioral symptoms in autistic children. *Journal of Autism and Developmental Disorders, 19,* 227–239.

Anderson, M. C., & Green, C. (2001). Suppressing unwanted memories by executive control. *Nature, 410,* 366–369.

Anderson, S., Hanson, R., Malecha, M., Oftelie, A., Erickson, C., & Clark, J. M. (1997). The effectiveness of naltrexone in treating task attending, aggression, self-injury, and stereotypic mannerisms of six young males with autism or pervasive developmental disorders. *Journal of Developmental and Physical Disabilities, 9,* 211–221.

Andreano, J. M., & Cahill, L. (2006). Glucocorticoid release and memory consolidation in men and women. *Psychological Science, 17,* 466–470.

Andreasen, N. C., Olsen, S. A., Dennert, J. W., & Smith, M. R. (1982). Ventricular enlargement in schizophrenia: Relationship to positive and negative symptoms. *American Journal of Psychiatry, 139,* 297–302.

Andrews, G., Charney, D. S., Sirovatka, P. J., & Regier, D. A. (Eds.). (2009). *Stress-induced and fear circuitry disorders.* Arlington, VA: American Psychiatric Association.

Andrews, G., Cuijpers, P., Craske, M. G., McEvoy, P., & Titov, N. (2010). Computer therapy for the anxiety and depressive disorders is effective, acceptable and practical health care: A meta-analysis. *PloS One, 5*(10), e13196. doi: 10.1371/journal.pone.0013196

Andrews, G., Hobbs, M. J., Borkovec, T. D., Beesdo, K., Craske, M. G., Heimberg, R. G., . . . Stanley, M. A. (2010). Generalized worry disorder: A review of DSM-IV generalized anxiety disorder and options for DSM-V. *Depression and Anxiety, 27*(2), 134–147. doi: 10.1002/da.20658

Anglin, M. D., Burke, C., Perrochet, B., Stamper, E., & Dawud-Noursi, S. (2000). History of the methamphetamine problem. *Journal of Psychoactive Drugs, 32,* 137–141.

Angold, A., Erkanli, A., Egger, H. L., & Costello, E. J. (2000). Stimulant treatment for children: A community perspective. *Journal of the American Academy of Child and Adolescent Psychiatry, 39,* 975–984.

Angrist, B., Lee, H. K., & Gershon, S. (1974). The antagonism of amphetamine-induced symptomatology by a neuroleptic. *American Journal of Psychiatry, 131,* 817–819.

Angst, F., Stassen, H. H., Clayton, P. J., & Angst, J. (2002). Mortality of patients with mood disorders: Follow-up over 34–38 years. *Journal of Affective Disorders, 68,* 167–181.

Angst, J. (1998). Sexual problems in healthy and depressed persons. *International Clinical Psychopharmacology, 13*(Suppl. 6), S1–S4.

Anthony, J. L., & Lonigan, C. L. (2004). The nature of phonological awareness: Converging evidence from four studies of preschool and early grade school children. *Journal of Educational Psychology, 96,* 43–55.

Appel, L. J., Moore, T. J., Obarzanek, E., Vollmer, W. M., Svetkey, L. P., Sacks, F. M., . . . Karanja, N., for the DASH Collaborative Research Group. (1997). A clinical trial of the effects of dietary patterns on blood pressure. *New England Journal of Medicine, 336,* 1117–1124.

Appelbaum, P. S. (2006). "Depressed? get out!": Dealing with suicidal students on college campuses. *Psychiatric Services, 57,* 914–916.

Appelbaum, P. S., & Grisso, T. (1995). The MacArthur Treatment Competence Study: 1. Mental illness and competence to consent to treatment. *Law and Human Behavior, 19,* 105–126.

Appelbaum, P. S., & Gutheil, T. (1991). *Clinical handbook of psychiatry and the law.* Baltimore: Williams & Wilkins.

Appignannesi, L. (2008). *Mad, bad, and sad: Women and the mind doctors.* New York: W. W. Norton.

Araujo, A. B., Durante, R., Feldman, H. A., Goldstein, I., & McKinley, J. B. (1998). The relationship between depressive symptoms and male erectile dysfunction: Cross-sectional results from the Massachusetts Male Aging Study. *Psychosomatic Medicine, 60,* 458–465.

Arbisi, P. A., Ben-Porath, Y. S., & McNulty, J. (2002). A comparison of MMPI-2 validity in African American and Caucasian psychiatric patients. *Psychological Assessment, 14,* 3–15.

Arentewicz, G., & Schmidt, G. (1983). *The treatment of sexual disorders: Concepts and techniques of couple therapy.* New York: Basic Books.

Arias, E., Anderson, R. N., Kung, H. C., Murphy, S. L., & Kochanek, K. D. (2003). *Deaths: Final reports, 52* (DHHS Publication No. 2003–1120). Hyattsville, MD: National Center for Health Statistics.

Arndt, I. O., Dorozynsky, L., Woody, G. E., McLellan, A. T., & O'Brien, C. P. (1992). Desipramine treatment of cocaine dependence in methadone-maintained patients. *Archives of General Psychiatry, 49,* 888–893.

Arnett, J. J. (2008). The neglected 95%: Why American psychology needs to become less American. *The American Psychologist, 63*(7), 602–614. doi: 10.1037/0003-066X.63.7.602

Arnold, E. H., O'Leary, S. G., & Edwards, G. H. (1997). Father involvement and self-reported parenting of children with attention deficit hyperactivity disorder. *Journal of Consulting and Clinical Psychology, 65,* 337–342.

Arnold, E. M., Kirk, R. S., Roberts, A. C., Griffith, D. P., Meadows, K., & Julian, J. (2003). Treatment of incarcerated, sexually-abused adolescent females: An outcome study. *Journal of Child Sexual Abuse, 12*(1), 123–139.

Arnold, L. E., Elliott, M., Sachs, L., et al. (2003). Effects of ethnicity on treatment attendance, stimulant response/dose, and 14-month outcome in ADHD. *Journal of Consulting and Clinical Psychology, 71,* 713–727.

Arnold, L. M., Keck, P. E., Jr., Collins J., Wilson, R., Fleck, D. E., Corey, K. B., . . . Strakowski, S. M. (2004). Ethnicity and first-rank symptoms in patients with psychosis. *Schizophrenia Research, 67,* 207–212.

Arnow, B., Kenardy, J., & Agras, W. S. (1992). Binge eating among the obese. *Journal of Behavioral Medicine, 15,* 155–170.

Aronson, E. (2004). *The social animal* (9th ed.). New York: Worth.

Arseneault, L., Cannon, M., Poulton, R., Murray, R., Caspi, A., & Moffitt, T. E. (2002). Cannabis use in adolescence and risk for adult psychosis: Longitudinal prospective study. *British Medical Journal, 325,* 1212–1213.

Artiles, A. J., & Trent, S. C. (1994). Overrepresentation of minority students in special education: A continuing debate. *Journal of Special Education, 27,* 410–437.

Ascher, E. A., Sturm, V. E., Seider, B. H., Holley, S. R., Miller, B. L., & Levenson, R. W. (2010). Relationship satisfaction and emotional language in frontotemporal dementia and Alzheimer disease patients and spousal caregivers. *Alzheimer's Disease & Associated Disorders, 24,* 49–55.

Ashbaugh, A. R., Antony, M. M., McCabe, R. E., Schmidt, L. A., & Swinson, R. P. (2005). Self-evaluative biases in social anxiety. *Cognitive Therapy and Research, 29,* 387–398.

Asmundson, G. J., Larsen, D. K., & Stein, M. B. (1998). Panic disorder and vestibular disturbance: An overview of empirical findings and clinical implications. *Journal of Psychosomatic Research, 44,* 107–120.

Asmundson, G. J., Stapleton, J. A., & Taylor, S. (2004). Are avoidance and numbing distinct PTSD symptom clusters? *Journal of Traumatic Stress, 17*(6), 467–475. doi: 10.1007/s10960-004-5795-7

Atha, M. J. (2005). Cannabis use in Britain. Independent Drug Monitoring Unit Ltd. Home Office Publications.

Attia, E., Haiman, C., Walsh, B. T., & Flater, S. R. (1998). Does fluoxetine augment the inpatient treatment of anorexia nervosa? *American Journal of Psychiatry, 155,* 548–551.

Attia, E., & Roberto, C. A. (2009). Should amenorrhea be a diagnostic criterion for anorexia nervosa? *International Journal of Eating Disorders, 42,* 581–589.

Aubry, J., Gervasoni, N., Osiek, C., Perret, G., Rossier, M. F., Bertschy, G., & Bondolfi, G. (2007). The DEX/CRH neuroendocrine test and the prediction of depressive relapse in remitted depressed outpatients. *Journal of Psychiatric Research, 41,* 290–294.

Audrain-McGovern, J., & Tercyak, K. P. (2011). Genes, enviroment, and adolescent smoking: Implications for prevention. In K. S. Kendler, S. R. Jaffee, & D. Romer (Eds.), *The dynamic genome and mental health* (pp. 294–321). New York: Oxford University Press.

Avissar, S., Nechamkin, Y., Barki-Harrington, L., Roitman, G., & Schreiber, G. (1997). Differential G protein measures in mononuclear leukocytes of patients with bipolar mood disorder are state dependent. *Journal of Affective Disorders, 43,* 85–93.

Avissar, S., Schreiber, G., Nechamkin, Y., Nehaus, I., Lam, G., Schwartz, P., . . . Rosenthal, N. E. (1999). The effects of seasons and light therapy on G protein levels in mononuclear leukocytes in patients with seasonal affective disorder. *Archives of General Psychiatry, 56,* 178–184.

Ayanian, J. Z., & Cleary, P. D. (1999). Perceived risks of heart disease and cancer among cigarette smokers. *Journal of the American Medical Association, 281,* 1019–1021.

Bach, A. K., Wincze, J. P., & Barlow, D. H. (2001). Sexual dysfunction. In D. H. Barlow (Ed.), *Clinical handbook of psychological disorders* (pp. 562–608). New York: Guilford.

Baer, R. A., & Sekirnjak, G. (1997). Detection of underreporting on the MMPI-II in a clinical population. Effects of information about validity scales. *Journal of Personality Assessment, 69,* 555–567.

Bagby, M. R., Nicholson, R. A., Bacchionchi, J. R., et al. (2002). The predictive capacity of the MMPI-2 and PAI validity scales and indexes to detect coached and uncoached feigning. *Journal of Personality Assessment, 78,* 69–86.

Bailey, A., LeCouteur, A., Gottesman, I., Bolton, P., Simonoff, E., Yuzda, E., & Rutter, M. (1995). Autism as a strongly genetic disorder: Evidence from a British twin study. *Psychological Medicine, 25,* 63–77.

Baker, J. H., Mitchell, K. S., Neale, M. C., & Kendler, K. S. (2010). Eating disorder symptomatology and substance use disorders: Prevalence and shared risk in a population based twin sample. *International Journal of Eating Disorders, 43,* 648–658.

Baker, L. A., Jacobson, K. C., Raine, A., Lozano, D. I., & Bezdjian, S. (2007). Genetic and environmental bases of childhood antisocial behavior: A multi-informant twin study. *Journal of Abnormal Psychology, 116,* 219–235.

Ball, J. C., & Ross, A. (1991). *The effectiveness of methadone maintenance treatment.* New York: Springer-Verlag.

Balsis, S., Carpenter, B. D., & Storandt, M. (2005). Personality change precedes clinical diagnosis of dementia of the Alzheimer type. *Journal of Gerontology, 60B*(2), 98–101.

Bancroft, J., Loftus, J., & Long, J. S. (2003). Distress about sex: A national survey of women in heterosexual relationships. *Archives of Sexual Behavior, 32,* 193–208.

Bandelow, B., Zohar, J., Hollander, E., Kasper, S., Moller, H. J., Allgulander, C., . . . Vega, J. (2008). World Federation of Societies of Biological Psychiatry (WFSBP) guidelines for the pharmacological treatment of anxiety, obsessive-compulsive and post-traumatic stress disorders—first revision. *World Journal of Biological Psychiatry, 9*(4), 248–312. doi: 10.1080/15622970802465807

Bandura, A., Blanchard, E. B., & Ritter, B. (1969). Relative efficacy of desensitization and modeling approaches for inducing behavioral, affective, and attitudinal changes. *Journal of Personality and Social Psychology, 13,* 173–199.

Bandura, A., & Menlove, F. L. (1968). Factors determining vicarious extinction of avoidance behavior through symbolic modeling. *Journal of Personality and Social Psychology, 8,* 99–108.

Banich, M. T., Passarotti, A. M., White, D. A., Nortz, M. J., & Steiner, R. D. (2000). Interhemispheric interaction during childhood: II. Children with early-treated phenylketonuria. *Developmental Neuropsychology, 18,* 53–71.

Bar-Haim, Y., Lamy, D., Lee, P., Bakermans-Kranenburg, M. J., & van Ijzendoorn, M. H. (2007). Threat-related attentional bias in anxious and nonanxious individuals: A meta-analytic study. *Psychological Bulletin, 133,* 1–24.

Bar-Haim, Y., Lamy, D., Pergamin, L., Bakermans-Kranenburg, M. J., & van Ijzendoorn, M. H. (2007). Threat-related attentional bias in anxious and nonanxious individuals: A meta-analytic study. *Psychological Bulletin, 133*(1), 1–24. doi: 10.1037/0033-2909.133.1.1

Barbato, A., & D'Avanzo, B. (2008). Efficacy of couple therapy as a treatment for depression: A meta-analysis. *Psychiatric Quarterly, 79,* 121–132.

Barber, C. (2008). *Comfortably numb.* New York: Pantheon.

Barbini, B., Benedetti, F., Colombo, C., Dotoli, D., Bernasconi, A., Cigala-Fulgosi, M., . . . Smeraldi, E. (2005). Dark therapy for mania: A pilot study. *Bipolar Disorders, 7,* 98–101.

Barch, D. M., Carter, C. S., Braver, T. S., et al. (2001). Selective deficits in prefrontal cortex function in medication naïve patients with schizophrenia. *Archives of General Psychiatry, 58,* 280–288.

Barch, D. M., Carter, C. S., MacDonald, A. W., Braver, T. S., & Cohen, J. D. (2003). Context processing deficits in schizophrenia: Diagnostic specificity, four-week course, and relationship to clinical symptoms. *Journal of Abnormal Psychology, 112,* 132–143.

Barch, D. M., Csernansky, J. G., Conturo, T., & Snyder, A. Z. (2002). Working and long-term memory deficits in schizophrenia: Is there a common prefrontal mechanism? *Journal of Abnormal Psychology, 111,* 478–494.

Bardone-Cone, A. M., Wonderlich, S. A., Frost, R. O., Bulik, C. M., Mitchell, J., et al. (2007). Perfectionism and eating disorders: Current status and future directions. *Clinical Psychology Review, 27,* a 384–405.

Barkley, R. A. (1981). *Hyperactive children: A handbook for diagnosis and treatment.* New York: Guilford.

Barkley, R. A. (1990). *Attention-deficit hyperactivity disorder: A handbook for diagnosis and treatment.* New York: Guilford.

Barkley, R. A. (1997). Behavioral inhibition, sustained attention, and executive function: Constructing a unifying theory of ADHD. *Psychological Bulletin, 121,* 65–94.

Barkley, R. A., DuPaul, G. J., & McMurray, M. B. (1990). A comprehensive evaluation of attention deficit disorder with and without hyperactivity defined by research criteria. *Journal of Consulting and Clinical Psychology, 58,* 775–789.

Barkley, R. A., Fischer, M., Smallish, L., & Fletcher, K. (2002). The persistence of attention-deficit hyperactivity disorder into young adulthood as a function of reporting source and definition of disorder. *Journal of Abnormal Psychology, 111,* 279–289.

Barkley, R. A., Fischer, M., Smallish, L., & Fletcher, K. (2003). Does the treatment of attention-deficit/hyperactivity disorder with stimulants contribute to drug use/abuse? A 13 year prospective study. *Pediatrics, 111,* 97–109.

Barkley, R. A., Grodzinsky, G., & DuPaul, G. J. (1992). Frontal lobe functions in attention deficit disorder with and without hyperactivity: A review and research report. *Journal of Abnormal Child Psychology, 20,* 163–188.

Barkley, R. A., Karlsson, J., & Pollard, S. (1985). Effects of age on the mother-child interactions of hyperactive children. *Journal of Abnormal Child Psychology, 13,* 631–638.

Barlow, D. H. (2004). *Anxiety and its disorders: The nature and treatment of anxiety and panic.* New York: Guilford.

Barlow, D. H., Blanchard, E. B., Vermilyea, J. A., Vermilyea, B. B., & DiNardo, P. A. (1986). Generalized anxiety and generalized anxiety disorder: Description and reconceptualization. *American Journal of Psychiatry, 143,* 40–44.

Barlow, D. H., Raffa, S. D., & Cohen, E. M. (2002). Psychosocial treatments for panic disorders, phobias, and generalized anxiety disorder. In J. M. Gorman & P. E. Nathan (Eds.), *A guide to treatments that work* (2nd ed., pp. 301–335). London: Oxford University Press.

Barsky, A. J., Fama, J. M., Bailey, E. D., & Ahern, D. K. (1998). A prospective 4 to 5-year study of DSM-III-R hypochondriasis. *Archives of General Psychiatry, 55,* 737–744.

Barsky, A. J., Orav, E. J., & Bates, D. W. (2005). Somatization increases medical utilization and costs independent of psychiatric and medical comorbidity. *Archives of General Psychiatry, 62,* 903–910.

Barth, J., Schumacher, M., & Herrmann-Lingen, C. (2004). Depression as a risk factor for mortality in patients with coronary heart disease: A meta-analysis. *Psychosomatic Medicine, 66,* 802–813.

Bartlik, B., & Goldberg, J. (2000). Female sexual arousal disorder. In S. R. Lieblum & R. C. Rosen (Eds.), *Principles and practice of sex therapy* (3rd ed., pp. 85–117). New York: Guilford.

Bass, E., & Davis, L. (1994). *The courage to heal: A guide for women survivors of child sexual abuse.* New York: HarperCollins.

Bassett, A. S., Scherer, S. W., & Brzustowicz, L. M. (2010). Copy number variations in schizophrenia: Critical review and new perspectives on concepts of genetics and disease. *American Journal of Psychiatry, 167,* 899–914.

Basson, R., Althof, S. A., Davis, S., Fugl-Meyer, K., Goldstein, I., Leiblum, S., . . . Wagner, G. (2004). Summary of the recommendations on sexual dysfunctions in women. *Journal of Sexual Medicine, 1*(1), 24–34.

Basson, R., Brotto, L. A., Laan, E., Redmond, G., & Utian, W. H. (2005). Assessment and management of women's sexual dysfunctions: Problematic desire and arousal. *Journal of Sexual Medicine, 2,* 291–300.

Bateman, A. W., & Fonagy, P. (2004). Mentalization-based treatment of BPD. *Journal of Personality Disorders, 18,* 36–51.

Baumeister, A. A., & Baumeister, A. A. (1995). Mental retardation. In M. Hersen & R. T. Ammerman (Eds.), *Advanced abnormal child psychology* (pp. 283–303). Hillsdale, NJ: Erlbaum.

Baumeister, R. F. (2000). Gender differences in erotic plasticity: The female sex drive as socially flexible and responsive. *Psychological Bulletin, 126*(3), 347–374.

Baumeister, R. F., & Butler, J. L. (1997). Sexual masochism: Deviance without pathology. In D. R. Laws & W. O'Donohue (Eds.), *Sexual deviance* (pp. 225–239). New York: Guilford.

Baumeister, R. F., Catanese, K. R., & Vohs, K. (2001). Is there a gender difference in strength of sex drive? Theoretical views, conceptual distinctions, and a review of relevant evidence. *Personality and Social Psychology Review, 5*(3), 242–273.

Baxter, L. R., Ackermann, R. F., Swerdlow, N. R., Brody, A., Saxena, S., Schwartz, J. M., et al. (2000). Specific brain system mediation of obsessive-compulsive disorder responsive to either medication or behavior therapy. In W. K. Goodman, M. V. Rudorfer, & J. D. Maser (Eds.), *Obsessive-compulsive disorder: Contemporary issues in treatment* (pp. 573–610). Mahwah, NJ: Erlbaum.

Beauchaine, T. P., Hinshaw, S. P., & Pang, K. L. (2010). Comorbidity of attention-deficit/hyperactivity disorder and early-onset conduct disorder: Biological, environmental, and developmental mechanisms. *Clinical Psychology: Science and Practice, 17,* 327–336.

Beck, A. T. (1967). *Depression: Clinical, experimental and theoretical aspects.* New York: Harper & Row.

Beck, A. T. (1976). *Cognitive therapy and the emotional disorders.* New York: International Universities Press.

Beck, A. T., & Freeman, A. (1990). *Cognitive therapy for personality disorders.* New York: Guilford.

Beck, A. T., Kovacs, M., & Weissman, A. (1975). Hopelessness and suicidal behavior: An overview. *Journal of the American Medical Association, 234,* 1146–1149.

Beck, A. T., & Rector, N. A. (2000). Cognitive therapy of schizophrenia: A new therapy for the new millennium. *American Journal of Psychotherapy, 54,* 291–300.

Beck, A. T., Rector, N., & Stolar, N. (2004, October). *The negative symptoms of schizophrenia: A cognitive perspective.* Paper presented at the Society for Research in Psychopathology, St. Louis, MO.

Beck, J. G. (1995). Hypoactive sexual desire disorder: An overview. *Journal of Consulting and Clinical Psychology, 63,* 919–927.

Beck, J. G., & Bozman, A. (1995). Gender differences in sexual desire: The effects of anger and anxiety. *Archives of Sexual Behavior, 24,* 595–612.

Becker, J. V., & Hunter, J. A. (1997). Understanding and treating child and adolescent sexual offenders. In T. H. Ollendick & R. J. Prinz (Eds.), *Advances in clinical child psychology* (pp. 177–196). New York: Plenum.

Beecher, H. K. (1966). Ethics and clinical research. *New England Journal of Medicine, 274,* 1354–1360.

Beesdo, K., Pine, D. S., Lieb, R., & Wittchen, H. U. (2010). Incidence and risk patterns of anxiety and depressive disorders and categorization of generalized anxiety disorder. *Archives of General Psychiatry, 67*(1), 47–57.

Beevers, C., Rohde, P., Stice, E., & Nolen-Hoeksema, S. (2007). Recovery from major depressive disorder among female adolescents: A prospective test of the scar hypothesis. *Journal of Consulting and Clinical Psychology, 75,* 888–900.

Bellack, A. S., & Hersen, M. (1998). *Behavioral assessment: A practical handbook* (4th ed.). Boston: Allyn & Bacon.

Ben-Porath, Y. S., & Butcher, J. N. (1989). The comparability of MMP-I and MMPI-2 scales and profiles. *Psychological Assessment, 1,* 345–347.

Bender, D., Morey, L. C., & Skodol, A. E. (2011). Toward a model for assessing level of personality functioning in DSM–5, Part I: A review of theory and methods. *Journal of Personality Assessment, 93*(4), 332–346.

Benkelfat, C., Ellenbogen, M. A., Dean, P., Palmour, R. M., & Young, S. N. (1994). Mood-lowering effect of tryptophan depletion: Enhanced susceptibility in young men at genetic risk for major affective disorders. *Archives of General Psychiatry, 51,* 687–700.

Benowitz, N. L., & Peng, M. W. (2000). Non-nicotine pharmacotherapy for smoking cessation. *CNS Drugs, 13,* 265–285.

Benowitz, N., Pérez-Stable, E., Herrera, B., & Jacob, P. (2002). Slower metabolism and reduced intake of nicotine from cigarette smoking in Chinese-Americans. *Journal of the National Cancer Institute, 94,* 108–115.

Bergen, A. W., Yeager, M., Welch, R. A., Haque, K., Ganjei, J. K., van den Bree, M. B. M., et al. (2005). Association of multiple DRD2 polymorphisms with anorexia nervosa. *Neuropsychopharmacology, 30,* 1703–1710.

Berkman, E. T., Falk, E. M., & Lieberman, M. D. (2011). In the trenches of real-world self-control: Neural correlates of breaking the link between craving and smoking. *Psychological Science, 22,* 498–506.

Berkman, L. F., Blumenthal, J., Burg, M., Carney, R. M., Catellier, D., Cowan, M. J., . . . Schneiderman, N. (2003). Effects of treating depression and low perceived social support on clinical events after myocardial infarction: The Enhancing Recovery in Coronary Heart Disease Patients (ENRICHD) Randomized Trial. *Journal of the American Medical Association, 289,* 3106–3116.

Bernal, M., Haro, J. M., Bernert, S., Brugha, T., de Graaf, R., Bruffaerts, R., . . . Alonso, J. (2007). Risk factors for suicidality in Europe: Results from the ESEMED study. *Journal of Affective Disorders, 101*(1–3), 27–34. doi: 10.1016/j.jad.2006.09.018

Berry, J. C. (1967). *Antecedents of schizophrenia, impulsive character and alcoholism in males.* Paper presented at the 75th annual convention of the American Psychological Association, Washington, DC.

Bertram, L., & Tanzi, R. E. (2009). Genome-wide association studies in Alzheimer's disease. *Human Molecular Genetics, 18*(R2), R137–R145. doi: 10.1093/hmg/ddp406

Beutler, L. E., Machado, P. P. P., & Neufeldt, S. A. (1994). Therapist variables. In S. L. Garfield & A. E. Bergin (Eds.), *Handbook of psychotherapy and behavior change* (pp. 229–269). Oxford, England: Wiley.

Bhugra, D., Popelyuk, D., & McMullen, I. (2010). Paraphilias across cultures: Contexts and controversies. *Journal of Sex Research, 47*(2), 242–256. doi: 10.1080/00224491003699833.

Bhutta, A. T., Cleves, M. A., Casey, P. H., Cradock, M. M., & Anand, K. J. (2002). Cognitive and behavioral outcomes of school-aged children who were born preterm: A meta-analysis. *Journal of the American Medical Association, 288,* 728–737.

Biederman, J., & Faraone, S. (2004). The Massachusetts General Hospital studies of gender influences on attention-deficit/hyperactivity disorder in youth and relatives. *Psychiatric Clinics of North America, 27,* 215–224.

Biederman, J., Faraone, S., Milberger, S., Curtis, S., Chen, L., Marrs, A., Ouellette, C., Moore, P., & Spencer, T. (1996). Predictors of persistence and remission of ADHD into adolescence: Results from a four-year prospective follow-up study. *Journal of the American Academy of Child and Adolescent Psychiatry, 35,* 343–351.

Biederman, J., Mick, E., Faraone, S. V., et al. (2000). Pediatric mania: A developmental subtype of bipolar disorder? *Biological Psychiatry, 48,* 458–466.

Biederman, J., Monuteasu, M. C., Mick, E., Spencer, T., Wilens, T. E., Silva, J. M., . . . Faraone, S. V. (2006). Young adult outcome of attention deficit hyperactivity disorder: A controlled 10-year follow-up study. *Psychological Medicine, 36,* 167–179.

Biederman, J., Petty, C. R., Monuteaux, M. C., Fried, R., Byrne, D., Mirto, T., . . . Faraone, S. V. (2010). Adult psychiatric outcomes of girls with attention deficit hyperactivity disorder: 11-year follow-up in a longitudinal case-control study. *American Journal of Psychiatry, 167,* 409–417.

Biederman, J., Rosenbaum, J. F., Hirshfeld, D. R., & Faraone, S. V. (1990). Psychiatric correlates of behavioral inhibition in young children of parents with and without psychiatric disorders. *Archives of General Psychiatry, 47,* 21–26.

Biglan, A., Hops, H., & Sherman, L. (1988). Coercive family processes and maternal depression. In R. J. McMahon & R. D. Peter (Eds.), *Marriages and families: Behavioral treatments and processes* (pp. 72–103). New York: Brunner/Mazel.

Binik, Y. M. (2010). The DSM diagnostic criteria for dyspareunia. *Archives of Sexual Behavior, 39*(2), 292–303. doi: 10.1007/s10508-009-9563-x

Birbaumer, N., Veit, R., Lotze, M., Erb, M., Hermann, C., Grodd, W., & Flor., H. (2005). Deficient fear conditioning in psychopathy: A functional magnetic resonance imaging study. *Archives of General Psychiatry, 62,* 799–805.

Birks, J. (2006). Cholinesterase inhibitors for Alzheimer's disease. *Cochrane Database of Systematic Reviews,* CD005593. doi: 10.1002/14651858.CD005593

Birnbaum, G. E., Reis, H. T., Mikulincer, M., Gillath, O., & Orpaz, A. (2006). When sex is more than just sex: Attachment orientations, sexual experience, and relationship quality. *Journal of Personality and Social Psychology, 91,* 929–943.

Bischkopf, J., Busse, A., & Angermeyer, M. C. (2002). Mild cognitive impairment: A review of prevalence, incidence and outcome according to current approaches. *Acta Psychiatrica Scandinavia, 106,* 403–414.

Bjornsson, A. S., Dyck, I., Moitra, E., Stout, R. L., Weisberg, R. B., Keller, M. B., & Phillips, K. A. (2011). The clinical course of body dysmorphic disorder in the Harvard/Brown Anxiety Research Project (HARP). *Journal of Nervous and Mental Disease, 199*(1), 55–57. doi: 10.1097/NMD.0b013e31820448f7

BJS. (1999). *Mental health and treatment of inmates and probationers.* Bureau of Justice Statistics Special Report. Department of Justice. NJC174463.

Blachman, D. R., & Hinshaw, S. P. (2002). Patterns of friendship among girls with and without attention-deficit/hyperactivity disorder. *Journal of Abnormal Child Psychology, 30,* 625–640.

Black, D. W., Baumgard, C. H., & Bell, S. E. (1995). A 16 to 45-year follow-up of 71 men with antisocial personality disorder. *Comprehensive Psychiatry, 36,* 130–140.

Blair, K. S., Shaywitz, J., Smith, B. W., Rhodes, R., Geraci, M., Jones, M., . . . Mondillo, K. (2008). Response to emotional expressions in generalized social phobia and generalized anxiety disorder: Evidence for separate disorders. *American Journal of Psychiatry, 165,* 1193–1202.

Blair, R. J. D., Jones, L., Clark, F., & Smith, M. (1997). The psychopathic individual: A lack of responsiveness to distress cues? *Psychophysiology, 34,* 192–198.

Blanchard, J. J., & Brown, S. B. (1998). Structured diagnostic interviews. In C. R. Reynolds (Ed.), *Comprehensive clinical psychology, Volume 3, Assessment* (pp. 97–130). New York: Elsevier.

Blanchard, J. J., & Cohen, A. S. (2006). The structure of negative symptoms within schizophrenia: Implications for assessment. *Schizophrenia Bulletin, 32,* 238–245.

Blanchard, J. J., Squires, D., Henry, T., Horan, W. P., Bogenschutz, M., et al. (1999). Examining an affect regulation model of substance abuse in schizophrenia: The role of traits and coping. *Journal of Nervous and Mental Disease, 187,* 72–79.

Blanco, C., Heimberg, R. G., Schneier, F. R., Fresco, D. M., Chen, H., Turk, C. L., . . . Liebowitz, M. R. (2010). A placebo-controlled trial of phenelzine, cognitive behavioral group therapy, and their combination for social anxiety disorder. *Archives of General Psychiatry, 67*(3), 286–295. doi: 10.1001/archgenpsychiatry.2010.11

Bloch, M. H., Landeros-Weisenberger, A., Sen, S., Dombrowski, P., Kelmendi, B., Coric, V., . . . Leckman, J. F. (2008). Association of the serotonin transporter polymorphism and obsessive-compulsive disorder: Systematic review. *American Journal of Medical Genetics. Part B, Neuropsychiatric Genetics: The Official Publication of the International Society of Psychiatric Genetics, 147B*(6), 850–858. doi: 10.1002/ajmg.b.30699

Blum, N., John, D. S., Pfohl, B., Stuart, S., McCormick, B., Allen, J. J., . . . Black, D. W. (2008). Systems training for emotional predictability and problem solving (STEPPS) for outpatients with borderline personality disorder: A randomized controlled trial and 1-year follow-up. *American Journal of Psychiatry, 165,* 468–478.

Boardman, J. D., Saint Onge, J. M., Haberstick, B. C., Timberlake, D. S., & Hewitt, J. K. (2008). Do schools moderate the genetic determinants of smoking? *Behavioral Genetics, 28,* 234–246.

Bockhoven, J. (1963). *Moral treatment in American psychiatry.* New York: Springer-Verlag.

Bockting, C. L. H., Schene, A. H., Spinhoven, P., Koeter, M. W. J., Wouters, L. F., Huyser, J., & Kamphuis, J. H. (2005). Preventing relapse/recurrence in recurrent depression with cognitive therapy: A randomized controlled trial. *Journal of Consulting and Clinical Psychology, 73,* 647–657.

Boegels, S. M., & Zigterman, D. (2000). Dysfunctional cognitions in children with social phobia, separation anxiety disorder, and generalized anxiety disorder. *Journal of Abnormal Child Psychology, 28,* 205–211.

Bohne, A., Keuthen, N. J., Wilhelm, S., Deckersbach, T., & Jenike, M. A. (2002). Prevalence of symptoms of body dysmorphic disorder and its correlates: A cross-cultural comparison. *Psychosomatics, 43,* 486–490.

Bolton, P., Bass, J., Neugebauer, R., Verdeli, H., Clougherty, K. F., Wickramaratne, P., . . . Weissman, M. (2003). Group interpersonal psychotherapy for depression in rural Uganda: A randomized controlled trial. *Journal of the American Medical Association, 289,* 3117–3124.

Bolton, P., MacDonald, H., Pickles, A., Rios, P., Goode, S., Crowson, M., . . . Rutter, M. (1994). A case control family history study of autism. *Journal of Child Psychology and Psychiatry, 35,* 877–900.

Bonanno, G. A. (2004). Loss, trauma, and human resilience: Have we underestimated the human capacity to thrive after extremely aversive events? *American Psychologist, 59,* 20–28.

Bonanno, G. A., Wortman, C. B., Lehman, D. R., Tweed, R. G., Haring, M., Sonnega, J., . . . Nesse, R. M. (2002). Resilience to loss and chronic grief: A prospective study from preloss to 18-months postloss. *Journal of Personality and Social Psychology, 83,* 1150–1164.

Bondy, B., Buettner, A., & Zill, P. (2006). Genetics of suicide. *Molecular Psychiatry, 11*(4), 336–351. doi: 10.1038/sj.mp.4001803

Bonta, J., Law, M., & Hanson, K. (1998). The prediction of criminal and violent recidivism among mentally disordered offenders. *Psychological Bulletin, 123,* 123–142.

Bookheimer, S., & Burggren, A. (2009). APOE-4 genotype and neurophysiological vulnerability to Alzheimer's and cognitive aging. *Annual Review of Clinical Psychology, 5,* 343–362. doi: 10.1146/annurev.clinpsy.032408.153625

Boos, H. B., Aleman, A., Cahn, W., Hulshoff, H., & Kahn, R. S. (2007). Brain volumes in relatives of patients with schizophrenia: A meta analysis. *Archives of General Psychiatry, 64,* 297–304.

Borch-Jacobsen, M. (1997, April 24). Sybil: The making of a disease? An interview with Dr. Herbert Spiegel. *New York Review of Books, 44*(7), 60.

Borduin, C. M., Mann, B. J., Cone, L. T., Henggeler, S. W., Fucci, B. R., Blaske, D. M., & Williams, R. A. (1995). Multisystemic treatment of serious juvenile offenders: Long-term prevention of criminality and violence. *Journal of Consulting and Clinical Psychology, 63,* 569–578.

Borkovec, T. D., Alcaine, O. M., & Behar, E. (2004). Clinical presentation and diagnostic features. In R. G. Heimberg, C. L. Turk, & D. S. Mennin (Eds.), *Generalized anxiety disorder* (pp. 77–108). New York: Guilford.

Borkovec, T. D., & Newman, M. G. (1998). Worry and generalized anxiety disorder. In P. Salkovskis (Ed.), *Comprehensive clinical psychology.* Oxford, England: Elsevier.

Bornstein, R. F. (2003). Behaviorally referenced experimentation and symptom validation: A paradigm for 21st century personality disorder research. *Journal of Personality Disorders, 17,* 1–18.

Boscarino, J. A. (2006). Posttraumatic stress disorder and mortality among U.S. Army veterans 30 years after military service. *Annals of Epidemiology, 16*(4), 248–256. doi: 10.1016/j.annepidem.2005.03.009

Bosquet, M., & Egeland, B. (2006). The development and maintenance of anxiety symptoms from infancy through adolescence in a longitudinal sample. *Development and Psychopathology, 18,* 517–550.

Botvin G. J. (1999). Prevention in schools. In: R. T. Ammerman and P. Ott, (eds). Prevention and Societal Impact of Drug and Alcohol Abuse. Mahwah, New Jersey: Lawrence Erlbaum Associates.

Botvin G. J. (2000). Preventing drug abuse in schools: social and competence enhancement approaches targeting individual-level etiologic factors. *Addictive Behaviors, 25,* 887–97.

Bouton, M. E., Mineka, S., & Barlow, D. H. (2001). A modern learning theory perspective on the etiology of panic disorder. *Psychological Review, 108,* 4–32.

Bouton, M. E., & Waddell, J. (2007). Some biobehavioral insights into persistent effects of emotional trauma. In L. J. Kirmayer, R. Lemelson, & M. Barad (Eds.), *Understanding trauma: Integrating biological, clinical, and cultural perspectives* (pp. 41–59). New York, NY: Cambridge University Press.

Bowden, C. L., Lecrubier, Y., Bauer, M., Goodwin, G., Greil, W., Sachs, G., & von Knorring, L. (2000). Maintenance therapies for classic and other forms of bipolar disorder. *Journal of Affective Disorders, 59,* S57–S67.

Bowers, W. A., & Ansher, L. S. (2008). The effectiveness of cognitive behavioral therapy on changing eating disorder symptoms and psychopathy of 32 anorexia nervosa patients at hospital discharge and one year follow-up. *Annals of Clinical Psychiatry, 20,* 79–86.

Boyle, M. (1991). *Schizophrenia: A scientific delusion?* New York: Routledge.

Bradley, L., & Bryant, P. E. (1985). *Rhyme and reason in reading and spelling.* Ann Arbor: University of Michigan Press.

Bradley, R., Greene, J., Russ, E., Dutra, L., & Westen, D. (2005). A multidimensional meta-analysis of psychotherapy for PTSD. *American Journal of Psychiatry, 162,* 214–227.

Brakoulias, V., Starcevic, V., Sammut, P., Berle, D., Milicevic, D., Moses, K., & Hannan, A. (2011). Obsessive-compulsive spectrum disorders: A comorbidity and family history perspective. *Australasian Psychiatry: Bulletin of Royal Australian and New Zealand College of Psychiatrists, 19*(2), 151–155. doi: 10.3109/10398562.2010.526718

Brandon, T. H., Collins, B. N., Juliano, L. M., & Lazev, A. B. (2000). Preventing relapse among former smokers: A comparison of minimal interventions through telephone and mail. *Journal of Consulting and Clinical Psychology, 68,* 103–113.

Brandon, T. H., Vidrine, J. I., & Litvin, E. B. (2007). Relapse and relapse prevention. *Annual Review of Clinical Psychology, 3,* 257–284.

Brandon, Y. H., Zelman, D. C., & Baker, T. B. (1987). Effects of maintenance sessions on smoking relapse: Delaying the inevitable? *Journal of Consulting and Clinical Psychology, 55,* 780–782.

Bransford, J. D., & Johnson, M. K. (1973). Considerations of some problems of comprehension. In W. G. Chase (Ed.), *Visual information processing.* New York: Academic Press.

Braswell, L., & Kendall, P. C. (1988). Cognitive-behavioral methods with children. In K. S. Dobson (Ed.), *Handbook of cognitive-behavioral therapies.* New York: Guilford.

Braun, J. M., Kahn, R. S., Froehlich, T., Auinger, P., & Lanphear, B. (2006). Exposures to environmental toxicants and attention deficit hyperactivity disorder in U.S. children. *Environmental Health Perspectives, 114,* 1904–1909.

Brecher, E. M., & the Editors of Consumer Reports. (1972). *Licit and illicit drugs.* Mount Vernon, NY: Consumers Union.

Bremner, J. D., Vythilingam, M., Vermetten, E., Southwick, S. M., McGlashan, T., Nazeer, A., . . . Charney, D. S. (2003). MRI and PET study of deficits in hippocampal structure and function in women with childhood sexual abuse and posttraumatic stress disorder. *American Journal of Psychiatry, 160,* 924–932.

Brems, C. (1995). Women and depression: A comprehensive analysis. In E. E. Beckham & W. Leber (Eds.), *Handbook of depression* (2nd ed., pp. 539–566). New York: Guilford.

Brennan, P. L., Schutte, K. K., & Moos, R. H. (1999). Reciprocal relations between stressors and drinking behavior: A three-wave panel study of late middle-aged and older women and men. *Addiction, 94,* 737–749.

Breslau, J., Aguilar-Gaxiola, A., Kendler, K. S., Su, M., Williams, D., & Kessler, R. (2006). Specifying race-ethnic differences in risk for psychiatric disorder in a USA national sample. *Psychological Medicine, 36,* 57–68.

Breslau, N., Brown, G. G., Del Dotto, J. E., Kumar, S., Ezhuthachan, S., Andreski, P., & Hufnagle, K. G. (1996). Psychiatric sequalae of low birth weight at 6 years of age. *Journal of Abnormal Child Psychology, 24,* 385–400.

Breslau, N., Chilcoat, H. D., Kessler, R. C., & Davis, G. C. (1999). Previous exposure to trauma and PTSD effects of subsequent trauma: Results from the Detroit Area Survey of Trauma. *American Journal of Psychiatry, 156,* 902–907.

Breslau, N., Davis, G. C., & Andreski, P. (1995). Risk factors for PTSD-related traumatic events: A prospective analysis. *American Journal of Psychiatry, 152,* 529–535.

Breslau, N., Lucia, V., & Alvarado, G. F. (2006). Intelligence and other predisposing factors in exposure to trauma and posttraumatic stress disorder: A follow-up study at age 17 years. *Archives of General Psychiatry, 63,* 1238–1245.

Brestan, E. V., & Eyberg, S. M. (1998). Effective psychosocial treatment of conduct disordered children and adolescents: 29 years, 82 studies, and 5275 kids. *Journal of Clinical Child Psychology, 27,* 180–189.

Breuer, J., & Freud, S. (1982). *Studies in hysteria* (J. Strachey, Trans. and Ed., with the collaboration of A. Freud). New York: Basic Books. (Original work published 1895).

Brewerton, T. D., Lydiard, B. R., Laraia, M. T., Shook, J. E., & Ballenger, J. C. (1992). CSF beta-endorphin and dynorphin in bulimia nervosa. *American Journal of Psychiatry, 149,* 1086–1090.

Brewin, C. R., Andrews, B., & Valentine, J. D. (2000). Metaanalysis of risk factors for posttraumatic stress disorder in trauma-exposed adults. *Journal of Consulting and Clinical Psychology, 68,* 748–766.

Brewin, C. R., & Holmes, E. A. (2003). Psychological theories of posttraumatic stress disorder. *Clinical Psychology Review, 23,* 339–376.

Brewin, C. R., Kleiner, J. S., Vasterling, J. J., & Field, A. P. (2007). Memory for emotionally neutral information in posttraumatic stress disorder: A meta-analytic investigation. *Journal of Abnormal Psychology, 116,* 448–463.

Brezo, J., Paris, J., & Turecki, G. (2006). Personality traits as correlates of suicidal ideation, suicide attempts, and suicide completions: A systematic review. *Acta Psychiatrica Scandinavica, 113,* 180–206.

Brickman, A. S., McManus, M., Grapentine, W. L., & Alessi, N. (1984). Neuropsychological assessment of seriously delinquent adolescents. *Journal of the American Academy of Child Psychiatry, 23,* 453–457.

Bridge, J. A., Iyengar, S., Salary, C. B., et al. (2007). Clinical response and risk for reported suicidal ideation and suicide attempts in pediatric antidepressant treatment: A meta-analysis of randomized controlled trials. *Journal of American Medical Association, 297,* 1683–1696.

Briere, J., Scott, C., & Weathers, F. (2005). Peritraumatic and persistent dissociation in the presumed etiology of PTSD. *American Journal of Psychiatry, 162,* 2295–2301.

Brody, A. L., Saxena, S., Stoessel, P., Gillies, L. A., Fairbanks, L. A., Alborzian, S., . . . Baxter, L. R. J. (2001). Regional brain metabolic changes in patients with major depression treated with either paroxetine or interpersonal therapy: Preliminary findings. *Archives of General Psychiatry, 58,* 631–640.

Brookes, K., Mill, J., Guindalini, C., Curran, S., Xu, X., Knight, J., . . . Asherson, P. (2006). A common haplotype of the dopamine transporter gene associated with attention-deficit/hyperactivity disorder and interacting with maternal use of alcohol during pregnancy. *Archives of General Psychiatry, 63,* 74–81.

Brooks, M. (2004). *Extreme measures: The dark visions and bright ideas of Francis Galton.* London: Bloomsbury.

Brooks, S., Prince, A., Stahl, D., Campbell, I. C., & Treasure, J. (2011). A systematic review and meta-analysis of cognitive bias to food stimuli in people with disordered eating behaviour. *Clinical Psychology Review, 31,* 37–51.

Brown, A. S. (2011). The environment and susceptibility to schizophrenia. *Progress in Neurobiology, 93,* 23–58.

Brown, A. S., Begg, M. D., Gravenstein, S., Schaefer, C. A., Wyatt, R. J., Bresnahan, M., . . . Susser, E. S. (2004). Serologic evidence of prenatal influenza in the etiology of schizophrenia. *Archives of General Psychiatry, 61,* 774–780.

Brown, A. S., Bottiglieri, T., Schaefer, C. A., Quesenberry, C. P., Jr., Liu, L., Bresnahan, M., & Susser, E. S. (2007). Elevated prenatal homocysteine levels as a risk factor for schizophrenia. *Archives of General Psychiatry, 64,* 31–39.

Brown, A. S., & Derkits, E. J. (2010). Prenatal infections and schizophrenia: A review of epidemiologic and translational studies. *American Journal of Psychiatry, 167,* 261–280.

Brown, A. S., Schaefer, C. A., Quesenberry, C. P., Jr., Liu, L., Babulas, V. P., & Susser, E. S. (2005). Maternal exposure to toxoplasmosis and risk of schizophrenia in adult offspring. *American Journal of Psychiatry, 162,* 767–773.

Brown, D., Scheflin, A. W., & Whitfield, C. L. (1999). Recovered memories: The current weight of the evidence in science and in the courts. *Journal of Psychiatry and Law, 27,* 5–156.

Brown, G. K., Beck, A. T., Steer, R. A., & Grisham, J. R. (2000). Risk factors for suicide in psychiatric outpatients: A 20-year prospective study. *Journal of Consulting and Clinical Psychology, 68,* 371–377.

Brown, G. K., Henriques, G. R., Ratto, C., & Beck, A. T. (2002). *Cognitive therapy treatment manual for suicide attempters.* Philadelphia: University of Pennsylvania Press.

Brown, G. K., Ten Have, T., Henriques, G. R., Xie, S. X., Hollander, J. E., & Beck, A. T. (2005). Cognitive therapy for the prevention of suicide attempts. *The Journal of the American Medical Association, 294,* 563–570.

Brown, G. W., & Andrews, B. (1986). Social support and depression. In R. Trumbull & M. H. Appley (Eds.), *Dynamics of stress: Physiological, psychological, and social perspectives* (pp. 257–282). New York: Plenum.

Brown, G. W., Bone, M., Dalison, B., & Wing, J. K. (1966). *Schizophrenia and social care.* London: Oxford University Press.

Brown, G. W., & Harris, T. O. (1978). *The Bedford College life events and difficulty schedule: Directory of contextual threat of events.* London: Bedford College, University of London.

Brown, G. W., & Harris, T. O. (1989a). Depression. In T. O. Harris & G. W. Brown (Eds.), *Life events and illness* (pp. 49–93). New York: Guilford.

Brown, G. W., & Harris, T. O. (1989b). *Life events and illness.* New York: Guilford.

Brown, R. J., Cardena, E., Nijenhuis, E., Sar, V., & Van Der Hart, O. (2007). Should conversion disorder be reclassified as dissociative disorder in DSM-5? *Psychosomatics, 48*(5), 369–378.

Brown, S. A., Vik, P. W., McQuaid, J. R., Patterson, T. L., Irwin, M. R., et al. (1990). Severity of psychosocial stress and outcome of alcoholism treatment. *Journal of Abnormal Psychology, 99,* 344–348.

Brown, T. A. (2007). Temporal course and structural relationships among dimensions of temperament and DSM-IV anxiety and mood disorder constructs. *Journal of Abnormal Psychology, 116*(2), 313–328. doi: 10.1037/0021-843X.116.2.313

Brown, T. A., Campbell, L. A., Lehman, C. L., Grisham, J. R., & Mancill, R. B. (2001). Current and lifetime comorbidity of the DSM-IV anxiety and mood disorders in a large clinical sample. *Journal of Abnormal Psychology, 110,* 585–599.

Brownell, K. D., & Horgen, K. B. (2003). *Food fight: The inside story of the food industry, America's obesity crisis, and what we can do about it.* Chicago: Contemporary Books.

Bruce, M. L., Ten Have, T. R., Reynolds, C. F., III, Katz, I. I., Schulberg, H. C., Mulsant, B. H., . . . Alexopoulos, G. S. (2004). Reducing suicidal ideation and depressive symptoms in depressed older primary care patients. *Journal of American Medical Association, 291,* 1081–1091.

Brugha, T. S., & Cragg, D. (1990). The list of threatening experiences: The reliability and validity of a brief life events questionnaire. *Acta Psychiatrica Scandinavica, 82,* 77–81.

Bryant, R. A., Creamer, M., O'Donnell, M. L., Silove, D., & McFarlane, A. C. (2008). A multisite study of the capacity of acute stress disorder diagnosis to predict posttraumatic stress disorder. *Journal of Clinical Psychiatry, 69*(6), 923–929.

Bryant, R. A., Mastrodomenico, J., Felmingham, K. L., Hopwood, S., Kenny, L., Kandris, E., . . . Creamer, M. (2008). Treatment of acute stress disorder: A randomized controlled trial. *Archives of General Psychiatry, 65,* 659–667.

Bryant, R. A., Sackville, T., Dang, S. T., Moulds, M., & Guthrie, R. (1999). Treating acute stress disorder: An evaluation of cognitive behavior therapy and supporting counseling techniques. *American Journal of Psychiatry, 156,* 1780–1786.

Buchanan, J. A., Christenson, A., Houlihan, D., & Ostrom, C. (2011). The role of behavior analysis in the rehabilitation of persons with dementia. *Behavior Therapy, 42*(1), 9–21.

Buchanan, R. W., Vladar, K., Barta, P. E., & Pearlson, G. D. (1998). Structural evaluation of the prefrontal cortex in schizophrenia. *American Journal of Psychiatry, 155,* 1049–1055.

Buchsbaum, M. S., Kessler, R., King, A., Johnson, J., & Cappelletti, J. (1984). Simultaneous cerebral glucography with positron emission tomography and topographic electroencephalography. In G. Pfurtscheller, E. J. Jonkman, & F. H. L. de Silva (Eds.), *Brain ischemia: Quantitative EEG and imaging techniques.* Amsterdam: Elsevier.

Budney, A. J., Moore, B. A., Rocha, H. L., & Higgens, S. T. (2006). Clinical trial of abstinence-based vouchers and cognitive behavior therapy for cannabis dependence. *Journal of Consulting and Clinical Psychology, 74,* 307–316.

Bulik, C. M., & Reichborn-Kjennerud, T. (2003). Medical morbidity in binge eating disorder. Published online in Wiley InterScience (http://www.interscience.wiley.com). doi: 10.1002/eat.10204

Bulik, C. M., Sullivan, P. F., Wade, T. D., & Kendler, K. S. (2000). Twin studies of eating disorders: A review. *International Journal of Eating Disorders, 27,* 1–20.

Bulik, C. M., Wade, T. D., & Kendler, K. S. (2000). Characteristics of monozygotic twins discordant for bulimia nervosa. *International Journal of Eating Disorders, 29,* 1–10.

Bullers, S., Cooper, M. L., & Russell, M. (2001). Social network drinking and adult alcohol involvement: A longitudinal exploration of the direction of influence. *Addictive Behaviors, 26,* 181–199.

Burke, B. L., Arkowitz, H., & Menchola, M. (2003). The efficacy of motivational interviewing: A meta-analysis of controlled clinical trials. *Journal of Consulting and Clinical Psychology, 71,* 843–861.

Burne, S. M., & McLean, N. J. (2002). The cognitive behavioral model of bulimia nervosa: A direct evaluation. *International Journal of Eating Disorders, 31,* 17–31.

Burris, K. D., Molski T. F., Xu, C., Ryan, E., Tottori, K., Kikuchi, T., . . . Molinoff, P. B. (2002). Aripiprazole, a novel antipsychotic, is a high-affinity partial agonist at human dopamine D2 receptors. *Journal of Pharmacology and Experimental Therapies, 302,* 381–389.

Burt, S. A. (2009). Are there meaningful etiological differences within antisocial behavior? Results of a meta-analysis. *Clinical Psychology Review, 29*(2), 163–178. doi: 10.1016/j.cpr.2008.12.004

Burt, S. A., & Donnellan, M. B. (2009). Development and validation of the Subtypes of Antisocial Behavior Questionnaire. *Aggressive Behavior, 35*(5), 376–398. doi: 10.1002/ab.20314

Bushman, B. J., & Cooper, H. M. (1990). Effects of alcohol on human aggression: An integrative research review. *Psychological Bulletin, 107*, 341–354.

Bustillo, J. R., Lauriello, J., Horan, W. P., & Keith, S. J. (2001). The psychosocial treatment of schizophrenia: An update. *American Journal of Psychiatry, 158*, 163–175.

Butcher, J. N., Dahlstrom, W. G., Graham, J. R., Tellegen, A., & Kraemer, B. (1989). *Minnesota Multiphasic Personality Inventory–2: Manual for administration and scoring.* Minneapolis: University of Minnesota Press.

Butler, L. D., Duran, R. E. F., Jasiukaitis, P., Koopman, C., & Spiegel, D. (1996). Hypnotizability and traumatic experience: A diathesis-stress model of dissociative symptomatology. *American Journal of Psychiatry, 153*, 42–63.

Butzlaff, R. L., & Hooley, J. M. (1998). Expressed emotion and psychiatric relapse: A meta-analysis. *Archives of General Psychiatry, 55*, 547–553.

Cadoret, R. J., Yates, W. R., Troughton, E., Woodworth, G., & Stewart, M. A. (1995). Adoption study demonstrating two genetic pathways to drug abuse. *Archives of General Psychiatry, 52*, 42–52.

Cahill, K., Stead, L., & Lancaster, T. (2007). Nicotine receptor partial agonists for smoking cessation. *Cochrane Database Systematic Reviews*, CD006103.

Caldwell, M. B., Brownell, K. D., & Wilfley, D. (1997). Relationship of weight, body dissatisfaction, and self-esteem in African American and white female dieters. *International Journal of Eating Disorders, 22*, 127–130.

Calhoun, V. D., Pekar, J. J., & Pearlson, G. D. (2004). Alcohol intoxication effects on simulated driving: Exploring alcohol-dose effects on brain activation using functional MRI. *Neuropsychopharmacology, 29*, 2197–2207.

Calvin, C. M., Deary, I. J., Fenton, C., Roberts, B. A., Der, G., Leckenby, N., et al. (2010). Intelligence in youth and all-cause-mortality: Systematic review with meta-analysis. *International Journal of Epidemiology, 40*, 626–644.

Calvo, R., Lázaro, L., Castro-Fornieles, J., Font, E., Moreno, E., & Toro, J. (2009). Obsessive-compulsive personality disorder traits and personality dimensions in parents of children with obsessive-compulsive disorder. *European Psychiatry, 24*(3), 201–206. doi: 10.1016/j.eurpsy.2008.11.003

Camí, J., & Farré, M. (2003). Drug addiction. *New England Journal of Medicine, 349*, 975–986.

Campbell, J., Stefan, S., & Loder, A. (1994). Putting violence in context. *Hospital and Community Psychiatry, 45*, 633.

Campbell, M., Armenteros, J. L., Malone, R. P., Adams, P. B., Eisenberg, Z. W., & Overall, J. E. (1997). Neuroleptic related dyskinesias in autistic children: A prospective, longitudinal study. *Journal of the American Academy of Child and Adolescent Psychiatry, 36*, 835–843.

Campbell, W.K., Bosson, J. K., Goheen, T. W., Lakey, C. E., & Kernis, M. H. (2007). Do narcissists dislike themselves "deep down inside"? *Psychological Science, 18*, 227–229.

Camus, V., Burtin, B., Simeone, I., Schwed, P., Gonthier, R., & Dubos, G. (2000). Factor analysis supports the evidence of existing hyperactive and hypoactive subtypes of delirium. *International Journal of Geriatric Psychiatry, 15*, 313–316.

Canivez, G. L., & Watkins, M. W. (1998). Long-term stability of the Wechsler Intelligence Scale for Children (3rd ed.). *Psychological Assessment, 10*, 285–291.

Cannon, T. D., Cadenhead, K., Cornblatt, B., Woods, S. W., Addington, J., Walker, E., . . . Heinssen, R. (2008). Prediction of psychosis in youth at high clinical risk: A multisite longitudinal study in North America. *Archives of General Psychiatry, 65*, 28–37.

Cannon, T. D., Kaprio, J., Lonnqvist, J., Huttunen, M., & Koskenvuo, M. (1998). The genetic epidemiology of schizophrenia in a Finnish twin cohort: A population based modeling study. *Archives of General Psychiatry, 55*, 67–74.

Cannon, T. D., & Mednick, S. A. (1993). The schizophrenia high-risk project in Copenhagen: Three decades of progress. *Acta Psychiatrica Scandanavica*, 33–47.

Cannon, T. D., Mednick, S. A., & Parnas, J. (1990). Antecedents of predominantly negative and predominantly positive-symptom schizophrenia in a high-risk population. *Archives of General Psychiatry, 47*, 622–632.

Cannon, T. D., van Erp, T. G., Rosso, I. M., et al. (2002). Fetal hypoxia and structural brain abnormalities in schizophrenic patients, their siblings, and controls. *Archives of General Psychiatry, 59*, 35–42.

Capaldi, D. M., & Patterson, G. R. (1994). Interrelated influences of contextual factors on antisocial behavior in childhood and adolescence for males. In D. C. Fowles, P. Sutker, & S. H. Goodman (Eds.), *Progress in experimental personality and psychopathology research* (pp. 165–198). New York: Springer-Verlag.

Capps, L., Losh, M., & Thurber, C. (2000). "The frog ate the bug and made his mouth sad": Narrative competence in children with autism. *Journal of Abnormal Child Psychology, 28*, 193–204.

Capps, L., Rasco, L., Losh, M., & Heerey, E. (1999). *Understanding of self-conscious emotions in high-functioning children with autism.* Paper presented at the biennial meeting of the Society for Research In Child Development.

Capps, L., Yirmiya, N., & Sigman, M. (1992). Understanding of simple and complex emotion in high-functioning children with autism. *Journal of Child Psychology and Psychiatry, 33*, 1169–1182.

Capron, A. M. (1999). Ethical and human rights issues in research on mental disorders that may affect decision making capacity. *New England Journal of Medicine, 340*, 1430–1434.

CAPT. (2000). Prisons: The nation's new mental institutions. *Outreach*, Retrieved from http://www.psych-health.com/mental8.htm

Cardno, A. G., Marshall, E. J., Coid, B., MacDonald, A. M., Ribchester, T. R., et al. (1999). Heritability estimates for psychotic disorders: The Maudsley Twin Psychosis Series. *Archives of General Psychiatry, 56*, 162–170.

Carey, B. (2011, June 23). Expert on mental illness reveals her own fight, *New York Times*, pA1.

Carey, K. B., Carey, M. P., Maisto, S. A., & Henson, J. M. (2006). Brief motivational interventions for heavy college drinkers: A randomized controlled trial. *Journal of Consulting and Clinical Psychology, 74*, 943–954.

Carlson, G. A., & Meyer, S. E. (2006). Phenomenology and diagnosis of bipolar disorder in children, adolescents, and adults: Complexities and developmental issues. *Development and Psychopathology, 18*, 939–969.

Carlsson, A., Hanson, L. O., Waters, N., & Carlsson, M. L. (1999). A glutamatergic deficiency model of schizophrenia. *British Journal of Psychiatry, 174*, 2–6.

Carney, R. M., Blumenthal, J. A., Freedland, K. E., Youngblood, M., Veith, R. C., Burg, M. M., . . . Jaffe, A. S. (2004). Depression and late mortality after myocardial infarction in the Enhancing Recovery in Coronary Heart Disease (ENRICHD) Study. *Psychological Medicine, 66*, 466–474.

Carpenter, W. T., Gold, J. M., Lahti, A. C., Queern, C. A., Conley, R. R., Bartko, . . . Appelbaum, P. S. (2000). Decisional capacity for informed consent in schizophrenia research. *Archives of General Psychiatry, 57*, 533–538.

Carpenter, W. T., & van Os, J. (2011). Should attenuated psychosis syndrome be a DSM–5 diagnosis? *American Journal of Psychiatry, 168*, 460–463.

Carpentieri, S. C., & Morgan, S. B. (1994). Brief report: A comparison of patterns of cognitive functioning of autistic and nonautistic retarded children on the Stanford-Binet (4th ed.). *Journal of Autism and Developmental Disorders, 24*, 215–223.

Carr, A. T. (1971). Compulsive neurosis: Two psychophysiological studies. *Bulletin of the British Psychological Society, 24*, 256–257.

Carr, D. (2008). *The night of the gun: A reporter investigates the darkest story of his life. His own.* New York: Simon & Schuster Adult Publishing Group.

Carr, E. G., Levin, L., McConnachie, G., Carlson, J. I., Kemp, D. C., & Smith, C. E. (1994). *Communication based intervention for problem behavior.* Baltimore: Brookes.

Carr, R. E. (1998). Panic disorder and asthma: Causes, effects, and research implications. *Journal of Psychosomatic Research, 44*, 43–52.

Carr, R. E. (1999). Panic disorder and asthma. *Journal of Asthma, 36*, 143–152.

Carrasco, J. L., Dyaz-Marsa, M., Hollander, E., Cesar, J., & Saiz-Ruiz, J. (2000). Decreased monoamine oxidase activity in female bulimia. *European Neuropsychopharmacology, 10*, 113–117.

Carroll, K. M., Ball, S. A., Nich, C., et al. (2001). Targeting behavioral therapies to enhance naltrexone treatment of opioid dependence: Efficacy of contingency management and significant other involvement. *Archives of General Psychiatry, 58*, 755–761.

Carroll, K. M., Easton, C. J., Nich, C., Hunkele, K. A., Neavins, T. M., et al. (2006). The use of contingency management and motivational/skills-building therapy to treat young adults with marijuana dependence. *Journal of Consulting and Clinical Psychology, 74*, 955–966.

Carroll, K. M., Rounsaville, B. J., Gordon, L. T., Nich, C., Jatlow, P., Bisighini, R. M., & Gawin, F. H. (1994). Psychotherapy and pharmacotherapy for ambulatory cocaine abusers. *Archives of General Psychiatry, 51*, 177–187.

Carroll, K. M., Rounsaville, B. J., Nich, C., Gordon, L. T., & Gawin, F. (1995). Integrating psychotherapy and pharmacotherapy for cocaine dependence: Results from a randomized clinical trial. In L. S. Onken, J. D. Blaine, & J. J. Boren (Eds.), *Integrating behavioral therapies with medications in the treatment of drug dependence* (pp. 19–36). Rockville, MD: National Institute on Drug Abuse.

Carstensen, L. L. (1996). Evidence for a life-span theory of socioemotional selectivity. *Current Directions in Psychological Science, 4*, 151–156.

Carter, F. A., McIntosh, V. V. W., Joyce, P. R., Sullivan, P. F., & Bulik, C. M. (2003). Role of exposure with response prevention in cognitive-behavioral therapy for bulimia nervosa: Three-year follow-up results. *International Journal of Eating Disorders, 33*, 127–135.

Carvalheira, A. A., Brotto, L. A., & Leal, I. (2010). Women's motivations for sex: Exploring the *Diagnostic and Statistical Manual*, fourth edition, text revision criteria for hypoactive sexual desire and female sexual arousal disorders. *Journal of Sexual Medicine, 7*(4, Pt 1), 1454–1463. doi: 10.1111/j.1743-6109.2009.01693.x

Carvalho, J., & Nobre, P. (2010). Biopsychosocial determinants of men's sexual desire: Testing an integrative model. *Journal of Sexual Medicine, 8,* 754–763. doi: 10.1111/j.1743-6109.2010.02156.x

Carver, C. S., Johnson, S. L., & Joormann, J. (2008). Serotonergic function, two-mode models of self-regulation, and vulnerability to depression: What depression has in common with impulsive aggression. *Psychological Bulletin, 134,* 912–943. doi: 910.1037/a0013740.

Caselli, R. J., & Yaari, R. (2008). Medical management of frontotemporal dementia. *American Journal of Alzheimer's Disease and Other Dementias, 22*(6), 489–498.

Casey, B. J., & Durston, S. (2006). From behavior to cognition to the brain and back: What have we learned from functional imaging studies of attention deficit hyperactivity disorder? *American Journal of Psychiatry, 163,* 957–960.

Casey, J. E., Rourke, B. P., & Del Dotto, J. E. (1996). Learning disabilities in children with attention deficit disorder with and without hyperactivity. *Child Neuropsychology, 2,* 83–98.

Caspi, A., & Moffitt, T. E. (2006). Gene–environment interactions in psychiatry: Joining forces with neuroscience. *Nature Reviews Neuroscience, 7,* 583–590.

Caspi, A., Hariri, A., Holmes, A, Uher, R., & Moffitt, T. E. (2010). Generic sensitivity to the environment: The case of the serotonin transporter gene and its implications for studying complex diseases and traits. *American Journal of Psychiatry, 167,* 509–527.

Caspi, A., McClay, J., Moffitt, T. E., Mill, J., Martin, J., Craig, I. W., . . . Poulton, R. (2002). Role of genotype in the cycle of violence in maltreated children. *Science, 297,* 851–854.

Caspi, A., Moffitt, T. E., Cannon, M., McClay, J., Murray, R., Harrington, H., . . . Craig, I. W. (2005). Moderation of the effect of adolescent-onset cannabis use on adult psychosis by a functional polymorphism in the catechol-O-methyltransferase gene: Longitudinal evidence of a gene-environment interaction. *Biological Psychiatry, 57,* 1117–1127.

Caspi, A., Sugden, K., Moffitt, T. E., Taylor, A., Craig, I. W., Harrington, H., . . . Poulton, R. (2003). Influence of life stress on depression: Moderation by a polymorphism in the 5-HTT gene. *Science, 301*(5631), 386–389.

Castellanos, F. X., Lee, P. P., Sharp, W., Jeffries, N. O., Greenstein, D. K., et al. (2002). Developmental trajectories of brain volume abnormalities in children and adolescents with attention-deficit/hyperactivity disorder. *Journal of the American Medical Association, 288,* 1740–1748.

Castellanos, F. X., Marvasti, F. F., Ducharme, J. L., Walter, J. M., Israel, M. E., Krain, . . . Hommer, D. W. (2000). Executive function oculomotor tasks in girls with ADHD. *Journal of the American Academy of Child and Adolescent Psychiatry, 39,* 644–650.

Castelli, F., Frith, C., Happe, F., & Frith, U. (2002). Autism, Asperger syndrome and brain mechanisms for the attribution of mental states to animated shapes. *Brain, 125,* 1839–1849.

Castells, X., Casas, M., Vidal, X., Bosch, R., Roncero, C., Ramos-Quiroga, J. A., et al. (2007). Efficacy of CNS stimulant treatment for cocaine dependence. A systematic review and meta-analysis of randomized controlled clinical trials. *Addiction, 102,* 1871–1887.

Celebucki, C. C., Wayne, G. F., Connolly, G. N., Pankow, J. F., & Chang, E. I. (2005). Characterization of measured menthol in 48 U.S. cigarette sub-brands. *Nicotine & Tobacco Research, 7,* 523–531.

Centre for Social Justice (2010). http://www.centreforsocialjustice.org.uk/client/downloads/CSJ_Green_paper_criminal_justice_07%2007_WEB.pdf

Centers for Disease Control and Prevention. (2006). Homicides and suicides—National violent death reporting system, United States, 2003–2004. *American Journal of Medicine, 296,* 506–510.

Centers for Disease Control and Prevention (CDC). (2009a). Prevalence of autism spectrum disorders—Autism and developmental disabilities monitoring network, 2006. *MMWR, 58,* 1–20.

Centers for Disease Control and Prevention. (2009b). *Sexually transmitted disease surveillance, 2008.* Atlanta, GA: Author.

Cerny, J. A., Barlow, D. H., Craske, M. G., & Himadi, W. G. (1987). Couples treatment of agoraphobia: A two year follow-up. *Behavior Therapy, 18,* 401–415.

CEWG. (2003). *Epidemiologic trends in drug abuse* (Vol. I, June 2003). National Institute of Drug Abuse.

Chabrol, H., Peresson, G., Milberger, S., Biederman, J., & Faraone, S. V. (1997). ADHD and maternal smoking during pregnancy. *American Journal of Psychiatry, 154,* 1177–1178.

Chaffin, M., Silovsky, J. F., & Vaughn, C. (2005). Temporal concordance of anxiety disorders and child sexual abuse: Implications for direct versus artifactual effects of sexual abuse. *Journal of Clinical Child and Adolescent Psychology, 34,* 210–222.

Chambers, R. A., Taylor, J. R., & Potenza, M. N. (2003). Developmental neurocircuitry of motivation in adolescence: A critical period of addiction vulnerability. *American Journal of Psychiatry, 160,* 1041–1052.

Chambless, D. L., Caputo, G. C., Bright, P., & Gallagher, R. (1984). Assessment of fear in agoraphobics: The body sensations questionnaire and the agoraphobic cognitions questionnaire. *Journal of Consulting and Clinical Psychology, 52*(6), 1090–1097.

Chambless, D. L., & Ollendick, T. H. (2001). Empirically supported psychological interventions: Controversies and evidence. *Annual Review of Psychology, 52,* 685–716.

Chang, L., Cloak, C. C., & Ernst, T. (2003). Magnetic resonance spectroscopy studies of GABA in neuropsychiatric disorders. *Journal of Clinical Psychiatry, 64*(Suppl. 3), 7–14.

Chang, S. M., Hahm, B., Lee, J., Shin, M. S., Jeon, H. J., Hong, J., . . . Cho, M. J. (2008). Cross-national difference in the prevalence of depression caused by the diagnostic threshold. *Journal of Affective Disorders, 106,* 159–167.

Chard, K. M. (2005). An evaluation of cognitive processing therapy for the treatment of posttraumatic stress disorder related to childhood sexual abuse. *Journal of Consulting and Clinical Psychology, 73,* 965–971.

Charuvastra, A., & Cloitre, M. (2008). Social bonds and posttraumatic stress disorder. *Annual Review of Psychology, 59,* 301–328.

Chase, A. (1980). *The legacy of Malthus.* Urbana: University of Illinois Press.

Chassin, L., Curran, P. J., Hussong, A. M., & Colder, C. R. (1996). The relation of parent alcoholism to adolescent substance abuse: A longitudinal follow-up. *Journal of Abnormal Psychology, 105,* 70–80.

Chassin, L., Pitts, S. C., DeLucia, C., & Todd, M. (1999). A longitudinal study of children of alcoholics: Predicting young adult substance use disorders, anxiety, and depression. *Journal of Abnormal Psychology, 108,* 106–119.

Chavira, D. A., Stein, M. B., & Malcarne, V. L. (2002). Scrutinizing the relationship between shyness and social phobia. *Journal of Anxiety Disorders, 16,* 585–598.

Chen, S., Boucher, H. C., & Parker Tapias, M. (2006). The relational self revealed: Integrative conceptualization

and implications for interpersonal life. *Psychological Bulletin, 132,* 151–179.

Chiariello, M. A., & Orvaschel, H. (1995). Patterns of parent–child communication: Relationship to depression. *Clinical Psychology Review, 15,* 395–407.

Chorpita, B. F., Brown, T. A., & Barlow, D. H. (1998). Perceived control as a mediator of family environment in etiological models of childhood anxiety. *Behavior Therapy, 29,* 457–476.

Chorpita, B. F., Vitali, A. E., & Barlow, D. H. (1997). Behavioral treatment of choking phobia in an adolescent: An experimental analysis. *Journal of Behavior Therapy and Experimental Psychiatry, 28,* 307–315.

Choy, Y., Fyer, A. J., & Lipsitz, J. D. (2007). Treatment of specific phobia in adults. *Clinical Psychology Review, 27,* 266–286.

Christakis, N., & Fowler, J. (2008). The collective dynamics of smoking in a large social network. *New England Journal of Medicine, 358,* 2249–2258.

Chronis, A. M., Jones, H. A., & Raggi, V. L. (2006). Evidence-based psychosocial treatments for children and adolescents with attention-deficit/hyperactivity disorder. *Clinical Psychology Review, 26,* 486–502.

Chu, J. A., Frey, L. M., Ganzel, B. L., & Matthews, J. A. (2000). Memories of childhood abuse: Dissociation, amnesia, and corroboration. *American Journal of Psychiatry, 156,* 749–755.

Chua, S. T., & McKenna, P. T. (1995). Schizophrenia—a brain disease? *British Journal of Psychiatry, 166,* 563–582.

Chung, J. C. C., & Lai, C. K. Y. (2009). Snoezelen for dementia. *Cochrane Database of Systematic Reviews* (4), CD003152. doi: 10.1002/14651858.CD003152

Cimbora, D. M., & McIntosh, D. N. (2003). Emotional responses to antisocial acts in adolescent males with conduct disorder: A link to affective morality. *Journal of Clinical Child and Adolescent Psychology, 32,* 296–301.

Cinciripini, P. M., Lapitsky, L. G., Wallfisch, A., Mace, R., Nezami, E., & Van Vunakis, H. (1994). An evaluation of a multicomponent treatment program involving scheduled smoking and relapse prevention procedures: Initial findings. *Addictive Behaviors, 19,* 13–22.

Cipriani, A., Pretty, H., Hawton, K., & Geddes, J. R. (2005). Lithium in the prevention of suicidal behavior and all-cause mortality in patients with mood disorders: A systematic review of randomized trials. *American Journal of Psychiatry, 162,* 1805–1819.

Clark, D. A. (1997). Twenty years of cognitive assessment: Current status and future directions. *Journal of Consulting and Clinical Psychology, 65,* 996–1000.

Clark, D. M. (1996). Panic disorder: From theory to therapy. In P. M. Salkovskis (Ed.), *Frontiers of cognitive therapy* (pp. 318–344). New York: Guilford.

Clark, D. M., Ehlers, A., Hackmann, A., McManus, F., Fennell, M., Grey, N., . . . Wild, J. (2006). Cognitive therapy versus exposure and applied relaxation in social phobia: A randomized controlled trial. *Journal of Consulting and Clinical Psychology, 74,* 568–578.

Clark, D. M., Ehlers, A., McManus, F., Hackmann, A., Fennell, M., Campbell, H., . . . Louis, B. (2003). Cognitive therapy versus fluoxetine in generalized social phobia: A randomized control trial. *Journal of Consulting and Clinical Psychology, 71,* 1058–1067.

Clark, D. M., Salkovskis, P. M., Hackmann, A., Wells, A., Ludgate, J., & Gelder, M. (1999). Brief cognitive therapy for panic disorder: A randomized controlled trial. *Journal of Consulting and Clinical Psychology, 67,* 583–589.

Clark, D. M., & Wells, A. (1995). A cognitive model of social phobia. In R. Heimberg, M. R. Liebowitz, D. A. Hope, & F. R. Schneier (Eds.), *Social phobia:*

Diagnosis, assessment and treatment (pp. 69–93). New York: Guilford.

Clark, L. A., & Livesley, W. J. (2002). Two approaches to identifying the dimensions of personality disorder: Convergence on the five-factor model. In T. A. Widiger & P. T. J. Costa (Eds.), *Personality disorders and the five-factor model of personality* (pp. 161–176). Washington, DC: American Psychological Association.

Clarkin, J. F., Levy, K. N., Lenzenweger, M. F., & Kernberg, O. F. (2007). Evaluating three treatments for borderline personality disorder: A multiwave study. *American Journal of Psychiatry, 164*, 922–928.

Classen, C., Koopman, C., Hales, R., & Spiegel, D. (1998). Acute stress disorder as a predictor of posttraumatic stress disorder. *American Journal of Psychiatry, 155*, 620–624.

Clayton, R. R., Catterello, A., & Walden, K. P. (1991). Sensation seeking as a potential mediating variable for school-based prevention intervention: A two-year follow-up of DARE. *Health Communication, 3*, 229–239.

Cleckley, H. (1976). *The mask of sanity* (5th ed.). St. Louis, MO: Mosby.

Cloninger, R. C., Martin, R. L., Guze, S. B., & Clayton, P. L. (1986). A prospective follow-up and family study of somatization in men and women. *American Journal of Psychiatry, 143*, 713–714.

Cloud, J. (1999, June 7). Mental health reform: What it would really take. *Time* pp. 54–56.

Cohen, H. W., Gibson, G., & Alderman, M. H. (2000). Excess risk of myocardial infarction in patients treated with antidepressant medications: Association with use of tricyclic agents. *American Journal of Medicine, 108*, 2–8.

Cohen, P. (2008, February 21). Midlife suicide rises, puzzling researchers, *New York Times*, pp. 1–4.

Cohen, P., Cohen, J., Kasen, S., et al. (1993). An epidemiological study of disorders in late childhood and adolescence: I. Age and gender-specific prevalence. *Journal of Child Psychology & Psychiatry, 34*, 851–867.

Cohen, R. M., Nordahl, T. E., Semple, W. E., Andreason, P., et al. (1997). The brain metabolic patterns of clozapine and fluphenazine-treated patients with schizophrenia during a continuous performance task. *Archives of General Psychiatry, 54*, 481–486.

Cohen, S., Frank, E., Doyle, W. J., Rabin, B. S., et al. (1998). Types of stressors that increase susceptibility to the common cold in healthy adults. *Health Psychology, 17*, 214–223.

Coie, J. D., & Dodge, K. A. (1998). Aggression and antisocial behavior. In W. Damon & N. Eisenberg (Eds.), *Handbook of child psychology: Vol. 3. Social emotional and personality development* (pp. 779–862). New York: Wiley.

Cole, D. A., Ciesla, J. A., Dallaire, D. H., et al. (2008). Emergence of attributional style and its relations to depressive symptoms. *Journal of Abnormal Psychology, 117*, 16–31.

Cole, D. A., Martin, J. M., Peeke, L. G., Seroczynski, A. D., & Hoffman, K. (1998). Are cognitive errors of underestimation predictive or reflective of depressive symptoms in children?: A longitudinal study. *Journal of Abnormal Psychology, 107*, 481–496.

Cole, D. A., Martin, J. M., Powers, B., & Truglio, R. (1990). Modeling causal relations between academic and social competence and depression: A multitrait-multimethod longitudinal study of children. *Journal of Abnormal Psychology, 105*, 258–270.

Cole, M. G. (2004). Delirium in elderly patients. *American Journal of Geriatric Psychiatry, 12*, 7–21.

Colom, F., Vieta, E., Reinares, M., Martinez-Aran, A., Torrent, C., Goikolea, J. M., & Gasto, C. (2003). Psychoeducation efficacy in bipolar disorders: Beyond compliance enhancement. *Journal of Clinical Psychiatry, 64*(9), 1101–1105.

Colombo, C., Benedetti, F., Barbini, B., Campori, E., & Smeraldi, E. (1999). Rate of switch from depression into mania after therapeutic sleep deprivation in bipolar depression. *Psychiatry Research, 86*, 267–270.

Comer, S. D., Hart, C. L., Ward, A. S., Haney, M., Foltin, R. W., & Fischman, M. W. (2001). Effects of repeated oral methamphetamine administration in humans. *Psychopharmacology, 155*, 397–404.

Compas, B. E., Haaga, D. A. F., Keefe, F. J., Leitenberg, H., & Williams, D. A. (1998). Sampling of empirically supported psychological treatments from health psychology: Smoking, chronic pain, cancer, and bulimia nervosa. *Journal of Consulting and Clinical Psychology, 66*, 89–112.

Compton, D. R., Dewey, W. L., & Martin, B. R. (1990). Cannabis dependence and tolerance production. *Advances in Alcohol and Substance Abuse, 9*, 129–147.

Compton, S. N., March, J. M., Brent, D., Albano, A. M., Weersing, R., & Curry, J. (2004). Cognitive-behavioral psychotherapy for anxiety and depressive disorders in children and adolescents: An evidence-based medicine review. *Journal of the American Academy of Child and Adolescent Psychiatry, 43*, 930–959.

Conceicao do Rosario-Campos, M., Leckman, J. F., Mercadante, M. T., Shavitt, R. G., Prado, H. S., Sada, P., . . . Miguel, E. C. (2001). Adults with early-onset obsessive-compulsive disorder. *American Journal of Psychiatry, 158*, 1899–1903.

Conley, R. R., Love, R. C., Kelly, D. L., & Bartko, J. J. (1999). Rehospitalization rates of patients recently discharged on a regimen of risperidone or clozapine. *American Journal of Psychiatry, 156*, 863–868.

Conley, R. R., & Mahmoud, R. (2001). A randomized double-blind study of risperidone and olanzapine in the treatment of schizophrenia or schizoaffective disorder. *American Journal of Psychiatry, 158*, 765–774.

Connelly, B. S., & Ones, D. S. (2010). Another perspective on personality: Meta-analytic integration of observers' accuracy and predictive validity. *Psychological Bulletin, 136*, 1092–1122.

Constantino, J. N., Zhang, Z., Frazier, T., Abbachi, A. M., & Law, P. (2010). Sibling recurrence and the genetic epidemiology of autism. *American Journal of Psychiatry, 167*, 1349–1356.

Cook, M., & Mineka, S. (1989). Observational conditioning of fear to fear-relevant versus fear-irrelevant stimuli in rhesus monkeys. *Journal of Abnormal Psychology, 98*, 448–459.

Cookson, W. O. C. M., & Moffatt, M. F. (1997). Asthma: An epidemic in the absence of infection? *Science, 275*, 41–42.

Cookson, W. O. C. M., & Moffatt, M. F. (2000). Genetics of asthma and allergic disease. *Human Molecular Genetics, 9*, 2359–2364.

Coons, P. M., & Bowman, E. S. (2001). Ten-year follow-up study of patients with dissociative identity disorder. *Journal of Trauma and Dissociation, 2*, 73–89.

Cooper, M. L., Frone, M. R., Russell, M., & Mudar, P. (1995). Drinking to regulate positive and negative emotion: A motivational model of alcoholism. *Journal of Personality and Social Psychology, 69*, 961–974.

Copolov, D. L., Mackinnon, A., & Trauer, T. (2004). Correlates of the affective impact of auditory hallucinations in psychotic disorders. *Schizophrenia Bulletin, 30*, 163–171.

Cornblatt, B., & Erlenmeyer-Kimling, L. E. (1985). Global attentional deviance in children at risk for schizophrenia: Specificity and predictive validity. *Journal of Abnormal Psychology, 94*, 470–486.

Corrigan, P. W., & Watson, A. C. (2005). Findings from the National Comorbidity Survey on the frequency of violent behavior in individuals with psychiatric disorders. *Psychiatry Research, 136*, 153–162.

Corrigan, P. W., Watson, A. C., Heyrman, J. D., Warpinski, A., Gracia, G., Slopen, N., & Hall, L. L. (2005). Structural stigma in state legislatures. *Psychiatric Services, 56*, 557–563.

Coryell, W., & Schlesser, M. (2001). The dexamethasone suppression test and suicide prevention. *Archives of General Psychiatry, 158*, 748–753.

Costa, P. T., Metter, E. J., & McCrae, R. R. (1994). Personality stability and its contribution to successful aging. *Journal of Geriatric Psychiatry, 27*, 41–59.

Costello, E. J., Costello, A. J., Edelbrock, C., Burns, B. J., Dulcan, M. K., Brent, D., & Janiszewski, S. (1988). Psychiatric disorders in pediatric primary care. *Archives of General Psychiatry, 45*, 1107–1116.

Costello, J. E., Erkanli, A., & Angold, A. (2006). Is there an epidemic of child or adolescent depression? *Journal of Child Psychology and Psychiatry, 47*, 1263–1271.

Cott, C. A., Dawson, P., Sidani, S., & Wells, D. (2002). The effects of a walking/talking program on communication, ambulation and functional status in residents with Alzheimer disease. *Alzheimer Disease and Associated Disorders, 16*, 81–87.

Cottler, L. B., Womack, S. B., Compton, W. M., et al. (2001). Ecstasy abuse and dependence among adolescents and young adults: applicability and reliability of DSM-IV criteria. *Human Psychopharmacology, Clinical and Experimental, 16*, 599–606.

Courchesne, E. (2004). Brain development in autism: Early overgrowth followed by premature arrests of growth. *Mental Retardation and Developmental Disabilities Research Reviews, 10*, 106–111.

Courchesne, E., Carnes, B. S., & Davis, H. R. (2001). Unusual brain growth patterns in early life in patients with autistic disorder: An MRI study. *Neurology, 57*, 245–254.

Courchesne, E., Carper, R., & Akshoomoff, N. (2003). Evidence of brain overgrowth in the first year of life in autism. *Journal of the American Medical Association, 290*, 337–344.

Cox, B. J., Clara, I. P., & Enns, M. W. (2002). Posttraumatic stress disorder and the structure of common mental disorders. *Depression and Anxiety, 15*, 168–171.

Coyne, J. C. (1976). Depression and the response of others. *Journal of Abnormal Psychology, 85*, 186–193.

Coyne, J. C. (1994). Self-reported distress: Analog or ersatz depression? *Psychological Bulletin, 116*, 29–45.

Craske, M. G., & Barlow, D. H. (2001). Panic disorder and agoraphobia. In D. H. Barlow (Ed.), *Clinical handbook of psychological disorders* (pp. 1–59). New York: Guilford.

Craske, M. G., Kircanski, K., Epstein, A., Wittchen, H. U., Pine, D. S., Lewis-Fernandez, R., & Hinton, D. (2010). Panic disorder: A review of DSM-IV panic disorder and proposals for DSM-V. *Depression and Anxiety, 27*(2), 93–112. doi: 10.1002/da.20654

Craske, M. G., Kircanski, K., Zelikowsky, M., Mystkowski, J., Chowdhury, N., & Baker, A. (2008). Optimizing inhibitory learning during exposure therapy. *Behaviour Research and Therapy, 46*(1), 5–27. doi: 10.1016/j.brat.2007.10.003

Craske, M. G., Maidenberg, E., & Bystritsky, A. (1995). Brief cognitive-behavioral versus nondirective therapy for panic disorder. *Journal of Behavior Therapy & Experimental Psychiatry, 26*, 113–120.

Craske, M. G., & Mystkowski, J. (2006). Exposure therapy and extinction: Clinical studies. In M. G. Craske, D. Hermans, & D. Vansteenwegen (Eds.), *Fear and learning from basic processes to clinical implications (pp. 217–233). Washington, DC: American Psychological Association.

Craske, M. G., Rauch, S. L., Ursano, R., Prenoveau, J., Pine, D. S., & Zinbarg, R. E. (2009). What is an anxiety disorder? *Depression and Anxiety, 26*(12), 1066–1085. doi: 10.1002/da.20633

Crawford, T. N., Cohen, P., Johnson, J. G., Kasen, S., First, M. B., Gordon, K., & Brook, J. S. (2005). Self-reported personality disorder in the children in the community sample: Convergent and prospective validity in late adolescence and adulthood. *Journal of Personality Disorders, 19,* 30–52.

Creamer, M., Burgess, P., & McFarlane, A. C. (2001). Posttraumatic stress disorder: Findings from the Australian national survey of mental health and well-being. *Psychological Medicine, 31,* 1237–1247.

Crick, N. R., & Dodge, K. A. (1994). A review and reformulation of social information-processing mechanisms in children's social adjustment. *Psychological Bulletin, 115,* 74–101.

Crime Survey, (2008). Drug Misuse Declared: Findings from the 2007/08. UK Home Office.

Critchley, H. D., Daly, E. M., Bullmore, E. T., Williams, S. C. R., Van Amelsvoort, T., Robertson, D. M., . . . Murphy, D. G. M. (2001). The functional neuroanatomy of social behaviour: Changes in cerebral blood flow when people with autistic disorder process facial expressions. *Brain, 123,* 2203–2212.

Crits-Christoph, P., & Barber, J. P. (2002). Psychological treatments for personality disorders. In P. E. Nathan & J. M. Gorman (Eds.), *A guide to treatments that work.* New York: Oxford University Press.

Crits-Christoph, P., Chambless, D. L., Frank, E., Brody, C., & Karp, J. F. (1995). Training in empirically validated treatments: What are clinical psychology students learning? *Professional Psychology: Research and Practice, 26,* 514–522.

Critser, G. (2003). *Fatland: How Americans became the fattest people in the world.* Boston: Houghton Mifflin.

Cronan, T. A., Cruz, S. G., Arriaga, R. I., & Sarkin, A. J. (1996). The effects of a community-based literacy program on young children's language and conceptual development. *American Journal of Community Psychology, 24,* 251–272.

Cronbach, L. J., & Meehl, P. E. (1955). Construct validity in psychological tests. *Psychological Bulletin, 52,* 281–302.

Crow, S. J., Peterson, C. B., Swanson, S. A., Raymond, N. C., Specker, S., Eckert, E. D., & Mitchell, J. E. (2009). Increased mortality in bulimia nervosa and other eating disorders. *American Journal of Psychiatry, 166,* 1342–1346.

Crow, T. J. (1980). Molecular pathology of schizophrenia: More than one disease process? *British Medical Journal, 280,* 784–788.

Crowell, N. A., & Burgess, A. W. (1996). *Understanding violence against women.* National Research Council, Commission on Behavioral and Social Sciences and Education, Committee on Law and Justice, Panel on Research on Violence Against Women, Washington, DC: National Academy Press.

Crozier, J. C., Dodge, K. A., Griffith, R., et al. (2008). Social information processing and cardiac predictors of adolescent antisocial behavior. *Journal of Abnormal Psychology, 117,* 253–267.

Cruts, M., Gijselinck, I., van der Zee, J., Engelborghs, S., Wils, H., Pirici, D., . . . Van Broeckhoven, C. (2006). Null mutations in progranulin cause ubiquitin-positive frontotemporal dementia linked to chromosome 17q21. *Nature, 442,* 920–924.

Curry, J. F. (2001). Specific psychotherapies for childhood and adolescent depression. *Biological Psychiatry, 49,* 1091–1100.

Curry, J., Silva, S., Rohde, P., Ginsburg, G., Kratochvil, C., Simons, A., Kirchner, J., May, D., Kennard, B., et al. (2011). Recovery and recurrence following treatment for adolescent major depression. *Archives of General Psychiatry, 68,* 263–270.

Curry, S. J., Mermelstein, R. J., & Sporer, A. K. (2009). Therapy for specific problems: Youth tobacco cessation. *Annual Review of Psychology, 60,* 229–255.

Curtin, J. J., Lang, A. R., Patrick, C. J., & Strizke, W. G. K. (1998). Alcohol and fear-potentiated startle: The role of competing cognitive demands in the stress-reducing effects of intoxication. *Journal of Abnormal Psychology, 107,* 547–557.

Curtis, L. H., Ostbye, T., Sendersky, V., Hutchison, S., Dans, P. E., Wright, A., . . . Schulman, K. A. (2004). Inappropriate prescribing for elderly Americans in a large outpatient population. *Archives of Internal Medicine, 164,* 1621–1625.

Dallery, J., Silverman, K., Chutuape, M. A., Bigelow, G. E., & Stitzer, M. (2001). Voucher-based reinforcement of opiate plus cocaine abstinence in treatment-resistant methadone patients: Effects of reinforcer magnitude. *Experimental & Clinical Psychopharmacology, 9,* 317–325.

Dallman, M. F., Pecoraro, N., Akana, S. F., La Fleur, S. E., Gomez, F., Houshyar, H., . . . Manalo, S. (2003). Chronic stress and obesity: A new view of comfort food. *Proceedings of the National Academy of Sciences, 100,* 11696–11701.

Dare, C., LeGrange, D., Eisler, I., & Rutherford, J. (1994). Redefining the psychosomatic family: Family process of 26 eating disordered families. *International Journal of Eating Disorders, 16,* 211–226.

Davidson, R. J., Pizzagalli, D., & Nitschke, J. B. (2002). The representation and regulation of emotion in depression: Perspectives from affective neuroscience. In C. L. Hammen & I. H. Gotlib (Eds.), *Handbook of depression* (pp. 219–244). New York: Guilford.

Davies, D. K., Stock, S. E., & Wehmeyer, M. (2003). Application of computer simulation to teach ATM access to individuals with intellectual disabilities. *Education & Training in Developmental Disabilities, 38,* 451–456.

Davila, J., Hammen, C. L., Burge, D., Paley, B., & Daley, S. E. (1995). Poor interpersonal problem solving as a mechanism of stress generation in depression among adolescent women. *Journal of Abnormal Psychology, 104,* 592–600.

Davis A. S., Malmbery, A., Brandt, L., Allebeck, P., & Lewis, G. (1997). IQ and risk for schizophrenia: A population-based cohort study. *Psychological Medicine, 27,* 1311–1323.

Davis, C. (1996). The interdependence of obsessive-compulsiveness, physical activity, and starvation: A model for anorexia nervosa. In W. F. Epling & W. D. Pierce (Eds.), *Activity nervosa: Theory, research, and treatment* (pp. 209–218). Mahwah, NJ: Erlbaum.

Davis, J. M. (1978). Dopamine theory of schizophrenia: A two-factor theory. In L. C. Wynne, R. L. Cromwell, & S. Matthysse (Eds.), *The nature of schizophrenia.* New York: Wiley.

Davis, J. M., Chen, N., & Glick, I. D. (2003). A meta-analysis of the efficacy of second-generation antipsychotics. *Archives of General Psychiatry, 60,* 553–564.

Davis, L., & Siegel, L. J. (2000). Posttraumatic stress disorder in children and adolescents: A review and analysis. *Clinical Child and Family Psychology Review, 3,* 135–153.

Davis, M. C., Matthews, K. A., & Twamley, E. W. (1999). Is life more difficult on Mars or Venus? A meta-analytic review of sex differences in major and minor life events. *Annals of Behavioral Medicine, 21,* 83–97.

Davis, K. L., Kahn, R. S., Ko, G., & Davidson, M. (1991). Dopamine and schizophrenia: A review and reconceptualization. *American Journal of Psychiatry, 148,* 1474–1486.

Davis, P. (2002, August 18). The faces of Alzheimer's. *Time.*

Davis, T. E., May, A., & Whiting, S. E. (2011). Evidence-based treatment of anxiety and phobia in children and adolescents: Current status and effects on the emotional response. *Clinical Psychology Review, 31,* 592–602.

Davison, T. E., McCabe, M., & Mellor, D. (2009). An examination of the "gold standard" diagnosis of major depression in aged-care settings. *American Journal of Geriatric Psychiatry, 17*(5), 359–367.

Dawson, G., Toth, K., Abbott, R., Osterling, J., Munson, J., Estes, A., & Liaw, J. (2004). Early social attention impairments in autism: Social orienting, joint attention, and attention to distress. *Developmental Psychology, 40,* 271–283.

Dawson, M. E., Schell, A. M., & Banis, H. T. (1986). Greater resistance to extinction of electrodermal responses conditioned to potentially phobic CSs: A noncognitive process? *Psychophysiology, 23,* 552–561.

Day, N. L., Leech, S. L., Richardson, G. A., Cornelius, M. D., Robles, N., & Larkby, C. (2004). Prenatal alcohol exposure predicts continued deficits in offspring size at 14 years of age. *Alcoholism: Clinical and Experimental Research, 26,* 1584–1591.

Day, N. L., & Richardson, G. A. (2004). An analysis of the effects of prenatal alcohol exposure on growth: A teratologic model. *American Journal of Medical Genetics Part C (Seminar in Medical Genetics), 127C,* 28–34.

Deacon, B. J., & Abramowitz, J. S. (2004). Cognitive and behavioral treatments for anxiety disorders: A review of meta-analytic findings. *Journal of Clinical Psychology, 60*(4), 429–441. doi: 10.1002/jclp.10255

Deacon, S., Minicchiello, V., & Plummer, D. (1995). Sexuality and older people: Revisiting the assumptions. *Educational Gerontology, 21,* 497–513.

Deary, I. J., & Johnson, W. (2010). Intelligence and education: Causal perceptions drive analytic processes and therefore conclusions. *International Journal of Epidemiology, 39,* 1362–1369.

Deckersbach, T., Savage, C. R., Phillips, K., Wilhelm, S., Buhlmann, U., Rauch, S., . . . Jenike, M. A. (2000). Characteristics of memory dysfunction in body dysmorphic disorder. *Journal of the International Neuropsychological Society, 6,* 673–681.

De Cuypere, G., Tsjoen, G., Beerten, R., Selvaggi, G., De Sutter, P., Hoebeke, P., . . . Rubens, R. (2005). Sexual and physical health after sex reassignment surgery. *Archives of Sexual Behavior, 34,* 679–690.

Deep, A. L., Lilenfeld, L. R., Plotnicov, K. H., Pollice, C., & Kaye, W. H. (1999). Sexual abuse in eating disorder subtypes and control women: The role of cormorbid substance dependence in bulimia nervosa. *International Journal of Eating Disorders, 25,* 1–10.

de Graaf, R., Bijl, R. V., Ravelli, A., Smit, F., & Vollenbergh, W. A. M. (2002). Predictors of first incidence of DSM-III-R psychiatric disorders in the general population: Findings from the Netherlands Mental Health Survey and Incidence Study. *Acta Psychiatrica Scandinavica, 106,* 303–313.

DeJong, W., & Kleck, R. E. (1986). The social psychological effects of overweight. In C. P. Herman, M. P. Zanna, & E. T. Higgins (Eds.), *Physical appearance, stigma, and social behavior.* Hillside, NJ: Erlbaum.

deLint, J. (1978). Alcohol consumption and alcohol problems from an epidemiological perspective. *British Journal of Alcohol and Alcoholism, 17,* 109–116.

Depression Guidlines Panel. (1993). *Depression in primary care: Vol 2. Treatment of major depression. Clinical practice guideline No. 5.* Rockville, MD: US Department of Health and Human Services Agency for Health Care Policy and Research.

Depue, R. A., Collins, P. F., & Luciano, M. (1996). A model of neurobiology: Environment interaction in developmental psychopathology. In M. F. Lenzenweger & J. J. Haugaard (Eds.), *Frontiers of developmental psychopathology* (pp. 44–76). New York: Oxford University Press.

Depue, R. A., & Iacono, W. G. (1989). Neurobehavioral aspects of affective disorders. In L. W. Porter & M. R. Rosenzweig (Eds.), *Annual review of psychology* (pp. 457–492). Palo Alto, CA: Annual Reviews Inc.

Derogatis, L. R., & Burnett, A. L. (2008). The epidemiology of sexual dysfunctions. *Journal of Sexual Medicine, 5*(2), 289–300. doi: 10.1111/j.1743-6109.2007.00668.x

DeRubeis, R. J. (2011). The gotcha moment: When science is taken out of context. *Observer, 24*(1), 13.

DeRubeis, R. J., & Crits-Christoph, P. (1998). Empirically supported individual and group psychological treatments for adult mental disorders. *Journal of Consulting and Clinical Psychology, 66,* 37–52.

DeRubeis, R. J., Gelfand, L. A., Tang, T. Z., & Simons, A. D. (1999). Medications versus cognitive behavior therapy for severely depressed outpatients: Mega-analysis of four randomized comparisons. *American Journal of Psychiatry, 156,* 1007–1013.

De Souza, E. B., Battaglia, G., & Insel, T. L. (1990). Neurotoxic effect of MDMA on brain serotonin neurons: Evidence from neurochemical and radioligand binding studies. *Annual Proceedings of the New York Academy of Science, 600,* 682–697.

de Wit, H., & Zacny, J. (2000). Abuse potential of nicotine replacement therapies. In K. J. Palmer (Ed.), *Smoking cessation* (pp. 79–92). Kwai Chung, Hong Kong: Adis International Publications.

Dick, D. M., Pagan, J. L., Viken, R., Purcell, S., Kaprio, J., Pulkinnen, L., et al. (2007). Changing environmental influencec on substance use across development. *Twin Research and Human Genetics, 10,* 315–326.

Dickerson, S. S., & Kemeny, M. E. (2004). Acute stressors and cortisol responses: A theoretical integration and synthesis of laboratory research. *Psychological Bulletin, 130,* 355–391.

Dickey, C. C., McCarley, R. W., & Shenton, M. E. (2002). The brain in schizotypal personality disorder: A review of structural MRI and CT findings. *Harvard Review of Psychiatry, 10,* 1–15.

Dickstein, D. P., & Leibenluft, E. (2006). Emotion regulation in children and adolescents: Boundaries between normalcy and bipolar disorder. *Development and Psychopathology, 18,* 1105–1131.

Didie, E. R., Menard, W., Stern, A. P., & Phillips, K. A. (2008). Occupational functioning and impairment in adults with body dysmorphic disorder. *Comprehensive Psychiatry, 49*(6), 561–569. doi: 10.1016/j.comppsych.2008.04.003

Dieserud, G., Roysamb, E., Braverman, M. T., Dalgard, O. S., & Ekeberg, O. (2003). Predicating repetition of suicide attempt: A prospective study of 50 suicide attempters. *Archives of Suicide Research, 7,* 1–15.

DiFranza, J. R., Richards, J. W., Paulman, P. M., Wolf-Gillespie, N., Fletcher, C., et al. (1991). RJR Nabisco's cartoon camel promotes Camel cigarettes to children. *Journal of the American Medical Association, 266,* 3149–3153.

Dimidjian, S., Barrera, M., Martell, C., Muñoz, R. F., & Lewinsohn, P. M. (2011). The origins and current status of behavioral activation treatments for depression. *Annual Review of Clinical Psychology, 7,* 1–38.

Dimidjian, S., Hollon, S. D., Dobson, K. S., Schmaling, K. B., Kohlenberg, R. J., Addis, M. E., . . . Jacobson, N. S. (2006). Randomized trial of behavioral activation, cognitive therapy, and antidepressant medication in the acute treatment of adults with major depression. *Journal of Consulting and Clinical Psychology, 74,* 658–670.

DiNardo, P. A., O'Brien, G. T., Barlow, D. H., Waddell, M. T., & Blanchard, E. B. (1993). Reliability of the DSM-III-R anxiety disorders categories using the Anxiety Disorders Interview Schedule-Revised (ADIS-R). *Archives of General Psychiatry, 50,* 251–256.

Dishion, T. J., & Andrews, D. W. (1995). Preventing escalation in problem behaviors with high-risk young adolescents: Immediate and 1-year outcomes. *Journal of Consulting and Clinical Psychology, 63,* 538–548.

Dishion, T. J., Patterson, G. R., & Kavanagh, K. A. (1992). An experimental test of the coercion model: Linking theory, measurement, and intervention. In J. McCord & R. E. Tremblay (Eds.), *Preventing antisocial behavior* (pp. 253–282). New York: Guilford.

Dixon, L. B., Dickerson, F., Bellack, A. S., Bennett, M., Dickinson, D., Goldberg, R. W., et al. (2010). The 2009 schizophrenia PORT psychosocial treatment recommendations and summary statements. *Schizophrenia Bulletin, 36,* 48–70.

Dobson, K. S., Hollon, S. D., Dimidjian, S., Schmaling, K. B., Kohlenberg, R. J., Gallop, R., . . . Jacboson, N. S. (2008). Randomized trial of behavioral activation, cognitive therapy, and antidepressent medication in the prevention of relapse and recurrence in major depression. *Journal of Consulting and Clinical Psychology, 76*(3), 468–477.

Dodge, K. A., & Frame, C. L. (1982). Social cognitive biases and deficits in aggressive boys. *Child Development, 53,* 620–635.

Doerr, P., Fichter, M., Pirke, K. M., & Lund, R. (1980). Relationship between weight gain and hypothalamic-pituitary-adrenal function in patients with anorexia nervosa. *Journal of Steroid Biochemistry, 13,* 529–537.

Dohrenwend, B. P. (2006). Inventorying stressful life events as risk factors for psychopathology: Toward resolution of the problem of intracategory variability. *Psychological Bulletin, 132,* 477–495.

Dohrenwend, B. P., Levav, P. E., Schwartz, S., Naveh, G., Link, B. G., Skodol, A. E., & Stueve, A. (1992). Socioeconomic status and psychiatric disorders: The causation-selection issue. *Science, 255,* 946–952.

Dohrenwend, B. S., Krasnoff, L., Askenasy, A. R., & Dohrenwend, B. P. (1978). Exemplification of method for scaling life events: The PERI life events scale. *Journal of Health and Social Behavior, 19,* 205–229.

Dolan, B. (1991). Cross-cultural aspects of anorexia and bulimia: A review. *International Journal of Eating Disorders, 10,* 67–78.

Dolder, C. R., Lacro, J. P., Dunn, L. B., & Jeste, D. V. (2002). Antipsychotic medication adherence: Is there a difference between typical and atypical agents? *American Journal of Psychiatry, 159,* 103–108.

Doll, H. A., & Fairburn, C. G. (1998). Heightened accuracy of self-reported weight in bulimia nervosa: A useful cognitive "distortion." *International Journal of Eating Disorders, 24,* 267–273.

Dougher, M. J. (1988). Clinical assessment of sex offenders. In B. K. Schwartz (Ed.), *A practitioner's guide to treating the incarcerated male sex offender* (pp. 77–84). Washington, DC: U.S. Department of Justice.

Douglas, K. S., Guy, L. S., & Hart, S. D. (2009). Psychosis as a risk factor for violence to others: A meta-analysis. *Psychological Bulletin, 135,* 679–706.

Doyle, P. M., Le Grange, D., Loeb, K., Doyle, A. C., & Crosby, R. D. (2010). Early response to family-based treatment for adolescent anorexia nervosa. *International Journal of Eating Disorders, 43,* 659–662.

Draguns, J. G. (1989). Normal and abnormal behavior in cross-cultural perspective: Specifying the nature of their relationships. In J. J. Berman (Ed.), *Nebraska symposium on motivation.* Lincoln: University of Nebraska Press.

Dreznick, M. T. (2003). Heterosocial competence of rapists and child molesters: A meta-analysis. *Journal of Sex Research, 40,* 170–178.

Drug Enforcement Administration. (2001). *Working to prevent the diversion and abuse of Oxycontin.* Drug Enforcement Administration, Office of Diversion Control, June 12.

Druglink, (2005). Street drug prices Sep.-Oct., 20(5), p. 32. (Druglink factsheet14).

Druglink, (2011). Heroine and other opiates. www.drugscope.org.uk

DrugScope, (2004). LSD. www.drugscope.org.uk

DrugScope, (2010) Cocaine and crack. www.drugscope.org.uk

DrugScope, (2011) Cocaine and crack. www.drugscope.org.uk

Drury, V., Birchwood, M., Cochrane, R., & Macmillan, R. (1996). Cognitive therapy and recovery from acute psychosis: A controlled trial. *British Journal of Psychiatry, 169,* 593–601.

Duffy, F. F., West, J. C., Wilk, J., Narrow, W. E., Hales, D., Thompson, J., et al. (2004). Mental health practitioners and trainees. In R. W. Manderscheid & M. J. Henderson (Eds.), *Mental health, United States, 2002* (DHHS Pub No.). Rockville, MD: Substance Abuse and Mental Health Services Administration.

Dugas, M. J., Brillon, P., Savard, P., Turcotte, J., Gaudet, A., Ladouceur, R., . . . Gervais, N. J. (2010). A randomized clinical trial of cognitive-behavioral therapy and applied relaxation for adults with generalized anxiety disorder. *Behavior Therapy, 41*(1), 46–58. doi: 10.1016/j.beth.2008.12.004

Dugas, M. J., Marchand, A., & Ladouceur, R. (2005). Further validation of a cognitive-behavioral model of generalized anxiety disorder: Diagnostic and symptom specificity. *Journal of Anxiety Disorders, 19,* 329–343.

Duman, R. S., Heninger, G. R., & Nestler, E. J. (1997). A molecular and cellular theory of depression. *Archives of General Psychiatry, 54,* 597–606.

Duman, R. S., Malberg, J., & Nakagawa, S. (2001). Regulation of adult neurogenesis by psychotropic drugs and stress. *Journal of Pharmacology and Experimental Therapeutics, 299,* 401–407.

DuPaul, G. J., & Henningson, P. N. (1993). Peer tutoring effects on the classroom performance of children with attention deficit hyperactivity disorder. *School Psychology Review, 22,* 134–143.

Dura, J. R., Stukenberg, K. W., & Kiecolt-Glaser, J. K. (1991). Anxiety and depressive disorders in adult children caring for demented parents. *Psychology and Aging, 6,* 467–473.

Dvoskin, J. A., & Steadman, H. J. (1994). Using intensive case management to reduce violence by mentally ill persons in the community. *Hospital and Community Psychiatry, 45,* 679–684.

Dworkin, R. H., & Lenzenwenger, M. F. (1984). Symptoms and the genetics of schizophrenia: Implications for diagnosis. *American Journal of Psychiatry, 141,* 1541–1546.

Dworkin, R. H., Lenzenwenger, M. F., & Moldin, S. O. (1987). Genetics and the phenomenology of schizophrenia. In P. D. Harvey & E. F. Walker (Eds.), *Positive and negative symptoms of psychosis.* Hillsdale, NJ: Erlbaum.

Eack, S. M., Greenwald, D. P., Hogarty, S. S., & Keshavan, M. S. (2010). One-year durability of the effects of cognitive enhancement therapy on functional outcome in early schizophrenia. *Schizophrenia Research, 120,* 210–216.

Eddy, K. T., Keel, P. K., Dorer, D. J., Delinksy, S. S., Franko, D. L., & Herzog, D. B. (2002). Longitudinal comparison of anorexia nervosa subtypes. *International Journal of Eating Disorders, 31,* 191–201.

Edelbrock, C., Rende, R., Plomin, T., & Thompson, L. A. (1995). A twin study of competence and problem behavior in childhood and early adolescence. *Journal of Child Psychology and Psychiatry and Allied Disciplines, 36,* 775–789.

Edenberg, H. J., Xuie, X., Chen, H-J., Tian, H., Weatherill, L. F., Dick, D. M., et al. (2006). Association of alcohol dehydrogenase genes with alcohol dependence: A comprehensive analysis. *Human Molecular Genetics, 15,* 1539–1549.

Eder, W., Ege, M. J., & von Mutius, E. (2006). The asthma epidemic. *New England Journal of Medicine, 355,* 2226–2235.

Edvardsen, J., Torgersen, S., Roysamb, E., Lygren, S., Skre, I., Onstad, S., & Oien, P. A. (2008). Heritability of bipolar spectrum disorders. Unity or heterogeneity? *Journal of Affective Disorders, 106*(3), 229–240.

Edwards, G. and Gross, M. (1976). Alcohol Dependence: provisional description of a clinical syndrome. *British Medical Journal, 1,* 1058–1061.

Ehlers, A., Mayou, R. A., & Bryant, B. (1998). Psychological predictors of chronic posttraumatic stress disorder after motor vehicle accidents. *Journal of Abnormal Psychology, 107,* 508–519.

Eley, T. C., Lichtenstein, P., & Moffitt, T. E. (2003). A longitudinal behavioral genetic analysis of the etiology of aggressive and nonaggressive antisocial behavior. *Development and Psychopathology, 15,* 383–402.

Elkin, I., Shea, M. T., & Shaw, B. F. (1996). Science is not a trial (but it can sometimes be a tribulation). *Journal of Consulting and Clinical Psychology, 64,* 92–103.

Elkin, I., Shea, M. T., Watkins, J. T., Imber, S. D., Sotsky, S. M., Collins, J. F., . . . Parloff, M. B. (1989). NIMH Treatment of Depression Collaborative Research Program: 1. General effectiveness of treatments. *Archives of General Psychiatry, 46,* 971–983.

Elkins, I., King, S. M., McGue, M., & Iacono, W. (2006). Personality traits and the development of alcohol, nicotine, and illicit drug disorders: Prospective links from adolescence to young adulthood. *Journal of Abnormal Psychology, 115,* 26–39.

Elkins, I., McGue, M., & Iacono, W. (2007). Prospective effects of attention-deficit/hyperactivity disorder, conduct disorder, and sex on adolescent substance use and abuse. *Archives of General Psychiatry, 64,* 1145–1152.

Elkis, H., Friedman, L., Wise, A., & Meltzer, H. T. (1995). Meta-analysis of studies of ventricular enlargement and cortical sulcal prominence in mood disorders. *Archives of General Psychiatry, 52,* 735–746.

Ellenberger, H. F. (1972). The story of "Anna O": A critical review with new data. *Journal of the History of the Behavioral Sciences, 8,* 267–279.

Ellis, A. (1991). The revised ABC's of rational-emotive therapy (RET). *Journal of Rational-Emotive and Cognitive Behavior Therapy, 9,* 139–172.

Ellis, A. (1993). Changing rational-emotive therapy (RET) to rational emotive behavior therapy (REBT). *The Behavior Therapist, 16,* 257–258.

Ellis, A. (1995). Changing rational-emotive therapy (RET) to rational emotive behavior therapy (REBT). *Journal of Rational-Emotive and Cognitive Behavior Therapy, 13,* 85–89.

Emmelkamp, P. M. G. (2004). Behavior therapy with adults. In M. J. Lambert (Ed.), *Bergin and Garfield's handbook of psychotherapy and behavior change* (5th ed., pp. 393–446). New York: Wiley.

Emmelkamp, P. M. G., Krijn, M., Hulsbosch, A. M., de Vries, S., Schuemie, M. J., & van der Mast, C. A. P. G. (2002). Virtual reality treatment versus exposure in vivo: A comparative evaluation in acrophobia. *Behaviour Research and Therapy, 40,* 509–516.

Emslie, G., & Mayes, T. N. (2001). Mood disorders in children and adolescents: Psychopharmacological treatment. *Biological Psychiatry, 49,* 1082–1090.

Engdahl, B., Dikel, T. N., Eberly, R., & Blank, A. (1997). Posttraumatic stress disorder in a community group of former prisoners of war: A normative response to severe trauma. *American Journal of Psychiatry, 154,* 1576–1581.

Enserink, M. (1999). Drug therapies for depression: From MAO inhibitors to substance. *Science, 284,* 239.

Epling, W. F., & Pierce, W. D. (1992). *Solving the anorexia puzzle.* Toronto, Canada: Hogrefe & Huber.

Epstein, J. A., Botvin, G. J., & Diaz, T. (2001). Linguistic acculturation associated with higher marijuana and polydrug use among Hispanic adolescents. *Substance Use & Misuse, 36,* 477–499.

Erdberg, P., & Exner, J. E., Jr. (1984). Rorschach assessment. In G. Goldstein & M. Hersen (Eds.), *Handbook of psychological assessment.* New York: Pergamon.

Erhardt, D., & Hinshaw, S. P. (1994). Initial sociometric impressions of attention-deficit hyperactivity disorder and comparison boys: Predictions from social behaviors and nonverbal behaviors. *Journal of Consulting and Clinical Psychology, 62,* 833–842.

Erickson, K. I., & Kramer, A. F. (2009). Aerobic exercise effects on cognitive and neural plasticity in older adults. *British Journal of Sports Medicine, 43*(1), 22–24. doi: 10.1136/bjsm.2008.052498

Erlenmeyer-Kimling, L. E., & Cornblatt, B. (1987). The New York high-risk project: A follow-up report. *Schizophrenia Bulletin, 13,* 451–461.

ESEMeD/MHEDEA 2000 investigators. (2004). Disability and quality of life impact of mental disorders in Europe: Results from the European study of the epidemiology of mental disorders (ESEMeD) project. *Acta Psychiatrica Scandinavica, 109,* 38–46. doi: 10.1111/j.1600-0047.2004.00329.x.

Essex, M. J., Klein, M. H., Slattey, M. J., Goldsmith, H. H., & Kalin, N. H. (2010). Early risk factors and developmental pathways to chronic high inhibition and social anxiety disorder in adolescence. *American Journal of Psychiatry, 167,* 40–46.

European Status Report on Alcohol and Health, (2010). www.euro.who.int/__data/assets/pdf_file/0004/128065/e94533.pdf

Evans, R. J. (2001). Social influences in etiology and prevention of smoking and other health threatening behaviors in children and adolescents. In A. Baum, T. A. Revenson, & J. E. Singer (Eds.), *Handbook of health psychology* (pp. 459–468). Mahwah, NJ: Erlbaum.

Everaerd, W., Laan, E., Both, S., & Van Der Velde, J. (2000). Female sexuality. In L. Szuchman & F. Muscarella (Eds.), *Psychological perspectives on human sexuality* (pp. 108–122). New York: Wiley.

Everett, F., Proctor, N., & Cartmell, B. (1989). Providing psychological services to American Indian children and families. In D. R. Atkinson, G. Morten, & D. W. Sue (Eds.), *Counseling American minorities* (3rd ed.). Dubuque, IA: Brown.

Everill, J. T., & Waller, G. (1995). Reported sexual abuse and eating psychopathology: A review of the evidence for a causal link. *International Journal of Eating Disorders, 18,* 1–11.

Exner, J. E. (1978). *The Rorschach: A comprehensive system: Vol. 2. Current research and advanced interpretation.* New York: Wiley.

Exner, J. E., Jr. (1986). *The Rorschach: A comprehensive system: Vol. 1. Basic foundations* (2nd ed.). New York: Wiley.

Fabrega, H., Jr. (2002). Evolutionary theory, culture and psychiatric diagnosis. In M. Maj & W. Gaebel (Eds.), *Psychiatric diagnosis and classification* (pp. 107–135). New York: Wiley.

Fairburn, C. G. (1985). Cognitive-behavioral treatment for bulimia. In D. M. Garner & P. E. Garfinkel (Eds.), *Handbook of psychotherapy for anorexia nervosa and bulimia* (pp. 160–192). New York: Guilford.

Fairburn, C. G. (1997). Eating disorders. In D. M. Clark & C. G. Fairburn (Eds.), *Science and practice of cognitive behavior therapy* (pp. 209–243). New York: Oxford University Press.

Fairburn, C. G., Agras, W. S., & Wilson, G. T. (1992). The research on the treatment of bulimia nervosa: Practical and theoretical implications. In G. H. Anderson & S. H. Kennedy (Eds.), *The biology of feast and famine: Relevance to eating disorders.* New York: Academic Press.

Fairburn, C. G., Cooper, A., Doll, H. A., O'Connor, M. E., Bohn, K., Hawker, D. M., . . . Palmer, R. L. (2009). Transdiagnostic cognitive-behavioral therapy for patients with eating disorders: A two-site trial with 60-week follow-up. *American Journal of Psychiatry, 166,* 311–319.

Fairburn, C. G., Cooper, Z., Doll, H. A., & Welch, S. L. (1999). Risk factors for anorexia nervosa: Three integrated case-control comparisons. *Archives of General Psychiatry, 56,* 468–478.

Fairburn, C. G., Doll, H. A., Welch, S. L., Hay, P. J., Davies, B. A., & O'Connor, M. E. (1998). Risk factors for binge eating disorder. *Archives of General Psychiatry, 55,* 425–432.

Fairburn, C. G., Jones, R., Peveler, R. C., Carr, S. J., Solomon, R. A., O'Connor, M. E., . . . Hope, R. A. (1991). Three psychological treatments for bulimia nervosa. *Archives of General Psychiatry, 48,* 463–469.

Fairburn, C. G., Jones, R., Peveler, R. C., Hope, R. A., & O'Connor, M. E. (1993). Psychotherapy and bulimia nervosa: The longer-term effects of interpersonal psychotherapy, behavior therapy, and cognitive therapy. *Archives of General Psychiatry, 50,* 419–428.

Fairburn, C. G., Marcus, M. D., & Wilson, G. T. (1993). Cognitive behaviour therapy for binge eating and bulimia nervosa: A comprehensive treatment manual. In C. G. Fairburn & G. T. Wilson (Eds.), *Binge eating: Nature, assessment, and treatment.* New York: Guilford.

Fairburn, C. G., Norman, P. A., Welch, S. L., O'Connor, M. E., Doll, H. A., & Peveler, R. C. (1995). A prospective study of outcome in bulimia nervosa and the long-term effects of three psychological treatments. *Archives of General Psychiatry, 52,* 304–312.

Fairburn, C. G., Shafran, R., & Cooper, Z. (1999). A cognitive behavioural theory of anorexia nervosa. *Behaviour Research and Therapy, 37,* 1–13.

Fairburn, C. G., Stice, E., Cooper, Z., Doll, H. A., Norman, P. A., & O'Connor, M. E. (2003). Understanding persistence in bulimia nervosa: A 5-year naturalistic study. *Journal of Consulting and Clinical Psychology, 71,* 103–109.

Fairburn, C. G., Welch, S. L., Doll, H. A., Davies, B. A., & O'Connor, M. E. (1997). Risk factors for bulimia nervosa: A community-based case-control study. *Archives of General Psychiatry, 54,* 509–517.

Fales, C. L., Barch, D. M., Rundle, M. M., Mintun, M. A., Snyder, A. Z., Cohen, J. D., . . . Sheline, Y. (2008). Altered emotional interference processing in affective and cognitive-control brain circuitry in major depression. *Biological Psychiatry, 63*(4), 377–384.

Falloon, I. R. H., Boyd, J. L., McGill, C. W., Razani, J., Moss, H. B., & Gilderman, A. N. (1982). Family management in the prevention of exacerbation of schizophrenia: A controlled study. *New England Journal of Medicine, 306,* 1437–1440.

Falloon, I. R. H., Boyd, J. L., McGill, C. W., Williamson, M., Razani, J., Moss, H. B., . . . Simpson, G. M. (1985). Family management in the prevention of morbidity of schizophrenia. *Archives of General Psychiatry, 42,* 887–896.

Fanous, A. H., Prescott, C. A., & Kendler, K. S. (2004). The prediction of thoughts of death or self-harm in a population-based sample of female twins. *Psychological Medicine, 34,* 301–312.

Faraone, S. V., Biederman, J., Jetton, J. G., & Tsuang, M. T. (1997). Attention deficit disorder and conduct disorder: Longitudinal evidence for a family subtype. *Psychological Medicine, 27,* 291–300.

Faraone, S. V., Biederman, J., & Mick, E. (2005). The age-dependent decline of attention deficit hyperactivity disorder: A meta-analysis of follow-up studies. *Psychological Medicine, 36,* 159–165.

Faraone, S. V., Biederman, J., Weber, W., & Russell, R. L. (1998). Psychiatric, neuropsychological, and psychosocial features of DSM-IV subtypes of attention-deficit/hyperactivity disorder: Results from a clinically referred sample. *Journal of the American Academy of Child and Adolescent Psychiatry, 37,* 185–193.

Faraone, S. V., Doyle, A. E., Mick, E., & Biederman, J. (2001). Meta-analysis of the association between the 7-repeat allele of the dopamine D(4) receptor gene and attention deficit hyperactivity disorder. *American Journal of Psychiatry, 158,* 1052–1057.

Faravelli, C., Salvatori, S., Galassi, F., & Aiazzi, L. (1997). Epidemiology of somatoform disorders: A community survey in Florence. *Social Psychiatry and Psychiatric Epidemiology, 32,* 24–29.

Farina, A. (1976). *Abnormal psychology.* Englewood Cliffs, NJ: Prentice Hall.

Faustman, W. O., Bardgett, M., Faull, K. F., Pfefferman, A., & Cseransky, J. G. (1999). Cerebrospinal fluid glutamate inversely correlates with positive symptom severity in unmedicated male schizophrenic/schizoaffective patients. *Biological Psychiatry, 45,* 68–75.

Favaro, A., & Santonastaso, P. (1997). Suicidality in eating disorders: Clinical and psychological correlates. *Acta Psychiatrica Scandanavica, 95,* 508–514.

Febbraro, G. A. R., & Clum, G. A. (1998). Meta-analytic investigation of the effectiveness of self-regulatory components in the treatment of adult behavior problems. *Clinical Psychology Review, 18,* 143–161.

Feingold, B. F. (1973). *Introduction to clinical allergy.* Springfield, IL: Thomas.

Feldman, R. S. et al., (1997). *Principles of Neuropsychopharmacology.* Sinauer.

Feldman, H. A., Goldstein, I., Hatzichristou, G., Krane, R. J., & McKinlay, J. B. (1994). Impotence and its medical and psychosocial correlates: Results of the Massachusetts male aging study. *Journal of Urology, 151,* 54–61.

Feldman, H. M., Kolmen, B. K., & Gonzaga, A. M. (1999). Naltrexone and communication skills in young children with autism. *Journal of the American Academy of Child and Adolescent Psychiatry, 38,* 587–593.

Feldman Barrett, L. (2003). So you want to be a social neuroscientist? *APS Observer, 16,* 5–7.

Ferguson, C. P., La Via, M. C., Crossan, P. J., & Kaye, W. H. (1999). Are SSRIs effective in underweight anorexia nervosa? *International Journal of Eating Disorders, 25,* 11–17.

Ferguson, S. B., Shiffman, S., & Gwaltney, C. J. (2006). Does reducing withdrawal severity mediate nicotine patch efficacy? A randomized clinical trial. *Journal of Consulting and Clinical Psychology, 74,* 1153–1161.

Fergusson, D. M., Boden, J. M., & Horwood, L. J. (2008). Exposure to childhood sexual and physical abuse and adjustment in early adulthood. *Child Abuse and Neglect, 32*(6), 607–619. doi: 10.1016/j.chiabu.2006.12.018

Fergusson, D. M., & Horwood, L. J. (2000). Does cannabis use encourage other forms of illicit drug use? *Addiction, 95,* 505–520.

Ferri, C. P., Prince, M., Brayne, C., Brodaty, H., & Lyketsos, C. G. (2005). Global prevalence of dementia: A delphi consensus study. *Lancet, 366,* 2112–2117.

Ferri, M., Amato, L., & Davoli, M. (2008). Alcoholics anonymous and other 12 step programmes for alcohol dependence (review). *Cochrane Database of Systematic Reviews,* Issue 3. Art. No.: CD005032. DOI: 10.1002/14561858.CD00532.pub2.

Fetkewicz, J., Sharma, V., & Merskey, H. (2000). A note on suicidal deterioration with recovered memory treatment. *Journal of Affective Disorders, 58,* 155–159.

Feusner, J. D., Phillips, K. A., & Stein, D. J. (2010). Olfactory reference syndrome: Issues for DSM-V. *Depression and Anxiety, 27*(6), 592–599. doi: 10.1002/da.20688

Fiellin, D. A., O'Connor, P. G., Chawarski, M., Pakes, J. P., Pantalon, M. V., & Schottenfeld, R. S. (2001). Methadone maintenance in primary care: A randomized controlled trial. *Journal of the American Medical Association, 286,* 1724–1731.

Fillmore, K. M. (1987). Prevalence, incidence and chronicity of drinking patterns and problems among men as a function of age: A longitudinal and cohort analysis. *British Journal of Addiction, 82,* 77–83.

Fillmore, K. M., & Caetano, R. (1980). *Epidemiology of occupational alcoholism.* Paper presented at the National Institute on Alcohol Abuse and Alcoholism's Workshop on Alcoholism in the Workplace, Reston, VA.

Fink, H. A., MacDonald, R., Rutks, I. R., Nelson, D. B., & Wilt, T. J. (2002). Sildenafil for male erectile dysfunction: A systematic review and meta-analysis. *Archives of Internal Medicine, 162*(12), 1349–1360.

Fink, P., Hansen, M. S., & Sondergaard, L. (2005). Somatoform disorders among firsttime referrals to a neurology service. *Psychosomatics, 46,* 540–548.

Finkelhor, D. (1983). Removing the child—Prosecuting the offender in cases of sexual abuse: Evidence from the national reporting system for child abuse and neglect. *Child Abuse and Neglect, 7,* 195–205.

Finkelstein, E. A., Trogdon, J. G., Cohen, J. W., & Dietz, W. (2009). Annual medical spending attributable to obesity: Payer- and service-specific estimates. *Health Affairs, 28,* w822-w831.

Finlay-Jones, R. (1989). Anxiety. In G. W. Brown & T. O. Harris (Eds.), *Life events and illness* (pp. 95–112). New York: Guilford.

Finney, J. W., & Moos, R. H. (1998). Psychosocial treatments for alcohol use disorders. In P. E. Nathan &

J. M. Gorman (Eds.), *A guide to treatments that work* (pp. 156–166). New York: Oxford University Press.

Fiorentine, R., & Hillhouse, M. P. (2000). Exploring the additive effects of drug misuse treatment and twelve step involvement: Does twelve-step ideology matter? *Substance Use and Misuse, 35,* 367–397.

First, M. B. (2010). Commentary on Krueger and Eaton's "Personality traits and the classification of mental disorders: Toward a more complete integration in DSM–5 and an empirical model of psychopathology": Real-world considerations in implementing an empirically based dimensional model of personality in DSM–5. *Personality Disorders: Theory, Research, and Treatment, 1*(2), 123–126.

Fischer, M. (1971). Psychoses in the offspring of schizophrenic monozygotic twins and their normal cotwins. *British Journal of Psychiatry, 118,* 43–52.

Fisher, J. E. (2011). Understanding behavioral health in late life: Why age matters. *Behavior Therapy, 42*(1), 143–149.

Fisher, J. E., & Noll, J. P. (1996). Anxiety disorders. In L. L. Carstensen, B. A. Edelstein, & L. Dornbrand (Eds.), *The practical handbook of clinical gerontology* (pp. 304–323). Thousand Oaks, CA: Sage.

Fisher, M., Holland, C., Merzenich, M. M., & Vinogradov, S. (2009). Using neuroplasticity-based auditory training to improve verbal memory in schizophrenia. *American Journal of Psychiatry, 166,* 805–811.

Fishler, K., Azen, C. G., Henderson, R., Friedman, E. G., & Koch, R. (1987). Psychoeducational findings among children treated for phenylketonuria. *American Journal of Mental Deficiency, 92,* 65–73.

Fitzgibbons, M. L., Spring, B., Avellone, M. E., Blackman, L. R., Pingitore, R., & Stolley, M. R. (1998). Correlates of binge eating in Hispanic, black, and white women. *International Journal of Eating Disorders, 24,* 43–52.

Fladung, A., Gron, G., Grammer, K., Herrnberger, B., Schilly, E., Grasteit, S., . . . von Wietersheim, J. (2010). A neural signature of anorexia nervosa in the ventral striatal reward system. *American Journal of Psychiatry, 167,* 206–212.

Flament, M. F., Whitaker, A., Rapoport, J. L., Davies, M., Berg, C. Z., Kalikow, K., et al. (1988). Obsessive compulsive disorder in adolescence: An epidemiological study. *Journal of the American Academy of Child and Adolescent Psychiatry, 27,* 764–771.

Flaum, M., Amador, X., Gorman, J., Bracha, H. S., Edell, W., McGlashan, T., et al. (1998). *DSM-IV field trial for schizophrenia and other psychotic disorders. DSM-IV sourcebook* (pp. 687–713). Washington, DC: American Psychological Association.

Flegal, K. M., Carroll, M. D., Ogden, C. L., & Curtin, L. R. (2010). Prevalence and trends in obesity among U.S. adults, 1999–2008. *Journal of the American Medical Association, 303,* 235–241.

Foa, E. B., Cahill, S. P., Boscarino, J. A., Hobfoll, S. E., Lahad, M., McNally, R. J., & Solomon, Z. (2005). Social, psychological, and psychiatric interventions following terrorist attacks: Recommendations for practice and research. *Neuropsychopharmacology: Official Publication of the American College of Neuropsychopharmacology, 30*(10), 1806–1817. doi: 10.1038/sj.npp.1300815

Foa, E. B., & Franklin, M. E. (2001). Obsessive-compulsive disorder. In D. H. Barlow (Ed.), *Clinical handbook of psychological disorders* (pp. 209–263). New York: Guilford.

Foa, E. B., Libowitz, M. R., Kozak, M. J., Davies, S., Campeas, R., Franklin, M. E., . . . Tu, X. (2005). Randomized, placebo-controlled trial of exposure and ritual prevention, clomipramine, and their combination in the treatment of obsessive-compulsive disorder. *American Journal of Psychiatry, 162*, 151–161.

Foa, E. B., & Meadows, E. A. (1997). Psychosocial treatments for posttraumatic stress disorder: A critical review. *Annual Review of Psychology, 48*, 449–480.

Foa, E. B., Riggs, D. S., Marsie, E. D., & Yarczower, M. (1995). The impact of fear activation and anger on the efficacy of exposure treatment for posttraumatic stress disorder. *Behavior Therapy, 26*, 487–499.

Folstein, S., & Rutter, M. (1977a). Genetic influences and infantile autism. *Nature, 265*, 726–728.

Folstein, S., & Rutter, M. (1977b). Infantile autism: A genetic study of 21 twin pairs. *Journal of Child Psychology and Psychiatry, 18*, 291–321.

Fontaine, N. M. G., McCrory, E. J. P., Boivin, M., Moffitt, T. E., & Viding, E. (2011). Predictors and outcomes of joint trajectories of callous-unemotional traits and conduct problems in childhood. *Journal of Abnormal Psychology*, advance online publication. doi: 10.1037/a0022620.

Food and Drug Administration. (2005). Deaths with antipsychotics in elderly patients with behavioral disturbances. Public Health Advisory.

Food and Drug Administration. (Jan 31, 2008). Serious Health Risks with Antiepileptic Drugs. Public Health Advisory available at www.fda.gov/consumer/updates/antiepileptic020508.html

Force, A. P. T. (2006). Evidence-based practice in psychology. *American Psychologist, 61*(4), 271–285. doi: 10.1037/0003-066X.61.4.271

Ford, C. S., & Beach, F. A. (1951). *Patterns of sexual behavior*. New York: Harper.

Ford, J. M., Mathalon, D. H., Whitfield, S., Faustman, W. O., & Roth, W. T. (2002). Reduced communication between frontal and temporal lobes during talking in schizophrenia. *Biological Psychiatry, 51*, 485–492.

Forhan, S. E., Gottlieb, S. L., Sternberg, M. R., Xu, F., Datta, S. D., Mcquillan, G. M., . . . Markowitz, L. E. (2009). Prevalence of sexually transmitted infections among female adolescents aged 14 to 19 in the United States. *Pediatrics, 124*, 1505–1512.

Foster, J. H., Marshall, E. J., & Peters, T. J. (2000). Outcome after in-patient detoxification for alcohol dependence: A naturalistic comparison of 7 versus 28 days stay. *Alcohol and Alcoholism, 36*, 580–586.

Foti, D. J., Kotov, R., Guey, L. T., & Bromet, E. J. (2010). Cannabis use and the course of schizophrenia: 10-year follow-up after first hospitalization. *American Journal of Psychiatry, 167*, 987–993.

Fournier, J. C., DeRubeis, R. J., Hollon, S. D., Dimidjian, S., Amsterdam, J. D., Shelton, R. C., & Fawcett, J. (2010). Antidepressant drug effects and depression severity: A patient-level meta-analysis. *Journal of the American Medical Association, 303*, 47–53.

Fowler, I. L., Carr, V. J., Carter, N. T., & Lewin, T. J. (1998). Patterns of current and lifetime substance use in schizophrenia. *Schizophrenia Bulletin, 24*, 443–455.

Frackiewicz, E. J., Sramek, J. J., Herrera, J. M., Kurtz, N. M., & Cutler, N. R. (1997). Ethnicity and antipsychotic response. *Annals of Pharmacotherapy, 31*, 1360–1369.

Fraley, R. C., & Shaver, P. R. (2000). Adult romantic attachment: Theoretical developments, emerging controversies, and unanswered questions. *Review of General Psychology, 4*, 132–154.

Francis, D., Diorio, J., Liu, D., & Meaney, M. J. (1999). Nongenomic transmission across generations of maternal behavior and stress responses in the rat. *Science, 286*, 1155–1158.

Frank, E., Kupfer, D. J., Perel, J. M., Cornes, C., Jarrett, D. B., Mallinger, A. G., . . . Grochocinski, V. (1990).

Three-year outcomes for maintenance therapies in recurrent depression. *Archives of General Psychiatry, 47*, 1093–1099.

Frank, E., Kupfer, D. J., Thase, M. E., Mallinger, A. G., Swartz, H. A., Fagiolini, A. M., . . . Monk, T. (2005). Two-year outcomes for interpersonal and social rhythm therapy in individuals with bipolar I disorder. *Archives of General Psychiatry, 62*, 996–1004.

Frank, E., Swartz, H. A., & Kupfer, D. J. (2000). Interpersonal and social rhythm therapy: Managing the chaos of bipolar disorder. *Biological Psychiatry, 48*, 593–604.

Franklin, J. C., Hessel, E. T., Aaron, R. V., Arthur, M. S., Heilbron, N., & Prinstein, M. J. (2010). The functions of nonsuicidal self-injury: Support for cognitive-affective regulation and opponent processes from a novel psychophysiological paradigm. *Journal of Abnormal Psychology, 119*(4), 850–862. doi: 10.1037/a0020896

Franklin, M. E., & Foa, E. B. (2011). Treatment of obsessive compulsive disorder. *Annual Review of Clinical Psychology, 7*, 229–243. doi: 10.1146/annurev-clinpsy-032210-104533

Franko, D. L., & Keel, P. K. (2006). Suicidality in eating disorders: Occurrence, correlates, and clinical implications. *Clinical Psychology Review, 26*, 769–782.

Frederick, R. I., Mrad, D. F., & DeMier, R. L. (2007). *Examinations of criminal responsibility: Foundations in mental health case law*. Sarasota, FL: Professional Resource Press.

Frederickson, B. L., & Carstensen, L. L. (1990). Choosing social partners: How old age and anticipated endings make people more selective. *Psychology and Aging, 5*, 335–347.

Fredrickson, B. L., & Roberts, T. A. (1997). Objectification theory: Toward understanding women's lived experience and mental health risks. *Psychology of Women Quarterly, 21*, 173–206.

Fredrickson, B. L., Roberts, T. A., Noll, S. M., Quinn, D. M., & Twenge, J. M. (1998). That swimsuit becomes you: Sex differences in self-objectification, restrained eating, and math performance. *Journal of Personality and Social Psychology, 78*, 269–284.

Fredrikson, M., Annas, P., & Wik, G. (1997). Parental history, aversive exposure and the development of snake and spider phobia in women. *Behaviour Research and Therapy, 35*, 23–28.

Freedman, R. (2003). Schizophrenia. *New England Journal of Medicine, 349*, 1738–1749.

Freeman, J. B., Choate-Summers, M. L., Moore, P. S., Garcia, A. M., Sapyta, J. J., Leonard, H. L., & Franklin, M. E. (2007). Cognitive behavioral treatment for young children with obsessive-compulsive disorder. *Biological Psychiatry, 61*, 337–343.

Freeston, M. H., Dugas, M. J., & Ladoceur, R. (1996). Thoughts, images, worry, and anxiety. *Cognitive Therapy and Research, 20*, 265–273.

Fremouw, W. J., De Perczel, M., & Ellis, T. E. (1990). *Suicide risk: Assessment and response guidelines*. New York: Pergamon.

French, S. A., Story, M., Neumark-Sztainer, D., Downes, B., Resnick, M., et al. (1997). Ethnic differences in psychosocial and health behavior correlates of dieting, purging, and binge eating in a population-based sample of adolescent females. *International Journal of Eating Disorders, 22*, 315–322.

Freud, A. (1966). *The ego and mechanisms of defense*. New York: International Universities Press. (Original work published 1946)

Freund, K. (1990). Courtship disorders. In W. L. Marshall, D. R. Laws & H. E. Barbaree (Eds.), *Handbook of sexual*

assault: *Issues, theories, and treatment* (pp. 195–207). New York: Plenum.

Freud, S. (1917/1950). Mourning and melancholia *Collected papers* (Vol. 4). London: Hogarth and the Institute of Psychoanalysis. (Original work published 1917)

Fried, P., Watkinson, B., James, D., & Gray, R. (2002). Current and former marijuana use: Preliminary findings of a longitudinal study of effects on IQ in young adults. *CMAJ, 166*, 887–891.

Friedmann, P. D., Lemon, S. C., & Stein, M. D. (2001). Transportation and retention in outpatient drug abuse treatment programs. *Journal of Substance Abuse Treatment, 21*, 97–103.

Friedrich, M. J. (2002). Epidemic of obesity expands its spread to developing countries. *Journal of the American Medical Association, 287*, 1382–1386.

Frieling, H., Romer, K. D., Scholz, S., Mittelbach, F., Wilhelm, J., De Zwaan, M., et al. (2010). Epigenetic dysregulation of dopaminergic genes in eating disorders. *International Journal of Eating Disorders, 43*, 577–583.

Friend, A., DeFries, J. C., Olson, R. K., & Penningon, B. F. (2009). Heritability of high reading ability and its interaction with parental education. *Behavior Genetics, 39*, 427–436.

Froehlich, T. E., Bogardus, S. T., & Inouye, S. K. (2001). Dementia and race: Are there differences between African Americans and Caucasians? *Journal of the American Gerontological Society, 49*, 477–484.

Frojdh, K., Hakansson, A., Karlsson, I., & Molarius, A. (2003). Deceased, disabled or depressed—a population-based 6-year followup study of elderly people with depression. *Social Psychiatry and Psychiatric Epidemiology, 38*, 557–562.

Fromm-Reichmann, F. (1948). Notes on the development of treatment of schizophrenics by psychoanalytic psychotherapy. *Psychiatry, 11*, 263–273.

Frost, D. O., & Cadet, J.-L. (2000). Effects of methamphetamine-induced toxicity on the development of neural circuitry: A hypothesis. *Brain Research Reviews, 34*, 103–118.

Frost, R., & Steketee, G. (2010). *Stuff: Compulsive hoarding and the meaning of things*: Houghton Mifflin Harcourt.

Frost, R., Steketee, G., & Greene, K. A. I. (2003). Cognitive and behavioral treatment of compulsive hoarding. *Brief Treatment and Crisis Intervention, 3*(3), 323–337.

Frost, R., Tolin, D., Steketee, G., Fitch, K., & Selbo-Bruns, A. (2009). Excessive acquisition in hoarding. *Journal of Anxiety Disorders, 23*(5), 632–639.

Fuller, R. K. (1988). Disulfiram treatment of alcoholism. In R. M. Rose & J. E. Barrett (Eds.), *Alcoholism: Treatment and outcome*. New York: Raven.

Fung, Y. K., & Lau, Y-S. (1989). Effects of prenatal nicotine exposure on rat striatal dopaminergic and nicotinic systems. *Pharmacology, Biochemistry and Behavior, 33*, 1–6.

Furnham, A., & Baguma, P. (1994). Cross-cultural differences in the evaluation of male and female body shapes. *International Journal of Eating Disorders, 15*, 81–89.

Gale, C. R., Batty, G. D., Tynelius, P., Deary, I. J., & Rasmussen, F. (2010). Intelligence in early adulthood and subsequent hospitalization for mental disorders. *Epidemiology, 21*, 70–77.

Galea, S., Ahern, J., Resnick, H., Kilpatrick, D., Bucuvalas, M., Gold, J., & Vlahov, D. (2002). Psychological sequelae of the September 11 terrorist attacks in New York City. *New England Journal of Medicine, 346*, 982–987.

Galea, S., Tracy, M., Hoggatt, K. J., Dimaggio, C., & Karpati, A. (2011). Estimated deaths attributable to social factors in the United States. *American Journal of Public Health, 101*, 1456–1465.

Galli, V., McElroy, S. L., Soutullo, C. A., Kizer, D., Raute, N., et al. (1999). The psychiatric diagnoses of twenty-two adolescents who have sexually molested children. *Comprehensive Psychiatry, 40,* 85–88.

Gallo, C. L., & Pfeffer, C. R. (2003). Children and adolescents bereaved by a suicidal death: Implications for psychosocial outcomes and interventions. In A. Apter & R. A. King (Eds.), *Suicide in Children and adolescents* (pp. 294–312). New York: Cambridge University Press.

Gallo, J. J., & Lebowitz, B. D. (1999). The epidemiology of common late-life mental disorders in the community: Themes for the new century. *Psychiatric Services, 50,* 1158–1166.

Ganellan, R. J. (1996). Comparing the diagnostic efficiency of the MMPI, MCMI-II, and Rorschach: A review. *Journal of Personality Assessment, 67,* 219–243.

Ganguli, M., Du, Y., Dodge, H. H., Ratcliff, G. G., & Chang, C. C. H. (2006). Depressive symptoms and cognitive decline in late life: A prospective epidemiological study. *Archives of General Psychiatry, 63,* 153–160.

Garand, L., Buckwalter, K. C., Lubaroff, D., Tripp-Reimer, T., Frantz, R. A., & Ansley, T. N. (2002). A pilot study of immune and mood outcomes of a community-based intervention for dementia caregivers: The PLST intervention. *Archives of Psychiatric Nursing, 16,* 156–167.

Garb, H. N. (2005). Clinical judgment and decision making. *Annual Review of Clinical Psychology, 1,* 67–89.

Garb, I. I. N. (1997). Race bias, social class bias, and gender bias in clinical judgment. *Clinical Psychology: Science and Practice, 4,* 99–120.

Garber, J. (2006). Depression in children and adolescents: Linking risk research and prevention. *American Journal of Preventative Medicine, 31,* 5104–5125.

Garber, J., Clarke, G. N., Weersing, V. R., Beardslee, W. R., Brent, D. A., Gladstone, T. R., et al. (2009). Prevention of depression in at-risk adolescents: A randomized controlled trial. *Journal of the American Medical Association, 301,* 2215–2224.

Garber, J., & Flynn, C. (2001). Vulnerability to depression in childhood and adolescence. In R. M. Ingram & J. M. Price (Eds.), *Vulnerability to psychopathology: Risk across the lifespan* (pp. 175–225). New York: Guilford.

Garber, J., Kelly, M. K., & Martin, N. C. (2002). Developmental trajectories of adolescents' depressive symptoms: Predictors of change. *Journal of Consulting and Clinical Psychology, 70,* 79–95.

Garbutt, J. C., Mayo, J. P., Little, K. Y., Gillette, G. M., Mason, G. A., Dew, B., & Prange, A. J. J. (1994). Dose-response studies with protirelin. *Archives of General Psychiatry, 51,* 875–883.

Gard, D. E., Kring, A. M., Germans Gard, M., Horan, W. P., & Green, M. F. (2007). Anhedonia in schizophrenia: Distinctions between anticipatory and consummatory pleasure. *Schizophrenia Research, 93,* 253–260.

Garety, P. A., Fowler, D., & Kuipers, E. (2000). Cognitive behavioral therapy for medication-resistant symptoms. *Schizophrenia Bulletin, 26,* 73–86.

Garfield, R. L., Zuvekas, S.H., Lave, J.R., & Donohue, J.M. (2011). The impact of national health care reform on adults with several mental disorders. *American Journal of Psychiatry, 168,* 486–494.

Garfinkel, P. E., Goering, E. L., Goldbloom, S. D., Kennedy, S., Kaplan, A. S., & Woodside, D. B. (1996). Should amenorrhea be necessary for the diagnosis of anorexia nervosa? *British Journal of Psychiatry, 168,* 500–506.

Garfinkel, P. E., Kennedy, S. H., & Kaplan, A. S. (1995). Views on classification and diagnosis of eating disorders. *Canadian Journal of Psychiatry, 40,* 445–456.

Garland, R. J., & Dougher, M. J. (1991). Motivational interviewing in the treatment of sex offenders. In W. R. Miller & S. Rollnick (Eds.), *Motivating interviewing: Preparing people to change addictive behavior* (pp. 303–313). New York: Guilford.

Garner, D. M., Garfinkel, P. E., Schwartz, D., & Thompson, M. (1980). Cultural expectation of thinness in women. *Psychological Reports, 47,* 483–491.

Garner, D. M., Olmsted, M. P., & Polivy, J. (1983). Development and validation of a multi-dimensional eating disorder inventory for anorexia nervosa and bulimia. *International Journal of Eating Disorders, 2,* 15–34.

Garner, D. M., Vitousek, K. M., & Pike, K. M. (1997). Cognitive-behavioral therapy for anorexia nervosa. In D. M. Garner & P. E. Garfinkel (Eds.), *Handbook of treatment for eating disorders* (pp. 94–144). New York: Guilford.

Gatchel, R. J., Peng, Y. B., Peters, M. L., Fuchs, P. N., & Turk, D. C. (2007). The biopsychosocial approach to chronic pain: Scientific advances and future directions. *Psychological Bulletin, 133,* 581–624.

Gatz, M., Reynolds, C. A., Fratiglioni, L., Johansson, B., Mortimer, J. A., Berg, S., . . . Pedersen, N. L. (2006). Roles of genes and environments for explaining Alzheimer disease. *Archives of General Psychiatry, 63,* 168–174.

Gaus, V. L. (2007). *Cognitive behavior therapy for adults with Asperger's syndrome.* New York: Guilford.

Gaw, A. C. (2001). *Concise guide to cross-cultural psychiatry.* Washington, DC: American Psychiatric Association.

Ge, X., Conger, R. D., Cadoret, R. J., Neiderhiser, J. M., Yates, W., Troughton, E., & Stewart, M. A. (1996). The developmental interface between nature and nurture: A mutual influence model of child antisocial behavior and parent behaviors. *Developmental Psychology, 32,* 574–589.

Geddes, J. R., Burgess, S., Hawton, K., Jamison, K., & Goodwin, G. M. (2004). Long-term lithium therapy for bipolar disorder: Systematic review and meta-analysis of randomized controlled trials. *American Journal of Psychiatry, 161,* 217–222.

Geddes, J. R., Carney, S. M., Davies, C., Furukawa, T. A., Frank, E., Kupfer, D. J., & Goodwin, G. (2003). Relapse prevention with antidepressant drug treatment in depressive disorders: A systematic review. *Lancet, 361,* 653–661.

Geller, B., Cooper, T. B., Graham, D., Fetner, H., Marstellar, F., & Wells, J. (1992). Pharmacokinetically designed double-blind placebo-controlled study of nortriptyline in 6 to 12-year-olds with major depressive disorder. *Journal of the American Academy of Child and Adolescent Psychiatry, 31,* 34–44.

Geller, J. L. (2006). A history of private psychiatric hospitals in the USA: From start to almost finished. *Psychiatric Quarterly, 77,* 1–41.

Gendall, K. A., Bulik, C. M., Joyce, P. R., McIntosh, V. V., & Carter, F. A. (2000). Menstrual cycle irregularity in bulimia nervosa: Associated factors and changes with treatment. *Journal of Psychosomatic Research, 49,* 409–415.

General Register Office. (1968). *A glossary of mental disorders.* London: HMSU.

Geracioti, T. D., Baker, D. G., Ekhator, N. N., West, S. A., Hill, K. K., Bruce, A. B., . . . Kasckow, J. W. (2001). CSF norepinephrine concentrations in posttraumatic stress disorder. *American Journal of Psychiatry, 158,* 1227–1230.

Geraerts, E., Schooler, J. W., Merckelbach, H., Jelicic, M., Hauer, B. J. A., & Ambadar, Z. (2007). The reality of recovered memories: Corroborating continuous and discontinuous memories of childhood sexual abuse. *Psychological Science, 18,* 564–568.

Gerlach, A. L., Wilhelm, F. H., Gruber, K., & Roth, W. T. (2001). Blushing and physiological arousability in social phobia. *Journal of Abnormal Psychology, 110,* 247–258.

Gernsbacher, M. A., Dawson, M., & Goldsmith, H. H. (2005). Three reasons not to believe in an autism epidemic. *Current Directions in Psychological Science, 14,* 55–58.

Gerra, G., Zaimovic, A., Ferri, M., Zambelli, U., Timpano, M., Neri, E., . . . Brambilla, F. (2000). Long-lasting effects of (6)3, 4-methylenedioxymethamphetamine (Ecstasy) on serotonin system function in humans. *Biological Psychiatry, 47,* 127–136.

Ghaemi, S. N., & Goodwin, F. K. (2003). Introduction to special issue on antidepressant use in bipolar disorder. *Bipolar Disorders, 5,* 385–387.

Ghosh, A., & Marks, I. (1987). Self-treatment of agoraphobia by exposure. *Behavior Therapy, 18*(1), 3–16.

Giancola, P., & Corman, M. (2007). Alcohol and aggression: A test of the attention-allocation model. *Psychological Science, 18,* 649–655.

Giancola, P. R., Martin, C. S., Tarter, R. E. et al. (1996) Executive cognitive functioning and aggressive behaviour in preadolescent boys at high risk for substance abuse/dependence. *Journal of Studies on Alcohol, 57,* 392–5.

Gibson, D. R. (2001). Effectiveness of syringe exchange programs in reducing HIV risk behavior and seroconversion among injecting drug users. *AIDS, 15,* 1329–1341.

Giesen-Bloo, J., van Dyck, R., Spinhoven, P., van Tilburg, W., Dirksen, C., van Asselt, T., . . . Arntz, A. (2006). Outpatient psychotherapy for borderline personality disorder: Randomized trial of schema-focused therapy vs transference-focused psychotherapy. *Archives of General Psychiatry, 63,* 649–658.

Gilbertson, M. W., Shenton, M. E., Ciszewski, A., Kasai, K., Lasko, N. B., Orr, S. P., & Pitman, R. K. (2002). Smaller hippocampal volume predicts pathologic vulnerability to psychological trauma. *Nature Neuroscience, 5,* 1242–1247.

Gilbody, S., Whitty, P., Grimshaw, J., & Thomas, R. (2003). Educational and organizational interventions to improve the management of depression in primary care: A systematic review. *Journal of American Medical Association, 289,* 3145–3151.

Gill, S., Bronskill, S. E., Normand, S. T., Anderson, G. M., Sykora, K., Lam, K., . . . Rochon, P. A. (2007). Antipsychotic drug use and mortality in older adults with dementia. *Annuals of Internal Medicine, 146,* 775–786.

Gillberg, C. (1991). Outcome in autism and autistic-like conditions. *Journal of the American Academy of Child and Adolescent Psychiatry, 30,* 375–382.

Gillespie, K., Duffy, M., Hackmann, A., & Clark, D. M. (2002). Community based cognitive therapy in the treatment of post-traumatic stress disorder following the Omaha bomb. *Behaviour Research and Therapy, 40,* 345–357.

Gillis, J. J., & DeFries, J. C. (1991). Confirmatory factor analysis of reading and mathematics performance measures in the Colorado Reading Project. *Behavior Genetics, 21,* 572–573.

Glass, C. R., & Arnkoff, D. B. (1997). Questionnaire methods of cognitive self-statement assessment. *Journal of Consulting and Clinical Psychology, 65,* 911–927.

Glassman, A. H., & Bigger, J. T. (2011). *Depression and cardiovascular disease: The safety of antidepressant drugs and their ability to improve mood and reduce medical morbidity.* New York: Wiley.

Glassman, A. H., O'Connor, C. M., Califf, R. M., Swedberg, K., Schwartz, P., Bigger, J. T., . . . Mclvor, M. (2002).

Sertraline treatment of major depression in patients with acute MI or unstable angina. *Journal of the American Medical Association, 288,* 701–709.

Glatt, S. J., Faraone, S. V., & Tsuang, M. (2003). Meta-analysis identifies an association between the dopamine D2 receptor gene and schizophrenia. *Molecular Psychiatry, 8,* 911–915.

Gleaves, D. H. (1996). The sociocognitive model of dissociative identity disorder: A reexamination of the evidence. *Psychological Bulletin, 120,* 42–59.

Glenn, A. L., Raine, A., Venables, P. H., & Mednick, S. A. (2007). Early temperamental and psychophysiological precursors of adult psychopathic personality. *Journal of Abnormal Psychology, 116,* 508–518.

Gloaguen, V., Cottraux, J., Cucherat, M., & Blackburn, I. M. (1998). A meta-analysis of the effects of cognitive therapy in depressed patients. *Journal of Affective Disorders, 49*(1), 59–72.

Godart, N. T., Flament, M. F., Lecrubier, Y., & Jeammet, P. (2000). Anxiety disorders in anorexia nervosa and bulimia nervosa: Co-morbidity and chronology of appearance. *European Psychiatry, 15,* 38–45.

Godart, N. T., Flament, M., Perdereau, F., & Jeammet, P. (2002). Comorbidity between eating disorders and anxiety disorders: A review. *International Journal of Eating Disorders, 32,* 253–270.

Goenjian, A. K., Walling, D., Steinberg, A. M., Karayan, I., Najarian, L. M., & Pynoos, R. (2005). A prospective study of posttraumatic stress and depressive reactions among treated and untreated adolescents 5 years after a catastrophic disaster. *American Journal of Psychiatry, 162,* 2302–2308.

Goldapple, K., Segal, Z., Garson, C., Lau, M., Bieling, P., Kennedy, S., & Mayberg, H. (2004). Modulation of cortical-limbic pathways in major depression. *Archives of General Psychiatry, 61,* 34–41.

Goldberg, T. E., & Weinberger, D. R. (2004). Genes and the parsing of cognitive processes. *Trends in Cognitive Sciences, 8,* 325–335.

Golden, C. J. (1981a). The Luria-Nebraska Children's Battery: Theory and formulation. In G. W. Hynd & J. E. Obrzut (Eds.), *Neuropsychological assessment and the school-age child: Issues and procedures.* New York: Grune & Stratton.

Golden, C. J. (1981b). A standardized version of Luria's neuropsychological tests: A quantitative and qualitative approach to neuropsychological evaluation. In S. B. Filskov & T. J. Boil (Eds.), *Handbook of clinical neuropsychology.* New York: Wiley.

Golden, C. J., Hammeke, T., & Purisch, A. (1978). Diagnostic validity of a standardized neuropsychological battery derived from Luria's neuropsychological tests. *Journal of Consulting and Clinical Psychology, 46,* 1258–1265.

Golden, R. N., Gaynes, B. N., Ekstrom, R. D., Hamer, R. M., Jacobsen, F. M., Suppes, T., . . . Nemeroff, C. B. (2005). The efficacy of light therapy in the treatment of mood disorders: A review and meta-analysis of the evidence. *American Journal of Psychiatry, 162*(4), 656–662.

Golding, J. M., Smith, G. R., & Kashner, T. M. (1991). Does somatization disorder occur in men? Clinical characteristics of women and men with unexplained somatic symptoms. *Archives of General Psychiatry, 48,* 231–235.

Goldman-Rakic, P. S., & Selemon, L. D. (1997). Functional and anatomical aspects of prefrontal pathology in schizophrenia. *Schizophrenia Bulletin, 23,* 437–458.

Goldstein, A. J., & Chambless, D. L. (1978). A reanalysis of agoraphobic behavior. *Behavior Therapy, 9,* 47–59.

Goldstein, A. J., de Beurs, E., Chambless, D. L., & Wilson, K. A. (2000). EMDR for panic disorder with agoraphobia: Comparison with waiting list and credible attention-placebo control conditions. *Journal of Consulting and Clinical Psychology, 68,* 947–956.

Goldstein, J. M., Buka, S. L., Seidman, L. J., & Tsuang, M. T. (2010). Specificity of familial transmission of schizophrenia psychosis spectrum and affective psychoses in the New England Family Study's high-risk design. *Archives of General Psychiatry, 67,* 458–467.

Gomez, F. C., Piedmont, R. L., & Fleming, M. Z. (1992). Factor analysis of the Spanish version of the WAIS: The Escala de Inteligencia Wechsler para Adultos (EIWA). *Psychological Assessment, 4,* 317–321.

Gonzalez, H. M., Vega, W. A., Williams, D. R., Tarraf, W., West, B. T., & Neighbors, H. W. (2010). Depression care in the United States: Too little for too few. *Archives of General Psychiatry, 67*(1), 37–46.

Goodkind, M. S., Gyurak, A., McCarthy, M., Miller, B. L., & Levenson, R. W. (2010). Emotion regulation deficits in frontotemporal lobar degeneration and Alzheimer's disease. *Psychological Aging, 25,* 30–37.

Goodman, G. S., Ghetti, S., Quas, J. A., Edelstein, R. S., Alexander, K. W., Redlich, A. D., . . . Jones, D. P. H. (2003). A prospective study of memory for child sexual abuse: New findings relevant to the repressed-memory controversy. *Psychological Science, 14,* 113–118.

Goodwin, F., & Jamison, K. (1990). *Manic-depressive illness.* New York: Oxford University Press.

Gopnik, A., Capps, L., & Meltzoff, A. N. (2000). Early theories of mind: What the theory can tell us about autism. In S. Baren-Cohen, H. Tager-Flusberg, & D. Cohen (Eds.), *Understanding other minds* (2nd ed., pp. 50–72). Oxford, England: Oxford University Press.

Gordon, K. H., Perez, M., & Joiner, T. E. (2002). The impact of racial stereotypes on eating disorder recognition. *International Journal of Eating Disorders, 32,* 219–224.

Gotlib, H., & Hamilton, J. P. (2008). Neuroimaging and depression: Current status and unresolved issues. *Current Directions in Psychological Science, 17*(2), 159–163.

Gotlib, H., & Joormann, J. (2010). Cognition and depression: Current status and future directions. *Annual Review of Clinical Psychology, 6,* 285–312.

Gottesman, I. I., & Goldsmith, H. H. (1994). Developmental psychopathology of antisocial behavior: Inserting genes into its ontogenesis and epigenesis. In C. A. Nelson (Ed.), *Threats to optimal development.* Hillside, NJ: Erlbaum.

Gottesman, I. I., Laursen, T. M., Bertelsen, A., & Mortensen, P. B. (2010). Severe mental disorders in offspring with 2 psychiatrically ill parents. *Archives of General Psychiatry, 67,* 252–257.

Gottesman, I. I., McGuffin, P., & Farmer, A. E. (1987). Clinical genetics as clues to the "real" genetics of schizophrenia. *Schizophrenia Bulletin, 13,* 23–47.

Goveas, J. S., Espeland, M. A., Woods, N. F., Wassertheil-Smoller, S., & Kotchen, J. M. (2011). Depressive symptoms and incidence of mild cognitive impairment and probable dementia in elderly women: The Women's Health Initiative Memory Study. *Journal of the American Geriatrics Society, 59*(1), 57–66.

Goyette, C. H., & Conners, C. K. (1977). *Food additives and hyperkinesis.* Paper presented at the 85th Annual Convention of the American Psychological Association.

Grabe, S., & Hyde, J. S. (2006). Ethnicity and body dissatisfaction among women in the United States: A meta-analyis. *Psychological Bulletin, 132,* 622–640.

Grady, D. (1999). A great pretender now faces the truth of illness. *New York Times.*

Graham, C. A. (2010). The DSM diagnostic criteria for female sexual arousal disorder. *Archives of Sexual Behavior, 39*(2), 240–255. doi: 10.1007/s10508-009-9535-1

Graham, J. R. (1988). *Establishing validity of the revised form of the MMPI.* Symposium presentation at the 96th annual convention of the American Psychological Association, Atlanta.

Graham, J. R. (1990). *MMPI-2: Assessing personality and psychopathology.* New York: Oxford University Press.

Grandin, T. (1986). *Emergence: Labeled autistic.* Novato, CA: Arena Press.

Grandin, T. (1995). *Thinking in pictures.* New York: Doubleday.

Grandin, T. (2008). *The way I see it: A personal look at autism and Asperger's.* Arlington, TX: Future Horizons.

Grant, B. F., & Dawson, D. A. (1997). Age of onset at alcohol use and its association with DSM-IV alcohol abuse and dependence: Results from the national longitudinal epidemiologic survey. *Journal of Substance Abuse, 9,* 103–110.

Green, J. G., McLaughlin, K. A., Berglund, P. A., Gruber, M. J., Sampson, N. A., Zaslavsky, A. M., & Kessler, R. C. (2010). Childhood adversities and adult psychiatric disorders in the National Comorbidity Survey Replication: Associations with first onset of DSM-IV disorders. *Archives of General Psychiatry, 67*(2), 113–123.

Green, M. F. (1996). What are the functional consequences of neurocognitive deficits in schizophrenia? *American Journal of Psychiatry, 153,* 321–330.

Green, M. F., Kern, R. S., Braff, D. L., & Mintz, J. (2000). Neurocognitive deficits and functional outcome in schizophrenia: Are we measuring the "right stuff"? *Schizophrenia Bulletin, 26,* 119–136.

Green, M. F., Marshall, B. D., Wirshing, W. C., Ames, D., Marder, S. R., McGurk, S., . . . Mintz, J. (1997). Does risperidone improve verbal working memory in treatment-resistant schizophrenia? *American Journal of Psychiatry, 154,* 799–804.

Green, R., & Fleming, D. T. (1990). Transsexual surgery follow-up: Status in the 1990s. In J. Bancroft, C. Davis, & D. Weinstein (Eds.), *Annual review of sex research* (pp. 163–174).

Griffin, M. G., Resick, P. A., & Mechanic, M. B. (1997). Objective assessment of peritraumatic dissociation: Psychophysiological indicators. *American Journal of Psychiatry, 154*(8), 1081–1088.

Grillon, C. (2002). Startle reactivity and anxiety disorders: Aversive conditioning, context, and neurobiology. *Biological Psychiatry, 52,* 958–975.

Grilo, C. M. (2007). Treatment of binge eating disorder. In S. Wonderlich, J. E. Mitchell, M. d. Zwaan, & H. Steiger (Eds.), *Annual review of eating disorders* (pp. 23–34). Oxford, England: Radcliffe.

Grilo, C. M., Shea, M. T., Sanislow, C. A., Skodol, A. E., Gunderson, J. G., Stout, R. L., . . . McGlashan, T. (2004). Two-year stability and change of schizotypal, borderline, avoidant, and obsessive-compulsive personality disorders. *Journal of Consulting and Clinical Psychology, 72,* 767–775.

Grilo, C. M., Shiffman, S., & Carter-Campbell, J. T. (1994). Binge eating antecedents in normal weight nonpurging females: Is there consistency? *International Journal of Eating Disorders, 16,* 239–249.

Grinker, R. R., & Spiegel, J. P. (1944). *Management of neuropsychiatric casualties in the zone of combat: Manual of military neuropsychiatry.* Philadelphia: Saunders.

Grinspoon, L., & Bakalar, J. B. (1995). Marijuana as medicine: A plea for reconsideration. *Journal of the American Medical Association, 273*, 1875–1876.

Grippo, A. J. (2009). Mechanisms underlying altered mood and cardiovascular dysfunction: The value of neurobiological and behavioral research with animal models. *Neuroscience and Biobehavioral Reviews, 33*(2), 171–180. doi: 10.1016/j.neubiorev.2008.07.004

Grisham, J. R., Frost, R. O., Steketee, G., Kim, H. J., & Hood, S. (2006). Age of onset of compulsive hoarding. *Journal of Anxiety Disorders, 20*(5), 675–686. doi: 10.1016/j.janxdis.2005.07.004

Grisso, T., & Appelbaum, P. S. (1991). Mentally ill and non-mentally ill patients' abilities to understand informed consent disclosures for medication: Preliminary data. *Law and Human Behavior, 15*, 377–388.

Grisso, T., Davis, J., Vesselinov, R. Appelbaum, P. S. & Monahan, J. (2000). Violent thoughts and violent behavior following hospitalization for mental disorder. *Journal of Consulting and Clinical Psychology, 68*, 388–398.

Groesz, L. M., Levine, M. P., & Murnen, S. K. (2002). The effect of experimental presentation of thin media images on body dissatisfaction: A meta-analytic review. *International Journal of Eating Disorders, 31*, 1–16.

Gross, C., Zhuang, X., Stark, K., Ramboz, S., Oosting, R., Kirby, L., . . . Hen, R. (2002). Serotonin 1A receptor acts during development to establish normal anxiety-like behaviour in the adult. *Nature, 416*, 396–400.

Grossman, D. (1995). *On killing: The psychological cost of learning to kill in war and society.* Boston: Little, Brown.

Guastella, A. J., Richardson, R., Lovibond, P. F., Rapee, R. M., Gaston, J. E., Mitchell, P., & Dadds, M. R. (2008). A randomized controlled trial of D-cycloserine enhancement of exposure therapy for social anxiety disorder. *Biological Psychiatry, 63*, 544–549.

Gum, A. M., King-Kallimanis, B., & Kohn, R. (2009). Prevalence of mood, anxiety, and substance-abuse disorders for older Americans in the National Comorbidity Survey–Replication. *American Journal of Psychiatry, 17*(9), 769–781.

Gump, B. S., Matthews, K. A., & Räikkönen, K. (1999). Modeling relationships among socioeconomic status, hostility, cardiovascular reactivity, and left ventricular mass in African American and white children. *Health Psychology, 18*, 140–150.

Gunn, J. (1993). Castration is not the answer. *British Medical Journal, 307*, 790–791.

Guo, X., Zhai, J., Liu, Z., Fang, M., Wang, B., Wang, C., Hu, B., Sun, X., et al. (2010). Effect of antipsychotic medication alone vs combined with psychosocial intervention on outcomes of early-stage schizophrenia. *Archives of General Psychiatry, 67*, 895–904.

Gur, R. E., & Pearlson, G. D. (1993). Neuroimaging in schizophrenia research. *Schizophrenia Bulletin, 19*, 337–353.

Gur, R. E., Turetsky, B. I., Cowell, P. E., et al. (2000). Temporolimbic volume reductions in schizophrenia. *Archives of General Psychiatry, 57*, 769–776.

Gustad, J., & Phillips, K. A. (2003). Axis I comorbidity in body dysmorphic disorder. *Comprehensive Psychiatry, 44*, 270–276.

Gutman, D. A., & Nemeroff, C. B. (2003). Persistent central nervous system effects of an adverse early environment: Clinical and preclinical studies. *Physiology and Behavior, 79*, 471–478.

Guyll, M., Matthews, K. A., & Bromberger, J. T. (2001). Discrimination and unfair treatment: Relationship to cardiovascular reactivity among African American and European American women. *Health Psychology, 20*, 315–325.

Haaga, D. A. F., Dyck, M. J., & Ernst, D. (1991). Empirical status of cognitive theory of depression. *Psychological Bulletin, 110*, 215–236.

Haaga, D. A. F., & Stiles, W. B. (2000). Randomized clinical trials in psychotherapy research: Methodology, design and evaluation. In R. E. Ingram & C. Snyder (Eds.), *Handbook of psychological change: Psychotherapy processes and practices for the 21st century* (pp. 14–39). New York: Wiley.

Haas, R. H., Townsend, J., Courchesne, E., Lincoln, A. J., Schreibman, L., & Yeung-Courchesne, R. (1996). Neurologic abnormalities in infantile autism. *Journal of Child Neurology, 11*, 84–92.

Hacking, I. (1998). *Mad travelers: Reflections on the reality of transient mental illness.* Charlottesville: University Press of Virginia.

Haddock, G., Tarrier, N., Spaulding, W., Yusupoff, L. K., & McCarthy, E. (1998). Individual cognitive-behavior therapy in the treatment of hallucinations and delusions: A review. *Clinical Psychology Review, 18*, 821–838.

Haedt-Matt, A. A., & Keel, P. K. (2011). Revisiting the affect regulation model of binge eating: A meta-analysis of studies using ecological momentary assessment. *Psychological Bulletin, 137*, 660–681.

Hagerman, R. (2006). Lessons from fragile X regarding neurobiology, autism, and neurodegeneration. *Developmental and Behavioral Pediatrics, 27*, 63–74.

Hall, G. C. (2001). Psychotherapy research with ethnic minorities: Empirical, ethical, and conceptual issues. *Journal of Consulting and Clinical Psychology, 69*(3), 502–510.

Hall, G. C., Hirschman, R., & Oliver, L. L. (1995). Sexual arousal and arousability to pedophilic stimuli in a community sample of normal men. *Behavior Therapy, 26*, 681–694.

Hallmayer, J., Cleveland, S., Torres, A., Phillips, J., Cohen, B., Torigoe, T., Miller, J., Fedele, A., et al. (2011). Genetic heritability and shared environmental factors among twin pairs with autism. *Archives of General Psychiatry*, E1-E8. doi:10.1001/archgenpsychiatry.2011.1076.

Halmi, K. A., Sunday, S. R., Strober, M., Kaplan, A., Woodside, D. B., Fichter, N., . . . Kaye, W. (2000). Perfectionism in anorexia nervosa: Variation by clinical subtype, obsessionality, and pathological eating behavior. *American Journal of Psychiatry, 157*, 1799–1805.

Hamer, M., & Chida, Y. (2009). Physical activity and risk of neurodegenerative disease: A systematic review of prospective evidence. *Psychological Medicine, 39*(1), 3–11. doi: 10.1017/S0033291708003681

Hammen, C. (1997). Children of depressed parents: The stress context. In S. A. Wolchik & I. N. Sandler (Eds.), *Handbook of children's coping: Linking theory and intervention. Issues in clinical child psychology* (pp. 131–157). New York: Plenum.

Hammen, C. (2009). Adolescent depression: Stressful interpersonal contexts and risk for recurrence. *Current Directions in Psychological Science, 18*, 200–204.

Hammen, C., & Brennan, P. (2001). Depressed adolescents of depressed and nondepressed mothers: Tests of an interpersonal impairment hypothesis. *Journal of Consulting and Clinical Psychology, 69*, 284–294.

Hankin, B. J., Abramson, L. Y., Moffitt, T. E., Silva, P. A., McGee, R., et al. (1998). Development of depression from preadolescence to young adulthood: Emerging gender differences in a 10-year longitudinal study. *Journal of Abnormal Psychology, 107*, 128–140.

Hankin, B. L., & Abramson, L. Y. (2001). Development of gender differences in depression: An elaborated cognitive vulnerability-transactional stress theory. *Psychological Bulletin, 127*, 773–796.

Hankin, B. L., Mermelstein, R., & Roesch, L. (2007). Sex differences in adolescent depression: Stress exposure and reactivity models. *Child Development, 78*, 279–295.

Hansen, W. B. (1992). School-based substance abuse prevention: A review of the state of the art in curriculum, 1980–1990. *Health Education Research: Theory and Practice, 7*, 403–430.

Hansen, W. B. (1993). School-based alcohol prevention programs. *Alcohol Health and Research World, 18*, 62–66.

Hansen, W. B., & Graham, J. W. (1991). Preventing alcohol, marijuana, and cigarette use among adolescents: Peer pressure resistance training versus establishing conservative norms. *Preventive Medicine, 20*, 414–430.

Hanson, R. K., & Bussiere, M. T. (1998). Predicting relapse: A meta-analysis of sexual offender recidivism studies. *Journal of Consulting and Clinical Psychology, 66*, 348–362.

Hanson, R. K., & Harris, A. J. R. (1997). Voyeurism: Assessment and treatment. In D. R. Laws & W. O'Donohue (Eds.), *Sexual deviance* (pp. 311–331). New York: Guilford.

Hardan, A. Y., Minshew, N. J., Harenski, K., & Keshavan, M. S. (2001). Posterior fossa magnetic resonance imaging in autism. *Journal of the American Academy of Child and Adolescent Psychiatry, 40*, 666–672.

Harden, K. P., Hill, J. E., Turkheimer, E., & Emery, R. E. (2008). Gene-environment correlation and interaction in peer effects on adolescent alcohol and tobacco use. *Behavior Genetics, 38*, 339–347.

Hare, R. D. (2003). *The Hare psychopathy checklist* (rev. ed.). Toronto, Canada: Multi-Health System.

Hare, R. D., & Neumann, C. N. (2006). The PCL-R assessment of psychopathy: Development, structural properties, and new directions. In C. Patrick (Ed.), *Handbook of psychopathy* (pp. 58–88). New York: Guilford.

Harenski, C. L., Harenski, K. A., Shane, M. S., & Kiehl, K. A. (2010). Aberrant neural processing of moral violations in criminal psychopaths. *Journal of Abnormal Psychology, 119*, 863–874.

Hariri, A. R., Drabant, E. M., Munoz, K. E., Kolachana, B. S., Mattay, V. S., Egan, M. F., & Weinberger, D. R. (2005). A susceptibility gene for affective disorders and the response of the human amygdala. *Archives of General Psychiatry, 62*, 146–152.

Harkin, A., Connor, T. J., Mulrooney, J., Kelly, J. P., & Leonard, B. E. (2001). Prior exposure to methylenedioxyamphetamine (MDA) induces serotonergic loss and changes in spontaneous exploratory and amphetamine-induced behaviors in rats. *Life Sciences, 68*, 1367–1382.

Harrington, A. (2008). *The cure within: A history of mind-body medicine.* New York: Norton.

Harris, J. L., Bargh, J. A. & Brownell, K. (2009). Priming effects of television food advertising on eating behavior. *Health Psychology, 28*, 404–413.

Harrison, P. J., & Weinberger, D. R. (2004). Schizophrenia genes, gene expression, and neuropathology: On the matter of their convergence. *Molecular Psychiatry, 10*, 1–29.

Harrow, M., Goldberg, J. F., Grossman, L. S., & Meltzer, H. Y. (1990). Outcome in manic disorders: A naturalistic follow-up study. *Archives of General Psychiatry, 47*, 665–671.

Hart, E. L., Lahey, B. B., Loeber, R., Applegate, B., & Frick, P. J. (1995). Developmental changes in attention-deficit hyperactivity disorder in boys: A four-year longitudinal study. *Journal of Abnormal Child Psychology, 23,* 729–750.

Hartl, T. L., Duffany, S. R., Allen, G. J., Steketee, G., & Frost, R. O. (2005). Relationships among compulsive hoarding, trauma, and attention-deficit/hyperactivity disorder. *Behaviour Research and Therapy, 43*(2), 269–276. doi: 10.1016/j.brat.2004.02.002

Hartmann, U., Heiser, K., Ruffer-Hesse, C., & Kloth, G. (2002). Female sexual desire disorders: Subtypes, classification, personality factors and new directions for treatment. *World Journal of Urology, 20,* 79–88.

Hartz, D. T., Fredrick-Osborne, S. L., & Galloway, G. P. (2001). Craving predicts use during treatment for methamphetamine dependence: A prospective repeated-measures, within-subjects analysis. *Drug and Alcohol Dependence, 63,* 269–276.

Harvard Mental Health Letter. (1995, July). Schizophrenia update—Part II, *12,* 1–5.

Harvey, A. G., & Bryant, R. A. (2002). Acute stress disorder: A synthesis and critique. *Psychological Bulletin, 128,* 886–902.

Harvey, A. G., Mullin, B. C., & Hinshaw, S. P. (2006). Sleep and circadian rhythms in children and adolescents with bipolar disorder. *Development and Psychopathology, 18,* 1147–1168.

Harvey, A. G., Watkins, E., Mansell, W., & Shafran, R. (2004). *Cognitive behavioural processes across psychological disorders: A transdiagnostic approach to research and treatment.* Oxford, England: Oxford University Press.

Harvey, P. D., Green, M. F., Keefe, R. S. I., & Velligan, D. (2004). Changes in cognitive functioning with risperidone and olanzapine treatment: A large-scale, double-blind, randomized study. *Journal of Clinical Psychiatry, 65,* 361–372.

Harvey, P. D., Green, M. F., McGurk, S., & Meltzer, H. Y. (2003). Changes in cognitive functioning with risperidone and olanzapine treatment: A large-scale, double-blind, randomized study. *Psychopharmacology, 169,* 404–411.

Hasin, D. S., Stinson, F. S., Ogburn, E., & Grant, B. F. (2007). Prevalence, correlates, disability, and comorbidity of DSM-IV alcohol abuse and dependence in the United States: Results from the National Epidemiologic Survey on Alcohol and Related Conditions. *Archives of General Psychiatry, 64,* 830–842.

Haslam, C., Brown, S., Atkinson, S., & Haslam, R. (2004). Patients' experiences of medication for anxiety and depression: Effects on working life. *Family Practice, 21,* 204–212.

Hathaway, S. R., & McKinley, J. C. (1943). *MMPI manual.* New York: Psychological Corporation.

Hawkins, J. D., Graham, J. W., Maguin, E., Abbott, R., et al. (1997). Exploring the effects of age of alcohol use initiation and psychosocial risk factors on subsequent alcohol misuse. *Journal of Studies on Alcohol, 58,* 280–290.

Hawton, K., Catalan, J., Martin, P., & Fagg, J. (1986). Long term outcome of sex therapy. *Behaviour Research and Therapy, 24,* 665–675.

Hayes, R. D., Dennerstein, L., Bennett, C. M., Sidat, M., Gurrin, L. C., & Fairley, C. K. (2008). Risk factors for female sexual dysfunction in the general population: Exploring factors associated with low sexual function and sexual distress. *Journal of Sexual Medicine, 5*(7), 1681–1693. doi:10.1111/j.1743-6109.2008.00838.x

Hayes, S. C. (2005). *Get out of your mind and into your life: The new acceptance and commitment therapy.* Oakland, CA: New Harbinger.

Hayes, S. C., Masuda, A., Bissett, R., Luoma, J., & Guerrero, L.F. (2004). DBT, FAR and ACT: How empirically

oriented are the new behavior therapy technologies? *Behavior Therapy, 35,* 35–54.

Haynes, S. N., & Horn, W. F. (1982). Reactivity in behavioral observation: A review. *Behavioral Assessment, 4,* 369–385.

Hazel, N. A., Hamman, C., Brennan, P. A., & Najman, J. (2008). Early childhood adversity and adolescent depression: The mediating role of continued stress. *Psychological Medicine, 38,* 581–589.

Hazlett, H. C., Poe, M. D., Gerig, G., Styner, M., Chappell, C., Smith, R. G., . . . Priven, J. (2011). Early brain overgrowth in autism associated with an increase in cortical surface area before age 2 years. *Archives of General Psychiatry, 68,* 467–476.

Heatherton, T. F., & Baumeister, R. F. (1991). Binge eating as escape from self-awareness. *Psychological Bulletin, 110,* 86–108.

Heatherton, T. F., Herman, C. P., & Polivy, J. (1991). Effects of physical threat and ego threat on eating behavior. *Journal of Personality and Social Psychology, 60,* 138–143.

Heinrichs, R. W., & Zakzanis, K. K. (1998). Neurocognitive deficits in schizophrenia: A quantitative review of the evidence. *Neuropsychology, 12,* 426–445.

Heinssen, R. K., Liberman, R. P., & Kopelowicz, A. (2000). Psychosocial skills training for schizophrenia: Lessons from the laboratory. *Schizophrenia Bulletin, 26,* 21–46.

Heiss, G., Wallace, R., Anderson, G. L., Aragaki, A., Beresford, S. A. A., et al. (2008). Health risks and benefits 3 years after stopping randomized treatment with estrogen and progestin. *Journal of the American Medical Association, 299,* 1036–1045.

Heller, T. L., Baker, B. L., Henker, B., & Hinshaw, S. P. (1996). Externalizing behavior and cognitive functioning from preschool to first grade: Stability and predictors. *Journal of Clinical Child Psychology, 25,* 376–387.

Helmuth, L. (2003). In sickness or in health? *Science, 302,* 808–810.

Henggeler, S. W., & Sheidow, A. J. Multisystemic therapy with substance abusing adolescents: A synthesis of the research. In N. Jainchill (Ed.), *Understanding and treating substance use disorders.* Kingston, NJ: Civic Research Institute.

Henggeler, S. W., Schoenwald, S. D., Borduin, C. M., Rowland, M. D., & Cunningham, P. B. (1998). *Multisystemic treatment of antisocial behavior in children and adolescents.* New York: Guilford.

Henningfield, J. E., Michaelides, T., & Sussman, S. (2000). Developing treatment for tobacco addicted youth—issues and challenges. *Journal of Child and Adolescent Substance Abuse, 9,* 5–26.

Henriques, G., Wenzel, A., Brown, G. K., & Beck, A. T. (2005). Suicide attempter's reaction to survival as a risk factor for eventual suicide. *American Journal of Psychiatry, 162,* 2180–2182.

Herbenick, D., Reece, M., Schick, V., Sanders, S. A., Dodge, B., & Fortenberry, J. D. (2010a). An event-level analysis of the sexual characteristics and composition among adults ages 18 to 59: Results from a national probability sample in the United States. *Journal of Sexual Medicine, 7* (Suppl. 5), 346–361. doi: 10.1111/j.1743-6109.2010.02020.x

Herbenick, D., Reece, M., Schick, V., Sanders, S. A., Dodge, B., & Fortenberry, J. D. (2010b). Sexual behavior in the United States: Results from a national probability sample of men and women ages 14–94. *Journal of Sexual Medicine, 7* (Suppl. 5), 255–265. doi: 10.1111/j.1743-6109.2010.02012.x

Herbert, M. A., Gerry, N. P., McQueen, I. M., Heid, A. P., Illig, T., et al. (2006). Common genetic variant is

associated with adult and childhood obesity. *Science, 312,* 279–312.

Herdt, G. H. (Ed.). (1984). *Ritualized homosexuality in Melanesia.* Berkeley: University of California Press.

Herman, C. P., Polivy, J., Lank, C., & Heatherton, T. F. (1987). Anxiety, hunger, and eating. *Journal of Abnormal Psychology, 96,* 264–269.

Herman, J. L., Perry, J. C., & van der Kolk, B. A. (1989). Childhood trauma in borderline personality disorder. *American Journal of Psychiatry, 146,* 490–495.

Hermans, D., Engelen, U., Grouwels, L., Joos, E., Lemmens, J., & Pieters, G. (2008). Cognitive confidence in obsessive-compulsive disorder: Distrusting perception, attention and memory. *Behaviour Research and Therapy, 46*(1), 98–113. doi: 10.1016/j.brat.2007.11.001

Herpetz, S. C., Dietrich, T. M., Wenning, B., Krings, T., Erberich, S. G., Willmes, K., . . . Sass, H. (2001). Evidence of abnormal amygdala functioning in borderline personality disorder: A functional MRI study. *Biological Psychiatry, 50,* 292–298.

Hersen, M., & Barlow, D. H. (1976). *Single case experimental designs: Strategies for studying behavior change.* New York: Pergamon.

Herzog, D. B., Greenwood, D. N., Dorer, D. J., Flores, A. T., Ekeblad, E. R., Richards, A., . . . Keller, M. B. (2000). Mortality in eating disorders: A descriptive study. *International Journal of Eating Disorders, 28,* 20–26.

Heston, L. L. (1966). Psychiatric disorders in foster home reared children of schizophrenic mothers. *British Journal of Psychiatry, 112,* 819–825.

Heston, L. L. and R. Heston, (1979). The medical casebook of Adolf Hitler: his illnesses, doctors and drugs. Kimber.

Hettema, J. M., Neale, M. C., & Kendler, K. S. (2001). A review and meta-analysis of the genetic epidemiology of the anxiety disorders. *American Journal of Psychiatry, 158,* 1568–1578.

Hettema, J. M., Prescott, C. A., Myers, J. M., Neale, M. C., & Kendler, K. S. (2005). The structure of genetic and environmental risk factors for anxiety disorders in men and women. *Archives of General Psychiatry, 62,* 182–189.

Heuser, I., Yassouridis, A., & Holsboer, F. (1994). The combined dexamethasone CRH test: A refined laboratory test for psychiatric disorders. *Journal of Psychiatric Research, 28,* 341–346.

Heyman, I., Fombonne, E., Simmons, H., Ford, T., Meltzer, H., & Goodman, R. (2003). Prevalence of obsessive-compulsive disorder in the British nationwide survey of child mental health. *International Review of Psychiatry, 15,* 178–184.

Heyn, P., Abreu, B. C., & Ottenbacher, K. J. (2004). Meta-analysis: The effects of exercise training on elderly persons with cognitive impairment and dementia: A meta-analysis. *Archives of Physical Medicine and Rehabilitation, 85,* 1694–1704.

Hibbeln, J. R., Nieminen, L. R. G., Blasbalg, T. L., Riggs, J. A., & Lands, W. E. M. (2006). Healthy intakes of n–3 and n–6 fatty acids: Estimations considering worldwide diversity. *Journal of Clinical Nutrition, 83,* 1483S–1493S.

Hietala, J., Syvalahti, E., Vuorio, K., Nagren, K., Lehikoinen, P., et al. (1994). Striatal D2 dopamine receptor characteristics in drug-naive schizophrenic patients studied with positive emission tomography. *Archives of General Psychiatry, 51,* 116–123.

Hill, A., Briken, P., Kraus, C., Strohm, K., & Berner, W. (2003). Differential pharmacological treatment of paraphilias and sex offenders. *International Journal of Offender Therapy and Comparative Criminology, 47*(4), 407–421.

Hingson, R. W., Edwards, E. M., Heeren, T., & Rosenbloom, D. (2009). Age of drinking onset and injuries, motor vehicle crashes, and physical fights after drinking and when not drinking. *Alcoholism, Clinical and Experimental Research, 33*, 783–790.

Hinshaw, S. P. (1987). On the distinction between attentional deficits/hyperactivity and conduct problems/aggression in child psychopathology. *Psychological Bulletin, 101*, 443–463.

Hinshaw, S. P. (2002). Preadolescent girls with attention-deficit/hyperactivity disorder: I. Background characteristics, comorbidity, cognitive and social functioning, and parenting practices. *Journal of Consulting and Clinical Psychology, 70*, 1086–1098.

Hinshaw, S. P. (2007). *The mark of shame: The stigma of mental illness and an agenda for change.* New York: Oxford University Press.

Hinshaw, S. P., Carte, E. T., Sami, N., Treuting, J. J., & Zupan, B. A. (2002). Preadolescent girls with attention-deficit/hyperactivity disorder: II. Neuropsychological performance in relation to subtypes and individual classification. *Journal of Consulting and Clinical Psychology, 70*, 1099–1111.

Hinshaw, S. P., & Lee, S. S. (2003). Oppositional defiant and conduct disorders. In E. J. Mash & R. A. Barkley (Eds.), *Child psychopathology* (2nd ed., pp. 144–198). New York: Guilford.

Hinshaw, S. P., & Melnick, S. M. (1995). Peer relationships in boys with attention-deficit hyperactivity disorder with and without comorbid aggression. *Development and Psychopathology, 7*, 627–647.

Hinshaw, S. P., Owens, E. B., Sami, N., & Fargeon, S. (2006). Prospective follow-up of girls with attention-deficit/hyperactivity disorder into adolescence: Evidence for continuing cross-domain impairment. *Journal of Consulting and Clinical Psychology, 74*, 489–499.

Hinshaw, S. P., Owens, E. B., Wells, K. C., et al. (2000). Family processes and treatment outcome in the MTA: Negative/Ineffective parenting practices in relation to multimodal treatment. *Journal of Abnormal Child Psychology, 28*, 555–568.

Hinshaw, S. P., Zupan, B. A., Simmel, C., Nigg, J. T., & Melnick, S. (1997). Peer status in boys with and without attention-deficit hyperactivity disorder: Predictions from overt and covert antisocial behavior, social isolation, and authoritative parenting beliefs. *Child Development, 68*, 880–896.

Hinton, D., Ba, P., Peou, S., & Um, K. (2000). Panic disorder among Cambodian refugees attending a psychiatric clinic. *General Hospital Psychiatry, 22*, 437–444.

Hinton, E., Um, K., & Ba, P. (2001). Kyol goeu ('wind overload') Part II: Prevalence, characteristics, and mechanisms of kyol goeu and near kyol goeu episodes of Khmer patients attending a psychiatric clinic. *Transcultural Psychiatry, 38*, 433–460.

Hirsch, C. R., & Clark, D. M. (2004). Mental imagery and social phobia. In J. Yiend (Ed.), *Cognition, emotion and psychopathology: Theoretical, empirical and clinical directions* (pp. 232–250). Cambridge, England: Cambridge University Press.

Ho, B. C., Milev, P., O'Leary, D. S., Librant, A., Flaum, M., Andreasen, N. C., & Wassink, T. (2006). Cognitive and magnetic resonance imaging brain morphometric correlates of brain-derived neurotrophic factor Val66Met gene polymorphism in patients with schizophrenia and healthy volunteers. *Archives of General Psychiatry, 63*, 731–740.

Ho, B. C., Nopoulos, P., Flaum, M., Arndt, S., & Andreasen, N. C. (1998). Two-year outcome in first-episode schizophrenia: Predictive value of symptoms for quality of life. *American Journal of Psychiatry, 155*, 1196–1201.

Hobson, R. P., & Lee, A. (1998). Hello and goodbye: A study of social engagement in autism. *Journal of Autism and Developmental Disorders, 28*, 117–127.

Hodges, E. L., Cochrane, C. E., & Brewerton, T. D. (1998). Family characteristics of binge-eating disorder patients. *International Journal of Eating Disorders, 23*, 145–151.

Hoebel, B. G., & Teitelbaum, P. (1966). Weight regulation in normal and hypothalamic hyperphagic rats. *Journal of Comparative and Physiological Psychology, 61*, 189–193.

Hoek, H. W., & van Hoeken, D. (2003). Review of the prevalence and incidence of eating disorders. *International Journal of Eating Disorders, 34*, 383–396.

Hoffman, E. J., & Mathew, S. J. (2008). Anxiety disorders: A comprehensive review of pharmacotherapies. *Mount Sinai Journal of Medicine, 75*, 248–262. doi: 10.1002/msj.2004110.1002/MSJ

Hofmann, S. G., Levitt, J. T., Hoffman, E. C., Greene, K., Litz, B. T., & Barlow, D. H. (2001). Potentially traumatizing events in panic disorder and other anxiety disorders. *Depression and Anxiety, 13*, 101–102.

Hofmann, S. G., Meuret, A. E., Smits, J. A. J., Simon, N. M., Pollack, M. H., Eisenmenger, K., . . . Otto, M. W. (2006). Augmentation of exposure therapy with D-cycloserine for social anxiety disorder. *Archives of General Psychiatry, 63*, 298–304.

Hofmann, S. G., & Smits, J. A. (2008). Cognitive-behavioral therapy for adult anxiety disorders: A meta-analysis of randomized placebo-controlled trials. *Journal of Clinical Psychiatry, 69*(4), 621–632.

Hogarty, G. E., Anderson, C. M., Reiss, D. J., Kornblith, S. J., Greenwald, D. P., et al. (1986). Family psychoeducation, social skills training, and maintenance chemotherapy in the aftercare treatment of schizophrenia: 1. One-year effects of a controlled study on relapse and expressed emotion. *Archives of General Psychiatry, 43*, 633–642.

Hogarty, G. E., Anderson, C. M., Reiss, D. J., Kornblith, S. J., Greenwald, D. P., Ulrich, R. F., Carter, M., & The Environmental-Personal Indicators in the Course of Schizophrenia (EPICS) Research Group. (1991). Family psychoeducation, social skills training, and maintenance chemotherapy in the aftercare treatment of schizophrenia. *Archives of General Psychiatry, 48*, 340–347.

Hogarty, G. E., Flesher, S., Ulrich, R., et al. (2004). Cognitive enhancement therapy for schizophrenia: Effects of a 2-year randomized trial on cognition and behavior. *Archives of General Psychiatry, 61*, 866–876.

Holder, H. D., Longabaugh, R., Miller, W. R., & Rubonis, A. V. (1991). The cost effectiveness of treatment for alcoholism: A first approximation. *Journal of Studies on Alcohol, 52*, 517–540.

Hollander, E., Allen, A., Kwon, J., Aronowitz, B., Schmeidler, J., Wong, C., & Simeon, D. (1999). Clomipramine vs desipramine crossover trial in body dysmorphic disorder: Selective efficacy of a serotonin reuptake inhibitor in imagined ugliness. *Archives of General Psychiatry, 56*(11), 1033–1039.

Hollingshead, A. B., & Redlich, F. C. (1958). *Social class and mental illness: A community study.* New York: Wiley.

Hollon, S. D., & DeRubeis, R. J. (2003). *Cognitive therapy for depression.* Paper presented at the annual conference of the American Psychiatric Association, Philadelphia.

Hollon, S. D., DeRubeis, R. J., Shelton, R. C., Amsterdam, J. D., Salomon, R. M., & O'Reardon, J. P. (2005). Prevention of relapse following cognitive therapy vs medications in moderate to severe depression. *Archives of General Psychiatry, 62*, 417–422.

Hollon, S. D., Haman, K. L., & Brown, L. L. (2002). Cognitive-behavioral treatment of depression. In C. L. Hammen & I. H. Gotlib (Eds.), *Handbook of depression* (pp. 383–403). New York: Guilford.

Hollon, S. D., Stewart, M. O., & Strunk, D. (2006). Enduring effects for cognitive behavior therapy in the treatment of depression and anxiety. *Annual Review of Psychology, 57*, 285–315. doi: 10.1146/annurev.psych.57.102904.190044

Hollon, S. D., Thase, M. E., & Markowitz, J. C. (2002). Treatment and prevention of depression. *Psychological Science in the Public Interest, 3*, 39–77.

Holm, V. A., & Varley, C. K. (1989). Pharmacological treatment of autistic children. In G. Dawson (Ed.), *Autism: Nature, diagnosis, and treatment* (pp. 386–404). New York: Guilford.

Holmes, C., Boche, D., Wilkinson, D., Yadegarfar, G., Hopkins, V., Bayer, A., . . . Nicoll, J. (2008). Long-term effects of Aβ42 immunisation in Alzheimer's disease: Follow-up of a randomised, placebo-controlled phase I trial. *Lancet, 372*(9634), 216–223. doi: 10.1016/s0140-6736(08)61075-2

Hope, D. A., Heimberg, R. G., & Bruch, M. A. (1995). Dismantling cognitive-behavioral group therapy for social phobia. *Behaviour Research and Therapy, 33*, 637–650.

Hopwood, C. J., & Zanarini, M. C. (2010). Borderline personality traits and disorder: Predicting prospective patient functioning. *Journal of Consulting and Clinical Psychology, 78*(4), 585–589. doi: 10.1037/a0019003

Horan, W. P., Kring, A. M., & Blanchard, J. J. (2006). Anhedonia in schizophrenia: A review of assessment strategies. *Schizophrenia Bulletin, 32*, 259–273.

Horan, W. P., Kring, A. M., Gur, R. E., & Blanchard, J. J. (2011). Development and psychometric evaluation of the clinical assessment interview for negative symptoms (CAINS). *Schizophrenia Research.*

Horowitz, J. L., & Garber, J. (2006). The prevention of depressive symptoms in children and adolescents: A meta-analytic review. *Journal of Consulting and Clinical Psychology, 74*, 401–415.

Horton, A. M. J. (2008). The Halstead-Reitan Neuropsychological Test Battery: Past, present, and future. In A. M. Horton & D. Wedding (Eds.), *The neuropsychology handbook* (3rd ed.,) (pp. 251–278). New York: Springer.

Horwitz, B., Ramsy, J. M., & Donahue, B. C. (1998). Functional connectivity of the angular gyrus in normal reading and dyslexia. *Proceedings of the National Academy of Science, 95*, 8939–8944.

Houenou, J., Frommberger, J., Carde, S., Glasbrenner, M., Diener, C., Leboyer, M., & Wessa, M. (2011). Neuroimaging-based markers of bipolar disorder: Evidence from two meta-analyses. *Journal of Affective Disorders, 132*(3), 344–355. doi: 10.1016/j.jad.2011.03.016

Houts, A. C. (2001). Harmful dysfunction and the search for value neutrality in the definition of mental disorder: Response to Wakefield, Part 2. *Behaviour Research and Therapy, 39*, 1099–1132.

Howlin, P., Goode, S., Hutton, J., & Rutter, M. (2004). Adult outcome or children with autism. *Journal of Child Psychology and Psychiatry, 45*, 212–229.

Howlin, P., Mawhood, L., & Rutter, M. (2000). Autism and developmental receptive language disorder—a follow-up comparison in early adult life. II. Social, behavioral, and psychiatric outcomes. *Journal of Child Psychiatry and Psychology, 41*, 561–578.

Hoza, B., Murray-Close, D., Arnold, L. E., Hinshaw, S. P., Hechtmen, L., & the MTA Cooperative Group. (2010). Time-dependent changes in positive illusory self-perceptions of children with attention-deficit/hyperactivity disorder: A developmental psychopathology perspective. *Developmental and Psychopathology, 22*, 375–390.

Hser, Y., Anglin, M. D., & Powers, K. (1993). A 24-year follow-up of California narcotics addicts. *Archives of General Psychiatry, 50*, 577–584.

Hsu, L. K. G. (1990). *Eating disorders.* New York: Guilford.

Hu, W. T., Seelaar, H., Josephs, K. A., Knopman, D. S., Boeve, B. F., Sorenson, E. J., . . . Grossman, M. (2009). Survival profiles of patients with frontotemporal dementia and motor neuron disease. *Archives of Neurology, 66*(11), 1359–1364. doi: 10.1001/archneurol.2009.253

Hudson, J. I., Hiripi, E., Pope, H. G., Jr, & Kessler, R. C. (2007). The prevalence and correlates of eating disorders in the National Comorbidity Survey Replication. *Biological Psychology, 61*, 348–358.

Hudson, J. I., Lalonde, J. K., Berry, J. M., Pindyck, L. J., Bulick, C., et al. (2006). Binge-eating disorder as a distinct familial phenotype in the obese. *Archives of General Psychology, 63*, 3138–3319.

Huesmann, L. R., & Miller, L. S. (1994). Long-term effects of repeated exposure to media violence in childhood. In L. R. Huesmann (Ed.), *Aggressive behavior: Current perspectives* (pp. 153–186). New York: Plenum.

Huether, G., Zhou, D., & Ruther, E. (1997). Causes and consequences of the loss of serotonergic presynapses elicited by the consumption of 3, 4-methylenedioxy-methamphetamine (MDMA, "Ecstasy") and its congeners. *Journal of Neural Transmission, 104*, 771–794.

Hughes, C., & Agran, M. (1993). Teaching persons with severe disabilities to use self-instruction in community settings: An analysis of applications. *Journal of the Association for Persons with Severe Handicaps, 18*, 261–274.

Hughes, C., Hugo, K., & Blatt, J. (1996). Self-instructional intervention for teaching generalized problem-solving within a functional task sequence. *American Journal on Mental Retardation, 100*, 565–579.

Hughes, J., Stead, L., & Lancaster, T. (2004). Antidepressants for smoking cessation. *Cochrane Database Systematic Reviews*, CD000031.

Hughes, J. R., Higgins, S. T., Bickel, W. K., Hunt, W. K., & Fenwick, J. W. (1991). Caffeine self-adminstration, withdrawal, and adverse effects among coffee drinkers. *Archives of General Psychiatry, 48*, 611–617.

Hughes, J. R., Higgins, S. T., & Hatsukami, D. K. (1990). Effects of abstinence from tobacco: A critical review. In L. T. Kozlowski, H. Annis, H. D. Cappell, F. Glaser, M. Goodstadt, Y. Israel, H. Kalant, E. M. Sellers, & J. Vingilis (Eds.), *Research advances in alcohol land drug problems.* New York: Plenum.

Huijbregts, S. C. J., de Sonneville, L. M. J., Licht, R., van Spronsen, F. J., Verkerk, P. H., & Sergeant, J. A. (2002). Sustained attention and inhibition of cognitive interference in treated phenylketonuria: Associations with concurrent and lifetime phenylalanine concentrations. *Neuropsychologia, 40*, 7–15.

Hulley, S., Grady, D., Bush, T., Furberg, C., Herrington, D., Riggs, B., & Vittinghoff, E. (1998). Randomized trial of estrogen plus progestin for secondary prevention of coronary heart disease in postmenopausal women. Heart and Estrogen/Progestin Replacement Study (HERS) Research Group. *Journal of the American Medical Association, 280*, 605–613.

Hulse, G. K., Ngo, H. T., & Tait, R. J. (2010). Risk factors for craving and relapse in heroin users treated with oral or implant naltrexone. *Biological Psychiatry, 68*, 296–302.

Human Genome Project. (2008). How many genes are in the human genome? Accessed online at http://www.ornl.gov/sci/techresources/Human_Genome/faq/genenumber.shtml

Hunsley, J., & Bailey, J. M. (1999). The clinical utility of the Rorschach: Unfulfilled promises and an uncertain future. *Psychological Assessment, 11*, 266–277.

Hunter, R., & Macalpine, I. (1963). *Three hundred years of psychiatry 1535–1860.* Oxford, England: Oxford University Press.

Huntjen, R. J. C., Postma, A., Peters, M. L., Woertman, L., & Van Der Hart, O. (2003). Interidentity amnesia for neutral, episodic information in dissociative identity disorder. *Journal of Abnormal Psychology, 112*, 290–297.

Hurlburt, R. T. (1979). Random sampling of cognitions and behavior. *Journal of Research on Personality, 13*, 103–111.

Hurlburt, R. T. (1997). Randomly sampling thinking in the natural environment. *Journal of Consulting and Clinical Psychology, 65*, 941–949.

Hussong, A. M., Hicks, R. E., Levy, S. A., & Curran, P. J. (2001). Specifying the relations between affect and heavy alcohol use among young adults. *Journal of Abnormal Psychology, 110*, 449–461.

Hustvedt, A. (2011). *Medical muses: Hysteria in nineteenth-century paris.* New York: Norton.

Hwang, J. P., Tsai, S. J., Yang, C. H., Liu, K. M., & Lirng, J. F. (1998). Hoarding behavior in dementia. A preliminary report. *American Journal of Geriatric Psychiatry: Official Journal of the American Association for Geriatric Psychiatry, 6*(4), 285–289.

Hyman, S. E. (2002). Neuroscience, genetics, and the future of psychiatric diagnosis. *Psychopathology, 35*, 139–144.

Hyman, S. E. (2010). The diagnosis of mental disorders: The problem of reification. *Annual Review of Clinical Psychology, 6*, 155–179.

Iervolino, A. C., Rijsdijk, F. V., Cherkas, L., Fullana, M. A., & Mataix-Cols, D. (2011). A multivariate twin study of obsessive-compulsive symptom dimensions. *Archives of General Psychiatry, 68*(6), 637–644. doi: 10.1001/archgenpsychiatry.2011.54

IMS Health. (2006). Top 10 therapeutic classes by U. S. dispensed prescriptions. http://www.hmshealth.com.

Indovina, I., Robbins, T. W., Nunez-Elizalde, A. O., Dunn, B. D., & Bishop, S. J. (2011). Fear-conditioning mechanisms associated with trait vulnerability to anxiety in humans. *Neuron, 69*(3), 563–571.

Inouye, S. K., Bogardus, S. T., Jr., Charpentier, P. A., Leo-Summers, L., Acampora, D., Holford, T. R., & Cooney, L. M., Jr. (1999). A multicomponent intervention to prevent delirium in hospitalized older patients. *New England Journal of Medicine, 340*, 669–676.

Insel, T. R., Scanlan, J., Champoux, M., & Suomi, S. J. (1988). Rearing paradigm in a nonhuman primate affects response to B-CCE challenge. *Psychopharmacology, 96*, 81–86.

Institute of Medicine. (1990). *Treating drug problems.* Washington, DC: National Academy Press.

Institute of Medicine. (1999). *Marijuana and medicine: Assessing the science base.* Washington, DC: National Academy Press.

Institute of Medicine. (2004). *Immunization safety review: Vaccines and autism.* Immunization Safety Review Board on Health Promotion and Disease Prevention. Washington, DC: National Academies Press.

Ipser, J. C., Sander, C., & Stein, D. J. (2009). Pharmacotherapy and psychotherapy for body dysmorphic disorder. *The Cochrane Library, Issue 1*, CD005332. doi: 10.1002/14651858.CD005332.pub2

Irvin, J. E., Bowers, C.A., Dunn, M.E., & Wang, M.C. (1999). Efficacy of relapse prevention: A meta-analytic review. *Journal of Consulting and Clinical Psychology, 67*, 563–570.

Irwin, M., Lovitz, A., Marder, S. R., Mintz, J., Winslade, W. J., van Putten, T., & Mills, M. J. (1985). Psychotic patients' understanding of informed consent. *American Journal of Psychiatry, 142*, 1351–1354.

Ishikawa, S. S., Raine, A., Lencz, T., Bihrle, S., & Lacasse, L. (2001). Autonomic stress reactivity and executive functions in successful and unsuccessful criminal psychopaths from the community. *Journal of Abnormal Psychology, 110*, 423–432.

Ito, T., Miller, N. & Pollock, V. (1996). Alcohol and aggression: A meta-analysis on the moderating effects of inhibitory cues, triggering events, and self-focused attention. *Psychological Bulletin, 120*, 60–82.

Ivanoff, A., Jang, S. J., Smyth, N. J., & Linehan, M. M. (1994). Fewer reasons for staying alive when you are thinking of killing yourself: The Brief Reasons for Living Inventory. *Journal of Psychopathology and Behavioral Assessment, 16*, 1–13.

Ivarsson, T., Råstam, M., Weitz, E., Gilberg, I. C., & Gilberg, G. (2000). Depressive disorders in teen-age-onset anorexia nervosa: A controlled longitudinal, partly community-based study. *Comprehensive Psychiatry, 41*, 398–403.

Jack, C. R., Jr., Albert, M. S., Knopman, D. S., McKhann, G. M., Sperling, R. A., Carrillo, M. C., . . . Phelps, C. H. (2011). Introduction to the recommendations from the National Institute on Aging-Alzheimer's Association workgroups on diagnostic guidelines for Alzheimer's disease. *Alzheimer's and Dementia : The Journal of the Alzheimer's Association, 7*(3), 257–262. doi: 10.1016/j.jalz.2011.03.004

Jackson, C. (1997). Testing a multi-stage model for the adoption of alcohol and tobacco behaviors by children. *Addictive Behaviors, 22*, 1–14.

Jackson, J. C., Gordon, S. M., Hart, R. P., Hopkins, R. O., & Ely, E. W. (2004). The association between delirium and cognitive decline: A review of the empirical literature. *Neuropsychology Review, 14*, 87–98.

Jackson, K. M., Sher, K. J., & Wood, P. K. (2000). Trajectories of concurrent substance use disorders: A developmental, typological approach to comorbidity. *Alcoholism: Clinical and Experimental Research, 24*, 902–913.

Jacobi, F., Wittchen, H. U., Holting, C., Hofler, M., Pfister, H., Muller, N., & Lieb, F. (2004). Prevalence, co-morbidity and correlates of mental disorders in the general population: Results from the German Health Interview and Examination Survey. *Psychological Medicine, 34*, 597–611.

Jacobsen, L. K., Southwick, S. M., & Kosten, T. R. (2001). Substance use disorders in patients with posttraumatic stress disorder: A review of the literature. *American Journal of Psychiatry, 158*, 1184–1190.

Jacobson, N. S., Dobson, K. S., Fruzzetti, A. E., & Schmaling, K. B. (1991). Marital therapy as a treatment for depression. *Journal of Consulting and Clinical Psychology, 59*, 547–557.

Jacobson, N. S., & Gortner, E. T. (2000). Can depression be de-medicalized in the 21st century?: Scientific revolutions, counter-revolutions and the magnetic field of normal science. *Behaviour Research and Therapy, 38*, 103–117.

Jacobson, N. S., Martell, C. R., & Dimidjian, S. (2001). Behavioral activation treatment for depression: Returning to contextual roots. *Clinical Psychology: Science and Practice, 8*, 255–270.

Jacobson, N. S., Roberts, L. J., Berns, S. B., & McGlinchey, J. B. (1999). Methods for defining and determining the clinical significance of treatment effects: Description, application, and alternatives. *Journal of Consulting and Clinical Psychology, 67*(3), 300–307.

Jaffe, J. H. (1985). Drug addiction and drug abuse. In Goodman & Gilman (Eds.), *The pharmacological basis of therapeutic behavior.* New York: Macmillan.

Jaffee, S. R., Moffitt, T. E., Caspi, A., Taylor, A., & Arseneault, L. (2002). Influence of adult domestic violence on children's internalizing and externalizing problems: An environmentally informative twin study. *Journal of the American Academy of Child and Adolescent Psychiatry, 41,* 1095–1103.

Jak, A. J., Bondi, M. W., Delano-Wood, L., Wierenga, C., Corey-Bloom, J., Salmon, D., & Delis, D. C. (2009). Quantification of five neuropsychological approaches to defining mild cognitive impairment. *American Journal of Geriatric Psychiatry, 17*(5), 368–375.

Jamison, K. R. (1992). *Touched with fire: Manic-depressive illness and the artistic temperament.* New York: Free Press.

Jampole, L., & Weber, M. K. (1987). An assessment of the behavior of sexually abused and nonsexually abused children with anatomically correct dolls. *Child Abuse and Neglect, 11,* 187–192.

Jansen, M. A., Glynn, T., & Howard, J. (1996). Prevention of alcohol, tobacco and other drug abuse. *American Behavioral Scientist, 39,* 790–807.

Jardri, R., Pouchet, A., Pins, D., & Thomas, P. (2011). Cortical activation during auditory verbal hallucinations in schizophrenia: A coordinate-based meta-analysis. *American Journal of Psychiatry, 168,* 73–81.

Jarrell, M. P., Johnson, W. G., & Williamson, D. A. (1986). *Insulin and glucose response in the binge purge episode of bulimic women.* Paper presented at the annual convention of the Association for Advancement of Behavior Therapy, Chicago.

Jeans, R. F. I. (1976). An independently validated case of multiple personality. *Journal of Abnormal Psychology, 85,* 249–255.

Jelicic, M., Geraerts, E., Merckelbach, H., & Guerrieri, R. (2004). Acute stress enhances memory for emotional words, but impairs memory for neutral words. *International Journal of Neuroscience, 114,* 1343–1351.

Jenike, M. A., & Rauch, S. L. (1994). Managing the patient with treatment-resistant obsessive-compulsive disorder: Current strategies. *Journal of Clinical Psychiatry, 55,* 11–17.

Jensen, P. S., Arnold, L. E., Swanson, J. M., et al. (2007). 3-year follow-up of the NIMH MTA study. *Journal of the American Academy of Child and Adolescent Psychiatry, 46,* 989–1002.

Jensen, P. S., Martin, D., & Cantwell, D. P. (1997). Comorbidity in ADHD: Implications for research, practice, and DSM-V. *Journal of the American Academy of Child and Adolescent Psychiatry, 36,* 1065–1079.

Jernigan, D. H., Ostroff, J., Ross, C., & O'Hara, J. A., III, (2004). Sex differences in adolescent exposure to alcohol advertising in magazines. *Archives of Pediatric and Adolescent Medicine, 158,* 702–704.

Jespersen, A. F., Lalumiere, M. L., & Seto, M. C. (2009). Sexual abuse history among adult sex offenders and non-sex offenders: A meta-analysis. *Child Abuse and Neglect, 33*(3), 179–192. doi: 10.1016/j.chiabu.2008.07.004

Jett, D., LaPorte, D. J., & Wanchism, J. (2010). Impact of exposure to pro-eating disorder websites on eating behaviour in college women. *European Eating Disorders Review, 18,* 410–416.

Jimerson, D. C., Lesem, M. D., Kate, W. H., & Brewerton, T. D. (1992). Low serotonin and dopamine metabolite concentrations in cerebrospinal fluid from bulimic patients with frequent binge episodes. *Archives of General Psychiatry, 49,* 132–138.

Jimerson, D. C., Wolfe, B. E., Metzger, E. D., Finkelstein, D. M., Cooper, T. B., et al. (1997). Decreased serotonin

function in bulimia nervosa. *Archives of General Psychiatry, 54,* 529–536.

Johnson, D. R. (1987). The role of the creative arts therapist in the diagnosis and treatment of psychological trauma. *The Arts in Psychotherapy, 14,* 7–13.

Johnson, J., Weissman, M. M., & Klerman, G. L. (1992). Service utilization and social morbidity associated with depressive symptoms in the community. *Journal of the American Medical Association, 267,* 1478–1483.

Johnson, S. L. (2005). Life events in bipolar disorder: Towards more specific models. *Clinical Psychology Review, 25*(8), 1008–1027.

Johnson, S. L., Cuellar, A. K., & Miller, C. (Eds.). (2010). *Bipolar and unipolar depression: A comparison of clinical phenomenology, biological vulnerability, and psychosocial predictors* (2nd ed.). New York: Guilford.

Johnson, S. L., Cuellar, A. K., Ruggero, C., Winett-Perlman, C., Goodnick, P., White, R., & Miller, I. (2008). Life events as predictors of mania and depression in bipolar I disorder. *Journal of Abnormal Psychology, 117*(2), 268–277. doi: 10.1037/0021-843X.117.2.268

Johnson, S. L., Sandrow, D., Meyer, B., Winters, R., Miller, I., Solomon, D., & Keitner, G. (2000). Increases in manic symptoms after life events involving goal attainment. *Journal of Abnormal Psychology, 109*(4), 721–727.

Johnson, W. G., Tsoh, J. Y., & Varnado, P. J. (1996). Eating disorders: Efficacy of pharmacological and psychological interventions. *Clinical Psychology Review, 16,* 457–478.

Johnston, C., & Marsh, E. J. (2001). Families of children with attention-deficit/hyperactivity disorder: Review and recommendations for future research. *Clinical Child and Family Psychology Review, 4,* 183–207.

Joiner, T. E. (1995). The price of soliciting and receiving negative feedback: Self-verification theory as a vulnerability to depression theory. *Journal of Abnormal Psychology, 104,* 364–372.

Joiner, T. E., Alfano, M. S., & Metalsky, G. I. (1992). When depression breeds contempt: Reassurance seeking, self-esteem, and rejection of depressed college students by their roommates. *Journal of Abnormal Psychology, 101,* 165–173.

Joiner, T. E. J., Brown, J. S., & Wingate, L. R. (2005). The psychology and neurobiology of suicidal behavior. *Annual Review of Psychology, 56,* 287–314.

Joiner, T. E., & Metalsky, G. I. (1995). A prospective test of an integrative interpersonal theory of depression: A naturalistic study of college roommates. *Journal of Personality and Social Psychology, 69,* 778–788.

Joiner, T. E., & Metalsky, G. I. (2001). Excessive reassurance-seeking: Delineating a risk factor involved in the development of depressive symptoms. *Psychological Science, 12,* 371–378.

Joiner, T. E., Voelz, Z. R., & Rudd, M. D. (2001). For suicidal young adults with comorbid depressive and anxiety disorders, problem-solving treatment may be better than treatment as usual. *Professional Psychology: Research and Practice, 32,* 278–282.

Jones, E., & Wessely, S. (2001). Psychiatric battle casualties: An intra- and interwar comparision. *British Journal of Psychiatry, 178,* 242–247.

Jones, P. B., Barnes, T. R. E., Davies, L., Dunn, G., Lloyd, H., et al. (2006). Randomized controlled trial of the effect on quality of life of second- vs first-generation antipsychotic drugs in schizophrenia: Cost Utility of the Latest Antipsychotic Drugs in Schizophrenia Study (CUtLASS 1). *Archives of General Psychiatry, 63,* 1079–1087.

Jordan, N. C. (2007). Do words count? Connections between mathematics and reading difficulties. In D. B.

Berch & M. M. M. Mazzocco (Eds.), *Why is math so hard for some children?* (pp. 107–120). Baltimore: Brooks.

Jorenby, D. E., Leischow, S. J., Nides, M. A., Rennard, S. I., Johnston, J. A., et al. (1999). A controlled trial of sustained-release buproprion, a nicotine patch, or both for smoking cessation. *New England Journal of Medicine, 340,* 685–691.

Jorm, A. F., Christensen, H., Henderson, A. S., Jacomb, P. A., Korten, A. E., & Rodgers, B. (2000). Predicting anxiety and depression from personality: Is there a synergistic effect of neuroticism and extraversion? *Journal of Abnormal Psychology, 109,* 145–149.

Josephs, K. A. (2008). Frontotemporal dementia and related disorders: Deciphering the enigma. *Annals of Neurology, 64*(1), 4–14. doi: 10.1002/ana.21426

Josephs, R. A., & Steele, C. M. (1990). The two faces of alcohol myopia: Attentional mediation of psychological stress. *Journal of Abnormal Psychology, 99,* 115–126.

Judd, L. L. (1997). The clinical course of unipolar depressive disorders. *Archives of General Psychiatry, 54,* 989–992.

Judd, L. L., Akiskal, H. S., Maser, J. D., Zeller, P. J., Endicott, J., Coryell, W., . . . Keller, M. B. (1998). A prospective 12-year study of subsyndromal and syndromal depressive symptoms in unipolar major depressive disorders. *Archives of General Psychiatry, 55,* 694–701.

Judd, L. L., Akiskal, H. S., Zeller, P. J., Paulus, M. P., Leon, A. C., Maser, J. D., . . . Keller, M. B. (2000). Psychosocial disability during the long-term course of unipolar major depressive disorder. *Archives of General Psychiatry, 57,* 375–380.

Jung, B., & Reidenberg, M. M. (2006). The risk of action by the Drug Enforcement Administration against physicians prescribing opioids for pain. *Pain Medicine, 7*(4), 353–357. doi: 10.1111/j.1526-4637.2006.00164.x

Just, N., & Alloy, L. B. (1997). The response styles theory of depression: Tests and an extension of the theory. *Journal of Abnormal Psychology, 106,* 221–229.

Kable, J. A., & Coles, C. D. (2004). The impact of prenatal alcohol exposure on neurophysiological encoding of environmental events at six months. *Alcoholism: Clinical and Experimental Research, 28,* 489–496.

Kadlic, D., Rawe, J., Park, A., Fonda, D., Cole, W., et al. (2004, May 3). The low carb frenzy. *Time.*

Kafka, M. P. (1997). Hypersexual desire in males: An operational definition and clinical implications for males with paraphilias and paraphilia-related disorders. *Archives of Sexual Behavior, 26*(5), 505–526.

Kafka, M. P. (2010). The DSM diagnostic criteria for fetishism. *Archives of Sexual Behavior, 39*(2), 357–362. doi: 10.1007/s10508-009-9558-7

Kafka, M. P., & Hennen, J. (2002). A DSM-IV axis I comorbidity study of males (*n* = 120) with paraphilias and paraphilia-related disorders. *Sexual Abuse: A Journal of Research and Treatment, 14*(4), 349–366. doi: 10.1177/107906320201400405

Kagan, J., & Snidman, N. (1999). Early childhood predictors of adult anxiety disorders. *Biological Psychiatry, 46,* 1536–1541.

Kandel, D. B. (2002). *Stages and pathways of drug involvement: Examining the gateway hypothesis.* New York: Cambridge University Press.

Kane, J., Honigfeld, G., Singer, J., Meltzer, H., & the Clozapine Collaborative Study Group. (1988). Clozapine for treatment resistant schizophrenics. *Archives of General Psychiatry, 45,* 789–796.

Kane, J. M., Marder, S. R., Schooler, N. R., et al. (2001). Clozapine and haloperidol in moderately refractory schizophrenia: A 6-month randomized and double-blind comparison. *Archives of General Psychiatry, 58,* 965–972.

Kane, P., & Garber, J. (2004). The relations among depression in fathers, children's psychopathology, and father–child conflict: A meta-analysis. *Clinical Psychology Review, 24,* 339–360.

Kanner, L. (1943). Autistic disturbances of affective contact. *Nervous Child, 2,* 217–250.

Kanner, L. (1973). *Childhood psychosis: Initial studies and new insights.* New York: Winston/Wiley.

Kapczinski, F., Lima, M. S., Souza, J. S., Cunha, A., & Schmitt, R. (2002). Antidepressants for generalized anxiety disorder. *Cochrane Database of Systematic Reviews*(2), CD003592. doi: 10.1002/14651858.CD003592

Kaplan, H. S. (1974). *The new sex therapy.* New York: Brunner/Mazel.

Kaplan, H. S. (1997). Sexual desire disorders (hypoactive sexual desire and sexual aversion). In G. O. Gabbard & S. D. Atkinson (Eds.), *Synopsis of treatments of psychiatric disorders* (2nd ed., pp. 771–780). Washington, DC: American Psychiatric Press.

Kaplan, M. S., & Kreuger, R. B. (1997). Voyeurism: Psychopathology and theory. In D. R. Laws & W. O'Donohue (Eds.), *Sexual deviance* (pp. 297–310). New York: Guilford.

Kaplow, J. B., & Widom, C. S. (2007). Age of onset of child maltreatment predicts long-term mental health outcomes. *Journal of Abnormal Psychology, 116,* 176–187.

Karg, K., Burmeister, M., Shedden, K., & Sen, S. (2011). The serotonin transporter promoter variant (5-HTTLPR), stress, and depression meta-analysis revisited: Evidence of genetic moderation. *Archives of General Psychiatry, 68,* 444–454.

Karkowski, L. M., Prescott, C.A., & Kendler, K.S. (2000). Multivariate assessment of factors influencing illicit substance use in twins from female-female pairs. *American Journal of Medical Genetics and Neuropsychiatric Genetics, 96,* 665–670.

Karon, B. P., & VandenBos, G. R. (1998). Schizophrenia and psychosis in elderly populations. In I. H. Nordhus, G. R. VandenBos, S. Berg, & P. Fromholt (Eds.), *Clinical geropsychology* (pp. 219–227). Washington, DC: American Psychological Association.

Kasari, C., Freeman, S., & Paparella, T. (2006). Joint attention and symbolic play in young children with autism: A randomized controlled intervention study. *Journal of Child Psychology and Psychiatry, 47,* 611–620.

Kasari, C., Paparella, T., Freeman, S., & Jahromi, L. B. (2008). Language outcome in autism: Randomized comparison of joint attention and play interventions. *Journal of Consulting and Clinical Psychology, 76,* 125–137.

Kashani, J. H., & Carlson, G. A. (1987). Seriously depressed preschoolers. *American Journal of Psychiatry, 144,* 348–350.

Kashani, J. H., Holcomb, W. R., & Orvaschel, H. (1986). Depression and depressive symptoms in preschool children from the general population. *American Journal of Psychiatry, 143,* 1138–1143.

Kashani, J. H., & Orvaschel, H. (1990). A community study of anxiety in children and adolescents. *American Journal of Psychiatry, 147,* 313–318.

Kashden, J., & Franzen, M. D. (1996). An interrater reliability study of the Luria-Nebraska Neuropsychological Battery Form-II quantitative scoring system. *Archives of Clinical Neuropsychology, 11,* 155–163.

Kassel, J. D., & Shiffman, S. (1997). Attentional mediation of cigarette smoking's effect on anxiety. *Health Psychology, 16,* 359–368.

Kassel, J. D., Stroud, L. R., & Paronis, C. A. (2003). Smoking, stress, and negative affect: Correlation, causation, and context across stages of smoking. *Psychological Bulletin, 129,* 270–304.

Kassel, J. D., & Unrod, M. (2000). Smoking, anxiety, and attention: Support for the role of nicotine in attentionally mediated anxiolysis. *Journal of Abnormal Psychology, 109,* 161–166.

Kassett, J. A., Gershon, E. S., Maxwell, M. E., et al. (1989). Psychiatric disorders in the first-degree relatives of probands with bulimia nervosa. *American Journal of Psychiatry, 146,* 1468–1471.

Kato, T. (2007). Molecular genetics of bipolar disorder and depression. *Psychiatry and Clinical Neurosciences, 61,* 3–19.

Katz, E. C., Gruber, K., Chutuape, M. A., & Stitzer, M. L. (2001). Reinforcement-based outpatient treatment for opiate and cocaine abusers. *Journal of Substance Abuse Treatment, 20,* 93–98.

Katz, I. R., Parmelee, P., & Brubaker, K. (1991). Toxic and metabolic encephalopathies in long-term care patients. *International Psychogeriatrics, 3,* 337–347.

Kawachi, I., Colditz, G. A., Ascherio, A., Rimm, E. B., Giovannucci, E., Stampfer, M. J., & Willett, W. C. (1994). Prospective study of phobic anxiety and risk of coronary heart disease in men. *Circulation, 89,* 1992–1997.

Kawakami, N., Shimizu, H., Haratani, T., Iwata, N., & Kitamura, T. (2004). Lifetime and 6-month prevalence of DSM-III-R psychiatric disorders in an urban community in Japan. *Psychiatry Research, 121,* 293–301.

Kaye, W. H., Ebert, M. H., Raleigh, M., & Lake, R. (1984). Abnormalities in CNS monoamine metabolism in anorexia nervosa. *Archives of General Psychiatry, 41,* 350–355.

Kaye, W. H., Greeno, C. G., Moss, H., Fernstrom, J., Lilenfeld, L. R., Wahlund, B., . . . Mann, J. J. L. (1998). Alterations in serotonin activity and platelet monoamine oxidase and psychiatric symptoms after recovery from bulimia nervosa. *Archives of General Psychiatry, 55,* 927–935.

Kazdin, A. E. (1985). *Treatment of antisocial behavior in children and adolescents.* Homewood, IL: Dorsey.

Kazdin, A. E. (2005). *Parent management training: Treatment for oppositional, aggressive, and antisocial behavior in children and adolescents.* New York: Oxford University Press.

Kazdin, A. E., & Weisz, J. R. (1998). Identifying and developing empirically supported child and adolescent treatments. *Journal of Consulting and Clinical Psychology, 66,* 19–36.

Keane, T. M., & Barlow, D. H. (2004). Posttraumatic stress disorder. In D. H. Barlow (Ed.), *Anxiety and its disorders: The nature and treatment of anxiety and panic* (pp. 418–454). New York: Guilford.

Keane, T. M., Fairbank, J. A., Caddell, J. M., & Zimering, R. T. (1989). Implosive (flooding) therapy reduces symptoms of PTSD in Vietnam combat veterans. *Behavior Therapy, 20,* 245–260.

Keane, T. M., Gerardi, R. J., Quinn, S. J., & Litz, B. T. (1992). Behavioral treatment of post-traumatic stress disorder. In S. M. Turner, K. S. Calhoun, & H. E. Adams (Eds.), *Handbook of clinical behavior therapy* (2nd ed., pp. 87–97). New York: Wiley.

Keane, T. M., Marshall, A. D., & Taft, C. T. (2006). Posttraumatic stress disorder: Etiology, epidemiology, and treatment outcome. *Annual Review of Clinical Psychology, 2,* 161–197.

Keane, T. M., Zimering, R. T., & Caddell, J. (1985). A behavioral formulation of posttraumatic stress disorder in Vietnam veterans. *The Behavior Therapist, 8,* 9–12.

Keefe, R. S. E., Bilder, R. M., Davis, S.M., Harvey, P.D., Palmer, B. W., et al. (2007). Neurocognitive effects of antipsychotic medications in patients with chronic

schizophrenia in the CATIE trial. *Archives of General Psychiatry, 64,* 633–647.

Keel, P. K., Baxter, M. G., Heatherton, T. F., & Joiner, T. E. (2007). A 20-year longitudinal study of body weight, dieting, and eating disorder symptoms. *Journal of Abnormal Psychology, 116,* 422–432.

Keel, P. K., & Brown, T. A. (2010). Update on course and outcome in eating disorders. *International Journal of Eating Disorders, 43,* 195–204.

Keel, P. K., Gravener, J. A., Joiner, T. E., Jr., & Haedt, A. A. (2010). Twenty-year follow-up of bulimia nervosa and related eating disorders not otherwise specified. *International Journal of Eating Disorders, 43,* 492–497.

Keel, P. K., & Klump, K. L. (2003). Are eating disorders culture-bound syndromes? Implications for conceptualizing their etiology. *Psychological Bulletin, 129,* 747–769.

Keel, P. K., & Mitchell, J. E. (1997). Outcome in bulimia nervosa. *American Journal of Psychiatry, 154,* 313–321.

Keel, P. K., Mitchell, J. E., Davis, T. L., & Crow, S. J. (2002). Long-term impact of treatment in women diagnosed with bulimia nervosa. *International Journal of Eating Disorders, 31,* 151–158.

Keel, P. K., Mitchell, J. E., Miller, K. B., Davis, T. L., & Crowe, S. J. (1999). Long-term outcome of bulimia nervosa. *Archives of General Psychiatry, 56,* 63–69.

Keilp, J. G., Sackeim, H. A., Brodsky, B. S., Oquendo, M. A., Malone, K. M., & Mann, J. J. (2001). Neuropsychological dysfunction in depressed suicide attempters. *Archives of General Psychiatry, 158,* 735–741.

Keller, M. B., Ryan, N. D., Strober, M., Klein, R. G., Kutcher, S. P., Birmaher, B., et al. (2001). Efficacy of paroxetine in the treatment of adolescent major depression: A randomized, controlled trial. *Journal of the American Academy of Child and Adolescent Psychiatry, 40,* 762–772.

Kellerman, J. (1989). *Silent partner.* New York: Bantam.

Kelley, M. L. (1990). *School-home notes: Promoting children's classroom success.* New York: Guilford.

Kellner, C. H., Fink, M., Knapp, R., Petrides, G., Husain, M., Rummans, T., . . . Malur, C. (2005). Relief of expressed suicidal intent by ECT: A consortium for research in ECT study. *American Journal of Psychiatry, 162,* 977–982.

Keltner, D., & Kring, A. M. (1998). Emotion, social function, and psychopathology. *Review of General Psychology, 2,* 320–342.

Kempster, N. (1996). Clinton orders tracking of sex offenders, *Los Angeles Times,* p. A20.

Kempton, M. J., Stahl, D., Williams, S. C., & DeLisi, L. E. (2010). Progressive lateral ventricular enlargement in schizophrenia: A meta-analysis of longitudinal MRI studies. *Schizophrenia Research, 120,* 54–62.

Kenardy, J., & Taylor, C. B. (1999). Expected versus unexpected panic attacks: A naturalistic prospective study. *Journal of Anxiety Disorders, 13,* 435–445.

Kendall, P. C., & Beidas, R. S. (2007). Trail for dissemination of evidence-based practices for youth: Flexibility within fidelity. *Professional Psychology: Research and Practice, 38,* 13–20.

Kendall, P. C., & Ingram, R. E. (1989). Cognitive-behavioral perspectives: Theory and research on depression and anxiety. In D. Watson & P. C. Kendall (Eds.), *Personality, psychopathology, and psychotherapy* (pp. 27–53). San Diego: Academic Press.

Kendall, P. C., Aschenbrand, S. G., & Hudson, J. L. (2003). Child-focused treatment of anxiety. In A. E. Kazdin & J. R. Weisz (Eds.), *Evidence-based psychotherapies for children and adolescents* (pp. 81–100). New York: Guilford.

Kendall, P. C., Flannery-Schroeder, E. C., Panichelli-Mindel, S., Southam-Gerow, M., Henin, A., & Warman,

M. (1997). Therapy for youths with anxiety disorders: A second randomized clinical trial. *Journal of Consulting and Clinical Psychology, 65,* 366–380.

Kendall, P. C., Haaga, D. A. F., Ellis, A., Bernard, M., DiGiuseppe, R., & Kassinove, H. (1995). Rational-emotive therapy in the 1990s and beyond: Current status, recent revisions, and research questions. *Clinical Psychology Review, 15,* 169–185.

Kendall, P. C., Hudson, J. L., Gosch, E., Flannery-Schroeder, E., & Suveg, C. (2008). Cognitive-behavioral therapy for anxiety disordered youth: A randomized clinical trial evaluating child and family modalities. *Journal of Consulting and Clinical Psychology, 76,* 282–297.

Kendall, P. C., Safford, S., Flannery-Schroeder, E., & Webb, A. (2004). Child anxiety treatment: Outcomes in adolescence and impact on substance use and depression at 7.4-year follow-up. *Journal of Consulting and Clinical Psychology, 72,* 276–287.

Kendler, K. S. (1997). The diagnostic validity of melancholic major depression in a population-based sample of female twins. *Archives of General Psychiatry, 54,* 299–304.

Kendler, K. S., & Baker, J. (2007). Genetic influences on measures of the environment: A systematic review. *Psychological Medicine, 37,* 615–626.

Kendler, K. S., & Gardner, C. O. (1998). Boundaries of major depression: An evaluation of DSM-IV criteria. *American Journal of Psychiatry, 155,* 172–177.

Kendler, K. S., Gatz, M., Gardner, C. O., & Pedersen, N. L. (2006). A Swedish national twin study of lifetime major depression. *American Journal of Psychiatry, 163,* 109–114.

Kendler, K. S., Hettema, J. M., Butera, F., Gardner, C. O., & Prescott, C. A. (2003). Life event dimensions of loss, humiliation, entrapment, and danger in the prediction of onsets of major depression and generalized anxiety. *Archives of General Psychiatry, 60,* 789–796.

Kendler, K. S., Jacobson, K., Myers, J. M., & Eaves L. J. (2008). A genetically informative developmental study of the relationship between conduct disorder and peer deviance in males. *Psychological Medicine, 38,* 1001–1011.

Kendler, K. S., Jacobson, K. C., Prescott, C. A., & Neale, M. C. (2003). Specificity of genetic and environmental risk factors for use and abuse/dependence of cannabis, cocaine, hallucinogens, sedatives, stimulants, and opiates in male twins. *American Journal of Psychiatry, 160,* 687–695.

Kendler, K. S., Karkowski-Shuman, L., & Walsh, D. (1996). Age of onset in schizophrenia and risk of illness in relatives. *British Journal of Psychiatry, 169,* 213–218.

Kendler, K. S., Myers, J., & Prescott, C. A. (2002). The etiology of phobias: An evaluation of the stress-diathesis model. *Archives of General Psychiatry, 59,* 242–249.

Kendler, K. S., Myers, J., Prescott, C. A., & Neale, M. C. (2001). The genetic epidemiology of irrational fears and phobias in men. *Archives of General Psychiatry, 58,* 257–267.

Kendler, K. S., & Prescott, C. A. (1998). Cannabis use, abuse, and dependence in a population-based sample of female twins. *American Journal of Psychiatry, 155,* 1016–1022.

Kendler, K. S., Prescott, C. A., Myers, J., & Neale, M. C. (2003). The structure of genetic and environmental risk factors for common psychiatric and substance use disorders in men and women. *Archives of General Psychiatry, 60,* 929–937.

Kennedy, E., Spence, S. H., & Hensley, R. (1989). An examination of the relationship between childhood depression and social competence amongst primary school children. *Journal of Child Psychology and Psychiatry, 30,* 561–573.

Kerns, J. G., & Berenbaum, H. (2002). Cognitive impairments associated with formal thought disorder in people with schizophrenia. *Journal of Abnormal Psychology, 111,* 211–224.

Kerns, J. G., & Berenbaum, H. (2003). The relationship between formal thought disorder and executive functioning component processes. *Journal of Abnormal Psychology, 112,* 339–352.

Keshavan, M. S., Rosenberg, D., Sweeney, J. A., & Pettegrew, J. W. (1998). Decreased caudate volume in neuroleptic-naive psychotic patients. *American Journal of Psychiatry, 155,* 774–778.

Kessler, D. A. (2009). *The end of overeating.* Emmaus, PA: Rodale.

Kessler, E. (2004, August 22). Dancing with Rose: A strangely beautiful encounter with Alzheimer's patients provides insights that challenge the way we view the disease. *LA Times Magazine.* http://www.articles.latimes.com.

Kessler, R. C. (2003). Epidemiology of women and depression. *Journal of Affective Disorders, 74*(1), 5–13.

Kessler, R. C., Akiskal, H. S., Angst, J., Guyer, M., Hirschfeld, R. M. A., Merikangas, K. R., & Stang, P. E. (2006). Validity of the assessment of bipolar spectrum disorders in the WHO CIDI 3.0. *Journal of Affective Disorders, 96,* 259–269.

Kessler, R. C., Berglund, P., Demler, O., Jin, R., Koretz, D., Merikangas, K. R., . . . Wang, P. S. (2003a). The epidemiology of major depressive disorder. *Journal of the American Medical Association, 289*(23), 3095–3105.

Kessler, R. C., Berglund, P., Demler, O., Jin, R., Koretz, D., Merikangas, K. R., . . . Wang, P. S. (2003b). The epidemiology of major depressive disorder: Results from the National Comorbidity Survey Replication (NCS-R). *Journal of the American Medical Association, 289*(23), 3095–3105. doi: 10.1001/jama.289.23.3095

Kessler, R. C., Berglund, P., Demler, O., Jin, R., Merikangas, K. R., & Walters, E. E. (2005). Lifetime prevalence and age-of-onset distributions of DSM-IV disorders in the National Comorbidity Survey Replication. *Archives of General Psychiatry, 62,* 593–602.

Kessler, R. C., Chiu, W. T., Jin, R., Ruscio, A. M., Shear, K., & Walters, E. E. (2006). The epidemiology of panic attacks, panic disorder, and agoraphobia in the National Comorbidity Survey Replication. *Archives of General Psychiatry, 63,* 415–424.

Kessler, R. C., Crum, R. M., Warner, L. A., Nelson, C. B., Schulenberg, J., & Anthony, J. C. (1997). Lifetime co-occurrence of DSM-IIIR alcohol dependence with other psychiatric disorders in the National Comorbidity Study. *Archives of General Psychiatry, 54,* 313–321.

Kessler, R. C., Heeringa, S., Lakoma, M. D., et al. (2008). Individual and society effects of mental disorders on earnings in the United States: Results from the National Comorbidity Survey Replication. *American Journal of Psychiatry, 165,* 703–711.

Kety, S. S., Rosenthal, D., Wender, P. H., & Schulsinger, F. (1976). Mental illness in the adoptive and biological families of adopted individuals who have become schizophrenic. In R. R. Fieve, D. Rosenthal, & H. Brill (Eds.), *Genetic research in psychiatry.* Baltimore: Johns Hopkins University Press.

Kety, S. S., Wender, P. H., Jacobsen, B., Ingraham, L. T., Jansson, L., et al. (1994). Mental illness in the biological and adoptive relatives of schizophrenic adoptees: Replication of the Copenhagen study in the rest of Denmark. *Archives of General Psychiatry, 51,* 442–468.

Keyes, K. M., Martins, S. S., Blanco, C., & Hasin, D. S. (2010). Telescoping and gender differences in alcohol dependence: New evidence from two national surveys. *American Journal of Psychiatry, 167,* 969–976.

Keys, A., Brozek, J., Hsu, L. K. G., McConoha, C. E., & Bolton, B. (1950). *The biology of human starvation.* Minneapolis: University of Minnesota Press.

Kiecolt-Glaser, J., Dura, J. R., Speicher, C. E., & Trask, O. (1991). Spousal caregivers of dementia victims: Longitudinal changes in immunity and health. *Psychosomatic Medicine, 54,* 345–362.

Kiecolt-Glaser, J. K., & Glaser, R. (2001). Stress and immunity: Age enhances the risks. *Current Directions in Psychological Science, 10,* 18–21.

Kiecolt-Glaser, J. K., & Glaser, R. (2002). Depression and immune function: Central pathways to morbidity and mortality. *Journal of Psychosomatic Research, 53,* 873–876.

Kieseppa, T., Partonen, T., Haukka, J., Kaprio, J., & Lonnqvist, J. (2004). High concordance of bipolar I disorder in a nationwide sample of twins. *American Journal of Psychiatry, 161,* 1814–1821.

Kiesler, C. A. (1991). Changes in general hospital psychiatric care. *American Psychologist, 46,* 416–421.

Kihlstrom, J. F. (1992). Dissociative and conversion disorders. In D. J. Stein & J. E. Young (Eds.), *Cognitive science and clinical disorders* (pp. 247–270). San Diego: Academic Press.

Kihlstrom, J. F., Tataryn, D. J., & Holt, I. P. (1993). Dissociative disorders. In P. B. Sutker & H. E. Adams (Eds.), *Comprehensive handbook of psychopathology* (pp. 203–234). New York: Plenum.

Killen, J. D., Fortmann, S. P., Murphy, G. M., Jr., Hayward, C., Arredondo, C., et al. (2006). Extended treatment with bupropion SR for cigarette smoking cessation. *Journal of Consulting and Clinical Psychology, 74,* 286–294.

Killen, J. D., Robinson, T. N., Haydel, K. F., Hayward, C., et al. (1997). Prospective study of risk factors for the initiation of cigarette smoking. *Journal of Consulting and Clinical Psychology, 65,* 1011–1016.

Killen, J. D., Taylor, C. B., Hayward, C., Haydel, K. F., Wilson, D. M., Hammer, L., . . . Strachowski, D. (1996). Weight concerns influence the development of eating disorders: A 4 year prospective study. *Journal of Consulting and Clinical Psychology, 64,* 936–940.

Killen, J. D., Taylor, C. B., Hayward, C., Wilson, D. M., Haydel, K. F., et al. (1994). Pursuit of thinness and onset of eating disorders in a community sample of adolescent girls. *International Journal of Eating Disorders, 16,* 227–238.

Kim, E. (2005). The effect of the decreased safety behaviors on anxiety and negative thoughts in social phobics. *Journal of Anxiety Disorders, 19,* 69–86.

Kim, E. D., & Lipshultz, L. I. (1997). Advances in the evaluation and treatment of the infertile man. *World Journal of Urology, 15,* 378–393.

Kim, H. J., Steketee, G., & Frost, R. O. (2001). Hoarding by elderly people. *Health and Social Work, 26*(3), 176–184.

Kim, M. J., Loucks, R. A., Palmer, A. L., Brown, A. C., Solomon, K. M., Marchante, A. N., & Whalen, P. J. (2011). The structural and functional connectivity of the amygdala: From normal emotion to pathological anxiety. *Behavioural Brain Research.* doi: 10.1016/j.bbr.2011.04.025

Kim, Y. S., Leventhal, B. L., Koh, Y.-J., Fombonne, E., Laska, E., Lim, E.-C., . . . Grinker, R. R. (2011). Prevalence of autism spectrum disorders in a total population sample. *American Journal of Psychiatry in Advance,* 1–9. doi: 10.1176/appi.ajp.2011.10101532.

Kim, Y., Zerwas, S., Trace, S. E., & Sullivan, P. F. (2011). Schizophrenia genetics: Where next? *Schizophrenia Bulletin, 37,* 456–463.

King, A. C., de Wit, H., McNamara, P. J., & Cao, D. (2011). Rewarding, stimulant, and sedative alcohol responses and relationship to future binge drinking. *Archives of General Psychiatry, 68,* 389–399.

Kinsey, A. C., Pomeroy, W. B., & Martin, C. E. (1948). *Sexual behavior in the human male.* Philadelphia: Saunders.

Kinzl, J. F., Traweger, C., Trefalt, E., Mangweth, B., & Biebl, W. (1999). Binge eating disorder in females: A population based investigation. *International Journal of Eating Disorders, 25,* 287–292.

Kirkbride, J. B., Fearon, P., Morgan, C., Dazzon, P., Morgan, K., et. al. (2006). Heterogeneity in the incidence of schizophrenia and other psychotic illnesses: Results from the 3-center Aesop study. *Archives of General Psychiatry, 63,* 250–258.

Kirkpatrick, B., Fenton, W., Carpenter, W.T., & Marder, S.R. (2006). The NIMH-MATRICS consensus statement on negative symptoms. *Schizophrenia Bulletin, 32,* 296–303.

Kirmayer, L. J. (2001). Cultural variations in the clinical presentation of depression and anxiety: Implications for diagnosis and treatment. *Journal of Clinical Psychiatry, 62* (Suppl. 13), 22–28.

Kirmayer, L. J., Robbins, J. M., & Paris, J. (1994). Somatoform disorders: Personality and social matrix of somatic distress. *Journal of Abnormal Psychology, 103,* 125–136.

Kirmayer, L. J., Thombs, B. D., Jurcik, T., Jarvis, G. E., & Guzder, J. (2008). Use of an expanded version of the DSM-IV outline for cultural formulation on a cultural consultation service. *Psychiatric Services, 59,* 683–686.

Kirsch, I. (2000). Are drug and placebo effects in depression additive? *Biological Psychiatry, 47,* 733–735.

Kirsch, I., Deacon, B. J., Huedo-Medina, T. B., Scoboria, A., Moore, T. J., & Johnson, B. T. (2008). Initial severity and antidepressant benefits: A meta-analysis of data submitted to the Food and Drug Administration. *PLoS Medicine, 5,* e45.

Kisiel, C. L., & Lyons, J. S. (2001). Dissociation as a mediator of psychopathology among sexually abused children and adolescents. *American Journal of Psychiatry, 158,* 1034–1039.

Kisley, M. A., Wood, S., & Burrows, C. L. (2007). Looking at the sunny side of life: Age-related change in an event-related potential measure of the negativity bias. *Psychological Science, 18,* 838.

Klein, D. N., Lewinsohn, P. M., Seeley, J. R., & Rohde, P. A. (2001). A family study of major depressive disorder in a community sample of adolescents. *Archives of General Psychiatry, 58,* 13–20.

Klein, D. N., Schwartz, J. E., Rose, S., & Leader, J. B. (2000). Five-year course and outcome of dysthymic disorder: A prospective, naturalistic follow-up study. *American Journal of Psychiatry, 157,* 931–939.

Klein, D. N., Shankman, S. A. M. A., & Rose, S. M. A. (2006). Ten-year prospective follow-up study of the naturalistic course of dysthymic disorder and double depression. *American Journal of Psychiatry, 163,* 872–880.

Kleinman, A. (1986). *Social origins of distress and disease: Depression, neurasthenia, and pain in modern China.* New Haven, CT: Yale University Press.

Klerman, G. L. (1988). Depression and related disorders of mood (affective disorders). In A. M. Nicholi, Jr. (Ed.), *The new Harvard guide to psychiatry.* Cambridge, MA: Harvard University Press.

Klerman, G. L., Weissman, M. M., Rounsaville, B. J., & Chevron, E. S. (1984). *Interpersonal psychotherapy of depression.* New York: Basic Books.

Kliem, S., Kröger, C., & Kosfelder, J. (2010). Dialectical behavior therapy for borderline personality disorder: A meta-analysis using mixed-effects modeling. *Journal of Consulting and Clinical Psychology, 78*(6), 936–951. doi: 10.1037/a0021015.supp

Klingberg, T., Hedehus, M., Temple, E., Salz, T., Gabrieli, J. D., Moseley, M. E., & Poldrack, R. A. (2000). Microstructure of temporo-parietal white matter as a basis for reading ability: Evidence from diffusion tensor magnetic resonance imaging. *Neuron, 25,* 493–500.

Klinger, E., Bouchard, S., Legeron, P., Roy, S., Lauer, F., Chemin, I., & Nugues, P. (2005). Virtual reality therapy versus cognitive behavior therapy for social phobia: A preliminary controlled study. *CyberPsychology and Behvaior, 8*(1), 76–88.

Klintsova, A. Y., Scamra, C., Hoffman, M., Napper, R. M. A., Goodlett, C. R., & Greenough, W. T. (2002). Therapeutic effects of complex motor training on motor performance deficits induced by neonatal binge-like alcohol exposure in rats: II. A quantitative stereological study of synaptic plasticity in female rat cerebellum. *Brain Research, 937,* 83–93.

Kloner, R. A., & Rezkalla, S. H. (2007). To drink or not to drink? That is the question. *Circulation, 116,* 1306–1317. doi: 1310.1161/CIRCULATIONAHA.1106.678375.

Klonsky, E. D., Oltmanns, T. F., & Turkheimer, E. (2002). Informant-reports of personality disorder: Relations to self-reports and future research directions. *Clinical Psychology: Science and Practice, 9,* 300–311.

Kluft, R. P. (1994). Treatment trajectories in multiple personality disorder. *Dissociation, 7,* 63–75.

Klump, K. L., McGue, M., & Iacono, W. G. (2000). Age differences in genetic and environmental influences on eating attitudes and behaviors in preadolescent and adolescent female twins. *Journal of Abnormal Psychology, 109,* 239–251.

Klump, K. L., McGue, M., & Iacono, W. G. (2002). Genetic relationships between personality and eating attitudes and behaviors. *Journal of Abnormal Psychology, 111,* 380–389.

Klunk, W. E., Engler, H., Nordberg, A., Wang, Y., Blomqvist, G., & Holt, D. P. (2004). Imaging brain amyloid in Alzheimer's disease with Pittsburgh compound-b. *Annuals of Neurology, 55,* 306–319.

Knight, B. G. (1996). *Psychotherapy with older adults* (2nd ed.). Thousand Oaks, CA: Sage.

Knox, K. L., Pflanz, S., Talcott, G. W., Campise, R. L., Lavigne, J. E., Bajorska, A., . . . Caine, E. D. (2010). The US Air Force suicide prevention program: Implications for public health policy. *American Journal of Public Health, 100*(12), 2457–2463.

Kochanek, K. D., Xu, J., Murphy, S. L., Minino, A. M., & Kung, H-S. (2011). *Deaths: Preliminary numbers for 2009.* National Vital Health Statistics Report, 59. Hyattsville, MD: National Center for Health Statistics.

Koegel, R. L., Bimbela, A., & Schreibman, L. (1996). Collateral effects of parent training on family interactions. *Journal of Autism and Developmental Disorders, 26,* 347–359.

Koegel, R. L., Koegel, L. K., & Brookman, L. I. (2003). Empirically supported pivotal response interventions with children with autism. In A. E. Kazdin & J. R. Weisz (Eds.), *Evidence-based psychotherapies for children and adolescents* (pp. 341–357). New York: Guilford.

Koegel, R. L., Schreibman, L., Britten, K. R., Burkey, J. C., & O'Neill, R. E. (1982). A comparison of parent training to direct child treatment. In R. L. Koegel, A. Rincover, & A. L. Egel (Eds.), *Educating and understanding autistic children.* San Diego: College-Hill.

Koenen, K. C., Moffitt, T. E., Poulton, R., Martin, J., & Caspi, A. (2007). Early childhood factors associated with the development of post-traumatic stress disorder: Results from a longitudinal birth cohort. *Psychological Medicine, 37*(2), 181–192. doi: 10.1017/S0033291706009019

Kohn, L. P., Oden, T., Munoz, R. F., Robinson, A., & Leavitt, D. (2002). Adapted cognitive behavioral group therapy for depressed low-income African American women. *Community Mental Health Journal, 38*(6), 497–504.

Kohn, M. L. (1968). Social class and schizophrenia: A critical review. In D. Rosenthal & S. S. Kety (Eds.), *The transmission of schizophrenia.* Elmsford, NY: Pergamon.

Kohut, H. (1971). *The analysis of the self.* New York: International Universities Press.

Kohut, H. (1977). *The restoration of the self.* New York: International Universities Press.

Koller, E. A., Cross, J. T., Doraiswamy, P. M., & Malozowski, S. N. (2003). Pancreatitis associated with atypical antipsychotics: From the Food and Drug Administration's MedWatch surveillance system and published reports. *Pharmacotherapy, 23,* 1123–1130.

Kolmen, B. K., Feldman, H. E., Handen, B. L., & Janosky, J. E. (1995). Naltrexone in young autistic children: A double-blind, placebo-controlled crossover study. *Journal of the American Academy of Child and Adolescent Psychiatry, 34,* 223–231.

Kong, L. L., Allen, J. J., & Glisky, E. L. (2008). Interidentity memory transfer in dissociative identity disorder. *Journal of Abnormal Psychology, 117*(3), 686–692. doi: 10.1037/0021-843X.117.3.686

Koob, G. F. (2008). A role for brain systems in addiction. *Neuron, 59,* 11–34.

Koob, G. F., & Le Moal. (2008). Addiction and the brain antireward system. *Annual Review of Psychology, 59,* 29–53.

Koob, G. F., Caine, B., Hyytia, P., Markou, A., Parsons, L. H., Roberts, A. J., et al. (1999). Neurobiology of drug addiction. In M. D. Glantz & C. R. Hartel (Eds.), *Drug abuse: Origins and interventions* (pp. 161–190). Washington, DC: American Psychological Association.

Kopelowicz, A., & Liberman, R. P. (1998). Psychosocial treatments for schizophrenia. In P. E. Nathan & J. M. Gorman (Eds.), *A guide to treatments that work* (pp. 190–211). New York: Oxford University Press.

Kopelowicz, A., Liberman, R. P., & Zarate, R. (2002). Psychosocial treatments for schizophrenia. In P. E. Nathan & J. M. Gorman (Eds.), *A guide to treatments that work* (pp. 201–229). New York: Oxford University Press.

Kornør, H., Winje, D., Ekeberg, Ø., Weisæth, L., Kirkehei, I., Johansen, K., & Steiro, A. (2008). Early traumafocused cognitive-behavioural therapy to prevent chronic post-traumatic stress disorder and related symptoms: A systematic review and meta-analysis. *Biological Medical Central Psychiatry, 8*(81), 1–8. doi: 10.1186/1471-244X-8-81

Kosten, T. R., Morgan, C. M., Falcione, J., & Schottenfeld, R. S. (1992). Pharmacotherapy for cocaine-abusing methadone-maintained patients using amantadine or desipramine. *Archives of General Psychiatry, 49,* 894–898.

Kotov, R., Gamez, W., Schmidt, F., & Watson, D. (2010). Linking "big" personality traits to anxiety, depressive, and substance use disorders: A meta-analysis. *Psychological Bulletin, 136*(5), 768–821. doi: 10.1037/a0020327

Kozak, M. J., Liebowitz, M., & Foa, E. B. (2000). Cognitive behavior therapy and pharmacotherapy for OCD: The NIMH-sponsored collaborative study. In W. K. Goodman, M. V. Rudorfer, & J. D. Maser (Eds.), *Obsessive compulsive disorder: Contemporary issues in treatment.* Mahwah, NJ: Erlbaum.

Kozel, N. J., & Adams, E. H. (1986). Epidemiology of drug abuse: An overview. *Science, 234,* 970–974.

Kozol, H., Boucher, R., & Garofalo, R. (1972). The diagnosis and treatment of dangerousness. *Crime and Delinquency, 18,* 37–92.

Kranzler, H. R., & Van Kirk, J. (2001). Efficacy of naltrexone and acamprosate for alcoholism treatment: A meta-analysis. *Alcoholism: Clinical and Experimental Research, 25*, 1335–1341.

Krause, K. H., Dresel, S. H., Krause, J., La Fougere, C., & Ackenheil, M. (2003). The dopamine transporter and neuroimaging in attention deficit hyperactivity disorder. *Neuroscience and Biobehavioral Reviews, 27*, 605–613.

Kremen, W. S., Jacobson, K. C., Xian, H., Eisen, S. A., Waterman, B., Toomey, R., et al. (2005). Heritability of word recognition in middle-aged men varies as a function of parental education. *Behavior Genetics, 35*, 417–433.

Kremen, W. S., Koenen, K. C., Boake, C., Purcell, S., Eisen, S. A., Franz, C. E., . . . Lyons, M. J. (2007). Pretrauma cognitive ability and risk for posttraumatic stress disorder. *Archives of General Psychiatry, 64*, 361–368.

Kreslake, J. M., Wayne, G. F., Alpert, H. R., Koh, H. K., & Connolly, G. N. (2008). Tobacco industry control of menthol in cigarettes and targeting of adolescents and young adults. *American Journal of Public Health, 98*, 1685–1692.

Kreyenbuhl, J., Zito, J. M., Buchanan, R. W., Soeken, K. L., & Lehman, A. F. (2003). Racial disparity in the pharmacological management of schizophrenia. *Schizophrenia Bulletin, 29*, 183–193.

Kring, A. M. (1999). Emotion in schizophrenia: Old mystery, new understanding. *Current Directions in Psychological Science, 8*, 160–163.

Kring, A. M. (2000). Gender and anger. In A. H. Fischer (Ed.), *Gender and emotion* (pp. 211–231). Cambridge, England: Cambridge University Press.

Kring, A. M., & Caponigro, J. M. (2010). Emotion in schizophrenia: Where feeling meets thinking. *Current Directions in Psychological Science, 19*, 255–259.

Kring, A. M., & Moran, E. K. (2008). Emotional response deficits in schizophrenia: Insights from affective science. *Schizophrenia Bulletin, 34*, 819–834.

Krinsley, K. E., Gallagher, J., Weathers, F. W., Kutter, C. J., & Kaloupek, D. G. (2003). Consistency of retrospective reporting about exposure to traumatic events. *Journal of Traumatic Stress, 16*, 399–409.

Krueger, R. B. (2010a). The DSM diagnostic criteria for sexual masochism. *Archives of Sexual Behavior, 39*(2), 346–356. doi: 10.1007/s10508-010-9613-4

Krueger, R. B. (2010b). The DSM diagnostic criteria for sexual sadism. *Archives of Sexual Behavior, 39*(2), 325–345. doi: 10.1007/s10508-009-9586-3

Krueger, R. F. (1999). Personality traits in late adolescence predict mental disorders in early adulthood: A prospective-epidemiological study. *Journal of Personality, 67*, 39–65.

Krueger, R. F., Eaton, N. R., Derringer, J., Markon, K. B., Watson, D., & Skodol, A. E. (2011). Personality in DSM–5: Helping delineate personality disorder content and framing the metastructure. *Journal of Personality Assessment, 93*, 325–331.

Krueger, R. F., Markon, K. E., Patrick, C. J., & Iacono, W. G. (2005). Externalizing psychopathology in adulthood: A dimensional-spectrum conceptualization and its implications for DSM-V. *Journal of Abnormal Psychology, 114*, 537–550.

Krystal, J. H., Cramer, J. A., Krol, W. F., et al. (2001). Naltrexone in the treatment of alcohol dependence. *New England Journal of Medicine, 345*, 1734–1739.

Kubzansky, L. D. (2007). Sick at heart: The pathophysiology of negative emotions. *Cleveland Clinic Journal of Medicine, 74* (Suppl 1), S67–S72.

Kuehnle, K. (1998). Child sexual abuse evaluations: The scientist-practitioner model. *Behavioral Sciences and the Law, 16*, 5–20.

Kuhn, T. S. (1970). *The structure of scientific revolutions*. Chicago: University of Chicago Press. (Original work published 1962)

Kunkel, D., Wilcox, B. L., Cantor, J., Palmer, E., Linn, S., & Dowrick, P. (2004). Report of the APA Task Force on Advertising and Children. Washington, DC: American Psychological Association.

Kupfer, D. J. (2005). The increasing medical burden in bipolar disorder. *Journal of the American Medical Association, 293*, 2528–2530.

Kurian, B. T., Ray, W. A., Arbogast, P. G., Fuchs, D. C., Dudley, J. A., & Cooper, W. O. (2007). Effect of regulatory warnings on antidepressant prescribing for children and adolescents. *Archives of General Psychiatry, 161*, 690–696.

Laan, E., Everaerd, W., & Both, S. (2005). Female sexual arousal. In R. Balon & R. T. Segraves (Eds.), *Handbook of sexual dysfunctions and paraphilias*. Boca Raton, FL: Taylor & Francis.

Ladoceur, R., Dugas, M. J., Freeston, M. H., Leger, E., Gagnon, F., & Thibodeua, N. (2000). Efficacy of a new cognitive-behavioral treatment for generalized anxiety disorder: Evaluation in a controlled clinical trial. *Journal of Consulting and Clinical Psychology, 68*, 957–996.

Lahey, B. B., Loeber, R., Burke, J. D., & Applegate, B. (2005). Predicting future antisocial personality disorder in males from a clinical assessment in childhood. *Journal of Consulting and Clinical Psychology, 73*, 389–399.

Lahey, B. B., Loeber, R., Hart, E. L., Frick, P. J., Applegate, B., Zhang, Q., . . . Russo, M. F. (1995). Four year longitudinal study of conduct disorder in boys: Patterns and predictors of persistence. *Journal of Abnormal Psychology, 104*, 83–93.

Lahey, B. B., McBurnett, K., & Loeber, R. (2000). Are attention-deficit/hyperactivity disorder and oppositional defiant disorder developmental precursors to conduct disorder? In A. J. Sameroff, M. Lewis, et al. (Eds.), *Handbook of developmental psychopathology* (2nd ed., pp. 431–446). New York: Kluwer Academic/Plenum.

Lahey, B. B., Miller, T. L., Gordon, R. A., & Riley, A. W. (1999). Developmental epidemiology of the disruptive behavior disorders. In H. C. Quay & A. Hogan (Eds.), *Handbook of disruptive behavior disorders* (pp. 23–48). New York: Plenum.

Lalumiere, M. L., & Quinsey, V. L. (1994). The discriminability of rapists from nonsex offenders using phallometric measures. *Criminal Justice and Behavior, 21*, 150–175.

Lam, D. H., Bright, J., Jones, S., Hayward, P., Schuck, N., Chisholm, D., & Sham, P. (2000). Cognitive therapy for bipolar illness—a pilot study of relapse prevention. *Cognitive Therapy and Research, 24*, 503–520.

Lam, R. W., Levitt, A. J., Levitan, R. D., Enns, M. W., Morehouse, R., Michalak, E. E., & Tam, E. M. (2006). The Can-SAD study: A randomized controlled trial of the effectiveness of light therapy and fluoxetine in patients with winter seasonal affective disorder. *American Journal of Psychiatry, 163*, 805–812.

Lamb, H. R., Weinberger, L. E., & DeCuir, W. J. (2002). The police and mental health. *Psychiatry Services, 53*, 1266–1271.

Lambert, M. J. (2004). Psychotherapeutically speaking—updates from the Division of Psychotherapy (29). Retrieved August 2008 from http://www.apa.org/about/division/div29.aspx

Lambert, M. J., & Ogles, B. M. (2004). The efficacy and effectiveness of psychotherapy. In M. J. Lambert (Ed.), *Bergin and Garfield's handbook of psychotherapy and behavior change* (5th ed., pp. 139–193). Hoboken, NJ: Wiley.

Lambrou, C., Veale, D., & Wilson, G. (2011). The role of aesthetic sensitivity in body dysmorphic disorder. *Journal of Abnormal Psychology, 120*(2), 443–453. doi: 10.1037/a0022300

Landa, R. J., Holman, K. C., & Garrett-Mayer, E. (2007). Social and communication development in toddlers with early and later diagnosis of autism spectrum disorders. *Archives of General Psychiatry, 64*, 853–864.

Landerl, K., Fussenegger, B., Moll, K., & Willburger, E. (2009). Dyslexia and dyscalculia: Two learning disorders with different cognitive profiles. *Journal of Experimental Child Psychology, 103*, 309–324.

Landgrebe, M., Barta, W., Rosengarth, K., Frick, U., Hauser, S., Langguth, B., . . . Eichhammer, P. (2008). Neuronal correlates of symptom formation in functional somatic syndromes: A fMRI study. *NeuroImage, 41*, 1336–1344.

Lane, E. A., & Albee, G. W. (1965). Childhood intellectual differences between schizophrenic adults and their siblings. *American Journal of Orthopsychiatry, 35*, 747–753.

Lang, A. R., Goeckner, D. J., Adessor, V. J., & Marlatt, G. A. (1975). Effects of alcohol on aggression in male social drinkers. *Journal of Abnormal Psychology, 84*, 508–518.

Langa, K. M., Larson, E. B., Karlawish, J. H., Cutler, D. M., Kabeto, M. U., Kim, S. Y., & Rosen, A. B. (2008). Trends in the prevalence and mortality of cognitive impairment in the United States: Is there evidence of a compression of cognitive morbidity? *Alzheimer's and Dementia: The Journal of the Alzheimer's Association, 4*, 134–144.

Langstrom, N. (2010). The DSM diagnostic criteria for exhibitionism, voyeurism, and frotteurism. *Archives of Sexual Behavior, 39*(2), 317–324. doi: 10.1007/s10508-009-9577-4

Langstrom, N., & Seto, M. C. (2006). Exhibitionistic and voyeuristic behavior in a Swedish national population survey. *Archives of Sexual Behavior, 35*(4), 427–435. doi: 10.1007/s10508-006-9042-6

Lantz, P. M., House, J. S., Lepkowski, J. M., Williams, D. R., et al. (1998). Socioeconomic factors, health behaviors, and mortality. *Journal of the American Medical Association, 279*, 1703–1708.

Larsson, H., Andershed, H., & Lichtenstein, P. (2006). A genetic factor explains most of the variance in psychopathic personality. *Journal of Abnormal Psychology, 115*, 221–230.

Larsson, H., Tuvblad, C., Rijsdijk, F. V., Andershed, H., Grann, M., & Lichtenstein, P. (2007). A common genetic factor explains the association between psychopathic personality and antisocial behavior. *Psychological Medicine, 37*, 15–26.

Lau, J. Y. F., Gregory, A. M., Goldwin, M. A., Pine, D. S., & Eley, T. C. (2007). Assessing gene–environment interactions on anxiety symptom subtypes across childhood and adolescence. *Development and Psychopathology, 19*, 1129–1146.

Laugesen, N., Dugas, M. J., & Bukowski, W. M. (2003). Understanding adolescent worry: The application of a cognitive model. *Journal of Abnormal Child Psychology, 31*, 55–64.

Laumann, E. O., Gagnon, J. H., Michael, R. T., & Michaels, S. (1994). *The social organization of sexuality*. Chicago: University of Chicago Press.

Laumann, E. O., Nicolosi, A., Glasser, D. B., Paik, A., Gingell, C., Moreira, E., & Wang, T. (2005). Sexual problems among women and men aged 40–80 y: Prevalence and correlates identified in the global study of sexual attitudes and behaviors. *International Journal of Impotence Research, 17*, 39–57.

Laumann, E. O., Paik, A., & Rosen, R. C. (1999). Sexual dysfunction in the United States: Prevalence and predictors. *Journal of the American Medical Association, 281(6),* 537–544.

Lauril, J. V., Pitkala, K. H., Strandberg, T. E., & Tilvis, R. S. (2004). Detection and documentation of dementia and delirium in acute geriatric wards. *General Hospital Psychiatry, 26,* 31–35.

Lavoie, K. L., Miller, S. B., Conway, M., & Fleet, R. P. (2001). Anger, negative emotions, and cardiovascular reactivity during interpersonal conflict in women. *Journal of Psychosomatic Research, 15,* 503–512.

Law, M., & Tang, J. L. (1995). An analysis of the effectiveness of interventions intended to help people stop smoking. *Archives of Internal Medicine, 155,* 1933–1941.

Lawton, M., Kleban, M. H., Dean, J., & Rajagopal, D. (1992). The factorial generality of brief positive and negative affect measures. *Journals of Gerontology, 47,* P228–P237.

Le Couteur, A., Bailey, A., Goode, S., Pickles, A., Robertson, S., Gottesman, I., & Rutter, M. (1996). A broader phenotype of autism: The clinical spectrum in twins. *Journal of Child Psychology and Psychiatry and Allied Disciplines, 37,* 785–801.

Le Grange, D., & Lock, J. A. (2005). The dearth of psychological treatment studies for anorexia nervosa. *International Journal of Eating Disorders, 37,* 79–91.

Le Grange, D., Crosby, R. D., Rathouz, P. J., & Leventhal, B. L. (2007). A randomized controlled comparison of family-based treatment and supportive psychotherapy for adolescent bulimia nervosa. *Archives of General Psychiatry, 64,* 1049–1056.

Leahy, R. L. (2003). *Cognitive therapy techniques: A practitioner's guide.* New York: Guilford.

LeBeau, R. T., Glenn, D., Liao, B., Wittchen, H. U., Beesdo-Baum, K., Ollendick, T., & Craske, M. G. (2010). Specific phobia: A review of DSM-IV specific phobia and preliminary recommendations for DSM-V. *Depression and Anxiety, 27(2),* 148–167. doi: 10.1002/da.20655

Lee, H.-C., Lin, H.-C., & Tsai, S.-Y. (2008). Severely depressed young patients have over five times increased risk for stroke: A 5-year follow-up study. *Biological Psychiatry, 64,* 912–915.

Lee, S. (1991). Anorexia nervosa in Hong Kong: A Chinese perspective. *Psychological Medicine,* 703–711.

Lee, S. S., Lahey, B., Owens, E. B., & Hinshaw, S. P. (2008). Few preschool boys and girls with ADHD are well-adjusted during adolescence. *Journal of Abnormal Child Psychology, 36,* 373–383.

Lee, S., Lee, A. M., Ngai, E., Lee, D. T. S., & Wing, Y. K. (2001). Rationale for food refusal in Chinese patients with anorexia nervosa. *International Journal of Eating Disorders, 29,* 224–229.

Lee, S., Ng, K. L., Kwok, K., & Fung, C. (2010). The changing profile of eating disorders at a tertiary psychiatric clinic in Hong Kong (1987–2007). *International Journal of Eating Disorders, 43,* 307–314.

Lee, V. E., Brooks-Gunn, J., & Shnur, E. (1988). Does Head Start work? A 1-year follow-up comparison of disadvantaged children attending Head Start, no preschool, and other preschool programs. *Developmental Psychology, 24,* 210–222.

Legido, A., Tonyes, L., Carter, D., Schoemaker, A., DiGeorge, A., & Grover, W. D. (1993). Treatment variables and intellectual outcome in children with classic phenylketonuria: A single-center-based study. *Clinical Pediatrics, 32,* 417–425.

Lehman, A. F., Kreyenbuhl, J., Buchanan, R. W., et al. (2004). The schizophrenia patient outcomes research team (PORT): Updated treatment recommendations 2003. *Schizophrenia Bulletin, 30,* 193–217.

Leibenluft, E., & Rich, B. A. (2008). Pediatric bipolar disorder. *Annual Review of Clinical Psychology, 4,* 163–187.

Leiblum, S. R. (1997). Sexual pain disorders. In G. O. Gabbard & S. D. Atkinson (Eds.), *Synopsis of treatments of psychiatric disorders* (2nd ed., pp. 805–810). Washington, DC: American Psychiatric Press.

Leischow, S. J., Ranger-Moore, J., & Lawrence, D. (2000). Addressing social and cultural disparities in tobacco use. *Addictive Behaviors, 25,* 821–831.

Leit, R. A., Gray, J. J., & Pope, H. G. (2002). The media's presentation of the ideal male body: A cause for muscle dysmorphia? *International Journal of Eating Disorders, 31,* 334–338.

Leit, R. A., Pope, H. G., & Gray, J. J. (2001). Cultural expectations of muscularity in men: The evolution of Playgirl centerfolds. *International Journal of Eating Disorders, 29,* 90–93.

Lenzenweger, M. F., Dworkin, R. H., & Wethington, E. (1991). Examining the underlying structure of schizophrenic phenomenology: Evidence for a 3-process model. *Schizophrenia Bulletin, 17,* 515–524.

Lenzenweger, M. F., Lane, M. C., Loranger, A. W., & Kessler, R. C. (2007). DSM-IV personality disorders in the National Comorbidity Survey Replication. *Biological Psychiatry, 62,* 553–564.

Leon, A. C., Portera, L., & Weissman, M. M. (1995). The social costs of anxiety disorders. *British Journal of Psychiatry, 166* (Suppl. 27), 19–22.

Leon, G. R., Fulkerson, J. A., Perry, C. L., & Early-Zald, M. B. (1995). Prospective analysis of personality and behavioral vulnerabilities and gender influences in the later development of disordered eating. *Journal of Abnormal Psychology, 104,* 140–149.

Leon, G. R., Fulkerson, J. A., Perry, C. L., Peel, P. K., & Klump, K. L. (1999). Three to four year prospective evaluation of personality and behavioral risk factors for later disordered eating in adolescent girls and boys. *Journal of Youth and Adolescence, 28,* 181–196.

Leon & McCambridge, (2006). Liver cirrhosis mortality rates in Britain from 1950 to 2002: an analysis of routine data. Lancet. 25, 367(9511):650.

Lerman, C., Caporaso, N. E., Audrain, J., Main, D., Bowman, E. D., et al. (1999). Evidence suggesting the role of specific genetic factors in cigarette smoking. *Health Psychology, 18,* 14–20.

Leslie, D. L., & Rosenheck, R. A. (2004). Incidence of newly diagnosed diabetes attributable to atypical antipsychotic medications. *American Journal of Psychiatry, 161,* 1709–1711.

Lester, D. (1995). Which nations establish suicide prevention centers? *Psychological Reports, 77,* 1298.

Leucht, S., Komossa, K., Rummel-Kluge, C., Corves, C., Hunger, H., Schmid, F., . . . Davis, J. M. (2009). A meta-analysis of head-to-head comparisons of second-generation antipsychotics in the treatment of schizophrenia. *American Journal of Psychiatry, 166,* 152–163.

Levav, I., Kohn, R., Golding, J. M., & Weissman, M. M. (1997). Vulnerability of Jews to major depression. *American Journal of Psychiatry, 154,* 941–947.

Levenson, R. W., Carstensen, L. L., & Gottman, J. M. (1994). Influence of age and gender on affect, physiology, and their interrelations: A study of long-term marriages. *Journal of Personality and Social Psychology, 67,* 56–68.

Levenson, R. W., & Miller, B. L. (2007). Loss of cells—Loss of self: Frontotemporal lobar degeneration and human emotion. *Current Directions in Psychological Science, 16,* 289–294.

Levenston, G. K., Patrick, C. J., Bradley, M. M., & Lang, P. J. (2000). The psychopath as observer: Emotion and attention in picture processing. *Journal of Abnormal Psychology, 109,* 373–385.

Leventhal, B. L., Cook, E. H., Morford, M., Ravitz, A. J., Heller, W., & Freedman, D. X. (1993). Clinical and neurochemical effects of fenfluramine in children with autism. *Journal of Neuropsychiatry and Clinical Neurosciences, 5,* 307–315.

Levitan, R. D., Kaplan, A. S., Joffe, R. T., Levitt, A. J., & Brown, G. M. (1997). Hormonal and subjective responses to intravenous meta-chlorophenylpiperazine in bulimia nervosa. *Archives of General Psychiatry, 54,* 521–528.

Levy, F., Hay, D. A., McStephen, M., Wood, C., & Waldman, I. (1997). Attention-deficit hyperactivity disorder: A category or a continuum? Genetic analysis of a large-scale twin study. *Journal of the American Academy of Child and Adolescent Psychiatry, 36,* 737–744.

Lewinsohn, P. M. (Ed.). (1974). *A behavioral approach to depression.* New York: Springer.

Lewinsohn, P. M., & Clarke, G. N. (1999). Psychosocial treatments for adolescent depression. *Clinical Psychology Review, 19,* 329–342.

Lewinsohn, P. M., Joiner, T. E., & Rohde, P. (2001). Evaluation of cognitive diathesis-stress models in predicting major depressive disorder. *Journal of Abnormal Psychology, 110,* 203–215.

Lewinsohn, P. M., Petit, J. W., Joiner, T. E., & Seeley, J. R. (2003). The symptomatic expression of major depressive disorder in adolescents and young adults. *Journal of Abnormal Psychology, 112,* 244–252.

Lewinsohn, P. M., Roberts, R. E., Seeley, J. R., Rohde, P., Gotlib, I. H., & Hops, H. (1994). Adolescent psychopathology: 2. Psychosocial risk factors for depression. *Journal of Abnormal Psychology, 103,* 302–315.

Lewinsohn, P. M., Rohde, P., Seeley, J. R., Klein, D. N., & Gotlib, I. H. (2000). Natural course of adolescent major depressive disorder in a community sample: Predictors of recurrence in young adults. *American Journal of Psychiatry, 157,* 1584–1591.

Lewis, D. O., Yeager, C. A., Swica, Y., Pincus, J. H., & Lewis, M. (1997). Objective documentation of child abuse and dissociation on 12 murderers with dissociative identity disorder. *American Journal of Psychiatry, 154,* 1703–1710.

Lewis, S. W., Barnes, T. R. E., Davies, L., Murray, R. M., Dunn, G., et al. (2006). Randomized controlled trial of effect of quality of life of prescription of clozapine vs other second generation antipsychotic drugs in resistant schizophrenia. *Schizophrenia Bulletin, 32,* 715–723.

Lewis-Fernandez, R., Hinton, D. E., Laria, A. J., Patterson, E. H., Hofmann, S. G., Craske, M. G., . . . Liao, B. (2010). Culture and the anxiety disorders: Recommendations for DSM-V. *Depression and Anxiety, 27(2),* 212–229. doi: 10.1002/da.20647

Li, F., Duncan, T. E., & Hops, H. (2001). Examining developmental trajectories in adolescent alcohol use using piecewise growth mixture modeling analysis. *Journal of Studies on Alcohol, 62,* 199–210.

Liberman, R. P., Eckman, T. A., Kopelowicz, A., & Stolar, D. (2000). *Friendship and intimacy module.* Camarillo, CA: Psychiatric Rehabilitation Consultants, PO Box 2867, Camarillo CA 93011.

Liberman, R. P., Wallace, C. J., Blackwell, G., Kopelowicz, J. V., et al. (1998). Skills training versus psychosocial occupational therapy for persons with persistent schizophrenia. *American Journal of Psychiatry, 155,* 1087–1091.

Liberto, J. G., Oslin, D. W., & Ruskin, P. E. (1996). Alcoholism in the older population. In L. L. Carstensen, B. A. Edelstein, & L. Dornbrand (Eds.), *The practical handbook of clinical gerontology* (pp. 324–348). Thousand Oaks, CA: Sage.

Lichenstein, P., & Annas, P. (2000). Heritability and prevalence of specific fears and phobias in childhood. *Journal of Child Psychology and Psychiatry and Allied Disciplines, 41,* 927–937.

Lichtenstein, P., Carlstrom, E., Ramstam, M., Gillberg, C., & Anckarsater, H. (2010). The genetics of autism spectrum disorders and related neuropsychiatric disorders in childhood. *American Journal of Psychiatry, 167,* 1357–1363.

Liddle, H. A. (1999). Theory development in a family-based therapy for adolescent drug abuse. *Journal of Clinical Child Psychology, 28,* 521–532.

Lieb, R., Meinlschmidt, G., & Araya, R. (2007). Epidemiology of the association between somatoform disorders and anxiety and depressive disorders: An update. *Psychosomatic Medicine, 69,* 860–863.

Lieberman, J. A. (2006). Comparing effectiveness of antipsychotic drugs. *Archives of General Psychiatry, 63,* 1069–1072.

Lieberman, J. A., Stroup, T. S., et al. (2005). Effectiveness of antipsychotic drugs in patients with chronic schizophrenia. *New England Journal of Medicine, 353,* 1209–1223.

Liebowitz, M. R., Heimberg, R. G., Fresco, D. M., Travers, J., & Stein, M. B. (2000). Social phobia or social anxiety disorder: What's in a name? *Archives of General Psychiatry, 57,* 191–192.

Liechti, M. E., Baumann, C., Gamma, A., & Vollenweider, F. X. (2000). Acute psychological effects of 3, 4-methylenedioxymethamphetamine (MDMA, 'Ecstasy') are attenuated by the serotonin uptake inhibitor citalopram. *Neuropsychopharmacology, 22,* 513–521.

Lief, H. I., & Hubschman, L. (1993). Orgasm in the postoperative transsexual. *Archives of Sexual Behavior, 22,* 145–155.

Lieverse, R., Van Someren, E. J. W., Nielen, M. M. A., Uitdehaag, B. M. J., Smit, J. H., & Hoogendijk, W. J. (2011). Bright light treatment in elderly patients with nonseasonal major depressive disorder: A randomized placebo-controlled trial. *Archives of General Psychiatry, 68*(1), 61–70.

Lilenfeld, L. R., Kaye, W. H., Greeno, C. G., Merikangas, K. R., Plotnicov, K., et al. (1998). A controlled family study of anorexia nervosa and bulimia nervosa: Psychiatric disorders in first-degree relatives and effects of proband comorbidity. *Archives of General Psychiatry, 55,* 603–610.

Lilienfeld, S. O. (2007). Psychological treatments that cause harm. *Perspectives on Psychological Science, 2,* 53–70.

Lilienfeld, S. O., Lynn, S. J., Kirsch, I., Chaves, J. F., Sarbin, T. R., & Ganaway, G. K. (1999). Dissociative identity disorder and the sociogenic model: Recalling lessons from the past. *Psychological Bulletin, 125,* 507–523.

Lilienfeld, S. O., Lynn, S. J., Ruscio, J., & Beyerstein, B. L. (2010). Sad, mad, and bad: Myths about mental illness. In S. O. Lilienfeld, S. J. Lynn, J. Ruscio, & B. L. Beyerstein (Eds.), *50 great myths of popular psychology: Shattering widespread misconceptions about human behavior* (pp. 181–208). Wiley.

Lilienfeld, S. O., & Marino, L. (1999). Essentialism revisited: Evolutionary theory and the concept of mental disorder. *Journal of Abnormal Psychology, 108,* 400–411.

Lilienfeld, S. O., Wood, J. M., & Garb, H. N. (2000). The scientific status of projective techniques. *Psychological Science in the Public Interest, 1,* 27–66.

Lilly, R., Quirk, A., Rhodes, T., & Stimson, G. V. (2000). Sociality in methadone treatment: Understanding methadone treatment and service delivery as a social process. *Drugs: Education, Prevention and Policy, 7,* 163–178.

Lim, K. O., Adalsteinssom, E., Spielman, D., Sullivan, E. V., Rosenbloom, M. J., & Pfefferman, A. (1998). Proton magnetic resonance spectroscopic imaging of cortical gray and white matter in schizophrenia. *Archives of General Psychiatry, 55,* 346–353.

Lindau, S. T., Schumm, L. P., Laumann, E. O., Levinson, W., O'Muircheartaigh, C. A., & Waite, L. J. (2007). A study of sexuality and health among older adults in the United States. *New England Journal of Medicine, 357,* 762–774.

Lindemann, E., & Finesinger, I. E. (1938). The effect of adrenalin and mecholyl in states of anxiety in psychoneurotic patients. *American Journal of Psychiatry, 95,* 353–370.

Linehan, M. M. (1987). Dialectical behavior therapy for borderline personality disorder. *Bulletin of the Menninger Clinic, 51,* 261–276.

Linehan, M. M. (1997). Behavioral treatments of suicidal behaviors: Definitional obfuscation and treatment outcomes. In D. M. Stoff & J. J. Mann (Eds.), *Neurobiology of suicide* (pp. 302–327). New York: Annals of the New York Academy of Sciences.

Linehan, M. M., Goodstein, J. L., Nielsen, S. L., & Chiles, J. A. (1983). Reasons for staying alive when you are thinking of killing yourself. *Journal of Consulting and Clinical Psychology, 51,* 276–286.

Linehan, M. M., & Heard, H. L. (1999). Borderline personality disorder: Costs, course, and treatment outcomes. In N. E. Miller & K. M. Magruder (Eds.), *Cost-effectiveness of psychotherapy: A guide for practitioners, researchers, and policymakers* (pp. 291–305). London: Oxford Univeristy Press.

Linehan, M. M., Heard, H. L., & Armstrong, H. E. (1993). Naturalistic follow-up of a behavioral treatment for chronically parasuicidal borderline patients. *Archives of General Psychiatry, 50,* 971–974.

Linehan, M. M., & Shearin, E. N. (1988). Lethal stress: A social-behavioral model of suicidal behavior. In S. Fisher & J. Reason (Eds.), *Handbook of life stress, cognition, and health.* New York: Wiley.

Links, P., Steiner, M., Boiago, I., & Irwin, D. (1990). Lithium therapy for borderline patients: Preliminary findings. *Journal of Personality Disorders, 4,* 173–181.

Linnet, K. M., Dalsgaard, S., Obel, C., et al. (2003). Maternal lifestyle factors in pregnancy risk of attention deficit hyperactivity disorder and associated behaviors: Review of the current evidence. *American Journal of Psychiatry, 160,* 1028–1040.

Lipsitz, J. D., Mannuzza, S., Klein, D. F., Ross, D. C., & Fyer, A. J. (1999). Specific phobia 10–16 years after treatment. *Depression and Anxiety, 10,* 105–111.

Lissek, S., Powers, A. S., McClure, E. B., Phelps, E. A., Woldehawariat, G., Grillon, C., & Pine, D. S. (2005). Classical fear conditioning in the anxiety disorders: A meta-analysis. *Behaviour Research and Therapy, 43*(11), 1391–1424. doi: 10.1016/j.brat.2004.10.007

Litrownik, A. F., & Castillo-Canez, I. (2000). Childhood maltreatment: Treatment of abuse and incest survivors. In C. R. Snyder & R. E. Ingram (Eds.), *Handbook of psychological change* (pp. 520–545). New York: Wiley.

Litz, B. T., Gray, M. J., Bryant, R. A., & Adler, A. B. (2002). Early intervention for trauma: Current status and future directions. *Clinical Psychology: Science and Practice, 9,* 112–134.

Livingston, G., Johnston, K., Katona, C., Paton, J., & Lyketsos, C. G. (2005). Systematic review of psychological approaches to the management of neuropsychiatric symptoms of dementia. *American Journal of Psychiatry, 162,* 1996–2021.

Lock, J., & Le Grange, D. (2001). Can family-based treatment of anorexia nervosa be manualized? *Journal of Psychotherapy Practice and Research, 10,* 253–261.

Lock, J., Le Grange, D., Agras, W. S., & Dare, C. (2001). *Treatment manual for anorexia nervosa: A family-based approach.* New York: Guilford.

Lock, J., Le Grange, D., Agras, S., Moye, A., Bryson, S. W., & Jo, B. (2011). Randomized clinical trial comparing family-based treatment with adolescent-focused individual therapy for adolescents with anorexia nervosa. *Archives of General Psychiatry, 67,* 1025–1032.

Lockwood, K. A., Alexopoulos, G. S., Kakuma, T., & van Gorp, W. G. (2000). Subtypes of cognitive impairment in depressed older adults. *American Journal of Geriatric Psychiatry, 8,* 201–208.

Loeb, K. L., Walsh, B. T., Lock, J., Le Grange, D., Jones, J., Marcus, S., et al. (2007). Open trial of family-based treatment for full and partial anorexia nervosa in adolescence: Evidence of successful dissemination. *Journal of the American Academy of Child and Adolescent Psychiatry, 46,* 792–800.

Loeber, R., Burke, J. D., Lahey, B. B., Winters, A., & Zera, M. (2000). Oppositional defiant and conduct disorder: A review of the past 10 years, Part I. *Journal of the American Academy of Child and Adolescent Psychiatry, 39,* 1468–1484.

Loeber, R., & Farrington, D. P. (1998). *Serious and violent juvenile offenders: Risk factors and successful interventions.* Thousand Oaks, CA: Sage.

Loeber, R., & Hay, D. (1997). Key issues in the development of aggression and violence from childhood to early adulthood. *Annual Review of Psychology, 48,* 371–410.

Loeber, R., & Keenan, K. (1994). Interaction between conduct disorder and its comorbid conditions: Effects of age and gender. *Clinical Psychology Review, 14,* 497–523.

Loftus, E. F. (1993). The reality of repressed memories. *American Psychologist, 48,* 518–537.

Logsdon, R. G., McCurry, S. M., & Teri, L. (2007). Evidence-based psychological treatments for disruptive behaviors in individuals with dementia. *Psychology and Aging, 22*(1), 28–36. doi: 10.1037/0882-7974.22.1.28

Lohr, J., Tolin, D. F., & Lilienfeld, S. O. (1998). Efficacy of eye movement desensitization and reprocessing: Implications for behavior therapy. *Behavior Therapy, 29,* 123–156.

London, P. (1964). *The modes and morals of psychotherapy.* New York: Holt, Rinehart and Winston.

Lonergan, E., Britton, A. M., & Luxenberg, J. (2007). Antipsychotics for delirium. *Cochrane Database of Systematic Reviews*(2), CD005594. doi: 10.1002/14651858.CD005594.pub2

Long, P., Forehand, R., Wierson, M., & Morgan, A. (1994). Does parent training with young noncompliant children have long-term effects? *Behaviour Research and Therapy, 32,* 101–107.

Longshore, D., Hawken, A., Urada, D., & Anglin, M. (2006). *Evaluation of the Substance Abuse and Crime Prevention Act: SACPA Cost-Analysis Report (First and Second Years).* Retrieved from http://www.uclaisap.org/prop36/html/reports.html

Longshore, D., Urada, D., Evans, E., Hser, Y. I., Prendergast, M., & Hawken, A. (2005). *Evaluation of the Substance Abuse and Crime Prevention Act: 2004 report.* Sacramento: Department of Alcohol and Drug Programs, California Health and Human Services Agency.

Longshore, D., Urada, D., Evans, E., Hser, Y. I., Prendergast, M., Hawken, A., . . . Ettner, S. (2003). *Evaluation of the Substance Abuse and Crime Prevention Act.* Retrieved from http://www.uclaisap.org/prop36/html/reports.html

Lonigan, C. J., Phillips, B. M., & Hooe, E. S. (2003). Relations of positive and negative affectivity to anxiety and depression in children: Evidence from a latent variable longitudinal study. *Journal of Consulting and Clinical Psychology, 71,* 465–481.

Looman, J. (1995). Sexual fantasies of child molesters. *Canadian Journal of Behavioural Science, 27,* 321–332.

Looney, S. W., & el-Mallakh, R. S. (1997). Meta-analysis of erythrocyte NA, K-ATPase activity in bipolar illness. *Depression and Anxiety, 5,* 53–65.

Looper, K. J., & Kirmayer, L. J. (2002). Behavioral medicine approaches to somatoform disorders. *Journal of Consulting and Clinical Psychology, 70,* 810–827.

Lopez, S. R. (1989). Patient variable biases in clinical judgment: Conceptual overview and methodological considerations. *Psychological Bulletin, 106,* 184–203.

Lopez, S. R. (1994). Latinos and the expression of psychopathology: A call for direct assessment of cultural influences. In C. Telles & M. Karno (Eds.), *Latino mental health: Current research and policy perspectives.* Los Angeles: UCLA.

Lopez, S. R. (1996). Testing ethnic minority children. In B. B. Wolman (Ed.), *The encyclopedia of psychology, psychiatry, and psychoanalysis.* New York: Holt.

Lopez, S. R. (2002). Teaching culturally informed psychological assessment: Conceptual issues and demonstrations. *Journal of Personality Assessment, 79,* 226–234.

Lopez, S. R., Garcia, J. I. R., Ullman, J. B., Kopelowicz, A., Jenkins, J., Breitborde, N. J. K., & Placencia, P. (2009). Cultural variability in the manifestation of expressed emotion. *Family Process, 48,* 179–194.

Lopez, S. R., Lopez, A. A., & Fong, K. T. (1991). Mexican Americans' initial preferences for counselors: The role of ethnic factors. *Journal of Counseling Psychology, 38,* 487–496.

Lopez, S. R., Nelson, K. A., Snyder, K. S., & Mintz, J. (1999). Attributions and affective reactions of family members and course of schizophrenia. *Journal of Abnormal Psychology, 108,* 307–314.

Lopez Leon, S., Croes, E. A., Sayed-Tabatabaei, F. A., Claes, S., Van Broekhoven, C., & van Duijn, C. M. (2005). The dopamine D4 receptor gene 48-base-pair repeat polymorphism and mood disorders: A meta-analysis. *Biological Psychiatry, 57,* 999–1003.

Lopez-Ibor, J. J., Jr. (2003). Cultural adaptations of current psychiatric classifications: Are they the solution? *Psychopathology, 36,* 114–119.

Lopiccolo, J., & Hogan, D. R. (1979). Multidimensional treatment of sexual dysfunction. In O. F. Pomerleau & J. P. Brady (Eds.), *Behavioral medicine: Theory and practice.* Baltimore, MD: Williams & Wilkins.

Lopiccolo, J., & Lobitz, W. C. (1972). The role of masturbation in the treatment of orgasmic dysfunction. *Archives of Sexual Behavior, 2,* 163–171.

Lorber, M. F. (2004). Psychophysiology of aggression, psychopathy, and conduct problems: A meta-analysis. *Psychological Bulletin, 130,* 531–552.

Lord, C., Risi, S., DiLavore, P. S., Shulman, C. Thurm, A., & Pickles, A. (2006). Autism from 2 to 9 years of age. *Archives of General Psychiatry, 63,* 694–701.

Lovaas, O. I. (1987). Behavioral treatment and normal educational and intellectual functioning in young autistic children. *Journal of Consulting and Clinical Psychology, 55,* 3–9.

Ludwig, D. S., & Currie, J. (2010). The association between pregnancy weight gain and birthweight: A within-family comparison. *Lancet, 376,* 984–990.

Luo, F., Florence, C. S., Quispe-Agnoli, M., Ouyang, L., & Crosby, A. E. (2011). Impact of business cycles on US suicide rates, 1928–2007. *American Journal of Public Health, 101*(6), 1139–1146.

Lykken, D. T. (1957). A study of anxiety in the sociopathic personality. *Journal of Abnormal and Social Psychology, 55,* 6–10.

Lynam, D., & Henry, B. (2001). The role of neuropsychological deficits in conduct disorders. In J. Hill & B. Maughan (Eds.), *Conduct disorders in childhood and adolescence* (pp. 235–263). New York: Cambridge University Press.

Lynam, D., Moffitt, T. E., & Stouthamer-Loeber, M. (1993). Explaining the relation between IQ and delinquency: Race, class, test motivation, school failure, or self-control. *Journal of Abnormal Psychology, 102,* 187–196.

Lynch, T. R., Rosenthal, M. Z., Kosson, D. S., Cheavens, J. S., Lejuez, C. W., & Blair, R. J. R. (2006). Heightened sensitivity to facial expressions of emotion in borderline personality disorder. *Emotion, 6,* 647–655.

Lynn, S. J., Lock, T., Loftus, E. F., Krackow, E., & Lilienfeld, S. O. (2003). The remembrance of things past: Problematic memory recovery techniques in psychotherapy. In S. J. Lynn & S. O. Lilienfeld (Eds.), *Science and pseudoscience in clinical psychology* (pp. 205–239). New York: Guilford.

Lyons, M. J., True, W. R., Eisen, S. A., et al. (1995). Differential heritability of adult and juvenile antisocial traits. *Archives of General Psychiatry, 52,* 906–915.

Lynskey, M. T. and Hall, W. (2001). Attention deficit hyperactivity disorder and substance use disorders: is there a causal link? *Addiction, 96,* 815–22.

Ma, S. H., & Teasdale, J. D. (2004). Mindfulness-based cognitive therapy for depression: Replication and exploration of differential relapse prevention effects. *Journal of Consulting and Clinical Psychology, 72,* 31–40.

Maarlatt, G. A. and Gordon, J. R., (1985)(Eds). Relapse Prevention: Maintenance Strategies in the Treatment of Addictive Behaviors. New York: Guilford Press.

MacDonald, A. W., III, & Carter, C. S. (2003). Event-related fMRI study of context processing in dorsolateral prefrontal cortex of patients with schizophrenia. *Journal of Abnormal Psychology, 112,* 689–697.

MacDonald, A. W., III, & Chafee, D. (2006). Translational and developmental perspective on N-methyl-D-aspartate synaptic deficits in schizophrenia. *Development and Psychopathology, 18,* 853–876.

MacDonald, V. M., Tsiantis, J., Achenbach, T. M., Motti-Stefanidi, F., & Richardson, C. (1995). Competencies and problems reported by parents of Greek and American children, ages 6–11. *European Child and Adolescent Psychiatry, 4,* 1–13.

MacGregor, M. W. (1996). Multiple personality disorder: Etiology, treatment, and techniques from a psychodynamic perspective. *Psychoanalytic Psychology, 13,* 389–402.

Mackenzie, I. R., Neumann, M., Bigio, E. H., Cairns, N. J., Alafuzoff, I., Kril, J., . . . Mann, D. M. (2009). Nomenclature for neuropathologic subtypes of frontotemporal lobar degeneration: Consensus recommendations. *Acta Neuropathologica, 117*(1), 15–18. doi: 10.1007/s00401-008-0460-5

Mackin, P., Targum, S. D., Kalali, A., Rom, D., & Young, A. H. (2006). Culture and assessment of manic symptoms. *British Journal of Psychiatry, 189,* 379–380.

Madonna, P. G., Van Scoyk, S., & Jones, D. B. (1991). Family interactions within incest and nonincest families. *American Journal of Psychiatry, 148,* 46–49.

Maffei, C., Fossati, A., Agostini, I., Barraco, A., et al. (1997). Interrater reliability and internal consistency of the Structured Clinical Interview for Axis II Personality Disorders (SCID-II), Version 2.0. *Journal of Personality Disorders, 11,* 279–284.

Maidment, I., Fox, C., & Boustani, M. (2006). Cholinesterase inhibitors for Parkinson's disease dementia. *Cochrane Database of Systematic Reviews, 1,* CD004747. doi: 10.1002/14651858.CD004747.pub2

Main, M., Kaplan, K., & Cassidy, J. (1985). Security in infancy, childhood, and adulthood: A move to the level of representation. *Monographs of the Society for Research in Child Development, 50,* (1–2, Serial No. 209).

Maj, M., Pirozzi, R., Magliano, L., & Bartoli, L. (1998). Long-term outcome of lithium prophylaxis in bipolar disorder: A 5-year prospective study of 402 patients at a lithium clinic. *American Journal of Psychiatry, 155*(1), 30–35.

Malamuth, N. M. (1998). An evolutionary-based model integrating research on the characteristics of sexually coercive men. In J. G. Adair & D. Belanger (Ed.), *Advances in psychological science: Vol. 1. Social, personal, and cultural aspects* (pp. 151–184). Hove, England: Psychology Press/Erlbaum.

Malamuth, N. M., & Brown, L. M. (1994). Sexually aggressive men's perceptions of women's communications: Testing three explanations. *Journal of Personality and Social Psychology, 67,* 699–712.

Malamuth, N. M., & Check, J. V. P. (1983). Sexual arousal to rape depictions: Individual differences. *Journal of Abnormal Psychology, 92,* 55–67.

Malaspina, D., Goetz, R. R., Yale, S., et al. (2000). Relation of familial schizophrenia to negative symptoms but not to the deficit syndrome. *American Journal of Psychiatry, 157,* 994–1003.

Malcolm, R., Herron, J. E., Anton, R. F., Roberts, J., & Moore, J. (2000). Recurrent detoxification may elevate alcohol craving as measured by the Obsessive Compulsive Drinking Scale. *Alcohol, 20,* 181–185.

Maletzky, B. M. (1997). Exhibitionism: Assessment and treatment. In D. R. Laws & W. O'Donohue (Eds.), *Sexual deviance* (pp. 40–74). New York: Guilford.

Maletzky, B. M. (2000). Exhibitionism. In M. Hersen & M. Biaggio (Eds.), *Effective brief therapy: A clinician's guide* (pp. 235–257). New York: Plenum.

Maletzky, B. M. (2002). The paraphilias: Research and treatment. In P. E. Nathan & J. M. Gorman (Eds.), *A guide to treatments that work* (pp. 525–558). New York: Oxford University Press.

Malizia, A. L. (2003). Brain imaging and anxiety disorders. In D. Nutt & J. Ballenger (Eds.), *Anxiety disorders* (pp. 201–228). Malden, MA: Blackwell.

Malkoff-Schwartz, S., Frank, E., Anderson, B. P., Hlastala, S. A., Luther, J. F., Sherrill, J. T., . . . Kupfer, D. J. (2000). Social rhythm disruption and stressful life events in the onset of bipolar and unipolar episodes. *Psychological Medicine, 30*(5), 1005–1016.

Malone, K. M., Oquendo, M. A., Haas, G. L., Ellis, S. P., Li, S., & Mann, J. J. (2000). Protective factors against suicidal acts in major depression: Reasons for living. *American Journal of Psychiatry, 157,* 1084–1088.

Mangweth, B., Hausmann, A., Walch, T., Hotter, A., Rupp, C. I., Biebl, W., et al. (2004). Body-fat perception in men with eating disorders. *International Journal of Eating Disorders, 35,* 102–108.

Manji, H. K., Chen, G., Shimon, H., Hsiao, J. K., Potter, W. Z., & Belmaker, R. H. (1995). Guanine nucleotide-binding proteins in bipolar affective disorder: Effects of long-term lithium treatment. *Archives of General Psychiatry, 52,* 135–144.

Mann, J. J., Huang, Y. Y., Underwood, M. D., Kassir, S. A., Oppenheim, S., & Kelly, T. M. (2000). A serotonin transporter gene promoter polymorphism (5-HTTLPR) and prefrontal cortical binding in major depression and suicide. *Archives of General Psychiatry, 57,* 729–738.

Mann, V. A., & Brady, S. (1988). Reading disability: The role of language deficiencies. *Journal of Consulting and Clinical Psychology, 56,* 811–816.

Mannuzza, S., Klein, R. G., Bonagura, N., Malloy, P., Giampino, T. L., & Addalli, K. A. (1991). Hyperactive boys almost grown up: 5. Replication of psychiatric status. *Archives of General Psychiatry, 48,* 77–83.

Mannuzza, S., Klein, R. G., & Moulton, J. L. (2003). Does stimulant medication place children at risk for adult substance abuse? A controlled, prospective follow-up study. *Journal of Child and Adolescent Psychopharmacology, 13,* 273–282.

Maramba, G. G., & Nagayama-Hall, G. C. (2002). Metaanalyses of ethnic match as a predictor of dropout, utilization, and level of functioning. *Cultural Diversity and Ethnic Minority Psychology, 8,* 290–297.

Marcantonio, E. R., Flacker, J. M., Wright, R. J., & Resnick, N. M. (2001). Reducing delirium after hip fracture: A randomized trial. *Journal of the American Geriatrics Society, 49,* 516–522.

March, J., Silva, S., Petrycki, S., et al. (2004). Fluoxetine, cognitive-behavioral therapy, and their combination for adolescents with depression: Treatment for adolescents with depression study (TADS) randomized controlled trial. *Journal of the American Medical Association, 292,* 807–820.

Marchand, W. R., & Yurgelun-Todd, D. (2010). Striatal structure and function in mood disorders: A comprehensive review. *Bipolar Disorders, 12*(8), 764–785.

Marcus, J., Hans, S. L., Nagier, S., Auerbach, J. G., Mirsky, A. F., & Aubrey, A. (1987). Review of the NIMH Israeli kibbutz-city and the Jerusalem infant development study. *Schizophrenia Bulletin, 13,* 425–438.

Marder, S. R., Wirshing, W. C., Glynn, S. M., Wirshing, D. A., Mintz, J., & Liberman, R. P. (1999). Risperidone and haloperidol in maintenance treatment. Interactions with psychosocial treatments. *Schizophrenia Research, 36,* 288.

Marengo, J., & Westermeyer, J. F. (1996). Schizophrenia and delusional disorder. In L. L. Carstensen, B. A. Edelstein, & L. Dornbrand (Eds.), *The practical handbook of clinical gerontology* (pp. 255–273). Thousand Oaks, CA: Sage.

Margraf, J., Ehlers, A., & Roth, W. T. (1986). Sodium lactate infusions and panic attacks: A review and critique. *Psychosomatic Medicine, 48,* 23–51.

Markowitz, J. C. (1994). Psychotherapy of dysthymia. *American Journal of Psychiatry, 151,* 1114–1121.

Marks, I. (1995). Advances in behavioral-cognitive therapy of social phobia. *Journal of Clinical Psychiatry, 56,* 25–31.

Marks, I., & Cavanagh, K. (2009). Computer-aided psychological treatments: Evolving issues. *Annual Review of Clinical Psychology, 5,* 121–141. doi: 10.1146/annurev.clinpsy.032408.153538

Marks, I., Lovell, K., Noshirvani, H., Livanou, M., & Thrasher, S. (1998). Treatment of posttraumatic stress disorder by exposure and/or cognitive restructuring: A controlled study. *Archives of General Psychiatry, 55,* 317.

Marlatt, G. A. (1983). The controlled drinking controversy: A commentary. *American Psychologist, 38,* 1097–1110.

Marlatt, G. A., & Gordon, J. R. (Eds.). (1985). *Relapse prevention: Maintenance strategies in the treatment of addictive behaviors.* New York: Guilford.

Marques, J. K., Wiederanders, M., Day, D. M., Nelson, C., & Van Ommeren, A. (2005). Effects of a relapse prevention program on sexual recidivism: Final results from California's Sex Offender Treatment and Evaluation Project (SOTEP). *Sexual Abuse: A Journal of Research and Treatment, 17*(1), 79–107. doi: 10.1177/107906320501700108

Marrazzi, M. A., & Luby, E. D. (1986). An auto-addiction model of chronic anorexia nervosa. *International Journal of Eating Disorders, 5,* 191–208.

Marsh, A. A., & Blair, R. J. R. (2008). Deficits in facial affect recognition among antisocial populations: A meta-analysis. *Neuroscience and Biobehavioral Reviews, 32,* 454–465.

Marshall, L. A., & Cooke, D. J. (1999). The childhood experiences of psychopaths: A retrospective study of familial and societal factors. *Journal of Personality Disorders, 13,* 211–225.

Marshall, W. L. (1997). Pedophilia: Psychopathology and theory. In D. R. Laws & W. O'Donohue (Eds.), *Sexual deviance* (pp. 152–174). New York: Guilford.

Marshall, W. L., Barbaree, H. E., & Christophe, D. (1986). Sexual offenders against female children: Sexual preferences for age of victims and type of behaviour. *Canadian Journal of Behavioural Science, 18,* 424–439.

Marson, D. C. (2001). Loss of competency in Alzheimer's disease: Conceptual and psychometric approaches. *International Journal of Law and Psychiatry, 24,* 267–283.

Marson, D. C., Huthwaite, J. S., & Hebert, K. (2004). Testamentary capacity and undue influence in the elderly: A jurisprudent therapy perspective. *Law and Psychology Review, 28,* 71–96.

Martell, B. A., Orson, F. M., Poling, J., Mitchell, E., Rossen, R. D., Gardner, T., et al. (2009). Cocaine vaccine for the treatment of cocaine dependence in methadone-maintained patients: A randomized, double-blind, placebo-controlled efficacy trial. *Archives of General Psychiatry, 66,* 1116–1123.

Martell, C. R., Addis, M. E., & Jacobson, N. S. (2001). *Ending depression one step at a time: The new behavioral activation approach to getting your life back.* New York: Oxford University Press.

Martinez, C., & Eddy, M. (2005). Effects of culturally adapted parent management training on Latino youth behavioral health outcomes. *Journal of Consulting and Clinical Psychology, 73,* 841–851.

Martini, D. R., Ryan, C., Nakayama, D., & Ramenofsky, M. (1990). Psychiatric sequelae after traumatic injury: The Pittsburgh regatta accident. *Journal of the American Academy of Child and Adolescent Psychiatry, 29,* 70–75.

Mason, B. J. (2001). Treatment of alcohol-dependent outpatients with acamprosate: A clinical review. *Journal of Clinical Psychiatry, 62,* 42–48.

Mason, F. L. (1997). Fetishism: Psychopathology and theory. In D. R. Laws & W. O'Donohue (Eds.), *Sexual deviance* (pp. 75–91). New York: Guilford.

Masters, W. H., & Johnson, V. E. (1966). *Human sexual response.* Boston: Little, Brown.

Masters, W. H., & Johnson, V. E. (1970). *Human sexual inadequacy.* Boston: Little, Brown.

Mataix-Cols, D., Frost, R. O., Pertusa, A., Clark, L. A., Saxena, S., Leckman, J. F., . . . Wilhelm, S. (2010). Hoarding disorder: A new diagnosis for DSM-V? *Depression and Anxiety, 27*(6), 556–572. doi: 10.1002/da.20693

Mataix-Cols, D., Marks, I. M., Greist, J. H., Kobak, K. A., & Baer, L. (2002). Obsessive-compulsive symptom dimensions as predictors of compliance with and response to behaviour therapy: Results from a controlled trial. *Psychotherapy and Psychosomatics, 71*(5), 255–262.

Mather, M., Canli, T., English, T., Whitfield, S., Wais, P., Ochsner, K., . . . Carstensen, L. L. (2004). Amygdala responses to emotionally valenced stimuli in older and younger adults. *Psychological Science, 15,* 259–263.

Mathews, A., & MacLeod, C. (2002). Induced processing biases have causal effects on anxiety. *Cognition and Emotion, 16,* 331–354.

Matsuda, L. A., Lolait, S. J., Brownstein, M. J., Young, A. C., & Bonner, T. I. (1990). Structure of a cannabinoid receptor and functional expression of the cloned cDNA. *Nature, 346,* 561–564.

Matthews, K. A., Owens, J. F., Kuller, L. H., Sutton-Tyrrell, K., & Jansen-McWilliams, L. (1998). Are hostility and anxiety associated with carotid atherosclerosis in healthy postmenopausal women? *Psychosomatic Medicine, 60,* 633–638.

Maugh T. H., II (2002, October 18). "Sobering" state report calls autism an epidemic. *Los Angeles Times,* pp. A1, A25.

Mayberg, H. S., Lozano, A. M., Voon, V., McNeely, H. E., Seminowicz, D., Hamani, C., . . . Kennedy, S. H. (2005). Deep brain stimulation for treatment-resistant depression. *Neuron, 45*(5), 651–660.

Mayer, E. A., Berman, S., Suyenobu, B., Labus, J., Mandelkern, M. A., Naliboff, B. D., & Chang, L. (2005). Differences in brain responses to visceral pain between patients with irritable bowel syndrome and ulcerative colitis. *Pain, 115,* 398–409.

Mayes, V., Cochran, S., & Barnes, N. W. (2007). Race, race-based discrimination, and health outcomes among African Americans. *Annual Review of Psychology, 58,* 201–225.

McBride, P. A., Anderson, G. M., & Shapiro, T. (1996). Autism research: Bringing together approaches to pull apart the disorder. *Archives of General Psychiatry, 53,* 980–983.

McCabe, R. E., McFarlane, T., Polivy, J., & Olmsted, M. (2001). Eating disorders, dieting, and the accuracy of self-reported weight. *International Journal of Eating Disorders, 29,* 59–64.

McCall, W. V., Reboussin, D. M., Weiner, R. D., & Sackeim, H. A. (2000). Titrated moderately suprathreshold vs fixed high-dose right unilateral electroconvulsive therapy: Acute antidepressant and cognitive effects. *Archives of General Psychiatry, 57,* 438–444.

McCann, D., Barrett, A., Cooper, A., et al. (2007). Food additives and hyperactive behaviour in 3-year-old and 8/9-year-old children in the community: A randomised, double-blinded, placebo-controlled trial. *Lancet, 370,* 1560–1567.

McCarthy, B. W. (1986). A cognitive-behavioral approach to understanding and treating sexual trauma. *Journal of Sex and Marital Therapy, 12,* 322–329.

McCarthy, D. E., Piasecki, T. M., Fiore, M. C., & Baker, T. (2006). Life before and after quitting smoking: An electronic diary study. *Journal of Abnormal Psychology, 115,* 454–466.

McCarty, D., Caspi, Y., Panas, L., Krakow, M., & Mulligan, D. H. (2000). Detoxification centers: Who's in the revolving door? *Journal of Behavioral Health Services and Research, 27,* 245–256.

McClellan, J., Kowatch, R., & Findling, R. L. (2007). Practice parameter for the assessment and treatment of children and adolescents with bipolar disorder. *Journal of the American Academy of Child and Adolescent Psychiatry, 46,* 107–125.

McCleod, B. D., Weisz, J. R., & Wood, J. J. (2007). Examining the association between parenting and childhood anxiety: A meta-analysis. *Clinical Psychology Review, 27*, 155–172.

McClure, M. M., Barch, D. M., Flory, J. D., Harvey, P. D., & Siever, L. J. (2008). Context processing in schizotypal personality disorder: Evidence of specificity of impairment to the schizophrenia spectrum. *Journal of Abnormal Psychology, 117*(2), 342–354. doi: 10.1037/0021-843X.117.2.342

McCormick, N. B. (1999). When pleasure causes pain: Living with interstitial cystitis. *Sexuality and Disability, 17*, 7–18.

McCrady, B. S., & Epstein, E. E. (1995). Directions for research on alcoholic relationships: Marital and individual-based models of heterogeneity. *Psychology of Addictive Behaviors, 9*, 157–166.

McCrae, R. R., & Costa, P. T., Jr. (1990). *Personality in adulthood.* New York: Guilford.

McCullough, J. P., Klein, D. N., Keller, M. B., Holzer, C. E., Davis, S. M., Korenstein, S. G., . . . Harrison, W. M. (2000). Comparison of DSM-III major depression and major depression superimposed on dysthymia (double depression): Validity of the distinction. *Journal of Abnormal Psychology, 109*, 419–427.

McCurry, S. M., Logsdon, R. G., Teri, L., & Vitiello, M. V. (2007). Evidence-based psychological treatments for insomnia in older adults. *Psychology and Aging, 22*(1), 18–27. doi: 10.1037/0882-7974.22.1.18

McCusker, J., Cole, M., & Abrahamowicz, M. (2002). Delirium predicts 12-month mortality. *Archives of Internal Medicine, 162*, 457–463.

McDonough, M., & Kennedy, N. (2002). Pharmacological management of obsessive-compulsive disorder: A review for clinicians. *Harvard Review of Psychiatry, 10*, 127–137.

McEachin, J. J., Smith, T., & Lovaas, O. I. (1993). Longterm outcome for children with autism who received early intensive behavioral treatment. *American Journal on Mental Retardation, 97*, 359–372.

McElwee, G. (2010). ManAlive.Ulster Cancer Foundation. www.ulstercancer.org

McEvoy, J. P., Johnson, J., Perkins, D., Lieberman, J. A., Hamer, R. M., Keefe, R. S. E., et al. (2006). Insight in first episode psychosis. *Psychological Medicine, 36*, 1385–1393.

McEwan, B., & Sapolsky, R. (1995). Stress and cognitive function. *Current Opinion in Neurobiology, 5*(2), 205–216.

McFall, R. M., & Hammen, C. L. (1971). Motivation, structure, and self-monitoring: Role of nonspecific factors in smoking reduction. *Journal of Consulting and Clinical Psychology, 37*, 80–86.

McFarlane, T., Polivy, J., & Herman, C. P. (1998). Effects of false weight feedback on mood, self-evaluation, and food intake in restrained and unrestrained eaters. *Journal of Abnormal Psychology, 107*, 312–318.

McFarlane, W. R., Lukens, E., Link, B., Dushay, R., Deakins, S., Newmark, M., . . . Toran, J. (1995). Multiple-family groups and psychoeducation in the treatment of schizophrenia. *Archives of General Psychiatry, 52*, 679–687.

McGhie, A., & Chapman, I. S. (1961). Disorders of attention and perception in early schizophrenia. *British Journal of Medical Psychology, 34*, 103–116.

McGlashan, T. H., Grilo, C. M., Sanislow, C. A., Ralevski, E., Morey, L. C., Gunderson, J. G., . . . Pagano, M. E. (2005). Two-year prevalence and stability of individual criteria for schizotypal, borderline, avoidant, and obsessive-compulsive personality disorders. *American Journal of Psychiatry, 162*, 883–889.

McGlashan, T. H., Grilo, C. M., Skodol, A. E., Gunderson, J. G., Shea, M. T., Morey, L. C., . . . Stout, R. L. (2000). The collaborative longitudinal personality disorders study: Baseline axis I/II and II/II diagnostic co-occurrence. *Acta Psychiatrica Scandinavica, 102*, 256–564.

McGlashan, T. H., & Hoffman, R. E. (2000). Schizophrenia as a disorder of developmentally reduced synaptic connectivity. *Archives of General Psychiatry, 57*, 637–648.

McGovern, C. W., & Sigman, M. (2005). Continuity and change from early childhood to adolescence in autism. *Journal of Child Psychology and Psychiatry, 46*, 401–408.

McGue, M., Pickens, R. W., & Svikis, D. S. (1992). Sex and age effects on the inheritance of alcohol problems: A twin study. *Journal of Abnormal Psychology, 101*, 3–17.

McGuire, P. K., Bench, C. J., Frith, C. D., & Marks, I. M. (1994). Functional anatomy of obsessive-compulsive phenomena. *British Journal of Psychiatry, 164*, 459–468.

McGuire, P. K., Shah, G. M. S., & Murray, R. M. (1993). Increased blood flow in Broca's area during auditory hallucinations in schizophrenia. *Lancet, 346*, 596–600.

McGuire, P. K., Silbersweig, D. A., & Frith, C. D. (1996). Functional neuroanatomy of verbal self-monitoring. *Brain, 119*, 907–917.

McGurk, S. R., Twamley, E. W., Sitzer, D. I., McHugo, G. J., & Mueser, K. T. (2007). A meta-analysis of cognitive remediation in schizophrenia. *American Journal of Psychiatry, 164*, 1791–1802.

McHugh, R. K., & Barlow, D. H. (2010). The dissemination and implementation of evidence-based psychological treatments. A review of current efforts. *American Psychologist, 65*(2), 73–84. doi: 10.1037/a0018121

McIntyre-Kingsolver, K., Lichtenstein, E., & Mermelstein, R. J. (1986). Spouse training in a multicomponent smoking-cessation program. *Behavior Therapy, 17*, 67–74.

McKeith, I. G., Dickson, D. W., Lowe, J., Emre, M., O'Brien, J. T., Feldman, H., . . . Burn, D. J. (2005). Diagnosis and management of dementia with Lewy bodies; third report of the DLB consortium. *Neurology, 65*, 1863–1872.

McKeller, J., Stewart, E., & Humphreys, K. (2003). Alcoholics Anonymous involvement and positive alcohol related outcomes: Cause, consequence, or just a correlate? A prospective 2-year study of 2,319 alcohol dependent men. *Journal of Consulting and Clinical Psychology, 71*, 302–308.

McKhann, G. M., Knopman, D. S., Chertkow, H., Hyman, B. T., Jack, C. R., Jr., Kawas, C. H., . . . Phelps, C. H. (2011). The diagnosis of dementia due to Alzheimer's disease: Recommendations from the National Institute on Aging-Alzheimer's Association work groups on diagnostic guidelines for Alzheimer's disease. *Alzheimer's and Dementia: The Journal of the Alzheimer's Association, 7*(3), 263–269. doi: 10.1016/j.jalz.2011.03.005

McKim, W. A. (1991). *Drugs and behavior: An introduction to behavioral pharmacology.* Englewood Cliffs, NJ: Prentice Hall.

McKinley, N. M., & Hyde, J. S. (1996). The objectified body consciousness scale: Development and validation. *Psychology of Women Quarterly, 20*, 181–216.

McKown, C., & Weinstein, R. S. (2003). The development and consequences of stereotype consciousness in middle childhood. *Child Development, 74*, 498–515.

McLeod, B. D., Wood, J. J., & Weisz, J. R. (2007). Examining the association between parenting and childhood anxiety: A meta-analysis. *Clinical Psychology Review, 27*, 155–172.

McMahon, C. G., Althof, S. E., Kaufman, J. M., Buvat, J., Levine, S. B., Aquilina, J. W., . . . Porst, H. (2011). Efficacy and safety of dapoxetine for the treatment of premature ejaculation: Integrated analysis of results from five phase 3 trials. *Journal of Sexual Medicine, 8*(2), 524–539. doi: 10.1111/j.1743-6109.2010.02097.x

McMahon, C. G., Althof, S. E., Waldinger, M. D., Porst, H., Dean, J., Sharlip, I. D., . . . Segraves, R. (2008). An evidence-based definition of lifelong premature ejaculation: Report of the International Society for Sexual Medicine (ISSM) ad hoc committee for the definition of premature ejaculation. *Journal of Sexual Medicine, 5*(7), 1590–1606. doi: 10.1111/j.1743-6109.2008.00901.x

McMullen, S., & Rosen, R. C. (1979). Self-administered masturbation training in the treatment of primary orgasmic dysfunction. *Journal of Consulting and Clinical Psychology, 47*, 912–918.

McNally, R. J. (1987). Preparedness and phobias: A review. *Psychological Bulletin, 101*, 283–303.

McNally, R. J. (1997). Atypical phobias. In G. C. L. Davey (Ed.), *Phobias: A handbook of theory, research and treatment* (pp. 183–199). Chichester, England: Wiley.

McNally, R. J. (2003). *Remembering trauma.* Cambridge, MA: Belknap Press/Harvard University Press.

McNally, R. J. (2009). Can we fix PTSD in DSM-V? *Depression and Anxiety, 26*(7), 597–600. doi: 10.1002/da.20586

McNally, R. J., Caspi, S. P., Riemann, B. C., & Zeitlin, S. B. (1990). Selective processing of threat cues in posttraumatic stress disorder. *Journal of Abnormal Psychology, 99*, 398–402.

McNally, R. J., Lasko, N. B., Clancy, S. A., Macklin, M. L., Pitman, R. K., & Orr, S. P. (2004). Psychophysiological responding during script-driven imagery in people reporting abduction by space aliens. *Psychological Science, 15*, 493–497.

McNally, R. J., Ristuccia, C. S., & Perlman, C. A. (2005). Forgetting trauma cues in adults reporting continuous or recovered memories of childhood sexual abuse. *Psychological Science, 16*, 336–340.

McNeil, T. F., Cantor-Graae, E., & Weinberger, D. R. (2000). Relationship of obstetric complications and differences in size of brain structures in monozygotic twin pairs discordant for schizophrenia. *American Journal of Psychiatry, 157*, 203–212.

McQuaid, J. R., Monroe, S. M., Roberts, J. R., & Johnson, S. L., et al. (1992). Toward the standardization of life stress assessment: Definitional discrepancies and inconsistencies in methods. *Stress Medicine, 8*, 47–56.

Meagher, D. J. (2001). Delirium: Optimizing management. *British Medical Journal, 322*, 144–149.

Meagher, D. J. (2007). Phenomenology of delirium: Assessment of 100 adult cases using standardised measures. *British Journal of Psychiatry, 190*, 135–141.

Meana, M., Binik, I., Khalife, S., & Cohen, D. (1997). Dyspareunia: Sexual dysfunction or pain syndrome? *Journal of Nervous and Mental Disease, 185*, 561–569.

Meana, M., Binik, I., Khalife, S., & Cohen, D. (1998). Affect and marital adjustment in women's ratings of dyspareunic pain. *Canadian Journal of Psychiatry, 43*, 381–385.

Meaney, M. J., Brake, W., & Gratton, A. (2002). Environmental regulation of the development of mesolimbic dopamine systems: A neurobiological mechanism for vulnerability to drug abuse? *Psychoneuroendocrinology, 27*, 127–148.

Mednick, S. A., Huttonen, M. O., & Machon, R. A. (1994). Prenatal influenza infections and adult schizophrenia. *Schizophrenia Bulletin, 20*, 263–268.

Mednick, S. A., Machon, R., Hottunen, M. O., & Bonett, D. (1988). Fetal viral infection and adult schizophrenia. *Archives of General Psychiatry, 45*, 189–192.

Mednick, S. A., & Schulsinger, F. (1968). Some premorbid characteristics related to breakdown in children with schizophrenic mothers. In D. Rosenthal & S. S. Kety (Eds.), *The transmission of schizophrenia.* Elmsford, NY: Pergamon.

Mehler, P. S. (2011). Medical complications of bulimia nervosa and their treatments. *International Journal of Eating Disorders, 44,* 95–104.

Meier, B. (2003). *Pain killer: A "wonder" drug's trail of addiction and death.* Emmaus, PA: Rodale.

Melamed, B. G., & Siegel, L. J. (1975). Reduction of anxiety in children facing hospitalization and surgery by use of filmed modeling. *Journal of Consulting and Clinical Psychology, 43,* 511–521.

Mellinger, G. D., Balter, M. B., & Uhlenhuth, E. H. (1985). Insomnia and its treatment. *Archives of General Psychiatry, 42,* 225–232.

Melnik, T., Soares, B. G. O., & Nasello, A. G. (2008). The effectiveness of psychological interventions for the treatment of erectile dysfunction: Systematic review and meta-analysis, including comparisons to sildenafil treatment, intracavernosal injection, and vacuum devices. *Journal of Sexual Medicine, 5,* 2562–2574.

Meltzer, H. Y. (2003). Suicide in schizophrenia. *Journal of Clinical Psychiatry, 64,* 1122–1125.

Meltzer, H. Y., Cola, P., & Way, L. E. (1993). Cost effectiveness of clozapine in neuroleptic-resistant schizophrenia. *American Journal of Psychiatry, 150,* 1630–1638.

Melville, J. D., & Naimark, D. (2002). Punishing the insane: The verdict of guilty but mentally ill. *Journal of the American Academy of Psychiatry and the Law, 30,* 553–555.

Mendez, M. F., Lauterbach, E. C., & Sampson, S. M. (2008). An evidence-based review of the psychopathology of frontotemporal dementia: A report of the ANPA committee on research. *Journal of Neuropsychiatry and Clinical Neurosciences, 20*(2), 130–149. doi: 10.1176/appi.neuropsych.20.2.130

Menezes, N. M., Arenovich, T., & Zipursky, R. B. (2006). A systematic review of longitudinal outcome studies of first-episode psychosis. *Psychological Medicine, 36,* 1349–1362.

Meng, Y.-Y., Babey, S. H., Hastert, T. A., Lombardi, C., & Brown, E. R. (2008). *Uncontrolled asthma means missed work and school, emergency department visits for many Californians.* Los Angeles: UCLA Center for Health Policy Research.

Mennin, D. S., Heimberg, R. G., & Turk, C. L. (2004). Clinical presentation and diagnostic features. In R. G. Heimberg, C. L. Turk, & D. S. Mennin (Eds.), *Generalized anxiety disorder* (pp. 3–28). New York: Guilford.

Mennin, D. S., Heimberg, R. G., Turk, C. L., & Fresco, D. M. (2002). Applying an emotion regulation framework to integrative approaches to generalized anxiety disorder. *Clinical Psychology: Science and Practice, 9,* 135–141.

Menzies, L., Chamberlain, S. R., Laird, A. R., Thelen, S. M., Sahakian, B. J., & Bullmore, E. T. (2008). Integrating evidence from neuroimaging and neuropsychological studies of obsessive-compulsive disorder: The orbitofronto-striatal model revisited. *Neuroscience and Biobehavioral Reviews, 32*(3), 525–549. doi: 10.1016/j.neubiorev.2007.09.005

Mercer, C. H., Fenton, K. A., Johnson, A. M., Wellings, K., Macdowall, W., Mcmanus, S., . . . Erens, B. (2003). Sexual function problems and help seeking behaviour in Britain: National probability sample survey. *British Medical Journal, 327,* 426–427.

Merckelbach, H., Dekkers, T., Wessel, I., & Roefs, A. (2003). Dissociative symptoms and amnesia in Dutch concentration camp survivors. *Comprehensive Psychiatry, 44,* 65–69.

Merikangas, K. R., Akiskal, H. S., Angst, J., Greenberg, P. E., Hirschfeld, R. M. A., Petukhova, M., & Kessler, R. C. (2007). Lifetime and 12-month prevalence of bipolar spectrum disorder in the National Comorbidity Survey Replication. *Archives of General Psychiatry, 64,* 543–552.

Merikangas, K. R., Jin, R., He, J. P., Kessler, R., Lee, S., Sampson, N., . . . Zarkov, Z. (2011). Prevalence and correlates of bipolar spectrum disorder in the World Mental Health Survey Initiative. *Archives of General Psychiatry, 68*(3), 241–251.

Merkin, D. (2009, May 10). A long journey in the dark, *New York Times Magazine,* pp. 28–48.

Merzenich, M. M., Jenkins, W. M., Johnson, P., Schreiner, C., Miller, S. L., & Tallal, P. (1996). Temporal processing deficits of language-learning impaired children ameliorated by training. *Science, 271,* 77–81.

Messinger, J. W., Tremeau, F., Antonius, D., Mendelsohn, E., Prudent, V., Stanore, A. D., & Malaspina, D. (2011). Avolition and expressive deficits capture negative symptom phenomenology: Implications for the DSM–5 and schizophrenia research. *Clinical Psychology Review, 31,* 161–168.

Meston, C., & Buss, D. (2009). *Why women have sex: Women reveal the truth about their sex lives, from adventure to revenge (and everything in between).* New York: St. Martin's Press.

Meston, C. M., & Gorzalka, B. B. (1995). The effects of sympathetic activation on physiological and subjective sexual arousal in women. *Behaviour Research and Therapy, 33,* 651–664.

Meyer, B., Johnson, S. L., & Winters, R. (2001). Responsiveness to threat and incentive in bipolar disorder: Relations of the BIS/BAS scales with symptoms. *Journal of Psychopathology and Behavioral Assessment, 23,* 133–143.

Meyer, G. J., & Archer, R. P. (2001). The hard science of Rorschach research: "What do we know and where do we go?" *Psychological Assessment, 13,* 486–502.

Meyer, J. K. (1995). Paraphilias. In H. I. Kaplan & B. J. Sadock (Eds.), *Comprehensive textbook of psychiatry* (pp. 1334–1347). Baltimore, Williams & Wilkins.

Meyer, V. (1966). Modification of expectations in cases with obsessional rituals. *Behaviour Research and Therapy, 4,* 273–280.

Meyer, V., & Chesser, E. S. (1970). *Behavior therapy in clinical psychiatry.* Baltimore: Penguin.

Mezzich, J. E., Fabrega, H., Jr., Coffman, G. A., & Haley, R. (1989). DSM-III disorders in a large sample of psychiatric patients: Frequency and specificity of diagnoses. *The American Journal of Psychiatry, 146*(2), 212–219.

Michael, T., Blechert, J., Vriends, N., Margraf, J., & Wilhelm, F. H. (2007). Fear conditioning in panic disorder: Enhanced resistance to extinction. *Journal of Abnormal Psychology, 116,* 612–617.

Mikami, A. Y., Hinshaw, S. P., Arnold, L. E., Hoza, B., Hechtman, L., Newcorn, J. H., & Abikoff, H. B. (2010). Bulimia nervosa symptoms in the multimodal treatment study of children with ADHD. *International Journal of Eating Disorders, 43,* 248–259.

Mikami, A. Y., Huang-Pollack, C. L., Pfiffner, L. J., McBurnett, K., & Hangai, D. (2007). Social skills differences among attention-deficit/hyperactivity disorder types in a chat room assessment task. *Journal of Abnormal Child Psychology, 35,* 509–521.

Miklowitz, D. J., George, E. L., Richards, J. A., Simoneau, T. L., & Suddath, R. L. (2003). A randomized study of family-focused psychoeducation and pharmacotherapy in the outpatient management of bipolar disorder. *Archives of General Psychiatry, 60,* 904–912.

Miklowitz, D. J., & Goldstein, M. J. (1997). *Bipolar disorder: A family-focused treatment approach.* New York: Guilford.

Miklowitz, D. J., Otto, M. W., Frank, E., Reilly-Harrington, N. A., Wisniewski, S. R., Kogan, J. N., . . . Sachs, G. S. (2007). Psychosocial treatments for bipolar depression: A 1-year randomized trial from the systematic treatment enhancement program. *Archives of General Psychiatry, 64,* 419–427.

Miklowitz, D. J., & Taylor, D.O. (2005). *Family-focused treatment of the suicidal bipolar patient.* Unpublished manuscript.

Milberger, S., Biederman, J., Faraone, S. V., & Chen, L. (1996). Is maternal smoking during pregnancy a risk factor for attention deficit hyperactivity disorder in children? *American Journal of Psychiatry, 153,* 1138–1142.

Miller, B. L., Ikonte, C., Ponton, M., & Levy, M. (1997). A study of the Lund Manchester research criteria for frontotemporal dementia: Clinical and single-photon emission CT correlations. *Neurology, 48,* 937–942.

Miller, D. D., Caroff, S. N., Davis, S. M., et al. (2008). Extrapyramidal side-effects of antipsychotics in a randomised trial. *British Journal of Psychiatry, 193,* 279–288.

Miller, M., & Hinshaw, S. P. (2010). Does childhood executive function predict adolescent functional outcomes in girls with ADHD? *Journal of Abnormal Childhood Psychology, 38,* 315–326.

Miller, T. J., McGlashan, T. H., Rosen, J. L., et al. (2002). Prospective diagnosis of the initial prodrome for schizophrenia based on the Structured Interview for Prodromal Syndromes: Preliminary evidence of interrater reliability and predictive validity. *American Journal of Psychiatry, 159,* 863–865.

Miller, T. Q., & Volk, R. J. (1996). Weekly marijuana use as a risk factor for initial cocaine use: Results from a six wave national survey. *Journal of Child and Adolescent Substance Abuse, 5,* 55–78.

Miller, W. R., & Rollnick, S. (Eds.). (1991). *Motivational interviewing: Preparing people to change addictive behavior.* New York: Guilford.

Millon, T. (1996). *Disorders of personality: DSM-IV and beyond* (2nd ed.). New York: Wiley.

Milrod, B., Leon, A. C., Busch, F., Rudden, M., Schwalberg, M., Clarkin, J., . . . Shear, M. K. (2007). A randomized controlled clinical trial of psychoanalytic psychotherapy for panic disorder. *American Journal of Psychiatry, 164,* 265–272.

Mineka, S., & Öhman, A. (2002). Born to fear: Nonassociative vs. associative factors in the etiology of phobias. *Behaviour Research and Therapy, 40,* 173–184.

Mineka, S., & Sutton, J. (2006). Contemporary learning theory perspectives on the etiology of fear and phobias. In M. G. Craske, D. Hermans, & D. Vansteenwegen (Eds.), *Fear and learning: From basic processes to clinical implications* (pp. 75–97). Washington, DC: American Psychological Association.

Mineka, S., & Zinbarg, R. (1998). Experimental approaches to the anxiety and mood disorders. In J. G. Adair, D. Belanger, & K. L. Dion (Eds.), *Advances in psychological science: Vol. 1. Social, personal, and cultural aspects.* (pp. 429–454), Psychology Press, East Sussex, UK.

Mineka, S., & Zinbarg, R. (2006). A contemporary learning theory perspective on the etiology of anxiety disorders: It's not what you thought it was. *American Psychologist, 61*(1), 10–26. doi: 10.1037/0003–066X.61.1.10

Minzenberg, M. J., Fan, J., New, A. S., Tang, C. Y., & Siever, L. J. (2007). Fronto-limbic dysfunction in response to facial emotion in borderline personality disorder: An event-related fMRI study. *Psychiatry Research, 115*(3), 231–243.

Minzenberg, M. J., Fan, J., New, A. S., Tang, C. Y., & Siever, L. J. (2008). Frontolimbic structural changes in borderline personality disorder. *Journal of Psychiatric Research, 42*(9), 727–733.

Miranda, J., Bernal, G., Lau, A., Kohn, L., Hwang, W., & LaFromboise, T. (2005). State of the science on psychosocial interventions for ethnic minorities. *Annual Review of Psychology, 1*, 113–142.

Miranda, J., Green, B. L., Krupnick, J. L., Chung, J., Siddique, J., Belin, T., & Revicki, D. (2006). One-year outcomes of a randomized clinical trial treating depression in low-income minority women. *Journal of Consulting and Clinical Psychology, 74*, 99–111.

Mishkind, M. E., Rodin, J., Silberstein, L. R., & Striegel-Moore, R. H. (1986). The embodiment of masculinity: Cultural, psychological, and behavioral dimensions. *American Behavioral Scientist, 29*, 545–562.

Mitchell, J. E. (1992). Subtyping of bulimia nervosa. *International Journal of Eating Disorders, 11*, 327–332.

Mitchell, J. T., & Everly, G. S., Jr. (2000). Critical incident stress management and critical incident stress debriefings: Evolutions, effects and outcomes. In J. P. Wilson & B. Raphael (Eds.), *Psychological debriefing: Theory, practice and evidence* (pp. 71–90). New York: Cambridge University Press.

Mitte, K. (2005). Meta-analysis of cognitive-behavioral treatments for generalized anxiety disorder: A comparison with pharmacotherapy. *Psychological Bulletin, 131*, 785–795.

Mittelman, M. S., Brodaty, H., Wallen, A. S., & Burns, A. (2008). A three-country randomized controlled trial of a psychosocial intervention for caregivers combined with pharmacological treatment for patients with Alzheimer disease: Effects on caregiver depression. *American Journal of Geriatric Psychiatry: Official Journal of the American Association for Geriatric Psychiatry, 16*(11), 893–904. doi: 10.1097/JGP.0b013e3181898095

Modestin, J. (1992). Multiple personality disorder in Switzerland. *American Journal of Psychiatry, 149*, 88–92.

Modrego, P. J. (2010). Depression in Alzheimer's disease. Pathophysiology, diagnosis, and treatment. *Journal of Alzheimer's Disease, 21*(4), 1077–1087.

Moffitt, T. E. (1993). Adolescence-limited and life-course-persistent antisocial behavior: A developmental taxonomy. *Psychological Review, 100*, 674–701.

Moffitt, T. E. (2005). The new look of behavioral genetics in developmental psychopathology: Gene–environment interplay in antisocial behaviors. *Psychological Bulletin, 131*, 533–554.

Moffitt, T. E. (2007). A review of research on the taxonomy of life-course persistent versus adolescence-limited antisocial behavior. In D. J. Flannery, A. T. Vazsonyi, & I. D. Waldman (Eds.), *The Cambridge handbook of violent behavior and aggression* (pp. 49–74). New York: Cambridge University Press.

Moffitt, T. E., & Caspi, A. (2001). Childhood predictors differentiate life-course persistent and adolescence-limited antisocial pathways among males and females. *Development and Psychopathology, 13*, 355–375.

Moffitt, T. E., Caspi, A., Harrington, H., & Milne, B. J. (2002). Males on the life-course persistent and adolescence-limited antisocial pathways: Follow-up at age 26. *Development and Psychopathology, 14*, 179–207.

Moffitt, T. E., Caspi, A., Harrington, H., Milne, B. J., Melchior, M., Goldberg, D., & Poulton, R. (2007). Generalized anxiety disorder and depression: Childhood risk factors in a birth cohort followed to age 32. *Psychological Medicine, 37*(3), 441–452. doi: 10.1017/S0033291706009640

Moffitt, T. E., Lynam, D., & Silvia, P. A. (1994). Neuropsychological tests predict persistent male delinquency. *Criminology, 32*, 101–124.

Moffitt, T. E., & Silvia, P. A. (1988). IQ and delinquency: A direct test of the differential detection hypothesis. *Journal of Abnormal Psychology, 97*, 330–333.

Molina, B. S. G., Hinshaw, S. P., Swanson, J. M., Arnold, L. E., Vitiello, B., Jensen, P. S., et al. (2009). The MTA at 8 years: Prospective follow-up of children treated for combined-type ADHD in a multisite study. *Journal of the American Academy of Child and Adolescent Psychiatry, 48*, 484–500.

Molnar, B. E., Buka, S. L., & Kessler, R. C. (2001). Child sexual abuse and subsequent psychopathology: Results from the National Comorbidity Survey. *American Journal of Public Health, 91*(5), 753–760.

Monahan, J. (1973). The psychiatrization of criminal behavior. *Hospital and Community Psychiatry, 24*, 105–107.

Monahan, J. (1976). The prevention of violence. In J. Monahan (Ed.), *Community mental health and the criminal justice system*. Elmsford, NY: Pergamon.

Monahan, J. (1984). The prediction of violent behavior: Toward a second generation of theory and policy. *American Journal of Psychiatry, 141*, 10–15.

Monahan, J. (1992). Mental disorder and violent behavior: Perceptions and evidence. *American Psychologist, 47*, 511–521.

Monahan, J., & Steadman, H. (1994). Toward a rejuvenation of risk assessment research. In J. Monahan & H. Steadman (Eds.), *Violence and mental disorder: Developments in risk assessment*. Chicago: University of Chicago Press.

Moniz, E. (1936). *Tentatives operatoires dans le traitement de ceretaines psychoses*. Paris: Mason.

Monk, C. S., Nelson, E. E., McClure, E. B., Mogg, K., Bradley, B. P., Leibenluft, E., . . . Pine, D. (2006). Ventrolateral prefrontal cortex activation and attentional bias in response to angry faces in adolescents with generalized anxiety disorder. *American Journal of Psychiatry, 163*, 1091–1097.

Monroe, S. M., & Harkness, K. L. (2005). Life stress, the "kindling" hypothesis, and the recurrence of depression: Considerations from a life stress perspective. *Psychological Review, 112*, 417–445.

Monuteaux, M., Faraone, S. V., Gross, L., & Biederman, J. (2007). Predictors, clinical characteristics, and outcome of conduct disorder in girls with attention-deficit/ hyperactivity disorder: A longitudinal study. *Psychological Medicine, 37*, 1731–1741.

Moos, R. H., & Humphreys, K. (2004). Long-term influence of duration and frequency of participation in Alcoholics Anonymous on individuals with alcohol use disorders. *Journal of Consulting and Clinical Psychology, 72*, 81–90.

Moos, R. H., & Moos, B. S. (2006). Participation in treatment and Alcoholics Anonymous: A 16-year follow-up of initially untreated individuals. *Journal of Clinical Psychology, 62*, 735–750.

Mora, S., Redberg, R. F., Cui, Y., Whiteman, M. K., Flaws, J. A., Sharrett, A. R., & Blumenthal, R. S. (2003). Ability of exercise testing to predict cardiovascular and all-cause death in asymptomatic women: A 20-year follow-up of the lipid research clinics prevalence study. *Journal of the American Medical Association, 290*, 1600–1607.

Moran, M. (1991). Psychological factors affecting pulmonary and rheumatological diseases: A review. *Psychosomatics, 32*, 14–23.

Moreau, D., Mufson, L., Weissman, M. M., & Klerman, G. L. (1992). Interpersonal psychotherapy for adolescent depression: Description of modification and preliminary application. *Journal of the Academy of Child and Adolescent Psychiatry, 30*, 642–651.

Moreland, K., Wing, S., Diez Roux, A., & Poole, C. (2002). Neighborhood characteristics associated with the location of food stores and food services places. *American Journal of Preventive Medicine, 22*, 23–29.

Morenz, B., & Becker, J. V. (1995). The treatment of youthful sexual offenders. *Applied and Preventive Psychology, 4*, 247–256.

Morey, L. C. (1988). Personality disorders in DSM-III and DSM-IIIR: Convergence, coverage, and internal consistency. *American Journal of Psychiatry, 145*, 573–577.

Morey, L. C., Berghuis, H., Bender, D., Verheul, R., Krueger, R. F., & Skodol, A. E. (2011). Toward a model for assessing level of personality functioning in DSM–5, Part II: Empirical articulation of a core dimension of personality pathology. *Journal of Personality Assessment, 93*(4), 347–353.

Morf, C.C., & Rhodewalt, F. (2001). Unraveling the paradoxes of narcissim: A dynamic self-regulatory processing model. *Psychological Inquiry, 12*, 177–196.

Morgan, C. A., III., Hazlett, G., Wang, S., Richardson, E. G. J., Schnurr, P., & Southwick, S. M. (2001). Symptoms of dissociation in humans experiencing acute, uncontrollable stress: A prospective investigation. *American Journal of Psychiatry, 158*, 1239–1247.

Morgan, M. J. (2000). Ecstasy (MDMA): A review of its possible persistent psychological effects. *Psychopharmacology, 152*, 230–248.

Morgenstern, J., Blanchard, K. A., Morgan, T. J., Labouvie, E., & Hayaki, J. (2001). Testing the effectiveness of cognitive-behavioral treatment for substance abuse in a community setting: Within treatment and posttreatment findings. *Journal of Consulting and Clinical Psychology, 69*, 1007–1017.

Morgenstern, J., Langenbucher, J., Labouvie, E., & Miller, K. J. (1997). The comorbidity of alcoholism and personality disorders in a clinical population: Prevalence rates and relation to alcohol typology variables. *Journal of Abnormal Psychology, 106*, 74–84.

Morokoff, P. J., & Gilliland, R. (1993). Stress, sexual functioning, and marital satisfaction. *Journal of Sex Research, 30*, 43–53.

Moroney, J. T., Tang, M. X., Berglund, L., Small, S., Merchant, C., Bell, K., . . . Mayeux, R. (1999). Low-density lipoprotein cholesterol and the risk of dementia with stroke. *Journal of the American Medical Association, 282*, 254–260.

Morriss, R. K., Faizal, M. A., Jones, A. P., Williamson, P. R., Bolton, C., & McCarthy, J. P. (2007). Interventions for helping people recognise early signs of recurrence in bipolar disorder. *Cochrane Database of Systematic Reviews, Issue 1*, CD004854. doi: 10.1002/14651858.CD004854.pub2

Morrow, J., & Nolen-Hoeksema, S. (1990). Effects of responses to depression on the remediation of depressive affect. *Journal of Personality and Social Psychology, 58*, 519–527.

Morse, S. J. (1982). A preference for liberty: The case against involuntary commitment of the mentally disordered. *California Law Review, 70*, 54–106.

Morse, S. J. (1992). The "guilty mind": Mens rea. In D. K. Kagehiro & W. S. Laufer (Eds.), *Handbook of psychology and law* (pp. 207–229). New York: Springer-Verlag.

Moscicki, E. K. (1995). Epidemiology of suicidal behavior. In M. M. Silverman & R. W. Maris (Eds.), *Suicide prevention: Toward the year 2000* (pp. 22–35). New York: Guilford.

Moser, C., & Levitt, E. E. (1987). An exploratory descriptive study of a sadomasochistically oriented sample. *Journal of Sex Research, 23*, 322–337.

Moses, J. A., & Purisch, A. D. (1997). The evolution of the Luria-Nebraska Battery. In G. Goldstein & T. Incagnoli (Eds.), *Contemporary approaches to neuropsychological assessment* (pp. 131–170). New York: Plenum.

Moses, J. A., Schefft, B. A., Wong, J. L., & Berg, R. A. (1992). Interrater reliability analyses of the Luria-Nebraska Neuropsychological Battery, Form II. *Archives of Clinical Neurology, 7,* 251–269.

Mowrer, O. H. (1947). On the dual nature of learning: A reinterpretation of "conditioning" and "problem-solving." *Harvard Educational Review, 17,* 102–148.

MTA Cooperative Group. (1999a). A 14-month randomized clinical trial of treatment strategies for attention-deficit/hyperactivity disorder. *Archives of General Psychiatry, 56,* 1073–1086.

MTA Cooperative Group. (1999b). Moderators and mediators of treatment response for children with attention-deficit/hyperactivity disorder. *Archives of General Psychiatry, 56,* 1088–1096.

Muehlenhard, C. L., & Shippee, S. K. (2010). Men's and women's reports of pretending orgasm. *Journal of Sex Research, 47*(6), 552–567. doi: 10.1080/00224490903171794

Mueser, K. T., Bond, G. R., Drake, R. E., & Resnick, S. G. (1998). Models of community care for severe mental illness: A review of research on case management. *Schizophrenia Bulletin, 24,* 37–74.

Mufson, L., Weissman, M. M., Moreau, D., & Garfinkel, R. (1999). Efficacy of interpersonal psychotherapy for depressed adolescents. *Archives of General Psychiatry, 56,* 573–579.

Multon, K. D., Kivlighan, D. M., & Gold, P. B. (1996). Changes in counselor adherence over the course of training. *Journal of Counseling Psychology, 43,* 356–363.

Mulvey, E. P. (1994). Assessing the evidence of a link between mental illness and violence. *Hospital and Community Psychiatry, 45,* 663–668.

Mundle, G., Bruegel, R., Urbaniak, H., Laengle, G., Buchkremer, G., & Mann, K. (2001). Kurzund mittelfristige Erfolgsraten ambulanter Entwoehnungsbehandlungen fuer alkoholabhaengige Patienten. *Fortschritte der Neurologie Psychiatrie, 69,* 374–378.

Mundo, E., Maina, G., & Uslenghi, C. (2000). Multicentre, double-blind comparison of fluvoxamine and clomipramine in the treatment of obsessive-compulsive disorder. *International Clinical Psychopharmacology, 15,* 69–76.

Munetz, M. R., Grande, T., Kleist, J., & Peterson, G. A. (1996). The effectiveness of outpatient civil commitment. *Psychiatric Services, 47,* 1251–1253.

Munro, S., Thomas, K. L., & Abu-Shaar, M. (1993). Molecular characterization of a peripheral receptor for cannabinoids. *Nature, 365,* 61–65.

Munson, J., Dawson, G., Abbott, R., et al. (2006). Amygdalar volume and behavioral development in autism. *Archives of General Psychiatry, 63,* 686–693.

Muntner, P., He, J., Cutler, J. A., Wildman, R. P., & Whelton, P. K. (2004). Trends in blood pressure among adolescents and children. *Journal of the American Medical Association, 291,* 2107–2113.

Murphy, J. (1976). Psychiatric labeling in cross-cultural perspective. *Science, 191,* 1019–1028.

Murray, C. J. L., & Lopez, A. D. (1996). *The global burden of disease: A comprehensive assessment of disease, injuries, and risk factors in 1990 and projected to 2020.* Cambridge, MA: Harvard University Press.

Murray, G., & Harvey, A. G. (2010). Circadian rhythms and sleep in bipolar disorder. *Bipolar Disorders, 12*(5), 459–472.

Murray-Close, D., Hoza, B., Hinshaw, S. P., Arnold, L. E., Swanson, J., Jensen, P. S., . . . Wells, K. (2010). Developmental processes in peer problems of children with attention-deficit/hyperactivity disorder in the Multimodal Treatment Study of Children With ADHD: Developmental cascades and vicious cycles. *Developmental and Psychopathology, 22,* 785–802.

Mustonen, T. K., Spencer, S. M., Hoskinson, R. A., Sachs, D. P. L., & Garvey, A. J. (2005). The influence of gender, race, and menthol content on tobacco exposure measures. *Nicotine and Tobacco Research, 7,* 581–590.

Myin-Germeys, I., van Os, J., Schwartz, J. E., et al. (2001). Emotional reactivity to daily life stress in schizophrenia. *Archives of General Psychiatry, 58,* 1137–1144.

Mykletun, A., Bjerkeset, O., Overland, S., Prince, M., Dewey, M., & Stewart, R. (2009). Levels of anxiety and depression as predictors of mortality: The HUNT study. *British Journal of Psychiatry: The Journal of Mental Science, 195*(2), 118–125. doi: 10.1192/bjp.bp.108.054866

Nacewicz, B. M., Dalton, K. M., Johnstone, T., et al. (2006). Amygdala volume and nonverbal social impairment in adolescent and adult males with autism. *Archives of General Psychiatry, 63,* 1417–1448.

Naranjo, C. A., Tremblay, L. K., & Busto, U. E. (2001). The role of the brain reward system in depression. *Progress in Neuro-Psychopharmacology and Biological Psychiatry, 25,* 781–823.

Nasser, M. (1988). Eating disorders: The cultural dimension. *Social Psychiatry and Psychiatric Epidemiology, 23,* 184–187.

Nasser, M. (1997). *Culture and weight consciousness.* London: Routledge.

Nathan, P. E., & Gorman, J. M. (Eds.). (2002). *A guide to treatments that work* (2nd ed.). London: Oxford University Press.

National Academy on an Aging Society. (1999). Challenges for the 21st century: Chronic and disabling conditions. Retrieved from http://www.agingsociety.org/agingsociety/publications/chronic/index.html

National Center for Chronic Disease Prevention and Health Promotion. (2010). Tobacco use: Targeting the nation's leading killer: At a glance 2010. Atlanta, GA Centers for Disease Control.

National Center for Health Statistics. (2004). *Healthy people, 2004.* Retrieved from: http://www.cdc.gov/nchs/hus.htm

National Center for Justice. (2003). *National crime victimization survey.* (Document NCJ 206348) National Center for Justice. Washington, DC.

National Center for Victims of Violent Crime. (2004). Sexual violence. Unpublished document number 32291. Retrieved from http://www.ncvc.org/ncvc/main.aspx?dbID=DBStatistics584

National Drug Treatment Monitoring System in England, 2001/02 and 2002/03 (Department of Health, 2007). www.dh.gov.uk

National Highway Transportation Safety Administration. (2010). *Traffic safety facts 2010, early edition: A compilation of motor vehicle crash data from the fatality analysis reporting system and the general estimates* (DOT Publication No. HS 811 402). National Center for Statistics and Analysis, U.S. Department of Transportation. Bethesda, MD.

National Institute of Child Health and Human Development. (2000). *Report of the National Reading Panel. Teaching children to read: An evidence-based assessment of the scientific research literature on reading and its implications for reading instruction.* Retrieved from http://www.nichd.nih.gov/publications/nrp/smallbook.htm

National Institute on Alcohol Abuse and Alcoholism. (2001). *Alcohol alert no. 51: Economic perspectives in alcoholism research.* Rockville, MD (Also available online at http://www.niaaa.nih.gov/publications/aa51-text.htm)

National Institute on Drug Abuse. (2004). *NIDA InfoFacts: Crack and cocaine.* National Institute on Drug Abuse, National Institute of Health, U.S. Department of Health and Human Services. Bethesda, MD. Retrieved from http://www.drugabuse.gov

National Institutes of Health, The Ad Hoc Group of Experts (1997, August). *Workshop on the medical utility of marijuana: Report to the director.* Bethesda, MD.

National Survey on Children's Health. (2003). Retrieved from: http://www.nschdata.org/Content/Default.aspx

National Treatment Agency for Substance Misuse (2010): Guidence for adult alcohols treatment providers. NHS. www.nta.nhs.uk/

National Treatment Agency for Substance Misuse (2011): National and regional estimates of the prevalence of opiate and/or crack cocaine use 2009-10: A summary of key findings. NHS. www.nta.nhs.uk/

NCHS. (2004). NCHS data on Alzheimer's disease. Atlanta, GA: Author.

Neale, J. M., & Liebert, R. M. (1986). *Science and behavior: An introduction to methods of research* (3rd ed.). Englewood Cliffs, NJ: Prentice Hall.

Neale, J. M., & Oltmanns, T. (1980). *Schizophrenia.* New York: Wiley.

Neisser, U. (1976). *Cognition and reality.* San Francisco: Freeman.

Nelson, E. C., Heath, A. C., Madden, P. A. F., Cooper, L., Dinwiddie, S. H., Bucholz, K. K., . . . Martin, N. G. (2002). Association between self-reported childhood sexual abuse and adverse psychosocial outcomes: A twin study. *Archives of General Psychiatry, 59,* 139–145.

Nelson, J. C. (2006). The STAR*D study: A four-course meal that leaves us wanting more. *American Journal of Psychiatry, 163*(11), 1864–1866. doi: 10.1176/appi.ajp.163.11.1864

Nelson, J. C., & Davis, J. M. (1997). DST studies in psychotic depression: A meta-analysis. *American Journal of Psychiatry, 154,* 1497–1503.

Nelson, M. D., Saykin, A. J., Flashman, L. A., & Riordin, H. J. (1998). Hippocampal volume reduction in schizophrenia as assessed by magnetic resonance imaging: A meta analytic study. *Archives of General Psychiatry, 55,* 433–440.

Nelson, R. O., Lipinski, D. P., & Black, J. L. (1976). The reactivity of adult retardates' self-monitoring: A comparison among behaviors of different valences, and a comparison with token reinforcement. *Psychological Record, 26,* 189–201.

Nemeroff, C. B., & Schatzberg, A. F. (1998). Pharmacological treatment of unipolar depression. In P. E. Nathan & J. M. Gorman (Eds.), *A guide to treatments that work* (pp. 212–225). New York: Oxford University Press.

Nestle, M. (2002). *Food politics: How the food industry influences nutrition and health.* Berkeley: University of California Press.

Neugebauer, R. (1979). Mediaeval and early modern theories of mental illness. *Archives of General Psychiatry, 36,* 477–484.

Neuman, R. J., Lobos, E., Reich, W., Henderson, C. A., Sun, L. W., & Todd, R. D. (2007). Prenatal smoking exposure and dopaminergic genotypes interact to cause a severe ADHD subtype. *Biological Psychiatry, 61,* 1320–1328.

Neumeister, A., Konstantinidis, A., Stastny, J., Schwarz, M. J., Vitouch, O., Willeit, M., . . . Kasper, S. (2002). Association between the serotonin transporter gene promoter polymorphism (5-HTTLPR) and behavioral responses to tryptophan depletion in healthy women with and without family history of depression. *Archives of General Psychiatry, 59,* 613–620.

Neuner, F., Schauer, M., Klaschik, C., Karunakara, U., & Ebert, T. (2004). A comparison of narrative exposure therapy, supportive counseling, and psychoeducation for treating posttraumatic stress disorder in an African refugee settlement. *Journal of Consulting and Clinical Psychology, 72*, 579–587.

New, A. S., Hazlett, E. A., Buchsbaum, M. S., Goodman, M., Mitelman, S. A., Newmark, R., . . . Siever, L. J. (2007). Amygdala-prefrontal disconnection in borderline personality disorder. *Neuropsychopharmacology: Official Publication of the American College of Neuropsychopharmacology, 32*(7), 1629–1640. doi: 10.1038/sj.npp.1301283

Newman, D. L., Moffitt, T. E., Caspi, A., & Silva, P. A. (1998). Comorbid mental disorders: Implications for treatment and sample selection. *Journal of Abnormal Psychology, 107*, 305–311.

Newman, J. P., Patterson, C. M., & Kosson, D. S. (1987). Response perseveration in psychopaths. *Journal of Abnormal Psychology, 96*, 145–149.

Newman, J. P., Schmitt, W. A., & Voss, W. D. (1997). The impact of motivationally neutral cues on psychopathic individuals: Assessing the generality of the response modulation hypothesis. *Journal of Abnormal Psychology, 196*, 563–575.

NHBLI. (2009). *Asthma at a glance* (NIH publication 09–7429). Bethesda, MD. National Heart, Blood, and Lung Institute. National Institutes of Health.

NHBLI. (2010). *Take action: Stop asthma today!* (NIH publication 10–7542). Bethesda, MD. National Heart, Blood, and Lung Institute. National Institutes of Health.

Nicholls, L. (2008). Putting the new view classification scheme to an empirical test. *Feminism & Psychology, 18*(4), 515–526. doi: 10.1177/0959353508096180

Nicholson, A., Kuper, H., & Hemingway, H. (2006). Depression as an aetiologic and prognostic factor in coronary heart disease: A meta-analysis of 6362 events among 146,538 participants in 54 observational studies. *European Heart Journal, 27*, 2763–2774.

Niederdeppe, J., Farrelly, M. C., & Haviland, M. L. (2004). Confirming "truth": More evidence of a successful tobacco countermarketing campaign in Florida. *American Journal of Public Health, 94*, 255–257.

Nielssen, O., Bourget, D., Laajasalo, T., Liem, M., Labelle, A., Hakkanen-Nyholm, H., et al. (2011). Homicide of strangers by people with a psychotic illness. *Schizophrenia Bulletin, 37*, 572–579.

Nietzel, M. T., & Harris, M. J. (1990). Relationship of dependency and achievement/ autonomy to depression. *Clinical Psychology Review, 10*, 279–297.

Nigg, J. T. (2001). Is ADHD a disinhibitory disorder? *Psychological Bulletin, 127*, 571–598.

Nigg, J. T., & Casey, B. J. (2005). An integrative theory of attention-deficit/ hyperactivity disorder based on the cognitive and affective neurosciences. *Development and Psychopathology, 17*, 785–806.

Nigg, J. T., & Goldsmith, H. H. (1994). Genetics of personality disorders: Perspectives from personality and psychopathology research. *Psychological Bulletin, 115*, 346–380.

Nigg, J. T., Knotterus, G. M., Martel, M. M., Nikolas, M. Cavanagh, K., Karmaus, W., & Rappley, M. D. (2008). Low blood lead levels associated with clinically diagnosed attention deficit hyperactivity disorder (ADHD) and mediated by weak cognitive control. *Biological Psychiatry, 63*, 325–331.

Nigg, J. T., Nikolas, M., Knottnerus, G. M., Cavanagh, K., & Friderici, K. (2010). Confirmation and extension of association of blood lead with attention deficit hyperactivity disorder (ADHD) and AHDH symptom dimensions at population typical exposure levels. *Journal of Psychology and Psychiatry, 51*, 58–65.

Noble, E. P. (2003). D2 dopamine receptor gene in psychiatric and neurologic disorders and its phenotypes. *American Journal of Medical Genetics, 116B*, 103–125.

Nobler, M. S., Oquendo, M. A., Kegeles, L. S., Malone, K. M., Campbell, C., Sackheim, H. A., & Mann, J. J. (2001). Decreased regional brain metabolism after ECT. *American Journal of Psychiatry, 158*, 305–308.

Nobre, P. J., & Pinto-Gouveia, J. (2008). Cognitions, emotions, and sexual response: Analysis of the relationship among automatic thoughts, emotional responses, and sexual arousal. *Archives of Sexual Behavior, 37*(4), 652–661. doi: 10.1007/s10508–007–9258–0

Nock, M. K. (2009). Why do people hurt themselves? New insights into the nature and function of self-injury. *Current Directions in Psychological Science, 18*, 78–83.

Nock, M. K. (2010). Self-injury. *Annual Review of Clinical Psychology, 6*, 339–363. doi: 10.1146/annurev. clinpsy.121208.131258

Nock, M. K., Kazdin, A. E., Hiripi, E., & Kessler, R. C. (2006). Prevalence, subtypes, and correlates of DSM-IV conduct disorder in the National Comorbidity Survey Replication. *Psychological Medicine, 36*, 699–710.

Nock, M. K., & Mendes, W. B. (2008). Physiological arousal, distress tolerance, and social problem-solving deficits among adolescent self-injurers. *Journal of Consulting and Clinical Psychology, 76*, 28–38.

Nock, M. K., & Prinstein, M. J. (2004). A functional approach to the assessment of self-mutilative behavior. *Journal of Consulting and Clinical Psychology, 72*, 885–890.

Nock, M. K., Prinstein, M. J., & Sterba, S. K. (2009). Revealing the form and functions of self-injurious thoughts and behaviors: A real-time ecological assessment study among adolescents and young adults. *Journal of Abnormal Psychology, 118*, 816–827.

Nolen-Hoeksema, S. (1991). Responses to depression and their effects on the duration of depressive episodes. *Journal of Abnormal Psychology, 100*, 569–582.

Nolen-Hoeksema, S. (2000). The role of rumination in depressive disorders and mixed anxiety/depressive symptoms. *Journal of Abnormal Psychology, 109*, 504–511.

Nolen-Hoeksema, S. (2001). Gender differences in depression. *Current Directions in Psychological Science, 10*, 173–176.

Nolen-Hoeksema, S., Wisco, B., & Lyubomirsky, S. (2008). Rethinking rumination. *Perspectives on Psychological Science, 3*, 400–424.

Noll, S. M., & Fredrickson, B. L. (1998). A mediational model linking self-objectification, body shame, and disordered eating. *Psychology of Women Quarterly, 22*, 623–636.

Nordin, V., & Gillberg, C. (1998). The long-term course of autistic disorders: Update on follow-up studies. *Acta Psychiatrica Scandinavica, 97*, 99–108.

Norman, R. M., Malla, A. K., McLean, R. S., McIntosh, E. M., Neufeld, R. W., et al. (2002). An evaluation of a stress management program for individuals with schizophrenia. *Schizophrenia Research, 58*, 292–303.

North West Public Health Observatory, 2010. www.nwph.net

Norton, G. R., Cox, B. J., & Malan, J. (1992). Non-clinical panickers: A critical review. *Clinical Psychology Review, 12*, 121–139.

Norton, M. C., Skoog, I., Toone, L., Corcoran, C., Tschanz, J. T., Lisota, R. D., . . . Steffens, D. C. (2006). Three-year incidence of first-onset depressive syndrome in a population sample of older adults: The Cache County Study. *American Journal of Geriatric Psychiatry, 14*, 237–245.

Norton, P. J., & Price, E. C. (2007). A meta-analytic review of adult cognitive-behavioral treatment outcome across the anxiety disorders. *Journal of Nervous and Mental Disease, 195*(6), 521–531. doi: 10.1097/01. nmd.000023843.70149.9a

Noyes, R. (1999). The relationship of hypochondriasis to anxiety disorders. *General Hospital Psychiatry, 21*, 8–17.

O'Brien, W. H., & Haynes, S. N. (1995). Behavioral assessment. In L. A. Heiden & M. Hersen (Eds.), *Introduction to clinical psychology* (pp. 103–139). New York: Plenum.

Ockene, J. K., Mermelstein, R. J., Bonollo, D. S., Emmons, K. M., Perkins, K. A., Voorhees, C. C., & Hollis, J. F. (2000). Relapse and maintenance issues for smoking cessation. *Health Psychology, 19*, 17–31.

Odgers, C. L., Caspi, A., Broadbent, J. M., Dickson, N., Hancox, R. J., Harrington, H., . . . Moffitt, T. E. (2007). Prediction of differential adult health burden by conduct problem subtypes in males. *Archives of General Psychiatry, 64*, 476–484.

Odgers, C. L., Moffitt, T. E., Broadbent, J. M., Dickson, N., Hancox, R. J., Harrington, H., . . . Caspi, A. (2008). Female and male antisocial trajectories: From childhood origins to adult outcomes. *Developmental and Psychopathology, 20*, 673–716.

O'Donnell, P., & Grace, A. A. (1998). Dysfunctions in multiple interrelated systems as the neurobiological bases of schizophrenic symptom clusters. *Schizophrenia Bulletin, 24*, 267–283.

O'Donohue, W. (1993). The spell of Kuhn on psychology: An exegetical elixir. *Philosophical Psychology, 6*, 267–287.

O'Donohue, W., & Plaud, J. J. (1994). The conditioning of human sexual arousal. *Archives of Sexual Behavior, 23*, 321–344.

O'Donohue, W., Dopke, C. A., & Swingen, D. N. (1997). Psychotherapy for female sexual dysfunction: A review. *Clinical Psychology Review, 17*, 537–566.

Oei, T. P. S., & Dingle, G. (2008). The effectiveness of group cognitive behaviour therapy for unipolar depressive disorders. *Journal of Affective Disorders, 107*, 5–21.

Oetting, E. R., Deffenbacher, J. L., Taylor, M. J., Luther, N., Beauvais, F., & Edwards, R. W. (2000). Methamphetamine use by high school students: Recent trends, gender and ethnicity differences, and use of other drugs. *Journal of Child and Adolescent Substance Abuse, 10*, 33–50.

O'Farrell, T. J., & Fals-Stewart, W. (2000). Behavioral couples therapy for alcoholism and drug abuse. *Journal of Substance Abuse Treatment, 18*, 51–54.

Öberga, O., Woodwardb, A., Jaakkolac, M. S., Perugad, A. and Prüss-Ustün, A., (2010). Global estimate of the burden of disease from second-hand smoke. WHO: www.who.int

Office of Applied Studies. (2002). *Results from the 2001 National Household Survey on Drug Abuse: Vol. I. Summary of national findings* (DHHS Publication No. SMA 02–3758 NHSDA Series H–17). Rockville, MD: Substance Abuse and Mental Health Services Administration.

Ogden, C. L., Carroll, M.D., & Flegal, K. M. (2008). High body mass index for age among US children and adolescents, 2003–2006. *Journal of the American Medical Association, 299*, 2401–2405.

Ogden, T., & Halliday-Boykins, C. A. (2004). Multisystemic treatment of antisocial adolescents in Norway: Replication of clinical outcomes outside the U.S. *Child and Adolescent Mental Health Volume, 9*, 77–83.

Ogrodniczuk, J. S., & Piper, W. E. (2001). Day treatment for personality disorders: A review of research findings. *Harvard Review of Psychiatry, 9*, 105–117.

O'Hara, M. W., & Swain, A. M. (1996). Rates and risk of postpartum depression meta-analysis. *International Reviews of Psychiatry, 8*(37), 37–54.

O'Hara, M. W., Stuart, S., Gorman, L. L., & Wenzel, A. (2000). Efficacy of interpersonal psychotherapy for postpartum depression. *Archives of General Psychiatry, 57*(11), 1039–1045.

Öhman, A., Flykt, A., & Esteves, F. (2001). Emotion drives attention: Detecting the snake in the grass. *Journal of Experimental Psychology: General, 137*, 466–478.

Öhman, A., & Mineka, A. (2003). The malicious serpent: Snakes as a prototypical stimulus for an evolved module of fear. *Current Directions in Psychological Science, 12*, 5–9.

Öhman, A., & Soares, J. J. F. (1994). "Unconscious anxiety": Phobic responses to masked stimuli. *Journal of Abnormal Psychology, 103*, 231–240.

O'Kearney, R. T., Anstey, K. J., & von Sanden, C. (2006). Behavioural and cognitive behavioural therapy for obsessive compulsive disorder in children and adolescents. *Cochrane Database of Systematic Reviews 2006*, Issue 4.

Olabi, B., Ellison-Wright, I., McIntosh, A. M., Wood, S. J., Bullmore, E., & Lawrie, S. M. (2011). Are there progressive brain changes in schizophrenia? A meta-analysis of structural magnetic resonance imaging studies. *Biological psychiatry, 70*, 88–96.

Olatunji, B. O., Cisler, J. M., & Tolin, D. F. (2007). Quality of life in the anxiety disorders: A meta-analytic review. *Clinical Psychology Review, 27*, 572–581.

O'Leary, D. S., Block, R. I., Flaum, M., Schultz, S. K., Ponto, L. L., Boles, Watkins, G. L., . . . Hichwa, R. D. (2000). Acute marijuana effects on rCBF and cognition: A PET study. *Neuroreport: For Rapid Communication of Neuroscience Research, 11*, 3835–3841.

O'Leary, K. D., & Wilson, G. T. (1987). *Behavior therapy: Application and outcome.* Englewood Cliffs, NJ: Prentice Hall.

Olff, M., Langeland, W. L., Draijer, N., & Gersons, B. P. R. (2007). Gender differences in posttraumatic stress disorder. *Psychological Bulletin, 133*, 183–204.

Olfson, M., Blanco, C., Liu, L., Moreno, C., & Laje, G. (2006). National trends in the outpatient treatment of children and adolescents with antipsychotic drugs. *Archives of General Psychiatry, 63*, 679–687.

Olfson, M., & Marcus, S. C. (2010). National trends in outpatient psychotherapy. *American Journal of Psychiatry, 167*, 1456–1463.

Olivardia, R., Pope, H. G., Mangweth, B., & Hudson, J. I. (1995). Eating disorders in college men. *American Journal of Psychiatry, 152*, 1279–1284.

O'Loughlin, J. O., Paradis, G., Kim, W., DiFranza, J., Meshefedjian, G., McMillan-Davey, E., . . . Tyndale, R. F. (2005). Genetically decreased CYP2A6 and the risk of tobacco dependence: A prospective study of novice smokers. *Tobacco Control, 13*, 422–428.

Olsson, A., Nearing, K. I., & Phelps, E. A. (2007). Learning fears by observing others: The neural systems of social fear transmission. *Social Cognitive and Affective Neuroscience Advances in Assessment, 2*, 3–11.

O'Neal, J. M. (1984). First person account: Finding myself and loving it. *Schizophrenia Bulletin, 10*, 109–110.

Ono, Y., Yoshimura, K., Sueoka, R., Yamauchi, K., Mizushima, H., Momose, T., . . . Asai, M. (1996). Avoidant personality disorder and taijin kyoufu: Sociocultural implications of the WHO/ADAMHA International Study of Personality Disorders in Japan. *Acta Psychiatrica Scandinavica, 93*(3), 172–176.

Orr, S. P., Metzger, L. J., Lasko, N. B., Macklin, M. L., Hu, F. B., Shalev, A. Y., & Pitman, R. K. (2003). Physiologic responses to sudden, loud tones in monozygotic twins discordant for combat exposure: Association with post-traumatic stress disorder. *Archives of General Psychiatry, 60*, 283–288.

Ortiz, J., & Raine, A. (2004). Heart rate level and antisocial behavior in children and adolescents: A meta-analysis. *Journal of the American Academy of Child and Adolescent Psychiatry, 43*, 154–162.

Ory, M., Hoffman, R. R., Yee, J. L., Tennstedt, S., & Schulz, R. (1999). Prevalence and impact of caregiving: A detailed comparison between dementia and nondementia caregivers. *The Gerontologist, 39*, 177–185.

Osby, U., Brandt, L., Correia, N., Ekbom, A., & Sparen, P. (2001). Excess mortality in bipolar and unipolar disorder in Sweden. *Archives of General Psychiatry, 58*, 844–850.

Osterling, J., & Dawson, G. (1994). Early recognition of children with autism: A study of first birthday home videotapes. *Journal of Autism and Developmental Disorders, 24*, 247–257.

Otto, M. W., Teachman, B. A., Cohen, L. S., Soares, C. N., Vitonis, A. F., & Harlow, B. L. (2007). Dysfunctional attitudes and episodes of major depression: Predictive validity and temporal stability in never-depressed, depressed, and recovered women. *Journal of Abnormal Psychology, 116*, 475–483.

Otto, M. W., Tolin, D. F., Simon, N. M., Pearlson, G. D., Basden, S., Meunier, S. A., . . . Pollack, M. H. (2010). Efficacy of d-cycloserine for enhancing response to cognitive-behavior therapy for panic disorder. *Biological Psychiatry, 67*(4), 365–370. doi: 10.1016/j.biopsych.2009.07.036

Otway, L. J., & Vignoles, V. L. (2006). Narcissim and childwood recollection: A quantitative test of psychoanalytic predictions. *Personality and Social Psychology Bulletin, 32*, 104–116.

Ouimette, P. C., Finney, J. W., & Moos, R. H. (1997). Twelve-step and cognitive-behavioral treatment for substance abuse: A comparison of treatment effectiveness. *Journal of Consulting and Clinical Psychology, 65*, 230–240.

Owen, M. J., Craddock, N., & O'Donovan, M. C. (2010). Suggestion of roles for both common and rare risk variants in genome-wide studies of schizophrenia. *Archives of General Psychiatry, 67*, 667–673.

Owen, M. J., Williams, N. M., & O'Donovan, M. C. (2004). The molecular genetics of schizophrenia: New findings promise new insights. *Molecular Psychiatry, 9*, 14–27.

Owen, P. P., & Laurel-Seller, E. (2000). Weight and shape ideals: Thin is dangerously in. *Journal of Applied Social Psychology, 54*, 682–687.

Ozer, D. J., & Benet-Martinez, V. (2006). Personality and the prediction of consequential outcomes. *Annual Review of Psychology, 57*, 401–421. doi: 10.1146/annurev.psych.57.102904.190127

Ozer, E. J., Best, S. R., Lipsey, T. L., & Weiss, D. S. (2003). Predictors of posttraumatic stress disorder and symptoms in adults: A meta-analysis. *Psychological Bulletin, 129*(1), 52–73.

Pagnin, D., de Querioz, V., Pini, S., & Cassano, G. B. (2004). Efficacy of ECT in depression: A meta-analytic review. *Journal of Electroconvulsive Therapy, 20*, 13–20.

Pantelis, C., Velakoulis, D., McGorry, P. D., et al. (2003). Neuroanatomical abnormalities before and after onset of psychosis: A cross-sectional and longitudinal MRI comparison. *Lancet, 361*, 281–288.

Paris, J. (2002). Implications of long-term outcome research for the management of patients with borderline personality disorder. *Harvard Review of Psychiatry, 10*, 315–323.

Parsons, T. D., & Rizzo, A. A. (2008). Affective outcomes of virtual reality exposure therapy for anxiety and specific phobias: A meta-analysis. *Journal of Behavior Therapy and Experimental Psychiatry, 39*(3), 250–261. doi: 10.1016/j.jbtep.2007.07.007

Patil, S. T., Zhang, L., Martenyi, F., Lowe, S. L., Jackson, K. A., et al. (2007). Activation of mGlu2/3 receptors as a new approach to treat schizophrenia: A randomized Phase 2 clinical trial. *Nature Medicine, 13*, 1102–1107.

Patronek, G. J., & Nathanson, J. N. (2009). A theoretical perspective to inform assessment and treatment strategies for animal hoarders. *Clinical Psychology Review, 29*(3), 274–281. doi: 10.1016/j.cpr.2009.01.006

Patterson, C. M., & Newman, J. P. (1993). Reflectivity and learning from aversive events: Toward a psychological mechanism for the syndromes of disinhibition. *Psychological Review, 100*, 716–736.

Patterson, G. R. (1982). *Coercive family process.* Eugene, OR: Castilia.

Patterson, G. R., Crosby, L., & Vuchinich, S. (1992). Predicting risk for early police arrest. *Journal of Quantitative Criminology, 8*, 335–355.

Paulhus, D. L. (1998). Interpersonal and intrapsychie adaptiveness of trait self-enhancement: A mixed blessing? *Jounal of Personality and Social Psychology, 74*, 1197–1208.

Paulus, M. P., Tapert, S. F., & Schuckit, M. A. (2005). Neural activation patterns of methamphetamine-dependent subjects during decision making predict relapse. *Archives of General Psychiatry, 62*, 761–768.

Paxton, S. J., Schutz, H. K., Wertheim, E. H., & Muir, S. L. (1999). Friendship clique and peer influences on body image concerns, dietary restraint, extreme weight-loss behaviors, and binge eating in adolescent girls. *Journal of Abnormal Psychology, 108*, 255–264.

Peat, C., Mitchell, J. E., Hoek, H. W., & Wonderlich, S. A. (2009). Validity and utility of subtyping anorexia nervosa. *International Journal of Eating Disorders, 42*, 590–594.

Peeples, F., & Loeber, R. (1994). Do individual factors and neighborhood context explain ethnic differences in juvenile delinquency? *Journal of Quantitative Criminology, 10*, 141–157.

Pelham, W. E., Gnagy, E. M., Greiner, A. R., Hoza, B., Hinshaw, S. P., Swanson, J. M., . . . McBurnett, K. (2000). Behavioral versus behavioral plus pharmacological treatment for ADHD children attending a summer treatment program. *Journal of Abnormal Child Psychology, 28*, 507–525.

Pendlebury, S. T., & Rothwell, P. M. (2009). Prevalence, incidence, and factors associated with pre-stroke and post-stroke dementia: A systematic review and meta-analysis. *Lancet Neurology, 8*(11), 1006–1018. doi: 10.1016/S1474-4422(09)70236-4

Penn, D. L., Chamberlin, C., & Mueser, K. T. (2003). The effects of a documentary film about schizophrenia on psychiatric stigma. *Schizophrenia Bulletin, 29*, 383–391.

Penn, D. L., & Mueser, K. T. (1996). Research update on the psychosocial treatment of schizophrenia. *American Journal of Psychiatry, 153*, 607–617.

Pennebaker, J. W., Kiecolt-Glaser, J. K., & Glaser, R. (1988). Disclosure of traumas and immune function: Health implications for psychotherapy. *Journal of Consulting and Clinical Psychology, 56*, 239–245.

Pennington, B. F. (1995). Genetics of learning disabilities. *Journal of Child Neurology, 10*, S69–S77.

Penzes, P., Cahill, M. E., Jones, K. A., VanLeeuwen, J. E., & Woolfrey, K. M. (2011). Dendritic spine pathology in neuropsychiatric disorders. *Nature Neuroscience, 14*, 285–293.

Peplau, L. A. (2003). Human sexuality: How do men and women differ? *Current Directions in Psychological Science, 12*, 37–40.

Perez, M., & Joiner, T. E. (2003). Body image dissatisfaction and disordered eating in black and white women. *International Journal of Eating Disorders, 33,* 342–350.

Perez, M., Voelz, Z. R., Pettit, J. W., & Joiner, T. E. (2002). The role of acculturative stress and body dissatisfaction in predicting bulimic symptomatology across ethnic groups. *International Journal of Eating Disorders, 31,* 442–454.

Perkins, D. D. (1995). Speaking truth to power: Empowerment ideology as social intervention and policy. *American Journal of Community Psychology, 23,* 765–794.

Perkins, K. A., Ciccocioppo, M., Conklin, C. A., Milanek, M. E., Grottenthaler, A., & Sayette, M. A. (2008). Mood influences on acute smoking responses are independent of nicotine intake and dose expectancy. *Journal of Abnormal Psychology, 117,* 79–93.

Perkins, K. A., Karelitz, J. L., Conklin, C. A., Sayette, M. A., & Giedgowd, G. E. (2010). Acute negative affect relief from smoking depends on the affect situation and measure but not on nicotine. *Biological Psychiatry, 67,* 707–714.

Perkonigg, A., Pfister, H., Stein, M. B., Hofler, M., Lieb, R., Maercker, A., & Wittchen, H. U. (2005). Longitudinal course of posttraumatic stress disorder and posttraumatic stress. *American Journal of Psychiatry, 162,* 1320–1327.

Perlin, M. L. (1994). *Law and mental disability.* Charlottesville, VA: Michie Company.

Perry, J. C., Banon, E., & Ianni, F. (1999). Effectiveness of psychotherapy for personality disorders. *American Journal of Psychiatry, 156,* 1312–1321.

Perry, R., Campbell, M., Adams, P., Lynch, N., Spencer, E. K., Curren, E. L., & Overall, J. E. (1989). Longterm efficacy of haloperidol in autistic children: Continuous versus discontinuous administration. *Journal of the American Academy of Child and Adolescent Psychiatry, 28,* 87–92.

Persing, J. S., Stuart, S. P., Noyes, R., & Happel, R. L. (2000). Hypochondriasis: The patient's perspective. *International Journal of Psychiatry in Medicine, 30,* 329–342.

Persons, J. B., Bostrom, A., & Bertagnolli, A. (1999). Results of randomized controlled trials of cognitive therapy for depression generalize to private practice. *Cognitive Therapy Research, 23,* 535–548.

Perugi, G., Akiskal, H. S., Giannotti, D., Frare, F., Di Vaio, S., & Cassano, G. B. (1997). Gender-related differences in body dysmorphic disorder. *Journal of Nervous and Mental Disease, 185,* 578–582.

Pescosolido, B. A., Martin, J. K., Long, J. S., Medina, T. R., Phelan, J. C., & Link, B. G. (2010). "A disease like any other?" A decade of change in public relations to schizophrenia, depression and alcohol dependence. *American Journal of Psychiatry, 167,* 1321–1330.

Peterson, C. B., Mitchell, J. E., Crow, S. J., Crosby, R. D., & Wonderlich, S. A. (2009). The efficacy of self-help group treament and therapist-led group treatment for binge eating disorder. *American Journal of Psychiatry, 166,* 1347–1354.

Petry, N. M., Alessi, S. M., & Hanson. (2007). Contingency management improves abstinence and quality of life in cocaine abusers. *Journal of Consulting and Clinical Psychology, 75,* 307–315.

Petry, N. M., Alessi, S. M., Marx, J., Austin, M., & Tardif, M. (2005). Vouchers versus prizes: Contingency management treatment of substance abusers in community settings. *Journal of Consulting and Clinical Psychology, 73,* 1005–1014.

Pettinati, H. M., Oslin, D. W., Kampman, K. M., Dundon, W. D., Xie, H., Gallis, T. L., et al. (2010). A double-blind, placebo-controlled trial combining sertraline and naltrexone for treating co-occuring depression and alcohol dependence. *American Journal of Psychiatry, 167,* 668–675.

Phillips, D. P. (1974). The influence of suggestion on suicide: Substantive and theoretical implications of the Werther effect. *American Sociological Review, 39,* 340–354.

Phillips, D. P. (1985). The Werther effect. *The Sciences, 25,* 33–39.

Phillips, K. A. (2005). *The broken mirror: Understanding and treating body dysmorphic disorder.* New York: Oxford University Press.

Phillips, K. A. (2006). "I look like a monster": Pharmacotherapy and cognitive-behavioral therapy for body dysmorphic disorder. In R. L. Spitzer, M. B. First, J. B. W. Williams, & M. Gibbon (Eds.), *DSM-IV-TR case book (Vol. 2) experts tell how they treated their own patients* (pp. 263–276). Washington, DC: American Psychiatric Publishing.

Phillips, K. A., McElroy, S. L., Dwight, M. M., Eisen, J. L., & Rasmussen, S. A. (2001). Delusionality and response to open-label fluvoxamine in body dysmorphic disorder. *Journal of Clinical Psychiatry, 62,* 87–91.

Phillips, K. A., Pagano, M. E., Menard, W., & Stout, R. L. (2006). A 12-month follow-up study of the course of body dysmorphic disorder. *American Journal of Psychiatry, 163,* 907–912.

Phillips, K. A., Stein, D. J., Rauch, S. L., Hollander, E., Fallon, B. A., Barsky, A., . . . Leckman, J. (2010). Should an obsessive-compulsive spectrum grouping of disorders be included in DSM-V? *Depression and Anxiety, 27*(6), 528–555. doi: 10.1002/da.20705

Phillips, K. A., Wilhelm, S., Koran, L. M., Didie, E. R., Fallon, B. A., Feusner, J., & Stein, D. J. (2010). Body dysmorphic disorder: Some key issues for DSM-V. *Depression and Anxiety, 27*(6), 573–591. doi: 10.1002/da.20709

Phillips, L. J., Francey, S.M., Edwards, J., & McMurray, N. (2007). Stress and psychosis: Towards the development of new models of investigation. *Clinical Psychology Review, 27,* 307–317.

Phillips, M. L., Ladouceur, C. D., & Drevets, W. C. (2008a). A neural model of voluntary and automatic emotion regulation: Implications for understanding the pathophysiology and neurodevelopment of bipolar disorder. *Molecular Psychiatry, 13,* 833–857.

Phillips, M. L., Ladouceur, C. D., & Drevets, W. C. (2008b). A neural model of voluntary and automatic emotion regulation: Implications for understanding the pathophysiology and neurodevelopment of bipolar disorder. *Molecular Psychiatry, 13*(9), 833–857.

Piasecki, T. M. (2006). Relapse to smoking. *Clinical Psychology Review, 26,* 196–125.

Pierce, J. M., Petry, N. M., Stitzer, M. L., Blaine, J., Kellog, S., et al. (2006). Effects of lower-cost incentives on stimulant abstinence in methadone maintenance treatment. *Archives of General Psychiatry, 63,* 201–208.

Pierce, J. P., Choi, W. S., Gilpin, E. A., Farkas, A. J., & Berry, C. C. (1998). Tobacco ads, promotional items linked with teen smoking. *Journal of the American Medical Association, 279,* 511–515.

Pierce, K., & Courchesne, E. (2001). Evidence for a cerebellar role in reduced exploration and stereotyped behavior in autism. *Biological Psychiatry, 49,* 655–664.

Pierce, K., Haist, F., Sedaghadt, F., & Corchesne, E. (2004). The brain response to personally familiar faces in autism: Findings of fusiform activity and beyond. *Brain, 127,* 1–14.

Pierce, K., Muller, R. A., Ambrose, J., Allen, G., & Courchesne, E. (2001). Face processing occurs outside the fusiform 'face area' in autism: Evidence from functional MRI. *Brain, 124,* 2059–2073.

Pietromonaco, P. R., & Barrett, L. F. (1997). Working models of attachment and daily social interactions. *Journal of Personality and Social Psychology, 73,* 1409–1423.

Pike, K. M., Dohm, F., Striegel-Moore, R. H., Wilfley, D. E., & Fairburn, C. M. (2001). A comparison of black and white women with binge eating disorder. *American Journal of Psychiatry, 158,* 1455–1460.

Pilling, S., Bebbington, P., Kuipers, E., Garety, P., Geddes, L., Martindale, B., . . . Morgan, C. (2002). Psychological treatments in schizophrenia: II. Meta-analyses of randomized controlled trials of social skills training and cognitive remediation. *Psychological Medicine, 32,* 783–791.

Pincus, H. A., Frances, A., Davis, W. W., First, M. B., & Widiger, T. A. (1992). DSM-IV and new diagnostic categories: Holding the line on proliferation. *American Journal of Psychiatry, 149,* 112–117.

Pineles, S. L., & Mineka, S. (2005). Attentional biases to internal and external sources of potential threat in social anxiety. *Journal of Abnormal Psychology, 114,* 314–318.

Piper, A., Jr., Pope, H. G., Jr., & Borowiecki J. J., I. (2000). Custer's last stand: Brown, Schefln, and Whitfiled's latest attempt to salvage "dissociative amnesia." *Journal of Psychiatry and the Law, 28,* 149–213.

Pitman, R. K., Orr, S. P., Altman, B., & Longpre, R. E. (1996). Emotional processing during eye movement desensitization and reprocessing therapy of Vietnam veterans with chronic posttraumatic stress disorder. *Comprehensive Psychiatry, 37,* 419–429.

Piven, J., Arndt, S., Bailey, J., & Andreasen, N. (1996). Regional brain enlargement in autism: A magnetic resonance imaging study. *Journal of the American Academy of Child and Adolescent Psychiatry, 35,* 530–536.

Piven, J., Arndt, S., Bailey, J., Havercamp, S., Andreasen, N. C., & Palmer, P. (1995). An MRI study of brain size in autism. *American Journal of Psychiatry, 152,* 1145–1149.

Placidi, G. P., Oquendo, M. A., Malone, K. M., Huang, Y. Y., Ellis, S. P., & Mann, J. J. (2001). Aggressivity, suicide attempts, and depression: Relationship to cerebrospinal fluid monoamine metabolite levels. *Biological Psychiatry, 50,* 783–791.

Plomin, R. (1999). Genetics and general cognitive ability. *Nature, 402,* C25–C29.

Plomin, R., DeFries, J. C., Craig, I. W., & McGuffin, P. (2003). *Behavioral genetics in the postgenomic era.* Washington, DC: APA Books.

Plomin, R., & Kovas, Y. (2005). Generalist genes and learning disabilities. *Psychological Bulletin, 131,* 592–617.

Pole, N., Gone, J. P., & Kulkarni, M. (2008). Posttraumatic stress disorder among ethnoracial minorities in the United States. *Clinical Psychology Science and Practice, 15,* 35–61.

Pole, N., Neylan, T. C., Otte, C., Henn-Hasse, C., Metzler, T. J., & Marmar, C. R. (2009). Prospective prediction of posttraumatic stress disorder symptoms using fear potentiated auditory startle responses. *Biological Psychiatry, 65*(3), 235–240. doi: 10.1016/j.biopsych.2008.07.015

Polich, J. M., Armor, D. J., & Braiker, H. B. (1980). Patterns of alcoholism over four years. *Journal of Studies on Alcohol, 41,* 397–415.

Polivy, J. (1976). Perception of calories and regulation of intake in restrained and unrestrained eaters. *Addictive Behaviors, 1,* 237–244.

Polivy, J., Heatherton, T. F., & Herman, C. P. (1988). Self esteem, restraint and eating behavior. *Journal of Abnormal Psychology, 97,* 354–356.

Polivy, J., & Herman, C. P. (1985). Dieting and binging: A causal analysis. *American Psychologist, 40,* 193–201.

Polivy, J., Herman, C. P., & Howard, K. (1980). The Restraint Scale. In A. Stunkard (Ed.), *Obesity.* Philadelphia: Saunders.

Polivy, J., Herman, C. P., & McFarlane, T. (1994). Effects of anxiety on eating: Does palatability moderate distress induced overeating in dieters? *Journal of Abnormal Psychology, 103*, 505–510.

Polonsky, D. C. (2000). Premature ejaculation. In R. C. Rosen & S. R. Leiblum (Eds.), *Principles and practice of sex therapy* (3rd ed., pp. 305–332). New York: Guilford.

Pomerleau, O. F., Collins, A. C., Shiffman, S., & Pomerleau, C. S. (1993). Why some people smoke and others do not: New perspectives. *Journal of Consulting and Clinical Psychology, 61*, 723–731.

Poole, D. A., Lindsay, D. S., Memon, A., & Bull, R. (1995). Psychotherapy and the recovery of memories of childhood sexual abuse: U.S. and British practitioners' opinions, practices and experiences. *Journal of Consulting and Clinical Psychology, 63*, 426–437.

Pope, H. G. J., Lalonde, J. K., Pindyck, L. J., Walsh, B. T., Bulik, C. M., et al. (2006). Binge eating disorder: A stable syndrome. *American Journal of Psychology, 163*, 2181–2183.

Pope, H. G., Jr., Oliva, P. S., Hudson, J. I., Bodkin, J. A., & Gruber, A. J. (1999). Attitudes toward DSM-IV dissociative disorders diagnoses among board-certified American psychiatrists. *American Journal of Psychiatry, 156*(2), 321–323.

Pope, H. G. Jr., Poliakoff, M. B., Parker, M. P., Boynes, M., & Hudson, J. J. (2006). Is dissociative amnesia a culture-bound syndrome? Findings from a survey of historical literature. *Psychological Medicine, 37*, 1067–1068.

Pope, K. S. (1998). Pseudoscience, cross-examination, and scientific evidence in the recovered memory controversy. *Psychology, Public Policy, and Law, 4*, 1160–1181.

Porter, S., Yuille, J. C., & Lehman, D. R. (1999). The nature of real, implanted, and fabricated memories for emotional childhood events: Implications for the recovered memory debate. *Law and Human Behavior, 23*, 415–537.

Posey, M. J., & McDougle, C. M. (2000). The pharmacotherapy of target symptoms associated with autistic disorder and other pervasive developmental disorders. *Harvard Review of Psychiatry, 8*, 45–63.

Potkin, S. G., Alva, G., Fleming, K., et al. (2002). A PET study of the pathophysiology of negative symptoms in schizophrenia. *American Journal of Psychiatry, 159*, 227–237.

Powell, R. A., & Gee, T. L. (2000). "The effects of hypnosis on dissociative identity disorder: A reexamination of the evidence": Reply. *Canadian Journal of Psychiatry, 45*, 848–849.

Powers, E., Saultz, J., & Hamilton, A. (2007). Which lifestyle interventions effectively lower LDL cholesterol? *Journal of Family Practice, 56*, 483–485.

Prechter, G. C., & Shepard, J. W. J. (1990). Sleep and sleep disorders in the elderly. In R. J. Martin (Ed.), *Cardiorespiratory disorders during sleep* (pp. 365–386). Armonk, NY: Futura.

Prentky, R., & Burgess, A. W. (1990). Rehabilitation of child molesters: A cost-benefit analysis. *American Journal of Orthopsychiatry, 60*(1), 108–117.

Prevention, C.F.D.C.A. (2011). *HIV surveillance report: Diagnoses of HIV infection and AIDS in the United States and dependent areas, 2009*. Atlanta: CDC. Retrieved from http://www.cdc.gov/hiv/surveillance/resources/reports

Price, D. D., Craggs, J. G., Zhou, Q., Verne, G. N., Perlstein, W. M., & Robinson, M. E. (2009). Widespread hyperalgesia in irritable bowel syndrome is dynamically maintained by tonic visceral impulse input and placebo/nocebo factors: Evidence from human psychophysics, animal models, and neuroimaging. *NeuroImage, 47*, 995–1001.

Prien, R. F., & Potter, W. Z. (1993). Maintenance treatment for mood disorders. In D. L. Dunner (Ed.), *Current psychiatric therapy*. Philadelphia: Saunders.

Prieto, S. L., Cole, D. A., & Tageson, C. W. (1992). Depressive self-schemas in clinic and nonclinic children. *Cognitive Therapy and Research, 16*, 521–534.

Primack, B. A., Bost, J. E., Land, S. R., & Fine, M. J. (2007). Volume of tobacco advertising in African American markets: Systematic review and meta-analysis. *Public Health Reports, 122*, 607–615.

Prinz, P., & Raskind, M. (1978). Aging and sleep disorders. In R. Williams & R. Karacan (Eds.), *Sleep disorders: Diagnosis and treatment*. New York: Wiley.

Pryor, T., Wiederman, M. W., & McGilley, B. (1996). Clinical correlates of anorexia subtypes. *International Journal of Eating Disorders, 19*, 371–379.

Przeworski, A., & Newman, M. G. (2006). Efficacy and utility of computer-assisted cognitive behavioural therapy for anxiety disorders. *Clinical Psychologist, 10*, 43–53.

Pujols, Y., Seal, B. N., & Meston, C. M. (2010). The association between sexual satisfaction and body image in women. *Journal of Sexual Medicine, 7*(2 Pt 2), 905–916. doi: 10.1111/j.1743-6109.2009.01604.x

Pukall, C. F., Payne, K. A., Kao, A., Khalife', S., & Binik, Y. M. (2005). Dyspareunia. In R. Balon & R. T. Segraves (Eds.), *Handbook of sexual dysfunctions and paraphilias*. Boca Raton, FL: Taylor & Francis.

Purdie, F. R., Honigman, T. B., & Rosen, P. (1981). Acute organic brain syndrome: A view of 100 cases. *Annals of Emergency Medicine, 10*, 455–461.

Putnam, F. W. (1993). Dissociative disorders in children: Behavioral profiles and problems. *Child Abuse and Neglect, 17*, 39–45.

Putnam, F. W. (1996). A brief history of multiple personality disorder. *Child and Adolescent Psychiatric Clinics of North America, 5*, 263–271.

Putnam, F. W., Guroff, J. J., Silberman, E. K., Barban, L., & Post, R. M. (1986). The clinical phenomenology of multiple personality disorder: Review of 100 recent cases. *Journal of Clinical Psychiatry, 47*, 285–293.

Qato, D. M., Alexander, G. C., Conti, R. M., Johnson, M., Schumm, P., & Lindau, S. T. (2008). Use of prescription and over-the-counter medications and dietary supplements among older adults in the United States. *Journal of the American Medical Association, 300*(24), 2867–2878.

Qualls, S. H., Segal, D. L., Norman, S., Niederehe, G., & Gallagher-Thompson, D. (2002). Psychologists in practice with older adults: Current patterns, sources of training, and need for continuing education. *Professional Psychology: Research and Practice, 33*, 435–442.

Quinsey, V. L., Harris, G. T., Rice, M. E., & Cormier, C. A. (2006). *Violent offenders: Appraising and managing risk* (2nd ed.). Washington, DC: American Psychological Association.

Rachman, S. (1977). The conditioning theory of fear acquisition: A critical examination. *Behaviour Research and Therapy, 15*, 375–387.

Rachman, S., & DeSilva, P. (1978). Abnormal and normal obsessions. *Behaviour Research and Therapy, 16*, 233–248.

Rachman, S. J. (1966). Sexual fetishism: An experimental analogue. *Psychological Record, 16*, 293–296.

Rachman, S. J., & Wilson, G. T. (1980). *The effects of psychological therapy* (2nd ed.). Elmsford, NY: Pergamon.

Rademaker, A. R., van Zuiden, M., Vermetten, E., & Geuze, E. (2011). Type D personality and the development of PTSD symptoms: A prospective study. *Journal of Abnormal Psychology, 120*(2), 299–307.

Raine, A. (2006). Schizotypal personality: Neurodevelopmental and psychosocial trajectories. *Annual Review of Clinical Psychology, 2*, 291–326. doi: 10.1146/annurev.clinpsy.2.022305.095318

Raine, A., Venables, P. H., & Williams, M. (1990). Relationships between central and autonomic measures of arousal at age 15 years and criminality at age 24 years. *Archives of General Psychiatry, 47*, 1003–1007.

Raine, A., & Yang, Y. (2007). The neuroanatomical bases of psychopathy. A review of brain imaging findings. In C. J. Patrick (Ed.), *Handbook of psychopathy* (pp. 278–295). New York: Guilford.

Raistrick, D., Heather, N. and Godfrey, C. (2006) Review of the effectiveness of treatment for alcohol problems. National Treatment Agency for Substance Misuse.www.nta.nhs.uk

Raj, B. A., Corvea, M. H., & Dagon, E. M. (1993). The clinical characteristics of panic disorder in the elderly: A retrospective study. *Journal of Clinical Psychiatry, 54*, 150–155.

Rao, Y., Hoffmann, E., Zia, M., et al. (2000). Duplications and defects in the CYP2A6 gene: Identification, genotyping, and in vivo effects on smoking. *Molecular Pharmacology, 58*, 747–755.

Rapee, R., Mattick, R., & Murrell, E. (1986). Cognitive mediation in the affective component of spontaneous panic attacks. *Journal of Behavior Therapy and Experimental Psychiatry, 17*, 245–253.

Rapee, R. M., Abbott, M., & Lyneham, H. (2006). Bibliotherapy for children with anxiety disorders using written materials for parents: A randomized controlled trial. *Journal of Consulting and Clinical Psychology, 74*, 436–444.

Rapee, R. M., Schniering, C. A., & Hudson, J. L. (2009). Anxiety disorders during childhood adolescence: Origins and treatment. *Annual Review of Clinical Psychology, 5*, 311–341.

Rapin, I. (1997). Autism. *New England Journal of Medicine, 337*, 97–104.

Rapoport, J. L., Swedo, S. E., & Leonard, H. L. (1992). Childhood obsessive compulsive disorder. *Journal of Clinical Psychiatry, 53* (Suppl-4), 11–16.

Rapp, M. A., Schnaider-Beeri, M., Grossman, H. T., Sano, M., Perl, D. P., Purohit, D. P., Gorman, J. M., & Haroutunian, V. (2006). Increased hippocampal plaques and tangles in patients with Alzheimer disease with a lifetime history of major depression. *Archives of General Psychiatry, 63*, 161–167.

Rascovsky, K., et al., 2011. Sensitivity of revised diagnostic criteria for the behavioral variant of frontotemporal dementia. *Brain, 134*, 2456–2477.

Raskind, W. H. (2001). Current understanding of the genetic basis of reading and spelling disability. *Learning Disability Quarterly, 24*, 141–157.

Rassin, E., Muris, P., Schmidt, H., & Merckelbach, H. (2000). Relationships between thought-action fusion, thought suppression and obsessive-compulsive symptoms: A structural equation modeling approach. *Behaviour Research and Therapy, 38*, 889–897.

Rather, B. C., Goldman, M. S., Roehrich, L., & Brannick, M. (1992). Empirical modeling of an alcohol expectancy memory network using multidimensional scaling. *Journal of Abnormal Psychology, 101*, 174–183.

Rauch, S. L., Whalen, P. J., Shin, L. M., McInerney, S. C., Macklin, M. L., Lasko, N. B., . . . Pitman, R. K. (2000). Exaggerated amygdala response to masked facial stimuli in posttraumatic stress disorder: A functional MRI study. *Biological Psychiatry, 47*, 769–776.

Rawson, R. A., Martinelli-Casey, P., Anglin, M. D., et al. (2004). A multi-site comparison of psychosocial approaches for the treatment of methamphetamine dependence. *Addiction, 99*, 708–717.

Reas, D. L., Williamson, D. A., Martin, C. K., & Zucker, N. L. (2000). Duration of illness predicts outcome for bulimia nervosa: A long-term follow-up study. *International Journal of Eating Disorders, 27*, 428–434.

Rector, N. A., Beck, A. T., & Stolar, N. (2005). The negative symptoms of schizophrenia: A cognitive perspective. *Canadian Journal of Psychiatry, 50*, 247–257.

Redding, N. (2009). *Methland: The death and life of an American small town*. New York: Bloomsbury USA.

Redmond, D. E. (1977). Alterations in the function of the nucleus locus coeruleus. In I. Hanin & E. Usdin (Eds.), *Animal models in psychiatry and neurology*. New York: Pergamon.

Regeer, E. J., ten Have, M., Rosso, M. L., van Roijen, L. H., Vollebergh, W., & Nolen, W. A. (2004). Prevalence of bipolar disorder in the general population: A reappraisal study of the Netherlands mental health survey and incidence study. *Acta Psychiatrica Scandinavica, 110*, 374–382.

Regier, D. A., Boyd, J. H., Burke, J. D., & Rae, D. S. (1988). One-month prevalence of mental disorders in the United States: Based on five epidemiologic catchment area sites. *Archives of General Psychiatry, 45*, 977–986.

Regier, D. A., Narrow, W. E., Rae, D. S., & Manderscheid, R. W. (1993). The de facto US mental and addictive disorders service system: Epidemiologic catchment area prospective 1-year prevalence rates of disorders and services. *Archives of General Psychiatry, 50*, 85–94.

Regland, B., Johansson, B.V., Grenfeldt, B., Hjelmgren, L.T., & Medhus, M. (1995). Homocysteinemia is a common feature of schizophrenia. *Journal of Neural Transmission: General Section, 100*, 165–169.

Reich, D., & Zanarini, M. C. (2001). Developmental aspects of borderline personality disorder. *Harvard Review of Psychiatry, 9*, 294–301.

Reich, J. (2000). The relationship of social phobia to avoidant personality disorder: A proposal to reclassify avoidant personality disorder based on clinical empirical findings. *European Psychiatry, 15*, 151–159.

Reichborn-Kjennerud, T., Czajkowski, N., Neale, M. C., Ørstavik, R. E., Torgersen, S., Tambs, K., . . . Kendler, K. S. (2007). Genetic and environmental influences on dimensional representations of DSM-IV cluster C personality disorders: A population-based multivariate twin study. *Psychological Medicine, 37*, 645–653.

Reichborn-Kjennerud, T., Czajkowski, N., Torgersen, S., Neale, M. C., Orstavik, R. E., Tambs, K., & Kendler, K. S. (2007). The relationship between avoidant personality disorder and social phobia: A population-based twin study. *American Journal of Psychiatry, 164*, 1722–1728.

Reichenberg, A., Avshalom, C., Harrington, H., Houts, R., Keefe, R. S. E., Murray, R. M., . . . Moffitt, T. E. (2010). Static and dynamic cognitive deficits in childhood preceding adult schizophrenia: A 30-year study. *American Journal of Psychiatry, 167*, 160–169.

Reid, D. H., Wilson, P. G., & Faw, G. D. (1991). Teaching self-help skills. In J. L. Matson & J. A. Mulick (Eds.), *Handbook of mental retardation*. New York: Pergamon.

Reilly-Harrington, N. A., Alloy, L. B., Fresco, D. M., & Whitehouse, W. G. (1999). Cognitive styles and life events interact to predict bipolar and unipolar symptomatology. *Journal of Abnormal Psychology, 108*, 567–578.

Reimherr, F. W., Strong, R. E., Marchant, B. K., Hedges, D. W., & Wender, P. H. (2001). Factors affecting return of symptoms 1 year after treatment in a 62-week controlled study of fluoxetine in major depression. *Journal of Clinical Psychiatry, 62*, 16–23.

Reiss, D., Heatherington, E. M., Plomin, R., Howe, G. W., Simmens, S. J., Henderson, S. H., . . . Law, T. (1995). Genetic questions for environmental studies: Differential parenting and psychopathology in adolescence. *Archives of General Psychiatry, 52*, 925–936.

Reissing, E. D., Binik, Y. M., & Khalife, S. (1999). Does vaginismus exist? A critical review of the literature. *Journal of Nervous and Mental Disease, 187*, 261–274.

Renneberg, B., Goldstein, A. J., Phillips, D., & Chambless, D. L. (1990). Intensive behavioral group treatment of avoidant personality disorder. *Behavior Therapy, 21*, 363–377.

Renshaw, D. C. (2001). Women coping with a partner's sexual avoidance. *Family Journal—Counseling and Therapy for Couples & Families, 9*, 11–16.

Resick, P. A., Nishith, P., & Griffin, M. G. (2003). How well does cognitive-behavioral therapy treat symptoms of complex PTSD? An examination of child sexual abuse survivors within a clinical trial. *CNS Spectrums, 8*, 351–355.

Resick, P. A., Nishith, P., Weaver, T. L., Astin, M. C., & Feuer, C. A. (2002). A comparison of cognitive-processing therapy with prolonged exposure and a waiting condition for the treatment of chronic posttraumatic stress disorder in female rape victims. *Journal of Consulting and Clinical Psychology, 70*, 867–879.

Ressler, K. J., & Nemeroff, C. B. (1999). Role of norepinephrine in the pathophysiology and treatment of mood disorders. *Biological Psychiatry, 46*, 1219–1233.

Ressler, K. J., Rothbaum, B. O., Tannenbaum, L., Anderson, P., Graap, K., Zimand, E., . . . Davis, M. (2004). Cognitive enhancers as adjuncts to psychotherapy: Use of D-cycloserine in phobic individuals to facilitate extinction of fear. *Archives of General Psychiatry, 61*, 1136–1144.

Rey, J. M., Martin, A., & Krabman, P. (2004). Is the party over? Cannabis and juvenile psychiatric disorder: The past 10 years. *Journal of the American Academy of Child and Adolescent Psychiatry, 43*, 1194–1205.

Reynolds, C. R., Chastain, R. L., Kaufman, A. S., & McLean, J. E. (1997). Demographic characteristics and IQ among adults: Analysis of the WAIS-R standardization sample as a function of the stratification variables. *Journal of School Psychology, 25*, 323–342.

Rhee, S. H., & Waldman, I. D. (2002). Genetic and environmental influences on antisocial behavior: A meta-analysis of twin and adoption studies. *Psychological Bulletin, 128*, 490–529.

Rhode, P., Seeley, J. R., Kaufman, N. K, Clarke, G. N., & Stice, E. (2006). Predicting time to recovery among depressed adolescents treated in two psychosocial group interventions. *Journal of Consulting and Clinical Psychology, 74*, 80–88.

Richards, P. S., Baldwin, B. M., Frost, H. A., Clark-Sly, J. B., Berrett, M. E., & Hardman, R. K. (2000). What works for treating eating disorders? Conclusions of 28 outcome reviews. *Eating Disorders, 8*, 189–206.

Richards, R. L., Kinney, D. K., Lunde, I., Benet, M., & Merzel, A. (1988). Creativity in manic-depressives, cyclothymes, their normal relatives, and control subjects. *Journal of Abnormal Psychology, 97*, 281–288.

Richters, J., De Visser, R. O., Rissel, C. E., Grulich, A. E., & Smith, A. M. (2008). Demographic and psychosocial features of participants in bondage and discipline, "sadomasochism"or dominance and submission (BDSM): Data from a national survey. *Journal of Sexual Medicine, 7*, 1660–1668.

Ricks, D. M. (1972). *The beginning of vocal communication in infants and autistic children*. Unpublished doctoral dissertation, University of London.

Ridenour, T. A., Miller, A. R., Joy, K. L., & Dean, R. S. (1997). "Profile" analysis of the personality characteristics of child molesters using the MMPI–2. *Journal of Clinical Psychology, 53*, 575–586.

Ridker, P. M., Cook, N. R., Lee, I.-M., Gordon, D., Gaziano, J. M., Manson, J. E., . . . Buring, J. E. (2005). A randomized trial of low-dose aspirin in the primary prevention of cardiovascular disease in women. *Journal of the American Medical Association, 352*, 1293–1304.

Ridley, M. (2003). *Nature via nurture: Genes, experience, and what makes us human*. Great Britain: HarperCollins.

Rieder, R. O., Mann, L. S., Weinberger, D. R., van Kammen, D. P., & Post, R. M. (1983). Computer tomographic scans in patients with schizophrenia, schizoaffective, and bipolar affective disorder. *Archives of General Psychiatry, 40*, 735–739.

Rief, W., & Broadbent, E. (2007). Explaining medically unexplained symptoms—models and mechanisms. *Clinical Psychology Review, 27*(7), 821–841. doi: 10.1016/j.cpr.2007.07.005

Rief, W., Buhlmann, U., Wilhelm, S., Borkenhagen, A., & Brähler, E. (2006). The prevalence of body dysmorphic disorder: A population-based survey. *Psychological Medicine, 36*, 877–885.

Riegel, D. L. (2004). Effects on boy-attracted pedosexual males of viewing boy erotica. *Archives of Sexual Behavior, 33*(4), 321–323.

Riley, A. J., & Riley, E. J. (1978). A controlled study to evaluate directed masturbation in the management of primary orgasmic failure in women. *British Journal of Psychiatry, 133*, 404–409.

Rimland, B. (1964). *Infantile autism*. New York: Appleton-Century-Crofts.

Rind, B., Tromovitch, P., & Bauserman, R. (1998). A metaanalytic examination of assumed properties of child sexual abuse using college students. *Psychological Bulletin, 124*, 22–53.

Ringwalt, C., Ennett, S. T., & Holt, K. D. (1991). An outcome evaluation of Project DARE (Drug Abuse Resistance Education). *Health Education Research, 6*, 327–337.

Rinne, T., van den Brink, W., Wouters, L., & van Dyck, R. (2002). SSRI treatment of borderline personality disorder: A randomized, placebo-controlled clinical trial for female patients with borderline personality disorder. *American Journal of Psychiatry, 159*, 2048–2054.

Ritsher, J. B., Struening, E. L., Hellman, F., & Guardino, M. (2002). Internal validity of an anxiety disorder screening instrument across five ethnic groups. *Psychiatry Research, 111*, 199–213.

Ritvo, E. R., Freeman, B. J., Geller, E., & Yuwiler, A. (1983). Effects of fenfluramine on 14 outpatients with the syndrome of autism. *Journal of the American Academy of Child Psychiatry, 22*, 549–558.

Roan, S. (1992, October 15). Giving up coffee tied to withdrawal symptoms. *Los Angeles Times*, p. A26.

Robbins, S. J., Ehrman, R. N., Childress, A. R., Cornish, J. W., & O'Brien, C. P. (2000). Mood state and recent cocaine use are not associated with levels of cocaine cue reactivity. *Drug and Alcohol Dependence, 59*, 33–42.

Roberts, B. W., Kuncel, N. R., Shiner, R., Caspi, A., & Goldberg, L. R. (2007). The power of personality: The comparative validity of personality traits, socioeconomic status, and cognitive ability for predicting important life outcomes. *Perspectives on Psychological Science, 2*, 313–345.

Robiner, W. N. (2006). The mental health professions: Workforce supply and demand, issues, and challenges. *Clinical Psychology Review, 26*, 600–625.

Robinson, D. N. (1996). *Wild beasts and idle humours: The insanity defense from antiquity to the present*. Cambridge, MA: Harvard University Press.

Robinson, L. A., Klesges, R. C., Zbikowski, S. M., & Glaser, R. (1997). Predictors of risk for different stages of adolescent smoking in a biracial sample. *Journal of Consulting and Clinical Psychology, 65,* 653–662.

Robinson, N. S., Garber, J., & Hillsman, R. (1995). Cognitions and stress: Direct and moderating effects on depression versus externalizing symptoms during the junior high school transition. *Journal of Abnormal Psychology, 104,* 453–463.

Robinson, T. E., & Berridge, K. C. (1993). The neural basis of drug craving: An incentive sensitization theory of addiction. *Brain Research Reviews, 18,* 247–191.

Robinson, T. E., & Berridge, K. C. (2003). Addiction. *Annual Review of Psychology, 54,* 25–53.

Robinson-Whelan, S., Tada, Y., McCallum, R. C., McGuire, L., & Kiecolt-Glaser, J. K. (2001). Long-term caregiving: What happens when it ends? *Journal of Abnormal Psychology, 110,* 573–584.

Rodin, J., McAvay, G., & Timko, C. (1988). A longitudinal study of depressed mood and sleep disturbances in elderly adults. *Journal of Gerontology: Psychological Sciences, 43,* 45–53.

Roehrig, J. P., & McLean, C. P. (2010). A comparison of stigma toward eating disorders versus depression. *International Journal of Eating Disorders, 43,* 671–674.

Roemer, L., Lee, J. K., Salters-Pedneault, K., Erisman, S. M., Orsillo, S. M., & Mennin, D. S. (2009). Mindfulness and emotion regulation difficulties in generalized anxiety disorder: Preliminary evidence for independent and overlapping contributions. *Behavior Therapy, 40*(2), 142–154. doi: 10.1016/j.beth.2008.04.001

Roemer, L., Molina, S., & Borkovec, T. D. (1997). An investigation of worry content among generally anxious individuals. *Journal of Nervous and Mental Disease, 185,* 314–319.

Roemer, L., Orsillo, S. M., & Barlow, D. H. (2004). Generalized anxiety disorder. In D. H. Barlow (Ed.), *Anxiety and its disorders: The nature and treatment of anxiety and panic* (pp. 477–515). New York: Guilford.

Rogler, L. H., & Hollingshead, A. B. (1985). *Trapped: Families and schizophrenia* (3rd ed.). Maplewood, NJ: Waterfront.

Rohan, K. J., Roecklein, K. A., Lindsey, K. T., Johnson, L. G., Lippy, R. D., Lacy, T. J., & Barton, F. B. (2007). A randomized controlled trial of cognitive-behavioral therapy, light therapy, and their combination for seasonal affective disorder. *Journal of Consulting and Clinical Psychology, 75,* 489–500.

Romans, S. E., Gendall, K. A., Martin, J. L., & Mullen, P. E. (2001). Child sexual abuse and later disordered eating: A New Zealand epidemiological study. *International Journal of Eating Disorders, 29,* 380–392.

Root, T. L., Pinheiro, A. P., Thornton, L., Strober, M., Fernandez-Aranda, F., Brandt, H., et al. (2010). Substance use disorders in women with anorexia nervosa. *International Journal of Eating Disorders, 43,* 14–21.

Rosa-Alcazar, A. I., Sanchez-Meca, J., Gomez-Conesa, A., & Marin-Martinez, F. (2008). Psychological treatment of obsessive-compulsive disorder: A meta-analysis. *Clinical Psychology Review, 28*(8), 1310–1325. doi: 10.1016/j.cpr.2008.07.001

Rose, J. E., Brauer, L. H., Behm, F. M., Cramblett, M., Calkins, K., & Lawhon, D. (2004). Psychopharmacological interactions between nicotine and ethanol. *Nicotine and Tobacco Research, 6,* 133–144.

Rosen, L. N., Targum, S. D., Terman, M., Bryant, M. J., Hoffman, H., Kasper, S. F., . . . Rosenthal, N. E. (1990). Prevalence of seasonal affective disorder at four latitudes. *Psychiatry Research, 31,* 131–144.

Rosen, R. C. (2000). Medical and psychological interventions for erectile dysfunction: Toward a combined treatment approach. In S. R. Lieblum & R. C. Rosen (Eds.), *Principles and practice of sex therapy* (pp. 276–304). New York: Guilford.

Rosen, R. C., & Leiblum, S. R. (1995). Treatment of sexual disorders in the 1990s: An integrated approach. *Journal of Consulting and Clinical Psychology, 63,* 877–890.

Rosen, R. C., Leiblum, S. R., & Spector, I. (1994). Psychologically based treatment for male erectile disorder: A cognitive-interpersonal model. *Journal of Sex and Marital Therapy, 20,* 67–85.

Rosen, R. C., & Rosen, L. (1981). *Human sexuality.* New York: Knopf.

Rosenfarb, I. S., Goldstein, M. J., Mintz, J., & Neuchterlein, K. H. (1994). Expressed emotion and subclinical psychopathology observable within transactions between schizophrenics and their family members. *Journal of Abnormal Psychology, 104,* 259–267.

Rosenheck, R., Cramer, J., Allan, E., Erdos, J., Frisman, J., et al. (1999). Cost-effectivness of clozapine in patients with high and low levels of hospital use. *Archives of General Psychiatry, 56,* 565–572.

Rosman, B. L., Minuchin, S., & Liebman, R. (1975). Family lunch session: An introduction to family therapy in anorexia nervosa. *American Journal of Orthopsychiatry, 45,* 846–852.

Rosman, B. L., Minuchin, S., & Liebman, R. (1976). Input and outcome of family therapy of anorexia nervosa. In J. L. Claghorn (Ed.), *Successful psychotherapy.* New York: Brunner/Mazel.

Ross, C. A. (1989). *Multiple personality disorder: Diagnosis, clinical features, and treatment.* New York: Wiley.

Ross, C. A. (1991). Epidemiology of multiple personality disorder and dissociation. *Psychiatric Clinics of North America, 14,* 503–517.

Ross, C. A. (2008). Case report: A convicted sex offender with dissociative identity disorder. *Journal of Trauma and Dissociation : The Official Journal of the International Society for the Study of Dissociation, 9*(4), 551–562.

Ross, G. J., Waller, G., Tyson, M., & Elliott, P. (1998). Reported sexual abuse and subsequent psychopathology among women attending psychology clinics: The mediating role of dissociation. *British Journal of Clinical Psychology, 37,* 313–326.

Rossello, J., Bernal, G., & Rivera-Medina, C. (2008). Individual and group CBT and IPT for Puerto Rican adolescents with depressive symptoms. *Cultural Diversity and Ethnic Minority Psychology, 14,* 234–245.

Rossiter, E. M., & Agras, W. S. (1990). An empirical test of the DSM-IIIR definition of binge. *International Journal of Eating Disorders, 9,* 513–518.

Rotge, J. Y., Guehl, D., Dilharreguy, B., Tignol, J., Bioulac, B., Allard, M., . . . Aouizerate, B. (2009). Meta-analysis of brain volume changes in obsessive-compulsive disorder. *Biological Psychiatry, 65*(1), 75–83. doi: 10.1016/j.biopsych.2008.06.019

Rothbaum, B. O., Anderson, P., Zimand, E., Hodges, L., Lang, D., & Wilson, J. (2006). Virtual reality exposure therapy and standard (in vivo) exposure therapy in the treatment of fear of flying. *Behavior Therapy, 37*(1), 80–90. doi: 10.1016/j.beth.2005.04.004

Rothbaum, B. O., & Foa, E. B. (1993). Subtypes of posttraumatic stress disorder and duration of symptoms. In J. R. T. Davidson & E. B. Foa (Eds.), *Post-traumatic stress disorder: DSM-IV and beyond* (pp. 23–35). Washington, DC: American Psychiatric Press.

Rothbaum, B. O., Foa, E. B., Murdock, T., Riggs, D. S., & Walsh, W. (1992). A prospective examination of posttraumatic stress disorder in rape victims. *Journal of Traumatic Stress, 5,* 455–475.

Rothbaum, B. O., Hodges, L., Alarcon, R., Ready, D., Shahar, F., Graap, K., . . . Baltzell, D. (1999). Virtual reality exposure therapy for PTSD Vietnam veterans: A case study. *Journal of Traumatic Stress, 12*(2), 263–271.

Roughgarden, J. (2004). *Evolution's rainbow: Diversity, gender and sexuality in nature and people.* Los Angeles CA: University of California Press.

Rouleau, C. R., & von Ranson, K. M. (2011). Potential risks of pro-eating disorder websites. *Clinical Psychology Review, 31,* 525–531.

Rowland, D. L., Cooper, S. E., & Slob, A. K. (1996). Genital and psychoaffective responses to erotic stimulation in sexually functional and dysfunctional men. *Journal of Abnormal Psychology, 105,* 194–203.

Roy, A. (1982). Suicide in chronic schizophrenia. *British Journal of Psychiatry, 141,* 171–180.

Roy, A. (1994). Recent biologic studies on suicide. *Suicide and Life Threatening Behaviors, 24,* 10–24.

Roy, A. (1995). Suicide. In H. I. Kaplan & B. J. Sadock (Eds.), *Comprehensive textbook of psychiatry* (pp. 1739–1752). Baltimore: Williams & Wilkins.

Roy-Byrne, P. P., Davidson, K. W., Kessler, R. C., Asmundson, G. J., Goodwin, R. D., Kubzansky, L., . . . Stein, M. B. (2008). Anxiety disorders and comorbid medical illness. *General Hospital Psychiatry, 30*(3), 208–225. doi: 10.1016/j.genhosppsych.2007.12.006

Roy-Byrne, P. P., Katon, W., Cowley, D. S., & Russo, J. (2001). A randomized effectiveness trial of collaborative care for patients with panic disorder in primary care. *Archives of General Psychiatry, 58,* 869–876.

Royal College of Physicians (1992) Smoking and the young. London: Royal College of Physicians.

Rubia, K., Overmeyer, S., Taylor, E., Brammer, M., Williams, S. C. R., et al. (1999). Hypofrontality in attention deficit hyperactivity disorder during higher-order motor control: A study with functional MRI. *American Journal of Psychiatry, 156,* 891–896.

Rubinstein, T. B., McGinn, A. P., Wildman, R. P., & Wylie-Rosett, J. (2010). Disordered eating in adulthood is associated with reported weight loss attempts in childhood. *International Journal of Eating Disorders, 43,* 663–666.

Rude, S. S., Valdez, C. R., Odom, S., & Ebrahimi, A. (2003). Negative cognitive biases predict subsequent depression. *Cognitive Therapy and Research, 27,* 415–429.

Rummel-Kluge, C., Komossa, K., Schwarz, S., Hunger, H., Schmid, F., Lobos, C. A., et al. (2010). Head to head comparisons of metabolic side effects of second generation antipsychotics in the treatment of schizophrenia: A systematic review and meta-analysis. *Schizophrenia Research, 123,* 225–233.

Ruscio, A. M., Brown, T. A., Chiu, W. T., Sareen, J., Stein, M. B., & Kessler, R. C. (2008). Social fears and social phobia in the USA: Results from the National Comorbidity Survey Replication. *Psychological Medicine, 38*(1), 15–28. doi: 10.1017/S0033291707001699

Ruscio, A. M., Stein, D. J., Chiu, W. T., & Kessler, R. C. (2010). The epidemiology of obsessive-compulsive disorder in the National Comorbidity Survey Replication. *Molecular Psychiatry, 15*(1), 53–63. doi: 10.1038/mp.2008.94

Rush, A. J., Trivedi, M., Wisniewski, S. R., Nierenberg, A. A., Stewart, J. W., Warden, D., . . . Fava, M. (2006). Acute and longer-term outcomes in depressed outpatients requiring one or several treatment steps: A STARD report. *American Journal of Psychiatry, 163,* 1905–1917.

Rutherford, M. J., Cacciola, J. S., & Alterman, A. I. (1999). Antisocial personality disorder and psychopathy in cocaine-dependent women. *American Journal of Psychiatry, 156,* 849–856.

Rutledge, T., Reis, S. E., Olson, M., Owens, J., Kelsey, S. F., Pepine, C. J., . . . Matthews, K. A. (2001). Psychosocial variables are associated with atherosclerosis risk factors among women with chest pain: The WISE study. *Psychosomatic Medicine, 63,* 282–288.

Rutter, M. (1983). Cognitive deficits in the pathogenesis of autism. *Journal of Child Psychology and Psychiatry, 2,* 513–531.

Rutter, M., Caspi, A., Fergusson, D., Horwood, L. J., Goodman, R., Maughan, B., . . . Carroll, J. (2004). Sex differences in developmental reading disability: New findings from 4 epidemiological studies. *Journal of the American Medical Association, 291,* 2007–2012.

Rutter, M., & Silberg, J. (2002). Gene-environment interplay in relation to emotional and behavioral disturbance. *Annual Review of Psychology, 53,* 463–490.

Sabo, S. Z., Nelson, M. L., Fisher, C., Gunzerath, L., Brody, C. L., et al. (1999). A genetic association for cigarette smoking behavior. *Health Psychology, 18,* 7–13.

Sacco, R. L., Elkind, M., Boden-Albala, B., Lin, I., Kargman, D. E., et al. (1999). The protective effect of moderate alcohol consumption on ischemic stroke. *Journal of the American Medical Association, 281,* 53–60.

Sachs, G. S., Nierenberg, A. A., Calabrese, J. R., Marangell, L. B., Wisniewski, S. R., & Gyulai, L. (2007). Effectiveness of adjunctive antidepressant treatment for bipolar depression. *New England Journal of Medicine, 356,* 1711–1722.

Sachs, G. S., & Thase, M. E. (2000). Bipolar disorder therapeutics: Maintenance treatment. *Biological Psychiatry, 48,* 573–581.

Sackeim, H. A., & Lisanby, S. H. (2001). Physical treatments in psychiatry: Advances in electroconvulsive therapy, transcranial magnetic stimulation, and vagus nerve stimulation. In M. M. Weissman (Ed.), *Treatment of depression: Bridging the 21st century* (pp. 151–174). Washington, DC: American Psychiatric Publishing.

Sackeim, H. A., Prudic, J., Fuller, R., Keilp, J., Lavori, P. W., & Olfson, M. (2007). The cognitive effects of electroconvulsive therapy in community settings. *Neuropsychopharmacology, 32,* 244–254.

Sacks, F. M., Bray, G. A., Carey, V. J., Smith, S. R., Ryan, D. H., Anton, S. D., . . . Williamson, D. A. (2009). Comparison of weight-loss diets with different compositions of fat, protein, and carbohydrates. *New England Journal of Medicine, 360,* 859–873.

Sacks, O. (1995). *An anthropologist on Mars.* New York: Knopf.

Saczynski, J. S., Beiser, A., Seshadri, S., Auerbach, S., Wolf, P. A., & Au, R. (2010). Depressive symptoms and risk of dementia. *Neurology, 75,* 35–41.

Saffer, H. (1991). Alcohol advertising bans and alcohol abuse: An international perspective. *Journal of Health Economics, 10,* 65–79.

Saha, S., Chant, D., & McGrath, J. (2007). A systematic review of mortality in schizophrenia: Is the differential mortality gap worsening over time? *Archives of General Psychiatry, 64,* 1123–1131.

Sakel, M. (1938). The pharmacological shock treatment of schizophrenia. *Nervous and Mental Disease Monograph, 62.*

Saks, E. R. (1997). *Jekyll on trial: Multiple personality disorder and criminal law.* New York: New York University Press.

Saks, E. R. (2007). *The center cannot hold: My journey through madness.* New York: Hyperion.

Salamone, J. D. (2000). A critique of recent studies on placebo effects of antidepressants: Importance of research on active placebos. *Psychopharmacology, 152,* 1–6.

Salan, S. E., Zinberg, N. E., & Frei, E. (1975). Antiemetic effect of delta–9-THC in patients receiving cancer chemotherapy. *New England Journal of Medicine, 293,* 795–797.

Salekin, R. T. (2002). Psychopathy and therapeutic pessimism: Clinical lore or clinical reality? *Clinical Psychology Review, 22,* 79–112.

Salem, J. E., & Kring, A. M. (1998). The role of gender differences in the reduction of etiologic heterogeneity in schizophrenia. *Clinical Psychology Review, 18,* 795–819.

Salkovskis, P. M. (1996). Cognitive-behavioral approaches to understanding obsessional problems. In R. M. Rapee (Ed.), *Current controversies in anxiety disorders.* New York: Guilford.

Salter, D., McMillan, D., Richards, M., Talbot, T., Hodges, J., Bentovim, A., . . . Skuse, D. (2003). Development of sexually abusive behaviour in sexually victimised males: A longitudinal study. *Lancet, 361*(9356), 471–476.

Samuel, D. B., & Widiger, T. A. (2008). A meta-analytic review of the relationships between the five-factor model and DSM-IV-TR personality disorders: A facet level analysis. *Clinical Psychology Review, 28*(8), 1326–1342. doi: 10.1016/j.cpr.2008.07.002

Samuels, J., Bienvenu, O., Pinto, A., Fyer, A., McCracken, J., Rauch, S., . . . Knowles, J. (2007). Hoarding in obsessive-compulsive disorder: Results from the OCD Collaborative Genetics Study. *Behaviour Research and Therapy, 45*(4), 673–686. doi: 10.1016/j.brat.2006.05.008

Samuels, J., Eaton, W. W., Bienvenu, O. J. I., Brown, C., Costa, P. T. J., & Nestadt, G. (2002). Prevalence and correlates of personality disorders in a community sample. *British Journal of Psychiatry, 180,* 536–542.

Sanchez, D. T., & Kiefer, A. K. (2007). Body concerns in and out of the bedroom: Implications for sexual pleasure and problems. *Archives of Sexual Behavior, 36,* 808–820.

Sandberg, S., Järvenpää, S., Paton, J. Y., & McCann, D.C. (2004). Asthma exacerbations in children immediately following stressful life events: A Cox's hierarchical regression. *Thorax, 49,* 1046–1051.

Santarelli, L., Saxe, M., Gross, C., Surget, A., Battaglia, F., Dulawa, S., . . . Hen, R. (2003). Requirement of hippocampal neurogenesis for the behavioral effects of antidepressants. *Science, 301,* 805–809.

Sar, V., Akyuz, G., Kundakci, T., Kiziltan, E., & Dogan, O. (2004). Childhood trauma, dissociation, and psychiatric comorbidity in patients with conversion disorder. *American Journal of Psychiatry, 161*(12), 2271–2276. doi: 10.1176/appi.ajp.161.12.2271

Sareen, J., Cox, B. J., Afifi, T. O., de Graaf, R., Asmundson, G. J. G., ten Have, M., & Stein, M. B. (2005). Anxiety disorders and risk for suicidal ideation and suicide attempts: A population-based longitudinal study of adults. *Archives of General Psychiatry, 62,* 1249–1257.

Sartorius, N., Jablensky, A., Korten, A., Ernberg, G., et al. (1986). Early manifestations and first-contact incidence of schizophrenia in different cultures: A preliminary report on the initial evaluation phase of the WHO Collaborative Study on Determinants of Outcome of Severe Mental Disorders. *Psychological Medicine, 16,* 909–928.

Sartorius, N., Shapiro, R., & Jablonsky, A. (1974). The international pilot study of schizophrenia. *Schizophrenia Bulletin, 2,* 21–35.

Saxena, S., Brody, A. L., Maidment, K. M., & Baxter, L. R. J. (2007). Paroxetine treatment of compulsive hoarding. *Journal of Psychiatric Research, 41*(6), 481–487.

Sbrocco, T., Weisberg, R. B., Barlow, D. H., & Carter, M. M. (1997). The conceptual relationship between panic disorder and male erectile dysfunction. *Journal of Sex and Marital Therapy, 23,* 212–220.

Scarborough, H. S. (1990). Very early language deficits in dyslexic children. *Child Development, 61,* 128–174.

Schaefer, H. S., Putnam, K. M., Benca, R. M., & Davidson, R. J. (2006). Event-related functional magnetic resonance imaging measures of neural activity to positive social stimuli in pre- and post-treatment depression. *Biological Psychiatry, 60,* 974–986.

Schaie, K. W., & Hertzog, C. (1982). Longitudinal methods. In B. B. Wolman (Ed.), *Handbook of developmental psychology.* Englewood Cliffs, NJ: Prentice Hall.

Schalock, R. L., Luckasson, R. A., & Shogren, K. A., et al. (2007). The renaming of mental retardation: Understanding the change to the term intellectual disability. *Intellectual and Developmental Disabilities, 45,* 116–124.

Schecter, R., & Grether, J. K. (2008). Continuing increases in autism reported to California's Developmental Services System. *Archives of General Psychiatry, 65,* 19–24.

Scherk, H., Pajonk, F. G., & Leucht, S. (2007). Second-generation antipsychotic agents in the treatment of acute mania: A systematic review and meta-analysis of randomized controlled trials. *Archives of General Psychiatry, 64,* 442–455.

Schilder, P. (1953). *Medical psychology.* New York: International Universities Press.

Schleifer, M. (1995). Should we change our views about early childhood education? *Alberta Journal of Educational Research, 41,* 355–359.

Schlundt, D. G., & Johnson, W. G. (1990). *Eating disorders: Assessment and treatment.* Needham Heights, MA: Allyn & Bacon.

Schmidt, E., Carns, A., & Chandler, C. (2001). Assessing the efficacy of rational recovery in the treatment of alcohol/drug dependency. *Alcoholism Treatment Quarterly, 19,* 97–106.

Schmidt, F. L., & Hunter, J. E. (1998). The validity and utility of selection methods in personnel psychology: Practical and theoretical implications of 85 years of research findings. *Psychology Bulletin, 124,* 262–274.

Schmidt, N. B., Lerew, D. R., & Jackson, R. J. (1999). Prospective evaluation of anxiety sensitivity in the pathogenesis of panic: Prospective evaluation of spontaneous panic attacks during acute stress. *Journal of Abnormal Psychology, 106,* 355–364.

Schmidt, N. B., Richey, J. A., Buckner, J. D., & Timpano, K. R. (2009). Attention training for generalized social anxiety disorder. *Journal of Abnormal Psychology, 118*(1), 5–14. doi: 10.1037/a0013643

Schmidt, N. B., Woolaway-Bickel, K., & Bates, M. (2000). Suicide and panic disorder: Integration of the literature and new findings. In M. D. Rudd & T. E. Joiner (Eds.), *Suicide science: Expanding the boundaries* (pp. 117–136). New York: Kluwer Academic/Plenum.

Schmitt, D. P., Alcalay, L., Allik, J., Ault, L., Austers, I., Bennett, K. L., . . . Durkin, K. (2003). Universal sex differences in the desire for sexual variety: Tests from 52 nations, 6 continents and 13 islands. *Journal of Personality and Social Psychology, 85,* 85–104.

Schnab, D. W., & Trinh, N. G. (2004). Do artificial food colors promote hyperactivity in children with hyperactive syndromes? A meta-analysis of double-blind placebo-controlled trials. *Journal of Developmental and Behavioral Pediatrics, 25,* 425–434.

Schneck, C. D., Miklowitz, D. J., Miyahara, S., Araga, M., Wisniewski, S. R., Gyulai, L., . . . Sachs, G. S. (2008). The prospective course of rapid-cycling bipolar disorder: Findings from the STEP-BD. *American Journal of Psychiatry, 165,* 370–376.

Schoeneman, T. J. (1977). The role of mental illness in the European witch-hunts of the sixteenth and seventeenth centuries: An assessment. *Journal of the History of the Behavioral Sciences, 13,* 337–351.

Schopler, E., Short, A., & Mesibov, G. (1989). Relation of behavioral treatment to "normal functioning": Comment on Lovaas. *Journal of Consulting and Clinical Psychology, 57*, 162–164.

Schreiber, F. L. (1973). *Sybil*. Chicago: Regnery.

Schuckit, M. A. (2009). Alcohol-use disorders. *Lancet, 373*, 492–501.

Schuckit, M. A. (2009). An overview of genetic influences in alcoholism. *Journal of Substance Abuse Treatment, 36*, S5–14.

Schuckit, M. A., Daeppen, J. B., Tipp, J. E., Hesselbrock, M., & Bucholz, K. K. (1998). The clinical course of alcohol-related problems in alcohol dependent and non-alcohol dependent drinking women and men. *Journal of Studies on Alcohol, 59*, 581–590.

Schuckit, M. A., Smith, T. L., Danko, G. P., Bucholz, K. K., Reich, T., & Bierut, L. (2001). Five-year clinical course associated with DSM-IV alcohol abuse or dependence in a large group of men and women. *American Journal of Psychiatry, 158*, 1084–1090.

Schumacher, J. E., Milby, J. B., Wallace, D., Meehan, D. C., Kertesz, S., et al. (2007). Meta-analysis of day treatment and contingency-management dismantling research: Birmingham homeless cocaine studies (1990–2005). *Journal of Consulting and Clinical Psychology, 75*, 823–828.

Schwartz, M. B., Chambliss, O. H., Brownell, K. D., Blair, S., & Billington, C. (2003). Weight bias among health professionals specializing in obesity. *Obesity Research, 11*, 1033–1039.

Schweizer, E., Rickels, K., Case, G., & Greenblatt, D. J. (1990). Long-term therapeutic use of benzodiazepines: Effects of gradual taper. *Archives of General Psychiatry, 47*, 908–915.

Schwitzgebel, R. L., & Schwitzgebel, R. K. (1980). *Law and psychological practice*. New York: Wiley.

Scorolli, C., Ghirlanda, S., Enquist, M., Zattoni, S., & Jamnini, E. A. (2007). Relative prevalence of different fetishes. *International Journal of Impotence Research, 19*, 432–437.

Scroppo, J. C., Drob, S. L., Weinberger, J. L., & Eagle, P. (1998). Identifying dissociative identity disorder: A self-report and projective study. *Journal of Abnormal Psychology, 107*, 272–284.

Seedat, S., & Matsunaga, H. (2006). Cross-national and ethnic issues in OC spectrum disorders. *CNS Spectrum, 12*, 392–400.

Seedat, S., Scott, K. M., Angermeyer, M., Berglund, P., Bromet, E., Brugha, T., . . . Kessler, R. (2009). Cross-national associations between gender and mental disorders in the World Health Organization world mental health surveys. *Archives of General Psychiatry, 66*(7), 785–795.

Segal, Z. V., Kennedy, S., Gemar, M., Hood, K., Pedersen, R., & Buis, T. (2006). Cognitive reactivity to sad mood provocation and the prediction of depressive relapse. *Archives of General Psychiatry, 63*, 749–755.

Segal, Z. V., Williams, J. M., & Teasdale, J. D. (2001). *Mindfulness-based cognitive therapy for depression*. New York: Guilford.

Segal, Z. V., Williams, J. M. G., & Teasdale, J. D. (2003). Mindfulness-based cognitive therapy for depression: A new approach to preventing relapse. *Psychotherapy Research, 13*, 123–125.

Segraves, K. B., & Segraves, R. T. (1991). Hypoactive sexual desire disorder: Prevalence and comorbidity in 906 subjects. *Journal of Sex and Marital Therapy, 17*, 55–58.

Segraves, R. T. (2003). Recognizing and reversing sexual side effects of medications. In S. B. Levine, C. B. Candace, et al. (Eds.), *Handbook of clinical sexuality for mental health professionals* (pp. 377–391). New York: Brunner-Routledge.

Segraves, R. T. (2010). Considerations for a better definition of male orgasmic disorder in DSM V. *Journal of Sexual Medicine, 7*(2 Pt 1), 690–695. doi: 10.1111/j.1743–6109.2009.01683.x

Segraves, R. T., & Althof, S. (1998). Psychotherapy and pharmacotherapy of sexual dysfunctions. In P. E. Nathan & J. M. Gorman (Eds.), *A guide to treatments that work*. New York: Oxford.

Segurado, R., Detera-Wadleigh, S. D., Levinson, D. F., Lewis, C. M., Gill, M., Nurnberger, J. I., et al. (2003). Genome scan meta-analysis of schizophrenia and bipolar disorder, part III: Bipolar disorder. *American Journal of Human Genetics, 73*, 49–62.

Seidler, G. H., & Wagner, F. E. (2006). Comparing the efficacy of EMDR and trauma-focused cognitive-behavioral therapy in the treatment of PTSD: A meta-analytic study. *Psychological Medicine, 36*, 1515–1522.

Seligman, M. E. P. (1971). Phobias and preparedness. *Behavior Therapy, 2*, 307–320.

Seligman, M. E., Maier, S. F., & Geer, J. H. (1968). Alleviation of learned helplessness in the dog. *Journal of Abnormal Psychology, 73*, 256–262.

Selkoe, D. J. (2002). Alzheimer's disease is a synaptic failure. *Science, 298*, 789–791.

Selling, L. S. (1940). *Men against madness*. New York: Greenberg.

Selwood, A., Johnson, K., Katona, C., Ilyketsos, C., & Livingson, G. (2007). Systematic review of the effect of psychological interventions on family caregivers of people with dementia. *Journal of Affective Disorders, 101*, 75–89.

Sensky, T., Turkington, D., Kingdon, D., et al. (2000). A randomized controlled trial of cognitive-behavioural therapy for persistent symptoms in schizophrenia resistant to medication. *Archives of General Psychiatry Psychiatry, 57*, 165–172.

Serdula, M. K., Mokdad, A. H., Williamson, D. F., Galuska, D. A., et al. (1999). Prevalence of attempting weight loss and strategies for controlling weight. *Journal of the American Medical Association, 282*, 1353–1358.

Seto, M. C. (2009). Pedophilia. *Annual Review of Clinical Psychology, 5*, 391–407. doi: 10.1146/annurev.clinpsy032408.153618

Sexton, T. L., Alexander, J. F., & Mease, A. L. (2004). Levels of evidence for the models and mechanisms of therapeutic change in family and couple therapy. In M. J. Lambert (Ed.), *Bergin and Garfield's handbook of psychotherapy and behavior change* (5th ed., pp. 590–646). Hoboken, NJ: Wiley.

Shachnow, J., Clarkin, J., DiPalma, C. S., Thurston, F., Hull, J., & Shearin, E. (1997). Biparental psychopathology and borderline personality disorder. *Psychiatry—Interpersonal and Biological Processes, 60*, 171–181.

Shaffer, D., Fisher, P., Lucas, C. P., et al. (2000). NIMH Diagnostic Interview for Children Version IV (NIMH DISC-IV): Description, differences from previous versions, and reliability of some common diagnoses. *Journal of the American Academy of Child and Adolescent Psychiatry, 39*, 28–38.

Shaper, A. G. (1990). Alcohol and mortality: A review of prospective studies. *British Journal of Addiction, 85*, 837–847.

Shapiro, F. (1999). Eye movement desensitization and reprocessing (EMDR) and the anxiety disorders: Clinical and research implications of an integrated psychotherapy treatment. *Journal of Anxiety Disorders, 13*, 35–67.

Sharkansky, E. J., King, D. W., King, L. A., Wolfe, J., Erickson, D. J., & Stokes, L. R. (2000). Coping with Gulf War combat stress: Mediating and moderating effects. *Journal of Abnormal Psychology, 109*, 188–197.

Shaw, D. S., Dishion, T. J., Supplee, L., Gardner, F., & Arnds, K. (2006). Randomized trial of a family-centered approach to the prevention of early conduct problems: 2-year effects of the family check-up in early childhood. *Journal of Consulting and Clinical Psychology, 74*, 1–9.

Shaw, L. J., Bairy Merz, C. N., Pepine. C. J., Reis, S. E., Bittner, V. E., et al. (2006). Insights from the NHLBI-sponsored Women's Ischemia Syndrome Evaluation (WISE) study. Part I: Gender differences in traditional and novel risk factors symptom evaluation and gender-optimized diagnostic strategies. *Journal of the American College of Cardiology, 47*, 4S–20S.

Shaywitz, B. A., Shaywitz, S. E., Blachman, B. A., et al. (2004). Development of left occipitotemporal systems for skilled reading in children after a phonologically-based intervention. *Biological Psychiatry, 55*, 926–933.

Shaywitz, B. A., Shaywitz, S. E., Pugh, K. R., et al. (2002). Disruption of posterior brain systems for reading in children with developmental dyslexia. *Biological Psychiatry, 52*, 101–110.

Shaywitz, S. E., Shaywitz, B. A., Fletcher, J. M., & Escobar, M. D. (1990). Prevalence of reading disability in boys and girls. *Journal of the American Medical Association, 264*, 998–1002.

Shaywitz, S. E., Shaywitz, B. A., Fulbright, R. K., et al. (2003). Neural systems for compensation and persistence: Young adult outcome of childhood reading disability. *Biological Psychiatry, 54*, 25–33.

Shea, M. T., Stout, R., Gunderson, J., Morey, L. C., Grilo, C. M., McGlashan, T., . . . Keller, M. B. (2002). Short-term diagnostic stability of schizotypal, borderline, avoidant, and obsessive-compulsive personality disorders. *American Journal of Psychiatry, 159*, 2036–2041.

Sheline, Y. (2000). 3D MRI studies of neuroanatomic changes in unipolar major depression: The role of stress and medical comorbidity. *Biological Psychiatry, 48*, 791–800.

Sheline, Y., Barch, D., Donnelly, J. M., Ollinger, J. M., Snyder, A. Z., & Mintun, M. A. (2001). Increased amygdala response to masked emotional faces in depressed subjects resolves with antidepressant treatment: An fMRI study. *Biological Psychiatry, 50*, 651–658.

Shelton, R. C., Mainer, D. H., & Sulser, F. (1996). cAMP-dependent protein kinase activity in major depression. *American Journal of Psychiatry, 153*, 1037–1042.

Shen, G. H. C., Sylvia, L. G., Alloy, L. B., Barrett, F., Kohner, M., Iacoviello, B., & Mills, A. (2008). Lifestyle regularity and cyclothymic symptomatology. *Journal of Clinical Psychology, 64*, 482–500.

Shenk, D. (2010). *The genius is in all of us: Why everything you've been told about genetics, talent, and IQ is wrong*. New York: Doubleday.

Sher, K. J., Grekin, E. R., & Williams, N. A. (2005). The development of alcohol use disorders. *Annual Review of Clinical Psychology, 1*, 493–523.

Sher, K. J., Walitzer, K. S., Wood, P. K., & Brent, E. F. (1991). Characteristics of children of alcoholics: Putative risk factors, substance use and abuse, and psychopathology. *Journal of Abnormal Psychology, 100*, 427–448.

Sher, K. J., Wood, M. D., Wood, P. K., & Raskin, G. (1996). Alcohol outcome expectancies and alcohol use: A latent variable cross-lagged panel study. *Journal of Abnormal Psychology, 105*, 561–574.

Shergill, S. S., Brammer, M. J., Williams, S. C., Murray, R. M., & McGuire, P. K. (2000). Mapping auditory hallucinations in schizophrenia using functional magnetic resonance imaging. *Archives of General Psychiatry, 57,* 1033–1038.

Sherman, D. K., Iacono, W. G., & McGue, M. K. (1997). Attention-deficit hyperactivity disorder dimensions: A twin study of inattention and impulsivity-hyperactivity. *Journal of the American Academy of Child and Adolescent Psychiatry, 36,* 745–753.

Shiffman, S., Gwaltney, C. J., Balabanis, M. H., Liu, K. S., Paty, J. A., Kassel, J. D., . . . Gnys, M. (2002). Immediate antecedents of cigarette smoking: An analysis from ecological momentary assessment. *Journal of Abnormal Psychology, 111,* 531–545.

Shiffman, S., Paty, J. A., Gwaltney, C. J., & Dang, Q. (2004). Immediate antecedents of cigarette smoking: An analysis of unrestricted smoking patterns. *Journal of Abnormal Psychology, 113,* 166–171.

Shiffman, S., & Waters, A. J. (2004). Negative affect and smoking lapses: A prospective analysis. *Journal of Consulting and Clinical Psychology, 72,* 192–201.

Shifren, J. L., Monz, B. U., Russo, P. A., Segreti, A., & Johannes, C. B. (2008). Sexual problems and distress in United States women: Prevalence and correlates. *Obstetrics and Gynecology, 112*(5), 970–978.

Shih, J. H., Eberhart, N., Hammen, C., & Brennan, P. A. (2006). Differential exposure and reactivity to interpersonal stress predict sex differences in adolescent depression. *Journal of Clinical Child and Adolescent Psychology, 35,* 103–115.

Shin, L. M., Rauch, S. L., & Pitman, R. K. (2006). Amygdala, medial prefrontal cortex, and hippocampal function in PTSD. *Annals of the New York Academy of Sciences, 1071,* 67–79. doi: 10.1196/annals.1364.007

Shin, L. M., Wright, C. I., Cannistraro, P. A., Wedig, M. M., McMullin, K., Martis, B., . . . Rauch, S. L. (2005). A functional magnetic resonance imaging study of amygdala and medial prefrontal cortex responses to overtly presented fearful faces posttraumatic stress disorder. *Archives of General Psychiatry, 62,* 273–281.

Shin, M., Besser, L. M., Kucik, J. E., Lu, C., Siffel, C., & Correa, A. (2009). Prevalence of Down syndrome among children and adolescents in 10 regions of the United States. *Pediatrics, 124,* 1565–1571.

Shneidman, E. S. (1973). Suicide. In E. Britannica (Ed.), *Encyclopedia Britannica.* Chicago: Encyclopedia Britannica.

Shneidman, E. S. (1987). A psychological approach to suicide. In G. R. VandenBos & B. K. Bryant (Eds.), *Cataclysms, crises, and catastrophes: Psychology in action.* Washington, DC: American Psychological Association.

Shobe, K. K., & Kihlstrom, J. F. (1997). Is traumatic memory special? *Current Directions in Psychological Science, 6,* 70–74.

Siegle, G. J., Thompson, W., Carter, C. S., Steinhauer, S. R., & Thase, M. E. (2007). Increased amygdala and decreased dorsolateral prefrontal BOLD responses in unipolar depression: Related and independent features. *Biological Psychiatry, 61,* 198–209.

Siegler, I. C., & Costa, P. T., Jr. (1985). Health behavior relationships. In J. E. Birren & K. W. Schaie (Eds.), *Handbook of the psychology of aging* (2nd ed.). New York: Van Nostrand-Reinhold.

Siever, L. J. (2000). Genetics and neurobiology of personality disorders. *European Psychiatry : The Journal of the Association of European Psychiatrists, 15*(1), 54–57.

Siever, L. J., & Davis, K. L. (2004). The pathophysiology of schizophrenia disorders: Perspectives from the spectrum. *American Journal of Psychiatry, 161*(3), 398–413.

Sigman, M. (1994). What are the core deficits in autism? In S. H. Broman & J. Grafman (Eds.), *Atypical cognitive deficits in developmental disorders: Implications for brain function* (pp. 139–157). Hillsdale, NJ: Erlbaum.

Sigman, M., Ungerer, J. A., Mundy, P., & Sherman, T. (1987). Cognition in autistic children. In D. J. Cohen, A. M. Donnellan, & R. Paul (Eds.), *Handbook of autism and pervasive developmental disorders* (pp. 103–120). New York: Wiley.

Silberg, J., Pickles, A., Rutter, M., Hewitt, J., Simonoff, E., et al. (1999). The influence of genetic factors and life stress on depression among adolescent girls. *Archives of General Psychiatry, 56,* 225–232.

Silbersweig, D., Clarkin, J. F., Goldstein, M., Kernberg, O. F., Tuescher, O., Levy, K. N., . . . Stern, E. (2007). Failure of frontolimbic inhibitory function in the context of negative emotion in borderline personality disorder. *American Journal of Psychiatry, 164,* 1832–1841.

Silverman, K., Evans, S. M., Strain, E. C., & Griffiths, R. R. (1992). Withdrawal syndrome after the double-blind cessation of caffeine consumption. *New England Journal of Medicine, 327,* 1109–1114.

Silverman, K., Higgins, S. T., Brooner, R. K., Montoya, I. D., Cone, E. J., Schuster, C. R., & Preston, K. I. (1996). Sustained cocaine abstinence in methadone maintenance patients through voucher-based reinforcement therapy. *Archives of General Psychiatry, 53,* 409–413.

Simeon, D. (2009). Depersonalization disorder. In P. F. Dell & J. A. O'Neil (Eds.), *Dissociation and dissociative disorders: DSM–5 and beyond* (pp. 441–442). New York: Routledge.

Simeon, D., Gross, S., Guralnik, O., Stein, D. J., Schmeidler, J., & Hollander, E. (1997). Feeling unreal: 30 cases of DSM-III-R depersonalization disorder. *American Journal of Psychiatry, 154,* 1107–1112.

Simeon, D., Guralnik, O., Schmeidler, J., Sirof, B., & Knutelska, M. (2001). The role of childhood interpersonal trauma in depersonalization disorder. *American Journal of Psychiatry, 158*(7), 1027–1033.

Simon, G., Ormel, J., VonKroff, M., & Barlow, W. (1995). Health care costs associated with depressive and anxiety disorders in primary care. *American Journal of Psychiatry, 152,* 352–357.

Simon, G. E. (1998). Management of somatoform and factitious disorders. In P. E. Nathan & J. M. Gorman (Eds.), *A guide to treatments that work* (pp. 408–422). New York: Oxford University Press.

Simon, G. E., Goldberg, D. P., Von Korff, M., & Ustun, T. B. (2002). Understanding cross-national differences in depression prevalence. *Psychological Medicine, 32,* 585–594.

Simon, G. E., & Gureje, O. (1999). Stability of somatization disorder and somatization symptoms among primary care patients. *Archives of General Psychiatry, 56,* 90–95.

Simon, G. E., Ludman, E. J., Bauer, M. S., Unutzer, J., & Operskalski, B. (2006). Long-term effectiveness and cost of a systematic care program for bipolar disorder. *Archives of General Psychiatry, 63*(5), 500–508.

Simon, G. E., Von Korff, M., Piccinelli, M., Fullerton, C., & Ormel, J. (1999). An international study of the relation between somatic symptoms and depression. *New England Journal of Medicine, 341,* 1329–1335.

Simon, G. E., Von Korff, M., Rutter, C. M., & Peterson, D. A. (2001). Treatment process and outcomes for managed care patients receiving new antidepressant prescriptions from psychiatrists and primary care physicians. *Archives of General Psychiatry, 58,* 395–401.

Simon, R. J., & Aaronson, D. E. (1988). *The insanity defense: A critical assessment of law and policy in the post-Hinckley era.* New York: Praeger.

Simon, W. (2009). Follow-up psychotherapy outcome of patients with dependent, avoidant and obsessive-compulsive personality disorders: A meta-analytic review. *International Journal of Psychiatry in Clinical Practice, 13*(2), 153–165. doi: doi:10.1080/13651500802570972

Simonoff, E. (2001). Genetic influences on conduct disorder. In J. Hill & B. Maughan (Eds.), *Conduct disorders in childhood and adolescence* (pp. 202–234). Cambridge, England: Cambridge University Press.

Sinha, S. S., Mohlman, J., & Gorman, J. M. (2004). Neurobiology. In R. G. Heimberg, C. L. Turk, & D. S. Mennin (Eds.), *Generalized anxiety disorder* (pp. 187–218). New York: Guilford.

Siok, W. T., Perfetti, C. A., Lin, Z., & Tan, L. H. (2004). Biological abnormality of impaired reading is constrained by culture. *Nature, 431,* 71–76.

Skeem, J. L., & Monahan, J. (2011). Current directions in violence risk assessment. *Current Directions in Psychological Science, 20,* 38–42.

Skinstad, A. H., & Swain, A. (2001). Comorbidity in a clinical sample of substance abusers. *American Journal of Drug and Alcohol Abuse, 27,* 45–64.

Skodol, A. E., Bender, D. S., Oldham, J. M., Clark, L. A., Morey, L. C., Verheul, R., . . . Siever, L. J. (2011). Proposed changes in personality and personality disorder assessment and diagnosis for DSM–5 Part II: Clinical application. *Personality Disorders: Theory, Research, and Treatment, 2*(1), 23–40. doi: 10.1037/a0021892

Skodol, A. E., Clark, L. A., Bender, D. S., Krueger, R. F., Morey, L. C., Verheul, R., . . . Oldham, J. M. (2011). Proposed changes in personality and personality disorder assessment and diagnosis for DSM–5 Part I: Description and rationale. *Personality Disorders: Theory, Research, and Treatment, 2*(1), 4–22. doi: 10.1037/a0021891

Skodol, A. E., Oldham, J. M., Hyler, S. E., Stein, D. J., Hollander, E., Gallaher, P. E., & Lopez, A. E. (1995). Patterns of anxiety and personality disorder comorbidity. *Journal of Psychiatric Research, 29*(5), 361–374. doi: 10.1016/0022–3956(95)00015-w

Skoog, G., & Skoog, I. (1999). A 40-year follow-up of patients with obsessive-compulsive disorder. *Archives of General Psychiatry, 56,* 121–130.

Slater, E. (1961). The thirty-fifth Maudsley lecture: Hysteria 311. *Journal of Mental Science, 107,* 358–381.

Slevec, J. H., & Tiggemann, M. (2011). Predictors of body dissatisfaction and disordered eating in middle-aged women. *Clinical Psychology Review, 31,* 515–524.

Slutske, W. S., Heath, A. C., Dinwiddie, S. H., Madden, P. A. F., Bucholz, K. K., Dunne, M. P., . . . Martin, N. G. (1997). Modeling genetic and environmental influences in the etiology of conduct disorder: A study of 2,682 adult twin pairs. *Journal of Abnormal Psychology, 106,* 266–279.

Small, B. J., Fratiglioni, L., Viitanen, M., Winblad, B., & Backman, L. (2000). The course of cognitive impairment in preclinical Alzheimer disease. *Archives of Neurology, 57,* 839–844.

Smart, R. G., & Ogburne, A. C. (2000). Drug use and drinking among students in 36 countries. *Addictive Behaviors, 25,* 455–460.

Smith, G. T., Goldman, M. S., Greenbaum, P. E., & Christiansen, B. A. (1995). Expectancy for social facilitation from drinking: The divergent paths of high expectancy and low expectancy adolescents. *Journal of Abnormal Psychology, 104,* 32–40.

Smith, M. L., Glass, G. V., & Miller, T. I. (1980). *The benefits of psychotherapy.* Baltimore: Johns Hopkins University Press.

Smith, S. M., Stinson, F. S., Dawson, D. A., Goldstein, R., Huang, B., & Grant, B. F. (2006). Race/ethnic differences in the prevalence and co-occurrence of substance use disorders and independent mood and anxiety disorders: Results from the National Epidemiologic Survey on Alcohol and Related Conditions. *Psychological Medicine, 36,* 987–998.

Smith, T., Groen, A., & Wynn, J. W. (2000). Randomized trial of intensive early intervention for children with pervasive developmental disorder. *Research in Developmental Disabilities, 21,* 297–309.

Smoller, J. W., Pollack, M. H., Wassertheil-Smoller, S., Jackson, R. D., Oberman, A., Wong, N. D., & Sheps, D. (2007). Panic attacks and risk of incident cardiovascular events among postmenopausal women in the women's health initiative observational study. *Archives of General Psychiatry, 64,* 1153–1160.

Smyth, J., Wonderlich, S. A., Heron, K. E., Sliwinski, M. J., Crosby, R. D., et al. (2007). Daily and momentary mood and stress are associated with binge eating and vomiting in bulimia nervosa patients in the natural environment. *Journal of Consulting and Clinical Psychology, 75,* 629–638.

Snyder, D. K., Castellani, A. M., & Whisman, M. A. (2006). Current status and future directions in couple therapy. *Annual Review of Psychology, 57,* 317–344.

Sobczak, S., Honig, A., Nicolson, N. A., & Riedel, W. J. (2002). Effects of acute tryptophan depletion on mood and cortisol release in first-degree relatives of type I and type II bipolar patients and healthy matched controls. *Neuropsychopharmacology, 27,* 834–842.

Sobell, L. C., & Sobell, M. B. (1996). *Timeline followback user's guide: A calendar method for assessing alcohol and drug use.* Toronto, Canada: Addiction Research Foundation.

Sobell, L. C., Sobell, M. B., & Agrawal, S. (2009). Randomized controlled trial of a cognitive-behavioral motivational intervention in a group versus individual format for substance use disorders. *Psychology of Addictive Behaviors: Journal of the Society of Psychologists in Addictive Behaviors, 23,* 672–683.

Sobell, L. C., Toneatto, A., & Sobell, M. B. (1990). Behavior therapy. In A. S. Bellack & M. Hersen (Eds.), *Handbook of comparative treatments for adult disorders* (pp. 479–505). New York: Wiley.

Sobell, M. B., & Sobell, L. C. (1976). Second-year treatment outcome of alcoholics treated by individualized behavior therapy: Results. *Behaviour Research and Therapy, 14,* 195–215.

Sobell, M. B., & Sobell, L. C. (1993). *Problem drinkers: Guided self-change treatment.* New York: Guilford.

Soloff, P. H., Meltzer, C. C., Greer, P. J., Constantine, D., & Kelly, T. M. (2000). A fenfluramine-activated FDG-PET study of borderline personality disorder. *Biological Psychiatry, 47,* 540–547.

Solomon, D. A., Keller, M. B., Leon, A. C., Mueller, T. I., Lavori, P. W., Shea, M. T., . . . Endicott, J. (2000). Multiple recurrences of major depressive disorder. *American Journal of Psychiatry, 157,* 229–233.

Soomro, G. M., Altman, D., Rajagopal, S., & Oakley-Browne, M. (2008). Selective serotonin re-uptake inhibitors. *The Cochrane Collaboration Cochrane Reviews, Issue 1,* CD001765. doi: 10.1002/14651858. CD001765.pub3

Soyka, M., Horak, M., Morhart, V., & Moeller, H. J. (2001). Modellprojekt "Qualifizierte ambulante Entgiftung" [Qualified outpatient detoxification]. *Nervenarzt, 72,* 565–569.

Spanos, N. P. (1994). Multiple identity enactments and multiple personality disorder: A sociocognitive perspective. *Psychological Bulletin, 116,* 143–165.

Spanos, N. P., Weekes, J. R., & Bertrand, L. D. (1985). Multiple personality: A social psychological perspective. *Journal of Abnormal Psychology, 94,* 362–376.

Spar, J. E., & LaRue, A. (1990). *Geriatric psychiatry.* Washington, DC: American Psychiatric Press.

Specialist Clinical Addiction Network, 2006.

Spek, V., Cuijpers, P., Nyklicek, I., Riper, H., Keyzer, J., & Pop, V. (2007). Database of abstracts of reviews of effects (DARE)—short record display: Internet-based cognitive behaviour therapy for symptoms of depression and anxiety: A meta-analysis. *Psychological Medicine, 37,* 319–328.

Spencer, S. J., Steele, C. M., & Quinn, D. M. (1999). Stereotype threat and women's math performance. *Journal of Experimental Social Psychology, 35,* 4–28.

Spencer, T., Biederman, J., Wilens, T., Harding, M., O'Donnell, D., & Griffin, S. (1996). Pharmacotherapy of attention-deficit hyperactivity disorder across the life cycle. *Journal of the American Academy of Child and Adolescent Psychiatry, 35,* 409–432.

Spengler, A. (1977). Manifest sadomasochism of males: Results of an empirical study. *Archives of Sexual Behavior, 6,* 441–456.

Sperling, R. A., Aisen, P. S., Beckett, L. A., Bennett, D. A., Craft, S., Fagan, A. M., . . . Phelps, C. H. (2011). Toward defining the preclinical stages of Alzheimer's disease: Recommendations from the National Institute on Aging-Alzheimer's Association workgroups on diagnostic guidelines for Alzheimer's disease. *Alzheimer's and Dementia: The Journal of the Alzheimer's Association, 7*(3), 280–292. doi: 10.1016/j.jalz.2011.03.003

Spezio, M. L., Adolphs, R., Hurley, R. S., & Piven, J. (2007). Abnormal use of facial information in high-functioning autism. *Journal of Autism and Developmental Disorders, 37,* 929–939.

Spitzer, R. L., Gibbon, M., & Williams, J. B. W. (1996). *Structured clinical interview of DSM-IV Axis I disorders.* New York: N. Y. State Psychiatric Institute, Biometrics Research Department.

Spitzer, R. L., Gibbon, M., Skodol, A. E., Williams, J. B. W., & First, M. B. (Eds.). (1994). *DSM-IV casebook: A learning companion to the Diagnostic and Statistical Manual of Mental Disorders* (4th ed.). Washington, DC: American Psychiatric Press.

Spitzer, R. M., Stunkard, A., Yanovski, S., Marcus, M. D., Wadden, T., et al. (1993). Binge eating disorders should be included in DSM-IV. *International Journal of Eating Disorders, 13,* 161–169.

Spoth, R. A., Guyll, M., & Day, S. X. (2002). Universal family-focused interventions in alcohol-use prevention: Cost-benefit analyses of two interventions. *Journal of Studies on Alcohol, 63,* 219–228.

Spoth, R. A., Redmond, C., Shin, C., & Azevedo, K. (2004). Brief family intervention effects on adolescent substance initiation: School-level growth curve analyses 6 years following baseline. *Journal of Consulting and Clinical Psychology, 72,* 535–542.

Sprich, S., Biederman, J., Crawford, M. H., Mundy, E., & Faraone, S. V. (2000). Adoptive and biological families of children and adolescents with ADHD. *Journal of the American Academy of Child and Adolescent Psychiatry, 39,* 1432–1437.

Stack, S. (2000). Media impacts on suicide: A quantitative review of 293 findings. *Social Science Quarterly, 81,* 957–971.

Stacy, A. W., Newcomb, M. D., & Bentler, P. M. (1991). Cognitive motivation and drug use: A 9-year longitudinal study. *Journal of Abnormal Psychology, 100,* 502–515.

Stahl, S. (2006). *Essential psychopharmacology: The prescriber's guide* (rev and updated ed.). Cambridge, England: Cambridge University Press.

Staugaard, S. R. (2010). Threatening faces and social anxiety: A literature review. *Clinical Psychology Review, 30*(6), 669–690. doi: 10.1016/j.cpr.2010.05.001

Stead, L. F., Perera, R., Bullen, C., Mant, D., & Lancaster, T. (2008). Nicotine replacement therapy for smoking cessation. *Cochrane Database of Systematic Reviews,* No.: CD000146. doi: 000110.001002/14651858. CD14000146.pub14651853

Steadman, H. J. (1979). *Beating a rap: Defendants found incompetent to stand trial.* Chicago: University of Chicago Press.

Steadman, H. J., McGreevy, M. A., Morrissey, J. P., Callahan, L. A., Robbins, P. C., & Cirincione, C. (1993). *Before and after Hinckley: Evaluating insanity defense reform.* New York: Guilford.

Steadman, H. J., Mulvey, E. P., Monahan, J., Robbins, P. C., Appelbaum, P. S., Grisso, T., . . . Silver, E. (1998). Violence by people discharged from acute psychiatric inpatient facilities and by others in the same neighborhoods. *Archives of General Psychiatry, 55,* 393–401.

Steele, A. L., Bergin, J., & Wade, T. D. (2011). Self-efficacy as a robust predictor of outcome in guided self-help treatment for broadly defined bulimia nervosa. *International Journal of Eating Disorders, 44,* 389–396.

Steele, C. M., & Josephs, R. A. (1988). Drinking your troubles away: 2. An attention-allocation model of alcohol's effects on psychological stress. *Journal of Abnormal Psychology, 97,* 196–205.

Steen, R. G., Mull, C., McClure, R., Hamer, R. M., & Lieberman, J. A. (2006). Brain volume in first-episode schizophrenia: Systematic review and meta-analysis of magnetic resonance imaging studies. *British Journal of Psychiatry, 188,* 510–518.

Steiger, H., Gauvin, L., Jabalpurwala, S., & Séguin, J. R. (1999). Hypersensitivity to social interactions in bulimic syndromes: Relationship to binge eating. *Journal of Consulting and Clinical Psychology, 67,* 765–775.

Stein, D. J., Ipser, J. C., & Balkom, A. J. (2004). Pharmacotherapy for social anxiety disorder. *Cochrane Database of Systematic Reviews*(4), CD001206. doi: 10.1002/14651858.CD001206.pub2

Stein, D. J., Ipser, J. C., & Seedat, S. (2000). Pharmacotherapy for post traumatic stress disorder (PTSD). *Cochrane Database of Systematic Reviews, Issue 4,* CD002795. doi: 10.1002/14651858.CD002795.pub2

Stein, D. J., Phillips, K. A., Bolton, D., Fulford, K. W., Sadler, J. Z., & Kendler, K. S. (2010). What is a mental/psychiatric disorder? From DSM-IV to DSM-V. *Psychological Medicine, 40,* 1759–1765.

Stein, E. A., Pankiewicz, J., Harsch, H. H., Cho, J. K., Fuller, S. A., et al. (1998). Nicotine-induced limbic cortical activation in the human brain: A functional MRI study. *American Journal of Psychiatry, 155,* 1009–1015.

Stein, L. I., & Test, M. A. (1980). Alternative to mental hospital treatment: I. Conceptual model, treatment program, and clinical evaluation. *Archives of General Psychiatry, 37,* 392–397.

Stein, M. B. (1998). Neurobiological perspectives on social phobia: From affiliation to zoology. *Biological Psychiatry, 44,* 1277–1285.

Steinhausen, H. C., & Metzke, C. W. (1998). Youth self-report of behavioral and emotional problems in a Swiss epidemiological study. *Journal of Youth and Adolescence, 27,* 429–441.

Steinhausen, H., & Weber, S. (2009). The outcome of bulimia nervosa: Findings from one-quarter century of research. *American Journal of Psychiatry, 166,* 1331–1341.

Steketee, G., & Barlow, D. H. (Eds.). (2004). *Obsessive-compulsive disorder.* New York: Guilford.

Steketee, G., & Frost, R. (2003). Compulsive hoarding: Current status of the research. *Clinical Psychology Review, 23,* 905–927.

Steketee, G., & Frost, R. O. (1998). Obsessive-compulsive disorder. In A. S. Bellack & M. Herse (Eds.), *Comprehensive clinical psychology: Vol. 6. Adults: Clinical formulation and treatment.*

Steketee, G., Frost, R. O., Tolin, D. F., Rasmussen, J., & Brown, T. A. (2010). Waitlist controlled trial of cognitive behavior therapy for hoarding disorder. *Depression and Anxiety, 27,* 476-484.

Stephens, R. S., Roffman, R. A., & Simpson, E. E. (1993). Adult marijuana users seeking treatment. *Journal of Consulting and Clinical Psychology, 61,* 1100–1104.

Stern, R. S., & Cobb, J. P. (1978). Phenomenology of obsessive-compulsive neurosis. *British Journal of Psychiatry, 132,* 233–234.

Stevenson, J., & Jones, I. H. (1972). Behavior therapy technique for exhibitionism: A preliminary report. *Archives of General Psychiatry, 27,* 839–841.

Stewart, W. F., Ricci, J. A., Chee, E., Hahn, S. R., & Morganstein, D. (2003). Cost of lost productive work time among US workers with depression. *Journal of the American Medical Association, 289,* 3135–3144.

Stice, E. (2001). A prospective test of the dual-pathway model of bulimic pathology: Mediating effects of dieting and negative affect. *Journal of Abnormal Psychology, 110,* 124–135.

Stice, E., & Agras, W. S. (1999). Subtyping bulimics along dietary restraint and negative affect dimensions. *Journal of Consulting and Clinical Psychology, 67,* 460–469.

Stice, E., Barrera, M., & Chasin, L. (1998). Prospective differential prediction of adolescent alcohol use and problem use: Examining the mechanisms of effect. *Journal of Abnormal Psychology, 107,* 616–628.

Stice, E., Burton, E. M., & Shaw, H. (2004). Prospective relations between bulimic pathology, depression, and substance abuse: Unpacking comorbidity in adolescent girls. *Journal of Consulting and Clinical Psychology, 72,* 62–71.

Stice, E., Marti, C. N., Spoor, S., Presnell, K., & Shaw, H. (2008). Dissonance and healthy weight eating disorder prevention programs: Long-term effects from a randomized efficacy trial. *Journal of Consulting and Clinical Psychology, 76,* 329–240.

Stice, E., Shaw, H., & Marti, C. N. (2007). A meta-analytic review of eating disorder prevention programs: Encouraging findings. *Annual Review of Clinical Psychology, 3,* 207–231.

Stinson, F. S., Ruan, W. J., Pickering, R., & Grant, B. F. (2006). Cannabis use disorders in the U.S.A.: Prevalence, correlates, and comorbidity. *Psychological Medicine, 36,* 1447–1460.

Stone, A. A., Schwartz, J., Neale, J. M., Shiffman, S., Marco, C. A., et al. (1998). A comparison of coping assessed by ecological momentary assessment and retrospective recall. *Journal of Personality and Social Psychology, 74,* 1670–1680.

Stone, A. A., & Shiffman, S. (1994). Ecological momentary assessment (EMA) in behavioral medicine. *Annals of Behavioral Medicine, 16,* 199–202.

Stone, G. (1982). *Health Psychology,* a new journal for a new field. *Health Psychology, 1,* 1–6.

Stone, J., Lafrance, W. C., Jr., Levenson, J. L., & Sharpe, M. (2010). Issues for DSM–5: Conversion disorder. *American Journal of Psychiatry, 167(6),* 626–627. doi: 10.1176/appi.ajp.2010.09101440

Stone, M. H. (1993). *Abnormalities of personality. Within and beyond the realm of treatment.* New York: Norton.

Stopa, L., & Clark, D. M. (2000). Social phobia and interpretation of social events. *Behaviour Research and Therapy, 38,* 273–283.

Stormer, S. M., & Thompson, J. K. (1996). Explanations of body image disturbance: A test of maturational status, negative verbal commentary, and sociological hypotheses. *International Journal of Eating Disorders, 19,* 193–202.

Story, M., French, S. A., Resnick, M. D., & Blum, R. W. (1995). Ethnic/racial and socioeconomic differences in dieting behaviors and body image perceptions in adolescents. *International Journal of Eating Disorders, 18,* 173–179.

Stoving, R. K., Hangaard, J., Hansen-Nord, M., & Hagen, C. (1999). A review of endocrine changes in anorexia nervosa. *Journal of Psychiatric Research, 33,* 139–152.

St. Pourcain, B., Wang, K., Glessner, J. T., Golding, J., Steer, C., Ring, S. M., . . . & Smith, G. D. (2010). Association between a high-risk autism locus on 5p14 and social communication spectrum phenotypes in the general population. *American Journal of Psychiatry, 167,* 1364–1372.

Strain, E. C., Bigelow, G. E., Liebson, I. A., & Stitzer, M. L. (1999). Moderate- vs low-dose methadone in the treatment of opioid dependence. *Journal of the Medical Association, 281,* 1000–1005.

Strakowski, S. M., Sax, K. W., Setters, M. J., Stanton, S. P., & Keck, P. E. (1997). Lack of enhanced behavioral response to repeated d-amphetamine challenge in first-episode psychosis: Implications for sensitization model of psychosis in humans. *Biological Psychiatry, 42,* 749–755.

Strauss, J. S., Carpenter, W. T., & Bartko, J. J. (1974). The diagnosis and understanding of schizophrenia: Part 3. Speculations on the processes that underlie schizophrenic signs and symptoms. *Schizophrenia Bulletin, 1,* 61–69.

Strauss, M. E., & Ogrocki, P. K. (1996). Confirmation of an association between family history of affective disorder and the depressive syndrome in Alzheimer's disease. *American Journal of Psychiatry, 153,* 1340–1342.

Streeton, C., & Whelan, G. (2001). Naltrexone, a relapse prevention maintenance treatment of alcohol dependence: A meta-analysis of randomized controlled trials. *Alcohol and Alcoholism, 36,* 544–552.

Striegel-Moore, R. H., Cachelin, F. M., Dohm, F. A., Pike, K. M., Wilfely, D. E., & Fairburn, C. G. (2001). Comparison of binge eating disorder and bulimia nervosa in a community sample. *International Journal of Eating Disorders, 29,* 157–165.

Striegel-Moore, R. H., & Franco, D. L. (2003). Epidemiology of binge eating disorder. *International Journal of Eating Disorders, 34,* S19–S29.

Striegel-Moore, R. H., & Franco, D. L. (2008). Should binge eating disorder be included in the DSM-V? A critical review of the state of the evidence. *Annual Review of Clinical Psychology, 4,* 305–324.

Striegel-Moore, R. H., Garvin, V., Dohm, F. A., & Rosenheck, R. (1999). Psychiatric comorbidity of eating disorders in men: A national study of hospitalized veterans. *International Journal of Eating Disorders, 25,* 399–404.

Striegel-Moore, R. H., Schreiber, G. B., Lo, A., Crawford, P., Obarzanek, E., & Rodin, J. (2000). Eating disorder symptoms in a cohort of 11 to 16-year-old black and white girls: The NHLBI growth and health study. *International Journal of Eating Disorders, 27,* 49–66.

Striegel-Moore, R. H., Wilson, G. T., Wilfley, D. E., Elder, K. A., & Brownell, K. D. (1998). Binge eating in an obese community sample. *International Journal of Eating Disorders, 23,* 27–36.

Stritzke, W. G. K., Patrick, C. J., & Lang, P. J. (1995). Alcohol and emotion: A multidimensional approach incorporating startle probe methodology. *Journal of Abnormal Psychology, 104,* 114–122.

Strober, M., Freeman, R., Lampert, C., Diamond, J., & Kaye, W. (2000). Controlled family study of anorexia nervosa and bulimia nervosa: Evidence of shared liability and transmission of partial syndromes. *American Journal of Psychiatry, 157,* 393–401.

Strober, M., Freeman, R., Lampert, C., Diamond, J., & Kaye, W. (2001). Males with anorexia nervosa: A controlled study of eating disorders in first-degree relatives. *International Journal of Eating Disorders, 29,* 264–269.

Strober, M., Freeman, R., & Morrell, W. (1997). The long-term course of severe anorexia nervosa in adolescents: Survival analysis of recovery, relapse, and outcome predictors over 10–15 years in a prospective study. *International Journal of Eating Disorders, 22,* 339–360.

Strober, M., Lampert, C., Morrell, W., Burroughs, J., & Jacobs, C. (1990). A controlled family study of anorexia nervosa: Evidence of family aggregation and lack of shared transmission with affective disorders. *International Journal of Eating Disorders, 9,* 239–253.

Stroud, C. B., Davila, J., Hammen, C., & Vrsheck-Schallhorn, S. (2011). Severe and nonsevere events in first onsets and recurrences of depression: Evidence for stress sensitization. *Journal of Abnormal Psychology, 120,* 142–154.

Strub, R. L., & Black, F. W. (1981). *Organic brain syndromes: An introduction to neurobehavioral disorders.* Philadelphia: Davis.

Struckman-Johnson, C. (1988). Forced sex on dates: It happens to men, too. *Journal of Sex Research, 24,* 234–241.

Stuart, G. A., & Llienfeld, S. O. (2007). The evidence missing from evidence-based practice. *American Psychologist, 62(6),* 615–616.

Styron, W. (1992). *Darkness visible: A memoir of madness.* New York: Vintage.

Substance Abuse and Mental Health Services Administration. (2004). *Overview of Findings from the 2003 National Survey on Drug Use and Health* (Office of Applied Studies, NSDUH Series H–24, DHHS Publication No. SMA 04–3963). Rockville, MD.

Substance Abuse and Mental Health Services Administration. (2007). *Results from the 2006 National Survey on Drug Use and Health: National Findings* (Office of Applied Studies, NSDUH Series H–32, DHHS Publication No. SMA 07–4293). Rockville, MD.

Substance Abuse and Mental Health Services Administration. (2010). *Results from the 2009 National Survey on Drug Use and Health: Vol. I. Summary of national findings.* (Office of Applied Studies, NSDUH Series H–38A, HHS Publication No. SMA 10–4856 Findings). Rockville, MD.

Substance Abuse and Mental Health Services Administration, Center for Behavioral Health Statistics and Quality. (2011). *Drug Abuse Warning Network, 2008: National Estimates of Drug-Related Emergency Department Visits* (HHS Publication No. SMA 11-4618). Rockville, MD.

Suddath, R. L., Christison, G. W., Torrey, E. F., Cassonova, M. F., Weinberger, D. R., et al. (1990). Anatomical abnormalities in the brains of monozygotic twins discordant for schizophrenia. *New England Journal of Medicine, 322,* 789–793.

Sue, D. W., & Sue, D. (2008). *Counseling the culturally different: Theory and practice* (5th ed.). Oxford, England: Wiley.

Sugarman, P., Dumughn, C., Saad, K., Hinder, S., & Bluglass, S. (1994). Dangerousness in exhibitionists. *Journal of Forensic Psychiatry, 5,* 287–296.

Sullivan, J. M. (2000). Cellular and molecular mechanisms underlying learning and memory impairments produced by cannabinoids. *Learning and Memory, 7*, 132–139.

Sullivan, P. F. (1995). Mortality in anorexia nervosa. *American Journal of Psychiatry, 152*, 1073–1075.

Sullivan, P. F., Neale, M. C., & Kendler, K. S. (2000). Genetic epidemiology of major depression: Review and meta-analysis. *American Journal of Psychiatry, 157*, 1552–1562.

Suls, J., & Bunde, J. (2005). Anger, anxiety, and depression as risk factors for cardiovascular disease: The problems and implications of overlapping affective dispositions. *Psychological Bulletin, 131*, 260–300.

Surles, R. C., Blanch, A. K., Shern, D. L., & Donahue, S. A. (1992). Case management as a strategy for systems change. *Health Affairs, 11*, 151–163.

Surtees, P. G., Wainwright, N. W., Luben, R. N., Wareham, N. J., Bingham, S. A., & Khaw, K.-T. (2008). Depression and ischemic heart disease mortality: Evidence from the EPIC-Norfolk United Kingdom prospective cohort study. *American Journal of Psychiatry, 165*, 515–523.

Susser, E., Neugebauer, R., Hoek, H. W., Brown, A. S., Lin, S., et al. (1996). Schizophrenia after prenatal famine: Further evidence. *Archives of General Psychiatry, 53*, 25–31.

Sussman, S. (1996). Development of a school-based drug abuse prevention curriculum for high-risk youth. *Journal of Psychoactive Drugs, 28*, 169–182.

Sussman, S., Dent, C. W., McAdams, L., Stacy, A. W., Burton, D., & Flay, B. R. (1994). Group self-identification and adolescent cigarette smoking: A 1-year prospective study. *Journal of Abnormal Psychology, 103*, 576–580.

Sussman, S., Dent, C. W., Simon, T. R., Stacy, A. W., Galaif, E. R., Moss, M. A., . . . Johnson, C. A. (1995). Immediate impact of social influence-oriented substance abuse prevention curricula in traditional and continuation high schools. *Drugs and Society, 8*, 65–81.

Sussman, S., Stacy, A. W., Dent, C. W., Simon, T. R., & Johnson, C. A. (1996). Marijuana use: Current issues and new research directions. *Journal of Drug Issues, 26*, 695–733.

Sussman, T., Dent, C. W., & Lichtman, K. L. (2001). Project EX: Outcomes of a teen smoking cessation program. *Addictive Behaviors, 26*, 425–438.

Sutcliffe, J. P., & Jones, J. (1962). Personal identity, multiple personality, and hypnosis. *International Journal of Clinical and Experimental Hypnosis, 10*, 231–269.

Sutker, P. B., & Adams, H. E. (2001). *Comprehensive handbook of psychopathology* (3rd ed.). New York: Kluwer Academic/Plenum.

Sutker, P. B., Uddo, M., Brailey, K., Vasterling, J. J., & Errera, P. (1994). Psychopathology in war-zone deployed and nondeployed Operation Desert Storm troops assigned grave registration duties. *Journal of Abnormal Psychology, 103*, 383–390.

Suwaki, H. et al. (1997). Methamphetamine abuse in Japan: its 45 year history and the current situation. In: H. Klee (ed.) *Amphetamine misuse: international perspectives on current trends.* Harwood Academic.

Suzuki, K., Takei, N., Kawai, M., Minabe, Y., & Mori, N. (2003). Is taijin kyofusho a culture-bound syndrome? *American Journal of Psychiatry, 160*(7), 1358.

Swain, J., Koszycki, D., Shlik, J., & Bradwein, J. (2003). In D. Nutt & J. Ballenger (Eds.), *Anxiety disorders* (pp. 269–295). Malden, MA: Blackwell.

Swanson, J., Hinshaw, S. P., Arnold, L. E., Gibbons, R., Marcus, S., Hur, K., et al. (2007). Secondary evaluations of MTA 36-month outcomes: Propensity score and growth mixture model analyses. *Journal of the American Academy of Child and Adolescent Psychiatry, 46*, 1002–1013.

Swanson, J., Kinsbourne, M., Nigg, J., et al. (2007). Etiologic subtypes of attention-deficit/hyperactivity disorder: Brain imaging, molecular genetic and environmental factors and the dopamine hypothesis. *Neuropsychology Review, 17*, 39–59.

Swanson, J., McBurnett, K., Christian, D. L., & Wigal, T. (1995). Stimulant medications and the treatment of children with ADHD. In T. H. Ollendick & R. J. Prinz (Eds.), *Advances in clinical child psychology* (Vol. 17, pp. 265–322). New York: Plenum.

Swanson, J. W., Holzer, C. E., Ganju, V. K., & Jono, R. T. (1990). Violence and psychiatric disorder in the community: Evidence from the Epidemiological Catchment Area surveys. *Hospital and Community Psychiatry, 41*, 761–770.

Sweet, J. J., Carr, M. A., Rossini, E., & Kasper, C. (1986). Relationship between the Luria-Nebraska Neuropsychological Battery and the WISC-R: Further examination using Kaufman's factors. *International Journal of Clinical Neuropsychology, 8*, 177–180.

Sweet, R. A., Mulsant, B. H., Gupta, B., Rifai, A. H., Pasternak, R. E., et al. (1995). Duration of neuroleptic treatment and prevalence of tardive dyskinesia in late life. *Archives of General Psychiatry, 52*, 478–486.

Szasz, T. S. (1999). *Fatal freedom: The ethics and politics of suicide.* Westport, CT: Praeger.

Szczypka, M. S., Kwok, K., Brot, M. D., Marck, B. T., Matsumoto, A. M., Donahue, B. A., & Palmiter, R. D. (2001). Dopamine production in the caudate putamen restores feeding in dopamine-deficient mice. *Neuron, 30*, 819–828.

Szechtman, H., & Woody, E. (2004). Obsessive-compulsive disorder as a disturbance of security motivation. *Psychological Review, 111*, 111–127.

TADS team. (2007). The treatment for adolescents with depression study (TADS): Long term effectiveness and safety outcomes. *Archives of General Psychiatry, 64*, 1132–1144.

Tallal, P., Merzenich, M., Miller, S., & Jenkins, W. (1998). Language learning impairment: Integrating research and remediation. *Scandinavian Journal of Psychology, 39*, 197–199.

Tallal, P., Miller, S. L., Bedi, G., Byma, G., Wang, X., Nagarajan, S. S., . . . Merzenich, M. M. (1996). Language comprehension in language learning impaired children improved with acoustically modified speech. *Science, 271*, 81–84.

Tallmadge, J., & Barkley, R. A. (1983). The interactions of hyperactive and normal boys with their mothers and fathers. *Journal of Abnormal Child Psychology, 11*, 565–579.

Tambs, K., Czajkowsky, N., Roysamb, E., Neale, M. C., Reichborn-Kjennerud, T., Aggen, S. H., . . . Kendler, K. S. (2009). Structure of genetic and environmental risk factors for dimensional representations of DSM-IV anxiety disorders. *The British Journal of Psychiatry: Journal of Mental Science, 195*(4), 301–307. doi: 10.1192/bjp.bp.108.059485

Tannock, R. (1998). Attention deficit hyperactivity disorder: Advances in cognitive, neurobiological, and genetic research. *Journal of Child Psychology and Psychiatry, 39*, 65–100.

Tapert, S. F. and Brown, S. A., (2000). Substance dependence, family history of alcohol dependence and neuropsychological functioning in adolescence. *Addiction 95*, 1043–53.

Tarrier, N., Taylor, K., & Gooding, P. (2008). Cognitive-behavioral interventions to reduce suicide behavior. *Behavior Modification, 32*(1), 77–108.

Task Force on Promotion and Dissemination of Psychological Procedures. (1995). Training in and dissemination of empirically-validated psychological treatments: Report and recommendations. *The Clinical Psychologist, 48*, 3–23.

Taylor, A., & Kim-Cohen, J. (2007). Meta-analysis of gene–environment interactions in developmental psychopathology. *Development and Psychopathology, 19*, 1029–1037.

Taylor, C. B., Hayward, C., King, R., Ehlers, A., Margraf, J., Maddock, R., . . . Agras, W. S. (1990). Cardiovascular and symptomatic reduction effects of alprazolam and imipramine in patients with panic disorder: Results of a double-blind, placebo-controlled trial. *Journal of Clinical Psychopharmacology, 10*, 112–118.

Taylor, C. T., & Alden, L. E. (2011). To see ourselves as others see us: An experimental integration of the intra- and interpersonal consequences of self-protection in social anxiety disorder. *Journal of Abnormal Psychology, 120*, 129–141.

Taylor, J., Iacono, W. G., & McGue, M. (2000). Evidence for a genetic etiology of early-onset delinquency. *Journal of Abnormal Psychology, 109*, 634–643.

Taylor, J., Loney, B. R., Bobadilla, L., Iacono, W. G., & McGue, M. (2003). Genetic and environmental influences on psychopathy trait dimensions in a community sample of male twins. *Journal of Abnormal Child Psychology, 31*, 633–645.

Taylor, S., Jang, K. L., & Asmundson, G. J. (2010). Etiology of obsessions and compulsions: A behavioral-genetic analysis. *Journal of Abnormal Psychology, 119*(4), 672–682. doi: 10.1037/a0021132

Teachman, B. A., & Allen, J. P. (2007). Development of social anxiety: Social interaction predictors of implicit and explicit fear of negative evaluation. *Journal of Abnormal Child Psychology, 35*, 63–78.

Teasdale, J. D. (1988). Cognitive vulnerability to persistent depression. *Cognition and Emotion, 2*, 247–274.

Teasdale, J. D., Segal, Z. V., Williams, J. M. G., Ridgeway, V. A., Soulsby, J. M., & Lau, M. A. (2000). Prevention of relapse/recurrence in major depression by mindfulness based cognitive therapy. *Journal of Consulting and Clinical Psychology, 68*, 615–623.

Tedeschi, R. G., Park, C. L., & Calhoun, L. G. (1998). Posttraumatic growth: Conceptual issues. In R. G. Tedeschi, C. L. Park, & L. G. Calhoun (Eds.), *Posttraumatic growth: Positive changes in the aftermath of trauma* (pp. 1–22). Thousand Oaks, CA: Sage.

Telch, M. J., & Harrington, P. J. (1992). *Anxiety sensitivity and unexpectedness of arousal in mediating affective response to 35% carbon dioxide inhalation.* Unpublished manuscript.

Telch, M. J., Shermis, M. D., & Lucas, J. A. (1989). Anxiety sensitivity: Unitary personality trait or domain-specific appraisals? *Journal of Anxiety Disorders, 3*, 25–32.

Temple, E., Poldrack, R. A., Salidas, J., Deutsch, G. K., Tallal, P., Merzenich, M. M., & Gabrieli, J. D. E. (2001). Disrupted neural responses to phonological and orthographic processing in dyslexic children: An fMRI study. *Neuroreport, 12*, 299–307.

Teper, E., & O'Brien, J. T. (2008). Vascular factors and depression. *International Journal of Geriatric Psychiatry, 23*(10), 993–1000. doi: 10.1002/gps.2020

Teri, L., Gibbons, L. E., McCurry, S. M., Logsdon, R. G., Buchner, D. M., Barlow, W. E., . . . Larson, E. B. (2003). Exercise plus behavioral management in patients with Alzheimer disease: A randomized controlled trial. *Journal of the American Medical Association, 290*, 2015–2022.

Terry, R. D. (2006). Alzheimer's disease and the aging brain. *Journal of Geriatric Psychiatry and Neurology, 19*, 125–128.

Thapar, A., Fowler, T., Rice, F., et al. (2003). Maternal smoking during pregnancy and attention deficit hyperactivity disorder symptoms in offspring. *American Journal of Psychiatry, 160*, 1985–1989.

Thapar, A., Langley, K., Owen, M. J., & O'Donovan, M. C. (2007). Advances in genetic findings on attention deficit hyperactivity disorder. *Psychological Medicine, 37*, 1681–1692.

Thase, M. E., & Rush, A. J. (1997). When at first you don't succeed: Sequential strategies for antidepressant nonresponders. *Journal of Clinical Psychiatry, 58*(Suppl. 13), 23–29.

Thase, M. E., Jindal, R., & Howland, R. H. (2002). Biological aspects of depression. In C. L. Hammen & I. H. Gotlib (Eds.), *Handbook of depression* (pp. 192–218). New York: Guilford.

The Information Centre, (2006). Drug use, smoking and drinking among young people in England, 2004. Leeds: NHS. www.ic.nhs.uk

The Information Centre, (2010). Drug use, smoking and drinking among young people in England, 2004. Leeds: NHS. www.ic.nhs.uk

The Information Centre, (2010). Statistics on Drug Misuse: England, 2010. NHS. www.ic.nhs.uk

The Information Centre, (2011). Statistics on Alcohol: England, 2011. NHS. www.ic.nhs.uk

Theobald, H., Bygren, L. O., Carstensen, J., & Engfeldt, P. A. (2000). Moderate intake of wine is associated with reduced total mortality and reduced mortality from cardiovascular disease. *Journal of Studies on Alcohol, 61*, 652–656.

Thibaut, F., De La Barra, F., Gordon, H., Cosyns, P., & Bradford, J. M. (2010). The World Federation of Societies of Biological Psychiatry (WFSBP) guidelines for the biological treatment of paraphilias. [Practice Guideline]. *The World Journal of Biological Psychiatry: The Official Journal of the World Federation of Societies of Biological Psychiatry, 11*(4), 604–655. doi: 10.3109/15622971003671628

Thiruvengadam, A. P., & Chandrasekaran, K. (2007). Evaluating the validity of blood-based membrane potential changes for the identification of bipolar disorder I. *Journal of Affective Disorders, 100*, 75–82.

Thoits, P. A. (1985). Self-labeling processes in mental illness: The role of emotional deviance. *American Journal of Sociology, 92*, 221–249.

Thomas, G., Reifman, A., Barnes, G. M., Farrell, & M. P. (2000). Delayed onset of drunkenness as a protective factor for adolescent alcohol misuse and sexual risk taking; A longitudinal study. *Deviant Behavior, 21*, 181–200.

Thompson, G. O. B., Raab, G. M., Hepburn, W. S., Hunter, R., Fulton, M., & Laxen, D. P. H. (1989). Blood-lead levels and children's behaviour: Results from the Edinburgh lead study. *Journal of Child Psychology and Psychiatry, 30*, 515–528.

Thompson, P. M., Hayashi, H. M., Simon, S. L., et al. (2004). Structural abnormalities in the brains of human subjects who use methamphetamine. *Journal of Neuroscience, 24*, 6028–6036.

Tiefer, L. (2001). A new view of women's sexual problems: Why new? Why now? *Journal of Sex Research, 38*, 89–96.

Tiefer, L. (2003). Female sexual dysfunction (FSD): Witnessing social construction in action. *Sexualities, Evolution and Gender, 5*, 33–36.

Tiefer, L., Hall, M., & Tavris, C. (2002). Beyond dysfunction: A new view of women's sexual problems. *Journal of Sex and Marital Therapy, 28*, 225–232.

Tienari, P., Wynne, L. C., Laksy, K., Moring, J., Nieminen, P., Sorri, A., . . . Wahlberg, K.-E. (2003). Genetic boundaries of the schizophrenia spectrum: Evidence from the Finnish adoptive family study of schizophrenia. *American Journal of Psychiatry, 160*, 1587–1594.

Tienari, P., Wynne, L. C., Moring, J., et al. (1994). The Finnish adoptive family study of schizophrenia: Implications for family research. *British Journal of Psychiatry, 164*, 20–26.

Tienari, P., Wynne, L. C., Moring, J., et al. (2000). Finnish adoptive family study: Sample selection and adoptee DSM-III diagnoses. *Acta Psychiatrica Scandinavica, 101*, 433–443.

Tihonen, J., Kuikka, J., Rasanen, P., Lepola, U., Kopenen, H., Liuska, A., . . . Karhu, J. (1997). Cerebral benzodiazepine receptor binding and distribution in generalized anxiety disorder: A fractal analysis. *Molecular Psychiatry, 2*, 463–471.

Timko, C., Moos, R. H., Finney, J. W., & Lesar, M. D. (2001). Long-term outcomes of alcohol use disorders: Comparing untreated individuals with those in Alcoholics Anonymous and formal treatment. *Journal of Studies on Alcohol, 61*, 529–540.

Tobin, D. L., Griffing, A., & Griffing, S. (1997). An examination of subtype criteria for bulimia nervosa. *International Journal of Eating Disorders, 22*, 179–186.

Tobler, N. S., Roona, M. A., Ochshorn, P., Marshall, D. G., Streke, A. V., & Stackpole, K. M. (2000). School-based adolescent drug prevention programs: 1998 metaanalysis. *Journal of Primary Prevention, 20*, 275–336.

Toffers, J., Völlm, B., Rücker, G., Timmer, A., Huband, N., & Lieb, K. (2010). Pharmacological interventions for borderline personality disorder. *Cochrane Database of Systematic Reviews, Issue 6*, CD005653. doi: DOI: 10.1002/14651858.CD005653.pub2

Tolin, D. F., & Foa, E. B. (2006). Sex differences in trauma and posttraumatic stress disorder: A quantitative review of 25 years of research. *Psychological Bulletin, 132*, 959–992.

Tolin, D. F., Frost, R. O., Steketee, G., Gray, K. D., & Fitch, K. E. (2008). The economic and social burden of compulsive hoarding. *Psychiatry Research, 160*(2), 200–211. doi: 10.1016/j.psychres.2007.08.008

Tompkins, M. A., & Hartl, T. L. (2009). *Digging out: Helping your loved one manage clutter, hoarding, and compulsive acquiring*: Oakland, CA, New Harbinger.

Tondo, L., Vazquez, G., & Baldessarini, R. J. (2010). Mania associated with antidepressant treatment: Comprehensive meta-analytic review. *Acta Psychiatrica Scandinavica, 121*(6), 404–414.

Tonigan, J. S., Miller, W. R., & Connors, G. J. (2000). Project MATCH client impressions about Alcoholics Anonymous: Measurement issues and relationship to treatment outcome. *Alcoholism Treatment Quarterly, 18*, 25–41.

Tonstad, S., Tonnesen, P., Hajek, P., Williams, K. E., Billing, C. B., & Reeves, K. R. (2006). Varenicline Phase 3 Study Group. Effect of maintenance therapy with varenicline on smoking cessation: A randomized controlled trial. *Journal of the American Medical Association, 296*, 64–71.

Torgersen, S. (1986). Genetics of somatoform disorder. *Archives of General Psychiatry, 43*, 502–505.

Torgersen, S., Lygren, S., Øien, P. A., Skre, I., Onstad, S., Edvardsen, J., . . . Kringlen, E. (2000). A twin study of personality disorders. *Comprehensive Psychiatry, 41*, 416–425.

Torres, A. R., Prince, M. J., Bebbington, P. E., Bhurga, D., Brugha, T. S., Farrell, M., . . . Singleton, N. (2006). Obsessive-compulsive disorder: Prevalence, comorbidity, impact, and help-seeking in the British National Psychiatric Morbidity Survey of 2000. *American Journal of Psychiatry, 163*, 1978–1985.

Torrey, E. F. (1996). *Out of the shadows: Confronting America's mental health crisis*. New York: Wiley.

Torti, F. M., Gwyther, L. P., Reed, S. D., Friedman, J. Y., & Schulman, K. A. (2004). A multinational review of recent trends and reports in dementia caregiver burden. *Alzheimer's, Disease and Associated Disorders, 18*, 99–109.

Toseland, R. W., McCallion, P., Smith, T., & Banks, S. (2004). Supporting caregivers of frail older adults in an HMO setting. *American Journal of Orthopsychiatry, 74*, 349–364.

Totterdell, P., & Kellett, S. (2008). Restructuring mood in cyclothymia using cognitive behavior therapy: An intensive time-sampling study. *Journal of Clinical Psychology, 64*, 501–518.

Toufexis, A., Blackman, A., & Drummond, T. (1996, April 29). Why Jennifer got sick. *Time*.

Tran, G. Q., Haaga, D. A. F., & Chambless, D. L. (1997). Expecting that alcohol will reduce social anxiety moderates the relation between social anxiety and alcohol consumption. *Cognitive Therapy and Research, 21*, 535–553.

Treadway, M. T., & Zald, D. H. (2011). Reconsidering anhedonia in depression: Lessons from translational neuroscience. *Neuroscience and Biobehavioral Reviews, 35*(3), 537–555. doi: 10.1016/j.neubiorev.2010.06.006

Treat, T. A., & Viken, R. J. (2010). Cognitive processing of weight and emotional information in disordered eating. *Current Directions in Psychological Science, 19*, 81–85.

Treynor, W., Gonzalez, R., & Nolen-Hoeksema, S. (2003). Rumination reconsidered: A psychometric analysis. *Cognitive Therapy and Research, 27*, 247–259.

Trierweiler, S. J., Neighbors, H. W., Munday, C., Thompson, E. E., Binion, V. J., & Gomez, J. P. (2000). Clinician attributions associated with the diagnosis of schizophrenia in African American and non-African American patients. *Journal of Consulting and Clinical Psychology, 68*, 171–175.

Trimpey, J., Velten, E., & Dain, R. (1993). Rational recovery from addictions. In W. Dryden & L. K. Hill (Eds.), *Innovations in rational-emotive therapy* (pp. 253–271). Thousand Oaks, CA: Sage.

Trinder, H., & Salkovaskis, P. M. (1994). Personally relevant intrusions outside the laboratory: Long-term suppression increases intrusion. *Behaviour Research and Therapy, 32*, 833–842.

Trivedi, M. H., Rush, A. J., Wisniewski, S. R., Nierenberg, A. A., Warden, D., Ritz, L., . . . Team, S. D. S. (2006). Evaluation of outcomes with citalopram for depression using measurement-based care in STAR*D: Implications for clinical practice. *American Journal of Psychiatry, 163*, 28–40.

True, W. R., Rice, J., Eisen, S. A., Heath, A. C., Godlberg, J., Lyons, M. J., & Nowak, J. (1993). A twin study of genetic and environmental contributions to liability for posttraumatic stress symptoms. *Archives of General Psychiatry, 50*, 257–264.

True, W. R., Xiam, H., Scherrer, J. F., Madden, P., Bucholz, K. K., et al. (1999). Common genetic vulnerability for nicotine and alcohol dependence in men. *Archives of General Psychiatry, 56*, 655–662.

Trull, T. J., Jahng, S., Tomko, R. L., Wood, P. K., & Sher, K. J. (2010). Revised NESARC personality disorder diagnoses: Gender, prevalence, and comorbidity with substance dependence disorders. *Journal of Personality Disorders, 24*(4), 412–426. doi: 10.1521/pedi.2010.24.4.412

Trull, T. J., Solhan, M. B., Tragesser, S. L., Jahng, S., Wood, P. K., Piasecki, T. M., & Watson, D. (2008). Affective instability: Measuring a core feature of borderline personality disorder with ecological momentary assessment. *Journal of Abnormal Psychology, 117*(3), 647–661. doi: 10.1037/a0012532

Tsai, D. C., & Pike, P. L. (2000). Effects of acculturation on the MMPI–2 scores of Asian American students. *Journal of Personality Assessment, 74,* 216–230.

Tsai, G., Parssani, L. A., Slusher, B. S., Carter, R., Baer, L., et al. (1995). Abnormal excitatory neurotransmitter metabolism in schizophrenic brains. *Archives of General Psychiatry, 52,* 829–836.

Tsai, G. E., Ragan, P., Chang, R., Chen, S., Linnoila, M. I., & Coyle, J. T. (1998). Increased glutamatergic neurotransmission and oxidative stress after alcohol withdrawal. *American Journal of Psychiatry, 155,* 726–732.

Tsai, J. L. (2007). Ideal affect: Cultural causes and behavioral consequences. *Perspectives on Psychological Science, 2,* 242–259.

Tsai, J. L., Butler, J. N. Vitoustk, K.,& Munoz, R. (2001). Culture, ethnicity, and psychopathology. In H. E. Adams & P.B. Sutkey (Eds). *Comprehensive handbook of psychopathology* (3rd. ed., pp. 105–127). New York: Kluwer Academic/Plenum.

Tsai, J. L., Knutson, B. K., & Fung, H. H. (2006). Cultural variation in affect valuation. *Journal of Personality and Social Psychology, 90,* 288–307.

Tsai, J. L., Knutson, B., & Rothman, A. (2007). The pursuit of ideal affect: Variation in mood-producing behavior. *Journal of Personality and Social Psychology, 90,* 288–307.

Tsuang, M. T., Lyons, M. J., Meyer, J. M., Doyle, T., Eisen, S. A., et al. (1998). Co-occurrence of abuse of different drugs in men: The role of drug-specific and shared vulnerabilities. *Archives of General Psychiatry, 55,* 967–972.

Tully, L. A., Arseneault, L., Caspi, A., Moffitt, T. E., & Morgan, J. (2004). Does maternal warmth moderate the effects of birth weight on twins' attention-deficit/hyperactivity disorder (ADHD) symptoms and low IQ? *Journal of Consulting and Clinical Psychology, 72,* 218–226.

Tune, L. E., Wong, D. F, Pearlson, G. D., Strauss, M. E., Young, T., et al. (1993). Dopamine D2 receptor density estimates in schizophrenia: A positron-emission tomography study with "C-methylspiperone." *Psychiatry Research, 49,* 219–237.

Turk, D. C. (2001). Treatment of chronic pain: Clinical outcomes, cost-effectiveness, and cost benefits. *Drug Benefit Trends, 13,* 36–38.

Turkheimer, E. (1998). Heritability and biological explanation. *Psychological Review, 105,* 782–791.

Turkheimer, E. (2000). Three laws of behavior genetics and what they mean. *Current Directions in Psychological Science, 9,* 160–164.

Turkheimer, E., Haley, A., Waldron, M., D'Onofrio, B., & Gottesman, I. I. (2003). Socioeconomic status modifies the heritability of IQ in young children. *Psychological Science, 6,* 623–628.

Turkington, D., Kingdom, D., & Turner, T. (2002). Effectiveness of a brief cognitive-behavioural intervention in the treatment of schizophrenia. *British Journal of Psychiatry, 180,* 523–527.

Turner, C. F, Ku, S. M., Rogers, L. D., Lindberg, J. H., & Pleck, F. L. (1998). Adolescent sexual behavior, drug use, and violence: Increased reporting with computer survey technology. *Science, 280,* 867–873.

Turner, C. M. (2006). Cognitive-behavioural theory and therapy for obsessive-compulsive disorder in children and adolescents: Current status and future directions. *Clinical Psychology Review, 26,* 912–948.

Turner, E. H., Matthews, A. M., Linardatos, E., Tell, R. A., & Rosenthal, R. (2008). Selective publication of antidepressant trials and its influence on apparent efficacy. *New England Journal of Medicine, 358,* 252–260.

Turner, S. M., Beidel, D. C., & Townsley, R. M. (1990). Social phobia: Relationship to shyness. *Behaviour Research and Therapy, 28,* 297–305.

Twamley, E. W., Jeste, D. V., & Bellack, A. S. (2003). A review of cognitive training in schizophrenia. *Schizophrenia Bulletin, 29,* 359–382.

Twigg, L., Moon, G. and Walker, S. (2004) The smoking epidemic in England 2004. Health Development Agency. www.erpho.org.uk

Tyrka, A. R., Waldron, I., Graber, J. A., & Brooks-Gunn, J. (2002). Prospective predictors of the onset of anorexic and bulimic syndromes. *International Journal of Eating Disorders, 32,* 282–290.

Uchinuma, Y., & Sekine, Y. (2000). Dissociative identity disorder (DID) in Japan: A forensic case report and the recent increase in reports of DID. *International Journal of Psychiatry in Clinical Practice, 4,* 155–160.

Uher, R., & McGuffin, P. (2010). The moderation by the serotonin transporter gene of environmental adversity in the etiology of depression: 2009 update. *Molecular Psychiatry, 15*(1), 18–22. doi: 10.1038/mp.2009.123

UK ECT Review Group. (2003). Efficacy and safety of electro-convulsive therapy in depressive disorders: A systematic review and meta-analysis. *Lancet, 361,* 799–808.

Unger, J. B., Boley Cruz, T., Schuster, D., Flora, J. A., & Anderson Johnson, C. (2001). Measuring exposure to pro and anti-tobacco marketing among adolescents: Intercorrelations among measures and associations with smoking status. *Journal of Health Communication, 6,* 11–29.

Urada, D., Evans, E., Yang, J., & Conner, B. T., et al. (2009). Evaluation of proposition 36: The substance abuse and crime prevention act of 2000: 2009 report. Retrieved from http://www.uclaisap.org/prop36/html/reports.html

U.S. Bureau of the Census, Population Division. (2010). Population estimates.

U.S. Bureau of the Census. (1999). *Current population reports, special studies.* Washington, DC: U.S. Government Printing Office.

U.S. Department of Health and Human Services. (1998). *NHLBLI report of the Task Force on Behavioral Research in Cardiovascular, Lung, and Blood Health and Disease.* Washington, DC: U.S. Government Printing Office.

U.S. Department of Health and Human Services. (1999). Mental health: A report of the Surgeon General— Executive summary, Rockville, MD: U.S. Department of Health and Human Services, Substance Abuse and Mental Health Services Administration, Center for Mental Health Services, National Institutes of Health, National Institute of Mental Health.

U.S. Department of Health and Human Services. (2001). *Mental health: Culture, race, and ethnicity—a supplement to mental health: A report of the Surgeon General.* Rockville, MD: U.S. Department of Health and Human Services, Substance Abuse and Mental Health Services Administration, Center for Mental Health Services.

U.S. Department of Health and Human Services. (2002). *Supplement to mental health: a report of the Surgeon General* (SMA–01–3613). Retrieved July 2, 2002, from http://www.mentalhealth.org/Publications/allpubs/SMA01–3613/sma–01–3613.pdf

U.S. Department of Health and Human Services. (2004). HHS announces revised Medicare obesity coverage policy. News releases of the Centers for Medicare and Medicaid Services, Washington, D.C., July 15, 2004. Retrieved July 14, 2008, from http://hhs.gov/news/press/2004pres/20040715.html

U.S. Department of Health and Human Services. (2004). *The health consequences of smoking: A report of the Surgeon General.* Atlanta, GA: Department of Health and Human Services, Centers for Disease Control and Prevention, Coordinating Center for Health Promotion.

U.S. Department of Health and Human Services. (2006). *The health consequences of involuntary exposure to tobacco smoke: A report of the Surgeon General.* Atlanta, GA: Department of Health and Human Services, Centers for Disease Control and Prevention, Coordinating Center for Health Promotion.

U. S. Department of Health and Human Services. (2008). *2008 national healthcare disparities report. Table 15-3-1.1b.*

U.S. Department of Health and Human Services, Administration for Children and Families. (2010). *Head Start impact study.* Final Report. Washington, DC.

Vacha-Haase, T., Kogan, L. R., Tani, C. R., & Woodall, R. A. (2001). Reliability generalization: Exploring variation of reliability coefficients of MMPI clinical scale scores. *Educational and Psychological Measurement, 61,* 45–49.

Vaglenova, J., Birru, S., Pandiella, N. M., & Breese, C. R. (2004). An assessment of the long-term developmental and behavioral teratogenicity of prenatal nicotine exposure. *Behavioural Brain Research, 150,* 159–170.

Valencia, M., Racon, M. L., Juarez, F., & Murow, E. (2007). A psychosocial skills training approach in Mexican outpatients with schizophrenia. *Psychological Medicine, 37,* 1393–1402.

Valenti, A. M., Narendran, R., & Pristach, C. A. (2003). Who are patients on conventional antipsychotics? *Schizophrenia Bulletin, 29,* 195–200.

Valenzuela, M. J., & Sachdev, P. (2006). Brain reserve and dementia: A systematic review. *Psychological Medicine, 36,* 441–454.

Van Ameringen, M. A., Lane, R. M., Walker, J. R., et al. (2001). Sertreline treatment of generalized social phobia: A 20-week, double-blind, placebo-controlled study. *American Journal of Psychiatry, 158,* 275–281.

Vance, S., Cohen-Kettenis, P., Drescher, J., Meyer-Bahlburg, H., Pfafflin, F., & Zucker, K. (2010). Opinions about the DSM gender identity disorder diagnosis: Results from an international survey administered to organizations concerned with the welfare of transgender people. *International Journal of Transgenderism, 12*(1), 1–14. doi: 10.1080/15532731003749087

van den Broucke, S., Vandereycken, W., & Vertommen, H. (1995). Marital communication in eating disorders: A controlled observational study. *International Journal of Eating Disorders, 17,* 1–23.

van der Kolk, B. A., Spinazzola, J., Blaustein, M. E., Hopper, J. W., Hopper, E. K., Korn, D. L., & Simpson, W. B. (2007). Randomized, placebo-controlled trial of exposure and ritual prevention, clomipramine, and their combination in the treatment of obsessive-compulsive disorder. *Journal of Clinical Psychiatry, 68*(1), 37–46.

van der Sande, R., Buskens, E., Allart, E., van der Graaf, Y., & van Engeland, H. (1997). Psychosocial intervention following suicide attempt: A systematic review of treatment interventions. *Acta Psychiatrica Scandinavica, 96,* 43–50.

van der Veen, F. M., Evers, E. A., Deutz, N. E., & Schmitt, J. A. (2007). Effects of acute tryptophan depletion on mood and facial emotion perception related brain activation and performance in healthy women with and without a family history of depression. *Neuropsychopharmacology, 32,* 216–224.

van Elst, L. T. (2003). Frontolimbic brain abnormalities in patients with borderline personality disorder: A volumetric magnetic resonance imaging study. *Biological Psychiatry, 54*, 163–171.

van Elst, L. T., Thiel, T., Hesslinger, B., Lieb, K., Bohus, M., Hennig, J., & Ebert, D. (2001). Subtle prefrontal neuropathology in pilot magnetic resonance spectroscopy study in patients with borderline personality disorder. *Journal of Neuropsychiatry and Clinical Neuroscience, 13*, 511–514.

van Erp, T. G. M., Saleh, P. A., Huttunen, M., et al. (2004). Hippocampal volumes in schizophrenic twins. *Archives of General Psychiatry, 61*, 346–353.

Van Etten, M. L., Higgins, S. T., Budney, A. J. et al., (1998). Comparison of the frequency and enjoyability of pleasant events in cocaine abusers vs non-abusers using a standardized behavioral inventory. *Addiction 93*, 1669–80.

van Hoeken, D., Veling, W., Sinke, S., Mitchell, J. E., Hoek, H. W., & Walsh, B. T. (2009). The validity and utility of subtyping bulimia nervosa. *International Journal of Eating Disorders, 42*, 595–602.

van Kammen, W. B., Loeber, R., & Stouthamer-Loeber, M. (1991). Substance use and its relationship to conduct problems and delinquency in young boys. *Journal of Youth and Adolescence, 20*, 399–413.

Van Oppen, P., de Haan, E., Van Balkom, A. J. L. M., Spinhoven, P., Hoogdiun, K., & van Dyck, R. (1995). Cognitive therapy and exposure in vivo in the treatment of obsessive compulsive disorder. *Behaviour Research and Therapy, 33*, 379–390.

van Orden, K. A., Cukrowicz, K. C., Witte, T. K., Braithwaite, S. R., & Joiner, T. E. (2010). The interpersonal theory of suicide. *Psychological Review, 117*(2), 575–600.

van Orden, K. A., Witte, T. K., Gordon, K. H., Bender, T. W., & Joiner, T. E. (2008). Suicidal desire and the capability for suicide: Tests of the interpersonal-psychological theory of suicidal behavior among adults. *Journal of Consulting and Clinical Psychology, 76*(1), 72–83.

van Os, J., Kenis, G., & Rutten, B. P. (2010). The environment and schizophrenia. *Nature, 468*, 203–212.

van Praag, H., Plutchik, R., & Apter, A. (Eds.). (1990). *Violence and suicidality*. New York: Brunner/Mazel.

Veale, D. (2000). Outcome of cosmetic surgery and "DIY" surgery in patients with body dysmorphic disorder. *Psychiatric Bulletin, 24*, 218–221.

Veale, D. (2004). Advances in a cognitive behavioural model of body dysmorphic disorder. *Body Image, 1*(1), 113–125. doi: 10.1016/s1740–1445(03)00009–3

Vega, W. A., Kolody, B., Aguilar-Gaxiola, S., Adlerete, E., Catalana, R., & Caraveo-Anduaga, J. (1998). Lifetime prevalence of DSM-III-R psychiatric disorders among urban and rural Mexican Americans in California. *Archives of General Psychiatry, 55*, 771–778.

Velakoulis, D., Pantelis, C., McGorry, P. D., Dudgeon, P., Brewer, W., et al. (1999). Hippocampal volume in first episode psychoses and chronic schizophrenia: A high-resolution magnetic resonance imaging study. *Archives of General Psychiatry, 56*, 133–141.

Velting, O. N., Setzer, N. J., & Albano, A. M. (2004). Update on and advances in assessment and cognitive-behavioral treatment of anxiety disorders in children and adolescents. *Professional Psychology: Research and Practice, 35*, 42–54.

Ventura, J., Neuchterlein, K. H., Lukoff, D., & Hardesty, J. D. (1989). A prospective study of stressful life events and schizophrenic relapse. *Journal of Abnormal Psychology, 98*, 407–411.

Vickrey, B. G., Mittman, B. S., Connor, K. I., Pearson, M., L., Della Penna, R. D., Ganiats, T. G., . . . Lee, M. (2006). The effect of a disease management intervention on quality and outcomes of demential care: A randomized, controlled trial. *Annuals of Internal Medicine, 145*, 713–726.

Videbech, P., & Ravnkilde, B. (2004). Hippocampal volume and depression: A meta-analysis of MRI studies. *American Journal of Psychiatry, 161*(11), 1957–1966.

Vieta, E., Martinez-De-Osaba, M. J., Colom, F., Martinez-Aran, A., Benabarre, A., & Gasto, C. (1999). Enhanced corticotropin response to corticotropin-releasing hormone as a predictor of mania in euthymic bipolar patients. *Psychological Medicine, 29*, 971–978.

Vinkers, D. J., Gussekloo, J., Stek, M. L., Westendorp, R. G. J., & van der Mast, R. C. (2004). Temporal relation between depression and cognitive impairment in old age: Prospective population based study. *British Medical Journal, 329*, 881.

Virtanen, M., Vahtera, J., Batty, G. D., Tuisku, K., Pentti, J., Oksanen, T., et al. (2011). Overcrowding in psychiatric wards and physical assaults on staff: Data-linked longitudinal study. *British Journal of Psychiatry: The Journal of Mental Science, 198*, 149–155.

Virués-Ortega, J. (2010). Applied behavior analytic intervention for autism in early childhood: Meta-analysis, meta-regression and dose–response meta-analysis of multiple outcomes. *Clinical Psychology Review, 30*, 387–399.

Vitaliano, P. P., Zhang, J., & Scanlan, J. M. (2003). Is caregiving hazardous to one's physical health? A meta-analysis. *Psychological Bulletin, 129*, 946–972.

Vitousek, K., & Manke, F. (1994). Personality variables and disorders in anorexia nervosa and bulimia nervosa. *Journal of Abnormal Psychology, 103*, 137–147.

Vittengl, J. R., Clark, L. A., Dunn, T. W., & Jarrett, R. B. (2007). Reducing relapse and recurrence in unipolar depression: A comparative meta-analysis of cognitive-behavior therapy's effects. *Journal of Consulting and Clinical Psychology, 75*, 475–488.

Volk, D. W., Austin, M. C., Pierri, J. N., et al. (2000). Decreased glutamic acid decarboxylase67 messenger RNA expression in a subset of prefrontal cortical gamma-aminobutyric acid neurons in subjects with schizophrenia. *Archives of General Psychiatry, 57*, 237–248.

Volkmar, F. R., Szatmari, P., & Sparrow, S. S. (1993). Sex differences in pervasive developmental disorders. *Journal of Autism and Developmental Disorders, 23*, 579–591.

Volkow, N. D., Chang, L., Wang, G. J., Fowler, J. S., Leonido-Lee, M., Franceschi, D., . . . Ding, Y. S. (2001). Association of dopamine transporter reduction with psychomotor impairment in methamphetamine abusers. *American Journal of Psychiatry, 158*, 377–382.

Volkow, N. D., Wang, G. J., Fischman, M. W., & Foltin, R. W. (1997). Relationship between subjective effects of cocaine and dopamine transporter occupancy. *Nature, 386*, 827–830.

Volkow, N. D., Wang, G. J., Fowler, J. S., Logan, J., Jayne, M., Franceschi, D., . . . Pappas, N. (2002). "Nonhedonic" food motivation in humans involves dopamine in the dorsal striatum and methylphenidate amplifies this effect. *Synapse, 44*, 175–180.

Volpicelli, J. R., Rhines, K. C., Rhines, J. S., Volpicelli, L. A., et al. (1997). Naltrexone and alcohol dependence: Role of subject compliance. *Archives of General Psychiatry, 54*, 737–743.

Volpicelli, J. R., Watson, N. T., King, A. C., Shermen, C. E., & O'Brien, C. P. (1995). Effects of naltrexone on alcohol "high" in alcoholics. *American Journal of Psychiatry, 152*, 613–617.

Von Knorring, A.-L., & Hagloff, B. (1993). Autism in northern Sweden: A population based follow-up study: Psychopathology. *European Child and Adolescent Psychiatry, 2*, 91–97.

Von Krafft-Ebing, R. (1902). *Psychopathia sexualis*. Brooklyn, NY: Physicians and Surgeons Books.

Wade, T. D., Bulik, C. M., Neale, M., & Kendler, K. S. (2000). Anorexia nervosa and major depression: Shared genetic and environmental risk factors. *American Journal of Psychiatry, 157*, 469–471.

Wade, W. A., Treat, T. A., & Stuart, G. A. (1998). Transporting an empirically supported treatment for panic disorder to a service clinic setting: A benchmarking strategy. *Journal of Consulting and Clinical Psychology, 66*, 231–239.

Wahl, O. F. (1999). Mental health consumers' experience of stigma. *Schizophrenia Bulletin, 25*, 467–478.

Wahlbeck, K., Cheine, M., Essali, A., & Adams, C. (1999). Evidence of clozapine's effectiveness in schizophrenia: A systemic review and meta-analysis of randomized trials. *American Journal of Psychiatry, 156*, 990–999.

Wakefield, J. (1992). Disorder as dysfunction: A conceptual critique of DSM-III-R's definition of mental disorder. *Psychological Review, 99*, 232–247.

Wakefield, J. C. (1999). Philosophy of science and the progressiveness of DSM's theory—neutral nosology: Response to Follette and Houts, Part 1. *Behaviour Research and Therapy, 37*, 963–969.

Wakefield, M., & Chaloupka, R. (2000). Effectiveness of comprehensive tobacco control programmes in reducing teenage smoking in the USA. *Tobacco Control, 9*, 177–186.

Waldman, I. D., Rowe, D. C., Abramowitz, A., Kozel, S. T., Mohr, J. H., Sherman, S. L., . . . Stever, C. (1998). Association and linkage of the dopamine transporter gene and attention-deficit hyperactivity disorder in children: Heterogeneity owing to diagnostic subtype and severity. *American Journal of Human Genetics 63*, 1767–1776.

Walitzer, K. S., & Dearing, R. L. (2006). Gender differences in alcohol and substance use relapse. *Clinical Psychology Review, 26*, 128–148.

Walker, E. F., & Tessner, K. (2008). Schizophrenia. *Perspectives on Psychological Science, 3*, 30–37.

Walker, E. F., Davis, D. M., & Savoie, T. D. (1994). Neuromotor precursors of schizophrenia. *Schizophrenia Bulletin, 20*, 441–451.

Walker, E. F., Grimes, K. E., Davis, D. M., & Adina, J. (1993). Childhood precursors of schizophrenia: Facial expressions of emotion. *American Journal of Psychiatry, 150*, 1654–1660.

Walker, E. F., Mittal, V., & Tessner, K. (2008). Stress and the hypothalamic pituitary adrenal axis in the developmental course of schizophrenia. *Annual Review of Clinical Psychology, 4*, 189–216.

Walker, E., Kestler, L., Bollini, A., & Hochman, K. (2004). Schizophrenia: Etiology and course. *Annual Review of Psychology, 55*, 401–430.

Walkup, J. T., Albano, A. M., Piacentini, J., Birmaher, B., Comptom, S. N., Sherrill, J. T., et al. (2008). Cognitive behavioral therapy, sertaline, or a combination in childhood anxiety. *New England Journal of Medicine, 359*, 2753–2766.

Waller, D. A., Kiser, S., Hardy, B. W., Fuchs, I., & Feigenbaum, L. P. (1986). Eating behavior and plasma betaendorphin in bulimia. *American Journal of Clinical Nutrition, 4*, 20–23.

Walsh, B. T., Agras, S. W., Devlin, M. J., et al. (2000). Fluoxetine for bulimia nervosa following poor response to psychotherapy. *American Journal of Psychiatry, 157*, 1332–1334.

Walsh, B. T., Seidman, S. N., Sysko, R., & Gould, M. (2002). Placebo response in studies of major depression: Variable, substantial, and growing. *Journal of the American Medical Association, 287*, 1840–1847.

Walsh, B. T., Wilson, G. T., Loeb, K. L., Devin, M. J., et al. (1997). Medication and psychotherapy in the treatment of bulimia nervosa. *American Journal of Psychiatry, 154*, 523–531.

Walsh, T., McClellan, J. M., McCarthy, S. E., Addington, A. M., Pierce, S. B., et al. (2008). Rare structural variants disrupt genes in neurodevelopmental pathways in schizophrenia. *Science, 320*, 539–543.

Walters, G. L., & Clopton, J. R. (2000). Effect of symptom information and validity scale information on the malingering of depression on the MMPI–2. *Journal of Personality Assessment, 75*, 183–199.

Wang, C.-Y., Xiang, Y-T., Cai, Z-J., Bo, Q-J., Zhao, J-P., Liu, T-Q., Wang, G-H., Weng, S-M., et al. (2010). Risperidone maintenance treatment in schizophrenia: a randomized, controlled trial. *American Journal of Psychiatry, 167*, 676–685.

Wang, K., Zhang, H., Ma, D., Bucan, M., Glassner, J. T., Abrahams, B. S., Salyakina, D., et al. (2009). Common genetic variants on 5p14.1 associate with autism spectrum disorders. *Nature, 459*, 528–533.

Wang, M. Q., Fitzhugh, E. C., Eddy, J. M., Fu, Q., et al. (1997). Social influences on adolescents' smoking progress: A longitudinal analysis. *American Journal of Health Behavior, 21*, 111–117.

Wang, P. S., Demler, O., & Kessler, R. C. (2002). Adequacy of treatment for serious mental illness in the United States. *American Journal of Public Health, 92*, 92–98.

Wang, P. S., Simon, G. E., Avorn, J., Azocar, F., Ludman, E. J., McCulloch, J., . . . Kessler, R. C. (2007). Telephone screening, outreach and care management for depressed workers and impact on clinical and work productivity outcomes: A randomized trial. *Journal of the American Medical Association, 298*, 1401–1411.

Wansink, B., & Payne, C.R. (2009). The *Joy of Cooking* too much: 70 years of calorie increases in classic recipes. *Annals of Internal Medicine, 150*, 291.

Waters, A., Hill, A., & Waller, G. (2001). Internal and external antecedents of binge eating episodes in a group of women with bulimia nervosa. *International Journal of Eating Disorders, 29*, 17–22.

Watkins, E. R. (2008). Constructive and unconstructive repetitive thought. *Psychological Bulletin, 134*(2), 163–206.

Watkins, P. C. (2002). Implicit memory bias in depression. *Cognition and Emotion, 16*, 381–402.

Watson, D. (2005). Rethinking the mood and anxiety disorders: A qualitative hierarchical model for DSM-V. *Journal of Abnormal Psychology, 114*(4), 522–536.

Watson, D. (2009). Differentiating the mood and anxiety disorders: A quadripartite model. *Annual Review of Clinical Psychology, 5*, 221–247.

Watson, D., O'Hara, M. W., & Stuart, S. (2008). Hierarchical structures of affect and psychopathology and their implications for the classification of emotional disorders. *Depression and Anxiety, 25*, 282–288.

Watson, J. B., & Rayner, R. (1920). Conditioned emotional reactions. *Journal of Experimental Psychology, 3*, 1–14.

Watson, S., Thompson, J. M., Ritchie, J. C., Ferrier, I. N., & Young, A. H. (2006). Neuropsychological impairment in bipolar disorder: The relationship with glucocorticoid receptor function. *Bipolar Disorders, 8*, 85–90.

Watt, N. F. (1974). Childhood and adolescent roots of schizophrenia. In D. Ricks, A. Thomas, & M. Roll (Eds.), *Life history research in psychopathology* (Vol. 3). Minneapolis: University of Minnesota Press.

Watt, N. F., Stolorow, R. D., Lubensky, A. W., & McClelland, D. C. (1970). School adjustment and behavior of children hospitalized for schizophrenia as adults. *American Journal of Orthopsychiatry, 40*, 637–657.

Watters, E. (2010). *Crazy like us: The globalization of the American psyche*. New York: Simon & Schuster.

Weaver, I. C. G., Cervoni, N., Champagne, F. A., D'Allesio, A. C., Shakti, S., Seck, J. R., . . . Meaney, J. J. (2004). Epigenetic programming by maternal behavior. *Nature Neuroscience, 7*, 847–854.

Webster, C., Douglas, K., Eaves, D., & Hart, S. (1997). *HCR–20: Assessing risk for violence* (Version 2). Vancouver, British Columbia, Canada: Simon Fraser University.

Webster, J. J., & Palmer, R. L. (2000). The childhood and family background of women with clinical eating disorders: A comparison with women with major depression and women without psychiatric disorder. *Psychological Medicine, 30*, 53–60.

Webster, R., & Holroyd, S. (2000). Prevalence of psychotic symptoms in delirium. *Psychosomatics, 41*, 519–522.

Webster-Stratton, C. (1998). Preventing conduct problems in Head Start children: Strengthening parenting competencies. *Journal of Consulting and Clinical Psychology, 66*, 715–730.

Webster-Stratton, C., Reid, M. J., & Hammond, M. (2001). Preventing conduct problems, promoting social competence: A parent and teacher training partnership in Head Start. *Journal of Clinical Child Psychology, 30*, 283–302.

Wechsler, D. (1968). *Escala de Inteligencia Wechsler para Adultos*. New York: Psychological Corporation.

Wegner, D. M., Schneider, D. J., Carter, S. R., & White, T. L. (1987). Paradoxical effects of thought suppression. *Journal of Personality and Social Psychology, 53*, 5–13.

Wehr, T. A., Duncan, W. C., Sher, L., Aeschbach, D., Schwartz, P. J., Turner, E. H., . . . Rosenthal, N. E. (2001). A circadian signal of change of season in patients with seasonal affective disorder. *Archives of General Psychiatry, 58*, 1108–1114.

Wehr, T. A., Turner, E. H., Shimada, J. M., Lowe, C. H., Baker, C., & Leibenluft, E. (1998). Treatment of a rapidly cycling bipolar patient by using extended bed rest and darkness to stabilize the timing and duration of sleep. *Biological Psychiatry, 43*, 822–828.

Weickert, C. S., Straub, R. E., McClintock, B. W., et al. (2004). Human dysbindin (DTNBP1) gene expression in normal brain and in schizophrenic prefrontal cortex and mid brain. *Archives of General Psychiatry, 61*, 544–555.

Weierich, M. R., & Nock, M. K. (2008). Posttraumatic stress symptoms mediate the relation between childhood sexual abuse and nonsuicidal self-injury. *Journal of Consulting and Clinical Psychology, 76*(1), 39–44. doi: 10.1037/0022-006X.76.1.39

Weinberger, D. R. (1987). Implications of normal brain development for the pathogenesis of schizophrenia. *Archives of General Psychiatry, 44*, 660–669.

Weinberger, D. R., Berman, K. F., & Illowsky, B. P. (1988). Physiological dysfunction of dorsolateral prefrontal cortex in schizophrenia: 3. A new cohort and evidence for a monoaminergic mechanism. *Archives of General Psychiatry, 45*, 609–615.

Weinberger, D. R., Cannon-Spoor, H. E., Potkin, S. G., & Wyatt, R. J. (1980). Poor premorbid adjustment and CT scan abnormalities in chronic schizophrenia. *American Journal of Psychiatry, 137*, 1410–1413.

Weiner, B., Frieze, L., Kukla, A., Reed, L., Rest, S., & Rosenbaum, R. M. (1971). *Perceiving the causes of success and failure*. New York: General Learning Press.

Weiner, D. B. (1994). Le geste de Pinel: The history of psychiatric myth. In M. S. Micale & R. Porter (Eds.), *Discovering the history of psychiatry*. New York: Oxford University Press.

Weinstein, H. (2002, February 19). Killer's sentence of death debated. *Los Angeles Times*, pp. A1, A14.

Weintraub, S., Prinz, R., & Neale, J. M. (1978). Peer evaluations of the competence of children vulnerable to psychopathology. *Journal of Abnormal Child Psychology, 6*, 461–473.

Weisberg, R. B., Brown, T. A., Wincze, J. P., & Barlow, D. H. (2001). Causal attributions and male sexual arousal: The impact of attributions for a bogus erectile difficulty on sexual arousal, cognitions, and affect. *Journal of Abnormal Psychology, 110*, 324–334.

Weisberg, R. W. (1994). Genius and madness? A quasiexperimental test of the hypothesis that manic-depression increases creativity. *Psychological Science, 5*, 361–367.

Weisman, A. G., Nuechterlein, K. H., Goldstein, M. J., & Snyder, K. S. (1998). Expressed emotion, attributions, and schizophrenia symptom dimensions. *Journal of Abnormal Psychology, 107*, 355–359.

Weisman, C. S., & Teitelbaum, M. A. (1985). Physician gender and the physician–patient relationship: Recent evidence and relevant questions. *Social Science and Medicine, 20*, 1119–1127.

Weiss, G., & Hechtman, L. (1993). *Hyperactive children grown up* (2nd ed.). New York: Guilford.

Weiss, L. A., Shen, Y., Korn, J. M., et al. (2008). Association between microdeletion and microduplication at 16p11.2 and autism. *New England Journal of Medicine, 358*, 667–675.

Weissman, A. N., & Back, A. T. (1978). *Development and validation of the Dysfunctional Attitude Scale: A preliminary investigation*. Paper presented at the annual meeting of the American Educational Research Association, Toronto.

Weissman, M., & Olfson, M. (1995). Depression in women: Implications for health care research. *Science, 269*, 799–801.

Weissman, M. M., Bland, R. C., Canino, G. J., Faravelli, C., Greenwald, S., Hwu, H. G., . . . Yeh, E. K. (1996). Cross-national epidemiology of major depression and bipolar disorder. *Journal of the American Medical Association, 276*(4), 293–299.

Weisz, J. R., McCarty, C. A., & Valeri, S. M. (2006). Effects of psychotherapy for depression in children and adolescents: A meta-analysis. *Psychological Bulletin, 132*, 132–149.

Weisz, J. R., Sigman, M., Weiss, B., & Mosk, J. (1993). Parent reports of behavioral and emotional problems among children in Kenya, Thailand and the United States. *Child Development, 64*, 98–109.

Weisz, J. R., Suwanlert, S. C., Wanchai, W., & Bernadette, R. (1987). Over-and undercontrolled referral problems among children and adolescents from Thailand and the United States: The wat and wai of cultural differences. *Journal of Consulting and Clinical Psychology, 55*, 719–726.

Weisz, J. R., Weiss, B., Suwanlert, S., & Wanchai, C. (2003). Syndromal structure of psychopathology in children of Thailand and the United States. *Journal of Consulting and Clinical Psychology, 71*, 375–385.

Wells, A. (1998). Cognitive therapy of social phobia. In N. Tarrier, A. Wells, & G. Haddock (Eds.), *Treating complex cases: The cognitive-behavioural approach* (pp. 1–26). Chichester, England: Wiley.

Wells, C. E., & Duncan, G. W. (1980). *Neurology for psychiatrists*. Philadelphia: F. A. Davis, Co.

Wells, K. C., Epstein, J. N., Hinshaw, S. P., et al. (2000). Parenting and family stress treatment outcomes in attention deficit hyperactivity disorder (ADHD): An empirical analysis in the MTA study. *Journal of Abnormal Child Psychology, 28*, 543–553.

Welsh, R., Burcham, B., DeMoss, K., Martin, C., & Milich, R. (1997). *Attention deficit hyperactivity disorder diagnosis and management: A training program for teachers.* Frankfurt: Kentucky Department of Education.

Wender, P. H., Kety, S. S., Rosenthal, D., Schulsinger, F., Ortmann, J., & Lunde, I. (1986). Psychiatric disorders in the biological and adoptive families of adopted individuals with affective disorders. *Archives of General Psychiatry, 43*, 923–929.

Westen, D. (1998). The scientific legacy of Sigmund Freud: Toward a psychodynamically informed psychological science. *Psychological Bulletin, 124*, 333–371.

Westen, D., Novotny, C. M., & Thompson-Brenner, H. (2004). The empirical status of empirically supported psychotherapies: Assumptions, findings, and reporting in controlled clinical trials. *Psychological Bulletin, 130*, 631–663.

Westen, D., Weinberger, J., & Bradley, R. (2007). Motivation, decision making, and consciousness: From psychodynamics to subliminal priming and emotional constraint satisfaction. In M. Moscovitch & P. D. Zelazo (Eds.), *The Cambridge handbook of consciousness* (pp. 673–702). Cambridge, England: Cambridge University Press.

Whalen, C. K. (1983). Hyperactivity, learning problems, and the attention deficit disorders. In T. H. Ollendick & M. Hersen (Eds.), *Handbook of child psychopathology*. New York: Plenum.

Whalen, C. K., & Henker, B. (1985). The social worlds of hyperactive (ADHD) children. *Clinical Psychology Review, 5*, 447–478.

Whalen, C. K., & Henker, B. (1991). Therapies for hyperactive children: Comparisons, combinations, and compromises. *Journal of Consulting and Clinical Psychology, 59*, 126–137.

Whisman, M. A. (2007). Marital distress and DSM-IV psychiatric disorders in a population-based national survey. *Journal of Abnormal Psychology, 116*, 638–643.

Whisman, M. A., & Bruce, M. L. (1999). Marital dissatisfaction and incidence of major depressive episode in a community sample. *Journal of Abnormal Psychology, 108*, 674–678.

Whisman, M. A., & Uebelacker, L. A. (2006). Impairment and distress associated with relationship discord in a national sample of married or cohabiting adults. *Journal of Family Psychology, 20*, 369–377.

Whitaker, A. H., van Rossen, R., Feldman, J. F., Schonfeld, I. S., Pinto-Martin, J. A., Torre, C., . . . Paneth, N. (1997). Psychiatric outcomes in low birth weight children at age 6 years: Relation to neonatal cranial ultrasound abnormalities. *Archives of General Psychiatry, 54*, 847–856.

Whitaker, R. (2002). *Mad in America*. Cambridge, MA: Perseus.

White, C. N., Gunderson, J. G., Zanarini, M. C., & Hudson, J. I. (2003). Family studies of borderline personality disorder: A review. *Harvard Review of Psychiatry, 12*, 118–119.

White, K. S., & Barlow, D. H. (2004). Panic disorder and agoraphobia. In D. H. Barlow (Ed.), *Anxiety and its disorders: The nature and treatment of anxiety and panic* (pp. 328–379). New York: Guilford.

White, S. W., Oswald, D., Ollendick, T., & Scahill, L. (2009). Anxiety in children and adolescents with autism spectrum disorders. *Clinical Psychology Review, 29*, 216–229.

Whitmore, E. A., Mikulich, S. K., Thompson, L. L., Riggs, P. D., Aarons, G. A., & Crowley, T. J. (1997). Influences on adolescent substance dependence: Conduct disorder, depression, attention deficit hyperactivity disorder, and gender. *Drug and Alcohol Dependence 47*, 87–97.

Whittal, M. L., Agras, S. W., & Gould, R. A. (1999). Bulimia nervosa: A meta-analysis of psychosocial and pharmacological treatments. *Behavior Therapy, 30*, 117–135.

WHO (2002): Public health science and the global strategy on alcohol. www.euro.who.int/

WHO (2010): World No Tobacco Day. www.euro.who.int/

WHO (2011): Report on the global tobacco epidemic-www.euro.who.int/en/what-we-do/data-and-evidence/health-evidence-network-hen/publications/hen-summaries-of-network-members-reports/is-low-dose-alcohol-exposure-during-pregnancy-harmful

WHO World Mental Health Survey Consortium. (2004). Prevalence, severity, and unmet need for treatment of mental disorders in the World Health Organization world mental health surveys. *Journal of the American Medical Association, 291*, 2581–2590. doi: 2510.1001/jama.2291.2521.2581.

Wiborg, I. M., & Dahl, A. A. (1996). Does brief dynamic psychotherapy reduce the relapse rate of panic disorder? *Archives of General Psychiatry, 53*, 689–694.

Widiger, T. A., Frances, A., & Trull, T. J. (1987). A psychometric analysis of the social-interpersonal and cognitive-perceptual items for schizotypal personality disorder. *Archives of General Psychiatry, 44*, 741–745.

Widiger, T. A., & Samuel, D. B. (2005). Diagnostic categories or dimensions? A question for the Diagnostic and Statistical Manual of Mental Disorders—Fifth Edition. *Journal of Abnormal Psychology, 114*, 494–504.

Wildes, J. E., Emery, R. E., & Simons, A. D. (2001). The roles of ethnicity and culture in the development of eating disturbance and body dissatisfaction: A meta-analytic review. *Clinical Psychology Review, 21*, 521–551.

Wilfley, D. E., Welch, R. R, Stein, R. I., Spurrell, E. B., Cohen, L. R., et al. (2002). A randomized comparison of group cognitive-behavioral therapy and group interpersonal psychotherapy for the treatment of overweight individuals with binge eating disorder. *Archives of General Psychiatry, 59*, 713–721.

Wilhelm, S., Buhlmann, U., Hayward, L. C., Greenberg, J. L., & Dimaite, R. (2010). A cognitive-behavioral treatment approach for body dysmorphic disorder. *Cognitive and Behavioral Practice, 17*, 241–247.

Wille, R., & Boulanger, H. (1984). 10 years' castration law in Schleswig-Holstein. *Beitrage zur gerichtlichen Medizin, 42*, 9–16.

Willemsen-Swinkels, S. H. N., Buitelaar, J. K., & van Engeland, H. (1996). The effects of chronic naltrexone treatment in young autistic children: A double-blind placebo-controlled crossover study. *Biological Psychiatry, 39*, 1023–1031.

Willemsen-Swinkels, S. H. N., Buitelaar, J. K., Weijnen, F. G., & van Engeland, H. (1995). Placebo-controlled acute dosage naltrexone study in young autistic children. *Psychiatry Research, 58*, 203–215.

Willford, J. A., Richardson, G. A., Leech, S. L., & Day, N. L. (2004). Verbal and visuospatial learning and memory function in children with moderate prenatal alcohol exposure. *Alcoholism: Clinical and Experimental Research, 28*, 497–507.

Williams, C. J. (1999, May 27). In Kosovo, rape seen as awful as death. *Los Angeles Times*, pp. A1, A18.

Williams, J. (2003). Dementia and genetics. In R. Plomin, J. D. DeFries, et al. (Eds.), *Behavioral genetics in the postgenomic era* (pp. 503–527). Washington, DC: American Psychological Association.

Williams, J., Hadjistavropoulos, T., & Sharpe, D. (2006). A meta-analysis of psychological and pharmacological treatments for body dysmorphic disorder. *Behaviour Research and Therapy, 44*(1), 99–111. doi: 10.1016/j.brat.2004.12.006

Williams, J. B. W., Gibbon, M., First, M. B., Spitzer, R. L., Davies, M., et al. (1992). The Structured Clinical Interview for DSM-III-R (SCID): 2. Multisite test-retest reliability. *Archives of General Psychiatry, 49*, 630–636.

Williams, J. M. G., Watts, F. N., MacLeod, C., & Mathews, A. (1997). *Cognitive psychology and emotional disorders* (2nd ed.). New York: Wiley.

Williams, J. W., Plassman, B. L., Burke, J., Holsinger, T., & Benjamin, S. (2010). *Preventing Alzheimer's disease and cognitive decline* (Evidence Report/Technology Assessment No. 193). Rockville, MD: Duke Evidence-Based Practice Center.

Williams, P. A., Allard, A., Spears, L., Dalrymple, N., & Bloom, A. S. (2001). Brief report: Case reports on naltrexone use in children with autism: Controlled observations regarding benefits and practical issues in medication management. *Journal of Autism and Developmental Disorders, 31*, 103–108.

Willis, S. L., Tennstedt, S. L., Marsiske, M., Ball, K., Elias, J., Koepke, K. M., . . . Wright, E. (2006). Long-term effects of cognitive training on everyday functional outcomes in older adults. *Journal of the American Medical Association, 296*(23), 2805–2814.

Wills, T. A., & Cleary, S. D. (1999). Peer and adolescent substance use among 6th–9th graders: Latent growth analysis of influence versus selection mechanisms. *Health Psychology, 18*, 453–463.

Wills, T. A., DuHamel, K., & Vaccaro, D. (1995). Activity and mood temperament as predictors of adolescent substance use: Test of a self-regulation model. *Journal of Personality and Social Psychology, 68*, 901–916.

Wills, T. A., Sandy, J. M., & Yaeger, A. M. (2002). Stress and smoking in adolescence: A test of directional hypotheses. *Health Psychology, 21*, 122–130.

Wills, T. A., Sandy, J. M., Shinar, O., & Yaeger, A. (1999). Contributions of positive and negative affect to adolescent substance use: Test of a bidimensional model in a longitudinal study. *Psychology of Addictive Behaviors, 13*, 327–338.

Wilsnack, R. W., Vogeltanz, N. D., & Wilsnack, S. C., et al. (2000). Gender differences in alcohol consumption and adverse drinking consequences: Cross-cultural patterns. *Addiction, 95*, 251–265.

Wilson, A. J., & Dehaene, S. (2007). Number sense and developmental dyscalculia. In D. Coch et al. (Eds.), *Human behavior, learning and the developing brain: Atypical development* (pp. 212–238). New York: Guilford.

Wilson, D. (2011, April 13). As generics near, makers tweak erectile drugs. *NewYork Times*, p. B1.

Wilson, G. T. (1995). Psychological treatment of binge eating and bulimia nervosa. *Journal of Mental Health (UK), 4*, 451–457.

Wilson, G. T., & Fairburn, C. G. (1998). Treatments for eating disorders. In P. Nathan & J. M. Gorman (Eds.), *A guide to treatments that work* (pp. 501–530). London: Oxford University Press.

Wilson, G. T., Loeb, K. L., Walsh, B. T., Labouvie, E., Petkova, E., Liu, X., & Waternaux, C. (1999). Psychological and pharmacological treatment of bulimia nervosa: Predictors and processes of change. *Journal of Consulting and Clinical Psychology, 67*, 451–459.

Wilson, G. T., & Pike, K. M. (1993). Eating disorders. In D. H. Barlow (Ed.), *Clinical handbook of psychological disorders* (pp. 278–317). New York: Guilford.

Wilson, G. T., & Pike, K. M. (2001). Eating disorders. In D. H. Barlow (Ed.), *Clinical handbook of psychological disorders* (3rd ed., pp. 332–375). New York: Guilford.

Wilson, G. T., & Sysko, R. (2009). Frequency of binge eating episodes in bulimia nervosa and binge eating disorder: Diagnostic considerations. *International Journal of Eating Disorders, 42*, 603–610.

Wilson, G. T., Wilfley, D. E., Agras, S., & Bryson, S. W. (2010). Psychological treatments of binge eating disorder. *Archives of General Psychiatry, 67*, 94–101.

Wilson, R. S., Scherr, P. A., Schneider, J. A., Tang, Y., & Bennett, D. A. (2007). Relation of cognitive activity to risk of developing Alzheimer disease. *Neurology, 69*, 1191–1920.

Wimo, A., Winblad, B., Aguero-Torres, A., & von Strauss, E. (2003). The magnitude of dementia occurrence in the world. *Alzheimer Disease and Associated Disorders, 17*, 63–67.

Winchel, R. M., Stanley, B., & Stanley, M. (1990). Biochemical aspects of suicide. In S. J. Blumenthal & D. J. Kupfer (Eds.), *Suicide over the life cycle: Risk factors, assessment and treatment of suicidal patterns* (pp. 97–126). Washington, DC: American Psychiatric Press.

Wincze, J. P., & Barlow, D. H. (1997). *Enhancing sexuality: A problem-solving approach.* Boulder, Co: Graywind.

Wincze, J. P., Steketee, G., & Frost, R. O. (2007). Categorization in compulsive hoarding. *Behaviour Research and Therapy, 45*(1), 63–72. doi: 10.1016/j.brat.2006.01.012

Wingfield, N., Kelly, N., Serdar, K., Shivy, V. A., & Mazzeo, S. E. (2011). College students' perceptions of individuals with anorexia and bulimia nervosa. *International Journal of Eating Disorders, 44*, 369–375.

Winick, B. J. (1997). *The right to refuse mental health treatment.* Washington, DC: American Psychological Association.

Winkleby, M. A., Cubbin, C., Ahn, D. K., & Kraemer, H. C. (1999). Pathways by which SES and ethnicity influence cardiovascular risk factors. In N. E. Adler & M. Marmot (Eds.), *Socioeconomic status and health in industrialized nations: Social, psychological, and biological pathways* (Vol. 896). New York: New York Academy of Sciences.

Winkleby, M. A., Kraemer, H. C., Ahn, D. K., & Varady, A. N. (1998). Ethnic and socioeconomic differences in cardiovascular disease risk factors. *Journal of the American Medical Association, 280*, 356–362.

Wirshing, D. W., Wirshing, W. C., Marder, S. R., Liberman, R. P., & Mintz, J. (1998). Informed consent: Assessment of comprehension. *American Journal of Psychiatry, 155*, 1508–1511.

Wirz-Justice, A., Quinto, C., Cajochen, C., Werth, E., & Hock, C. (1999). A rapid-cycling bipolar patient treated with long nights, bedrest and light. *Biological Psychiatry, 45*, 1075–1077.

Witlox, J., Eurelings, L. S. M., de Jonghe, J. F. M., Kalisvaart, K. J., Eikelenboom, P., & van Gool, W. A. (2010). Delirium in elderly patients and the risk of postdischarge mortality, institutionalization, and dementia. *Journal of the American Medical Association, 304*, 443–451.

Wittchen, H. U., Gloster, A. T., Beesdo-Baum, K., Fava, G. A., & Craske, M. G. (2010). Agoraphobia: A review of the diagnostic classificatory position and criteria. *Depression and Anxiety, 27*(2), 113–133. doi: 10.1002/da.20646

Wittchen, H. U., & Jacobi, F. (2005). Size and burden of mental disorders in Europe—a critical review and appraisal of 27 studies. *European Neuropsychopharmacology, 15*, 357–376.

Wittchen, H. U., Nocon, A., Beesdo, K., Pine, D. S., Hofler, M., Lieb, R., & Gloster, A. T. (2008).

Agoraphobia and panic. Prospective-longitudinal relations suggest a rethinking of diagnostic concepts. *Psychotherapy and Psychosomatics, 77*(3), 147–157. doi: 10.1159/000116608

Wolf, M., Bally, H., & Morris, R. (1986). Automaticity, retrieval processes, and reading: A longitudinal study in average and impaired readers. *Child Development, 57*, 988–1000.

Wolfe, V. V. (1990). Sexual abuse of children. In A. S. Bellack, M. Hersen, & A. E. Kazdin (Eds.), *International handbook of behavior modification and therapy* (2nd ed., pp. 707–729). New York: Plenum.

Wolitzky, D. (1995). Traditional psychoanalytic psychotherapy. In A. S. Gurman & S. B. Messer (Eds.), *Essential psychotherapies: Theory and practice.* New York: Guilford.

Wolkowitz, O. M., Epel, E. S., Reus, V. I., & Mellon, S. H. (2010). Depression gets old fast: Do stress and depression accelerate cell aging? *Depression and Anxiety, 27*(4), 327–338. doi: 10.1002/da.20686

Wolpe, J. (1958). *Psychotherapy by reciprocal inhibition.* Stanford, CA: Stanford University Press.

Wolraich, M. L., Wilson, D. B., & White, J. W. (1995). The effect of sugar on behavior or cognition in children: A meta-analysis. *Journal of the American Medical Association, 274*, 1617–1621.

Women's Health Initiative Screening Committee. (2004). Effects of conjugated equine estrogen in postmenopausal women with hysterectomy: The women's health initiative randomized controlled trial. *Journal of the American Medical Association, 291*, 1701–1712.

Wonderlich, S. A., Crosby, R. D., Mitchell, J. E., Thompson, K. M., Redlin, J., Demuth, G., . . . Haseltine, B. (2001). Eating disturbance and sexual trauma in childhood and adulthood. *International Journal of Eating Disorders, 30*, 401–412.

Wonderlich, S. A., Gordon, K. H., Mitchell, J. E., Crosby, R. D., Engel, S. G., & Walsh, B. T. (2009). The validity and clinical utility of binge eating disorder. *International Journal of Eating Disorders, 42*, 687–705.

Wonderlich, S. A., Wilsnack, R. W., Wilsnack, S. C., & Harris, T. R. (1996). Childhood sexual abuse and bulimic behavior in a nationally representative sample. *American Journal of Public Health, 86*, 1082–1086.

Wong, D. F., Wagner, H. N., Tune, L. E., Dannals, R. F., Pearlson, G. D., Links, J. M., et al. (1986). Positron emission tomography reveals elevated D2 dopamine receptors in drug-naive schizophrenics. *Science, 234*, 1558–1562.

Woo, J. S., Brotto, L. A., & Gorzalka, B. B. (2011). The role of sex guilt in the relationship between culture and women's sexual desire. *Archives of Sexual Behavior, 40*(2), 385–394. doi: 10.1007/s10508–010–9609–0

Woodberry, K. A., Giuliano, A. J., & Seidman, L. J. (2008). Premorbid IQ in schizophrenia: A meta-analytic review. *American Journal of Psychiatry, 165*, 579–587.

Woodmansee, M. A. (1996). The guilty but mentally ill verdict: Political expediency at the expense of moral principle. *Notre Dame Journal of Law, Ethics and Public Policy, 10*, 341–387.

Woods, S. W., Addington, J., Cadenhead, K. S., Cannon, T. D., Cornblatt, B. A., Heinssen, R., et al. (2009). Validity of the prodromal risk syndrome for first psychosis: Findings from the North American Prodrome Longitudinal Study. *Schizophrenia Bulletin, 35*, 894–908.

Woodside, D. B., Bulik, C. M., Halmi, K. A., et al. (2002). Personality, perfectionism, and attitudes towards eating in parents of individuals with eating

disorders. *International Journal of Eating Disorders, 13*, 290–299.

Woodside, D. B., Shekter-Wolfson, L. F., Garfinkel, P. E., & Olmsted, M. P. (1995). Family interactions in bulimia nervosa: Study design, comparisons to established population norms and changes over the course of an intensive day hospital treatment program. *International Journal of Eating Disorders, 17*, 105–115.

Woody, E. Z., & Szechtman, H. (2011). Adaptation to potential threat: The evolution, neurobiology, and psychopathology of the security motivation system. *Neuroscience and Biobehavioral Reviews, 35*(4), 1019–1033. doi: 10.1016/j.neubiorev.2010.08.003

World Health Organization. (2001). *World health report: New understanding, new hope.* Geneva: Author.

Wouda, J. C., Hartman, P. M., Bakker, R. M., Bakker, J. O., Van De Wiel, H. B. M., & Schultz, W. C. (1998). Vaginal plethysmography in women with dyspareunia. *Journal of Sex Research, 35*, 141–147.

Wright, I. A., Rabe-Hesketh, S., Woodruff, P. W., Davis, A. S., Murray, R. M., & Bullmore, E. T. (2000). Meta-analysis of regional brain volumes in schizophrenia. *American Journal of Psychiatry, 157*, 16–25.

Wright, M. J. (1991). Identifying child sexual abuse using the Personality Inventory for Children. *Dissertation Abstracts International, 52*, 1744.

Writing Group for the Women's Health Initiative Investigators. (2002). Risks and benefits of estrogen plus progestin in healthy postmenopausal women. Principle results from the Women's Health Initiative randomized controlled trial. *Journal of the American Medical Association, 288*, 321–333.

Wu, L. T., Pilowsky, D. J., & Schlenger, W. E. (2004). Inhalant abuse and dependence among adolescents in the United States. *Journal of the American Academy of Child and Adolescent Psychiatry, 43*, 1206–1214.

Wykes, T., Huddy, V., Cellard, C., McGurk, S., & Czobor, P. (2011). A meta-analysis of cognitive remediation for schizophrenia: Methodology and effect sizes. *American Journal of Psychiatry, 168*, 472–485.

Wykes, T., Steel, C., Everitt, T., & Tarrier, N. (2008). Cognitive behavior therapy for schizophrenia: Effect sizes, clinical models, and methodological rigor. *Schizophrenia Bulletin, 34*, 523–537.

Wylie, K. R. (1997). Treatment outcome of brief couple therapy in psychogenic male erectile disorder. *Archives of Sexual Behavior, 26*, 527–545.

Wylie, K., & MacInnes, I. (2005). Erectile dysfunction. In R. Balon & R. T. Segraves (Eds.), *Handbook of sexual dysfunctions and paraphilias.* Boca Raton, FL: Taylor & Francis.

Xia, J., Merinder, L. B., & Belgamwar, M. R. (2011). Psychoeducation for schizophrenia. *Schizophrenia Bulletin, 37*, 21–22.

Yaffe, K., Fiocco, A. J., Lindquist, K., Vittinghoff, E., Simonsick, E. M., Newman, A. B., . . . Harris, T. B. (2009). Predictors of maintaining cognitive function in older adults. *Neurology, 72*, 2029–2035.

Yan, L. J., Hammen, C., Cohen, A. N., Daley, R. M., & Henry, R. M. (2004). Expressed emotion versus relationship quality variable in the prediction of recurrence in bipolar patients. *Journal of Affective Disorders, 83*, 199–206.

Yanovski, S. Z. (2003). Binge eating disorder and obesity in 2003: Could treating an eating disorder have a positive effect on the obesity epidemic? *International Journal of Eating Disorders, 34* (Suppl), S117–S120.

Yehuda, R., & LeDoux, J. (2007). Response variation following trauma: A translational neuroscience approach to understanding PTSD. *Neuron, 56*(1), 19–32. doi: 10.1016/j.neuron.2007.09.006

Yen, S., Shea, M. T., Pagano, M., Sanislow, C. A., Grilo, C. M., McGlashan, T. H., . . . Morey, L. C. (2003). Axis I and Axis II disorders as predictors of prospective suicide attempts: Findings from the collaborative longitudinal personality disorders study. *Journal of Abnormal Psychology, 112*(3), 375–381.

Yerkes, R. M., & Dodson, J. D. (1908). The relation of strength of stimulus to rapidity of habit formation. *Journal of Comparative and Neurological Psychology, 18*, 459–482.

Yildiz, A., Guleryuz, S., Ankerst, D. P., Öngür, D., & Renshaw, P. F. (2008). Protein kinase C inhibition in the treatment of mania: A double-blind, placebo-controlled trial of tamoxifen. *Archives of General Psychiatry, 65*, 255–263.

Yirmiya, N., & Sigman, M. (1991). High functioning individuals with autism: Diagnosis, empirical findings, and theoretical issues. *Clinical Psychology Review, 11*, 669–683.

Yoast, R., Williams, M. A., Deitchman, S. D., & Champion, H. C. (2001). Report of the Council on Scientific Affairs: Methadone maintenance and needle-exchange programs to reduce the medical and public health consequences of drug abuse. *Journal of Addictive Diseases, 20*, 15–40.

Yonkers, K. A., Dyck, I. R., Warshaw, M., & Keller, M. B. (2000). Factors predicting the clinical course of generalised anxiety disorder. *British Journal of Psychiatry, 176*, 544–549.

Young, A. S., Niv, N., Cohen, A. N., Kessler, C., & McNagny, K. (2010). The appropriateness of routine medication treatment for schizophrenia. *Schizophrenia Bulletin, 36*, 732–739.

Young, J., Goey, A., Minassian, A., Perry, W., Paulus, M., & Geyer, M. (2010). GBR 12909 administration as a mouse model of bipolar disorder mania: Mimicking quantitative assessment of manic behavior. *Psychopharmacology, 208*(3), 443–454. doi: 10.1007/s00213-009-1744-8

Younglove, J. A., & Vitello, C. J. (2003). Community notification provisions of "Megan's law" from a therapeutic jurisprudence perspective: A case study. *American Journal of Forensic Psychology, 21*, 25–38.

Youngstrom, E. A., Arnold, L. E., & Frazier, T. W. (2010). Bipolar and ADHD comorbidity: Both artifact and

outgrowth of shared mechanisms. *Clinical Psychology: Science and Practice, 17*, 350–359.

Youngstrom, E. A., Freeman, A. J., & Jenkins, M. M. (2009). The assessment of children and adolescents with bipolar disorder. *Child and Adolescent Psychiatric Clinics of North America, 18*, 353–390. doi:310.1016/j.chc.2008.1012.1002

Yung, A. R., McGorry, P. D., McFarlane, C. A., & Patton, G. (1995). The PACE Clinic: Development of a clinical service for young people at high risk of psychosis. *Australia Psychiatry, 3*, 345–349.

Yung, A. R., Nelson, B., Thompson, A. D., & Wood, S. J. (2010). Should a "risk syndrome for psychosis" be included in the DSMV? *Schizophrenia Research, 120*, 7–15.

Yung, A. R., Phillips, L. J., Hok, P. Y., & McGorry, P. D. (2004). Risk factors for psychosis in an ultra high-risk group: Psychopathology and clinical features. *Schizophrenia Research, 67*, 131–142.

Zanarini, M. C., Frankenburg, F. R., Hennen, J., Reich, D. B., & Silk, K. R. (2004). Axis I comorbidity in patients with borderline personality disorder: 6-year follow-up and prediction of time to remission. *American Journal of Psychiatry, 161*, 2108–2114.

Zanarini, M. C., Frankenburg, F. R., Hennen, J., Reich, D. B., & Silk, K. R. (2006). Prediction of the 10-year course of borderline personality disorder. *American Journal of Psychiatry, 163*, 827–832.

Zanarini, M. C., Skodol, A. E., Bender, D., Dolan, R., Sanislow, C., Schaefer, E., et al. (2000). The Collaborative Longitudinal Personality Disorders Study: Reliability of Axis I and II diagnoses. *Journal of Personality Disorders, 14*, 291–299.

Zane, M. D. (1984). Psychoanalysis and contextual analysis of phobias. *Journal of the American Academy of Psychoanalysis, 12*, 553–568.

Zapf, P. A., & Roesch, R. (2011). Future directions in the restoration of competency to stand trial. *Current Directions in Psychological Science, 20*, 43–47.

Zarit, S. H. (1980). *Aging and mental disorders: Psychological approaches to assessment and treatment.* New York: Free Press.

Zarit, S. H., & Zarit, J. M. (1998). *Mental disorders in older adults: Fundamentals of assessment and treatment.* New York: Guilford.

Zatzick, D. F., Marmer, C. R., Weiss, D. S., Browner, W. S., Metzler, T. J., Golding, J. M., . . . Wells, K. B. (1997).

Posttraumatic stress disorder and functioning and quality of life in a nationally representative sample of male Vietnam veterans. *American Journal of Psychiatry, 154*, 1690–1695.

Zellner, D. A., Harner, D. E., & Adler, R. L. (1989). Effects of eating abnormalities and gender on perceptions of desirable body shape. *Journal of Abnormal Psychology, 98*, 93–96.

Zhang, T. Y., & Meaney, M. J. (2010). Epigenetics and the environmental regulation of the genome and its function. *Annual Review of Psychology, 61*, 439–466.

Zheng, H., Sussman, S., Chen, X., Wang, Y., Xia, J., Gong, J., . . . Johnson, C. A. (2004). Project EX—a teen smoking cessation initial study in Wuhan, China. *Addictive Behaviors, 29*, 1725–1733.

Zilboorg, G., & Henry, G. W. (1941). *A history of medical psychology.* New York: Norton.

Zimmer, D. (1987). Does marital therapy enhance the effectiveness of treatment for sexual dysfunction? *Journal of Sex and Marital Therapy, 13*, 193–209.

Zimmer, L., & Morgan, J. P. (1995). *Exposing marijuana myths: A review of the scientific evidence.* New York: The Lindemith Center.

Zimmerman, M., & Mattia, J. I. (1999). Differences between clinical and research practices in diagnosing borderline personality disorder. *American Journal of Psychiatry, 156*, 1570–1574.

Zimmerman, M., Rothschild, L., & Chelminski, I. (2005). The prevalence of DSM-IV personality disorders in psychiatric outpatients. *American Journal of Psychiatry, 162*, 1911–1918.

Zinbarg, R., Barlow, D. H., Liebowitz, M. R., Street, L., Broadhead, E., Katon, W., . . . Richards, J. (1994). The DSM-IV field trial for mixed anxiety depression. *American Journal of Psychiatry, 151*(8), 1153–1162.

Zlotnick, C., Johnson, S. L., Miller, I. W., Pearlstein, T., & Howard, M. (2001). Postpartum depression in women receiving public assistance: Pilot study of an interpersonal therapy-oriented group intervention. *American Journal of Psychiatry, 158*, 638–640.

Zohar, A. H., & Felz, L. (2001). Ritualistic behavior in young children. *Journal of Abnormal Child Psychology, 29*(2), 121–128.

Zubin, J., & Spring, B. (1977). Vulnerability: A new view of schizophrenia. *Journal of Abnormal Psychology, 86*, 103–126.

Quotation and Illustration Credits

Page 33, Figure 2.4. Adapted from Caspi et al. (2002). *Science*, 301, 387.

Page 78, Figure 3.7. Adapted from University of Minnesota Press.

Page 82, Figure 3.8. From New York State Psychiatric Institute, Biometrics Research Division. Copyright © 1996 by the Board of Trustees of Leland Stanford University.

Page 117, Figure 4.5. Drawn from Lambert, M.J. (2004). Psychotherapeutically speaking-updates from the Division of Psychotherapy (29). Available by web at http://www.divisionofpsychotherapy.org/updates.php

Page 126, Figure 4.6. From Chorpita et al. "Behavioral treatment of choking phobia in an adolescent: An experimental analysis," *Journal of Behavioral Therapy and Experimental Psychiatry*, 38, 307–315, copyright © 1997.

Page 146, Figure 5.5. Adapted from Snyder (1986) p. 106.

Page 147, Figure 5.6. Adapted from *Annual Review of Review of Psychology*, Vol. 53, copyright © 2002 by Annual Reviews, www.annualreviews.org.

Page 155, Figure 5.11. Adapted from Caspi et al. (2002). *Science*, 301, 387, AAAS.

Page 158, Quotation drawn from Geahy (2003) Guilford Press.

Page 159, Clinical case quotation drawn from Leahy (2003), Guilford Press.

Page 168, Figure 5.12. From Arias, E., Andress R.N., Kung, H.C., Murphy, S.L., Kochanek, K. (2003) *Deaths: Final Data for 2001*. Hyattsville, Maryland: National Center for Deals Statistics, 52.

Page 193, Figure 6.7. Adapted from Clark, D.M. (1997). Panic disorder and social phobia. [In D.M. Clark and C.G. Fairburn (Eds.), Science and Practice of Cognitive Behaviour Therapy (pp. 121–153)], Oxford University Press.

Page 245, Figure 8.5. Adapted from Looper, K.J., & Kirmayer, L.J. (2002). Behavioral medicine approaches to somatoform disorders. *Journal of Consulting and Clinical Psychology*, 70, 810–827.

Page 255, quotation: McGhie, A. & Chapman, J.S. (1961). Disorders of attention and perception in early schizophrenia. *British Journal of Medical Psychology*, 34, 103–116, British Psychological Society.

Page 373, Figure 12.5. Adapted from Masters, W.H. & Johnson, V.E. (1970). *Human sexual inadequacy*, Masters & Johnson Institute.

Page 408, Figure 13.3. Adapted from Blumstein, A., Cohen, J., & Farrington, D.P. *Criminology*, 26, 11. Copyright © 1988. The American Society of Criminology.

Page 427, Table 13.4. Adapted from American Association on Mental Retardation.

Page 436, Focus on Discovery 13.6, quotation: Sacks, O. (1995). Excerpts from An Anthropologist on Mars. Copyright © 1995, Random House, Inc.

Name Index

S

Sabo, S. Z., 310
Sacco, R. L., 293
Sachdev, P., 455
Sachs, G. S., 164
Sachs, L., 405
Sackeim, 246
Sackeim, H. A., 161, 169
Sacks, F. M., 349
Sacks, O., 436, 437
Sackville, T., 224
Saczynski, J. S., 455
Saffer, H., 316
Safford, S., 422
Saha, S., 253
Saint Onge, J. M., 309
Sakel, M., 15
Saks, E. R., 281, 508
Salamone, J. D., 121
Salan, S. E., 298
Salary, C. B., 417
Saleh, P. A., 270
Salekin, R. T., 489
Salem, J. E., 276
Salidas, J., 425
Salkovskis, 249
Salkovskis, P. M., 47, 187, 210
Salter, D., 386
Salvatori, S., 242
Samaritans Information Resource
    Pack, 517
Sami, N., 401
Sammut, P., 204
Sampson, S. M., 456
Samuel, D. B., 467
Samuels, 211
Samuels, J., 208, 467, 468
Sanchez, D. T., 363
Sanchez-Meca, J., 213
Sandberg, S., 399
Sander, C., 213
Sandy, J. M., 309, 312
Sanislow, C. A., 468
Santarelli, L., 165
Santonastaso, P., 338
Sar, V., 234, 242
Sareen, J., 175
Sartorius, N., 73, 254–256
Saultz, J., 293
Savage, C. R., 211
Savard, P., 198
Savoie, T. D., 274
Sax, K. W., 146
Saxe, M., 165
Saxena, S., 165, 212
Sayed-Tabatabaei, F. A., 145
Saykin, A. J., 270
Sbrocco, T., 374
Scahill, L., 436
Scamra, C., 293
Scanlan, J., 188

Scanlan, J. M., 459
Scarborough, H. S., 425
Schaefer, C. A., 268, 270
Schaefer, H. S., 147
Schaie, K. W., 447
Schalock, R. L., 427
Schatzberg, A. F., 162
Schauer, M., 223
Schell, A. M., 190
Schene, A. H., 157
Scherer, S. W., 265
Scherk, H., 164
Scherr, P. A., 455
Scherrer, J. F., 309
Schick, V., 363
Schilder, P., 232
Schlenger, W. E., 307
Schlesser, M., 169
Schlundt, D. G., 346
Schmeidler, J., 232
Schmid, F., 279
Schmidt, E., 320
Schmidt, F., 151, 468
Schmidt, G., 370
Schmidt, N. B., 168, 188, 193
Schmitt, D. P., 365
Schmitt, W. A., 182, 483
Schnab, D. W., 404
Schnaider-Beeri, M., 455
Schneck, C. D., 143
Schneider, J. A., 455
Schneier, F. R., 200
Schniering, C. A., 418
Schoeneman, T. J., 10
Schoenwald, S. D., 413
Schooler, N. R., 278
Schopler, E., 440
Schreiber, F. L., 234
Schreiber, G., 165
Schreibman, L., 440
Schuckit, M. A., 288, 289, 304,
    318
Schulsinger, F., 263
Schumacher, J. E., 326
Schumacher, M., 138
Schumm, L. P., 446
Schuster, D., 331
Schutte, K. K., 312
Schwartz, J. E., 138, 271
Schwartz, M. B., 350
Schwartz, S., 272
Schwartz, S. A., 215
Schwarz, S., 279
Schweizer, E., 199
Schwitzgebel, R. K., 506, 512
Schwitzgebel, R. L., 506, 512
Scorolli, C., 379
Scott, C., 221
Scott, K. M., 136
Scroppo, J. C., 233
Seagraves, R. T., 376

Seal, B. N., 375
Sedaghadt, F., 434
Seedat, S., 136, 199, 205, 222
Seelaar, H., 456
Seeley, J. R., 415, 416
Segal, D. L., 445
Segal, Z., 165
Segal, Z. V., 48, 153, 159
Segraves, K. B., 368, 371
Segraves, R. T., 368, 371, 372,
    374, 378
Seider, B. H., 456
Seidler, G. H., 223
Seidman, L. J., 264, 274
Seidman, S. N., 121
Sekine, Y., 234
Sekirnjak, G., 86
Selemon, L. D., 269
Seligman, M. E., 124
Seligman, M. E. P., 190
Selkoe, D. J., 453
Selling, L. S., 11
Selwood, A., 460
Selye, 83
Semple, W. E., 267
Sen, S., 205
Sendersky, V., 447
Seneca, N., 146
Sensky, T., 283
Serdula, M. K., 349
Seshadri, S., 455
Seto, M. C., 379, 382, 386
Setters, M. J., 146
Setzer, N. J., 422
Sexton, T. L., 54
Shaffer, D., 81
Shafran, R., 346
Shah, G. M. S., 255
Shane, M. S., 483
Shankman, S. A. M. A., 135
Shaper, A. G., 450
Shapiro, F., 223
Shapiro, R., 254
Shapiro, T., 438
Sharkansky, E. J., 221
Sharma, V., 237
Sharp, W., 403
Sharpe, D., 213
Shaver, P. R., 56
Shaw, B. F., 163
Shaw, D. S., 412
Shaw, H., 338, 359
Shaw, L. J., 53
Shaywitz, B. A., 424, 425
Shaywitz, J., 186
Shaywitz, S. E., 424, 425
Shea, M. T., 157, 163, 468, 484
Shearin, E. N., 169
Sheline, Y., 40, 146, 147
Shelton, R. C., 38, 163
Shelton, T., 406

Shen, G. H. C., 109
Shen, Y., 438
Shenk, D., 30, 31
Shenton, M. E., 220, 477
Shepard, J. W. J., 446
Sher, K. J., 309, 310, 314
Sher, L., 137
Shergill, S. S., 255
Sherman, D. K., 403
Shermis, M. D., 193
Shern, D. L., 284
Shiffman, S., 92, 310, 312, 313,
    316, 324, 338
Shifren, J. L., 368
Shih, J. H., 416
Shimizu, H., 183
Shimon, H., 165
Shin, L. M., 186, 220
Shin, M., 429
Shinar, O., 309
Shiner, R., 311, 468
Shippee, S. K., 372
Shlik, J., 192
Shneidman, E. S., 168, 170
Shobe, K. K., 229
Shogren, K. A., 427
Short, A., 440
Sidani, S., 459
Siegel, L. J., 24, 421, 422
Siegle, G. J., 147
Siegler, I. C., 445
Siever, L. J., 477, 485
Sigman, M., 397, 434, 437
Silberg, J., 30, 35
Silberman, E. K., 237
Silbersweig, D., 485
Silbersweig, D. A., 255
Silovsky, J. F., 187
Silva, P. A., 182
Silva, S., 417
Silverman, K., 302, 320, 325
Silvia, P. A., 410
Simeon, D., 232
Simeone, I., 461
Simmel, C., 400, 404
Simmons, H., 421
Simon, 249
Simon, G., 175
Simon, G. E., 121, 135, 136, 156,
    165, 237, 240, 248, 250
Simon, N. M., 200
Simon, R. J., 501, 502n.2
Simon, S. L., 304
Simon, T. R., 330
Simon, W., 163
Simonoff, E., 409
Simons, A. D., 352
Simpson, E. E., 297
Singer, J., 278
Sinha, S. S., 186
Siok, W. T., 426

Subject Index

DSM-IV-TR Classification Axes I and II

Axis I

DISORDERS USUALLY FIRST DIAGNOSED IN INFANCY, CHILDHOOD, OR ADOLESCENCE

Learning Disorders
Reading Disorder / Mathematics Disorder / Disorder of Written Expression

Motor Skills Disorder
Developmental Coordination Disorder

Pervasive Developmental Disorders
Autistic Disorder / Rett's Disorder / Childhood Disintegrative Disorder / Asperger's Disorder

Attention-deficit and Disruptive Behavior Disorders
Attention-deficit/Hyperactivity Disorder / Oppositional Defiant Disorder / Conduct Disorder

Feeding and Eating Disorders of Infancy or Early Childhood
Pica / Rumination Disorder / Feeding Disorder of Infancy or Early Childhood

Tic Disorders
Tourette's Disorder / Chronic Motor or Vocal Tic Disorder / Transient Tic Disorder

Communication Disorders
Expressive Language Disorder / Mixed Receptive/Expressive Language Disorder / Phonological Disorder / Stuttering

Elimination Disorders
Encopresis / Enuresis

Other Disorders of Infancy, Childhood, or Adolescence
Separation Anxiety Disorder / Selective Mutism / Reactive Attachment Disorder of Infancy or Early Childhood / Stereotypic Movement Disorder

DELIRIUM, DEMENTIA, AMNESTIC, AND OTHER COGNITIVE DISORDERS

Delirium
Delirium Due to a General Medical Condition / Substance-intoxicated Delirium / Substance-withdrawal Delirium / Delirium Due to Multiple Etiologies

Dementias
Dementia of the Alzheimer's Type; with Early Onset: if onset at age 65 or below; with Late Onset if onset after age 65 / Vascular Dementia / Dementias Due to Other General Medical Conditions / Substance-induced Persisting Dementia / Dementia Due to Multiple Etiologies

Amnestic Disorders
Amnestic Disorder Due to a General Medical Condition / Substance-induced Persisting Amnestic Disorder (refer to specific substance for code)

SUBSTANCE-RELATED DISORDERS

Alcohol-related Disorders
Amphetamine-related Disorders
Caffeine-related Disorders
Cannabis-related Disorders
Cocaine-related Disorders
Hallucinogen-related Disorders
Inhalant-related Disorders
Nicotine-related Disorders
Opioid-related Disorders
Phencyclidine (or Related Substance)-related Disorders
Sedative, Hypnotic, or Anxiolytic-related Disorders
Polysubstance-related Disorder

SCHIZOPHRENIA AND OTHER PSYCHOTIC DISORDERS

Schizophrenia
Paranoid Type / Disorganized Type / Catatonic Type / Undifferentiated Type / Residual Type

Schizophreniform Disorder
Schizoaffective Disorder
Delusional Disorder
Brief Psychotic Disorder
Shared Psychotic Disorder (Folie à Deux)
Psychotic Disorder Due to a General Medical Condition
With delusions / with hallucinations / Substance-induced Psychotic Disorder

MOOD DISORDERS

Depressive Disorders
Major Depressive Disorder / Dysthymic Disorder

Bipolar Disorders
Bipolar I Disorder / Bipolar II Disorder (Recurrent Major Depressive Episodes with Hypomania) / Cyclothymic Disorder

Mood Disorder Due to a General Medical Condition
Substance-induced Mood Disorder

ANXIETY DISORDERS

Panic Disorder
without Agoraphobia / with Agoraphobia

Agoraphobia without History of Panic Disorder
Specific Phobia
Social Phobia (Social Anxiety Disorder)
Obsessive-Compulsive Disorder
Posttraumatic Stress Disorder
Acute Stress Disorder
Generalized Anxiety Disorder
Anxiety Disorder Due to a General Medical Condition
Substance-induced Anxiety Disorder

SOMATOFORM DISORDERS

Somatization Disorder
Conversion Disorder
Hypochondriasis
Body Dysmorphic Disorder
Pain Disorder

FACTITIOUS DISORDERS

Factitious Disorder

DISSOCIATIVE DISORDERS

Dissociative Amnesia
Dissociative Fugue
Dissociative Identity Disorder (Multiple Personality Disorder)
Depersonalization Disorder

SEXUAL AND GENDER IDENTITY DISORDERS

Sexual Dysfunctions
Sexual Desire Disorders: Hypoactive Sexual Desire Disorder; Sexual Aversion Disorder / Sexual Arousal Disorders: Female Sexual Arousal Disorder; Male Erectile Disorder / Orgasmic Disorders: Female Orgasmic Disorder; Male Orgasmic Disorder; Premature Ejaculation / Sexual Pain Disorders: Dyspareunia; Vaginismus / Sexual Dysfunction Due to a General Medical Condition / Substance-induced Sexual Dysfunction
Paraphilias
Exhibitionism / Fetishism / Frotteurism / Pedophilia / Sexual Masochism / Sexual Sadism / Voyeurism / Transvestic Fetishism
Gender Identity Disorders
Gender Identity Disorder: in Children; in Adolescents or Adults

EATING DISORDERS

Anorexia Nervosa
Bulimia Nervosa

SLEEP DISORDERS

Primary Sleep Disorders
Dyssomnias: Primary Insomnia; Primary Hypersomnia; Narcolepsy; Breathing-related Sleep Disorder; Circadian Rhythym Sleep Disorder (Sleep-Wake Schedule Disorder) / Parasomnias; Nightmare Disorder (Dream Anxiety Disorder); Sleep Terror Disorder; Sleepwalking Disorder / Sleep Disorders Related to Another Mental Disorder
Sleep Disorder Due to a General Medical Condition
Substance-induced Sleep Disorder

IMPULSE CONTROL DISORDERS NOT ELSEWHERE CLASSIFIED

Intermittent Explosive Disorder
Kleptomania
Pyromania
Pathological Gambling
Trichotillomania

ADJUSTMENT DISORDERS

Adjustment Disorder
With Anxiety / with Depressed Mood / with Disturbance of Conduct / with Mixed Disturbance of Emotions and Conduct / with Mixed Anxiety and Depressed Mood

Axis II

MENTAL RETARDATION

Mild Mental Retardation / Moderate Mental Retardation / Severe Mental Retardation / Profound Mental Retardation

PERSONALITY DISORDERS

Paranoid Personality Disorder
Schizoid Personality Disorder
Schizotypal Personality Disorder
Antisocial Personality Disorder
Borderline Personality Disorder
Histrionic Personality Disorder
Narcissistic Personality Disorder
Avoidant Personality Disorder
Dependent Personality Disorder
Obsessive-Compulsive Personality Disorder

OTHER CONDITIONS THAT MAY BE A FOCUS OF CLINICAL ATTENTION

Psychological Factors Affecting Medical Condition/ Medication-Induced Movement Disorders/Relational Problems
Relational Problem Related to a Mental Disorder or General Medical Condition / Parent-Child Relational Problem / Partner Relational Problem / Sibling Relational Problem
Problems Related to Abuse or Neglect
Physical Abuse of Child / Sexual Abuse of Child / Neglect of Child / Physical Abuse of Adult / Sexual Abuse of Adult
Additional Conditions That May Be a Focus of Clinical Attention
Bereavement / Borderline Intellectual Functioning / Academic Problem / Occupational Problem / Child or Adolescent Antisocial Behavior / Adult Antisocial Behavior / Malingering / Phase of Life Problem / Noncompliance with Treatment / Identity Problem / Religious or Spiritual Problem / Acculturation Problem / Age-related Cognitive Decline